INTERNATIONAL
LAW REPORTS

VOLUME 143

Volumes published under the title:

ANNUAL DIGEST AND REPORTS
OF PUBLIC INTERNATIONAL LAW CASES

Vol. 1 (1919-22)
Vol. 2 (1923-24) } Edited by Sir John Fischer Williams, K.C., and H. Lauterpacht, LL.D.

Vol. 3 (1925-26)
Vol. 4 (1927-28) } Edited by Arnold D. McNair, C.B.E., LL.D., and H. Lauterpacht, LL.D.

Vol. 5 (1929-30)
Vol. 6 (1931-32)
Vol. 7 (1933-34)
Vol. 8 (1935-37)
Vol. 9 (1938-40)
Vol. 10 (1941-42) } Edited by H. Lauterpacht, Q.C., LL.D., F.B.A.
Vol. 11 (1919-42)
Vol. 12 (1943-45)
Vol. 13 (1946)
Vol. 14 (1947)
Vol. 15 (1948)
Vol. 16 (1949)

Volumes published under the title:

INTERNATIONAL LAW REPORTS

Vol. 17 (1950)
Vol. 18 (1951)
Vol. 19 (1952)
Vol. 20 (1953) } Edited by Sir Hersch Lauterpacht, Q.C., LL.D., F.B.A.
Vol. 21 (1954)
Vol. 22 (1955)
Vol. 23 (1956)

Vol. 24 (1957)   Edited by Sir Hersch Lauterpacht, Q.C., LL.D., F.B.A., and E. Lauterpacht

Vol. 25 (1958-I)
Vol. 26 (1958-II) } Edited by E. Lauterpacht, Q.C.

Vols. 27-68 *and* Consolidated Tables and Index to Vols. 1-35 *and* 36-45
Edited by E. Lauterpacht, Q.C.

Vols. 69-143 *and* Consolidated Index and Consolidated Tables of Cases and Treaties to Vols. 1-80, Vols. 81-100 *and* Vols. 1-125
Edited by Sir Elihu Lauterpacht, C.B.E., Q.C., and Sir Christopher Greenwood, C.M.G., Q.C.

Lauterpacht Centre for International Law
University of Cambridge

INTERNATIONAL LAW REPORTS

VOLUME 143

Edited by

SIR ELIHU LAUTERPACHT, CBE QC
Honorary Professor of International Law, University of Cambridge
Bencher of Gray's Inn

SIR CHRISTOPHER GREENWOOD, CMG QC
Judge of the International Court of Justice
Bencher of Middle Temple

and

KAREN LEE
Assistant Editor
Fellow of the Lauterpacht Centre for International Law, University of Cambridge
Fellow of Girton College, Cambridge

GROTIUS PUBLICATIONS
CAMBRIDGE UNIVERSITY PRESS

CAMBRIDGE UNIVERSITY PRESS
Cambridge, New York, Melbourne, Madrid, Cape Town,
Singapore, São Paulo, Delhi, Tokyo, Mexico City

Cambridge University Press
The Edinburgh Building, Cambridge CB2 8RU, UK

Published in the United States of America by Cambridge University Press, New York

www.cambridge.org
Information on this title: www.cambridge.org/9780521198011

© Sir Elihu Lauterpacht 2011

This publication is in copyright. Subject to statutory exception
and to the provisions of relevant collective licensing agreements,
no reproduction of any part may take place without the written
permission of Cambridge University Press.

First published 2011

Printed in the United Kingdom at the University Press, Cambridge

A catalogue record for this publication is available from the British Library

ISBN 978-0-521-19801-1 Hardback

Cambridge University Press has no responsibility for the persistence or
accuracy of URLs for external or third-party internet websites referred to
in this publication, and does not guarantee that any content on such
websites is, or will remain, accurate or appropriate.

CONTENTS

	Page
Preface	vii
Editorial Note	ix
Table of Cases (alphabetical)	xiii
Table of Cases (according to courts and countries)	xv
Digest (main headings)	xvii
Digest of Cases Reported in Volume 143	xix
Table of Treaties	xxxiii
Reports of Cases	1
Index	729

PREFACE

The present volume contains the judgments of the International Tribunal for the Law of the Sea on the application for prompt release in the *Hoshinmaru* and *Tomimaru* cases. It also contains decisions from the courts of Australia (*Tang*), Canada (*Hape, Khadr (No 1)* and *(No 2)*), Denmark (*Thule Tribe Case*), Kenya (*RM, Al-Dahas* and *Sitamze*), Singapore (*Yong*), South Africa (*Fuel Retailers, Van Zyl* and *Von Abo*) and Uganda (*Kigula*).

There are many people, to all of whom the Editors are most grateful, whose work has made this volume possible. Ms Karen Lee, Assistant Editor, wrote the summaries of the *Hoshinmaru* and *Tomimaru* cases, *Tang, Hape, Van Zyl* and *Kigula* and saw the volume through the press. Ms Tara Grant prepared the summaries of the cases from Kenya and *Fuel Retailers*, the Tables of Cases and Digest and provided general and secretarial assistance. The Danish case was summarized by Mr Andrew Oppenheimer. Thanks are also due to the Danish Ministry of Justice for permitting us to use its translation of the *Thule Tribe Case* and to Dr Ole Spiermann for supplying it. Miss Maureen MacGlashan, CMG compiled the Table of Treaties and the Index. Mrs Diane Ilott checked the copy and Mr Ian Pickett read the proofs.

Finally, our thanks go to all the others who have worked to complete this volume, particularly our publishers, Cambridge University Press, and typesetters, Aptara, and their staff.

E. LAUTERPACHT

LAUTERPACHT CENTRE
   FOR INTERNATIONAL LAW,
UNIVERSITY OF CAMBRIDGE

C. J. GREENWOOD

THE PEACE PALACE,
THE HAGUE

June 2011

EDITORIAL NOTE

The *International Law Reports* endeavour to provide within a single series of volumes comprehensive access in English to judicial materials bearing on public international law. On certain topics it is not always easy to draw a clear line between cases which are essentially ones of public international law interest and those which are primarily applications of special domestic rules. For example, in relation to extradition, the *Reports* will include cases which bear on the exception of "political offences" or the rule of double criminality, but will restrict the number of cases dealing with purely procedural aspects of extradition. Similarly, while the general rules relating to the admission and exclusion of aliens, especially of refugees, are of international legal interest, cases on the procedure of admission usually are not. In such borderline areas, and sometimes also where there is a series of domestic decisions all dealing with a single point in essentially the same manner, only one illustrative decision will be printed and references to the remainder will be given in an accompanying note.

DECISIONS OF INTERNATIONAL TRIBUNALS

The *Reports* seek to include so far as possible the available decisions of every international tribunal, e.g. the International Court of Justice, or *ad hoc* arbitrations between States. There are, however, some jurisdictions to which full coverage cannot be given, either because of the large number of decisions (e.g. the Administrative Tribunal of the United Nations) or because not all the decisions bear on questions of public international law (e.g. the Court of Justice of the European Union). In these instances, those decisions are selected which appear to have the greatest long-term value.

Human rights cases. The number of decisions on questions of international protection of human rights has increased considerably in recent years and it is now impossible for the *Reports* to cover them all. As far as decisions of international jurisdictions are concerned, the *Reports* will continue to publish decisions of the European Court of Human Rights and of the Inter-American Court of Human Rights, as well as "views" of the United Nations Committee on Human Rights. Decisions of national courts on the application of conventions on human rights will not be published unless they deal with a major point of substantive human rights law or a matter of wider interest to public international lawyers such as the relationship of international law and national law, the extent of the right of derogation or the principles of the interpretation of treaties.

International arbitrations. The *Reports* of course include arbitral awards rendered in cases between States which involve an application of public international law. Beyond this, however, the selection of arbitral decisions is more open to debate. As these *Reports* are principally concerned with matters of public international law, they will not include purely private law commercial arbitrations even if they are international in the sense that they arise between parties of different nationality and even if one of them is a State. (For reports of a number of such awards, see *Yearbook Commercial Arbitration* (ed. Albert Jan van den Berg, under the auspices of the International Council for Commercial Arbitration).) But where there is a sufficient point of contact with public international law then the relevant parts of the award will be reported. Examples of such points of contact are cases in which the character of a State as a party has some relevance (e.g. State immunity, stabilization clauses, *force majeure*) or where there is a choice of law problem involving discussion of international law or general principles of law as possible applicable laws. The same criteria will determine the selection of decisions of national courts regarding the enforcement of arbitral awards.

Decisions of National Tribunals
A systematic effort is made to collect from all national jurisdictions those judicial decisions which have some bearing on international law.

Editorial Treatment of Materials
The basic policy of the Editors is, so far as possible, to present the material in its original form. It is no part of the editorial function to impose on the decisions printed in these volumes a uniformity of approach or style which they do not possess. Editorial intervention is limited to the introduction of the summary and of the bold-letter rubric at the head of each case. This is followed by the full text of the original decision or of its translation. Normally, the only passages which will be omitted are those which contain either statements of fact having no bearing on the points of international law involved in the case or discussion of matters of domestic law unrelated to the points of international legal interest. The omission of material is usually indicated either by a series of dots or by the insertion of a sentence in square brackets noting the passages which have been left out.

PRESENTATION OF MATERIALS
The material in the volume has been typeset for this volume. The source of all such material is indicated by the reference to the "Report" in square brackets at the end of the case. The language of the original decision is also mentioned there. The bold figures in square brackets in the body of the text in non-English cases indicate the pagination of the original report.

NOTES
Footnotes. Footnotes enclosed in square brackets are editorial insertions. All other footnotes are part of the original report.

Other notes. References to cases deemed not to be sufficiently substantial to warrant reporting will occasionally be found in editorial notes either at the end of a report of a case on a similar point or under an independent heading.

DIGEST OF CASES
With effect from Volume 75 the decisions contained in the *Reports* are no longer arranged according to the traditional classification scheme. Instead a Digest of Cases is published at the beginning of each volume. The main headings of the Digest are arranged alphabetically. Under each heading brief details are given of those cases reported in that volume which contain points covered by that heading. Each entry in the Digest gives the name of the case concerned and the page reference, the name of the tribunal which gave the decision and an indication of the main points raised in the case which relate to that particular heading of the Digest. Where a case raises points which concern several different areas of international law, entries relating to that case will appear under each of the relevant headings in the Digest. A list of the main headings used in the Digest is set out at p. xvii.

CONSOLIDATED INDEX AND TABLES
A Consolidated Index and a Consolidated Tables of Cases and Treaties for volumes 1-80 were published in two volumes in 1990 and 1991. A further volume containing the Consolidated Index and Consolidated Tables of Cases and Treaties for volumes 81-100 was published in 1996. A Consolidated Index, a Consolidated Tables of Cases and a Consolidated Table of Treaties for volumes 1-125 were published in 2004. Volume 140 contains Consolidated Tables of Cases for volumes 126-140.

TABLE OF CASES REPORTED
ALPHABETICAL

(Cases which are reported only in a note are distinguished from cases which are reported in full by the insertion of the word "note" in parentheses after the page number of the report.)

Al-Dahas v. Attorney-General and Others 331

Attorney-General (Uganda) v. Kigula and Others 667

Death Penalty Constitutionality Case 667

Fuel Retailers Association of Southern Africa v. Director-General Environmental Management, Department of Agriculture, Conservation and Environment, Mpumalanga Province and Others 426

Hape v. The Queen (Attorney-General of Ontario intervening) 140

Hingitaq 53, Petersen and Others v. Office of the Prime Minister of Denmark 277, 298 (note)

The Hoshinmaru (Japan v. Russian Federation) (Application for Prompt Release) 1

Kenya (Sitamze) v. Minister for Home Affairs and Others 349

Khadr v. Canada (No 1) 212
Khadr v. Canada (No 2) 225
Kigula Case 667

R v. Hape 140
R v. Tang 76
RM (a minor, through next friend JK) v. Attorney-General 299

Sitamze Case 349

Tang Case 76
Thule Tribe Case 277
The Tomimaru (Japan v. Russian Federation) (Application for Prompt Release) 36

Van Zyl and Others v. Government of Republic of South Africa and Others 473
Von Abo v. Republic of South Africa and Others 577, 666 (note)

Yong Vui Kong v. Public Prosecutor 374

TABLE OF CASES REPORTED
ARRANGED ACCORDING TO COURTS AND
TRIBUNALS (INTERNATIONAL CASES) AND
COUNTRIES (MUNICIPAL CASES)

(Cases which are reported only in a note are distinguished from cases which are reported in full by the insertion of the word "note" in parentheses after the page number of the report.)

I. DECISIONS OF INTERNATIONAL TRIBUNALS

International Tribunal for the Law of the Sea

2007
The Hoshinmaru (Japan v. Russian Federation) (Application for Prompt Release) 1

The Tomimaru (Japan v. Russian Federation) (Application for Prompt Release) 36

II. DECISIONS OF MUNICIPAL COURTS

Australia

2008
R v. Tang 76

Canada

2007
Hape v. Her Majesty the Queen (Attorney-General of Ontario intervening) 140

2008
Khadr v. Canada (No 1) 212

2009
Khadr v. Canada (No 2) 225, 228

2010
Khadr v. Canada (No 2) 225, 264

Denmark

2003
Hingitaq 53, Petersen and Others v. Office of the Prime Minister of Denmark 277, 298 (note)

Kenya

2006
RM (a minor, through next friend JK) v. Attorney-General 299

2007
Al-Dahas v. Attorney-General and Others 331

2008
Republic of Kenya v. Minister for Home Affairs and Others, *ex parte* Sitamze 349

Singapore

2010
Yong Vui Kong v. Public Prosecutor 374

South Africa

2005
Van Zyl and Others v. Government of Republic of South Africa and Others 473, 478

2007

Fuel Retailers Association of Southern Africa v. Director-General Environmental Management, Department of Agriculture, Conservation and Environment, Mpumalanga Province and Others 426

Van Zyl and Others v. Government of Republic of South Africa and Others 473, 545

2008

Von Abo v. Republic of South Africa and Others 577, 581

2009

Von Abo v. Republic of South Africa and Others 577, 624

2010

Von Abo v. Republic of South Africa and Others 577, 643

2011

Republic of South Africa and Others v. Von Abo 577, 666 (note)

Uganda

2009

Attorney-General v. Kigula and Others 667

DIGEST OF CASES
List of Main Headings

(Those headings for which there are entries in the present volume are printed in italics. For a guide to the Digest, see the Editorial Note at p. xi.)

Air	*International Tribunals*
Aliens	*Jurisdiction*
Arbitration	Lakes and Landlocked Seas
Canals	*Nationality*
Claims	Recognition
Comity	Relationship of International Law and Municipal Law
Conciliation	Reprisals and Countermeasures
Consular Relations	Rivers
Damages	*Sea*
Diplomatic Relations	Sources of International Law
Economics, Trade and Finance	Space
Environment	State Immunity
Expropriation	State Responsibility
Extradition	State Succession
Governments	States
Human Rights	*Territory*
International Court of Justice	Terrorism
International Criminal Law	*Treaties*
International Organizations	*War and Armed Conflict*

DIGEST OF CASES
REPORTED IN VOLUME 143

Page

Claims

Exhaustion of local remedies — Diplomatic protection — Exhaustion of local remedies rule for international delict — Whether effective local remedies available — South Africa, High Court (Transvaal Provincial Division), Constitutional Court and High Court (North Gauteng Division)

Von Abo v. Republic of South Africa and Others   577

Exhaustion of local remedies — Diplomatic protection — Exhaustion of local remedies rule for international delict — Whether exhaustion of local remedies rule disqualifying South African Government from affording diplomatic protection to appellants — Whether Lesotho courts rectifying wrongs — South Africa, High Court and Supreme Court of Appeal

Van Zyl and Others v. Government of Republic of South Africa and Others   473

Comity

Comity of nations as interpretative principle — Appropriateness of comity — Whether any clear violations of international law — Canada, Supreme Court

Khadr v. Canada (No 1)   212

Comity of nations as interpretative principle — Appropriateness of comity — Whether any clear violations of international law — Canada, Supreme Court

Hape v. Her Majesty the Queen (Attorney-General of Ontario intervening)   140

Diplomatic Relations

Diplomatic protection — Appellants requesting diplomatic protection from Government of South Africa against Government of Lesotho — Whether State having obligation to provide diplomatic protection — Position under international law — Whether South Africa entitled to afford appellants diplomatic protection —

xix

Diplomatic Relations (*cont.*)

Whether appellants having right to diplomatic protection under South African law — South African Constitution — Responsibility of executive for conducting foreign relations — Discretion of executive with respect to diplomatic relations — Principle of equal sovereignty of States — Policy considerations — Lesotho cancelling and revoking mining leases without payment of compensation — Whether international delict — Whether violating international minimum standards — Whether expropriation — Nationality requirement — Exhaustion of local remedies requirement — Whether claim admissible before international tribunal — South Africa, High Court and Supreme Court of Appeal

Van Zyl and Others v. Government of Republic of South Africa and Others 473

Diplomatic protection — Applicant requesting diplomatic protection from Government of South Africa against Government of Zimbabwe — Whether applicant entitled to diplomatic protection — Whether State having obligation to provide diplomatic protection — Position under international law — Whether South Africa entitled to afford diplomatic protection — South African Constitution — Responsibility of executive for conducting foreign relations — Discretion of executive with respect to diplomatic relations — Zimbabwean expropriation of farmland — Whether violating international minimum standards — South Africa, High Court (Transvaal Provincial Division), Constitutional Court and High Court (North Gauteng Division)

Von Abo v. Republic of South Africa and Others 577

Environment

Protection of the environment — Relationship between the protection of the environment and development — Concept of sustainable development — Recognition of sustainable development by the international community — Principle of integration of environmental protection and socio-economic development — International environmental law and sustainable development — Concept of sustainable development in the law of South Africa — South Africa, Constitutional Court

Fuel Retailers Association of Southern Africa v. Director-General Environmental Management, Department of Agriculture, Conservation and Environment, Mpumalanga Province and Others 426

DIGEST OF CASES xxi

Human Rights

Discrimination — Grounds for non-discrimination in international and domestic law — Convention on the Rights of the Child, 1989 — African Charter on the Rights and Welfare of the Child, 1990 — Constitution of Kenya — Children Act 2001 of Kenya, Section 24(3) — Parental responsibility — Whether part of *jus cogens* — Parental responsibility for children born out of wedlock — Whether non-discrimination provisions under the Constitution and the Children Act 2001 of Kenya inconsistent — Whether non-discrimination provisions under Constitution and international obligations inconsistent — Whether vesting parental responsibility in mother in first instance discriminatory — Principle of equality and non-discrimination — Margin of appreciation — Whether distinction for legitimate purpose — Whether distinction reasonable in light of legitimate aim — Kenya, High Court

 RM (a minor, through next friend JK) v. Attorney-General 299

Economic, social and cultural rights — Right of everyone to safe and clean environment — Inter-generational and intra-generational equity — Constitution of South Africa, Section 24 — Environment Conservation Act 1989 — National Environmental Management Act 1998 — Obligation to protect environment and promote economic and social development — Interrelationship between environment and development — Environmental authorities — Nature and scope of obligation on environmental authorities to consider socio-economic factors — Delegation of duties to local council — Whether environmental authorities fulfilled their statutory duty — Whether environmental authorities had properly considered impact of proposed development on socio-economic conditions — South Africa, Constitutional Court

 Fuel Retailers Association of Southern Africa v. Director-General Environmental Management, Department of Agriculture, Conservation and Environment, Mpumalanga Province and Others 426

Indigenous peoples — Property rights — Recognition of indigenous land rights — Indigenous Inughuit population of Thule in Greenland — ILO Convention No 169 concerning Indigenous and Tribal Peoples in Independent Countries, 1989 — Whether Inughuit constituting distinct indigenous people separate from main population within meaning of Convention —

Human Rights (*cont.*)

Forced resettlement in 1953 to make way for United States air base — Right to return — Right to compensation — United States–Denmark Agreement concerning the Defence of Greenland, 1951 — Whether providing adequate legal basis for expropriation and resettlement under municipal and international law — Whether satisfying requirements for legality under Danish Constitution — Denmark, Supreme Court

Hingitaq 53, Petersen and Others v. Office of the Prime Minister of Denmark   277

Inhuman treatment — Protection of fundamental human rights when Canadian officers operating abroad — Requirement that Canadian officials follow foreign laws and procedures — Comity — Whether foreign procedures violating fundamental human rights — Whether Canadian Charter of Rights and Freedoms applicable extraterritorially — Canadian officials interviewing Canadian national detained at Guantánamo Bay — National subjected to sleep deprivation by United States authorities — Whether engaging responsibility of Canada — Convention against Torture, 1984 — Convention on the Rights of the Child, 1989 — Remedies — Canada, Federal Court of Appeal and Supreme Court

Khadr v. Canada (No 2)   225

Protection of fundamental human rights when Canadian officers investigating abroad — Effective participation in fight against transnational crime — Requirement that Canadian officials follow foreign laws and procedures — Comity — Whether foreign procedures violating fundamental human rights — Balance — Whether international law or Canadian Charter of Rights and Freedoms appropriate vehicle to achieve balance — Whether Charter applying extraterritorially — Canada, Supreme Court

Hape v. Her Majesty the Queen (Attorney-General of Ontario intervening)   140

Protection of fundamental human rights when Canadian officers operating abroad — Requirement that Canadian officials follow foreign laws and procedures — Comity — Whether foreign procedures violating fundamental human rights — Whether Canadian Charter of Rights and Freedoms applicable extraterritorially — Canada, Supreme Court

Khadr v. Canada (No 1)   212

Refugees — Immigration Act, Sections 3 and 8 — Detention of prohibited immigrants — Repatriation — Whether extended detention contrary to rights under Constitution and international conventions — Whether failed repatriation rendered deportation orders invalid — Whether Sections 3 and 8 of Immigration Act contrary to provisions of Constitution — Whether continued detention of applicant unlawful — Kenya, High Court

Al-Dahas v. Attorney-General and Others   331

Refugees — Rights of refugees under international law and municipal law — Constitution of Kenya, Section 70(a) — United Nations Convention Relating to the Status of Refugees, 1951, Articles 31, 32 and 33 — Organization of African Unity Convention Governing the Specific Aspects of Refugee Problems in Africa, 1969 — Obligations of States in refugee protection — Limitation of individual rights in international and municipal law — Obligations of asylum seekers to contact authorities in receiving State — Kenya, High Court

Al-Dahas v. Attorney-General and Others   331

Right to life — Death penalty — Constitutionality of death penalty — International instruments — Whether abolishing death penalty — Freedom from torture, cruel, inhuman or degrading punishment — Whether two issues to be dealt with separately — Whether imposition of death penalty in Uganda constituting cruel, inhuman or degrading punishment — Whether framers of Constitution of Uganda purposefully providing for death penalty — Constitutional interpretation — Reading death penalty provisions as whole and in relation to relevant international instruments — Uganda's history and background — Punishment for political purposes — Whether conflict between Articles 22(1) and 44(a) of Constitution of Uganda — Whether death penalty inconsistent with Articles 20, 21, 22(1), 24, 28, 44(a) and 45 of Constitution of Uganda — Uganda, Supreme Court

Attorney-General v. Kigula and Others   667

Right to life — Death penalty — Constitutionality of mandatory death penalty — Inherency of individual's right — Right to equality before and under law — Right to fair, speedy and public hearing before independent and impartial tribunal — Right to legal representation at State's expense for offence carrying death sentence — Whether sentencing part of trial — Whether Ugandan laws providing for mandatory death sentence inconsistent with Articles 20,

Human Rights (*cont.*)

21, 22, 24, 28 and 44(a) of Constitution of Uganda — Uganda, Supreme Court

    Attorney-General v. Kigula and Others   667

Right to life — Death penalty — Long delay between death sentence pronouncement and execution — Whether unreasonable delay rendering execution unconstitutional — Death-row syndrome — Whether constituting cruel, inhuman and degrading treatment contrary to Articles 24 and 44 of Constitution — Uganda, Supreme Court

    Attorney-General v. Kigula and Others   667

Right to life — Death penalty — Mode of hanging — Constitutionality — Whether causing excessive pain and suffering — Whether constituting cruel, inhuman and degrading treatment contrary to Articles 24 and 44 of Constitution — Uganda, Supreme Court

    Attorney-General v. Kigula and Others   667

Right to life — Inhuman treatment and punishment — Mandatory death penalty — Whether contrary to customary international law — Whether inhuman — Constitution of Singapore — Whether prohibiting inhuman punishment — Equal protection of the laws — Whether violated by mandatory death penalty for trafficking more than specified quantity of drugs — Singapore, Court of Appeal

    Yong Vui Kong v. Public Prosecutor   374

Right to work and right to family life — Protection of rights to work and to family life under Constitution of Kenya 1963 and international human rights instruments — Enforceability of rights by non-nationals — Refusal of work permit — Whether refusal of work permit to non-national married to Kenyan national a breach of right to work and right to family life — Protection of fundamental rights in accordance with domestic law — Sections 5 and 8 of Immigration Act 1967 — Whether abuse of discretionary powers by executive — Whether reason and effect of denial of work permit a breach of applicant's rights — Separation of powers — Role of executive in maintaining public order and acting in the public interest — Kenya, High Court

    Republic of Kenya v. Minister for Home Affairs and Others, ex parte Sitamze   349

International Criminal Law

Offences against humanity — International Convention to Suppress the Slave Trade and Slavery, 1926 — Slavery — Definition — Definition of slavery in Australian Criminal Code (Cth) deriving from definition in Article 1 of Convention — Whether respondent possessing and using complainants as slaves — Whether proof of intention required — Sections 270.1 and 270.3(1)(a) of Code — Meaning and constitutional validity — Convictions in Australia of slavery offences contrary to Section 270.3(1)(a) of Code — Provisions in Chapter 8 of Code dealing with offences against humanity — Australia, High Court

R v. Tang   76

International Tribunals

International Tribunal for the Law of the Sea — Jurisdiction and admissibility — United Nations Convention on the Law of the Sea, 1982, Article 292 — Japan filing Application against Russian Federation for prompt release of vessel — Whether Tribunal having jurisdiction — Whether Application admissible — Whether Russian Federation breaching obligations under Article 73(2) of Convention — International Tribunal for the Law of the Sea

The Hoshinmaru (Japan v. Russian Federation) (Application for Prompt Release)   1

International Tribunal for the Law of the Sea — Jurisdiction and admissibility — United Nations Convention on the Law of the Sea, 1982, Article 292 — Japan filing Application against Russian Federation for prompt release of vessel — Whether Tribunal having jurisdiction — Whether Application admissible — Whether Russian Federation breaching obligations under Article 73(2) of Convention — Domestic proceedings before Russian courts — Russian Federation confiscating vessel — Effect of confiscation — Whether confiscation rendering application for prompt release of vessel under Article 292 of Convention without object — International Tribunal for the Law of the Sea

The Tomimaru (Japan v. Russian Federation) (Application for Prompt Release)   36

Jurisdiction

Principles of jurisdiction — Principles arising from sovereign equality and duty of non-intervention — Bases of jurisdiction — Interplay between various forms and bases of jurisdiction —

Jurisdiction (*cont.*)

Whether extraterritorial exercise of jurisdiction permissible — Enforcement jurisdiction — Limits on extraterritorial jurisdiction based on sovereign equality, non-intervention and territoriality principle — Principle of consent — Whether Canada permitted to exercise enforcement jurisdiction over matter outside Canadian territory without consent of other State — Whether Canadian Charter of Rights and Freedoms having extraterritorial application — Whether Section 32 of Charter having territorial limitations — Canada, Supreme Court

Hape v. Her Majesty the Queen (Attorney-General of Ontario intervening)   140

Nationality

Diplomatic protection — Nationality requirement for international delict — Whether nationality rule disqualifying South African Government from affording diplomatic protection to appellants — Continuous nationality rule — South Africa, High Court and Supreme Court of Appeal

Van Zyl and Others v. Government of Republic of South Africa and Others   473

Diplomatic protection — Nationality requirement for international delict — Whether nationality rule disqualifying South African Government from affording diplomatic protection to applicant — Applicant sole shareholder in companies incorporated in Zimbabwe — Whether expropriation of property of companies by Zimbabwe capable of giving rise to diplomatic protection by South Africa — South Africa, High Court (Transvaal Provincial Division), Constitutional Court and High Court (North Gauteng Division)

Von Abo v. Republic of South Africa and Others   577

Relationship of International Law and Municipal Law

Canadian Charter of Rights and Freedoms — Interpretation and application — Interpretation of Section 32(1) of Charter — Jurisdictional scope — Extraterritorial application — Canada's obligations under international law — Canadian national detained at Guantánamo Bay — Whether Charter of Rights and Freedoms applicable to extent of Canadian participation in detention and proposed trial — Remedies for violation of Charter rights — Conduct of foreign relations by the Government — Justiciability — Whether appropriate for Court to order that Government request United States authorities to repatriate Canadian national detained at Guantánamo Bay — Canada, Federal Court of Appeal and Supreme Court

Khadr v. Canada (No 2)   225

Canadian Charter of Rights and Freedoms — Interpretation and application — Interpretation of Section 32(1) of Charter — Jurisdictional scope — Extraterritorial application — Canada's obligations under international law — Domestic reception of international law — Doctrine of adoption — Prohibitive rules of customary international law as interpretative aid — Principle of respect for sovereignty of foreign States — Principle of non-intervention — Principle of respect for territorial sovereignty of foreign States — Comity as interpretative principle — Presumption of conformity of Canadian legislation to international law — Investigatory actions by Canadian law enforcement officials in Turks and Caicos Islands — Whether Section 8 of Charter applying to searches and seizures by Canadian police outside Canada — Canada, Supreme Court

Hape v. Her Majesty the Queen (Attorney-General of Ontario intervening)   140

Canadian Charter of Rights and Freedoms — Interpretation and application — Interpretation of Section 32(1) of Charter — Jurisdictional scope — Extraterritorial application — Canada's obligations under international law — Principle of respect for sovereignty of foreign States — Principle of respect for territorial sovereignty of foreign States — Comity — Whether Charter of Rights and Freedoms applicable to acts of Canadian officials in territory under the jurisdiction of a foreign State — Whether applicability affected by fact that foreign State's actions contrary to international law binding upon Canada — Canadian national detained at Guantánamo Bay — Whether Charter of Rights and Freedoms applicable to extent of Canadian participation in detention and proposed trial — Canada, Supreme Court

Khadr v. Canada (No 1)   212

Conduct of foreign relations — Whether justiciable in municipal court — South Africa, High Court and Supreme Court of Appeal

Van Zyl and Others v. Government of Republic of South Africa and Others   473

Relationship of International Law and Municipal Law (*cont.*)

Conduct of foreign relations — Whether justiciable in municipal court — Nature of protection — Whether court entitled to question efficacy of steps taken by South African Government — South Africa, High Court (Transvaal Provincial Division), Constitutional Court and High Court (North Gauteng Division)

Von Abo v. Republic of South Africa and Others   577

Customary international law — Whether part of the law of Singapore — Requirement that customary international law be adopted by the Singapore courts before forming part of Singapore law — Alleged customary international law rule prohibiting mandatory death penalty — Inconsistency with Singapore legislation — Singapore, Court of Appeal

Yong Vui Kong v. Public Prosecutor   374

Environmental law — International law on environmental protection — Relevance in interpreting and applying domestic environmental law — South Africa, Constitutional Court

Fuel Retailers Association of Southern Africa v. Director-General Environmental Management, Department of Agriculture, Conservation and Environment, Mpumalanga Province and Others   426

Treaties — Effect in municipal law — International Convention to Suppress the Slave Trade and Slavery, 1926 — Sections 270.1 and 270.3(1)(a) of Australian Criminal Code (Cth) — Construction and application of Code — Relevant provisions introducing into Australian municipal law offences deriving from 1926 Slavery Convention — Constitutional validity of Sections 270.1 and 270.3(1)(a) of Code — Australia, High Court

R v. Tang   76

Treaties — International human rights treaties and instruments — International Covenant on Economic, Social and Cultural Rights, 1966 — International Covenant on Civil and Political Rights, 1966 — Declaration of Human Rights of Individuals Who Are Not Nationals of the Country In Which They Live, 1985 — Constitution of Kenya 1963 — Interpretation — Whether Constitution of Kenya capable of giving effect to provisions of international human rights instruments to which Kenya a State party — Whether Constitution capable of giving effect to rights not expressly mentioned — Enforceability of rights by non-nationals — Kenya, High Court

Republic of Kenya v. Minister for Home Affairs and Others, ex parte Sitamze   349

Treaties — Ratification without reservation of international instrument — Incorporation in domestic legislation — Whether States obliged to mirror provisions of international instruments in domestic legislation — Margin of appreciation — Constitution of Kenya — Conflict between international law and domestic law — Bangalore Principles, 1989 — Supremacy of Constitution where clear and unambiguous — Inability of court to expand provisions of Constitution where clear and unambiguous — Kenya, High Court

RM (a minor, through next friend JK) v. Attorney-General   299

Treaty obligations — Effect under municipal law — United States–Denmark Agreement concerning the Defence of Greenland, 1951 — Obligations of State in relation to private claimants — Memorandum of Understanding between States Parties to Agreement — Effect on rights of private claimants — Interpretation of treaties — ILO Convention No 169 concerning Indigenous and Tribal Peoples in Independent Countries, 1989 — Denmark, Supreme Court

Hingitaq 53, Petersen and Others v. Office of the Prime Minister of Denmark   277

United Nations Convention on the Law of the Sea, 1982 — Decisions of courts of Russian Federation — Confiscation of fishing vessel — Issues of ownership and nationality — Whether confiscation having impact on nationality of the vessel — Role of flag State — Whether confiscation rendering application for prompt release of vessel under Article 292 of Convention without object — Object and purpose of prompt release procedure — Article 292(3) of Convention — Decision of Russian Federation Supreme Court concluding domestic court proceedings — Encroachment upon national competences — Article 292(3) of Convention — International Tribunal for the Law of the Sea

The Tomimaru (Japan v. Russian Federation) (Application for Prompt Release)   36

Sea

Exclusive economic zone ("EEZ") — Environment — Arrest and detention of Japanese vessel fishing in EEZ of Russian Federation with valid licence — Application for prompt release — Alleged offence of false record of catch of fish — Gravity of offence — Conservation and management of fish stocks in Russian EEZ — Bilateral cooperation between Japan and Russian Federation — International Tribunal for the Law of the Sea

The Hoshinmaru (Japan v. Russian Federation) (Application for Prompt Release)   1

Sources of International Law

Customary international law — Requirement of extensive and virtually uniform State practice — Whether rule of customary international law prohibiting the mandatory death penalty — Retention of mandatory death penalty by thirty-one States — Significance — Singapore, Court of Appeal

Yong Vui Kong v. Public Prosecutor   374

Territory

Territorial sovereignty — Customary international law — Principle of respect for sovereignty of foreign State — Principle of sovereign equality — Article 2(1) of United Nations Charter — 1970 UN General Assembly Declaration applying principle to non-UN Member States — Principle of non-intervention — Principle of respect for territorial sovereignty of foreign States — Whether extraterritorial application of Canadian Charter of Rights and Freedoms interfering with sovereign authority of foreign State — Canada, Supreme Court

Hape v. Her Majesty the Queen (Attorney-General of Ontario intervening)   140

Territorial sovereignty — Customary international law — Principle of respect for sovereignty of foreign State — Principle of sovereign equality — Whether extraterritorial application of Canadian Charter of Rights and Freedoms interfering with sovereign authority of foreign State — Canada, Supreme Court

Khadr v. Canada (No 1)   212

Treaties

Interpretation and application — United Nations Convention on the Law of the Sea, 1982 — Articles 73(2) and 292 — Whether Respondent complying with Article 73(2) of Convention — Whether Respondent providing for prompt release of vessel and crew upon posting of a reasonable bond or financial security — Time-limit for setting bond — Whether bond reasonable — Relevant factors — Facts and circumstances of case — Document concerning bond calculation communicated by Russia to Japan within framework of Russian–Japanese Commission on Fisheries — Whether Japan tacitly consenting — Whether bond of 22 million roubles reasonable — Determination by Tribunal of amount, nature and form of bond or other financial security to be posted — Article 113(2) of Rules of Tribunal — Article 293 of Convention — Applicability of Convention provisions and other international law rules not incompatible with Convention — International Tribunal for the Law of the Sea

The Hoshinmaru (Japan v. Russian Federation) (Application for Prompt Release)   1

War and Armed Conflict

Combatants — Detention and trial of enemy combatants — Detention of persons captured in Afghanistan conflict — Guantánamo Bay — Whether detention and proposed trial by military commission contrary to international law — Canada, Supreme Court

Khadr v. Canada (No 1)   212

Combatants — Detention and trial of enemy combatants — Detention of persons captured in Afghanistan conflict — Guantánamo Bay — Whether detention and proposed trial by military commission contrary to international law — Canada, Federal Court of Appeal and Supreme Court

Khadr v. Canada (No 2)   225

TABLE OF TREATIES

This table contains a list, in chronological order according to the date of signature, of the treaties referred to in the decisions printed in the present volume. It has not been possible to draw a helpful distinction between treaties judicially considered and treaties which are merely cited.

In the case of bilateral treaties, the names of the parties are given in alphabetical order. Multilateral treaties are referred to by the name by which they are believed commonly to be known. References to the texts of treaties have been supplied, including wherever possible at least one reference to a text in the English language. The full titles of the abbreviated references will be found in the list of Abbreviations and Sources printed in the volume containing the Consolidated Table of Treaties to Volumes 1-125.

1890
July 2   General Act of the Brussels Conference relative to the African Slave Trade, and Declaration (17 Martens NRG, 2nd ser. 345; 82 BFSP 55; 2 US Treaties 1964; 18 Traités 496; 19 Hertslet 278; 173 CTS 293)
　　　　　Preamble 88

1919
Sept. 10   Convention of St Germain revising the General Act of Berlin, 1885 and the General Act and Declaration of Brussels, 1890 (112 BFSP 901; UKTS 18 (1919); 3 US Treaties 3739; 225 CTS 501)
　　　　　Art. 2 88

1926
Sept. 25   International Convention for the Abolition of Slavery and the Slave Trade (60 LNTS 253; 3 Hudson 2010; 4 US Treaties 5022; USTS 778; UKTS 16 (1927)) 101-2, 113-14, 117
　　　　　Preamble 88
　　　　　Art. 1 .... 88-94, 105, 108, 122-3
　　　　　Art. 1(1) 88-90, 129-30
　　　　　Art. 2 88

1945
June 26   Charter of the United Nations (9 Hudson 327; UKTS 67 (1946), Cmd 7015; 145 BFSP 805; USTS 993; 1 Peaslee 1288; 59 Stat 1031; 1 UNTS 16; 39 AJIL (1945) Supp. 190;

JOF 13 January 1946; 3 Bevans 1153; Blackstone's *International Law Documents*, 8th edn 9 (amended version))
Chapter I
Art. 2(1) 156-8, 528

June 26   Statute of the International Court of Justice (9 Hudson 510; UKTS 67 (1946), Cmd 7015; USTS 993; 145 BFSP 832; 1 Peaslee 1322; 3 Bevans 1179; 1945 CanTS 7; 39 AJIL (1945) Supp. 215n; JOF 13 January 1946; 59 Stat 1031)
Chapter II
Art. 38(1)(d) 417-18

1950
Nov. 4   European Convention for the Protection of Human Rights and Fundamental Freedoms, First Protocol (20 March 1952) (213 UNTS 262; 159 BFSP 355; UKTS 46 (1954), Cmd 9221; ETS 9; Blackstone's *International Law Documents*, 8th edn 55)
Art. 1 .... 475 n. 3

1951
July 28   Convention Relating to the Status of Refugees (Geneva Convention) (189 UNTS 150; UKTS 39 (1954), Cmd 9171; 158 BFSP 499; ATS 5 (1954); NZTS 2 (1961); JOF 29 October 1954; 3 Vert A 28; Blackstone's *International Law Documents*, 8th edn 69) 338-9
Chapter I
Art. 2 340-1
Art. 3 340-1
Chapter V
Art. 31 340-1
Art. 31(1) 345-8
Art. 32 340-1
Art. 33 340-1
Art. 33(1) 462

1956
Sept. 7   Supplementary Convention for the Abolition of Slavery, the Slave Trade and Institutions and Practices Similar to Slavery (266 UNTS 3; UKTS 59 (1957); 162 BFSP 759) 101-2, 105, 108
Art. 1 .... 91, 125 n. 139
Art. 1(a) .... 124 n. 137
Art. 7 88-9
Art. 7(b) .... 124 n. 137

1957
Mar. 25 Treaty Establishing the European Economic Community (Treaty of Rome) (as amended by the Treaties of Amsterdam and Nice) (TEC) (2002 OJ C 325/1)
Art. 307(1) 106-7

1965
Mar. 18 Convention on the Settlement of Investment Disputes between States and Nationals of Other States (ICSID) (575 UNTS 159; UKTS 25 (1967), Cmnd 3255; 17 UST 1270; TIAS 6090; 1966 UNJYB 196; 60 AJIL (1966) 892; 4 ILM 532 (1965)) 490-1, 583-5, 586-91, 596, 603-4
615, 623, 626, 652, 656
Art. 25 .... 520-1, 566-7, 569

1966
Dec. 16 International Covenant on Civil and Political Rights (999 UNTS 171; UKTS 6 (1977), Cmnd 6702; JOF 30 June 1981; 50 Vert A 683; 6 ILM 368 (1967); 1966 UNJYB 178; 1966 YBHR 442; 30 ZaöRV 365; Brownlie, *Basic Documents in International Affairs*, 3rd edn 270; Blackstone's *International Law Documents*, 8th edn 108) .... 385, 475 n. 3, 496-7
Art. 2 340
Art. 6(1) 678
Art. 6(4) 678
Art. 6(5) 325
Art. 7 .... 361-3, 679, 684-5, 716, 723, 728

Dec. 16 International Covenant on Economic, Social and Cultural Rights (993 UNTS 3; UKTS 6 (1977), Cmnd 6702; 6 ILM 360 (1967); 1966 UNJYB 170; Blackstone's *International Law Documents*, 8th edn 101) .... 369-71, 372, 475 n. 3, 496-7
Preamble 366-7, 369-70
Art. 1 .... 360, 370-2
Art. 2 370-1
Art. 6(1) 363-4, 365, 367
Art. 6(2) 352, 355, 363-4, 365, 367

1969
Sept. 10 OAU Convention Governing the Specific Aspects of Refugee Problems in Africa (OAU Doc. No CAB/LEG/24.3) 335, 346
Art. 8 345

Nov. 22   American Convention on Human Rights (1144 UNTS 123; PAULTS 36; 9 ILM 673 (1970); 65 AJIL (1971) 679; Blackstone's *International Law Documents*, 8th edn 146)
          Art. 21(2) 495

1979
Dec. 18   Convention on the Elimination of All Forms of Discrimination Against Women (CEDAW) (1249 UNTS 13; Parl. Papers, Misc 1 (1982), 8444; 19 ILM 33 (1980); 21 IndJIL 155; UKTS 2 (1989), Cm 643)
          Art. 2(f) 306-7
          Art. 16(1)(d) 307

1980
May 20   Convention on the Conservation of Antarctic Marine Living Resources (CCAMLR) (UKTS 48 (1982), Cmnd 8714; TIAS 10240; 19 ILM 841 (1980); 33 UST 3476) 35

1981
June 26   African Charter on Human and Peoples' Rights (Banjul Charter) (27 RevICJ 64; 21 ILM 58 (1982); Blackstone's *International Law Documents*, 8th edn 191)
          Art. 4 681
          Art. 14 495
          Art. 15 365

1982
Dec. 10   UN Convention on the Law of the Sea (UNCLOS) (21 ILM 1261 (1982); Misc 11 (1983), 8941; 1833 UNTS 3 (1994); Brownlie, *Basic Documents in International Affairs*, 3rd edn 129)
          Part V
          Art. 73(1) 61-2
          Art. 73(2) 8, 9-10, 17-18, 19, 20-6, 28, 30-5,
                                              43-4, 51, 64-5, 69-70
          Art. 73(3) 61
          Part VII, Section 1
          Art. 94 54
          Part XV, Section 2
          Art. 292 .... 5-35, 41-75
          Art. 292(1) 19-21, 22, 32-4, 51-2, 62-3
          Art. 292(2) 32-3
          Art. 292(3) 21, 24-5, 29-30, 52, 55, 56, 57-8, 62, 68-9
          Art. 292(4) 30

1984

Dec. 7 Japan–USSR, Agreement on Mutual Relations in the Field of Fisheries off the Coast of Both Countries 34

Dec. 10 UN Convention against Torture and Other Cruel, Inhuman and Degrading Treatment or Punishment (New York Convention) (UKTS 107 (1991), Cm 1775; 1465 UNTS 85; 23 ILM 1027 (1984); 24 ILM 535 (1985); 6 EHRR 259; Blackstone's *International Law Documents*, 8th edn 309) ... 238, 245, 252, 256
    Part I
    Art. 1 680

Dec. 10 UN Convention against Torture and Other Cruel, Inhuman and Degrading Treatment or Punishment (New York Convention), Optional Protocol of 18 December 2002 (2375 UNTS 237; UNGA resolution A/RES/57/199 of 9 January 2003) 680-1

1985

May 12 Japan–USSR, Agreement on Cooperation in the Field of Fisheries 34

1989

June 27 Indigenous and Tribal Peoples in Independent Countries (ILO Convention 169)
    Art. 1(1) 295-6
    Art. 1(1)(a) 293
    Art. 1(1)(b) 292, 293
    Art. 12 292
    Art. 14 292
    Art. 16 292
    Art. 16(3) 296

Nov. 20 Convention on the Rights of the Child (1577 UNTS 3; UKTS 44 (1992), Cm 1976; 28 ILM 1448 (1989); Blackstone's *International Law Documents*, 5th edn 344) 250-1, 252, 256, 309, 314
    Preamble 305
    Art. 2 301
    Art. 2(1) 305
    Art. 3 301
    Art. 18(1) 305-6
    Art. 37(a) 245

Nov. 20   Convention on the Rights of the Child (1577 UNTS 3; UKTS 44 (1992), Cm 1976; 28 ILM 1448 (1989); Blackstone's *International Law Documents*, 5th edn 344), Optional Protocol on the Involvement of Children in Armed Conflict (25 May 2000) (2220 UNTS 161; 2002 CanTS 5) 252, 256

1990
July 11   African Charter on the Rights and Welfare of the Child (CAB/LEG/24.9/49 (1990)) 309, 314
    Art. 2 301
    Art. 3 .... 301, 306
    Art. 4 306
    Art. 18(3) 306
    Art. 20(1) 306

1997
Dec. 18   UN–International Tribunal for the Law of the Sea Agreement on Cooperation and Relationship (ITLOS) (available at www.itlos.org) 6, 42

1998
July 17   Rome Statute of the International Criminal Court (2187 UNTS 90; 37 ILM 999 (1998); Blackstone's *International Law Documents*, 8th edn 428; Schabas, *An Introduction to the International Criminal Court* (2001))
    Art. 7(2)(c) 89

Nov. 1   European Convention for the Protection of Human Rights and Fundamental Freedoms (1950) as amended by Protocol 11, effective as of 1 November 1998 (ETS 5; Blackstone's *International Law Documents*, 8th edn 46)
    Art. 2(1) 715
    Art. 3 .... 400, 714-15, 720-2
    Art. 8 371-2
    Art. 14 371
    Art. 63 402

International tribunals — International Tribunal for the Law of the Sea — Jurisdiction and admissibility — United Nations Convention on the Law of the Sea, 1982, Article 292 — Japan filing Application against Russian Federation for prompt release of vessel — Whether Tribunal having jurisdiction — Whether Application admissible — Whether Russian Federation breaching obligations under Article 73(2) of Convention

Treaties — Interpretation and application — United Nations Convention on the Law of the Sea, 1982 — Articles 73(2) and 292 — Whether Respondent complying with Article 73(2) of Convention — Whether Respondent providing for prompt release of vessel and crew upon posting of a reasonable bond or financial security — Time-limit for setting bond — Whether bond reasonable — Relevant factors — Facts and circumstances of case — Document concerning bond calculation communicated by Russia to Japan within framework of Russian–Japanese Commission on Fisheries — Whether Japan tacitly consenting — Whether bond of 22 million roubles reasonable — Determination by Tribunal of amount, nature and form of bond or other financial security to be posted — Article 113(2) of Rules of Tribunal — Article 293 of Convention — Applicability of Convention provisions and other international law rules not incompatible with Convention

Sea — Exclusive economic zone ("EEZ") — Environment — Arrest and detention of Japanese vessel fishing in EEZ of Russian Federation with valid licence — Application for prompt release — Alleged offence of false record of catch of fish — Gravity of offence — Conservation and management of fish stocks in Russian EEZ — Bilateral cooperation between Japan and Russian Federation

THE HOSHINMARU[1]

(JAPAN v. RUSSIAN FEDERATION)

(APPLICATION FOR PROMPT RELEASE)

International Tribunal for the Law of the Sea. 6 August 2007

---

[1] For a list of counsel, see para. 18 of the judgment.

(Wolfrum, *President*; Akl, *Vice-President*; Caminos, Marotta Rangel, Yankov, Kolodkin, Park, Nelson, Chandrasekhara Rao, Treves, Ndiaye, Jesus, Cot, Lucky, Pawlak, Yanai, Türk, Kateka and Hoffmann, *Judges*)

SUMMARY: *The facts*:—On 1 June 2007, the *Hoshinmaru*, a fishing vessel flying the flag of Japan, owned by a Japanese company and whose Master and crew members were of Japanese nationality, was boarded and inspected by Russian Federation officials while fishing in the exclusive economic zone of the Russian Federation off the eastern coast of the Kamchatka Peninsula. The vessel and crew were arrested for contravening the terms of the fishing licence by substituting species for reporting purposes, which resulted in an illegal catch of sockeye salmon. The Master and crew failed to cooperate. On 3 June, the *Hoshinmaru* was escorted to the Russian port of Petropavlovsk-Kamchatskii for judicial proceedings and detained.

On 6 July 2007, Japan ("the Applicant") filed an Application with the International Tribunal for the Law of the Sea under Article 292 of the United Nations Convention on the Law of the Sea, 1982 ("the Convention")[2] against the Russian Federation ("the Respondent") for the prompt release of the *Hoshinmaru* and its crew. The Applicant contended that the Tribunal had jurisdiction, that the Application was admissible, that the allegation was well founded, and that the Respondent had breached its obligations under Article 73(2) of the Convention.[3] The Applicant sought an order that the *Hoshinmaru* be released upon terms and conditions considered reasonable by the Tribunal. The Respondent challenged the admissibility of the Application; in the alternative, it claimed that it had fulfilled its obligations under Article 73(2) of the Convention.

On 13 July 2007, the Respondent set the bond at 25 million roubles, adjusted to 22 million roubles (approximately US $862,000) due to a revised estimate of the value of the vessel. The Respondent argued that the Application was thereby rendered moot since it had no object.

Held (unanimously):—(1) The Tribunal had jurisdiction to entertain the Application under Article 292 of the Convention. Japan and the Russian Federation were both States Parties to the Convention. Japan was the flag State of the *Hoshinmaru*. The *Hoshinmaru*, its Master and crew remained in the port of Petropavlovsk-Kamchatskii. The Applicant alleged that the Respondent had not complied with Article 73(2) of the Convention for the prompt release of the vessel and its crew upon the posting of a reasonable bond or other financial security. The Parties did not agree to submit the question of release of the vessel to another court or tribunal within ten days from the time of detention. Japan made the Application in accordance with Articles 110 and 111 of the Rules of the Tribunal (paras. 52-9).

---

[2] For the text of Article 292 of the Convention, see para. 52 of the judgment.
[3] Article 73(2) provided that: "Arrested vessels and their crews shall be promptly released upon the posting of reasonable bond or other security."

(2) The Application for release was admissible.

(a) As required by Article 292(1) of the Convention, the Application was based on an allegation that the detaining State had not complied with Convention provisions for the prompt release of a vessel and crew upon the posting of a reasonable bond or other financial security (para. 60).

(b) The setting of the bond by the Respondent did not render the Application without object. A State might make an application under Article 292 of the Convention not only where no bond had been set but also where it considered the bond set to be unreasonable. It was for the Tribunal to decide whether a bond was reasonable under Article 292. While the nature of the dispute had not changed, its scope had narrowed to the reasonableness of the bond (paras. 61-6).

(c) The Application could be properly considered by the Tribunal; it was not too general. It was based on Article 292 read in conjunction with Article 73(2) of the Convention. The Tribunal was asked to exercise its power under Article 292(3), to order the release of the vessel and its crew upon the posting of a reasonable bond or other financial security (paras. 67-9).

(3) In the circumstances of the case, the Respondent had not complied with Article 73(2) of the Convention. Since the Application was well founded, the Respondent must release promptly the *Hoshinmaru*, including the catch on board and its crew.

(a) Although there was no precise time-limit for setting a bond in the Convention, it should be reasonable given the object and purpose of Article 292 of the Convention. Neither was there a specific time by which the flag State was required to file an application after the detention of the vessel or its crew; the earliest date was ten days from detention pursuant to Article 292(1) (paras. 70-80).

(b) The bond fixed had to be reasonable in light of the objective assessment of relevant factors, which included the gravity of the alleged offences, penalties under the laws of the detaining State and the amount and form of bond imposed by that State (para. 82).

(c) While an agreed procedure between States with long-standing relations regarding fisheries was helpful, and the Protocol or minutes of a commission such as the Russian–Japanese Commission on Fisheries could be the source of rights and obligations between parties, there was no evidence of acquiescence by Japanese representatives in the procedure contained in Russia's bond calculation document communicated to Japan within the framework of that Commission (paras. 83-7).

(d) While confined to the question of release, the Tribunal was not prevented from examining the facts and circumstances of the case to the extent necessary for a proper appreciation of the reasonableness of the bond as set by the Respondent. In so doing it was not acting as a court of appeal (paras. 88-9).

(e) The bond of 22 million roubles (approximately US $862,000) was not reasonable. While a violation of the rules on reporting might be sanctioned by the detaining State, a bond should not be set on the basis of the maximum penalties applicable to the owner and the Master. Neither should it be calculated on the basis of the confiscation of the vessel, given the circumstances of this case (paras. 90-4).

(4) The bond should amount to 10 million roubles in the form of a payment into a bank account or a bank guarantee. Although the *Hoshinmaru* held a valid fishing licence and the offence was committed within a broadly satisfactory cooperative framework in respect of the conservation and management of fish stocks in the Russian EEZ, it was not a minor or purely technical offence. The monitoring of catches, requiring accurate reporting, was essential for managing marine living resources (paras. 95-101).

Declaration of Judge Kolodkin: The bond issued by the Tribunal did not conform to the relevant legal arrangements between Japan and the Russian Federation. It did not take into account the gravity of the offence and its calculation was inconsistent with the Tribunal's practice of including the vessel's value in the bond (p. 29).

Declaration of Judge Treves: The provision in the operative part that the Master and crew were free to leave without conditions, even though they had not been considered as "detained", was not unnecessary since it preserved the efficacy of the judgment for the release of the vessel (pp. 29-30).

Declaration of Judge Lucky: The relevant meaning of the word "bond" was legal; the amount should not be punitive since guilt had not been established. In fixing a bond, the interests of the coastal State and flag State had to be balanced. The gravity of the alleged offence had to be weighed in the same manner as a national judge determining urgent applications. The bond should constitute sufficient security to ensure implementation of a court decision at the end of proceedings. A reasonable bond was less than that fixed by the Respondent (pp. 30-1).

Declaration of Judge Türk: While the Convention in Article 73(2) wisely avoided setting a precise time-limit for a bond, preserving necessary flexibility according to circumstances, it had to be borne in mind that the prompt release procedure was designed to be expeditious. As such, a bond was to be set as early as possible, varying according to the complexity of the detaining State's investigations. A maximum period of one month after detention seemed reasonable. International litigation should be a last resort in settling a dispute (pp. 31-3).

Separate Opinion of Judge Yanai: The bond should have been set at a lower level, given that the offence was not very grave. The falsely recorded amount of catch was within the limits set in the licence. It did not damage the conservation of the high level of salmon and trout resources in the Russian EEZ, for which there was long-standing bilateral cooperation between Japan and Russia as for fishery matters generally (pp. 33-5).

The texts of the judgment and the declarations and opinion are set out as follows:

	page
Judgment on the Application for Prompt Release	5
Declaration of Judge Kolodkin	29
Declaration of Judge Treves	29
Declaration of Judge Lucky	30
Declaration of Judge Türk	31
Separate Opinion of Judge Yanai	33

The following is the text of the judgment of the Tribunal:

TABLE OF CONTENTS

	paragraphs
Introduction	1-26
Factual background	27-51
Jurisdiction	52-9
Admissibility	60-9
Non-compliance with article 73, paragraph 2, of the Convention	70-94
Amount and form of the bond or other financial security	95-101
Operative provisions	102

INTRODUCTION

1. On 6 July 2007, an Application under article 292 of the United Nations Convention on the Law of the Sea (hereinafter "the Convention") was filed by electronic mail with the Registry of the Tribunal by Japan against the Russian Federation concerning the release of the *88th Hoshinmaru* (hereinafter "the *Hoshinmaru*") and its crew. The Application was accompanied by a letter dated 6 July 2007 from Mr Ichiro Komatsu, Director-General, International Legal Affairs Bureau, Ministry of Foreign Affairs of Japan, which transmitted a communication from the Minister for Foreign Affairs of Japan, notifying the Registrar of the Tribunal of the appointment of Mr Komatsu as Agent of Japan. By the same letter, the Registrar was notified of the appointment of Mr Tadakatsu Ishihara, Consul-General of Japan in Hamburg, as Co-Agent. The original of the Application and of the letter of the Agent of Japan were delivered on 9 July 2007.

2. A copy of the Application was sent on 6 July 2007, by electronic mail and facsimile, to the Embassy of the Russian Federation in Berlin. A

certified copy of the original of the Application was sent to the Embassy of the Russian Federation in Berlin on 10 July 2007.

3. By a note verbale from the Registrar dated 6 July 2007, the Minister of Foreign Affairs of the Russian Federation was informed that the Statement in Response of the Russian Federation, in accordance with article 111, paragraph 4, of the Rules of the Tribunal (hereinafter "the Rules") could be filed no later than 96 hours before the opening of the hearing.

4. In accordance with article 112, paragraph 3, of the Rules, the President of the Tribunal, by Order dated 9 July 2007, fixed 19 July 2007 as the date for the opening of the hearing with respect to the Application. Notice of the Order was communicated forthwith to the parties.

5. The Application was entered in the List of cases as Case No 14 and named the *"Hoshinmaru" Case.*

6. In accordance with article 24, paragraph 3, of the Statute of the Tribunal (hereinafter "the Statute"), States Parties to the Convention were notified of the Application by a note verbale from the Registrar dated 9 July 2007.

7. In accordance with articles 45 and 73 of the Rules, the President held consultations with representatives of the parties on 10 July 2007, during which he ascertained their views with regard to questions of procedure. Japanese representatives were present at the consultations while the Russian representative participated via telephone.

8. Pursuant to the Agreement on Cooperation and Relationship between the United Nations and the International Tribunal for the Law of the Sea of 18 December 1997, the Secretary-General of the United Nations was notified by the Registrar on 11 July 2007 of the receipt of the Application.

9. On 11 July 2007, the Registrar was notified by a letter of the same date from the First Deputy Minister of Foreign Affairs of the Russian Federation of the appointment of Mr Evgeny Zagaynov, Deputy Director, Legal Department, Ministry of Foreign Affairs of the Russian Federation, as Agent of the Russian Federation. By the same letter, the Registrar was notified of the appointment of Mr Sergey Ganzha, Consul-General of the Russian Federation in Hamburg, as Co-Agent.

10. By letter from the Registrar dated 12 July 2007, the Co-Agent of Japan was requested to complete the documentation, in accordance with article 63, paragraph 1, and article 64, paragraph 3, of the Rules. On 18 July 2007, the Applicant submitted documents, copies of which were communicated to the other party.

11. On 13, 17 and 18 July 2007, the Applicant sent additional documents in support of its Application, copies of which were communicated to the other party.

12. On 15 July 2007, the Russian Federation filed its Statement in Response, a copy of which was transmitted forthwith to the Co-Agent of Japan. On 16 and 19 July 2007, the Russian Federation submitted additional documents in support of its Statement in Response. Copies of these documents were communicated to the other party.

13. On 17 July 2007, the Agent of the Russian Federation transmitted to the Tribunal two corrections to the Statement in Response. These corrections, being of a formal nature, were accepted by leave of the President in accordance with article 65, paragraph 4, of the Rules.

14. By letters from the Registrar dated 18 and 21 July 2007, the Co-Agent of the Russian Federation was requested to complete the documentation in accordance with article 63, paragraph 1, and article 64, paragraph 3, of the Rules. On 24 July 2007, the Agent of the Russian Federation submitted documents, copies of which were communicated to the other party pursuant to article 71 of the Rules.

15. Prior to the opening of the oral proceedings, the Tribunal held initial deliberations on 17 July 2007, in accordance with article 68 of the Rules.

16. On 18 and 19 July 2007, the President held consultations with the Agents of the parties in accordance with articles 45 and 73 of the Rules. During the consultations on 18 July 2007, the President communicated to the Agents a list of points or issues which the Tribunal wished the parties specially to address.

17. Pursuant to article 67, paragraph 2, of the Rules, copies of the pleadings and documents annexed thereto were made accessible to the public on the date of the opening of the oral proceedings.

18. Oral statements were presented at four public sittings held on 19, 20 and 23 July 2007 by the following:

On behalf of Japan: Mr Ichiro Komatsu, Agent,
  Mr Vaughan Lowe, Advocate,
  Mr Shotaro Hamamoto, Advocate.

On behalf of the   Mr Evgeny Zagaynov, Agent,
  Russian Federation: Mr Alexey Monakhov, Deputy Agent,
  Mr Vladimir Golitsyn, Counsel.

19. On 20 July 2007, Mr Alexey Monakhov, Deputy Agent for the Russian Federation, delivered his statement in Russian. The necessary

arrangements were made for the statement of Mr Monakhov to be interpreted into the official languages of the Tribunal in accordance with article 85 of the Rules.

20. During the oral proceedings, the representatives of the parties addressed the points or issues referred to in paragraph 16. Written responses were subsequently submitted by the Applicant on 19 and 21 July 2007.

21. On 20 July 2007, a list of questions which the Tribunal wished the parties to address was communicated to the Agents. Written responses to these questions were subsequently submitted by the Applicant on 23 July 2007 and by the Respondent on 24 July 2007.

22. In the Application of Japan and in the Statement in Response of the Russian Federation, the following submissions were presented by the parties:

On behalf of Japan,
in the Application:

Pursuant to Article 292 of the United Nations Convention on the Law of the Sea (hereinafter "the Convention"), the Applicant requests the International Tribunal for the Law of the Sea (hereinafter "the Tribunal"), by means of a judgment:

(a) to declare that the Tribunal has jurisdiction under Article 292 of the Convention to hear the application concerning the detention of the vessel and the crew of the *88th Hoshinmaru* (hereinafter "the *Hoshinmaru*") in breach of the Respondent's obligations under Article 73(2) of the Convention;
(b) to declare that the application is admissible, that the allegation of the Applicant is well-founded, and that the Respondent has breached its obligations under Article 73(2) of the Convention; and
(c) to order the Respondent to release the vessel and the crew of the *Hoshinmaru*, upon such terms and conditions as the Tribunal shall consider reasonable.

On behalf of the Russian Federation,
in the Statement in Response:

The Russian Federation requests the Tribunal to decline to make the orders sought in paragraph 1 of the Application of Japan. The Russian Federation requests the Tribunal to make the following orders:

(a) that the Application of Japan is inadmissible;
(b) alternatively, that the allegations of the Applicant are not well-founded and that the Russian Federation has fulfilled its obligations under paragraph 2 of Article 73 of the United Nations Convention on the Law of the Sea.

23. Following the submission of its Application, the Applicant, by letter dated 18 July 2007, filed an additional statement which reads as follows:

For the sake of clarity, the Government of Japan wishes to make plain that its Application in the *88th Hoshinmaru* case, made under Articles 73 and 292 of UNCLOS, relates to the failure of the Russian Federation to comply with the provisions of the Convention for the prompt release of a vessel or its crew upon the posting of a reasonable bond or other financial security. A bond has been belatedly set for the release of the *88th Hoshinmaru*; but Japan does not consider the amount set to be reasonable.

Accordingly, the setting of that bond does not resolve the dispute over the failure of the Russian Federation to comply with the provisions of the Convention for the prompt release of a vessel or its crew upon the posting of a reasonable bond or other financial security. While it is now unnecessary for Japan to include in its oral pleadings any submissions relating specifically to circumstances in which there is a complete failure to set any bond, Japan will address all other aspects of its Application.

24. On 19 July 2007, before the opening of the oral proceedings, the Respondent filed an additional statement which reads as follows:

With respect to the clarification provided by the Agent for Japan on the *Hoshinmaru* case we would like to state that Russia does not accept allegations contained therein. Contrary to the statement of the Applicant the bond was set not belatedly but within a reasonable period of time. We take note of the statement of the Applicant that "it is now unnecessary to include in its oral pleadings any submissions relating specifically to circumstances in which there is a complete failure to set any bond". But this statement implies that there is at least partial failure of the Respondent to comply with its obligations under the relevant provisions of the UNCLOS. We [cannot] agree with it.

25. In accordance with article 75, paragraph 2, of the Rules, the following final submissions were presented by the parties at the end of the hearing on 23 July 2007:

On behalf of Japan,

The Applicant requests the International Tribunal for the Law of the Sea (hereinafter "the Tribunal"), by means of a judgment:

(a) to declare that the Tribunal has jurisdiction under Article 292 of the United Nations Convention on the Law of the Sea (hereinafter "the Convention") to hear the application concerning the detention of the vessel of the *88th Hoshinmaru* (hereinafter "the *Hoshinmaru*") in breach of the Respondent's obligations under Article 73(2) of the Convention;

(b) to declare that the application is admissible, that the allegation of the Applicant is well-founded, and that the Respondent has breached its obligations under Article 73(2) of the Convention; and
(c) to order the Respondent to release the vessel of the *Hoshinmaru*, upon such terms and conditions as the Tribunal shall consider reasonable.

On behalf of the Russian Federation,

The Russian Federation requests the International Tribunal for the Law of the Sea to decline to make the orders sought in paragraph 1 of the Application of Japan. The Russian Federation requests the Tribunal to make the following orders:

(a) that the Application of Japan is inadmissible;
(b) alternatively, that the allegations of the Applicant are not well-founded and that the Russian Federation has fulfilled its obligations under paragraph 2 of Article 73 of the United Nations Convention on the Law of the Sea.

26. By letter dated 25 July 2007, the Agent of Japan requested the correction of an error in the original version of the final submissions in subparagraphs (a) and (c) of which the words "and the crew" had been omitted purely by clerical error. This correction was accepted by leave of the President in accordance with article 65, paragraph 4, of the Rules.

FACTUAL BACKGROUND

27. The *Hoshinmaru* is a fishing vessel flying the flag of Japan. Its owner is Ikeda Suisan, a company incorporated in Japan. The Master of the *Hoshinmaru* is Mr Shoji Takahashi. The 17 crew members of the *Hoshinmaru* including the Master are of Japanese nationality.

28. According to the Certificate of Registration, the *Hoshinmaru* was entered in the State Ship's Registry of Nyuzen-machi, Shimoniikawa-gun, Toyama Prefecture, in Japan on 24 March 2004. On 14 May 2007, the Russian Federation provided the *Hoshinmaru* with a fishing licence for drift net salmon and trout fishing in three different areas of the exclusive economic zone of the Russian Federation. According to the fishing licence, the *Hoshinmaru* was authorized to fish, from 15 May until 31 July 2007, the following: 101.8 tons of sockeye salmon; 161.8 tons of chum salmon; 7 tons of sakhalin trout; 1.7 tons of silver salmon; and 2.7 tons of spring salmon.

29. On 1 June 2007, the *Hoshinmaru* was fishing in the exclusive economic zone of the Russian Federation off the eastern coast of the Kamchatka Peninsula when it was ordered to stop by a Russian

patrol boat. Subsequently, the *Hoshinmaru* was boarded by an inspection team of the State Sea Inspection of the Northeast Border Coast Guard Directorate of the Federal Security Service of the Russian Federation (hereinafter the "State Sea Inspection"). According to the Applicant, at the time of boarding, the *Hoshinmaru* was at the position 56° 09'N, 165° 28'E, which is a point located within the exclusive economic zone of the Russian Federation and where the vessel was licensed to fish.

30. After boarding the vessel, an inspection team of the State Sea Inspection examined it. A protocol of inspection No 003483 drawn up on 1 June 2007 by a senior state coastguard inspector recorded the following:

[Translation from Russian provided by the Respondent]

During the inspection of holds No 10 and No 11 the inspectors of the State [Sea] Inspection found out that under the upper layer of chum salmon sockeye salmon is kept.

Therefore an offence is detected: substitution of output of one kind (*chum salmon*) with the other kind (*sockeye salmon*) and, thus, concealment of part of sockeye salmon catch in the Exploitation area No 1; misrepresentation of data in a fishing log and daily vessel report (*SSD*).

31. On 2 June 2007, a protocol of detention was drawn up by an officer of the Frontier Service of the Federal Security Service of the Russian Federation which recorded the detention of the *Hoshinmaru* on the basis of the following reasons:

[Translation from Russian provided by the Respondent]

transmitting of untrue inadequate operational accounts in the form of SSD [daily vessel report], creating in the course of checking a difference between the amount permitted for catching by the license and the actual catch on board, incorrect reflecting of inadequate information on catching in the vessel's logbook, substitution of biological resources species.

32. The protocol of detention recorded that the Master refused to lead the vessel to Petropavlovsk-Kamchatskii and to sign the said protocol.

33. By a letter dated 2 June 2007, the Northeast Border Coast Guard Directorate of the Federal Security Service of the Russian Federation informed the Consul-General of Japan in Vladivostok of the inspection and detention of the *Hoshinmaru*. According to that letter, "[t]he falsification of the species composition of the fish products . . . was discovered and consequently, about 14 tons of raw sockeye salmons were illegally captured". The letter also stated that the actions of the Master were in

violation of article 12, paragraph 2, of the Federal Law of the Russian Federation No 191-FZ of 17 December 1998 on the exclusive economic zone of the Russian Federation, articles 35, paragraph 3, and 40, paragraph 2, of the Federal Law of the Russian Federation No 52-FZ of 24 April 1995 on Wildlife, and articles 3.5.1, 3.5.5, 3.5.6, 7, 14.1, 14.2 and 19 of the regulation on the operation of the anadromous stocks living in the rivers of the Russian Federation approved by the Protocol dated 19 March 2007 of the 23rd Session of the Russian–Japanese Commission on Fisheries.

34. On 3 June 2007, the vessel was escorted for the purpose of judicial proceedings to the port of Petropavlovsk-Kamchatskii.

35. On 4 June 2007, administrative proceedings were instituted against the owner of the *Hoshinmaru* by a Decision of the Military Prosecutor's Office of Garrison, which reads, *inter alia*, as follows:

[Translation from Russian provided by the Respondent]

taking into consideration the existence of sufficient evidence of the Ikeda Suisan company's guilt in committing the administrative offence, punishable under article 8.17, part 2, of the Code on Administrative Offences of the Russian Federation and being guided by articles 25.11, 28.1, 28.4, 28.7 of the Code and Article 25 of the Federal Law "On the Office of Prosecutor of the Russian Federation"
Decided as follows:

1. To institute the administrative proceedings under article 8.17, part 2, of the Code on Administrative Offences of the Russian Federation with regard to the "Ikeda Suisan" company.
2. To operate administrative investigation with regard to the "Ikeda Suisan" company and to entrust the Northeast Border Coast Guard Directorate of the Federal Security Service of the Russian Federation to operate such investigation.
3. To inform interested parties about this Decision.

36. Article 8.17, paragraph 2, of the Code on Administrative Offences of the Russian Federation reads as follows:

[Translation from Russian provided by the Respondent]

Violating the rules of catching (fishing) aquatic biological (living) resources and of protection thereof, or the terms and conditions of a license for water use, or of a permit (license) to catch aquatic biological (living) resources of the internal sea waters, or of the territorial sea, or of the continental shelf and (or) the exclusive economic zone of the Russian Federation—shall entail the imposition of an administrative fine on citizens in the amount of from half the cost to the full cost of aquatic biological (living) resources, which have become the subject of the administrative offence, with or without confiscation of the vessel and of other instruments of committing the administrative offence; on officials in the amount of from one to one and a half times the cost of aquatic biological (living) resources, which have become the subject of the administrative offence, with or without confiscation of the vessel and of other instruments of committing the administrative offence; and on legal entities in the amount of from twofold to threefold the cost of aquatic biological (living) resources which have become the subject of the administrative offence with or without confiscation of the vessel and of other instruments of committing the administrative offence.

37. On 7 June 2007, the cargo on board the *Hoshinmaru* was inspected by officials of the State Sea Inspection. According to the Application, "the allegedly illegal catch of the *Hoshinmaru* was seized and is held in custody by the authorities of the Respondent, and the rest of the catch is conserved in the vessel of the *Hoshinmaru*".

38. The Respondent alleges that the Master of the *Hoshinmaru* refused to take the vessel for safekeeping. The Respondent further states that a senior inspector of the State Sea Inspection decided, on 8 June 2007, to transfer the *Hoshinmaru* with all its facilities and equipment for safekeeping to the company Kamchatka Logistic Centre.

39. On 13 June 2007, the chief inspector of the State Sea Inspection decided to request documentation from the owner of the vessel with a view to facilitating the administrative proceedings. According to the Respondent, documents were received on 4 July 2007.

40. On 26 June 2007, a criminal case No 700518 against the Master of the *Hoshinmaru* was instituted by the investigation authority of the Northeast Border Coast Guard Directorate for the criminal act stipulated in article 256, paragraph 1(a) and (b), of the Criminal Code of the Russian Federation concerning "illegal fishing with grave damages and with the use of self-propelled mode of transport". According to the provisional investigation, the Master had failed to fulfil the requirements contained, *inter alia*, in the following regulations:

(a) Articles 3.5.1, 3.5.5, 7, 14.1, 14.2 and 19 of the regulation on the operation of the anadromous stocks living in the rivers of the Russian Federation approved by the Protocol dated 19 March 2007 of the 23rd Session of the Russian–Japanese Commission on Fisheries;
(b) Article 12 of the Federal Law of the Russian Federation No 191-FZ of 17 December 1998 on the exclusive economic zone of the Russian Federation;
(c) Article 40, paragraph 2, of the Federal Law of the Russian Federation No 52-FZ of 24 April 1995 on the Wildlife.

41. Articles 3.5.1, 3.5.5, 7, 14.1, 14.2 and 19 of the regulation on the operation of the anadromous stocks living in the rivers of the Russian Federation approved by the Protocol dated 19 March 2007 of the 23rd Session of the Russian–Japanese Commission on Fisheries read as follows:

[Translation from Russian provided by the Applicant]

3.5.1 To observe the regulations on the fishing (catch) and the restrictions on the fishing (catch) of stipulated living resources as well as to fulfil the requirements set out in the operation license (permission) on the living resources.

3.5.5 To submit a daily, ten-day and monthly report on the result of the operation in accordance with the Attachment I-4, I-5 and I-6 of this regulation.

3.5.6 To keep an operation log (Attachment I-7 and I-8). The log shall be strapped and authenticated by means of the seal and signature of the owner of the vessel.

7. The operation is permitted for the licensed amount in the licensed area during the licensed period by using a drift net. Other fishing gear and fishing methods are prohibited.

14.1 The calculation of the consumption of the fishing allocation in the salmon-trout operation by the drift-net fishing shall be carried out on each fishing vessel, by the weight of the caught salmon/trout and its number, species by species.

14.2 All caught fish shall be classified and weighed out, the result of which shall be recorded on the operation log of the drift-net fishing vessel to an accuracy of 1 kg and 1 fish.

19. It is prohibited to keep the various species of salmon/trout together in a hold. When the various species of salmon/trout are kept together in a hold, they must be clearly separated by each species (vertical partition).

42. Article 12, paragraph 2, of the Federal Law of the Russian Federation No 191-FZ of 17 December 1998 on its exclusive economic zone reads as follows:

[Law of the Sea Bulletin No 46, United Nations (2001), pp. 46-7]

2. Licence holders shall be obliged:

– To observe the established rules for catching (harvesting) living resources and the limits on their catch (harvest), and to comply with the conditions of the licence (permit) for the commercial exploitation of living resources;
– To make the payments stipulated in a timely fashion;
– To prevent the degradation of the natural conditions of the habitat of living resources;

- To prevent illegal acclimatization of species of living resources and to comply with the requirements of the quarantine regime;
- To ensure unimpeded access to a commercial fishing vessel by officials of protection agencies;
- To ensure, at their own expense, optimum working conditions for officials of protection agencies;
- To submit to the specially empowered federal executive body for the border service, federal executive body for fisheries, federal executive body for environmental protection, federal executive body for customs matters, federal executive body for currency and export control and federal executive body for taxation readily and without charge reports, including computer printouts, on the volumes of the catch (harvest) and the periods, types and areas of commercial exploitation of living resources, including information on the quantity, quality and species of living resources and products derived therefrom loaded onto or from other vessels and on the quantity, quality and species of living resources and products derived therefrom unloaded or loaded in foreign ports;
- To maintain regular contact with the coastal services of the Russian Federation and, if appropriate equipment is available, to transmit, at the main international synoptical times, to the nearest radiometeorological centre of the Russian Federation, operational data on meteorological and hydrological observations in accordance with the standard procedures of the World Meteorological Organization and urgent information on oil pollution of the marine environment if observed;
- To keep a commercial fishing logbook in the format stipulated by the specially empowered federal executive body for fisheries;
- To have special distinguishing marks;
- To mark set fishing (harvesting) gear at both ends with the name of the vessel (for foreign vessels, the name of the flag country), the number of the licence (permit) for the commercial exploitation of living resources and the index number for the fishing (harvesting) gear.

43. Article 40, paragraph 2, of the Federal Law of the Russian Federation No 52-FZ of 24 April 1995 on the Wildlife reads as follows:

[Translation from Russian provided by the Applicant]

2. License holders for the use of wildlife shall have the (following) obligations:

To use wildlife only in the forms described in the license;
To comply with the prescribed rules, regulations, and periods concerning the use of wildlife;
To apply methods, when using the wildlife, that will not cause damage to the integrity of the natural world;
To prevent the destruction or degradation of the natural habitat of the wildlife;

To calculate the quantity and assess the current conditions of the utilizable wildlife, and also to assess the condition of their natural habitat;
To take the necessary measures for ensuring the reproduction of the wildlife;
To support state authorities in accomplishing the protection of the wildlife;
To ensure the protection and reproduction of the wildlife, including rare and endangered species;
To apply humane methods when using the wildlife;

Rules, periods, and a list of instruments and methods for catching the wildlife that were permitted for application, shall be formulated by state authorities, which have been given special authorization to protect, control and regulate the utilization of the wildlife and their natural habitat, and approved by the Government of the Russian Federation or the agencies of executive power of the subjects of the Russian Federation.

44. According to the investigation authority, the charge against the Master was as follows:

[Translation from Russian provided by the Applicant]

[the Master] caught 6,343 sockeye salmon (total weight 20,063.80 kg) ... without the necessary license ... , and subsequently processed them into 1,057 gutted, headed, gilled and salted sockeye salmon (total weight 15,199.85 kg). He recorded these products on the daily logbook and the daily ship reports as chum [salmon] which are cheaper products than sockeye [salmon]. This caused serious damages equivalent to not less than 7 million rubles against the living aquatic resources in the Russian Federation.

...

A criminal case is established for the suspicion of the criminal act stipulated in Article 256(1)(a) and (b) of the Criminal Code of the Russian Federation.

45. Article 256, paragraph 1(a) and (b), of the Criminal Code of the Russian Federation reads as follows:

[Translation from Russian provided by the Applicant]

1. Illegal catching of fish, [marine mammals] and other aquatic animals or harvesting of sea plants, if these acts have been committed:

(a) resulting in large damage;
(b) with the use of a self-propelled transport floating craft or explosives, chemicals, electric current ... ;

shall be punishable by a fine from one hundred thousand to three hundred thousand roubles or in the amount of the wages or other income of the convicted for a period from one year to two years or by corrective labour for a term of up to two years, or by placing under arrest for a term of four to six months.

46. In a letter addressed to the Consulate-General of Japan in Vladivostok dated 11 July 2007, the Inter-district Prosecutor's Office confirmed that damage equivalent to 7,927,500 roubles had been caused to the living aquatic resources by the illegal catch.

47. By a note verbale dated 6 June 2007 addressed to the Ministry of Foreign Affairs of the Russian Federation, the Embassy of Japan in the Russian Federation requested that the *Hoshinmaru* and its crew be released upon the posting of a reasonable bond in accordance with article 73, paragraph 2, of the Convention. Similar notes were sent to the Ministry of Foreign Affairs of the Russian Federation on 8 June 2007, and to the Embassy of the Russian Federation in Japan on 12 June 2007.

48. Examination procedures to evaluate the vessel were instituted by a decision of 29 June 2007 of a senior coastguard inspector of the State Sea Inspection. In a letter dated 6 July 2007 addressed to a representative of the owner of the *Hoshinmaru*, the State Sea Inspection requested information on the estimated value of the vessel necessary for the determination of the amount of the bond. According to the Respondent, no reply was received.

49. By a note verbale dated 6 July 2007, addressed to the Embassy of Japan in the Russian Federation, the Ministry of Foreign Affairs of the Russian Federation informed the Embassy of Japan that the detained vessel *Hoshinmaru* and its crew would be promptly released upon the posting of a bond, the amount of which was in the process of being determined.

50. Subsequently, by a note verbale dated 13 July 2007, the Ministry of Foreign Affairs of the Russian Federation informed the Embassy of Japan that the bond was set at 25,000,000 roubles including the amount of damages equivalent to 7,927,500. The note verbale stated that after the posting of the bond the *Hoshinmaru* and its crew, including the Master, would be able to promptly leave the Russian Federation.

51. The Respondent initially set the bond at 25,000,000 roubles; the amount was changed during the hearing to 22,000,000 roubles, owing to a revised estimate of the value of the vessel. According to the Respondent, the bond was calculated to take into account: the maximum fine imposable on the Master, i.e. 500,000 roubles (legal basis: article 256 of the Criminal Code of the Russian Federation); the maximum fine imposable on the owner: 2,001,364.05 roubles (method of calculation: value of the illegal catch (33.25 roubles/kilo x 20,063.8 kilos) x 3; legal basis: article 8.17, part 2, of the Code on Administrative Offences of the Russian Federation); the procedural costs of 240,000 roubles (in accordance with article 24.7 of the Code on Administrative Offences of the Russian Federation); penalty for damages caused by illegal fishing

or harvesting of protected marine living resources: 7,927,500 roubles (method of calculation: 1,250 roubles (value of 1 piece of sockeye salmon x 6,342), legal basis: articles 1064 and 1068 of the Civil Code of the Russian Federation; articles 4, 40, 55, 56 and 58 of the federal law on wildlife, Regulation No 724/2000); and the value of the vessel of 11,350,000 roubles.

JURISDICTION

52. The Tribunal must, at the outset, examine whether it has jurisdiction to entertain the Application. The requirements to be satisfied in order to found the jurisdiction of the Tribunal are provided for in article 292 of the Convention, which reads as follows:

Article 292

Prompt release of vessels and crews

1. Where the authorities of a State Party have detained a vessel flying the flag of another State Party and it is alleged that the detaining State has not complied with the provisions of this Convention for the prompt release of the vessel or its crew upon the posting of a reasonable bond or other financial security, the question of release from detention may be submitted to any court or tribunal agreed upon by the parties or, failing such agreement within 10 days from the time of detention, to a court or tribunal accepted by the detaining State under article 287 or to the International Tribunal for the Law of the Sea, unless the parties otherwise agree.

2. The application for release may be made only by or on behalf of the flag State of the vessel.

3. The court or tribunal shall deal without delay with the application for release and shall deal only with the question of release, without prejudice to the merits of any case before the appropriate domestic forum against the vessel, its owner or its crew. The authorities of the detaining State remain competent to release the vessel or its crew at any time.

4. Upon the posting of the bond or other financial security determined by the court or tribunal, the authorities of the detaining State shall comply promptly with the decision of the court or tribunal concerning the release of the vessel or its crew.

53. Japan and the Russian Federation are both States Parties to the Convention. Japan ratified the Convention on 20 June 1996 and the Convention entered into force for Japan on 20 July 1996. The Russian Federation ratified the Convention on 12 March 1997 and the Convention entered into force for the Russian Federation on 11 April 1997.

54. The status of Japan as the flag State of the *Hoshinmaru* is not disputed by the Respondent.

55. The *Hoshinmaru*, its Master and its crew remain in the port of Petropavlovsk-Kamchatskii.

56. The Applicant alleges that the Respondent has not complied with the provisions of article 73, paragraph 2, of the Convention for the prompt release of the vessel and its crew upon the posting of a reasonable bond or other financial security.

57. The parties did not agree to submit the question of release of the vessel to another court or tribunal within 10 days from the time of detention.

58. The Tribunal is of the view that the Application for the prompt release of the vessel was made by the Government of Japan in accordance with articles 110 and 111 of the Rules.

59. For these reasons, the Tribunal finds that it has jurisdiction under article 292 of the Convention.

ADMISSIBILITY

60. Article 292, paragraph 1, of the Convention provides that an application for release must be based on an allegation that the detaining State has not complied with the provisions of the Convention for the prompt release of a vessel and its crew upon the posting of a reasonable bond or other financial security. In the present case this requirement for admissibility is satisfied as such allegation is set forth in the Application of Japan. The parties disagree on other aspects of the admissibility of the Application.

61. The Respondent maintains that this Application for prompt release is inadmissible for two reasons.

62. First, the Respondent claims that the application became moot on 13 July 2007, when the competent Russian authorities informed the Applicant that the bond had been set in the amount of 25,000,000 roubles (approximately US $980,000) and that upon payment of it the vessel and its crew, including the Master, would be allowed to leave the territory of the Russian Federation. The Respondent maintains that events subsequent to the filing of an application may render an application without object.

63. The Applicant contends that "the setting of that bond does not resolve the dispute over the failure of the Russian Federation to comply with the provisions of the Convention for the prompt release of a vessel or its crew upon the posting of a reasonable bond or other financial security". Clarifying its original submission, on 18 July 2007,

after receiving the Statement in Response, it claims that the amount of the bond set by the Respondent on 13 July 2007 is unreasonable and that the bond does not meet the requirements of article 292 of the Convention. It further maintains that the bond was not set promptly.

64. While the Tribunal takes the view that, in principle, the decisive date for determining the issues of admissibility is the date of the filing of an application, it acknowledges that events subsequent to the filing of an application may render an application without object (*Nuclear Tests (Australia v. France), Judgment, ICJ Reports 1974*, p. 253, at p. 272, para. 62; *Border and Transborder Armed Actions (Nicaragua v. Honduras), Jurisdiction and Admissibility, Judgment, ICJ Reports 1988*, p. 69, at p. 95, para. 66; *Arrest Warrant of 11 April 2000 (Democratic Republic of the Congo v. Belgium), Provisional Measures, Order of 8 December 2000, ICJ Reports 2000*, p. 182, at p. 197, para. 55).

65. However, in the present case, the Tribunal considers that the setting of the bond by the Respondent does not render the Application without object. In the *M/V "SAIGA" Case*, the Tribunal held that a State may make an application under article 292 of the Convention not only where no bond has been set but also where it considers that the bond set by the detaining State is unreasonable (*ITLOS Reports 1997*, p.16, at p. 35, para. 77). The Tribunal reaffirms this jurisprudence and emphasizes that it is for the Tribunal to decide whether a bond is reasonable under article 292 of the Convention.

66. The Tribunal considers that the nature of the dispute between the parties has not changed. It notes, however, that the scope of the dispute has narrowed and that the legal dispute between the parties concerning the release of the vessel now turns on the reasonableness of the bond.

67. Secondly, the Respondent maintains that the Applicant's submission in paragraph 1(c) is too vague and too general. In its view, it is so unspecific that it neither allows the Tribunal to consider it properly, nor the Respondent to reply to it. Moreover, the Respondent alleges that the Tribunal does not have competence under article 292 of the Convention to determine the terms and conditions upon which the arrested vessel should be released. The Respondent further states that, according to article 113, paragraph 2, of the Rules, the Tribunal only has to determine the amount, nature and form of the bond or financial security to be posted for the release of the vessel and the crew.

68. The Tribunal finds that there is no merit in these arguments. The Tribunal considers that the Application is based on article 292 read in conjunction with article 73, paragraph 2, of the Convention.

The Applicant asks the Tribunal to exercise its power under article 292, paragraph 3, of the Convention, to order the release of the vessel and its crew upon the posting of a reasonable bond or other financial security.

69. Accordingly, the Tribunal holds that the Application is admissible.

NON-COMPLIANCE WITH ARTICLE 73, PARAGRAPH 2, OF THE CONVENTION

70. The Applicant requests the Tribunal to declare that the Respondent has not complied with article 73, paragraph 2, of the Convention because it has not provided for the prompt release of the vessel and its crew upon the posting of a reasonable bond or financial security.

71. Article 73, paragraph 2, reads as follows:

Arrested vessels and their crews shall be promptly released upon the posting of reasonable bond or other security.

72. The *Hoshinmaru* was ordered to stop on 1 June 2007 and was boarded in the exclusive economic zone of the Russian Federation by a team of inspectors from a patrol boat of the State Sea Inspection of the Northeast Border Coast Guard Directorate of the Federal Security Service of the Russian Federation. It was escorted by the patrol boat to the Respondent's port of Petropavlovsk-Kamchatskii, where the vessel and its crew have since remained.

73. A bond for the release of the vessel and its crew was not set by the Respondent until 13 July 2007, seven days after the Application for the prompt release of the *Hoshinmaru* was filed and more than five weeks after the vessel was arrested. The Respondent did not react to several requests from the Applicant to have the vessel and its crew released upon the posting of a reasonable bond or other financial security made since 6 June 2007. The Respondent, for its part, argues that the delay was due to the lack of cooperation of the Master and the owner of the vessel.

74. The parties disagree as to whether the Master and the crew are being detained along with the vessel.

75. The Applicant contends that the Master and the crew of the *Hoshinmaru* remain in detention, that crew members need to be present on board for the proper maintenance of the vessel and that the release of the crew cannot be separated entirely from the release of the vessel.

76. The Respondent argues that the members of the crew, with the exception of the Master, have never actually been detained and that, if crew members do not have formal permission to enter the Russian Federation and to leave the country, this is not due to the offence

committed but to the fact that the owner of the vessel is required to apply to the competent authorities for such permission—a common and simple procedure applicable to all foreign sailors arriving in Russian ports.

77. The Tribunal notes the statement by the Respondent that the restrictions on the free movement of the Master were lifted on 16 July 2007. The Tribunal further notes that the Master and the crew still remain in the Russian Federation.

78. The Applicant maintains that contrary to article 73, paragraph 2, of the Convention the bond was not set promptly. This allegation is denied by the Respondent.

79. However, both parties agree in principle that a bond should be set within a reasonable time, taking into account the complexity of the given case.

80. The Tribunal notes that the Convention does not set a precise time-limit for setting a bond (*"Camouco"*, *ITLOS Reports 2000*, p. 10, at p. 28, para. 54). The Tribunal further notes that, given the object and purpose of article 292 of the Convention, the time required for setting a bond should be reasonable. It observes that article 292 of the Convention does not require the flag State to file an application at any particular time after the detention of a vessel or its crew and that the earliest date for initiating such procedure before the Tribunal is, in accordance with paragraph 1 of that provision, 10 days from the time of detention.

81. The Tribunal will now turn to the reasonableness of the bond set by the Respondent.

82. The Tribunal has expressed its views on the reasonableness of the bond in a number of its judgments. In the *"Camouco" Case* it stated: "the Tribunal considers that a number of factors are relevant in an assessment of the reasonableness of bonds or other financial security. They include the gravity of the alleged offences, the penalties imposed or imposable under the laws of the detaining State, the value of the detained vessel and of the cargo seized, the amount of the bond imposed by the detaining State and its form" (*ITLOS Reports 2000*, p. 10, at p. 31, para. 67). In the *"Monte Confurco" Case* it added that: "This is by no means a complete list of factors. Nor does the Tribunal intend to lay down rigid rules as to the exact weight to be attached to each of them" (*ITLOS Reports 2000*, p. 86, at p. 109, para. 76). In the *"Volga" Case* it stated that: "In assessing the reasonableness of the bond or other security, due account must be taken of the terms of the bond or security set by the detaining State, having regard to all the circumstances of the particular case" (*ITLOS Reports 2002*, p. 10, at p. 32, para. 65). In the *"Juno Trader" Case* the

Tribunal further declared that: "The assessment of the relevant factors must be an objective one, taking into account all information provided to the Tribunal by the parties" (*ITLOS Reports 2004*, p. 17, at p. 41, para. 85).

83. In justifying the amount of the bond of 22,000,000 roubles (approximately US $862,000) as indicated in paragraph 51, the Respondent puts forward several arguments. It states that in the last two sessions of the Russian–Japanese Commission on Fisheries the Russian representatives had informed the Japanese representatives about the procedure that would be applied for the purpose of prompt release in cases of the detention of Japanese fishing vessels in the Russian exclusive economic zone. The Respondent further states that the criteria to be applied for the assessment of a bond in such cases were also specified during these sessions. The Respondent refers, in paragraph 65 of the Statement in Response, to documents contained in Annex 10 to the Protocol of the 23rd Session of the Russian–Japanese Commission on Fisheries dated 14 December 2006, as well as in Annex 4-2 of the Protocol of Russian–Japanese intergovernmental consultations on issues of harvesting of Russian originated salmon by Japanese fishing vessels in the 200-mile zone of the Russian Federation signed on 26 April 2007. According to those documents, the bond should be comparable to the amount of potential fines, compensation for damage caused, cost of illegally harvested living resources, products of their processing and instruments of illegal fishing (i.e. vessel, equipment, etc.). The Respondent expresses the opinion that such criteria and such procedure are consistent with the criteria elaborated by the Tribunal. The Respondent states that the Japanese representatives had not raised any objections to this methodology and that it can be inferred that they had acquiesced in it.

84. The Applicant, for its part, maintains that the Japanese Government had not given its consent, even tacitly, to a method of calculating a bond for prompt release which would include the value of the vessel. Further it contends that it had not given its consent to the Russian text of Annex 10 to the Protocol of the 23rd Session of the Russian–Japanese Commission on Fisheries dated 14 December 2006. In particular, the Applicant objects to the Respondent's interpretation that the value of the vessel would always be included in the bond.

85. The Tribunal is of the view that, especially between States that have long-standing relations as regards fisheries, an agreed procedure for setting bonds in the event of the detention of fishing vessels may contribute to mutual confidence, help resolve misunderstandings and prevent disputes. In the present case, however, the Tribunal does not consider that the information submitted to it is sufficient to establish that

the Japanese representatives had acquiesced in the procedure contained in the Respondent's document concerning the calculation of the bond communicated to Japan within the framework of the Russian–Japanese Commission on Fisheries.

86. The Protocol or minutes of a joint commission such as the Russian–Japanese Commission on Fisheries may well be the source of rights and obligations between Parties. In the case concerning *Maritime Delimitation and Territorial Questions between Qatar and Bahrain (Jurisdiction and Admissibility, Judgment, ICJ Reports 1994*, p. 112), the International Court of Justice admitted this possibility, but added, quoting its judgment in the *Aegean Sea Continental Shelf Case*, that "the Court must have regard above all to its actual terms and to the particular circumstances in which it was drawn up" (*Judgment, ICJ Reports 1978*, p. 3, at p. 39, para. 96). In the case concerning *Maritime Delimitation and Territorial Questions between Qatar and Bahrain*, the Court considered:

The Minutes are not a simple record of a meeting . . . ; they do not merely give an account of discussions and summarize points of agreement and disagreement. They enumerate the commitments to which the Parties have consented. They thus create rights and obligations in international law for the Parties. They constitute an international agreement. (*Judgment, ICJ Reports 1994*, p. 112, at p. 121, para. 25)

87. The Tribunal notes that, while on some matters the Protocols of the meetings mention agreed views, this is not the case as regards the criteria notified by the Russian side as to the setting of the bond. In this context, tacit consent or acquiescence cannot be presumed. The situation is not one where Japan would have been under an obligation to react according to the rule: *qui tacet consentire videtur si loqui debuisset ac potuisset* (*Temple of Preah Vihear, Merits, Judgment, ICJ Reports 1962*, p. 6, at p. 23).

88. The Tribunal is of the view that the amount of a bond should be proportionate to the gravity of the alleged offences. Article 292 of the Convention is designed to ensure that the coastal State, when fixing the bond, adheres to the requirement stipulated in article 73, paragraph 2, of the Convention, namely that the bond it fixes is reasonable in light of the assessment of relevant factors.

89. The proceedings under article 292 of the Convention, as clearly provided in paragraph 3 thereof, can deal only with the question of release, without prejudice to the merits of any case before the appropriate domestic forum against the vessel, its owner or its crew. Nevertheless, in the proceedings before it, the Tribunal is not prevented from examining

the facts and circumstances of the case to the extent necessary for a proper appreciation of the reasonableness of the bond as set by the Respondent (*"Monte Confurco", ITLOS Reports 2000*, p. 86, at pp. 108-9, para. 74). However, the Tribunal wishes to emphasize that in so doing it is by no means acting as a court of appeal (*"Monte Confurco", ITLOS Reports 2000*, p. 86, at p. 108, para. 72).

90. As the Respondent explained, the bond of 22,000,000 roubles for the release of the *Hoshinmaru* was calculated on the basis of the potential fines imposable upon the Master and the owner of the vessel, a penalty calculated on the basis of the amount of sockeye salmon allegedly taken illegally, the value of the vessel and administrative expenses incurred by the Russian authorities for carrying out the investigation.

91. The Applicant maintains that for the bond to be reasonable its level must reflect certain factors, in particular the gravity of the offence. This would exclude setting bonds at a level reflecting the highest possible fines. The Applicant considers it unreasonable to take account of the value of the vessel when calculating the bond since the alleged offence was not of the same degree of gravity as overfishing or fishing without a licence. Under Russian law, confiscation is one of the possible penalties. However, the Applicant is of the view that, taking into account the lesser degree of gravity of the offence, it would be unreasonable to consider it as a likely outcome of domestic proceedings which might justify including the value of the ship in the calculation of the reasonable bond. According to the Applicant the amount of the bond should not be more than 8,000,000 roubles (approximately US $313,000) considering the potential penalties in this case.

92. The Respondent, for its part, argues that fishing can be legal only when it is carried out in compliance with all the applicable rules and norms established by the coastal State, including timely and full reporting of data on species and amounts of the catch to its competent bodies. It considers the offence to be of a nature of sufficient gravity to justify the confiscation of the vessel and the imposition of the maximum fine. Finally, it states that the bond includes an amount of damages which is calculated in accordance with the law of the Russian Federation.

93. The Tribunal does not consider the bond of 22,000,000 roubles (approximately US $862,000) to be reasonable. Although the Tribunal is of the view that a violation of the rules on reporting may be sanctioned by the detaining State, it does not consider it reasonable that a bond should be set on the basis of the maximum penalties which could be

applicable to the owner and the Master, nor does it consider it reasonable that the bond should be calculated on the basis of the confiscation of the vessel, given the circumstances of this case. The Tribunal notes in this respect that the applicable Russian regulations do not foresee automatic inclusion of the value of the arrested vessel in the assessment of the bond.

94. For these reasons and in view of the circumstances of the case, the Tribunal finds that the Respondent has not complied with article 73, paragraph 2, of the Convention, that the Application is well-founded, and that, consequently, the Russian Federation must release promptly the *Hoshinmaru,* including the catch on board and its crew in accordance with paragraph 102.

AMOUNT AND FORM OF THE BOND OR OTHER FINANCIAL SECURITY

95. The Tribunal must now determine the amount, nature and form of the bond or other financial security to be posted, as laid down in article 113, paragraph 2, of the Rules. In accordance with article 293 of the Convention, the Tribunal must apply the provisions of this Convention and other rules of international law not incompatible with the Convention.

96. The Tribunal notes that the Respondent considers the offence committed by the Master of the *Hoshinmaru* to be a grave one. The Respondent maintains that the Master of the *Hoshinmaru* had declared 20 tons of raw sockeye salmon as the cheaper chum salmon. If the substitution of the species on the *Hoshinmaru* had not been revealed by the competent authorities of the Russian Federation, the 20 tons of sockeye salmon would simply have been stolen and taken illegally out of the exclusive economic zone of the Russian Federation. This amount of marine living resources could not have been accounted for by the competent bodies of the Russian Federation in exercising control over the percentage of total allowable catch of the species, i.e. sockeye salmon. In the view of the Respondent this was a classic manifestation of illegal, unreported and unregulated fishing. In the view of the Respondent, the gravity of the offence justifies the bond of 22,000,000 roubles.

97. The Applicant maintains that the alleged offence is not fishing without a licence or overfishing but falsely recording a catch that the vessel was entitled to take under its licence. Further, the Applicant argues that, since the amount of sockeye salmon on board the *Hoshinmaru* was well within the limit the vessel was licensed to fish, the sockeye salmon stock could not be considered to have been damaged or endangered.

98. The Tribunal notes that the present case is different from cases it has previously dealt with, since this case does not entail fishing without a licence. The *Hoshinmaru* held a valid fishing licence and was authorized to be present and to fish in the Russian exclusive economic zone. The Tribunal further notes that Russia and Japan cooperate closely in respect of fishing activities in the area in question. They have even established an institutional framework for consultations concerning the management and conservation of fish stocks which also deals with the enforcement of the applicable rules on the management and conservation of fish stocks in the exclusive economic zone of the Russian Federation in the Pacific. They have been cooperating in order to promote the conservation and reproduction of salmon and trout of Russian origin in the exclusive economic zone of the Russian Federation. The Tribunal notes that Japan expresses the wish to continue to endeavour ensuring that the crews of fishing vessels flying its flag respect local laws and regulations.

99. The offences considered here may be seen as transgressions within a broadly satisfactory cooperative framework. At the same time, the Tribunal is of the view that the offence committed by the Master of the *Hoshinmaru* should not be considered as a minor offence or an offence of a purely technical nature. Monitoring of catches, which requires accurate reporting, is one of the most essential means of managing marine living resources. Not only is it the right of the Russian Federation to apply and implement such measures but the provisions of article 61, paragraph 2, of the Convention should also be taken into consideration to ensure through proper conservation and management measures that the maintenance of the living resources in the exclusive economic zone is not endangered by over-exploitation.

100. On the basis of these considerations, the Tribunal is of the view that the security should be in the total amount of 10,000,000 roubles. The security should take the form either of a payment made to the bank account indicated by the Respondent, or of a bank guarantee, if the Applicant prefers this alternative.

101. The bank guarantee should, among other things, state that it is issued in consideration of the Russian Federation releasing the *Hoshinmaru* in relation to incidents that occurred in the exclusive economic zone of the Russian Federation on 1 June 2007, and that the issuer undertakes and guarantees to pay the Russian Federation such sum, up to 10,000,000 roubles, as may be determined by a final judgment or decision of the appropriate domestic forum in the Russian Federation or by agreement of the parties. Payment under the guarantee would be due promptly after receipt by the issuer of a written demand by

the competent authority of the Russian Federation, accompanied by a certified copy of the final judgment or decision or agreement.

OPERATIVE PROVISIONS

102. For these reasons, the Tribunal,

(1) Unanimously,
Finds that the Tribunal has jurisdiction under article 292 of the Convention to entertain the Application made by Japan.

(2) Unanimously,
Finds that the Application with respect to the allegation of non-compliance with article 73, paragraph 2, of the Convention is admissible.

(3) Unanimously,
Finds that the allegation made by the Applicant that the Respondent has not complied with the provisions of article 73, paragraph 2, of the Convention for the prompt release of the *Hoshinmaru* and its crew upon the posting of a reasonable bond or other financial security is well-founded.

(4) Unanimously,
Decides that the Russian Federation shall promptly release the *Hoshinmaru*, including its catch on board, upon the posting of a bond or other security as determined by the Tribunal, and that the Master and the crew shall be free to leave without any conditions.

(5) Unanimously,
Determines that the bond shall amount to 10,000,000 roubles.

(6) Unanimously,
Determines that the bond of 10,000,000 roubles shall be in the form either of a payment into the bank account indicated by the Respondent, or, if the Applicant so prefers, of a bank guarantee from a bank present in the Russian Federation or having corresponding arrangements with a Russian bank.

Done in English and in French, both texts being authoritative, in the Free and Hanseatic City of Hamburg, this sixth day of August, two thousand and seven, in three copies, one of which will be placed in the archives of the Tribunal and the others transmitted to the

Government of Japan and the Government of the Russian Federation, respectively.

DECLARATION OF JUDGE KOLODKIN

Notwithstanding my vote, I feel it necessary to make the following points.

The bond issued by the Tribunal is not in conformity with the relevant legal arrangements between Japan and the Russian Federation. It does not take into account the gravity of the offence. Moreover, its calculation is inconsistent with the practice of the Tribunal, which, as a rule, includes the value of the vessel in the bond.

DECLARATION OF JUDGE TREVES

In paragraph 77 of the Judgment, the Tribunal, faced with the opposing contentions of the parties as to whether the Master and the crew are detained along with the vessel, after observing that the restrictions imposed on the free movement of the Master had been lifted on 16 July 2007, notes that "the Master and crew still remain in the Russian Federation". In the operative part the Tribunal decides that the Russian Federation shall promptly release the *Hoshinmaru* "and that the Master and the crew shall be free to leave without any conditions". This operative provision might seem questionable, as the Tribunal does not state that the Master and the crew are "detained" under article 292, paragraph 1, of the Convention.

In my view, the observation concerning the Master—whose situation up to 16 July 2007 was similar to that of *contrôle judiciaire* under French law, which the Tribunal has considered as corresponding to "detention" in its judgment on the *"Camouco" Case* (*ITLOS Reports 2000*, p. 10, paragraph 71)—seems to imply that, in the opinion of the Tribunal, neither the Master nor the crew is "detained", as does the mild statement that Master and crew "still remain in the Russian Federation". Limitations to their liberty to leave Russia depending on the need to apply for permission under rules applicable to all foreign sailors (paragraph 76), or on the need for crew members to be present on board to ensure the proper maintenance of the ship (paragraph 75), can hardly, in my view, qualify as restrictions to freedom that can be considered as "detention", even when such notion is broadly interpreted as the Tribunal correctly did in the *"Camouco" Case*. So, why provide that Master and crew "shall be free to leave without conditions"?

In my view, this provision should not be read as concerning the release of the Master and crew from detention. It ought to be read, instead, as a complement to the provision for the release of the vessel. Its function is to prevent resort to conditions of any kind, bureaucratic or otherwise, concerning the departure of Master and crew, that might delay the departure of the vessel. A possible obstacle to the effectiveness of the "prompt" release of the vessel after the posting of the bond set by the Tribunal, as provided in article 292, paragraph 4, of the Convention, is thus eliminated.

The provision in the operative part that the Master and crew are free to leave without conditions, even though they have not been considered as "detained", is not unnecessary. It serves to preserve the efficacy of the judgment of the Tribunal for the release of the vessel.

DECLARATION OF JUDGE LUCKY

I agree with the reasoning in the Judgment; however, I wish to add a few comments in respect of the amount of the bond.

In the context of article 73 of the Convention, the relevant meaning of the word "bond" must be taken as a legal one and as such should be given the meaning ascribed to it in the language of criminal law and procedure. The bond in this context is similar to bail bonds in criminal proceedings which are defined as:

Written undertakings executed by the defendant... that the defendant will, while at liberty as a result of an order fixing bail and of the execution of a bail bond in satisfaction thereof, appear in a designated criminal action or proceeding when his attendance is required.
Black's Law Dictionary, eighth edition

The primary purpose of bail is to ensure the attendance of a person at court proceedings. There is no evidence that the owner (the Ikeda Suisan Co., a Japanese registered company with a given address) is not well known or is likely to become insolvent, the undisputed evidence being that it was willing to post a reasonable bond. The amount of the bond must not be punitive because the essence of the rule of law is that a person should be punished for crimes he has committed, not when a charge for a criminal offence is pending and the person has not admitted guilt.

In fixing a bond, the interests of the coastal State and of the flag State should be balanced. The bond should secure the coastal State's interest in imposing penalties that take account of the gravity of the alleged offences and in policing its fisheries and marine environment.

In paragraph 67 of the judgment in the "*Camouco*" *Case* (*Panama v. France*), *ITLOS Reports* 2000, p. 31, the Tribunal set out the criteria for determining the reasonableness of a bond or security. The Tribunal repeated that dictum in paragraph 79 of the *"Monte Confurco"* judgment in which the Tribunal added that the list of factors was not complete.

In my separate opinion in the *"Juno Trader" Case* I said:

It appears to me that in order to consider the gravity of the alleged offence the Tribunal would have to weigh the gravity in the same manner as a national judge determining urgent applications, for example in injunctive proceedings, and find whether a *prima facie* case has been made. In carrying out that exercise, the Tribunal will not be making any finding on the merits *per se* but will be determining whether or not the detaining State violated the provisions of article 73 of the Convention or whether the vessel of the applicant State violated the fisheries legislation of the detaining State.

I still subscribe to the above view.

Article 292 specifies in part that the "court or tribunal shall deal without delay with the application and shall deal only with the question of release, without prejudice to the merits of any case before the appropriate domestic forum against the vessel, its owner or its crew".

In prompt release cases the bond should constitute sufficient security that would ensure implementation of a court decision at the end of the proceedings.

In these proceedings the question is whether or not the bond sought for the release of the vessel and crew is reasonable.

For the reasons set out above I am of the opinion that the bond fixed by the Respondent is on the high side. I am in favour of a bond which is less than that fixed by the Respondent.

DECLARATION OF JUDGE TÜRK

1. In the present case the vessel was detained on 2 June 2007 and the bond was set by the Respondent on 13 July 2007. The Applicant maintained that contrary to article 73, paragraph 2, of the Convention the bond was not set promptly. This allegation was denied by the Respondent. However, both parties agreed in principle that a bond should be set within a reasonable time, taking into account the complexity of the given case (see paras. 78 and 79 of the Judgment).

2. In paragraph 80 of the Judgment the Tribunal notes that the Convention does not set a precise time-limit for setting a bond. The Tribunal further notes that, given the object and purpose of article 292 of the Convention, the time required for setting a bond should be reasonable. It observes that article 292 of the Convention does not require the flag State to file an application at any particular time after the

detention of a vessel or its crew and that the earliest date for initiating such procedure before the Tribunal is, in accordance with article 292, paragraph 1 of that provision, 10 days from the time of detention.

3. I fully agree with the position of the Tribunal set forth in paragraph 80 of the Judgment; the matter, however, calls for some further observations:

The Convention in article 73, paragraph 2, wisely avoids laying down a precise time-limit for the setting of a bond or other financial security, thus maintaining the necessary flexibility for dealing with the particular circumstances of each individual case. As the Tribunal already stated in the "*Camouco*" *Case* (*ITLOS Reports 2000*, p. 28, para. 54) and reiterated in paragraph 80 of the present Judgment, the Convention also does not require the flag State to file an application at any particular time after the detention of a vessel or its crew.

It must, however, be borne in mind that the prompt release procedure is designed as an expeditious procedure with the objective of ensuring that a detained vessel is not immobilized until the completion of the domestic administrative or criminal procedures of the detaining State, which might take many months. Furthermore, important humanitarian considerations must be taken into account for shortening, as far as possible, the time during which the crew of the detained vessel is not permitted to leave the detaining State.

In keeping with the fundamental objective and purpose of the prompt release procedure a bond or other financial security should be set at the earliest possible point in time. The due diligence which may in this regard be expected from the detaining State, however, also applies to the shipowner and the flag State. The shipowner should take prompt action in complying with the bond set by the detaining State, unless it considers the bond not to be "reasonable"—as required by articles 292, paragraph 1, and 73, paragraph 2, of the Convention. In such case the prompt release procedure under article 292 should, as soon as possible, be initiated through the flag State or, as the case may be, on its behalf.

The exact time-period for the setting of a bond will certainly depend on the degree of complexity of the investigations carried out by the detaining State and will thus have to vary from case to case. Nevertheless the ten-day time-frame enshrined in article 292, paragraph 1, of the Convention for seizing the Tribunal in prompt release cases, the requirement of article 292, paragraph 2, for the competent court or tribunal to deal without delay with an application for release and the stringent time-limits imposed on the Tribunal by its Rules for dealing with such an application and the rendering of a judgment should be taken into consideration. Thus, a maximum period of approximately one month after the detention of a vessel and its crew would seem reasonable for the setting of the bond. In case the flag State engages the prompt release procedure under article 292, if it considers the bond or other financial security not to be reasonable, the time of detention of the vessel and/or its crew would then altogether not exceed approximately two months.

Although the flag State has the right to initiate a prompt release procedure already after ten days from the time of detention of vessel and crew, international litigation should, in general, be considered a last rather than a first resort for the settling of a dispute.

SEPARATE OPINION OF JUDGE YANAI

I voted in favour of the Judgment since I substantially agree with its findings but I have reservations as to the way in which the amount of the bond was calculated.

1. The *Hoshinmaru* was licensed by the Russian Federation to catch certain limited quantities of sockeye salmon, chum salmon, sakhalin trout, silver salmon and spring salmon in the Russian exclusive economic zone from 15 May to 31 July 2007. When the *Hoshinmaru* was stopped and boarded by Russian officials on 1 June 2001, it was fishing with a valid licence in the area where it was licensed to fish and the fish on board corresponded to the species specified in the licence, namely, sockeye salmon, chum salmon and spring salmon. The amount of the three species on board was well within the limits set in the licence. Specifically, it is said that the *Hoshinmaru* had caught about 45,000 kg of sockeye salmon, of which approximately 20,000 kg had been recorded as cheaper chum salmon. However, the *Hoshinmaru* was licensed to catch 85,700 kg of sockeye salmon—which is more than four times the amount that was said to be falsely recorded—and 85,200 kg of chum salmon—which is again far more than said to be falsely recorded. So the alleged offence is not fishing without a licence or over-fishing; the alleged offence is falsely recording a catch that the vessel was entitled to take (Professor Lowe, Thursday, 19 July 2007, p.m., *ITLOS/PV.07/1*, p. 14).

2. The Respondent included in its calculation of the bond an amount of 7,927,500 roubles as compensation for damage allegedly caused by the *Hoshinmaru* to salmon and trout resources in the Russian exclusive economic zone. Thus this amount forms part of the bond amounting to 22,000,000 roubles proposed by the Respondent. I am not in a position to challenge the way the amount of compensation for the alleged damage was calculated under the internal laws and regulations of the Russian

Federation. Nevertheless, I am not prevented from examining the facts and circumstances of the case to the extent necessary for a proper appreciation of the reasonableness of the bond as set by the Respondent. In my view, the following three factors are relevant to such an examination (paragraph 89 of the Judgment):

First, as stated in paragraph 1 above, the *Hoshinmaru* was fishing with a valid licence, and the falsely recorded amount of catch was well within the limits set in the licence. In this sense, the "*Hoshinmaru*" *Case* is different from cases the Tribunal has previously dealt with (paragraph 98 of the Judgment). When the competent authorities of the Russian Federation issued the licence to the *Hoshinmaru* on 14 May 2007, they must have ascertained that the amount of catch allocated to the *Hoshinmaru*, together with quotas for other national and foreign vessels, would not cause damage to salmon and trout resources in the Russian exclusive economic zone, let alone its environment. So I find it difficult to believe that the offence the *Hoshinmaru* committed by falsely recording the catch would cause damage to the conservation of salmon and trout resources in the Russian exclusive economic zone.

Secondly, as the Agent of the Respondent recognized, Japan and Russia have a long history of bilateral cooperation in fishery matters under the two agreements concluded between them in 1984 and 1985 (Mr Zagaynov, Friday, 20 July 2007, a.m., *ITLOS/PV.07/2*, p. 2). Japanese vessels fish salmon and trout in the Russian exclusive economic zone within this bilateral framework. In the conservation and management of anadromous stocks, both countries cooperate under the agreement of 1985, specifically through the Joint Commission established by it. In this connection, the Agent of the Applicant referred to this cooperation in the following statement:

I would like to point out, in this regard, the fact that Japan has been actively cooperating in order to promote the conservation and the reproduction of salmon and trout of Russian origin within the framework of a bilateral treaty with the Russian Federation. Japan has been providing, for example, a sizable amount of equipment for the good functioning of hatchery and nursery for salmon and trout in the Russian Federation and the scientists of both countries are in agreement that the salmon-trout resources in the exclusive economic zone of the Russian Federation where this incident occurred are conserved at a high level (Mr Komatsu, Thursday, 19 July 2007, p.m., *ITLOS/PV.07/1*, p. 6).

The Tribunal also notes the long-standing bilateral cooperation between Japan and Russia in the field of fisheries including the conservation and reproduction of salmon and trout of Russian origin in the Russian exclusive economic zone (paragraph 98 of the Judgment).

Thirdly, I would like to shed light on another aspect of fishing resources by comparing the present case with the *"Monte Confurco" Case* and the *"Volga" Case*. The *Monte Confurco*, a vessel flying the flag of the Applicant (Seychelles), was allegedly engaged in the unlicensed fishing of toothfish in the exclusive economic zone of the Kerguelen Islands in the French Southern and Antarctic Territories. The *Volga*, a vessel flying the flag of the Applicant (the Russian Federation), was allegedly fishing Patagonian toothfish without licence in the Australian exclusive economic zone. Both cases were considered to involve illegal, unregulated and unreported fishing, and the respective Respondents, France and Australia, expressed concern about the depletion of these stocks as a result of continuing illegal fishing in the area covered by the Convention on the Conservation of Antarctic Marine Living Resources (CCAMLR) (*The "Monte Confurco" Case, Judgment, ITLOS Reports 2000*, p. 110, paragraph 79; *The "Volga" Case, Judgment, ITLOS Reports 2002*, p. 33, paragraph 67). While a depletion of toothfish and Patagonian toothfish stocks is a matter of international concern and conservation measures have been taken under CCAMLR, salmon and trout resources in the Russian exclusive economic zone are conserved at a high level as mentioned above.

3. In light of the foregoing, the offence committed by the *Hoshinmaru* which is the false recording of the catch within the limits set in the valid licence cannot be considered as causing damage to salmon and trout resources in the Russian exclusive economic zone. If this relatively low degree of gravity of the offence and the above-mentioned aspects of fishing resources concerned had been adequately taken into account in the determination of the bond, its amount in the present case would have been set at a lower level.

[Report: Transcript]

International tribunals — International Tribunal for the Law of the Sea — Jurisdiction and admissibility — United Nations Convention on the Law of the Sea, 1982, Article 292 — Japan filing Application against Russian Federation for prompt release of vessel — Whether Tribunal having jurisdiction — Whether Application admissible — Whether Russian Federation breaching obligations under Article 73(2) of Convention — Domestic proceedings before Russian courts — Russian Federation confiscating vessel — Effect of confiscation — Whether confiscation rendering application for prompt release of vessel under Article 292 of Convention without object

Relationship of international law and municipal law — United Nations Convention on the Law of the Sea, 1982 — Decisions of courts of Russian Federation — Confiscation of fishing vessel — Issues of ownership and nationality — Whether confiscation having impact on nationality of the vessel — Role of flag State — Whether confiscation rendering application for prompt release of vessel under Article 292 of Convention without object — Object and purpose of prompt release procedure — Article 292(3) of Convention — Decision of Russian Federation Supreme Court concluding domestic court proceedings — Encroachment upon national competences — Article 292(3) of Convention

THE TOMIMARU[1]

(JAPAN v. RUSSIAN FEDERATION)

(APPLICATION FOR PROMPT RELEASE)

International Tribunal for the Law of the Sea. 6 August 2007

(Wolfrum, *President*; Akl, *Vice-President*; Caminos, Marotta Rangel, Yankov, Kolodkin, Park, Bamela Engo, Nelson, Chandrasekhara Rao, Treves, Ndiaye, Jesus, Cot, Lucky, Pawlak, Yanai, Türk, Kateka and Hoffmann, *Judges*)

SUMMARY: *The facts:*—On 31 October 2006, the *Tomimaru*, a fishing vessel flying the flag of Japan, owned and operated by a Japanese company, was boarded and inspected by Russian Federation officials while fishing in the

[1] For a list of counsel, see para. 17 of the judgment.

exclusive economic zone ("EEZ") of the Russian Federation in the western Bering Sea. The officials found on board an unaccounted amount of walleye pollack and some illegal catches in breach of the terms of the fishing licence. The *Tomimaru* was escorted to Avachinskiy Bay for further investigation and detained.

Criminal and administrative proceedings were instituted against the Master and owner of the *Tomimaru* for the exploitation of living marine resources. The owner's request for the setting of a reasonable bond for the *Tomimaru* was rejected. The order to confiscate the *Tomimaru* was confirmed by the Kamchatka District Court on 24 January 2007. The owner applied to the Russian Federation Supreme Court under the supervisory review procedure.

On 6 July 2007, Japan ("the Applicant") filed an Application with the International Tribunal for the Law of the Sea under Article 292 of the United Nations Convention on the Law of the Sea, 1982 ("the Convention")[2] against the Russian Federation ("the Respondent") for the prompt release of the *Tomimaru* and its crew. The Applicant contended that the Tribunal had jurisdiction, that the Application was admissible, that the allegation was well founded, and that the Respondent had breached its obligations under Article 73(2) of the Convention.[3] The Applicant sought an order that the *Tomimaru* be released upon terms and conditions considered reasonable by the Tribunal. The Respondent challenged the admissibility of the Application; in the alternative, it claimed that it had fulfilled its obligations under Article 73(2) of the Convention.

The Respondent argued that the Tribunal had no competence to examine an application for prompt release according to Article 292(3) of the Convention. The change of ownership of the *Tomimaru*, by way of confiscation, rendered the Application without object. The case had been considered before the appropriate domestic forum on its merits; the decision entered into force upon delivery and executed; the supervisory procedure application constituted a complaint rather than an appeal. The Applicant maintained that the confiscation was not final since the matter was pending before the Supreme Court. Irrespective of ownership, the *Tomimaru* remained a Japanese vessel; Japan was entitled to bring a prompt release application in respect of it regardless of its owner's nationality.

After the hearing's closure, on 26 July 2007, the Respondent informed the Tribunal that the Supreme Court had dismissed the application concerning the review of the decision on confiscation.

Held (unanimously):—Since the Application no longer had any object, no decision was required.

(1) With respect to jurisdiction under Article 292 of the Convention, Japan and the Russian Federation were both States Parties to the Convention. While the Respondent did not dispute that Japan was the flag State of the *Tomimaru*, it

---

[2] For the text of Article 292 of the Convention, see para. 48 of the judgment.
[3] Article 73(2) provided that: "Arrested vessels and their crews shall be promptly released upon the posting of reasonable bond or other security."

argued that the change of ownership rendered the Application without object. The *Tomimaru* was detained in Avachinskiy Bay. The Applicant alleged that the Respondent had not complied with Article 73(2) of the Convention for the prompt release of the vessel upon the posting of a reasonable bond or other financial security. The Parties did not agree to submit the question of release of the vessel to another court or tribunal within ten days from the time of detention. Japan made the Application in accordance with Articles 110 and 111 of the Rules of the Tribunal (paras. 48-55).

(2) As required by Article 292(1) of the Convention, the Application was based on an allegation that the detaining State had not complied with Convention provisions for the prompt release of a vessel and crew upon the posting of a reasonable bond or other financial security. The Application was based on Article 292 read in conjunction with Article 73(2) of the Convention. The Tribunal was asked to exercise its power under Article 292(3) to order the release of vessel and crew upon the posting of a reasonable bond or other financial security (paras. 56-8).

(3) Although the decision of the Russian Federation Supreme Court was taken after the closure of the hearing, it was appropriate to take this fact into consideration (para. 68).

(4) The confiscation of a vessel changed a vessel's ownership. It did not result *per se* in an automatic change of the flag or in its loss since the nationality of a vessel was a different issue to its ownership. It was for each State to establish conditions for the granting of its nationality to ships according to Article 91 of the Convention. The flag State had important functions described in Article 94 and played a pivotal role in initiating the prompt release procedure under Article 292 (paras. 69-70).

(5) In determining whether the confiscation of a fishing vessel rendered an application for prompt release under Article 292 of the Convention without object, account had to be taken of the object and purpose of that procedure and of Article 292(3) of the Convention. There was no reference in Article 73 to confiscation. The confiscation of a fishing vessel was not to be used in such a manner as to upset the balance of the interests of the flag State and of the coastal State established in the Convention; that a judgment under Article 292 did not prejudice the merits of any case before the appropriate domestic forum against the vessel or its crew was a factor (paras. 71-5).

(6) A decision to confiscate eliminated the provisional character of the vessel's detention, rendering the procedure for its prompt release without object. It was not to be taken so as to prevent the shipowner from having recourse to available domestic judicial remedies, to prevent the flag State from resorting to the Convention's prompt release procedure, through proceedings inconsistent with international due process standards, or in unjustified haste (para. 76).

(7) Considering the objective of Article 292 of the Convention, the flag State was to act in a timely manner. The shipowner and the flag State had to take action within reasonable time either to have recourse to the national

judicial system of the detaining State or to initiate the prompt release procedure under Article 292 (para. 77).

(8) Considering the object and purpose of the prompt release procedure, a decision to confiscate the vessel did not prevent consideration of a prompt release application while proceedings were still before the domestic courts of the detaining State. The decision of the Russian Federation Supreme Court had, however, concluded domestic court proceedings. A decision under Article 292 of the Convention to release the vessel would contradict that decision, encroaching national competences in contravention of Article 292(3) (paras. 78-81).

Declaration of Judge Nelson: (1) The mechanism for prompt release was designed to isolate the prompt release proceedings from those in the domestic forum. The Tribunal was not a court of appeal (p. 57).

(2) Facts could only be examined where strictly necessary to assess the reasonableness of measures taken by the arresting State. Utmost restraint was to be exercised in making statements that might imply criticisms of procedures and decisions of domestic courts. The suggestion in paragraph 76 of the judgment that the Tribunal had the power *inter alia* to examine whether the shipowner was prevented from having recourse to available domestic procedures ran the risk of straying into the local court's territory (pp. 57-8).

Declaration of Judge Yanai: (1) The two factors that complicated the case were the delay by the flag State in filing the Application and the intricacy of procedures concerning the release of detained foreign fishing vessels and the bond system in the Russian Federation (p. 58).

(2) It was the duty of coastal States to exercise their sovereign rights in their EEZs in accordance with the Convention and to ensure that national legislation and procedure conformed to the Convention so that the international law of the sea regime, including the prompt release procedure, could function properly. Bond or other security under national laws should be unified. National prompt release procedure, including bond, should be simple and transparent. The amount of bond should be decided upon and communicated reasonably promptly. National prompt release procedure should be based on due process of law (pp. 59-60).

Separate Opinion of Judge Jesus: (1) Under Article 73 the coastal State, in exercising its sovereign rights, was entitled to take measures to protect the living resources in its EEZ in the most effective way to prevent their depletion. The confiscation of vessels as a penalty was consistent with Article 73(1), as supported by undisputed State practice (pp. 60-1).

(2) A fishing vessel could be confiscated immediately after its arrest or detention. Confiscation was a matter of the merits, outside the Tribunal's jurisdiction. A State's laws and judicial decisions were facts. The prompt release procedure did not prevent the detaining State from confiscating a vessel at any

stage of its detention; it was a means of avoiding the unnecessary immobilization of a vessel pending the decision of the domestic forum on the merits. The flag State, to avoid early confiscation, could apply to the Tribunal for prompt release immediately after the ten days from the time of detention had elapsed upon satisfying Article 292(1) of the Convention (pp. 61-3).

Separate Opinion of Judge Lucky: The Application was inadmissible.
(1) The period between the detention of the vessel and the filing of the Application was too long; the due process of law in the Russian judicial system had already been set in train. An order for prompt release could be deemed as interference with the State's judicial system (pp. 67-9).

(2) There was no evidence of abuse of process. The Application was not too vague but it was moot because the Respondent had complied with Article 73(2) on 12 December 2006 by setting a bond and informing the owner. The confiscation of the vessel prevented the Tribunal from entertaining the case. National courts had determined and confirmed the merits of the case. The Applicant could have applied to the Tribunal after it was advised that a bond had been set by the Respondent but did not. The vessel had been confiscated in judicial proceedings in accordance with the laws and regulations of the Respondent. The Tribunal could not circumvent or intervene in the due process of national courts. Even if the Supreme Court had not given its decision, the Application would have still been inadmissible (pp. 69-75).

The texts of the judgment and the declarations and opinions are set out as follows:

	page
Judgment on the Application for Prompt Release	40
Declaration of Judge Nelson	56
Declaration of Judge Yanai	58
Separate Opinion of Judge Jesus	60
Separate Opinion of Judge Lucky	63

The following is the text of the judgment of the Tribunal:

TABLE OF CONTENTS

	paragraphs
Introduction	1-21
Factual background	22-47
Jurisdiction	48-55
Admissibility	56-8
Effects of confiscation	59-81
Operative provision	82

INTRODUCTION

1. On 6 July 2007, an Application under article 292 of the United Nations Convention on the Law of the Sea (hereinafter "the Convention") was filed by electronic mail with the Registry of the Tribunal by Japan against the Russian Federation concerning the release of the *53rd Tomimaru* (hereinafter "the *Tomimaru*"). The Application was accompanied by a letter of 6 July 2007 from Mr Ichiro Komatsu, Director-General, International Legal Affairs Bureau, Ministry of Foreign Affairs of Japan, which transmitted a communication from the Minister of Foreign Affairs of Japan, notifying the Registrar of the Tribunal of the appointment of Mr Komatsu as Agent of Japan. By the same letter, the Registrar was notified of the appointment of Mr Tadakatsu Ishihara, Consul-General of Japan in Hamburg, as Co-Agent. The original of the Application and of the letter of the Agent of Japan were delivered on 9 July 2007.

2. A copy of the Application was sent on 6 July 2007, by electronic mail and facsimile, to the Embassy of the Russian Federation in Berlin. A certified copy of the original of the Application was sent to the Embassy of the Russian Federation in Berlin on 10 July 2007.

3. By a note verbale from the Registrar dated 6 July 2007, the Minister of Foreign Affairs of the Russian Federation was informed that the Statement in Response of the Russian Federation, in accordance with article 111, paragraph 4, of the Rules of the Tribunal (hereinafter "the Rules"), could be filed no later than 96 hours before the opening of the hearing.

4. In accordance with article 112, paragraph 3, of the Rules, the President of the Tribunal, by Order dated 9 July 2007, fixed 21 July 2007 as the date for the opening of the hearing with respect to the Application. Notice of the Order was communicated forthwith to the parties.

5. The Application was entered in the List of cases as Case No 15 and named the *"Tomimaru" Case*.

6. In accordance with article 24, paragraph 3, of the Statute of the Tribunal (hereinafter "the Statute"), States Parties to the Convention were notified of the Application by a note verbale from the Registrar dated 9 July 2007.

7. In accordance with articles 45 and 73 of the Rules, the President held consultations with the representatives of the parties on 10 July 2007, during which he ascertained their views with regard to questions of procedure. The Japanese representatives were present at the consultations while the Russian representative participated via telephone.

8. Pursuant to the Agreement on Cooperation and Relationship between the United Nations and the International Tribunal for the Law of the Sea of 18 December 1997, the Secretary-General of the United Nations was notified by the Registrar on 11 July 2007 of the receipt of the Application.

9. On 11 July 2007, the Registrar was notified by a letter of the same date from the First Deputy Minister of Foreign Affairs of the Russian Federation of the appointment of Mr Evgeny Zagaynov, Deputy Director, Legal Department, Ministry of Foreign Affairs of the Russian Federation, as Agent of the Russian Federation. By the same letter, the Registrar was notified of the appointment of Mr Sergey Ganzha, Consul-General of the Russian Federation in Hamburg, as Co-Agent.

10. On 12, 18 and 21 July 2007, the Agent of Japan transmitted additional documents in support of its Application, copies of which were transmitted to the other party.

11. On 17 July 2007, the Russian Federation filed its Statement in Response, a copy of which was transmitted forthwith to the Agent of Japan. On the same date, the Russian Federation submitted additional documents in support of its Statement in Response, copies of which were transmitted to the other party.

12. By letters from the Registrar dated 9, 12 and 13 July 2007, the Co-Agent of Japan was requested to complete the documentation, in accordance with article 63, paragraph 1, and article 64, paragraph 3, of the Rules. On 11 and 13 July 2007, the Co-Agent of Japan, and on 18 July 2007, the Agent of Japan, submitted documents, copies of which were forwarded to the other party.

13. In accordance with articles 45 and 73 of the Rules, the President held consultations with the Agents of the parties on 18 July 2007, during which he ascertained their views regarding the order and duration of the presentation by each party and the evidence to be produced during the oral proceedings.

14. Prior to the opening of the oral proceedings, the Tribunal held initial deliberations on 20 July 2007, in accordance with article 68 of the Rules.

15. Prior to the opening of the oral proceedings, the Agent of Japan and the Agent of the Russian Federation communicated information required under paragraph 14 of the Guidelines concerning the Preparation and Presentation of Cases before the Tribunal.

16. Pursuant to article 67, paragraph 2, of the Rules, copies of the pleadings and documents annexed thereto were made accessible to the public on the date of the opening of the oral proceedings.

17. Oral statements were presented at four public sittings held on 21 and 23 July 2007 by the following:

On behalf of Japan:	Mr Ichiro Komatsu, Agent,
	Mr Vaughan Lowe, Advocate,
	Mr Shotaro Hamamoto, Advocate.
On behalf of the Russian Federation:	Mr Evgeny Zagaynov, Agent,
	Mr Vadim Yalovitskiy, Deputy Agent,
	Mr Vladimir Golitsyn, Counsel.

18. On 21 July 2007, Mr Vadim Yalovitskiy, Deputy Agent for the Russian Federation, delivered his statement in Russian. The necessary arrangements were made for his statement to be interpreted into the official languages of the Tribunal in accordance with article 85 of the Rules.

19. On 21 July 2007, a list of questions which the Tribunal wished the parties to address was communicated to the Agents. Written responses to these questions were subsequently submitted by the Applicant on 21 July 2007 and by the Respondent on 24 July 2007.

20. In the Application of Japan and in the Statement in Response of the Russian Federation, the following submissions were presented:

On behalf of Japan,
in the Application:

Pursuant to Article 292 of the United Nations Convention on the Law of the Sea (hereinafter "the Convention"), the Applicant requests the International Tribunal for the Law of the Sea (hereinafter "the Tribunal"), by means of a judgment:

(a) to declare that the Tribunal has jurisdiction under Article 292 of the Convention to hear the application concerning the detention of the vessel the *53rd Tomimaru* (hereinafter "the *Tomimaru*") in breach of the Respondent's obligations under Article 73(2) of the Convention;
(b) to declare that the application is admissible, that the allegation of the Applicant is well-founded, and that the Respondent has breached its obligation under Article 73(2) of the Convention; and
(c) to order the Respondent to release the vessel of the *Tomimaru*, upon such terms and conditions as the Tribunal shall consider reasonable.

On behalf of the Russian Federation,
in the Statement in Response:

The Russian Federation requests the Tribunal to decline to make the orders sought in paragraph 1 of the Application of Japan. The Russian Federation requests the Tribunal to make the following orders:

(a) that the Application of Japan is inadmissible;
(b) alternatively, that the allegations of the Applicant are not well-founded and that the Russian Federation has fulfilled its obligations under paragraph 2 of Article 73 of the United Nations Convention on the Law of the Sea.

21. In accordance with article 75, paragraph 2, of the Rules, the following final submissions were presented by the parties at the end of the hearing on 23 July 2007:

On behalf of Japan,

The Applicant requests the International Tribunal for the Law of the Sea (hereinafter "the Tribunal"), by means of a judgment:

(a) to declare that the Tribunal has jurisdiction under Article 292 of the United Nations Convention on the Law of the Sea (hereinafter "the Convention") to hear the application concerning the detention of the vessel the *53rd Tomimaru* (hereinafter "the *Tomimaru*") in breach of the Respondent's obligations under Article 73(2) of the Convention;
(b) to declare that the application is admissible, that the allegation of the Applicant is well-founded, and that the Respondent has breached its obligation under Article 73(2) of the Convention; and
(c) to order the Respondent to release the vessel the *Tomimaru*, upon such terms and conditions as the Tribunal shall consider reasonable.

On behalf of the Russian Federation,

The Russian Federation requests the International Tribunal for the Law of the Sea to decline to make the orders sought in paragraph 1 of the Application of Japan. The Russian Federation requests the Tribunal to make the following orders:

(a) that the Application of Japan is inadmissible;
(b) alternatively, that the allegations of the Applicant are not well-founded and that the Russian Federation has fulfilled its obligations under paragraph 2 of Article 73 of the United Nations Convention on the Law of the Sea.

FACTUAL BACKGROUND

Boarding and Inspection of the Tomimaru

22. The trawler *Tomimaru* is a fishing vessel owned and operated by Kanai Gyogyo Co., a company registered in Japan. At the time of detention, the *Tomimaru* was flying the flag of Japan.

23. According to the fishing licence issued to the *Tomimaru* by the competent Russian authorities, the ship was authorized to fish walleye

pollack and herring, from 1 October to 31 December 2006, in an area of the western Bering Sea located in the exclusive economic zone of the Respondent. The quota allowances fixed by the fishing licence were 1,163 tons of walleye pollack and 18 tons of herring.

24. On 31 October 2006, the *Tomimaru* was fishing in the area of the Respondent's exclusive economic zone designated above when it was boarded by officers from the patrol boat *Vorovskii* and inspected by officials from the Northeast Border Coast Guard Directorate of the Federal Security Service of the Russian Federation. According to the letter of 5 November 2006 from the Northeast Border Coast Guard Directorate to the Inter-district Prosecutor's Office for Nature Protection in Kamchatka, the examination of the holds of the vessel revealed that there was an unaccounted amount of 5.5 tons of walleye pollack. The vessel was then re-routed and escorted to Avachinskiy Bay for further investigation.

25. By a note verbale dated 9 November 2006 from the Representative Office of the Ministry of Foreign Affairs of the Russian Federation in Petropavlovsk-Kamchatskii, the Consulate-General of Japan in Vladivostok was informed that, as a result of the inspection of the *Tomimaru* on 8 November 2006, not less than 20 tons of gutted walleye pollack, that was not listed in the logbook, were found on board the vessel, and "some kinds of fish products which are forbidden to catch, i.e. not less than 19.5 tons of various sorts of frozen halibut, 3.2 tons of ray, 4.9 tons of cod as well as not less than 3 tons of other kinds of bottom fish". Later, by a letter dated 22 December 2006, the Inter-district Prosecutor's Office for Nature Protection in Kamchatka informed the Consulate-General of Japan in Vladivostok that the accurate quantity of fish illegally caught was "established at 62,186.9 kg and the damage to the living [marine] resources in the Russian Federation amount[ed] to 8,800,000 rubles" (approximately US $345,000).

Institution of Proceedings by the Detaining State

26. According to the letter of 1 December 2006 from the Public Prosecutor's Office of the Russian Federation to the Consulate-General of Japan in Vladivostok, a criminal case was instituted against the Master of the *Tomimaru* on 8 November 2006 for "exploitation without permission of the natural resources in the exclusive economic zone of the Russian Federation, causing enormous environmental damages to the living [marine] resources equivalent to not less than 8,500,000 rubles", a crime stipulated in article 253, paragraph 2, of the Criminal Code of the Russian Federation. The Master was ordered to stay in

Petropavlovsk-Kamchatskii until the completion of the preparatory examination and the examination for the trial of the criminal case.

27. Article 253, paragraph 2, of the Criminal Code of the Russian Federation reads as follows:

[Translation from Russian provided by the Applicant]

Research, search, prospecting and exploitation of the natural resources of the continental shelf of the Russian Federation or of the exclusive economic zone of the Russian Federation, conducted without appropriate permits, shall be punished by imposing a fine from one hundred thousand to five hundred thousand roubles or in the amount of the wages or other income of the convicted for a period from one year to three years or by corrective labour for a term of up to two years, with the deprivation of the right to hold certain duties or to engage in certain activities for a term of up to three years, or without such deprivation.

28. The *Tomimaru* was considered material evidence in the criminal proceedings under article 82 of the Code of Criminal Procedure of the Russian Federation and detained in Avachinskiy Bay.

29. According to the Application, the allegedly illegal portion of the catch of the *Tomimaru* was confiscated by the authorities of the Respondent. The rest of the catch was sold by the agent of the vessel owner and its value was returned to the owner.

30. It is not disputed by the parties that the other members of the crew were allowed to leave the Russian Federation after the completion of the investigation.

31. Administrative proceedings were instituted against the owner on 14 November 2006 for violation of article 8.17, paragraph 2, of the Code of Administrative Offences of the Russian Federation.

32. Article 8.17, paragraph 2, of the Code of Administrative Offences provides as follows:

[Translation from Russian provided by the Respondent]

Violating the rules of catching (fishing) aquatic biological (living) resources and of protection thereof, or the terms and conditions of a license for water use, or of a permit (license) to catch aquatic biological (living) resources of the internal sea waters, or of the territorial sea, or of the continental shelf and (or) the exclusive economic zone of the Russian Federation—shall entail the imposition of an administrative fine on citizens in the amount of from half the cost to the full cost of aquatic biological (living) resources, which have become the subject of the administrative offence, with or without confiscation of the vessel and of other instruments of committing the administrative offence; on officials in the amount of from one to one and a half times the cost of aquatic biological (living) resources, which have become the subject of the administrative offence, with or without confiscation of the vessel and of other instruments of committing the administrative offence; and on legal entities in the amount of from twofold to threefold the cost of aquatic biological (living) resources which have become the subject of the administrative offence with or without confiscation of the vessel and of other instruments of committing the administrative offence.

Petition for the Determination of a Bond

33. On 30 November 2006, a representative of the company Yokei Suisan, the owner of another detained trawler—the *Youkeimaru*—wrote to the Northeast Border Coast Guard Directorate regarding the cases instituted against three Japanese corporations, including the owner of the *Tomimaru* ("Kanai Gyogyo"). The letter stated: "We apologize for the actions of our masters and guarantee payment of all appropriate penalties provided for in the Russian legislation" and requested that "the possibility of release of our vessels upon posting the bond, which will be set by the Russian side" be considered. In response to this request, the Northeast Border Coast Guard Directorate wrote to the Consulate-General of Japan in Vladivostok on 14 December 2006 and asked the Consulate-General to notify the representatives of the companies concerned that the matter was being handled by the Inter-district Prosecutor's Office for Nature Protection in Kamchatka.

34. In a letter dated 1 December 2006 sent to the Consulate-General of Japan in Vladivostok, the Inter-district Prosecutor's Office for Nature Protection in Kamchatka observed that "the owner of the vessel, who bears responsibility for unlawful actions of the Master, has not until now applied to provide a bond commensurate to the amount of incurred damage". The letter added: "As to the decision regarding the release of the detained vessels, it will be taken after the bond has been posted to include the judicial costs in respect of the cases on the administrative offences against the legal entities, i.e. ship owners."

35. On 8 December 2006, the owner sent a petition to the Inter-district Prosecutor's Office for Nature Protection to request that a bond be fixed for the release of the vessel.

36. The owner was informed by a letter dated 12 December 2006 from the Inter-district Prosecutor's Office that "[a]ccording to the estimation of the damage, the amount of the damage to the Russian Federation is equivalent to 8,800,000 rubles. The free use of the trawler '53rd' *Tomimaru* will not be prevented by the Inter-district Prosecutor's Office once the bond is paid to the deposit account ...". The amount of 8,800,000 roubles (approximately US $345,000) was not paid.

37. On 14 December 2006, the owner sent a "petition concerning the case of administrative offences" to the Northeast Border Coast Guard Directorate, in which he noted that the Inter-district Prosecutor's Office for Nature Protection "has set the amount of a bond upon the posting of which the vessel will be released, within the criminal case established against the Master of the '*53rd' Tomimaru*" and then added: "[c]onsidering the aforementioned fact, I request the amount of a bond be set for the case of administrative offences established against the owner of the '*53rd' Tomimaru*".

38. After the owner had been informed that the matter was being handled by the Federal Court of Petropavlovsk-Kamchatskii, he made a similar request for a bond to the Petropavlovsk-Kamchatskii City Court with respect to the administrative proceedings.

39. By a decision dated 19 December 2006, the City Court rejected the petition for the setting of a reasonable bond for the *Tomimaru* for the following reasons:

[Translation from Russian provided by the Applicant]

the measures to ensure the proceedings on administrative offences have been taken in accordance with Articles 27.1 and 27.14 of the Code of the Administrative Offences of the Russian Federation by means of detention of the vessel ...

The provisions of the Code of Administrative Offences of the Russian Federation do not provide the possibility of releasing a property after posting the amount of bond by the accused on the case of administrative offences.

In accordance with Article 29.10(3) of the Code of Administrative Offences ..., the problems concerning the property of detention ... taken into custody shall be solved at the resolution of the case of administrative offences taken as the result of administrative offences.

40. Article 29.10(3) of the Code of Administrative Offences provides as follows:

[Translation from Russian provided by the Applicant]

A decision with regard to a case concerning an administrative offence should settle the questions concerning seized items and documents, as well as items under arrest, if an administrative penalty in the form of confiscation or compensated seizure has not been imposed or may not be imposed in respect of them ...

41. In addition to the action taken by the owner of the vessel, several requests have been made by the Government of Japan through its Consulate-General in Vladivostok (notes and letters dated 27 November 2006, 28 November 2006, 19 December 2006, 21 December 2006,

22 December 2006, 26 December 2006 and 27 December 2006) or its Embassy in Moscow (notes verbales dated 23 January 2007 and 7 March 2007) for the prompt release of the vessel and its Master.

Further Developments in Proceedings before the Courts of the Detaining State

42. The Petropavlovsk-Kamchatskii City Court delivered its judgment in the proceedings instituted against the owner on 28 December 2006. In its judgment, the court made the following ruling:

> *[Translation from Russian provided by the Respondent]*
> To recognize that the corporate entity Kanai Gyogyo Co. (6-3-25, Irifune, Kushiro city, Hokkaido, Japan) is responsible for committing an administrative offence under Article 8.17, Section 2, of the Russian Federation Code of Administrative Offences and to impose an administrative penalty in the form of a fine totalling double the cost of biological (living) aquatic resources that were the subject of the administrative offence in the amount of 2,865,149 rubles and 50 kopecks and to confiscate the *53rd Tomimaru* vessel with all its technical and other equipment, communications facilities, salvage appliances and installations.

43. The owner of the vessel then filed an appeal at the Kamchatka District Court on 6 January 2007. The Kamchatka District Court confirmed on 24 January 2007 the decision of the Petropavlovsk-Kamchatskii City Court concerning the confiscation of the *Tomimaru*. The owner then took action under the supervisory review procedure regarding the decision of the Kamchatka District Court on 26 March 2007. The procedure was pending before the Supreme Court of the Russian Federation at the time of filing of the Application.

44. By Order No 158-r of 9 April 2007 of the Federal Agency on Management of Federal Property, the *Tomimaru* was "seized by the State as beneficiary" and was entered in the Federal Property Register as property of the Russian Federation.

45. The Petropavlovsk-Kamchatskii City Court decided on 15 May 2007 to impose a fine of 500,000 roubles (approximately US $19,600) and to award damages of 9,000,000 roubles (approximately US $353,000) against the Master. The Master paid the fine but not the damages and on 30 May 2007 was allowed to leave Petropavlovsk-Kamchatskii for Japan. According to the Applicant, an appeal in this case is pending before the Kamchatka District Court.

46. After the closure of the hearing, on 26 July 2007 the Respondent informed the Tribunal that the Supreme Court of the Russian

Federation had dismissed the complaint concerning the confiscation of the *Tomimaru* since "... there are no grounds for review of the Judgment on the basis of the arguments of the complaint".

47. Invited by the Tribunal to comment on the information from the Respondent, the Agent of the Applicant transmitted a communication on 27 July 2007 in which he made, *inter alia*, the following observation:

[Japan] hopes that the Tribunal will consider the request made by counsel for Japan in the second round of hearings in the *Tomimaru* case that the Tribunal addresses in its judgment at least certain important matters of principle concerning prompt release obligations.

JURISDICTION

48. The requirements to be satisfied in order to found the jurisdiction of the Tribunal are provided for in article 292 of the Convention, which reads as follows:

Article 292

Prompt release of vessels and crews

1. Where the authorities of a State Party have detained a vessel flying the flag of another State Party and it is alleged that the detaining State has not complied with the provisions of this Convention for the prompt release of the vessel or its crew upon the posting of a reasonable bond or other financial security, the question of release from detention may be submitted to any court or tribunal agreed upon by the parties or, failing such agreement within 10 days from the time of detention, to a court or tribunal accepted by the detaining State under article 287 or to the International Tribunal for the Law of the Sea, unless the parties otherwise agree.

2. The application for release may be made only by or on behalf of the flag State of the vessel.

3. The court or tribunal shall deal without delay with the application for release and shall deal only with the question of release, without prejudice to the merits of any case before the appropriate domestic forum against the vessel, its owner or its crew. The authorities of the detaining State remain competent to release the vessel or its crew at any time.

4. Upon the posting of the bond or other financial security determined by the court or tribunal, the authorities of the detaining State shall comply promptly with the decision of the court or tribunal concerning the release of the vessel or its crew.

49. Japan and the Russian Federation are both States Parties to the Convention. Japan ratified the Convention on 20 June 1996 and the Convention entered into force for Japan on 20 July 1996. The

Russian Federation ratified the Convention on 12 March 1997 and the Convention entered into force for the Russian Federation on 11 April 1997.

50. The status of Japan as the flag State of the *Tomimaru* is not disputed by the Respondent. However, the Respondent is of the opinion that the change of ownership of the vessel, by way of confiscation, renders the Application without object.

51. The *Tomimaru* was detained in Avachinskiy Bay.

52. The Applicant alleges that the Respondent has not complied with article 73, paragraph 2, of the Convention regarding the prompt release of the vessel upon the posting of a reasonable bond or other financial security and that the Application therefore falls within the scope of application of article 292 of the Convention.

53. Article 73, paragraph 2, of the Convention reads as follows:

Arrested vessels and their crews shall be promptly released upon the posting of reasonable bond or other security.

54. The parties did not agree to submit the question of the release of the vessel to another court or tribunal within 10 days from the time of detention.

55. The Application for the prompt release of the vessel was made by the Government of Japan in accordance with articles 110 and 111 of the Rules.

ADMISSIBILITY

56. Article 292, paragraph 1, of the Convention provides that an application for release must be based on an allegation that the detaining State has not complied with the provisions of the Convention for the prompt release of a vessel and its crew upon the posting of a reasonable bond or other financial security. In the present case, such allegation is set forth in the Application of Japan.

57. The Respondent maintains that this Application for prompt release is inadmissible because the Applicant's submission in subparagraph 1(c) is too vague and general. In its view it is so unspecific that it allows neither the Tribunal to consider it properly nor the Respondent to reply to it. Moreover, the Respondent alleges that the Tribunal does not have competence under article 292 of the Convention to determine the terms and conditions upon which the arrested vessel should be released. The Respondent further states that, according to article 113, paragraph 2, of the Rules, the Tribunal only has to determine the amount, nature

and form of the bond or other financial security to be posted for the release of the vessel and the crew.

58. The Tribunal notes that the Application is based on article 292 read in conjunction with article 73, paragraph 2, of the Convention. The Applicant asks the Tribunal to exercise its power under article 292, paragraph 3, of the Convention, to order the release of the vessel and the crew upon the posting of a reasonable bond or other financial security.

EFFECTS OF CONFISCATION

59. The Respondent maintains that the judgment of the Kamchatka District Court confirming the confiscation of the *Tomimaru* renders the Application under article 292 of the Convention without object. The Respondent argues that, according to article 292, paragraph 3, of the Convention, when examining applications for release, the Tribunal should deal only with the question of release, without prejudice to the merits of any case before the appropriate domestic forum against the vessel, its owner or its crew. The Respondent states that the case has been considered before the appropriate domestic forum on the merits; that the decision rendered by that forum has already entered into force and, moreover, has been executed. As a consequence, the Tribunal has no competence to examine an application for prompt release.

60. In support of this argument the Respondent states that on 28 December 2006 the Petropavlovsk-Kamchatskii City Court decided that the vessel should be confiscated and a fine of 2,865,149.5 roubles (approximately US $112,000) should be paid by the owner. This judgment was upheld on 24 January 2007 by the Kamchatka District Court, to which the owner had appealed. In this context the Respondent draws the attention of the Tribunal to a letter from the Supreme Court of the Russian Federation, dated 20 August 2003, providing clarification with regard to the entry into force of decisions and judgments concerning administrative offences in cases which have gone on appeal. According to this letter, if a matter has been considered by a magistrate judge or a judge of equal standing, its decision or judgment may be appealed in accordance with articles 30.2-30.8 of the Code of Administrative Offences of the Russian Federation.

61. The Respondent states that, in the light of the clarifications provided in the above-mentioned letter of the Supreme Court of the Russian Federation, the decision of the Kamchatka District Court entered into force immediately upon its delivery, i.e. on 24 January 2007. The Respondent further states that, following the completion

of the above procedures and entry into force of the judgment of the Petropavlovsk-Kamchatskii City Court, the Federal Agency on Management of Federal Property in the Kamchatskii District by implementing act No 158-p of 9 April 2007 had included the *Tomimaru*, confiscated in accordance with the judgment of the court, in the Federal Property Register as property of the Russian Federation.

62. The Applicant is of the view that the confiscation cannot be regarded as final. It draws the attention of the Tribunal to the fact that the owner of the *Tomimaru* had lodged a complaint in accordance with the supervisory review procedure regarding that judgment of the Kamchatka District Court and that the matter was pending before the Supreme Court of the Russian Federation.

63. As far as the case before the Supreme Court of the Russian Federation is concerned, the Respondent maintains that this is not an appeal but a complaint lodged by the owner of the vessel in accordance with the supervisory review procedure exercised by the Supreme Court. In essence the Respondent maintains that such complaint does not suspend the effect of the judgment of the Kamchatka District Court. The Respondent states that the principal purpose of the supervisory procedure is to guarantee uniformity in the application of legal norms. Decisions upheld in the course of an appeal may be annulled at a supervisory stage if they violate human and civil rights and freedoms proclaimed by universally recognized principles and norms of international law and international treaties to which the Russian Federation is party. Furthermore, such decisions can be annulled if they violate the rights and legitimate interests of an indefinite number of people or other public interests.

64. The Applicant maintains that, regardless of the manner in which the procedure before the Supreme Court of the Russian Federation is qualified, this case is still pending. The Applicant stresses, referring in that respect to the Statement in Response, that the Supreme Court of the Russian Federation may annul the decision of the Kamchatka District Court of 24 January 2007.

65. The Applicant further stresses that the position concerning the nationality of the *Tomimaru* would be the same even if it had been confiscated by the Russian Federation. If the confiscation of arrested vessels were allowed to prevent the Tribunal exercising its prompt release jurisdiction, the prompt release obligations and procedures under the Convention would lose all practical meaning. The Applicant maintains, in any event, that ownership of a vessel is distinct from a change of nationality of a vessel. In the view of the Applicant the *Tomimaru* remains a Japanese ship and, because the *Tomimaru* is a Japanese ship,

Japan is entitled to bring a prompt release application in respect of it regardless of the nationality of its owner.

66. As indicated in paragraph 46, after the closure of the hearing, on 26 July 2007, the Respondent informed the Tribunal that the Supreme Court of the Russian Federation had dismissed the complaint concerning the review of the decision on the confiscation of the *Tomimaru*.

67. The Tribunal also takes note of the comment made by the Applicant on the information from the Respondent, as referred to in paragraph 47.

68. The decision of the Supreme Court of the Russian Federation was taken after the closure of the hearing in this case. Nevertheless, the Tribunal considers it appropriate to take this fact into consideration.

69. The Tribunal emphasizes that two questions have to be distinguished: (i) whether confiscation may have an impact on the nationality of a vessel; and (ii) whether confiscation renders an application for the prompt release of a vessel without object.

70. As regards the first question, the Tribunal states that the confiscation of a vessel does not result *per se* in an automatic change of the flag or in its loss. Confiscation changes the ownership of a vessel but ownership of a vessel and the nationality of a vessel are different issues. According to article 91 of the Convention, it is for each State to establish the conditions for the granting of its nationality to ships and for the registration of ships. The State of nationality of the ship is the flag State or the State whose flag the ship is entitled to fly. The juridical link between a State and a ship that is entitled to fly its flag produces a network of mutual rights and obligations, as indicated in article 94 of the Convention. In view of the important functions of the flag State as referred to in article 94 of the Convention and the pivotal role played by the flag State in the initiation of the procedure for the prompt release of a ship under article 292 of the Convention, it cannot be assumed that a change in ownership automatically leads to the change or loss of its flag. The Tribunal notes that the Respondent has not claimed to have initiated procedures leading to a change or loss of the flag of the *Tomimaru*.

71. The Tribunal now turns its attention to the second question: whether the confiscation of a vessel renders an application for its prompt release under article 292 of the Convention without object.

72. The Tribunal notes that article 73 of the Convention makes no reference to confiscation of vessels. The Tribunal is aware that many States have provided for measures of confiscation of fishing vessels in their legislation with respect to the management and conservation of marine living resources.

73. In considering whether confiscation renders an application for the prompt release of a vessel without object the Tribunal has to take into account the object and purpose of the prompt release procedure. Account has to be taken also of article 292, paragraph 3, of the Convention which reads:

The court or tribunal shall deal without delay with the application for release and shall deal only with the question of release, without prejudice to the merits of any case before the appropriate domestic forum against the vessel, its owner or its crew.

74. As the Tribunal already stated in its judgment in the "*Monte Confurco*" *Case* (*ITLOS Reports 2000*, p. 86, at p. 108, para. 70), article 73 of the Convention establishes a balance between the interests of the coastal State in taking appropriate measures as may be necessary to ensure compliance with the laws and regulations adopted by it on the one hand and the interest of the flag State in securing prompt release of its vessels and their crew upon the posting of a bond or other security on the other. The Tribunal wishes to emphasize that a judgment under article 292 of the Convention must be "without prejudice to the merits of any case" ("*sans préjudice de la suite qui sera donnée à toute action*") before the appropriate domestic forum against the vessel or its crew and that this, too, is a factor in maintaining the balance between the interests of the coastal State and of the flag State.

75. It is the view of the Tribunal that confiscation of a fishing vessel must not be used in such a manner as to upset the balance of the interests of the flag State and of the coastal State established in the Convention.

76. A decision to confiscate eliminates the provisional character of the detention of the vessel rendering the procedure for its prompt release without object. Such a decision should not be taken in such a way as to prevent the shipowner from having recourse to available domestic judicial remedies, or as to prevent the flag State from resorting to the prompt release procedure set forth in the Convention; nor should it be taken through proceedings inconsistent with international standards of due process of law. In particular, a confiscation decided in unjustified haste would jeopardize the operation of article 292 of the Convention.

77. In this context, the Tribunal emphasizes that, considering the objective of article 292 of the Convention, it is incumbent upon the flag State to act in a timely manner. This objective can only be achieved if the shipowner and the flag State take action within reasonable time either to have recourse to the national judicial system of the detaining State or to initiate the prompt release procedure under article 292 of the Convention.

78. The Tribunal emphasizes that, considering the object and purpose of the prompt release procedure, a decision to confiscate a vessel does not prevent the Tribunal from considering an application for prompt release of such vessel while proceedings are still before the domestic courts of the detaining State.

79. The Tribunal notes that the decision of the Supreme Court of the Russian Federation brings to an end the procedures before the domestic courts. This has not been contested by the Applicant. After being informed of that decision, the Applicant did not maintain its argument that the confiscation of the *Tomimaru* is not final. The Tribunal notes also that no inconsistency with international standards of due process of law has been argued and that no allegation has been raised that the proceedings which resulted in the confiscation were such as to frustrate the possibility of recourse to national or international remedies.

80. The Tribunal considers that a decision under article 292 of the Convention to release the vessel would contradict the decision which concluded the proceedings before the appropriate domestic fora and encroach upon national competences, thus contravening article 292, paragraph 3, of the Convention.

81. For the reasons which it has given, the Tribunal does not consider it necessary to pronounce expressly upon the several submissions of the parties, in the form in which they have been cast, and considers that the Application is without object.

OPERATIVE PROVISION

82. For these reasons, the Tribunal,
Unanimously,
Finds that the Application of Japan no longer has any object and that the Tribunal is therefore not called upon to give a decision thereon.

Done in English and in French, both texts being authoritative, in the Free and Hanseatic City of Hamburg, this sixth day of August, two thousand and seven, in three copies, one of which will be placed in the archives of the Tribunal and the others transmitted to the Government of Japan and the Government of the Russian Federation, respectively.

DECLARATION OF JUDGE NELSON

I take this opportunity to make some brief remarks on paragraph 76 of the Judgment. The paragraph reads as follows:

A decision to confiscate eliminates the provisional character of the detention of the vessel rendering the procedure for its prompt release without object. Such a decision should not be taken in such a way as to prevent the shipowner from having recourse to available domestic judicial remedies, or as to prevent the flag State from resorting to the prompt release procedure set forth in the Convention; nor should it be taken through proceedings inconsistent with international standards of due process of law. In particular, a confiscation decided in unjustified haste would jeopardize the operation of article 292 of the Convention.

This provision brings very much into play article 292, paragraph 3, of the Convention which states:

The court or tribunal shall deal without delay with the application for release and shall deal only with the question of release, without prejudice to the merits of any case before the appropriate domestic forum against the vessel, its owner or its crew. The authorities of the detaining State remain competent to release the vessel or its crew at any time.

This mechanism for prompt release is designed to isolate the prompt release proceedings from those taking place in the domestic forum and this must be a logical consequence arising from the very nature of the proceedings. As the Tribunal has itself asserted, it provides for an independent remedy and not an appeal against a decision of a national court (*"Camouco"*, para. 59). In other words, it is not the business of the Tribunal to act as a court of appeal.

To what extent does the Tribunal have the power to examine the facts of the case? It will be recalled that in the *"Monte Confurco" Case* the Tribunal had this to say on the matter:

[T]he proceedings under article 292 of the Convention, as clearly provided in paragraph 3 thereof, can deal only with the question of release, without prejudice to the merits of any case before the appropriate domestic forum against the vessel, its owner or its crew. Nevertheless, in the proceedings before it, the Tribunal is not precluded from examining the facts and circumstances of the case to the extent necessary for a proper appreciation of the reasonableness of the bond. Reasonableness cannot be determined in isolation from facts.
(*"Monte Confurco" (Seychelles* v. *France), Prompt Release, Judgment, ITLOS Reports 2000*, para. 74)

Judge Mensah, in his Declaration, warned, correctly in my view, "that any 'examination' of the facts must be limited to what is strictly necessary for an appreciation of the reasonableness or otherwise of the measures taken by the authorities of the arresting State". He proceeded pertinently to add that "the Tribunal should exercise *utmost restraint* in making statements that might plausibly imply criticism of the procedures and decisions of the domestic courts" (emphasis added) (Mensah, Separate Opinion, *"Monte Confurco"*, p. 121. To the same effect see also Jesus, Separate Opinion, *ibid.*, p. 140, para. 10).

The Judgment in paragraph 76 seems to suggest that this Tribunal has the power to examine whether the shipowner was prevented from having recourse to available domestic judicial procedures, to find out whether the proceedings were inconsistent with due process of law and so on.

The approach taken by the Tribunal in this paragraph runs the risk of "straying into territory which more properly belongs to the local court".[1] Perhaps these are not matters to be dealt with within the system contained in article 292.

DECLARATION OF JUDGE YANAI

I concur with the Judgment rendered in the *"Tomimaru"* Case but I would like to make some observations on the question of proper functioning of the prompt release procedure.

1. The central issue in the *"Tomimaru"* Case was the effect of the confiscation of the vessel on the prompt release procedure under the United Nations Convention on the Law of the Sea. However, as the Supreme Court of the Russian Federation finalized the confiscation on 26 July 2007, the Tribunal "finds that the Application of Japan no longer has any object and that the Tribunal is therefore not called upon to give a decision thereon" (the operative provision of the Judgment). As a result, the Tribunal did not have the opportunity to express its views on other aspects of the case, particularly the question of the bond. So I would like to offer my observations on some of these aspects, other than the reasonableness of the amount of bond.

2. There are two factors that complicated the *"Tomimaru" Case*. First, the flag State, Japan, waited too long before filing the Application at the Tribunal. The vessel was boarded and inspected by Russian officers on 31 October 2006 in the Russian exclusive economic zone and detained thereafter, but the Application was not filed until 6 July 2007. During this extended period of time, the procedure on the confiscation of the vessel went ahead in the Russian Federation.

Another factor is the intricacy of the procedures concerning the release of detained foreign fishing vessels and the bond system in the Russian Federation.

---

[1] Lowe, "International Tribunal for the Law of the Sea: Survey for 2000", (2001) *16 International Journal of Marine and Coastal Law*, p. 549 [at] 566.

The owner of the *Tomimaru* was informed by a letter dated 12 December 2006 from the Russian authorities concerned that the amount of the damages caused by the vessel to the Russian Federation was equivalent to 8,800,000 roubles and that the Russian authorities would not prevent the free use of the vessel once the bond were paid (paragraph 36 of the Judgment). The owner did not pay this amount because he had reason to believe that his vessel would not be released upon payment of this bond, which was considered to be a bond relating only to the criminal case and did not cover the case of the administrative offences established against the owner of the vessel. So he requested the Petropavlovsk-Kamchatskii City Court to set the amount of a bond for the case of the administrative offences. The City Court rejected the petition on 19 December 2006, stating that the Code of Administrative Offences of the Russian Federation does not provide for the possibility of releasing a property after posting the amount of bond by the accused in the case of administrative offences (paragraph 39 of the Judgment).

In short, a bond was set for the criminal case but no bond was fixed for the administrative case, owing to the lack of relevant provisions in the Code of Administrative Offences. So there was a fragmentation of bond.

Another difficulty the owner of the vessel faced was that the nature of the sum of 8,800,000 roubles requested by the Russian authorities was not clear at that time, December 2006. It was explained to the owner to be a voluntary compensation for the damage caused by the *Tomimaru*, although during the pleadings, the Respondent referred to this as a bond. The owner and the Master encountered other administrative or procedural difficulties but I refrain from going into further details.

3. Coastal States should exercise their sovereign rights in their exclusive economic zones in accordance with the relevant provisions of the Convention and ensure that their national legislations and procedures are in conformity with the Convention, so that the international law of the sea regime, including the prompt release procedure, can function properly. The purpose of my observations is not to criticize any particular State or its national legislation but for the better functioning of the prompt release procedure under the Convention. Bearing this in mind and based on the experience gained in the *"Tomimaru" Case* and the *"Hoshinmaru" Case*, I would like to submit the following points:

(a) Bond or other security under national laws should be unified and not be fragmented. In other words, arrested vessels and their crews shall be promptly released upon the posting of a reasonable bond or other security without being subjected to parallel bonds or other conditions.

(b) National prompt release procedure, including bond or other security, should be simple and transparent, so that the owners of arrested vessels and their flag States can easily understand the relevant procedures of the coastal States concerned. This will prevent conflicts between detaining States and flag States.

(c) The detaining States should decide on the amount of bond or other security and communicate it to the owners of vessels and other interested persons with reasonable promptness, since undue delay in the implementation of prompt release procedure will cause economic damage to the owners of vessels and humanitarian problems for their crew.

(d) National prompt release procedure should be based on the principle of due process of law in order to ensure fairness in its implementation.

SEPARATE OPINION OF JUDGE JESUS

1. Although I voted in favour of the Judgment of the Tribunal, I feel compelled, nonetheless, to file this separate opinion to highlight my understanding of the issue of confiscation of fishing vessels by the detaining State for violation of fishing laws and regulations, since I do not share some of the tenets of the doctrinal construction built into the decision of the Tribunal on this case. The intention is not to deal with the legitimacy of the confiscation of vessels for fisheries-related violations *per se*, but only to underline certain aspects of it that may have a bearing on the outcome of prompt release cases.

2. Faced with an increase in illegal, unreported and unregulated fishing in their waters, coastal States have been resorting to harsh measures, in order to better protect their resources from being plundered and to avoid over-exploitation. In many cases, it is believed that fines imposed have not acted as a significant deterrent, as might have been expected, for effectively controlling and preventing illegal fishing.

3. As a result, one of the measures taken, not so infrequently, by a vast number of coastal States is confiscation of the fishing vessel because of illegal fishing. Confiscation is generally treated by the fisheries laws and regulations of the detaining State as a penalty or as a result of failure to pay fines imposed within the due time.

4. Article 73 of the Convention seems to give a clear direction as to the nature of the measures the coastal State may take to protect its

sovereign rights over living resources in its exclusive economic zone (EEZ). Indeed, paragraph 1 of that article states that

in the exercise of its sovereign rights to explore, exploit, conserve and manage the living resources in the exclusive economic zone, [the coastal State may] take such measures ... as may be necessary to ensure compliance with the laws and regulations adopted by it in conformity with the Convention.

5. It would appear, from a careful reading of the provision of article 73 quoted above, that, whatever measure the coastal State takes to protect the living resources in its EEZ, it is a measure that the coastal State is entitled to take in exercising its sovereign rights over such resources, in order to secure the most effective protection of them from those who are plundering them, and prevent their depletion.

6. The penalty of confiscation of fishing vessels, in this regard, appears to be consistent with the provision of article 73, paragraph 1, of the Convention, for there is nothing in the Convention that would exclude the penalty of confiscation from those measures that, in accordance with this article, the coastal State is entitled to take against a vessel engaged in illegal fishing in its EEZ. This understanding seems to be supported by undisputed State practice.

7. Measures of the coastal States that would not be in conformity with the Convention are, for example, those referred to in paragraph 3 of article 73, that is to say, the imposition of the penalty of imprisonment, in the absence of agreements to the contrary by the States concerned, or any other form of corporal punishment, for fisheries violations committed in the EEZ. If such measures were to be taken by a detaining State, they would be considered, as referred to in paragraph 1 of article 73 of the Convention, as not being in conformity with the Convention. By the same token, if the intention of the Convention was to exclude confiscation of fishing vessels for violations of fisheries laws and regulations from the panoply of measures that the coastal State may take to protect its marine living resources, then the provision of paragraph 3 of article 73 would have said so, explicitly, as it did in relation to imprisonment and other forms of corporal punishment.

8. While not questioning the right of the coastal State to confiscate fishing vessels, this decision of the Tribunal includes a certain amount of elaboration which may imply that coastal States should not confiscate a fishing vessel immediately after its arrest or detention, so as to give time for the flag State to apply for its release upon the posting of a bond. This view seems to have found support in paragraph 76 of the decision of the Tribunal, *in fine*. In assessing the balance that should exist

between the interests of the detaining State and of the flag State on the issue of prompt release, that paragraph declares that "[i]n particular, a confiscation decided in unjustified haste would jeopardize the operation of article 292 of the Convention".

9. I do not share this view, for the following reasons:

(a) Firstly, confiscation of fishing vessels on account of illegal fishing is imposed as a penalty and, as such, confiscation is a matter to be considered part and parcel of the merits of a case, which is excluded from the jurisdiction of the Tribunal when seized of an application for the prompt release of fishing vessels, as set out in article 292, paragraph 3, of the Convention. Indeed, this article and paragraph, as mentioned before, make it clear that the prompt release procedure "is without prejudice to the merits of any case before the appropriate domestic forum against the vessel, its owner or its crew".

(b) Secondly, the Tribunal has held, and rightly so, that laws and judicial decisions of States are to be considered by it as facts. Therefore national legislation and decisions should not be the object of a value judgment or qualification in a prompt release case.

(c) Thirdly, the prompt release procedure does not seem to prevent the detaining State from confiscating a vessel at any stage of its detention. The timing of the adoption of the measure of confiscation of a fishing vessel is an issue germane only to the consideration of the merits of the case. Whether the coastal State confiscates the vessel immediately after its detention or at a later stage, confiscation of detained fishing vessels is a matter that falls totally within the competence of the appropriate forum of the coastal State and should not, therefore, be a consideration of the Tribunal when it is dealing with a case concerning the prompt release of a fishing vessel. If the process leading to confiscation is tainted by irregularities or illegalities, the proper forum for seeking redress for such irregularities and illegalities is to be found in the local remedies available and not in the Tribunal, since it should consider only the application for release. It is to be noted in this regard that the imposition of penalties involving the confiscation of the vessel lies at the very core of any merits case, since the very purpose of such a case is to decide whether or not penalties of one sort or another should be imposed. Therefore, the Tribunal, while seized of a prompt release case, is not called upon, for lack of competence, to make inroads into what is or is not confiscation properly exercised, whether or not it be exercised in a justifiably or unjustifiably hasty manner. Since confiscation, as stated before, is an issue that is relevant to the merits of the case, issues pertaining to the inappropriateness of confiscation, the justification or non-justification of the hasty manner in which it is carried out by the detaining State, and the absence of procedures that guarantee the due process of the law, among others, are issues whose relevance may be pursued in the appropriate domestic forum, but certainly not by the Tribunal in the context of a prompt release procedure.

(d) Fourthly, as conceived and translated into article 292 of the Convention, the prompt release procedure is rather a means of avoiding a fishing vessel that is detained on account of violations of fisheries laws and regulations being left unnecessarily immobilized, pending the decision of the domestic forum on the merits. Its prompt release, therefore, presupposes that the vessel is still detained. Indeed, article 292, paragraph 1, states that "the question of release *from detention* may be submitted to any court or tribunal" (emphasis added). If, as a result of the automatic operation of the law or a domestic judicial decision or a decision of any other competent authority of the arresting State, the vessel has been the object of an irrevocable decision of confiscation by the arresting State, then the vessel is no longer detained within the meaning of article 292 of the Convention. Therefore the issue of prompt release becomes moot. This is, after all, the conclusion of paragraph 76 of the Judgment of the Tribunal in the present case, when it states that "A decision to confiscate eliminates the provisional character of the detention of the vessel rendering the procedure for its prompt release without object."

(e) Lastly, if the flag State wants its vessel released promptly from detention, then in order to avoid early confiscation of the fishing vessel, the flag State may, after satisfying the requirements of paragraph 1 of article 292 of the Convention, apply to the Tribunal for prompt release immediately after the 10 days from the time of the vessel's detention have elapsed.

SEPARATE OPINION OF JUDGE LUCKY

Although I voted in favour of the Judgment of the Tribunal, I deemed it necessary to view this case from another perspective. Consequently, I have written a separate opinion.

In its Application to the International Tribunal for the Law of the Sea ("the Tribunal") the Applicant requests the Tribunal to:

(a) declare that the Tribunal has jurisdiction under article 292 of the United Nations Convention on the Law of the Sea ("the Convention") to hear the Application concerning the detention of the vessel of the *53rd Tomimaru* ("the *Tomimaru*"), in breach of the Respondent's obligations under Article 73(2) of the Convention;
(b) declare that the Application is admissible, that the Application is well-founded, and that the Respondent has breached its obligation under Article 73(2) of the Convention; and,
(c) order the Respondent to release the *Tomimaru* upon such terms and conditions as the Tribunal shall consider reasonable.

The Respondent requests the Tribunal to make the following orders:

(a) that the Application of Japan is inadmissible;
(b) alternatively, that the allegations of the Applicant are not well-founded and that the Russian Federation has fulfilled its obligations under paragraph 2 of article 73 of the United Nations Convention on the Law of the Sea.

The facts (briefly)

The Applicant pleads that on 31 October 2006 the *Tomimaru* ("the vessel") was boarded by officials of the Respondent and ordered to sail to the port of Petropavlovsk-Kamchatskii where the vessel and crew were detained. No charge or allegation of any violation of the Respondent's laws was made upon boarding. During the voyage to the port, an official of the Respondent indicated that the actual amount of the fish transported by the vessel appeared to differ from the amount stated in the logbook and that the difference was about 5 tons. The vessel arrived at the port on 5 November 2006. On 5 November 2006 an inspection was carried out by officials of the Northeast Border Coast Guard Directorate of the Federal Security Service of the Respondent.

The Respondent pleads that on 1 November 2006 four vessels, including the *Tomimaru*, that were fishing in the Respondent's EEZ, were checked. In order to examine the actual catch of each vessel more thoroughly, the vessels were escorted to Avachinskiy Bay.

On 8 November 2006 the examination of the amount of catch was completed. The examination revealed a grave breach of the Respondent's national legislation, as well as serious damage to the environmental balance and security of the biological resources of the Respondent's

EEZ. The breach is set out in a note verbale dated 9 November 2006 from the Representative Office of the Ministry of Foreign Affairs of the Russian Federation in Petropavlovsk-Kamchatskii to the Consulate-General of Japan in Vladivostok.

It is not disputed that:

(a) Japan ("the Applicant") and the Russian Federation ("the Respondent") are both Parties to the Convention;
(b) The *Tomimaru* is a fishing vessel owned and operated by Kanai Gyogyo, a Japanese company;
(c) The *Tomimaru* was flying the Japanese flag at the time it was detained by the relevant authorities of the Respondent;
(d) The *Tomimaru* was licensed to fish in the EEZ of the Respondent at the time of the detention;
(e) Apart from the Master of the vessel, members of the crew were allowed to leave the Russian Federation after completion of the investigation.

The time-frame

The time-frame is important in order to demonstrate the conduct of the Parties prior to the submission of the application for prompt release. The time-frame is set out below:

On 8 November 2006 criminal proceedings were instituted against the Master of the vessel.

On 9 November 2006 a note verbale was issued by a representative of the Ministry of Foreign Affairs of the Respondent at the port; the note sets out the charge against the Master and the results of the inspection.

The Applicant states that:

The *Tomimaru* itself was *registered as evidence* in the proceedings and was detained in the port of Petropavlovsk-Kamchatskii. (Emphasis added.)

The alleged illegal portion of the catch of the vessel was confiscated by the authorities of the Respondent. It was transferred to the National Treasury of the Respondent. The rest of the catch was sold by the agent of the owner of the vessel and its value returned to the owner (there is no evidence that the owner objected to the confiscation and sale or refused to accept the monies raised from the sale).

The events following the above are crucial.

1. The Applicant states that "the owner of the *Tomimaru* has at all times been ready and willing to post a bond or other security in respect of all proceedings in order to secure the release of the vessel and its Master and crew provided that the amount and the conditions for their payment were reasonable". (The Respondent submits that a reasonable bond was fixed on 12 December 2006 but the owner did not post a bond, instead seeking relief in the national courts.)

2. On 14 November 2006 administrative proceedings were instituted against the owner for violation of article 8.17, paragraph 2, of the Code of Administrative Offences of the Russian Federation.

3. On 30 November 2006 and 8 December 2006 the owner of the *Tomimaru* petitioned the Prosecutor, presumably, at the Inter-district Prosecutor's Office for Nature Protection in Kamchatka for a bond to be fixed so as to enable the vessel to leave for Japan. After a bond had been set, the owner made a similar petition to the Northeast Border Coast Guard Directorate. In response to the petition, the owner was informed that this case had been filed with the Petropavlovsk-Kamchatskii City Court and that the Directorate had no authority to deal with the petition.

4. On 15 December 2006 the owner made a petition to the said City Court during the administrative proceedings to release the *Tomimaru* upon the posting of a bond or other security. The petition was refused by the Court.

5. On 28 December 2006 the administrative case was heard. The Court decided to confiscate the *Tomimaru* and imposed a fine on the owner (approximately US $111,000).

6. On 6 January 2007 the owner submitted an appeal against the decision to the Kamchatka District Court.

7. On 24 January 2007 the Kamchatka District Court confirmed the decision of the Petropavlovsk-Kamchatskii City Court on the confiscation of the *Tomimaru*.

The owner lodged a written objection to the decision on 12 February 2007. The objection was dismissed.

8. On 26 March 2007 the owner appealed to the Federal Supreme Court of the Russian Federation for judicial review.

The Applicant claims that:

as at the time of filing this Application (6 July 2007) no bond or other security has been set and the vessel has not been released.

The Respondent admits that on 8 December 2006 the owner of the vessel submitted a request to the District Prosecutor's Office and the Northeast Border Coast Guard Directorate to determine a bond. In response, the owner was advised that the proper body for determining bonds was the Inter-district Prosecutor's Office for Nature Protection in Kamchatka.

The Respondent submits that on 12 December 2006 the said Office duly set a reasonable bond and specified in a letter to the owner of the vessel that the Prosecutor's Office would allow the vessel to operate freely upon payment of the bond, which was fixed at 8,800,000 roubles. It claims that it has satisfied the provisions of article 73 of the Convention. The Respondent contends that the bond has never been paid or contested by the owner.

In view of the applicant's contention, it appears to me that there is no concrete evidence to support the claim that the owner was always willing to pay a fixed bond.

9. On 19 December 2006 Judge I. V. Bazdnikin of the Petropavlovsk-Kamchatskii City Court rejected the vessel owner's petition for a reasonable bond to be set on the grounds that:

The provisions of the Code of Administrative Offences of the Russian Federation do not provide the possibility of releasing a property after posting the amount of bond by the accused on the case of administrative offences. (See paragraph 17 of Response.)

This ruling has never been contested by attorneys of the owner of the vessel. The Respondent submits that from a legal point of view such an opportunity existed.

10. On 28 December 2006 the Petropavlovsk City Court decided that the vessel should be confiscated and a fine of 2,865,149.5 roubles paid by the owner.

Delay in making the Application

I have referred to the relevant dates above in order to demonstrate that the ensuing period between the detention of the vessel and the filing of the Application is one of the reasons why the Application is inadmissible. In my opinion this period is too long. During that period, the due process of law in the Russian judicial system was set in train in order to resolve the matter. After the hearing at which all the facts were considered, the City Court made an order *inter alia* for confiscation. The owner appealed to the City Court, but the City Court upheld its decision.

Following the order of the Court, the vessel was registered as the property of the Russian Federation. Whereas in the past the Tribunal has entertained applications made several months after the vessels in question had been detained, the circumstances in the present matter are different. In this case, the Application was made eight months after the detention of the vessel. What exacerbates the situation and makes the inadmissibility favourable to the Respondent is the conduct of the Applicant, owner and Master during the months between the vessel's detention and the submission of the Application. As I mentioned earlier, the vessel and crew were detained. On 31 October 2006 the vessel was taken to port and inspected after the flag State had been notified of the arrest and detention. On 12 December 2006 a bond was fixed. It appears to me, having assessed the documentary evidence, that no bond was posted in relation to the vessel.

The owner, presumably with the knowledge and consent of the flag State, chose to apply to the domestic court for relief. Being unable to obtain the relief sought, the owner appealed to the higher court. By so doing, the owner began a process under national jurisdiction during which the order for confiscation was confirmed and the vessel was deemed the property of the Russian Federation.

It was only on 6 July 2007 that an application under article 292 of the Convention was made to the Tribunal. At that time the matter had been engaging the attention of the domestic courts in Russia. Throughout the period in question neither the owner nor the flag State had asked for a stay of execution pending the hearings on appeal.

If the Tribunal makes an order for prompt release upon the posting of a bond, the Tribunal could be deemed to be interfering in the internal proceedings of a domestic legal system and proceedings in national courts. I do not think article 292 of the Convention envisages interference in the judicial system of a State while proceedings are in progress, particularly when orders for confiscation have been made. In fact confiscation is not mentioned in articles 292 and 73 of the Convention. Article 73, paragraph 3, specifies the sanctions which a detaining State may not apply for violations of its fisheries laws and regulations in its exclusive economic zone. Article 73, paragraph 3, reads:

Coastal State penalties for violations of fisheries laws and regulations in the exclusive economic zone may not include imprisonment, in the absence of agreements to the contrary by the States concerned, or any other form of corporal punishment.

If it was the intention of the relevant articles to cover the question of confiscation, specific reference to its exclusion would have been made therein. Unless there is cogent, compelling evidence and reasons to the contrary, it can be presumed that due process was adhered to and in the circumstances the legal maxim *omnia praesemuntur rite esse acta* is applicable. The judicial integrity of the Russian legal system has to be respected.

Due process

The crucial question is whether there was an abuse of process. There is no evidence indicating an abuse of due process and therefore it can be presumed that *omnia praesemuntur rite esse acta*.

It seems to me that the correct procedure was adhered to by the Court (there is no evidence to the contrary) and the vessel was confiscated in accordance with the decision of the Court and entered in the Federal Property register as property of the Russian Federation. In circumstances such as those surrounding the present case, the Tribunal cannot overrule that decision and ought not to interfere in the decisions of national courts through prompt release proceedings.

Assuming, but not admitting, that the Tribunal has jurisdiction, it should not imply in advance that the allegations made by the Applicant regarding non-compliance by the Respondent with the provisions of paragraph 2 of article 73 of the Convention are well-founded and therefore acceptable. In my opinion, the Respondent had complied with the requirements set out in that article. A bond was fixed and the owner was advised:

that if [the bond] was paid at the given address the Prosecutor's Office would allow the free operation of the vessel upon payment of the bond.

This could only mean that if the bond was posted by the owner, the vessel and crew would be free to leave for Japan.

Is the Application too vague?

I do not think so. My view is based on previous orders of the Tribunal and therefore it appears to me that the words have to be construed within the context of articles 292 and 73 of the Convention. This contention of the Respondent is *non sequitur*.

Is the Application moot?

I think that the Application is moot because, on 12 December 2006, the Respondent had complied with the provisions of article 73, paragraph 2.

A bond had been fixed and the owner informed. The owner neither objected to nor accepted the offer. It should be pointed out that the Applicant did not make an Application to the Tribunal to fix a reasonable bond within a reasonable time.

Confiscation

There are clear distinctions in the legal meanings of "detention" and "confiscation".

> *To confiscate* means to appropriate (property) as forfeited to the Government (*Black's Law Dictionary, eighth edition*) or
> *To appropriate* to the public treasury (as a penalty); adjudge to be forfeited to the State (*The New Oxford Dictionary*)
> *To detain* means: "keep in confinement or under restraint" (*The Oxford Concise English Dictionary, ninth edition*)

I think the confiscation of the vessel in the circumstances surrounding the case prevents the Tribunal from entertaining the case for the following reasons:

1. A bond had been fixed on 12 December 2006. On 19 December 2006 the Petropavlovsk-Kamchatskii City Court rejected the Petition of the owner of the *Tomimaru* for a reasonable bond to be set on the grounds that the provisions of the Code of Administrative Offences of the Russian Federation do not provide the possibility of releasing property after the amount of the bond has been posted by the accused with respect to administrative offences. The ruling was not contested by the attorneys of the owner of the vessel, although they could have done so.

2. On 28 December 2006 the said Court decided that the vessel should be confiscated and a fine of 2,865,149.5 roubles paid by the owner. The owner could have appealed within 10 days. It must be noted that during the proceedings the attorney representing the owner pleaded guilty and asked the Court to impose a fine equal to twice the damages without confiscation of the vessel because it was the owner's first offence and the company was willing to pay all the fines and to cover the costs of the current proceedings.

3. On 6 January 2007 the owner of the vessel submitted an appeal against the judgment of 28 December to the Kamchatka District Court, which upheld the decision of the City Court. Following the above decisions the Federal Agency on the Management of Federal Property in the Kamchatka District entered the *Tomimaru* (confiscated in accordance

with the decisions of the Courts) in the Federal Property Register as property of the Russian Federation.

I cannot agree with the view of the Tribunal expressed in paragraph 78 of the Judgment which reads as follows:

> The Tribunal emphasizes that, considering the object and purpose of the prompt release procedure, a decision to confiscate a vessel does not prevent the Tribunal from considering an application for prompt release of such vessel while proceedings are still before the domestic courts of the detaining State.

In my opinion this statement is not necessary in view of the decision in this case. In a case such as the instant case where the merits of the case against the owner of the vessel were dealt with by courts of competent jurisdiction under the applicable laws of the Russian Federation confiscation is a *fait accompli*. Therefore the Application lost its force even before the Supreme Court of the Russian Federation delivered its judgment. Under Russian legislation, the decision by a district court concerning administrative offences cannot be appealed and the decision entered into force immediately upon pronouncement. The penalty of confiscation was imposed in this case. I am of the view that the view expressed in paragraph 78 needs to be clarified. It seems to me that where the courts of a coastal State have confiscated a vessel for a breach of its laws the Tribunal could be prevented from considering an application for prompt release of a vessel.

The guilty plea

When a defendant pleads guilty to an offence, he is admitting the charges and accepting the facts presented by the prosecution. The court (judge) is not asked to make a finding of fact on the merits. In other words, the defendant in the present case, the owner, has admitted the wrongdoing and sought the mercy of the court with respect to sentencing, the merits having been determined and the sentence of the court pronounced. The learned judge pronounced his sentence, which was a fine and confiscation of the vessel. The owner appealed, presumably, the sentence of the Court.

The judge's order was confirmed by the appellate court, the Kamchatka [District] Court. Following that decision, as I said earlier, the confiscated vessel was entered in the Russian Property Register as property of the Russian Federation. The owner then appealed to the Supreme Court of the Russian Federation for judicial review, which could only mean that the court was being asked to review whether the courts followed the rule of law and due process. Bearing in mind the question of time-frame relating to this case as set out earlier in this opinion, the doctrine of *laches* seems applicable. There is nothing on record to show that the Applicant or the owner applied for a stay of execution of the order to confiscate.

As I stated earlier and I repeat for emphasis, the vessel was confiscated and has been entered in the Federal Property Register as the property of the Russian Federation. Therefore if the Tribunal were to order the release of the vessel, it would be interfering in the due process of the Russian national court and its legal system.

For the avoidance of doubt, I must add that there is a distinction between flag State registration and ownership of a vessel, i.e. between ownership and nationality. Therefore the ship can be de-registered by the new owners.

In my opinion the *Tomimaru* has been confiscated and the merits of the case have been determined and confirmed by the national courts. Further, although the Supreme Court of Russia has been asked by the owner to review the decision of the City Court, its function is of a supervisory nature and it will only consider the legality of the acts without examining the merits of the case.

The question of admissibility

Article 73 of the Convention reads:

1. The coastal State may, in the exercise of its sovereign rights to explore, exploit, conserve and manage the living resources in the exclusive economic zone, take such measures, including boarding, inspection, arrest and judicial proceedings, as may be necessary to ensure compliance with the laws and regulations adopted by it in conformity with this Convention.
2. Arrested vessels and their crews shall be promptly released upon the posting of reasonable bond or other security.
...

The Applicant submits that there were two sets of proceedings against the Master and the owner of the *Tomimaru* in the domestic courts of the Respondent:

(a) criminal proceedings against the Master in respect of which a bond of 8,800,000 roubles (approximately US $343,000) was set on 12 December 2006; and
(b) administrative proceedings against the owner of the *Tomimaru*, in respect of which no bond was fixed.

Counsel for the Applicant contends that the Applicant was in a predicament because he had to post two bonds, one for 8,800,000 roubles and another which had not been fixed in order to secure the release of the *Tomimaru*, its Master and its crew.

The Respondent argues that on 12 December 2006 a bond was fixed in the sum of 8,800,000 roubles. This bond was set for the release of the *Tomimaru*. The bond was never contested or paid by the owner. The Applicant contends that this bond was in respect of the criminal proceedings. The question is whether the bond, fixed on 12 December 2006, was for the release of the vessel, Master and crew, or, in respect of the Master in the criminal proceedings. It seems to me that the Applicant was aware that the bond of 12 December was in respect of the vessel and crew because in paragraph 16 of the Application the Applicant states:

According to the Master of the *Tomimaru*, a bond was set on 12 December 2006 with the amount of 8,800,000 roubles by the Inter-district Prosecutor's Office for Nature Protection in Kamchatka which mentioned that it would not hinder the vessel from *navigating freely on condition that the bond would be paid*.

Further, on 2 March 2007 the Master was fined 500,000 roubles, which he paid, and he was subsequently allowed to leave for Japan. This supports the view that the bond set on 12 December 2006 was in respect of the *Tomimaru*.

The bond was set by the Inter-district Prosecutor's Office for Nature Protection in Kamchatka which was authorized to fix a bond. But the owner did not post the bond. The owner requested the Petropavlovsk-Kamchatskii City Court to set a reasonable bond for the release of the said vessel. It is therefore apparent that the owner chose to ask the Court to fix a reasonable bond, ignoring what had been fixed by the Prosecutor.

The Applicant was advised that a bond in the sum of 8,800,000 roubles had been set by the Respondent. Yet even though the Applicant had the right to do so, an Application was not made to the Tribunal in accordance with article 292 of the Convention. That could have been an appropriate time to make an Application to the Tribunal for prompt release of the vessel. One would have thought that at that stage the Applicant would have made an Application to the Tribunal under article 292 of the Convention for the prompt release of the vessel and crew. It appears as though both the Applicant and the owner were content to approach the City Court for the fixing of a reasonable bond.

For the reasons set out above, I find the Application inadmissible.

Apart from the above, the Application is also inadmissible because the vessel has been confiscated in judicial proceedings, in accordance with the laws and regulations of the Respondent (the coastal State). The Applicant contends that the domestic judicial proceedings have not been exhausted and, in support of its arguments, submits that the question of confiscation is still engaging the attention of the Supreme Court of the Russian Federation because an application for judicial review of judgments of the City and District Courts which ordered and confirmed the decision to confiscate the *Tomimaru* was made to the said Court.

It is my view that the Tribunal should not envisage what the Supreme Court of the Russian Federation may do or may not do. The Tribunal ought to consider the documentary evidence and oral submissions in the matter. It seems clear to me that the domestic proceedings before the national courts have been concluded as regards the question of the merits and it is beyond the jurisdiction of the Tribunal to consider the merits. Article 292 of the Convention makes this quite clear. It reads in part:

> The court or tribunal shall deal without delay with the application for release and shall deal only with the question of release, without prejudice to the merits of any case before the appropriate domestic forum against the vessel, its owner or its crew . . .

It must be noted that the relevant articles of the Convention are silent with respect to confiscation by coastal States. The question may be posed: Does confiscation circumvent the application of article 292? However, I think the circumstances of each case will determine whether confiscation circumvents the Application for prompt release under article 292 of the Convention.

Reference was made to the *"Juno Trader"* Case but a difference has to be made with respect to that case. In the *"Juno Trader"* Case the vessel was confiscated by an administrative forum. That decision was suspended by a court, pending a hearing on the merits. In the present case, the matter was heard on the merits and the order of the court executed.

In support of his contention that the appropriate court proceedings were completed, Counsel for the Respondent referred to part of the arguments presented by the French Government in the *"Grand Prince" Case*, which he adopted as part of his arguments.

The French Government argued that:

> When the internal judicial proceedings have reached their conclusion and, in particular, when they have led to the pronouncement of a sentence of confiscation of the vessel, any possible resort to Article 292 procedure loses its reason for being. In such a case, the Application for prompt release is moot. As from the time when the national court has pronounced confiscation

of the vessel as the applicable sanction, the introduction of prompt release proceedings before the International Tribunal for the Law of the Sea is not only no longer possible but is not even conceivable.

I agree with the above passage and add that the "pronouncement" stands, even though there is an application for judicial review before the Federal Supreme Court of the Russian Federation. The matter is under the jurisdiction of the national courts and the admissibility of an application in internal judicial proceedings which the parties had accepted would be interfering in the judicial proceedings of the coastal State.

Therefore, the Tribunal cannot circumvent or intervene in the due process of national courts.

For the reasons stated I am of the view that the Application is inadmissible.

After the close of oral proceedings the Registrar of the Tribunal was advised that the Supreme Court of the Russian Federation had found that there were no grounds for judicial review of the judgment of the Kamchatka City Court given on 24 January 2007.

On 27 July 2007 the Agent of Japan states in part that:

Japan noted the contents of Russia's communication to the Registrar, dated 26 July 2007, concerning developments in Russia's Supreme Court in relation to the *Tomimaru* case.

Japan regrets that it has not had the opportunity to address this development before the close of the written and oral proceedings in the case, and should not be understood to accept the propositions set out in the Russian communication.

The judicial proceedings before the Russian domestic courts have been exhausted. The Supreme Court of the Russian Federation has found that there are no grounds for reversing the judicial decisions of the District and City Courts of Petropavlovsk-Kamchatskii (letter of 26 July to the Registrar of the Tribunal from the Agent of the Russian Federation).

Having considered all the relevant evidence in this case from another perspective, I remain convinced that, even if the Supreme Court of the Russian Federation had not given its decision, the Application would remain inadmissible.

[Report: 46 ILM 1185 (2007)]

International criminal law — Offences against humanity — International Convention to Suppress the Slave Trade and Slavery, 1926 — Slavery — Definition — Definition of slavery in Australian Criminal Code (Cth) deriving from definition in Article 1 of Convention — Whether respondent possessing and using complainants as slaves — Whether proof of intention required — Sections 270.1 and 270.3(1)(a) of Code — Meaning and constitutional validity — Convictions in Australia of slavery offences contrary to Section 270.3(1)(a) of Code — Provisions in Chapter 8 of Code dealing with offences against humanity

Relationship of international law and municipal law — Treaties — Effect in municipal law — International Convention to Suppress the Slave Trade and Slavery, 1926 — Sections 270.1 and 270.3(1)(a) of Australian Criminal Code (Cth) — Construction and application of Code — Relevant provisions introducing into Australian municipal law offences deriving from 1926 Slavery Convention — Constitutional validity of Sections 270.1 and 270.3(1)(a) of Code — The law of Australia

R *v.* TANG[1]

([2008] HCA 39)

Australia, High Court. 28 *August* 2008

(Gleeson CJ; Gummow, Kirby, Hayne, Heydon, Crennan and Kiefel JJ)

SUMMARY: *The facts*:—The complainants, five Thai women, had voluntarily come to Australia to work as prostitutes, having previously worked in the sex industry. They were treated as "owned" by those syndicate recruiters who had procured their passage to Australia and became "contract workers" for the respondent, Ms Tang, the owner of a licensed brothel. While there was no written contract, each complainant was to work in the brothel for six days per week without earnings, being allowed to keep the $50 per customer on the

---

[1] The appellant was represented by W. J. Abraham QC and R. R. Davis, instructed by the Director of Public Prosecutions (Cth). The respondent was represented by N. J. Young QC, M. J. Croucher and K. L. Walker, instructed by Slades & Parsons Solicitors. D. M. J. Bennett QC, Solicitor-General (Cth) and S. P. Donaghue, instructed by the Australian Government Solicitor, intervened on behalf of the Attorney-General (Cth). B. W. Walker SC and R. Graycar, instructed by the Human Rights and Equal Opportunity Commission, intervened on behalf of the Human Rights and Equal Opportunity Commission.

seventh "free" day each week to offset the contract debts incurred during the rest of the week.

The County Court of Victoria convicted the respondent of five offences of intentionally possessing a slave and five offences of intentionally exercising over a slave a power attaching to the right of ownership, namely the power to use, contrary to Section 270.3(1)(a) of the Criminal Code (Cth) ("the Code"),[2] and sentenced her to a lengthy term of imprisonment.

The Court of Appeal of the Supreme Court of Victoria upheld an appeal, quashed the convictions and ordered a new trial. It held that Sections 270.1 and 270.3(1)(a) of the Code were within the legislative power of the Commonwealth. It also found that the offences created by Section 270.3(1)(a) extended to this alleged behaviour and were not confined to situations akin to "chattel slavery" or in which the complainant was notionally owned by the accused or another at the relevant time. The prosecution, by special leave, appealed.

Held:—The appeal was allowed. The respondent's convictions were restored.[3]

Per Gleeson CJ (with whom Gummow, Hayne, Heydon, Crennan and Kiefel JJ agreed): (1) Sections 270.1 and 270.3(1)(a) of the Code were within the Commonwealth's legislative power. The offences created by Section 270.3(1)(a) extended to the behaviour alleged and were not confined to situations akin to "chattel slavery" or in which the complainant was notionally owned by the accused or another at the relevant time (paras. 19-20).

(2) The word "slave", which was not defined in Section 270.3(1)(a), took its meaning from the definition of "slavery" in Section 270.1. That definition was derived from Article 1 of the 1926 Slavery Convention,[4] which was taken up in

---

[2] Div. 270 of the Code dealt with "Slavery, sexual servitude and deceptive recruiting". It was included under Chapter 8 of the Code, which dealt with "Offences against humanity". Section 270.3 of the Code provided that: "(1) A person who, whether within or outside Australia, intentionally: (a) possesses a slave or exercises over a slave any of the other powers attaching to the right of ownership; . . . is guilty of an offence. Penalty: Imprisonment for 25 years . . . " After the alleged offences, a further offence of "debt bondage" was added to Chapter 8, in Section 271.8. For the text of the relevant provisions, see paras. 3-5 of the judgment.

[3] While the respondent was convicted of the twin offences of possessing a slave and of using a slave contrary to Section 270.3(1)(a) of the Code, the Court of Appeal of Victoria, on 17 August 2009, held that the offences overlapped when committed in relation to the same person and reduced the sentence accordingly, finding that complete concurrency between sentences for use and for possession did not answer a complaint of double punishment ([2009] VSCA 182, (2009) 233 FLR 399).

[4] For the text of Article 1 of the International Convention to Suppress the Slave Trade and Slavery, 1926 (212 UNTS 17), see para. 23 of the judgment. The definition of slavery in Article 1(1), that slavery was the status or condition of a person over whom any or all of the powers attaching to the right of ownership were exercised, was used in international instruments, such as the Rome Statute of the International Criminal Court.

Article 2 of the 1926 Slavery Convention contained an undertaking by the parties to bring about the complete abolition of slavery "in all its forms".

Article 7 of the 1956 Supplementary Convention.[5] The relevant provisions of Div. 270 were reasonably capable of being considered appropriate and adapted to give effect to Australia's obligations under the Convention (paras. 21-34).

(3) It was important not to trivialize crimes against humanity by giving slavery a meaning that extended beyond the limits set by the text, context and purpose of the 1926 Slavery Convention. Harsh and exploitative labour conditions did not of themselves amount to slavery; some factors, such as control of movement and of physical environment, involved questions of degree (para. 32).

(4) The factors accepted by the Trial and Appeals Chambers of the International Criminal Tribunal for the Former Yugoslavia in *Prosecutor* v. *Kunarac* were relevant to the application of Section 270.3(1)(a) of the Code.[6] Consent was not inconsistent with slavery. For the purpose of Section 270.3(1)(a), the commoditization of an individual by treating him or her as an object of sale and purchase, if it existed, was a material factor when a tribunal of fact assessed the circumstances of a case, and might involve the exercise of a power attaching to a right of ownership (paras. 28-35).

(5) There was cogent evidence of the intentional exercise of powers of such a nature and extent that they could reasonably be regarded as resulting in the condition of slavery, and the conduct, to which Section 270.3(1)(a) was directed (paras. 36-59).

Per Kirby J: (1) The provisions of the Code were constitutionally valid. Section 270.3(1)(a) of the Code gave effect to Australia's obligations under the 1926 Slavery Convention. The definition of "slavery" in Section 270.1 and the consequential offences in Section 270.3(1)(a) were reasonably proportionate to a law giving effect to those obligations (para. 84).

(2) The Court's task was to construe and apply the Code, an Australian statute which introduced into Australian municipal law offences derived substantially from the 1926 Convention. Slavery, like piracy, was a crime against humanity. Such offences arguably attracted obligations that attached to crimes of universal jurisdiction. As a *jus cogens* rule, slavery was prohibited as a peremptory norm from which no derogation was permitted. Given its seriousness, slavery needed to be defined carefully and precisely. That human trafficking, the movement, recruitment or receipt of persons, often by means of the threat or use of force, for the purpose of exploitation, commonly operated as part of slavery served to reinforce the serious nature of slavery. Slavery should not be overextended to apply to activities amounting to seriously oppressive employment

---

[5] The Supplementary Convention on the Abolition of Slavery, the Slave Trade, and Institutions and Practices similar to Slavery, 1956 (266 UNTS 3).

[6] Both the Trial Chamber and the Appeals Chamber adopted a view of the offence that was not limited to chattel slavery. The Trial Chamber concluded that enslavement as a crime against humanity in customary international law consisted of the exercise of any or all of the powers attaching to the right of ownership over a person; the actus reus of the violation being the exercise of any or all of such powers and the mens rea consisting in the intentional exercise of such powers.

relationships. The approach of the majority was inconsistent with this aim (paras. 110-17).

(3) To ensure that Australia remained in broad harmony with the law of similar countries, and particularly for universal crimes, the more stringent requirement of proof of intention should be adopted in respect of the slavery offences in Section 270.3(1)(a) of the Code. Neither should slavery offences be used to suppress lawful commercial sex work. While there was evidence upon which a reasonable jury, properly instructed, might have convicted the respondent of slavery offences, the fault element of intention had not been clearly explained to the jury, resulting in a miscarried trial (paras. 118-31).

Per Hayne J (with whom Gummow, Heydon, Crennan and Kiefel JJ agreed): (1) The definition of "slavery" adopted in Section 270.1 of the Code derived from the definition of slavery, as a condition, that was given in the 1926 Convention (paras. 135-7).

(2) "Ownership" and "powers attaching to the right of ownership" had to be understood as ordinary expressions applied in their context. Proof of the intentional exercise of any of the relevant powers over a person established that the victim was a slave and the accused had done that which was prohibited by legislation. Since the evidence permitted the conclusion that the respondent used and possessed each complainant as an item of property at the disposal of the purchaser irrespective of her wishes, it could be concluded that the respondent used and possessed each complainant as a slave (paras. 138-68).

The following is the text of the judgments delivered in the Court:

[201] 1. GLEESON **CJ.** Following a trial in the County Court of Victoria, before Judge McInerney and a jury, the respondent was convicted of five offences of intentionally possessing a slave, and five offences of intentionally exercising over [202] a slave a power attaching to the right of ownership, namely the power to use, contrary to s 270.3(1)(a) of the Criminal Code (Cth) (the Code). She was sentenced to a lengthy term of imprisonment. The Court of Appeal of the Supreme Court of Victoria upheld an appeal against each of the convictions, quashed the convictions and ordered a new trial on all counts.[1] The prosecution, by special leave, has appealed to this court. The respondent seeks special leave to cross-appeal against the order for a new trial.

2. The Court of Appeal rejected a number of grounds of appeal which, if upheld, would have resulted in an acquittal on all counts. It upheld one ground of appeal, which complained that the directions given to the jury were inadequate. The proposed cross-appeal raises three

---

[1] *R v. Tang* (2007) 16 VR 454; [2007] VSCA 134.

grounds. The first two grounds concern the meaning and constitutional validity of s 270.3(1)(a). Both grounds were rejected by the Court of Appeal. Logically, a consideration of those grounds should come before consideration of the Court of Appeal's decision on the directions given to the jury. Special leave to cross-appeal on those two grounds should be granted. It will be convenient to deal with them before turning to the prosecution appeal. It is also convenient to leave to one side for the moment the proposed third ground of cross-appeal, which is that the Court of Appeal erred in failing to hold that the jury verdicts were unreasonable or could not be supported having regard to the evidence.

The Legislation

3. Chapter 8 of the Code deals with "Offences against humanity". It includes Div. 270, which deals with "Slavery, sexual servitude and deceptive recruiting". Division 270, which was introduced by the Criminal Code Amendment (Slavery and Sexual Servitude) Act 1999 (Cth), was based on recommendations made by the Australian Law Reform Commission in 1990.[2] It includes the following:

270.1 *Definition of* slavery

For the purposes of this Division, *slavery* is the condition of a person over whom any or all of the powers attaching to the right of ownership are exercised, including where such a condition results from a debt or contract made by the person.

270.2 *Slavery is unlawful*

Slavery remains unlawful and its abolition is maintained, despite the repeal by the Criminal Code Amendment (Slavery and Sexual Servitude) Act 1999 of Imperial Acts relating to slavery.

270.3 *Slavery offences*

(1) A person who, whether within or outside Australia, intentionally:

(a) possesses a slave or exercises over a slave any of the other powers attaching to the right of ownership; or
(b) engages in slave trading; or
(c) enters into any commercial transaction involving a slave; or
(d) exercises control or direction over, or provides finance for:
   (i) any act of slave trading; or
   (ii) any commercial transaction involving a slave;

is guilty of an offence.
Penalty: Imprisonment for 25 years.

---

[2] Australian Law Reform Commission, "Criminal admiralty jurisdiction and prize", Report No 48, 1990, pp. 72-92.

(2) A person who:

(a) whether within or outside Australia:
   (i) enters into any commercial transaction involving a slave; or
   (ii) **[203]** exercises control or direction over, or provides finance for, any commercial transaction involving a slave; or
   (iii) exercises control or direction over, or provides finance for, any act of slave trading; and
(b) is reckless as to whether the transaction or act involves a slave, slavery or slave trading;

is guilty of an offence.
Penalty: Imprisonment for 17 years.
(3) In this section:
"slave trading" includes:

(a) the capture, transport or disposal of a person with the intention of reducing the person to slavery; or
(b) the purchase or sale of a slave.

(4) A person who engages in any conduct with the intention of securing the release of a person from slavery is not guilty of an offence against this section.
(5) The defendant bears a legal burden of proving the matter mentioned in subsection (4).

4. Later, at a time after the alleged offences the subject of these proceedings, a further offence described as "debt bondage" was added to Ch 8: s 271.8. That offence carries a lesser maximum penalty than an offence against s 270.3. It may be that the facts of this case would have fallen within s 271.8 had it been in force. If so, that is immaterial. There are many statutes, Commonwealth and state, which create offences of such a kind that particular conduct may fall within both a more serious and a less serious offence. There is a question, to be considered, whether the facts alleged in this case fall within s 270.3. If they had occurred at a later time, they might also have fallen within s 271.8. The two provisions are not mutually exclusive.

5. It is necessary also to refer to Ch 2 of the Code. It includes the following:

Chapter 2—General principles of criminal responsibility
Part 2.1—Purpose and application
Division 2
2.1 *Purpose*
   The purpose of this Chapter is to codify the general principles of criminal responsibility under laws of the Commonwealth. It contains all the general principles of criminal responsibility that apply to any offence, irrespective of how the offence is created.

...

Part 2.2—The elements of an offence
Division 3—General
3.1 *Elements*
(1) *An offence consists of physical elements and fault elements.*
(2) However, the law that creates the offence may provide that there is no fault element for one or more physical elements.
(3) The law that creates the offence may provide different fault elements for different physical elements.
3.2 Establishing guilt in respect of offences
In order for a person to be found guilty of committing an offence the following must be proved:

- (a) the existence of such physical elements as are, under the law creating the offence, relevant to establishing guilt;
- (b) in respect of each such physical element for which a fault element is required, one of the fault elements for the physical element.

...

[204] *Division 4—Physical elements*
4.1 *Physical elements*
(1) *A physical element of an offence may be:*

- (a) *conduct; or*
- (b) a result of conduct; or
- (c) a circumstance in which conduct, or a result of conduct, occurs.

(2) In this Code:
"*conduct*" means an act, an omission to perform an act or a state of affairs.
"*engage in conduct*" means:

- (a) do an act; or
- (b) omit to perform an act.

4.2 *Voluntariness*
(1) Conduct can only be a physical element if it is voluntary.
(2) Conduct is only voluntary if it is a product of the will of the person whose conduct it is.
...
4.3 *Omissions*
An omission to perform an act can only be a physical element if:

- (a) the law creating the offence makes it so; or
- (b) the law creating the offence impliedly provides that the offence is committed by an omission to perform an act that by law there is a duty to perform.

Division 5—Fault elements
5.1 *Fault elements*

(1) A fault element for a particular physical element may be intention, knowledge, recklessness or negligence.

(2) Subsection (1) does not prevent a law that creates a particular offence from specifying other fault elements for a physical element of that offence.

5.2 *Intention*

(1) A person has intention with respect to conduct if he or she means to engage in that conduct.

(2) A person has intention with respect to a circumstance if he or she believes that it exists or will exist.

(3) A person has intention with respect to a result if he or she means to bring it about or is aware that it will occur in the ordinary course of events.

5.3 *Knowledge*

A person has knowledge of a circumstance or a result if he or she is aware that it exists or will exist in the ordinary course of events.

5.4 *Recklessness*

(1) A person is reckless with respect to a circumstance if:

(a) he or she is aware of a substantial risk that the circumstance exists or will exist; and

(b) having regard to the circumstances known to him or her, it is unjustifiable to take the risk.

(2) A person is reckless with respect to a result if:

(a) he or she is aware of a substantial risk that the result will occur; and

(b) having regard to the circumstances known to him or her, it is unjustifiable to take the risk.

(3) The question whether taking a risk is unjustifiable is one of fact.

(4) If recklessness is a fault element for a physical element of an offence, proof of intention, knowledge or recklessness will satisfy that fault element.

5.5 *Negligence*

A person is negligent with respect to a physical element of an offence if his or her conduct involves:

(a) such a great falling short of the standard of care that a reasonable person would exercise in the circumstances; and

(b) such a high risk that the physical element exists or will exist;

[205] that the conduct merits criminal punishment for the offence.

5.6 *Offences that do not specify fault elements*

(1) If the law creating the offence does not specify a fault element for a physical element that consists only of conduct, intention is the fault element for that physical element.

(2) If the law creating the offence does not specify a fault element for a physical element that consists of a circumstance or a result, recklessness is the fault element for that physical element.

The Background

6. The respondent was the owner of a licensed brothel at 417 Brunswick St, Fitzroy known as Club 417. The ten counts in the indictment contained two charges (possessing and using) under s 270.3(1)(a) in relation to each of five women (sometimes described as the complainants). The women were Thai nationals. They all came to Australia to work as prostitutes. They had all previously worked in what was described as the sex industry. They became "contract workers". There was no written contract, but there were agreed conditions. Each complainant came to Australia voluntarily.

7. In an appeal to the Court of Appeal of Victoria by a woman, DS, who originally had been a co-accused of the respondent, Chernov JA described the practice that was followed:[3]

> 6. ... The organisers in Australia arranged for an appropriate visa to be issued to a [complainant], no doubt on the basis of false information being provided to the immigration authorities. Sometimes that required funds to be deposited temporarily in a bank account in the name of the [complainant] in order to ensure that her visa could be obtained. The woman was then flown to Sydney from Bangkok, "escorted" by one or two people, usually an elderly couple (so as not to arouse suspicion as to the [complainant's] real purpose in coming to Australia). Generally, once the [complainant] arrived here she was treated as being "owned" by those who had procured her passage. The [complainant] would be met at the airport by a representative of the Australian "owner", who would pay off the "escorts" and take the [complainant] to an apartment or hotel in Sydney and keep her there until a decision was made as to the brothel at which she was to work.

The "Purchase" of the Complainants and the "Debts" Incurred By Them

8. DS gave evidence at the trial of the respondent. DS's involvement included negotiating with people in Thailand who recruited the women and settling the women in brothels in Australia.[4] In her evidence in the trial of the respondent, DS described the process that was followed in relation to one of the complainants, once she had arrived in Australia. She gave a similar account in relation to three of the other complainants. After receiving a telephone call from the woman's "boss", DS collected this particular complainant from a hotel. She then contacted the respondent, who agreed to accept the complainant as a contract worker in her brothel, and who also agreed to take up a 70% interest in a syndicate which would "purchase" the woman, DS and her associates taking up

---

[3] *R* v. *DS* (2005) 191 FLR 337; [2005] VSCA 99 at para. 6 *(DS)*.   [4] *DS* at para. 7.

the other 30%. The syndicate agreed to pay the "boss" the sum of $20,000. That sum was described by DS as "the amount for this girl", "the amount of money we purchased this woman" and "the money for purchasing women from Thailand to come here". The $20,000 was sent to Thailand.

[206] 9. An amount of $110 was to be charged to customers for the complainant's services. It was agreed that the respondent would retain $43 in her capacity as brothel owner. The remaining $67 was divided between the "owners" of the complainant. In this case, the respondent retained 70% of $67 and DS and her associates took 30%.

10. The complainant acknowledged a "debt" to the syndicate in an amount of $45,000. For each customer serviced, the complainant's "debt" would be reduced by $50. In the particular case, the amount of the debt was the subject of subsequent negotiation between DS, the respondent and the complainant. DS said:

It was agreed in Sydney that the debt would be $45,000, but [the complainant] was not happy to pay that amount. So, I asked [the respondent] if she could review the amount on her. So, it was finally agreed that the amount would be I'm not sure $43,000 or $42,000.

It was also agreed that there would be a "free day" for the complainant. On that day, the complainant retained $50 per customer and $17 was divided between the syndicate members (70% to the respondent and 30% to DS and her associates). The respondent was also paid $43 per customer, in her capacity as owner of the brothel. Prior to coming to Australia the complainants were not always aware of the precise terms of the debt or of the living conditions in Australia.

11. There were five complainants. All of them consented to come to Australia to work, on the understanding that, once they had paid off their "debt", they would have the opportunity to earn money on their own account as prostitutes. Upon their arrival the women had very little, if any, money in their possession, spoke little, if any, English, and knew no one.

12. Four of the complainants went to work in the respondent's brothel in the circumstances described above. In respect of each of those four complainants, the respondent had a share in a syndicate which, according to DS, "purchased" the complainant for $20,000. The contract "debt" was $45,000, or, in the particular case earlier mentioned, $42,000 or $43,000. In his remarks on sentencing, which were based on the evidence that went to the jury, the trial judge said that this sum took account of the $20,000 paid to the recruiters in Thailand, as well as costs of travel and the complainant's living expenses during the term of the

contract. It included a profit margin, but the margin was not the subject of any calculation. The "debt" was a notional liability by reference to which aspects of the complainant's obligations were regulated. It was the amount she had to work off, at the rate of $50 per customer, under her "contract". Two of the complainants ultimately worked off their debts, and were thereafter paid for their prostitution.

13. The respondent herself paid nothing to the recruiters in the case of the fifth complainant. The evidence was that, after the fifth complainant was brought to Australia, she worked for others at a different brothel. Later, DS arranged for her to work at the respondent's brothel. The arrangements in relation to the fifth complainant were the same as for the other four, save that she had different "owners". DS's evidence was that, in relation to the $110 paid by each of the fifth complainant's customers, the respondent retained $43 as brothel owner and the remaining $67 would be paid to DS, who divided the amount between that complainant's owners. The fifth complainant's "debt" of $45,000 also was being worked off at the rate of $50 per customer.

[207] 14. In summary, then, while under contract, each complainant was to work in the respondent's brothel in Melbourne 6 days per week, serving up to 900 customers over a period of 4-6 months. The complainants earned nothing in cash while under contract except that, by working on the seventh "free" day each week, they could keep the $50 per customer that would, during the rest of the week, go to offset their contract debts.

The Conditions of the Complainants

15. The trial judge said in his sentencing remarks that he was satisfied on the evidence that the complainants were financially deprived and vulnerable upon arriving in Australia. He found that the complainants entered Australia on visas that were obtained illegally. Continued receipt of the benefits of the complainants' contracts depended on their not being apprehended by immigration authorities. The benefits were more certain to be obtained when the complainants were kept hidden.

16. While on contract, the complainants' passports and return airfares were retained by the respondent. This was done so that the passports could be produced to immigration authorities if necessary, and also so that the complainants could not run away. The complainants lived in premises arranged by the respondent, where they were lodged and fed, and their medical requirements attended to. The evidence was that the complainants were well provisioned, fed and provided for. The complainants were not kept under lock and key. Nevertheless, the trial judge

said that, in the totality of the circumstances, the complainants were effectively restricted to the premises. On rare occasions they ventured out with consent or under supervision. The circumstances to which the trial judge referred included the hours of work involved, as well as control by way of fear of detection from immigration authorities, fear of visa offences, advice to be aware of immigration authorities, advice to tell false stories to immigration authorities if apprehended and instructions not to leave their accommodation without the respondent, DS or the manager of the brothel. In the case of some of the contract workers, the regime became more relaxed as the contract progressed and, towards the end of their contracts, they were at liberty to go out as they wished. At work, the trial judge found that, while they were occasionally permitted to go out to shop, the complainants were, because of the nature and hours of their work, effectively restricted to the premises.

17. In the case of the two complainants who ultimately paid off their debts, the restrictions that had been placed on them were then lifted, their passports were returned and they were free to choose their hours of work, and their accommodation.

18. In addition to the restrictions that were placed on the complainants, the prosecution pointed to the demands placed upon them as to the numbers of clients they were required to service, their lack of payment and the days and hours they were required to work as demonstrating that their situation differed materially from that of other sex workers, who, however exploited they may have been, were not slaves. The Court of Appeal accepted that the evidence was capable of supporting the jury verdicts, which were held not to have been unreasonable.

[208] *The Meaning and Validity of s 270.3(1)(a)*

19. The first two grounds of the respondent's proposed cross-appeal are that:

(1) the Court of Appeal erred in holding that ss 270.1 and 270.3(1)(a) of the Code were within the legislative power of the Commonwealth; and
(2) the Court of Appeal erred in holding that the offences created by s 270.3(1)(a) extended to the behaviour alleged in the present case and that they were not confined to situations akin to "chattel slavery" or in which the complainant is notionally owned by the accused or another at the relevant time.

20. As to ground (1), the Court of Appeal held that the relevant provisions of the Code were enacted pursuant to, and sustained by, the power of the parliament to make laws with respect to external affairs

(s 51(xxix) of the Constitution). As to ground (2), the Court of Appeal held that s 270.3(1)(a) was not confined to what is sometimes called "chattel slavery". Presumably, the reference in ground (2) to "situations akin to" chattel slavery, and to notional ownership, was prompted by the consideration that chattel slavery is, in Australia, a legal impossibility. If s 270.3(1)(a), in its application to conduct within Australia, were confined to chattel slavery and legal ownership, it would have no practical operation. Section 270.2 would eliminate chattel slavery and ownership and s 270.3(1)(a) would be otiose. The Court of Appeal held that the facts alleged in the present case were capable of being regarded as within the scope of s 270.3(1)(a). For the reasons that follow, the decision of the Court of Appeal on these issues should be upheld.

21. The word "slave" in s 270.3(1)(a) is not defined. It takes its meaning from the definition of "slavery" in s 270.1. That definition, in turn, derives from, although it is not identical to, the definition of "slavery" in Art. 1 of the 1926 International Convention to Suppress the Slave Trade and Slavery (the 1926 Slavery Convention).[5] That definition was taken up in Art. 7 of the 1956 Supplementary Convention on the Abolition of Slavery, the Slave Trade, and Institutions and Practices similar to Slavery (the 1956 Supplementary Convention),[6] which dealt with institutions and practices similar to slavery "where they still exist and whether or not they are covered by the definition of slavery contained in article 1 of the [1926] Slavery Convention".[7]

22. The 1926 Slavery Convention, in its preamble, recited the declaration in the General Act of the Brussels Conference of 1889-90 of an intention to put an end to the traffic in African slaves, the intention, affirmed at the Convention of Saint-Germain-en-Laye of 1919, to secure the complete suppression of slavery in all its forms, and the need to prevent forced labour from developing into conditions analogous to slavery. Article 2 contained an undertaking by the parties to prevent and suppress the slave trade and to bring about the complete abolition of slavery "in all its forms".

23. Article 1 of the 1926 Slavery Convention was in the following terms:

Article 1
For the purpose of the present Convention, the following definitions are agreed upon:

(1) Slavery is the status or condition of a person over whom any or all of the powers attaching to the right of ownership are exercised.

---

[5] 212 UNTS 17.   [6] 266 UNTS 3.   [7] Article 1.

(2) **[209]** The slave trade includes all acts involved in the capture, acquisition or disposal of a person with intent to reduce him to slavery; all acts involved in the acquisition of a slave with a view to selling or exchanging him; all acts of disposal by sale or exchange of a slave acquired with a view to being sold or exchanged, and, in general, every act of trade or transport in slaves.

24. The definition in Art. 1(1) has continued to be used in international instruments. For example, the Rome Statute of the International Criminal Court, which entered into force in 2002, defined "enslavement", a crime against humanity, as "the exercise of any or all of the powers attaching to the right of ownership over a person . . . includ[ing] the exercise of such power in the course of trafficking in persons".[8]

25. The travaux préparatoires of the 1926 Slavery Convention are not especially illuminating as to the meaning of Art. I.[9] Nevertheless, certain observations may be made as to the text and context, including the purpose, of the Convention. First, in 1926, in the case of many of the parties to the Convention, including Australia, the legal status of slavery did not exist, and legal ownership by one person of another was impossible. (In Australia, the law on slavery was based on four nineteenth-century Imperial Acts,[10] a matter adverted to in s 270.2 of the Code.) Secondly, a principal object of the Convention was to bring about the same situation universally, as soon as possible. Thirdly, the definition of slavery in Art. 1 referred to the status or condition of a person. Status is a legal concept. Since the legal status of slavery did not exist in many parts of the world, and since it was intended that it would cease to exist everywhere, the evident purpose of the reference to "condition" was to cover slavery de facto as well as de jure. This is hardly surprising. The declared aim of the parties to the Convention was to secure the complete suppression of slavery in all its forms, and to prevent forced labour from developing into conditions analogous to slavery. They undertook to bring about "the complete abolition of slavery in all its forms". It would have been a pitiful effort towards the achievement of those ends to construct a Convention that dealt only with questions of legal status. The slave trade was not, and is

---

[8] 2187 UNTS 90, Art. 7(2)(c).

[9] J. Allain, "A Legal Consideration of 'Slavery' in Light of the Travaux Préparatoires of the 1926 Convention", paper delivered at the conference, "Twenty-First Century Slavery: Issues and Responses", 23 November 2006; J. Allain, "The Definition of 'Slavery' in General International Law and the Crime of Enslavement within the Rome Statute", paper delivered at the International Criminal Court, Guest Lecture Series of the Office of the Prosecutor, 26 April 2007; J. Allain, *The Slavery Conventions: The Travaux Préparatoires of the 1926 League of Nations Convention and the 1956 United Nations Convention*, Martinus Nijhoff Publishers, Leiden, 2008.

[10] The Slave Trade Act 1824 (Imp); the Slavery Abolition Act 1833 (Imp); the Slave Trade Act 1843 (Imp); and the Slave Trade Act 1873 (Imp).

not, something that could be suppressed merely by withdrawal of legal recognition of the incidents of slavery. It is one thing to withdraw legal recognition of slavery; it is another thing to suppress it. The Convention aimed to do both. Fourthly, the definition turns upon the exercise of power over a person. The antithesis of slavery is freedom. The kind of exercise of power that deprives a person of freedom to the extent that the person becomes a slave is said to be the exercise of any or all of the powers attaching to the right of ownership. As already noted, there was no legal right of ownership in many of the states which were parties to the Convention, and one purpose of the Convention was that there would be no such legal right anywhere.

[210] 26. In its application to the de facto condition, as distinct from the de jure status, of slavery, the definition was addressing the exercise over a person of powers of the kind that attached to the right of ownership when the legal status was possible; not necessarily all of those powers, but any or all of them. In a 1953 Memorandum, the Secretary-General of the United Nations[11] listed such powers as including the capacity to make a person an object of purchase, the capacity to use a person and a person's labour in a substantially unrestricted manner and an entitlement to the fruits of the person's labour without compensation commensurate to the value of the labour. Each of those powers is of relevance in the present case. On the evidence it was open to the jury to conclude that each of the complainants was made an object of purchase (although in the case of one of them the purchaser was not the respondent); that, for the duration of the contracts, the owners had a capacity to use the complainants and the complainants' labour in a substantially unrestricted manner; and that the owners were entitled to the fruits of the complainants' labour without commensurate compensation.

27. The reference to "chattel slavery" in the second ground of cross-appeal is a reference to the legal capacity of an owner to treat a slave as an article of possession, subject to the qualification that the owner was not allowed to kill the slave; power over "the slave's person, property, and limbs, life only excepted".[12] Without doubt, chattel slavery falls within the definition in Art. 1 of the 1926 Slavery Convention, but it would be inconsistent with the considerations of purpose, context and text referred to in the preceding paragraph to read the definition as limited to that form of slavery.

28. In the case of *Prosecutor* v. *Kunarac*, before the International Criminal Tribunal for the Former Yugoslavia, where the charges were

---

[11] United Nations Economic and Social Council, "Slavery, the Slave Trade, and Other Forms of Servitude, Report of the Secretary-General", UN Doc. E/2357, 1953, p. 28.

[12] *Somerset* v. *Stewart* (1772) Lofft 1 at 2; 98 ER 499 at 500. See also *Smith* v. *Gould* (1706) 2 Salk 666; 91 ER 567; *Forbes* v. *Cochrane* (1824) 2 B & C 448 at 471-2; 107 ER 450 at 459.

of "enslavement", both the Trial Chamber[13] and the Appeals Chamber[14] adopted a view of the offence that was not limited to chattel slavery. The Trial Chamber, after an extensive review of relevant authorities and materials, concluded that enslavement as a crime against humanity in customary international law consisted of the exercise of any or all of the powers attaching to the right of ownership over a person; the actus reus of the violation being the exercise of any or all of such powers and the mens rea consisting in the intentional exercise of such powers.[15] The Trial Chamber identified, as factors to be taken into account, control of movement, control of physical environment, psychological control, measures taken to prevent or deter escape, force, threat of force or coercion, duration, assertion of exclusivity, subjection to cruel treatment and abuse, control of sexuality and forced labour.[16] The Appeals Chamber agreed with those factors.[17] However, it preferred to leave open, as a matter that was unnecessary for decision in that case, the Trial Chamber's added factor of an ability to buy and [211] sell a person, and it disagreed with the Trial Chamber's view that lack of consent was an element of the offence, although accepting that it may be of evidential significance.[18]

29. It is unnecessary, and unhelpful, for the resolution of the issues in the present case, to seek to draw boundaries between slavery and cognate concepts such as servitude, peonage, forced labour or debt bondage. The 1956 Supplementary Convention in Art. 1 recognised that some of the institutions and practices it covered might also be covered by the definition of slavery in Art. 1 of the 1926 Slavery Convention. To repeat what was said earlier, the various concepts are not all mutually exclusive. Those who engage in the traffic in human beings are unlikely to be so obliging as to arrange their practices to conform to some convenient taxonomy.

30. In *Siliadin* v. *France*,[19] the European Court of Human Rights dealt with a complaint by a domestic worker that the French criminal law did not afford her sufficient and effective protection against "servitude", or at least "forced or compulsory" labour. Reference was made to legislative materials which used the term "modern slavery" to apply to some females, working in private households, who started out as migrant domestic workers, au pairs or "mail-order brides".[20] The court referred briefly and dismissively to the possibility that the applicant was

---

[13] Case No IT-96-23-T & IT-96-23/1-T, 22 February 2001 *(Kunarac* (Trial)).
[14] Case No IT-96-23 & IT-96-23/1-A, 12 June 2002 *(Kunarac* (Appeal)).
[15] *Kunarac* (Trial) at paras. 539-40.   [16] *Kunarac* (Trial) at para. 543.
[17] *Kunarac* (Appeal) at paras. 117-19.   [18] *Kunarac* (Appeal) at paras. 119-20.
[19] (2006) 43 EHRR 16 *(Siliadin).*   [20] *Siliadin* at para. 49.

a slave within the meaning of Art. 1 of the 1926 Slavery Convention, saying:[21]

[The Court] notes that this definition corresponds to the "classic" meaning of slavery as it was practised for centuries. Although the applicant was, in the instant case, clearly deprived of her personal autonomy, the evidence does not suggest that she was held in slavery in the proper sense, in other words that Mr and Mrs B exercised a genuine right of legal ownership over her, thus reducing her to the status of an "object".[22]

31. It is understandable, in the context of that case, that the definition of "slavery" was dealt with only in passing and briefly. Nevertheless, it is to be noted that the court did not refer to the definition's reference to condition in the alternative to status, or to powers as well as rights, or to the words "any or all". It may be assumed that there is, in France, no such thing as "a genuine right of legal ownership" of a person. That Mr and Mrs B did not exercise a genuine right of legal ownership over the applicant was self-evident, but it would not have been a complete answer if there had been a serious issue of slavery in the case.

32. It is important not to debase the currency of language, or to banalise crimes against humanity, by giving slavery a meaning that extends beyond the limits set by the text, context and purpose of the 1926 Slavery Convention. In particular it is important to recognise that harsh and exploitative conditions of labour do not of themselves amount to slavery. The term "slave" is sometimes used in a metaphorical sense to describe victims of such conditions, but that sense is not of present relevance. Some of the factors identified as relevant in *Kunarac*, such as control of movement and control of physical environment, involve questions of degree. An employer normally has some degree of control over the [212] movements, or work environment, of an employee. Furthermore, geographical and other circumstances may limit an employee's freedom of movement. Powers of control, in the context of an issue of slavery, are powers of the kind and degree that would attach to a right of ownership if such a right were legally possible, not powers of a kind that are no more than an incident of harsh employment, either generally or at a particular time or place.

33. Although the definition of "slavery" in s 270.1 of the Code is plainly based on the definition in Art. 1 of the 1926 Slavery Convention, the wording is not identical. First, s 270.1 refers to "condition", not

---

[21] *Siliadin* at para. 122 (emphasis added).
[22] In the authoritative French text, "c'est-à-dire que les époux B aient exercé sur elle, *juridiquement, un véritable droit de propriété*, la réduisant à l'état d'objet": *Affaire Siliadin c. France*, Requête No 73316/01, 26 July 2005 at para. 122 (emphasis added).

"status or condition". The explanation for the difference appears from s 270.2. There is no status of slavery under Australian law. Legal ownership of a person is impossible. Consequently s 270.1, in its application to conduct within Australia, is concerned with de facto slavery. In s 270.1, the reference to powers attaching to the right of ownership, which are exercised over a person in a condition described as slavery, is a reference to powers of such a nature and extent that they are attributes of effective (although not legal, for that is impossible) ownership.[23] Secondly, the concluding words of the definition in s 270.1 ("including where such a condition results from a debt or contract made by the person") do not alter the meaning of the preceding words because it is only where "such a condition" (that is, the condition earlier described in terms of the 1926 Slavery Convention) results that the words of inclusion apply. The words following "including", therefore, do not extend the operation of the previous words but make it plain that a condition that results from a debt or a contract is not, on that account alone, to be excluded from the definition, provided it would otherwise be covered by it. This is a common drafting technique, and its effect is not to be confused with that of cases where "including" is used as a term of extension.[24]

34. In the result, the definition of "slavery" in s 270.1 falls within the definition in Art. 1 of the 1926 Slavery Convention, and the relevant provisions of Div. 270 are reasonably capable of being considered appropriate and adapted to give effect to Australia's obligations under that convention.[25] They are sustained by the external affairs power. They are not limited to chattel slavery.

35. The factors accepted by both the Trial Chamber and the Appeals Chamber in *Kunarac* are relevant to the application of s 270.3(1)(a) of the Code. The Appeals Chamber was right to point out that consent is not inconsistent with slavery. In some societies where slavery was lawful, a person could sell himself into slavery. Peonage could be voluntary as well as involuntary, the difference affecting the origin, but not the character, of the servitude.[26] Consent may be factually relevant in a given case, although it may be necessary to make a closer examination of the circumstances and extent of the consent relied upon, but absence of consent is not a necessary element of the offence. On the point left open

---

[23] Allain, 2007, pp. 12-13.
[24] That this construction conforms to the legislative purpose appears from the minister's second reading speech: Cth Hansard, Senate, 24 March 1999, p. 3076; and Model Criminal Code Officers Committee of the Standing Committee of Attorneys-General, "Model Criminal Code, Ch 9, Offences Against Humanity: Slavery", Report, 1998, p. 29.
[25] Compare *Victoria* v. *Commonwealth*; (1996) 187 CLR 416 at 486-8; 138 ALR 129 at 146; [1995] HCA 45.
[26] *Clyatt* v. *United States* 197 US 207 (1905) at 215.

by the Appeals Chamber, it should be concluded that, for the purpose of s 270.3(1)(a) of the Code, the commodification of an individual by treating him **[213]** or her as an object of sale and purchase, if it exists, is a material factor when a tribunal of fact comes to assess the circumstances of a case, and may involve the exercise of a power attaching to a right of ownership. Having regard to all those matters, there was in the present case evidence to go to a jury that was capable of sustaining verdicts of guilty.

The Appeal

36. The Court of Appeal quashed the respondent's convictions, and ordered a new trial, substantially upon a single ground of criticism of the primary judge's directions to the jury. The point on which the Court of Appeal differed from the primary judge comes down to a question of the application of the provisions of Ch 2 of the Code to charges of breaches of s 270.3(1)(a). Before turning to those provisions, it is convenient to set out what was said in the Court of Appeal by Eames JA, with whom Maxwell P and Buchanan JA agreed.

37. Eames JA described as "the critical issue" one that "concerns the character of the exercise of power by the accused over the victim". He said that the prosecutor's argument and the trial judge's directions "did not, in terms, [invite or] direct the jury to consider the subjective intention of the [respondent]—her state of mind—when dealing with the complainants". This, he said, "was a critical element of the offence that had to be established if the [respondent] was to be convicted". The jurors, Eames JA held, "were not alerted as to the relevance, when considering the question of intention, of the belief which the [respondent] may have held as to the basis on which she was dealing with each of the complainants". What his Honour understood to be the relevance of that belief was made clear in his reasons. The primary judge had told the jury that, in order to convict, they had to find that the complainants were slaves in accordance with the statutory definition as he explained it to them, that the respondent knew the facts that brought the complainants within that definition (although not that she was aware of the legislation, or the legal definition of slavery) and that she intended to possess or use persons in the condition disclosed by those facts. (It may be noted that the elements of the offence as explained by the primary judge in his directions were somewhat similar to what the Trial Chamber in *Kunarac* identified as the actus reus and the mens rea for the crime of enslavement.)

38. Eames JA said that the critical element of the offence of possessing a slave, missing from the primary judge's directions, was "[the

respondent's] *appreciation* of the character of her own actions" (emphasis added). He described the element as follows (references omitted):

> 77. ... Fourthly, the accused must have possessed the worker in the intentional exercise of what constitutes a power attaching to a right of ownership, namely, the power of possession. For that to be the case the accused must be shown to have regarded the worker as though she was mere property, a thing, thereby intending to deal with her not as a human being who had free will and a right to liberty, but as though she was mere property. However harsh or oppressive her conduct was towards the worker it would not be sufficient for a conviction if, rather than having possessed the worker with the knowledge, intention, or in the belief that she was dealing with her as though she was mere property, the accused possessed her in the knowledge or belief that she was exercising some different right or entitlement to do so, falling short of what would amount to ownership, such as that of an employer, contractor, or manager.

[214] 39. In a footnote to his reasons on this point, Eames JA said that it was not necessary to prove that an offender knew that the power to possess or use property was an incident of the right of ownership. That is correct, but it is not easy to relate that to the concluding words of the paragraph just quoted, which seem to postulate, as exculpatory, a knowledge or belief that the offender was exercising some other right or entitlement. If it were not necessary to prove that the respondent knew what rights of ownership were, it would be curious if it were relevant to consider what she knew or believed about other rights or entitlements. One would have expected that a person could be convicted of the offence of possessing a slave without knowing, or caring, anything about possible alternative sources of rights or entitlements.

40. In a further footnote, Eames JA supported the above paragraph by references to s 5.2(2) and (3) of the Code, which, he said, were both relevant. This is a matter to which it will be necessary to return.

41. Later, Eames JA said (in a passage that also is difficult to reconcile with the first of the footnotes mentioned above):

> 124. ... What the judge omitted to state was that the Crown had to prove intention to exercise power over the slave in the knowledge or belief that the power that was being exercised was one attaching to ownership. That is, the power must have been intentionally exercised as an owner of property would exercise power over that property, acting in the knowledge or belief that the victim could be dealt with as no more than a chattel. It would not suffice for the power to have been exercised by the accused in the belief that she was dealing with the victim as her employee, albeit one in a subservient position and being grossly exploited.

42. These passages, notwithstanding the footnote, indicate that Eames JA had in mind that it was necessary for the prosecution to establish a certain state of knowledge or belief on the part of the respondent as to the source of the powers she was exercising, in addition to an intention to exercise those powers. They appear to require advertence by the respondent to the different capacities (owner or employer) by virtue of which she might have been able to exercise powers. This was made even clearer by the form of an answer which his Honour said should have been given to a question asked by the jury:

> 145. . . . You must be satisfied that the accused was intentionally exercising a power that an owner would have over property *and was doing so with the knowledge or in the belief that the complainant was no more than mere property.*
>
> If it is reasonably possible that the accused acted to possess or to use the complainant with the knowledge or in the belief that she was exercising her rights and entitlements as her employer or contractor and not in the belief that the complainant had no rights or free will, but was property, a thing, over whom she could exercise power as though she owned her then, however exploitative and unfair you may think her treatment of the complainant was, it would not constitute the offences of intentionally possessing or using a slave. [Emphasis added.]

43. This cannot be accepted. What the respondent knew or believed about her rights and entitlements as an employer or contractor, as distinct from rights of property, in the perhaps unlikely event that she knew or believed anything on that subject, was not something that the prosecutor had to establish or that the jury had to consider.

44. It seems likely that the Court of Appeal was, with good reason, concerned about a problem presented by s 270.3(1)(a), at least in a borderline case: how is a jury to distinguish between slavery, on the one hand, and harsh and exploitative [**215**] conditions of labour, on the other? The answer to that, in a given case, may be found in the nature and extent of the powers exercised over a complainant. In particular, a capacity to deal with a complainant as a commodity, an object of sale and purchase, may be a powerful indication that a case falls on one side of the line. So also may the exercise of powers of control over movement which extend well beyond powers exercised even in the most exploitative of employment circumstances, and absence or extreme inadequacy of payment for services. The answer, however, is not to be found in the need for reflection by an accused person upon the source of the powers that are being exercised. Indeed, it is probably only in a rare case that there would be any evidence of such consideration.

45. It should also be noted that the concluding words of the definition of slavery in s 270.1 of the Code show that the existence of a contract between an alleged offender and a complainant is not inconsistent with the commission of an offence. The legislation, in terms, accepts that a condition of slavery may result from a contract. The above reasoning appears to construct a false dichotomy between employment and effective ownership, in addition to importing a requirement of rights analysis by the offender which is unnecessary.

46. Chapter 2 of the Code does not provide support for the Court of Appeal's reasoning. In the case of both of the offences alleged in relation to each complainant, the physical element of the offence was conduct, which is defined to include both an act and a state of affairs. It was not suggested by the Court of Appeal that recklessness, as the default element in relation to circumstances, had a role to play.[27] As Brennan J pointed out in *He Kaw Teh* v. *R*,[28] having something in possession is more easily seen as a state of affairs that exists because of what the person who has possession does in relation to the thing possessed. Both possessing a slave and using a slave are conduct, and the prosecution had to establish the existence of the conduct and one of the fault elements specified in s 5.1(1). The prosecution case was conducted on the basis that the relevant fault element was intention. In a footnote earlier mentioned, Eames JA said that all of subss (1), (2) and (3) of s 5.2 were relevant. This is not easy to understand: subs (1) applies where the physical element is conduct; subs (2) applies where the physical element is a circumstance; and subs (3) applies where the physical element is a result. Section 4.1 says a physical element may be conduct or a result of conduct or a circumstance in which conduct or a result of conduct occurs.

47. The physical element was conduct (which includes a state of affairs); the fault element was intention. It was, therefore, s 5.2(1) that was relevant. A person has intention with respect to conduct if he or she means to engage in that conduct. Knowledge or belief is often relevant to intention.[29] If, for example, it is the existence of a state of affairs that gives an act its criminal character, then proof of knowledge of that state of affairs ordinarily will be the best method of proving that an accused meant to engage in the proscribed conduct.

48. The terms of s 270.3(1) reinforce the conclusion that intention is the relevant fault element. The offences in question were of intentionally possessing a slave or intentionally exercising over a slave another power

---

[27] Compare *R* v. *Saengsai-Or* (2004) 61 NSWLR 135; [2004] NSWCCA 108.
[28] (1985) 157 CLR 523 at 564; 60 ALR 449 at 478; [1985] HCA 43 *(He Kaw Teh)*.
[29] *He Kaw Teh* at CLR 570; ALR 483.

(here, using) attaching to the right of ownership. It is agreed on all sides that it was **[216]** unnecessary for the prosecution to prove that the respondent knew or believed that the complainant was a slave, or even that she knew what a slave was. Thus, Eames JA said that the respondent "does not have to have known the definition of a slave, nor even that there was an offence of slavery". So much is uncontroversial. If a person is known by an accused to possess the qualities that, by virtue of s 270.1, go to make that person a slave, then the state of knowledge relevant to intention, and therefore intention itself, may be established regardless of whether the accused appreciates the legal significance of those qualities. An accused does not have to know anything about the law in order to contravene s 270.3(1)(a).

49. In so far as a state of knowledge or belief is factually relevant to intention as the fault element of the offence, it is knowledge or belief about the facts relevant to possession or using, and knowledge or belief about the facts which determine the existence of the condition described in s 270.1. This is a condition that results from the exercise of certain powers. Whether the powers that are exercised over a person are "any or all of the powers attaching to the right of ownership" is for a jury to decide in the light of a judge's directions as to the nature and extent of the powers that are capable of satisfying that description. This is not to ignore the word "intentionally" in s 270.3(1). Rather, it involves no more than the common exercise of relating the fault element to the physical elements of the offence.[30]

50. In this case, the critical powers the exercise of which was disclosed (or the exercise of which a jury reasonably might find disclosed) by the evidence were the power to make the complainants an object of purchase, the capacity, for the duration of the contracts, to use the complainants and their labour in a substantially unrestricted manner, the power to control and restrict their movements and the power to use their services without commensurate compensation. As to the last three powers, their extent, as well as their nature, was relevant. As to the first, it was capable of being regarded by a jury as the key to an understanding of the condition of the complainants. The evidence could be understood as showing that they had been bought and paid for, and that their commodification explained the conditions of control and exploitation under which they were living and working.

51. It was not necessary for the prosecution to establish that the respondent had any knowledge or belief concerning the source of the powers exercised over the complainants, although it is interesting to

---

[30] Compare *He Kaw Teh* at CLR 568; ALR 482.

note that, in deciding to order a new trial, the Court of Appeal evidently took the view that the evidence was capable of satisfying a jury, beyond reasonable doubt, of the existence of the knowledge or belief that the Court of Appeal considered necessary.

52. The ground on which the Court of Appeal regarded the primary judge's directions as inadequate has not been sustained.

The Third Ground of Proposed Cross-Appeal

53. This ground is:

The Court of Appeal erred in failing to hold that the verdicts are unreasonable or cannot be supported having regard to the evidence.

[217] 54. The argument that the jury's verdict was unreasonable, because of the inadequacy of the evidence, was considered and rejected by the Court of Appeal, applying the principles stated by this court in *M* v. *R*.[31] Eames JA noted that much of the evidence in the case was uncontested, although there were some disputes of fact, especially in relation to some testimony as to aspects of the restraint applied to the movements of the complainants.

55. A cognate question was the subject of further argument and further reasons for judgment. When the Court of Appeal delivered its reasons for quashing the convictions (on the ground discussed earlier) it left open for further argument and consideration the question whether there should be an order for a new trial. After further argument, Eames JA said that his earlier reasons were intended to embrace a conclusion that the evidence in the case had sufficient cogency to justify a conviction. He said it did not follow automatically that there should be a new trial, but went on to deal with other relevant considerations. Finally, the Court of Appeal ordered a new trial.

56. It is likely that a good deal would have turned on the jury's assessment of DS and the complainants. Subject to that, there was cogent evidence of the intentional exercise of powers of such a nature and extent that they could reasonably be regarded as resulting in the condition of slavery, and the conduct, to which s 270.3(1)(a) was directed. There was no error of principle by the Court of Appeal on this aspect of the case, and it has not been shown that the interests of justice require a grant of special leave to cross-appeal on this ground.

---

[31] (1994) 181 CLR 487; 126 ALR 325; [1994] HCA 63.

Orders

57. I propose that the following orders be made:

(1) Appeal allowed.
(2) Special leave to cross-appeal on the first and second grounds in the proposed notice of cross-appeal granted. Cross-appeal on those grounds treated as instituted, heard instanter and dismissed.
(3) Special leave to cross-appeal on the third ground in the proposed notice of cross-appeal refused.
(4) Set aside orders 3, 4 and 5 of the orders of the Court of Appeal of the Supreme Court of Victoria made on 29 June 2007 and, in their place, order that the appeal to that court against conviction be dismissed.

58. Notwithstanding that these are criminal proceedings, the appellant, on the hearing of the application for special leave to appeal, undertook to pay the costs of the respondent of the application for special leave to appeal and of the appeal to this court. Consistently with that undertaking, the court should order that the appellant pay the respondent's costs of the application for special leave to appeal and of the appeal to this court.

59. There was also an application to the Court of Appeal for leave to appeal against sentence. Because the Court of Appeal allowed the appeal against conviction, it did not deal with the matter of sentence. The matter should be remitted to the Court of Appeal for its consideration of the application for leave to appeal against sentence.

60. GUMMOW J. I agree with the orders proposed by the Chief Justice and with his Honour's reasons. I agree also with the reasons of Hayne J.

[218] 61. KIRBY J. These proceedings arise out of convictions entered against Wei Tang (Ms Tang) following jury verdicts. The convictions are said to be the "first convictions in Australia" of "slavery offences" contrary to s 270.3(1)(a) of the Criminal Code (Cth) (the Code).[32] These offences are found in Ch 8 of the Code, dealing with "Offences against humanity".

62. Ms Tang sought, and obtained, leave to appeal against her convictions to the Court of Appeal of the Supreme Court of Victoria.[33] That court, while rejecting her submission that verdicts of acquittal should be entered, set aside the convictions and ordered a retrial of the charges.[34]

---

[32] *R v. Tang* (2007) 16 VR 454; [2007] VSCA 134 at para. 4 *(Tang)*.   [33] *Tang* at para. 200.
[34] *R v. Tang* [2007] VSCA 144 at paras. 13-14 *(Tang* (retrial judgment)). See *Tang* at paras. 199-200.

63. The prosecution, by special leave, has appealed to this court seeking restoration of Ms Tang's convictions. For her part, Ms Tang has sought special leave to cross-appeal on three grounds. If successful on the cross-appeal, Ms Tang again seeks the substitution of verdicts of acquittal.

64. The other members of this court[35] have concluded that the prosecution is entitled to succeed, its appeal should be allowed, the convictions of Ms Tang should be restored and the cross-appeal rejected. I agree with most of their reasons. However, upon what Eames JA, in the Court of Appeal, described as "the critical issue" in the proceedings,[36] I disagree with my colleagues. On that issue, in effect, I concur in the approach and conclusion expressed in the Court of Appeal by Eames JA (with whom Maxwell P and Buchanan JA agreed without additional reasons).[37]

65. The "critical issue" concerns the accuracy and adequacy of the directions given to the jury at the second trial of Ms Tang. (In the first trial, the jury failed to agree on verdicts in relation to Ms Tang.[38] The controversial point involves the meaning and application of the provisions of the Code that define the offences with which Ms Tang was charged and the content of the "fault elements"[39] (relevantly the "intention" aspect) necessary to constitute those offences. It concerns what the trial judge was obliged to tell the jury in that respect about the law governing these offences.

66. I concede that there is room for differences of opinion on the issue that separates my opinion from that reached by the majority in this court. Such differences may arise because of the difficulties in interpreting the novel provisions of the Code;[40] the absence of earlier explorations of those provisions by appellate decisions;[41] the necessary interaction of the applicable Australian law with the relevant provisions of international law—in particular, the Convention to Suppress the Slave Trade and Slavery (the 1926 Slavery Convention)[42] and the Supplementary Convention on the Abolition of Slavery, the Slave Trade, and Institutions and Practices Similar to Slavery (the 1956 **[219]** Supplementary

---

[35] Reasons of Gleeson CJ at para. 57 and reasons of Hayne J at para. 168. Gummow, Heydon, Crennan and Kiefel JJ agreeing with both.
[36] *Tang* at para. 66; see also reasons of Hayne J at para. 133.
[37] *Tang* at paras. 1 and 2.   [38] *Tang* at para. 17.
[39] Chapter 2, Div. 5, s 5.1 of the Code. The relevant provisions are set out in the reasons of Gleeson CJ at para. 5.
[40] See *Tang* at paras. 60 and 143.   [41] *Tang* at para. 93.
[42] Opened for signature in 1926 and entered into force in 1927. See [1927] ATS 11; 212 UNTS 17.

Convention);⁴³ and the mass of evidentiary material from the lengthy trial of Ms Tang. Such evidence was relevant for two purposes: first, as to the quality of the relationship between Ms Tang and the five women (the complainants) whom she was charged with possessing as "a slave" or using as "a slave" contrary to s 270.3(1)(a) of the Code; and secondly, as to the suggested "fault element" (intention) that the prosecution was required to prove in order to secure convictions.⁴⁴

67. While I agree that the other challenges mounted for Ms Tang fail, in my opinion the approach of the Court of Appeal to the "critical issue" was correct. That approach is more consonant with:

- the proper analysis of the Code;
- the basic doctrine of criminal law in Australia, against the background of which the Code is written, on the operation of "intention" in respect of serious criminal offences;
- the principles of interpretation applicable to the legislation in question;
- a proper view of the relationship between the Code provisions and the international law that they seek to apply in Australia; and
- the various other considerations of legal principle and policy to which regard may properly be had.

68. We do not advance the correct application in Australia of a contemporary statutory provision to tackle modern issues of "slavery" and trafficking in "sexual slaves" by distorting the essential ingredients of serious criminal offences as provided by the parliament. Nor do we do so by diminishing the elements that the prosecution must prove and that the trial judge must accurately explain to the jury. In this case, that element is the "intention" necessary to constitute such a serious offence, with the exposure that it brings, upon conviction, to special calumny and to extremely severe punitive consequences.

69. In a case such as the present, there is an inescapable dilemma in the operation of fundamental principles of human rights, reflected in the Code and in Australian law more generally. Protection of persons alleged to have been trafficked as "sexual slaves" is achieved in this country in a trial system that also provides fundamental legal protections for those who are accused of having been involved in such offences. As is often observed, the protection of the law becomes specially important when it is claimed by the unpopular and the despised accused of grave wrongdoing.⁴⁵

---

⁴³ Opened for signature in 1956 and entered into force in 1957. See [1958] ATS 3; 266 UNTS 3.
⁴⁴ Compare *Tang* at para. 157.
⁴⁵ Compare *Adelaide Company of Jehovah's Witnesses Inc.* v. *Commonwealth* (1943) 67 CLR 116 at 124; [1943] ALR 193 at 197; [1943] HCA 12 per Latham CJ.

70. In my opinion, the appeal fails and so does Ms Tang's attempt, by cross-appeal, to secure the substitution of verdicts of acquittal. As the Court of Appeal proposed, an order for a retrial, freed from the legal errors of the second trial, is the correct outcome.

The Facts

71. *The general background*: The general factual background is explained in the reasons of Gleeson CJ.[46] There were various points of difference in the extensive evidence called at the trial. For example, in respect of one of the complainants, there were differences as to the arrangements whereby she had **[220]** travelled to Australia from Thailand and as to the persons involved in making those arrangements. However, much of the evidence tendered against Ms Tang was not in dispute.[47] The battleground, instead, lay in the interpretation of that evidence and its legal effect. The relevant question was whether the evidence fell within the particular provisions of the Code governing, first, the "physical elements" of the offences provided in s 270.3(1) with which Ms Tang was charged, and secondly, the "fault elements" that also had to be proved in order to satisfy those charges.[48]

72. In this appeal, the novelty of the meaning of the "slavery offences" provided by s 270.3 of the Code gives rise to the first problem of interpretation. This country has never lawfully had "slavery" in the conventional meaning of that term and still does not. The novelty of the "general principles of criminal responsibility"[49] and the specification of the essential elements of an offence under the Code give rise to the second problem of interpretation. Those problems of interpretation must be made concrete by reference to the evidence at the trial. Such evidence will help to test whether the trial judge properly understood, and explained, the provisions of the Code so as to render the verdicts of the second jury (and the convictions that followed) both lawful and reasonable. The evidence will also help to answer the legal propositions advanced by the contesting parties.

73. At the outset, it is important to acknowledge that the evidence was by no means incontestable or clear-cut. There are two particular indications of this:

- first, upon basically the same evidence, the first jury summoned to try Ms Tang and a co-accused (Mr Paul Pick, who was the

---

[46] Reasons of Gleeson CJ at paras. 6-18. [47] *Tang* at para. 191.
[48] See ss 2.1, 3.1, 3.2 and 5.1 of the Code. These provisions are set out in the reasons of Gleeson CJ at para. 5.
[49] The chapter heading to Ch 2 of the Code. See reasons of Gleeson CJ at para. 5.

manager of the licensed brothel "Club 417") acquitted Mr Pick on eight counts. The jury were unable to agree on two further counts against him or upon any of the counts presented against Ms Tang. Mr Pick subsequently applied successfully for a nolle prosequi;[50] and

- secondly, following very extensive directions given by the trial judge to the jury in the second trial, the jury returned twice to seek judicial clarification about the requirements of intention. This became the "critical issue" in the Court of Appeal, as it is likewise in this court. What took place and the terms of the questions asked by the jury and directions given by the trial judge are explained in detail by Eames JA.[51]

74. The first question was asked on the first day of the jury's deliberations (after a charge that had proceeded over 3 days). The question was presented after the jury had already been deliberating for 5 hours. The second question was asked the following afternoon, after the jury had been deliberating for over a day. It will be necessary to return to these developments.[52]

75. For a complete understanding of my reasons, it is essential to appreciate how the questions emerged, the preceding complex and confusing instructions given to the jury on the subject, and the further instruction that followed, which, with respect, was partly non-responsive and partly added to the uncertainty and **[221]** confusion. This is all set out with admirable clarity by Eames JA. If nothing else, it indicates the confusion of the instructions given to the jury on the subject of the intention necessary to justify guilty verdicts, the correct focus that the jury themselves were giving to the "critical issue" and thus the great importance of that issue to their deliberations in the forensic circumstances of the second trial.

76. The successive questions from the jury indicate the significance that they were assigning to the quality and content of the "intention" of Ms Tang which the prosecution had to prove to secure guilty verdicts. The length of the jury's deliberations and their repeated questions on this issue also indicate (correctly in my view) that this jury, like the earlier jury in the first trial, did not find reaching their verdicts in these proceedings an easy task, considering the way in which the evidence emerged in the second trial.

77. In these reasons, I incorporate by reference the chronicle set out by Eames JA in the Court of Appeal. This includes the lengthy directions

---

[50] *Tang* at para. 17. [51] *Tang* at paras. 122-9. [52] See these reasons below at paras. 123-5.

given to the jury about the meaning of the words "possession" and "use" of a "slave", contrary to the Code, the jury's successive questions, the supplementary directions then given by the trial judge and the further supplementary directions given after trial counsel for Ms Tang took exception to aspects of the judge's first attempt.[53]

78. Although additional reference will be made below to these questions and the resulting redirections, because mine is a minority opinion in this court, I will not set the passages out seriatim. They are not set out in other reasons. Nevertheless, to understand the conclusion that Eames JA and the other members of the Court of Appeal reached, it is essential to appreciate the deficiencies in the directions given to the jury on the critical subject of "intention". No other course would do justice to Ms Tang's case or to the Court of Appeal's analysis.

79. *Evidence against statutory slavery*: Allowing, for the moment, that the Code expands somewhat the traditional definition of "slavery" in international law (and in more recent times under the 1926 Slavery Convention and the 1956 Supplementary Convention), and that it may do this in Australia in conformity with the Constitution, there was certainly evidence before the jury in the second trial that, in combination, could have supported the acquittal of Ms Tang:

(1) The trial was conducted on the footing that each of the complainants, in their country of nationality (Thailand), had earlier worked in the sex industry.[54] In this sense, they were not tricked into employment in Australia on a false premise or led to believe that they would be working in tourism, entertainment or other non-sexual activities.[55] While trafficking in persons for sexual or like purposes is an undeniable feature of modern population movements, equally, some such movements are undoubtedly economically motivated.[56] As such, they would not constitute "slavery" offences under s 270.3(1)(a) of the Code if undertaken with appropriate knowledge and consent by an adult person who was able to give such consent.

(2) **[222]** Each complainant was above the legal age of consent. It was not suggested (and it did not appear from the evidence) that they were in any way legally incompetent or that they had been subjected to coercion to persuade them to come to Australia

---

[53] This is set out, with extracts from the trial, in *Tang* at paras. 93-141.
[54] *Tang* at para. 5.
[55] Compare A. Dorevitch and M. Foster, "Obstacles on the Road to Protection: Assessing the Treatment of Sex-Trafficking Victims under Australia's Migration and Refugee Law", (2008) 9 *MJIL* 1, pp. 8 and 38.
[56] See Dorevitch and Foster, 2008, pp. 38-9.

to work in the sex industry. It was accepted that they came to this country voluntarily, knowing at least the general nature and incidents of the work they were agreeing to perform.[57]

(3) While the evidence revealed several offences against the Migration Act 1958 (Cth) and Regulations and perhaps state offences, the brothel in Melbourne in which the complainants worked as commercial sex workers and their work were not illegal under Victorian law. The brothel held a licence pursuant to the Prostitution Control Act 1994 (Vic).[58] Although activities of prostitution were previously illegal under Australian law (as they still are in many countries) they were not, without more, illegal in the subject brothel. Necessarily, Ms Tang's trial was unconcerned with any migration or other offences that she, the complainants or others might have committed. No such offences were before the jury.

(4) The evidence indicated that the complainants were not imprisoned in the brothel or in their place of residence. The largest evidentiary dispute at trial concerned the extent to which the complainants were able to move freely and whether their accommodation was subject to a deadlock controlling access and egress.[59] It is appropriate to accept the trial judge's finding on sentencing that the complainants were not kept under lock and key,[60] although initially they were "effectively restricted". In part, such restrictions were adopted because of the common objective of the complainants and Ms Tang to avoid detection by migration authorities and deportation from Australia as unlawful aliens present in the country without relevant visas.[61]

(5) The "fee" paid to the "recruiters" in Thailand who arranged for the complainants to travel to Australia (and eventually to Melbourne)[62] was never fully explained, still less justified, to the complainants. However, there was no doubt that some costs were incurred by the "recruiters". These included, by inference, procuring visas, arranging land and air transport,[63] providing return airfares for the complainants, arranging and paying for accompanying persons (usually an elderly couple so as to avoid detection at the border), providing initial and later accommodation and a "profit margin".[64] The "fee" extracted

---

[57] Reasons of Gleeson CJ at para. 6; reasons of Hayne J at para. 166.
[58] *Tang* at para. 8. [59] *Tang* at para. 191.
[60] *Tang* at para. 192. See also at para. 196. [61] *Tang* at para. 8.
[62] The "fee" varied but was about $20,000. See reasons of Gleeson CJ at para. 12.
[63] Reasons of Gleeson CJ at para. 8. [64] Reasons of Gleeson CJ at paras. 8 and 12.

would arguably fall to be considered (at least in part) in the context of the law, culture and economy of Thailand, where it was orally agreed. It would also arguably need to be judged in the context that the complainants voluntarily entered Australia aware of the type of work they were to perform, inferentially so as to make their lives better as a consequence **[223]** and appreciating that it would result in a debt to those who had made the necessary arrangements to facilitate their travel and relocation.[65]

(6) As was essential to their successful initiation into the sex industry in Australia, the complainants themselves participated in the subterfuge of pretending to visit Australia on a tourist visa.[66]

(7) After the complainants commenced work in the brothel, their passports and return air tickets were taken and retained in a secure place. It was stated that this was done to permit the nationality and identity of the complainants to be established, in the event of investigations by migration authorities. Also, it was done to avoid loss or theft of the documents. This is in addition to any motive to prevent the non-consensual departure of the complainants.

(8) It was agreed that the complainants enjoyed a "free day" each week, that each was credited with a notional sum of $50 per customer in the reduction of their outstanding debt and that, on the free day, each complainant could either rest or continue to work and receive $50 per customer for themselves.[67] The evidence also showed that the complainants were well fed and provided for.[68] Two had actually paid off their debts[69] within 6 months of arrival. Assuming that they worked every day of the week (as most did), this would mean attending to an average of five clients a day. The two who had paid off their debts stayed and continued to work in the brothel. This was strongly relied on as contradicting a relationship that could be characterised as "slavery" in any meaningful sense of that word. It was common ground that once the debt was paid, each complainant was completely free to choose for herself the hours of work and place of accommodation.[70] There was conflicting and unclear evidence about the freedom of movement permitted before the debt was paid, other than transfer between the brothel and the residence. Some evidence

---

[65] *Tang* at para. 149. [66] *Tang* at para. 6. [67] Reasons of Gleeson CJ at para. 14.
[68] Reasons of Gleeson CJ at para. 16.
[69] The debt varied but was about $45,000, inclusive of the "fee" paid or payable to the Thai "recruiters".
[70] Reasons of Gleeson CJ at paras. 12 and 17.

suggested that at least one complainant had formed a personal relationship which she pursued during that interval.

(9) Once the complainants and their migration status were discovered, they were, by law, subject to immediate detention and deportation from Australia. The availability of legal relief against that course was limited. One such form of relief, introduced soon after these events took place, was the provision of both temporary and longer-term visas to stay in Australia.[71] The latter were available only to permit a person, such as one or more of the complainants, to stay if they made a "significant contribution" to a prosecution of an accused offender for criminal offences.

(10) **[224]** There was no evidence that the complainants were subjected to rape, violence or other such offences.[72] This sometimes marks the predicament of those (generally women and children) who are trafficked for the purpose of sexual slavery and sexual debt bondage.[73]

80. *Evidence favouring statutory slavery*: The foregoing evidence was available to Ms Tang to contest the charge that she had "within ... Australia, intentionally ... possesse[d] a slave or exercise[d] over a slave any of the other powers attaching to the right of ownership".[74] However, as noted by the Court of Appeal, there was also evidence capable of supporting the conclusions that Ms Tang was guilty of the offences charged and that such verdicts were not unreasonable.[75]

81. The relevant evidence included:

(1) The meaning to be given to the language of Div. 270 of the Code is not controlled by considerations prevailing in the law, culture or economy of Thailand. The applicable Code provisions draw upon international law, specifically the 1926 Slavery Convention and the 1956 Supplementary Convention. They thus purport to express universal offences against humanity. However, ultimately it is the duty of an Australian court to give effect to the language stated in the Code, an Australian statute. It is to measure the evidence accepted against the standards expressed in the Code, as that law is understood in Australia.

---

[71] Dorevitch and Foster, 2008, p. 10: "Effective since 1 January 2004, the ... framework consists of four types of visa: a new Bridging Visa F (Subclass 060) ('BVF'); the existing Criminal Justice Stay Visa ('CJSV'); a Temporary Witness Protection (Trafficking) Visa ('TWPTV'); and a Permanent Witness Protection (Trafficking) Visa ('PWPTV')" (footnotes omitted).

[72] Compare J. Halley, "Rape in Berlin: Reconsidering the Criminalisation of Rape in the International Law of Armed Conflict", (2008) 9 *MJIL* 78, p. 113.

[73] Dorevitch and Foster, 2008, pp. 19-20.   [74] Section 270.3(1)(a) of the Code.

[75] Compare reasons of Gleeson CJ at para. 18.

In determining what constitutes employment conditions that are extremely harsh, unconscionable and oppressive but which do not answer to the defined description of "slavery", it is proper that the criteria expressed in the Code[76] should be given a meaning that reflects Australian understandings. The definition of "slavery" in the Code is not intended to attract merely harsh, unconscionable and oppressive employment conditions. As such, the discrimen for "slavery offences" will properly take into account the normal features of working conditions in Australia, and not working conditions that may exist in Thailand or elsewhere.

Such conditions in Australia are closely regulated by federal and state laws. They have been so regulated since colonial times. Commonly, the applicable laws are designed to ensure a "fair go all round".[77] (Some would argue the purpose of s 51 (xxxv) of the Constitution was to protect and entrench in law that basic feature of Australian society.) Measured against that feature, as this court may take judicial notice and as a jury would have been aware, the working conditions of the complainants were substantially different. The differences were most evident in the **[225]** hours, conditions and circumstances of the work; the closely restricted accommodation; and the onerous requirements for the reduction of the "employment" debts.

At trial, counsel for Ms Tang suggested analogies between the situation of the complainants and those of an oil rig employee or of students obliged to repay higher education contribution scheme debts. These comparisons are unconvincing when contrasted with the seriously exploitative conditions of the complainants that were revealed by the evidence. At the very least, in an Australian setting, it was open to the jury to conclude that such circumstances bore no comparison or analogy to (even harsh) employment conditions as understood in Australia.[78]

(2) If it be accepted that the complainants came voluntarily to Australia to work in the sex industry, the counts charging Ms Tang with offences against s 270.3(1)(a) of the Code still raised a critical question. That question was what happened to the complainants

---

[76] Section 270.1 of the Code (definition of slavery): "the condition of a person over whom any or all of the powers attaching to the right of ownership are exercised, including where such a condition results from a debt or contract made by the person".

[77] *Blackadder* v. *Ramsey Butchering Services Pty Ltd* (2005) 221 CLR 539; 215 ALR 87; [2005] HCA 22 at para. 30; citing *Re Loty and Holloway and Australian Workers' Union* [1971] AR (NSW) 95 at 99 per Sheldon J; compare *New South Wales* v. *Commonwealth* (2006) 229 CLR 1; 231 ALR 1; [2006] HCA 52 at para. 609.

[78] See *Tang* at paras. 8 and 12.

after they arrived at their place of employment and what was the quality and content of Ms Tang's intention in that regard. Allowing for the existence of some kind of agreement with the complainants before they left Thailand, the fact is that the agreement was not in writing; its terms were in some respects unclear and disputed; and the "fees" payable to the Thai "recruiters" and to Ms Tang were never fully explained or justified to the complainants. At the very least, the complainants were economically vulnerable in Thailand. They were particularly vulnerable once they arrived in Australia. In this country, they found themselves in an alien culture; were exposed to the possibility of sudden immigration expulsion; had severe practical restrictions affecting their movements, work and accommodation; had little skill in the English language; and had few, if any, local friends or acquaintances outside the brothel, its personnel and customers.

(3) The taking of the passports and return air tickets from the complainants can, it is true, be explained in other ways; likewise the confiscation of the funds lent to them to afford evidence upon arrival of an apparent capacity of self-support. However, the consequence of these steps was to remove from the complainants the wherewithal to inquire about or pursue their legal rights or to escape from the conditions in which they found themselves, if that was their desire.[79]

Particular employment arrangements, including in Australia, can sometimes seem oppressive to those engaged in conventional employment. Relevant here, however, was the work that the complainants had agreed to perform, the regime of effective discipline governing the complainants' place of employment and accommodation, their sleeping arrangements, the long hours of service and the effective contemplation of a seven-day week. These factors combine to portray a level of oppression having few analogies in contemporary consensual Australian employment conditions. The Court of Appeal did not err in reaching the opinion that it was open to the jury to so conclude.[80]

(4) **[226]** There was a lively dispute at the trial as to whether the arrangements with the Thai "recruiters" or the "syndicate" amounted to a "purchase [of] the women".[81] This is distinct from "purchasing the contracts" under which they allegedly agreed to travel to Australia to work in their own interests. However, at

---

[79] *Tang* paras. 192-3. See also at para. 155. [80] *Tang* at paras. 59, 155 and 193.
[81] *Tang* at para. 46.

least one witness used the term "we purchased this woman". To that extent, evidence was available that the jury could accept about the attitude of human purchase towards procuring the complainants' services for Ms Tang.[82]

(5) Not every exploitative employment arrangement will warrant the description of "slavery", including in its extended Australian statutory form under the Code. Making the distinction between harsh, unconscionable and oppressive employment and "slavery" may sometimes be difficult. The notion of "slavery" should not be debased by metaphorical applications to non-"slave" conditions. Nevertheless, it was open to the Court of Appeal to reach its conclusion that the burdens imposed on the complainants were different in kind from even the harshest conditions of "employment", as such, in contemporary Australia.[83] Upon this basis, it was competent for a properly instructed jury to conclude that the "employment" conditions of the complainants involved the exercise over them of at least some of the "powers attaching to the right of ownership". That expression is to be understood in the Australian context, where full ownership (in the sense of "chattel slavery") was unlawful under Imperial legislation dating back to colonial times and remains unlawful under the Code.[84]

(6) "Full ownership" of another human being (and thus "chattel slavery") is, and has always been, expressly excluded as a possibility under Australian law. This makes it clear that, in creating "slavery offences" as it does, s 270.3 of the Code provides such offences in another, different and extended (statutory) sense. Subject to any constitutional problems in so providing, it is therefore in this extended sense that the charges of "slavery offences" preferred against Ms Tang under the Code needed to be understood. This involved some awareness on the part of the court of important changes in international law since earlier times. It also involved responding to the evidence of new forms of people-trafficking and exploitation. Subject to the Constitution, there are good reasons why the "slavery offences" in s 270.3 of the Code should be given an operation that accords with the language in which the offences are expressed. The language of s 270.3 should not be artificially narrowed nor its application circumscribed when invoked for suggested application to new and emerging fact situations.

---

[82] *Tang* at para. 46.   [83] *Tang* at para. 59.   [84] Section 270.2 of the Code.

(7) It is possible that the complainants, especially when faced with the prospect of deportation as illegal immigrants, may have been motivated to cooperate with the prosecution of Ms Tang in order to obtain visas to remain in Australia.[85] However, such visas themselves present serious deficiencies. They are readily cancelled. Their provision does not found [227] an inference that the complainants falsely elaborated the circumstances of their living and working arrangements with Ms Tang simply to stay in Australia and to further the economic opportunities that allegedly motivated their journey to Australia in the first place.

82. *Conclusion—verdicts arguably available*: Subject therefore to what follows, to respond to the issues raised by the appeal and by Ms Tang's application for special leave to cross-appeal (including on constitutional grounds), no error has been demonstrated in the conclusion of the Court of Appeal that there was evidence available at the trial to support the second jury's guilty verdicts and the subsequent convictions of Ms Tang. As long as that trial was not flawed by inaccurate or imperfect directions on the applicable law, the resulting convictions must therefore stand.

The Legislation

83. The reasons of Gleeson CJ set out the relevant provisions of the legislation,[86] which I incorporate by reference. That legislation consists of the specific provisions of the Code in respect of the "slavery offences", introduced by the Criminal Code Amendment (Slavery and Sexual Servitude) Act 1999 (Cth), and the general provisions, under Ch 2 of the Code, that govern the required approach to the "general principles of criminal responsibility" under the laws of the Commonwealth (including the Code). It is unnecessary for me to repeat those provisions.

The Issues

84. The following issues are raised by these proceedings:

(1) *The meaning of "slavery" issue*: Upon consideration of Div. 270 of the Code and relevant provisions of international law, did the Court of Appeal err in the "slavery" definition that it adopted (and, by extension, the definition of "slave" in s 270.3(1)(a) of the

---

[85] Dorevitch and Foster, 2008, pp. 44-5.   [86] Reasons of Gleeson CJ at para. 5.

Code)? Should Ms Tang be granted special leave to cross-appeal to challenge the approach adopted by the Court of Appeal with respect to the stated ambit of the offence?

Before tackling propounded issues of constitutional validity, it is the conventional methodology of this court to identify first the meaning to be attributed to the impugned legislation.[87] Subject to what I have said in these reasons, I am in general agreement on this issue with Gleeson CJ[88] and Hayne J[89] about the meaning of "slavery" and "slave" in the Code. Accordingly, the order proposed by Gleeson CJ in respect of the first ground of Ms Tang's notice of cross-appeal should be made.

(2) *The constitutional validity issue*: The Court of Appeal rejected Ms Tang's challenge to the constitutional validity of the offences expressed in s 270.3(1)(a) under which Ms Tang had been charged. It affirmed the validity of the offences on the footing that the provisions give effect to Australia's obligations under the 1926 Slavery **[228]** Convention.[90] Did the Court of Appeal err in making such findings? Alternatively, was s 270.3(1)(a) constitutionally valid as within the powers of the Federal Parliament on any of the alternative bases propounded by the prosecution,[91] as supported by the Attorney-General of the Commonwealth intervening in this court?

The Court of Appeal did not err in concluding this issue as it did. The definition of "slavery" in s 270.1 of the Code, and the consequential offences expressed in s 270.3(1)(a) of the Code, are reasonably proportionate to a law giving effect to Australia's obligations under the 1926 Slavery Convention.[92] In any case, besides the constitutional support afforded by that treaty, other well-established foundations for constitutional validity exist in the present case. Following the decision of this court in

---

[87] *Bank of New South Wales* v. *Commonwealth* (1948) 76 CLR 1 at 186; [1948] 2 ALR 89 at 128; [1948] HCA 7 per Latham CJ; *Residual Assco Group Ltd* v. *Spalvins* (2000) 202 CLR 629; 172 ALR 366; 36 ACSR 1; [2000] HCA 33 at para. 81; *Northern Territory* v. *Arnhem Land Aboriginal Land Trust* (2008) 248 ALR 195; [2008] HCA 29 at para. 65.

[88] Reasons of Gleeson CJ at paras. 21-35. [89] Reasons of Hayne J at paras. 135-59.

[90] *Tang* at para. 24. [91] *Tang* at para. 23.

[92] The "reasonable proportionality" test is to be preferred to the opaque and partly circular "reasonably capable of being considered appropriate and adapted" test expressed in *Victoria* v. *Commonwealth* (1996) 187 CLR 416 at 486-9; 138 ALR 129 at 146-8; [1995] HCA 45. However, there is no basic difference in these two propounded tests of constitutional connection: *Lange* v. *Australian Broadcasting Corp.* (1997) 189 CLR 520 at 562 and 567 (fn 272); 145 ALR 96 at 108 and 112; [1997] HCA 25; *Mulholland* v. *Australian Electoral Commission* (2004) 220 CLR 181; 209 ALR 582; [2004] HC 41 at paras. 205-6.

XYZ v. Commonwealth,[93] I regard the challenge to the constitutional validity of the contested provisions of the Code as barely arguable. Even on the narrowest view expressed in that case, and assuming that the external affairs power in s 51 (xxix) of the Constitution does not support laws that are solely concerned with matters geographically external to Australia,[94] there is no such disqualifying defect in the present case. The provisions of the Code are valid. Accordingly the order proposed by Gleeson CJ, in relation to this ground, should also be made.

(3) *The accuracy of the judicial directions issue*: This is the "critical issue" presented by the appeal. It constitutes the ground upon which the Court of Appeal concluded that the second trial of Ms Tang had miscarried.[95] For reasons that I will explain, the Court of Appeal was right in its conclusion. Accordingly, subject to what follows, Ms Tang was entitled to have her convictions set aside. That order, and the consequential orders that followed, should be confirmed by this court.

(4) *The unreasonable verdicts issue*: Did the Court of Appeal err in concluding that the verdicts of the jury were not unreasonable or unsupported by the evidence so that (besides the allegedly inaccurate and inadequate directions on the applicable law) they should otherwise stand?[96]

For the reasons explained by the Court of Appeal,[97] by Gleeson CJ[98] and by myself,[99] the evidence before the jury was otherwise capable of sustaining the verdicts of guilty that the second jury returned against **[229]** Ms Tang. This ground of Ms Tang's application for special leave to cross-appeal therefore fails. The order proposed by Gleeson CJ in that respect should be made. It follows that the attempt by Ms Tang to persuade this court to substitute orders of acquittal, so as to spare her a further (third) trial, fails.

(5) *The miscarriage/proviso issue*: The Court of Appeal declined to apply the "proviso" stated in s 568(1) of the Crimes Act 1958 (Vic) with respect to the inaccurate and inadequate directions that it found the trial judge had given to the jury on the ingredients of the slavery offences.[100] Did the Court of Appeal err in so deciding? In this court, the prosecution ultimately contested an order for a retrial on the basis of the conclusion reached by the

---

[93] (2006) 227 CLR 532; 227 ALR 495; [2006] HCA 25 *(XYZ)*.
[94] *XYZ* at para. 226 per Callinan and Heydon JJ.   [95] *Tang* at para. 146.
[96] *Tang* at para. 194.   [97] *Tang* at paras. 190-3.   [98] Reasons of Gleeson CJ at para. 35.
[99] These reasons above at paras. 80-2.   [100] *Tang* at paras. 195-7.

Court of Appeal on the "essential issue" as it defined it. There was no error in the reasoning of that court.[101] If the conclusion of the Court of Appeal on the errors and inadequacies of the impugned directions is otherwise sustained by this court, the dispositive orders made below will likewise be upheld. This would result in a retrial of Ms Tang even though a third trial would be most unfortunate.[102] Any relief against a third trial would have to rest in the discretion of the prosecution.

85. From the foregoing it follows that all but one of the issues that have been propounded in these proceedings (including some that were not continued in this court)[103] fall away. That leaves only the accuracy of the judicial directions issue relating to the intention of Ms Tang necessary for her to be found guilty of the "slavery offences" charged. I turn to that issue to explain why I come to a conclusion different from my colleagues.

Remaining Issue: Judicial Directions on Intention

86. *The issue defined*: The issue that divides this court is whether, in the second trial, the trial judge gave sufficiently accurate and clear directions to the jury on the ingredients of the offences with which Ms Tang was charged.

87. Juries cannot be expected to know the law. They must rely on the judge, presiding in the trial, to explain to them, accurately and clearly, the legal ingredients of the offences with which the accused stands charged and of any defences that arise for consideration. It is not the duty of the judge to give the jury a general disquisition on the law or to burden them with immaterial or unnecessary directions.[104] However, unless the charges are explained to the jury accurately and clearly, with assistance on the application of the law to the facts as appropriate, a fundamental assumption of trial by jury is undermined.

[230] 88. As the Court of Appeal pointed out, the "trial judge had the misfortune to be the first judge in Australia called on to devise

---

[101] Compare *Weiss* v. *R* (2005) 224 CLR 300; 223 ALR 662; [2005] HCA 81 at paras. 45-6. See also *AK* v. *Western Australia* (2008) 243 ALR 409; 82 ALJR 534; [2008] HCA 8 at para. 59 per Gummow and Hayne JJ, para. 87 per Heydon J; and *CTM* v. *R* (2008) 247 ALR 1; 82 ALJR 978; [2008] HCA 25 at para. 132 *(CTM)*.

[102] See *Tang* (retrial judgment) at para. 10.

[103] For example, the ground complaining of lack of balance in the trial judge's charge to the jury and the ground complaining of excessive judicial intervention during cross-examination. See *Tang* at paras. 159-89.

[104] *Alford* v. *Magee* (1952) 85 CLR 437 at 466; [1952] ALR 101 at 116; [1952] HCA 3. See *Melbourne* v. *R* (1999) 198 CLR 1; 164 ALR 465; [1999] HCA 32 at para. 143 per Hayne J.

directions for these novel offences".[105] This is a reason to avoid overly pernickety approaches to Ms Tang's challenge to those directions. But it cannot be a reason for denying Ms Tang an accurate trial that conforms to the law as stated by the parliament.

89. The matter that concerned the Court of Appeal was the explanation given by the trial judge "as to the elements of the offences created by s 270.3(1)(a)". Relevantly, that issue concerns the character and quality of the exercise of power by the accused over the victim who is alleged to be a "slave".[106] In the Court of Appeal, Eames JA, a judge with much experience in criminal trials and law, concluded that the approach urged by the prosecution, and adopted by the judge at the trial, "did not correctly identify the elements of the offences which the [prosecution] had to establish". Specifically, by reference to s 5.2 of the Code (which contains the explanation of the general principles of criminal responsibility in respect of "intention"), Eames JA concluded that, to make good the offences in s 270.3(1)(a), the prosecution had to prove the following against Ms Tang:[107]

77. ... First, the worker must have been reduced to the condition that would constitute her a slave, as defined in the [Code]. The jury must be satisfied that she had had powers exercised over her as though she was mere property, with the result that she had been reduced to the status of mere property, a thing, over whom powers attaching to the right of ownership could be exercised.

Secondly, the accused must have known that the worker had been reduced to a condition where she was no more than property, a thing, over whom persons could exercise powers as though they owned her.

Thirdly, the accused must have intentionally possessed the worker, that is, must have intentionally held her in her custody or under her physical control.

Fourthly, the accused must have possessed the worker in the intentional exercise of what constitutes a power attaching to a right of ownership, namely, the power of possession. For that to be the case the accused must be shown to have regarded the worker as though she was mere property, a thing, thereby intending to deal with her not as a human being who had free will and a right to liberty, but as though she was mere property. However harsh or oppressive her conduct was towards the worker it would not be sufficient for a conviction if, rather than having possessed the worker with the knowledge, intention, or in the belief that she was dealing with her as though she was mere property, the accused possessed her in the knowledge or belief that she was exercising some different right or entitlement to do so, falling short of what would amount to ownership, such as that of an employer, contractor, or manager.

---

[105] *Tang* at para. 93. [106] *Tang* at para. 66.
[107] *Tang* at para. 77 (citations omitted). Eames JA explained that he would use the "neutral descriptor of 'worker'", inferentially instead of using the conclusory word "victim".

90. I do not take there to be a present dispute concerning the first three "elements of the offences" identified in the foregoing passage. There was also no disagreement over the trial judge's direction to the jury that it was not essential that Ms Tang should know that the "worker" was, in law, a "slave". Although ignorance of the law is no excuse, the provisions of s 270.3(1)(a) of the Code do not postulate that a person, such as Ms Tang, will necessarily be aware of the categories and classifications of Australian law. Still less would such a person be expected to know the provisions of an international treaty dating back to 1926. The Code, however, is intended to bring proved "physical" and "fault" elements **[231]** together in particular evidentiary circumstances to render a person answerable for "criminal responsibility under laws of the Commonwealth".[108] This befits a contemporary federal statute that imposes criminal liability on people for their acts and omissions within Australia.

91. The basic reason for adopting this view arises from the language and structure of the Code itself. That is the starting point for an analysis of the offences with which Ms Tang was charged. However, there are several other reasons that support the approach to the construction of the Code adopted by the Court of Appeal. In the balance of these reasons, I will explain what I consider to be the most important arguments favouring the approach that the Court of Appeal adopted.

92. *Analysis of the statute*: Relevant here are not only the "slavery offences" with which Ms Tang was charged under s 270.3(1)(a) of the Code but also the more general "physical" and "fault" element provisions under Ch 2 of the Code. These latter elements are declared by the parliament to be necessary in Australia for criminal responsibility under federal law.[109]

93. The starting point is the structure of s 270.3(1). In expressing the relevant "slavery offence", the word "intentionally" is placed in the chapeau, above the particular offences that follow. These include the provisions of para. (a) under which Ms Tang was charged. By the ordinary application of the principles of statutory construction, it must therefore be accepted that the adverb "intentionally" was designed to modify the entirety of the subsequent paragraphs. Thus, it is not enough for the accused to "possess" a slave or to "exercise" over a slave "any of the other powers attaching to the right of ownership". To be guilty of the offence provided by the Code, the accused must do these things, and all of them, "intentionally".

94. That paragraph contains descriptors of "physical elements", such as "possessing" a slave or "exercising" powers "attaching to the right of ownership" over a slave. However, the general principles of criminal

---

[108] Section 2.1 of the Code. See also s 3.1(1).   [109] Pursuant to ss 3.1(1) and 5.2(1) of the Code.

responsibility contained in Ch 2 of the Code also make it clear that such "physical elements" alone are not sufficient to secure a conviction. There must be a relevant combination of both "physical" and "fault" elements. In the present appeal (as was properly acknowledged by the prosecution in its conduct of Ms Tang's trial) it was common ground that the applicable "fault element" was the "intention" of the accused. This is clear enough because of the inclusion of the adverb "intentionally" in the chapeau to s 270.3(1).

95. Where "intention" is the applicable "fault element", as here, s 5.2(1) of the Code provides that "[a] person has intention with respect to conduct if he or she means to engage in that conduct". Quite apart from the introductory adverb in the language of s 270.3(1) of the Code, it is clear that the prosecution must prove beyond reasonable doubt that the accused had the "intention" to engage in the relevant conduct. Thus, in a case brought under s 270.3(1) of the Code, the "intention" is not simply an "intention" addressed to the "physical elements" concerned with "possession" or the exercise of powers attaching to the "right of ownership". It is also an intention directed to the underlying entitlement that gives rise to those elements. Without that ingredient of the offence, the word "intentionally" might just as well not have been present in s 270.3(1).

[232] 96. In effect, the construction urged by the prosecution (and now adopted by this court) either ignores the word "intentionally" at the head of the subsection or treats it as relevant only to the physical elements involved in the treatment of a person. It does not, as s 270.3(1)(a) indicates by its language and structure, also govern the quality and character of those physical elements so that they amount, in law, to "possession" or to "exercis[ing] over a slave any of the other powers attaching to the right of ownership".

97. Paragraph (a) of s 270.3(1) of the Code uses legal notions such as "possession" and "rights of ownership" preceded by the statutory requirement that such "physical elements" should be exercised "intentionally". This imports into the constituent elements of the offences charged an appreciation, belief or realisation by the accused (intentionally) of the entitlement to assert the "physical elements" that go to make up the offences.

98. *Relevant canons of construction*: A fundamental canon of construction that supports the Court of Appeal's approach is reflected in the acknowledgment, in extrinsic statutory material, that:[110]

---

[110] The revised explanatory memorandum to the Criminal Code Amendment (Slavery and Sexual Servitude) Bill 1999 (Cth), p. 4 cited by the Court of Appeal: *Tang* at para. 27.

... slavery is more than merely the exploitation of another. It is where the power a person exercises over another effectively amounts to the power a person would exercise over property he or she owns.

99. To exercise such a power, as if over property that the person owns or possesses, it is inherent that the person deploying that power does so based upon a notion of that person's entitlement to act as he or she does. What is done is not done mindlessly, thoughtlessly or carelessly. It is done out of a sense of power, founded on a sense of entitlement. Thus the language and structure of the legislation, and the terms of the explanatory memorandum, support the approach of the Court of Appeal. And basically that is enough.

100. Two additional considerations further reinforce the conclusion adopted by the Court of Appeal. The first, which Eames JA noted,[111] is that the Code comprises penal legislation which is conventionally construed strictly because of the consequences of serious punishment that may follow from a conviction.[112] To the extent that there is any residual doubt about the meaning and requirement of the provisions of the Code to Ms Tang's case, the Court of Appeal adopted such an approach and that approach is to be preferred.

101. Secondly, the introduction of "slavery offences" into the Code enacted novel crimes that have to be read together with general principles of the Code governing criminal responsibility. Those principles are, in turn, in some ways new. They must be given meaning according to their terms and in consideration of the context and purpose of the reforms they introduce. Nevertheless, these provisions are themselves written against the background of the basic doctrines of criminal law as they operate throughout Australia. It will generally be presumed that the language of a code that is designed to state criminal offences **[233]** applicable in Australia is intended generally to reflect, and not to depart from, long-observed basic principles of criminal liability.[113]

102. With respect, it is not persuasive to suggest[114] that the approach favoured by the majority is supported by the "common exercise of relating the fault element to the physical elements of the offence".[115] The ultimate duty of this court is to construe the language of the

---

[111] *Tang* at para. 85.
[112] Compare *He Kaw Teh* v. *R* (1985) 157 CLR 523 at 583; 60 ALR 449 at 492; [1985] HCA 43 *(He Kaw Teh)* per Brennan J; *Murphy* v. *Farmer* (1988) 165 CLR 19 at 28-9; 79 ALR 1 at 7; [1988] HCA 31.
[113] *R* v. *Barlow* (1997) 188 CLR 1 at 32; 144 ALR 317 at 340; [1997] HCA 19 *(Barlow)*. The passage cites *Vallance* v. *R* (1961) 108 CLR 56 at 75-6; [1963] ALR 461 at 474-5; [1961] HCA 42 and *Parker* v. *R* (1997) 186 CLR 494 at 517-19; 143 ALR 293 at 309-10; [1997] HCA 15.
[114] Reasons of Gleeson CJ at para. 49.
[115] Referring to *He Kaw Teh* at CLR 568; ALR 481.

Code.[116] This must be done by reference to the text of the Code and a consideration of the context of the relevant provisions and their purpose of expressing a new approach to the application of the "fault elements" of federal offences. When this approach is adopted, the language of the Code, and especially the structure of the provisions in which that language appears (the chapeau of s 270.3(1)), argue powerfully against the conclusion reached by the majority. This approach instead supports the analysis adopted by the Court of Appeal.

103. In any case, when considering basic principles of criminal law, one such principle is the common law presumption that no person will be punished criminally "for doing an act which he honestly and reasonably believes to be lawful and right".[117] To the extent that they are consistent with the Code, fundamental principles of criminal responsibility inform the construction of such statutory provisions.[118] It would require very clear statutory language to render the mere performance of an act criminally blameworthy, without regard being had to the "golden thread"[119] which has been present in Australian (and earlier English) criminal law for at least 70 years. In the present case, this is not to oblige (in effect) that the accused should know the precise terms of the statute or of antecedent treaties. It is simply to apply the statutory postulate of "intention" not only to the physical elements but also to their quality and the "circumstances [that] make [them] criminal".[120]

104. General considerations such as these[121] confirm the conclusion of the Court of Appeal in this case. The mere existence of what the Code now describes as "physical elements" (relevantly "possession" and "the right of ownership") does not, on conventional theory, ordinarily attract criminal liability to a person accused in Australia of a serious criminal offence. Something more is required. That something is the "mental element" (mens rea as formerly described) on the part of the accused or, as is now described in the Code, the "fault element". This **[234]** element is essential to constitute, with a "particular physical element", responsibility in law for an offence against federal criminal provisions.

---

[116] This is a special example of the general rule mandating the primacy of statutory language as the source of, and starting point for deriving, legislative obligations. Recent cases are set out in *Central Bayside General Practice Association Ltd* v. *Cmr of State Revenue (Vic)* (2006) 228 CLR 168; 229 ALR 1; [2006] HCA 43 at para. 84, fn 86. See also *Barlow* at CLR 31-3; ALR 339-41.

[117] *R* v. *Tolson* (1889) 23 QBD 168 at 182. See *CTM* at para. 4 per Gleeson CJ, Gummow, Crennan and Kiefel JJ and para. 61 of my own reasons.

[118] *CTM* at para. 5 per Gleeson CJ, Gummow, Crennan and Kiefel JJ, para. 61 of my own reasons and para. 146 per Hayne J.

[119] *Woolmington* v. *DPP* [1935] AC 462 at 481.

[120] *He Kaw Teh* at CLR 572; ALR 484 per Brennan J.

[121] Compare *CTM* at para. 6 per Gleeson CJ, Gummow, Crennan and Kiefel JJ and para. 108 of my own reasons.

105. The Court of Appeal's approach gives full force and effect to these basic notions of our criminal law. So much is required by the language and structure of the Code. However, if there were any ambiguity, this is the approach that this court should take. It conforms more closely to the "general principles of criminal responsibility" expressed in Ch 2 of the Code and also in the basic doctrines of contemporary Australian criminal law. It is against this background that the Code provisions were formulated and enacted.

106. *Further considerations in support*: A number of additional considerations lend still further support to the approach adopted by the Court of Appeal.

107. *Traditional approach to "intention"*: Having something in "possession" (or asserting over something "powers attaching to the right of ownership") will not ordinarily render a person liable for a criminal act unless the mind ("intention") of the person combines with the physical elements. Take, for example, someone who carries a suitcase containing a prohibited drug over a border. The physical elements involved in such "possession" of that drug (or the assertion of powers attaching to the "right of ownership" over the suitcase) would not, on conventional theory, alone be sufficient to render the carrier criminally liable. The prosecution would have to identify and prove that the accused was aware of the nature and quality of the control asserted over the import in question. It is not enough that the suitcase should, in physical fact, contain a prohibited drug. The prosecution must establish, to the requisite standard, that the accused knew that the drug was present and intended to perform the physical acts amounting to a criminal importation.[122]

108. Innocent parties fall outside the ambit of the offences provided by s 270.3(1) of the Code. This is precisely because the requirement of "intentionally", as expressed in the chapeau to the subsection, imports a necessity of consciousness of the quality, source and purported basis or justification of the "possession" and "right of ownership" being asserted. All of this is simply to insist that, under the Code, as conventionally at common law, the mere acts of "possession" or "ownership" alone are not enough to constitute the criminal offence. The necessary added ingredient is the presence of the intention to which s 270.3(1) refers, addressed to the quality and character of the acts charged.

109. The Court of Appeal correctly insisted upon the necessity of this ingredient. Correctly, it concluded that its absence from the directions of the trial judge to the jury constituted a serious omission in explaining to the jury the legal components of the offences charged.

---

[122] *He Kaw Teh* at CLR 585-6; ALR 494 per Brennan J.

110. *Conformability with international law*: The present task is to construe and apply the Code, an Australian statute. However, the ostensible purpose of the relevant provisions was to introduce into Australian municipal law offences derived substantially from the 1926 Slavery Convention.

111. The interpretation of s 270.3(1) favoured by the Court of Appeal is more consonant with that Convention and the extremely grave international crime that "slavery", so expressed, involves. As stated in the Code,[123] slavery, like **[235]** piracy,[124] is a crime against humanity.[125] Thus those who engage in "slavery", piracy and other special crimes are enemies of mankind.[126] Such offences arguably attract obligations that attach to crimes of universal jurisdiction.[127] As a rule [of] jus cogens,[128] slavery is prohibited as a peremptory norm from which no derogation is permitted.[129] This further reinforces the seriousness of slavery and hence the need to define it very carefully and precisely.

112. I therefore agree with Gleeson CJ that, without the clearest statutory authority, it is undesirable to banalise slavery crimes by applying them to circumstances that would amount to no more than a seriously exploitative employment relationship.[130] The approach of the Court of Appeal requires consideration by the decision-maker of the quality and extent of the accused's "intention". To that extent, in asserting "possession" and "rights of ownership" over another person as a "slave", the crimes provided by s 270.3(1) are reserved to indisputably serious offences containing a substantial, not trivial, intention element.

---

[123] Section 268.10 of the Code.

[124] G. Simpson, *Law, War and Crime: War Crimes Trials and the Reinvention of International Law*, Polity Press, Cambridge, 2007, p. 159.

[125] *Prosecutor* v. *Kunarac* Case No IT-96-23-T & IT-96-23/1-T, 22 February 2001 at paras. 522, 526, 537 and 539 (*Kunarac* (Trial)) and Case No IT-96-23 & IT-96-23/1-A, 12 June 2002 at para. 13 (*Kunarac* (Appeal)); R. Jennings and A. Watts (eds.), *Oppenheim's International Law*, 9th edn, Longman, London, 1992, vol. 1, Pts 2-4, §429; M. C. Bassiouni, "Enslavement as an International Crime", (1991) 23 *New York Univ J Int Law Polit* 445, p. 448. Some of the above references refer to the term "enslavement", which is nonetheless applicable in the present circumstances. As noted in *Kunarac* (Trial) at para. 539, "enslavement" consists of the "exercise of any or all of the powers attaching to the right of ownership over a person". Further, *Kunarac* (Appeal) at para. 123 equates the terms "slavery" and "enslavement".

[126] See Simpson, 2007, p. 159.

[127] Compare *R* v. *Bow Street Metropolitan Stipendiary Magistrate; Ex parte Pinochet Ugarte (No 3)* [2000] 1 AC 147 at 189, 200-4 and 278-9; [1999] 2 All ER 97 at 99, 109-13 and 178-80.

[128] L. Hannikainen, *Peremptory Norms (Jus Cogens) in International Law*, Finnish Lawyers' Pub. Co., Helsinki, 1988, pp. 446-7; T. Meron, *Human Rights and Humanitarian Norms as Customary Law*, Clarendon Press, Oxford, 1989, pp. 20-1; L. Henkin, *International Law: Politics and Values*, Martinus Nijhoff, Dordrecht, 1995, p. 39; O. Schachter, *International Law in Theory and Practice*, Martinus Nijhoff, Dordrecht, 1991, p. 343; S. Drew, "Human Trafficking: A Modern Form of Slavery?", (2002) 4 *EHRLR* 481, p. 481.

[129] Article 53 of the Vienna Convention on the Law of Treaties, 1969.

[130] Reasons of Gleeson CJ at para. 32.

113. To the extent that the intention element is restricted to conduct in relation to a person, with no attention being given to the perpetrator's intention, there is a serious risk of over-expansion of the notion of "slavery". The approach of the Court of Appeal is more rigorous. Such rigour is more appropriate to a crime defined by reference to the universal international offence of "slavery".

114. *Consistency with severe punishment*: All of the foregoing is yet further reinforced by a reflection upon the maximum penalty that the Code provides upon conviction of the s 270.3(1) slavery offences.

115. The maximum penalty of imprisonment for 25 years[131] is one of the highest now provided under Australian legislation. This feature helped to reinforce the conclusion of the Court of Appeal that the applicable "fault element" of "intention" should apply in the manner adopted by Eames JA.[132] His Honour remarked:[133]

[236] 84. ... Lack of control of the "slave" over her life, and her lack of personal liberty, may well suggest that she is being treated as though she were mere property—as a thing—but more is required to be proved for an offence under s 270.3(1)(a). And much more is required than that the person be shown to have been exploited, abused or humiliated, whether physically, emotionally or financially. To be a slave, the person must be in a state where he or she is dealt with by others as though he or she was mere property—a thing. For the exercise of the power to contravene s 270.3(1)(a) the accused must have knowingly treated the person as though he or she was the accused's property. Only when that state of mind exists is the exercise of power referable to a right of ownership, as the section requires.

116. *Comparison with human trafficking*: In a case such as the present it is important for the judicial decision-maker to be familiar with contemporary instances of human trafficking. Human trafficking involves the movement, recruitment or receipt of persons, often by means of the threat or use of force, for the purpose of exploitation.[134] As such, it commonly operates in conjunction with, or as part of, slavery.[135]

---

[131] *Tang* at para. 53.   [132] Compare *He Kaw Teh* at CLR 583; ALR 492 per Brennan J.
[133] *Tang* at para. 84.
[134] See Art. 3 of the Protocol to Prevent, Suppress and Punish Trafficking in Persons, Especially Women and Children, Supplementing the United Nations Convention Against Transnational Organized Crime, 2000; International Labour Office, "Trafficking in Human Beings: New Approaches to Combating the Problem", 2003, p. 6; International Labour Office (P. Belser, M. de Cock and F. Mehran), "ILO Minimum Estimate of Forced Labour in the World", 2005, pp. 4-6.
[135] See Art. 7(2)(c) of the Rome Statute of the International Criminal Court, 1998; United Nations Economic and Social Council, "Contemporary Forms of Slavery", UN Doc. E/CN.4/Sub.2/2000/3, 2000, para. 48; K. Tessier, "The New Slave Trade: The International Crisis of Immigrant Smuggling", (1995) 3 *Ind J Global Legal Studies* 261, pp. 261-2; M. C. Bassiouni, *Crimes Against Humanity in International Criminal Law*, 2nd rev edn, Kluwer Law International, The Hague, 1999, p. 212;

Women and children are particularly vulnerable to human trafficking and they are often subjected to sexual and other physical and emotional exploitation. This abhorrent activity commonly involves conditions of infancy, serious vulnerability, shocking living and working conditions and repeated violence, oppression and humiliation.

117. The close connection between human trafficking, as described, and "slavery" serves to reinforce the extremely serious nature of such "slavery offences". Given the nature of "slavery", as understood in international law, there is a great need to not over-extend "slavery offences" to apply to activities such as seriously oppressive employment relationships. The approach adopted by the Court of Appeal is more consistent with such an aim. The approach of the majority in this court is not.

118. *Distinguishing "slavery" from debt bondage*: Since the actions occurred for which Ms Tang was charged, the parliament has amended the Code to introduce into Australian law[136] a new and discrete offence of "debt bondage".[137] As Eames JA remarked:[138]

[237] 87. "Debt bondage" is defined in the Dictionary of the Code as arising when a person pledges personal services as security for a debt and the debt is manifestly excessive, or the reasonable value of the services provided is not applied in reduction of the debt, or the length and nature of the services are not limited and defined. Arguably, that offence would have been proved on the evidence in this case and, if so, it would have carried a maximum sentence of 12 months' imprisonment. There being no such provision, [Ms Tang] was charged with slavery offences, which carried a maximum sentence of 25 years... [S]he received a total effective sentence of 10 years' imprisonment with a non-parole period of six years, although she had no prior convictions.

119. Responding to a question asked during the hearing, the Attorney-General of the Commonwealth acknowledged that:

After examining the legislation of the United States, Canada, South Africa, New Zealand and the United Kingdom, we have not identified any provisions that implement the Convention in terms similar to those found in Australia's Criminal Code.

K. Levchenko, "Combat of Trafficking in Women for the Purpose of Forced Prostitution—Ukraine (Country Report)", 1999, p. 23. For a comprehensive analysis of the relationship between slavery and trafficking, see J. Hathaway, "The Human Rights Quagmire of 'Human Trafficking'", (2008) 49 *Va J Int'l L* 1.

[136] *Tang* at para. 86.

[137] Section 271.8 of the Code. "Slavery" and "debt bondage" are often treated separately in international instruments. See, for example, Arts. 1(a) and 7(b) of the 1956 Supplementary Convention ("debt bondage" as a "person of servile status") and Art. 7(a) (slavery).

[138] *Tang* at para. 87 (footnote omitted).

The closest analogy to the Australian provisions was said to be s 98(1) of the Crimes Act 1961 (NZ).[139]

120. None of the states mentioned above have implemented the Convention in a similar way to that of the Code here. This affords a further reason why, in respect of the "slavery offences" in s 270.3(1)(a) of the Code, this court should adopt the more stringent requirement of proof of intention favoured by the Court of Appeal. Doing so would ensure that Australian law remained in broad harmony with the law of similar countries. Especially in relation to crimes having a universal or transnational character; that is, a proper interpretive consideration.

121. *Shift in law on sex work*: As to the extension of "slavery" to adult consensual participation in the commercial sex industry, it is also important for courts such as this to give due weight to recent changes in Australian law (including in Victoria). Those changes reflect a recognition by parliament that adults (as the prosecution conceded before this court) are entitled to participate in the sex industry lawfully. This includes participation as sex workers, consensually, for economic reasons. Attempts to use "slavery offences" to suppress commercial sex work, based upon individual repugnance towards adult sexual behaviour, potentially contradict the law enacted by the Victorian Parliament. The simple fact is that some commercial sex workers have no desire to exit the industry. Some people may find that shocking; but it matters not. In Victoria, so long as the sex worker is a consenting adult with no relevant disability, that is a choice open to her or him. The contrary approach risks returning elements of the sex industry to operate, as was previously the case, covertly, corruptly and underground. This would undermine the fundamental objectives of the recent Australian legislation in this area, such as that of Victoria under which the brothel where the complainants worked was licensed.[140]

122. Such developments could also prove counterproductive to important purposes of the recent legislation. Specifically, such purposes include empowering sex workers to safeguard their own lives and well-being and thereby assisting in the reduction of the spread of sexually transmitted diseases, including **[238]** the human immunodeficiency virus.[141] These policy considerations (although not mentioned by the

---

[139] This section creates an offence of dealing with, using or detaining a person as a slave and defines "debt bondage" in terms similar to the 1956 Supplementary Convention (Art. 1). See also *R v. Decha-Iamsakun* [1993] 1 NZLR 141.

[140] Prostitution Control Act 1994 (Vic).

[141] See United Kingdom, Committee on Homosexual Offences and Prostitution, "Report of the Committee on Homosexual Offences and Prostitution", (1957) Cmnd 247, pp. 95-6 286 (the Wolfenden Report); N. Lacey, C. Wells and D. Meure, *Reconstructing Criminal Law,* Weidenfeld and

Court of Appeal) offer additional reasons of legal principle and policy to confine "sexual slavery" offences in Australia to cases where the specific element of "intention" includes exerting powers of possession or ownership over a person because of an established belief, on the part of the accused, that it is his or her right and entitlement to do so.

123. *The jury's repeated questions*: The Court of Appeal's approach on this issue was by no means an esoteric one. This is made clear by the questions which the jury in the second trial returned twice to ask. The first question was:[142]

122. ... "Does the defendant have to have known what the definition of a slave is 'to intentionally possess a slave' as stated in the indictment?"

124. The second question, presented the following afternoon, was:[143]

129. "To intentionally possess a slave is it necessary for the accused to have knowledge that her actions amount to slavery?
or
Is it sufficient that the accused only have knowledge of the conditions she has imposed (i.e. slavery has not entered her mind) and the law has decided those conditions amount to slavery?"

125. The members of the jury in the second trial were obviously puzzled over these questions and the members of the jury in the first trial were unable to reach verdicts. It is thus reasonable to infer that considerations as to the requisite intention of Ms Tang may be foremost in the minds of Australian jurors as they seek to differentiate activities that amount to seriously oppressive employment from those that justify conviction of "slavery offences" against s 270.3(1)(a) of the Code.

126. *Court of Appeal's answers*: Instead of the partly unresponsive, generally unclear and confusing answers given by the trial judge to the foregoing questions, the Court of Appeal (consistent with its approach) favoured the following answers. In my opinion, they are correct. They are not confusing. They respond precisely to the concern expressed by the jury about the "fault element" of "intention" that the Code requires to be proved to establish the "slavery offences". Eames JA said:[144]

145. With the benefit of hindsight, and the luxuries of time and the provision of comprehensive submissions of counsel on the appeal, I would respectfully suggest that the answers to the jury questions might have been along the following lines:

Nicolson, London, 1990, pp. 357-68; compare *Bodyline Spa and Sauna (Sydney) Pty Ltd* v. *South Sydney City Council* (1992) 77 LGRA 432 at 433-8; L. O. Gostin and Z. Lazzarini, *Human Rights and Public Health in the AIDS Pandemic*, Oxford University Press, New York, 1997, pp. 50-1, 124-5.
[142] *Tang* at para. 122.   [143] *Tang* at para. 129.   [144] *Tang* at para. 145.

[239] [As to the first question]
A—No, she does not have to have known the definition of a slave, nor even that there was an offence of slavery in the laws of Australia. Ignorance of the law is no defence.[145]

The Crown has to prove that she did know that in each case the worker had been reduced to a condition in which she was treated as though she was mere property, just a thing, who had no say in how she was treated.

[As to the second question]
A—It is not necessary for the accused to have knowledge that her actions amount, in law, to slavery.

For the offence of intentionally possessing a slave, the accused must have known that the complainant had been reduced to a condition where she was no more than property, merely a thing, over which the accused could exercise powers as though she owned the complainant.

Furthermore, the Crown must prove that in exercising the relevant power over a particular complainant (that is, possessing or using the complainant) the accused was treating that complainant as though she was property, as if she owned her, as if she could do with her whatever she chose to do. You must be satisfied that the accused was intentionally exercising a power that an owner would have over property and was doing so with the knowledge or in the belief that the complainant was no more than mere property.

If it is reasonably possible that the accused acted to possess or to use the complainant with the knowledge or in the belief that she was exercising her rights and entitlements as her employer or contractor and not in the belief that the complainant had no rights or free will, but was property, a thing, over whom she could exercise power as though she owned her then, however exploitative and unfair you may think her treatment of the complainant was, it would not constitute the offences of intentionally possessing or using a slave.

127. Such answers would have provided accurate and adequate instructions to the jury and clear responses to their questions. These suggested answers may be contrasted with the very confusing directions actually presented to the jury by the trial judge.[146]

128. *Conclusion—miscarriage of the trial*: I leave aside the justifiable criticisms by the Court of Appeal of the unresponsiveness, ambiguity and uncertainty of the directions given to the jury. These criticisms alone raise serious questions about the compliance of Ms Tang's trial with the standards established by this court for the comprehensibility and

---

[145] See s 9.3 of the Code.   [146] Set out at length by the Court of Appeal: *Tang* at paras. 122-39.

accuracy of jury directions.[147] The Court of Appeal considered authorities of this court and came to the correct conclusion on this "critical issue". It is the conclusion that I also reach. It leaves a continuing substantive operation for "slavery offences" under Australian law, as the valid provisions of s 270.3(1)(a) of the Code require. It allows such offences to apply in contemporary circumstances warranting the appellation of "slavery". It properly confines such offences to the grave affront to humanity that is "slavery" eo nomine, as expanded by statute in Australia to include modern instances, and not to employment deemed harsh, oppressive or repulsive.

[240] 129. As the Court of Appeal concluded, there was evidence upon which a reasonable jury, properly instructed, might have arrived at the decision that "slavery offences" of the kind provided for in the Code had been proved against Ms Tang. However, it was essential for the "fault element" of "intention" to be applied to all, and not just some, of the ingredients of the offences and to be accurately and clearly explained to the jury. Despite the jury's repeated questions, this was not done. The result is that Ms Tang's second trial miscarried. The outcome favoured by the Court of Appeal was then inevitable. There should be a new trial.

Orders

130. It follows that I agree with Gleeson CJ that special leave to cross-appeal on the first and second grounds in the proposed notice of cross-appeal should be granted. That cross-appeal should be treated as instituted and heard instanter and dismissed. I also agree with Gleeson CJ that special leave to cross-appeal on the third ground in the proposed notice of cross-appeal should be refused.

131. However, the appeal from the orders of the Court of Appeal of the Supreme Court of Victoria should be dismissed.

132. HAYNE J. I agree with Gleeson CJ that, for the reasons he gives, the appeal to this court should be allowed. I also agree with Gleeson CJ that, for the reasons he gives, orders should be made granting the respondent special leave to cross-appeal, limited to the first two proposed grounds of cross-appeal, but dismissing the cross-appeal. I agree that consequential orders should be made in the form proposed by Gleeson CJ.

133. Section 270.3(1)(a) of the Criminal Code (Cth) (the Code) makes it an offence intentionally to possess a slave or to exercise over

---

[147] *Ahern* v. *R* (1988) 165 CLR 87 at 103; 80 ALR 161 at 171; [1988] HCA 39; *Zoneff* v. *R* (2000) 200 CLR 234; 172 ALR 1; [2000] HCA 28 at paras. 65-7; *Doggett* v. *R* (2001) 208 CLR 343; 182 ALR 1; [2001] HCA 46 at para. 2 per Gleeson CJ.

a slave "any of the other powers attaching to the right of ownership". The central issue in the appeal concerns what directions should have been given to the jury at the respondent's trial about the mental element of the offences of possessing or using a slave. I agree with Gleeson CJ that, contrary to the holding of the Court of Appeal,[148] the prosecution did not have to prove that the respondent had any knowledge or belief about the source of the powers she exercised over the complainants. What was to be proved was the intentional possession and use of each complainant as a slave, which is to say as a person over whom any or all of the powers attaching to the right of ownership were exercised.

134. I agree with what Gleeson CJ has said about the application of Ch 2 of the Code to s 270.3(1). The relevant fault element of each of the offences with which the respondent was charged was intention.[149] The conduct, which is to say the act or state of affairs,[150] in question in this matter was possessing a slave or using a slave. To establish the relevant fault element in this case it was necessary to show that the respondent meant to engage in the conduct, in respect of each complainant, of exercising powers attaching to the right of ownership.

135. The remaining part of these reasons is directed to the meaning, and application in this case, of the terms "slavery" and "slave" when used in the relevant provisions of the Code. "Slavery" is defined[151] as follows:

[241] For the purposes of this Division, *slavery* is the condition of a person over whom any or all of the powers attaching to the right of ownership are exercised, including where such a condition results from a debt or contract made by the person.

"Slave" is not separately defined but must take its meaning from the definition of "slavery".

136. As Gleeson CJ has pointed out, the definition of "slavery" in the Code derives from, but is not identical with, the definition of "slavery" in Art. 1(1) of the 1926 International Convention to Suppress the Slave Trade and Slavery.[152] Because the purpose of the Convention was to suppress the slave trade and slavery it was directed to both the status of slavery and the condition of slavery. The status of slavery, in the context of the Convention, is to be understood as referring to a legal status created by or recognised under relevant municipal law. By contrast, the condition of slavery is to be understood as referring to a factual state of affairs which need not, but may, depend upon recognition by the relevant municipal legal system. Yet both that status and that

---

[148] *R* v. *Tang* (2007) 16 VR 454; [2007] VSCA 134 at paras. 77, 124 and 145 *(Tang)*.
[149] Sections 5.1 and 5.2 of the Criminal Code (Cth). [150] Section 4.1(2).
[151] Section 270.1. [152] [1927] ATS 11.

condition were defined in the Convention in identical terms: as a status or condition of a person over whom any or all of the powers attaching to the right of ownership are exercised.

137. The language of the Convention, whether in its definition of slavery or otherwise, cannot be read as if it gave effect to or reflected particular legal doctrines of ownership or possession developed in one or more systems of municipal law. Nothing in the preparatory materials relating to the Convention suggests that it was intended to embrace any particular legal doctrine of that kind, and the text of the Convention itself does not evidence any such intention. Rather, slavery (both as a legal status and as a factual condition) was defined only by a description that assumed an understanding, but did not identify the content, of "the powers attaching to the right of ownership". Yet for the purposes of creating particular norms of individual behaviour enforceable by application of the criminal law, the definition of "slavery" that is adopted in s 270.1 of the Code takes as its origin the definition of slavery, as a condition, that was given in the Convention.

138. What are the "powers attaching to the right of ownership"? How are they to be identified when the Code is applied, given that the Convention did not use the term "ownership", or the expression "powers attaching to the right of ownership", with a legal meaning that was anchored in any particular legal system? Both "ownership" and the "powers attaching to the right of ownership" must be understood as ordinary English expressions and applied having regard to the context in which they are to be applied. The chief feature of that context is that the subject of "ownership", the subject of the exercise of "powers attaching to the right of ownership", is a human being.

139. Because "ownership" cannot be read in s 270.1 of the Code as a technical legal term whose content is spelled out by a particular legal system, it is a word that must be read as conveying the ordinary English meaning that is captured by the expression "dominion over" the subject-matter. That is, it must be read as identifying a form of relationship between a person (the owner) and the subject-matter (another person) that is to be both described and identified by the powers that the owner has over that other.

[242] 140. "Ownership" ordinarily is to be understood as referring to a legal relationship between owner and subject-matter. An "owner" has an aggregation of powers that are recognised in law as the powers permissibly exercised over the subject-matter.[153] It is a term that connotes

---

[153] Compare *Yanner* v. *Eaton* (1999) 201 CLR 351; 166 ALR 258; [1999] HCA 53 at paras. 17 and 85-6.

at least an extensive aggregation of powers, perhaps the fullest and most complete aggregation that is possible. But s 270.1 cannot be read as requiring the identification of an aggregation of powers that the law permits to be exercised over a person because Australian law does not recognise, and never has recognised, the possibility that one person may own another. There is not, and never has been, legal endorsement in Australia for the creation or maintenance of such a concentration of legally recognised powers in one person over another as would amount to "ownership" of that person. In particular, Australian law does not recognise, and never has recognised, any right to "possess" a person.

141. It follows that neither the definition of slavery in s 270.1, nor the references to "a slave" in s 270.3, invite attention to what legal rights the "owner" has over the person who it is alleged is "a slave". Rather, the references in s 270.3(1)(a) of the Code to possessing a slave, and exercising over a slave "any of the other powers attaching to the right of ownership", invite attention to what the alleged offender has done. In particular, what powers has the alleged offender exercised over the person who is alleged to be a slave? And what the alleged offender has done must then be measured against a factual construct: the powers that an owner would have over a person if, contrary to the fact, the law recognised the right to own another person.

142. As explained earlier, to constitute "ownership", one person would have dominion over that other person. That is, the powers that an owner of another person would have would be the powers which, taken together, would constitute the complete subjection of that other person to the will of the first. Or to put the same point another way, the powers that an owner would have over another person, if the law recognised the right to own that other, would be powers whose exercise would not depend upon the assent of the person over whom the powers are exercised.

143. How are those abstract ideas to be given practical application? It is convenient to approach that question by reference to the particular allegations in this matter, where it was alleged that the respondent had "possessed" each complainant as a slave and that she had "used" each complainant as a slave.

144. The first step to take is to recognise that both the offence of possessing a slave, and the offence of exercising over a slave any of the powers attaching to the right of ownership, are cast in terms that appear to present two questions: first, did the accused possess, or exercise some other power attaching to the right of ownership over, the complainant and second, was the complainant a slave? But the two questions merge.

145. The condition that must be proved is that the person meets the description "a slave". The offence is intentionally to possess a slave or intentionally to exercise over a slave any of certain powers. The condition of slavery (which is what provides the content of the term "a slave") is defined as the condition of a person over whom any or all of the powers attaching to the right of ownership are exercised. It thus follows that proof of the intentional exercise of any of the **[243]** relevant powers over a person suffices to establish both that the victim is a slave and that the accused has done what the legislation prohibits.

146. The next step to take is to observe that the Code's definition of "slavery" in s 270.1 speaks of "the *powers* attaching to the *right* of ownership" (emphasis added). Section 270.3 of the Code shows that possessing a slave is one particular power attaching to the right of ownership. And it is also clear that possessing a slave is not the only power attaching to the right of ownership. So much is made clear by the use of the word "other" in the phrase "other powers attaching to the right of ownership". But s 270.1 does not further identify what those powers are.

147. As Brennan J said in *He Kaw Teh* v. *R*,[154] "'possession' is a term which implies a state of mind with respect to the thing possessed". In that case, Brennan J identified[155] the actus reus of possession of a prohibited import as being that the object of possession was physically in the custody or under the control of the accused. And as Dawson J pointed out in the same case,[156] "[p]ossession may be an intricate concept for some purposes, but the intricacies belong to the civil rather than the criminal law". That is why, in the criminal law, "possession" is best understood as a reference to a state of affairs in which there is[157] "the intentional exercise of physical custody or control over something". In considering s 270.3(1)(a) of the Code, however, it will also be important to recognise that the right to possess a subject-matter, coupled with a power to carve out and dispose of subsidiary possessory rights, is an important element in that aggregation of powers over a subject-matter that is commonly spoken of as "ownership".

148. Just as the word "ownership" evokes notions of the dominion of one person over another, to speak of one person possessing another (in the sense of having physical custody of or control over that other) connotes one person having dominion over the other. Or to put the same point in different words, possession, like ownership, refers to a

---

[154] (1985) 157 CLR 523 at 585; 60 ALR 449 at 494; [1985] HCA 43 *(He Kaw Teh)*.
[155] *He Kaw Teh* at CLR 585-6; ALR 494.   [156] *He Kaw Teh* at CLR 599; ALR 504.
[157] *He Kaw Teh* at CLR 599; ALR 504 per Dawson J.

state of affairs in which there is the complete subjection of that other by the first person.

149. One, and perhaps the most obvious, way in which to attempt to give practical content to the otherwise abstract ideas of ownership or possession (whether expressed by reference to subjection, dominion or otherwise) is to explore the antithesis of slavery. That is, because both the notion of ownership and of possession, when applied to a person, can be understood as an exercise of power over that person that does not depend upon the assent of the person concerned, it will be relevant to ask why that person's assent was irrelevant. Or, restating the proposition in other words, in asking whether there was the requisite dominion over a person, the subjection of that person, it will be relevant to ask whether the person concerned was deprived of freedom of choice in some relevant respect and, if so, what it was that deprived the person of choice. In that inquiry some assistance is to be had from United States decisions about legislation giving effect to the Thirteenth Amendment to the United States Constitution.

[244] 150. Those cases explore what is meant when it is said that a person had no choice but to continue to serve a person accused of holding the first in "involuntary servitude". And they show that a person may be deprived of choice to the requisite extent, not just by force or the threat of force, but also by threats to invoke the proper application of the law to the detriment of the person threatened. But examination of the cases will also show why analysis of who is "a slave" by reference only to freedom or absence of choice of the alleged victim, or by reference only to the nature of the coercion applied by an accused, is not determinative of that question.

151. The Thirteenth Amendment provides, in s 1, that:

Neither slavery nor involuntary servitude, except as a punishment for crime whereof the party shall have been duly convicted, shall exist within the United States, or any place subject to their jurisdiction.

Section 2 of the Amendment gives the Congress power to make appropriate laws to enforce the Amendment.

152. The prime purpose of outlawing "involuntary servitude" in the Thirteenth Amendment, and in statutes enacted to enforce it, was described by Judge Friendly, speaking for the plurality of the United States Court of Appeals for the Second Circuit in *United States* v. *Shackney*,[158] as being:

---

[158] 333 F 2d 475 (1964) at 485-6 *(Shackney)*.

... to abolish all practices whereby subjection having some of the incidents of slavery was legally enforced, either directly, by a state's using its power to return the servant to the master ... or indirectly, by subjecting persons who left the employer's service to criminal penalties.

But as Judge Friendly went on to point out, the Thirteenth Amendment is not addressed solely to state action. In the United States it has been held to apply in cases of physical restraint,[159] threats of imprisonment or physical violence.[160] In *Shackney*, the plurality held[161] that:

... a holding in involuntary servitude means to us *action by the master causing the servant to have, or to believe he has, no way to avoid continued service or confinement* ... not a situation where the servant knows he has a choice between continued service and freedom, even if the master has led him to believe that the choice may entail consequences that are exceedingly bad. [Emphasis added.]

The third member of that court, Judge Dimock, held[162] that servitude is involuntary only "[w]here the subjugation of the will of the servant is so complete as to render him incapable of making a rational choice".

153. Twenty years later, in 1984, the United States Court of Appeals for the Ninth Circuit expressed the test differently. In *United States v. Mussry*,[163] a case about Indonesian domestic workers, the Court of Appeals held that:

... A holding in involuntary servitude occurs when an individual *coerces another into his service by improper or wrongful conduct* that is intended to cause, and does cause, the other person to believe that he or she has no alternative but to perform the labor. [Emphasis added.]

[245] In that case the prosecution alleged that:[164]

[the defendants] knowingly placed [the Indonesian servants] in a strange country where [they] had no friends, had nowhere to go, did not speak English, had no work permit, social security card, or identification, no passport or return airline ticket to return to Indonesia, [were] here as ... illegal alien[s], with no means by which to seek other employment, and with insufficient funds to break [their] contract[s] by paying back to defendant[s] the alleged expenses incurred in getting ... here.

The court held that the conduct alleged by the prosecution, if proved, was sufficient to demonstrate improper or wrongful acts by the

---

[159] *Davis v. United States* 12 F 2d 253 (1926).
[160] *Bernal v. United States; Pierce v. United States* 146 F 2d 84 (1944); *United States v. Ingalls* 73 F Supp 76 (1947).
[161] *Shackney* at 486.   [162] *Shackney* at 488.
[163] 726 F 2d 1448 (1984) at 1453 *(Mussry)*.   [164] *Mussry* at 1453.

defendants intended to coerce the Indonesian servants into performing service for the defendants. The court further held[165] that "the use, or threatened use, of law or physical force is not an essential element of a charge of 'holding' in involuntary servitude". Other forms of coercion may also result in a violation of the involuntary servitude statutes.

154. Subsequently, the Supreme Court of the United States held in *United States* v. *Kozminski*[166] that the use, or threatened use, of physical or legal coercion was essential to proof of involuntary servitude.[167] The court rejected the view that the statute then in question extended to cases the court identified[168] as the compulsion of services "through psychological coercion". Such a test was rejected[169] as depending "entirely upon the victim's state of mind". Accordingly, while deprivation of the victim's will was essential, the court held that the deprivation must be enforced by the use or threatened use of the means identified. But as the reference to "legal coercion" reveals, the court held that involuntary servitude could be established in cases where the coercion applied was not in itself illegal. Thus, threatening an immigrant with deportation was identified[170] as one possible form of threatened legal coercion.

155. The discussion in the United States cases reveals three points of immediate relevance to the application of the provisions of the Code in issue in this case. First, they show that some assistance can be obtained in the practical application of the abstract concepts of ownership and possession by considering the antithesis of slavery and asking whether, and in what respects, the person alleged to be a slave was free. But the second point revealed by the United States cases is that to ask whether a person was "free", or to ask the more particular questions of when and how a person was deprived of will or freedom of choice, is in each case a question of fact and degree. And because that is the nature of the question, the answer may often be expressed using some word like "real" or "substantial" to describe the quality of the freedom or the denial of freedom that is identified. The third point that emerges from the United States cases is that to ask whether a person has been deprived of free choice presents two further questions. First there is the question: choice about what? Then there is the question: how is the deprivation effected? The United States cases that have been discussed explore choice about provision of labour, and deprivation by means other than close physical confinement. The detail of that discussion may or may **[246]** not be immediately relevant to the facts of a case brought under the provisions of the Code that are in issue in this case.

---

[165] *Mussry* at 1455.   [166] 487 US 931 (1988) *(Kozminski)*.   [167] *Kozminski* at 944 and 952.
[168] *Kozminski* at 949.   [169] *Kozminski* at 949.   [170] *Kozminski* at 948.

156. Asking what freedom a person had may shed light on whether that person was a slave. In particular, to ask whether a complainant was deprived of choice may assist in revealing whether what the accused did was exercise over that person a power attaching to the right of ownership. To ask how the complainant was deprived of choice may help to reveal whether the complainant retained freedom of choice in some relevant respect. And if the complainant retained freedom to choose whether the accused used the complainant, that freedom will show that the use made by the accused of the complainant was not as a slave. But it is essential to bear three points at the forefront of consideration.

157. First, asking what freedom a person had is to ask a question whose focus is the reflex of the inquiries required by ss 270.1 and 270.3 of the Code. It is a question that looks at the person who it is alleged was a slave, whereas the definition of slavery in s 270.1 looks to the exercise of power over that person. The question looks at freedom, but the Code requires a decision about ownership.

158. Secondly, what is proscribed by the Code is conduct of the accused. An absence of choice on the part of the complainant may be seen to result from the combined effect of multiple factors. Some of these, such as the complainant's immigration status or the conduct of third parties, may be present independently of the conduct of the accused. Such factors are part of the context in which the conduct of the accused falls to be assessed. However, it is that conduct which must amount to the exercise by the accused of a power attaching to the right of ownership for the offence to be made out.

159. Thirdly, because the Code requires consideration of whether the accused exercised any of the powers attaching to the right of ownership, it will be important to consider the particular power that it is alleged was exercised and the circumstances that bear upon whether the exercise of that power was the exercise of a power attaching to the right of ownership. To ask only the general question—was a complainant "free"—would not address the relevant statutory questions.

160. There were two aspects in the present case that were of critical importance in deciding whether the respondent possessed each complainant as a slave and used each as a slave. There was the evidence that each complainant came to Australia following a transaction described as purchase and sale. There was the evidence of how each complainant was treated in Australia, in particular evidence about the living and the working conditions of each. And a critical feature of that evidence was that each woman was treated as having incurred a debt that had to be repaid by working in the brothel. Although there was evidence that one of the complainants was able to secure a reduction in the amount of

her initial debt, there was no satisfactory explanation in the evidence of how the so-called debt of any of the complainants was calculated, or of what had been or was to be provided in return for the incurring of the obligation. To be put against this evidence about the purchase and sale of the women and their living and working conditions was the concession made by the prosecution at the outset of these proceedings that each complainant came to Australia voluntarily.

161. The evidence at trial showed that the respondent had bought a "share" in four of the five women. The fifth woman had also been bought by a syndicate but the respondent was not a member of that syndicate.

[247] 162. In argument at trial, and on appeal to the Court of Appeal, there was much attention given to what was meant by "buying" the women or a share in some of them. A deal of that debate appears to have proceeded by reference to a supposed distinction between the respondent buying a contract under which a person agreed to provide services, and buying the person.[171] The distinction asserted depends upon directing attention to the legal rights and duties of the parties affected by the transaction. But it is a distinction that is necessarily flawed. One of the asserted alternatives (buying a person) is legally impossible. It is a transaction that could not give rise to legal rights and duties. To the extent, therefore, that the comparison seeks to direct attention to legal rights and duties, it is of no assistance.

163. Yet because reference to buying or selling the complainants is to speak of what, in Australian law, is a legal impossibility, the significance that is to be attached to the transaction depends upon what the respondent did. And in that respect, each of the transactions identified as a syndicate "buying" one of the women had to take its significance in a context provided by all of the evidence. The way in which all five women were treated in Australia by setting them to work as they did, on the terms that they did, coupled with the restraints on their movement and freedom of other action, permitted a jury to conclude that what the respondent did, when she took up a "share" in four of the women, was to buy them as if they were articles of trade or commerce and thereafter possess and use them.

164. In the case of the fifth woman, where the respondent was not a member of the syndicate, the respondent's acceptance of that woman as a worker in her brothel on terms that payments were made to the syndicate members for her services was evidence which, when coupled with the evidence of her working conditions and restraints on movement

---

[171] See, for example, *Tang* at paras. 149-58.

and freedom, was again capable of demonstrating to a jury's satisfaction that the respondent possessed her as if she were an article of trade or commerce that others had bought and sold, and that the respondent thereafter possessed and used her. That is, what was done with respect to the fifth of the complainants could be understood as her "owners" giving the respondent the right to possess her and use her. Those who exercised over the fifth complainant the powers attaching to the right of ownership carved out of that "ownership", and disposed of to the respondent, subsidiary possessory "rights" over the woman.

165. What permitted the conclusion, in respect of each complainant, that she had been bought and sold as if an article of trade or commerce and thereafter possessed and used by the respondent was the combination of the evidence about the treatment of each in Australia with the evidence of sale and purchase in Thailand. The respondent's use of each woman in the respondent's business, coupled with the restraints on the freedom of action of the complainants, permitted the conclusion that the reference to their sale and purchase was an accurate reflection of the relationship that the respondent was to have with each complainant. That relationship was to be one in which the respondent was to have the possession and use of each as if the respondent owned her.

166. Accepting, as the prosecution did at the outset of the trial, that each of the women came to Australia voluntarily did not preclude the conclusion that each was possessed and used by the respondent as if owned by her. Taking the **[248]** concession at its highest (that each woman had consciously, freely and deliberately submitted herself to the conditions that she encountered in Australia), the evidence permitted the jury to conclude that none of the women thereafter retained any freedom to choose what was done with them in Australia. The practical impediments and economic consequences for each woman, if she refused to complete her performance of the arrangement, were such as permitted the jury to conclude that, if there were choices to be made about those matters, they were to be made by others. In this case the evidence permitted the conclusion that the respondent used and possessed each complainant as a slave because it permitted the conclusion, in each case, that the respondent used and possessed the complainant as an item of property at the disposal of those who had bought the complainant regardless of any wish she might have.

167. There is one further point to make about the evidence of purchase and sale. There was no evidence at trial about the circumstances in which the transactions were made. In particular, there was no evidence of how it came about that the "vendor" asserted the right to make the sales that were made. Exploration of those matters would very likely have

cut down, even eliminated altogether, the notion that the women came to Australia voluntarily. Not least is that so because it is possible, even probable, that examination of those matters would reveal not just great disparities of knowledge and power as between the "vendor" and each of the women concerned, but other circumstances touching the reality of the assent which it was accepted each had expressed. But assuming that each of the women was to be taken to have voluntarily agreed to be the subject of sale and purchase, her assent does not deny that the result of the transaction to which each agreed was her subjection to the dominion of her purchasers.

168. It was open to the jury at the respondent's trial to find that each complainant was a person over whom was exercised, by the respondent, one or more powers attaching to the right of ownership. The respondent's appeal to the Court of Appeal of Victoria against her convictions should have been dismissed.

169. **HEYDON J.** I agree with both Gleeson CJ and Hayne J.

170. **CRENNAN J.** I agree with the orders proposed by the Chief Justice, for the reasons given by his Honour. I agree also with the reasons given by Hayne J for concurring in those orders.

171. **KIEFEL J.** I agree with Gleeson CJ and with Hayne J.

Orders

(1) Appeal allowed.
(2) Special leave to cross-appeal on the first and second grounds in the proposed notice of cross-appeal granted. Cross-appeal on those grounds treated as instituted, heard instanter and dismissed.
(3) Special leave to cross-appeal on the third ground in the proposed notice of cross-appeal refused.
(4) Set aside orders 3, 4 and 5 of the orders of the Court of Appeal of the Supreme Court of Victoria made on 29 June 2007 and, in their place, order that the appeal to that court against conviction be dismissed.
(5) **[249]** The appellant to pay the respondent's costs of the application for special leave to appeal and of the appeal to this court.
(6) Remit the matter to the Court of Appeal of the Supreme Court of Victoria for that court's consideration of the application for leave to appeal against sentence.

[Reports: (2008) 249 ALR 200; 237 CLR 1; 187 Crim R 252; 82 ALJR 1334]

Relationship of international law and municipal law — Canadian Charter of Rights and Freedoms — Interpretation and application — Interpretation of Section 32(1) of Charter — Jurisdictional scope — Extraterritorial application — Canada's obligations under international law — Domestic reception of international law — Doctrine of adoption — Prohibitive rules of customary international law as interpretative aid — Principle of respect for sovereignty of foreign States — Principle of non-intervention — Principle of respect for territorial sovereignty of foreign States — Comity as interpretative principle — Presumption of conformity of Canadian legislation to international law — Investigatory actions by Canadian law enforcement officials in Turks and Caicos Islands — Whether Section 8 of Charter applying to searches and seizures by Canadian police outside Canada

Territory — Territorial sovereignty — Customary international law — Principle of respect for sovereignty of foreign State — Principle of sovereign equality — Article 2(1) of United Nations Charter — 1970 UN General Assembly Declaration applying principle to non-UN Member States — Principle of non-intervention — Principle of respect for territorial sovereignty of foreign States — Whether extraterritorial application of Canadian Charter of Rights and Freedoms interfering with sovereign authority of foreign State

Jurisdiction — Principles of jurisdiction — Principles arising from sovereign equality and duty of non-intervention — Bases of jurisdiction — Interplay between various forms and bases of jurisdiction — Whether extraterritorial exercise of jurisdiction permissible — Enforcement jurisdiction — Limits on extraterritorial jurisdiction based on sovereign equality, non-intervention and territoriality principle — Principle of consent — Whether Canada permitted to exercise enforcement jurisdiction over matter outside Canadian territory without consent of other State — Whether Canadian Charter of Rights and Freedoms having extraterritorial application — Whether Section 32 of Charter having territorial limitations

Human rights — Protection of fundamental human rights when Canadian officers investigating abroad — Effective participation in fight against transnational crime — Requirement that Canadian officials follow foreign laws and procedures — Comity — Whether foreign procedures violating fundamental human rights — Balance — Whether international law or Canadian Charter of Rights and Freedoms appropriate vehicle to achieve balance — Whether Charter applying extraterritorially

Comity — Comity of nations as interpretative principle — Appropriateness of comity — Whether any clear violations of international law — The law of Canada

Hape v. Her Majesty the Queen (Attorney-General of Ontario intervening)[1]

(2007 SCC 26)

Canada, Supreme Court. 7 *June* 2007

(McLachlin CJ; Bastarache, Binnie, LeBel, Deschamps, Fish, Abella, Charron and Rothstein JJ)

Summary: *The facts*:—The appellant, a Canadian businessman, was convicted by the Ontario Superior Court of Justice of money laundering contrary to Section 9 of the Controlled Drugs and Substances Act 1996. He appealed on the ground that evidence seized by Canadian police officers while searching company premises in the Turks and Caicos Islands should have been excluded pursuant to Section 24(2) of the Canadian Charter of Rights and Freedoms ("the Charter").

The appellant claimed that the Charter applied to the Canadian police officers even though they were operating outside Canada's territorial boundaries and that they had violated his right to be secure against unreasonable search and seizure under Section 8 of the Charter. The respondent maintained that the Charter was not applicable since the searches and seizures were conducted under the authority of the Turks and Caicos police. The appellant's convictions were upheld by the Ontario Court of Appeal. He appealed to the Supreme Court of Canada.

Held:—The appeal was dismissed. The convictions were affirmed.

---

[1] The appellant was represented by Alan D. Gold and Vanessa Arsenault, instructed by solicitors Gold & Associate, Toronto. The respondent was represented by John North and Robert W. Hubbard, instructed by the Attorney-General of Canada, Toronto. The intervener was represented by Michal Fairburn, instructed by the Attorney-General of Ontario, Toronto.

Per McLachlin CJ, LeBel, Deschamps, Fish and Charron JJ: (1) Section 32 of the Charter[2] did not impose any territorial limits on its application. Since the Charter's framers did not state its jurisdictional scope, courts were to interpret its jurisdictional reach and limits. Where application involved issues of extraterritoriality, interpretative aids included Canada's obligations under international law and the principle of the comity of nations (paras. 32-3).

(2) Following common law tradition, the doctrine of adoption operated in Canada such that prohibitive rules of customary international law were to be incorporated into domestic law in the absence of conflicting legislation. As the law of nations, international custom was also the law of Canada absent an express derogation by Canada in a valid exercise of its sovereignty (paras. 34-9).

(3) Respect for the sovereignty of foreign States was a key customary principle of international law, dictated by the maxim that all States were sovereign and equal. This principle of sovereign equality was recognized by Article 2(1) of the United Nations Charter, and its scope expanded to non-UN member States by the 1970 UN General Assembly Declaration.[3] Jurisdiction was one aspect of State sovereignty. The only limits on State sovereignty were those to which the State consented or that flowed from customary or conventional international law. Such limits had arisen from developments in international humanitarian law, international human rights law and international criminal law, particularly relating to crimes against humanity. The foundational principles of sovereign equality, including non-intervention and respect for territorial sovereignty of foreign States, were firmly established rules of customary international law. As such they were binding and could be adopted into the common law of Canada in the absence of conflicting legislation (paras. 40-6).

(4) Comity was a principle of interpretation where Canadian law affected other sovereign States; it reinforced sovereign equality and contributed to the functioning of the international legal system. Comity ceased to be appropriate where it undermined peaceable interstate relations and the international order, and considerations of comity could not be used to justify a violation of international law (paras. 47-52).

(5) Legislation was presumed to conform to international law. In interpreting the scope of the Charter, courts were to seek to ensure compliance with Canada's binding obligations under international law where the express words were capable of supporting such a construction (paras. 53-6).

(6) While extraterritorial jurisdiction—prescriptive, enforcement or adjudicative—existed under international law, it was subject to strict limits under international law based on sovereign equality, non-intervention and the territoriality principle. The principle of consent was central to assertions of extraterritorial enforcement jurisdiction (paras. 57-65).

---

[2] Section 32(1) of the Charter provided that: "(1) This Charter applies (a) to the Parliament and government of Canada in respect of all matters within the authority of Parliament including all matters relating to the Yukon Territory and Northwest Territories; and (b) to the legislature and government of each province in respect of all matters within the authority of the legislature of each province."

[3] 1970 Declaration on Principles of International Law concerning Friendly Relations and Cooperation among States in accordance with the Charter of the United Nations.

(7) Canadian law, whether statutory or constitutional, could not be enforced in another State's territory without its consent. Consistent with international law principles, this conclusion was also dictated by the words of the Charter itself. Since effect could not be given to Canadian law in the circumstances, the matter fell outside the authority of Parliament and the provincial legislatures. As such the Charter did not apply pursuant to its Section 32 (paras. 66-9).

(8) The Charter did not apply. Although the Canadian officers were State actors for the purposes of Section 32(1) of the Charter, it was not a matter within the authority of Parliament since the search was carried out in Turks and Caicos. There was no evidence of consent. Turks and Caicos clearly and consistently asserted its territorial jurisdiction in the conduct of the investigation within its borders. The investigation was under Turks and Caicos control and authority at all times. When investigations were carried out within another country's borders, the law of that country applied even if the effort was cooperative, involving police from different countries. International cooperation was necessary in the modern world due to the growing problem of transnational crime (paras. 70-121).

Per Bastarache, Abella and Rothstein JJ: (1) The Charter did apply to the search and seizures conducted by Canadian officers in the Turks and Caicos Islands. Its application need not jeopardize comity. The Charter was a flexible document, amenable to contextual interpretation and permitting reasonable justifications of limitations to fundamental rights. The appellant, however, had not established a breach of Section 8 of the Charter (paras. 123-6).

(2) While Section 32(1) of the Charter did not extend its application to the actions of foreign officials, there was no implication that it could not apply to Canadian police officials acting abroad. Since this was a matter of a Canadian criminal investigation involving Canadian police acting abroad, it was clearly a matter within the authority of Parliament or the provincial legislatures. The Charter's application to the actions of Canadian officials did not automatically interfere with the sovereign authority of foreign States (paras. 127-62).

(3) A principled and practical approach was for Canadian officers to assess the fundamental human rights protection offered by foreign procedures against principles guaranteed by the Charter. Minor differences could be justified by the need to fight transnational crime, and comity. Substantial differences required greater justifications, but there was still a favourable presumption for laws and procedures of democratic countries. The ultimate question was whether it was reasonable for Canadian officers to participate in the search authorized by Turks and Caicos law (paras. 163-75).

(4) While the Charter applied extraterritorially, the obligations created depended on the nature of the right at risk, the nature of the action of the police, the involvement of foreign authorities and the application of foreign laws. Consent was not a useful criterion since this existed if Canadian officers were operating in another country. Local laws had not been breached nor failed

to meet fundamental human rights standards; Turks and Caicos search and seizure laws offered similar protections to the Charter. Since the seizure was reasonable, the evidence should not be excluded (paras. 176-9).

Per Binnie J: It was not true that any extraterritorial effect of the Charter was objectionable. Given the importance of issues in the context of the "war on terror" due to confront Canadian courts, pronouncements restricting the application of the Charter to Canadian officials operating abroad in relation to Canadian citizens should be avoided. Flexibility was necessary for the evolution of the law of the Constitution (paras. 181-92).

The following is the text of the judgments delivered in the Court:

LeBel J

I. *Introduction*

A. *Overview*

1. At issue in this appeal is whether the Canadian Charter of Rights and Freedoms applies to extraterritorial searches and seizures by Canadian police officers. The appellant, Lawrence Richard Hape, is a Canadian businessman. He was convicted of two counts of money laundering contrary to s 9 of the Controlled Drugs and Substances Act, SC 1996, c 19. At his trial, the Crown adduced documentary evidence that the police had gathered from the records of the appellant's investment company while searching its premises in the Turks and Caicos Islands. The appellant sought to have that evidence excluded, pursuant to s 24(2) of the Charter, on the basis that the Charter applies to the actions of the Canadian police officers who conducted the searches and seizures and that the evidence was obtained in violation of his right under s 8 of the Charter to be secure against unreasonable search and seizure. For the reasons that follow, I would affirm the convictions and dismiss the appeal.

B. *Background*

2. In the spring of 1996, the RCMP commenced an investigation of the appellant for suspected money laundering activities. Sergeant Nicholson, an undercover operative, contacted the appellant in October 1996 posing as someone interested in laundering proceeds of narcotics trafficking. On February 2, 1998, Sergeant Nicholson provided C $252,000 of "sting money" to the appellant on the understanding

that the funds would be laundered through the appellant's investment company, the British West Indies Trust Company ("BWIT"), located in the Turks and Caicos Islands, and transferred to an account in the Netherlands. Unbeknownst to the appellant, the RCMP had set up the account. Sergeant Nicholson gave the appellant a further US $80,000 on November 11, 1998, instructing him to send the funds to the same account in the Netherlands. The RCMP hoped to obtain documentation confirming the transfers and determine whether the BWIT was involved in other money laundering activities.

3. RCMP officers sought permission to conduct parts of their investigation in Turks and Caicos. Detective Superintendent Lessemun of the Turks and Caicos Police Force was in charge of criminal investigations on the Islands. In November 1997, he met with the two Canadian officers in charge of the RCMP's investigation, Detective Sergeant Boyle and Corporal Flynn. He agreed to allow the RCMP to continue the investigation on Turks and Caicos territory, but warned the officers that he would be in charge and that the RCMP would be working under his authority. Because the appellant was well known on the Islands and Detective Superintendent Lessemun was concerned that he could not trust all Turks and Caicos police officers, the Canadian officers dealt exclusively with him while planning and preparing their operations.

4. The investigators planned a covert entry into the BWIT's office for March 1998. RCMP technical experts assisted with the planning, which began in Canada using technical information provided by Detective Superintendent Lessemun. The experts traveled to the Turks and Caicos Islands in February 1998 to obtain information about the office's door locks and burglar alarm systems.

5. Late in the nights of February 7 and 8, 1998, the RCMP officers and Detective Superintendent Lessemun surreptitiously entered the BWIT's premises. The technical experts examined the office's locks and alarm systems from outside the building. They recorded what they observed, using a video camera. Throughout this perimeter search, Detective Superintendent Lessemun was with the RCMP investigators as a lookout.

6. During the day on February 9, 1998, two RCMP technical experts entered the reception area of the BWIT's office to observe what they could of the interior locks and alarm system. They entered the office under a ruse and spent a few minutes speaking with the receptionist.

7. There were no warrants authorizing the RCMP to enter the BWIT's premises in February 1998. The RCMP investigators were aware of this, but they testified that they had relied on Detective

Superintendent Lessemun's expertise and advice regarding the legalities of investigations conducted on the Islands.

8. After the RCMP technical experts returned to Canada, they received further technical information from Detective Superintendent Lessemun to assist with the planning of the March 1998 covert entry. A briefing was held in the Bahamas on March 11, 1998, in preparation for the covert search. Present at the meeting were seven RCMP officers involved in the investigation and three American police officers. No Turks and Caicos officers were in attendance.

9. The investigators covertly entered the BWIT's office twice on March 14, 1998, once in the early hours of the morning and once shortly before midnight. The RCMP technical experts opened the locked doors of the office to enable the investigators to enter it. Detective Superintendent Lessemun entered the office with what the RCMP officers understood to be a warrant. He then took up a position outside the building to provide security around the perimeter and stop any Turks and Caicos police officers who might come by from jeopardizing the operation. Inside the office, the RCMP investigators downloaded information contained in the company's computer systems onto portable hard drives and electronically scanned documents from numerous client files, as well as company records and banking documents.

10. The RCMP officers testified at trial that they had understood separate warrants to be in place for each of the two covert entries of March 14, 1998. Officer Boyle said he saw a warrant for the first entry. Sergeant McDonagh, one of the technical experts, stated that after the first entry, but before the second, Detective Superintendent Lessemun had shown him a document that Sergeant McDonagh understood to be the warrant for the first entry. Sergeant McDonagh noted down the document's terms. Both Officer Boyle and Sergeant McDonagh understood from Detective Superintendent Lessemun that a warrant had been obtained for the second entry, but neither had any notes on this point or remembered having seen it. No warrants were introduced into evidence at trial. The Crown sought to introduce copies of two Turks and Caicos warrants, one dated March 13 and the other March 14, 1998. The purported warrants, issued to Robert Conway Lessemun, authorized entry into the BWIT's office to search for computer and office records linking Richard Hape to the laundering of proceeds of drug trafficking. The copies of the warrants had not been authenticated, and counsel for the appellant objected to their admission at trial.

11. RCMP officers returned to the Turks and Caicos Islands in February 1999. Beginning on February 16 and continuing over the

next three days, six RCMP officers, along with Detective Superintendent Lessemun and three other Turks and Caicos police officers, entered the BWIT's office and seized over one hundred banker's boxes of records. Officer Boyle testified that he had read a document he understood to be a warrant authorizing the entry and seizure, and had passed it to the other officers to read. Again, no warrant was entered into evidence at trial.

12. When the search was complete, the RCMP officers began loading the seized records onto their airplane with the intention of bringing them back to Canada. Detective Superintendent Lessemun informed the officers that they could not remove the records from the Islands. The boxes were unloaded. At trial, there was some suggestion that a Turks and Caicos court order had prevented the officers from removing the evidence from the jurisdiction, but no such order was admitted as evidence.

13. The RCMP returned to the Turks and Caicos Islands in March and October 1999. In the presence of Turks and Caicos police officers, the RCMP officers scanned thousands of the seized documents in order to bring electronic copies of them back to Canada. Ultimately, a number of the documents seized during the search became exhibits at the appellant's trial.

14. Money laundering charges were laid for the two transactions involving the funds Sergeant Nicholson had provided to the appellant. The appellant was also charged, along with a co-accused, Ross Beatty, with conspiring to launder funds. A lengthy and complex trial took place before Juriansz J (as he then was) of the Ontario Superior Court of Justice, sitting without a jury. Before the trial started, the appellant brought a Charter application to exclude the documentary evidence obtained from the BWIT's office on the basis of a violation of the s 8 guarantee against unreasonable search and seizure. The application was denied and the documents were admitted into evidence.

C. *Judicial history*

(1) *Ontario Superior Court of Justice*

15. The appellant called evidence on the s 8 application. The Crown, taking the position that the Charter does not apply to searches and seizures conducted outside Canada and that the appellant had not established that he had standing to bring the application, sought a ruling on these two issues in advance of its decision on introducing evidence. Juriansz J ruled on this application on January 17, 2002 ([2002] OJ No 3714 (QL)).

16. The application judge considered three decisions of this Court on the extraterritorial application of the Charter: *R* v. *Harrer*, [1995] 3 SCR. 562, *R* v. *Terry*, [1996] 2 SCR 207, and *R* v. *Cook*, [1998] 2 SCR 597. He noted that all those cases concerned the application of the s 10(*b*) right to counsel and that the question of the potential extraterritorial application of s 8 might raise different issues. Relying on the majority decision in *Cook*, the application judge held that his task was to determine whether applying the Charter to the activities of the RCMP officers in Turks and Caicos would "interfere with the sovereign authority of the foreign state and thereby generate an objectionable extra-territorial effect" (para. 20).

17. In his argument before the application judge, the appellant resisted the characterization of the RCMP's actions in the instant case as part of a "cooperative investigation", within the meaning of *Terry*, with Turks and Caicos authorities, because the searches and seizures were carried out by the RCMP officers with little or no involvement of the Turks and Caicos police. The application judge rejected the argument that a "cooperative investigation" must involve relatively equal contributions from the participants (para. 24).

18. Juriansz J made several key findings of fact that were relevant to his Charter ruling. He noted that Detective Superintendent Lessemun, who was with the Canadian police at all times, had played a role in the investigation by acting as a lookout, providing information, and obtaining warrants. The Turks and Caicos contributed police authority. The RCMP was required to seek and receive permission from Turks and Caicos authorities to conduct the investigation in that jurisdiction. The RCMP officers were operating under the authority of Detective Superintendent Lessemun. The fact that they were not permitted to remove the seized physical records from Turks and Caicos was a significant factor in the application judge's conclusion that they were subject to Turks and Caicos authority. The application judge found that all the RCMP's actions on the Turks and Caicos Islands were part of a "cooperative investigation" (para. 26).

19. As the next step in his analysis, Juriansz J considered whether the application of the Charter to the "cooperative investigation" would result in an objectionable extraterritorial effect. The application judge found that the propriety and legality of the entries into the BWIT's office were governed by Turks and Caicos criminal law and procedure and the supervisory authority of the Turks and Caicos courts. In light of that fact, he concluded that there was a potential conflict between the concurrent exercise of jurisdiction by Canada on the basis of nationality and by Turks and Caicos on the basis of territoriality. Juriansz J held,

as a result, that the Charter did not apply. He therefore dismissed the application without discussing whether the appellant had standing to bring the Charter application or whether the searches and seizures were conducted in accordance with the requirements of s 8.

20. The appellant had also applied under ss 7 and 24(1) of the Charter for a stay of proceedings on the basis that the police conduct had contravened fundamental notions of justice and that the ensuing trial would undermine the integrity of the justice system. In the alternative, the appellant requested an order excluding from evidence 26 documents seized from the BWIT. In his ruling on this application dated January 18, 2002, Juriansz J relied on the findings of fact he had made on the s 8 application. He noted that the RCMP officers had believed there were warrants for the entries that took place in March 1998 and February 1999 and had believed their actions to be lawful under Turks and Caicos law. No evidence to the contrary had been called. The burden of proving that the operations of the Canadian officers had violated Turks and Caicos law rested on the appellant. In refusing to grant the stay, Juriansz J gave the following explanation:

Considering that the applicant in this case has not established that the police conduct infringed a Charter right or was otherwise unlawful, and considering the police conduct as a whole, I have concluded that this is not one of those clearest of cases in which a stay ought to be granted.

Relying on *Harrer* and *Terry*, Juriansz J stated that the overriding consideration was whether the admission of the evidence would result in an unfair trial. He reasoned that since the documents constituted real, non-conscriptive evidence, their reliability as evidence was not affected by the manner in which they were obtained. As the admission of the evidence would not therefore render the trial unfair, he refused to grant the exclusionary order.

21. On June 10, 2002, Juriansz J found the appellant guilty beyond a reasonable doubt on both counts of money laundering ([2002] OJ No 5044 (QL)). The appellant was acquitted of the charge of conspiracy to launder funds.

(2) *Ontario Court of Appeal*

22. The appellant appealed his conviction to the Court of Appeal for Ontario on numerous grounds, one of which was that Juriansz J had erred in his rulings on ss 7 and 8 of the Charter. The appeal from the ruling on s 7 was not pursued at the oral hearing before the Court of Appeal, and the issue of trial fairness is not before this Court. The appellant also contested his sentence of 30 months' imprisonment. The

Crown cross-appealed on the trial judge's refusal to make a forfeiture order.

23. The Court of Appeal dismissed the appeal: (2005), 201 OAC 126. It held that the trial judge had made a finding of fact that the investigation was under the control of the Turks and Caicos authorities and that his finding was supported by the evidence. Referring to the decisions in *Terry* and *Cook*, the court concluded that the trial judge had correctly applied the law to his findings of fact. The Crown's cross-appeal was also dismissed. The appellant obtained leave to appeal from that judgment.

II. *Analysis*

A. *Issues*

24. The sole issue in this appeal is whether s 8 of the Charter applies to searches and seizures conducted by RCMP officers outside Canada. This issue requires the Court to consider the question of the extraterritorial application of the Charter. This in turn requires the Court to consider the more general question of the relationship between Canadian criminal and constitutional law, on the one hand, and public international law, on the other. In addition, although the issue is not before this Court, I feel that it will be helpful to comment on the use of ss 7 and 11(*d*) of the Charter to exclude evidence gathered outside Canada.

B. *Positions of the parties*

(1) *The appellant*

25. The appellant argues that the Charter applies to the actions of the RCMP officers in the course of their searches and seizures at the BWIT's office, notwithstanding that those actions took place outside Canada. He submits that Canadian authorities are subject to the Charter even when operating outside the territorial boundaries of Canada and that it can be seen from the evidence in the case at bar that the searches and seizures were the product of and were integral to an investigation that was completely planned by the RCMP. In the appellant's submission, Detective Superintendent Lessemun merely served as a host for the Canadian officials. He made no decisions, even if he provided ultimate control and legal authority. The actual searches and seizures were conducted by the RCMP, and they are the actions that are subject to Charter scrutiny. Given the almost non-existent role of the Turks

and Caicos authorities, the application of the Charter does not in any way interfere with that state's sovereign authority. The appellant argues that the courts below erred in concluding, on the basis of a finding that the RCMP's actions constituted a "cooperative investigation", that the Charter did not apply.

26. At the hearing, counsel for the appellant argued that, in *Cook*, this Court had specified two situations in which the application of the Charter would have an objectionable extraterritorial effect. The first would be if the Charter were applied to foreign officers, and the second would be if it were applied to foreign criminal proceedings. Aside from those two circumstances, extraterritorial application of the Charter would not, in the appellant's opinion, interfere with the sovereign authority of a foreign state. If it were physically impracticable to comply with the Charter, then Canadian officials acting abroad could either request that foreign officials undertake the activities that are inconsistent with the Charter or carry out the activities themselves and try to establish that the evidence obtained should not be excluded under s 24(2) of the Charter.

(2) *The Crown*

27. The Crown responds that the Charter does not apply because the searches and seizures in this case were conducted under the authority of the Turks and Caicos police. To impose Canada's Charter standards on the actions of the RCMP officers while they were operating in Turks and Caicos would produce an objectionable extraterritorial effect. The trial judge made a factual finding that the investigation in Turks and Caicos was under the control of the Turks and Caicos police force. The appellant has not demonstrated that this finding resulted from a palpable and overriding error; he is asking this Court to reweigh the evidence and substitute its view for that of the trial judge.

28. In the Crown's view, the fact that Canadian police officers participated in an international investigation does not, on its own, mean that the Charter is engaged. The Charter does not apply to conduct outside Canada unless the impugned action falls within the exception established in *Cook*, namely, where no conflict arises from the concurrent exercise of jurisdiction by Canada on the basis of nationality and by a foreign state on the basis of territoriality. The authority for all the RCMP's actions in Turks and Caicos was derived from Turks and Caicos law. It is clear from the evidence that the RCMP exercised no control over the Turks and Caicos police. Further, the appellant has not established that the RCMP's conduct violated Turks and Caicos law.

29. The Crown adds that it would be untenable to require that searches carried out in Turks and Caicos in accordance with the laws of that jurisdiction be consistent with the Charter or to subsequently scrutinize such searches for consistency with the Charter. In *Cook*, the Charter was applied on facts very different from those in the case at bar. In that case, it would have been easy for the Canadian police officers, in interviewing the accused, to comply with Charter standards in a way that did not interfere with the host state's procedures. Here, to apply the Charter to the investigation in Turks and Caicos would of necessity compel compliance by the foreign authorities, thus impinging on their sovereign authority.

30. According to the Crown, to hold that s 8 of the Charter does not apply to foreign searches is not to suggest that there are no controls over the actions of Canadian law enforcement officers involved in investigations in other countries. Where the admission of evidence would lead to an unfair trial, a court has the discretion to exclude evidence under s 7 of the Charter.

(3) *The intervener*

31. The Attorney General of Ontario intervened in this appeal. His submissions focused on the complexities and difficulties of applying s 8 of the Charter to searches and seizures outside Canada. The intervener emphasized the need to consider the nature and scope of s 8 rights in the host jurisdiction. He also drew the Court's attention to the need for international cooperation in criminal investigations as a practical matter, and to the importance of not hampering such investigations unduly by imposing Canadian standards on foreign jurisdictions.

C. *Scope of the Charter*

32. This case centres around the proper scope of application of the Charter, and in particular its territorial reach and limits. The analysis must begin with the wording of s 32(1) of the Charter, which reads as follows:

32. (1) This Charter applies

(a) to the Parliament and government of Canada in respect of all matters within the authority of Parliament including all matters relating to the Yukon Territory and Northwest Territories; and
(b) to the legislature and government of each province in respect of all matters within the authority of the legislature of each province.

Pursuant to s 32(1), the Charter serves to limit the legislative and executive powers of Canada and each of the provinces. The problem involved in establishing the Charter's scope has two aspects. First, s 32(1) determines who is bound by the Charter: Parliament and the federal government, and the provincial legislatures and governments, bear the burden of complying with the requirements of the Charter. Second, s 32(1) specifies what powers, functions or activities of those bodies and their agents are subject to the Charter: constitutional limitations are imposed "in respect of all matters within the authority of" Parliament or the provincial legislatures. Any action by the relevant body or its agents in relation to any matter within its legislative authority must be consistent with the Charter.

33. Section 32 does not expressly impose any territorial limits on the application of the Charter. By virtue of state sovereignty, it was open to the framers to establish the jurisdictional scope of the Charter. Had they done so, the courts of this country would have had to give effect to a clear expression of that scope. However, the framers chose to make no such statement. Consequently, as with the substantive provisions of the Charter, it falls upon the courts to interpret the jurisdictional reach and limits of the Charter. Where the question of application involves issues of extraterritoriality, and thereby necessarily implicates interstate relations, the tools that assist in the interpretation exercise include Canada's obligations under international law and the principle of the comity of nations. As I will explain, the issue of applying the Charter to activities that take place abroad implicates the extraterritorial enforcement of Canadian law. The principles of state jurisdiction are carefully spelled out under international law and must guide the inquiry in this appeal.

D. *Relationship between domestic law and international law*

34. In order to understand how international law assists in the interpretation of s 32(1), it is necessary to consider the relationship between Canadian domestic law and international law, as well as the principles of international law pertaining to territorial sovereignty, non-intervention and extraterritorial assertions of jurisdiction.

(1) *Relationship between customary international law and the common law*

35. As I will explain, certain fundamental rules of customary international law govern what actions a state may legitimately take outside its territory. Those rules are important interpretive aids for determining

the jurisdictional scope of s 32(1) of the Charter. The use of customary international law to assist in the interpretation of the Charter requires an examination of the Canadian approach to the domestic reception of international law.

36. The English tradition follows an adoptionist approach to the reception of customary international law. Prohibitive rules of international custom may be incorporated directly into domestic law through the common law, without the need for legislative action. According to the doctrine of adoption, the courts may adopt rules of customary international law as common law rules in order to base their decisions upon them, provided there is no valid legislation that clearly conflicts with the customary rule: I. Brownlie, *Principles of Public International Law* (6th edn 2003), at p. 41. Although it has long been recognized in English common law, the doctrine received its strongest endorsement in the landmark case of *Trendtex Trading Corp.* v. *Central Bank of Nigeria*, [1977] 1 QB 529 (CA). Lord Denning considered both the doctrine of adoption and the doctrine of transformation, according to which international law rules must be implemented by Parliament before they can be applied by domestic courts. In his opinion, the doctrine of adoption represents the correct approach in English law. Rules of international law are incorporated automatically, as they evolve, unless they conflict with legislation. He wrote, at p. 554:

It is certain that international law does change. I would use of international law the words which Galileo used of the earth: "But it does move." International law does change: and the courts have applied the changes without the aid of any Act of Parliament...

...Seeing that the rules of international law have changed—and do change—and that the courts have given effect to the changes without any Act of Parliament, it follows to my mind inexorably that the rules of international law, as existing from time to time, do form part of our English law. It follows, too, that a decision of this court—as to what was the ruling of international law 50 or 60 years ago—is not binding on this court today. International law knows no rule of stare decisis. If this court today is satisfied that the rule of international law on a subject has changed from what it was 50 or 60 years ago, it can give effect to that change—and apply the change in our English law—without waiting for the House of Lords to do it.

37. In Canada, this Court has implicitly or explicitly applied the doctrine of adoption in several cases. In *The Ship "North"* v. *The King* (1906), 37 SCR 385, at p. 394, Davies J wrote: "[T]he Admiralty Court when exercising its jurisdiction is bound to take notice of the law of nations... The right of hot pursuit... being part of the law of nations was properly judicially taken notice of and acted upon by the

learned judge in this prosecution." In *Reference as to Whether Members of the Military or Naval Forces of the United States of America are Exempt from Criminal Proceedings in Canadian Criminal Courts*, [1943] SCR 483, at p. 502, Kerwin J stated that the exemptions from territorial jurisdiction based on sovereign immunity "are grounded on reason and are recognized by civilized countries as being rules of international law which will be followed in the absence of any domestic law to the contrary". See also *Reference as to Powers to Levy Rates on Foreign Legations and High Commissioners' Residences*, [1943] SCR 208 ("*Re Foreign Legations*"). In *Saint John (Municipality of)* v. *Fraser-Brace Overseas Corp.*, [1958] SCR 263, Rand J accepted the doctrine of adoption, applying international law principles to exempt foreign sovereigns and their property from municipal taxation in Canada. He wrote, at pp. 268-9:

If in 1767 Lord Mansfield, as in *Heathfield* v. *Chilton* [(1767), 4 Burr. 2015, 98 ER 50], could say, "The law of nations will be carried as far in England, as any where", in this country, in the 20th century, in the presence of the United Nations and the multiplicity of impacts with which technical developments have entwined the entire globe, we cannot say any thing less.

The Court of Appeal for Ontario recently cited the doctrine of adoption in *Bouzari* v. *Islamic Republic of Iran* (2004), 71 OR (3d) 675, stating at para. 65 that "customary rules of international law are directly incorporated into Canadian domestic law unless explicitly ousted by contrary legislation" (leave to appeal refused, [2005] 1 SCR vi). See also *Mack* v. *Canada (Attorney General)* (2002), 60 OR (3d) 737 (CA), at para. 32 (leave to appeal refused, [2003] 1 SCR xiii).

38. In other decisions, however, the Court has not applied or discussed the doctrine of adoption of customary international law when it had the opportunity to do so: see, for example, *Gouvernement de la République démocratique du Congo* v. *Venne*, [1971] SCR 997; *Reference re Newfoundland Continental Shelf*, [1984] 1 SCR 86; *Reference re Secession of Quebec*, [1998] 2 SCR 217; *Suresh* v. *Canada (Minister of Citizenship and Immigration)*, [2002] 1 SCR 3, 2002 SCC 1.

39. Despite the Court's silence in some recent cases, the doctrine of adoption has never been rejected in Canada. Indeed, there is a long line of cases in which the Court has either formally accepted it or at least applied it. In my view, following the common law tradition, it appears that the doctrine of adoption operates in Canada such that prohibitive rules of customary international law should be incorporated into domestic law in the absence of conflicting legislation. The automatic incorporation of such rules is justified on the basis that international custom, as the

law of nations, is also the law of Canada unless, in a valid exercise of its sovereignty, Canada declares that its law is to the contrary. Parliamentary sovereignty dictates that a legislature may violate international law, but that it must do so expressly. Absent an express derogation, the courts may look to prohibitive rules of customary international law to aid in the interpretation of Canadian law and the development of the common law.

(2) *Principle of respect for sovereignty of foreign states as a part of customary international law and of Canadian common law*

40. One of the key customary principles of international law, and one that is central to the legitimacy of claims to extraterritorial jurisdiction, is respect for the sovereignty of foreign states. That respect is dictated by the maxim, lying at the heart of the international legal structure, that all states are sovereign and equal. Article 2(1) of the Charter of the United Nations, Can. TS 1945 No 7, recognizes as one of that organization's principles the "sovereign equality of all its Members". The importance and centrality of the principle of sovereign equality was reaffirmed by the General Assembly in the 1970 Declaration on Principles of International Law concerning Friendly Relations and Co-operation among States in accordance with the Charter of the United Nations, GA Res. 2625 (XXV), 24 October 1970, which expanded the scope of application of the principle to include non-UN member states. A renowned international law jurist, Antonio Cassese, writes that of the various principles recognized in the UN Charter and the 1970 Declaration

this is unquestionably the only one on which there is unqualified agreement and which has the support of all groups of States, regardless of ideologies, political leanings, and circumstances. It is safe to conclude that sovereign equality constitutes the linchpin of the whole body of international legal standards, the fundamental premise on which all international relations rest.

See A. Cassese, *International Law* (2nd edn 2005), at p. 48.

41. The principle of sovereign equality comprises two distinct but complementary concepts: sovereignty and equality. "Sovereignty" refers to the various powers, rights and duties that accompany statehood under international law. Jurisdiction—the power to exercise authority over persons, conduct and events—is one aspect of state sovereignty. Although the two are not coterminous, jurisdiction may be seen as the quintessential feature of sovereignty. Other powers and rights that fall under the umbrella of sovereignty include the power to use and dispose of the state's territory, the right to state immunity from the jurisdiction

of foreign courts and the right to diplomatic immunity. In his individual opinion in *Customs Regime between Germany and Austria* (1931), PCIJ Ser. A/B, No 41, at p. 57, Judge Anzilotti defined sovereignty as follows: "Independence... is really no more than the normal condition of States according to international law; it may also be described as *sovereignty* (*suprema potestas*), or *external sovereignty*, by which is meant that the State has over it no other authority than that of international law" (emphasis in original).

42. Sovereignty also has an internal dimension, which can be defined as "the power of each state freely and autonomously to determine its tasks, to organize itself and to exercise within its territory a 'monopoly of legitimate physical coercion'": L. Wildhaber, "Sovereignty and International Law", in R. St J. Macdonald and D. M. Johnston, eds., *The Structure and Process of International Law: Essays in Legal Philosophy, Doctrine and Theory* (1983), 425, at p. 436.

43. While sovereignty is not absolute, the only limits on state sovereignty are those to which the state consents or that flow from customary or conventional international law. Some such limits have arisen from recent developments in international humanitarian law, international human rights law and international criminal law relating, in particular, to crimes against humanity (R. Jennings and A. Watts, eds., *Oppenheim's International Law* (9th edn 1996), vol. I, at p. 125; K. Kittichaisaree, *International Criminal Law* (2001), at pp. 6 and 56; H. M. Kindred and P. M. Saunders, *International Law, Chiefly as Interpreted and Applied in Canada* (7th edn 2006), at p. 836; Cassese, at p. 59). Nevertheless, despite the rise of competing values in international law, the sovereignty principle remains one of the organizing principles of the relationships between independent states.

44. Equality is a legal doctrine according to which all states are, in principle, equal members of the international community: Cassese, at p. 52. It is both a necessary consequence and a counterpart of the principle of sovereignty. If all states were not regarded as equal, economically and politically weaker states might be impeded from exercising their rights of sovereignty. One commentator suggests the following rationales for the affirmation of the equality of states in their mutual relations: "to forestall factual inequities from leading to injustice, to ensure that one state should not be disadvantaged in relation to another state, and to preclude the possibility of powerful states dictating their will to weaker nations" (V. Pechota, "Equality: Political Justice in an Unequal World", in Macdonald and Johnston, 453, at p. 454). Although all states are not in fact equal in all respects, equality is, as a matter of principle, an axiom of the modern international legal system.

45. In order to preserve sovereignty and equality, the rights and powers of all states carry correlative duties, at the apex of which sits the principle of non-intervention. Each state's exercise of sovereignty within its territory is dependent on the right to be free from intrusion by other states in its affairs and the duty of every other state to refrain from interference. This principle of non-intervention is inseparable from the concept of sovereign equality and from the right of each state to operate in its territory with no restrictions other than those existing under international law. (For a discussion of these principles, see the comments of Arbitrator Huber in the *Island of Palmas Case (Netherlands* v. *United States)* (1928), 2 RIAA 829, at pp. 838-9.)

46. Sovereign equality remains a cornerstone of the international legal system. Its foundational principles—including non-intervention and respect for the territorial sovereignty of foreign states—cannot be regarded as anything less than firmly established rules of customary international law, as the International Court of Justice held when it recognized non-intervention as a customary principle in the *Case concerning Military and Paramilitary Activities In and Against Nicaragua (Nicaragua* v. *United States of America)*, [1986] ICJ Rep. 14, at p. 106. As the International Court of Justice noted on that occasion, the status of these principles as international customs is supported by both state practice and *opinio juris*, the two necessary elements of customary international law. Every principle of customary international law is binding on all states unless superseded by another custom or by a rule set out in an international treaty. As a result, the principles of non-intervention and territorial sovereignty may be adopted into the common law of Canada in the absence of conflicting legislation. These principles must also be drawn upon in determining the scope of extraterritorial application of the Charter.

(3) *Comity as an interpretive principle*

47. Related to the principle of sovereign equality is the concept of comity of nations. Comity refers to informal acts performed and rules observed by states in their mutual relations out of politeness, convenience and goodwill, rather than strict legal obligation: *Oppenheim's International Law*, at pp. 50-1. When cited by the courts, comity is more a principle of interpretation than a rule of law, because it does not arise from formal obligations. Speaking in the private international law context in *Morguard Investments Ltd* v. *De Savoye*, [1990] 3 SCR 1077, at p. 1095, La Forest J defined comity as "the deference and respect due by other states to the actions of a state legitimately taken within its territory". In *Re Foreign Legations*, both Duff CJ and Hudson J referred

in their reasons to *The Parlement Belge* (1880), 5 PD 197 (CA), in which Brett LJ commented, at pp. 214-15, that the principle of international comity "induces every sovereign state to respect the independence and dignity of every other sovereign state".

48. Where our laws—statutory and constitutional—could have an impact on the sovereignty of other states, the principle of comity will bear on their interpretation. One example is in the area of extradition. As this Court noted in *Kindler* v. *Canada (Minister of Justice)*, [1991] 2 SCR 779, at p. 844: "Extradition procedure, unlike the criminal procedure, is founded on the concepts of reciprocity, comity and respect for differences in other jurisdictions." In *United States of America* v. *Dynar*, [1997] 2 SCR 462, another extradition case, Cory and Iacobucci JJ, writing for the majority, stated, at para. 123:

> There is no doubt that the Charter applies to extradition proceedings. Yet s 32 of the Charter provides that it is applicable only to Canadian state actors. Pursuant to principles of international comity as well, the Charter generally cannot apply extraterritorially ...

In stating that the Charter cannot apply extraterritorially, Cory and Iacobucci JJ were speaking specifically of applying it to foreign authorities.

49. In other contexts as well, this Court has noted the importance of comity as a tool in the interpretation of Canadian law in situations where it affects other sovereign states. In *Zingre* v. *The Queen*, [1981] 2 SCR 392, Dickson J (as he then was), writing for the Court, stated, at pp. 400-1:

> As that great jurist, US Chief Justice Marshall, observed in *The Schooner Exchange* v. *M'Faddon & Others* [(1812), 7 Cranch's Reports 116], at pp. 136-7, the jurisdiction of a nation within its own territory is necessarily exclusive and absolute, susceptible of no limitation not imposed by itself, but common interest impels sovereigns to mutual intercourse and an interchange of good offices with each other.
>
> It is upon this comity of nations that international legal assistance rests.

Further, McLachlin J (as she then was) noted in *Terry*, at para. 16, that this Court "has repeatedly affirmed the territorial limitations imposed on Canadian law by the principles of state sovereignty and international comity". See also *Singh* v. *Minister of Employment and Immigration*, [1985] 1 SCR 177; *Libman* v. *The Queen*, [1985] 2 SCR 178, at p. 183.

50. The nature and limitations of comity need to be clearly understood. International law is a positive legal order, whereas comity, which is of the nature of a principle of interpretation, is based on a desire for

states to act courteously towards one another. Nonetheless, many rules of international law promote mutual respect and, conversely, courtesy among states requires that certain legal rules be followed. In this way, "courtesy and international law lend reciprocal support to one another": M. Akehurst, "Jurisdiction in International Law" (1972-3), 46 *Brit. YB Int'l L.* 145, at p. 215. The principle of comity reinforces sovereign equality and contributes to the functioning of the international legal system. Acts of comity are justified on the basis that they facilitate interstate relations and global cooperation; however, comity ceases to be appropriate where it would undermine peaceable interstate relations and the international order.

51. The principle of comity does not offer a rationale for condoning another state's breach of international law. Indeed, the need to uphold international law may trump the principle of comity (see for example the English Court of Appeal's decision in *Abbasi v. Secretary of State for Foreign and Commonwealth Affairs*, [2002] EWJ No 4947 (QL), [2002] EWCA Civ. 1598, in respect of a British national captured by US forces in Afghanistan who was transferred to Guantanamo Bay and detained for several months without access to a lawyer or a court).

52. In an era characterized by transnational criminal activity and by the ease and speed with which people and goods now cross borders, the principle of comity encourages states to cooperate with one another in the investigation of transborder crimes even where no treaty legally compels them to do so. At the same time, states seeking assistance must approach such requests with comity and respect for sovereignty. Mutuality of legal assistance stands on these two pillars. Comity means that when one state looks to another for help in criminal matters, it must respect the way in which the other state chooses to provide the assistance within its borders. That deference ends where clear violations of international law and fundamental human rights begin. If no such violations are in issue, courts in Canada should interpret Canadian law, and approach assertions of foreign law, in a manner respectful of the spirit of international cooperation and the comity of nations.

(4) *Conformity with international law as an interpretive principle of domestic law*

53. One final general principle bears on the resolution of the legal issues in this appeal. It is a well-established principle of statutory interpretation that legislation will be presumed to conform to international law. The presumption of conformity is based on the rule of judicial policy that, as a matter of law, courts will strive to avoid constructions of domestic law pursuant to which the state would be in violation of its

international obligations, unless the wording of the statute clearly compels that result. R. Sullivan, *Sullivan and Driedger on the Construction of Statutes* (4th edn 2002), at p. 422, explains that the presumption has two aspects. First, the legislature is presumed to act in compliance with Canada's obligations as a signatory of international treaties and as a member of the international community. In deciding between possible interpretations, courts will avoid a construction that would place Canada in breach of those obligations. The second aspect is that the legislature is presumed to comply with the values and principles of customary and conventional international law. Those values and principles form part of the context in which statutes are enacted, and courts will therefore prefer a construction that reflects them. The presumption is rebuttable, however. Parliamentary sovereignty requires courts to give effect to a statute that demonstrates an unequivocal legislative intent to default on an international obligation. See also P.-A. Côté, *The Interpretation of Legislation in Canada* (3rd edn 2000), at pp. 367-8.

54. The presumption of conformity has been accepted and applied by this Court on numerous occasions. In *Daniels* v. *White*, [1968] SCR 517, at p. 541, Pigeon J stated:

[T]his is a case for the application of the rule of construction that *Parliament is not presumed to legislate in breach of a treaty or in any manner inconsistent with the comity of nations and the established rules of international law* ... [I]f a statute is unambiguous, its provisions must be followed even if they are contrary to international law ... [Emphasis added.]

See also *Zingre*, at pp. 409-10; *Ordon Estate* v. *Grail*, [1998] 3 SCR 437, at para. 137; *Schreiber* v. *Canada (Attorney General)*, [2002] 3 SCR 269, 2002 SCC 62, at para. 50. The presumption applies equally to customary international law and treaty obligations.

55. This Court has also looked to international law to assist it in interpreting the Charter. Whenever possible, it has sought to ensure consistency between its interpretation of the Charter, on the one hand, and Canada's international obligations and the relevant principles of international law, on the other . For example, in *Slaight Communications Inc.* v. *Davidson*, [1989] 1 SCR 1038, at p. 1056, Dickson CJ, writing for the majority, quoted the following passage from his dissenting reasons in *Reference re Public Service Employee Relations Act (Alta.)*, [1987] 1 SCR 313, at p. 349:

The content of Canada's international human rights obligations is, in my view, an important indicia of the meaning of the "full benefit of the Charter's protection". I believe that the Charter should generally be presumed to provide protection at least as great as that afforded by similar provisions in international human rights documents which Canada has ratified.

Dickson CJ then stated that Canada's international obligations should also inform the interpretation of pressing and substantial objectives under s 1 of the Charter. (See also *Re BC Motor Vehicle Act*, [1985] 2 SCR 486, at p. 503; *Suresh*; *United States* v. *Burns*, [2001] 1 SCR 283, 2001 SCC 7; *Canadian Foundation for Children, Youth and the Law* v. *Canada (Attorney General)*, [2004] 1 SCR 76, 2004 SCC 4.)

56. In interpreting the scope of application of the Charter, the courts should seek to ensure compliance with Canada's binding obligations under international law where the express words are capable of supporting such a construction. In light of the foregoing principles—the direct application of international custom, territorial sovereignty and non-intervention as customary rules, and comity and the presumption of conformity as tools of construction—I will now turn to the point that is directly in issue in this appeal: the interpretation of s 32 of the Charter and the application of the Charter to searches and seizures outside Canada.

E. *Constitutional authority of Parliament to make laws with extraterritorial effects*

(1) *International law principles of jurisdiction*

57. In order to resolve the question of extraterritorial application of the Charter, the international law principles of jurisdiction and Parliament's authority to make laws with extraterritorial effects must be examined. As has already been mentioned, jurisdiction is distinct from, but integral to, the principle of state sovereignty. The principles relating to jurisdiction arise from sovereign equality and the corollary duty of non-intervention. Broadly speaking, jurisdiction refers to a state's power to exercise authority over individuals, conduct and events, and to discharge public functions that affect them: Cassese, at p. 49.

58. Jurisdiction takes various forms, and the distinctions between them are germane to the issue raised in this appeal. Prescriptive jurisdiction (also called legislative or substantive jurisdiction) is the power to make rules, issue commands or grant authorizations that are binding upon persons and entities. The legislature exercises prescriptive jurisdiction in enacting legislation. Enforcement jurisdiction is the power to use coercive means to ensure that rules are followed, commands are executed or entitlements are upheld. As stated by S. Coughlan et al. in "Global Reach, Local Grasp: Constructing Extraterritorial Jurisdiction

in the Age of Globalization" (2007), 6 *CJLT* 29, at p. 32, "*enforcement* or *executive* jurisdiction refers to the state's ability to act in such a manner as to give effect to its laws (including the ability of police or other government actors to investigate a matter, which might be referred to as *investigative jurisdiction*)" (emphasis in original). Adjudicative jurisdiction is the power of a state's courts to resolve disputes or interpret the law through decisions that carry binding force. See Cassese, at p. 49; Brownlie, at p. 297.

59. International law—and in particular the overarching customary principle of sovereign equality—sets the limits of state jurisdiction, while domestic law determines how and to what extent a state will assert its jurisdiction within those limits. Under international law, states may assert jurisdiction in its various forms on several recognized grounds. The primary basis for jurisdiction is territoriality: *Libman*, at p. 183. It is as a result of its territorial sovereignty that a state has plenary authority to exercise prescriptive, enforcement and adjudicative jurisdiction over matters arising and people residing within its borders, and this authority is limited only by the dictates of customary and conventional international law. The principle of territoriality extends to two related bases for jurisdiction, the objective territorial principle and the subjective territorial principle. According to the objective territorial principle, a state may claim jurisdiction over a criminal act that commences or occurs outside the state if it is completed, or if a constituent element takes place, within the state, thus connecting the event to the territory of the state through a sufficiently strong link: Brownlie, at p. 299. See also *Libman*, at pp. 212-13. Subjective territoriality refers to the exercise of jurisdiction over an act that occurs or has begun within a state's territory even though it has consequences in another state.

60. Territoriality is not the only legitimate basis for jurisdiction, however. In *The Case of the SS "Lotus"* (1927), PCIJ Ser. A, No 10, at p. 20, the Permanent Court of International Justice noted:

Though it is true that in all systems of law the principle of the territorial character of criminal law is fundamental, it is equally true that all or nearly all these systems of law extend their action to offences committed outside the territory of the State which adopts them, and they do so in ways which vary from State to State. The territoriality of criminal law, therefore, is not an absolute principle of international law and by no means coincides with territorial sovereignty.

Where a dispute is wholly contained within the territory of one state, jurisdiction is not an issue. However, disputes and events commonly have implications for more than one state, and competing claims for jurisdiction can arise on grounds other than territoriality, which are, of course, extraterritorial in nature. Of those bases for jurisdiction, the most common is the nationality principle. States may assert jurisdiction over acts occurring within the territory of a foreign state on the basis that their nationals are involved. For example, a state may seek to try and punish one of its nationals for a crime committed in another state. The nationality principle is not necessarily problematic as a justification for asserting prescriptive or adjudicative jurisdiction in order to attach domestic consequences to events that occurred abroad, but it does give rise to difficulties in respect of the extraterritorial exercise of enforcement jurisdiction. Under international law, a state may regulate and adjudicate regarding actions committed by its nationals in other countries, provided enforcement of the rules takes place when those nationals are within the state's own borders. When a state's nationals are physically located in the territory of another state, its authority over them is strictly limited. I will discuss this below.

61. There are other bases of extraterritorial jurisdiction that, although less widely recognized, are nonetheless cited from time to time as justifications for a state's assertion of jurisdiction. One example is the principle of universal jurisdiction, pursuant to which jurisdiction may be asserted over acts committed, in other countries, by foreigners against other foreigners. Assertions of universal jurisdiction are not based on any link of territoriality or nationality between the crime or the perpetrator and the state: L. Reydams, *Universal Jurisdiction: International and Municipal Legal Perspectives* (2003), at p. 5. For that reason, universal jurisdiction is confined to the most serious crimes and includes crimes under international law. Any state that obtains custody of accused persons may try and punish those who have committed crimes under international law: Brownlie, at p. 303.

62. The interplay between the various forms and bases of jurisdiction is central to the issue of whether an extraterritorial exercise of jurisdiction is permissible. At the outset, it must be borne in mind, first, that the exercise of jurisdiction by one state cannot infringe on the sovereignty of other states and, second, that states may have valid concurrent claims to jurisdiction. Even if a state can legally exercise extraterritorial jurisdiction, whether the exercise of such jurisdiction is proper and desirable is another question: Coughlan et al., at p. 31. Where two or more states have a legal claim to jurisdiction, comity dictates that a state ought to assume jurisdiction only if it has a real and substantial link to the event. As La Forest J noted in *Libman*, at p. 213, what constitutes a "real and substantial link" justifying jurisdiction may be "coterminous with the requirements of international comity".

63. In the classic example, Parliament might pass legislation making it a criminal offence for Canadian nationals to smoke in the streets of Paris, thereby exercising extraterritorial prescriptive jurisdiction on the basis of nationality. If France chooses to contest this, it may have a legitimate claim of interference with its territorial sovereignty, since Canada's link to smoking on the Champs-Élysées is less real and substantial than that of France. France's territorial jurisdiction collides with Canada's concurrent claim of nationality jurisdiction. The mere presence of the prohibition in the Criminal Code of Canada might be relatively benign from France's perspective. However, France's outrage might be greater if Canadian courts tried a Canadian national in Canada for violating the prohibition while on vacation in Paris. It would be greater still if Canadian police officers marched into Paris and began arresting Canadian smokers or if Canadian judges established a court in Paris to try offenders.

64. This example demonstrates the nuances of extraterritorial jurisdiction. It is not uncommon for states to pass legislation with extraterritorial effects or, in other words, to exercise extraterritorial prescriptive jurisdiction. This is usually done only where a real and substantial link with the state is evident. Similarly, comity is not necessarily offended where a state's courts assume jurisdiction over a dispute that occurred abroad (extraterritorial adjudicative jurisdiction), provided that the enforcement measures are carried out within the state's own territory. The most contentious claims for jurisdiction are those involving extraterritorial *enforcement* of a state's laws, even where they are being enforced only against the state's own nationals, but in another country. The fact that a state has exercised extraterritorial prescriptive jurisdiction by enacting legislation in respect of a foreign event is necessary, but not in itself sufficient, to justify the state's exercise of enforcement jurisdiction outside its borders: F. A. Mann, "The Doctrine of International Jurisdiction Revisited After Twenty Years", in W. M. Reisman, ed., *Jurisdiction in International Law* (1999), 139, at p. 154.

65. The Permanent Court of International Justice stated in the *Lotus* case, at pp. 18-19, that jurisdiction "cannot be exercised by a State outside its territory except by virtue of a permissive rule derived from international custom or from a convention". See also *Cook*, at para. 131. According to the decision in the *Lotus* case, extraterritorial jurisdiction is governed by international law rather than being at the absolute discretion of individual states. While extraterritorial jurisdiction—prescriptive, enforcement or adjudicative—exists under international law, it is subject to strict limits under international law that are based on sovereign equality, non-intervention and the territoriality

principle. According to the principle of non-intervention, states must refrain from exercising extraterritorial enforcement jurisdiction over matters in respect of which another state has, by virtue of territorial sovereignty, the authority to decide freely and autonomously (see the opinion of the International Court of Justice in the *Case concerning Military and Paramilitary Activities In and Against Nicaragua*, at p. 108). Consequently, it is a well-established principle that a state cannot act to enforce its laws within the territory of another state absent either the consent of the other state or, in exceptional cases, some other basis under international law. See Brownlie, at p. 306; *Oppenheim's International Law*, at p. 463. This principle of consent is central to assertions of extraterritorial enforcement jurisdiction.

(2) *Extraterritoriality in Canadian law*

66. This Court recognized the foregoing principles in *Terry*. At para. 15, McLachlin J wrote the following on behalf of the Court:

The principle that a state's law applies only within its boundaries is not absolute: *The Case of the SS "Lotus"* (1927), PCIJ Ser. A, No 10, at p. 20. States may invoke a jurisdiction to prescribe offences committed elsewhere to deal with special problems, such as those provisions of the Criminal Code, RSC 1985, c C-46, pertaining to offences on aircraft (s 7(1), (2)) and war crimes and other crimes against humanity (s 7(3.71)). A state may likewise formally consent to permit Canada and other states to enforce their laws within its territory for limited purposes.

The Statute of Westminster, 1931 (UK), 22 Geo. 5, c 4, s 3, conferred on Canada the authority to make laws having extraterritorial operation and Canada has enacted legislation with extraterritorial effects on several occasions. Some examples can be found in criminal legislation, including the Crimes Against Humanity and War Crimes Act, SC 2000, c 24, which addresses crimes of universal jurisdiction. Section 6(1) of that statute provides that every person who commits genocide, a crime against humanity or a war crime outside Canada is guilty of an indictable offence. Pursuant to s 8, such a person may be prosecuted in Canada: (a) if at the time of the offence the person was a Canadian citizen or a citizen of a state engaged in armed conflict against Canada, or the victim was a Canadian citizen or a citizen of a state allied with Canada in an armed conflict; or (b) if, after the time the offence was committed, the person is present in Canada. These provisions exemplify valid extraterritorial prescriptive jurisdiction, and any trial for such offences would constitute a legitimate exercise of extraterritorial adjudicative jurisdiction. But, importantly, they do not authorize Canada to enforce the prohibitions in a foreign state's territory by arresting the offenders there. Section 7 of the Criminal Code, RSC 1985, c C-46, contains a number of provisions that deem certain acts—including attacks on internationally protected persons or UN personnel, torture or hostage taking—to have been committed in Canada even though they took place in other countries. Although committed outside Canada, such an act will be deemed to have been committed in Canada if, *inter alia*, the person who committed it is a Canadian citizen or normally resides in Canada, it was committed on an aircraft registered in Canada or it was committed against a Canadian citizen.

67. On the other hand, it is recognized that there are limits to the extraterritorial application of Canadian law. Section 6(2) of the Criminal Code provides: "Subject to this Act or any other Act of Parliament, no person shall be convicted or discharged under section 730 of an offence committed outside Canada." As a general rule, then, Canadian criminal legislation is territorial unless specifically declared to be otherwise. Further, as noted by McLachlin J in *Terry*, at para. 18, bilateral treaties negotiated pursuant to the Mutual Legal Assistance in Criminal Matters Act, RSC 1985, c 30 (4th Supp.), provide that the actions requested of the assisting state are governed by that state's own laws, not by the laws of the requesting state.

68. Parliament has clear constitutional authority to pass legislation governing conduct by non-Canadians outside Canada. Its ability to pass extraterritorial legislation is informed by the binding customary principles of territorial sovereign equality and non-intervention, by the comity of nations, and by the limits of international law to the extent that they are not incompatible with domestic law. By virtue of parliamentary sovereignty, it is open to Parliament to enact legislation that is inconsistent with those principles, but in so doing it would violate international law and offend the comity of nations. However, in light of the foregoing discussion of the jurisdictional principles of customary international law, the prohibition on interference with the sovereignty and domestic affairs of other states, and this Court's jurisprudence, Canadian law can be *enforced* in another country only with the consent of the host state.

69. As the supreme law of Canada, the Charter is subject to the same jurisdictional limits as the country's other laws or rules. Simply put, Canadian law, whether statutory or constitutional, cannot be enforced in another state's territory without the other state's consent. This conclusion, which is consistent with the principles of international law, is also dictated by the words of the Charter itself. The Charter's territorial limitations are provided for in s 32, which states that the

Charter applies only to matters that are within the authority of Parliament or the provincial legislatures. In the absence of consent, Canada cannot exercise its enforcement jurisdiction over a matter situated outside Canadian territory. Since effect cannot be given to Canadian law in the circumstances, the matter falls outside the authority of Parliament and the provincial legislatures.

F. *External reach of the Charter*

70. In light of the context and interpretive assistance set out in the foregoing discussion, I will now turn to the specific issue raised in this appeal—the application of the Charter to investigations conducted by Canadian officers outside Canada.

(1) *Review of the Supreme Court of Canada jurisprudence:* Harrer, Terry, Cook *and* Schreiber

71. This Court has already considered the question of extraterritorial application of the Charter to evidence gathering abroad in a series of cases, beginning with *Harrer*. The accused in *Harrer* was questioned by United States marshals about possible criminal involvement in her boyfriend's escape from custody in Canada. The accused was tried in Canada on the basis of statements she had made to the marshals. During the interrogation, she had not been given a second right-to-counsel warning, which would have been required by the Charter but not by US law. At trial, the Crown sought to introduce statements that the accused had made to the marshals. The trial judge excluded the statement made after the second warning ought to have been given and this Court held that she erred in doing so. La Forest J noted that pursuant to s 32(1), the application of the Charter is confined to the governments of Canada, the provinces and the territories. The US marshals were not acting on behalf of those bodies, and the Charter consequently had no direct application to the interrogation. He wrote, at para. 15:

[I]t is obvious that Canada cannot impose its procedural requirements in proceedings undertaken by other states in their own territories. And I see no reason why evidence obtained in other countries in a manner that does not conform to our procedures should be rejected if, in the particular context, its admission would not make the trial unfair. For us to insist that foreign authorities have followed our internal procedures in obtaining evidence as a condition of its admission in evidence in Canada would frustrate the necessary cooperation between the police and prosecutorial authorities among the various states of the world.

McLachlin J, in concurring reasons, agreed that pursuant to s 32, the Charter does not apply to foreign authorities. Both La Forest J and McLachlin J mentioned that evidence obtained abroad can be excluded from a trial in Canada if its admission would jeopardize trial fairness. I will return to this point.

72. The next case in the series was *Terry*, which also involved interrogation by US authorities of an accused who was later tried in Canada. The accused was arrested in the US on an extradition warrant. Canadian police asked the US authorities to advise him of his American rights. Although the US police gave the "*Miranda* warning" required under American law, the accused was not advised forthwith upon his detention of his right to counsel as required by the Charter. He made a statement to the US police, and it was admitted at trial in Canada. The accused was convicted of second degree murder. McLachlin J, writing for the Court, found that the statement was admissible and upheld the conviction. She noted that despite the cooperation between Canadian and US police, the latter could not be governed by the requirements of Canadian law. Charter standards cannot be imposed on US authorities operating in their jurisdiction as that would undermine the principles of state sovereignty and international comity. In a passage that is particularly relevant to the facts of the case at bar, McLachlin J wrote, at para. 19:

Still less can the Charter govern the conduct of foreign police cooperating with Canadian police on an informal basis. The personal decision of a foreign officer or agency to assist the Canadian police cannot dilute the exclusivity of the foreign state's sovereignty within its territory, where its law alone governs the process of enforcement. The gathering of evidence by these foreign officers or agency is subject to the rules of that country and none other. Consequently, any cooperative investigation involving law enforcement agencies of Canada and the United States will be governed by the laws of the jurisdiction in which the activity is undertaken...

McLachlin J reaffirmed the position taken in *Harrer* that evidence gathered abroad may be excluded from a Canadian trial if it was gathered in a way that would undermine trial fairness as guaranteed by s 11(*d*) of the Charter or that violates the principles of fundamental justice.

73. The issue of extraterritorial application of the Charter arose once more in *Schreiber* v. *Canada (Attorney General)*, [1998] 1 SCR 841. Mr Schreiber, a Canadian citizen, had an interest in Swiss bank accounts. The federal Department of Justice sent a request to Swiss authorities seeking assistance in a Canadian criminal investigation. Switzerland accepted the request and ordered the seizure of documents and records

relating to Mr Schreiber's accounts. Prior to the request, no search warrant or other judicial authorization had been issued in Canada. The question before this Court was whether Canadian standards for the issuance of a search warrant had to be complied with before the request was made. The majority answered the question in the negative.

74. L'Heureux-Dubé J wrote the majority decision. She concluded that the sending of a letter of request to a foreign state does not attract scrutiny under s 8 of the Charter. Section 32 limits the application of the Charter to actions taken by Parliament, the government of Canada, a provincial legislature or a provincial government. As the sending of the letter of request was the only action authorized and undertaken by the government, it was the only one that could be assessed for Charter compliance. The sending of the letter did not engage s 8 of the Charter, and "[a]ll of those actions which rely on state compulsion in order to interfere with the respondent's privacy interests were undertaken in Switzerland by Swiss authorities. Neither the actions of the Swiss authorities, nor the laws which authorized their actions, are subject to Charter scrutiny" (para. 31).

75. Lamer CJ, in separate concurring reasons, found that the Charter applied to the actions of the Canadian officials who had prepared and sent the letter of request. He considered whether the searches and seizures carried out in Switzerland were consistent with s 8 of the Charter but found that there had been no violation, because Mr Schreiber had not had a reasonable expectation of privacy. He reasoned as follows, at paras. 22-3:

Of critical importance to this case is the fact that the records were located in Switzerland, and obtained in a manner consistent with Swiss law.

...a Canadian residing in a foreign country should expect his or her privacy to be governed by the laws of that country and, as such, a reasonable expectation of privacy will generally correspond to the degree of protection those laws provide. This, if anything, is more true for the person who decides to conduct financial affairs and keep records in a foreign state. It may be fairly assumed that such a person has made an informed choice about where to conduct business, and thereby to create corresponding records, particularly banking records.

76. Iacobucci J, in dissent, found that Mr Schreiber had had a reasonable expectation of privacy regarding the accounts and stated, in respect of the actions of the Canadian authorities in requesting the search and seizure, that "s 8 consequently applies in full force with all of its attendant guarantees and preventative measures" (para. 48).

77. This Court's most recent decision on the issue of extraterritorial Charter application was *Cook*. The accused in that case was an American arrested in the US by US authorities on a warrant issued in connection with a Canadian extradition request. While he was detained in the US, Vancouver police officers interrogated the accused. He was not properly advised of his right to counsel as required by s 10(*b*) of the Charter. At his trial in Canada, a statement he had made to the Canadian officers was admitted for the limited purpose of impeaching his credibility on cross-examination. A majority of this Court held that the Charter applied to the actions of the Canadian detectives and that there had been a violation of s 10(*b*). The evidence should have been excluded under s 24(2). A new trial was ordered.

78. Cory and Iacobucci JJ wrote the majority decision. They noted that the circumstances in which the Charter may apply to actions taken outside Canada will be rare. At para. 25, they suggested the following two factors to assist in identifying those circumstances: "(1) the impugned act falls within s 32(1) of the Charter; and (2) the application of the Charter to the actions of the Canadian detectives in the United States does not . . . interfere with the sovereign authority of the foreign state and thereby generate an objectionable extraterritorial effect". On the facts of the case, they found no interference with the sovereign authority of the US.

79. The majority considered jurisdiction under international law. Cory and Iacobucci JJ noted, at para. 26, that sovereign equality "generally prohibits extraterritorial application of domestic law since, in most instances, the exercise of jurisdiction beyond a state's territorial limits would constitute an interference under international law with the exclusive territorial jurisdiction of another state". However, the nationality of the person subject to the domestic law may also be invoked as a valid basis for jurisdiction, and nationality jurisdiction may operate concurrently with the territorial jurisdiction of the foreign state. The majority affirmed that the Charter cannot apply to the actions of foreign authorities but distinguished the facts of the case before them from those in *Harrer* and *Terry* on the basis that the interrogation had been conducted by Canadian officers rather than by foreign authorities. Since the officers who questioned the accused were Canadian nationals, s 32(1) extended the application of the Charter to their actions abroad pursuant to the nationality principle, provided there was no interference with the sovereign authority of the US. The majority concluded as follows, at para. 48: "[T]he Charter applies on foreign territory in circumstances where the impugned act falls within the scope of s 32(1) of the Charter on the jurisdictional basis of the nationality of the state law enforcement

authorities engaged in governmental action, and where the application of Charter standards will not conflict with the concurrent territorial jurisdiction of the foreign state." The majority took care to confine its holding to the facts before it, expressly acknowledging at para. 54 that the case might be different where "Canadian authorities participate, on foreign territory, in an investigative action undertaken by foreign authorities in accordance with foreign procedures".

80. Bastarache J wrote concurring reasons in which he reached the same result by means of a different analysis. To begin, he found that the wording of s 32(1) applies to the actions of Canadian police officers, since the police are constituted as part of the government and act under statutory authority. That statutory authority to exercise coercion will come into conflict with the jurisdiction of a foreign state when Canadian officers travel into the territory of that state; however, s 32(1) continues to apply to the Canadian officers regardless of whether they exercise governmental powers of coercion. At para. 126, Bastarache J stated that where an investigation abroad involves cooperation between Canadian officials and foreign officials, "the key issue ... is determining who was in control of the specific feature of the investigation which is alleged to constitute the Charter breach". If the foreign authority was in control of the circumstances leading to the Charter breach in obtaining the evidence, the activities in question are not subject to the Charter. If the Canadian authorities were primarily responsible for the breach, the Charter will apply to them and to the evidence. Bastarache J considered principles of jurisdiction under international law, including territoriality, the objective territorial principle and the importance of a real and substantial link where competing claims of jurisdiction are made. He determined that, in the circumstances of that case, there was a real and substantial connection between the criminal prosecution in Canada and the investigation outside Canada in which Canadian officers had taken part. He then discussed whether the application of the Charter would interfere with the jurisdictional integrity of the foreign state. At para. 143, he reasoned as follows:

[T]he nature of the rights contained in the relevant sections of the Charter are not mandatory, but rather conditional upon the occurrence of specified investigatory activities. Thus, if there is a rule of investigation in the foreign jurisdiction that directly contradicts a Charter provision, there is still no conflict. The reason for this is that the Charter does not impose any obligation to investigate; it simply requires that if an investigation is made by the officer, it must be conducted in accordance with certain conditions. It follows from this, moreover, that the application of the Charter to the Canadian official has no impact on the foreign legal system. At worst, the Canadian official may be obliged to cease taking a directing or primary role in the investigation in order to comply with the Charter.

81. L'Heureux-Dubé J dissented in *Cook*, and McLachlin J concurred in her reasons. According to L'Heureux-Dubé J's approach, before considering whether a case involves state action that may have infringed a Charter right, it must be asked whether the person claiming the Charter right in fact holds that right. If the claimant does hold a Charter right, the inquiry then moves to the question of state action. After reviewing the decisions in *Harrer, Terry* and *Schreiber*, L'Heureux-Dubé J identified two fundamental principles relating to the extraterritorial application of the Charter. First, the action allegedly in breach of the Charter must have been carried out by one of the state actors identified in s 32(1). Second, even an action by one of those state actors will fall outside the scope of the Charter if it is performed in cooperation with foreign officials on foreign soil. The key question to ask in order to determine whether the investigation is cooperative is whether Canadian officials have legal authority in the place where the actions occurred. Where the conduct of state actors falls under the authority of a foreign government, s 32 does not apply, since it is confined to matters "within the authority" of Parliament or a provincial legislature. At paras. 93-4, L'Heureux-Dubé J wrote the following:

> In my opinion, the Charter does not apply to any investigation where Canadian officials no longer have the legal attributes of "government"; this occurs whenever an investigation takes place under the sovereignty of another government.
>
> When Canadian officials work under the sovereignty of a foreign legal system, the investigation is necessarily cooperative. Foreign officials who permit Canadians to work with them, or to work on soil that is under their government's legal authority, are bound to follow that country's laws, and work within the procedural requirements of that system. So are the Canadian officials who work with them.

82. The dissent concluded that the Charter did not apply to the interrogation, and, consequently, that the statement was properly admitted at trial.

(2) Concerns in respect of the jurisprudence

83. The jurisprudence on the issue of extraterritorial application of the Charter as it stands after *Cook* is subject to a number of difficulties and criticisms, both practical and theoretical. The essence of the majority's holding in *Cook* is that the Charter will apply to acts of Canadian law enforcement authorities engaged in governmental action where the

application of Charter standards will not conflict with the concurrent territorial jurisdiction of the foreign state. When that holding is applied to facts such as those in the present case, problems arise. For one, the majority in *Cook* failed to distinguish prescriptive from enforcement jurisdiction. Second, practical and theoretical difficulties arise when its approach is applied to different facts (such as a search and seizure). Third, it failed to give due consideration to the wording of s 32(1).

84. Beginning with the first of these criticisms, the majority in *Cook* disregarded the important distinction between the powers of prescription and enforcement. It also failed to discuss the principle that Canadian law cannot be enforced in another state's territory without the other state's consent, regardless of the extent or degree of difference between the laws of Canada and the foreign state, or of whether there is any conflict at all. Criminal investigations in foreign countries by definition implicate foreign law and procedures. The choice of legal system inherently lies within the authority of each state as an exercise of its territorial sovereignty. Were Charter standards to be applied in another state's territory without its consent, there would by that very fact *always* be interference with the other state's sovereignty. *Cook* is also inconsistent with this Court's approval of the principle of consent in *Terry*.

85. The *Cook* approach therefore puts the focus in the wrong place, as it involves looking for a conflict between concurrent jurisdictional claims, whereas the question should instead be viewed as one of extraterritorial enforcement of Canadian law. The issue in these cases is the applicability of the Charter to the activities of Canadian officers conducting investigations abroad. The powers of prescription and enforcement are both necessary to application of the Charter. The Charter is prescriptive in that it sets out what the state and its agents may and may not do in exercising the state's powers. Prescription is not in issue in the case at bar, but even so, the Charter cannot be applied if compliance with its legal requirements cannot be enforced. Enforcement of compliance with the Charter means that when state agents act, they must do so in accordance with the requirements of the Charter so as to give effect to Canadian law as it applies to the exercise of the state power at issue. However, as has already been discussed, Canadian law cannot be enforced in another state's territory without that state's consent. Since extraterritorial enforcement is not possible, and enforcement is necessary for the Charter to apply, extraterritorial application of the Charter is impossible.

86. As for the second criticism, the circumstances of the instant case exemplify the theoretical and practical difficulties arising out of an

attempt to apply Charter standards outside Canada in fact situations other than the one in *Cook*. In Turks and Caicos, judicial authorization does not appear to be necessary for a perimeter search of private premises, such as the one that took place on the nights of February 7 and 8, 1998. Under Canadian law, in most circumstances a warrant would be required to conduct such a search. To comply with the Charter, the RCMP officers would have had to obtain a warrant that is unavailable under Turks and Caicos law. It would constitute blatant interference with Turks and Caicos sovereignty to require that country's legal system to develop a procedure for issuing a warrant in the circumstances simply to comply with the dictates of the Charter.

87. The theoretical and practical impediments to extraterritorial application of the Charter can thus be seen more clearly where the s 8 guarantee against unreasonable search and seizure is in issue than where the issue relates, as in the cases discussed above, to the right to counsel. Searches and seizures, because of their coerciveness and intrusiveness, are by nature vastly different from police interrogations. The power to invade the private sphere of persons and property, and seize personal items and information, is paradigmatic of state sovereignty. These actions can be authorized only by the territorial state. From a theoretical standpoint, the Charter cannot be applied, because its application would necessarily entail an exercise of the enforcement jurisdiction that lies at the heart of territoriality. As a result of the principles of sovereign equality, non-intervention and comity, Canadian law and standards cannot apply to searches and seizures conducted in another state's territory.

88. It is also evident from a practical standpoint that the Charter cannot apply to searches and seizures in other countries. How exactly would Charter standards operate in such circumstances? Lamer CJ suggested in *Schreiber* that it would be sufficient for Charter purposes for those conducting a search and seizure to comply with the domestic law of the foreign state, since an individual's reasonable expectation of privacy would be commensurate to the degree of protection provided by the law of the country in which she or he is located. If the only requirement were that the Canadian officers and their foreign counterparts comply with the foreign law, it is unclear what purpose would be served by applying the Charter, as it would carry no added protection in respect of a search and seizure. Moreover, in some cases, compliance with the foreign law would be directly contrary to the express wording of the Charter provisions guaranteeing the rights in question.

89. Conversely, it is in practice impossible to apply the full force of the Charter to searches and seizures in foreign territory. One example of this, as I mentioned earlier, is where the Charter would require

a warrant but the foreign law provides no procedure for obtaining or issuing such a warrant. The judicial authorities of a foreign state cannot be required under Canadian law to invent *ad hoc* procedures for the purposes of a cooperative investigation. Should that be a reason for prohibiting a search and seizure from taking place even though it is authorized by the law of the jurisdiction where it would occur? Further, it would be unrealistic, in a cooperative investigation, to require the various officers involved to follow different procedural and legal requirements. Searches and seizures require careful and detailed planning; where the investigation is a joint effort, it is bound to be unsuccessful if the participants are following two different sets of rules. This would be the result if the Charter applied to the Canadian officers only, and it clearly cannot apply to the foreign authorities: *Harrer* and *Terry*.

90. It is no more helpful to suggest that some third option other than the law of the host state or the full application of Charter standards might govern foreign investigations. Where would the standards to be applied come from? How would Canadian officials know what is required of them at the outset of an investigation? The only reasonable approach is to apply the law of the state in which the activities occur, subject to the Charter's fair trial safeguards and to the limits on comity that may prevent Canadian officers from participating in activities that, though authorized by the laws of another state, would cause Canada to be in violation of its international obligations in respect of human rights.

91. One possible response to the problem of enforcement outside Canada is that *ex post facto* scrutiny of the investigation by a Canadian court in a Canadian trial that might result in the exclusion of evidence gathered in breach of the Charter would not interfere with the sovereignty of the foreign state, since this would merely constitute an exercise of extraterritorial adjudicative jurisdiction. However, while it is true that foreign sovereignty is not engaged by a criminal process in Canada that excludes evidence by scrutinizing the manner in which it was obtained for compliance with the Charter, the purpose of the Charter is not simply to serve as a basis for an *ex post facto* review of government action. The Charter's primary role is to limit the exercise of government and legislative authority in advance, so that breaches are stopped before they occur. Canadian officers need to know what they are required to do as the investigation unfolds, so as to ensure that the evidence gathered will be admitted at trial. When a trial judge is considering a possible breach of the Charter by state actors, the ability of the state actors to comply with their Charter obligations must be relevant. The fact that the Charter could not be complied with during the investigation because the relevant state action was being carried out in a

foreign jurisdiction strongly intimates that the Charter does not apply in the circumstances. In any event, if the concern is really about the *ex post facto* review of investigations, that function is performed by ss 7 and 11(*d*) of the Charter, pursuant to which evidence may be excluded to preserve trial fairness. The inquiry under those provisions relates to the court's responsibility to control its own process and is fundamentally different from asking at trial whether the Canadian officer's conduct amounted to the violation of a particular Charter right.

92. The importance of considering the possibility of compliance with the Charter in advance is highlighted by the legal problems attendant upon the conduct of an interrogation abroad. Certain provisions setting out Charter rights require no more than that the accused be advised of something, such as the reasons for his or her arrest or detention (under s 10(*a*)). Other Charter rights provisions in the investigation context require more. For example, s 10(*b*) guarantees to everyone the right on arrest or detention *to be informed of* the right to retain and instruct counsel without delay; however, it also includes the right *to retain and instruct* counsel without delay. Consequently, while imposing an obligation on Canadian officers conducting an interrogation abroad to inform the accused of a right would not significantly interfere with the territorial sovereignty of the foreign state, interference would occur if the accused were to claim that right. At that point, Canadian officers would no longer be able to comply with their Charter obligations independently. As L'Heureux-Dubé J wrote in *Cook*, at para. 94: "In an investigation that takes place under foreign sovereignty, it is the foreign government that has legal authority over the mechanics of the investigation." For Charter rights to be effective, it must be possible to assert them.

93. Finally, the third criticism of the current jurisprudence is that proper regard has not been given to the wording of s 32(1) of the Charter. In setting out the two factors that were central to the conclusion that the Charter applied, the majority in *Cook* noted first that "the impugned act falls within s 32(1) of the Charter" (para. 25). In doing so, it made the error of assuming precisely what had to be decided. The purpose of the inquiry into the application of the Charter to investigations in other countries is to determine whether the act in fact falls under s 32(1). The words of s 32(1)—interpreted with reference to binding principles of customary international law—must ultimately guide the inquiry. In my view, there is little logic in an approach that first determines that the activity falls under s 32(1) and then questions at a second stage whether the Charter nonetheless ought not to apply because of some "objectionable extraterritorial effect". Rather, the extraterritorial

implications of applying the Charter are, in my view, central to the question whether the activity in question falls under s 32(1) in the first place. The inquiry begins and ends with s 32(1) of the Charter.

94. Section 32(1) puts the burden of complying with the Charter on Parliament, the government of Canada, the provincial legislatures and the provincial governments. While my colleague is correct in stating, at para. 161, that s 32(1) defines *to whom* the Charter applies and not *where* it applies, s 32(1) does more than that. It also defines *in what circumstances* the Charter applies to those actors. The fact that a state actor is involved is not in itself sufficient, as Bastarache J suggests. The activity in question must also fall within the "matters within the authority of" Parliament or the legislature of each province. A criminal investigation in the territory of another state cannot be a matter within the authority of Parliament or the provincial legislatures, because they have no jurisdiction to authorize enforcement abroad. Criminal investigations, like political structures or judicial systems, are intrinsically linked to the organs of the state, and to its territorial integrity and internal affairs. Such matters are clearly within the authority of Parliament and the provincial legislatures when they are in Canadian territory; it is just as clear that they lie outside the authority of those bodies when they are outside Canadian territory.

95. My colleague, Binnie J, recognizes that there are practical and theoretical difficulties with the application of the approach followed in *Cook* (para. 183). Nonetheless, in his view that approach should be preserved because of possible issues that may eventually end up before this Court in respect of international law and of its relationship with Canadian law. He refers to matters such as the "war on terror", the deployment of Canadian police officers in states with troubled histories and the Maher Arar inquiry. With respect, I do not think such matters belong to the issue put before our Court in this appeal, nor form part of the record in this case. We cannot always know what new issues might arise before the courts in the future, but we can trust that the law will grow and evolve as necessary and when necessary in response. But until those new issues are presented in live cases we ought not to abdicate our duty to rethink and refine today the law when confronted by jurisprudence that has demonstrated practical and theoretical weaknesses.

(3) *The globalization of criminal activities and the need for international cooperation*

96. The principles of international law and comity that I have discussed demonstrate why Charter standards cannot be applied to an

investigation in another country involving Canadian officers so as to require that the investigation conform to Canadian law. At the same time, there is no impediment to extraterritorial adjudicative jurisdiction pursuant to which evidence gathered abroad may be excluded from a Canadian trial, as this jurisdiction simply attaches domestic consequences to foreign events. The question flowing from those two propositions is whether the Charter can restrain Canadian officers from participating in a foreign investigation that does not meet Charter standards.

97. When it applies, the Charter imposes limits on the state's coercive power. It requires that state power be exercised only in accordance with certain restrictions. As a corollary, where those restrictions cannot be observed, the Charter prohibits the state from exercising its coercive power. Since the Charter does not authorize state action, but simply operates as a limit on such action, could it not be said that the Charter "applies" to extraterritorial investigations by prohibiting Canadian officers from participating in investigations abroad that do not conform to Canadian law? International law provides only part of the answer to this question. To prohibit Canadian officers from participating would indeed ensure conformity with both international law and the Charter; however, it would also mean that the investigation could not be conducted. This is a serious concern. The complete answer therefore lies both in international law and in the need to address the challenges of investigating and prosecuting transborder criminal activity.

98. Transnational crime is a growing problem in the modern world, as people, property and funds move fluidly across national borders. Some of the most costly, exploitative or dangerous crimes are committed on a worldwide scale, unconfined by state boundaries. The investigation and policing of such criminal activities requires cooperation between states. In a cooperative investigation, Canada cannot simply walk away when another country insists on following its own investigation and enforcement procedures rather than ours. That would fall short not only of Canada's commitment to other states and the international community to provide assistance in combatting transnational crime, but also of Canada's obligation to Canadians to ensure that crimes having a connection with Canada are investigated and prosecuted. As McLachlin J wrote in *Harrer*, at para. 55:

> It is not reasonable to expect [police forces abroad] to comply with details of Canadian law. To insist on conformity to Canadian law would be to insist on external application of the Charter in preference to the local law. It would render prosecution of offences with international aspects difficult if not impossible.

And it would undermine the ethic of reciprocity which underlies international efforts to control trans-border crime: *Argentina* v. *Mellino*, [1987] 1 SCR 536, at p. 551, *per* La Forest J. We live in an era when people, goods and information pass from country to country with great rapidity. Law enforcement authorities, if they are to do their job, must apprehend people and intercept goods and communications wherever they may be found. Often they find themselves working with officers in foreign jurisdictions; often they are merely the recipients of information gathered independently elsewhere... We need to accommodate the reality that different countries apply different rules to evidence gathering, rules which must be respected in some measure if we are to retain the ability to prosecute those whose crime and travel take them beyond our borders.

99. When individuals choose to engage in criminal activities that cross Canada's territorial limits, they can have no guarantee that they carry Charter rights with them out of the country. As this Court has noted in the past, individuals should expect to be governed by the laws of the state in which they find themselves and in which they conduct financial affairs—it is the individual's decision to go to or operate in another country that triggers the application of the foreign law: *Terry*, at paras. 24 and 26; *Schreiber*, at para. 23. Cooperation between states is imperative if transnational crimes are not to be committed with impunity because they fall through jurisdictional cracks along national borders. In *United States of America* v. *Cotroni*, [1989] 1 SCR 1469, in the context of drug trafficking, La Forest J stated the following, at p. 1485:

The only respect paid by the international criminal community to national boundaries is when these can serve as a means to frustrate the efforts of law enforcement and judicial authorities. The trafficking in drugs, with which we are here concerned, is an international enterprise and requires effective tools of international cooperation for its investigation, prosecution and suppression.

In order to foster such cooperation, and in the spirit of comity, Canada cannot either insist that the Charter be applied in other countries or refuse to participate. When Canadian authorities are guests of another state whose assistance they seek in a criminal investigation, the rules of that state govern.

100. It is clear that a balance must be struck "to achieve a just accommodation between the interests of the individual and those of the state in providing a fair and workable system of justice": *Harrer*, at para. 14. Individual rights cannot be completely disregarded in the interests of transborder cooperation. Sections 7 and 11(*d*) provide that everyone tried in Canada enjoys the same rights to a fair trial and not to

be deprived of life, liberty or security of the person except in accordance with the principles of fundamental justice. Where the Crown seeks at trial to adduce evidence gathered abroad, the Charter provisions governing trial processes in Canada ensure that the appropriate balance is struck and that due consideration is shown for the rights of an accused being investigated abroad.

101. Moreover, there is an argument that comity cannot be invoked to allow Canadian authorities to participate in activities that violate Canada's international obligations. As a general rule, Canadian officers can participate in investigations abroad, but must do so under the laws of the foreign state. The permissive rule that allows Canadian officers to participate even when there is no obligation to do so derives from the principle of comity; the rule that foreign law governs derives from the principles of sovereign equality and non-intervention. But the principle of comity may give way where the participation of Canadian officers in investigative activities sanctioned by foreign law would place Canada in violation of its international obligations in respect of human rights. In such circumstances, the permissive rule might no longer apply and Canadian officers might be prohibited from participating. I would leave open the possibility that, in a future case, participation by Canadian officers in activities in another country that would violate Canada's international human rights obligations might justify a remedy under s 24(1) of the Charter because of the impact of those activities on Charter rights in Canada.

(4) *A balancing methodology*

102. In light of the foregoing considerations, several issues arise with respect to the question of the application of the Charter to investigations. It will be necessary to consider each of them carefully in order to develop a principled approach to determining whether the Charter applies and avoid the uncertainties that now plague the question.

103. The court must first turn to s 32 in order to determine whether the actors are agents of government and then determine whether the activities fall within the scope of the legislative authority of Parliament or the provincial legislatures. It must begin by considering the wording of s 32(1) of the Charter, bearing in mind that provision's two distinct components. As a threshold question, it must be asked whether there is a state actor in the sense of a government agent or official possessing statutory authority or exercising a public function (see P. W. Hogg, *Constitutional Law of Canada* (loose-leaf edn), vol. 2, at pp. 34-13 to 34-15 and 34-16 to 34-18). Police officers are clearly government actors to whom, *prima facie*, the Charter would apply: "By its terms, s 32(1)

dictates that the Charter applies to the Canadian police by virtue of their identity as part of the Canadian government" (*Cook*, at para. 124). However, the inquiry does not end there. It is clear that s 32(1) applies to state actors "*in respect of all matters*" within the authority of Parliament or the provincial legislatures. The second part of the s 32(1) inquiry is essential in such cases.

104. Although, on the basis of nationality, Canada has some jurisdiction over Canadian agents acting abroad, that jurisdiction is subject to the caveat that the matter must be within the authority of Parliament or the provincial legislatures. Consequently, Canada's jurisdiction is circumscribed by the territorial jurisdiction of the state in which its agents are operating. For example, Canadian consular officials operating abroad have some immunity from local laws on the basis of nationality jurisdiction, but that does not mean they have the power to abide by Canadian laws and only Canadian laws when in the host state. Bastarache J correctly noted in *Cook* that a Canadian police officer is not stripped of his or her status as such on crossing the border into the US, but the officer's authority to exercise state powers is necessarily curtailed. Canada does not have authority over all matters respecting what the officer may or may not do in the foreign state. Where Canada's authority is limited, so too is the application of the Charter.

105. Neither Parliament nor the provincial legislatures have the power to authorize the enforcement of Canada's laws over matters in the exclusive territorial jurisdiction of another state. Canada can no more dictate what procedures are followed in a criminal investigation abroad than it can impose a taxation scheme in another state's territory. Criminal investigations implicate enforcement jurisdiction, which, pursuant to the principles of international law discussed above, cannot be exercised in another country absent the consent of the foreign state or the application of another rule of international law under which it can so be exercised. While concurrent jurisdiction over prosecutions of crimes linked with more than one country is recognized under international law, the same is not true of investigations, which are governed by and carried out pursuant to territorial jurisdiction as a matter inherent in state sovereignty. Any attempt to dictate how those activities are to be performed in a foreign state's territory without that state's consent would infringe the principle of non-intervention. And, as mentioned above, without enforcement, the Charter cannot apply.

106. In some cases, the evidence may establish that the foreign state consented to the exercise of Canadian enforcement jurisdiction within its territory. The Charter can apply to the activities of Canadian officers in foreign investigations where the host state consents. In such a case,

the investigation would be a matter within the authority of Parliament and would fall within the scope of s 32(1). Consent clearly is neither demonstrated nor argued on the facts of the instant appeal, so it is unnecessary to consider when and how it might be established. Suffice it to say that cases in which consent to the application of Canadian law in a foreign investigation is demonstrated may be rare.

107. If the court is not satisfied that the foreign state consented to the enforcement of Canadian law in its territory, it must turn to the final stage of the inquiry and consider how to ensure the fairness of a trial held in Canada. What is in issue at this stage is no longer whether the actions of state agents outside Canada were consistent with the Charter, but whether they affect the fairness of a trial inside Canada.

108. Any individual tried in Canada for an offence under Canadian law has, pursuant to s 11(*d*) and to centuries of common law, the right to a fair trial. In addition, everyone has the right to liberty and the right not to be deprived thereof except in accordance with the principles of fundamental justice (s 7). This Court has in fact held that the right to a fair trial is a principle of fundamental justice: *R v. Seaboyer*, [1991] 2 SCR 577, at p. 603. If evidence is gathered in a way that fails to meet certain minimum standards, its admission at trial in Canada may—regardless of where it was gathered—amount to a violation of either or both of those sections of the Charter. Judges have the discretion to exclude evidence that would result in an unfair trial. That discretion, long established at common law, has attained constitutional status by being entrenched in s 11(*d*) of the Charter. However, it does not automatically follow that a trial will be unfair or that the principles of fundamental justice will be infringed if evidence obtained in circumstances that do not meet Charter standards is admitted: *Harrer*, at para. 14.

109. The circumstances in which the evidence was gathered must be considered in their entirety to determine whether admission of the evidence would render a Canadian trial unfair. The way in which the evidence was obtained may make it unreliable, as would be true of conscriptive evidence, for example. The evidence may have been gathered through means, such as torture, that are contrary to fundamental Charter values. Such abusive conduct would taint the fairness of any trial in which the evidence was admitted: *Harrer*, at para. 46. La Forest J offered the following additional guidance in *Harrer*, at paras. 16-18:

The fact that the evidence was obtained in another country in accordance with the law of that country may be a factor in assessing fairness. Its legality at the place in question will necessarily affect all participants, including the police and the individual accused. More specifically, conformity with the law of a country with a legal system similar to our own has even more weight, for we know that a number of different balances between conflicting principles can be fair...

But the foreign law is not governing in trials in this country. For example, it may happen that the evidence was obtained in a manner that conformed with the law of the country where it was obtained, but which a court in this country would find in the circumstances of the case would result in unfairness if admitted at trial. On the other hand, the procedural requirements for obtaining evidence imposed in one country may be more onerous than ours. Or they may simply have rules that are different from ours but are not unfair. Or again we may not find in the particular circumstances that the manner in which the evidence was obtained was sufficiently objectionable as to require its rejection. In coming to a decision, the court is bound to consider the whole context.

At the end of the day, a court is left with a principled but fact-driven decision.

110. La Forest J and McLachlin J both found that admission of the evidence would not render the trial unfair in the circumstances of that case. McLachlin J noted in particular that the relevant circumstances included the expectations of the accused in the place where the evidence was taken, and that the police conduct was neither unfair nor abusive. She made the following comment, at para. 49: "The unfairness arises in large part from the accused's expectation that the police in Canada will comply with Canadian law. Where the [evidence] is [gathered] abroad, the expectation is otherwise."

111. Individuals can reasonably expect that certain basic standards will be adhered to in all free and democratic societies; where those standards are deviated from in gathering evidence, a Canadian trial that relies on that evidence may be unfair. In such instances, "[i]t may be that ... notwithstanding the suspect's submission to the law of the foreign jurisdiction, to admit the evidence would be so grossly unfair as to repudiate the values underlying our trial system and condone procedures which are anathema to the Canadian conscience" (*Harrer*, at para. 51). Whether the evidence was obtained in compliance with or in violation of the law of the foreign state may also be relevant. However, where commonly accepted laws are complied with, no unfairness results from variances in particular procedural requirements or from the fact that another country chooses to do things in a somewhat different way than Canada. Further, the failure to comply with a particular rule in a given case does not necessarily amount to an injustice. As La Forest J noted in *Harrer*, at para. 15, "we must be mindful that a constitutional rule may be adopted to ensure that our system of obtaining evidence is so devised as to ensure that a guaranteed right is respected as a matter

of course". The rule is directed not at the individual case alone, but rather at systemic fairness—a concern that does not arise in foreign investigations under foreign systems. Instead, the concern is to preserve the fundamental values of the Canadian trial process.

112. Despite the fact that the right to a fair trial is available only at the domestic level, after the investigation, it does provide an incentive for Canadian police officers to encourage foreign police to maintain high standards in the course of a cooperative investigation so as to avoid having the evidence excluded or a stay entered: *Terry*, at para. 26. In a similar vein, L'Heureux-Dubé J commented in *Cook*, at para. 103, that to the extent that it is possible to do so in the circumstances, Canadian police should strive to conduct investigations outside Canada in accordance with the letter and spirit of the Charter, even when its guarantees do not apply directly.

G. *Summary of the approach*

113. The methodology for determining whether the Charter applies to a foreign investigation can be summarized as follows. The first stage is to determine whether the activity in question falls under s 32(1) such that the Charter applies to it. At this stage, two questions reflecting the two components of s 32(1) must be asked. First, is the conduct at issue that of a Canadian state actor? Second, if the answer is yes, it may be necessary, depending on the facts of the case, to determine whether there is an exception to the principle of sovereignty that would justify the application of the Charter to the extraterritorial activities of the state actor. In most cases, there will be no such exception and the Charter will not apply. The inquiry would then move to the second stage, at which the court must determine whether evidence obtained through the foreign investigation ought to be excluded at trial because its admission would render the trial unfair.

H. *Application to the facts*

114. I will now apply the foregoing methodology to the facts of the instant case.

115. At the first stage, there is no question in the case at bar that the RCMP officers involved in the searches and seizures are state actors for the purposes of s 32(1). However, since the search was carried out in Turks and Caicos, it is not a matter within the authority of Parliament. Without evidence of consent, that is enough to conclude that the Charter does not apply. It is not reasonable to suggest that

Turks and Caicos consented to Canadian extraterritorial enforcement jurisdiction in the instant case. Nonetheless, I will say a few words on the factual circumstances of the investigation.

116. The trial judge made several significant findings of fact, and the appellant has not attempted to argue that they were based on a palpable and overriding error. Those findings are that:

- Detective Superintendent Lessemun "agreed to allow the RCMP to continue its investigation on the Islands, but was adamant he was going to be in charge, and that the RCMP would be working under his authority" (para. 4);
- "the RCMP officers were, and understood that they were, operating under the authority of Detective Superintendent Lessemun" (para. 25);
- the RCMP officers "were subject to Turks & Caicos authority" (para. 25);
- "the Canadian police, in this case, were operating under and subject to the authority of Detective Superintendent Lessemun" (para. 29); and
- "the propriety and legality of the entries into the private premises in the Turks & Caicos Islands ... are subject to Turks & Caicos criminal law and procedures and the superintending scrutiny of the Turks & Caicos courts" (para. 29).

As those findings demonstrate, Turks and Caicos clearly and consistently asserted its territorial jurisdiction in the conduct of the investigation within its borders. It controlled the investigation at all times, repeatedly making it known to the RCMP officers that, at each step, the activities were being carried out pursuant to Turks and Caicos authority alone. As found by the trial judge, the RCMP officers were well aware that, when operating in Turks and Caicos, they were working under the authority and direction of Detective Superintendent Lessemun. Although much of the planning took place in Canada, and Canada contributed much of the human and technological resources, Turks and Caicos law and procedure applied to all the searches: it applied to the perimeter searches in February 1998, to the covert entries in March 1998, and to the overt entries in February 1999. In his trial testimony, Officer Boyle explained this as follows:

I—I don't think there would have been any way, and certainly we would—I wasn't of the—I wasn't of the opinion that we would make [Detective Superintendent Lessemun] answerable to us in any way. We were—we were at his—it was at his discretion as to what we were allowed to do on that island. We were asking for his assistance as a Turks and Caicos police officer.

...

... I had no authority. None of our officers, myself or the RCMP officers, had any authority to conduct any investigations or searches on the island.

Finally, warrants were sought in Turks and Caicos courts, and that country's authorities prevented the seized documents from being removed to Canada.

117. The appellant took issue in this appeal with the trial judge's finding that the RCMP and Turks and Caicos officers were engaged in a "cooperative investigation". There is no magic in the words "cooperative investigation", because the issue relates not to who participated in the investigation but to the fact that it occurred on foreign soil and that consent was not given for the exercise of extraterritorial jurisdiction by Canada. When investigations are carried out within another country's borders, that country's law will apply. A cooperative effort involving police from different countries "does not make the law of one country applicable in the other country": *Terry*, at para. 18.

118. In short, although Canadian state actors were involved, the searches and seizures took place in Turks and Caicos and so were not matters within the authority of Parliament. The Charter does not apply.

119. The final recourse available to the appellant would be to demonstrate that the trial judge erred in admitting the evidence because doing so rendered the trial unfair. The trial judge determined that to admit the evidence would not result in an unfair trial and that it need not therefore be excluded, and the appellant did not argue trial fairness in this appeal. Nonetheless, I will consider this issue briefly.

120. There was some discussion at trial about the existence of warrants authorizing the March 14, 1998 entries. No warrants were admitted into evidence, and I must proceed on the basis that the searches were warrantless. However, considering all the circumstances, I cannot conclude that the admission of the documents obtained through the searches rendered the trial unfair. The evidence at issue consists of documents obtained from the BWIT's office. As Juriansz J found in his ruling on the application to exclude, it is not conscriptive evidence. The actions of the RCMP officers were not unreasonable or unfair, as they were acting under Detective Superintendent Lessemun's direction and had a genuine and reasonable belief that they were complying with Turks and Caicos law. They thought that search warrants had been obtained and that the investigation was lawful under Turks and Caicos law. The RCMP officers acted in good faith at all times. Their actions

were not improper. The way in which the evidence was obtained in no way undermines its reliability. Moreover, since he had chosen to conduct business in Turks and Caicos, the appellant's reasonable expectation should have been that Turks and Caicos law would apply to the investigation. Although no warrants were admitted at trial, I can find no evidence that the searches and seizures were conducted in a manner inconsistent with the requirements of Turks and Caicos law. Little evidence was presented on Turks and Caicos law. Foreign law must be proved. I see no basis for concluding that the procedural requirements for a lawful search and seizure under Turks and Caicos law fail to meet basic standards commonly accepted by free and democratic societies.

121. I do not think the circumstances demonstrate that this is a case where admission of the evidence would violate the appellant's right to a fair trial.

III. *Disposition*

122. For the foregoing reasons, I would dismiss the appeal and affirm the convictions.

The reasons of Bastarache, Abella and Rothstein were delivered by

123. BASTARACHE J:—This appeal is concerned with only one situation, investigatory actions undertaken by Canadian law enforcement officials in the Turks and Caicos Islands. It is argued that this Court's decision in *R* v. *Cook*, [1998] 2 SCR 597, left unclear whether the Canadian Charter of Rights and Freedoms will apply in such a case and that some clarification of the issue is required.

124. I have read the reasons of LeBel J and believe we agree on many points. We agree that Canadian officers must respect fundamental human rights when investigating abroad. We also see the need for Canadian officers to participate effectively in the fight against transnational crime and recognize that this will often require Canadian officials to follow foreign laws and procedures. We both recognize that, on one hand, comity demands respect for a foreign state's choice of criminal procedure, while on the other hand, there is the possibility that some foreign procedures may violate fundamental human rights. In essence, we both see the need to strike a balance between effective participation by Canadian officers in fighting transnational crime and the protection of fundamental human rights.

125. Where we disagree is on the Charter's role in this process. My colleague sees international law as the proper vehicle for achieving this balance. I prefer to continue to rely on the Charter, as this Court

attempted to do in *Cook*, though I recognize there are problems with the position of the majority in that case that must be dealt with. Constitutions operate to define the sphere of legitimate governmental action; the Charter imposes restraints on all conduct of Canadian government officials with respect to fundamental human rights. It is a flexible document, amenable to contextual interpretation and permitting reasonable justifications of limitations to fundamental rights. I am of the view that it can apply to Canadian officers operating in another country without jeopardizing the need for comity.

126. I would resolve this case by ruling that the Charter did apply to the search and seizures conducted by the RCMP in the Turks and Caicos Islands. I would however dismiss the appeal by finding that Hape has not established a breach of s 8 of the Charter.

I. *Background*

127. I generally agree with the summary of facts and judicial history of the case as set out by my colleague. However, I find it useful for the analysis that is to follow to set out the trial judge's ruling on the Charter and s 8 in greater detail.

128. The trial judge resolved Hape's Charter motion by reference to *Cook*. He first noted that the majority found the Charter did apply to the actions of Canadian law enforcement in foreign territory and then cited an excerpt from my concurring reasons as imposing a qualification based on the extent of control an officer exercises over the investigation ([2002] OJ No 3714 (QL)).

129. He then stated that both the majority and concurring reasons require more than just s 32 compliance, citing the majority's statement that the Charter will not apply where it "interfere[s] with the sovereign authority of the foreign state and thereby generate[s] an objectionable extra-territorial effect" (para. 20).

130. The trial judge went on to discuss alternative language used by the majority to express this requirement, specifically that "Charter standards could 'not conflict with the concurrent territorial jurisdiction of the foreign state'" (para. 21). He then quoted all of para. 54 of *Cook* where he found that the majority again stressed this limitation.

131. The trial judge then pointed out the majority's emphasis on the words "cooperative investigation" in para. 54, quoting Justice McLachlin's (as she then was) observation in *R v. Terry*, [1996] 2 SCR 207, that "any cooperative investigation involving law enforcement agencies of Canada and the United States will be governed by the laws of the jurisdiction in which the activity is undertaken".

132. Following this, the trial judge rejected the defence's argument that a "cooperative investigation" is one where the participants make relatively equal contributions. He found that the term did not connote the extent of participation of the parties except that they "wor[k] together to the same end" (para. 24).

133. He then proceeded to find that the RCMP officers in question were involved in a "cooperative investigation":

In any event, Detective Superintendent Lessemun was with the Canadian police at all times and did play a role in what they did by acting as a lookout, by providing information, and, the Canadian police believed, by obtaining warrants. While the Canadians may have made a larger contribution of officers, expertise and equipment, the Turks & Caicos contributed police authority in the jurisdiction. The RCMP sought and was granted permission from the Turks & Caicos authorities to conduct [an] investigation on the Island. I accept Officer Boyle's testimony that the RCMP officers were, and understood that they were, operating under the authority of Detective Superintendent Lessemun. The fact that the RCMP could not remove the seized records from the Island, as they had planned, makes apparent that they were subject to Turks & Caicos authority.

I find that all the actions of the RCMP on the Turks and Caicos Islands were part of a "cooperative investigation". [paras. 25-6]

134. Following this conclusion, the trial judge determined that it was for him to determine whether the application of the Charter to this "cooperative investigation" would result in an objectionable extraterritorial effect. He concluded that it would:

Cory J and Iacobucci J, in the majority judgment in *Cook*, indicated, at paragraphs 15 and 54, that there is an objectionable extraterritorial effect when Canadian criminal law standards are imposed on foreign officials and procedures. In *Cook*, the words which the Canadian police spoke to the accused were at their complete discretion. The conversation between the Canadian police and Cook, while it took place in a US jail, was not subject to American law and procedure. In that conversation, the Canadian police could have instructed the accused about his right to counsel in accordance with Canadian standards without implicating American criminal law or procedures.

This is a different case, because the Canadian police, in this case, were operating under and subject to the authority of Detective Superintendent Lessemun. Moreover, the propriety and legality of the entries into the private premises in the Turks & Caicos Islands, whether pursuant to warrants or not, are subject to Turks & Caicos criminal law and procedures and the superintending scrutiny of the Turks & Caicos courts. [paras. 28-9]

On this basis, the trial judge held that the Charter did not apply.

135. The Court of Appeal essentially endorsed the trial judge's ruling on s 8, finding that he considered the binding authorities (*Terry* and *Cook*) and correctly concluded on the basis of these authorities that the Charter did not apply ((2005), 201 OAC 126).

II. *Submissions of the Parties*

136. The appellant's argument is that the conduct of the Canadian police falls within the factual confines of *Cook*. He further argues that the courts below erred in not applying the Charter on the basis that the RCMP officer's actions were part of a "cooperative investigation". He submits that the passage in *Terry* that employs this term only emphasizes that the Charter will not apply to foreign authorities, not that the Charter cannot apply to Canadian authorities. The appellant asks that the conviction be quashed as a result of a violation of s 8 (though I note that he submits no argument on the alleged s 8 breach or s 24(2)).

137. The respondent takes the position that the trial judge correctly applied a "cooperation" test to determine the application of the Charter, and that the appellant is really only challenging his factual finding that the RCMP officers were cooperating with and under the control of Turks and Caicos officials. It argues that the decision of the trial judge is entitled to deference absent a palpable and overriding error and notes that no such error has been demonstrated. The respondent further argues that applying the Charter in this case would result in imposing the Charter [on] the laws and procedures of a foreign country, which *Cook* determined would constitute an interference with the sovereign authority of that country.

138. The intervener, Attorney General of Ontario, argues that cooperation *per se* precludes the application of the Charter in this case and supports the rulings of the courts below. The intervener does, however, make an alternative argument assuming Charter application. It argues that before determining whether Charter compliance will constitute an "objectionable extraterritorial effect", it is first necessary to determine the nature and scope of the s 8 Charter right in the location and jurisdiction searched. Essentially, the intervener cautions this Court against endorsing an approach that would permit wholesale application of s 8 to the activities of Canadian officials investigating abroad. It argues that protection consistent with the law of the foreign country is merited here and that this can be realized by adopting the approach of Lamer CJ in *Schreiber* v. *Canada (Attorney General)*, [1998] 1 SCR 841, or by relying on comments made by this Court in previous judgments that provide that the scope of s 8 is determined by a contextual approach.

The intervener also emphasizes that a wholesale approach to applying s 8 abroad would hamper international cooperation in fighting transnational crime.

III. *Analysis*

139. It is clear from this Court's jurisprudence (notably *Cook*, but also comments made by La Forest J in *R* v. *Harrer*, [1995] 3 SCR 562, at paras. 11 and 12, and by Lamer CJ in *Schreiber*, at para. 16) that the Charter's reach does not end at the "water's edge". It is less clear, however, when and how the Charter applies abroad.

A. *Solution(s) presented by the majority judgment in* Cook

140. At para. 25 of *Cook*, the majority set out two factors it identified as critical to its conclusion that the Charter applied to the activities of the Canadian police in that case on the basis of nationality: (1) the impugned act falls within s 32(1) of the Charter; and (2) the application of the Charter does not interfere with the sovereign authority of the foreign state and thereby generate an objectionable extraterritorial effect. These two factors have since been seen by many as the test for the application of the Charter abroad.

141. Applying this test to the facts in *Cook*, the majority held that s 10(*b*) of the Charter applied to the conduct of two Vancouver police officers in the United States. As to the first stage, the Court found that the officers involved were Canadians and thus the impugned act (failure to provide a proper counsel warning) fell within the scope of s 32(1). I would similarly find that the first branch of the test in *Cook* applies to the RCMP officers' actions in this case.

142. What remains unclear about the majority's decision in *Cook* is when the second branch of its test has been met. In my view, the majority decision in *Cook* does not provide a definitive answer. Rather, several possible approaches to the question, "When is there an interference with the sovereign authority of [a] foreign state?" appear possible on the basis of *Cook*. I review each of these below.

(1) *"Cooperation"*

143. The reference to Justice McLachlin's comments in *Terry* and the emphasis placed on "cooperation" at para. 54 of *Cook* suggest that cooperation is tantamount to interference with foreign jurisdiction if it involves the application of Canadian laws or procedures and that the determinative test for Charter application is therefore whether there is

"cooperation" between Canadian and foreign officials or not. This also suggests that there was no cooperation in *Cook*. However, in my view, there clearly had to have been "cooperation", at least in the form of consent, between the US and the Canadian law enforcement officers in order for the interrogation to take place. (See R. A. Harvie and H. Foster, "Let the Yanks Do It? The Charter, the Criminal Law and Evidence on a 'Silver Platter'" (2001), 59 *Advocate* 71, at pp. 75-6.)

144. The majority in *Cook* suggests, at para. 54, by citing the comments of McLachlin J in *Terry*, that once there is any cooperation, the door to the application of the Charter closes entirely. In the present appeal, the trial judge did not dispose of the Charter issue by simply finding that there was cooperation between the RCMP and Turks and Caicos police. He went on to find that applying the Charter to this particular "cooperative investigation" would result in imposing Canadian standards on foreign authorities, and therefore constitute an interference with foreign jurisdiction. This Court must now decide whether *Cook* actually created a test based on "cooperation" to determine Charter application.

145. In my opinion, using "cooperative investigation" language to determine whether there is an objectionable extraterritorial effect of Canadian law is not helpful. The first problem with this approach relates to the fact that cooperation with foreign officials in the context of Canadian investigations abroad will be inevitable in most, if not all cases. All Canadian officers investigating in a foreign territory, in order to fulfill their mandate, will have to cooperate with foreign officials and comply with foreign law. This principle of international law is stated in I. Brownlie, *Principles of Public International Law* (6th edn 2003), at p. 306:

The governing principle is that a state cannot take measures on the territory of another state by way of enforcement of national laws without the consent of the latter. Persons may not be arrested, a summons may not be served, police or tax investigations may not be mounted, orders for production of documents may not be executed, on the territory of another state, except under the terms of a treaty or other consent given.

It is repeated in S. Coughlan et al., "Global Reach, Local Grasp: Constructing Extraterritorial Jurisdiction in the Age of Globalization" (2007), 6 *CJLT* 29, at p. 32: "[S]tate officials such as police cannot exercise their executive powers on the territory of another state without that state's permission."

146. As well, in a paper on the extraterritorial application of the Fourth Amendment outside the United States, E. Bentley, writes:

[S]earches and seizures in foreign states are of necessity a cooperative endeavor, with United States agents routinely cast in the supporting role. In the "typical case", of which *Verdugo* provides an example, "the foreign officials are the ones who decide the scope and reasonableness of any proposed search", and United States agents "must comply with the demands of their hosts". The reasons for this are both legal and practical.

It is a settled principle of international law that law enforcement operations are exclusively entrusted to each state within its own jurisdiction, and that when one state sends police to another state to conduct a search, it may conduct the search only with the permission, and conforming to the laws, of the host state...

It is not only international law, but practical realities as well, that prevent the United States from conducting unilateral law enforcement operations in foreign states. United States law enforcement agents operating in a foreign state must try to accomplish their objectives while stripped of most of the powers of search and arrest that they wield in the United States. To accomplish anything, they generally must engage the cooperation of local authorities at one level or another. In attempting to do so, they face additional hurdles, in the form of alien legal and political systems, divergent law enforcement cultures, and diplomatic frictions.

As a result, United States extraterritorial law enforcement now takes place within an elaborate framework of international cooperation, at all levels of formality.

("Toward an International Fourth Amendment: Rethinking Searches and Seizures Abroad After *Verdugo-Urquidez*" (1994), 27 *Vand. J. Transnat'l L.* 329, at pp. 365-6 and 368)

147. Adopting a "cooperation" approach as the limit to Charter application will result in very few situations where the Charter can apply. This can be seen in the American experience. Bentley describes, at pp. 400-2, how the US "joint venture standard" used to determine constitutional protection abroad (which operates somewhat like a cooperation test in that it seeks to identify sufficient participation of US officials in foreign investigation to activate Fourth Amendment protection) has failed to be applied in a coherent fashion by US courts and has resulted in little constitutional protection:

To date, as noted above, courts have found United States participation in foreign searches sufficient to trigger the Fourth Amendment in only a handful of cases. Among the activities which have been held not to rise to the requisite level of participation are: requesting, but not participating in, a foreign search, or otherwise "triggering the interest" of foreign authorities who subsequently conduct a search and pass the evidence on to United States authorities; passing on tips which prompt foreign police to initiate an investigation; passing on information requested by foreign governments; joining foreign police in a foreign-initiated search; participating in foreign wiretaps, as long as United States agents do not "initiate, supervise, control or direct" them; using information from an illegal foreign wiretap to support a United States search warrant; and even, in a few cases, triggering and then participating in a foreign search.

If these decisions embody a coherent standard on joint participation, it is difficult to perceive. While most courts have followed the test set out in *Stonehill* v. *United States*—that "Federal agents so substantially participated in the raids so as to convert them into joint ventures"—or language essentially to that effect; they have failed to articulate what this test entails in any coherent fashion, instead applying the test in an ad hoc, apparently result-oriented manner to the facts of the case at hand ... Whatever factors courts have focused on, the result has been the same: courts have found insufficient United States participation in all but the most indisputable circumstances. If one had to judge by the few cases in which joint participation has been found, one would have to conclude that the Fourth Amendment does not apply abroad unless United States officials both initiate the search and then continue to participate actively as it unfolds.

This near-elimination of Fourth Amendment liability cannot have been intended by the Supreme Court when it formulated the doctrine on which the joint venture standard was based. [Emphasis deleted.]

148. A second problem with the "cooperation" approach, at least in my view, is the fact that cooperation as such which occurs between Canadian officials and foreign authorities tells us nothing about whether impermissible extraterritorial effects will occur. An objectionable territorial effect does not necessarily result from the mere fact of cooperation. On this basis, I think Justice McLachlin's comments in *Terry* are better characterized as a recognition of a state of affairs rather than a prescription of when there will be objectionable extraterritorial effects.

(2) *The "factors" approach to determining when there is interference with the sovereign authority of a foreign state*

149. At para. 50, the majority in *Cook* enumerates a number of factual elements that demonstrate why there is no interference with US territorial jurisdiction on the facts in that case. These are: (1) the arrest and interrogation were initiated by a Canadian extradition request; (2) the offence was committed exclusively in Canada and was to be prosecuted in Canada; (3) the US authorities did not become involved in the investigation; and (4) the interrogation was conducted solely by Canadian police officers. Harvie and Foster, at pp. 75-6, suggest that this is in fact *the* test advanced by the majority and criticize it as "a difficult and complex analysis", not straightforward enough, and difficult for lower courts to apply.

150. I have difficulty seeing how these factors establish a "test". Rather, this approach is based on a determination that seems as vague as "We will know what an interference is when we see one." Nevertheless, this is the type of "test" the appellant seems to suggest *Cook* stands for by arguing that his situation falls within the factual confines of *Cook*. There is clearly a need to define a more principled articulation of the rule governing the application of the Charter abroad.

(3) *Who initiates the investigation as determinative of when there is interference with the sovereign authority of a foreign state*

151. It has been suggested that the principle that can be distilled from the factors raised by the majority in *Cook* is that the Charter will apply when the Canadian investigation abroad occurs absent an independent foreign investigation (see Harvie and Foster, at p. 76). R. J. Currie, in "Charter Without Borders? The Supreme Court of Canada, Transnational Crime and Constitutional Rights and Freedoms" (2004), 27 *Dal. LJ* 235, at p. 242, states that the majority of the Court in *Cook* permitted Charter application to the interrogation in that case because "even though it occurred on US territory, [it] did not interfere with American sovereignty since it was directed at the activities of Canadian officers acting within the context of a Canadian investigation, aimed at the ultimate result of a criminal trial in Canada". Coughlan et al., at p. 57, footnote 58, identifies the basis for applying the Charter in *Cook* as follows: "The application of the Charter in this kind of case appears to turn on whether the Canadian police are conducting their own investigative activities with the consent of the foreign authorities to do so, or whether they are engaged in policing activities under the direction of the foreign police authority."

152. The statement in *Cook*, at para. 54, that "It may well be a different case where, for example, Canadian authorities participate, on foreign territory, in an investigative action *undertaken* by foreign authorities in accordance with foreign procedures" supports this view (emphasis added). "Undertaken" can be seen to refer to an investigation *initiated* by foreign authorities. Therefore, as long as the investigation is initiated by Canadians and the evidence is sought to be used in Canada, compliance with the test in *Cook* will be achieved. The facts of this case do tend to support the view that this was indeed an investigation initiated by Canadians and that the role played by Turks and Caicos authorities was merely one of facilitating the RCMP's investigation.

153. I see no principled basis why the Charter would not apply to Canadian officials who are actively involved in an investigation just because they did not initiate the investigation.

(4) *Foreign "control" over the investigation as the limit on the extraterritorial application of the Charter*

154. The approach I suggested in my concurring reasons in *Cook* offered a solution to the indeterminacy presented by the majority's "factors" or "cooperation" approaches. It would appear that the trial judge in this case interpreted my reasons to call for such a "control" test and found this test to be easily reconcilable with the majority reasons in *Cook*. This view of the "control" test has been summarized as follows: "On the one hand, no Charter breach occurs if the evidence is obtained by the host officers or under their supervision. On the other hand, the Charter does apply if the Canadian authorities are primarily responsible for obtaining the evidence" (Harvie and Foster, at p. 74). A "control" test would thus be seen as a precision on the "cooperation" test discussed above, but this overlooks the fact that in most foreign investigations foreign officers will be in "control" since Canadian officials must operate in the foreign territory under their consent and guidance, usually relying on their procedures.

(5) *Imposing Canadian standards as determinative of when there is an interference with the sovereign authority of a foreign state*

155. The majority reasons in *Cook* also suggest that the Charter will not apply where Canadian criminal law standards are imposed on foreign officials or where they would supplant foreign procedures (para. 54). I believe that this is what the trial judge in the case at bar concluded in his analysis. Above any other determination, in my view, his analysis emphasized the fact that the RCMP officers were subject to Turks and Caicos authority. This can be seen at para. 30, where, analysing the s 8 arguments of the defence, he notes a tacit recognition by the defence of "the inescapable conclusion that foreign criminal law and procedures are engaged".

156. Adopting this approach will no doubt help resolve the issue where Canadian officers act independently; they will have to satisfy their normal Charter obligations. The test rests on two assumptions: (1) that whenever the Charter does apply, Canadian standards are applied *wholesale*; and (2) that some investigations occurring in a foreign state will be regulated by Canadian law. When the Canadian officers can meet their Charter obligation *independently* (and not by consent, as argued by LeBel J), as was the case in *Cook*, there will be no interference. But when the assistance or authorization of foreign authorities is required, fulfilling Canadian standards for some Charter rights will always result in an interference if they are, as said earlier, applied *wholesale*, as if the investigation was being held in Canada. For example,

meeting Canadian s 8 standards abroad will then mean imposing warrant requirements and standards on Turks and Caicos and requiring a certain conduct of Turks and Caicos officials. This generates objectionable extraterritorial effects.

157. But this approach produces inconsistent application of the Charter's protection of legal rights because some rights, such as s 10(*b*), could apply, as in *Cook*, but s 8 and maybe s 9 never will. This sort of "patchwork" approach to the Charter seems quite unprincipled. I recognize that the majority in *Cook* having said that the Charter would only apply in "rare circumstances" (see para. 25) supports the opposite inference; but I prefer the contrary view of Lamer CJ in *Schreiber*, at para. 16, that "[Canadian] officials are clearly subject to Canadian law, including the Charter, within Canada, and in most cases, outside it" (cited in *Cook*, at para. 46).

B. *An alternative to the majority approach in* Cook

158. It thus appears that the various approaches to determining when there is an interference with the sovereign authority of a foreign state presented by this Court's decision in *Cook* are problematic. One solution is to revert to the dissenting position of L'Heureux-Dubé J in *Cook* and cut off the Charter's reach at the "water's edge" on the basis that comity requires it. But there is an alternative to this displacement of the Charter.

159. Section 32(1) provides as follows:

32. (1) This Charter applies

(a) to the Parliament and government of Canada in respect of all matters within the authority of Parliament including all matters relating to the Yukon Territory and Northwest Territories; and
(b) to the legislature and government of each province in respect of all matters within the authority of the legislature of each province.

These terms do not extend the application of the Charter to the actions of foreign officials. But they do not imply that the Charter cannot apply to Canadian police officials acting abroad. There can be no suggestion, therefore, that the Charter creates any legal consequences whatsoever for a foreign agent or for the application of foreign law.

160. I would disagree with LeBel J that if one cannot enforce Canadian law outside Canada the matter falls outside the authority of Parliament and the provincial legislatures under s 32(1) (para. 69). I think s 32(1) includes all actions of Canadian police officers precisely because s 32 does not distinguish between actions taken on Canadian soil and

actions taken abroad. It would also be unprincipled, in my view, to draw a distinction the moment a Canadian police officer's foot touches foreign soil. As I noted in *Cook*, at para. 120: "the status of a police officer as an officer of the state is not altered by crossing a jurisdictional border, even if he or she is deprived of all the coercive powers conferred by the home state... From the perspective of the home legal system... police officers are still representatives of their home government." The fact that Canadian law is not enforced in a foreign country does not mean that it cannot apply to a Canadian government official. I would note in particular that some Canadian laws apply on the basis of nationality wherever the crime is committed: see s 7(4.1) of the Criminal Code, RSC 1985, c C-46, on sex crimes committed outside Canada and ss 7(3.7) to 7(3.75) on crimes against humanity.

161. I do not think a restrictive interpretation of the words "matters that are within the authority of Parliament or the provincial legislatures", adopted at para. 69 of my colleague's reasons, is warranted in discussing the obligations of Canadian police officers operating in another country. I am uncomfortable with such a "reading down" of s 32(1) of the Charter. Section 32(1) of the Charter defines *who* acts, not *where* they act. In the instant case, the matter is a Canadian criminal investigation involving Canadian police acting abroad, which clearly makes it a matter within the authority of Parliament or the provincial legislatures. It appears strange to me that my colleague could see an investigation as falling under s 32(1) of the Charter in one case (in Canada) and not the other (outside Canada). If the investigative activities of Canadian police officers abroad do not fall under "matters that are within the authority of Parliament or the provincial legislatures", then the officers would have no jurisdiction whatsoever to be conducting investigations abroad. Clearly, they do, as found in *Libman* v. *The Queen*, [1985] 2 SCR 178.

162. The second thing that must be recognized is that the application of the Charter as such to the actions of Canadian officials does not automatically result in an interference with the sovereign authority of foreign states. In *Cook*, where I had adopted the "control" test, I found that there was no interference or "conflict" with sovereign authority when Canadian officials are subject to the Charter because the Charter does not mandate specific conduct, but rather imposes certain limits on the conduct of government officials:

[T]he nature of the rights contained in the relevant sections of the Charter are not mandatory, but rather conditional upon the occurrence of specified investigatory activities. Thus, *if there is a rule of investigation in the foreign jurisdiction that directly contradicts a Charter provision, there is still no conflict.*

The reason for this is that the Charter does not impose any obligation to investigate; it simply requires that if an investigation is made by the officer, it must be conducted in accordance with certain conditions. It follows from this, moreover, that the application of the Charter to the Canadian official has no impact on the foreign legal system.

...

As is clear from the discussion above, there is no question of a "conflict" between foreign procedures and Canadian procedures. If the compulsory foreign procedure adopted falls below the standard required by the Charter, then the Canadian officials may not take *a directing or primary role* in the part of the investigation involving those techniques. In essence, they may not exercise, even when invited to do so by the foreign authority, the powers purportedly conferred on them by the foreign investigatory procedures. This is no more complex than the obligation imposed by the Charter within Canada. [Emphasis added; paras. 143 and 150.]

By putting the onus squarely on Canadian authorities to not exercise control if the investigatory action is not Charter compliant, we never have to ask whether the application of the Charter results in an interference with sovereign authority of a foreign state. If the "control" test is not adopted, as prescribed by *Cook*, we must consider in what circumstances there will be interference in cases where Canadian officers simply cooperate with foreign authorities.

163. At para. 97 of his reasons, LeBel J concedes that international law does not prohibit Canada from imposing restraints on its own conduct and that of its officials. He admits that it is the policy consideration of Canadian participation in the fight against transnational crime that ultimately informs his conclusion:

Since the Charter does not authorize state action, but simply operates as a limit on such action, could it not be said that the Charter "applies" to extraterritorial investigations by prohibiting Canadian officers from participating in investigations abroad that do not conform to Canadian law? International law provides only part of the answer to this question. To prohibit Canadian officers from participating would indeed ensure conformity with both international law and the Charter; however, it would also mean that the investigation could not be conducted. This is a serious concern. The complete answer therefore lies both in international law and in the need to address the challenges of investigating and prosecuting transborder criminal activity.

I do not question the importance of this policy consideration and the need for Canada to participate in the fight against transnational crime. However, I fail to see how the Charter prevents us from taking into account this important societal need while holding Canadian officers to their obligation to respect fundamental Canadian values. Let me then examine more closely what Charter compliance demands of Canadian officials. For present purposes I will limit my examination to the Legal Rights set out in ss 7-14 of the Charter.

164. The Legal Rights provisions of the Charter are very different from the provisions one can find in the Criminal Code, although there are provisions of the Criminal Code that prohibit specific conduct by Canadian officials based on the recognition of fundamental human rights. Take, for example, s 269.1(1) which makes "[e]very official, or every person acting at the instigation of or with the consent or acquiescence of an official, who inflicts torture on any other person" liable of an indictable offence.

165. The Legal Rights provisions of the Charter are also very different from the provisions in the Criminal Code, or other statutes, that stipulate specific criminal procedures that must be followed in a given case. For example, the Criminal Code specifies the circumstances in which search or arrest warrants are necessary (see for example ss 487 to 489 and 495(2) of the Criminal Code), as well as those when they are not (see for example ss 117.02(1), (2), 199(2), 254(2) to (4), 462 and 495(1)). Police also have powers to search and detain without a warrant in certain circumstances at common law under the *Waterfield* test (*R* v. *Godoy*, [1999] 1 SCR 311, *R* v. *Mann*, [2004] 3 SCR 59, 2004 SCC 52, and *Dedman* v. *The Queen*, [1985] 2 SCR 2).

166. The Legal Rights provisions of the Charter neither mandate nor prohibit specific conduct by Canadian officials. Rather they lay down a number of fundamental principles—framed as general propositions regarding the treatment of individuals—that are used to scrutinize the legitimacy of the specific criminal procedures and conduct of Canadian officials. The principles embodied within these provisions are broadly worded and from these courts draw out further guiding principles. Consider s 8 of the Charter, which puts forth the principle that "[e]veryone has the right to be secure against unreasonable search or seizure". This general principle has engendered a number of further principles determining what constitutes a "reasonable" search. This Court has stated in previous cases that: (1) the purpose behind s 8 is to protect the privacy of individuals from unjustified state intrusion (*Hunter* v. *Southam Inc.*, [1984] 2 SCR 145); (2) this interest in privacy is, however, limited to a "reasonable expectation of privacy" (*R* v. *Evans*, [1996] 1 SCR 8); (3) wherever feasible, prior authorization must be obtained in order for a search and seizure to be reasonable (*Hunter*); (4) prior authorization must be given by someone who is neutral and impartial and who is capable of acting judicially (*Hunter*); (5) the person granting the authorization must be satisfied by objective evidence on oath that there are

reasonable and probable grounds for believing that an offence has been committed and that a search of the place for which the warrant is sought will find evidence related to that offence (*Hunter*); (6) a search is reasonable if it is authorized by law, if the law itself is reasonable and if the manner of the search is reasonable (*R* v. *Caslake*, [1998] 1 SCR 51).

167. It is the role of courts to interpret the general principles set out in the provisions of the Charter, draw out further principles, and apply these to the facts of a given case. That exercise is an ongoing process which has produced, up to now, a body of rules applicable within the Canadian legal system. The specific application of these principles to factual circumstances and the rules they create, however, should not be confused with the more abstract principles for which the Charter stands.

168. For example s 10(*b*), in the context of officers operating in Canada, has been interpreted to require that officers tell individuals upon detention, without delay, of their right to counsel and to provide reasonable access to counsel if the right is exercised. In the context of officers operating in a foreign country, unless it is a situation like that in *Cook* where the officers were acting independently, the officer will have to rely on the foreign authorities and their procedures. When the foreign officials are detaining and interrogating the individual, and where there is Canadian participation, the participating Canadian officer is not required to give a s 10(*b*) warning; detention and interrogation are governed by the local laws. Nor is the Canadian officer required to provide "a crash course" to foreign officials on how to give the accused his s 10(*b*) warning on the Canadian government's behalf. The Charter is not meant to be applied as if it were merely a code of criminal procedure.

169. In my view, adhering to fundamental principles that emanate from the Charter would simply require the Canadian officers to inform themselves of the rights and protections that exist under foreign law when dealing with the individual's legal rights on detention, and compare them to those guaranteed under the Charter in order to determine if they are consistent with fundamental human rights norms. It is not the case that the protections have to be identical. When the foreign procedure differs from the plain language of s 10(*b*) (the right to retain and instruct counsel is not provided without delay upon arrest or detention for example), there will be a *prima facie* breach of this provision. However, differences resulting from different legal regimes and different approaches adopted in other democratic societies will usually be justified given the international context, the need to fight transnational crime and the need to respect the sovereign authority of other states, coupled with the fact that it is impossible for Canadian officials to follow their own procedures in those circumstances. Flexibility in this case is

permitted by s 1 of the Charter. Trivial and technical differences will easily be discarded, more substantial differences between the protections that would be available in Canada and those available in the foreign state will require more in order to be justified.

170. Consider a further example that is closer to the facts at hand. In *R* v. *Kokesch*, [1990] 3 SCR 3, while investigating an illegal marijuana growing operation in British Columbia, police conducted a perimeter search of a dwelling, acting without reasonable grounds to justify a warrantless search under s 10(1)(*a*) of the Narcotic Control Act, RSC 1970, c N-1. The search not being authorized by statute, the Court found that the police had no common law power to conduct the perimeter search because the common law rights of property holders to be free of police intrusion can be restricted only by clear statutory language. The search was therefore deemed illegal, and hence in violation of s 8 of the Charter. But the case does not stand for the general rule that the Charter always prohibits warrantless perimeter searches. The case also does not mean that Canadian officers conducting such a search under the laws of a foreign state would have to obtain a warrant issued in Canada to be executed, for example, in the Turks and Caicos (this would be contrary to norms of international law, as earlier stated), or require Turks and Caicos officials to obtain an authorization that is not required under local law.

171. Under s 8 Charter principles, a warrantless perimeter search may be Charter compliant if authorized by law. On the facts of this case, we know that a warrantless perimeter [search] occurred and that such searches are permitted under Turks and Caicos law. Charter principles also require that a search permitted by law must be reasonable. The reasonableness test to be applied here is one that has regard to comity and the determination that the foreign law is not inconsistent with fundamental human rights. The ultimate question becomes, in reality: Was it reasonable for Canadian officers to participate in the search authorized by Turks and Caicos law?

172. I believe the Charter is flexible enough to permit a reasonable margin of appreciation for different procedures. Even between free and democratic societies, investigative procedures can vary and it is necessary, in order to foster continued cooperation between nations in the fight against transnational crime, to respect certain differences. As was noted by McLachlin J in *Harrer*, at para. 55:

We live in an era when people, goods and information pass from country to country with great rapidity. Law enforcement authorities, if they are to do their job, must apprehend people and intercept goods and communications wherever they may be found. Often they find themselves working with officers in foreign jurisdictions; often they are merely the recipients of information gathered independently elsewhere. The result is evidence gathered by rules which may differ from Canadian rules. We need to accommodate the reality that different countries apply different rules to evidence gathering, rules which must be respected in some measure if we are to retain the ability to prosecute those whose crime and travel take them beyond our borders. To insist on exact compliance with Canadian rules would be to insist universally on Canadian standards of procedures which, in the real world, may seldom be attained—an insistence which would make prosecution of many offences difficult, if not impossible.

173. The Charter permits the incorporation of legitimate justifications, sometimes within the right itself, as with s 8, or pursuant to ss 1 and 24(2). Both my colleague and I are prepared to accept that the need for Canadian officers to fight transnational crime, abide by foreign procedures and respect the sovereign authority of foreign states justifies Canada's participation in investigation procedures that are not identical to Canada's, *to a point*. For LeBel J, this point seems to be when Canadian authorities violate their international law obligations (para. 101). It may be that this proposition sounds appealing in theory, but I have difficulty in seeing how, in practice, Canadian officials will know when this point has been reached. Is the expectation that Canadian officers become knowledgeable in international customary law—an area of law whose content is uncertain and disputed? Practically speaking, I believe it is preferable to frame the fundamental rights obligations of Canadian officials working abroad in a context that officers are already expected to be familiar with—their obligations under the Charter. LeBel J's proposal of applying international law standards to the actions of Canadian officials working abroad introduces another new set of standards to the mix, which my colleague himself appears to recognize is difficult, at para. 90:

It is no more helpful to suggest that some third option other than the law of the host state or the full application of Charter standards might govern foreign investigations. Where would the standards to be applied come from? How would Canadian officials know what is required of them at the outset of an investigation?

The approach I am advocating is in my view far more practical. It is also consistent with this Court's approach in extradition and deportation cases: see for instance *United States of America* v. *Dynar*, [1997] 2 SCR 462, and *United States* v. *Burns*, [2001] 1 SCR 283, 2001 SCC 7. What I advocate is that Canadian officers assess the fundamental human rights protection offered by the foreign procedures against the principles guaranteed by the Charter; they may consider Charter compliance for guidance. Minor differences in protection can be justified on the basis [of] the need for Canadian officials to participate in fighting transnational crime, and comity. Substantial differences require greater justifications, but there will still be a favourable presumption for laws and procedures of democratic countries.

174. To summarize, in any challenge to the conduct of Canadian officials investigating abroad, the onus will be on the claimant to demonstrate that the difference between fundamental human rights protection given by the local law and that afforded under the Charter is inconsistent with basic Canadian values; the onus will then shift to the government to justify its involvement in the activity. In many cases, differences between protections guaranteed by Charter principles and the protections offered by foreign procedures will simply be justified by the need for Canada to be involved in fighting transnational crime and the need to respect the sovereign authority of foreign states. On account of this, courts are permitted to apply a rebuttable presumption of Charter compliance where the Canadian officials were acting pursuant to valid foreign laws and procedures. Unless it is shown that those laws or procedures are substantially inconsistent with the fundamental principles emanating from the Charter, they will not give rise to the breach of a Charter right. In my view, this is the most principled and practical way to strike an appropriate balance between effective participation by Canadian officers in fighting transnational crime and respect for fundamental human rights.

175. It can be argued that applying the Charter abroad in this fashion, at the end of the day, essentially achieves the same result as applying the Charter "*ex post facto*"; under that approach, the Charter never applies abroad, but evidence at a Canadian trial could be excluded on the basis of ss 7 and 11(*d*) of the Charter. The first problem I see with that approach is that it can only address situations where a s 24(2) remedy may be sought (i.e., the exclusion of evidence), and not situations where s 24(1) remedies may be sought. Though no such case has yet come before the Court, it is possible that at some future date an applicant may seek a declaration or some other remedy resulting from a Charter violation by Canadian officials acting abroad. It would be premature, in my view, to preclude this from occurring, without such a case being properly before the Court. The second problem with the ss 7 and 11(*d*) approach is that it curtails the use of the fundamental principles set out under the other provisions of the Charter. From an analytical standpoint, it is preferable to use the principles emanating

from s 8 of the Charter to assess whether evidence gathered from a search and seizure ought to be excluded from a trial in Canada than to refer to principles developed under s 7 to deal with the same issue.

C. *Conclusion on the proper approach to extraterritorial Charter application*

176. The main question here is to determine what are the Charter obligations of Canadian officers investigating in another country. In my view, *Cook* at least established that Canadian authorities must abide by standards set for actions taken in Canada when they act independently, i.e., where the foreign state takes absolutely no part in the action and does not subject the action to its laws. Where the host state takes part in the action by subjecting Canadian authorities to its laws, the Charter still applies to Canadian officers but there will be no Charter violation where the Canadian officers abide by the laws of the host state, subject to the exception discussed above. I believe this is the outcome contemplated in *Harrer* and *Terry*. This is also consistent with the approach taken by Lamer CJ in *Schreiber*, who found a person's expectation of privacy to be commensurate with legal protections provided in the host country; his approach was based on a contextual application of the Charter and also showed some deference to the laws of the foreign country where the search took place.

177. I cannot agree with LeBel J that the Charter is inapplicable or cannot be complied with outside Canadian territory. If s 8 of the Charter was inapplicable to a s 32(1) matter, as LeBel J argues, I fail to see why he would apply s 7 of the Charter as a control mechanism *ex post facto* (see para. 91) to the same matter, i.e. a Canadian investigation. There is, in my view, no meaningful distinction between *ex post facto* and *ex ante* application of the Charter to Canadian officials.

178. The Charter applies extraterritorially, but the obligations it creates in the circumstances will depend on the nature of the right at risk, the nature of the action of the police, the involvement of foreign authorities and the application of foreign laws. In the context of actions taken outside Canada, the search had to be conducted in conformity with the local laws. There is obviously consent to the participation of Canadian officers in all cases where they operate in another country. Thus, in my view, consent is not a useful criterion to determine Charter application. The main question is rather whether the foreign law applies. *Cook* was a rare instance where it did not. But even where the foreign law applies, there are potential Charter protections. As LeBel J recognizes

himself at para. 109, flagrant breaches of fundamental human rights, such as torture, would not be accepted even if authorized by local laws.

179. On the facts of this case, it is clear that the Canadian authorities were operating under the authority of Detective Superintendent Lessemun, that the local laws applied to the investigation and that there was no evidence that the local laws had been breached or did not meet fundamental human rights standards. Hape led no evidence to suggest there were any differences between the fundamental human rights protections available under Turks and Caicos search and seizure laws and what the protections the Charter guarantees under Canadian law that would raise serious concerns. The seizure of documents was thus reasonable in the context and the evidence should not be excluded.

IV. *Conclusion*

180. I would dismiss the appeal and affirm the convictions.

The following are the reasons delivered by
181. BINNIE J:—This appeal raises relatively straightforward issues arising out of a money laundering investigation. It should be dismissed. As my colleagues note, the searches and seizures of the appellant's bank records in the Turks and Caicos Islands were carried out under the authority of the local police in conformity with local powers of search and seizure. No prejudice to the appellant's right to a fair trial in Canada has been demonstrated. The appellant, having chosen to do his banking in the Turks and Caicos Islands, can be taken to have accepted the degree of privacy which the law of that jurisdiction affords. The record demonstrates that superimposing the Canadian law of search and seizure on top of that of the Turks and Caicos Islands would be unworkable. The appeal fails because the appellant cannot bring his case within the requirements adopted by the majority of this Court in *R* v. *Cook*, [1998] 2 SCR 597, at para. 25, namely that:

... (1) the impugned act falls within s 32(1) of the Charter; and (2) the application of the Charter to the actions of the Canadian [police in the Turks and Caicos Islands does] not, in this particular case, interfere with the sovereign authority of the foreign state and thereby generate an *objectionable* extraterritorial effect. [Emphasis added.]

182. My colleague LeBel J holds, in essence, that *any* extraterritorial effect is objectionable (para. 85). This effectively overrules *Cook* and would further limit the potential extraterritorial application of the Canadian Charter of Rights and Freedoms. With respect, I do not believe

that this case, or the narrowly focussed argument of the very experienced counsel for the appellant (a 12-page factum of which three pages were devoted to legal argument citing only four authorities), affords a proper springboard for such sweeping conclusions.

183. While the application of *Cook* is not without practical and theoretical difficulties, as my colleagues Bastarache and LeBel JJ show, there is sufficient flexibility in the notion of *objectionable* extraterritorial effect for such difficulties to be resolved over time in circumstances more challenging than those of the routine police investigations at issue here and in the four cases cited by the appellant, namely, *R* v. *Harrer*, [1995] 3 SCR 562; *R* v. *Terry*, [1996] 2 SCR 207; *Schreiber* v. *Canada (Attorney General)*, [1998] 1 SCR 841, and *Cook* itself. Routine Canadian police investigations in the United States (*Harrer, Terry* and *Cook*), Switzerland (*Schreiber*) and in the Turks and Caicos Islands (this case) are of course significant, but issues of more far-reaching importance will soon confront Canadian courts, especially in the context of the "war on terror" and its progeny. We should, in my view, avoid premature pronouncements that restrict the application of the Charter to Canadian officials operating abroad in relation to Canadian citizens.

184. In the 12 years since *Harrer*, serious questions of the utmost importance have arisen respecting the extent to which, if at all, a constitutional bill of rights follows the flag when state security and police authorities operate outside their home territory. In the United States, the issues are being debated in the context of "special renditions" of suspects by non-military US authorities to and between foreign countries and the rights of individuals held in camps said to be operated under the control of non-military US personnel outside the United States (quite apart from military installations such as Guantánamo Bay). It has been widely contended in that country that different standards apply to civilian as distinguished from military personnel and to citizens as distinguished from non-citizens. Canadian police and security officials have also been active recently in foreign "hot spots" as diverse as Haiti, Iraq and Afghanistan. In fact, since 1989, the RCMP has managed the deployment of over 2,000 Canadian police officers in at least 12 countries with troubled histories, including Kosovo, East Timor, Guinea, Sierra Leone, Bosnia and Herzegovina, Ethiopia, Haiti, Jordan, Iraq, the Democratic Republic of Congo, Côte d'Ivoire and Afghanistan (Royal Canadian Mounted Police, *RCMP International Peacekeeping Branch Review, 2004/2005* (2006)). In addition, RCMP "International Operations Branch" Officers work in 25 locations around the world (Royal Canadian Mounted Police, *RCMP Fact Sheet—International Operations Branch* (2005)) in circumstances that could give rise to Charter

challenges. Recently, claims have been launched in Canadian courts by human rights activists (including Amnesty International Canada and British Columbia Civil Liberties Association) against the federal government asking the courts to extend Charter protections (as well as international human rights and humanitarian law) to individuals detained by the Canadian Forces operating in Afghanistan. It is not known to what extent Canadian citizens were among the detainees in question, although there is some evidence that there are Canadians among the Taliban. The allegation against the Minister of National Defence and the Attorney General of Canada (both civilian authorities) is that detainees were given into the custody of the security personnel of the government of Afghanistan without adequate safeguards (see Federal Court File Number T-324-07). We have no idea if there is any merit in any of these claims, but at some point we are likely to be called upon to address them. The Maher Arar Inquiry disclosed serious issues about Canadian police conduct in relation to the extraterritorial apprehension of a Canadian citizen in the United States which led to his incarceration and torture in Syria. The work of Canadian security personnel other than the RCMP may give rise to other issues, some of which may relate to the extraterritorial treatment of Canadian citizens. I mention these matters simply to illustrate the sort of issues that may eventually wind up before us and on which we can expect to hear extensive and scholarly argument in relation to the extraterritorial application of the Charter. Traditionally, common law courts have declined to make far-reaching pronouncements before being required by the facts before them to do so, heeding the cautionary words of the poet:

There are more things in heaven and earth, Horatio, Than are dreamt of in your philosophy.

(*Hamlet*, Act I, Scene v, 11. 166-7)

185. Justice LeBel places great emphasis on the remedial potential of s 24(2) of the Charter under which evidence may, in certain circumstances, be excluded from a Canadian trial, but the allegations now coming before our courts may not result in a trial in Canada. Indeed even the *right* to an ordinary trial may become an issue here as it has in the United States. Such serious Charter issues should be resolved only after full argument and debate in this Court, which we did not receive (and had no reason to expect) in this case.

186. My colleague LeBel J draws a number of very broad propositions from his analysis of certain aspects of international law and takes a more attenuated view of s 32(1) of the Charter than was adopted by the majority in *Cook*. LeBel J concludes that:

Since extraterritorial enforcement [of Canadian law] is not possible, and enforcement is necessary for the Charter to apply, *extraterritorial application of the Charter is impossible*. [Emphasis added; para. 85.]

I accept, of course, that enforcement is a central issue, but at this stage I would not treat difficulties in that regard as conclusive. My colleague adds at para. 100 that "[i]ndividual rights cannot be *completely* disregarded in the interests of transborder co-operation" (emphasis added). In an effort to fill the gap created by his rejection of Charter applicability, LeBel J would substitute Canada's "international human rights obligations", as a source of limitation on state power. The content of such obligations is weaker and their scope is more debatable than Charter guarantees. Specifically, LeBel J writes, at para. 101, that relief may be available "where the participation of Canadian officers in investigative activities sanctioned by foreign law would place Canada in violation of its international obligations in respect of human rights". The proposal is that international human rights obligations should become the applicable "extraterritorial" standard in substitution for Charter guarantees even as between the Canadian government and Canadian citizens.

187. This is not the case, in my respectful view, for the Court to determine whether Canadian citizens harmed by the extraterritorial conduct of Canadian authorities should be denied Charter relief (except if faced with a criminal trial in Canada) and be left to arguments about Canada's international law obligations. The Crown and the intervener, the Attorney General of Ontario, sought no such limitation. Neither the parties nor the intervener asked that *Cook* be revisited, much less overruled. Counsel were not at all dismissive of the relevance of the Charter in holding to account "extraterritorial" conduct of Canadian officials in relation to Canadian citizens, accepting (in my view correctly) that in Charter terms the denial of "*objectionable* extraterritorial effect" is a very different thing from the denial of *any* extraterritorial effect.

188. So too my colleague LeBel J writes, at para. 101:

I would leave open the possibility that, in a future case, participation by Canadian officers in activities in another country that would violate Canada's international human rights obligations might justify a remedy under s 24(1) of the Charter because of the impact of those activities on Charter rights in Canada.

However, the scope of this possible exception is unclear, given the fact that the conduct at issue would necessarily be outside Canada and, according to my colleague, ought not to be judged by the Charter standards because "extraterritorial application of the Charter is impossible" (para. 85).

189. I would therefore resolve this appeal on the basis of *Harrer, Terry, Schreiber* and *Cook*. I would retain for the present *Cook*'s "objectionable extraterritorial effect" principle while leaving the door open to future developments in assessing the extraterritorial application of the Charter. Our grasp of the potential ramifications of different approaches would be sharpened by the challenging fact situations and fresh perspectives presented in cases now working their way through the system. Constitutional pronouncements of such far-reaching implications as are laid down by my colleague ("extraterritorial application of the Charter is impossible") were not even on the radar screen of the parties and intervener to this appeal, all of whom were represented by able and experienced counsel. The Court should decline to resolve such important questions before they are ripe for decision.

190. Since writing the above, my colleague LeBel J has joined issue with this lone protest with the following comment:

We cannot always know what new issues might arise before the courts in the future, but we can trust that the law will grow and evolve as necessary and when necessary in response. [para. 95]

191. The law of the Constitution can only "grow and evolve" if the Court leaves it the flexibility to do so. It is precisely because of the uncertainty about future developments, some of which are now in the litigation pipeline, that I believe the Court should not in this case substitute rigidity for flexibility and, prematurely (and unnecessarily), foreclose Charter options that are now open to it under the flexible principles enunciated in *Cook*.

192. I would dismiss the appeal and affirm the convictions.

[Reports: [2007] 2 SCR 292; 280 DLR (4th) 385; 22 BHRC 585; 220 CCC (3d) 161; 47 CR (6th) 96]

Relationship of international law and municipal law — Canadian Charter of Rights and Freedoms — Interpretation and application — Interpretation of Section 32(1) of Charter — Jurisdictional scope — Extraterritorial application — Canada's obligations under international law — Principle of respect for sovereignty of foreign States — Principle of respect for territorial sovereignty of foreign States — Comity — Whether Charter of Rights and Freedoms applicable to acts of Canadian officials in territory under the jurisdiction of a foreign State — Whether applicability affected by fact that foreign State's actions contrary to international law binding upon Canada — Canadian national detained at Guantánamo Bay — Whether Charter of Rights and Freedoms applicable to extent of Canadian participation in detention and proposed trial

Territory — Territorial sovereignty — Customary international law — Principle of respect for sovereignty of foreign State — Principle of sovereign equality — Whether extraterritorial application of Canadian Charter of Rights and Freedoms interfering with sovereign authority of foreign State

Human rights — Protection of fundamental human rights when Canadian officers operating abroad — Requirement that Canadian officials follow foreign laws and procedures — Comity — Whether foreign procedures violating fundamental human rights — Whether Canadian Charter of Rights and Freedoms applicable extraterritorially

Comity — Comity of nations as interpretative principle — Appropriateness of comity — Whether any clear violations of international law

War and armed conflict — Combatants — Detention and trial of enemy combatants — Detention of persons captured in Afghanistan conflict — Guantánamo Bay — Whether detention and proposed trial by military commission contrary to international law — The law of Canada

Khadr v. Canada (No 1)[1]

(2008 SCC 28)

Canada, Supreme Court. 23 May 2008

(McLachlin CJ; Bastarache, Binnie, LeBel, Deschamps, Fish, Abella, Charron and Rothstein JJ)

SUMMARY: *The facts*:—The applicant was a Canadian national who was taken prisoner by United States forces in Afghanistan in 2002, when he was fifteen years old. He was sent to the detention centre at Guantánamo Bay. The United States authorities accused him of having thrown a grenade which had killed a United States soldier during fighting in Afghanistan and proposed to put him on trial before a military commission. In 2003 he was interviewed at Guantánamo Bay by Canadian officials, including members of the Canadian Security Intelligence Service. Information concerning that interview was later given to the United States authorities. The applicant commenced proceedings in Canada seeking the disclosure of all information, including the records of the 2003 interview, in the possession of Canada which might assist in the preparation of his defence for the trial in the United States. He relied upon Section 7 of the Canadian Charter of Rights and Freedoms ("the Charter"), which, he claimed, had been applicable to the conduct of the Canadian officials in interviewing him at Guantánamo Bay and subsequently disclosing the results of that interview. The Federal Court dismissed his application. The Federal Court of Appeals allowed his appeal and ordered disclosure. The Crown appealed to the Supreme Court of Canada, contending that the Charter was not applicable to the conduct of Canadian officials in a foreign country.

Held (unanimously):—The appeal was dismissed but the order for disclosure was modified.

(1) The Charter was not normally applicable to the acts of Canadian officials which took place on the territory of a foreign State, because principles of international law militated against the extraterritorial application of domestic laws and comity implied acceptance of foreign laws and procedures when Canadian officials were operating in another country. However, these

---

[1] For related proceedings, see 143 ILR 225. The appellant was represented by Robert Frater, Sharlene Telles-Langdon and Doreen Mueller, instructed by the Attorney-General of Canada, Ottawa. The respondent was represented by Nathan Whitling and Dennis Edney, instructed by Parlee McLaws, Edmonton. The British Columbia Civil Liberties Association, intervening, was represented by Joseph Arvay QC, Sujit Choudhry and Paul Champ, instructed by Arvay Finlay, Vancouver. The Criminal Lawyers Association (Ontario), intervening, was represented by John Norris and Brydie Bethell, instructed by Ruby and Edwardh, Toronto. The University of Toronto, Faculty of Law—International Human Rights Clinic and Human Rights Watch, intervening, was represented by Audrey Macklin, Tom Friedland and Gerald Chan, instructed by Goodmans, Toronto.

considerations could not be used to justify Canadian participation in activities of a foreign State which were contrary to the international legal obligations of Canada. If Canadian officials participated in such activities, the Charter was applicable to the extent of that participation (paras. 15-20).

(2) The United States Supreme Court had held that the detention of inmates at Guantánamo Bay without recourse to an independent legal procedure to determine their status was contrary to United States law and international law. The United States Supreme Court had also held that the system of trial by military commissions was contrary to the requirements of the Geneva Conventions. It followed that the detention and proposed trial of the applicant were contrary to international law obligations which were binding on Canada. No question of a duty of deference to foreign law arose because the activity in question had been held to be incompatible with the relevant foreign law by the highest judicial authority in that country. The Charter was, therefore, applicable to the extent of the participation by Canadian officials in the detention and trial process (paras. 21-7).

(3) Section 7 of the Charter imposed a duty to disclose, the scope of which was defined by the nature of Canada's participation in the detention and proposed trial of the applicant. The order of the Federal Court of Appeal would be modified to take account of the nature of that participation (paras. 28-41).

The following is the text of the judgment of the Court:

1. This appeal raises the issue of the relationship between Canada's domestic and international human rights commitments. Omar Khadr currently faces prosecution on murder and other charges before a US Military Commission in Guantánamo Bay, Cuba. Mr Khadr asks for an order under s 7 of the Canadian Charter of Rights and Freedoms that the appellants be required to disclose to him all documents relevant to these charges in the possession of the Canadian Crown, including interviews conducted by Canadian officials with him in 2003 at Guantánamo Bay. The Minister of Justice opposes the request, arguing that the Charter does not apply outside Canada and hence did not govern the actions of Canadian officials at Guantánamo Bay.

2. We conclude that Mr Khadr is entitled to disclosure from the appellants of the records of the interviews and of information given to US authorities as a direct consequence of conducting the interviews. The principles of international law and comity of nations, which normally require that Canadian officials operating abroad comply with local law, do not extend to participation in processes that violate Canada's international human rights obligations.

3. The process in place at the time Canadian officials interviewed Mr Khadr and passed the fruits of the interviews on to US officials has been found by the United States Supreme Court to violate US domestic law and international human rights obligations to which Canada is party. In light of these decisions by the United States Supreme Court that the process at Guantánamo Bay did not comply with either US domestic or international law, the comity concerns that would normally justify deference to foreign law do not apply in this case. Consequently, the Charter applies, and Canada is under a s 7 duty of disclosure. The content of this duty is defined by the nature of Canada's participation in the process that violated Canada's international human rights obligations. In the present circumstances, this duty requires Canada to disclose to Mr Khadr records of the interviews conducted by Canadian officials with him, and information given to US authorities as a direct consequence of conducting the interviews, subject to claims for privilege and public interest immunity.

4. We thus uphold the Federal Court of Appeal's conclusion that Mr Khadr is entitled to a remedy under s 7 of the Charter. However, because we reach this conclusion on different grounds than those relied on by the Court of Appeal, we vary the Court of Appeal's order as it relates to the scope of disclosure to which Mr Khadr is entitled as remedy. Like the Court of Appeal, we make this order subject to the balancing of national security and other considerations as required by ss 38 ff. of the Canada Evidence Act, RSC 1985, c C-5.

1. *Factual Background*

5. Omar Khadr is a Canadian citizen who has been detained by US forces at Guantánamo Bay, Cuba, for almost six years. Mr Khadr was taken prisoner on July 27, 2002 in Afghanistan, as part of military action taken against Taliban and Al Qaeda forces after the September 11, 2001 attacks in New York City and Washington. He was 15 years old at the time. The United States alleges that near the end of the battle at which he was taken prisoner, Mr Khadr threw a grenade which killed an American soldier. The United States also alleges that Mr Khadr conspired with members of Al Qaeda to commit acts of murder and terrorism against US and coalition forces. Mr Khadr is currently facing charges relating to these allegations, which are being tried by a US Military Commission at Guantánamo Bay.

6. The Guantánamo Bay detention camp was established by Presidential Military Order in 2001 (66 FR 57833) for the detention and prosecution of non-US citizens believed to be members of Al Qaeda

or otherwise involved in international terrorism. The Order conferred exclusive jurisdiction upon military commissions for the trial of "any and all offences triable by military commission", and stipulated pursuant to 10 USC s 836 that applying normal rules of criminal procedure to such trials "is not practicable". The Order further provided that an individual subject to the order "shall not be privileged to seek any remedy or maintain any proceeding ... or to have any such remedy or proceeding sought on the individual's behalf, in (i) any court of the United States, or any State thereof, (ii) any court of any foreign nation, or (iii) any international tribunal". Subsequent orders purported to remove protections of the Geneva Conventions of 1949 (75 UNTS 31, 85, 135 and 287) and established procedural rules for the military commissions that departed from normal rules of criminal procedure as to the type of evidence that may be admitted, the right to counsel and disclosure of the case to meet, and judicial independence.

7. On several occasions, including in February and September of 2003, Canadian officials, including agents of the Canadian Security Intelligence Service (CSIS), attended at Guantánamo Bay and interviewed Mr Khadr for intelligence and law enforcement purposes. The CSIS agents questioned Mr Khadr with respect to matters connected to the charges he is now facing, and shared the product of these interviews with US authorities.

8. After formal charges were laid against Mr Khadr in November 2005, he sought disclosure of all documents relevant to these charges in the possession of the Canadian Crown, including the records of the interviews, invoking *R v. Stinchcombe*, [1991] 3 SCR 326. The appellants formally refused Mr Khadr's request in January 2006. Mr Khadr then applied for an order of mandamus in the Federal Court, which was dismissed, *per* von Finckenstein J ((2006), 290 FTR 313, 2006 FC 509). The Federal Court of Appeal allowed Mr Khadr's appeal ([2008] 1 FCR 270, 2007 FCA 182), and ordered that unredacted copies of all relevant documents in the possession of the Crown be produced before the Federal Court for review under ss 38 ff. of the Canada Evidence Act. The Minister of Justice now appeals to this Court, asking that the order of the Federal Court of Appeal be set aside.

2. *The Fresh Evidence Applications*

9. Mr Khadr has filed two applications to admit fresh evidence before this Court. We deal with the applications to admit fresh evidence at the outset.

10. The first application concerns primarily evidence that is part of a related proceeding brought by Mr Khadr in the Federal Court (file

T-536-04), in which Mr Khadr is seeking a remedy for alleged violations of his Charter rights at Guantánamo Bay. This evidence relates primarily to the general situation at Guantánamo Bay, Mr Khadr's particular circumstances, and Canadian participation in interviewing Mr Khadr at Guantánamo Bay. It includes affidavits filed as part of that proceeding from Canadian officials at CSIS and the Department of Foreign Affairs and International Trade, and from Muneer Ahmad, who was counsel for Mr Khadr in *habeas corpus* proceedings taking place in the United States. The record includes the exhibits that were attached to these affidavits.

11. Also included in the first application is an affidavit from Lt Cdr William Kuebler, Mr Khadr's defence counsel in the military commission proceedings, updating the Court on developments in relevant US law.

12. The second application relates to an additional affidavit from Lt Cdr Kuebler, as well as exhibits filed under seal with the consent of the US Deputy Assistant Secretary of Defense for Detainee Affairs.

13. The appellants' primary argument against admitting the fresh evidence is that the evidence from the related proceeding was filed as part of an interlocutory motion in which the appellants chose not to lead certain evidence in response: *Khadr* v. *Canada*, [2006] 2 FCR 505, 2005 FC 1076. The appellants maintain that the nature of the evidence they led was tailored to the specific context of that motion and that this evidence should not be imported into the different context of this proceeding. Furthermore, the T-536-04 proceeding has not yet gone to trial, and so the appellants have not yet had an opportunity to present a complete evidentiary record. The appellants argue that it would be unfair to admit the fresh evidence, because, the appellants allege, they were not given an adequate opportunity to respond to it.

14. We find that the fresh evidence is admissible. The fresh evidence amplifies and significantly clarifies the record as it relates to Canadian officials' interviews with Mr Khadr and Canada's participation in handing over the products of these interviews to US authorities. As the basic facts are not contested, the appellants are not disadvantaged by the admission of the material.

3. *The Application for Disclosure*

(i) *Does the Charter apply?*

15. As discussed, CSIS, a Canadian government organization, interviewed Mr Khadr at his prison in Guantánamo Bay and shared the contents of these interviews with US authorities. Mr Khadr seeks an

order that the appellants be required to disclose to him all documents in the possession of the Canadian Crown relevant to the charges he is facing, for the purpose of his defence.

16. Had the interviews and process been in Canada, Mr Khadr would have been entitled to full disclosure under the principles in *Stinchcombe*, which held that persons whose liberty is at risk as a result of being charged with a criminal offence are entitled to disclosure of the information in the hands of the Crown under s 7 of the Charter. The Federal Court of Appeal applied *Stinchcombe* to Mr Khadr's situation and ordered disclosure.

17. The government argues that this constituted an error, because the Charter does not apply to the conduct of Canadian agents operating outside Canada. It relies on *R* v. *Hape*, [2007] 2 SCR 292, 2007 SCC 26, where a majority of this Court held that Canadian agents participating in an investigation into money laundering in the Caribbean were not bound by Charter constraints in the manner in which the investigation was conducted. This conclusion was based on international law principles against extraterritorial enforcement of domestic laws and the principle of comity which implies acceptance of foreign laws and procedures when Canadian officials are operating abroad.

18. In *Hape*, however, the Court stated an important exception to the principle of comity. While not unanimous on all the principles governing extraterritorial application of the Charter, the Court was united on the principle that comity cannot be used to justify Canadian participation in activities of a foreign state or its agents that are contrary to Canada's international obligations. It was held that the deference required by the principle of comity "ends where clear violations of international law and fundamental human rights begin" (*Hape*, at para. 52, *per* LeBel J; see also paras. 51 and 101). The Court further held that in interpreting the scope and application of the Charter, the courts should seek to ensure compliance with Canada's binding obligations under international law (para. 56, *per* LeBel J).

19. If the Guantánamo Bay process under which Mr Khadr was being held was in conformity with Canada's international obligations, the Charter has no application and Mr Khadr's application for disclosure cannot succeed: *Hape*. However, if Canada was participating in a process that was violative of Canada's binding obligations under international law, the Charter applies to the extent of that participation.

20. At this point, the question becomes whether the process at Guantánamo Bay at the time that CSIS handed the products of its interviews over to US officials was a process that violated Canada's binding obligations under international law.

21. Issues may arise about whether it is appropriate for a Canadian court to pronounce on the legality of the process at Guantánamo Bay under which Mr Khadr was held at the time that Canadian officials participated in that process. We need not resolve those issues in this case. The United States Supreme Court has considered the legality of the conditions under which the Guantánamo detainees were detained and liable to prosecution during the time Canadian officials interviewed Mr Khadr and gave the information to US authorities, between 2002 and 2004. With the benefit of a full factual record, the United States Supreme Court held that the detainees had illegally been denied access to *habeas corpus* and that the procedures under which they were to be prosecuted violated the Geneva Conventions. Those holdings are based on principles consistent with the Charter and Canada's international law obligations. In the present appeal, this is sufficient to establish violations of these international law obligations, to which Canada subscribes.

22. In *Rasul* v. *Bush*, 542 US 466 (2004), the United States Supreme Court held that detainees at Guantánamo Bay who, like Mr Khadr, were not US citizens, could challenge the legality of their detention by way of the statutory right of *habeas corpus* provided for in 28 USC s 2241. This holding necessarily implies that the order under which the detainees had previously been denied the right to challenge their detention was illegal. In his concurring reasons, Kennedy J noted that "the detainees at Guantánamo Bay are being held indefinitely, and without benefit of any legal proceeding to determine their status" (pp. 487-8). Mr Khadr was detained at Guantánamo Bay during the time covered by the *Rasul* decision, and Canadian officials interviewed him and passed on information to US authorities during that time.

23. At the time he was interviewed by CSIS officials, Mr Khadr also faced the possibility of trial by military commission pursuant to Military Commission Order No 1. In *Hamdan* v. *Rumsfeld*, 126 S Ct 2749 (2006), the United States Supreme Court considered the legality of this Order. The court held that by significantly departing from established military justice procedure without a showing of military exigency, the procedural rules for military commissions violated both the Uniform Code of Military Justice (10 USC s 836) and Common Article 3 of the Geneva Conventions. Different members of the majority of the United States Supreme Court focused on different deviations from the Geneva Conventions and the Uniform Code of Military Justice. But the majority was unanimous in holding that, in the circumstances, the deviations were sufficiently significant to deprive the military commissions of the status of "a regularly constituted court, affording all the judicial

guarantees which are recognized as indispensable by civilized peoples", as required by Common Article 3 of the Geneva Conventions.

24. The violations of human rights identified by the United States Supreme Court are sufficient to permit us to conclude that the regime providing for the detention and trial of Mr Khadr at the time of the CSIS interviews constituted a clear violation of fundamental human rights protected by international law.

25. Canada is a signatory of the four Geneva Conventions of 1949, which it ratified in 1965 (Can. TS 1965 No 20) and has incorporated into Canadian law with the Geneva Conventions Act, RSC 1985, c G-3. The right to challenge the legality of detention by *habeas corpus* is a fundamental right protected both by the Charter and by international treaties. It follows that participation in the Guantánamo Bay process which violates these international instruments would be contrary to Canada's binding international obligations.

26. We conclude that the principles of international law and comity that might otherwise preclude application of the Charter to Canadian officials acting abroad do not apply to the assistance they gave to US authorities at Guantánamo Bay. Given the holdings of the United States Supreme Court, the *Hape* comity concerns that would ordinarily justify deference to foreign law have no application here. The effect of the United States Supreme Court's holdings is that the conditions under which Mr Khadr was held and was liable for prosecution were illegal under both US and international law at the time Canadian officials interviewed Mr Khadr and gave the information to US authorities. Hence no question of deference to foreign law arises. The Charter bound Canada to the extent that the conduct of Canadian officials involved it in a process that violated Canada's international obligations.

(ii) *Participation in the process*

27. By making the product of its interviews of Mr Khadr available to US authorities, Canada participated in a process that was contrary to Canada's international human rights obligations. Merely conducting interviews with a Canadian citizen held abroad under a violative process may not constitute participation in that process. Indeed, it may often be essential that Canadian officials interview citizens being held by violative regimes to provide assistance to them. Nor is it necessary to conclude that handing over the fruits of the interviews in this case to US officials constituted a breach of Mr Khadr's s 7 rights. It suffices to note that at the time Canada handed over the fruits of the interviews to US officials, it was bound by the Charter, because at that point it

became a participant in a process that violated Canada's international obligations.

(iii) *Implications of participation in the process*

28. Having concluded that the Charter applied to Canadian officials when they participated in the Guantánamo Bay process by handing over the fruits of its interviews with Mr Khadr, the next question concerns what obligations, if any, this entails.

29. With Mr Khadr's present and future liberty at stake, s 7 of the Charter required that CSIS conduct itself in conformity with the principles of fundamental justice. The principles of fundamental justice are informed by Canada's international human rights obligations: *Suresh* v. *Canada (Minister of Citizenship and Immigration)*, [2002] 1 SCR 3, 2002 SCC 1, at para. 60; *United States* v. *Burns*, [2001] 1 SCR 283, 2001 SCC 7, at paras. 82-92; *Hape*, at paras. 55-6.

30. In the domestic context, the principles of fundamental justice impose a duty on the prosecuting Crown to provide disclosure of relevant information in its possession to the accused whose liberty is in jeopardy: *Stinchcombe*. In a domestic prosecution, the Crown has put the accused's liberty at risk, which engages s 7 of the Charter and the attendant duty of disclosure.

31. To the extent that Canadian officials operating abroad are bound by s 7 of the Charter, as we have earlier concluded was the case in this appeal, they are bound by the principles of fundamental justice in an analogous way. Where, as in this case, an individual's s 7 right to liberty is engaged by Canada's participation in a foreign process that is contrary to Canada's international human rights obligations, s 7 of the Charter imposes a duty on Canada to provide disclosure to the individual. Thus, s 7 imposes a duty on Canada to provide disclosure of materials in its possession arising from its participation in the foreign process that is contrary to international law and jeopardizes the liberty of a Canadian citizen.

32. It is not necessary to define for all fact situations the scope of the duty of disclosure, when the Charter is engaged by the actions of Canadian officials abroad, but it may differ from the scope of the duty of disclosure in a domestic criminal prosecution. In this case, although Canada participated in the US process by giving the product of its interviews with Mr Khadr to US authorities, it did not by virtue of that action step into the shoes of the US prosecutors. The scope of the disclosure obligation in this context is defined by the nature of Canada's participation in the foreign process. The crux of that participation was

providing information to US authorities in relation to a process which is contrary to Canada's international human rights obligations. Thus, the scope of the disclosure obligation must be related to the information provided to US authorities.

33. As noted at the outset, the appellants formally refused Mr Khadr's request for disclosure in January 2006. This refusal of disclosure has put the appellants in breach of s 7 of the Charter and entitles Mr Khadr to a remedy.

34. Canada has an obligation under s 7 to provide disclosure to Mr Khadr to mitigate the effect of Canada's participation by passing on the product of the interviews to US authorities. It is not clear from the record before this Court if all portions of all of the interviews were given to US authorities. If Mr Khadr is given only partial disclosure of the interviews on the ground that only parts of the interviews were shared with US authorities, it may be impossible for him to evaluate the significance of the parts of the interviews that are disclosed to him. For example, by analogy with *Stinchcombe*, disclosure of an inculpatory statement shared with the US authorities might require disclosure of an exculpatory statement not shared to permit Mr Khadr to know his jeopardy and prepare his defence. It would seem to follow that fairness requires disclosure of all records in any form of the interviews themselves—whether or not passed on to US authorities—including any transcripts, recordings or summaries in Canada's possession. For similar reasons, it would seem to follow that Mr Khadr is entitled to disclosure of information given to US authorities as a direct consequence of Canada's having interviewed him.

35. In making these observations, we are acutely aware that the record before us is incomplete. As this Court does not have the information given to US authorities before it, we are unable to assess precisely what information is so connected to the shared information that it in fairness must be disclosed to Mr Khadr. The designated judge of the Federal Court who hears the application under s 38 of the Canada Evidence Act may be expected to have a fuller picture of what was shared with the US authorities and what other material, if any, should be disclosed, bearing in mind the reasons of this Court and the principles enunciated in *Stinchcombe*. The ultimate process against Mr Khadr may be beyond Canada's jurisdiction and control. However, to the extent that Canada has participated in that process, it has a constitutional duty to disclose information obtained by that participation to a Canadian citizen whose liberty is at stake.

36. The Minister of Justice has argued that Mr Khadr's right to disclosure is confined to disclosure from the US authorities who are

prosecuting him. We disagree. The remedy of disclosure being granted to Mr Khadr is for breach of a constitutional duty that arose when Canadian agents became participants in a process that violates Canada's international obligations. Whether or not he is given similar disclosure by US officials, he is entitled to a remedy for the Canadian government's failure to provide disclosure to him after having given US authorities access to the product of the interviews, in circumstances that engaged s 7 of the Charter.

4. *Conclusion*

37. In reaching its conclusions on disclosure, the Federal Court of Appeal held that the *Stinchcombe* disclosure regime should apply, and consequently held that the scope of disclosure extended to all materials in the Crown's possession which might be relevant to the charges against the appellant, subject to ss 38 ff. of the Canada Evidence Act. Our holding is not based on applying *Stinchcombe* directly to these facts. Rather, as described above, the s 7 duty of disclosure to Mr Khadr is triggered on the facts of this case by Canadian officials giving US authorities access to interviews conducted at Guantánamo Bay with Mr Khadr. As a result, the disclosure order we make is different in scope than the order of the Federal Court of Appeal. The appellants must disclose (i) all records in any form of the interviews conducted by Canadian officials with Mr Khadr, and (ii) records of any information given to US authorities as a direct consequence of Canada's having interviewed him. This disclosure is subject to the balancing of national security and other considerations as required by ss 38 ff. of the Canada Evidence Act.

38. As noted above, it is not possible on the record before this Court to determine what specific records should be disclosed to Mr Khadr. In order to assess what specific documents must be disclosed as falling within the group of documents described in para. 37, a designated judge of the Federal Court must review the documents. The designated judge will also consider any privilege or public interest immunity claim that is raised, including any claim under ss 38 ff. of the Canada Evidence Act.

39. The Federal Court of Appeal ordered that the appellants produce unredacted copies of all documents, records and other materials in their possession which might be relevant to the charges against Mr Khadr to a designated judge of the Federal Court. In view of the fact that production has already been made pursuant to the Court of Appeal's order and this Court's order of January 23, 2008, we see no reason to interfere with this order.

40. The designated judge will review the material and receive submissions from the parties, and decide which documents fall within the categories set out in para. 37 above. In particular, the designated judge will determine which records fall within the scope of the disclosure obligation as being (i) records of the interviews conducted by Canadian officials with Mr Khadr, or (ii) records of information given to US authorities as a direct consequence of Canada's having interviewed Mr Khadr.

41. Pursuant to s 38.06 of the Canada Evidence Act, the designated judge will then consider whether disclosure of the records described in (i) and (ii) to Mr Khadr would be injurious to international relations or national defence or national security, and whether the public interest in disclosure outweighs in importance the public interest in non-disclosure. The designated judge will decide whether to authorize the disclosure of all the information, a part or summary of the information, or a written admission of facts relating to the information, subject to any conditions that the judge considers appropriate. We note that this review is currently ongoing pursuant to this Court's order of January 23, 2008.

42. Subject to these variations, we would dismiss the appeal with costs in this Court, and issue an order directing that:

(a) the Minister of Justice and Attorney General of Canada, the Minister of Foreign Affairs, the Director of the Canadian Security Intelligence Service and the Commissioner of the Royal Canadian Mounted Police produce to a "judge" as defined in s 38 of the Canada Evidence Act unredacted copies of all documents, records and other materials in their possession which might be relevant to the charges against Mr Khadr;

and

(b) the "judge" as defined in s 38 of the Canada Evidence Act shall consider any privilege or public interest immunity claim that is raised, including any claim under ss. 38 ff. of the Act, and make an order for disclosure in accordance with these reasons.

[Reports: [2008] 2 SCR 125; 293 DLR (4th) 629; 232 CCC (3d) 101; 56 CR (6th) 255; 172 CRR (2d) 1; 72 Admin LR (4th) 1]

Human rights — Inhuman treatment — Protection of fundamental human rights when Canadian officers operating abroad — Requirement that Canadian officials follow foreign laws and procedures — Comity — Whether foreign procedures violating fundamental human rights — Whether Canadian Charter of Rights and Freedoms applicable extraterritorially — Canadian officials interviewing Canadian national detained at Guantánamo Bay — National subjected to sleep deprivation by United States authorities — Whether engaging responsibility of Canada — Convention against Torture, 1984 — Convention on the Rights of the Child, 1989 — Remedies

Relationship of international law and municipal law — Canadian Charter of Rights and Freedoms — Interpretation and application — Interpretation of Section 32(1) of Charter — Jurisdictional scope — Extraterritorial application — Canada's obligations under international law – Canadian national detained at Guantánamo Bay — Whether Charter of Rights and Freedoms applicable to extent of Canadian participation in detention and proposed trial — Remedies for violation of Charter rights — Conduct of foreign relations by the Government — Justiciability — Whether appropriate for Court to order that Government request United States authorities to repatriate Canadian national detained at Guantánamo Bay

War and armed conflict — Combatants — Detention and trial of enemy combatants — Detention of persons captured in Afghanistan conflict — Guantánamo Bay — Whether detention and proposed trial by military commission contrary to international law — The law of Canada

KHADR *v.* CANADA (NO 2)[1]

(2009 FCA 246 and 2010 SCC 3)

Canada, Federal Court of Appeal. 14 *August* 2009

[1] For related proceedings, see 143 ILR 212. Before the Federal Court of Appeal, Mr Khadr was represented by Nathan Whitling and Dennis Edney, instructed by Parlee McLaws, Edmonton, and Edney, Dennis Professional Corporation, Edmonton. Canada was represented by Doreen Mueller and Jonathan Martin, instructed by the Deputy Attorney-General of Canada. Before the Supreme Court, Mr Khadr was represented by Nathan Whitling and Dennis Edney, instructed by Parlee

(Nadon, Evans and Sharlow JJA)

Supreme Court. 29 *January* 2010

(McLachlin CJ; Binnie, LeBel, Deschamps, Fish, Abella, Charron, Rothstein and Cromwell JJ)

SUMMARY: *The facts*:—The applicant was a Canadian national who was taken prisoner by United States forces in Afghanistan in 2002, when he was fifteen years old. He was sent to the detention centre at Guantánamo Bay. The United States authorities accused him of having thrown a grenade which had killed a United States soldier during fighting in Afghanistan and proposed to put him on trial before a military commission. In 2003 he was interviewed at Guantánamo Bay by Canadian officials, including members of the Canadian Security Intelligence Service. Information concerning that interview was later given to the United States authorities. In *Khadr* v. *Canada (No 1)* (referred to in the judgments in the present case as "*Khadr 2008*"), the Supreme Court of Canada held that Canadian participation in the detention and proposed trial of the applicant rendered the Canadian Charter of Rights and Freedoms ("the Charter") applicable to the actions of Canadian officials in interviewing the applicant and disclosing information from those interviews to the United States. The Supreme Court ordered Canada to disclose to the applicant the records of the interviews.

In the light of the information disclosed to him following the judgment of 2008, the applicant commenced fresh proceedings, claiming that Canada had violated his rights under Section 7 of the Charter.[2] The Federal Court

---

McLaws, Edmonton. Canada was represented by Robert Frater, Doreen Mueller and Jeffrey Johnston, instructed by the Department of Justice, Ottawa. Amnesty International (Canadian Section, English Branch), intervening, was represented by Sacha Paul, Vanessa Gruben and Michael Bossin, instructed by Thompson Dorfman Sweatman, Winnipeg. Human Rights Watch, the University of Toronto, Faculty of Law—International Human Rights Program and the David Asper Center for Constitutional Rights, intervening, were represented by John Norris, Brydie Bethell and Audrey Macklin. The Canadian Coalition for the Rights of Children and Justice for Children and Youth, intervening, was represented by Emily Chan and Martha MacKinnon. The British Columbia Civil Liberties Association, intervening, was represented by Joseph Arvay QC and Sujit Choudhry, instructed by Arvay Finlay, Vancouver. The Criminal Lawyers Association (Ontario), intervening, was represented by Brian Greenspan, instructed by Greenspan Humphrey Lavine, Toronto. The Canadian Bar Association, intervening, was represented by Lorne Waldman and Jacqueline Swaisland, instructed by Waldman and Associates, Toronto. Lawyers without Borders Canada, the Barreau du Québec and Group d'étude en droits et libertés de la Faculté de droit de l'Université Laval, intervening, were represented by Simon Potter, Pascal Paradis, Sylvie Champagne and Fannie Lafontaine, instructed by McCarthy Tétrault, Montréal. The Canadian Civil Liberties Association, intervening, was represented by Marlys Edwardh, Adriel Weaver and Jessica Orkin, instructed by Arlys Edwardh barristers Professional Corporation, Toronto. The National Council for the Protection of Canadians Abroad were represented by Dean Peroff, Chris Macleod and Scott Fairley, instructed by Theall Group, Toronto, and Amsterdam and Peroff, Toronto.

[2] See para. 42 of the Judgment of the Federal Court of Appeal.

held that Canada had violated the applicant's rights under Section 7, had failed to protect him and was under an obligation to request the United States authorities to repatriate him. The Crown appealed.

Held (by the Federal Court of Appeal, Nadon JA dissenting):—The appeal was dismissed.

(1) The Charter applied to constrain the conduct of Canadian authorities when they participated in a foreign process that was contrary to Canada's international human rights obligations (para. 26).

(2) The principles of fundamental justice reflected in the Convention against Torture, 1984, and the Convention on the Rights of the Child, 1989, did not permit the questioning of a prisoner after he had been subjected to cruel and abusive treatment to induce him to talk, whether the abuse was inflicted by the questioner or by some other person with the questioner's knowledge. The applicant was a minor, who had been detained without trial in an adult detention facility and subjected to sleep deprivation. Canada could not avoid responsibility for its participation in the process at Guantánamo Bay by relying on the fact that it had been United States officials who had mistreated the applicant, because Canadian officials knew of that abuse and sought to take advantage of it when questioning the applicant. Canada had violated the applicant's rights under Section 7 of the Charter (paras. 46-60).

(3) Section 1 of the Charter[3] did not justify the breach of Section 7. There was no law which required—either expressly or by necessary implication—the treatment of the applicant, nor had Canada shown that relations with the United States would be injured by requesting the applicant's return or that that return would jeopardize Canada's security (paras. 61-5).

(4) The appropriate remedy for the violation of the applicant's rights was to order Canada to request the United States to return the applicant to Canada. The fact that United States reaction to such a request could not be predicted did not make it inappropriate to order that such a request be made (paras. 66-74).

Per Nadon JA (dissenting): In view of the extensive steps which Canada had taken to secure the welfare of the applicant, there had been no failure to protect him. Even if there had been such a failure, the remedy ordered was inappropriate. It was for the executive to conduct foreign relations, not the courts (paras. 76-119).

Canada appealed to the Supreme Court.

Held (by the Supreme Court, unanimously):—The appeal was allowed in part. The appropriate remedy was a declaration that, through the conduct of Canadian officials in the course of interrogations in 2003-4, Canada had actively participated in a process contrary to Canada's international human rights obligations and contributed to the applicant's ongoing detention so as

---

[3] See para. 61 of the Judgment of the Federal Court of Appeal.

to deprive him of his right to liberty and security of the person guaranteed by Section 7 of the Charter, contrary to the principles of fundamental justice. That declaration would provide the legal framework for the executive to exercise its functions and consider what actions to take in respect of the applicant in conformity with the Charter.

(1) Although there had been significant changes to the regime under which the applicant was detained at Guantánamo Bay since 2003-4, the applicant's claim was based upon events which predated those changes and the Charter was applicable to the actions of Canadian officials during that earlier period (paras. 14-18).

(2) The participation of Canadian officials, in particular their action in sharing with the United States authorities information from the interviews they had conducted, had contributed to the continued detention of the applicant under what was at the time an illegal regime (paras. 19-21).

(3) The conduct of Canadian officials did not conform with the principles of fundamental justice. Canadian participation in the questioning of a minor who had been detained under an unlawful regime and subjected to sleep deprivation, in the knowledge that the results of the interviews with him would be made known to the United States authorities and might be used in a trial before a military commission, was a violation of Section 7 of the Charter (paras. 22-6).

(4) The necessary connection between the violation and the remedy sought was established. However, the decision not to request the applicant's repatriation had been made in the exercise of the prerogative power to conduct foreign relations. While the exercise of that power was not beyond scrutiny by the courts, the executive was better placed than the courts to assess what action to take and had to have flexibility in determining how its duties under the prerogative power were to be discharged. The order that the Government should request the applicant's repatriation gave too little weight to the responsibility of the executive in the context of complex and ever-changing circumstances. That order was not appropriate. The appropriate remedy was a declaration that there had been a violation of the Charter. It would then be for the executive to determine how to proceed in the light of that declaration (paras. 27-47).

The judgment of the Supreme Court of Canada commences at p. 264. The dissenting opinion of Nadon JA in the Federal Court of Appeal commences at p. 250. The following is the text of the judgment of the Federal Court of Appeal, delivered by Evans and Sharlow JJA:

JUDGMENT OF THE FEDERAL COURT OF APPEAL

1. EVANS and SHARLOW JJA:—Since 2002, the respondent Omar Ahmed Khadr has been imprisoned by the United States at Guantánamo Bay pending his trial before a United States military commission or a United States federal court. In *Khadr* v. *Canada (Prime Minister)*, 2009

FC 405, [2010] 1 FCR. 34, Justice O'Reilly of the Federal Court found that Canadian officials breached Mr Khadr's rights under section 7 of the Canadian Charter of Rights and Freedoms [being Part I of the Constitution Act, 1982, Schedule B, Canada Act 1982, 1982, c 11 (UK) [RSC, 1985, Appendix II, No 44]] when they interviewed Mr Khadr at the Guantánamo Bay prison and shared the resulting information with the United States. As a remedy pursuant to subsection 24(1) of the Charter, Justice O'Reilly ordered the Crown to request the United States to return Mr Khadr to Canada as soon as practicable. The Crown has appealed. At the root of the Crown's appeal is its argument that the Crown should have the unfettered discretion to decide whether and when to request the return of a Canadian citizen detained in a foreign country, a matter within its exclusive authority to conduct foreign affairs. For the reasons that follow, we have concluded that the Crown's appeal should be dismissed with costs.

Preliminary Issues

Appeal books

2. In accordance with the usual practice of this Court, the parties agreed to the contents of an appeal book and the Crown, as appellant, prepared and filed appeal books that conformed to that agreement. Later, counsel for Mr Khadr noticed that the agreement excluded a number of documents that were exhibits to the affidavit of Lieutenant-Commander (LCdr) William C. Kuebler sworn on August 4, 2008, as well as the affidavit of April Bedard sworn on August 8, 2008. Both of those affidavits, with all of their exhibits, were filed in the Federal Court on behalf of Mr Khadr and were before Justice O'Reilly when he rendered the judgment under appeal.

3. Counsel for Mr Khadr sought the consent of the Crown to file a supplementary appeal book containing the excluded documents. The Crown agreed to the filing of a supplementary appeal book but objected to the inclusion of some of the exhibits to the affidavits.

4. With leave of this Court, counsel for Mr Khadr prepared and filed two volumes of a supplementary appeal book so that the merits of the Crown's objection could be determined by the panel hearing the appeal. Volume I contains the previously excluded documents that the Crown agrees are properly part of the appeal book. Volume II contains the previously excluded documents that the Crown argues should not be part of the appeal book.

5. The Crown objects to the inclusion of the documents in Volume II of the supplementary appeal book because they were not footnoted

in the memorandum of fact and law submitted on behalf of Mr Khadr at the hearing in the Federal Court. This objection is not well founded. The documents in Volume II were before Justice O'Reilly. Even if counsel for Mr Khadr did not refer to them in his argument in the Federal Court, it is appropriate that they be available to this Court for reference if the need arises, either in the course of the hearing or during the Court's deliberations. For that reason, both volumes of the supplementary appeal book have been accepted as part of the appeal book.

Evidence ruled inadmissible

6. The appeal book contains the supplemental affidavit of April Bedard sworn on October 22, 2008. Appended as an exhibit to that affidavit is a DVD copy of a documentary entitled "The US vs Omar Khadr" [Canadian Broadcasting Corporation. *Doc Zone*, October 16, 2008]. Justice O'Reilly concluded at paragraph 90 of his reasons that the recording was not relevant to the proceeding, and as a result he did not admit it as evidence. That ruling has not been challenged in this appeal. Therefore, although the appeal book includes the recording, no reference has been made to it.

Background

7. Mr Khadr is a citizen of Canada. He was born in Canada in 1986. He moved to Pakistan with his family in 1990. In 1995 his father was arrested in Pakistan for alleged involvement in the bombing of the Egyptian embassy in Islamabad, after which the rest of the family returned to Canada. They moved back to Pakistan in 1996 when Mr Khadr's father was released. In 2001 the family returned to Canada for a few months, and then moved to Afghanistan.

8. After the attacks on New York and Washington DC on September 11, 2001, Mr Khadr's father and older brothers attended training camps associated with Al-Qaida. Counsel for Mr Khadr says that, contrary to a statement in paragraph 5 of Justice O'Reilly's reasons, there is no evidence that Mr Khadr attended those camps. Counsel for the Crown has not suggested that the record contains evidence that Mr Khadr attended an Al-Qaida training camp.

9. Mr Khadr was taken into custody by the United States in July of 2002 following a firefight in Afghanistan. The United States alleges that during that fight, Mr Khadr threw a grenade that killed a United States soldier. Mr Khadr was detained by the United States at Bagram

Airbase in Afghanistan, where he received medical treatment for injuries he suffered in the fight. At that time Mr Khadr was 15 years of age.

10. In diplomatic notes dated August 30 and September 13, 2002, Canada asked the United States for consular access to Mr Khadr at Bagram. That request was refused. The United States has continued to deny Canada consular access to Mr Khadr with the exception of "welfare visits" beginning in 2005, which are described later in these reasons.

11. The August 30, 2002 diplomatic note mentioned that Mr Khadr was a minor, and that a request had been made to United States intelligence contacts that Mr Khadr not be transferred to the Guantánamo Bay prison. The September 13, 2002 diplomatic note also urged the United States to consider that Mr Khadr was a minor. It pointed out that the laws of Canada and the United States require special treatment for minors with respect to legal and judicial processes, and that because Mr Khadr was a minor, it would not be appropriate for him to be detained at the prison at Guantánamo Bay.

12. Canada continued its diplomatic efforts on behalf of Mr Khadr during 2003. The documentary evidence of those efforts may be summarized as follows:

> Diplomatic note July 9, 2003
> Request for special consideration of Mr Khadr's status as a minor and an expression of concern that he was not being treated like other juvenile detainees.
> Minister's letter October 6, 2003
> Expression of concern that Mr Khadr could face the death penalty, indicating that Canada would seek assurances that the death penalty would not be imposed.
> Diplomatic note November 11, 2003
> Request that Canadian detainees at the Guantánamo Bay prison be informed prior to their release of their right to return to Canada if they wish, and that they be given the opportunity to exercise that right.
> Diplomatic note November 12, 2003
> Request for assurances that Mr Khadr was receiving medical treatment for his injuries.

13. The record contains no formal responses to any of these communications. There is no record of any assurance by the United States that the death penalty would not be sought or imposed, that Mr Khadr would be informed of his right to return to Canada if released, or that he would be permitted to exercise that right.

14. Despite Canada's diplomatic efforts on Mr Khadr's behalf, the United States sent him to the prison at the United States Naval Base in Guantánamo Bay in October of 2002, when he was 16 years of age. There he remains to this day. Despite his age, Mr Khadr has been detained either alone or with adult detainees, and never in the part of the prison that at one time was set apart for minors. As of the end of March 2004, Mr Khadr had not been permitted to contact his family. It is not clear whether family contact was permitted later, and if so when. Mr Khadr was given no access to legal counsel until November of 2004.

15. Mr Khadr is awaiting trial before a United States military commission or a United States federal court on a number of serious charges, including murder. The trial has been delayed. Counsel for Mr Khadr does not know whether or when the trial will continue.

16. In February and September of 2003, and on March 30, 2004, officials from the Canadian Security Intelligence Service (CSIS) and the Department of Foreign Affairs and International Trade (DFAIT) interviewed Mr Khadr at the prison at Guantánamo Bay. All of the interviews were monitored and recorded by United States officials. As noted by Justice O'Reilly at paragraph 17 of his reasons, at the time of the last of these interviews on March 30, 2004, Mr Khadr was "a 17-year-old minor, who was being detained without legal representation, with no access to his family and with no Canadian consular assistance".

17. The interviews were held for the purpose of gathering intelligence and not for the purpose of gathering evidence to assist the United States in its prosecution of Mr Khadr (see *Khadr* v. *Canada*, 2005 FC 1076, [2006] 2 FCR 505, at paragraphs 23 and 24; and *Khadr* v. *Canada (Attorney General)*, 2008 FC 807, 59 CR (6th) 284, at paragraph 73). However, the fruits of the interviews were shared with the United States officials, and no request was made to limit their use of that information.

18. The record contains reports of the interviews prepared by Canadian officials. Except for the report of the interview of March 30, 2004, the reports are heavily redacted. It is not possible to determine whether any of the information that Canadian officials obtained from Mr Khadr would be of assistance to the United States prosecution.

19. In *Canada (Justice)* v. *Khadr*, 2008 SCC 28, [2008] 2 SCR 125 (*Khadr* 2008), the Supreme Court of Canada made the following comments about the legal regime governing Mr Khadr's detention and trial, between 2002 and 2004 (at paragraphs 21-4):

The United States Supreme Court has considered the legality of the conditions under which the Guantánamo detainees were detained and liable to prosecution during the time Canadian officials interviewed Mr Khadr and gave the information to US authorities, between 2002 and 2004. With the benefit of a full factual record, the United States Supreme Court held that the detainees had illegally been denied access to *habeas corpus* and that the procedures under which they were to be prosecuted violated the Geneva Conventions. Those holdings are based on principles consistent with the Charter and Canada's international law obligations. In the present appeal, this is sufficient to establish violations of these international law obligations, to which Canada subscribes.

In *Rasul* v. *Bush*, 542 US 466 (2004), the United States Supreme Court held that detainees at Guantánamo Bay who, like Mr Khadr, were not US citizens, could challenge the legality of their detention by way of the statutory right of *habeas corpus* provided for in 28 USC s 2241. This holding necessarily implies that the order under which the detainees had previously been denied the right to challenge their detention was illegal. In his concurring reasons, Kennedy J noted that "the detainees at Guantánamo Bay are being held indefinitely, and without benefit of any legal proceeding to determine their status" (pp. 487-8). Mr Khadr was detained at Guantánamo Bay during the time covered by the *Rasul* decision, and Canadian officials interviewed him and passed on information to US authorities during that time.

At the time he was interviewed by CSIS officials, Mr Khadr also faced the possibility of trial by military commission pursuant to Military Commission Order No 1. In *Hamdan* v. *Rumsfeld*, 126 S Ct 2749 (2006), the United States Supreme Court considered the legality of this Order. The court held that by significantly departing from established military justice procedure without a showing of military exigency, the procedural rules for military commissions violated both the Uniform Code of Military Justice (10 USC s 836) and Common Article 3 of the Geneva Conventions. Different members of the majority of the United States Supreme Court focused on different deviations from the Geneva Conventions and the Uniform Code of Military Justice. But the majority was unanimous in holding that, in the circumstances, the deviations were sufficiently significant to deprive the military commissions of the status of "a regularly constituted court affording all the judicial guarantees which are recognized as indispensable by civilized peoples", as required by Common Article 3 of the Geneva Conventions.

The violations of human rights identified by the United States Supreme Court are sufficient to permit us to conclude that the regime providing for the detention and trial of Mr Khadr at the time of the CSIS interviews constituted a clear violation of fundamental human rights protected by international law.

20. In addition to these issues about the lawfulness of the regime governing Mr Khadr's detention and trial, Mr Khadr alleges that he has been subjected to various kinds of torture during his detention. The affidavit of his United States counsel, LCdr Kuebler, provides support for those allegations. Justice O'Reilly did not consider it necessary to determine whether all of Mr Khadr's allegations of torture were true.

However, he noted that it was uncontested that on March 30, 2004, when Canadian officials interviewed Mr Khadr at the Guantánamo Bay prison, they were aware that he had been subjected to a particular form of sleep deprivation known as the "frequent flyer program". According to the report of that interview prepared by a DFAIT official on April 24, 2004, the purpose of that particular form of mistreatment was to make Mr Khadr "more amenable and willing to talk". That report describes the mistreatment of Mr Khadr in the present tense, from which it is reasonable to infer that it began at some point before the March 30, 2004 interview and was continuing as of that date.

21. Shortly before the March 30, 2004 interview, an action was commenced in the Federal Court on behalf of Mr Khadr alleging a number of breaches of Mr Khadr's rights under the Charter. In that action, which is pending, Mr Khadr is seeking an award of damages and an injunction against further interrogation by Canadian agents. The Crown's motion to strike the statement of claim was dismissed by Justice von Finckenstein (*Khadr* v. *Canada (Attorney General)*, 2004 FC 1394, 245 DLR (4th) 556).

22. On August 8, 2005, Justice von Finckenstein granted the motion of Mr Khadr for an interlocutory injunction against further interviews with Mr Khadr until the conclusion of the trial of his action for damages (*Khadr* v. *Canada*, 2005 FC 1076). An exception was made for consular visits. By a further order dated October 17, 2005, that exception was clarified to permit "welfare visits", defined as meetings between Mr Khadr and officials of DFAIT who are not involved in security matters as part of their regular duties, for the purpose of observing Mr Khadr, listening to his impressions about his confinement and treatment, gaining an impression of his apparent health status, and inquiring about his ability to carry out religious observances. That order required that a report of each welfare visit be provided to Mr Khadr's counsel within 30 days of the visit. Welfare visits occurred in March of 2005, December of 2005, July of 2006, June, August and November of 2007, and monthly from February to June of 2008.

23. On March 31, 2004, an application for judicial review was commenced in the Federal Court on behalf of Mr Khadr seeking, among other things, an order requiring DFAIT to provide consular services to Mr Khadr. The Crown moved to strike the application. Justice von Finckenstein struck the portion of the application that duplicated the relief sought in Mr Khadr's action, but permitted the remainder of the application to continue because he concluded that Mr Khadr had an arguable case (*Khadr* v. *Canada (Minister of Foreign Affairs)*, 2004 FC 1145, 123 CRR (2d) 7). The Crown appealed that decision but

discontinued the appeal in March of 2005. Mr Khadr discontinued his application in February of 2009.

24. Between June of 2004 and April of 2006, Canadian officials sent further diplomatic notes to the United States. Those diplomatic notes may be summarized as follows:

Diplomatic note June 7, 2004
General request for assurances that the treatment of detainees at the prison at Guantánamo Bay is in accordance with international humanitarian law and human rights law.

Diplomatic note July 9, 2004
Request for assurances that Mr Khadr would be provided in the near future with a judicial review of his detention by a regularly constituted court affording all judicial guarantees in accordance with due process and international law, and repeating the request that Mr Khadr be provided with the option of returning to Canada if he is released.

Diplomatic note January 13, 2005
Repetition of the request that Canadian officials be permitted access to Mr Khadr to confirm his well-being, that he be provided with an independent medical assessment, and that his most recent medical reports be released to his family.

Expression of concern that Mr Khadr was not getting adequate legal representation because the procedures governing access and information-sharing prevented his Canadian counsel from getting access to him, and from being fully briefed by his United States counsel.

Diplomatic note February 11, 2005
Expression of concern about Mr Khadr's allegations of mistreatment, and a request that Canadian officials be given access to Mr Khadr to verify his welfare, and that Mr Khadr be given an independent medical assessment, to be shared with Canada and Mr Khadr's legal counsel.

Request for formal assurances that the death penalty will not be applied to Mr Khadr, and reminding the United States that he was only 15 years of age when first detained.

Diplomatic note July 12, 2005
Request for medical report and for permission for a medical visit by a Canadian physician, and for permission for him to speak to his family by telephone.

Diplomatic note November 10, 2005
Acknowledgement of communication from United States authorities that the evidence currently available does not support the death penalty, noting that this stops short of the unequivocal assurances

that Canada has repeatedly sought that, given Mr Khadr's status as a minor at the time of the alleged offence, the prosecution will not seek the death penalty and Mr Khadr will not be subject to a capital sentence by the Military Commission.

Further request that Mr Khadr be given the opportunity to respond in full to the allegations against him with a process that safeguards the right of due process to which he is entitled, including independent judicial oversight of the Military Commission, recognition of his status as a minor at the time of the alleged offence, choice of counsel, and a clear distinction between the prosecutorial and judicial roles.

Request for immediate welfare access to Mr Khadr, consistent with Article 36 of the Vienna Convention on Consular Relations [April 24, 1963, [1974] Can. TS No 25].

Statement of Canada's intention to attend as far as possible the proceedings against Mr Khadr as observers, and request for permission that other independent observers be permitted to attend, and that Canada receive timely notice of hearings.

Diplomatic note April 17, 2006

Further requests for an independent medical assessment, and for assurances that Mr Khadr will be permitted access to counsel of his choice, including Canadian counsel, without delay.

25. On January 3, 2006, Mr Khadr commenced an application in the Federal Court for judicial review of the decision of the Minister of Justice not to respond to Mr Khadr's request for disclosure of all the information in the Crown's possession that might be relevant to the United States charges pending against him. This Court ordered disclosure on the basis of the standard in *R* v. *Stinchcombe*, [1991] 3 SCR 326, subject to a review of the documents by a Federal Court judge pursuant to section 38 [sections 38 to 38.16 inclusive (as enacted by SC 2001, c 41, ss 43, 141)] of the Canada Evidence Act, RSC, 1985, c C-5 (*Khadr* v. *Canada (Minister of Justice)*, 2007 FCA 182, [2008] 1 FCR 270). The Crown appealed to the Supreme Court of Canada, which allowed the appeal in part (*Khadr* 2008, cited above). The Court agreed that Mr Khadr was entitled to disclosure, but of a narrower scope than ordered by this Court. Disclosure was ordered of "(i) records of the interviews conducted by Canadian officials with Mr Khadr, or (ii) records of information given to US authorities as a direct consequence of Canada's having interviewed Mr Khadr" (*Khadr* 2008, at paragraph 40).

26. The general principle established by *Khadr* 2008 is that the Charter applies to constrain the conduct of Canadian authorities when they participate in a foreign legal process that is contrary to Canada's

international human rights obligations (see also *R* v. *Hape*, 2007 SCC 26, [2007] 2 SCR 292). In addition, a number of specific determinations made in *Khadr* 2008 are applicable to this case. Those determinations are discussed later in these reasons.

27. In *Khadr* 2008, the Supreme Court of Canada expressly declined to determine whether Canadian officials breached Mr Khadr's rights under section 7 of the Charter when they interviewed Mr Khadr and gave the fruits of the interviews to United States authorities because they did not consider it necessary to do so. *Khadr* 2008 dealt only with an application for disclosure of information.

28. On June 25, 2008, Justice Mosley conducted a review of the documents pursuant to section 38 [and following] of the Canada Evidence Act (*Khadr* v. *Canada (Attorney General)*, 2008 FC 807). His review led him to make the following comments that are pertinent to this appeal (at paragraphs 72-4, 85-9):

As is now well known, in February 2003 three CSIS officials and one officer of the DFAIT Foreign Intelligence Division were authorized by the US Department of Defence to visit Guantánamo Bay. They interviewed Mr Khadr over four days; February 13-16, 2003. CSIS and DFAIT officials subsequently returned to Guantánamo to interview the applicant in September 2003. A DFAIT official went again in March 2004. The purpose of these visits was primarily to collect intelligence information. The interview notes and reports prepared by the Canadian officials were shared with the RCMP. US agencies were subsequently provided with edited versions of those reports.

Questions have arisen in these proceedings as to whether the visits had a law enforcement aspect, about which there is some dispute between the Attorney General and Mr Khadr's counsel. The former Deputy Director of Operations for CSIS was cross-examined on the point in the course of earlier proceedings. From what I have seen, it appears clear that the interviews were not conducted for the purpose of assisting the US authorities with their case against Mr Khadr or for building a case against him in Canada. I note that no law enforcement personnel were authorized to attend at that time. The information collected during the interviews was provided to the RCMP for intelligence purposes. However, it is equally clear that the US authorities were interested in having Canada consider whether Khadr could be prosecuted here and provided details about the evidence against him to Canadian officials for that purpose. Nonetheless, the interviews by Canadian officials were conducted for intelligence collection and not evidence gathering.

The interviews were monitored by US officials on each occasion the Canadian officials visited Guantánamo. An audio and video record was made of the February 2003 interviews. It is not clear in which format they were originally recorded but they are described as videotapes. CSIS was subsequently provided with copies of the February videotapes. Copies were filed with the Court as exhibits in DVD format. The evidence before me was that Canadian officials do not have copies of any recordings that may have been made of the September 2003 or March 2004 interviews.

...

The report of the March 2004 visit to Guantánamo prepared by the DFAIT official who went on that occasion is included in the collection as document 168. The version served on the applicant is almost entirely unredacted. The respondent seeks to protect a paragraph on page 2 of the report as it contains information provided in confidence by a member of the US military regarding steps taken by the Guantánamo authorities to prepare the applicant for the Canadian visit. There is also a side comment by the DFAIT official that the Attorney General wishes to protect as potentially harmful to Canada–US relations.

As indicated in a recently published report of the Office of the Inspector General of the US Department of Justice, during the period in question detainees at Guantánamo were subjected to a number of harsh interrogation techniques that would not have been permissible under American law for law enforcement purposes and have since been prohibited for use by the military.

Canada's international human rights obligations include the United Nations Convention against Torture and Other Cruel, Inhuman or Degrading Treatment or Punishment, Can. TS 1987 No 36 ("UNCAT"), to which the US is also a signatory. The application of this Convention to specific types of interrogation practices employed by military forces against detainees was discussed by the Supreme Court of Israel in *Public Committee against Torture in Israel* v. *Israel* 38 ILM 1471 (1999). The practice of using these techniques to lessen resistance to interrogation was found to constitute cruel and inhuman treatment within the meaning of the Convention.

The practice described to the Canadian official in March 2004 was, in my view, a breach of international human rights law respecting the treatment of detainees under UNCAT and the 1949 Geneva Conventions. Canada became implicated in the violation when the DFAIT official was provided with the redacted information and chose to proceed with the interview.

Canada cannot now object to the disclosure of this information. The information is relevant to the applicant's complaints of mistreatment while in detention. While it may cause some harm to Canada–US relations, that effect will be minimized by the fact that the use of such interrogation techniques by the US military at Guantánamo is now a matter of public record and debate. In any event, I am satisfied that the public interest in disclosure of this information outweighs the public interest in non-disclosure.

29. On May 13, 2009, Justice Mosley granted Mr Khadr leave to amend the statement of claim in his action for damages to seek relief for a breach of section 12 of the Charter, based on the evidence that when he was interviewed by Canadian officials, they were aware that he

had been subjected to sleep deprivation in preparation for the interview (*Khadr* v. *Canada*, 2009 FC 497, at paragraph 14).

30. The laws of the United States governing the detention and trial of Mr Khadr have changed since 2004 because of the decisions of the United States Supreme Court in *Rasul* v. *Bush*, 542 US 466 (2004) and *Hamdan* v. *Rumsfeld*, 548 US 557 (2006). In response to those decisions, the Military Commissions Act of 2006, Pub. L No 109-366, 120 Stat. 2600 was enacted. It appears that under the current legal regime, Mr Khadr has certain legal rights initially denied to him, including the right to bring an application for *habeas corpus* in the United States federal courts. Such an application was commenced on Mr Khadr's behalf, but the proceedings have been stayed.

31. It is not clear whether evidence of statements made by Mr Khadr as a result of his interrogation by United States officials and others would be admissible at his trial before a United States military commission. It would appear that a military judge may admit a statement where the degree of coercion is disputed, but only if "the totality of the circumstances renders the statement reliable and possessing sufficient probative value" and "the interests of justice would best be served by admission of the statement into evidence" (s 948r(c) of the Military Commissions Act of 2006, quoted at paragraph 48 of the affidavit of LCdr Kuebler).

The Current Litigation

32. On August 8, 2008, Mr Khadr filed in the Federal Court the application for judicial review that resulted in this appeal. He was seeking to challenge the Crown's decision and policy not to request his repatriation. His application was granted by Justice O'Reilly, who found that Canadian officials had breached Mr Khadr's rights under section 7 of the Charter and ordered, as a remedy under subsection 24(1) of the Charter, that Canada request the United States to return Mr Khadr to Canada as soon as practicable. The Crown has appealed that order.

Discussion

Preliminary points

33. Two preliminary observations are required to put this appeal into context.

34. First, the legal issues raised in this case are narrow and the facts are highly unusual. Justice O'Reilly did not decide that Canada is obliged to request the repatriation of any Canadian citizen detained abroad. He

did not decide that Canada is obliged to request Mr Khadr's repatriation because the conditions of his imprisonment breach international human rights norms. He did not decide that Canada must provide a remedy for anything done by the United States. These issues do not arise in this case and it would not be appropriate for this Court to express any opinion on them.

35. Justice O'Reilly focussed on specific conduct of Canadian officials, namely their interviewing Mr Khadr at the prison at Guantánamo Bay for the purpose of obtaining information from him, and giving the fruits of those interviews to United States authorities without attempting to control their use of that information. That was potentially detrimental to Mr Khadr's liberty and personal security and, most importantly, it occurred at a time when Canadian officials knew that Mr Khadr was an imprisoned minor without the benefit of consular assistance, legal counsel, or contact with his family, who had been subjected to abusive sleep deprivation techniques in order to induce him to talk. The issue before this Court is whether Justice O'Reilly erred in law in finding that conduct of Canadian officials, in those circumstances, to be a breach of Mr Khadr's rights under section 7 of the Charter.

36. Second, it is not legally relevant that in both *Khadr* 2008 and in this case, the same conduct of Canadian officials was found to breach Mr Khadr's rights under section 7 of the Charter. That is because the two cases concern two different decisions of the Canadian government affecting Mr Khadr or more precisely, separate legal challenges to two different government decisions. An application for judicial review normally may be made in respect of only one decision (see Federal Courts Rules, SOR/98-106 [r 1 (as amended by SOR/2004-283, s 1)], rule 302).

37. In *Khadr* 2008, Mr Khadr was challenging the Crown's decision not to disclose certain documents. The Supreme Court of Canada intervened in that decision because of the Crown's breach of Mr Khadr's rights under section 7 of the Charter, and as a remedy for that breach ordered the disclosure of some of the documents that Mr Khadr sought.

38. The disclosure of those documents provided evidence upon which Mr Khadr could challenge the Crown's decision not to request Mr Khadr's repatriation. He did so in a new application for judicial review. Justice O'Reilly intervened in that decision essentially because of the same conduct of Canadian officials that was the subject of *Khadr* 2008, viewed in the light of the new evidence. The Crown does not allege in its notice of appeal that *Khadr* 2008 rendered the issues raised in this proceeding *res judicata*. Nor does the Crown challenge Justice

O'Reilly's rejection of the Crown's argument that there was no "decision" that the Federal Court could review.

39. The following analysis of the issues raised in this appeal begins with an outline of the constitutional and legal background, followed by a discussion of whether there was a breach of section 7 of the Charter, and if so whether the breach was justified, and if it was not whether the remedy ordered was appropriate.

Constitutional and legal background

40. The decision to request the repatriation of a Canadian citizen detained in a foreign country is an aspect of the conduct of foreign affairs within the mandate of the Minister of Foreign Affairs and International Trade pursuant to section 10 [as amended by SC 1995, c 5, s 7(F)] of the Department of Foreign Affairs and International Trade Act, RSC, 1985, c E-22. That provision reads as follows:

10. (1) The powers, duties and functions of the Minister extend to and include all matters over which Parliament has jurisdiction, not by law assigned to any other department, board or agency of the Government of Canada, relating to the conduct of the external affairs of Canada, including international trade and commerce and international development.

(2) In exercising his powers and carrying out his duties and functions under this Act, the Minister shall

- (*a*) conduct all diplomatic and consular relations on behalf of Canada;
- (*b*) conduct all official communication between the Government of Canada and the government of any other country and between the Government of Canada and any international organization;
- (*c*) conduct and manage international negotiations as they relate to Canada;
- (*d*) coordinate Canada's international economic relations;
- (*e*) foster the expansion of Canada's international trade and commerce;
- (*f*) have the control and supervision of the Canadian International Development Agency;
- (*g*) coordinate the direction given by the Government of Canada to the heads of Canada's diplomatic and consular missions;
- (*h*) have the management of Canada's diplomatic and consular missions;
- (*i*) administer the foreign service of Canada;
- (*j*) foster the development of international law and its application in Canada's external relations; and
- (*k*) carry out such other duties and functions as are by law assigned to him.

41. There is no statute or regulation governing the exercise of the Minister's mandate under section 10 of the Department of Foreign

Affairs and International Trade Act or the Minister's authority to determine whether and when to request the repatriation of a Canadian citizen detained in a foreign country.

42. Mr Khadr's application relies on the Charter which, as part of the Constitution of Canada, constrains the exercise of governmental authority against individuals. Mr Khadr has alleged breaches of his rights under sections 7 and 12 of the Charter, which read as follows:

7. Everyone has the right to life, liberty and security of the person and the right not to be deprived thereof except in accordance with the principles of fundamental justice.
...
12. Everyone has the right not to be subjected to any cruel and unusual treatment or punishment.

43. Mr Khadr invoked the authority of the Federal Court to grant a remedy pursuant to subsection 24(1) of the Charter, which reads as follows:

24. (1) Anyone whose rights or freedoms, as guaranteed by this Charter, have been infringed or denied may apply to a court of competent jurisdiction to obtain such remedy as the court considers appropriate and just in the circumstances.

44. As mentioned above, Justice O'Reilly found that Canadian officials interviewed Mr Khadr at the prison at Guantánamo Bay for the purpose of obtaining information from him, and gave the fruits of those interviews to United States authorities without attempting to control their use of that information. At that time, the Canadian officials knew the circumstances of Mr Khadr's imprisonment. In particular, they knew that Mr Khadr had been subjected to serious mistreatment in order to induce him to talk. Justice O'Reilly found that Mr Khadr's rights under the Charter had been breached. As a remedy for that breach, Justice O'Reilly ordered the Crown to request the United States to return Mr Khadr to Canada as soon as practicable. Enforcement of the judgment has been stayed on consent pursuant to the order of Chief Justice Richard dated May 13, 2009.

45. In this appeal, the Crown argues that Mr Khadr's Charter rights were not breached, and alternatively, if there was a breach, that it can be justified by section 1 of the Charter. The Crown also argues that, if there was an unjustified breach of Mr Khadr's Charter rights, the remedy granted is not appropriate.

Whether there was a breach of section 7 of the Charter

46. It is necessary at this point to refer to the specific determinations from *Khadr* 2008 that must be applied in this case. Those determinations may be summarized as follows. When Canadian officials interviewed Mr Khadr and gave the resulting information to the United States authorities, they were participating in a process that was illegal under the laws of the United States and contrary to Canada's international human rights obligations. For that reason, the Charter was engaged by their conduct. Because Mr Khadr's liberty was at stake, section 7 of the Charter required Canadian officials to conduct themselves in conformity with the principles of fundamental justice in relation to those interviews. Section 7 is quoted above but is repeated here for ease of reference:

> 7. Everyone has the right to life, liberty and security of the person and the right not to be deprived thereof except in accordance with the principles of fundamental justice.

47. Given *Khadr* 2008, the Crown must accept that the conduct of Canadian officials abroad may in certain circumstances affect the rights of an individual to such an extent that the Charter is engaged. In *Khadr* 2008, the Charter was engaged when Canadian officials interviewed Mr Khadr at the Guantánamo Bay prison. Their conduct was found to be participation in the process at that prison, in breach of Mr Khadr's Charter right to liberty and security of the person. Therefore, Justice O'Reilly was bound to conclude that Canadian officials participated in the process at the Guantánamo Bay prison as it related to Mr Khadr, and that the Charter was engaged when they did so. It is not open to this Court to reach a different conclusion on those points.

48. When *Khadr* 2008 was decided, Mr Khadr had not yet been provided with the evidence that when he was interviewed by Canadian officials, they knew of his mistreatment by sleep deprivation. That evidence became available only as a result of the disclosure of the documents reviewed by Justice Mosley following *Khadr* 2008. That evidence indicates that Canadian officials not only participated in a process that did not conform to international human rights norms, but they did so knowingly.

49. The Crown objects strongly to the suggestion that Canadian officials participated in the mistreatment of Mr Khadr. They argue that any mistreatment suffered by Mr Khadr was at the hands of officials of the United States, not Canada. That argument is untenable in the face of *Khadr* 2008, but even without the authority of that case it cannot

be accepted. It is true that the United States is primarily responsible for Mr Khadr's mistreatment. However, the purpose of the sleep deprivation mistreatment was to induce Mr Khadr to talk, and Canadian officials knew that when they interviewed Mr Khadr to obtain information for intelligence purposes. There can be no doubt that their conduct amounted to knowing participation in Mr Khadr's mistreatment.

50. Questioning a prisoner to obtain information after he has been subjected to cruel and abusive treatment to induce him to talk does not accord with the principles of fundamental justice. That is well illustrated by the following comments of the Supreme Court of Canada in *Suresh* v. *Canada (Minister of Citizenship and Immigration)*, 2002 SCC 1, [2002] 1 SCR 3, at paragraphs 50-1:

It can be confidently stated that Canadians do not accept torture as fair or compatible with justice. Torture finds no condonation in our Criminal Code; indeed the Code prohibits it (see, for example, s 269.1). The Canadian people, speaking through their elected representatives, have rejected all forms of state-sanctioned torture. Our courts ensure that confessions cannot be obtained by threats or force ... While we would hesitate to draw a direct equation between government policy or public opinion at any particular moment and the principles of fundamental justice, the fact that successive governments and Parliaments have refused to inflict torture and the death penalty surely reflects a fundamental Canadian belief about the appropriate limits of a criminal justice system.

When Canada adopted the Charter in 1982, it affirmed the opposition of the Canadian people to government-sanctioned torture by proscribing cruel and unusual treatment or punishment in s 12. A punishment is cruel and unusual if it "is so excessive as to outrage standards of decency": see *R* v. *Smith*, [1987] 1 SCR 1045, at pp. 1072-3, *per* Lamer J (as he then was). It must be so inherently repugnant that it could never be an appropriate punishment, however egregious the offence. Torture falls into this category. The prospect of torture induces fear and its consequences may be devastating, irreversible, indeed, fatal. Torture may be meted out indiscriminately or arbitrarily for no particular offence. Torture has as its end the denial of a person's humanity; this end is outside the legitimate domain of a criminal justice system: see, generally, E. Scarry, *The Body in Pain: The Making and Unmaking of the World* (1985), at pp. 27-59. Torture is an instrument of terror and not of justice. As Lamer J stated in *Smith*, *supra*, at pp. 1073-4, "some punishments or treatments will always be grossly disproportionate and will always outrage our standards of decency: for example, the infliction of corporal punishment". As such, torture is seen in Canada as fundamentally unjust.

51. Subsection 269.1(1) [as enacted by RSC, 1985 (3rd Supp.), c 10, s 2] of the Criminal Code, RSC, 1985, c C-46, referred to in the passage quoted above, makes it an offence for a peace officer or public officer to

inflict torture on another person. In that provision, "torture" is defined to include any act by which severe pain or suffering is intentionally inflicted on a person for the purpose of obtaining information or for the purpose of intimidating or coercing the person. Subsection 269.1(1) reflects the recognition of Parliament that freedom from such intentional mistreatment is a basic human right (see paragraph 164 of *R. v. Hape*, cited above).

52. Canada is also a party to the Convention against Torture and other Cruel, Inhuman or Degrading Treatment or Punishment, December 10, 1984, [1987] Can. TS No 36 (entered into force June 26, 1987). It is not necessary in this case to determine whether the Convention against Torture confers any enforceable legal rights on Canadian citizens. It is enough to say that, by becoming a party to the Convention against Torture, Canada expressed in the clearest possible way its acceptance of the general prohibition on cruel, inhuman or degrading treatment as a principle of fundamental justice, which must inform any consideration of the scope of section 7 of the Charter. It is also worth noting the discussion in paragraphs 61 to 64 of *Suresh* (cited above) explaining the basis for finding that the absolute prohibition on torture is a peremptory norm of customary international law, or *jus cogens*.

53. In addition, the Charter breach resulting from the conduct of the Canadian officials is exacerbated by the fact that, at the relevant time, the officials knew that Mr Khadr was a "child" as defined in the Convention on the Rights of the Child, November 20, [1992] Can. TS No 3 (entered into force 2 September 1990). It is reasonable to infer that when Canada became a party to that Convention, it was accepting that the most important international norms stated in that Convention are principles of fundamental justice. Article 37(a) of that Convention reads in relevant part as follows:

Article 37

States Parties shall ensure that:

(a) No child shall be subjected to torture or other cruel, inhuman or degrading treatment or punishment.

54. As stated above, the principles of fundamental justice do not permit the questioning of a prisoner to obtain information after he has been subjected to cruel and abusive treatment to induce him to talk. That must be so whether the abuse was inflicted by the questioner or by some other person with the questioner's knowledge. Canada cannot avoid responsibility for its participation in the process at the Guantánamo Bay prison by relying on the fact that Mr Khadr was mistreated by officials

of the United States, because Canadian officials knew of the abuse when they conducted the interviews and sought to take advantage of it.

55. Consequently, the rights of Mr Khadr under section 7 of the Charter were breached when Canadian officials interviewed him at the prison at Guantánamo Bay and shared the resulting information with United States officials.

56. At paragraph 50 of his reasons, Justice O'Reilly considered whether the circumstances of Mr Khadr's detention, and Canadian officials' questioning of him, gave rise to an obligation on the part of Canada to take steps to protect Mr Khadr from further abuse. Justice O'Reilly reasoned that the only protection the Crown could offer Mr Khadr at that point was to request his repatriation, which the Crown has refused to do, and therefore the refusal to request his repatriation was a breach of Mr Khadr's rights under section 7 of the Charter.

57. The Crown has not offered an acceptable basis for concluding that Justice O'Reilly erred in this logical extension of his principal conclusion. The Crown's challenge to this aspect of Justice O'Reilly's reasons is a variation on its main theme, namely that the conduct of foreign affairs is a matter of Crown prerogative and thus within the sole purview of the Executive. However, the Crown's position on this point is not consistent with the principle that in Canada the rule of law means that all government action is potentially subject to the Charter and the individual rights it guarantees. The Supreme Court of Canada has already decided in *Khadr* 2008 that the Charter was engaged because the conduct of Canadian officials in the United States towards Mr Khadr amounted to participation by Canada in the unlawful process at the Guantánamo Bay prison.

58. Further, Crown prerogative in the conduct of foreign affairs has already been held to be subject to the Charter. For instance, when Canada is asked pursuant to a treaty to extradite a Canadian citizen to stand trial in another country for an offence punishable by death, the Minister of Justice must refuse the request in the absence of an assurance from the prosecuting authorities that they will not seek the death penalty. Thus, in *United States* v. *Burns*, 2001 SCC 7, [2001] 1 SCR 283, the Court reviewed the constitutionality of the Minister's decision to surrender Burns, saying (at paragraph 38):

We affirm that it is generally for the Minister, not the Court, to assess the weight of competing considerations in extradition policy, but the availability of the death penalty, like death itself, opens up a different dimension.

Similarly, the knowing involvement of Canadian officials in the mistreatment of Mr Khadr in breach of international human rights law, in particular by interviewing him knowing that he had been deprived of sleep in order to induce him to talk, "opens up a different dimension" of a constitutional and justiciable nature.

59. Finally, there is no factual basis for the Crown's argument that a court order requiring the government to request the return of Mr Khadr is a serious intrusion into the Crown's responsibility for the conduct of Canada's foreign affairs. The Crown adduced no evidence that requiring it to request Mr Khadr's return would damage Canada's relations with the United States (see *Burns*, at paragraph 136). Indeed, when pressed in oral argument, counsel for the Crown conceded that the Crown was not alleging that requiring Canada to make such a request would damage its relations with the United States.

60. Justice O'Reilly did not err in law or fact when he concluded that, in the particular circumstances of this case, the Crown's refusal to request Mr Khadr's repatriation is a breach of Mr Khadr's rights under section 7 of the Charter.

Whether the breach was justified by section 1 of the Charter

61. The Crown argues that if there was a breach of Mr Khadr's rights under section 7, the breach was justified by section 1 of the Charter. Section 1 reads as follows (emphasis added):

1. The Canadian Charter of Rights and Freedoms guarantees the rights and freedoms set out in it subject only to such reasonable limits *prescribed by law* as can be demonstrably justified in a free and democratic society.

62. For its justification of the Charter breach, the Crown relies on section 10 of the Department of Foreign Affairs and International Trade Act, quoted above. The Crown's argument is that, given the breadth of the Minister's mandate as described in section 10, and the absence of any statutory or regulatory constraints on the exercise of the Minister's discretion, any decision of the Minister that comes within the scope of section 10 justifies a Charter breach if it is rationally connected to the advancement of Canada's international interests, including its interest in combating international terrorism. The explanation offered for the Minister's decision not to request the repatriation of Mr Khadr is that Canada's interests are best served if any such decision is deferred until after Mr Khadr is tried by a United States military commission or a United States federal court. The Crown's argument must be rejected.

63. First, since a reviewing court will already have taken competing state interests into account when determining the content of the principles of fundamental justice for the purpose of section 7, there is generally

little scope for the kind of balancing exercise required under section 1. The Supreme Court of Canada [in *Re BC Motor Vehicle Act*, [1985] 2 SCR 486, at page 518] has said that only in exceptional circumstances, including "natural disasters, the outbreak of war, epidemics, and the like", could a breach of section 7 be validated under section 1: see Peter W. Hogg, *Constitutional Law of Canada*, 5th edn supplemented, Vol. 2 (Toronto: Thomson/Carswell, 2007), at page 38-46. The Crown has not alleged or adduced evidence that Canada's relations with the United States would be injured by requesting Mr Khadr's return or that his return would pose a threat to Canada's security. For that reason, it cannot plausibly be argued that "exceptional conditions" exist on the facts of this case so as to require a section 1 analysis of whether the breach of his section 7 rights is justified.

64. Second, neither legislation nor Crown prerogative expressly or by necessary implication obliged Canadian officials to interview Mr Khadr in the circumstances in which he found himself, or to refuse to request Mr Khadr's return, in violation of his Charter rights. Mr Khadr is challenging the government's decision not to request his repatriation, not the validity of the law under which that decision was made. Therefore, any section 1 justification must be found in the decision itself (*Slaight Communications Inc.* v. *Davidson*, [1989] 1 SCR 1038, at pages 1077-80). There is no legal or factual foundation upon which this Court can conclude that the decision not to request Mr Khadr's repatriation is justified as a reasonable limit on his Charter rights.

65. Justice O'Reilly made no error when he said, at paragraph 91 of his reasons, that the Crown did not offer any basis for its section 1 argument. Nor did he err in finding that the breach of Mr Khadr's Charter rights was not justified by section 1 of the Charter.

Whether the remedy is appropriate

66. Once Justice O'Reilly found that Canada had an obligation in the unusual circumstances of this case to request Mr Khadr's repatriation, the most obvious remedy was to order Canada to discharge its obligation. In these circumstances, the Crown has a heavy onus to discharge in persuading the Court that Justice O'Reilly abused his broad remedial discretion under subsection 24(1) by failing to select a remedy other than the most obvious.

67. Judicial discretion in the award of an appropriate and just remedy for a violation of Charter rights must be guided by the considerations set out in *Doucet-Boudreau* v. *Nova Scotia (Minister of Education)*, 2003 SCC 62, [2003] 3 SCR 3. Although Justice O'Reilly does not cite

Doucet-Boudreau, it is clear that he addressed all relevant considerations raised by the Crown.

68. First, Justice O'Reilly considered the effectiveness of the remedy. He addressed, at paragraph 88 of his reasons, the Crown's argument that ordering Canada to request Mr Khadr's repatriation was not an effective remedy because there was only a remote possibility that the United States would comply. Justice O'Reilly rejected that argument on the basis of an affidavit by Mr Khadr's United States counsel, LCdr Kuebler. Paragraph 52 of that affidavit reads as follows:

> Based on discussions with Omar's Canadian counsel, I am aware that the US government has undertaken efforts to have the Canadian government accept the return of Omar to Canada to face a prosecution in Canada, and has shared evidence against Omar with the Government of Canada to help facilitate this repatriation process. I believe that the US government would release Omar from Guantánamo Bay and allow his repatriation should the Canadian government request that this happen.

69. The Crown has offered no basis upon which Justice O'Reilly should have rejected this evidence. The assertion of the Crown in oral argument that there is "one chance in a million" that the United States will comply with a request from Canada for the return of Mr Khadr is not supported by any evidence. It is also contradicted by the fact that the United States has complied with requests from all other western countries for the return of their nationals from detention in the prison at Guantánamo Bay.

70. The record provides no basis for predicting with certainty how the United States will respond to a request for Mr Khadr's repatriation. However, the fact that Canada has no control over the response of the United States does not mean that it is inappropriate to order the request to be made. In the circumstances of this case, making the request is the most appropriate remedy Canada can offer Mr Khadr that has the potential to mitigate the effects of the Charter violation. The Crown argues that an effective alternative remedy would be a declaration that Mr Khadr's Charter rights have been breached. That would leave Mr Khadr without even a chance at the vindication of his rights.

71. Second, Justice O'Reilly considered whether the remedy he proposed would result in undue prejudice or hardship to Canada's interests. At paragraphs 84 to 86 of his reasons he discussed whether the remedy would cause any harm to Canada's foreign relations, particularly its relations with the United States. He found no evidence of any such harm. He also addressed the Crown's argument that the remedy proposed by Mr Khadr was inappropriate because it involved an improper judicial

intrusion into the Crown prerogative over foreign affairs. Again, he noted that he was given no evidence on this point. The lack of evidence of potential harm to Canada's interests is the basis for Justice O'Reilly's comment that he was imposing a remedy that was "minimally intrusive" on the Crown's prerogative (paragraph 89 of his reasons). In the unusual circumstances of this case, it was reasonable for him to conclude that being ordered to make such a request of a close ally is a relatively small intrusion into the conduct of international relations.

72. Third, Justice O'Reilly considered whether the remedy he proposed would exceed the competence of the courts, and concluded that it would not. That conclusion is reasonable in the circumstances of this case. Justice O'Reilly's order is precise and specific, requires no special knowledge not possessed by courts, and calls for no ongoing judicial supervision. In the absence of indications to the contrary, the Federal Court is entitled to presume that the government will comply in good faith with a judicial order to request Mr Khadr's return.

73. Contrary to the submission of the Crown, Justice O'Reilly's order does not require the Attorney General to prosecute Mr Khadr in Canada. If Mr Khadr is returned, it will be for the Attorney General to decide, in the exercise of his or her discretion, whether to institute criminal proceedings in Canada against Mr Khadr. While Canada may have preferred to stand by and let the proceedings against Mr Khadr in the United States run their course, the violation of his Charter rights by Canadian officials has removed that option.

74. When the *Doucet-Boudreau* factors and Justice O'Reilly's reasons are considered as a whole, the remedy that he awarded did not constitute an abuse of discretion. In fashioning the remedy, Justice O'Reilly considered the relevant factors in order to tailor the remedy to the facts, and cannot be said to have weighed them in such a manner as to reach an unreasonable outcome.

Conclusion

75. For these reasons, this appeal should be dismissed with costs.

The following are the reasons for judgment rendered in English by

76. NADON JA (dissenting):—I have read, in draft, the reasons of my colleagues Evans and Sharlow JJA in which they conclude that the appeal ought to be dismissed. Specifically, my colleagues propose that we endorse the conclusion reached by O'Reilly J of the Federal Court at paragraphs 91 and 92 of his reasons in *Khadr* v. *Canada (Prime Minister)*, 2009 FC 405, [2010] 1 FCR 34:

I find that the Government of Canada is required by section 7 of the Charter to request Mr Khadr's repatriation to Canada in order to comply with a principle of fundamental justice, namely, the duty to protect persons in Mr Khadr's circumstances by taking steps to ensure that their fundamental rights, recognized in widely accepted international instruments such as the Convention on the Rights of the Child, are respected. The respondents did not offer any basis for concluding that the violation of Mr Khadr's rights was justified under section 1 of the Charter.

The ongoing refusal of Canada to request Mr Khadr's repatriation to Canada offends a principle of fundamental justice and violates Mr Khadr's rights under section 7 of the Charter. To mitigate the effect of that violation, Canada must present a request to the United States for Mr Khadr's repatriation to Canada as soon as practicable.

77. At paragraph 35 of their reasons, my colleagues formulate the issue before us in this appeal in the following terms:

Justice O'Reilly focussed on specific conduct of Canadian officials, namely their interviewing Mr Khadr at the prison at Guantánamo Bay for the purpose of obtaining information from him, and giving the fruits of those interviews to United States authorities without attempting to control their use of that information. That was potentially detrimental to Mr Khadr's liberty and personal security and, most importantly, it occurred at a time when Canadian officials knew that Mr Khadr was an imprisoned minor without the benefit of consular assistance, legal counsel, or contact with his family, who had been subjected to abusive sleep deprivation techniques in order to induce him to talk. The issue before this Court is whether Justice O'Reilly erred in law in finding that conduct of Canadian officials, in those circumstances, to be a breach of Mr Khadr's rights under section 7 of the Charter. [Emphasis added.]

78. My colleagues conclude that O'Reilly J did not err in fact or in law in holding that the Government of Canada's (Canada) refusal to request Mr Khadr's repatriation was a breach of his rights under section 7 of the Canadian Charter of Rights and Freedoms (the Charter). They then go on to find that O'Reilly J made no error in determining that the breach of Mr Khadr's Charter rights was not justified by section 1 of the Charter. Finally, Evans and Sharlow JJA conclude that the remedy awarded by O'Reilly J does not constitute an abuse of his discretion.

79. I cannot subscribe to my colleagues' point of view and I therefore dissent. In my view, the appeal should be allowed. However, before setting out my reasons, a brief review of the rationale which led O'Reilly J to his ultimate conclusion will be useful.

80. O'Reilly J held that Canada's decision not to request Mr Khadr's repatriation could be judicially reviewed. Although he recognized that Canada's decisions regarding foreign affairs fell to the Executive, he

emphasized the fact that the Executive's prerogative in that area was subject to review under the Charter. At paragraph 49 of his reasons, O'Reilly J concludes on this point as follows:

The government's decision is amenable to judicial review under the Charter but, at the same time, its view as to how best to deal with matters that affect international relations and foreign affairs is entitled to "particular weight".

81. O'Reilly J then turned to the question of whether the Charter applied in the circumstances of this case. On the basis of the Supreme Court of Canada's decision in *Canada (Justice)* v. *Khadr*, 2008 SCC 28, [2008] 2 SCR 125, he found that the Charter did apply to Canada's agents who had travelled to Guantánamo Bay to question Mr Khadr, to the extent that their conduct involved Canada in a process that violated Canada's international obligations. At paragraph 52 of his reasons, O'Reilly J concluded that Canada's "knowing involvement in the mistreatment of Mr Khadr" constituted a compelling basis for the application of the Charter through the conduct of those officials who conducted the interviews with Mr Khadr at Guantánamo Bay.

82. O'Reilly J then addressed the issue raised under section 7 of the Charter. He first determined whether the principles of fundamental justice required Canada to protect Mr Khadr. After reviewing various international instruments—namely, the Convention against Torture and other Cruel, Inhuman or Degrading Treatment or Punishment, the Convention on the Rights of the Child and the Optional Protocol to the Convention on the Rights of the Child on the involvement of Children in Armed Conflict [May 25, 2000, [2002] Can. TS No 5]—and Mr Khadr's particular circumstances, he concluded that the "duty to protect persons in Mr Khadr's circumstances" was a principle of fundamental justice (see paragraph 71 of his reasons). He further found that the "principles of fundamental justice obliged Canada to protect Mr Khadr by taking appropriate steps to ensure that his treatment accorded with international human rights norms" (see paragraph 75 of his reasons).

83. By reason of his conclusion that Canada was in breach of Mr Khadr's rights under section 7 of the Charter, O'Reilly J then proceeded to determine the appropriate remedy. More particularly, he sought to determine the remedy which would "mitigate the effect of the involvement of Canadian officials in the mistreatment of Mr Khadr at Guantánamo Bay" (see paragraph 77 of his reasons). He concluded that the appropriate remedy in the circumstances was to require Canada

to request Mr Khadr's repatriation to Canada, adding that no other remedy appeared to be capable of mitigating the effects of Canada's Charter violations "or accord with the government's duty to promote Mr Khadr's physical, psychological and social rehabilitation and reintegration" (see paragraph 78 of his reasons). In so concluding, O'Reilly J pointed out that Canada had not "identified any particular harm that might flow from requesting Mr Khadr's repatriation" (see paragraph 86 of his reasons).

84. Finally, because of his conclusion regarding section 7 of the Charter, O'Reilly J did not address the arguments made by Mr Khadr regarding sections 6 and 12 of the Charter.

85. In my view, O'Reilly J erred in concluding as he did. First, he erred in determining that Canada had failed to protect Mr Khadr. Second, he erred in regard to the appropriate remedy.

86. Although I am far from convinced that Canada had a duty to protect Mr Khadr, I need not address that issue in view of the conclusion which I have reached with regard to the steps taken by Canada to protect him. In my opinion, Canada has taken all necessary means at its disposal to protect Mr Khadr during the whole period of his detention at Guantánamo Bay. Consequently, assuming that Canada had a duty under section 7 of the Charter to protect Mr Khadr, it did not breach that duty in the circumstances of the case.

87. In determining whether Canada met its obligations to protect Mr Khadr, it is, in my respectful view, of great importance to keep in mind that he was arrested by the United States military (the US military) in Afghanistan in July 2002, that the US military transferred him to Guantánamo Bay in October 2002 and that he has been imprisoned thereat since that time by the US military. Canada did not participate either in his arrest, transfer or detention, nor was it consulted at any time in regard thereto by the US military or the US government.

88. I now turn to the steps taken by Canada to protect Mr Khadr from the time it learned of his arrest in Afghanistan. At paragraphs 59 and 60 of its memorandum of fact and law, Canada sets out the various steps that it took to protect Mr Khadr. As the facts which are related therein are not disputed by Mr Khadr, it will be easier for me to reproduce them rather than attempt a summary thereof. Canada has outlined the steps taken in reference to a number of topics, namely, Mr Khadr's youth, his need for medical care, his lack of education, his lack of access to consular access, his lack of access to legal counsel, his inability to challenge his detention or conditions of confinement at Guantánamo Bay in a court of law and his mistreatment by US officials:

59. ...
a. The Respondent's youth [the Respondent is Mr Khadr]
   * In 2002 Canada asked the US not to transfer the Respondent to Guantánamo Bay given his age.
   * After the respondent was transferred to Guantánamo Bay, Canada again expressed concern to the US that consideration be given to his age in his detention, requesting urgent consideration be given to having him transferred to a facility for juvenile enemy combatants.
b. The Respondent's need for medical care:
   * Canadian interviewers asked that the Respondent be seen by a medic or doctor in February 2003.
   * Later in 2003, Canada sought assurances that the Respondent was receiving adequate medical attention.
   * On several occasions in 2005 and 2006, Canada requested that the Respondent be provided with an independent medical assessment. Continued communication with US authorities through welfare visits allowed Canadian officials to follow up on various medical and dental issues for the Respondent.
c. The Respondent's lack of education:
   * Through welfare visits, Canadian officials provided educational materials, books and magazines to the Respondent and attempted to facilitate the provision of educational opportunities to him in communications with US officials.
d. The Respondent's lack of access to consular access:
   * Although the US has refused consular access since 2002, Canada obtained permission to conduct regular "welfare visits" with the Respondent starting in March 2005 and has since conducted over 10 visits.
e. The Respondent's lack of access to legal counsel:
   * Canada expressed concerns to the US with regard to the adequacy of the Respondent's counsel of choice in 2005 and assisted his Canadian counsel in ultimately obtaining access to the Respondent.
f. The Respondent's inability to challenge his detention or conditions of confinement in a court of law:
   a) On July 9, 2004, Canada advised the US of its expectation that the Respondent be provided with a judicial review of his detention by a regularly constituted court according all judicial guarantees in accordance with due process and international law.
   b) In 2007, the US [adopted] a new Military Commission Act to address the concerns identified in *Hamdan* v. *Rumsfeld* [126 S Ct 2749 (2006)].
   c) In 2008, the US Supreme Court confirmed in *Boumediene* v. *Bush* [553 US 723 (2008) 128 S Ct 2229] that detainees have the constitutional privilege of *habeas corpus*.
g. The Respondent's presence in a remote prison with no family contact:
   * Canada has facilitated communication with family members.

60. In addition, with regard to the Respondent's mistreatment by US officials, Canada took a number of steps:

a. Canada asked for and received assurances in 2003 that the Respondent was being treated humanely and in a manner consistent with the principles of the Third Geneva Convention of 1949.
b. On June 7, 2004, Canada delivered a diplomatic note seeking assurances from the US that the treatment of detainees in Guantánamo Bay would be in accordance with international humanitarian law and human rights law.
c. In January 2005, Canada sent a further diplomatic note reiterating its position that allegations of mistreatment should be investigated and perpetrators brought to justice.
d. Canada followed up with another note in February 2005 expressing extreme concerns regarding allegations of abuse against the Respondent and requesting information regarding the allegations and assurances that [*sic*] is being treated humanely.
e. In the initial welfare [visit] in March 2005, the DFAIT official asked US authorities specific questions in connection with adherence to the Standard Minimum Rules for the Treatment of Prisoners from the Office of the High Commissioner for Human Rights. Welfare visit reports from 2005 through 2008 reflect that the Respondent has generally been in good health.

89. Canada says that in identifying the relevant factors that should be considered in determining the scope of the principles of fundamental justice at issue, O'Reilly J erred in failing to find that the steps taken by Canada through diplomatic channels had, in fact, addressed these factors or that these factors had changed since Mr Khadr had been arrested in Afghanistan by the US military. In making this assertion, Canada refers, *inter alia*, to paragraph 70 of O'Reilly J's reasons, where he states:

In Mr Khadr's case, relevant factors to consider are his youth; his need for medical attention; his lack of education; access to consular assistance and legal counsel; his inability to challenge his detention or conditions of confinement in a court of law; and his presence in an unfamiliar, remote and isolated prison, with no family contact.

90. I agree entirely with Canada that the Judge erred. More particularly, the Judge not only failed to find that the steps taken by Canada had indeed addressed the factors which he had identified, he never turned his mind to the question as to whether these steps were sufficient for Canada to meet its duty to protect Mr Khadr. I believe the Judge erred because of the way in which he determined and defined Canada's duty.

91. At paragraph 54 of his reasons, the Judge indicated that he had to decide whether the principles of fundamental justice required Canada to protect Mr Khadr. In attempting to make this determination, he turned to the international instruments which I have already listed above. First, he reviewed the Convention against Torture and other Cruel, Inhuman or Degrading Treatment or Punishment. This led him to find that by providing to US authorities "the fruits of its interrogation of Mr Khadr", Canada had failed to prevent the possibility that statements made by Mr Khadr would be used against him in legal proceedings (see paragraph 57 of his reasons). In so finding, O'Reilly J referred to article 15 of the aforesaid Convention.

92. O'Reilly J then considered the Convention on the Rights of the Child. This led him to a number of findings and, more particularly, those found at paragraphs 63, 64 and 65 of his reasons, which I reproduce below:

The CRC [the Convention on the Rights of the Child] imposes on Canada some specific duties in respect of Mr Khadr. Canada was required to take steps to protect Mr Khadr from all forms of physical and mental violence, injury, abuse or maltreatment. We know that Canada raised concerns about Mr Khadr's treatment, but it also implicitly condoned the imposition of sleep deprivation techniques on him, having carried out interviews knowing that he had been subjected to them.

Canada had a duty to protect Mr Khadr from being subjected to any torture or other cruel, inhuman or degrading treatment or punishment, from being unlawfully detained, and from being locked up for a duration exceeding the shortest appropriate period of time. In Mr Khadr's case, while Canada did make representations regarding his possible mistreatment, it also participated directly in conduct that failed to respect Mr Khadr's rights, and failed to take steps to remove him from an extended period of unlawful detention among adult prisoners, without contact with his family.

Canada had a duty to take all appropriate measures to promote Mr Khadr's physical, psychological and social recovery.

93. The Judge then examined the Optional Protocol to the Convention on the Rights of the Child on the involvement of Children in Armed Conflict. As a result, he made the following remarks at paragraph 68 of his reasons:

Clearly, Canada was obliged to recognize that Mr Khadr, being a child, was vulnerable to being caught up in armed conflict as a result of his personal and social circumstances in 2002 and before. It cannot resile from its recognition of the need to protect minors, like Mr Khadr, who are drawn into hostilities before they can apply mature judgment to the choices they face.

94. Finally, at paragraph 70 of his reasons, which I have already reproduced, he considered a number of additional factors which he felt were relevant to his determination.

95. O'Reilly J then went on to consider whether the duty to protect Mr Khadr was a principle of fundamental justice. He answered that question in the affirmative and, at paragraph 75 of his reasons, he concluded that Canada had an obligation to "protect Mr Khadr by taking appropriate steps to ensure that his treatment accorded with international human rights norms". However, nowhere in his reasons does the Judge consider the steps taken by Canada, nor does he, in my respectful opinion, consider the context of Mr Khadr's detention and the extent to which Canada's ability to protect him was limited. More particularly, in imposing obligations on Canada, on the basis of international instruments to which Canada is a party, O'Reilly J failed to recognize the territorial limitation of these instruments.

96. It is apparent from the Judge's reasons that he has couched Canada's duty to protect Mr Khadr in the most absolute terms, without regard to the actual circumstances of his detention. As a result, I find it impossible to understand how Canada could ever fulfill the duty of protection which O'Reilly J has determined, more specifically at paragraph 64 of his reasons. For example, how could Canada prevent Mr Khadr from being unlawfully detained by the US military in Guantánamo Bay? Also, how could Canada prevent the US from detaining Mr Khadr "for a duration exceeding the shortest appropriate period of time"? And how could Canada remove Mr Khadr from "an extended period of unlawful detention among adult prisoners"?

97. I must confess that I have serious doubts about the soundness of O'Reilly J's assertion, found at paragraph 65 of his reasons, that Canada was bound "to take all appropriate measures to promote Mr Khadr's physical, psychological and social recovery". With respect, the Judge again appears to have forgotten that Mr Khadr was and is detained at Guantánamo Bay by the US military.

98. The statements made by O'Reilly J explain, in my view, why he did not give serious consideration to the steps taken by Canada from the moment it learned of Mr Khadr's arrest in Afghanistan. In my view, these steps, when considered in their proper context, are sufficient for me to conclude that Canada met its duty to protect Mr Khadr. In other words, the only possible steps that Canada could take, looking at the matter fairly and realistically, are the ones that it took through the diplomatic channel which I have outlined at paragraph 88 of these reasons. To this I would add that there were, in my view, no specific means by which Canada was bound to act. As the only means available to Canada were

through the diplomatic channel, the means to be employed could only be determined by Canada in the exercise of its powers regarding matters of foreign policy and national interest.

99. In summary, Canada sought consular access for Mr Khadr, which the US refused. It also requested [that] the US not transfer Mr Khadr to Guantánamo Bay, given his age, but to no avail. Further, Canada, on a separate occasion, attempted to convince the US that Mr Khadr, given his age, should be transferred to a facility for juvenile enemy combatants. In the fall of 2003, Canada expressed its concerns to the US that Mr Khadr could be subject to the death penalty and sought assurances with regard to his medical situation. In June 2004, Canada sought assurances from the US that detainees in Guantánamo Bay would be treated in accordance with international humanitarian and human rights laws. Further, throughout 2004, Canada continued to monitor Mr Khadr's situation and kept in contact with US officials in that regard. In July 2004, Canada informed the US that it expected that Mr Khadr would be entitled to judicial review of his detention before a court of law, in accordance with due process and international law. In January 2005, upon receipt of reports that physical and psychological coercion was being used against detainees at Guantánamo Bay, Canada made it known to the US that it expected detainees to be treated humanely and that perpetrators of mistreatment would be brought to justice.

100. During 2005 and 2006, Canada requested that Mr Khadr be provided with independent medical attention. Although the US continued to refuse consular access to Mr Khadr during 2005, it permitted Canadian officials to conduct welfare visits with Mr Khadr in Guantánamo Bay. Such visits were made in March and December 2005, in July 2006, in June, August and November of 2007, as well as in February through June of 2008.

101. Other than the fact that Canada, as determined by the Supreme Court of Canada in *Khadr*, above, should not have proceeded with interviews in 2003 and 2004 and should not have provided the information obtained therefrom to US authorities, I cannot see how Canada's conduct can be criticized. Thus, in the end, it appears that what has given rise to the Judge's order is the fact that Canadian officials questioned Mr Khadr in 2003 and 2004. That breach, in my respectful view, has been remedied by the order made by the Supreme Court in *Khadr*, above. Hence, notwithstanding the fact that the interviews should not have taken place, and considering the reality of Mr Khadr's detention, I am satisfied that the steps taken by Canada from 2002 to 2008 are sufficient to satisfy Canada's duty to protect Mr Khadr. The scope of Canada's duty, as I have attempted to explain, must necessarily depend

on the circumstances of the case, and in the present matter, on the circumstances of Mr Khadr's detention.

102. I would add that I also cannot agree with the statement made by O'Reilly J, at paragraph 52 of his reasons, that, by questioning Mr Khadr, Canada had been knowingly involved in his mistreatment. In my view, that determination cannot find any basis in the evidence before us. The fact that Canada had been made aware that US authorities were using sleep deprivation as an interrogation technique cannot, *per se*, lead to the conclusion that Canada participated therein or was somehow culpable in regard thereto. Canadian officials did not participate in or condone Mr Khadr's mistreatment. Nor, in my view, can it be seriously said that Canada either directly or indirectly intended to mistreat Mr Khadr. On the contrary, as the evidence clearly shows, Canada took a number of steps, which I have already outlined, to insure Mr Khadr's security. It should also be borne in mind that at the time that the interviews were conducted, the US neither permitted consular access nor had it yet authorized welfare visits. In fact, both before and after the interviews, Canadian officials pressed the US to have access to Mr Khadr in order to assess his welfare. Also, various requests were made by Canada to the US regarding Mr Khadr's treatment. It was only in March 2005 that Canadian officials were allowed to conduct welfare visits with Mr Khadr.

103. I therefore conclude that if section 7 of the Charter imposed a duty on Canada to protect Mr Khadr, Canada has fulfilled that duty.

104. I now turn to the remedy granted by O'Reilly J, which, in my view, constitutes his second error.

105. Canada argues, and I agree, that the redress granted by O'Reilly J appears to be an attempt by him to address the fact that Canada had knowledge of his mistreatment in 2004. As I have already stated, Canada's knowledge does not constitute participation in Mr Khadr's mistreatment. I will therefore say no more on that point.

106. In my opinion, the remedy granted by O'Reilly J exceeds the role of the Federal Court and is not within the power of the Court to grant. Ordering Canada to request the repatriation of Mr Khadr constitutes, in my view, a direct interference into Canada's conduct of its foreign affairs. It is clear that Canada has decided not to seek Mr Khadr's repatriation at the present time. Why Canada has taken that position is, in my respectful view, not for us to criticize or inquire into. Whether Canada should seek Mr Khadr's repatriation at the present is a matter best left to the Executive. In other words, how Canada should conduct its foreign affairs, including the management of its relationship with the US and the determination of the means by which it should

advance its position in regard to the protection of Canada's national interest and its fight against terrorism, should be left to the judgment of those who have been entrusted by the democratic process to manage these matters on behalf of the Canadian people.

107. In support of this view I wish to refer to two English decisions. The first one is *Abbasi & Anor, R (on the application of)* v. *Secretary of State for Foreign & Commonwealth Affairs & Secretary of State for the Home Department*, [2002] EWCA Civ 1598. In that case, the issue before the Court of Appeal was whether the Foreign Office could be compelled to make representations on behalf of Mr Abbasi, a British national captured by the US military in Afghanistan and detained since January 2002 at Guantánamo Bay, or to take other appropriate action on his behalf. In dismissing Mr Abbasi's judicial review application, the Court, at paragraph 106 of its reasons, made the following points:

We would summarise our views as to what the authorities establish as follows:

i. It is not an answer to a claim for judicial review to say that the source of the power of the Foreign Office is the prerogative. It is the subject matter that is determinative.
ii. *Despite extensive citation of authority there is nothing which supports the imposition of an enforceable duty to protect the citizen.* The European Convention on Human Rights does not impose any such duty. Its incorporation into the municipal law cannot therefore found a sound basis on which to consider the authorities binding on this court.
iii. *However the Foreign Office has discretion whether to exercise the right, which it undoubtedly has, to protect British citizens.* It has indicated in the ways explained what a British citizen may expect of it. The expectations are limited and the discretion is a very wide one but there is no reason [why] its decision or inaction should not be reviewable if it can be shown that the same were irrational or contrary to legitimate expectations; but the court cannot enter the forbidden areas, including decisions affecting foreign policy.
iv. *It is highly likely that any decision of the Foreign and Commonwealth Office, as to whether to make representations on a diplomatic level, will be intimately connected with decisions relating to this country's foreign policy, but an obligation to consider the position of a particular British citizen and consider the extent to which some action might be taken on his behalf, would seem unlikely itself to impinge on any forbidden area.*
v. The extent to which it may be possible to require more than that the Foreign Secretary give due consideration to a request for assistance will depend on the facts of the particular case. [Emphasis added.]

108. I wish to emphasize more particularly point Nos iii, iv and v, where the Court states that it cannot interfere with decisions affecting

foreign policy, that decisions made by the Foreign and Commonwealth Office as to whether representations should be made on behalf of a citizen "will be intimately connected with decisions relating to this country's foreign policy", and that requiring the Foreign Secretary to do more than give due consideration to a request "will depend on the facts of a particular case".

109. The fact that Canadian officials conducted interviews which ought not to have been conducted does not allow us, in my respectful view, to enter what the English Court of Appeal has characterized as constituting "the forbidden areas". The existence of circumstances much more exceptional than those of this case would be required for us to consider intruding into matters of foreign policy and national interest.

110. In a subsequent decision, *Al Rawi & Ors, R (on the application of)* v. *Secretary of State for Foreign & Commonwealth Affairs & Anor*, [2006] EWCA Civ 1279, the English Court of Appeal reiterated the view which it had expressed in *Abbasi*, above. There, three of the appellants were residents of the United Kingdom and were detained at Guantánamo Bay. They requested the Foreign Secretary to ask the US government to release them. Following a negative answer, the appellants sought an order of the High Court ordering the Foreign Secretary to make such a request. The evidence before the Court was that the Foreign Secretary was of the view that such a request should not be made. As the Court puts it at paragraph 1 of its reasons:

The evidence is that it is against her [the Foreign Secretary's] ... better judgment to do so. She considers that it would probably be seen by the United States as unjustified special pleading by the United Kingdom, and would be likely to be both ineffective and counterproductive.

111. In addition to reiterating the view expressed in *Abbasi*, above, the Court of Appeal, at paragraphs 147 and 148, made the following remarks:

For present purposes, we would approach the matter as follows. The courts have a special responsibility in the field of human rights. It arises in part from the impetus of the HRA, in part from the common law's jealousy in seeing that intrusive State power is always strictly justified. *The elected government has a special responsibility in what may be called strategic fields of policy, such as the conduct of foreign relations and matters of national security.* It arises in part from considerations of competence, in part from the constitutional imperative of electoral accountability. In *Secretary of State for the Home Department* v. *Rehman* [2003] 1 AC 153 Lord Hoffmann said at paragraph 62:

It is not only that the executive has access to special information and expertise in these matters. *It is also that such decisions, with serious potential results for the community, require a legitimacy which can be conferred only by entrusting them to persons responsible to the community through the democratic process.* If the people are to accept the consequences of such decisions, they must be made by persons whom the people have elected and whom they can remove.

This case has involved issues touching both the government's conduct of foreign relations, and national security: pre-eminently the former. In those areas the common law assigns the duty of decision upon the merits to the elected arm of government; all the more so if they combine in the same case. This is the law for constitutional as well as pragmatic reasons, as Lord Hoffmann has explained. *The court's role is to see that the government strictly complies with all formal requirements, and rationally considers the matters it has to confront. Here, because of the subject-matter, the law accords to the executive an especially broad margin of discretion.* This conclusion betrays no want of concern for the plight of the appellants. At the outset we described the case as acute on its facts, and so it is. But it is the court's duty to decide where lies the legal edge between the executive and judicial functions. That exercise has been this appeal's principal theme. [Emphasis added.]

112. In the present matter, I can find absolutely no basis to justify the remedy granted by O'Reilly J. The fact that Canada has refused to request Mr Khadr's repatriation and that Canada has not "pointed to any particular harm that would result" from granting such a remedy is, in my respectful view, an irrelevant consideration. The remedy awarded by O'Reilly J simply cannot be justified. In the circumstances, we must necessarily, as O'Reilly J recognized earlier in his reasons, allow considerable discretion to the Executive in dealing with matters such as the one now before us. Canada has considered the question of whether repatriation should be requested and it has decided that it should not. That, in my view, should end the matter.

113. I am also of the view that the remedy granted by O'Reilly J is inappropriate in that it bears no connection to Canada's alleged breach of Mr Khadr's rights under section 7 of the Charter. To repeat, it is the fact that Canadian officials interviewed Mr Khadr in 2003 and 2004 and provided the information which they obtained to US authorities coupled with O'Reilly J's finding that Canada was knowingly involved in Mr Khadr's mistreatment which has led to the granting of the remedy.

114. With respect, I cannot see the link between the inappropriateness of the interviews and the remedy of repatriation, a remedy which is, in my view, totally disproportionate in the circumstances. In *Khadr*, above, the Supreme Court dealt with Canada's breach by ordering that

it provide Mr Khadr with the information which it had passed on to US authorities. Perhaps an order could have issued prohibiting Canada from using the information obtained from Mr Khadr, should Canada ever decide to prosecute him in Canada. That remedy would have at least some connection to the alleged breach. It might also suffice, in the circumstances, for the Court to grant, as Canada suggests, a declaration indicating which actions of Canada are unconstitutional.

115. I would add that the fact that O'Reilly J believed that Canada's request for repatriation "would likely be granted by the United States" (see paragraph 88 of his reasons) is an irrelevant consideration and, in any event, is pure speculation on the part of the Judge. As I have attempted to make clear, the decision as to whether such a request should be made is one which ought to be made by Canada and not by O'Reilly J or this Court. It is up to Canada, in the exercise of its powers over foreign policy, to determine the most appropriate course of action in dealing with the US with regard to Mr Khadr's situation.

116. One final matter. Because O'Reilly J found that Mr Khadr's rights under section 7 had been breached, he did not address the other grounds raised by Mr Khadr, who argued that his rights under sections 6 and 12 of the Charter had been breached.

117. In my view, as neither one of these sections was breached, Canada cannot be required thereunder to request Mr Khadr's repatriation. Section 6 of the Charter provides that every citizen of Canada "has the right to enter, remain in and leave Canada". However, Canadian officials have not deprived Mr Khadr of this right to enter the country; rather, it is US officials who are detaining him in Guantánamo Bay. If or when Mr Khadr is released by the US, he will retain his constitutional right to enter Canada. In fact, Canada says that if he is convicted by the US Military Commission, he may make an application under the International Transfer of Offenders Act, SC 2004, c 21 to serve his sentence in Canada.

118. Section 12 of the Charter provides that "[e]veryone has the right not to be subjected to any cruel and unusual treatment or punishment". However, the mistreatment suffered by Mr Khadr in Guantánamo Bay was imposed by US officials, not by Canadian agents, and section 12 of the Charter is not applicable to charges or punishments under foreign law (see *Kindler v. Canada (Minister of Justice)*, [1991] 2 SCR 779, at pages 846-7; see also Peter W. Hogg, *Constitutional Law of Canada*, 5th edn supplemented, Vol. 2 (Toronto: Thomson/Carswell, 2007), at page 47-25). The fact that Canadian officials interviewed Mr Khadr cannot amount to cruel and unusual treatment, even if these officials were aware that Mr Khadr had been deprived of sleep. Mere knowledge

of Mr Khadr's mistreatment cannot be equated with participation in such mistreatment.

119. For these reasons, I would allow the appeal with costs and I would dismiss Mr Khadr's judicial review application, also with costs.

[Reports: [2010] 1 FCR 73; 310 DLR (4th) 462]

The following is the text of the judgment of the Supreme Court:

JUDGMENT OF THE SUPREME COURT

I. *Introduction*

1. Omar Khadr, a Canadian citizen, has been detained by the United States government at Guantánamo Bay, Cuba, for over seven years. The Prime Minister asks this Court to reverse the decision of the Federal Court of Appeal requiring the Canadian government to request the United States to return Mr Khadr from Guantánamo Bay to Canada.

2. For the reasons that follow, we agree with the courts below that Mr Khadr's rights under s 7 of the Canadian Charter of Rights and Freedoms were violated. However, we conclude that the order made by the lower courts that the government request Mr Khadr's return to Canada is not an appropriate remedy for that breach under s 24(1) of the Charter. Consistent with the separation of powers and the well-grounded reluctance of courts to intervene in matters of foreign relations, the proper remedy is to grant Mr Khadr a declaration that his Charter rights have been infringed, while leaving the government a measure of discretion in deciding how best to respond. We would therefore allow the appeal in part.

II. *Background*

3. Mr Khadr was 15 years old when he was taken prisoner on July 27, 2002, by US forces in Afghanistan. He was alleged to have thrown a grenade that killed an American soldier in the battle in which he was captured. About three months later, he was transferred to the US military installation at Guantánamo Bay. He was placed in adult detention facilities.

4. On September 7, 2004, Mr Khadr was brought before a Combatant Status Review Tribunal which affirmed a previous determination that he was an "enemy combatant". He was subsequently charged with

war crimes and held for trial before a military commission. In light of a number of procedural delays and setbacks, that trial is still pending.

5. In February and September 2003, agents from the Canadian Security Intelligence Service ("CSIS") and the Foreign Intelligence Division of the Department of Foreign Affairs and International Trade ("DFAIT") questioned Mr Khadr on matters connected to the charges pending against him and shared the product of these interviews with US authorities. In March 2004, a DFAIT official interviewed Mr Khadr again, with the knowledge that he had been subjected by US authorities to a sleep deprivation technique, known as the "frequent flyer program", in an effort to make him less resistant to interrogation. During this interview, Mr Khadr refused to answer questions. In 2005, von Finckenstein J of the Federal Court issued an interim injunction preventing CSIS and DFAIT agents from further interviewing Mr Khadr in order "to prevent a potential grave injustice" from occurring: *Khadr* v. *Canada*, 2005 FC 1076, [2006] 2 FCR 505, at para. 46. In 2008, this Court ordered the Canadian government to disclose to Mr Khadr the transcripts of the interviews he had given to CSIS and DFAIT in Guantánamo Bay, under s 7 of the Charter: *Canada (Justice)* v. *Khadr*, 2008 SCC 28, [2008] 2 SCR 125 ("*Khadr 2008*").

6. Mr Khadr has repeatedly requested that the Government of Canada ask the United States to return him to Canada: in March 2005 during a Canadian consular visit; on December 15, 2005, when a welfare report noted that "[Mr Khadr] wants his government to bring him back home" (Report of Welfare Visit, Exhibit "L" to Affidavit of Sean Robertson, December 15, 2005 (JR, vol. IV, at p. 534)); and in a formal written request through counsel on July 28, 2008.

7. The Prime Minister announced his decision not to request Mr Khadr's repatriation on July 10, 2008, during a media interview. The Prime Minister provided the following response to a journalist's question, posed in French, regarding whether the government would seek repatriation:

[Translation] The answer is no, as I said the former Government, and our Government with the notification of the Minister of Justice had considered all these issues and the situation remains the same ... We keep on looking for [assurances] of good treatment of Mr Khadr.

(http://watch.ctv.ca/news/clip65783#clip65783, at 3'3", referred to in Affidavit of April Bedard, August 8, 2008 (JR, vol. II, at pp. 131-2).)

8. On August 8, 2008, Mr Khadr applied to the Federal Court for judicial review of the government's "ongoing decision and policy" not

to seek his repatriation (Notice of Application filed by the respondent, August 8, 2008 (JR, vol. II, at p. 113)). He alleged that the decision and policy infringed his rights under s 7 of the Charter, which states:

7. Everyone has the right to life, liberty and security of the person and the right not to be deprived thereof except in accordance with the principles of fundamental justice.

9. After reviewing the history of Mr Khadr's detention and applicable principles of Canadian and international law, O'Reilly J concluded that in these special circumstances, Canada has a "duty to protect" Mr Khadr (2009 FC 405, 341 FTR 300). He found that "[t]he ongoing refusal of Canada to request Mr Khadr's repatriation to Canada offends a principle of fundamental justice and violates Mr Khadr's rights under s 7 of the Charter" (para. 92). Also, he held that "[t]o mitigate the effect of that violation, Canada must present a request to the United States for Mr Khadr's repatriation to Canada as soon as practicable" (para. 92).

10. The majority judgment of the Federal Court of Appeal (*per* Evans and Sharlow JJA) upheld O'Reilly J's order, but defined the s 7 breach more narrowly. The majority of the Court of Appeal found that it arose from the March 2004 interrogation conducted with the knowledge that Mr Khadr had been subject to the "frequent flyer program", characterized by the majority as involving cruel and abusive treatment contrary to the principles of fundamental justice: 2009 FCA 246, 310 DLR (4th) 462. Dissenting, Nadon JA reviewed the many steps the government had taken on Mr Khadr's behalf and held that since the Constitution conferred jurisdiction over foreign affairs on the executive branch of government, the remedy sought was beyond the power of the courts to grant.

III. *The Issues*

11. Mr Khadr argues that the government has breached his rights under s 7 of the Charter, and that the appropriate remedy for this breach is an order that the government request the United States to return him to Canada.

12. Mr Khadr does not suggest that the government is obliged to request the repatriation of all Canadian citizens held abroad in suspect circumstances. Rather, his contention is that the conduct of the government of Canada in connection with his detention by the US military in Guantánamo Bay, and in particular Canada's collaboration with the US government in 2003 and 2004, violated his rights under the Charter, and requires as a remedy that the government now request his return

to Canada. The issues that flow from this claim may be summarized as follows:

A. Was there a breach of section 7 of the Charter?

1. Does the Charter apply to the conduct of Canadian state officials alleged to have infringed Mr Khadr's s 7 Charter rights?
2. If so, does the conduct of the Canadian government deprive Mr Khadr of the right to life, liberty or security of the person?
3. If so, does the deprivation accord with the principles of fundamental justice?

B. Is the remedy sought appropriate and just in all the circumstances?

13. We will consider each of these issues in turn.

A. *Was there a breach of section 7 of the Charter?*

1. *Does the Canadian Charter apply to the conduct of the Canadian state officials alleged to have infringed Mr Khadr's section 7 Charter rights?*

14. As a general rule, Canadians abroad are bound by the law of the country in which they find themselves and cannot avail themselves of their rights under the Charter. International customary law and the principle of comity of nations generally prevent the Charter from applying to the actions of Canadian officials operating outside of Canada: *R.* v. *Hape*, 2007 SCC 26, [2007] 2 SCR 292, at para. 48, *per* LeBel J, citing *United States of America* v. *Dynar*, [1997] 2 SCR 462, at para. 123. The jurisprudence leaves the door open to an exception in the case of Canadian participation in activities of a foreign state or its agents that are contrary to Canada's international obligations or fundamental human rights norms: *Hape*, at para. 52, *per* LeBel J; *Khadr 2008*, at para. 18.

15. The question before us, then, is whether the rule against the extraterritorial application of the Charter prevents the Charter from applying to the actions of Canadian officials at Guantánamo Bay.

16. This question was addressed in *Khadr 2008*, in which this Court held that the Charter applied to the actions of Canadian officials operating at Guantánamo Bay who handed the fruits of their interviews over to US authorities. This Court held, at para. 26, that "the principles of international law and comity that might otherwise preclude application of the Charter to Canadian officials acting abroad do not apply to

the assistance they gave to US authorities at Guantánamo Bay", given holdings of the Supreme Court of the United States that the military commission regime then in place constituted a clear violation of fundamental human rights protected by international law: see *Khadr 2008*, at para. 24; *Rasul* v. *Bush*, 542 US 466 (2004), and *Hamdan* v. *Rumsfeld*, 548 US 557 (2006). The principles of fundamental justice thus required the Canadian officials who had interrogated Mr Khadr to disclose to him the contents of the statements he had given them. The Canadian government complied with this Court's order.

17. We note that the regime under which Mr Khadr is currently detained has changed significantly in recent years. The US Congress has legislated and the US courts have acted with the aim of bringing the military processes at Guantánamo Bay in line with international law. (The Detainee Treatment Act of 2005, Pub. L 109-148, 119 Stat. 2739, prohibited inhumane treatment of detainees and required interrogations to be performed according to the Army field manual. The Military Commissions Act of 2006, Pub. L 109-366, 120 Stat. 2600, attempted to legalize the Guantánamo regime after the US Supreme Court's ruling in *Hamdan* v. *Rumsfeld*. However, on June 12, 2008, in *Boumediene* v. *Bush*, 128 S Ct 2229 (2008), the US Supreme Court held that Guantánamo Bay detainees have a constitutional right to *habeas corpus*, and struck down the provisions of the Military Commissions Act of 2006 that suspended that right.)

18. Though the process to which Mr Khadr is subject has changed, his claim is based upon the same underlying series of events at Guantánamo Bay (the interviews and evidence-sharing of 2003 and 2004) that we considered in *Khadr 2008*. We are satisfied that the rationale in *Khadr 2008* for applying the Charter to the actions of Canadian officials at Guantánamo Bay governs this case as well.

2. *Does the conduct of the Canadian government deprive Mr Khadr of the right to life, liberty or security of the person?*

19. The United States is holding Mr Khadr for the purpose of trying him on charges of war crimes. The United States is thus the primary source of the deprivation of Mr Khadr's liberty and security of the person. However, the allegation on which his claim rests is that Canada has also contributed to his past and continuing deprivation of liberty. To satisfy the requirements of s 7, as stated by this Court in *Suresh* v. *Canada (Minister of Citizenship and Immigration)*, 2002 SCC 1, [2002] 1 SCR 3, there must be "a sufficient causal connection between [the Canadian] government's participation and the deprivation [of liberty and security of the person] ultimately effected" (para. 54).

20. The record suggests that the interviews conducted by CSIS and DFAIT provided significant evidence in relation to these charges. During the February and September 2003 interrogations, CSIS officials repeatedly questioned Mr Khadr about the central events at issue in his prosecution, extracting statements from him that could potentially prove inculpatory in the US proceedings against him (CSIS Document, Exhibit "U" to Affidavit of Lt Cdr William Kuebler, November 7, 2003 (JR, vol. II, at p. 280); Interview Summary, Exhibit "AA" to Affidavit of Lt Cdr William Kuebler, February 24, 2003 (JR, vol. III, at p. 289); Interview Summary, Exhibit "BB" to Affidavit of Lt Cdr William Kuebler, February 17, 2003 (JR, vol. III, at p. 292); Interview Summary, Exhibit "DD" to Affidavit of Lt Cdr William Kuebler, April 20, 2004 (JR, vol. III, at p. 296)). A report of the Security Intelligence Review Committee titled *CSIS's Role in the Matter of Omar Khadr* (July 8, 2009) further indicated that CSIS assessed the interrogations of Mr Khadr as being "highly successful, as evidenced by the quality intelligence information" elicited from Mr Khadr (p. 13). These statements were shared with US authorities and were summarized in US investigative reports (Report of Investigative Activity, Exhibit "AA" to Affidavit of Lt Cdr William Kuebler, February 24, 2003 (JR, vol. III, at pp. 289 ff.)). Pursuant to the relaxed rules of evidence under the US Military Commissions Act of 2006, Mr Khadr's statements to Canadian officials are potentially admissible against him in the US proceedings, notwithstanding the oppressive circumstances under which they were obtained: see *United States of America* v. *Jawad*, Military Commission, September 24, 2008, D-008 Ruling on Defense Motion to Dismiss—Torture of the Detainee (online: http://www.defense.gov/news/Ruling%20D-008.pdf). The above interrogations also provided the context for the March 2004 interrogation, when a DFAIT official, knowing that Mr Khadr had been subjected to the "frequent flyer program" to make him less resistant to interrogations, nevertheless proceeded with the interrogation of Mr Khadr (Interview Summary, Exhibit "DD" to Affidavit of Lt Cdr William Kuebler, April 20, 2004 (JR, vol. III, at p. 296)).

21. An applicant for a Charter remedy must prove a Charter violation on a balance of probabilities (*R* v. *Collins*, [1987] 1 SCR 265, at p. 277). It is reasonable to infer from the uncontradicted evidence before us that the statements taken by Canadian officials are contributing to the continued detention of Mr Khadr, thereby impacting his liberty and security interests. In the absence of any evidence to the contrary (or disclaimer rebutting this inference), we conclude on the record before us that Canada's active participation in what was at the time an illegal

regime has contributed and continues to contribute to Mr Khadr's current detention, which is the subject of his current claim. The causal connection demanded by *Suresh* between Canadian conduct and the deprivation of liberty and security of person is established.

3. *Does the deprivation accord with the principles of fundamental justice?*

22. We have concluded that the conduct of the Canadian government is sufficiently connected to the denial of Mr Khadr's liberty and security of the person. This alone, however, does not establish a breach of Mr Khadr's s 7 rights under the Charter. To establish a breach, Mr Khadr must show that this deprivation is not in accordance with the principles of fundamental justice.

23. The principles of fundamental justice "are to be found in the basic tenets of our legal system": *Re BC Motor Vehicle Act*, [1985] 2 SCR 486, at p. 503. They are informed by Canadian experience and jurisprudence, and take into account Canada's obligations and values, as expressed in the various sources of international human rights law by which Canada is bound. In *R.* v. *DB*, 2008 SCC 25, [2008] 2 SCR 3, at para. 46, the Court (Abella J for the majority) restated the criteria for identifying a new principle of fundamental justice in the following manner:

(1) It must be a legal principle.
(2) There must be a consensus that the rule or principle is fundamental to the way in which the legal system ought fairly to operate.
(3) It must be identified with sufficient precision to yield a manageable standard against which to measure deprivations of life, liberty or security of the person.

24. We conclude that Canadian conduct in connection with Mr Khadr's case did not conform to the principles of fundamental justice. That conduct may be briefly reviewed. The statements taken by CSIS and DFAIT were obtained through participation in a regime which was known at the time to have refused detainees the right to challenge the legality of detention by way of *habeas corpus*. It was also known that Mr Khadr was 16 years old at the time and that he had not had access to counsel or to any adult who had his best interests in mind. As held by this Court in *Khadr 2008*, Canada's participation in the illegal process in place at Guantánamo Bay clearly violated Canada's binding international obligations (*Khadr 2008*, at paras. 23-5; *Hamdan* v. *Rumsfeld*). In conducting their interviews, CSIS officials had control over the questions asked and the subject matter of the interviews (Transcript

of cross-examination on Affidavit of Mr Hooper, Exhibit "GG" to Affidavit of Lt Cdr William Kuebler, March 2, 2005 (JR, vol. III, p. 313, at p. 22)). Canadian officials also knew that the US authorities would have full access to the contents of the interrogations (as Canadian officials sought no restrictions on their use) by virtue of their audio and video recording (*CSIS's Role in the Matter of Omar Khadr*, at pp. 11-12). The purpose of the interviews was for intelligence gathering and not criminal investigation. While in some contexts there may be an important distinction between those interviews conducted for the purpose of intelligence gathering and those conducted in criminal investigations, here, the distinction loses its significance. Canadian officials questioned Mr Khadr on matters that may have provided important evidence relating to his criminal proceedings, in circumstances where they knew that Mr Khadr was being indefinitely detained, was a young person and was alone during the interrogations. Further, the March 2004 interview, where Mr Khadr refused to answer questions, was conducted knowing that Mr Khadr had been subjected to three weeks of scheduled sleep deprivation, a measure described by the US Military Commission in *Jawad* as designed to "make [detainees] more compliant and break down their resistance to interrogation" (para. 4).

25. This conduct establishes Canadian participation in state conduct that violates the principles of fundamental justice. Interrogation of a youth to elicit statements about the most serious criminal charges while detained in these conditions and without access to counsel, and while knowing that the fruits of the interrogations would be shared with the US prosecutors, offends the most basic Canadian standards about the treatment of detained youth suspects.

26. We conclude that Mr Khadr has established that Canada violated his rights under s 7 of the Charter.

B. *Is the remedy sought appropriate and just in all the circumstances?*

27. In previous proceedings (*Khadr 2008*), Mr Khadr obtained the remedy of disclosure of the material gathered by Canadian officials against him through the interviews at Guantánamo Bay. The issue on this appeal is whether the breach of s 7 of the Charter entitles Mr Khadr to the remedy of an order that Canada request of the United States that he be returned to Canada. Two questions arise at this stage: (1) Is the remedy sought sufficiently connected to the breach? and (2) Is the remedy sought precluded by the fact that it touches on the Crown prerogative power over foreign affairs?

28. The judge at first instance held that the remedy sought was open to him. The Federal Court of Appeal held that he did not abuse his remedial discretion. On the basis of our answer to the second of the foregoing questions, we conclude that the trial judge, on the record before us, erred in the exercise of his discretion in granting the remedy sought.

29. First, is the remedy sought sufficiently connected to the breach? We have concluded that the Canadian government breached Mr Khadr's s 7 rights in 2003 and 2004 through its participation in the then illegal military regime at Guantánamo Bay. The question at this point is whether the remedy now being sought—an order that the Canadian government ask the United States to return Mr Khadr to Canada—is appropriate and just in the circumstances.

30. An appropriate and just remedy is "one that meaningfully vindicates the rights and freedoms of the claimants": *Doucet-Boudreau* v. *Nova Scotia (Minister of Education)*, 2003 SCC 62, [2003] 3 SCR 3, at para. 55. The first hurdle facing Mr Khadr, therefore, is to establish a sufficient connection between the breaches of s 7 that occurred in 2003 and 2004 and the order sought in these judicial review proceedings. In our view, the sufficiency of this connection is established by the continuing effect of these breaches into the present. Mr Khadr's Charter rights were breached when Canadian officials contributed to his detention by virtue of their interrogations at Guantánamo Bay knowing Mr Khadr was a youth, did not have access to legal counsel or *habeas corpus* at that time and, at the time of the interview in March 2004, had been subjected to improper treatment by the US authorities. As the information obtained by Canadian officials during the course of their interrogations may be used in the US proceedings against Mr Khadr, the effect of the breaches cannot be said to have been spent. It continues to this day. As discussed earlier, the material that Canadian officials gathered and turned over to the US military authorities may form part of the case upon which he is currently being held. The evidence before us suggests that the material produced was relevant and useful. There has been no suggestion that it does not form part of the case against Mr Khadr or that it will not be put forward at his ultimate trial. We therefore find that the breach of Mr Khadr's s 7 Charter rights remains ongoing and that the remedy sought could potentially vindicate those rights.

31. The acts that perpetrated the Charter breaches relied on in this appeal lie in the past. But their impact on Mr Khadr's liberty and security continue to this day and may redound into the future. The impact of the breaches is thus perpetuated into the present. When past acts violate present liberties, a present remedy may be required.

32. We conclude that the necessary connection between the breaches of s 7 and the remedy sought has been established for the purpose of these judicial review proceedings.

33. Second, is the remedy sought precluded by the fact that it touches on the Crown prerogative over foreign affairs? A connection between the remedy and the breach is not the only consideration. As stated in *Doucet-Boudreau*, an appropriate and just remedy is also one that "must employ means that are legitimate within the framework of our constitutional democracy" (para. 56) and must be a "judicial one which vindicates the right while invoking the function and powers of a court" (para. 57). The government argues that courts have no power under the Constitution of Canada to require the executive branch of government to do anything in the area of foreign policy. It submits that the decision not to request the repatriation of Mr Khadr falls directly within the prerogative powers of the Crown to conduct foreign relations, including the right to speak freely with a foreign state on all such matters: P. W. Hogg, *Constitutional Law of Canada* (5th edn Supp.), at p. 1-19.

34. The prerogative power is the "residue of discretionary or arbitrary authority, which at any given time is legally left in the hands of the Crown": *Reference as to the Effect of the Exercise of the Royal Prerogative of Mercy Upon Deportation Proceedings*, [1933] SCR 269, at p. 272, per Duff CJ, quoting A. V. Dicey, *Introduction to the Study of the Law of the Constitution* (8th edn 1915), at p. 420. It is a limited source of non-statutory administrative power accorded by the common law to the Crown: Hogg, at p. 1-17.

35. The prerogative power over foreign affairs has not been displaced by s 10 of the Department of Foreign Affairs and International Trade Act, RSC 1985, c E-22, and continues to be exercised by the federal government. The Crown prerogative in foreign affairs includes the making of representations to a foreign government: *Black* v. *Canada (Prime Minister)* (2001), 199 DLR (4th) 228 (Ont. CA). We therefore agree with O'Reilly J's implicit finding (paras. 39, 40 and 49) that the decision not to request Mr Khadr's repatriation was made in the exercise of the prerogative over foreign relations.

36. In exercising its common law powers under the royal prerogative, the executive is not exempt from constitutional scrutiny: *Operation Dismantle* v. *The Queen*, [1985] 1 SCR 441. It is for the executive and not the courts to decide whether and how to exercise its powers, but the courts clearly have the jurisdiction and the duty to determine whether a prerogative power asserted by the Crown does in fact exist and, if so, whether its exercise infringes the Charter (*Operation Dismantle*) or

other constitutional norms (*Air Canada* v. *British Columbia (Attorney General)*, [1986] 2 SCR 539).

37. The limited power of the courts to review exercises of the prerogative power for constitutionality reflects the fact that in a constitutional democracy, all government power must be exercised in accordance with the Constitution. This said, judicial review of the exercise of the prerogative power for constitutionality remains sensitive to the fact that the executive branch of government is responsible for decisions under this power, and that the executive is better placed to make such decisions within a range of constitutional options. The government must have flexibility in deciding how its duties under the power are to be discharged: see, e.g., *Reference re Secession of Quebec*, [1998] 2 SCR 217, at paras. 101-2. But it is for the courts to determine the legal and constitutional limits within which such decisions are to be taken. It follows that in the case of refusal by a government to abide by constitutional constraints, courts are empowered to make orders ensuring that the government's foreign affairs prerogative is exercised in accordance with the constitution: *United States* v. *Burns*, 2001 SCC 7, [2001] 1 SCR 283.

38. Having concluded that the courts possess a narrow power to review and intervene on matters of foreign affairs to ensure the constitutionality of executive action, the final question is whether O'Reilly J misdirected himself in exercising that power in the circumstances of this case (*R* v. *Bjelland*, 2009 SCC 38, [2009] 2 SCR 651, at para. 15; *R* v. *Regan*, 2002 SCC 12, [2002] 1 SCR 297, at paras. 117-18). (In fairness to the trial judge, we note that the government proposed no alternative (trial judge's reasons, at para. 78).) If the record and legal principle support his decision, deference requires we not interfere. However, in our view that is not the case.

39. Our first concern is that the remedy ordered below gives too little weight to the constitutional responsibility of the executive to make decisions on matters of foreign affairs in the context of complex and ever-changing circumstances, taking into account Canada's broader national interests. For the following reasons, we conclude that the appropriate remedy is to declare that, on the record before the Court, Canada infringed Mr Khadr's s 7 rights, and to leave it to the government to decide how best to respond to this judgment in light of current information, its responsibility for foreign affairs, and in conformity with the Charter.

40. As discussed, the conduct of foreign affairs lies with the executive branch of government. The courts, however, are charged with adjudicating the claims of individuals who claim that their Charter rights have

been or will be violated by the exercise of the government's discretionary powers: *Operation Dismantle*.

41. In some situations, courts may give specific directions to the executive branch of the government on matters touching foreign policy. For example, in *Burns*, the Court held that it would offend s 7 to extradite a fugitive from Canada without seeking and obtaining assurances from the requesting state that the death penalty would not be imposed. The Court gave due weight to the fact that seeking and obtaining those assurances were matters of Canadian foreign relations. Nevertheless, it ordered that the government seek them.

42. The specific facts in *Burns* justified a more specific remedy. The fugitives were under the control of Canadian officials. It was clear that assurances would provide effective protection against the prospective Charter breaches: it was entirely within Canada's power to protect the fugitives against possible execution. Moreover, the Court noted that no public purpose would be served by extradition without assurances that would not be substantially served by extradition with assurances, and that there was nothing to suggest that seeking such assurances would undermine Canada's good relations with other states: *Burns*, at paras. 125 and 136.

43. The present case differs from *Burns*. Mr Khadr is not under the control of the Canadian government; the likelihood that the proposed remedy will be effective is unclear; and the impact on Canadian foreign relations of a repatriation request cannot be properly assessed by the Court.

44. This brings us to our second concern: the inadequacy of the record. The record before us gives a necessarily incomplete picture of the range of considerations currently faced by the government in assessing Mr Khadr's request. We do not know what negotiations may have taken place, or will take place, between the US and Canadian governments over the fate of Mr Khadr. As observed by Chaskalson CJ in *Kaunda* v. *President of the Republic of South Africa*, [2004] ZACC 5, 136 ILR 452, at para. 77: "The timing of representations if they are to be made, the language in which they should be couched, and the sanctions (if any) which should follow if such representations are rejected are matters with which courts are ill-equipped to deal." It follows that in these circumstances, it would not be appropriate for the Court to give direction as to the diplomatic steps necessary to address the breaches of Mr Khadr's Charter rights.

45. Though Mr Khadr has not been moved from Guantánamo Bay in over seven years, his legal predicament continues to evolve. During the hearing of this appeal, we were advised by counsel that the US

Department of Justice had decided that Mr Khadr will continue to face trial by military commission, though other Guantánamo detainees will now be tried in a federal court in New York. How this latest development will affect Mr Khadr's situation and any ongoing negotiations between the United States and Canada over his possible repatriation is unknown. But it signals caution in the exercise of the Court's remedial jurisdiction.

46. In this case, the evidentiary uncertainties, the limitations of the Court's institutional competence, and the need to respect the prerogative powers of the executive, lead us to conclude that the proper remedy is declaratory relief. A declaration of unconstitutionality is a discretionary remedy: *Operation Dismantle*, at p. 481, citing *Solosky* v. *The Queen*, [1980] 1 SCR 821. It has been recognized by this Court as "an effective and flexible remedy for the settlement of real disputes": *R* v. *Gamble*, [1988] 2 SCR 595, at p. 649. A court can properly issue a declaratory remedy so long as it has the jurisdiction over the issue at bar, the question before the court is real and not theoretical, and the person raising it has a real interest to raise it. Such is the case here.

47. The prudent course at this point, respectful of the responsibilities of the executive and the courts, is for this Court to allow Mr Khadr's application for judicial review in part and to grant him a declaration advising the government of its opinion on the records before it which, in turn, will provide the legal framework for the executive to exercise its functions and to consider what actions to take in respect of Mr Khadr, in conformity with the Charter.

IV. Conclusion

48. The appeal is allowed in part. Mr Khadr's application for judicial review is allowed in part. This Court declares that through the conduct of Canadian officials in the course of interrogations in 2003-4, as established on the evidence before us, Canada actively participated in a process contrary to Canada's international human rights obligations and contributed to Mr Khadr's ongoing detention so as to deprive him of his right to liberty and security of the person guaranteed by s 7 of the Charter, contrary to the principles of fundamental justice. Costs are awarded to Mr Khadr.

Appeal allowed in part with costs to the respondent.

[Reports: [2010] 1 SCR 44; 315 DLR (4th) 1; 251 CCC (3d) 435; 206 CRR (2d) 1]

Human rights — Indigenous peoples — Property rights — Recognition of indigenous land rights — Indigenous Inughuit population of Thule in Greenland — ILO Convention No 169 concerning Indigenous and Tribal Peoples in Independent Countries, 1989 — Whether Inughuit constituting distinct indigenous people separate from main population within meaning of Convention — Forced resettlement in 1953 to make way for United States air base — Right to return — Right to compensation — United States–Denmark Agreement concerning the Defence of Greenland, 1951 — Whether providing adequate legal basis for expropriation and resettlement under municipal and international law — Whether satisfying requirements for legality under Danish Constitution

Relationship of international law and municipal law — Treaty obligations — Effect under municipal law — United States–Denmark Agreement concerning the Defence of Greenland, 1951 — Obligations of State in relation to private claimants — Memorandum of Understanding between States Parties to Agreement — Effect on rights of private claimants — Interpretation of treaties — ILO Convention No 169 concerning Indigenous and Tribal Peoples in Independent Countries, 1989 — The law of Denmark

HINGITAQ 53, PETERSEN AND OTHERS v. OFFICE OF THE PRIME MINISTER OF DENMARK[1]

(THULE TRIBE CASE)

Denmark, Supreme Court.   28 November 2003

(Hermann, Pedersen, Melchior, Blok, Grubbe, Hojgaard Pedersen and Stokholm JJ)

SUMMARY: *The facts*:—The claimants were members and descendants of the "Thule Tribe" or Inughuit who had lived in the settlement of Uummannaq in Thule in Northern Greenland. In 1951 the United States and Denmark concluded an Agreement concerning the Defence of Greenland which provided

---

[1] The claimants were represented by Christian Harlang. The defendants were represented by Hagel Sorensen.

the framework for the construction of a large United States Air Base in Thule beside the settlement in question. In June 1951 the new base came into use and adversely affected the hunting conditions and livelihood of the inhabitants. In May 1953 the Danish authorities ordered the immediate resettlement of the Inughuit resident in Thule. They were moved to modern accommodation 120 kilometres to the north, but no other compensation was paid and their claims for losses from poorer hunting conditions were not addressed by the Danish authorities.

In December 1996 proceedings were instituted before the Eastern High Court of Denmark. The claimants sought to establish (1) that they had a right to live in and use the settlement from which they had been expelled and to move about and hunt in the surrounding area, and (2) that they were entitled to compensation collectively and individually for the interference with their rights since 1953. The High Court found in favour of the claimants, characterizing the resettlement as a serious interference with the rights of the population, rejecting the position of the Danish Government that the population had itself requested the resettlement and awarding compensation. Following the judgment, the Danish Prime Minister made a statement acknowledging that the resettlement had been an unlawful act and conceding that the State would not appeal. The claimants, however, appealed to the Supreme Court, arguing in particular that the amount of compensation awarded was inadequate and that the High Court had been wrong to reject their argument that ILO Convention No 169 concerning Indigenous and Tribal Peoples in Independent Countries, 1989, gave them a right to return to their former lands. Denmark had been party to the Convention since 1997.

Held:—The appeal was dismissed and the judgment of the lower court was confirmed.

(1) The assessment of whether or not the Thule Tribe was a distinct indigenous people in the sense of the ILO Convention should be based on current conditions. In Greenland, regional variations still existed in terms of language, business conditions and rules of law deriving in part from the country's size, communications and transport structure, and natural local conditions. Based on an overall assessment of the available evidence, for all practical purposes the population of the Thule district shared the same conditions as the rest of the Greenland people and did not differ from it in any other relevant aspect. The information produced concerning the difference between the languages spoken in Qaanaaq and in West Greenland, and the Thule Tribe's perception of itself as a distinct indigenous people, could not lead to any other conclusion. Accordingly, the Thule Tribe did not "retain some of or all their own social, economic, cultural and political institutions" and consequently the Thule Tribe was not a distinct indigenous people within the meaning of Article 1(1)(b) of the ILO Convention (pp. 292-3).

(2) According to Article 1(1)(a), the ILO Convention also protected "tribal populations in independent countries whose social, cultural and economic

conditions distinguish them from other sections of the national community, and whose status is regulated wholly or partially by their own customs or traditions or by special laws or regulations". By reason of the above considerations, the Thule Tribe did not fall within the scope of this provision of the Convention. This interpretation was consistent with the declaration made by the Danish Government and subscribed to by the Greenland Home Rule Government at the time of the ratification of the ILO Convention. According to this Declaration, Denmark had "only one indigenous people" in the sense of the Convention, namely the indigenous population in Greenland or the Inuit (p. 293).

(3) In its decision of March 2001, the Governing Body of the ILO had reached the same conclusion as the Supreme Court. The Governing Body thereby endorsed the Report dated 23 March 2001 of the ILO Committee considering the complaint submitted by a Greenland trade union ("SIK") on behalf of the Thule Tribe, concerning Denmark's alleged contravention of the Convention. The Report stated that "there is no basis for considering the inhabitants of the community in question to be a 'people' separate and different from other Greenlanders" and that "the land traditionally occupied by the *Inuit* people has been identified and consists of the entire territory of Greenland". Taking into account that, pursuant to Article 1(1) of the ILO Convention, the Thule Tribe did not constitute a tribal people or a distinct indigenous people within or co-existing with the Greenlandic people as a whole, the Thule Tribe had no independent rights under the Convention (p. 294).

(4) The Thule Air Base had been established under the Defence Agreement of 1951, adopted by the Danish Parliament pursuant to Article 18 of the Constitution then in force. As such, there was a proper constitutional basis for the establishment of the Base and the Agreement was also valid under international law. The decisions to restrict hunting in the Thule area in 1951 and to relocate the population of Thule in 1953 amounted to acts of expropriation, had been lawfully carried out under the 1951 Defence Agreement and had not required specific statutory authority. The claims that the Thule tribe members had a right to live in and use the abolished settlement and a right to access, occupy and hunt in the entire Thule district therefore failed for the simple reason that the acts of expropriation had validly curtailed these rights of enjoyment in the areas affected (pp. 294-6).

(5) This conclusion applied even though, in February 2003, in application of their 1951 Defence Agreement, the United States and Denmark, acting together with the Greenland Home Rule Government, had signed a Memorandum of Understanding regarding the removal from the Thule Defence Area of Dundas, the area in which the settlement and colony were situated. In this connection, it should be stressed that the Thule Tribe which, as stated above, could not be considered a tribal people or a distinct indigenous people in the sense of the ILO Convention, could not claim privileges regarding Dundas under Article 16(3) of the Convention.

Equally the customary law of Greenland did not give rise to such privileges (p. 296).

The following is the text of the relevant part of the judgment of the Court:

This is an appeal against the judgment delivered on 20 August 1999 by the Third Eastern Division of the High Court. The appeal is brought by the Thule Tribe and the following 422 out of the total of 598 Thule Tribe members who were individual plaintiffs before the High Court: Nos 2, 4-5, 7-13, 15-23, 25-41, 43-8, 50-65, 68-78, 80-8, 90-3, 96-7, 99, 101-3, 111, 119-26, 129, 135-6, 138-9, 141-8, 152-3, 156-7, 159, 161-2, 169, 171-3, 180-1, 183-8, 190-5, 197-203, 207-9, 211-13, 215-16, 220-4, 228-43, 245, 247-9, 251, 253-4, 258-60, 262-4, 266-71, 274-7, 279-82, 288-93, 295-1, 305-6, 308-9, 311-15, 317-18, 328-35, 337, 339-41, 343, 350-70, 376-84, 391, 393, 395, 409, 411-17, 421, 423-6, 432-55, 457, 459-67, 469, 471-5, 477-8, 480, 482-94, 496-503, 506-11, 513, 515-23, 525-9, 533, 535-56, 558-9, 563, 566-71, 575, 578, 581, 585, 587, 590-9, 601 and 604-11. The names of these persons, some of whom have since passed away, appear in the judgment of the High Court.

The Thule Tribe and the individual appellants repeat their first and second claims, lodged before the High Court. The Thule Tribe has increased its claim for compensation (third claim) from DK (Danish Kroner) 25,000,000 to DK 235,114,290. Of this amount it is claimed that litigation interest on DK 25,000,000 should be paid in the same manner as claimed before the High Court, and that litigation interest on the increase of DK 210,114,290 should be paid from 15 August 2002. In the alternative, the Thule Tribe claims that it should be awarded compensation of DK 136,200,000 with the addition of interest as stated above, and in the further alternative, a smaller amount. Of the individual appellants affected by the relocation in 1953, 77 (Nos 2, 4-5, 7-13, 15-41, 43-8, 50-65, 68-78, 81 and 83-8), or the estates of each of these appellants, have repeated their claims for payment of DK 250,000 to each of them (fourth claim).

Regarding the first and second claims, the Prime Minister's Office has repeated its claim for dismissal and, in the alternative, for the judgment delivered by the High Court to be upheld. Regarding the Thule Tribe's claim for compensation (third claim), the Prime Minister's Office has made a claim for dismissal and, in the alternative, for the judgment delivered by the High Court to be upheld. Regarding the individual claims of the 77 appellants (fourth claim), the Prime Minister's Office asks for the judgment delivered by the High Court to be upheld. As regards the claims for dismissal brought by the Prime Minister's Office, the appellants ask for the Supreme Court to hear the first, second and third claims on their merits.

The amounts of compensation awarded by the High Court in its judgment have all been paid. The Prime Minister's Office has declared that it will not claim repayment of the amount of compensation of DK 500,000 even if it succeeds in its claims for dismissal.

The Thule Tribe has calculated its claim for compensation of DK 235,114,290 on the basis of the following figures: The Treasury paid compensation in connection with the establishment of the Thule weather station in 1946 in the form of an annual amount of DK 200. According to the appellants the base covered an area of 2,743 square km, or 26,183.81 times larger than the area covered by the weather station which, according to the appellants, comprised 0.105 square km. The annual compensation at today's values therefore amounts to DK 200 multiplied by 26,183.81, or DK 5,224,762. For the forty-five-year period between the establishment of the Thule Air Base in 1951 and the institution of proceedings in 1996 the amount claimed therefore amounts to DK 235,114,290. The Thule Tribe's alternative claim of DK 136,200,000 has been calculated as stated at the end of paragraphs 1 and 5.4 of the High Court judgment.

As regards the first and second claims, the appellants have submitted that the Memorandum of Understanding concluded in February 2003 between the Danish Government, the Home Rule Government of Greenland, and the Government of the United States of America regarding the Dundas area is illegal in relation to the appellants, because Article 4(3) provides that the Danish/Greenland authorities must ensure that non-residents of Qaanaaq Municipality are not permitted in Dundas on a permanent basis or allowed to enter the defence area without permission. In this connection, reference is made to Article 16(3) of the ILO Convention.

The Prime Minister's Office has stated, notably in support of its claims for dismissal, that according to its own definition the Thule Tribe is delimited in such a way that persons who have moved to the Thule district after 1921 are not part of the tribe and that the tribe includes members who were neither born nor are resident in Greenland. In support of the claim for dismissal of the Thule Tribe's claim for compensation (third claim) the Prime Minister's Office has further submitted that the Thule Tribe cannot bring a collective claim for compensation because, as litigant before the Supreme Court, the Thule Tribe is no longer a representative spokesman. The Prime Minister's Office has not disputed that the 422 persons regard themselves as belonging to the Thule Tribe.

The Prime Minister's Office has accepted the Joint Declaration made on 2 September 1999 by Prime Minister Poul Nyrup Rasmussen and Greenland Prime Minister Jonatan Motzfeldt, in which the Danish Government acknowledged that the relocation was decided and implemented in a manner and under circumstances that caused serious disruption for, and represented an unlawful act against, the population.

The Prime Minister's Office has not raised any argument before the Supreme Court that the Thule Tribe and its members have forfeited their claims through limitation of actions or inactivity.

For the proceedings before the Supreme Court, further details have been obtained and new evidence has been submitted.

The Home Rule Act (No 577 of 29 November 1978) contains the following provisions:

1. (1) Greenland is a distinct community within the Kingdom of Denmark. Within the framework of the Unity of the Realm, the Greenland Home Rule authorities shall conduct Greenland affairs in accordance with the provisions laid down in this Act.

(2) The Greenland Home Rule authorities shall consist of an assembly, elected in Greenland, to be called the *Landsting*, and an administration headed by a *Landsstyre*.

8. (1) The resident population of Greenland has fundamental rights to Greenland's natural resources.

9. (1) Greenlandic shall be the principal language. Thorough instruction in Danish must be provided.

11. (1) The central authorities of the Realm shall have jurisdiction in questions affecting the international relations of the Realm.

When the proposal for parliamentary approval was introduced in the Danish Parliament on the occasion of the conclusion of the United States–Denmark Defence Agreement, 1951, Ole Bjørn Kraft, Minister of Foreign Affairs, stated, *inter alia* (Parliamentary Debates 1950-1, column 3671):

Initially, only very few joint defence areas will be established and, for the time being, they will be under US command. However, the Agreement provides that these areas may be transferred to Denmark at a later date or to joint defence areas under Danish command, if such a transfer is expedient under the circumstances.

In this connection I would like to point out at once that it is obviously impossible for me to give a detailed account of the establishment of the joint defence areas.

The House will understand that it would be contrary to the measures adopted to protect the military information of the Atlantic Powers if, in this forum, I explained in detail the measures that are to be taken.

Background and Submissions Concerning the Claim for Compensation for the Thule Tribe

Attorney Harlang's submission dated 26 February 1999 to the High Court was as follows:

In these proceedings, the collective claim for compensation is made by Hingitaq 53 acting for the Thule Tribe. For the purpose of the management of this claim, I can inform you that, on 1 February 1999, the organization adopted statutes of a Foundation named "Tukumeq", clause 3 of which provides as follows:

> 3. The Purpose of the Foundation is charitable and consists of supporting the *Inughuit* community in the following areas:
> 1. Child-care centres;
> 2. Education for children, young people and adults;
> 3. Business development, primarily the re-establishment of hunting potential and measures to safeguard the survival of the hunting trade;
> 4. Care of the elderly.

On 20 August 1999, on the same day as the High Court judgment was delivered, Prime Minister Poul Nyrup Rasmussen made the following statement:

The case regarding the events that took place almost 50 years ago has now been resolved. The High Court has held that the relocation of the Thule population in 1953 took place in a manner that was unlawful.

We take note of the High Court's decision. It is fitting that the historical course of events that has affected the lives of many people in Thule from that time has been clarified. The Government does not intend to bring the case before the Supreme Court. The case has gone on long enough.

On 2 September 1999, the Danish Prime Minister [Poul Nyrup Rasmussen] and Greenland Prime Minister Jonathan Motzfeldt issued the following "Joint Statement: A Unity of the Realm of mutual respect":

From the outset, the Unity of the Realm has been built on equal status, mutual respect and cohesion.

Denmark and Greenland have a common history which we must accept, even when the history is unpleasant and when it shows disregard for people's self-respect.

On 20 August 1999, the High Court delivered its judgment in the case concerning the 1953 relocation of the Thule population. The High Court holds that, at the time, the Danish authorities acted unlawfully. The relocation was decided and implemented in a manner and under circumstances that caused serious disruption for the population. We cannot change the course of history but we must accept and respect the events which occurred because the judgment limits the degree to which a government can disrupt a population group.

No one today can be held responsible for the acts committed by former generations almost 50 years ago. But in the spirit of the Unity of the Realm and with due respect for Greenland and the Thule population, the Government, on behalf of the Danish State, would like to offer its apologies—*utoqqatserpugut*—to *Inughuit*, the Thule population, and all of Greenland for the manner in which the relocation was decided and implemented in 1953.

We wish to continue and strengthen the cooperation and cohesion between Denmark and Greenland. In future, Danish–Greenland cooperation within the Unity of the Realm must also be built on mutual respect.

When the Danish Constitution was amended in 1953, the citizens of Greenland were given the same rights as Danish citizens. The introduction of home rule in 1979 gave Greenland its own parliament and enabled decisions to be made closer to the citizens of the Greenland democracy. A recurrence of the events in 1953 is therefore ruled out.

We acknowledge the results achieved through our cooperation and cohesion during the years that have passed since the events of 1953. The Unity of the Realm has undergone a very positive, humane, social and economic development for the benefit of the populations of both Greenland and Denmark.

The Danish Government wants to strengthen Greenland's participation in foreign and security policy issues which relate in particular to Greenland's interests. Dialogue on these issues has been initiated in part on the basis of the report of the "Anorak" Committee.

As part of the expansion of our cooperation, representatives of the Greenland Home Rule Government will be involved in the negotiation process when new agreements relating especially to Greenland interests are concluded between the Danish Government and foreign States.

On 17 November 1999, the Greenland trade union *Sulinermik Inuussutissarsiutequartut Kattuffiat* ("SIK") filed a complaint with the International Labour Organization ("ILO") claiming that Denmark had not taken adequate measures to observe the ILO Convention. The complaint was occasioned by the relocation of the *Uummannaq* settlement in 1953. A Report issued by the ILO Committee set up to consider the complaint states *inter alia*:

33. The Committee notes that the parties to this case do not dispute that the *Inuit* residing in *Uummannaq* at the time of the relocation are of the same origin as the *Inuit* in other areas of Greenland, that they speak the same language (Greenlandic), engage in the same traditional hunting, trapping and

fishing activities as other inhabitants of Greenland and identify themselves as Greenlanders (*Kalaalit*). The Committee notes that, prior to 1953, the residents of the *Uummannaq* community were at times isolated from other settlements in Greenland due to their remote location; however, with the development of modern communications and transportation technology, the Thule District is no longer cut off from other settlements in Greenland. The Committee notes that these persons share the same social, economic, cultural and political conditions as the rest of the inhabitants of Greenland (see Article 1(1) of the Convention), conditions which do not distinguish the people of the *Uummaannaq* community from other Greenlanders, but which do distinguish Greenlanders as a group from the inhabitants of Denmark and the Faroe Islands. As concerns Article 1(2) of the Convention, while self-identification is a fundamental criterion for defining the groups to which the Convention shall apply, this relates specifically to self-identification as indigenous or tribal, and not necessarily to a feeling that those concerned are a "people" different from other members of the indigenous or tribal population of the country, which together may form a people. The Committee considers there to be no basis for considering the inhabitants of the *Uummannaq* community to be a "people" separate and apart from other Greenlanders. This does not necessarily appear relevant to the determination of this representation, however, for there is nothing in the Convention that would indicate that only distinct peoples may make land claims, especially as between different indigenous or tribal groups.

34. With regard to the pending claims for compensation for lost hunting and trapping rights and other consequential damages incurred by the residents of the *Uummannaq* community as a result of the 1953 relocation, the Committee points out that the ILO cannot resolve individual land disputes under the Convention, including issues of valuation of compensation. The Committee considers that its essential task in such cases is not to offer an alternative venue for parties dissatisfied with the outcome of a claim for compensation before the national administrative or judicial bodies, but rather to ensure that the appropriate procedures for resolving land disputes have been applied and that the principles of the Convention have been taken into account in dealing with the issues affecting indigenous and tribal peoples.

35. Article 14(2) of the Convention provides that: "Governments shall take steps as necessary to identify the lands which the peoples concerned traditionally occupy, and to guarantee effective protection of their rights of ownership and possession."

36. The Committee points out that Article 14(2), on which the complainant organization bases its allegations, must be interpreted in the light of the general policy set forth in Article 2(1) of the Convention, which requires Governments to develop, with the participation of the peoples concerned, "coordinated and systematic action to protect the rights of these peoples and to guarantee respect for their integrity".

37. The Committee considers that the land traditionally occupied by the *Inuit* people has been identified and consists of the entire territory of

Greenland. Section 8(1) of the Home Rule Act of 1978 establishes that "the resident population of Greenland has fundamental rights to the natural resources of Greenland". Noting that Greenlanders have the collective right to use the territory of Greenland and continue to have access to the land for their subsistence and traditional hunting and fishing activities, the Committee considers that the situation in Greenland is not inconsistent with the principles established in Article 14 of the Convention.

38. The Committee observes that Article 14(3) requires Governments to establish adequate procedures within the national legal system to resolve land claims by indigenous and tribal peoples. The Committee observes that there are procedures in place to resolve land disputes, that these procedures have in fact been invoked by the peoples concerned and that the land claims have been and are continuing to be examined in depth by the competent national authorities. It therefore concludes that the Government of Denmark has complied in this respect with Article 14(3).

39. The Committee is aware of the difficulties entailed in resolving conflicting land claims, particularly where there are different and opposing viewpoints with respect to the relationship which different communities have to the land, their cultural and spiritual attachment to lands which they traditionally occupy, as well as to the activities that they traditionally carry out on the land, such as hunting, trapping and fishing. The Committee is aware that the former residents of the *Uummannaq* community were forcibly relocated in 1953 under difficult circumstances, with little or no prior consultation, and that they have not been able to return to their settlement.

40. The Committee also notes, however, that the former residents of the *Uummannaq* community have been awarded compensation for lost hunting and trapping rights, as well as for damages incurred as a result of the relocation. It also notes that, almost 50 years later, the persons concerned, and their children, have now resettled in other sections of Greenland or in Denmark. Under the particular circumstances of this case, the Committee considers that to call for a demarcation of lands within Greenland for the benefit of a specific group of Greenlanders would run counter to the well-established system of collective land rights based on Greenlandic tradition and maintained by the Greenland Home Rule Authorities. This conclusion should be seen in the light of Article 17(1) of the Convention, which provides that "procedures established by the peoples concerned for the transmission of land rights among members of these peoples shall be respected", noting that traditionally no individual land rights are recognized among Greenlanders.

41. The Committee also refers to Articles 16(3) and (4) of the Convention, which relate directly to the consequences of relocation of indigenous and tribal peoples.

These provisions of Article 16 are as follows:

> 3. Whenever possible, these peoples shall have the right to return to their traditional lands, as soon as the grounds for relocation cease to exist.

4. When such return is not possible, as determined by agreement or, in the absence of agreement, through appropriate procedures, these peoples shall be provided in all possible cases with lands of quality and legal status at least equal to that of the lands previously occupied by them, suitable to provide for their present needs and further development. Where the peoples concerned express a preference for compensation in money or in kind, they shall be so compensated under appropriate guarantees.

42. The Committee considers that the measures taken by the Government are not inconsistent with Articles 16(3) and (4).

43. In general, the Committee concludes that the measures taken in this respect since 1997 by the Government are consistent with the Convention. Noting the spirit of consultation and participation that is the hallmark of this instrument, it urges the Government and the groups most directly affected to continue their common search for solutions.

In March 2001, the Governing Body of ILO adopted the Committee's Report and thereby closed the examination of SIK's complaint.

On 20 February 2003, the Danish Government, the Home Rule Government of Greenland and the Government of the United States of America signed a Memorandum of Understanding regarding the relinquishment of Dundas from the Thule defence area. The Agreement, which appears in Executive Order No 23 dated 21 August 2003, includes the following provisions:

Article I

1. This Memorandum of Understanding regulates cooperation between the Government of the Kingdom of Denmark (including the Home Rule Government of Greenland) and the Government of the United States of America, which has been agreed upon in connection with the Exchange of Notes this day between the Danish and United States Governments regarding the relinquishment of Dundas from the Thule defence area.

2. With reference also to the NATO Status of Forces Agreement, this Memorandum is in implementation of the United States–Denmark Agreement Concerning the Defence of Greenland, dated 27 April 1951 (hereinafter referred to as "the 1951 Agreement"), and related agreements . . .

Article III

1. Except as otherwise agreed in the Permanent Committee, there shall be no settlement of persons or erection of permanent structures in Dundas for three years from the date of the Exchange of Notes regarding the relinquishment of Dundas from the Thule defence area. This does not prevent restoration which does not alter the original size and essential character of existing buildings. For an additional period of three years the United States authorities will

be consulted no later than six months in advance in case any initiative should be taken that would alter the original size and essential character of existing buildings . . .

Article IV

. . .

3. Danish/Greenland authorities shall ensure that non-residents of the *Qaanaaq* Municipality are not permitted in Dundas on a permanent basis and that such non-residents do not enter the Thule defence area from Dundas without permission of competent United States authorities at Thule Air Base.

The case documents regarding the Ministry of Greenland's consideration of the claim for compensation raised by the Hunters' Council in 1959 have been supplied to the Court. It appears from official statistics regarding the population in *Qaanaaq* on 1 January 2000 that 864 persons are resident in the Municipality of *Qaanaaq*. Of these, 179 were born elsewhere and 319 people who were born in *Qaanaaq* live in another municipality in Greenland or Denmark.

In an article, "Ethnic Identity in Greenland", *Inuit Studies*, 2001, vol. 25 (1-2), pp. 319 ff., Professor Robert Petersen states, *inter alia*:

Because it is my opinion that group or regional identity still exists in different local and regional communities, I think it is important to put clear questions to people, when we ask them about their feelings of identity. One colleague claimed several years ago that the *Inughuit* thought of themselves more as *Inughuit* than as Greenland *Inuit*. I am not convinced of this claim, however, because both Polar *Inuit* and East Greenlanders are part of the Greenland community and utilize (and benefit from) this membership. But they are also quick to stress the dialectal and other differences between the West Greenlanders and themselves. I am not quite sure that this is so different from the *Upernavik* people, or speakers of the Cape Farewell dialect. One of the elements which united Greenland *Inuit*, at least in creating a common self-image, was the [religious] mission. The Greenland administration in Copenhagen originally allowed only the Lutheran and Moravian missions to work in Greenland, and from 1900 to 1953, this right was extended only to the Lutheran mission. This resulted in, among other things, a common identity based on membership in the Lutheran Church, a claim substantiated by Greenland *Inuit* elders who, in speaking about their identity, always mention that Christianity is one of the common traits.

The political reform of 1908 established two provincial councils, one in the northern part of West Greenland and the other in the southern part. At some point around 1950, the two councils merged into one, forming the *National Council*. This merging contributed to other initiatives within education and information . . .

Another trend that contributed to the formation of a national identity was the different associations, including sport associations, cultural associations and trade unions (or their equivalents in Greenland), that established umbrella organizations. These organizations had to work together in order to gain support from the Greenland Information Service, established in 1957. Another important development was *Aasivik*, a series of meetings organized by several youth groups that combined cultural events and political debate. They were attended by *Inuit* from all over Greenland.

Improvement of the infrastructure also made it easier to gather people together than was possible previously. The introduction of the telephone enabled individuals separated by hundreds if not thousands of miles to speak to each other. These changes also made it possible to establish political parties based on common political goals, rather than local interests, and in this way, the movement towards the establishment of a Greenland Home Rule Government gained momentum.

The Greenland policy advocating Home Rule (i.e. the creation of a separate Nation-State) was based on the idea that not only were Denmark and Greenland separated by a vast geographical distance, but they were separated by ethnic and cultural differences as well, manifested clearly in Greenland's use of a distinct language and by the fact that Greenland possessed a different occupational structure than Denmark. But Greenlanders were also by definition Danish citizens. This situation was probably appreciated by the founders of Home Rule, as the Home Rule Commission included both Danes and Greenland *Inuit*. The Act creating Greenland Home Rule was therefore based on democratic principles valid for all citizens in Greenland (*Loven om Hjemmestyret* 1979). This meant that Danes who lived in Greenland were therefore citizens of Greenland and entitled to the same cultural and political rights as Greenland *Inuit*.

But many Greenland *Inuit* consider their ethnic identity to be similar today to what it was in the colonial period, before the introduction of Home Rule (cf. *Lidegaard* 2000: pp. 21 ff.). Most academics, administrators, health services professionals and professionals in other sectors are still ethnic Danes. They normally do not speak *Inuit*, even if many understand it. They have good salaries. Many of the private firms are owned by immigrant Danes. Many Greenlandic *Inuit* have a low level of formal education and low paying jobs. This asymmetry between Danes and Greenland *Inuit* has led them to be treated as two separate ethnic/social units, a theme that inspired the political debates of the 1960s.

Petersen [in oral testimony] has explained that he has a background as an Eskimologist. He was a professor at the University of Copenhagen during the period 1975-83. He was appointed rector with a view to building up the University of Nuuk in 1983 and left the position when he retired in 1995. He is of Greenland origin and comes from Sukkertoppen.

The subject Eskimology consisted originally of the Eskimo languages, including *Inuit*, and culture. Other than in Greenland, *Inuit* live in Northern Canada and Alaska, and on the Chukotka peninsula in Northern Siberia. The people who live in these areas all call themselves *Inuit*. The designation Eskimo covers the same population group.

In Northern Greenland, there are people living north-west of parallel 75. From 1921 until today, settlements have existed towards the south in Savigsiviq. No permanent settlements existed in Kap York, but this area was occasionally used for hunting. The northernmost settlement was situated in Siorapaluk, just north of Qaanaaq. In air route terms, this is an area of some 150 km. The small group that lived south of Kap York in 1921 left in 1926. Since then, the only settlements south of Kap York have been in the area around Upernavik in West Greenland, situated some 300 km towards the south as the crow flies. East of this area is the ice cap, and there have been no settlements further north since the time of Knud Rasmussen.

The population of the area mentioned calls itself *Inughuit*. This is a grouping under the *Inuit*, which is largely determined by the use of the affix language. The words of an affix language consist of a root and an affix which constitutes the endings of the words. The endings of the *Inughuit* affix are different from those used in ordinary *Inuit*. Other grouping criteria are hunting culture, social norms and oral tradition, but the language affiliation is still the primary criterion. The population's own designation as *Inughuit* was becoming more widely used when Robert Petersen left Greenland in 1995. Other Greenlanders had also started using it, and it is likewise used today by Danish professionals. He does not know exactly how the use of the designation *Inughuit* developed after he left Greenland. The population differs in various ways from the rest of the Greenland population. This was already the case at the time of Knud Rasmussen. The language of the population differs from Western Greenlandic, in particular grammatically but also phonetically. It also contains words and expressions not used anywhere else in Greenland or by the *Inuit* in Canada.

The community remained undiscovered until 1818. Scientific research into the history of the population before that time assumes that the population originates from Victoria Island, an island in Northern Canada, east of the Mackenzie delta. Here are houses that correspond to those that were built in Thule. As regards the time after 1818, Knud Rasmussen assumed there was a severe epidemic in the area, which caused many deaths, especially of old people. This led to the dying out of the oral tradition of passing on information about peoples' origins. In 1860, there were probably about 100 people left.

In the 1860s a small group of people, probably around 20 from the northern Baffin Island, arrived in the area. They had walked all the way north to Thule. Several expeditions met them on the way. This is the population which, together with the remaining "old population", constituted the main tribe discovered by Knud Rasmussen. According to Knud Rasmussen, the people from Canada stuck to their hunting culture. The children of new arrivals adopted the language of the original population. The linguistic difference or distance to the language spoken in West Greenland is similar to the difference between Western Jutland dialect and Scanian.

The music played in Thule differs from the music of West and East Greenland. The Thule tunes are characterized partly by the original population's origins in the Victoria Island Copper Eskimos, and partly by the kind of tunes played at Baffin Island, where the Canadian *Inuit* settlers came from in the 1860s. The two different types of tune or music forms are performed in parallel by the Thule Tribe.

The *Inughuit* business culture also differs from that of West Greenland. Until the great epidemic, kayak hunting was used. This was a hunting culture that originated from the original population. No research exists regarding the development of means of communication and the importance of radio and TV for the linguistic development in the Thule district. There is no doubt about the importance of the introduction of school attendance, but in addition to this the language is strongly influenced by old phonetic and grammatical conditions.

Greenland has only one written language, Western Greenlandic. In East Greenland, however, there is a strong interest in promoting an actual Eastern Greenlandic written language as well. Along the west coast, four different sub-dialects are spoken, which can be traced back to Upernavik, the Disko Bay, Central-West Greenland and South Greenland. As regards the Disko Bay, Central-West Greenland and South Greenland, the dialectal difference is modest and relates to different pronunciation of certain letters. The Upernavik dialect differs slightly more from the other dialects.

Kaj Søby [in oral testimony] has explained that he has been a district judge in Qaanaaq since 1994. Before that, he had been a lay judge for many years. To a certain extent, customs form part of the law applied in the adjudication of civil cases and probate cases in particular. This is the case in hunting, sharing of catches, dog teams, compensation, marriage, divorce, fostering, adoption and probate cases. He is not aware if these customs differ from customs applied in the remainder of Greenland. In the course of his term of office, the district court has convened hunters to explain about hunting law and the sharing of catches. Efforts are being made to include these customs in municipal by-laws, but centralized and international legislation is making this increasingly difficult.

Avva Mathiassen has explained that until September 2003, he was chief executive of the Municipality of Qaanaaq. The Municipality adheres to several rules that are particular to Qaanaaq and have applied for many years. Only in Qaanaaq, for example, is it required that narwhal and beluga be harpooned from a kayak. Fjords may not be navigated with motor boats during the narwhal's breeding or feeding seasons. He is not entirely sure what the source of these regulations is, but they have applied throughout the entire existence of Qaanaaq. Qaanaaq has maintained provisions regarding, for example, traffic on the ice that are more restrictive than those of other Greenland municipalities.

Axel Lund Olsen, senior head teacher in Qaanaaq, has explained that in 2003 there were 186 children in the school in Qaanaaq and 39 children distributed among four village schools. The children speak the Thule language among themselves, with their parents and their Greenland teachers. The children's language is affected by whether they were born in the municipality, but not by whether their parents and their ancestors lived in Qaanaaq for several generations. The Thule area, including Qaanaaq, has no written language. The school does not give its pupils the opportunity of learning to read and write in their own local language. He believes that the difference between the Thule language and Western Greenlandic is the same as the difference between Danish and Swedish. The Thule language is also used in official oral communication.

Two maps produced are attached as appendices to the judgment, one of which shows the Thule district and the other the extent of the Thule Air Base in 1951. [The maps are not reproduced in the *International Law Reports*.]

Grounds of the Judgment

The ILO Convention

Regarding the claims for dismissal made by the Prime Minister's Office and in support of its own claims, the Thule Tribe has referred, as a principal allegation, to the provisions of the International Labour Organization Convention (No 169) of 27 June 1989 concerning Indigenous and Tribal Peoples in Independent Countries ("the ILO Convention"), particularly Articles 1, 12, 14 and 16. The Thule Tribe has argued, pursuant to Article 1(1)(b), that the Tribe is considered a distinct indigenous people separate from the rest of the Greenland population. The

Convention became operative for Denmark on 22 February 1997. On ratification, it was assumed that the Greenland people as a whole is an indigenous people in the sense of the Convention.

In support of its status as an indigenous people, the Thule Tribe has specifically argued that its members descend from people that lived in the Thule district at the time of the colonization in 1921 and that its members retain some of their own social, economic, cultural and political institutions. According to its own definition, the Thule Tribe encompasses all descendants of this indigenous population and the descendants' spouses irrespective of where they were born and live. The members of the Tribe see themselves as belonging to a distinct indigenous people.

The assessment of whether or not the Thule Tribe is a distinct indigenous people in the sense of the ILO Convention should be based on current conditions. In Greenland, regional variations still exist in terms of language, business conditions and rules of law deriving in part from the country's size, communication and transport structure, and local natural conditions. Based on an overall assessment of the available evidence, the Supreme Court finds that, for all practical purposes, the population in the Thule district shares the same conditions as the rest of the Greenland people and does not differ from it in any other relevant respects. The information produced concerning the difference between the languages spoken in Qaanaaq and in West Greenland and the Thule Tribe's perception of itself as a distinct indigenous people cannot lead to any other conclusion. The Supreme Court therefore finds that the Thule Tribe does not "retain some of or all their own social, economic, cultural and political institutions" and, therefore, the Thule Tribe is not a distinct indigenous people within the meaning of Article 1(1)(b) of the ILO Convention.

According to Article 1(1)(a), the ILO Convention also includes "tribal populations in independent countries whose social, cultural and economic conditions distinguish them from other sections of the national community, and whose status is regulated wholly or partially by their own customs or traditions or by special laws or regulations". By reason of the above conclusions, the Supreme Court finds that, under this provision also, the Thule Tribe does not fall within the scope of the Convention. This interpretation is consistent with the declaration made by the Danish Government, subscribed to by the Greenland Home Rule Government, in connection with the ratification of the ILO Convention. According to this Declaration, Denmark has "only one indigenous people" in the sense of the Convention, namely the indigenous population in Greenland or the *Inuit*.

In its decision of March 2001, the Governing Body of the ILO reached the same conclusion. The Governing Body thus endorsed the Report dated 23 March 2001 from the ILO Committee considering the complaint submitted by the Greenland trade union *Sulinermik Inuussutissarsiutequartut Kattuffiat* ("SIK") concerning Denmark's alleged contravention of the Convention. The Report states that "there is no basis for considering the inhabitants of the *Uummannaq* community to be a 'people' separate and different from other Greenlanders" and that "the land traditionally occupied by the *Inuit* people has been identified and consists of the entire territory of Greenland".

Taking into account that, pursuant to Article 1(1) of the ILO Convention, the Thule Tribe does not constitute a tribal people or a distinct indigenous people within or co-existing with the Greenlandic people as a whole, the Thule Tribe has no independent rights under the Convention.

The claims for dismissal made by the Prime Minister's Office

The fact that the Thule Tribe cannot be considered as a tribal or distinct indigenous people in the sense of the ILO Convention does not rule out the possibility that the Thule Tribe may be entitled to take legal action according to the related general rules. The Prime Minister's Office has not disputed that the Hingitaq 53 organization may represent the Thule Tribe. As stated by the High Court, the Thule Tribe must be considered a sufficiently clearly defined group of individuals. This is not altered by the fact that only 422 of the original approximately 600 individual plaintiffs have joined as individual appellants before the Supreme Court. The objection raised by the Prime Minister's Office that the Thule Tribe is not entitled to pursue the claims and that consequently the Tribe is not the rightful plaintiff does not give rise to dismissal. According to their substance, the first and second claims are not so vague that they cannot form the basis of adjudication of the case.

On these grounds, the Supreme Court upholds the dismissal by the High Court of the claims for dismissal regarding the Thule Tribe's first and second claims. On the same grounds, the Supreme Court disallows the claim for dismissal regarding the third claim. The Supreme Court further upholds the dismissal by the High Court below of the claim for dismissal regarding the individual appellants' first and second claims.

Occupation, access and hunting rights (first and second claims)

In addition to the reference to the ILO Convention, in support of the first and second claims, the Thule Tribe has argued that the Thule

Air Base was established illegally, in part because the United States–Denmark Defence Agreement of 1951 is invalid under constitutional and international law. The Thule Tribe has also argued that no legal decision to move the settlement was made.

As stated by the High Court in paragraph 7.3 of its judgment, the Thule Air Base was established under the Defence Agreement of 1951. The Agreement was adopted by the *Rigsdag* [Danish Parliament until 1953] pursuant to Article 18 of the Danish Constitution in force at the time.

The Supreme Court finds that, after that time, a constitutionally valid approval to establish the Base existed, although the technical appendix to the Agreement was not submitted to the *Rigsdag*. For this very reason, the Agreement is also valid under international law.

The significant restriction on hunting and catches caused by the establishment of the Thule Air Base in 1951 cannot, on the grounds stated by the High Court in paragraph 7.4, be considered a regulatory measure involving no compensation, but is rather an act of expropriation. As stated by the High Court in paragraph 7.3, this expropriation could be carried out without statutory authority.

On the grounds stated by the High Court, the Supreme Court therefore finds:

> that the substantive law provisions of the Danish Constitution in force at the time, including section 80 on the inviolability of property, did not extend to Greenland;
> that the Act on the Administration of Greenland did not include any claim for statutory authority;
> and that the question of establishing the Base did not fall within the competence of the Hunters' Council.

As stated by the High Court in paragraph 7.4, the intervention regarding the *Uummannaq* settlement proper and the Thule colony that took place in connection with the decision in 1953 to move the population must also be considered an act of expropriation. This intervention too is considered as having being carried out under the 1951 Defence Agreement and the implied expropriation could therefore take place without statutory authority. It should also be noted that any inadequate provision of information to the Hunters' Council in 1951 and 1953 does not give rise to invalidity.

The Supreme Court therefore finds that both the intervention in 1951 in the access to hunting and the intervention in 1953 to relocate the settlement were legal and valid. In this context, it is unnecessary to decide whether or not the population in the Thule District at the time constituted a tribal people or a distinct indigenous people in the terms of the current definitions of Article 1(1) of the ILO Convention.

The substance of the Thule Tribe's first and second claims is that the tribe members have a right to live in and use the abolished settlement and a right to access, occupy and hunt in the entire Thule district. For the simple reason that the acts of expropriation prevent or curtail this right of enjoyment in the areas affected by the acts of expropriation, the appellants' first and second claims are disallowed.

This applies as regards the first claim even though, in February 2003, in continuation of their 1951 Defence Agreement, the USA and Denmark, including the Greenland Home Rule Government, signed a Memorandum of Understanding regarding the relinquishment of Dundas, the area in which the settlement and colony were situated, from the Thule defence area. In this connection, it should be noted that the Thule Tribe which, as stated above, cannot be considered a tribal people or a distinct indigenous people in the sense of the ILO Convention, cannot claim privileges regarding Dundas with reference to Article 16(3) of the Convention, nor does Greenland customary law give cause for such privileges.

The Supreme Court therefore upholds the dismissal by the High Court of the appellants' first and second claims against the Prime Minister's Office.

The Thule Tribe's claim for compensation (third claim)

The primary claim for compensation of just over DK 235 million refers first of all to the Thule Tribe's damage suffered as a result of lost and impaired hunting grounds following the establishment of the Base and relocation of the population from the *Uummannaq* settlement.

On the grounds stated by the High Court in paragraph 7.4, the Supreme Court finds that compensation for this loss should be paid according to the principles of Section 80 of the Danish Constitution in force at the time, although this provision was not directly applicable to Greenland.

After an overall assessment and weighing up of the factors for and against, the High Court set the level of compensation at an estimated DK 500,000. The Prime Minister's Office merely asked for the decision of the High Court to be upheld.

On the grounds stated by the High Court, the Supreme Court finds that the claim for proof of the loss must be relaxed somewhat.

In fixing the level of compensation, importance cannot be attached to the calculations on which the Thule Tribe's claims are based. These calculations use factors that, to a large extent, must be considered arbitrary, while various matters that ought to have been included in the assessment are disregarded. The calculations are not based on developments in the size of catches. The primary claim for just over DK 235 million is calculated on the basis of the size of the confiscated land without clarifying the correlation between area size and catch potential. The calculation covers 45 years without taking into account the substantial reduction in the base area in 1986 and the general limitation of the indemnity period. These calculation factors are related to an annual compensation of DK 200 granted on the establishment of the Thule weather station in 1946, the specific basis of which remains undisclosed. The alternative claim for just over DK 136 million is mainly based on a presumed cost increase due to longer hunting distances without taking into account that, according to the survey report, there has not been a general increase in the distances to the most important hunting grounds (Reply 23). Adaptation of the catches to the changed conditions has not been taken into consideration. The number of hunters included, approximately half the number of original plaintiffs, has no connection with the number of hunters affected by the interventions.

The Supreme Court concurs, on the whole, in the High Court's assessment of the facts to be considered when fixing compensation, including the character of the confiscated hunting grounds, distances to the most important hunting grounds, general catch pattern developments (in particular the decreasing importance of fox and increasing importance of narwhal) and the limitation of the period to be included in the calculation.

After an overall assessment, the Supreme Court finds no grounds for increasing the compensation of DK 500,000 fixed by the High Court. On the grounds stated by the High Court, separate compensation for the church cannot be granted.

The Supreme Court therefore allows the plea by the Prime Minister's Office for the decision of the High Court in respect of the Thule Tribe's third claim to be upheld.

Individual claims (fourth claim)

The appellants under this claim are members of the Thule Tribe affected by the relocation in 1953 and their estates. They have repeated their claim for compensation of DK 250,000 to be paid to each of them individually.

As stated by the High Court in paragraph 7.4, the inhabitants of *Uummannaq* must be considered to have received full compensation for relinquishing their houses by being granted replacement houses. Having been provided with free goods and equipment from the store, they must furthermore be considered to have received full compensation for special expenses incurred in connection with the actual relocation.

Accordingly, the claims under the fourth claim refer solely to compensation for injury to the feelings of the persons concerned owing to the circumstances of the relocation.

The Prime Minister's Office has admitted to the Supreme Court that the relocation of the population of *Uummannaq*, as described by the High Court in paragraph 7.1, was decided and implemented in a manner and under circumstances that caused serious disruption for, and represented an unlawful act against, the population of *Uummannaq*. Against this background, the Prime Minister's Office has accepted the amounts of compensation fixed by the High Court.

In assessing the amounts of compensation, the Supreme Court concurs in the High Court's statements in paragraph 7.5 on the matters to be taken into consideration. The Supreme Court also accepts that the inhabitants' age on relocation should carry weight as described by the High Court, so that persons aged 18 or more at the time of the relocation are granted higher compensation than younger people and that persons who were under 4 years of age should receive no compensation.

The Supreme Court finds no grounds for increasing the amounts of compensation fixed by the High Court. The plea by the Prime Minister's Office for the decision by the High Court in respect of the fourth claim to be upheld is therefore allowed.

Ruling:

The Supreme Court upholds the judgment of the High Court in its entirety. No order is made as to costs.

[Report: *Ugeskrift for Retsvaesen*, 2004, p. 382 (in Danish). Unofficial translation provided by the Danish Ministry of Justice]

NOTE.—A commentary on the above decision by Ole Spiermann is printed in 98 *American Journal of International Law*, 2004, p. 1.

Relationship of international law and municipal law — Treaties — Ratification without reservation of international instrument — Incorporation in domestic legislation — Whether States obliged to mirror provisions of international instruments in domestic legislation — Margin of appreciation — Constitution of Kenya — Conflict between international law and domestic law — Bangalore Principles, 1989 — Supremacy of Constitution where clear and unambiguous — Inability of court to expand provisions of Constitution where clear and unambiguous

Human rights — Discrimination — Grounds for non-discrimination in international and domestic law — Convention on the Rights of the Child, 1989 — African Charter on the Rights and Welfare of the Child, 1990 — Constitution of Kenya — Children Act 2001 of Kenya, Section 24(3) — Parental responsibility — Whether part of *jus cogens* — Parental responsibility for children born out of wedlock — Whether non-discrimination provisions under the Constitution and the Children Act 2001 of Kenya inconsistent — Whether non-discrimination provisions under Constitution and international obligations inconsistent — Whether vesting parental responsibility in mother in first instance discriminatory — Principle of equality and non-discrimination — Margin of appreciation — Whether distinction for legitimate purpose — Whether distinction reasonable in light of legitimate aim — The law of Kenya

RM (A MINOR, THROUGH NEXT FRIEND JK) *v.*
ATTORNEY-GENERAL[1]

Kenya, High Court. 1 *December* 2006

(Nyamu and Ibrahim JJ)

SUMMARY: *The facts*:—The application was brought on behalf of RM, a minor, by her mother JK, claiming that Section 24(3) of the Children Act No 8 of 2001 of Kenya ("the Children Act"), which bestowed parental responsibility

---

[1] The applicant was represented by Kajwang. The respondent was represented by Mwangi Njoroge. The first interested party, CRADLE, was represented by Millie Odhiambo and Jane Kamangu; the second interested party, the Coalition on Violence Against Women (COVAW), was represented by Mrs Arasa; the third interested party, the Federation of Women Lawyers Kenya (FIDA), was represented by Hellen Kwamboka.

for children born out of wedlock on the mother, should be struck out because it was discriminatory, inconsistent with the Constitution of Kenya and various international obligations and failed to take into account the best interests of the child.

RM had been born out of wedlock to parents who were cohabiting. The father, who had allegedly named RM and paid the hospital expenses when she was born, left a few months after the birth and, within a year, had effectively disappeared. RM was left without any paternal support or provision for her upkeep.

It was argued that placing parental responsibility only on the mother in the first instance put RM in a disadvantaged position compared to children born within wedlock and amounted to discrimination on the grounds of social origin, birth or other status, which was prohibited by the Convention on the Rights of the Child, 1989 ("the CRC")[2] and the African Charter on the Rights and Welfare of the Child, 1990 ("the African Children's Charter").[3] It was argued that since the State had not lodged any reservations at the time it ratified the CRC, the Children Act should have implemented the CRC provisions without reservation. Further, Section 24(3) actually imposed discriminatory statutory criteria that were both inconsistent with Section 82(1) and (2) of the Constitution and in breach of customary international law.

Held:—The application was dismissed. Section 24(3) and, by extension, Section 25 of the Children Act were not discriminatory or unconstitutional and did not offend the principle of equality and non-discrimination either by themselves or in their effect.

(1) The Constitution was the supreme law of Kenya and its provisions under Section 82 were clear and unambiguous. As such, and in accordance with the Bangalore Principles, the provisions of the Constitution took precedence over the provisions of international agreements. Expanding the anti-discrimination categories in Section 82 of the Constitution to accord with those of the CRC or African Children's Charter would be *ultra vires* and a usurpation of the legislative function (pp. 316-17, 328).

(2) In enacting legislation to implement the provisions of international obligations, States had a margin of appreciation that enabled them to take account of their own local laws, traditions and circumstances. Parliament was under no obligation to enact the exact provisions of the CRC or African Children's Charter (pp. 327-9).

(3) Article 2 of the Universal Declaration of Human Rights, 1948, entitled everyone to protection from discrimination. However, not all distinctions amounted to discrimination and there was an accepted principle of international law that differentiation based on reasonable and objective criteria did not amount to prohibited discrimination. Distinctions made between people

---

[2] Convention on the Rights of the Child, signed 20 November 1989, entered into force 2 September 1990, 1577 UNTS 3.

[3] Organization of African Unity, African Charter on the Rights and Welfare of the Child, 11 July 1990, CAB/LEG/24.9/49 (1990).

were justified provided they were reasonable and imposed for objective and legitimate purposes (pp. 323-9).

(4) The aim of Section 24(3) was both legitimate and proportionate. Parental responsibility was the cornerstone of protecting the interests of the child and the aim of the provision was to ensure parental responsibility in all possible relationships and without delay. Vesting parental responsibility in the unmarried mother in the first instance was in the best interests of the child (pp. 326-9).

(5) The rights at issue were not part of *jus cogens*. The right to life was closest in classification but since the provisions at issue were designed to protect and promote the rights of the child, they could not be said to threaten the right to life (pp. 314-16).

The following is the text of the judgment of the Court:

This is an application brought by way of an Originating Summons dated and filed on 12 August 2002. It has been brought by RM (a minor through next friend JK her mother) and CRADLE, a Non-Governmental Children['s] Foundation as the 1st Interested Party. The 2nd Interested Party is COVAW (Coalition on Violence Against Women). The 3rd Interested Party is FIDA (Federation of Women Lawyers Kenya). The application was brought for the determination of the following questions.

1. Is Section 24(3) of the Children Act an abrogation of the plaintiff's human right; to wit, protection from discrimination to the extent that it negates the Constitution, international conventions and charters of which Kenya is a signatory, in particular, Articles 2 and 3 of the Convention on the Rights of the Child and Articles 2 and 3 of the African Charter on the Rights and Welfare of the Child by expressly discriminating against children born out of wedlock and failing to take into account the best interest of the child?
2. Is Section 24(3) of the Children Act either of itself or in its effect discriminatory to the extent that it expressly or constructively prescribes that a father of a child who is neither married to nor has subsequently married the child's [mother] bears no parental responsibility in relation to that child?
3. Is Section 24(3) of the Children Act inconsistent with Section 82(2) of the Constitution of Kenya concerning a child whose parents were not married to each other at the time of the child's birth to the extent that it permits a father of such child to discharge parental responsibility to the child by virtue of its provision?

4. Has the applicant been treated in a discriminatory manner by [her] father who, acting by virtue of Section 24(3) of the Children Act, has refused to assume parental responsibility on her behalf?
5. Does Section 24(3) of the Children Act impose statutory criteria which discriminate [against] children whose parents were not married to each other at the time of their birth as against all other children; which criteria are inconsistent with Section 82(1) and (2) of the Constitution of Kenya making the same therefore null and void?
6. Who shall pay costs of this summons?

The factual background is that RM was born on 16 September 2000 through a relationship between the mother and another man [*sic*]. It is alleged that the father worked with a local company as a mechanic. At the time of birth the mother depones that she was cohabiting both before the date of birth and up to 3 January 2001 with the alleged father who duly paid hospital expenses at the hospital where RM was born. On 3 January 2001 the alleged father disappeared or avoided the mother completely in April 2001.

On 16 September 2000 the mother depones that the alleged father came to the matrimonial home [*sic*] and named the child after his mother (RM) and shaved her head after one week as per his tribe's customary law, i.e. Kisii.

She depones that he has failed to give any parental support to both the mother and the child and that both entirely depend on good Samaritans for their upkeep.

She laments that the law does not place any parental responsibility on the plaintiff's father since she is not married and had she married him the plaintiff's father would have had parental responsibility towards the plaintiff just like the mother.

She finally depones that she has been advised that the law, i.e. s 24(3) of the Children Act, is discriminatory as it puts the plaintiff [in] a disadvantaged position vis-à-vis other children whose fathers have married or subsequently married their mothers. Such children do not therefore have to contend with the question of who will take responsibility on their behalf. And therefore the plaintiff should be accorded equal treatment with those children whose parents are married or have subsequently married by placing parental responsibility on both the father and mother.

Counsel for all the parties including Interested Parties hereinafter called IPs have since filed affidavits and have also filed and relied on written skeleton arguments with lists of authorities which we have duly considered in preparing this judgment

ANALYSIS

According to the format of the Originating Summons, s 82 of the Constitution of Kenya has been mentioned in prayers 3 and 5 of the Originating Summons and because the Constitution is the supreme law of the land, we consider it important to start with it by setting out relevant parts in extenso. Section 82(1), (2), (3), (4) and (6) reads:

82 (1) Subject to subsections (4), (5) and (8), no law shall make any provision that is discriminatory either of itself or in its effect.

(2) Subject to subsections (6), (8) and (9) no person shall be treated in a discriminatory manner by a person acting by virtue of any written law or in the performance of the functions of a public office or a public authority.

(3) In this section the expression "discriminatory" means affording different treatment to different persons attributable wholly or mainly to their respective descriptions by race, tribe, place of origin or residence or other local connection, political opinions, colour, creed or sex whereby persons of one such description are subjected to disabilities or restrictions to which persons of another such description are not made subject or are accorded privileges or advantages which are not accorded to persons of another such description.

(4) Subsection (1) shall not apply to any law so far as the law makes provision—

- (a) with respect to persons who are not citizens of Kenya;
- (b) with respect to adoption, marriage, divorce, burial, devolution of property on death or other matters of personal law;
- (c) for the application in the case of members of a particular race or tribe of customary law with respect to any matter to the exclusion of any law with respect to that matter which is applicable in the case of other persons; or
- (d) whereby persons of a description mentioned in subsection (3) may be subjected to a disability or restriction or may be accorded a privilege or advantage which, having regard to its nature and to special circumstances pertaining to those persons or to persons of any other such description, is reasonably justifiable in a democratic society.

...

(6) Subsection (2) shall not apply to:

- (a) anything which is expressly or by necessary implication authorized to be done by a provision of law referred to in subsection (4); or
- (b) [not relevant]

We also consider it important to set out in full the relevant sections of the Children Act 2001 of Kenya, that is the sections which have given rise to this suit.

24 (1) Where a child's father and mother were married to each other at the time of his birth, they shall have parental responsibility for the child and neither the father nor the mother of the child shall have superior right or claim against the other in exercise of such parental responsibility.

(2) Where a child's father and mother were not married to each other at the time of the child's birth and have subsequently married each other, they shall have parental responsibility for the child and neither the father nor the mother of the child shall have a superior right or claim against the other in the exercise of such parental responsibility.

(3) Where a child's father and mother were not married to each other at the time of the child's birth and have not subsequently married each other—

(a) the mother shall have parental responsibility at the first instance;
(b) the father shall subsequently acquire parental responsibility for the child in accordance with the provisions of section 25.

(4) More than one person may have parental responsibility for the same child at the same time.

(5) A person who has parental responsibility for a child at any time shall not cease to have that responsibility for the child.

(6) [not relevant]
(7) [not relevant]
(8) [not relevant]

The marginal note to [Section] 24 states:

Who has parental responsibility

Section 25 states:

25 (1) Where a child's father and mother were not married at the time of his birth—

(a) the court may, on application of the father, order that he shall have parental responsibility for the child; or
(b) the father and mother may by agreement ("a parental responsibility agreement") provide for the father to have parental responsibility for the child.

(2) Where a child's father and mother were not married to each other at the time of his birth but have subsequent to such birth cohabited for a period or periods which amount to not less than twelve months, or where the father has acknowledged paternity of the child or has maintained the child, he shall have acquired parental responsibility for the child, notwithstanding that a parental responsibility agreement has not been made by the mother and father of the child.

It is strongly contended that s 24(3) of the Children Act also violates the Convention on the Rights of the Child and in particular its preamble which provides:

Recognising that the United Nations has, in the Universal Declaration of Human Rights and in the International Covenants on Human Rights, proclaimed and agreed that everyone is entitled to all the rights and freedoms set forth therein, without distinction of any kind such as race, colour, sex, language, religion, political or other opinion, national or social origin, property, birth or other status.

It has been argued that s 24(3) of the Children Act is discriminatory against children born out of wedlock whose parents are not married to each other either at the time of the child's birth or subsequently thereafter. The argument is that the discrimination is on social origin, birth or other status which is that the child cannot benefit and enjoy parental responsibility from both the mother and father because of the status of the mother, a single mother. For this reason the court is urged to hold that s 24(3) is inconsistent with the United Nations Convention on the Rights of the Child which Convention was intended to be domesticated by the passage of the Children Act. It is submitted that the section should be declared discriminatory and null and void.

Article 2(1) of the United Nations Convention on the Rights of the Child has also been relied on by the applicant. It states:

States Parties shall respect and ensure the rights set forth in the present Convention to each child within their jurisdiction without discrimination of any kind, irrespective of the child's or his or her parents' or legal guardian's race, colour, sex, language, religion, political or other opinion, national, ethnic or social origin, property, disability, birth or other status.

The argument presented to court on the above is that excluding children born out of wedlock from automatically receiving support from their fathers is discriminating [against] them on the grounds of their social origin, birth and status. Status here being that the child's parents were not married to each other at the time of the child's birth and or subsequently thereto. Reliance has also been placed on Article 18(1) of the same Convention which reads:

States Parties shall use their best efforts to ensure recognition of the principle that both parents have common responsibilities for the upbringing and development of the child... The best interests of the child will be their basic concern.

The argument by the applicant is that Article 18(1) envisages the principle that both parents have joint primary responsibility for bringing up their children. There should be no distinction that the child is born within or out of wedlock. Thus children born out of wedlock are being victimized for something they have no control over, the children cannot decide whether they want to be born either within or out of a subsisting or subsequent marriage of their parents. Kenya should therefore as a State implement the provisions of the Convention without any reservations because she did not seek any when she ratified the Convention.

The applicant and the IPs have also reinforced their argument by citing Article 3 of the African Charter on the Rights and Welfare of the Child which provides:

Every child shall be entitled to the enjoyment of the rights and freedoms recognized and guaranteed in this Charter irrespective of the child's or his/her parents' or legal guardians' race, ethnic group, colour, sex, language, religion, political or other opinion, national and social origin, fortune, birth or other status.

Article 4 of the same Charter states:

In all actions concerning the child undertaken by any person or authority the best interests of the child shall be the primary consideration.

Article 18(3) of the same Charter declares:

No child shall be deprived of maintenance by reference to the parents' marital status.

And finally on the Charter Article 20(1) provides:

Parents or other persons responsible for the child shall have the primary responsibility for the upbringing and development of the child....

The applicant has also relied on the provisions of the Convention on the Elimination of All Forms of Discrimination Against Women (CEDAW), 1979. Discrimination against women is defined as:

any distinction, exclusion or restriction made on the basis of sex which has the effect or purpose of impairing or nullifying the recognition, enjoyment or exercise by women, irrespective of their marital status, on a basis of equality of men and women, of human rights and fundamental freedoms in the political, economic, social, cultural, civil or any other field.

It has been submitted that the States by ratifying the Convention undertook to incorporate the principle of equality of men and women in their legal systems and to abolish all discriminatory laws and adopt appropriate ones prohibiting discrimination against women. For this argument the court's attention has been drawn to Article 2(f) of CEDAW which reads:

To take all appropriate measures, including legislation, to modify or abolish existing laws, regulations, customs and practices which constitute discrimination against women.

Article 16(1)(d) provides:

The same rights and responsibilities as parents, irrespective of their marital status, in matters relating to their children; in all cases the interests of the children shall be paramount.

POSITION OF INTERNATIONAL CONVENTIONS AND THE STATE CONSTITUTIONS

Having set out above the relevant Conventions and the constitutional provisions including the challenged sections of the municipal law, we consider it important to touch on the relationship between the two—namely the Conventions and the state law including the Constitution.

The general principle unless there is a provision in the local law of automatic domestication of a Convention or Treaty is that a Convention does not automatically become municipal law unless by virtue of ratification.

The position has been very ably articulated in the Bangalore Principles, 1989 as follows:

It is within the proper nature of the judicial process and well-established judicial functions for national courts to have regard to international obligations which a country undertakes—whether or not they have been incorporated into domestic law—for the purpose of removing ambiguity or uncertainty from national constitutions, legislation or common law.

On the other hand where the national law is clear and inconsistent with the international obligation, in common law countries, the national court is obliged to give effect to national law. And in such cases the court should draw such inconsistencies to the attention of the appropriate authorities since the supremacy of the national law in no way mitigates a breach of an international legal obligation which is undertaken by a country. From this analysis the court does adopt the reasoning of Justice Musumali of the Zambian High Court in his holding in the case cited by the applicants and Interested Parties' counsel, namely *Sara Longwe* v. *International Hotels* [1993] 4 LRC 221, where [it was] held:

Ratification of such [instruments] by a nation State without reservations is a clear testimony of the willingness by the State to be bound by the provisions of such (a Treaty). Since there is that willingness, if an issue comes before this court which would not be covered by local legislation but would be covered by international instruments, I would take judicial notice of that Treaty or Convention in my resolution of the dispute.

We shall shortly revert to analysis of the Kenyan position vis-à-vis the relevant Conventions with particular reference to the Bangalore Principles as set out above, after analysing the respondent's submissions on the issue of parental responsibility, what discrimination is, and what the Kenyan Constitution stipulates. Before we turn to the respondent's arguments however it is important to reproduce the definition of parental responsibility as per the Children Act.

Section 23(1) defines parental responsibility as under:

In this Act, "parental responsibility" means all the duties, rights, powers, responsibilities and authority which by law a parent of a child has in relation to the child and the child's property in a manner consistent with the evolving capacities of the child.

Section 23(2) sets out the actual responsibilities.

It is also significant to ascertain who is a parent. The *Concise Oxford English Dictionary* 11th Edition Oxford University Press defines the word "parent" as under:

(1) a father or mother, an animal or plant from which younger ones are derived—derivatives—parental (adj) and parenthood (n)

The Attorney-General who is the respondent has put forward the following arguments:

(1) The application does not set out in precise terms the actual provisions in the Constitution which are violated by s 24(3) of the Children Act.
(2) No specific grievance or injury, specific to the infant, has been demonstrated. The court cannot pursue a matter which is of academic value only.
(3) The applicant has no cause of action.
(4) An applicant in an application under s 84(1) of the Constitution is obliged to state his complaint, the provision of the Constitution he considers has been infringed in relation to him and the manner in which he believes they have been infringed. Those allegations are the ones which if pleaded with particularity invoke the jurisdiction of this Court under the section. It is not enough to allege infringement without particularizing the details and the manner of infringement: see
   (a) *Matiba* v. *Attorney-General* NB HC Misc 613 of 1990
   (b) *Anarita Karimi Njeru* v. *R (No 1)* 1979 KLR 154
   (c) *Cyprian Kubai* v. *Mwenda* NBI HC Misc 615 of 2002 UR

The respondent argues that no specific prayer has been sought against him or any violation attributable to the Attorney-General and that no case can stand without any particular grievance. The respondent further contends that *loci standi* of a party need not be assumed. Under s 84 of the Constitution the violation of the right must be personal to the applicant, which he has suffered over and above others. On the contrary in this case the alleged contravention is only in respect of the parents and their marital status and it is not the parents who have brought the Originating Summons but the child. Sections 23, 24 and 25 deal with parents and not the child. A person must sue on his own behalf.

(5) A child cannot effectively claim that the effect of a parent's classification would discriminate [against] her or him, as the criteria under s 82 do not include "age" and marital status: see *Attorney-General* v. *Lawrence* [1985] LRC 921 at page 930D. The test is whether the applicant has been directly affected by the impugned statute.

(6) That issues against the respondent have not been adequately or properly addressed or the jurisdiction of the court properly invoked.

(7) When considering whether or not s 24(3) is discriminatory, the court must take into account the history and social economic context of the legislation or in other words the environment in which the legislature enacted the statute. Thus the Act repealed and consolidated all statutes on child legislation—the Children and Young Persons Act, the Adoption Act and the Guardianship of Infants Act. In addition principles in the International Convention on the Rights of the Child and the African Charter on the Rights and Welfare of the Child were taken into consideration. In children matters the tendency is to define what is good for the child by reference to the parents. Generally the Act views a child as an individual member of the family. The Children Act achieved this principle by giving the child the right to protection from discrimination, child labour, abuse, economic and sexual exploitation, to live and be cared for by his parents, to basic education and identity.

(8) It is quite clear that s 24(3) merely states that such responsibility for a child born out of wedlock shall vest in the mother in the first instance. The essential feature of s 24(3) is that it does not prohibit a father of a child born out of wedlock from claiming parental responsibility. The steps to be followed by the father to achieve the status of a parent with responsibility over that child

are set out. By following the outlined steps the uncertain status of the father is changed.

(9) The respondent has identified three issues related to the above for determination, namely:

(a) Whether s 24(3) of the Act is discriminatory of itself; and
(b) Whether s 24(3) has introduced discriminatory statutory criteria to illegitimate children against all other children; [and]
(c) Whether the national law is subject to the International Convention or Charters.

The respondent has powerfully argued that if the court were to hold that s 24(3) affords different treatment for the children in its effects then the criteria [to] which that alleged differential treatment [gives rise have] to be one of those provided for under section 82(3) of the Constitution in order to be discriminatory in terms of the Constitution. Discrimination is defined in the Kenya Constitution and the court must be guided by this in its determination.

(10) Even if the court were to find that there is discrimination as per the definition in the Constitution it has been argued that should not be the end of the matter. The court should go a step further and consider whether the difference in treatment has an objective and reasonable justification and for such justification to be established it has to be shown that the difference in treatment:

(i) pursues a legitimate aim;
(ii) bears a reasonable relationship of proportionality between the aim sought to be realized and the means used to achieve it—see the case of *R (Morris)* v. *Westminster City Council and First Secretary of State* [2004] EWHC 2191.

It has been argued for the respondent that s 82(3) does not prohibit Kenya from adjusting its legislation to differences or forbid classification at all. It only requires that the classification be reasonable, justifiable and necessary. It has also been stressed that s 82 of the Constitution does not demand that things that are different be treated as though they were the same. What is forbidden is the differences based wholly or mainly on race, colour or as specified in s 82 of the Constitution. The respondent has with a touch of humour given two illustrations why not every difference in fact violates s 82 of the Constitution. Thus, it cannot be unconstitutional when employing nurses to observe that women appear to have a natural advantage over men in this area. Similarly one would be entitled to classify people on the basis that there are more [male] night-guards than [female ones] in real life. This kind of thinking would not be unconstitutional or discriminatory because you are not treating the classification on account of one of the specified descriptions or classifications mentioned in s 82. The additional reason is that although in the humorous examples on sex as illustrated above, "sex" is one of the forbidden classifications, the employer is not wholly employing on the basis of sex. There is a justifiable and objective reason for the difference—there are situations where nature must have an edge in real life. By analogy a child born out of wedlock is not being addressed in the Children Act only in the capacity of an illegitimate child, rather he is being treated as one at whose birth it is likely that the father might not be known or immediately available to fend for him, yet the child's immediate needs [for] parental responsibility which is absolutely necessary at the moment of birth cannot reasonably be expected to await for example a Legitimacy Act suit or a paternity suit under the Children's Act or any other law that regulates the maintenance of children. Reason demands that the law apportions parental responsibility in the first instance because parental responsibility can in certain situations vest in only one parent because of the overriding interest of the child and this is what it has done. The mother or any other person with the *loci standi* can thereafter cause the parental responsibility to be shared thereafter and the child would be at par in terms of parental responsibility with the child born within wedlock. In other words the law places parental responsibility on the unmarried mother because she is the only one immediately available at birth where there is no marriage and the needs of the child have to be paramount or overriding at any given time. The differentiation is not wholly or mainly on her status or that of the child. It is the mother who in the first instance has a clear and undisputed linkage to the child. The respondent has also contended that it is the opposite situation which would be unreasonable and unconstitutional—which is to allow a mother to point at the nearest man in the street and baptize him a father of the child without according him the right of hearing or producing proof of paternity.

The respondent concludes that the exclusion of marital status or age in s 82 is clear proof that any legislation that provides for such classification is not and cannot be unconstitutional.

The applicant has on the other hand urged the court to adopt a broad and purposeful interpretation of s 82 and find that although marital status is not specified in s 82 we should, all the same, hold that it is so included, because the framers of the Constitution could not have contemplated or foreseen all possible categories on which discrimination ought to have been forbidden at the time the Kenyan Constitution was being drafted. Alternatively, we have been urged to adjudicate in terms of the Conventions reproduced above, and which have specifically included the term "other status". In support of this the applicants have quoted the Canadian case of *Andrews* v. *Law Society of British Columbia* [1989] 1 SCR 143 where it was held that the enumerated heads of discrimination in Article 15(1) of the Canadian Charter, "race, national or ethnic origin, colour, religion, sex, age or mental or physical disability" were not a complete listing of categories of discrimination. The invitation to the court is that we go beyond the categories set out in s 82 of the Constitution, namely *race, tribe, place of origin or residence or other local connection, political opinions, colour, creed or sex.* We shall be touching on this aspect later on in this judgment. Wilson J in the *Andrews* case (*supra*) defined discrimination as follows:

Distinction which, whether intentional or not but based on grounds relating to personal characteristics of the individual or group, has an effect which imposes disadvantages not imposed upon others or which withholds or limits access to advantages available to other members of society.

At page 127 in *Botswana* v. *Unity Dow* the learned Judge held:

I do not think that [the framers of the Constitution] intended to declare that the categories mentioned in that definition were forever closed ... other groups or classes needing protection would arise ... In that sense, the classes or groups itemized in the definition would be, and in my opinion are, by way of example of what the framers of the Constitution thought worth mentioning as potentially some of the most likely areas of possible discrimination ... Sex was not specified in the Constitution of Botswana.

Although the suit is filed on behalf of the child an argument has been presented on behalf of mothers as follows:

A mother of a child born within wedlock on the other hand or one who subsequently marries the father of her child does not go through this process of proof. She enjoys obvious advantages, as the law imposes a duty on the father to have parental responsibility towards the child/children. She does not have to shoulder parental responsibility on her own. This means that the law on one hand treats unmarried mothers differently from married mothers and thereby discriminates on the basis of marital status and on the other hand discriminates on the basis of sex by making mothers of children born out of wedlock have sole parental responsibility in the first instance.

The case of *R (Morris)* v. *Westminster City Council and First Secretary of State* [2004] EWHC 2191 (Admin) has been relied on by the applicant for the principle that when a State legislates on a Convention or domesticates it, [it] cannot do so discriminatively. The argument is that s 24(3) should be on all fours with the relevant Convention.

In determining whether or not the provisions under the Children Act are discriminatory when tested against the Conventions and the Constitutional provisions, we were urged to consider the five questions posed in *Wandsworth London Borough Council* v. *Michalak* [2003] 1 WLR 617, when Brooke LJ posited that if the answer to any of the questions is "no", then the claim is likely to fail. The questions are:

1. Do the facts fall within the ambit of one or more of the substantive Convention rights (European Convention for the Protection of Human [Rights and Fundamental] Freedoms)?
2. If so, was there different treatment as respects that right between the complainant on the one hand and the other person put forward for comparison?
3. Were the chosen comparators in an analogous situation to the complainant's situation?
4. If so, did the difference in that treatment have an objective and reasonable justification? Did it pursue a legitimate aim and did the differential treatment bear a reasonable relationship of proportionality to the aim sought to be achieved?
5. If so, was the difference in treatment on one or more of the prohibited grounds under Article 14?

Personal Law

While conceding that discrimination or distinction is allowed in relation to matters of personal law, the applicant and counsel for the other Interested Parties (IPs) contend that the framers could not have allowed discrimination that encompasses the entire spectrum of a person's life. The applicant defines personal law as the law of religion, tribe or other personal factors. The applicant again drew the court's attention to the definition of personal law in *Botswana* v. *Unity Dow* where the learned judge observed that the words "other matters of personal law" in section 15(4)(c) of the Botswana Constitution referred to personal transactions determined by the law of his tribe, religious groups or other personal factors as distinct from the territorial law of the country. Thus at page 652, Amissah JP held that citizenship which is conferred by Statute on a state-wide basis is not a matter of personal law. Thus, if there is a matter that is legislated on a state-wide basis, the same cannot then be subject to personal law otherwise this would make mockery and nonsense of modern law. Tribal and religious laws have clear provision in relation to women and children that are often inimical to written law and which encompass their economic, political, social and cultural lives. It was therefore argued that parental responsibility is conferred by the Children Act on a state-wide basis and for this reason it cannot be treated as a matter of personal law which deals with laws of tribe, religions or communities. Children or women are not a homogenous group subject to the same personal law everywhere.

Conflicts in the Children Act

The applicant has argued that Part II of the Act and in particular s 5 prohibits discrimination on the basis of birth or other status among other grounds. This is in conflict with s 24(3) of the same Act. As the Act was meant to domesticate the Convention on the Rights of the Child and the African Charter, the court has been invited to hold that Part II must prevail in the face of the apparent conflict.

JUS COGENS

It has also been argued that discrimination against the child born out of wedlock or their mother by the State through legislation forms part of *jus cogens* which is the technical name now given to the basic principles of international law, which States are not allowed to contract out of—otherwise known as "peremptory norms of general international law"—and that there is such a general recognition of use of force, of genocide, slavery, gross violations of the right of people to self-determination and of racial discrimination and prohibition on torture as *jus cogens*.

A consistent pattern of gross violations of internationally recognized human rights if practised, encouraged or conducted by the government of a State as official policy constitutes a violation in the category of *jus cogens*. It has therefore been argued that the court should regard the discrimination [against] the child in terms of parental responsibility as [a] breach of customary international law.

FINDINGS

(a) Locus Standi

We find that the applicant has *locus* in public law because he is affected by the subject matter of the suit, namely parental responsibility, but the mother had no *locus* to attempt in the course of the proceedings to articulate the position of mothers generally including herself. Any alleged violation of a Constitution has to be made personally unless the relevant right can be asserted by a corporate body or unincorporated association: see s 84 and s 123 of the Constitution for the definition of a "person". On this point we respectfully depart from that great judgment of Ringera J in the *Njoya* case.

(b) *Personal Law*

The court does not accept the definition of personal law as outlined by the applicant. They have only captured part of the definition and left out the rest: *Black's Law Dictionary* 8th Edition defines personal law at p. 1180 as follows:

The law that governs a person's family matters usually regardless of where the person goes. In common law systems, personal law refers to the law of the person's domicile. In civil law systems it refers to the law of the individual's nationality (and is sometimes called *lex patriae*). Cf territorial law.

The idea of the personal law is based on the conception of man as a social being, so that those transactions of his daily life which affect him most closely in a personal sense, such as marriage, divorce, legitimacy, many kinds of capacity and succession, may be governed universally by that purpose. Although the law of domicile is the chief criteri[on] adopted by English courts for the personal law, it lies within the power of any man of full age and capacity to establish his domicile in any country he chooses and thereby automatically to make the law of that country his personal law.

In view of the above it is quite clear that the definition of personal law is wider than what the applicant has contended in this matter and we would not accept [the restriction of its meaning to that] under the Constitution and we opt to give it its widest meaning as defined above. We are therefore unable to find for the applicant on this point in the face of the above definition and the constitutional provision excepting personal law under s 82(4) of the Constitution. It is one field of law where the Constitution gives the Legislature some latitude to create suitable laws that are in keeping with the peculiar needs and values of the society at any given time.

(c) Jus Cogens

On this, a perusal of the authoritative sources and international jurisprudence reveals that although the applicants are correct in the definition of *jus cogens* as outlined above and its current classifications, it has not yet embraced parental responsibility and the rights associated with it. The closest linkage is the right to life and we are not convinced that the challenged section(s) threaten the right to life. On the contrary the provisions endeavour to provide for the gaps that have hitherto existed in the law so that the overriding interest of the child is satisfied even where the status of the parents is uncertain. The provisions have in our view been crafted in a fairly objective and reasonable manner. There is therefore nothing which we could apply to Kenya by way of *jus cogens* except the recognized classifications set out above. In enacting ss 24 and 25 we find that the Legislature invoked the provisions of s 82 of the Constitution.

(d) *Conflict between the Provisions of the Children Act*

We accept that s 5 is worded in broader terms in terms of the definition of discrimination because it includes "birth" and status. However, in so far as Part II purports to go contrary to s 82 of the Constitution (although this has not arisen for determination in this case because Part II and in particular section 5 have not been challenged) it would be void to the extent of the conflict. As held elsewhere, we have a serious duty to uphold the provisions of the Constitution and nothing has been established to justify the invitation either to add to or to subtract from what appears to us to be very clear unambiguous, unequivocal provisions of the Constitution. Neither an Act of Parliament nor a provision in any ordinary Act of Parliament can alter the Constitution.

(e) *Invitation to Expand on the Antidiscrimination Categories Set Out in s 82 of the Constitution*

We reject the invitation to blindly follow *Attorney General of Botswana* v. *Dow* (above) where the court unilaterally added "sex" to the Botswana Constitution. Firstly with all due respect we consider that if we did the same in Kenya it would amount to usurpation of the work of the Constitution framers. We would have no reason to add or to subtract in the face of what is, to us, very clear provisions. Moreover in the context of Kenya, in 1997 the country deliberately came up with a constitutional amendment to include the classification of "sex" [in] the section so as to bring in line the constitutional provision with the emerging jurisprudence contained in the relevant Convention. Failure to expand to other categories was in our view deliberate and *inter alia* took into account the limitations already contained in s 82 and in particular subsection 4. Any other approach would amount to unacceptable judicial activism. Similarly the invitation that we call a woman's "womb" "a place of origin" strains the language or the wording used in the Constitution and we would have no reason to embark on such a course. In this regard while conceding that some of the reasoning in the case of *Republic* v. *El Mann*

[1969] EA 357 has been substantially overtaken, especially in the interpretation of the Constitution, one important principle remains intact, that the words of the Constitution or a statute should be accorded their natural and ordinary sense. This is the path we have chosen in the circumstances of this case. We further endorse Potter J's holding in *Ngobit Estate Ltd* v. *Carnegie* (1982) KLR 137:

The function of the judiciary is to interpret the statute law, not to make it. Where the meaning of a statute is plain and unambiguous, no question of interpretation or construction arises. It is the duty of the judge to apply such a law as it stands. To do otherwise would be to usurp the legislative functions of parliament.

(f) *Other status etc.*

Even if we adopted the *Andrews* case or the *Westminster* or the *Dow* cases (*supra*) and expanded the constitutional categories and definition we would still not find for the applicant because of what we have said elsewhere in this judgment concerning the non-restrictive approach adopted by the United Nations monitoring bodies in interpreting the Universal Declaration and the Covenant on Civil and Political Rights. The additional reason for not taking the path of the cases relied on above is that in our view they fail to recognize "*the States' margin of appreciation*" as defined in the ever expanding international jurisprudence – see the *Belgian Linguistic* case 1968 (*ibid*) and . . . the *Constitution of Costa Rica* case 1984 OC-4/84 (*ibid.*).

Finally, we cannot uphold the applicant in the face of the Bangalore Principles concerning the position of the Conventions vis-à-vis the States' Constitutions. Where there is no ambiguity the clear provisions of the Constitution prevail over the International Conventions.

Principles 6, 7 and 8 as per the Reprint Commonwealth Secretariat Developing Human Rights Jurisprudence Vol. 3 151 read:

P6
While it is desirable for the norms contained in the international human rights instruments to be still more widely recognized and applied by national courts, this process must take fully into account local laws, traditions, circumstances and needs.

P7
It is within the proper nature of the judicial process and well-established judicial functions for national courts to have regard to international obligations which a country undertakes—whether or not they have been incorporated into domestic law—for the purpose of removing ambiguity or uncertainty from national constitutions, legislation or common law.

P8
However, where national law is clear and inconsistent with the international obligation of the state concerned, in common law countries the national court is obliged to give effect to national law. In such cases the court should draw such inconsistency to the attention of the appropriate authorities since the supremacy of national law in no way mitigates a breach of an international legal obligation which is undertaken by a country.

In *Cheney* v. *Conn* [1968] 1 WLR 242 at page 245E and G-H it was held that the Conventions, Treaties and Charters need not bind its Legislature.

Returning to the *El Mann* case we have great sympathy for the principle expressed in the case as under:

We have said enough to show that in our opinion sub-section (7) of s 21 of the Constitution means no more and no less than it is to be gathered from the plain words of the provision and is not to be given an extended meaning which cannot be spelt out of the words used without doing violence to the language of the subsection.

Of course the *El Mann* principles have quite rightly been buffeted or shaken by the powerful winds of broad and purposive approach in interpreting the Constitution together with the living tree principle of interpreting the Constitution, but except in exceptional cases where these two approaches apply, the above principle still reigns supreme. The situation where a living spirit has to be injected into the constitutional provisions includes where the language used is likely to lead to unjust situations. Even where the living tree principle of construction is invoked the nourishment given must originate from the roots, the trunk and the natural branches. The court would not be entitled to disregard the roots, the trunk and the natural branches in the name of giving flesh to the Constitution, or to graft in its own artificial branches. The living tree is sustained by the tree and any graftings are likely to be rejected. By all means let the courts be innovative and take into account the contemporary situation of each age but let the innovations be supported by the roots.

In this regard we endorse fully the presumption of constitutionality which was powerfully expressed by the Supreme Court of India in *Hamdard Dawakhana* v. *Union of India* 1960 AIR 554 where the respected Court stated:

In examining the constitutionality of a statute it must be assumed that the legislature understands and appreciates the need of the people and the law it enacts are directed to problems which are made manifest by experience and the elected representatives assembled in a legislature enact laws which they consider to be reasonable for the purpose for which they are enacted. Presumption is therefore, in favour of the constitutionality of an enactment.

Nothing has been shown to us that can lead us to upset the presumption that s 24(3) and by extension s 25 were not enacted for a reasonable purpose and for a need the Legislature felt had to be addressed. Indeed it has not been demonstrated to us by the applicant that the striking out or declaring the section unconstitutional would be in the interest of the intended beneficiary or the overriding interest of the child which is the aim of the legislation. On the contrary, the child's interest would be subverted by the prayers sought. In addition it has not been demonstrated how the contended equality could be achieved by law in a situation where parental responsibility is wholly shared by both parents in the case of married couples and split only where one of them is not available in the first instance because of the uncertain status of the father. In our view the Legislature has provided for all possible situations in order to address the aim of parental responsibility. We would of course have agreed with the applicant's contention on inequality and discrimination if for example it is the government which was charged with parental responsibility and it dishes better treatment to a child born within wedlock and dishes out bad or inferior treatment to that born out of wedlock. There would be an ironcast case for inequality and discrimination. However, the definition of a parent includes both parents when immediately available or one of them when the other is not available—see the meaning of "parent" as set out above. The court in sustaining the constitutionality of the section must carefully analyse the relationship under scrutiny and all the underlying circumstances which necessitated differential treatment. We would therefore wish to associate ourselves with the holding in the *Hamdard Dawakhana* case *supra* where the court observed:

that in order to sustain the presumption of constitutionality the court may take into consideration matters of common knowledge, the history of the times and may assume every state of facts which can be conceived existing at the time of legislation.

We further approve the holding in the same decision on what the function of the court is when an enactment is impugned on the ground that it is ultra vires and unconstitutional:

As already stated when an enactment is impugned on the ground that it is ultra vires and unconstitutional what has to be ascertained is the true character of the legislation and for that purpose regard must be had to the enactment as a whole, to its objects, purpose and true intention and the scope and effect of its provisions or what they are directed against and what they aim at.

While there is no contention that the impugned section(s) are ultra vires it is contended that s 24(3) is unconstitutional and we as a court have the mandate as expressed above. As crafted the Children Act is a milestone in entrenching and securing the rights of the child and s 24(3) is in our view a big improvement of the uncoordinated laws which dealt with parental responsibility before its enactment. Scrapping it from our law would go against the objects of the Act and the State responsibility to endeavour to create laws, aimed at securing the best interests of the child.

(g) *Equal Protection of Laws*

Equal protection of laws means subjection to equal laws applying to all in the same circumstances.

In the circumstances presented to us the child born within wedlock has the immediate support of the two parents. In the case of the child born out of wedlock there is only one parent available in the first instance. The difference in terms of the two otherwise equal situations arises because the status of the father in the latter case is not immediately ascertainable and the law goes on to provide for the process of ascertainment and to allow the sharing of responsibility upon ascertainment of status or acceptance by the father. The law does not prevent or frustrate paternity or legitimacy suits. They are contemplated by the section or other applicable laws. The question is, does the right of equal protection under the Constitution prevent the Legislature from legislating differently in the two situations? The answer in our view is "no". The principle of equal protection of the laws does not prevent the Legislature or the State from adjusting its legislation to differences in situations or forbid classification in that connection, but it does require that the classification be not arbitrary, but based on a *"real and substantial difference, having a reasonable relation to the subject or aim of the particular legislation"*.

The equal protection provisions do not in our view require things which are different in fact or in law to be treated as though they are the same. Indeed, the reasonableness of a classification would depend upon the purpose for which the classification is made. There is nothing wrong in providing differently in situations that are factually different.

The intelligible differentia in the case before us is the uncertain status of the father in the first instance. The differentia is not arbitrary because it has a nexus to attachment of parental responsibility and it recognizes that the process of ascertainment of the status will take time. Surely there is a substantial distinction between the two situations and the law has handled the distinction in a reasonable manner and with the object of parental responsibility and the objects of the Act in view. By way of analogy we wish to quote with approval the holdings of Mahajan J and Das J respectively in the Indian case of *State of West Bengal* v. *Anwar Ali* [1952] SCR 284 and 335.

The classification permissible, however, must be based on some real and substantial distinction bearing a just and reasonable relation to the objects sought to be attained and cannot be made arbitrarily and without any substantial basis. ... Thus the Legislature may fix the age at which persons shall be deemed competent to contract between themselves, but no one will claim that competency to contract can be made to depend upon the stature or colour of the hair. "Such a classification for such a purpose would be arbitrary and a piece of legislative despotism."

And Das J put it:

The classification must not be arbitrary but must be rational, that is to say, it must not only be based on some qualities or characteristics which are to be found in all the persons grouped together and not in others who are left out but those qualities or characteristics must have a reasonable relation to the object of the legislation. In order to pass the test, two conditions must be fulfilled, namely:

1. that the classification must be founded on an intelligible differentia which distinguishes those that are grouped together from others and
2. that that differentia must have a rational relation to the object sought to be achieved by the Act.

In this case, child born within wedlock etc. and out of wedlock is the differentia and parental responsibility is the nexus. Unwedded mothers and their children are grouped together for the purpose of locating parental responsibility. This cannot be said to be an arbitrary or unreasonable differentia—because how else can parental responsibility be located in the two situations? To reinforce this point permit us to quote from the American Supreme Court decision in *Tigner* v. *State of Texas* (1940) 310 US 141:

The Fourteenth Amendment enjoins "the equal protection of the laws", and laws are not abstract propositions. They do not relate to abstract units A, B and C, but are expressions of policy arising out of specific difficulties, addressed to the attainment of specific ends by the use of specific remedies. The Constitution does not require things which are different in fact or opinion to be treated in law as though they were the same.

And to answer the question we have posed above, as to whether the law could have handled or dealt with the situation in any other way, the decision in the American Supreme Court decision in *Buck* v. *Bell* (1927) 274 US 200 (208) is to the point:

The law does all that is needed when it does all that it can, indicates a policy, applies it to all within the lines, and seeks to bring within the lines all similarly situated so far and so fast as its means allow.

To conclude this important point we recognize that the American jurisprudence has extensively covered the rule of equality since the case of *Magoun* v. *Illinois Trust Bank* (1898) 170 US 283 to *Bayside Fish Flour Co.* v. *Gentry* (1936) 297 US 422 (429) as follows:

The rule of equality permits many practical inequalities. And necessarily so. In a classification for governmental purposes, there cannot be any exact exclusion or inclusion of persons and things.

In other words, a classification having some reasonable basis, does not offend against the clause merely because it is not made with mathematical nicety, or because, in practice, it results in some inequality.

Government is not a simple thing. It encounters and must deal with the problems which come from persons in an infinite variety of relations. Classification is recognition of those relations and, in making it, a legislature must be allowed a wide latitude of discretion and judgment.

In applying the dangerously wide and vague language of the equality clause to the concrete facts of life, a doctrinaire approach should be avoided.

When a law is challenged as offending against equal protection the question for determination by the court is not whether it has resulted in inequality, but whether there is some difference which bears a just and reasonable relation to the object of the legislation.

As the Supreme Court of India has observed in the case of *Kedar Nath Bajoria* v. *State of West Bengal* [1954] SCR 30:

Mere differentia or inequality of treatment does not per se amount to discrimination within the inhibition of the equal protection clause. To attract the operation of the clause it is necessary to show that the selection or differentiation is unreasonable or arbitrary: that it does not rest on any rational basis having regard to the object which the legislature has in view.

Finally by analogy we turn to the American case of *Lalli* v. *Lalli* 439 US 259 (1978).

A state was permitted to condition an illegitimate's inheritance from his father on a judicial determination of paternity during the father's lifetime.

The section recognizes the child's right to parental support at all stages provided paternity is established and even where it is not an agreement of parental responsibility has been allowed. We find no unreasonableness in the way the legislation has provided for the situations which arise, in this personal law relationship.

We therefore conclude that the differentia in ss 24(3) and 25 is not arbitrary and cannot be said to lack a rational basis having regard to the objects of the Act and in particular locating parental responsibility.

CONSTITUTIONAL POSITION TO PREVAIL AS PER THE BANGALORE PRINCIPLES

After analysing the case law cited to us by the applicant's counsel including the Interested Parties' counsel we prefer reinforcing the three relevant Bangalore Principles set out elsewhere in this judgment to the effect that the State's clear constitutional provisions should prevail over those of the Conventions. It follows that the clear provisions of s 82 and the limitations must prevail and we so hold. It is only where an Act intended to bring a Treaty into effect is itself ambiguous or one interpretation is compatible with the term of the treaty while others are not that the former will be adopted. This is in recognition of a presumption in our law that legislation is to be construed to avoid a conflict with international law. In this regard we endorse as good law Lord Diplock's comments in the English case of *Salomon* v. *Commissioner of Customs* [1967] 2 QB 116 cited elsewhere in the judgment where he said:

Parliament does not intend to act in breach of international law, including therein specific treaty obligations.

However, where the words of Constitution or statute are unambiguous the courts have no choice other than to enforce the local law irrespective of any conflict with international agreements. Where not domesticated, Treaties may be taken into account in seeking to interpret ambiguous provisions in the municipal law: see *R* v. *Chief Immigration Officer, Heathrow Airport, ex p Bibi* [1976] 3 All ER 843.

POSITION AS PER INTERNATIONAL INSTRUMENTS—STATES PERMITTED TO TAKE INTO ACCOUNT SPECIAL CIRCUMSTANCES

The Universal Declaration of Human Rights, 1948, Articles 1, 2 and 7 state the following about human rights, equality before the law and discrimination:

Article 1
All human beings are born free and equal in dignity and rights . . .

Article 2
Everyone is entitled to all the rights and freedoms set forth in this Declaration, without distinction of any kind, such as race, colour, sex, language, religion, political or other opinion, national or social origin, property, birth or other status . . .

Article 7
All are equal before the law and are entitled without any discrimination to equal protection of the law. All are entitled to equal protection against any discrimination in violation of this Declaration and against any incitement to such discrimination.

It is strikingly clear that Article 2 of the Universal Declaration prohibits distinction of any kind. The obvious interpretation is that no differences at all can be legally accepted. However, the situation on the ground does not support such a restrictive interpretation of the Declaration in that the monitoring bodies have not supported any such interpretation and some of the Constitutions of the Member States, including that of Kenya, do not support the position as stated in Article 2. The Member States have claimed and have been allowed "*a margin of appreciation*" because differences in real life are inevitable and they are not necessarily negative. Indeed, international jurisprudence and supporting case law demonstrates that not all distinctions between persons and groups of persons can be regarded as discrimination in the strict sense or true sense of the term. Thus General Comment No 18 in the United Nations Compilation of General Comments, p. 134 para. 1, lays [down] what appears to be a peremptory international norm (*jus cogens*) in these words:

Non-discrimination, together with equality before the law and equal protection of the law without any discrimination, constitute a basic and general principle relating to the protection of human rights.

The second principle which is now generally accepted and which does not support a restrictive interpretation is that *distinctions made between people are justified provided that they are, in general terms, reasonable and imposed for an objective and legitimate purpose.*

To amplify on this we wish to borrow again from the Human Rights Committee General Comments (*supra*) at page 135 para. 7 in its definition of "discrimination":

that the term "discrimination" as used in the Covenant (International Covenant on Civil and Political Rights) should be understood to imply any distinction, exclusion, restriction or preference which is based on any ground such as race, colour, sex, language, religion, political or other opinion, national or social origin, property, birth or other status, and which has the purpose or effect of nullifying or impairing the recognition, enjoyment or exercise by all persons, on an equal footing, of all rights and freedoms.

The Human Rights Committee has commented that the enjoyment of rights and freedoms on an equal footing does not mean identical treatment in every instance. Taking the ICCPR as an example, Article 6(5) prohibits the death sentence from being imposed on persons below 18 years of age and from being carried out on pregnant women. The other obvious example is affirmative action which is aimed at diminishing or eliminating conditions likely to perpetuate inequality or discrimination in fact. Such a corrective action constitutes or is termed legitimate differentiation under the ICCPR.

It is therefore an accepted international principle of law that differentiation based on *reasonable* and *objective criteria* does not amount to prohibited discrimination. A State which complies with these criteria would not be faulted in practice or in its formulation of a supporting law provided these criteria are adhered to. To explain the position further, the universality of the 1948 Declaration of Human Rights is based on a common heritage of humankind which is the oneness of the human family and the essential dignity of the individual. It is from these two universally shared traits [that] the notion of equality finds its stem or base.

INTERDEPENDENCY AND INDIVISIBILITY OF HUMAN RIGHTS

In this particular case the court has deliberately declined to stretch the natural meaning of the words set out in s 82 of the Constitution of Kenya for the reasons given herein. However, we must clarify that we are acutely aware that the role of the Court in determining the values and principles of our Constitution is vast in that in the hitherto neglected field of economic, social and cultural rights the courts have the critical role of harmonizing these rights with the civil and political rights. The reason for this is that the two sets of rights are interdependent and indivisible. A good recent example is this court's broad interpretation of the right to life in the case of *PK Waweru* v. *Attorney-General and Others*. This was in the field of environmental law. And the court ruled that life was more than soul and body. In this decade and beyond, one of the greatest challenges in the courts will be finding a lasting place for economic, social and cultural rights in our jurisprudence.

The challenge in this case is however different and we decline to pave a new path—because the facts and the law have not sufficiently energized us to pave such a path in the circumstances.

NO DISCRIMINATION WHERE THE DIFFERENCE HAS A LEGITIMATE PURPOSE

It is clear to the court that what ss 24(3) and 25 are seeking to achieve is to have the parental responsibility shared in the case of the married couples or where there is a consensual parental agreement or the responsibility split between individuals if there is no marriage and also to locate parental responsibility permanently where an unmarried father has had a 12-month history of giving maintenance to the child. In cases outside these situations the law initially locates the parental responsibility on the mother of the child because firstly there cannot be a gap in parental responsibility in the first instance and the best interests of the child is for the identified parent to take up the responsibility. The law assumes that the process of identifying the father outside marriage is likely to take time, e.g. paternity or legitimacy suits are likely to take time where instituted, yet the needs of the child cannot be held in abeyance even for a moment. Taking the facts of the case before the court as an illustration, the next friend of the child has claimed that the child's head was "shaven" by the father pursuant to the Kisii customary tradition. Yet she has not explained why she has not pursued this claim in a court of law. A constitutional court is not the right forum for such a claim. Customary African marriages are recognized by our law. Thus in the event of a successful claim under the customary law, s 24(3) could still be invoked to ensure that parental responsibility is shared between the two. The section is not tied to statutory marriages only.

In the circumstances we have no hesitation in finding that the challenged subsection 24(3) on the mother's initial responsibility and the father in the situations described in the subsection and s 25 have a legitimate purpose and are based on the realities of the relationships and the rights of all those concerned. A law that does not recognize the right of all concerned including those disputing paternity would be unrealistic and unreasonable and would be contrary to justice, to reason and to the nature of things.

This is why this Court agrees with the [*Constitution of Costa Rica* case OC-4/84] paras. 55-7, and we take the liberty of reproducing [para. 57]:

> 57. Accordingly, no discrimination exists if the difference in treatment has a legitimate purpose and if it does not lead to situations which are contrary

to justice, to reason or to the nature of things. It follows that there would be no discrimination in differences in treatment of individuals by a State when the classifications selected are based on substantial factual differences and there exists a reasonable relationship of proportionality between these differences and the aims of the legal rule under review. These aims may not be unjust or unreasonable, that is, they may not be arbitrary, capricious, despotic or in conflict with the essential oneness and dignity of human kind.

Thus we find that since the aim of the section is to provide for parental responsibility, locating it initially in the mother and providing for a shared responsibility taking into account all possible relationships that spring from the birth, the section has handled the situation with a reasonable proportionality between the difference of the one set of children (generally born within) and those born out of wedlock since the aim is to provide for parental responsibility in both situations as far as it is practically possible in the latter situation. We find that the balance struck by the challenged section cannot be said to be unreasonable or unjust. The difference between the two sets of situations cannot in our view be said not to have *an objective and reasonable justification*.

A MARGIN OF APPRECIATION IS IN CERTAIN SITUATIONS PERMITTED

Although, as is clear from s 82 of the Constitution of Kenya, our Constitution does allow departure from the non-discrimination rule, in cases of marriage and areas of personal law, the courts are obliged to apply the law as it is at the moment, even in those situations where birth, age or marital status are categories in the Constitution (or as we were being persuaded to agree with our brother Judges in Zambia where the court appears to have extended the categories), because the local legislation does not have to be on all fours with the Convention. We are persuaded to hold that even in these situations each State has a certain margin of appreciation which she can exercise in the legislating as has happened in Kenya as regards Sections 24(3) and 25 by extension. In the case before us, we would be more inclined to agree with the finding of the Inter-American Court of Human Rights in its advisory opinion on the case of *Proposed Amendments to the Naturalization Provisions of the Constitution of Costa Rica* OC-4/84 of 19 January 1984, Series A No 4 p. 104, where it gave this opinion:

58. Although it cannot be denied that a given factual context may make it more or less difficult to determine whether or not one has encountered the situation described in the foregoing paragraph, it is equally true that, starting

with the notion of the essential oneness and dignity of the human family, it is possible to identify circumstances in which considerations of public welfare may justify departures to a greater or lesser degree from the standards articulated above. One is here dealing with values which take on concrete dimensions in the face of those real situations in which they have to be applied and which permit in each case a certain margin of appreciation in giving expression to them.

While the ideal situation may be holy matrimony or the other legally recognized marriage status, in terms of parental responsibility the law as crafted has gone beyond this in order to locate and provide parental responsibility so as to achieve it, this being a cornerstone of the overriding interest of the child. If a State or the courts were to blindly apply the rule of the thumb and hold that there cannot be legitimate distinction in the situation before us, then what is the case of the single mothers who would have nothing to do with the father by choice? Should the law wipe them from the face of the earth or should it not try and do social engineering by providing for each situation using the best criteria available to secure the rights and obligations of all in the interest of justice, reason and equity?

In interpreting our Constitution we consider ourselves bound by its provisions in the matter before us, namely s 82 and its limitations. Perhaps it is important to point out at the outset, that following the great momentum of gender equity in the 80s and 90s, s 82 of the Kenya Constitution was amended in 1997 and the prohibited category expanded to include "sex". Age and marital status were not added. At the moment one can only conclude that the exclusion was deliberate and we do not consider that it is the function of the court to fill the gaps. It must not be forgotten that modern Constitutions are being negotiated with the people directly or indirectly by way of Constituent Assemblies and Referendums and it would not be proper for the courts to take their places by filling in fundamental gaps in the Constitutions. The life of society has other important actors such as Parliament and other organs which must be left to play their role to the full. In this regard we would like to borrow from one of the holdings by the European Court of Human Rights in the *Belgian Linguistic* case Judgment of 23 July 1968, Series A No 6 p. 33, [B para. 10], where it held:

In attempting to find out in a given case, whether or not there has been an arbitrary distinction, the Court cannot disregard those legal and factual features which characterize the life of the society in the State which, as a Contracting Party, has to answer for the measure in dispute. In so doing it cannot assume the role of the competent national authorities [in our case read the people,

Constituent Assembly or Referendum and Parliament], for it would thereby lose sight of the subsidiary nature of the international machinery of collective enforcement established by the Convention. The national authorities remain free to choose the measures which they consider appropriate in those matters which are governed by the Convention. Review by the Court concerns only the conformity of these measures with the requirements of the Convention.

Thus, in the case of our Parliament it did address the measures set out in the cited Conventions and choose only those measures which are considered suitable to the local situation. Parliament had no obligation to adopt, line, hook and sinker, the provision of the Conventions in formulating the Children Act. It had a margin of appreciation reserved to the State as defined above. On the other hand the role of the court is to uphold the provisions of the Constitution by recognizing the prohibited categories in s 82. The situations which would justify a constitutional court in adopting a broad view or using the living tree principle of the interpretation of the Constitution is where there is ambiguity, inconsistencies, unreasonableness, lack of legislative purpose or obvious imbalance or lack of proportionality or absurd situations. In all these situations a court would be justified in breathing life into any such provisions in order to achieve situations which are not contrary to justice, to reason or to the nature of things. Any other approach would in our view be usurpation of the role of the Constitution framers and other law makers. Any spirit or nourishment to constitutional provisions by the court must spring directly from the roots and cannot justifiably be grafted from outside the living tree.

To sum up, we find and hold that s 23(4) and by extension s 25 do not offend the principle of equality and non-discrimination either by themselves or in their effect. We further hold that the principle of equality and non-discrimination does not mean that all distinctions between people are illegal. Distinctions are legitimate and hence lawful provided they satisfy the following:

(1) pursue a legitimate aim such as affirmative action to deal with factual inequalities; and
(2) are reasonable in the light of their legitimate aim.

The challenged difference does satisfy both criteria in our view. At the moment we find no other better option of dealing with the situation other than as set out in the sections. It must be recalled that the Act took the best provisions of the repealed Children and Young Persons Act, Guardianship—Adoption of Infants Act and other laws affecting children and the relevant International Conventions among others and codified them as one. The Act including the challenged section(s) captures the issue of parental responsibility in a manner never done before in the history of the rights of the child in this country and it would be a great tragedy for the court to accept the invitation to strike them out or to hold that the subsection is unconstitutional. If the court were to do so, the gap in meeting the overriding interest of the child would be immediately retrogressive and unforgivable.

The suit is dismissed with no order as to costs as the suit had been brought on behalf of a child.

[Report: Transcript]

Human rights — Refugees — Rights of refugees under international law and municipal law — Constitution of Kenya, Section 70(a) — United Nations Convention Relating to the Status of Refugees, 1951, Articles 31, 32 and 33 — Organization of African Unity Convention Governing the Specific Aspects of Refugee Problems in Africa, 1969 — Obligations of States in refugee protection — Limitation of individual rights in international and municipal law — Obligations of asylum seekers to contact authorities in receiving State

Human rights — Refugees — Immigration Act, Sections 3 and 8 — Detention of prohibited immigrants — Repatriation — Whether extended detention contrary to rights under Constitution and international conventions — Whether failed repatriation rendered deportation orders invalid — Whether Sections 3 and 8 of Immigration Act contrary to provisions of Constitution — Whether continued detention of applicant unlawful — The law of Kenya

AL-DAHAS v. ATTORNEY-GENERAL AND OTHERS[1]

Kenya, High Court. 1 March 2007

(Emukule J)

SUMMARY: *The facts*:—The applicant filed an application with the High Court under Section 84 of the Constitution of Kenya seeking enforcement of his fundamental rights and freedoms. The applicant, who had previously been recognized as a refugee by the United Nations High Commission for Refugees (the "Interested Party"), claimed that his continued detention without charge was unlawful and a violation of his fundamental rights and freedoms as enshrined in Section 70(a)[2] of the Constitution of Kenya and numerous international human rights instruments to which Kenya was party. The applicant sought various declarations from the Court recognizing his treatment as unlawful and unconstitutional, and effecting his release from State custody into that of the Interested Party.

The respondents replied that the applicant was not in Kenya as a refugee but as a prohibited immigrant as defined by Section 3(1), subsections (f), (h) and (k), of the Immigration Act.[3] The respondents argued that, since the

---

[1] The applicant was represented by Mr Otieno, instructed by Swaleh Kanyeki & Co., Advocates; the respondents were represented by Mr Kaka.
[2] Set out at p. 336 of the judgment.   [3] Set out at p. 337 of the judgment.

applicant was in Kenya unlawfully, the Minister was empowered under Section 8(1) of the Immigration Act to order his removal, and that, under Section 8(2) of the Act,[4] the applicant could be lawfully detained until his departure from the State.

Held:—The application was dismissed. The acts of the respondents were not unconstitutional and had not breached the applicant's fundamental rights under either the Constitution or international human rights instruments. Each party was to bear their own costs and, unless Kenya accepted the applicant as a refugee, the Interested Party was to find a third country to host the applicant in the terms of the United Nations Convention Relating to the Status of Refugees ("RC").[5]

(1) Sections 3 and 8 of the Immigration Act were not inconsistent with Section 3 of the Constitution of Kenya. The orders made under the Immigration Act and Section 26 of the Penal Code for the applicant's removal remained valid and enforceable in accordance with their terms. The failed attempts to repatriate the applicant had not affected the validity of the orders since an order for the removal of a prohibited immigrant was only completed when the prohibited immigrant had either been handed over to a third country as a refugee or placed under the authorities of his country of origin (p. 344).

(2) International human rights instruments not only imposed stringent obligations on host and receiving States but also considered the needs of those States to maintain security and public order. International conventions such as the RC and the OAU Convention Governing the Specific Aspects of Refugee Problems in Africa[6] imposed strict positive obligations upon asylum seekers which the applicant had failed to meet.

(a) The theory and practice of international law, as demonstrated by Article 31(1) of the RC,[7] required that a person fleeing his own country at the first instance upon entering another country present himself to the immigration or security agents of that State and show good cause for being there. The applicant had failed to report his presence in Kenya to any of the Kenyan authorities and had evaded and avoided the Kenyan authorities until his arrest for immigration offences some time after he first entered the country (pp. 340-3).

(b) The fundamental rights and freedoms granted under the Constitution and various United Nations and African Union Conventions relating to refugees were universal. However, all individual rights were subject to the enjoyment of those rights by other individuals and the public interest and so were not absolute. As a non-national in Kenya, the applicant was entitled

---

[4] Set out at pp. 337-8 of the judgment.

[5] 1951 United Nations Convention Relating to the Status of Refugees, signed 28 July 1951, entered into force 22 April 1954, 189 UNTS 150.

[6] 1969 Organization of African Unity Convention Governing the Specific Aspects of Refugee Problems in Africa, signed 10 September 1969, entered into force 20 June 1974, OAU Doc. No CAB/LEG/24.3.

[7] Set out at p. 340 of the judgment.

to the protection of his fundamental rights and freedoms subject only to the limitations as stated in Section 70 of the Constitution (pp. 345-7).

(c) The applicant had been kept in lawful custody within the terms of Section 8(2)(b) of the Immigration Act and in accordance with Section 70 of the Constitution pending the finding of a suitable third country by the Interested Party. The respondents had not contravened any provisions of the Bill of Rights in the Constitution of Kenya or any provisions of human rights or refugee conventions (pp. 344-8).

The following is the text of the judgment of the Court:

I. THE APPLICATION

By an Application brought by way of an Originating Summons pursuant to the provisions of the Constitution of Kenya (Protection of Fundamental Rights and Freedoms of the the Individual) High Court Practice and Procedure Rules, 2001 (now revoked by the Constitution of Kenya (Supervisory Jurisdiction and Protection of Fundamental Rights and Freedoms of the Individual) Practice and Procedure Rules 2006 (LN No 6 of 2006)), one Adel Mohammed Abdukader Al-Dahas (the Applicant) sought the declarations following against the Hon. the Attorney-General (1st Respondent), the Principal Immigration Officer (2nd Respondent) and the Minister of State for Provincial Administration and National Security (3rd Respondent). The United Nations High Commission for Refugees (UNHCR) was joined as an Interested Party. The declarations sought are namely—

(a) A declaration that the Declaration of the Minister of State dated 25 May 2001 declaring that the entry and presence of the Applicant (in Kenya) is contrary to the national interests (of Kenya) is unconstitutional to the extent that it is not based on any facts at all;
(b) A declaration that the Declaration by the Minister of State dated 25 May 2001 declaring that the Applicant be immediately removed from Kenya to his country of origin, Iraq, is in breach of the United Nations Convention Relating to the Status of Refugees;
(c) A declaration that the Universal Declaration of Human Rights (UDHR), 1948 bars the Respondents from continued infringement of the rights of the Applicant;
(d) A declaration to the extent that the Applicant was removed from Kenya on 6 October 2001 and remained outside Kenya until

8 October 2001 by the Minister's declaration of 21 May 2001 ceased to have effect;
(e) A declaration that the continued detention of the Applicant at Kileleswa Police Station or any other police station or prison is unconstitutional to the extent that there is no lawful order for his continued detention;
(f) A declaration that the Respondents forthwith release the Applicant to the Interested Party; and
(g) An order that the Applicant's costs of the Application be borne by the Respondents.

The Originating Summons was supported by the Affidavit of the Applicant sworn on 10 November 2001 and filed with the Application on 11 November 2001, and the following grounds—

(a) the Ministerial declaration made on 25 May 2001 under Section 3 of the Immigration Act (Cap. 172, Laws of Kenya) is unconstitutional,
(b) the Ministerial Declaration made on 25 May 2001 under Section 8 of the Immigration Act (Cap. 172) has been spent and has ceased to have any effect,
(c) the Applicant has been unlawfully detained in police custody for an inordinately long period without charge,
(d) that the Applicant has already been accorded refugee status by the Interested Party herein and ought to be in their custody,
(e) save for being a refugee in this country, the Applicant has not committed any offence,
(f) the incarceration of the Applicant in the circumstances is a flagrant violation of his fundamental rights enshrined in the Constitution of Kenya, and in the numerous international human rights instruments to which Kenya is a party, particularly the United Nations Convention Relating to the Status of Refugees.

In addition to the grounds and the Supporting Affidavit of the Applicant, the Applicant's counsel Mr Otieno, instructed by the firm of Swaleh Kanyeki & Co. Advocates, also filed Skeleton Arguments dated 31 May 2005, together also with decided cases some of which I shall refer to in due course.

On their part, the Respondents through the Attorney-General filed a Replying Affidavit sworn on 24 March 2005 by one Evans Kinyanjui, an Immigration Officer attached to the Department of Immigration headquarters at Nairobi. The Attorney-General also prepared and filed on 30 October 2006 Skeleton Arguments dated 11 October 2006.

When this matter came for hearing before me on 20 November 2006, the Applicant was represented by Mr Otieno, while the Respondents were all represented by Mr Kaka, State counsel.

The Applicant's Case

The Applicant's case is that he is a refugee, and he is entitled to all the fundamental rights and freedoms as envisaged in the Universal Declaration of Human Rights 1948, the International Covenant on Civil and Political Rights, the United Nations Charter, the 1951 Convention Relating to the Status of Refugees and the 1969 OAU Convention on Specific Aspects of Refugee Problems in Africa, and more specifically as those rights are enshrined under Chapter V—Fundamental Rights and Freedoms of the Individual of the Kenya Constitution. Mr Otieno argued that detention of the Applicant after unsuccessful efforts to deport him was a breach of the Applicant's fundamental rights under the said Chapter of the Constitution, and that the Court should so find, and grant the several declarations sought as outlined above.

The Respondents' Case

The Respondents' case was, as expected, quite to the opposite. Mr Kaka, learned State counsel, argued that in essence, the Applicant's counsel's case was one seeking orders of *habeas corpus*—production of the Applicant and his release from police custody. Although Mr Otieno, the Applicant's counsel, in reply protested against this argument, in essence this was the Applicant's counsel's case, the release of the Applicant to the Interested Party, the United Nations High Commission for Refugees, Nairobi Office.

ANALYSIS OF THE APPLICATION

I will consider this application at two levels. Firstly in its narrow aspect, namely on the declarations sought that Sections 3 and 8 of the Immigration Act are in light of Sections 3, 47 and 123 of the Constitution inconsistent with the Constitution and are to the extent of such inconsistency void.

The second level of consideration of the application is what Mr Otieno, learned counsel for the Applicant, argued in his submissions to the court, namely that the Application was based upon the provisions of Section 84(1) of the Constitution which empowers any person who alleges that any fundamental rights and freedoms of the individual as enshrined in Sections 70–83 (inclusive) of the Constitution have been contravened or are threatened with contravention in relation to him, or in respect of a detained person, to file an application in the High Court and seek a redress and the court has wide discretion under Section 84(2) of the Constitution. Where appropriate the court has exercised its wide discretion and granted damages. Such was the case in *Marete* v. *Attorney-General* [1987] KLR 690, where Shields J awarded the Applicant his lost wages, as well as his capitalized pension, and also general damages. Such was also the case in *Dominic Arony Amolo* v. *Attorney-General* (HC Misc. Application No 494 of 2003) (unreported) where the three-judge bench awarded the Applicant damages, costs and interest.

These cases, as I shall presently show in discussing the first, and what I refer to as the narrow aspect of this Application, have no recourse to the Applicant's case. The Applicant does not seek any such redress of damages for his incarceration in police custody. The Applicant's contention is merely that his continued detention is unconstitutional in the sense that it is contrary to the provisions of Section 70(a) of the Constitution, although the application was vague and did not, contrary to the precedent in these matters that a party who alleges contravention of his fundamental rights or freedoms must state which right had been contravened, and the manner of such contravention, [state details of the contravention]. Section 70(a) provides as follows—

70. Whereas every person in Kenya is entitled to the fundamental rights and freedoms of the individual, that is to say, the right whatever his race, tribe, place of origin or residence or other local connection, political opinions, colour, creed or sex, but subject to the respect for the rights and freedoms of others and for the public interest, to each and all of the following, namely—

(a) life, liberty, security of the person and the protection of the law,
(b) . . .
(c) . . .

the provisions of this Chapter shall have effect for the purpose of affording protection to those rights and freedoms subject to such limitations of that protection as are contained in those provisions, being limitations designed to ensure that the enjoyment of those rights and freedoms by any individual does not prejudice the rights and freedoms of others or the public interest.

In this context the only issue to determine is whether the continued detention of the Applicant at the Kileleswa Police Station after aborted efforts to deport him is contrary to the said provisions of Section 70(a) of the Constitution.

Answer to the Narrow Issue

To answer this wider issue I will first revert to the narrow issue as set out above, and in the application, whether Sections 3 and 8 of the Immigration Act are contrary to the provisions of the Constitution and therefore void for being contrary to Section 3 of the Constitution which declares the supremacy of the Constitution and voids any other statute or law to the extent of the inconsistency. Section 3(1)(a)-(l) of the Immigration Act set out twelve incidences or descriptions of a prohibited immigrant. Section 3(1)(f), (h) and (k) are the most relevant in the case of the Applicant. Under those subsections, a prohibited immigrant means a person who is not a citizen of Kenya and who is—

(f) a person who, in consequence of information received from any government or from any other source considered by the Minister to be reliable, is considered by the Minister to be an undesirable immigrant;
(h) a person who, upon entering or seeking to enter Kenya, fails to produce a valid passport to an immigration officer on demand or within such time as that officer may allow;
(k) a person in respect of whom there is in force an order made or deemed to be made under Section 8 directing that such person shall be removed from and remain out of Kenya.

Although Section 3(3) of the Immigration Act confers upon an immigration officer power to issue a prohibited immigrant's pass to a prohibited immigrant, subsection 2 of the said Section prescribes that the entry and presence in Kenya of a prohibited immigrant is unlawful, and permission shall be refused to a person who is a prohibited immigrant whether or not he is in possession of any document which, were it not for this provision, would entitle him to enter Kenya.

Section 8(1) of the Immigration Act empowers the Minister to remove persons unlawfully in Kenya in these terms—

8(1) The Minister may, by order in writing, direct that any person whose presence in Kenya was, immediately before the making of that order, unlawful under this Act, or in respect of whom a recommendation has been made to him under Section 26A of the Penal Code, shall be removed from and remain out of Kenya either indefinitely or for such period as may be specified in the order.

(2) A person to whom an order made under this section relates shall—

(a) be removed to the place from whence he came, or *with the approval of the Minister, to a place in the country to which he belongs, or to any place to which he consents to be removed if the Government of that place consents to receive him*;

(b) if the Minister so directs, be kept in prison or in police custody until his departure from Kenya, and while so kept shall be deemed to be in lawful custody; ...
(4) any order made or directions given under this section may at any time be varied or revoked by the Minister by further order in writing; ...
(8) [until a decision has been made under this section *(for the removal of any person unlawfully in Kenya)*] the court may order that such person be detained in prison or in police custody for a period not exceeding fourteen days pending a decision by the Minister.

Mr Otieno, learned counsel for the Applicant, argued passionately in both his submissions and skeletal written arguments that the Application herein was brought against the backdrop of human rights, the spirit of upholding our own Constitution as outlined in Section 70 thereof, the protection of fundamental rights and freedoms of the individual and [embodying] all the tenets and/or characteristics of human rights, that is, universality, non-discrimination, inalienability, rights are equal and indivisible, internationally guaranteed, legally protected, protect[ing] both individuals and oblig[ing] State[s] and State actors as well as non-State actors.

HUMAN RIGHTS INSTRUMENTS IN INTERNATIONAL LAW

I have already made reference to the relevant provisions of the Constitution and the law of Kenya. I will now refer to the relevant instruments in international law on human rights and in particular in relation to the protection of refugees.

The Republic of Kenya (Kenya) is a player in the comity of nations, Kenya is an active member of the United Nations Organization and being a member thereof is also a member of its specialized agencies. By being a former Colony of Britain, Kenya is bound by the treaties and conventions made by Britain as a colonial power for itself and its erstwhile Colonies, Dominions and Overseas Territories. Such instruments include the Charter of the United Nations itself established as a consequence of the United Nations Conference on International Organization held at San Francisco and was brought into force on 26 June 1945 and the Statutes of the International Court of Justice, the 1948 Universal Declaration of Human Rights (described in the human rights field as the mother of all human rights documents), the 1951 Convention Relating to the Status of Refugees.

Kenya is, after Independence from Britain, a signatory to the 1967 Optional Protocol on the Status of Refugees, a member of the Charter of the Organization of African Unity and now the African Union and also a signatory to the 1969 OAU Convention on Specific Aspects of Refugee Problems in Africa.

These conventions, treaties and protocols all have one theme, the promotion and protection of human rights and with particular reference to the status of persons who for reasons of race, nationality, religion, colour, sex, language, political or other opinion, national or social origin, property, birth or other status are forced or obliged by circumstances to flee their homes and countries of origin. I will take a few examples.

1. *Universal Declaration of Human Rights (1948)*

Preamble
The General Assembly proclaims this Universal Declaration of Human Rights as a common standard of achievement for all peoples and all nations, to the end that every individual and every organ of society, keeping this Declaration constantly in mind, shall strive by teaching and education to promote respect for these rights and freedoms and by progressive measures, national and international, to secure their universal and effective recognition and observance, both among the peoples of Member States themselves and among the peoples of territories under their jurisdiction.

After the said preamble, Articles 1, 2, 3 and 9 provide—

Article 1
All human beings are born free and equal in dignity and rights. They are endowed with reason and conscience and should act towards one another in a spirit of brotherhood.

Article 2
Everyone is entitled to all the rights and freedoms set forth in this Declaration, without distinction of any kind, such as race, colour, sex, language, religion, political or other opinion, national or social origin, property, birth or other status. Furthermore, no distinction shall be made on the basis of the political, jurisdictional or international status of the country or territory to which a person belongs, whether it be independent, trust, non-self-governing or under any other limitation of sovereignty.

Article 3
Everyone has the right to life, liberty and security of person.

Article 9
No one shall be subjected to arbitrary arrest, detention or exile.

2. *International Covenant on Civil and Political Rights*

Article 2

Reiterates the provisions of the Universal Declaration of Human Rights above, as to non-discrimination, of any person within a State's territory on any ground, and

Article 2(3)(a)

Each State Party to the present Covenant undertakes—

(a) to ensure that any person whose rights or freedoms as herein recognized are violated shall have an effective remedy, notwithstanding that the violation has been committed by persons acting in an official capacity.

3. *Convention Relating to the Status of Refugees*

This Convention was adopted on 28 July 1951 by the UN Conference of Plenipotentiaries on the Status of Refugees and Stateless Persons convened under the General Assembly resolution 429(V) of 14 December 1950 and entered into force on 22 April 1954 in accordance with Article 43 thereof. For the purposes of this judgment the relevant provisions are Articles 3 (Non-discrimination), 31(1) and (2) (regarding refugees unlawfully in the country of refuge), 32 (Expulsion) and 33 (Prohibition of expulsion or return ("*refoulement*")), which I set out in full—

(1) *Article 3—Non-discrimination*

The Contracting States shall apply the provisions of this Convention to refugees without discrimination as to race, religion or country of origin.

(2) *Article 31—Refugees unlawfully in the country*

(1) The Contracting States shall not impose penalties, on account of their illegal entry or presence, on refugees who, coming directly from a territory where their life or freedom was threatened in the sense of Article 1, enter or are present in their territory without authorization, *provided they present themselves without delay to the authorities and show good cause for their illegal entry or presence* (emphasis mine).

(2) The Contracting States shall not apply to the movements of such refugees restrictions other than those which are necessary and such restrictions shall only be applied until their status in the country is regularized or they obtain admission into another country. The Contracting States shall allow

such refugees a reasonable period and all the necessary facilities to obtain admission into another country.

Article 32—Expulsion

(1) The Contracting States shall not expel a refugee lawfully in their territory save on grounds of national security or public order.
(2) The expulsion of such a refugee shall be only in pursuance of a decision reached in accordance with due process of law. Except where compelling reasons of national security otherwise require, the refugee shall be allowed to submit evidence to clear himself, and to appeal to and be represented for the purpose before competent authority or a person or persons specially designated by the competent authority.
(3) The Contracting States shall allow such a refugee a reasonable period within which to seek legal admission into another country. *The Contracting States reserve the right to apply during that period such internal measures as they may deem necessary* (emphasis mine).

Article 33—Prohibition of expulsion or return ("refoulement")

(1) No Contracting State shall expel or return ("*refouler*") a refugee in any manner whatsoever to the frontiers of territories where his life or freedom would be threatened on account of his race, religion, nationality, membership of a particular social group or political opinion.
(2) The benefit of the present provision may not, however, be claimed by a refugee whom there are reasonable grounds for regarding as a *danger to the security of the country in which he is, or who, having been convicted by a final judgment of a particularly serious crime, constitutes a danger to the community of that country* (emphasis mine).

ANALYSIS OF THE LAW AND FACTS

Those are the relevant provisions of the Constitution, the statute law of Kenya as well as the applicable articles of the relevant UN and OAU international conventions. The facts are not in dispute. They are set out in both the Supporting Affidavit of the Applicant which is somewhat skewed to the Applicant's situation, but more succinctly in the Replying Affidavit of Evans Kinyanjui, an Immigration Officer, a person charged with both the administration [and] implementation of the Immigration Act under the overall direction and supervision of the Principal Immigration Officer under the provisions of the Immigration Act, with specific statutory functions under Sections 3 and 8 of the said Act being reserved for the Minister responsible for matters relating to immigration. These are the facts—

(1) The Applicant did not arrive in Kenya as a refugee or an asylum seeker. He slipped into Kenya and failed to report to any immigration authorities of Kenya, or seek asylum, instead [he] approached the Interested Party, and sought to be accorded refugee status on the grounds that he was being persecuted in Iraq (paragraphs 5-6).

(2) Between 13 December 1999 and 21 April 2001, a period of approximately 678 days [*sic*], the Applicant went underground, until he was traced following receipt of information by the Immigration authorities to a Madrasa School in Eastleigh, a suburb of Nairobi, on 21 April 2001 (*paragraph 7*).

(3) Upon the Applicant's arrest the Applicant was found to be in possession of a Passport No 100604262, originating from Denmark, issued in the name of one Najjir Sharbebi Essa, not the Applicant (*paragraph 8*).

(4) Subsequent inquiries by the Kenyan authorities with the Royal Danish Embassy confirmed that the said passport had been lost in Denmark and that as such the Applicant had in his possession a forged document (*paragraph 9*).

(5) Further subsequent investigations carried out by the Kenyan Police and other security agencies established that the Applicant together with nine (9) other Iraq nationals had visited Somalia for reasons unknown and not referred to in the Applicant's supporting Affidavit, and the nine subsequently entered Kenya singly and illegally (*paragraph 10*).

(6) Following the Applicant's arrest, he was charged with the following offences—

(a) being in possession of a forged document;
(b) being unlawfully present in Kenya;
(c) failing to register as an alien;
(d) failing to report his entry into Kenya to the nearest Immigration Office.

(7) The Applicant pleaded guilty to the said offences, and was sentenced to four (4) months' imprisonment or a fine of Kshs 8,000 which the Applicant paid (paragraph 7 of the Applicant's Supporting Affidavit).

(8) The Applicant was placed under police custody pending the carrying out of the repatriation order (paragraphs 9, 11, 12 and 13 of the Replying Affidavit of Evans Kinyanjui).

(9) The Respondent's efforts to repatriate the Applicant to his country of origin, Iraq, were unsuccessful and the Applicant remained in police custody.

Those being the facts, the narrow and simple issue is whether the acts of the Respondents were contrary to the Constitution. The answer to this issue must clearly be in the negative. The facts and the relevant law clearly point to that conclusion.

The Applicant was a runaway fugitive from his country, Iraq, and the reasons whether he was fleeing from persecution for his political views or [whether] he was a criminal fugitive are really irrelevant for the purpose of this conclusion. The theory and practice in international law requires that a person fleeing his own country for whatever reason to another, or foreign, country will at the first instance upon entering that other country with or without proper entry papers (passport with or without visa, or appropriate endorsement) present himself to the immigration or security agents of that State. For instance, a soldier will show and surrender his weapon or firearm. A civilian will show his identity. The host or receiving country's authorities will usually keep such person under some protective custody or quarantine pending the determination of such person's status.

In notorious cases such as the erstwhile failed State of Somalia, and the war-ravaged Southern Sudan, the Kenya authorities would send such person or persons to the already established refugee camps, pending the processing of applications for refugee status, and find them countries willing to take such persons.

The Applicant's case is different from that scenario. The Applicant slipped into Kenya and failed to report his presence in Kenya to any of the Kenyan authorities responsible for refugees or political asylum seekers. He swears that he arrived in Kenya on 13 December 1999, that he presented himself to the UN Refugee Agency. The Agency did not report his presence in Kenya to any of the Kenyan authorities. The Applicant did not report to any of the Kenyan authorities responsible for immigration matters or registration of aliens. For the period 13 December 1999 to 14 September 2001 (when the Applicant was granted refugee status by the UN Refugee Agency), that is more than two-and-a-half years later [*sic*], the Applicant evaded and avoided the Kenyan authorities, until he was traced to an Islamic Madrasa School in the Eastleigh suburbs of Nairobi. Now to my mind, that is not a model refugee whatever the Applicant thought of his host country as a possible host for him as an asylum seeker.

Once found, and charged, the Applicant readily pleaded guilty to the charges, he was sentenced to imprisonment of four months, or a fine in lieu of such imprisonment. Having opted to pay the fine, he was not a free man. The other order of Court was for his repatriation to his country of origin. That order coupled with the Minister's declarations under Sections 3 and 8 of the Immigration Act that the Applicant was a prohibited immigrant could not be carried out. There were several reasons for this hitch. Iraq, the Applicant's country of origin, was suffering under the sanctions imposed by the United Nations Security Council. There were no direct flights between Kenya and that country. Worse still, the Applicant had conveniently no vital travel documents, and for which the Respondent had to arrange. The Applicant was denied transit through the United Arab Emirates, on 8 October 2001, and further attempts to remove the Applicant through the Hashemite Kingdom of Jordan in the year 2004 were also not successful.

The Applicant's counsel's argument that once attempts to repatriate the Applicant through the United Arab Emirates had failed, and that Applicant was returned to Kenya, then the Minister's order for removal lapsed, cannot be correct. I think it needs no interpretation of law to say that an order for removal of a prohibited immigrant is only completed when a prohibited immigrant has either been handed over to a third country which has agreed to take him as a refugee, or he has been placed under the authorities of his country of origin. This has not been done, or has not happened in the case of the Applicant. In making the orders for repatriation of the Applicant, the Minister was acting not merely pursuant to the provisions of Sections 3 and 8 of the Immigration Act but also of the Court orders of May 2001 made pursuant to Section 26A of the Penal Code which says—

26A. Where a person who is not a citizen of Kenya is convicted of an offence punishable with imprisonment... the court by which he is convicted, or any court to which his case is brought by way of appeal against conviction or sentence, may... recommend to the Minister... responsible for immigration that an order for removal from Kenya be made in accordance with section 8 of the Immigration Act.

In this case the Applicant having pleaded guilty, and having paid the fine in lieu of the full term of four months, there was hardly any question for an appeal, and there was also no application for stay of the order of repatriation. The effect of this is that both the orders of court and the Minister's order for removal of the Applicant from Kenya remain valid and are enforceable in accordance with their terms.

THE ANSWER TO THE NARROW CONSTITUTIONAL QUESTION

The answer to the narrow question whether or not Sections 3 and 8 of the Immigration Act are inconsistent with Section 3 of the Constitution must as stated above be in the negative. The answer further whether the Applicant's fundamental rights and freedoms of the individual have been contravened must also be in the negative as I shall presently show on the wider issue of human rights and the UN Convention Relating to the Status of Refugees.

OF HUMAN RIGHTS AND CONVENTIONS ON REFUGEES

Commencing perhaps within the Continent of Africa, the OAU (or now, the African Union) Convention Governing Specific Aspects of Refugee Problems in Africa is by Article 8 thereof declared to be an effective regional complement in Africa of the 1951 United Nations Convention on the Status of Refugees. Article 8 enjoins African States to cooperate with the office of the United Nations High Commission for Refugees. Article 5 allows voluntary repatriation of a refugee, but no refugee may be repatriated to his country of origin against his will.

I have already alluded to the prime theme of these conventions, namely the universal promotion or upholding and protection of human rights across the globe wherever human beings may be found irrespective of their stage of development or in particular of persons seeking asylum in foreign countries. The other equally important and complementary theme is the public interest and the need to maintain security and public order in the host State or State receiving asylum seekers whether on ground of religious persecution, their race (as happened in the infamous mass expulsion of citizens of Asian origin by Idi Amin in Uganda in the 1970s), nationality, social group or political opinion.

Whereas the United Nations Convention Relating to the Status of Refugees and indeed the Convention Governing Specific Aspects of Refugee Problems in Africa impose stringent obligations upon States not to turn away asylum seekers, even those who enter and remain in the State illegally, the conventions equally impose strict positive obligations upon an asylum seeker who is present in the country unlawfully, that is without the authorization of the relevant authorities of such country, or more specifically who fails to present himself without delay to the authorities and show good cause for his or their unlawful entry into the country, and their failure to present themselves, or himself, to such authorities (Article 31(1) of the United Nations Convention Relating to the Status of Refugees).

Now, in my book, any person not being a citizen of Kenya entering Kenya, without the necessary authorization, or in terms of the Immigration Act, without a valid visa or other permit or pass, and who fails to regularize his stay or presence in Kenya at the earliest possible opportunity does not qualify to be a refugee, that is, a person deprived of protection of his country of origin on account of persecution for reasons of race, religion, nationality, because of internal upheaval or breakdown of law and order, or aggression and occupation by foreign powers, [who] is unable to obtain such protection, and is for those reasons unwilling to return to his country of origin.

In my opinion, any person purporting to be a refugee, and who enters Kenya unlawfully, and fails to present himself to the relevant authorities of Kenya at the earliest [opportunity] does not qualify to be a refugee. Such a person is in my judgement a fugitive from his country of origin, and from the law of Kenya, and indeed the United Nations Convention Relating to the Status of Refugees and if he were a person from a member country of the former Organization of African Unity, and now the African Union, in contravention of the OAU Convention Governing the Specific Aspects of Refugee Problems in Africa. He is, or they are, prohibited immigrants under Section 3(1)(h) of the Immigration Act, and is liable, on conviction, to be repatriated to the country of origin under Section 26A of the Penal Code.

Speaking therefore from the point of view of the Constitution, these are persons whose rights have been limited and circumscribed in terms of Section 70(a) of the Constitution, and subjected to the rights of others and to the public interest. The public interest includes the right to life in a secure environment without fear of the loss of one's life or property by the ordinary citizens of the host or receiving State. The government of the host or receiving State, whose primary duty is the security of its citizens and their property, is bound to treat with extra caution any asylum seeker who sneaks into its country unannounced and plays a hide and seek game with such country's security personnel until he is caught and prosecuted, and ordered to be repatriated.

In that regard I would endorse and adopt the speech of Lord Pearce in *Chandler* v. *Director of Public Prosecutions* [1964] AC 763 (HL) where he said at page 813

Questions of defence policy are vast, complicated, confidential and wholly unsuited for ventilation before a jury. In such a context the interest of the state must in my judgement mean interests of the state according to the policies laid down for it by its recognized organs of government and authority, the policies of the state as they are, not as they ought, in the opinion of the jury, to be. Anything which prejudices those policies is within the meaning of the Act "prejudicial to the interests of the state".

In our context in the present case, questions of security and public order loom large, and are complicated and confidential, unsuitable for ventilation in public at large. In such context therefore, the primary policies of the government of the host country are as laid down in the Constitution (that all individual rights are subject to the enjoyment of those rights by other individuals and the public interest and are therefore not absolute) and the existing laws. Anything done by any person, and any person who acts contrary to those policies as set out in the law and the Constitution, acts in a manner prejudicial to the public interest within the meaning of the Constitution and the relevant law, in this case, the Immigration Act.

On both the narrow and wider issue whether the Respondents have contravened the fundamental rights and freedoms of the Applicant contrary to the provisions of Chapter V (the Bill of Rights) of the Constitution of Kenya, and the various United Nations and the African Union (successor to the Organization of African Unity) conventions relating to refugees, I am of the considered view that whereas the fundamental rights and freedoms are universal and the Constitution of Kenya does not make a distinction in the application of the Bill of Rights, as between citizen and non-citizen, that the Applicant (a foreigner and not a citizen of Kenya) is entitled to the protection of his fundamental rights and freedoms, subject only to the limitations as stated in Section 70 of the Constitution. The Respondents have neither contravened any provision of the Bill of Rights as set out in the Constitution of Kenya, nor contravened any provision of the said human rights conventions or conventions relating to status of refugees.

On the contrary, and it ought to be observed to the credit of the Respondents, the Applicant has, despite the standing orders of court for the repatriation of the Applicant, been accorded ample opportunity (over three years) to find a third country to host the Applicant. In the meantime, the Applicant has been kept in lawful custody (in terms of Section 8(2)(b) of the Immigration Act), again pending the finding by the Interested Party, the United Nations High Commission for Refugees, of a suitable third country which would accept and grant the Applicant a home as a refugee.

Besides, over the years of the Applicant's presence in Kenya following the Applicant's conviction for unlawful presence in Kenya and other offences on the Applicant's own plea of guilty, the Respondents have relaxed restrictions upon the Applicant. In those circumstances I am unable to say, as the Applicant prayed, that his fundamental rights and freedoms have been contravened contrary to the relevant provisions of the Constitution of Kenya. Having come to this conclusion, no constitutional law question arises for interpretation of the Constitution under Section 123 thereof, and reference to Section 47 of the Constitution (alteration of the Constitution) had no relevance.

For those reasons, I find no merit whatsoever with the Applicant's Originating Summons dated 9 November 2004, and the same is hereby dismissed with a direction that unless Kenya does accept to host the

Applicant as refugee, the Interested Party should find a third country to host the Applicant in terms of the United Nations Convention on the Status of Refugees.

On humanitarian grounds, and taking into account the Interested Party's correspondence with the Respondents that the Applicant may indeed have been a victim of persecution (in his country of origin) within the meaning of the relevant international instruments and in particular the United Nations Convention and its 1967 Protocol Relating to the Status of Refugees, I direct that each party, the Applicant, the Respondents and Interested Party shall bear their respective costs.

There shall be orders accordingly.

[Report: Transcript]

Relationship of international law and municipal law — Treaties — International human rights treaties and instruments — International Covenant on Economic, Social and Cultural Rights, 1966 — International Covenant on Civil and Political Rights, 1966 — Declaration of Human Rights of Individuals Who Are Not Nationals of the Country In Which They Live, 1985 — Constitution of Kenya 1963 — Interpretation — Whether Constitution of Kenya capable of giving effect to provisions of international human rights instruments to which Kenya a State party — Whether Constitution capable of giving effect to rights not expressly mentioned — Enforceability of rights by non-nationals

Human rights — Right to work and right to family life — Protection of rights to work and to family life under Constitution of Kenya 1963 and international human rights instruments — Enforceability of rights by non-nationals — Refusal of work permit — Whether refusal of work permit to non-national married to Kenyan national a breach of right to work and right to family life — Protection of fundamental rights in accordance with domestic law — Sections 5 and 8 of Immigration Act 1967 — Whether abuse of discretionary powers by executive — Whether reason and effect of denial of work permit a breach of applicant's rights — Separation of powers — Role of executive in maintaining public order and acting in the public interest — The law of Kenya

REPUBLIC OF KENYA v. MINISTER FOR HOME AFFAIRS AND OTHERS, *ex parte* SITAMZE

Kenya, High Court. 18 *April* 2008

(Nyamu J)

SUMMARY: *The facts*:—The applicant, a national of Cameroon married to a Kenyan woman, sought judicial review of the Ministry of Immigration's decision to refuse him a work permit required by foreign nationals wanting to engage in economic activity in Kenya. Permits were granted by immigration officers acting with discretionary powers provided by Section 5 of the Immigration Act 1967 (amended 1972).

The grant of the permit had been refused by the Principal Immigration Officer and, following the lack of a timely appeal, a deportation order had been issued against the applicant. Although the deportation order was subsequently challenged successfully in court, the applicant's passport and travel documents had been confiscated by the police, who he complained had subjected him to intimidation, harassment and inhuman treatment on the pretext of his apparent failure to possess valid immigration documents.

The applicant sought an order of *mandamus* to compel the grant of the permit and an order of prohibition to prevent the police from harassing him or hindering his free movement in Kenya. The applicant claimed that the refusal to grant the permit was discriminatory, unjust and unfair and affected his right to the enjoyment of his property under Section 75 of the Constitution of Kenya 1963 ("the Constitution"), his right to found a family under Article 5 of the Declaration of the Human Rights of Individuals Who Are Not Nationals of the Country In Which They Live (1985) ("the Declaration")[1] and his right to work as protected by Article 6(2) of the International Covenant on Economic, Social and Cultural Rights, 1966 ("the ICESCR").[2] He further contended that the confiscation of his passport was also in breach of his right to property under Section 75 of the Constitution and that his treatment by the police amounted to inhuman and degrading treatment contrary to Section 74(1) of the Constitution, Article 5 of the Declaration and Article 17 of the International Covenant on Civil and Political Rights, 1966 ("the ICCPR").[3]

The respondents replied that the discretionary powers under Section 5 of the Immigration Act entitled the Immigration Officer to refuse the applicant a permit. Since no appeal had been made, the Minister was entitled under Section 8 of the Act to declare the applicant a prohibited immigrant for the purposes of his removal from Kenya. The respondents also produced a classified document claiming the applicant was a threat to national security.

Held:—The application was dismissed.

(1) The Constitution of Kenya could be generously interpreted to recognize and give effect to fundamental rights provided for under international instruments or other treaties to which Kenya was a State party. However, these rights were not unlimited and, in the absence of express incorporation, international instruments or treaties could only be applied where ambiguities or gaps in the domestic law existed and where the instruments or treaties were not inconsistent with the Constitution (pp. 364-71).

(2) The respondents were entitled to use the discretionary powers under Section 5 of the Immigration Act to deny the applicant a permit. In doing so, they had not breached his right to work or to a family life.

(a) Under a broad interpretation of the Constitution and under Article 5(1)(d) of the Declaration, Article 6(1) of the ICESCR and other international instruments, the applicant had the right to work as regulated by domestic law (pp. 364-5).

(b) As a non-national, the applicant did not have an absolute right to a work permit, which had to be issued in accordance with domestic law (p. 367).

---

[1] United Nations General Assembly Resolution 40/144 (1985), UN Doc. A/RES/40/144.
[2] 16 December 1966, entered into force 3 January 1976, 993 UNTS 3.
[3] 16 December 1966, entered into force 23 March 1976, 999 UNTS 171, UN Doc. A/6316.

(c) The executive was best placed to take account of the State's national interests, including security concerns, and to regulate immigration matters. Under the Immigration Act, the Immigration Officer was entitled to a margin of appreciation on the issuance of work permits and the respondents had sufficiently demonstrated to the Court via the classified document that the applicant posed a security risk (pp. 367-70, 373).

(d) Although not expressly mentioned therein, the applicant's right to a family life was protected by the Kenyan Constitution. However, the effect of the denial of the work permit by the respondent had not constituted a breach of the applicant's right to a family life because the applicant could choose to emigrate to his country of origin and live there with his family (pp. 367-8, 371-2).

(3) Although the applicant was entitled to protection under Section 74(1) of the Constitution and Article 7 of the ICCPR, there was no evidence of torture or inhuman treatment by the Kenyan police. The right under the Constitution and ICCPR not to be subjected to torture or to cruel, inhuman or degrading treatment or punishment applied to all persons in Kenya, not just Kenyan citizens. However, the applicant had failed to show that the alleged infringement was tangible or had amounted to torture or inhuman treatment as envisaged by the Constitution or the ICCPR (pp. 361-3, 372).

(4) The applicant's passport was part of the right to liberty and the freedom of movement covered by Sections 72(1) and 81(1) of the Constitution. The confiscation of the passport was not therefore a breach of the applicant's right to property under Section 75 of the Constitution as claimed (pp. 363, 372).

The following is the text of the judgment of the Court:

The application before the court is dated 16 December 2004. The Applicant is a Cameroonian national married to a Kenyan lady. As a foreigner, the Applicant can only engage in economic interests after obtaining a work permit from the Ministry of Immigration. According to the statement, the Applicant has complied with the requirements of Rule 22 of the Immigration Act Chapter 172 Laws of Kenya.

The Minister for Home Affairs and the Principal Immigration Officer have refused to positively consider the Applicant's request for a class "H" permit.

The Applicant contends that he has been running his company Sileo Company Kenya Ltd with the aid of his wife Josephine Nyambura Thuo as exhibited by the trading licence, Articles of Association and certificate of analysis produced in this case. The Applicant's company has employed many Kenyans and it is financially healthy. The Applicant was also issued with a certificate of good conduct on 23 June 2003 by the Kenya police and as such the 1st Respondent has no good reason to deny the Applicant the class "H" permit.

The Applicant has also been constantly intimidated, harassed and subjected to inhuman treatment by the police on the pretext of failure to possess valid immigration documents.

The grounds upon which the reliefs are sought are:

1. The decision by the 1st and 3rd Respondents is discriminatory, unfair and unjust.
2. The Applicant has been deprived of his right to enjoy his property quietly in contravention of Section 75 of the Constitution of Kenya.
3. The Applicant shall be deprived of his right to found a family if he is deported, which is in contravention of Article 5 of the Declaration of Human Rights of Individuals Who Are Not Nationals of the Country In Which They Live.
4. The harassment and arrest of the Applicant by the 2nd Respondent amounts to inhuman and degrading treatment contrary to Section 74 of the Constitution as well as Article 5 of the Declaration of Human Rights.
5. The decision by the 1st Respondent to refuse the Applicant a class "H" permit contravenes Article 6(2) of the International Covenant on Economic, Social and Cultural Rights.
6. The Applicant has been deprived of his right to own and retain his property in contravention of Article 9 of the Declaration of Human Rights.
7. The decision of the 1st Respondent contravenes Article 1 of the Code of Conduct for Law Enforcement Officials.

The Applicant has sought reliefs as follows:

(a) An order of *mandamus* to compel the 1st Respondent to issue the Applicant with a class "H" work permit to enable the applicant to carry out his business lawfully.
(b) An order of prohibition to forbid the 2nd Respondent by himself and/or his servants and agents from intimidating, harassing, arresting and or hindering the Applicant's free movement on pretext of not being in possession of valid immigration documents.

The application is opposed by the Minister for Home Affairs, the Commissioner of Police and the Principal Immigration Officer, who are the three Respondents. All the parties have filed their written arguments and lists of authorities.

The Respondents' response relies heavily on the Immigration Act, especially Sections 5 and 8.

Section 5(1) states that there shall be classes of entry permits specified in the Schedule. Section 5(2) states that where a person, other than a prohibited immigrant, has made [an] application in the prescribed manner for an entry permit of a particular class, and has satisfied an immigration officer that he belongs to that class and that the conditions specified in the Schedule in relation to that class are fulfilled, the immigration officer may, in his discretion, issue an entry permit of that class to that person.

Section 5(3) states that any person who has applied for an entry permit of any of the classes E to M (inclusive) and who is aggrieved by a decision refusing him an entry permit may, in the manner and within the time prescribed, appeal against that decision to the Minister, whose decision shall be final and shall not be questioned in any court.

Section 8(1) states that the Minister may, by order in writing, direct that any person whose presence in Kenya was, immediately before the making of that order, unlawful under this Act, or in respect of whom a recommendation has been made to him under Section 26A of the Penal Code, shall be removed from and remain out of Kenya either indefinitely or for such period as may be specified in the order.

The Respondents contend the decision of the Immigration [officer] is made pursuant to Section 5(2) of the Immigration Act while the decision of the Minister is made pursuant to Section 8 of the said Act. The Respondents further contend that the quashing of the Minister's decision contained in the letter dated 1 April 2004 does not entitle the Applicant to seek orders of *mandamus* to compel the Immigration Officer to issue him with a permit as it amounts to urging the court to usurp the powers of the Executive/Immigration in issuing an entry permit.

The Respondents further contend that Section 5(2) of the said Act gives the Immigration Officer discretion to issue an entry permit when an application is made in a prescribed manner satisfying certain conditions. According to the Respondents, prayer (1) of the Applicant's Notice of Motion is misplaced and wholly bad in law for the reasons hereinunder:

(a) The Court cannot compel the doing of an act which is discriminatory upon the concerned public officer.
(b) The Court cannot exercise its powers of judicial review over merits of the decision by a public officer but rather the process of making the challenged decision.
(c) The Court cannot act as an appellate body over the decision made by the Immigration Officer to refuse the applicant a class "H" permit.
(d) The application is *res judicata* because although the Applicant had the knowledge that he had been refused an entry permit on

23 February 2004, he did not include a prayer for *certiorari* to quash the notification refusing him the entry permit.

The Respondents contend that the issue as to whether the Applicant should be mandatorily granted a class "H" permit or have the same renewed ought to have been canvassed in *Misc. Civil Application No 430 of 2004*. The Court has had the occasion to go through the pleadings and judgment of Hon. Justice J. B. Ojwang in the aforementioned case. The Applicant had sought prayers as follows:

(a) An order of *certiorari* to remove into the Court for the purposes of being quashed, the decision and order of the Minister for Home Affairs as contained in his letter dated 1 April 2004.
(b) An order of prohibition prohibiting the Respondents, by themselves or their agents, from deporting the Applicant.
(c) An order of *mandamus* compelling the 2nd Respondent to return the property of the Applicant seized on 20 March 2004.

The case was heard on merit and Hon. Justice J. B. Ojwang made the following orders:

(a) That an order of *certiorari* be and is hereby issued to remove into the court and quash the decision and order of the Minister for Home Affairs as contained in his letter dated 1 April 2004.
(b) That an order of prohibition be and is hereby issued prohibiting the Respondents by themselves or their agents from deporting the Applicant on the basis of the decision and order already quashed by the order set out hereinabove.
(c) That an order of *mandamus* be and is hereby issued, compelling the 2nd Respondent to return the property of the Applicant seized on 20 March 2004.

The Respondents contend that the decision to refuse the work permit or its renewal had been made by the 3rd Respondent as at the time of Honourable Mr Justice Ojwang's judgment and had not been quashed and the Applicant's prayer for an order of *mandamus* is intended to circumvent the law and its procedural requirements and further that the *mandamus* now being sought is *res judicata*.

The Respondents have further argued that the application before court is *res judicata* because although the Applicant knew that he had been refused an entry permit on 23 February 2004, he did not include a prayer for *certiorari* to quash the notification refusing him the permit. The Respondents contend that the issue of whether the Applicant should be mandatorily granted a class "H" permit or have the same renewed ought to have been canvassed in the aforementioned case, *Misc. Civil Application No 430 of 2004*.

In consideration of the above contention by the Respondents, it is not demonstrated to the Court how this instant application is *res judicata*. As I have earlier stated, the Court has had the advantage of going through the proceedings in *Misc. Application No 430 of 2004*. The Applicant in the aforesaid case was fighting against deportation which had already been ordered by the 1st Respondent. If the Applicant was deported everything else would have been overtaken by events. The Applicant's failure to apply for *certiorari* and *mandamus* in *Misc. Civil Application No 430 of 2004* cannot be a ground for alleging that the matter is *res judicata* for the following reasons. First, the Applicant can be lawfully in Kenya without necessarily requiring a work permit and as such one may not link his being in Kenya purely for working reasons and that is why he challenged the order to deport him. Secondly, the Applicant is seeking to enforce his right to work under the Constitution, International Covenant on Economic, Social and Cultural Rights, 1966 and the Declaration on the Human Rights of Individuals Who Are Not Nationals of the Country In Which They Live.

Therefore, going by the facts of the *Misc. Civil Application No 430 of 2004*, the argument that the application herein is *res judicata* has no merit. The prayers in both previous and instant case are quite distinct and the Court has jurisdiction to proceed and determine the prayers sought by the Applicant. The Respondents have cited the Court of Appeal decision in *Mburu Kinyua* v. *Gachini Tuti* [1978] KLR 69-82 where the Court quoted the Privy Council in *Yat Tung Investment Co. Ltd* v. *Dao Heng Bank Ltd* [1975] AC 581, 590 [quoting]:

> ... where a given matter becomes the subject of litigation in, and of adjudication by, a court of competent jurisdiction, the court requires the parties to that litigation to bring forward their whole case, and will not (except under special circumstances) permit the same parties to open the same subject of litigation in respect of the matter which might have been brought forward as part of the subject in contest, but which was not brought forward, only because they have, from negligence, inadvertence or even accident, omitted part of their case. The plea of *res judicata* applies, except in special cases, not only to points upon which the court was actually required by the parties to form an opinion and pronounce a judgment, but to every point which properly belonged to the subject of litigation, and which the parties, exercising reasonable diligence, might have brought forward at the time.

As earlier noted, this instant application is not *res judicata* because Hon. Justice J. B. Ojwang did not consider the issues of the Applicant's right to work as well as his passport and no judgment was pronounced on the two issues. However, even if the Court was to find that *certiorari* and *mandamus* orders ought to have been sought in the *Misc. Civil Application No 430 of 2004*, there are special circumstances in this case which would necessitate the reopening in this case. Since Hon. Justice J. B. Ojwang quashed the deportation of the Applicant, who runs a company, which is lawfully registered in Kenya, there is no way he could have enjoyed the fruits of his earlier judgment without the orders sought herein. Further, in the *Misc. Civil Application No 430 of 2004*, the Applicant was faced with imminent deportation and the day he was declared a prohibited immigrant is the day he came to court under certificate of urgency. The Court has noted that even the pleadings in *Misc. Civil Application No 430 of 2004* were filed by M/s Kathambi Kinoti Advocates and later the case was prosecuted by Dr Khaminwa on behalf of the Applicant. Whichever way one looks at this case, the Respondents' argument on *res judicata* must fail and the Court finds that it has no merit.

The Respondents urge this Honourable Court to refer to its earlier decision in *Republic* v. *Judicial Service Commission, ex parte Pareno* [2004] KLR 1 at pages 212-13, wherein the Court held that judicial review is principally concerned with the decision-making process and not the merit of a decision.

The Respondents contend that prayer 2 of the Notice of Motion is also misplaced, misconceived and wholly bad in law for the following reasons:

(i) The orders are abstracts and unenforceable.
(ii) The Applicant is seeking Court orders to prohibit the Respondents from implementing the law thereby urging the Court to partake in an illegality.

The Respondents urge the Court to depart from the decision of Hon. Justice J. B. Ojwang in *Misc. Civil Application No 430 of 2004* to the extent that it addressed the merits of the decision which is the subject matter of the Judicial Review instead of the process through which the decision was reached. However, this Court rejects the invitation firstly [because] it cannot review another judge's judgment on any point and secondly because the new circumstances affecting the application were never canvassed before Hon. Justice Ojwang. Courts in judicial review have sometimes to deal with the same matter but under different circumstances.

The Respondents contend that Section 5 of the Act gives discretionary powers to the Immigration Officer and provides room for appeal against the refusal to grant an entry permit by the Minister. When a person has been refused an entry permit by an immigration officer and no appeal is filed in the prescribed manner and within the prescribed time, the person becomes a prohibited immigrant and the Minister is right under Section 8 of the Immigration Act to declare such a person a prohibited immigrant for purposes of his removal from Kenya. The Applicant has confirmed that he did not appeal to the Minister against the refusal to grant him or renew the entry permit which renders him a prohibited immigrant.

The Respondents have further argued that the Applicant has not filed a constitutional petition to declare the provisions of the Immigration Act unconstitutional for breach of fundamental rights or as being inconsistent with the values and principles of the United Nations Millennium Declarations or any treaty and as such they are irrelevant to the Applicant's case.

The Applicant has relied on two lists of authorities dated 27 April and 27 July 2007. The latter is a supplementary one. The two lists of authorities cite thirty-one (31) authorities which inter alia include the Immigration Act, local cases, international instruments and judicial colloquium.

The Applicant, who is a foreigner, contends that he has complied with all the requirements of Rule 22 of the Immigration Act Chapter 172 Laws of Kenya and should have been therefore positively considered by the 1st Respondent for the issuance of a class "H" permit. The Immigration Act at the Schedule states:

A person who intends to engage, whether alone or in partnership, in a specific trade, business or profession (other than a prescribed profession) in Kenya, and who:

(a) has obtained, or is assured of obtaining, any licence, registration or other authority or permission that may be necessary for the purpose, and
(b) has in his own right and at his full and free disposition sufficient capital and other resources for the purpose, and whose engagement in that trade, business or profession will be to the benefit of Kenya.

The Applicant has suffered great losses arising from the refusal of the 1st Respondent to issue him with the said permit because he cannot attend to his business without breaking the law.

The *Judicial Review of Administrative Action* by S. A. de Smith (2nd Edition) page 462 gives an insight as to why the Applicant has sought the order of *mandamus* against the 1st Respondent, and it reads as follows:

In mandamus cases it is recognized that when a statutory duty is cast upon a crown servant in his official capacity and the duty is one owed not to the crown but to the public, any person having a sufficient legal interest in the performance of the duty may apply to the courts for an order of mandamus to enforce it . . .

The Supreme Court Practice 1979 53/1 14/4 commonly known as the White Book also outlines the principles to be followed when considering an application for the order of *mandamus*. The Applicant contends that the order is discretionary but it is made where there is a legal right to the act and no other specific and equally convenient or effective remedy against officers of the State who are obliged by statute to do some ministerial act in favour of the person applying.

The Applicant contends that in deciding whether or not to issue the order of *mandamus*, the Court should be in a position to answer the five (5) questions outlined hereinbelow:

1. Is the Applicant eligible [for] a class "H" permit?
2. Has the Applicant met all the requirements of Rule 22 of Cap 172 of the Laws of Kenya?
3. Does the Applicant have a criminal record?
4. Is the Applicant's company self-sustaining?
5. Did the Minister use his discretionary powers as he should have?

The Applicant further argues that he applied for orders of prohibition against the 2nd Respondent because he and his family have been subject of arbitrary and abusive treatment at their home and place of business on several occasions. The Applicant's honour and reputation have been subjected to unlawful attack by the 2nd Respondent without any lawful reason, which amounts to inhuman and degrading treatment.

The Applicant relies on Supreme Court Practice 1979 to urge his prayer for order of prohibition.

An order of prohibition lies to restrain an inferior court from exceeding its jurisdiction. For this purpose any body of persons is a court if it has legal authority to determine questions affecting the right of subjects and is under a duty to act judicially [*R* v. *Electricity Commissioners* [1924] 1 KB 171 Atkin LJ at page 204] . . . Excess of jurisdiction includes a case where the error of the inferior court involves doing something which is contrary to the general laws of the land or so vicious as to violate some fundamental principles of justice.

The Applicant contends that the police have exceeded their jurisdiction or are exercising jurisdiction not vested in them because their duty to maintain law and order cannot be interpreted to mean that they can harass, mistreat and arbitrarily arrest the Applicant on suspicion that he is illegally in Kenya purely because he is a foreigner. The Applicant further submits that the Court has discretion on whether or not to make the order and the order should be made in favour of the person directly affected by the proceedings of the inferior tribunal whether the defect is latent or not.

The Applicant also relies on both local and international laws which protect the fundamental rights of an individual which the Applicant alleges have been interfered with by the police through his constant harassment. Section 74(1) of the Constitution of Kenya has been cited and it provides that:

No person shall be subject to torture or to inhuman treatment or degrading punishment or other treatment.

Article 17 of the International Covenant on Civil and Political Rights (1966), also relied upon by the Applicant, depicts the importance of the fundamental right of the individual and is couched as follows:

(1) No one shall be subjected to arbitrary or unlawful interference with his privacy, family, home or correspondence, nor to unlawful attacks on his honour and reputation.
(2) Everyone has the right to the protection of the law against such interference or attacks.

The Applicant further relies on Article 2(3)(a) and (b) of the same Covenant, which states:

Each State Party to the present Covenant undertakes:

(a) To ensure that any person whose rights or freedoms as herein recognized are violated shall have an effective remedy, notwithstanding that the violation has been committed by persons acting in an official capacity;
(b) To ensure that any person claiming such a remedy shall have his right thereto determined by competent judicial, administrative or legislative authorities, or by any other competent authority provided for by the legal system of the State, and to develop the possibilities of judicial remedy.

The Applicant urges that this Honourable Court is the only authority that can aid him to realize his rights. He has been deprived of his passport and other travel documents, which is in contravention of Section 75(1) of the Constitution of Kenya which provides:

No property of any description shall be compulsorily taken possession of, and no interest in or right over property of any description shall be compulsorily acquired, except where the following conditions are satisfied ...

The Applicant argues that the Respondents have not only kept in their possession vital travel documents but that the 1st Respondent's refusal to issue him with a class "H" permit has interfered with his property in that he is unable to use, enjoy or dispose of it as he wills. The Applicant submits that the need to protect an individual's right of ownership of property is underscored by the reason that even international bodies have come up with laws to govern these rights. He has cited the International Covenant on Economic, Social and Cultural Rights of 1966, Article 1 of which states:

(1) All peoples have the right of self-determination. By virtue of that right they freely determine their political status and freely pursue their economic, social and cultural development.
(2) All peoples may, for their own ends, freely dispose of their natural wealth and resources without prejudice to any obligations arising out of international economic cooperation, based upon the principle of mutual benefit, and international law. In no case may a people be deprived of its own means of subsistence.

The Minister for Home Affairs is mandated under the Immigration Act Chapter 172 to issue work permits to foreigners who have complied with all the requirements thereof and the Applicant is one of such foreigners. In discharging his mandate as per the Act, it must be appreciated that the 1st Respondent is the best judge of merit pertaining to issuance of work permits. Parliament clearly vests the aforesaid mandate to the 1st Respondent and it would be wrong in the view of this Court to intervene with the merits of the decision by the 1st Respondent. This Court can only intervene in the following situations:

1. Where there is abuse of discretion.
2. Where the decision maker exercises discretion for an improper purpose.
3. Where the decision maker is in breach of the duty to act fairly.
4. Where the decision maker has failed to exercise statutory discretion reasonably.
5. Where the decision maker acts in a manner to frustrate the purpose of the Act donating the power.
6. Where the decision maker fetters the discretion given.
7. Where the decision maker fails to exercise discretion.
8. Where the decision is irrational and unreasonable.

Turning on to the orders of prohibition, as the Court has already noted, some decisions are best made by the persons or bodies mandated to do so. The duty to maintain law and order or to prevent commission of crime is vested in the Kenya police under Section 14 of the Police Act Chapter 84, which states:

The Force shall be employed in Kenya for the maintenance of law and order, the preservation of peace, the protection of life and property, the prevention and detection of crime, the apprehension of offenders, and the enforcement of all laws and regulations with which it is charged.

In discharging the mandate given to the Kenya police force, by Section 14 of the Police Act, similarly, the best judge of merit pertaining to maintenance of law and order as well as prevention and detection of crime is the 2nd Respondent and not the courts. It would be wrong for the Court to interfere with the merit of the decision by the police. Again this Court can only intervene in the following situations:

1. Where there is abuse of discretion by the police in discharging the same.
2. Where the police exercise their discretion for an improper purpose.
3. Where the police are in breach of the duty to act fairly.
4. Where the police act in a manner to frustrate the intentions of the Act donating the power.
5. Where the police act in an irrational and unreasonable manner while discharging their duties.

As the Court has noted, the case herein deals with an Applicant who is a foreigner and before addressing the above-mentioned issues, the Court must first settle the following:

(i) Is the Applicant as a foreigner entitled to the benefits and protection which accrue to the Kenyan citizens under the Constitution of Kenya as regards the provisions cited?
(ii) If the Applicant cannot rely on the Constitution of Kenya to enforce his rights, can he count on international law to achieve the same end?

The Applicant alleges contravention of Sections 74 and 75 of the Constitution. The case presents a new challenge to the Court as the Applicant is a foreigner. Section 74(1) of the Constitution prohibits torture or inhuman treatment or degrading punishment or other treatment. Although the Applicant as a foreigner may not have the same standing as the Kenyan citizens in respect of some of the rights in the Constitution, Section 74(1) is available to protect the Applicant because it applies to all persons and it echoes human rights which are recognized by all modern and democratic societies and Kenya is one of such States.

Further, the provisions of Section 74(1) of the Constitution of Kenya are echoed in Article 7 of the International Covenant on Civil and Political Rights, 1966, which states:

No one shall be subjected to torture or to cruel, inhuman or degrading treatment or punishment ...

The Kenyan provision applies to all persons and not only to citizens.

As demonstrated both by Section 74(1) of the Constitution of Kenya and Article 7 of the International Covenant on Civil and Political Rights, 1966, the Applicant has a right as a foreigner not to be subjected to torture, inhuman or degrading treatment or punishment both under the Constitution and also under the Covenant on Civil and Political Rights. The right cuts across the board, and it is inherent in mankind. However, the Applicant must demonstrate that Section 74(1) has been infringed in relation to him.

The onus of demonstrating that Section 74(1) of the Constitution has been infringed is purely on the Applicant. Although the Applicant's right under Section 74(1) of the Constitution is guaranteed, evidence must be availed to the Court to determine if there is any infringement. In order to determine whether the Applicant's rights under Section 74(1) of the Constitution have been infringed, the Court must define the meaning of torture, inhuman treatment or degrading punishment.

According to *Black's Law Dictionary* 8th Edition, torture means "infliction of intense pain to the body or mind to punish, to extract a confession or information or to obtain sadistic pleasure". The said dictionary has also quoted another definition by James Heath in his text, *Torture and English Law* 3 (1982):

By torture I mean infliction of physically founded suffering or the threat to immediately inflict it, where such infliction or threat is intended to elicit, or such infliction is incidental to means adopted to elicit, matter of intelligence or forensic proof and the motive is one of military, civic or ecclesiastical interest.

In the case of *Ireland* v. *United Kingdom* (1978) 2 EHRR 25 (Eur. Ct of Human Rights), the court referred to torture as deliberate inhuman treatment causing very serious and cruel suffering.

Further, the said dictionary defines inhuman treatment as physical or mental cruelty so severe that it endangers life or health. Inhuman treatment was for the first time in International Humanitarian Law defined by the [ICTY] Trial Chamber in the *Čelebići Camp Case* [No IT-96-21-T at para. 543] as an intentional act or omission, that is an act which, judged objectively, is deliberate and not accidental, which causes serious mental or physical suffering or injury or constitutes a serious attack on human dignity.

I have considered the facts of this case and in particular the averments of the Applicant. There is absolutely no evidence of torture or inhuman treatment by the Kenya police. As earlier noted, all rights have their limitations. The alleged infringement of Section 74(1) of the Constitution must be tangible and not imagined or deduced from the existing circumstances. The Applicant's evidence falls far below what torture or inhuman treatment envisage either in the Constitution of Kenya or under the International Covenant on Civil and Political Rights, 1966 (ICCPR).

The Applicant has also relied on Section 75 of the Constitution. He alleges that his passport has been compulsorily taken away from him in contravention of Section 75 of the Constitution. The application is misconceived as regards the status of a passport which is described as property. A passport is not a property for purposes and intent of Section 75 of the Constitution. This Court has already made a decision on the issue of a passport. In *Deepak Chamanlal Kamani* v. *Principal Immigration Officer and Two Others*, Petition No 199 of 2007, the Court held that a passport is part of the right to liberty and the right of movement under Sections 72(1) and 81(1) of the Constitution. I therefore, without going further, find that the passport is not property and that the Applicant has not demonstrated in the least sense how his property has been compulsorily taken away from him. The Applicant has also offended the rules contained in Legal Notice No 6 of 2006 and which Rules were in turn made pursuant to s 84(6) of the Constitution. The Applicant has come before the Court under a Judicial Review application instead of a Constitutional Application and the Court cannot conclusively deal with the passport which as earlier observed is a part of right to liberty and right of movement. The upshot is that the application before the Court is incompetent.

I have addressed the application of international instruments and in particular the International Covenant on Economic, Social and Cultural Rights, 1966 (ICESCR) vis-à-vis the right to work. Kenya has ratified the Covenant and the Court cannot just wish away an Applicant who insists on his rights guaranteed in the instrument. Article 6 of the Covenant states:

(1) The States Parties to the present Covenant recognize the right to work, which includes the right of everyone to the opportunity to gain his living by

work which he freely chooses or accepts, and will take appropriate steps to safeguard this right.

(2) The steps to be taken by a State Party to the present Covenant to achieve the full realization of this right shall include technical and vocational guidance and training programmes, policies and techniques to achieve steady economic, social and cultural development and full and productive employment under conditions safeguarding fundamental political and economic freedoms to the individual.

Under the International Covenant on Economic, Social and Cultural Rights, 1966, the right to work is one of the fundamental rights. It is necessary not only for the material well being of the Applicant but also for the harmonious development of his personality. This area of human rights has grown at a faster speed and our Constitution is somehow behind. However, since Kenya is a State that is a party to the aforesaid Covenant, the Court must rise to the occasion in addressing, recognizing and giving remedies under the Covenant. To give effect to the human rights provided for under the International Covenant on Economic, Social and Cultural Rights, 1966, the Court should interpret the Constitution generously to reflect a dynamic and progressive society. The Court should bear in mind that the rights under the Covenant are intended to be guaranteed by each party State and effectively redressed whenever infringed. The Constitution of Kenya at Section 1A states that the Republic of Kenya shall be a multiparty democratic State. Section 1 also provides that Kenya is a sovereign State. Sovereignty is internally vested in the people of Kenya. Multiparty democracies are modern and progressive States which are evolving every day towards making the world a universal entity in terms of social, economic and political issues. With the above provisions in mind, the Court is inclined to hold the view that social, economic and cultural rights are part and parcel of a multiparty democracy and particularly because Kenya has ratified the instrument. There is no doubt that under a broad interpretation, the Applicant is entitled to the right to work under the Constitution of Kenya and can seek redress if the same is infringed. However, the Applicant as a foreigner is also subject to the Declaration on the Human Rights of Individuals Who Are Not Nationals of the Country In Which They Live, 1985. The Applicant is also relying on the instrument to enforce his rights. Article 5(1)(d) states:

Aliens shall enjoy in accordance with domestic law . . . in particular the right to choose a spouse, to marry, to found a family.

I have no doubt that the Applicant is entitled to found a family under the aforementioned instrument but as earlier noted all rights are subject to limitations. Even considering Article 5(1)(d) quoted above, a non-national such as the Applicant can only enjoy his rights in accordance with the domestic law. A closer look at the preceding Article 4 captures the spirit and the scope of enjoyment of rights by foreigners. Article 4 states:

Aliens shall observe the laws of the State in which they reside or are present and regard with respect the customs and traditions of the people of that State.

In the context of the case before the Court, the applicant cannot demonstrate and has not demonstrated any discrimination in the application of the municipal immigration laws of Kenya to him. The Kenyan immigration law is not in conflict with any of the Covenants relied on or the provisions of the Constitution.

FINDINGS

1. Our Constitution is silent on the right to work as is the case with the other economic, social and cultural rights.
2. This Court has no doubt that the right to work is the first of the specific rights recognized in the International Covenant on Economic, Social and Cultural Rights (ICESCR). Thus under Article 6(1) the Covenant provides for the right to work which includes "the right of everyone to the opportunity to gain his living by work" and the Article further provides that the full realization of the right shall include technical and vocational guidance and training programmes.
3. Article 23 of the Universal Declaration of Human Rights (UDHR) guarantees everyone "the right to work, to free choice of employment, to just and favourable conditions of work and to protection against unemployment".
4. Article 1(2) of ILO Convention No 122 states that each member shall ensure that there is work for all who are available for and seeking work.
5. Article 15 of the African Charter on Human and Peoples' Rights provides:

    Every individual shall have the right to work under equitable and satisfactory conditions, and shall receive equal pay for equal work.

6. It is clear to the Court that the language of the Covenant on Economic, Social and Cultural Rights is inclusive and that the rights of the Covenant are granted to everyone and the rights

in the Covenant are not restricted to the nationals of the State Parties.
7. In the *R* v. *RM* suing through Kavindo HCC 1351 of 2002 a two-judge bench of the High Court made a finding that international human rights instruments and other treaties apply even without specific domestication where there are ambiguities or gaps in the domestic law and where the instruments are not inconsistent with the Constitution. The High Court dealt at length with the relevance and application of the Bangalore Principles as well. It is not intended to restate the law again in this decision. It is however useful to reproduce Articles 7 and 8 of the Bangalore Principles.

P7
It is within the proper nature of the judicial process and well-established judicial functions for national courts to have regard to international obligations which a country undertakes—whether or not they have been incorporated into domestic law—for the purpose of removing ambiguity or uncertainty from national constitutions, legislation or common law.

P8
However, where national law is clear and inconsistent with the international obligation of the State concerned, in common law countries the national court is obliged to give effect to national law. In such cases the court should draw such inconsistency to the attention of the appropriate authorities since the supremacy of national law in no way mitigates a breach of an international legal obligation which is undertaken by a country.

I have no intention of restating the position here except to repeat the same findings. I find that there is nothing in the Constitution that prevents the Court from upholding the right to work, especially where the individual has created the right as in the case before me, where the applicant's company has generated employment for himself and others. Constitutions speak to the people, their vision, their values, their obligations and aspirations.

8. Again in the case of *Rogers Mwema* v. *Attorney-General* (*Titanium Case II*) I did make an observation concerning the extent of State obligations in human rights under international instruments and the Bill of Rights, where I set aside a draft bill of costs in the issue of shs 200 million in a human rights case.

In this case, I think it is apt to restate the State obligation as regards economic, social and cultural rights. The treatment which

States owe to non-nationals (and nationals) under the ICESCR have been conceptualized as covering three levels of State obligations:

- the duty to respect;
- the duty to protect;
- the duty to fulfil.

The obligation to respect requires the State to abstain from interfering with the freedom of the individual. The obligation to protect requires the State to prevent other individuals from interfering with the rights of the individual. The obligation to fulfil requires the State to take necessary measures to ensure satisfaction of the needs of the individual that cannot be secured by the personal efforts of that individual alone. The latter obligation is central to economic, social and cultural rights and is the basis of the State's duty to progressively realize the rights of the ICESCR.

9. I therefore uphold the Applicant's counsel's contention and citations of the international human rights instruments with special emphasis on the right to work. Work might not exist for everyone but shall progressively become a State obligation to provide directly or by creating an enabling environment. No doubt, the State party cannot frustrate a non-national or a national who has created work for himself and others as in this case, because she would be in breach of the ICESCR and as expounded herein also in breach of the Constitution. In situations such as set out in the facts where the applicant has created employment the State obligation is both to respect and protect the right to work.

10. Having made the observation in 9 above, I wish to add that work permits are not an automatic entitlement and have to be issued in accordance with the domestic law and each State does have a margin of appreciation to take into account local needs and circumstances before granting them. Each application has to be considered on its merits and in accordance with the provisions of the Immigration Act. A temporary residence permit or work permit or any other permit specified in the Immigration Act to an alien or non-national spouse could be refused on reasonable grounds and in the national interest.

11. Although the current Constitution does not expressly mention the right to family life, I find that following its recognition in international treaties and its protection under the treaties in a variety of ways, it is constitutionally protected in Kenya taking

into account the central position the family occupies in the hierarchy of values in the Kenyan society as a whole and because of deep cultural roots the family unit has occupied since time immemorial in the Kenyan societies.

Marriage and family are of vital importance to nearly all the societies on earth and Kenyan society is one of them. Human dignity is of fundamental importance to any society including Kenya and is indeed a foundational value which informs the interpretation of many and perhaps all other fundamental rights. It follows therefore [that] the right to enter into and sustain permanent intimate relationships is part of the human dignity. Entering into and sustaining a marriage relationship is of defining significance for many people, including the applicant. In turn the central aspect of marriage is cohabitation and the right and duty to live together. Any limitation on this right must therefore be based on some law and it must be reasonable, proportionate and aimed at addressing a pressing social need. Permits must therefore be issued to applicants who qualify as per the requirements of the domestic law as defined therein except where there are pressing social needs to the contrary or where grant, extension, or renewal of the permits constitutes a real threat to the public.

12. In the case of the Applicant the State has, using a classified document, demonstrated that the presence of the Applicant and any such issue or renewal of a permit [poses] a threat to national security or interest and the State is entitled to a margin of appreciation in denying any such issue or extension on grounds of national security on the ground that its grant, renewal or extension would pose a real threat to the public and the Court is so satisfied. The State is entitled to take into account security concerns when administering the immigration laws. I am satisfied that such a threat does exist. In terms of entitlement to work permits, I adopt the reasoning in the South African case of *Dawood and Another* v. *Minister of Home Affairs* and, as regards respect for family life, I adopt the reasoning of the Strasbourg Court in the case of *Abdulaziz, Cabales and Balkandali* v. *United Kingdom* to the effect that contracting parties/States enjoy a wide margin of appreciation in determining the steps to be taken in ensuring compliance with the convention or treaties with regard to the needs and resources of the community and of the individual and, above all, I dare add, considerations of national security or threats [posed] to the State by the residence of a non-national such as the Applicant cannot be ignored by the Court.

DUTY OF COURT

While it is clear to the Court that economic, social and cultural rights including the right to work are not specifically mentioned in the Constitution, it is equally clear that under s 75 of the Constitution some rights and interests are recognized and have been enforced by the High Court as the Constitutional Court over the years. It is also not lost to the Court that in the recent past the High Court has given an expanded meaning to the meaning of life under s 71 of the Constitution. In addition, this Court recognizes the principle of indivisibility of human rights and their interdependency. As it is not disputed that Kenya is a signatory to the International Covenant on Economic, Social and Cultural Rights, and therefore in so far as the Covenant rights are not inconsistent with the Constitution the Court has a duty to recognize them and apply them where appropriate, as Kenya as a member State has specific obligations under the Covenant, which obligations, in turn, demand both judicial interpretation and in some cases judicial remedies. It follows therefore the Covenant's rights cannot be said to be outside the Court's role or mandate and in my view they are justiciable. The principle of indivisibility of human rights and interpency alluded to above means that since the fundamental rights and freedoms under Chapter 5 of the Constitution on Civil and Political Rights share that indivisibility and interdependence the rights are inseparable.

The other good reason for the Court not to abdicate its role is that the Covenant (ICESCR) of 1966 does in a singular way express the reasons why democracies and progressive governments exist. Governmental power is largely aimed at achieving social justice. Justice Hedge expressed the same point in the Indian case of [*Chandra Bhavan Boarding* v. *State of Mysore* 1970 2 SCR 600] as follows:

The mandate of the Constitution is to build a welfare society in which justice, social, economical and political, shall inform all institutions of our national life. The hopes and aspirations aroused by the Constitution will be belied if the minimum needs of the lowest of our citizens are not met.

Thus, despite the fact that many States especially the developing States face many economic and social problems, the rights expressed in the Covenant have been and remain a legal tool, aimed at achieving a steady improvement in the living conditions of the people in each State regardless of the means and resources available. A State's ability to direct its policy to achieving even the barest minimum in satisfying the Covenant rights is necessary. Governmental powers and governance must of necessity and in practical terms be directed to fulfilling the rights set out both in the Political and Civil Rights (ICCPR) and the Economic, Social and Cultural Rights (ICESCR) Covenants in order to in turn achieve governmental development goals. It follows therefore [that] although the civil and political rights have been largely and specifically provided for in the Constitution in (Chapter 5), the ICESCR rights do in my view constitute foundational values in any democracy and would be covered as attributes of a democratic society as contemplated in s 1 and s 1A of the Constitution. A democratic society has been defined to include a society which respects human rights. The ICESCR rights constitute in my view foundational values under s 1 and s 1A of the Constitution quite apart from constituting international State obligations for Kenya. In Kenya a good example of the State's recognition of these rights is the recently introduced compulsory primary education—this is indeed one of the (ICESCR) Covenant's rights. The Government itself took an executive decision to introduce the project. What is now left is legislation to provide for sanctions for default in the primary education project. Granted that in practice most (ICESCR) rights demand both administrative action and remedies, this does not oust the Court's role.

The reality on the ground is that the Covenant's rights entail both a legal duty of immediate enforcement to achieve the basic minimum (subject to resource availability) and an allowance for progressive realization of the rights which cannot be immediately enforced due to resource constraints, for example in developing countries.

In order to underscore the scope of [the] (ICESCR) Covenant it is important to reproduce herein the relevant Article which does embrace the requirements as outlined above.

Article 2 of the International Covenant on Economic, Social and Cultural Rights, 1966 (ICESCR) reads as follows:

(1) Each State Party to the present Covenant undertakes to take steps, individually and through international assistance and co-operation, especially economic and technical, to the maximum of its available resources, with a view to achieving progressively the full realization of the rights recognized in the present Covenant by all appropriate means, including particularly the adoption of legislative measures.

(2) The State Parties to the present Covenant undertake to guarantee that the rights enunciated in the present Covenant will be exercised without discrimination of any kind as to race, colour, sex, language, religion, political or other opinion, national or social origin, property, birth or other status.

(3) Developing countries, with due regard to human rights and their national economy, may determine to what extent they would guarantee the economic rights recognized in the present Covenant to non-nationals.

It is therefore evident that the Covenant rights apply to both nationals and non-nationals pursuant to this Article. Thus under provision (3) above Kenya would be perfectly entitled to regulate the issue of work permits by law and she has a margin of appreciation, that has to take into account the needs of her nationals and also take into account the national interest including security concerns. A non-national such as the Applicant cannot properly argue that the right is absolute because it is subject to the margin of appreciation accorded to each State and also subject to the national interest including security concerns. The need to comply with the requirements of the immigration laws and regulations is embraced by the Article.

Finally, on justiciability of the Covenant rights it is pertinent to observe that whereas in many cases administrative remedies are contemplated as the effective remedies, where a (ICESCR) Covenant right cannot be made fully effective without some role of the judiciary, judicial remedies would still be necessary and the courts must be involved.

Turning to the facts of the case before me, I find that it would not be right for Kenya to discriminate against a non-national where he has created legitimate employment for himself and his family but where there are national security concerns—the Respondent would be entitled to decline to issue a work permit or to renew or extend the same. Such a rejection would in my view not constitute a violation of the Covenant's right to work or any constitutional foundational value and in particular the right to work and the right to family life. The applicant has a choice to emigrate to his country of origin and to move there with his family.

In the case of *Abdulaziz, Cabales and Balkandali* v. *United Kingdom* the European Court of Human Rights had to decide whether the United Kingdom immigration laws violated the right to respect for family life guaranteed by Article 8 of the European Convention taken either alone or in conjunction with the non-discrimination provision contained in Article 14 of the European Convention on Human Rights. The case involved three women who wanted to establish residence in the United Kingdom with their respective husbands. The women were of Malawian, Philippine and Egyptian origins and their husbands were from Portugal, the Philippines and Turkey respectively, and all wanted to settle in the United Kingdom. It was held inter alia:

> The duty imposed by Article 8 cannot be considered as extending to a general obligation on the part of a Contracting State to respect the choice by married couples of the country of their matrimonial residence and to accept the non-national spouses for settlement in that country. In the present case, the applicants have not shown that there were obstacles to establishing family

life in their own or their husbands' home countries or that there were special reasons why that could not be expected of them.

I am persuaded by the decision of *Balkandali*, above, and I find no contravention of any of the Chapter 5 fundamental rights and freedoms or s 1 and s 1A of the Constitution or the relevant International Covenant on Economic, Social and Cultural Rights (ICESCR). In addition I find no violation of the Immigration Act or regulations in the circumstances.

I am sufficiently convinced that there are great similarities here with the holding in the *Balkandali* case and this one before me, in that it has not been shown that it is impossible for the family to move to the husband's country of origin. In addition, hovering over the Applicant's head are matters of national security as set out in the classified document shown to the Court and which raise security concerns and I find that the Respondents are entitled to enforce the immigration law as regards the Applicant.

As regards the detention of the Applicant's passport, he is entitled to it as the passport has been held to be part of the right to liberty under s 72 and therefore a constitutional right unless it is otherwise lawfully held, e.g. for deportation purposes. However, as regards freedom of movement in Kenya, this right is specifically accorded to Kenyan citizens under s 81 of the Constitution and there is no constitutional reference on this. However, as the applicant sought to move the Court by way of a judicial review application, I cannot give any order or declaration under s 72 and s 81 of the Constitution as he should have moved the Court under s 84(6) and LN 6/2001.

Since the right to a passport is part of liberty, reference to s 75 of the Constitution is a misdirection and this is rejected. Concerning s 74 on alleged inhuman and degrading treatment, on the facts no contravention has been shown or proven as per the definition of the right as outlined above and this too is rejected.

On the issue of the right to family life, the Court finds no breach on the part of the Respondent since on the facts there is no such proof of breach of the Covenant and, in any event, the demand of national interest must prevail.

Finally, on the issue of national security and the Court's handling of such matters, I wish to rely on the decision in the case of *The Zamora* [1916] 2 AC 77 at p. 107 where Lord Parker observed:

Those who are responsible for the national security must be the sole judges of what the national security requires. It would be obviously undesirable that such matters should be made the subject of evidence in a court of law or otherwise discussed in public.

The Judicial Committee were there asserting what I have already sought to say, namely that some matters of which national security is one are not amenable to the judicial process.

In the case of *Council of Civil Service Unions* v. *Minister for Civil Service* [1985] AC 374 Lord Scarman held that the Minister's opinion on security ought to be accepted unless no reasonable minister could in the circumstances reach such a conclusion.

Again in the case of *R* v. *Secretary of State for the Home Department, ex parte Ruddock* [1987] 1 WLR 1482, at page 1490, the court observed that credible evidence was required in support of a plea of national security before judicial investigation of a factual issue is precluded. Taylor J accepted that in an extreme case where there was "cogent", "very strong and specific" evidence of potential damage to national security flowing from the trial of the issues a court might have to decline to try factual issues.

In this matter the Respondent has sufficiently demonstrated to the Court, [via] the classified document seen by the Court, that it is entitled to take into account national concerns as regards the grant of the permit and also as regards the Applicant's immigration status. Consequently, even on this ground alone, the application would stand dismissed.

For the above reasons I would dismiss the application but give no order as to costs in the circumstances.

[Report: Transcript]

Human rights — Right to life — Inhuman treatment and punishment — Mandatory death penalty — Whether contrary to customary international law — Whether inhuman — Constitution of Singapore — Whether prohibiting inhuman punishment — Equal protection of the laws — Whether violated by mandatory death penalty for trafficking more than specified quantity of drugs

Relationship of international law and municipal law — Customary international law — Whether part of the law of Singapore — Requirement that customary international law be adopted by the Singapore courts before forming part of Singapore law — Alleged customary international law rule prohibiting mandatory death penalty — Inconsistency with Singapore legislation

Sources of international law — Customary international law — Requirement of extensive and virtually uniform State practice — Whether rule of customary international law prohibiting the mandatory death penalty — Retention of mandatory death penalty by thirty-one States — Significance — The law of Singapore

Yong Vui Kong v. Public Prosecutor[1]

Singapore, Court of Appeal.   14 May 2010

(Chan CJ; Phang and Rajah JJA)

Summary: *The facts*:—The appellant was convicted of drug trafficking, which carried the mandatory death penalty under the law of Singapore. He appealed against sentence of death, contending that the mandatory death penalty was unconstitutional. He argued that the mandatory death penalty was contrary to Article 9(1) of the Singapore Constitution,[2] which guaranteed the right to life, on the ground that it was inhuman, and contrary to Article 12(1),[3] which guaranteed equal protection before the law, because it arbitrarily singled out a particular group of convicted persons. In support of these submissions, he maintained that customary international law prohibited the mandatory death penalty, that customary international law formed part of the law of Singapore

---

[1] The appellant was represented by M. Ravi of L. F. Violet Netto. The respondent was represented by Walter Woon SC, Jaswant Singh, Davinia Aziz and Chua Ying-Hong of the Attorney-General's Chambers.
[2] See p. 379 below.   [3] See p. 418 below.

and that the Singapore courts were required, so far as possible, to interpret the Constitution and legislation in accordance with Singapore's international legal obligations.

Held (unanimously):—The appeal was dismissed.

(1) So far as possible, Singapore legislation, including the Constitution, should be interpreted in accordance with Singapore's international legal obligations. Nevertheless, there were inherent limits in the extent to which the courts could refer to international human rights norms for this purpose. Reference to such norms was not appropriate where the express wording of the Constitution was not amenable to the incorporation of those international norms. In such cases, it was necessary for Parliament to legislate or amend the Constitution to give effect to the norms in question (para. 59).

(2) It was not possible to read Article 9(1) of the Constitution as including a prohibition of inhuman punishments. The constitutional history of Singapore was different from that of the various Caribbean States whose constitutions, modelled upon the European Convention on Human Rights, had been interpreted as including such a prohibition. In particular, a specific proposal to incorporate such a prohibition in the Constitution had been made by an official commission in 1966 and been rejected (paras. 60-86).

(3) Customary international law was incorporated in Singapore law by the courts in so far as it was not inconsistent with domestic rules which had been enacted by statute or finally declared by the courts. A rule of customary international law had to be accepted and adopted by the courts of Singapore before it became part of the law of Singapore. A rule of customary international law was not self-executing. Since Singapore statute law provided for the mandatory death penalty as the sentence for a number of crimes, the courts of Singapore could not treat any rule of customary international law prohibiting such a sentence as part of the law of Singapore. Moreover, since Singapore had rejected the proposal to incorporate into the Constitution a prohibition of inhuman punishment in general, a rule of customary international law specifically prohibiting the mandatory death penalty as inhuman could not be incorporated into Singapore law without usurping the role of the legislature (paras. 87-92).

(4) Customary international law did not contain a rule prohibiting the mandatory death penalty. The creation of a rule of customary international law required extensive and virtually uniform practice by States, together with *opinio juris*. Since thirty-one States retained the mandatory death penalty for some offences, the State practice necessary for the creation of a prohibition of the mandatory death penalty was lacking (paras. 93-9).

(5) Differences in sentencing for different categories of defendants would violate the equal protection provision in Article 12(1) of the Constitution only if the basis for differentiating between the defendants was arbitrary. The provision of a mandatory death penalty for those convicted of trafficking a specified quantity of drugs while no such mandatory penalty restricted sentencing in the case of persons trafficking lesser quantities was not an arbitrary distinction and did not violate Article 12(1) (paras. 100-19).

The following is the text of the judgment of the Court, delivered by Chan CJ:

[495] *Introduction*

1. The appellant, Yong Vui Kong ("the Appellant"), was convicted of trafficking in 47.27g of diamorphine, a controlled drug, and sentenced to death (see *Public Prosecutor* v. *Yong Vui Kong* [2009] SGHC 4). He appealed against the conviction and the sentence, but later withdrew that appeal. Four days before the sentence was to be carried out, he filed Criminal Motion No 41 of 2009 ("CM 41/2009") seeking leave to pursue his appeal. This court granted him leave to do so (see *Yong Vui Kong* v. *Public Prosecutor* [2010] 2 SLR 192). In the present proceedings, the Appellant's counsel, Mr M. Ravi ("Mr Ravi"), has confirmed that the Appellant is appealing against only his sentence, and not his conviction.

[496] *The Issues Raised in this Appeal*

2. The general issue in this appeal is whether the *mandatory* death penalty ("the MDP") is permitted by the Constitution of the Republic of Singapore (1985 rev. edn, 1999 reprint). The specific issue is whether the MDP imposed under certain provisions of the Misuse of Drugs Act (Cap 185, 2001 rev. edn), in particular, is permitted by the Constitution of the Republic of Singapore.

3. In this judgment, the cases to be considered and the legal points to be discussed relate to different revised editions of both the Constitution of the Republic of Singapore and the Misuse of Drugs Act. For simplicity, we shall hereafter refer to the particular revised edition of the statute that is relevant to the case or legal point being discussed as "the Singapore Constitution" (*vis-à-vis* the Constitution of the Republic of Singapore) and "the MDA" (*vis-à-vis* the Misuse of Drugs Act).

4. The Appellant is challenging the constitutional validity of s 33 read with the Second Schedule to the MDA (collectively referred to hereafter as "the MDP provisions in the MDA"), under which he was sentenced to suffer the MDP. This challenge against the MDP for drug-related offences is not new. It was made in 1980 before the Privy Council in *Ong Ah Chuan* v. *Public Prosecutor* [1981] AC 648 ("*Ong Ah Chuan*") and in 2004 before this court in *Nguyen Tuong Van* v. *PP* [2005] 1 SLR(R) 103 ("*Nguyen*"). In both cases, it was contended that the MDP prescribed by the MDA for the offence in question (*viz.*, trafficking in controlled drugs in *Ong Ah Chuan* and importation of controlled drugs in *Nguyen*) was unconstitutional because it infringed

Arts. 9(1) and 12(1) of the Singapore Constitution. In both cases, the constitutional challenge to the MDP was dismissed.

5. Notwithstanding the decisions in *Ong Ah Chuan* and *Nguyen*, both of which affirm the constitutionality of the MDP provisions in the MDA, we gave leave to the Appellant in CM 41/2009 to pursue the present appeal and argue both the general issue and the specific issue delineated at para. 2 above because Mr Ravi said that he had new arguments based on new materials to show that both *Ong Ah Chuan* and *Nguyen* were wrongly decided at the relevant time, and that, today, this court should depart from those decisions and declare the MDP unconstitutional in view of Art. 9(1) and/or Art. 12(1) of the Singapore Constitution.

6. We should point out at this juncture that the issue of whether the death penalty *per se* (*i.e.*, the death penalty as a form of punishment for an offence) is unconstitutional does not arise in this appeal since the Appellant (as Mr Ravi has emphasised) is only challenging the constitutional validity of the MDP. It is not surprising that the Appellant has adopted this stance because Art. 9(1) expressly allows a person to be deprived of his life "in accordance with law"; *i.e.*, it expressly sanctions the death penalty. This precludes the Appellant from challenging the constitutionality of the death **[497]** penalty *per se* (see in this regard the observations of the Privy Council in *Ong Ah Chuan* at 672 as quoted at para. 20 below). The Appellant has thus chosen to argue that:

(a) as the MDP is an inhuman punishment, any legislation that prescribes the MDP as the punishment for an offence (referred to hereafter as "MDP legislation" generically) violates the right to life set out in Art. 9(1) and, therefore, is not "law" for the purposes of this provision;

(b) MDP legislation is also not "law" for the purposes of Art. 9(1) because the term "law" therein includes customary international law ("CIL"), which prohibits the MDP as an inhuman punishment; and

(c) the differentia employed in the MDA for determining when the MDP is to be imposed is arbitrary, thus making the MDP provisions in the MDA inconsistent with the right under Art. 12(1) of equal protection of the law.

7. The Appellant's challenge to the MDP based on Art. 9(1) ("the Article 9(1) challenge") is targeted at the mandatory nature of the MDP. It rests on the premise that, because MDP legislation does not give the court any discretion to decide (in view of the circumstances of the case at hand) whether or not to impose the death penalty, such legislation "treats

all persons convicted of a designated offense not as uniquely individual human beings, but as members of a faceless, undifferentiated mass to be subjected to the blind infliction of the penalty of death" (*per* Stewart J in *Woodson et al.* v. *North Carolina* 428 US 280 (1976) ("*Woodson*") at 304). From this perspective, MDP legislation is regarded as being inhuman and, thus, antithetical to the right to life set out in Art. 9(1). The Article 9(1) challenge, if successful, will affect the constitutionality of not only the MDP provisions in the MDA, but also all other MDP legislation, such as:

(a) s 302 of the Penal Code (Cap 224, 2008 rev. edn) ("the Singapore Penal Code") *vis-à-vis* the offence of murder;
(b) s 4 of the Arms Offences Act (Cap 14,2008 rev. edn) *vis-à-vis* the offence of using or attempting to use arms;
(c) s 4A of the Arms Offences Act *vis-à-vis* the offence of using or attempting to use arms to commit or to attempt to commit an offence listed in the Schedule to the Act; and
(d) s 58(1) of the Internal Security Act (Cap 143, 1985 rev. edn) *vis-à-vis* the offence of having or carrying, without lawful excuse and without lawful authority, any firearm, ammunition or explosive in a security area (as defined in s 2 of that Act).

8. In contrast, the Appellant's challenge to the MDP based on Art. 12(1) ("the Article 12(1) challenge"), if successful, will affect only the MDP **[498]** provisions in the MDA. In other words, the Appellant's argument on Art. 12(1) is specific to the MDP provisions in the MDA and does not impinge on the constitutional validity of other MDP legislation. The Appellant's submission in this regard is that the MDP provisions in the MDA, in making the quantity of controlled drugs trafficked the sole determinant of when the MDP is to be imposed, draw arbitrary distinctions between offenders who traffic in different amounts of controlled drugs. (In the case of trafficking in diamorphine specifically, the MDP provisions in the MDA state that the MDP applies so long as more than 15g of diamorphine is trafficked. For convenience, we shall hereafter refer to this criterion as "the 15g differentia".)

9. Although the Article 9(1) challenge and the Article 12(1) challenge are different in so far as they pertain to two different constitutional provisions, they are at the same time related in that the Appellant does not need to rely on the Article 12(1) challenge if he succeeds on the Article 9(1) challenge. In other words, if the MDP provisions in the MDA violate Art. 9(1) because, in making the death penalty *mandatory*, they lay down an inhuman punishment, they would be unconstitutional

regardless of whether or not they also, contrary to Art. 12(1), draw arbitrary distinctions between offenders who traffic in different amounts of controlled drugs. For this reason, we shall address the Article 9(1) challenge first before the Article 12(1) challenge.

The Article 9(1) Challenge: Whether the MDP is Consistent with the Right to Life in Article 9(1)

10. To understand the parties' arguments on Art. 9(1) of the Singapore Constitution, it is necessary to appreciate the legal context of those arguments. We shall set out this legal context first, followed by the parties' arguments and then our decision on the Article 9(1) challenge.

The legal context of the Article 9(1) challenge

11. Article 9(1) of the Singapore Constitution provides as follows:

No person shall be deprived of his life or personal liberty save in accordance with law.

The expression "law" is defined in Art. 2(1) as follows:

"law" includes written law and any legislation of the United Kingdom or other enactment or instrument whatsoever which is in operation in Singapore and the common law in so far as it is in operation in Singapore and any custom or usage having the force of law in Singapore . . .

In this regard, the expression "written law" means (see likewise Art. 2(1)):

. . . this Constitution and all Acts and Ordinances and subsidiary legislation for the time being in force in Singapore.

[499] 12. *Prima facie*, the MDA, being legislation in force in Singapore, is "written law" and is thus "law" as defined in Art. 2(1); the same applies to other MDP legislation currently in force in Singapore. The meaning of the term "law" was considered by the Privy Council in *Ong Ah Chuan* (para. 4 *supra*) and by this court in *Nguyen* (para. 4 *supra*). Before we turn to examine these two decisions, we note in passing that, although Art. 2(1) defines the expression "law" to include "custom or usage" (*per* Art. 2(1)), Mr Ravi has not argued that these words are intended to include CIL. If such an argument had been made, we would have rejected it because, in our view, the phrase "custom or usage" in Art. 2(1) refers to local customs and usages which (in the words of this provision) "[have] the force of law in Singapore", that is to say, local customs and usages which are already part of our domestic law.

The decision in Ong Ah Chuan

13. In *Ong Ah Chuan*, the appellants were convicted of the offence of drug trafficking and sentenced to death. They appealed against their convictions on, *inter alia*, the ground that the rebuttable presumption of trafficking which arose under the MDA upon proof of possession of controlled drugs exceeding the stipulated quantity was a violation of due process of law and was therefore not "in accordance with law" for the purposes of Art. 9(1).

14. The Prosecution in that case argued that, since the expression "law" was defined in Art. 2(1) to include written law and since "written law" included all Acts of Parliament, the requirements of Art. 9(1) were satisfied so long as the deprivation of life or personal liberty complained of was carried out in accordance with provisions contained in "any Act passed by the Parliament of Singapore, *however arbitrary or contrary to fundamental rules of natural justice* the provisions of such Act [might] be" [emphasis added] (see *Ong Ah Chuan* at 670). The Privy Council rejected this argument (which was characterised as "extreme" in the later Privy Council decision of *Haw Tua Tau* v. *PP* [1981-2] SLR(R) 133 at para. 7) for the following reasons (see *Ong Ah Chuan* at 670-1):

In a Constitution founded on the Westminster model and particularly in that part of it that purports to assure to all individual citizens the continued enjoyment of fundamental liberties or rights, *references to "law" in such contexts as "in accordance with law", "equality before the law", "protection of the law" and the like, in their Lordships' view, refer to a system of law which incorporates those fundamental rules of natural justice that had formed part and parcel of the common law of England that was in operation in Singapore at the commencement of the [Singapore] Constitution.* It would have been taken for granted by the makers of the [Singapore] Constitution that the "law" to which citizens could have recourse for the protection of fundamental liberties assured to them by the [Singapore] Constitution would be a system of law that did not flout those fundamental rules. If it were otherwise it would be [a] **[500]** misuse of language to speak of law as something which affords "protection" for the individual in the enjoyment of his fundamental liberties, and the purported entrenchment (by article 5) of articles 9(1) and 12(1) would be little better than a mockery. [emphasis added]

15. Having set out its interpretation of the expression "law", the Privy Council in *Ong Ah Chuan* tested the provisions of the MDA against that interpretation to determine their constitutional validity,

and held that they did not breach the fundamental rules of natural justice. Hence, the Privy Council rejected the appellants' constitutional challenge to the statutory presumption of trafficking in the MDA.

16. We should point out that, at the hearing before the Privy Council, the Board (*per* Lord Diplock) specifically asked counsel for the Prosecution whether he was contending that, so long as a statute was an Act of Parliament, it would be justified by Art. 9(1), however unfair, absurd or oppressive it might be (see *Ong Ah Chuan* at 659). When counsel answered that the Prosecution was not advancing that argument and that it was unnecessary for him to rely on that argument since the Prosecution considered its case against each appellant to be plain on its facts, Lord Diplock replied (likewise at 659):

Their Lordships cannot accept that because they will have to deal with the point. They are not disposed to find that article 9(1) justifies all legislation whatever its nature.

However, beyond what was actually decided in *Ong Ah Chuan* itself, it is not clear what the Privy Council had in mind vis-à-vis the kind of legislation that would not qualify as "law" for the purposes of Art. 9(1). Perhaps, the Privy Council had in mind colourable legislation which purported to enact a "law" as generally understood (*i.e.*, a legislative rule of general application), but which in effect was a legislative judgment, that is to say, legislation directed at securing the conviction of particular known individuals (see *Don John Francis Douglas Liyanage* v. *The Queen* [1967] 1 AC 259 at 291), or legislation of so absurd or arbitrary a nature that it could not possibly have been contemplated by our constitutional framers as being "law" when they crafted the constitutional provisions protecting fundamental liberties (*i.e.*, the provisions now set out in Pt IV of the Singapore Constitution).

17. In this connection, it is useful to put in context the following statement by Yong Pung How CJ (delivering the judgment of this court) in *Jabar bin Kadermastan* v. *PP* [1995] 1 SLR(R) 326 ("*Jabar*") at para. 52:

Any law which provides for the deprivation of a person's life or personal liberty ... is valid and binding so long as it is validly passed by Parliament. *The court is not concerned with whether it is also fair, just and reasonable as well.* [emphasis added]

[501] 18. Upon a first reading, Yong CJ's statement may appear to contradict the Privy Council's interpretation of the expression "law" in *Ong Ah Chuan* (para. 4 *supra*) at 670-1 (see the extract quoted at para. 14 above). In our view, however, there is in fact no such contradiction. Yong

CJ's statement was made in the context of a case where the appellant argued, in reliance on *Earl Pratt* v. *Attorney-General for Jamaica* [1994] 2 AC 1 ("*Pratt*"), that Art. 9(1) of the Singapore Constitution was applicable to render the execution of the death sentence imposed on him unconstitutional as he had been incarcerated on death row for more than five years since his conviction. In *Pratt*, the Privy Council held that a prolonged delay in the execution of a death sentence constituted inhuman punishment and contravened s 17(1) of the Constitution of Jamaica, which stated that no person should be subjected to "torture or to inhuman or degrading punishment or other treatment". This ruling was rejected in *Jabar* by this court, which preferred the decision in *Willie Lee Richmond* v. *Samuel A. Lewis* 948 F 2d 1473 (1990). In that case, the US Court of Appeals, Ninth Circuit, held that the carrying out of a death sentence after the offender had spent 16 years on death row did not constitute cruel and unusual punishment in contravention of the Eighth and the Fourteenth Amendments to the US Constitution where the delay was occasioned by the offender initiating unmeritorious legal proceedings.

19. The issue raised in *Jabar* concerned the constitutionality of *carrying out the MDP*, given the period of time which had lapsed since the appellant's conviction, and not the constitutionality of the MDP *per se*. That was why this court held that the question of whether the relevant MDP legislation (which, on the facts of *Jabar*, was s 302 of the Penal Code (Cap 224, 1985 rev. edn)) was fair, just and reasonable was not relevant. Yong CJ's statement should be read in this context, and not as a definitive interpretation of the term "law" in Art. 9(1); otherwise, that statement would be inconsistent with the approach taken in *Nguyen* (para. 4 *supra*), where this court (Yong CJ presiding) affirmed (at para. 82) the Privy Council's interpretation of "law" in *Ong Ah Chuan*.

20. Returning to the facts of *Ong Ah Chuan*, the appellants, apart from challenging the constitutionality of the statutory presumption of trafficking (see para. 13 above), also disputed the constitutionality of the MDP. The Privy Council made the following observations about the death penalty in general (at 672):

It was not suggested on behalf of the [appellants] that capital punishment is unconstitutional per se. Such an argument is foreclosed by the recognition in article 9(1) of the [Singapore] Constitution that a person may be deprived of life "in accordance with law".

21. With regard to the MDP specifically, the Privy Council commented (at 672-3):

[502] ... As their Lordships understood the argument presented to them on behalf of the [appellants], it was that the mandatory nature of the sentence, in the case of an offence so broadly drawn as that of trafficking created by section 3 of the [MDA], rendered it arbitrary since it debarred the court in punishing offenders from discriminating between them according to their individual blameworthiness. This, it was contended, was arbitrary and not "in accordance with law" as their Lordships have construed that phrase in article 9(1); alternatively it offends against the principle of equality before the law entrenched in the [Singapore] Constitution by article 12(1), since it compels the court to condemn to the highest penalty of death an addict who has gratuitously supplied an addict friend with 15 grammes of heroin from his own private store, and to inflict a lesser punishment upon a professional dealer caught selling for distribution to many addicts a total of 14.99 grammes.

Their Lordships would emphasise that in their judicial capacity they are in no way concerned with arguments for or against capital punishment or its efficacy as a deterrent to so evil and profitable a crime as trafficking in addictive drugs. Whether there should be capital punishment in Singapore and, if so, for what offences, are questions for the legislature of Singapore which, in the case of drugs offences, it has answered by section 29 and Schedule 2 of the [MDA]. A primary object of imposing a death sentence for offences that society regards with particular abhorrence is that it should act as a deterrent; particularly where the offence is one that is committed for profit by an offender who is prepared to take a calculated risk. There is nothing unusual in a capital sentence being mandatory. Indeed its efficacy as a deterrent may be to some extent diminished if it is not. At common law all capital sentences were mandatory; under the Penal Code of Singapore [*i.e.*, the Penal Code (Cap 103, 1970 rev. edn)] the capital sentence for murder and for offences against the President's person still is. If it were valid the argument for the [appellants] would apply to every law which imposed a mandatory fixed or minimum penalty even where it was not capital—an extreme position which counsel was anxious to disclaim. [emphasis added]

The decision in Nguyen

22. Moving on to *Nguyen* (para. 4 *supra*), the appellant in that case was convicted of importing 396.2g of diamorphine into Singapore without authorisation, an offence under s 7 of the MDA, and was, pursuant to the MDP provisions in the MDA, sentenced to suffer the MDP. He appealed against both his conviction and his sentence, contending that those provisions were unconstitutional because they violated Arts. 9(1), 12(1) and 93 of the Singapore Constitution (these Articles concern, respectively, the right to life, the right to equal protection of the law and the judicial power of Singapore).

23. For present purposes, we shall examine only the appellant's argument based on Art. 9(1) and this court's decision on that argument. The appellant's argument was that: (a) the MDP was arbitrary because

it [503] precluded proportional and individualised sentencing, which form of sentencing was protected by the prohibition against cruel and inhuman treatment or punishment; and (b) even if the MDP were not arbitrary, execution by hanging amounted to cruel and inhuman punishment. In making this argument, the appellant took the position that the expression "law" in Art. 9(1) incorporated CIL, specifically, the CIL prohibition against cruel, inhuman, degrading or unusual treatment or punishment. (In this regard, we shall hereafter refer to such treatment or punishment as "inhuman punishment" generically since Mr Ravi has, in his arguments, emphasised the prohibition against *inhuman* treatment or punishment in particular; it should, however, be noted that the terms "cruel", "inhuman", "degrading" and "unusual" do not share the exact same meaning.)

24. The way in which the appellant in *Nguyen* framed his argument on Art. 9(1) was probably influenced by post-*Ong Ah Chuan* Privy Council decisions on the constitutional validity of the MDP under the Constitutions of other Commonwealth States, principally the Caribbean States. Counsel for the appellant cited those cases in an attempt to persuade this court that either *Ong Ah Chuan* (para. 4 *supra*) had been wrongly decided at the material time or, alternatively, the Privy Council would have decided the case differently in 2004. The decisions which counsel referred to were:

(a) *Reyes* v. *The Queen* [2002] 2 AC 235 ("*Reyes*"), an appeal from a decision of the Court of Appeal of Belize;
(b) *Boyce* v. *The Queen* [2005] 1 AC 400 ("*Boyce*"), an appeal from a decision of the Court of Appeal of Barbados;
(c) *Matthew* v. *State of Trinidad and Tobago* [2005] 1 AC 433 ("*Matthew*"), an appeal from a decision of the Court of Appeal of Trinidad and Tobago; and
(d) *Watson* v. *The Queen* (*Attorney General for Jamaica intervening*) [2005] 1 AC 472 ("*Watson*"), an appeal from a decision of the Court of Appeal of Jamaica.

25. In considering whether the MDP provided for under the MDA was arbitrary, this court affirmed in *Nguyen* (at para. 82) as established law the Privy Council's decision in *Ong Ah Chuan* at 670-1 (quoted at para. 14 above) on the meaning of the phrase "in accordance with law" in Art. 9(1). The court noted that the Privy Council had ruled in both *Watson* and *Reyes* that "the [MDP] in respect of certain classes of murder was ... unconstitutional as a violation of the prohibition against cruel or inhuman treatment or punishment" (see *Nguyen* at para. 83),

and opined (likewise at para. 83) that the Privy Council would have ruled in the same way in *Matthew* and *Boyce* "but for certain 'saving provisions' in the relevant national Constitutions which preserved pre-existing national laws".

[504] 26. In *Reyes*, the Privy Council held that the MDP was unconstitutional under s 7 of the Constitution of Belize (Laws of Belize, c 4) ("the Belize Constitution"), which specifically prohibited, *inter alia*, inhuman punishment. The Privy Council (*per* Lord Bingham of Cornhill) observed thus (at para. 43):

To deny the offender the opportunity, before sentence is passed, to seek to persuade the court that in all the circumstances to condemn him to death would be disproportionate and inappropriate is to treat him as no human being should be treated and thus to deny his basic humanity, the core of the right which section 7 [of the Belize Constitution] exists to protect.

27. In *Nguyen*, this court held (at para. 84) that the Privy Council's reasoning in *Reyes* as to why the MDP was unconstitutional was not applicable to Singapore because neither the Singapore Constitution nor any other Singapore statute contained an equivalent of s 7 of the Belize Constitution. The court also pointed out (at para. 85 of *Nguyen*) that *Reyes* was decided "in the light of the various international norms that had been 'accepted by Belize as consistent with the fundamental standards of humanity'", such as those encapsulated in the Universal Declaration of Human Rights (10 December 1948), GA Res. 217A (III), UN Doc. A/810 ("the UDHR") and the International Covenant on Civil and Political Rights (19 December 1966), 999 UNTS 171.

28. With regard to *Watson*, this court distinguished it in *Nguyen* (at para. 86) on the same grounds as those outlined in the preceding paragraph. At the same time, this court acknowledged (likewise at para. 86) the following comments by Lord Hope of Craighead, who delivered the judgment of the majority in *Watson* (at paras. 29-30):

Their Lordships consider that the mandatory death penalty which is imposed under section 3 of the Act [*i.e.*, the Offences against the Person Act 1864 (Laws of Jamaica, c 268), as amended by the Offences against the Person (Amendment) Act 1992 (No 14)] is open to the same constitutional objections as those that were identified in *Reyes* v. *The Queen*. It is no longer acceptable, nor is it any longer possible to say, as Lord Diplock did on behalf of the Board in *Ong Ah Chuan* v. *Public Prosecutor* [1981] AC 648, 674, that there is nothing unusual in a death sentence being mandatory. As Lord Bingham pointed out in *Reyes's* case [2002] 2 AC 235, 244, para. 17, the mandatory penalty of death on conviction of murder long predated any international arrangements for the protection of human rights. The decision in that case was made at a time when international jurisprudence on human rights was rudimentary ...

The march of international jurisprudence on this issue [*viz*, the constitutionality of the MDP] began with the Universal Declaration of Human Rights which was adopted by a resolution of the General Assembly of the United Nations on 10 December 1948 (Cmd 7662). It came to be recognised that among the fundamental rights which must be protected are the right to life and the right not to be subjected to cruel, inhuman or **[505]** degrading treatment or punishment: see articles 3 and 5 of the Universal Declaration; articles I and XXVI of the American Declaration of the Rights and Duties of Man which was adopted by the Ninth International Conference of American States on 2 May 1948; articles 2 and 3 of the European Convention for the Protection of Human Rights and Fundamental Freedoms (1953) (Cmd 8969); articles 6(1) and 7 of the International [Covenant] on Civil and Political Rights which was adopted by a resolution of the General Assembly of the United Nations on 16 December 1966 and [which] entered into force on 23 March 1976 (1977) (Cmnd 6702); and articles 4.1 and 5.2 of the American Convention on Human Rights which was signed on 22 November 1969 and [which] came into force on 18 July 1978. So the practice was adopted, as many of the former British colonies achieved independence, of setting out in their Constitutions a series of fundamental rights and freedoms which were to be protected under the Constitution. The history of these developments is fully set out in *Reyes* [2002] 2 AC 235. It is as relevant to the position under the Constitution of Jamaica as it was in that case to Belize. There is a common heritage. In *Minister of Home Affairs* v. *Fisher* [1980] AC 319, 328 Lord Wilberforce referred to the influence of the European Convention in the drafting of the constitutional instruments during the post-colonial period, including the Constitutions of most Caribbean territories. That influence is clearly seen in Chapter III of the Constitution of Jamaica.

29. Ultimately, in *Nguyen*, this court upheld the constitutionality of the MDP in view of two factors, namely: (a) the difference between the wording of the applicable constitutional provisions in *Reyes* and *Watson* and that of the relevant provisions of the Singapore Constitution; and (b) the difference between the constitutional history of the States from which those two Privy Council appeals arose (namely, Belize where *Reyes* was concerned, and Jamaica where *Watson* was concerned) and the constitutional history of Singapore. In so ruling, this court effectively distinguished *Reyes*, *Watson* and other like cases on the ground that Art. 9(1) of the Singapore Constitution did not contain any words prohibiting inhuman punishment.

30. To complete this account of the decision in *Nguyen*, we should add that the basis on which this court distinguished *Reyes* and *Watson* was *in pari materia* with the basis on which the Privy Council in

Bowe v. The Queen [2006] 1 WLR 1623 ("*Bowe*"), an appeal from the Commonwealth of the Bahamas ("the Bahamas"), distinguished *Ong Ah Chuan*, namely, the Bahamian Constitution expressly prohibited inhuman punishment whereas the Singapore Constitution contained no such express prohibition. In *Bowe*, the Privy Council observed thus (at para. 41):

Ong Ah Chuan... concerned mandatory death sentences in Singapore for possession of more than 15 grammes of heroin. The constitutionality of that sentence was challenged, and in giving the judgment of the Board rejecting the challenge Lord Diplock made observations... approbatory of the mandatory death sentence for murder, while suggesting... that the moral **[506]** blameworthiness of those convicted of murder might vary more widely than in the case of drug traffickers. He pointed to the prerogative of mercy as a means of mitigating the rigidity of the law. *But the [Singapore] Constitution... contained no provision comparable with sections of the 1963 and 1969 Constitutions [of the Bahamas], or the eighth amendment to the US Constitution, or article 3 of the European Convention, [all of which prohibit subjecting a person to torture or inhuman punishment].* The decision... is not authority on the compatibility of a mandatory death sentence with a constitution containing such a provision, particularly where (contrary to the situation said by counsel to prevail in the case of drug traffickers in Singapore...) the sentence is frequently commuted. [emphasis added]

31. With regard to the argument by the appellant in *Nguyen* that death by hanging was inhuman punishment and that the prohibition against such punishment was incorporated in the expression "law" in Art. 9(1) of the Singapore Constitution, this court said (at paras. 91-2) that while it was widely accepted that the prohibition against inhuman punishment amounted to a rule of CIL, there was insufficient evidence of state practice to demonstrate that the content of this CIL prohibition was such as to prohibit hanging as a mode of execution. This court also noted that there was no CIL prohibition against the death penalty *per se*.

32. The above summary of what was decided in *Ong Ah Chuan* and *Nguyen* forms the legal backdrop to the form and structure of the arguments advanced by Mr Ravi in this appeal. We shall now consider the Article 9(1) challenge proper.

The two limbs of the Article 9(1) challenge

33. As indicated at para. 6 above, there are two limbs to the Article 9(1) challenge, namely:

(a) MDP legislation is not "law" for the purposes of Art. 9(1) as it prescribes the MDP, which is an inhuman punishment, as the punishment for an offence; and
(b) the MDP is prohibited under CIL, which is included in the expression "law" in Art. 9(1), and, accordingly, the MDP is prohibited by Art. 9(1).

For convenience, we shall hereafter refer to the first limb as "the 'inhuman punishment' limb" and the second limb as "the 'contrary to CIL' limb".

The parties' arguments on the "inhuman punishment" limb

The Appellant's submissions

34. With regard to the "inhuman punishment" limb of the Article 9(1) challenge, Mr Ravi contends that the MDP is an inhuman punishment because it has been held to be so in a long string of Privy Council cases decided post-*Ong Ah Chuan* and/or post-*Nguyen*, as well as in cases **[507]** emanating from the US Supreme Court, the Supreme Court of India, the Supreme Court of Uganda and the High Court of Malawi. The cases cited by Mr Ravi in this regard (collectively, "the Appellant's Art. 9(1) cases") and the constitutional provisions on which the respective decisions in these cases were based are as follows:

(a) *Reyes* (para. 24 *supra*), which concerned the stipulation in s 7 of the Belize Constitution that "[n]o person shall be subjected to torture or to inhuman or degrading punishment or other treatment";
(b) *Fox* v. *The Queen* [2002] 2 AC 284, which concerned the stipulation in s 7 of the Constitution of Saint Christopher and Nevis that "[a] person shall not be subjected to torture or to inhuman or degrading punishment or other like treatment";
(c) *Regina* v. *Hughes* [2002] 2 AC 259 ("*Hughes*"), which concerned the stipulation in s 5 of the Constitution of Saint Lucia that "[n]o person shall be subjected to torture or to inhuman or degrading punishment or other treatment";
(d) *Boyce* (para. 24 *supra*), which concerned the stipulation in s 15(1) of the Constitution of Barbados that "[n]o person shall be subjected to torture or to inhuman or degrading punishment or other treatment";

(e) *Watson* (para. 24 *supra*), which concerned the stipulation in s 17(1) of the Constitution of Jamaica that "[n]o person shall be subjected to torture or to inhuman or degrading punishment or other treatment";

(f) *Matthew* (para. 24 *supra*), which concerned the stipulation in s 5(2)(b) of the Constitution of Trinidad and Tobago that the Parliament could not "impose or authorise the imposition of cruel and unusual treatment or punishment";

(g) *Bowe* (para. 30 *supra*), which concerned the stipulation in s 3 of the 1963 and the 1969 Constitutions of the Bahamas (and, subsequently, s 17 of the 1973 Constitution of the Bahamas) that "[n]o person shall be subjected to torture or to inhuman or degrading treatment or punishment";

(h) *Bernard Coard* v. *The Attorney General* [2007] UKPC 7, which concerned the stipulation in s 5(1) of the Constitution of Grenada that "[n]o person shall be subjected to torture or to inhuman or degrading punishment or other treatment";

(i) *Woodson* (para. 7 *supra*), which concerned the scope of the Eighth Amendment to the US Constitution prohibiting excessive bail, excessive fines and cruel and unusual punishment;

(j) *Attorney General* v. *Susan Kigula* Constitutional Appeal No 3 of 2006 (21 January 2009), which concerned the stipulation in Art. 24 of the Constitution of Uganda that "[n]o person shall be subjected to any **[508]** form of torture or cruel, inhuman or degrading treatment or punishment";

(k) *Francis Kafantayeni* v. *Attorney General* Constitutional Case No 12 of 2005 (27 April 2007), which concerned the stipulation in s 19(3) of the Constitution of Malawi that no person should be subjected to torture of any kind or to cruel, inhuman or degrading treatment or punishment; and

(l) *Mithu* v. *State of Punjab* AIR 1983 SC 473 ("*Mithu*"), which concerned the Indian equivalent of Arts. 9(1) and 12(1) of the Singapore Constitution (namely, Arts. 21 and 14 respectively of the Constitution of India ("the Indian Constitution")).

It may be noted that many of the above cases were decided prior to *Nguyen* (para. 4 *supra*), and were considered and distinguished by this court in *Nguyen*. To this extent, Mr Ravi is traversing old ground.

35. Mr Ravi's argument before this court is that the Appellant's Art. 9(1) cases cast doubt on the correctness of the decisions in *Ong Ah Chuan* (para. 4 *supra*) and *Nguyen*, and support the view that the MDP

dehumanises the offender by debarring the trial judge from considering, during the sentencing process, any and all mitigating circumstances as to why the offender should not suffer death. In this respect, three of the Appellant's Art. 9(1) cases should be noted in particular.

36. The first is the Privy Council case of *Reyes*. In that case, the appellant was convicted of two counts of murder for shooting his neighbour and his neighbour's wife in a dispute over the neighbour's attempt to build a fence 2ft from the back of the appellant's house. Under s 102(3)(b) of the Criminal Code of Belize (Laws of Belize, c 84) ("the Belize Criminal Code"), murder by shooting was classified as a "class A" murder, and, under s 102(1) of the same statute, it attracted the MDP. The appellant appealed against his sentence, contending that s 102 of the Belize Criminal Code was contrary to s 7 of the Belize Constitution. The Privy Council, in allowing the appeal, made the following observations (at para. 43):

For [the] purposes of this appeal the Board need not consider the constitutionality of any mandatory penalty other than death, nor the constitutionality of a mandatory death penalty imposed for any murder other than by shooting. In the absence of adversarial argument it is undesirable to decide more than is necessary to resolve this appeal. The Board is however satisfied that the provision requiring sentence of death to be passed on the defendant on his conviction of murder by shooting subjected him to inhuman or degrading punishment or other treatment incompatible with his right under section 7 of the [Belize] Constitution in that it required sentence of death to be passed and precluded any judicial consideration of the humanity of condemning him to death. The use of firearms by dangerous and aggressive criminals is an undoubted social evil and, so long as the death penalty is retained, there may well be murders by shooting which justify the **[509]** ultimate penalty. But there will also be murders of quite a different character (for instance, murders arising from sudden quarrels within a family, or between neighbours, involving the use of a firearm legitimately owned for no criminal or aggressive purpose) in which the death penalty would be plainly excessive and disproportionate. In a crime of this kind there may well be matters relating both to the offence and the offender which ought properly to be considered before sentence is passed. *To deny the offender the opportunity, before sentence is passed, to seek to persuade the court that in all the circumstances to condemn him to death would be disproportionate and inappropriate is to treat him as no human being should be treated and thus to deny his basic humanity, the core of the right which section 7 exists to protect.* [emphasis added]

37. The second case which we wish to highlight is *Woodson* (para. 7 *supra*), where the US Supreme Court (by a majority of 5:4) struck down MDP legislation as unconstitutional in view of the prohibition

against (*inter alia*) "cruel and unusual punishments" set out in the Eighth Amendment to the US Constitution. Stewart J, who delivered the judgment of the majority, said in a passage at 303-5 (which was later cited with approval by Lord Bingham at para. 34 of *Reyes*):

[D]eath is a punishment different from all other sanctions in kind rather than degree... *A process that accords no significance to relevant facets of the character and record of the individual offender or the circumstances of the particular offense excludes from consideration in fixing the ultimate punishment of death the possibility of compassionate or mitigating factors stemming from the diverse frailties of humankind. It treats all persons convicted of a designated offense not as uniquely individual human beings, but as members of a faceless, undifferentiated mass to be subjected to the blind infliction of the penalty of death.*

This Court has previously recognized that "[f]or the determination of sentences, justice generally requires consideration of more than the particular acts by which the crime was committed and that there be taken into account the circumstances of the offense together with the character and propensities of the offender". *Pennsylvania ex rel Sullivan v. Ashe*, 302 US 51, 55 (1937). Consideration of both the offender and the offense in order to arrive at a just and appropriate sentence has been viewed as a progressive and humanizing development... While the prevailing practice of individualizing sentencing determinations generally reflects simply enlightened policy rather than a constitutional imperative, we believe that in capital cases the fundamental respect for humanity underlying the Eighth Amendment... requires consideration of the character and record of the individual offender and the circumstances of the particular offense as a constitutionally indispensable part of the process of inflicting the penalty of death.

This conclusion rests squarely on the predicate that the penalty of death is qualitatively different from a sentence of imprisonment, however long. Death, in its finality, differs more from life imprisonment than a 100-year prison term differs from one of only a year or two. Because of that qualitative **[510]** difference, there is a corresponding difference in the need for reliability in the determination that death is the appropriate punishment in a specific case. [emphasis added]

38. It should be noted that, although Stewart J highlighted in the above passage the qualitative difference between the death sentence and a sentence of imprisonment (because of the finality of death) and the "corresponding difference in the need for reliability in the determination that death [would be] the appropriate punishment in a specific case" (see *Woodson* at 305), he did not say that the possibility of error in making this determination rendered the MDP dehumanising. Instead, he held that it was the exclusion of judicial discretion—specifically, the exclusion of "the character and record of the individual offender and the circumstances of the particular offense" (see *Woodson* at 304)

from the court's consideration—which made the MDP dehumanising. Stewart J also added that if every offender convicted of murder were punished with death, the law would be treating all such offenders as "a faceless, undifferentiated mass" (see *Woodson* at 304) and would be dehumanising them; from that perspective, the MDP was an inhuman punishment.

39. The third of the Appellant's Art. 9(1) cases which we wish to draw attention to is *Mithu* (para. 34 *supra*). Several extracts of the Indian Supreme Court's judgment in that case were cited in a passage at para. 36 of *Reyes* (para. 24 *supra*). That passage ("the composite passage from *Mithu*") comprises certain observations made by Y. V. Chandrachud CJ (at paras. 12 and 16) and Chinnappa Reddy J (at para. 25) on s 303 of the Penal Code 1860 (Act 45 of 1860) (India) ("the Indian Penal Code"), which imposes the MDP on a person who commits murder while under a sentence of life imprisonment. The passage reads as follows:

12. ... [A] provision of law which deprives the Court of the use of its wise and beneficent discretion in a matter of life and death, without regard to the circumstances in which the offence was committed and, therefore, without regard to the gravity of the offence, cannot but be regarded as harsh, unjust and unfair ...

...

16. Thus, there is no justification for prescribing a mandatory sentence of death for the offence of murder committed inside or outside the prison by a person who is under the sentence of life imprisonment. A standardized mandatory sentence, and that too in the form of a sentence of death, fails to take into account the facts and circumstances of each particular case. It is those facts and circumstances which constitute a safe guideline for determining the question of sentence in each individual case ...

...

25. ... Section 303 [of the Indian Penal Code] excludes judicial discretion. The scales of justice are removed from the hands of the Judge so soon as he pronounces the accused guilty of the offence. So final, so irrevocable and so **[511]** irrestitutable is the sentence of death that no law which provides for it without involvement of the judicial mind can be said to be fair, just and reasonable. Such a law must necessarily be stigmatised as arbitrary and oppressive. Section 303 is such a law and it must go the way of all bad laws ...

Mr Ravi has referred to para. 12 of *Mithu* in his submissions, but not to paras. 16 and 25 of that judgment.

40. In addition to the Appellant's Art. 9(1) cases, Mr Ravi has also relied on the opinions of two experts on international human rights

law to contend that the MDP is an inhuman punishment. The first of these experts is Ms Asma Jilani Jahangir ("Ms Jahangir"), Special Rapporteur of the UN Commission on Human Rights on extrajudicial, summary or arbitrary executions (from August 1998 to July 2004), who, in her report to the UN General Assembly, expressed the view that "the death penalty should *under no circumstances* be mandatory, regardless of the charges involved" [emphasis added] (see *Interim Report of the Special Rapporteur of the Commission on Human Rights on Extrajudicial, Summary or Arbitrary Executions*, UN Doc. A/55/288 (11 August 2000) at para. 34). The second of the abovesaid experts is Mr Philip Alston ("Mr Alston"), the current Special Rapporteur of the UN Commission on Human Rights on extrajudicial, summary or arbitrary executions. In a critique of the decision in *Nguyen* (para. 4 *supra*) (see "Expert on arbitrary executions calls on Singapore Government not to carry out mandatory death sentence" (15 November 2005)), Mr Alston expressed the view that, in *Nguyen*, this court failed to examine *Boyce* (para. 24 *supra*), where the dissenting members of the Privy Council (*viz.*, Lord Bingham, Lord Nicholls of Birkenhead, Lord Steyn and Lord Walker of Gestingthorpe) accepted the submission (at para. 81) that:

No international human rights tribunal anywhere in the world has ever found a mandatory death penalty regime compatible with international human rights norms . . .

41. Mr Ravi argues that in view of the post-*Ong Ah Chuan* and/or post-*Nguyen* decisions from other Commonwealth jurisdictions condemning the MDP as an inhuman punishment, coupled with the opinions of Ms Jahangir and Mr Alston as mentioned in the preceding paragraph, this court should declare that Art. 9(1) of the Singapore Constitution prohibits the MDP.

The Prosecution's response

42. In response to Mr Ravi's submission that the MDP is an inhuman punishment and that MDP legislation is therefore not "law" for the purposes of Art. 9(1), the then Attorney-General, Prof. Walter Woon SC ("the AG"), who appeared in his capacity as the Public Prosecutor, has pointed out that the Privy Council in *Ong Ah Chuan* (para. 24 *supra*) and this court in *Nguyen* decided otherwise. The AG submits that the position laid down in *Ong Ah Chuan* and *Nguyen* holds good, and that [512] the Privy Council's decisions in post-*Ong Ah Chuan* and/or post-*Nguyen* cases should not be followed because the Privy Council does not dictate human rights standards for the rest of humanity.

The parties' arguments on the "contrary to CIL" limb

The Appellant's submissions

43. Turning now to the "contrary to CIL" limb of the Article 9(1) challenge, Mr Ravi's submission is that CIL is part of the expression "law" in Art. 9(1). It should be noted that Mr Ravi has not cited any authority for this proposition, although, with regard to the contention that there is a CIL rule prohibiting the MDP as an inhuman punishment, he has pointed to the fact that there are a diminishing number of States which still retain the MDP for drug-related offences. According to Mr Ravi, at last count, only 14 States still retain the MDP for such offences (*cf* the figure given by the AG as to the number of States which still retain the MDP for drug-related *and other* serious offences (see para. 45 below)). This, Mr Ravi asserts, demonstrates the existence of a CIL prohibition against the MDP as an inhuman punishment. In our view, Mr Ravi's argument is not devoid of merit, but it does not explain why the expression "law" in Art. 9(1) should be interpreted to include CIL, in particular, the CIL rule prohibiting inhuman punishment.

The Prosecution's response

44. In response to the Appellant's argument that the word "law" in Art. 9(1) includes CIL, the AG has submitted that there are two possible interpretations of this word: the first is that it refers only to statutes and the common law as applied in Singapore; the second is that it also includes CIL in addition to statutes and the common law as applied locally. When asked to clarify his position as to which was the preferred interpretation, the AG said that, in principle, the expression "law" should be interpreted to include CIL. We do not think that the AG, by this reply, was conceding that the expression "law" in Art. 9(1) includes CIL in the sense that "law" has been defined to include CIL, with the consequence that, once it is shown that there is a rule of CIL prohibiting the MDP as an inhuman punishment, that CIL rule automatically becomes part of "law" for the purposes of Art. 9(1). Indeed, the constitutional definition of "law" in Art. 2(1) is quite different (see para. 11 above). Besides, such a concession would be contrary to the decision in *Nguyen* (para. 4 *supra*), where this court held at para. 94, citing (*inter alia*) the Privy Council case of *Chung Chi Cheung* v. *The King* [1939] AC 160 ("*Chung Chi Cheung*"), that in the event of a conflict between a rule of CIL and a domestic statute, the latter would prevail. From his other submissions, it seems clear enough to us that what the AG meant when he said that the expression "law" should be interpreted to include CIL was that **[513]** this expression would include a CIL rule

which had already been recognised and applied by a domestic court as part of Singapore law.

45. The AG disagrees with Mr Ravi's contention that the MDP violates the CIL prohibition against inhuman punishment. In this regard, the AG has submitted that the post-*Ong Ah Chuan* and/or post-*Nguyen* Privy Council decisions cited by Mr Ravi ("the Privy Council cases relating to Art. 9(1)") merely reflect a change in the Privy Council's attitude towards the MDP and, like the rest of the Appellant's Art. 9(1) cases, do not reflect an international consensus that the MDP is prohibited as a rule of CIL. The AG has also pointed out that since there are 31 States which continue to impose the MDP for drug-related and other serious offences, the widespread state practice and the *opinio juris sive necessitatis* ("*opinio juris*") necessary to establish the prohibition of that penalty as a rule of CIL are lacking.

Our decision on the Article 9(1) challenge

The "inhuman punishment" limb

46. We shall first consider the "inhuman punishment" limb of the Article 9(1) challenge, which rests on the premise that the expression "law" in Art. 9(1) should be interpreted as excluding MDP legislation because such legislation lays down an inhuman punishment (*viz.*, the MDP). Article 9(1), which we set out earlier at para. 11 above and which we reproduce again below for ease of reference, provides as follows:

No person shall be deprived of his life or personal liberty save in accordance with law.

47. In view of the wording of Art. 9(1), the key issue in the Article 9(1) challenge is whether the MDP deprives a person of his life "in accordance with law". This, in turn, raises the question of what the word "law" as used in Art. 9(1) means (in this regard, see paras. 13-19 above, where we set out our local jurisprudence on the meaning of "law" in Art. 9(1)). Mr Ravi accepts (in keeping with the case law which he has referred to) that any law (*i.e.*, any common law rule or any legislation properly enacted by the Legislature) that provides for the death penalty as a form of punishment is, *prima facie*, "law" for the purposes of Art. 9(1). Hence, he accepts—correctly—that the death penalty *per se* does not violate Art. 9(1) (in this regard, see also para. 6 above). What he argues (in reliance on the Appellant's Art. 9(1) cases as defined at para. 34 above) is, instead, that *MDP* legislation violates Art. 9(1) because such legislation prescribes an inhuman punishment (*i.e.*, the MDP) for an offence. As alluded to at para. 7 above, Mr Ravi's contention is that it

is the taking away of judicial discretion as to whether or not to impose the death penalty which makes the MDP an inhuman punishment as each offender is then treated in the same way as any other offender convicted of **[514]** the same offence, regardless of the circumstances in which he committed the offence and, thus, regardless of his personal culpability.

48. Significantly, all of the Appellant's Art. 9(1) cases concern the offence of murder, unlike the offence in issue in this appeal, which is the offence of drug trafficking. Hence, the rationale underlying those cases has no direct application to the present appeal. In this regard, it is pertinent to note the following comments made by Lord Diplock in *Ong Ah Chuan* at 674 (these comments, although made in relation to Art. 12(1), are also relevant to the present discussion on Art. 9(1)):

Wherever a criminal law provides for a mandatory sentence for an offence there is a possibility that there may be considerable variation in moral blameworthiness, despite the similarity in legal guilt of offenders upon whom the same mandatory sentence must be passed. In the case of murder, a crime that is often committed in the heat of passion, the likelihood of this is very real; *it is perhaps more theoretical than real in the case of large scale trafficking in drugs, a crime [for] which the motive is cold calculated greed.* [emphasis added]

49. With regard to the offence of drug trafficking, what is an appropriate threshold of culpability for imposing the MDP is, in our view, really a matter of policy, and it is for Parliament to decide, having regard to public interest requirements, how the scale of punishment ought to be calibrated. This is *par excellence* a policy issue for the Legislature and/or the Executive, and not a judicial issue for the Judiciary. The MDA does not recognise any gradations in culpability in drug trafficking offences except in terms of the amount of controlled drugs trafficked. In this regard, it is a matter of common sense that the larger the amount trafficked, the greater the likelihood of harm done to society. Accordingly, even if the Appellant's Art. 9(1) cases bear out the conclusion that the MDP is an inhuman punishment when it is prescribed as the punishment for murder, it does not necessarily follow that the MDP, when prescribed as the punishment for drug trafficking, is likewise an inhuman punishment. In any event, whatever might be the merits of the argument (based on the Appellant's Art. 9(1) cases) that the MDP imposed for the offence of murder is an inhuman punishment and is thus unconstitutional, this argument has been foreclosed by constitutional developments in Singapore (see paras. 61-72 below).

50. It should also be noted that the Appellant's Art. 9(1) cases (leaving aside *Mithu* (para. 34 *supra*)) were decided in a different *textual*

context. All of those cases (save for *Mithu*) involved Constitutions which *expressly* prohibited inhuman punishment. The key issue in those cases was thus interpretative in nature, *i.e.*: in relation to the constitutional prohibition against inhuman punishment, was the MDP an inhuman punishment? The decisions in the Appellant's Art. 9(1) cases (apart from *Mithu*) are therefore technically decisions on the question of what kind of punishment would **[515]** constitute inhuman punishment and, strictly speaking, are *not* relevant to the meaning of the expression "law" in Art. 9(1) of the Singapore Constitution. Hence, these cases are not direct authority on the question of whether the MDP provisions in the MDA constitute "law" for the purposes of Art. 9(1).

51. That the Appellant's Art. 9(1) cases (other than *Mithu*) concern interpretative issues can be seen from the following comments by Lord Bingham in *Reyes* (para. 24 *supra* at paras. 25-6):

25. In a modern liberal democracy it is ordinarily the task of the democratically elected legislature to decide what conduct should be treated as criminal, so as to attract penal consequences, and to decide what kind and measure of punishment such conduct should attract or be liable to attract. The prevention of crime, often very serious crime, is a matter of acute concern in many countries around the world, and prescribing the bounds of punishment is an important task of those elected to represent the people. *The ordinary task of the courts is to give full and fair effect to the penal laws which the legislature has enacted. This is sometimes described as deference shown by the courts to the will of the democratically-elected legislature. But it is perhaps more aptly described as the basic constitutional duty of the courts which, in relation to enacted law, is to interpret and apply it.*

26. *When (as here) an enacted law is said to be incompatible with a right protected by a Constitution, the court's duty remains one of interpretation.* If there is an issue (as here there is not) about the meaning of the enacted law, the court must first resolve that issue. Having done so it must interpret the Constitution to decide whether the enacted law is incompatible or not ... As in the case of any other instrument, the court must begin its task of constitutional interpretation by carefully considering the language used in the Constitution. But it does not treat the language of the Constitution as if it were found in a will or a deed or a charterparty. A generous and purposive interpretation is to be given to constitutional provisions protecting human rights. *The court has no licence to read its own predilections and moral values into the Constitution, but it is required to consider the substance of the fundamental right at issue and ensure contemporary protection of that right in the light of evolving standards of decency that mark the progress of a maturing society* ... [emphasis added]

52. In this appeal, Mr Ravi is arguing that, as a matter of interpretation, Art. 9(1) of the Singapore Constitution should be read as

incorporating some form of prohibition against inhuman punishment similar to the prohibition expressed in the various Constitutions at issue in the Appellant's Art. 9(1) cases (apart from *Mithu*). In other words, what Mr Ravi is seeking to argue is that the expression "law" in Art. 9(1) *excludes* a law that provides for an inhuman punishment. We must emphasise that Mr Ravi is not arguing that Art. 9(1) *expressly* prohibits inhuman punishment. He cannot make that argument on the face of Art. 9(1) without asking the court to (in effect) legislate those words into Art. 9(1). What he is **[516]** arguing, instead, is that Art. 9(1) should be interpreted generously to prohibit a law that prescribes an inhuman punishment because human values have changed and legal norms should also change to reflect such changed human values. Mr Ravi's argument, really, is that the world has changed and so have the civilised norms of humanity, with the result that the MDP is no longer acceptable, and, thus, this court should depart from *Ong Ah Chuan* (para. 4 *supra*) and *Nguyen* (para. 4 *supra*).

53. Indeed, Mr Ravi has argued that the world had already changed by the time *Ong Ah Chuan* was decided in 1980, with the MDP being widely recognised by then as an inhuman punishment which was not "in accordance with law" for the purposes of Art. 9(1), but the Privy Council in *Ong Ah Chuan* failed to recognise or understand this. In this connection, Mr Ravi has referred to *Bowe* (para. 30 *supra*), where the Privy Council held that the Bahamian courts had made a similar mistake in failing to recognise, prior to the coming into force of the 1973 Constitution of the Bahamas, the incompatibility of the MDP with the constitutional prohibition against (*inter alia*) inhuman punishment (this prohibition was first set out in s 3 of the 1963 Constitution of the Bahamas; it was subsequently reproduced as, respectively, s 3 of the 1969 Constitution of the Bahamas and s 17 of the 1973 Constitution of the Bahamas). Lord Bingham said (at para. 42):

It is ... clear that it took some time for the legal effect of entrenched human rights guarantees to be appreciated, not because the meaning of the rights changed but because the jurisprudence on human rights and constitutional adjudication was unfamiliar and, by some courts, resisted. The task of the court today is not to conduct a factual inquiry into the likely outcome had the present challenge been presented on the eve of the 1973 Constitution [when the 1969 Constitution of the Bahamas was still in force]. That would be an inappropriate exercise for any court to adopt, perhaps turning on personalities and judicial propensities. The task is to ascertain what the law, correctly understood, was at the relevant time, unaffected by later legal developments, since that is plainly the law which should have been declared had the challenge been presented then. As it is, all the building blocks of a correct constitutional exposition were in place well before 1973. It matters little what lawyers and judges might have thought in their own minds: in the context of a codified Constitution, what matters is what the Constitution says and what it has been interpreted to mean. In 1973 there was no good authority contrary to the appellants' argument [*viz.*, that the MDP was an inhuman punishment and thus contravened the constitutional prohibition against such punishment], and much to support it. In the final resort, the most important consideration is that those who are entitled to the protection of human rights guarantees should enjoy that protection. The appellants should not be denied such protection because, a quarter century before they were condemned to death, the law was not fully understood.

54. We do not accept Mr Ravi's criticism of *Ong Ah Chuan*. There may be good reasons why Lord Bingham held in *Bowe* that the Bahamian courts had made the mistake outlined in the preceding paragraph (we should add **[517]** that his Lordship's holding was based on the constitutional development of the Bahamas from colonial times until the Bahamas became an independent State in 1973 (see paras. 13-21 of *Bowe*)). But, where the Singapore Constitution is concerned, Mr Ravi's criticism of *Ong Ah Chuan* borders on the fanciful as it suggests *incorrectly* that: (a) Lord Diplock did not understand the nature of the MDP and thus failed to recognise it as an inhuman punishment (when his Lordship had specifically said (at 673 of *Ong Ah Chuan*) that there was nothing unusual about a capital sentence being mandatory and that the efficacy of a capital sentence as a deterrent might to some extent be diminished if it were not mandatory); and (b) our courts (in post-*Ong Ah Chuan* decisions) did not understand the term "law" as interpreted by the Privy Council in *Ong Ah Chuan*.

55. Mr Ravi has made much of the Privy Council cases relating to Art. 9(1) (as defined at para. 45 above) in attempting to buttress his case that Art. 9(1) should be read as prohibiting inhuman punishment, including the MDP. His argument implies that even though there is no express prohibition against inhuman punishment in the Singapore Constitution, it does not follow that Art. 9(1), which sets out the right to life, cannot be interpreted as prohibiting such punishment. In this regard, Mr Ravi points to *Reyes* (para. 34 *supra*), where the Privy Council stated that, given its decision that the MDP provided for under s 102(1) of the Belize Criminal Code *vis-à-vis* the offence of "class A" murder violated s 7 of the Belize Constitution, it was unnecessary to analyse the compatibility of that provision with ss 3 and 4 of the Belize Constitution (apropos the right to life), but "[that] should not ... be taken as a rejection of the defendant's arguments based on

those sections" (at para. 48). Another case which Mr Ravi has relied on is *Matthew* (para. 24 *supra*), where the Privy Council, although focusing its analysis on the issue of whether the MDP was cruel and unusual punishment and, thus, inconsistent with the prohibition against such punishment in s 5(2)(b) of the Constitution of Trinidad and Tobago, also stated (in addition to finding that the MDP was inconsistent with that constitutional provision) that the MDP was inconsistent with s 4(a) of the Constitution of Trinidad and Tobago (which sets out "the right of the individual to life, liberty, security of the person and enjoyment of property and the right not to be deprived thereof except by *due process of law*" [emphasis added]).

56. Mr Ravi has further submitted that international human rights norms are relevant in interpreting the Singapore Constitution as our courts, to the extent that is permitted by the language of the Singapore Constitution, will be slow to interpret constitutional provisions as being inconsistent with Singapore's international legal obligations. In this regard, Mr Ravi argues that, even though the Singapore Constitution does not expressly prohibit inhuman punishment, this court should, following the path made on Caribbean soil by the Privy Council in cases such as *Reyes* and *Matthew*, **[518]** likewise read the moral bases of human rights—which include the right to be protected from inhuman punishment—into the expression "law" in Art. 9(1). This right (*i.e.*, the right to be protected from inhuman punishment), Mr Ravi emphasises, is recognised in, *inter alia*, Art. 5 of the UDHR, which provides that "[n]o one shall be subjected to torture or to cruel, inhuman or degrading treatment or punishment", and Art. 3 of the European Convention on Human Rights (4 November 1950), 213 UNTS 221 ("the ECHR"), which provides that "[n]o one shall be subjected to torture or to inhuman or degrading treatment or punishment".

57. In his book *The Idea of Justice* (Allen Lane, 2009), Prof. Amartya Sen ("Prof. Sen") points out (at p. 359):

The framers of the [UDHR] in 1948 clearly hoped that the articulated recognition of human rights would serve as a kind of a template for new laws that would be enacted to legalize those human rights across the world. The focus was on fresh legislation, and not just on more humane interpretation of existing legal protections.

58. In this regard, Prof. Sen agrees (at p. 363) with Herbert Hart's view that moral rights (which would include human rights) should be seen as "*parents of law*" [emphasis in original]—*i.e.*, as motivators of specific legislation—rather than as "child[ren] of law" (see, likewise, p. 363), which was Jeremy Bentham's view. This observation has

resonance in the following comments by Lord Bingham in *Reyes* at paras. 27-8 (although it should be noted that his Lordship's comments were made for a different purpose):

27. In considering what norms have been accepted by Belize as consistent with the fundamental standards of humanity, it is relevant to take into account the international instruments incorporating such norms to which Belize has subscribed ... By becoming a member of the Organisation of American States Belize proclaimed its adherence to rights which, although not listed in the Charter of the Organisation, are expressed in the Declaration [*i.e.*, the American Declaration of the Rights and Duties of Man adopted in 1948 at the Ninth International Conference of American States]. With some differences of wording, all these instruments prohibit "cruel, inhuman or degrading treatment or punishment", words equivalent in meaning to those used in this Constitution [*i.e.*, the Belize Constitution]. As more fully discussed below, the requirement of humanity has been read as incorporating the precept that consideration of the culpability of the offender and of any potentially mitigating circumstances of the offence and the individual offender should be regarded as a sine qua non of the humane imposition of capital punishment.

28. In interpreting the Constitution of Belize it is also relevant to recall that for 28 years preceding independence the country was covered by the [ECHR], the provisions of which were in large measure incorporated into Part II of the [Belize] Constitution ... [But this] does not mean that in interpreting the Constitution of Belize effect need be given to treaties not incorporated into **[519]** the domestic law of Belize or non-binding recommendations or opinions made or given by foreign courts or human rights bodies. *It is open to the people of any country to lay down the rules by which they wish their state to be governed* and they are not bound to give effect in their Constitution to norms and standards accepted elsewhere, perhaps in very different societies. [emphasis added]

59. We agree that domestic law, including the Singapore Constitution, should, as far as possible, be interpreted consistently with Singapore's international legal obligations. There are, however, inherent limits on the extent to which our courts may refer to international human rights norms for this purpose. For instance, reference to international human rights norms would not be appropriate where the express wording of the Singapore Constitution is not amenable to the incorporation of the international norms in question, or where Singapore's constitutional history is such as to militate against the incorporation of those international norms (in this regard, see further paras. 61-72 below). In such circumstances, in order for our courts to give full effect to international human rights norms, it would be necessary for Parliament to first enact new laws (as the drafters of the UDHR hoped States would do) or even amend the Singapore Constitution to expressly

provide for rights which have not already been incorporated therein. Both of these measures are, as Lord Bingham observed in *Reyes* at para. 28 (reproduced in the preceding paragraph), well within the prerogative of a sovereign State. In short, the point which we seek to make is this: where our courts have reached the limits on the extent to which they may properly have regard to international human rights norms in interpreting the Singapore Constitution, it would not be appropriate for them to legislate new rights into the Singapore Constitution under the guise of interpreting existing constitutional provisions.

60. Where the Singapore Constitution is concerned, we are of the view that it is not possible to incorporate a prohibition against inhuman punishment through the interpretation of existing constitutional provisions (in this case, Art. 9(1)) for two reasons.

61. First, unlike the Constitutions of the Caribbean States, the Singapore Constitution does not contain any express prohibition against inhuman punishment. Our constitutional history is quite different from that of the Caribbean States. Belize and the other Caribbean States modelled their Constitutions after the ECHR, whereas the Singapore Constitution—specifically, Pt IV thereof on fundamental liberties—was derived (albeit with significant modifications) from Pt II of the 1957 Constitution of the Federation of Malaya ("the 1957 Malayan Constitution"), which formed the basis of what we shall hereafter refer to as "the 1963 Malaysian Constitution" (*viz.*, the Constitution of Malaysia that came into effect when Malaysia (comprising the Federation of Malaya, Singapore, Sabah and Sarawak) was formed on 16 September 1963). It is a little known legal fact **[520]** that the ECHR was made applicable to Singapore and the Federation of Malaya in 1953 just as it was made applicable to Belize and several other British colonies by virtue of the UK's declaration under Art. 63 of the ECHR (see Karel Vasak, "The European Convention of Human Rights Beyond the Frontiers of Europe" (1963) 12 ICLQ 1206 at p. 1210). The ECHR ceased to apply in the respective British colonies upon their independence (in the case of Singapore, the ECHR ceased to apply when we became a constituent State of Malaysia in 1963), but Belize and many other former British colonies (especially those in the Caribbean) modelled their Constitutions after the ECHR. As a result, the Constitutions of these countries included a prohibition against inhuman punishment. This was not the case for either Malaysia or Singapore.

62. When the 1957 Malayan Constitution was drafted (pursuant to advice from the Federation of Malaya Constitutional Commission chaired by Lord Reid ("the Reid Commission")), no reference was made to a prohibition against inhuman punishment in any provision of the

draft Constitution; *i.e.*, the Reid Commission did not recommend the incorporation of such a prohibition. Given that the Reid Commission's report (*viz., Report of the Federation of Malaya Constitutional Commission 1957* (11 February 1957)) was published in 1957 when the prohibition against inhuman punishment already existed in the ECHR (which applied to the Federation of Malaya prior to its independence), the omission of a similar prohibition from the 1957 Malayan Constitution was clearly not due to ignorance or oversight on the part of the Reid Commission. The prohibition against inhuman punishment was likewise omitted from the 1963 Malaysian Constitution.

63. When Singapore separated from Malaysia and became an independent sovereign republic on 9 August 1965, we inherited a state Constitution (*i.e.*, the Constitution of the State of Singapore set out in Schedule 3 to the Sabah, Sarawak and Singapore (State Constitutions) Order in Council 1963 (GN No SI of 1963)) and many provisions of the 1963 Malaysian Constitution, including (*inter alia*) the provisions on fundamental liberties that are now Arts. 9-16 in Pt IV of the Singapore Constitution. As a result of the aforesaid developments in our constitutional history, the Singapore Constitution, unlike many other Commonwealth Constitutions, is not modelled after the ECHR and does not contain an express prohibition against inhuman punishment. This weakens Mr Ravi's contention that the Singapore Constitution should be read as incorporating an implied prohibition to this effect.

64. The second and more important reason why it is not possible to interpret the Singapore Constitution as incorporating a prohibition against inhuman punishment is that a proposal to add an *express* constitutional provision to this effect was made to the Government in 1966 by the constitutional commission chaired by Wee Chong Jin CJ ("the Wee **[521]** Commission"), but that proposal was ultimately rejected by the Government. The Wee Commission was appointed to look into (among other things) the protection of minority rights in Singapore after we became an independent sovereign republic. To this end, the Wee Commission studied the constitutional texts of some 40 different British colonies and dominions and newly independent nations as well as non-Commonwealth Constitutions (see *Evolution of a Revolution: Forty Years of the Singapore Constitution* (Li-ann Thio & Kevin Y. L. Tan eds.) (Routledge Cavendish, 2009) at pp. 11-12), and, in its written report (*viz., Report of the Constitutional Commission 1966* (27 August 1966) ("the 1966 Report")), went out of its way to recommend, *inter alia*, the inclusion of a constitutional provision prohibiting torture or inhuman punishment.

65. The Wee Commission gave the following reasons for its recommendation (see the 1966 Report at para. 40):

In looking at other written Constitutions[,] we find *a fundamental human right* which is acknowledged and protected in all of them but which is not written into the Constitution of Malaysia [*i.e.*, the 1963 Malaysian Constitution, certain provisions of which continued in force in Singapore after 9 August 1965 by virtue of the Republic of Singapore Independence Act 1965 (Act 9 of 1965)]. This is the right of every individual not to be subjected to torture or inhuman treatment. We think it is beneficial if this right is written into the Constitution of Singapore as a fundamental right and accordingly we recommend a new Article as follows—

> 13. —(1) *No person shall be subjected to torture or to inhuman or degrading punishment or other treatment.*
>
> (2) Nothing contained in or done under the authority of any law shall be held to be inconsistent with or in contravention of this Article to the extent that the law in question authorises the infliction of any punishment or the administration of any treatment that was lawful immediately before the coming into force of this Article.

[emphasis added]

For convenience, we shall hereafter refer to the new Article proposed by the Wee Commission as "the proposed Art. 13", and to the two subsections of this proposed Article as, respectively, "the proposed Art. 13(1)" and "the proposed Art. 13(2)".

66. Three things may be noted about the proposed Art. 13. The first is that the proposed Art. 13(1) is effectively word for word the same as both Art. 3 of the ECHR and s 7 of the Belize Constitution (which was the subject matter of the decision in *Reyes* (para. 24 *supra*)). The second is that the proposed Art. 13(1) and the proposed Art. 13(2) are *in pari materia* with: (a) ss 15(1) and 15(2) respectively of the Constitution of Barbados (which provisions were commented on by the Privy Council in *Boyce* (para. 24 *supra*) at, *inter alia*, para. 28); and (b) ss 17(1) and 17(2) respectively of the Constitution of Jamaica (which Constitution was construed in *Pratt* (para. 18 **[522]** *supra*), a decision rejected by this court in *Jabar* (para. 17 *supra*) (see para. 18 above)). Third, the proposed Art. 13(2), which is essentially a savings clause to preserve the validity *of punishments* existing before the coming into force of the proposed Art. 13 (regardless of whether or not such punishments are inhuman), is also substantially the same as para. 10 of Schedule 2 to the Saint Lucia Constitution Order 1978 (SI 1978/1901) ("the Saint Lucia savings clause").

67. The Saint Lucia savings clause reads as follows:

Nothing contained in or done under the authority of any law shall be held to be inconsistent with or in contravention of section 5 of the Constitution [of Saint Lucia] to the extent that the law in question authorises the infliction of any description of punishment that was lawful in Saint Lucia immediately before 1 March 1967 (being the date on which Saint Lucia became an associated state).

68. In *Hughes*, the Privy Council held that the above clause was inadequate to save the MDP imposed for murder under s 178 of the Criminal Code of Saint Lucia as revised in 1992 ("Saint Lucia's Criminal Code") from unconstitutionality (in terms of violating the constitutional prohibition against inhuman punishment set out in s 5 of the Constitution of Saint Lucia). The Privy Council, relying on the word "authorises" (which is also used in the proposed Art. 13(2)), stated (at para. 47 of *Hughes* (para. 34 *supra*)):

[T]here is a world of difference between a law that *requires* a judge to impose the death penalty in all cases of murder and a law that merely *authorises* him to do so. More particularly, it is because the law requires, rather than merely authorises, the judge to impose the death sentence that there is no room for mitigation and no room for the consideration of the individual circumstances of the defendant or of the murder. [emphasis added]

Proceeding on this basis, the Privy Council held that s 178 of Saint Lucia's Criminal Code fell outside the scope of the Saint Lucia savings clause "to the extent that it... require[d] the infliction of the death penalty in all cases of murder" (at para. 48). In other words, the Saint Lucia savings clause saved only the discretionary death penalty, but not the MDP.

69. Since the proposed Art. 13 is not part of the Singapore Constitution, the Privy Council's decision in *Hughes*, which turned on the interpretation of the word "authorises" in the Saint Lucia savings clause, is not relevant in the present appeal. Nevertheless, we wish to add that, whatever the legislative intent of the Saint Lucia savings clause was, we find it difficult to believe that when the Wee Commission raised the proposed Art. 13(2) for the Government's consideration, it intended to exclude from the protection of this provision all punishments "required" by law, such as the MDP for murder, mandatory caning for other offences as well as the various mandatory minimum punishments prescribed under the then existing criminal statutes (for example, the Vandalism Act 1966 (Act 38 of 1966), **[523]** which came into force on 16 September 1966). It seems to us that the converse

was more likely, *i.e.*, the Wee Commission intended the proposed Art. 13(2) to prevent the raising of any argument that any pre-existing lawful punishment of whatever nature would be in violation of the proposed Art. 13(1) upon the proposed Art. 13 taking effect.

70. In this regard, we note that the word "requires" was not used in the proposed Art. 13(2). The word used was, instead, "authorises". It is an established principle of interpretation that the meaning of a word is derived from the context in which that word is used. The purpose of a savings clause in the nature of the proposed Art. 13(2) is clearly to save from possible unconstitutionality all existing punishments that were lawful prior to the coming into effect of a new constitutional right (such as that set out in the proposed Art. 13(1)). If the word "authorises" in such a savings clause is indeed intended to exclude existing punishments that are "required" to be imposed (*i.e.*, mandatory punishments such as the MDP), it would be far easier to simply abrogate all those punishments so as to conform to the new constitutional right in question, instead of leaving the constitutional validity of those punishments in doubt until a court decides, long after the event, which of the "required" punishments are saved and which are not. It seems to us rather surprising that a punishment which the court is "required" to impose for a particular offence (*e.g.*, the MDP) can be construed as falling outside the ambit of "authorised" punishments. This is because, if the court is "required" to inflict a particular punishment, it is *a fortiori* authorised to inflict that punishment.

71. Returning to the Wee Commission's recommendations as set out in the 1966 Report, the Government accepted many of those recommendations in their entirety. There were other recommendations which the Government agreed to in principle, but not with regard to the details; and there were yet other recommendations which the Government found to be unacceptable. In respect of the proposed Art. 13, the Government accepted *in principle* that no individual should be subjected to torture, but it omitted any reference to protection from inhuman punishment (see *Singapore Parliamentary Debates, Official Report* (21 December 1966) vol. 25 at cols. 1052-3) (Mr E. W. Barker, Minister for Law and National Development)). Ultimately, the Government did not include the proposed Art. 13 in the amendments to the Singapore Constitution, and the Constitution (Amendment) Act 1969 (Act 19 of 1969), which was passed to give effect to provisions of the 1966 Report that the Government accepted, provided for only the establishment of what is now the Presidential Council for Minority Rights to, *inter alia*, serve as "an additional check on ... matters which might affect the minorities" (see the 1966 Report at para. 16).

72. The Government's rejection of the proposed Art. 13 was unambiguous, whatever the reasons for such rejection were. This **[524]** development, in our view, forecloses Mr Ravi's argument that it is open to this court to interpret Art. 9(1) of the Singapore Constitution as incorporating a prohibition against inhuman punishment. We may reasonably assume that the Wee Commission recommended the inclusion of the proposed Art. 13 in the Singapore Constitution because Art. 9(1) did not deal with the same subject matter as that of the proposed Art. 13(1) (*viz.*, prohibition of inhuman punishment); otherwise, Art. 9(1) would have been redundant. The Government's rejection of the proposed Art. 13(1)—the content of which forms the basis of the ruling in the Privy Council cases relating to Art. 9(1) that the MDP is an inhuman punishment—makes it impossible for the Appellant to now challenge the constitutionality of the MDP by relying on these Privy Council cases. It is not legitimate for this court to read into Art. 9(1) a constitutional right which was decisively rejected by the Government in 1969, especially given the historical context in which that right was rejected. We therefore conclude that Mr Ravi's proposed interpretation of Art. 9(1) as incorporating a prohibition against inhuman punishment is an interpretation which our courts are barred from adopting.

73. In this connection, we wish to highlight Lord Bingham's observation in *Reyes* (para. 24 *supra*) at para. 28 (quoted at para. 58 above) that States are not bound to give effect in their Constitutions to norms and standards accepted elsewhere, perhaps in very different societies. It is also pertinent to refer to the judgment of Lord Nicholls in *Matthew* (para. 24 *supra*), where his Lordship said:

> 73. . . . . If the requisite legislative support for a change in the Constitution is forthcoming, a deliberate departure from fundamental human rights may be made, profoundly regrettable although this may be. That is the prerogative of the legislature.
> 74. If departure from fundamental human rights is desired, that is the way it should be done. The Constitution should be amended explicitly . . .

74. In our view, the reasoning of Lord Nicholls in the above quotation is equally apt to apply to the Government's decision in 1969 to reject the proposed Art. 13, with the result that the right to freedom from inhuman punishment was not elevated to a constitutional right. There is, in substance, no difference between *repealing* an existing constitutional provision prohibiting inhuman punishment and *deliberately deciding not to enact* such a constitutional provision in the first place. On this ground alone, there is no legitimate basis for this court to now

expand, via an interpretative exercise, the scope of Art. 9(1) so as to include a prohibition against inhuman punishment.

75. This conclusion does not mean that, because the proposed Art. 13 included a prohibition against torture, an Act of Parliament that permits torture can form part of "law" for the purposes of Art. 9(1). Currently, no domestic legislation permits torture. In any case, torture is not the issue **[525]** before us. All that is necessary is for us to reiterate the Privy Council's position in *Ong Ah Chuan* (para. 4 *supra* at 659 (quoted at para. 16 above)) that Art. 9(1) does not justify all legislation, whatever its nature. It also bears mention that the Government has expressed the view that torture is wrong (see *Singapore Parliamentary Debates, Official Report* (29 July 1987) vol. 49 at cols. 1491-2 (Prof. S. Jayakumar, Minister for Home Affairs)). This explicit recognition by the Government that torture is wrong in the local context stands in sharp contrast to the absence of any statement on its part (in the context of our national policy on combating drug trafficking in Singapore) that the MDP is an inhuman punishment. In addition, torture, in so far as it causes harm to the body with criminal intent, is already criminalised under ch XVI of the Singapore Penal Code, which sets out the types of offences affecting the human body.

76. We shall now consider the Appellant's reliance on *Mithu* (para. 34 *supra*) to support the contention that Art. 9(1) of the Singapore Constitution should be read as incorporating a prohibition against inhuman punishment. Mr Ravi has submitted that, in *Mithu*, the Supreme Court of India ruled that the MDP was unconstitutional as it violated Arts. 14 and 21 of the Indian Constitution (*viz.*, the Indian equivalent of, respectively, Arts. 12(1) and 9(1) of the Singapore Constitution).

77. Articles 14 and 21 of the Indian Constitution read as follows:

> 14. The State shall not deny to any person equality before the law or the equal protection of the laws within the territory of India.
>
> . . .
>
> 21. No person shall be deprived of his life or personal liberty except *according to procedure established by law.* [emphasis added]

The issue in *Mithu* was whether s 303 of the Indian Penal Code (which, as mentioned at para. 39 above, lays down the MDP for the offence of murder committed by a person whilst under a sentence of life imprisonment) infringed these two Articles of the Indian Constitution. The Supreme Court of India held that s 303 infringed Art. 14 as there was no rational justification for making a distinction between the punishment imposed on a person who committed murder whilst under a sentence of life imprisonment and the punishment imposed on a person who committed murder under other circumstances.

78. With regard to Art. 21, the Indian Supreme Court held that the phrase "procedure established by law" meant "according to fair, just and reasonable procedure established by valid law" (see *Mithu* at para. 6). On this basis, the Supreme Court held, further, that:

(a) **[526]** it was harsh, unjust and unfair to condemn a murderer to death without taking into account the circumstances in which he committed the murder (at para. 12); and
(b) a provision which precluded the court from exercising judicial discretion as to whether or not the MDP should be imposed was arbitrary and oppressive (at para. 25).

In short, what the Indian Supreme Court objected to in *Mithu* was the fact that, under s 303 of the Indian Penal Code (at para. 25):

The scales of justice are removed from the hands of the Judge so soon as he pronounces the accused guilty of the offence [and] ... the sentence of death ... [is] provide[d] for ... without involvement of the judicial mind ...

79. In our view, there are three reasons why, contrary to what Mr Ravi advocated, we cannot apply the reasoning in *Mithu* to interpret Art. 9(1) of the Singapore Constitution as prohibiting inhuman punishment generally and the MDP in particular. The first reason is that the test for the constitutional validity of laws under Art. 9(1) of the Singapore Constitution is different from the test under Art. 21 of the Indian Constitution. *Mithu* was not a case about inhuman punishment (*cf* the decisions in the rest of the Appellant's Art. 9(1) cases), although Chandrachud CJ did say in his judgment (at para. 6) that "[a] savage sentence [was] anathema to the civilized jurisprudence of Article 21" (in this regard, the learned Chief Justice gave the example of cutting off the offender's hands as a punishment for theft). The issue before the court was not whether the MDP was inhuman, but whether s 303 of the Indian Penal Code was procedurally "fair, just and reasonable" (at para. 6) when it "deprive[d] the Court of the use of its wise and beneficent discretion in a matter of life and death" (at para. 12). What we now have to consider is whether this test of fair, just and reasonable procedure employed by the Indian Supreme Court ("the 'fair, just and reasonable procedure' test") for the purposes of determining the constitutional validity of laws under Art. 21 of the Indian Constitution is applicable in our local context to Art. 9(1) of the Singapore Constitution.

80. As stated earlier (at paras. 11 and 46 above), Art. 9(1) of the Singapore Constitution provides as follows:

No person shall be deprived of his life or personal liberty save *in accordance with law*. [emphasis added]

Although the expression "law" may include substantive law as well as procedural law, it does not follow that any procedural law must be "fair, just and reasonable" (see *Mithu* (para. 34 *supra*) at para. 6) before it can constitute "law" for the purposes of Art. 9(1). Article 9(1) contains no such qualification; nor can such a qualification be implied from its context or its wording. It must also be noted that the Privy Council in *Ong Ah Chuan* (para. 4 *supra*) did not adopt the "fair, just and reasonable procedure" test as the **[527]** criterion for determining the constitutional validity of laws under Art. 9(1) (because that would have been too vague a test of constitutionality). Such a test hinges on the court's view of the reasonableness of the law in question, and requires the court to intrude into the legislative sphere of Parliament as well as engage in policy making. Thus, in *Ong Ah Chuan*, the Privy Council only required, for the purposes of Art. 9(1), that any law depriving a person of his life or personal liberty must be consistent with "fundamental principles of natural justice" (at 670).

81. Our second reason for rejecting Mr Ravi's submissions on *Mithu* is that the Indian Supreme Court in that case paid no regard to the overall context of Art. 21 of the Indian Constitution, which applies not only to deprivation of life, but also deprivation of personal liberty. The court declared the MDP as provided for under s 303 of the Indian Penal Code to be inconsistent with Art. 21 without reference to the context of that Article, which (as just mentioned) also allows for derogation from the right to personal liberty. If the objection to the MDP is the absence of judicial discretion to calibrate the sentence according to the circumstances of the case, then all mandatory sentences (and, indeed, all fixed minimum and maximum sentences prescribed by the Legislature) will contravene Art. 21. It may be that this is the law in India. But, it is not the law in Singapore. In *Ong Ah Chuan*, this was an extreme position which the appellants' counsel refrained from taking (see *Ong Ah Chuan* at 673 (as reproduced at para. 21 above)). Mr Ravi has also not taken this position before this court.

82. It may well be that the Indian Supreme Court in *Mithu* considered that the death penalty was qualitatively different from other punishments (a view also expressed by Stewart J in *Woodson* (para. 7 *supra*) at 305 (quoted at para. 37 above)), and, thus, a *different* standard

must be adhered to in terms of the *procedure* for imposing the death penalty. With respect, we do not think this reasoning is applicable to Art. 9(1) of the Singapore Constitution. While we agree that it is beyond doubt that the death penalty is qualitatively different from other lesser punishments, the relevant question in this appeal is whether Parliament's power to legislate for the imposition of the death penalty as the *mandatory* punishment for a serious offence is circumscribed because of this qualitative difference. In our view, the plain wording of Art. 9(1) does not support the conclusion that Parliament cannot make the death penalty mandatory. We do not think that we can give to Art. 9(1) of the Singapore Constitution the same expansive interpretation as that which the Indian Supreme Court has given to Art. 21 of the Indian Constitution.

83. Our third reason for not applying the reasoning in *Mithu* to Art. 9(1) of the Singapore Constitution is that the Indian Supreme Court has given Art. 21 of the Indian Constitution pride of place in India's constitutional framework. The expansive interpretation of Art. 21 was established progressively in three cases, namely, *Smt Maneka Gandhi* v. *Union of India* AIR 1978 SC 597, *Sunil Batra* v. *Delhi Administration* AIR 1978 SC 1675 **[528]** and *Bachan Singh* v. *State of Punjab* AIR 1980 SC 898. The decision in *Mithu* is entirely understandable, having regard to the economic, social and political conditions prevailing in India and the proactive approach of the Indian Supreme Court in matters relating to the social and economic conditions of the people of India. In this regard, since its decision in *Mithu*, the Indian Supreme Court has expanded the scope of Art. 21 even further to include numerous rights relating to life, such as the right to education, the right to health and medical care and the right to freedom from noise pollution (see generally *Shorter Constitution of India* (A. R. Lakshmanan *et al.* eds.) (LexisNexis Butterworths Wadhwa Nagpur, 14th edn, 2009) at vol. 1, pp. 364-414).

84. In our view, it is not possible for this court to interpret Art. 9(1) of the Singapore Constitution in the same way that the Indian Supreme Court has interpreted Art. 21 of the Indian Constitution. Although the right to life is the most basic of human rights, Art. 9(1) of the Singapore Constitution expressly allows a person's life to be taken away in accordance with law. The MDP is provided by law. With regard to the offence of murder, the MDP has been the punishment prescribed by our penal legislation since 14 March 1883, when what is now s 302 of the Singapore Penal Code was enacted via s 1 of the Penal Code Amendment Ordinance 1883 (Ordinance 2 of 1883) ("the Penal Code Amendment

Ordinance"). The MDP was not abolished by the UK government during the period when the ECHR applied in Singapore (see para. 61 above), and it survived under the 1963 Malaysian Constitution as well as the Singapore Constitution. The constitutional validity of the MDP was affirmed by the Privy Council in 1980 in *Ong Ah Chuan* (para. 4 *supra*) and also by this court in 2004 in *Nguyen* (para. 4 *supra*). Since the latter decision, there has been no change in the legal matrix (including CIL (see paras. 87-99 below)) that requires this court to give a different interpretation to the expression "law" in Art. 9(1) and declare that MDP legislation is not "law" for the purposes of this provision. The development in human rights jurisprudence as manifested in the Privy Council cases relating to Art. 9(1) is not relevant to the interpretation of Art. 9(1) as those cases all concern the meaning of express constitutional prohibitions against inhuman punishment.

85. For the foregoing reasons, we reject Mr Ravi's submissions on *Mithu* and, in turn, the Appellant's argument on the "inhuman punishment" limb of the Article 9(1) challenge.

86. We would add that, in so far as this limb of the Article 9(1) challenge rests on the argument that the objectionable element in MDP legislation is the absence of judicial discretion in imposing the punishment prescribed by law (from the viewpoint that MDP legislation requires the courts to impose the MDP in an arbitrary, absurd or mindless manner on different offenders regardless of the different circumstances of each offender's case), it raises an issue which is, in essence, no different from the question of whether MDP **[529]** legislation is consistent with the right under Art. 12(1) of the Singapore Constitution, *i.e.*, the right to equal protection of the law. In other words, Mr Ravi's objection to the MDP provisions in the MDA on the ground that these provisions are arbitrary and thus inconsistent with Art. 12(1) overlaps with the objection based on Art. 9(1) (*viz.*, that Art. 9(1) does not sanction an arbitrary law that takes away an individual's life). In the context of Art. 9(1), the argument is that the MDP provisions in the MDA impose the MDP on convicted drug traffickers in so arbitrary and absurd a manner that these provisions cannot constitute "law". In the context of Art. 12(1), the argument is that the MDP provisions in the MDA, which make the 15g differentia the only criterion, to the exclusion of all other considerations, for determining whether or not the MDP is to be imposed for trafficking in diamorphine, are arbitrary and thus do not accord to convicted drug traffickers equal protection of the law. We shall address this point below (at paras. 111-19) when we consider the Article 12(1) challenge.

The "contrary to CIL" limb

87. We now turn to the "contrary to CIL" limb of the Article 9(1) challenge, which is based on the proposition that CIL prohibits the MDP as an inhuman punishment and, because CIL is "law" for the purposes of Art. 9(1) of the Singapore Constitution, the MDP is unconstitutional. This limb of the Article 9(1) challenge is quite different from the "inhuman punishment" limb, which centres on interpreting the expression "law" in Art. 9(1) to exclude any law providing for inhuman punishment. On his part, the AG expressed his agreement that the expression "law" should be given a liberal, rather than a restrictive, interpretation to include CIL (see para. 44 above). However, as we pointed out earlier (likewise at para. 44 above), we do not think that the AG meant to agree that so long as it can be shown to the satisfaction of the court that a particular rule has become part of CIL, that rule automatically becomes "law" for the purposes of Art. 9(1) in the sense that it becomes part of Singapore law by operation of either the common law or Art. 9(1) itself. Be that as it may, even if the AG did agree with Mr Ravi's proposition that "law" in Art. 9(1) includes CIL, this court is free to reject this submission. As a general principle, the court is not obliged to accept as the law what the parties agree should be the law, even in a case such as the present, where one of the parties concerned is the AG acting in his capacity as the Public Prosecutor. Thus, in the present case, we can—and, indeed, must—still consider whether the interpretation advanced by Mr Ravi (*viz.*, that CIL is part of "law" for the purposes of Art. 9(1)) is an interpretation which is legally correct.

88. Let us first consider the effect of the proposition that the expression "law" in Art. 9(1) includes CIL. If this proposition were accepted, it would mean that any rule of CIL would be cloaked with constitutional status and would override any existing MDP legislation, such as s 302 of the Singapore **[530]** Penal Code, which, as mentioned at para. 84 above, can be traced back to 1883 (see s 1 of the Penal Code Amendment Ordinance).

89. Ordinarily, in common law jurisdictions, CIL is incorporated into domestic law by the courts as part of the common law in so far as it is not inconsistent with domestic rules which have been enacted by statutes or finally declared by the courts. (A rule of CIL may, of course, also be incorporated by statute, but, in that situation, the rule in question will become part of domestic legislation and will be enforced as such; *i.e.*, it will no longer be treated as a rule of CIL.) The classic exposition of the principle delineating when a CIL rule becomes part of domestic common law is set out in the Privy Council case of *Chung Chi*

Cheung (para. 44 supra) (cited by this court in *Nguyen* (para. 4 supra) at para. 94), where Lord Atkin explained (at 167-8):

[S]o far, at any rate, as the Courts of this country are concerned, international law has no validity save in so far as its principles are accepted and adopted by our own domestic law. There is no external power that imposes its rules upon our own code of substantive law or procedure. The Courts acknowledge the existence of a body of rules which nations accept amongst themselves. On any judicial issue they seek to ascertain what the relevant rule is, and, having found it, they will treat it as incorporated into the domestic law, so far as it is not inconsistent with rules enacted by statutes or finally declared by their tribunals.

Other authorities which illustrate this principle include *Collco Dealings Ltd* v. *Inland Revenue Commissioners* [1962] AC 1 (likewise referred to in *Nguyen* at para. 94); Ian Brownlie, *Principles of Public International Law* (Oxford University Press, 7th edn, 2008) at p. 44; *Oppenheim's International Law, Volume 1: Peace* (Robert Jennings and Arthur Watts eds.) (Longman, 9th edn, 1992) at p. 56; and Peter Malanczuk, *Akehurst's Modern Introduction to International Law* (Routledge, 7th rev. edn, 1997) at p. 69.

90. The principle enunciated by Lord Atkin in *Chung Chi Cheung* entails that, at common law, a CIL rule must first be accepted and adopted as part of our domestic law before it is valid in Singapore— *i.e.*, a Singapore court would need to determine that the CIL rule in question is consistent with "rules enacted by statutes or finally declared by [our] tribunals" (*per* Lord Atkin in *Chung Chi Cheung* at 168) and either declare that rule to be part of Singapore law or apply it as part of our law. Without such a declaration or such application, the CIL rule in question would merely be floating in the air. Once that CIL rule has been incorporated by our courts into our domestic law, it becomes part of the common law. The common law is, however, subordinate to statute law. Hence, ordinarily, CIL which is received via the common law is subordinate to statute law. If we accept Mr Ravi's submission that the expression "law" in Art. 9(1) includes CIL, the hierarchy of legal rules would be reversed: any rule of CIL that is received via the common law would be cloaked with constitutional status **[531]** and would nullify any statute or any binding judicial precedent which is inconsistent with it.

91. In our view, a rule of CIL is not self-executing in the sense that it cannot become part of domestic law until and unless it has been applied as or definitively declared to be part of domestic law by a domestic court. The expression "law" is defined in Art. 2(1) to include the common law only "in so far as it is in operation in Singapore". It must therefore

follow that until a Singapore court has applied the CIL rule prohibiting the MDP as an inhuman punishment (if such a rule exists) or has declared that rule as having legal effect locally, that rule will not be in operation in Singapore. In the present case, given the existence of the MDP in several of our statutes, our courts cannot treat the alleged CIL rule prohibiting inhuman punishment as having been incorporated into Singapore law, and, therefore, this alleged CIL rule would not be "law" for the purposes of Art. 9(1). We might add that (as noted at para. 44 above), in *Nguyen*, this court held (at para. 94) that in the event of any conflict between a rule of CIL and a domestic statute, the latter would prevail.

92. There is an even stronger reason why, even if we accept that "law" in Art. 9(1) includes CIL, the specific CIL rule prohibiting the MDP as an inhuman punishment (assuming there is such a rule) cannot be regarded as part of "law" for the purposes of this provision. As mentioned earlier (at paras. 64-5 and 71 above), the Wee Commission had in 1966 recommended adding a prohibition against inhuman punishment (in the form of the proposed Art. 13) to the Singapore Constitution, but that recommendation was rejected by the Government. Given that the Government deliberated on but consciously rejected this suggestion of incorporating into the Singapore Constitution an express prohibition against *inhuman punishment generally*, a CIL rule prohibiting such punishment—let alone a CIL rule prohibiting *the MDP specifically* as an inhuman punishment—cannot now be treated as "law" for the purposes of Art. 9(1). In other words, given the historical development of the Singapore Constitution, it is not possible for us to accept Mr Ravi's submission on the meaning of the expression "law" in Art. 9(1) without acting as legislators in the guise of interpreters of the Singapore Constitution.

93. In any event, there is one other crucial threshold which Mr Ravi must cross before he can make out a case that "law" in Art. 9(1) includes the CIL prohibition against the MDP (assuming this prohibition does indeed exist), namely, he must show that the content of the CIL rule prohibiting inhuman punishment is such as to prohibit the MDP specifically. To this question, we now turn.

94. In attempting to show that the prohibition against the MDP has become part and parcel of the CIL rule prohibiting inhuman punishment, Mr Ravi has relied on the following evidence:

(a) **[532]** first, the fact that only 14 countries in the world (*i.e.*, approximately 7% of the countries in the world) still retain the MDP for drug-related offences;

(b) second, the plethora of decisions (including the Privy Council cases relating to Art. 9(1)) which hold the MDP to be an inhuman punishment; and
(c) third, the opinions of Ms Jahangir and Mr Alston on the status of the MDP (see para. 40 above).

By way of rebuttal, the AG has pointed out that there are in fact 31 States which still retain the MDP for drug-related and other serious offences (see para. 45 above).

95. In an extensive survey of the status of the death penalty worldwide, Roger Hood and Carolyn Hoyle, the learned authors of *The Death Penalty: A Worldwide Perspective* (Oxford University Press, 4th edn, 2008) ("*The Death Penalty*"), make the following observations on the MDP in relation to drug-related offences specifically (at pp. 137-8):

Many countries in Asia, the Middle East, and North Africa, and in a few other parts of the world, have responded to international concern about the growth of illicit trafficking in "dangerous" drugs by introducing the death penalty for both importation and "possession for sale" of certain amounts of such drugs, or by making the death penalty mandatory for such offences where it was previously optional. According to a survey in 1979, the death penalty could be imposed for drug trafficking in 10 countries. Just six years later, in 1985, a United Nations survey revealed that such offences could, in certain circumstances, be punished by death in 22 countries. By the end of 2006 the number was at least 31 . . .

. . . A number of these countries have made the death penalty mandatory, especially for recidivist drug offenders and trading on a large scale. Others, such as Iran (1969), Thailand (1979), Singapore (1975 and 1989), and Malaysia (1983) have made capital punishment mandatory for possession of even relatively small amounts . . .

The learned authors then continue as follows (at pp. 279-80):

The death penalty is still mandatory for some crimes in less than a third (31) of the 95 retentionist and abolitionist *de facto* countries that at present (December 2007) retain the death penalty on their statute books, even if no persons have been, or are very rarely, executed for them. Whilst it is usually only mandatory for "capital murder", it is still the only sentence available for armed robbery in several African countries, including Kenya (ADF [abolitionist *de facto*]), Nigeria, Tanzania (ADF), and Zambia. Further, 12 of the 26 countries which introduced the death penalty for producing, or trading in, illicit drugs have made it mandatory on conviction of possessing quantities over certain prescribed (and sometimes relatively modest) amounts. This is the case in Brunei Darussalam (ADF), Egypt, Guyana **[533]** (ADF), India, Iran, Jordan, Malaysia, Qatar, Saudi Arabia, Singapore, Thailand and the United Arab Emirates . . .

96. Of the States referred to in the two passages quoted above, the practice in India is inconclusive. Despite the Supreme Court of India's decision in *Mithu* (para. 34 *supra*) (discussed at paras. 76-85 above) that s 303 of the Indian Penal Code was unconstitutional, subsequent to that decision, the Indian legislature passed the Narcotics Drugs and Psychotropic Substances Act 1985 (Act 61 of 1985) (India) and the Scheduled Castes and the Scheduled Tribes (Prevention of Atrocities) Act 1989 (Act 33 of 1989) (India), both of which provide for the MDP. Also, some of the other States referred to in the above extracts from *The Death Penalty* are abolitionist *de facto*, which means that they retain the MDP on their statute books, but in practice do not carry out that penalty. Leaving aside those States and India, this still leaves a significant number of States which impose, both in law and in practice, the MDP for drug-related and other serious offences. As a result, although the majority of States in the international community do not impose the MDP for drug trafficking, this does not make the prohibition against the MDP a rule of CIL. Observance of a particular rule by a majority of States is not equivalent to extensive and virtually uniform practice by all States (see further para. 98 below). The latter, together with *opinio juris*, is what is needed for the rule in question to become a rule of CIL.

97. As for the Privy Council cases relating to Art. 9(1) and the expert opinions of Ms Jahangir and Mr Alston, they are relevant, but they are not in themselves sources of CIL. Instead, they are a *subsidiary* means for determining the existence or otherwise of rules of CIL. This well-established proposition is encapsulated in Art. 38(1)(d) of the Statute of the International Court of Justice (26 June 1945), 33 UNTS 993 ("the ICJ Statute"), which provides that:

1. The Court, whose function is to decide in accordance with international law such disputes as are submitted to it, shall apply:

   a. international conventions, whether general or particular, establishing rules expressly recognized by the contesting states;
   b. international custom, as evidence of a general practice accepted as law;
   c. the general principles of law recognized by civilized nations;
   d. subject to the provisions of Article 59, judicial decisions and the teachings of the most highly qualified publicists of the various nations, as *subsidiary means* for the determination of rules of law. [emphasis added]

98. Hence, although "judicial decisions and the teachings of the most highly qualified publicists of the various nations" (*per* Art. 38(1)(d) of the ICJ Statute) are relevant in determining the existence of rules of CIL, [534] they are relevant only as a subsidiary means for such

determination (see generally Andreas Zimmermann, Christian Tomuschat and Karin Oellers-Frahm, *The Statute of the International Court of Justice: A Commentary* (Oxford University Press, 2006) at paras. 298-324). In the final analysis, as the International Court of Justice observed in *Case Concerning the Continental Shelf (Libyan Arab Jamahiriya v. Malta)* [1985] ICJ 13 at para. 27, the substance of CIL "is to be looked for primarily in the actual practice and *opinio juris* of States". To establish a rule of CIL, the state practice accompanying the *opinio juris* of States must be "both extensive and virtually uniform" (see the seminal decision of the International Court of Justice on CIL in *North Sea Continental Shelf Cases (Federal Republic of Germany v. Denmark; Federal Republic of Germany v. Netherlands)* [1969] ICJ 3 at para. 74; see also *Case Concerning Right of Passage over Indian Territory (Portugal v. India)* [1960] ICJ 6 at 40 and *Asylum Case (Colombia v. Peru)* [1950] ICJ 266 at 276-7). As we stated above (at para. 96), there is a lack of extensive and virtually uniform state practice to support Mr Ravi's contention that CIL prohibits the MDP as an inhuman punishment.

99. For these reasons, we are unable to accept Mr Ravi's contention that the content of the CIL rule prohibiting inhuman punishment is such as to prohibit the MDP. In our view, there does not presently exist a rule of CIL prohibiting the MDP as an inhuman punishment. Accordingly, we also reject Mr Ravi's arguments on the "contrary to CIL" limb of the Article 9(1) challenge. The Article 9(1) challenge therefore fails.

The Article 12(1) Challenge: Whether the MDP Provisions in the MDA are Consistent with the Right to Equal Protection in Article 12(1)

The Appellant's arguments

100. Turning now to the Article 12(1) challenge, this is a challenge to the constitutional validity of the MDP provisions in the MDA on the ground that these provisions, in using the 15g differentia (as defined at para. 8 above) to determine when the MDP is to be imposed, cause arbitrary distinctions to be drawn between offenders who traffic in different amounts of controlled drugs and thus violate Art. 12(1) of the Singapore Constitution.

101. Article 12(1) reads as follows:

Equal protection

12. —(1) All persons are equal before the law and entitled to the equal protection of the law.

In *Ong Ah Chuan* (para. 4 *supra*), the Privy Council commented on this provision (at 673-4) as follows:

What article 12(1) of the [Singapore] Constitution assures to the individual is the right to equal treatment with other individuals in similar circumstances. It prohibits laws which require that some individuals within a single class **[535]** should be treated by way of punishment more harshly than others; it does not forbid discrimination in punitive treatment between one class of individuals and another class in relation to which there is some difference in the circumstances of the offence that has been committed.

... The questions whether [a] dissimilarity in circumstances justifies any differentiation in the punishments imposed upon individuals who fall within one class and those who fall within the other, and, if so, what are the appropriate punishments for each class, are questions of social policy. Under the [Singapore] Constitution, which is based on the separation of powers, these are questions which it is the function of the legislature to decide, not that of the judiciary. *Provided that the factor which the legislature adopts as constituting the dissimilarity in circumstances is not purely arbitrary but bears a reasonable relation to the social object of the law, there is no inconsistency with article 12(1) of the [Singapore] Constitution.* [emphasis added]

102. In relation to the specific drug trafficking offence which the Appellant was charged with (*i.e.*, the offence of trafficking in diamorphine), Mr Ravi has advanced six arguments as to why the 15g differentia bears no reasonable connection to the object of the MDA and is arbitrary.

103. Mr Ravi's first argument is that the application of the 15g differentia entails that the death penalty is mandatory for trafficking where the offender traffics in just slightly more than 15g of diamorphine (*e.g.*, 15.01g), but is unavailable altogether where the offender traffics in just under 15g of diamorphine (*e.g.*, 14.99g). This distinction, so Mr Ravi submits, is illogical, and, even if there is a quantitative and incremental increase in guilt or social mischief associated with trafficking in an additional 0.02g of diamorphine (taking the example just outlined), it is inappropriate for our sentencing regime to respond to this by a qualitative and non-incremental increase in the penalty prescribed for the offence.

104. The second argument advanced by Mr Ravi is that the death penalty is also unavailable altogether where an offender has multiple convictions for trafficking in less than 15g of diamorphine. In other words, if the offender is convicted of two counts of trafficking in 14.99g of diamorphine, the death penalty is unavailable even though the offender has demonstrated a more conscious assumption of risk and greater imperviousness to deterrence than a one-time offender who traffics in

just slightly more than 15g of diamorphine (and, as a result, faces the MDP).

105. Mr Ravi's third argument is that the MDP, which precludes the court from considering, for sentencing purposes, the circumstances in which the offence came to be committed, denies the Prosecution and the public the benefit of having information on the type of offenders who are more likely to re-offend. This impedes the Legislature's determination of whether the MDP is necessary or whether it is in fact superfluous.

[536] 106. The fourth argument put forth by Mr Ravi is that the sentencing regime under the MDA is too rigid because it denies the court the opportunity to consider any major factual differences between different cases of drug trafficking.

107. Mr Ravi's fifth argument is that the sentencing regime, although predicated on considerations of general deterrence, does not allow the court to take into account whether the offender in question voluntarily assumed the risk of trafficking in controlled drugs. It is contended that, since whether or not the 15g differentia is satisfied depends on the amount of pure diamorphine contained in the substance trafficked, it is unlikely that a drug courier would ever know whether the substance which he traffics contains the requisite amount of pure diamorphine needed to satisfy the 15g differentia and thus attract the MDP.

108. The sixth and final argument by Mr Ravi is that the sentencing regime fails to differentiate between an offender who traffics in just slightly more than 15g of diamorphine and one who traffics in multiple times that quantity since both offenders will, if convicted, be sentenced to death.

The Prosecution's response

109. In response to Mr Ravi's arguments, the AG has referred to *Nguyen* (para. 4 *supra*), where this court set out (at para. 70) the two-step "reasonable classification" test for determining the validity under Art. 12(1) of a differentiating factor prescribed by the Legislature for distinguishing between different classes of offenders for sentencing purposes, *viz.*:

A "differentiating measure" such as the 15g differentia is valid if:

(a) the classification is founded on an *intelligible* differentia; and
(b) the differentia bears a *rational relation* to the *object* sought to be achieved by the law in question. [emphasis in original]

In this connection, the AG has submitted that the 15g differentia is an intelligible differentia which bears a rational relation to the social object sought to be achieved by the MDA (which is to deter large-scale drug traffickers from plying their trade in or through Singapore).

110. We shall now consider these arguments in turn.

Our analysis of the Appellant's arguments

111. With regard to Mr Ravi's first argument as set out at para. 103 above, we agree that the difference between the punishment for trafficking in just slightly more than 15g of diamorphine and that for trafficking in just slightly under 15g of this drug is stark. This, however, does not mean that the 15g differentia is therefore arbitrary. The test for whether this differentia violates Art. 12(1) is, as the AG has rightly pointed out, the two-step **[537]** "reasonable classification" test outlined at para. 70 of *Nguyen*. Specifically, what we are concerned with in this appeal is the "rational relation" limb of this test (referred to hereafter as "the 'rational relation' test" for short), *viz.*: is there a *rational* relation between the 15g differentia (which is based on the quantity of diamorphine trafficked) and the social object of the MDA? (This test is, for all intents and purposes, the same as the "reasonable relation" test enunciated by Lord Diplock in *Ong Ah Chuan* (para. 4 *supra*) at 673-4 (reproduced at para. 101 above).) Mr Ravi contends that, in applying this test, the court cannot take the view that so long as the 15g differentia goes *some* distance towards advancing the social object of the MDA, a rational relation will be found. If that were the case, Mr Ravi submits, even purely arbitrary differentiating factors could survive the "rational relation" test. For instance, it would be permissible to use the length of the offender's hair as the criterion for determining when the MDP is applicable because imposing the death penalty on all drug traffickers with short hair would go *some* distance towards eradicating the illicit drug trade. We agree with Mr Ravi on this point. The test is one of *rational* relation precisely to exclude the use of purely arbitrary differentiating factors. To take Mr Ravi's example, the length of the drug trafficker's hair clearly does not bear any rational relation to the social object of the MDA.

112. Where the MDA is concerned, it cannot be said that the 15g differentia is purely arbitrary. In *Ong Ah Chuan*, the Privy Council said (at 674) in relation to the question of whether the 15g differentia bore a "reasonable relation" (at 674) to the social object of the MDA:

The social object of the [MDA] is to prevent the growth of drug addiction in Singapore by stamping out the illicit drug trade and, in particular, the trade in those most dangerously addictive drugs, heroin and morphine. The social evil caused by trafficking which the [MDA] seeks to prevent is broadly proportional to the quantity of addictive drugs brought on to [*sic*] the illicit market. There is nothing unreasonable in the legislature's holding the view that an illicit dealer on the wholesale scale who operates near the apex of the distributive pyramid requires a stronger deterrent to his transactions and deserves more condign punishment than do dealers on a smaller scale who operate nearer the base of the pyramid. It is for the legislature to determine in the light of the information that is available to it about the structure of the illicit drug trade in Singapore, and the way in which it is carried on, where the appropriate quantitative boundary lies between these two classes of dealers.

We agree with this observation. We would also add that the quantity of addictive drugs trafficked is not only broadly proportionate to the quantity of addictive drugs brought onto the illicit market, but also broadly proportionate to the scale of operations of the drug dealer and, hence, broadly proportionate to the harm likely to be posed to society by the offender's crime. For these reasons, we find that the 15g differentia bears a rational relation to the social object of the MDA.

[538] 113. Our finding that there is a rational relation between the 15g differentia and the social object of the MDA should not, however, be taken to mean that this differentia is the best and that there is no other better differentia which would further the social object of the MDA. In this regard, we appreciate the points made in Mr Ravi's second, third and fourth arguments at paras. 104-6 above, all of which suggest possible reasons for expanding the differentia to take into account something more than just the quantity of controlled drugs trafficked. We should also point out that although a differentia which takes into account something more than merely the quantity of controlled drugs trafficked may be a better differentia than the 15g differentia, what is a better differentia is a matter on which reasonable people may well disagree. This question is, in truth, a question of social policy, and, as the Privy Council stated in *Ong Ah Chuan* at 673 (quoted at para. 101 above), it lies within the province of the Legislature, not the Judiciary. Our judiciary has to respect the constitutional role of our legislature as delineated in the Singapore Constitution (under Art. 38), and this is why our courts will only act to ensure that the differentia employed in the MDA for determining when the MDP is to be imposed bears a rational relation to the social object of that statute. As mentioned in the preceding paragraph, we find that the 15g differentia does satisfy this test.

114. With regard to the fifth argument canvassed by Mr Ravi at para. 107 above, we do not agree that a drug courier who does not know the amount of pure diamorphine contained in the substance which he traffics is one who has not voluntarily assumed the risk of trafficking. There is no need for a drug courier to know the precise amount of pure

diamorphine contained in the substance which he traffics in order to know that his act causes harm to society and is illegal, and that he will be punished if he is caught and convicted.

115. With regard to Mr Ravi's sixth argument at para. 108 above, we do not think it can be taken seriously. If this argument were accepted, it would apply even if the 15g differentia is changed such that a far greater amount of diamorphine must be trafficked before the MDP becomes applicable. For instance, if the MDP were to be imposed only if the amount of diamorphine trafficked exceeds 100kg, Mr Ravi would still be able to argue that the sentencing regime fails to differentiate between an offender who traffics in just slightly more than 100kg of diamorphine and one who traffics in multiple times that quantity. The reason why a more severe sentence is not imposed for a more egregious violation of our drug trafficking laws (in terms of trafficking in a larger quantity of controlled drugs) is that the death penalty is the ultimate punishment and there exists no punishment which is more severe. Parliament has set 15g of diamorphine as the threshold for imposing the MDP where the offence of trafficking in this drug is concerned; *i.e.*, it has decided that trafficking in any quantity of diamorphine more than 15g is sufficiently serious to warrant the imposition of the MDP. **[539]** Hence, even though trafficking in even larger quantities of diamorphine (as compared to, say, just 15.01g of diamorphine) would be a more egregious violation of the law, there is no more severe punishment which may be imposed.

116. Before we conclude our analysis of the Article 12(1) challenge, we should briefly mention another argument made by Mr Ravi which has some bearing (albeit only tangentially) on the question of whether the MDP provisions in the MDA are consistent with Art. 12(1) of the Singapore Constitution. This argument is that the MDP has in fact only a limited deterrent effect on drug couriers. To buttress this argument, Mr Ravi filed Criminal Motion No 7 of 2010 ("CM 7/2010") seeking leave for the Appellant to adduce an affidavit by Prof. Jeffrey Pagan dated 3 March 2010 ("Prof. Pagan's affidavit"), which states that the deterrent effect of the MDP for drug trafficking has not been established and that the utility of this penalty as a deterrence is limited where drug couriers are concerned. Mr Ravi sought to rely on this affidavit to argue that the imposition of the MDP on all offenders who traffic in more than 15g of diamorphine is of limited deterrent effect. In this regard, the AG has produced statistics (compiled by the UN Office on Drugs and Crime for the year 2008) to show that Singapore has one of the lowest drug addiction rates internationally, which suggests that the MDP does have a deterrent effect on drug trafficking here.

117. It is not within the purview of this court to determine the efficacy or otherwise of the MDP as a deterrent *vis-à-vis* the offence of drug trafficking. In *Ong Ah Chuan* (para. 4 *supra*), the Privy Council addressed this very point when it said (at 672-3):

Their Lordships would emphasise that in their judicial capacity they are in no way concerned with arguments for or against capital punishment or its efficacy as a deterrent to so evil and profitable a crime as trafficking in addictive drugs.

118. We would add that, although there is room for arguing that there is insufficient evidence that the MDP deters serious offences like murder, it can equally be said that there is insufficient evidence that the MDP does not have such a deterrent effect. Surveys and statistical studies on this issue in one country can never be conclusive where another country is concerned. The issue of whether the MDP has a deterrent effect is a question of policy and falls within the purview of Parliament rather than that of the courts. Therefore, Prof. Fagan's affidavit is of little practical relevance in this appeal. Accordingly, CM 7/2010 is unnecessary and we make no order on it.

119. Given our ruling that the 15g differentia bears a rational relation to the social object of the MDA, this differentia is not arbitrary and, thus, not inconsistent with Art. 12(1). In this regard, we note that the Privy Council in *Ong Ah Chuan* likewise found that a "reasonable relation" (at 674) existed **[540]** between the 15g differentia and the social object of the MDA; we have no reason to disagree with its finding. For these reasons, the Article 12(1) challenge also fails.

Conclusion

120. To summarise, our ruling on the issues raised in this appeal is as follows:

(a) Article 9(1) of the Singapore Constitution cannot be interpreted as impliedly including a prohibition against inhuman punishment because of our constitutional history (in particular, because of the Government's conscious decision not to incorporate such a prohibition into the Singapore Constitution notwithstanding the recommendation of the Wee Commission);
(b) in view of our ruling in the preceding sub-paragraph, it is unnecessary for us to decide whether the MDP is an inhuman punishment;
(c) the expression "law" in Art. 9(1) does not include CIL which has yet to be incorporated into domestic law;

(d) even if the word "law" in Art. 9(1) includes CIL which has yet to be incorporated into domestic law, we are not persuaded that the CIL rule prohibiting inhuman punishment includes a prohibition against the MDP specifically;
(e) in view of our findings at sub-paras. (a) and (d) above, the MDP is not contrary to the right to life set out in Art. 9(1); and
(f) the 15g differentia in the MDP provisions in the MDA does not draw arbitrary distinctions between offenders who traffic in different amounts of drugs and thus does not violate the right under Art. 12(1) of equal protection of the law.

121. It follows that the MDP is not unconstitutional as it does not contravene either Art. 9(1) or Art. 12(1). In view of this conclusion, it is unnecessary for us to consider Mr Ravi's submission as to the effect which the President's power to grant clemency under Art. 22P of the Singapore Constitution has on the constitutionality of the MDP.

122. Finally, we would reiterate that, in the light of our constitutional history since Singapore became an independent sovereign republic on 9 August 1965, there is no room for the argument that MDP legislation is unconstitutional because it is not "law" for the purposes of Art. 9(1). In our view, whether or not our existing MDP legislation should have been enacted and/or whether such legislation should be modified or repealed are policy issues that are for Parliament to determine in the exercise of its legislative powers under the Singapore Constitution. It is for Parliament, **[541]** and not the courts, to decide on the appropriateness or suitability of the MDP as a form of punishment for serious criminal offences. In view of the decisive rejection of a constitutional prohibition against inhuman punishment in the evolution of the Singapore Constitution (see paras. 61-72 above), any changes in CIL and any foreign constitutional or judicial developments in relation to the MDP as an inhuman punishment will have no effect on the scope of Art. 9(1). If any change in relation to the MDP (or the death penalty generally) is to be effected, that has to be done by Parliament and not by the courts under the guise of constitutional interpretation.

123. In the result, we dismiss the present appeal.

[Reports: [2010] 3 SLR 489; [2011] 1 LRC 642]

Environment — Protection of the environment — Relationship between the protection of the environment and development — Concept of sustainable development — Recognition of sustainable development by the international community — Principle of integration of environmental protection and socio-economic development — International environmental law and sustainable development — Concept of sustainable development in the law of South Africa

Human rights — Economic, social and cultural rights — Right of everyone to safe and clean environment — Inter-generational and intra-generational equity — Constitution of South Africa, Section 24 — Environment Conservation Act 1989 — National Environmental Management Act 1998 — Obligation to protect environment and promote economic and social development — Interrelationship between environment and development — Environmental authorities — Nature and scope of obligation on environmental authorities to consider socio-economic factors — Delegation of duties to local council — Whether environmental authorities fulfilled their statutory duty — Whether environmental authorities had properly considered impact of proposed development on socio-economic conditions

Relationship of international law and municipal law — Environmental law — International law on environmental protection — Relevance in interpreting and applying domestic environmental law — The law of South Africa

FUEL RETAILERS ASSOCIATION OF SOUTHERN AFRICA *v.* DIRECTOR-GENERAL ENVIRONMENTAL MANAGEMENT, DEPARTMENT OF AGRICULTURE, CONSERVATION AND ENVIRONMENT, MPUMALANGA PROVINCE AND OTHERS[1]

---

[1] The applicant was represented by M. C. Erasmus SC and J. De Beer, instructed by Swanepoel and Partners Inc. The first to sixth respondents (respectively the Director-General Environmental Management, Department of Agriculture, Conservation and Environment, Mpumalanga Province; the MEC Department of Agriculture, Conservation and Environment, Mpumalanga Province; the Department of Agriculture, Conservation and Environment, Mpumalanga Province; the Minister of Water Affairs and Forestry; the Regional Director, Department of Water Affairs and Forestry; and MEC Department of Transport and Public Works, Mpumalanga Province) were represented by J. Du Plessis and S. P. Mothle, instructed by the State Attorney, Pretoria. The seventh to twelfth Respondents (respectively Mbombela Local Municipality; Sophia Lekeisang Inama No; Matebogo Maria Inama No; Podudu Owen Inama No; Archibald Inama No; and Lowveld Motors (Pty) Ltd) were represented by M. M. Rip SC and C. M. Rip, instructed by De Swart Vögel and Mahlafonya.

South Africa, Constitutional Court. 7 *June* 2007

(Moseneke DCJ; Madala, Mokgoro, Ngcobo, Nkabinde, O'Regan, Sachs, Skweyiya and Van der Westhuizen JJ; Navsa AJ)

SUMMARY: *The facts*:—The applicant brought proceedings against the respondents to overturn approval of an application seeking authorization for the construction of a filling station on a property in the Mpumalanga region. The applicant, who represented the interests of fuel retailers, contended that, in granting the authorization, the first, second and third respondents[2] ("the environmental authorities") had failed in their statutory duty to consider the need, desirability and sustainability of the proposed petrol station, including its impact on the sustainability of existing filling stations in the area.

The environmental authorities agreed that the socio-economic impact of the proposed development had to be considered as part of the authorization process. However, they contended that, consistent with local practice, there had been no need to assess the need, desirability and sustainability of the proposed development themselves because it had already been considered by the local authority as part of the rezoning application for the property. Rezoning also formed part of the authorization process and reconsideration would have amounted to a duplication of the functions of the local council and the environmental agencies.

The applicant responded that the two processes were distinct and separate and that the local authority considered an application for rezoning from a town planning perspective whereas the environmental authorities were required to consider the impact of the proposed development on environmental and socio-economic conditions.

The High Court and Supreme Court of Appeal dismissed the applicant's claims and upheld the practice of the environmental authorities of leaving the consideration of need, desirability and sustainability to the local authority. The applicant appealed to the Constitutional Court.

Held:—The decision granting authorization for the construction of the filling station was reviewed and set aside. The application for authorization was remitted for reconsideration to the first, second and third respondents, who were also ordered to pay costs.

(1) Sustainable development was an evolving concept of international law that had received considerable endorsement from the international community. The principles of inter-generational and intra-generational equity and of integration of environmental protection and socio-economic development

---

[2] The first respondent was the Director-General Environmental Management, Department of Agriculture, Conservation and Environment, Mpumalanga Province; the second respondent was the MEC Department of Agriculture, Conservation and Environment, Mpumalanga Province; the third respondent was the Department of Agriculture, Conservation and Environment, Mpumalanga Province.

were internationally acknowledged as being fundamental to the concept of sustainable development (paras. 46-59).

(2) The concept of sustainable development in South African law had to be construed and understood in line with its development in international law. Sustainable development had a significant role to play in the resolution of environmentally related disputes under South African law and provided an important framework for the resolution of tensions between the need to protect the environment and the need for socio-economic development (paras. 44-5, 56-62).

(3) Section 24 of the Constitution guaranteed the right of everyone to a healthy environment and the Environment Conservation Act 1989 ("ECA")[3] and the National Environmental Management Act 1998 ("NEMA")[4] were legislation giving effect to that constitutional provision. The proper interpretation and nature of the obligations imposed by these provisions on the environmental authorities raised constitutional issues (paras. 40-5).

(4) The Constitution, ECA and NEMA imposed a continuing and evolving obligation on the environmental authorities to ensure the sustainability of the development and to protect the environment (paras. 71-82).

(5) The environmental authorities had misconstrued the obligations imposed on them by NEMA and unlawfully delegated their duties to the local authority. The environmental authorities had failed properly to consider the cumulative effect of the proliferation of filling stations on the aquifer and the impact of the proposed petrol station on socio-economic conditions in violation of their statutory duty (paras. 83-100, 105).

(6) The role of the courts was especially important in the context of the protection of the environment and in giving effect to the principle of sustainable development. Environmental protection was vital to the enjoyment of other rights contained in the Bill of Rights and the environment had to be protected for the benefit of present and future generations (paras. 100-4).

Per Sachs J (dissenting in part): (1) The failure by the environmental authorities had formal rather than substantive significance and was not sufficiently material to initiate judicial review proceedings under Section 6(2) of the Promotion of Administrative Justice Act 2000[5] (paras. 109-12).

(2) The essence of sustainable development was the balanced integration of socio-economic development and environmental priorities and norms. The applicant's argument was based on economic factors that, on the facts, did not truly engage the principles of sustainable development. Commercial sustainability only gained significance under NEMA to the extent that it presented an actual or potential threat to the environment (paras. 113-19).

The text of the judgments delivered in the Court commences on the opposite page.

---

[3] Act 72 of 1989. [4] Act 107 of 1998.
[5] Act 3 of 2000. The text of Section 6(2) is provided at para. 36, n 35 of the judgment.

[7] Ngcobo J

Introduction

1. This application for leave to appeal against the decision of the Supreme Court of Appeal concerns the nature and scope of the obligations of environmental authorities when they make decisions [8] that may have a substantial detrimental impact on the environment.[1] In particular, it concerns the interaction between social and economic development and the protection of the environment. It arises out of a decision by the Department of Agriculture, Conservation and Environment, Mpumalanga province (the Department), the third respondent, to grant the Inama Family Trust (the Trust)[2] authority in terms of section 22(1) of the Environment Conservation Act 1989 (ECA)[3] to construct a filling station on a property in White River, Mpumalanga (the property).

2. Section 22(1) of ECA forbids any person from undertaking an activity that has been identified in terms of section 21(1) as one that may have a substantial detrimental impact on the environment without written authorisation by the competent authority.[4] It was not disputed that the MEC Agriculture, Conservation and Environment, Mpumalanga (the MEC), the second respondent, is the competent authority designated by the Minister.[5] Before authorisation can be granted, a report concerning the impact of the proposed development on the environment

---

[1] The decision of the Supreme Court of Appeal is reported as *Fuel Retailers Association of SA (Pty) Ltd v. Director-General, Environmental Management, Mpumalanga, and Others* 2007 (2) SA 163 (SCA).

[2] The Trust was represented in the proceedings by its trustees who are the eighth to eleventh respondents.

[3] Act 73 of 1989.

[4] Section 22 of ECA provides:

(1) No person shall undertake an activity identified in terms of section 21(1) or cause such an activity to be undertaken except by virtue of a written authorization issued by the Minister or by a competent authority or local authority or an officer, which competent authority, authority or officer shall be designated by the Minister by notice in the *Gazette*.

(2) The authorization referred to in subsection (1) shall only be issued after consideration of reports concerning the impact of the proposed activity and of alternative proposed activities on the environment, which shall be compiled and submitted by such persons and in such manner as may be prescribed.

(3) The Minister or the competent authority, or a local authority or officer referred to in subsection (1), may at his or its discretion refuse or grant the authorization for the proposed activity or an alternative proposed activity on such conditions, if any, as he or it may deem necessary.

(4) If a condition imposed in terms of subsection (3) is not being complied with, the Minister, any competent authority or any local authority or officer may withdraw the authorization in respect of which such condition was imposed, after at least 30 days' written notice was given to the person concerned.

[5] These proceedings were conducted on the footing that Dr Batchelor and Mr Hlatshwayo were duly designated by the Minister for the purposes of considering applications for authorisation in terms of section 22(1).

must be furnished. The relevant authority has a discretion to grant or refuse such authorisation. In granting it, the relevant authority may impose such conditions as may be necessary to ensure the protection of the environment.

3. Section 21(1) of ECA empowers the Minister of Environmental Affairs and Tourism (the Minister) to identify activities which in his or her opinion may have a substantial detrimental effect on the environment.[6] **[9]** Subsection (2) sets out some of these activities and they include land use and transformation.[7] In Schedule 1 of GN R1182, dated 5 September 1997, the Minister identified the activities that may have a substantial detrimental effect on the environment. These include the construction or upgrading of "transportation routes and structures, and manufacturing, storage, handling or processing facilities for any substance which is dangerous or hazardous and is controlled by national legislation".[8] It is common cause that the construction of a filling station falls within this category and thus requires the authorisation contemplated in section 22(1) of ECA.

4. The decision to grant or refuse authorisation in terms of section 22(1) of ECA must be made in the light of the provisions of the National Environmental Management Act 1998 (NEMA).[9] One of the declared purposes of NEMA is to establish principles that will guide organs of state in making decisions that may affect the environment. One of these principles requires environmental authorities to consider the social,

---

[6] Section 21 of ECA provides:

(1) The Minister may by notice in *the Gazette* identify those activities which in his opinion may have a substantial detrimental effect on the environment, whether in general or in respect of certain areas.

(2) Activities which are identified in terms of subsection (1) may include any activity in any of the following categories, but are not limited thereto:

(a) land use and transformation;
(b) water use and disposal;
(c) resource removal, including natural living resources;
(d) resource renewal;
(e) agricultural processes;
(f) industrial processes;
(g) transportation;
(h) energy generation and distribution;
(i) waste and sewage disposal;
(j) chemical treatment;
(k) recreation.

(3) The Minister identifies an activity in terms of subsection (1) after consultation with—

(a) the Minister of each department of State responsible for the execution, approval or control of such activity;
(b) the Minister of State Expenditure; and
(c) the competent authority of the province concerned.

[7] Section 21(2)(a).   [8] Schedule 1 item 1(c).   [9] Act 107 of 1998.

economic and environmental impact of a proposed activity including its "disadvantages and benefits".[10]

5. The Fuel Retailers Association of Southern Africa (incorporated in terms of section 21 of the Companies Act), the applicant, challenged the decision to grant authorisation in the Pretoria High Court on various grounds. However, the only ground that concerns us in this application is that the environmental authorities in Mpumalanga had not considered the socio-economic impact of constructing the proposed filling station, a matter which they were obliged to consider. In resisting the application **[10]** on this ground the Department contended that need and desirability were considered by the local authority when it decided the rezoning application of the property for the purposes of constructing the proposed filling station. Therefore it did not have to reassess these considerations.

6. The High Court upheld the contention of the Department and dismissed the application. So did the Supreme Court of Appeal. Hence this application for leave to appeal.

7. The Director-General, Environmental Management in the Department, the first respondent, as well as the Department and the MEC are opposing the application. For convenience they are referred to as the environmental authorities. The Trust represented by its trustees and Lowveld Motors (Pty) Ltd are also opposing the application.[11]

Factual Background

8. During July 2000, the Trust, through an environmental consultant firm, Globecon Environmental Management Services (Globecon), applied to the Department for authorisation to construct a filling station on the property in terms of these provisions.[12] A scoping report, a geotechnical and geohydrological report (the Geo3 report) were submitted in support of the application.[13] The scoping report dealt with, among other matters, socio-economic factors and the presence of an

---

[10] Section 2(4)(i).

[11] The Trust subsequently sold its interest in the proposed development to Lowveld Motors (Pty) Ltd.

[12] The application was made on a prescribed form which is called a Plan of Study for Scoping.

[13] A scoping report is an environmental impact report that must be submitted in support of an application for authorisation under section 22(1) of ECA. Section 26, which empowers the Minister to make regulations concerning the scope and content of the environmental reports envisaged in section 22(1), contemplates that reports will include matters such as the identification of the economic and social interests which may be affected by the proposed activity; the extent and the nature of the effect of the proposed activity on social and economic interests; and how the adverse impact is to be minimised. By regulations regarding activities identified under section 21(1), GN R1 183 of 5 September 1997, the Minister published the regulations concerning the scope and the contents of

aquifer in the property. In addition, the scoping report contained an evaluation of the impact of the proposed filling station, identified certain areas of concern and proposed recommendations to address these concerns.

9. Under the heading "Socio-Economic Components", the scoping report referred to the implications of the proposed filling station for noise, visual impacts, traffic, municipal services, safety and crime, and cultural and historical sites. It also dealt with the feasibility of the proposed filling station and stated that—

Various other locations do exist for the proposed development, as the [11] positioning of a filling station is dictated by traffic flow, visibility, availability of land and the location of other filling stations in the area.

As the proposed filling station is directly targeting traffic moving between White River, Hazy view and the Numbi Gate of the Kruger National Park, a specific location along the said route was identified. Once the site was identified a feasibility study was done based on locating the filling station at the specific site. Once the feasibility of the filling station on the specific site was identified, and the availability of the property was confirmed, no other options were considered.

10. One of the issues identified in the report as requiring attention was the protection of an existing aquifer, a significant clean groundwater resource below the surface of the property. In the past this aquifer had been used to augment the water supply in White River. The report noted that the aquifer needed protection from pollution. The report recommended that the water quality of the aquifer through the borehole should be tested bi-annually. It proposed that if the Department of Water Affairs and Forestry (Water Affairs and Forestry) required it, an impermeable layer should be installed in the base of the pit to ensure that no contaminants from the tanks reach the aquifer. In addition, it recommended that a reconciliation programme should be in place to detect any leakage. These recommendations were made in the light of the Geo3 report.

11. The applicant, through its environmental consultants, Ecotechnik, objected to the construction of the proposed filling station on several grounds, one being that the quality of the water in the aquifer might be contaminated. Ecotechnik submitted an evaluation report which criticised the consideration of alternatives to the development as

---

reports. These reports have come to be known as "scoping reports". The provisions of ECA relating to the nature and scope of the environmental authority's obligation when considering an application for authorisation under section 22(1), as well as the scope and contents of the report that must be submitted in support of such application, must be understood in the light of the provisions of NEMA.

being vague and non-specific and pointed out that "demand and activity alternatives were not investigated". The report also took issue with the manner in which the public participation process had been conducted, pointing out that there were interested persons who had not had the opportunity to express their views on a proposed filling station that might affect them.

12. There was a further exchange of reports by the opposing consultants which dealt with the adequacy or otherwise of the proposed measures for the prevention of the contamination of the aquifer.[14] In the light of these [12] reports and, in particular, the existence of the aquifer, the Department referred the Geo3 report together with the objections raised by the applicant to Water Affairs and Forestry for comment.

13. In a very brief response, Water Affairs and Forestry accepted the Geo3 report and, on the issue of underground water, required "[t]he proposed developer [to] ensure that no pollution of the groundwater... take[s] place. And [that it] must be monitored as set out in the report and in accordance [with] all the relevant Regulations as set out by the Dept of Water Affairs and Forestry." Nothing was said about the installation of an impermeable layer, which according to the scoping report was to be installed if Water Affairs and Forestry required this. However, it subsequently transpired that the Water Quality Management and Water Utilization divisions of Water Affairs and Forestry had neither received nor commented on the Geo3 report.

14. The application was considered in the first instance by Mr Hlatshwayo, the Deputy-Director in the Department. On 9 January 2002 authorisation was granted over the objection of the applicant. A record of decision was issued, which contained the decision and conditions upon which authorisation was granted. This decision authorised the construction of a filling station, three fuel tanks, a convenience store, a canopy, ablution facilities and driveways providing access to and from

---

[14] In relation to the contamination of underground water, Globecon reiterated that if required by Water Affairs and Forestry, an impermeable layer would be installed at the base of the pit and that this would ensure that no contaminants from the tanks reach the aquifer. In relation to the public participation process, it acknowledged that the neighbours referred to in the Ecotechnik evaluation report had not been notified but blamed this on the local authority which "did not supply the consultant with all the relevant information". In a further response Ecotechnik criticised the installation of an impermeable layer at the base of the pit and the leak detection system as inadequate. It pointed out that leaks not only occur from tanks but also from pipes. It added that in any event, given the present day construction methods, "it is unlikely ... [that] constructing impermeable layers ... can be guaranteed to be 100% leak proof". It questioned the adequacy of the contamination safeguards suggested in the geological report. It expressed the opinion that if an impermeable layer is to be used it "would have to be provided not only below but on the sides as well".

the nearby streets. The record of decision was signed by Dr Batchelor, the Director of Environmental Management in the Department.

15. One of the conditions of the authorisation was that the necessary permits or approvals must be obtained from other government departments such as Water Affairs and Forestry. The record of decision sets out "key factors" which presumably influenced the decision. It noted that the property had "been rezoned from 'special' to 'Business 1'" and that all identified and perceived impacts were satisfactorily dealt with in the scoping report.

16. The applicant lodged an appeal against this decision. One of the grounds of appeal was that the need, desirability and sustainability of the proposed filling station had not been considered. It was alleged that this aspect was not addressed in the scoping report submitted by Globecon. It was also pointed out that the proposed filling station was within a radius of five kilometres from six other filling stations that adequately served the needs of the community. The applicant alleged that there had recently been a decline in the growth of fuel consumption in White River. The viability of existing filling stations would be affected and this had been exacerbated by the introduction of three new filling stations in the area.

17. In support of its ground of appeal based on need and desirability, the applicant relied on the Gauteng Provincial Government Guidelines [13] (Gauteng Guidelines)[15] which were developed by the Gauteng province to ensure that its responsibilities in respect of the protection of the environment are carried out in an efficient and considered manner. One of the general guidelines provides that new filling stations will generally not be approved where they will be "within three (3) kilometres of an existing filling station in urban, built-up or residential areas".[16] This limitation on the distance between filling stations was influenced by international experience, views of interested persons and the legislative obligations under ECA and NEMA.[17]

18. A further ground of appeal related to the inadequacy of the Geo3 report concerning measures to prevent fuel leaks. The applicants submitted a report by De Villiers and Cronje, a firm of consulting engineering geologists, which evaluated the Geo3 report and expressed the following opinion—

It is ... highly probable that the residual granitic material at the level of the fuel tanks will have geo-mechanical properties that could be conducive to the

---

[15] Gauteng Provincial Government, Agriculture, Conservation, Environmental and Land Affairs EIA Administrative Guideline: Guideline for the Construction and Upgrade of Filling Stations and Associated Tank Installations (March 2002).
[16] Id. at para. 2.1.   [17] Id. at para. 1.

spread of petro-chemical pollution into the underlying major aquifer should a leak occur in the fuel tanks. This could then contaminate the aquifer system beyond further utilization.

It concluded that—

It is therefore of the greatest importance that, in the absence of detail[ed] soil test results of all the sub-surface material at and below the level of the fuel tanks, the current and future value and intended utilization of the water from the aquifer be evaluated (as well as the presence of any other water borehole situated on the same aquifer).

19. The appeal was considered and dismissed by Dr Batchelor. It is not clear how Dr Batchelor could have considered the appeal as he had signed the record of decision. No point was taken in this regard and nothing more need be said about this issue. The reasons for dismissal are very scanty, and they are recorded in a letter. In relation to need, desirability and sustainability of the proposed filling station the letter states that these matters had been considered by the local authority.

The Review Proceedings

20. The applicant subsequently launched proceedings in the High Court, seeking an order reviewing and setting aside the decision to grant authorisation. The applicant alleged that its cause of action arose from [14] section 36 of ECA,[18] alternatively the common law, alternatively the Promotion of Administrative Justice Act 2000 (PAJA).[19]

21. The decision to grant authorisation was attacked on eleven grounds. One of the grounds was the failure to take into consideration or to properly consider the requirements of need, desirability and sustainability in relation to the proposed filling station, and another, the failure to obtain the recommendations of Water Affairs and Forestry in view of the existence of the aquifer. As pointed out earlier, the only ground of review persisted with in this Court is the one relating to need, desirability and sustainability. It is therefore this ground only that need concern us.

---

[18] Section 36 of ECA provides:

(1) Notwithstanding the provisions of section 35, any person whose interests are affected by a decision of an administrative body under this Act, may within 30 days after having become aware of such decision, request such body in writing to furnish reasons for the decision within 30 days after receiving the request.

(2) Within 30 days after having been furnished with reasons in terms of subsection (1), or after the expiration of the period within which reasons had to be so furnished by the administrative body, the person in question may apply to a division of the Supreme Court having jurisdiction, to review the decision.

[19] Act 3 of 2000.

22. Both Dr Batchelor and Mr Hlatshwayo deposed to affidavits explaining how they dealt with the application. Their evidence is substantially to the same effect. It amounts to this: need and desirability are factors that are considered by the local authority when it approves the rezoning of a property for the purposes of erecting a proposed development. As Mr Hlatshwayo put it, the requirements of need and desirability must be considered by the local authority whenever applicants apply for the rezoning of land under the Town-Planning and Townships Ordinance 1986 (the Ordinance).[20] The Department does not reconsider these factors. It is sufficient for an applicant for authorisation to state that the property has been rezoned for the construction of the proposed development. And if there is no reason to doubt this, based on this statement, the Department will ". . . accept that need and desirability has indeed been considered by the Local Councils . . . ".

23. Ms Muller, a town planner, who specialises in the lodging of applications for the rezoning of properties for filling stations, confirmed this practice. She accepted that environmental issues must be addressed, but added that it ". . . is not necessary nor desirable to duplicate functions between the Local Council and the different Departments of Agriculture, Conservation and Environment of the different provinces". In the instant case, she has no personal knowledge of the information that was placed before the town-planning authorities or of the decision that was made by the town-planning authorities in relation to need and desirability. In short, the environmental authorities did not themselves consider need and desirability nor did they check to consider whether it was in fact dealt with by the local authority.

[15] 24. It is necessary to pause here to explain the phrase "need, desirability and sustainability". The parties referred to this phrase when they were referring to socio-economic considerations. This phrase does not appear in ECA or NEMA. However, the phrase "need and desirability" is used in Schedule 7 of the Regulations promulgated under the Ordinance.[21] It is one of the factors that the local authority is required

---

[20] Ordinance 15 of 1986.
[21] Schedule 7 of the Regulations made under the Ordinance contains a specimen application form to be completed by a person who wishes to apply for an amendment of a town-planning scheme in terms of section 56 of the Ordinance. Part C of Schedule 7 lists documents and reports that must be submitted together with the application. Item C requires the applicant to enclose a report which—

(a) explains the proposed maps, annexures and schedules, if any;
(b) provides information on the geotechnical conditions and use of the land as well as traffic, including public transport, roads and parking facilities, where applicable;
(c) contains a motivation for the need and desirability of the amendment proposed.

to consider when approving the rezoning of a property. It is this factor which the environmental authorities contended must be considered by the local authority in the context of an application for authorisation under section 22(1) of ECA. Having regard to the provisions of ECA and NEMA, the proper reference must be to socio-economic considerations. Whether the phrase "need and desirability" in Schedule 7 bears the same meaning as socio-economic considerations in the context of ECA and NEMA is an issue that is dealt with later in this judgment.[22]

The Decision of the High Court

25. The High Court upheld the submission of the environmental authorities that the questions of need, desirability and sustainability are matters that must be considered by the local authority when an application for rezoning is made and that it is unnecessary for the environmental authorities to consider these factors. It held that the practice of leaving the consideration of need and desirability to the local authority is consistent with the principle of intergovernmental co-ordination and harmonisation of policies, legislation and actions relating to the environment.[23] Having found that there was no merit in the other grounds either, the High Court dismissed the application with costs, but granted the applicant leave to appeal to the Supreme Court of Appeal.

The Decision of the Supreme Court of Appeal

26. The Supreme Court of Appeal accepted that socio-economic considerations are a relevant consideration when making decisions under section 22 of ECA. Indeed, it accepted that the environment may "... be adversely affected by unneeded, and thus unsustainable, filling stations [16] that become derelict...".[24] However, it found that there was no evidence to suggest that there was a possibility of this happening.

27. Like the High Court, the Supreme Court of Appeal upheld the practice of the environmental authorities of leaving the consideration of need, desirability and sustainability to the local authority. It reasoned

---

[22] At para. 82.
[23] This is apparently a reference to section 2(4)(1) of NEMA which provides:

There must be intergovernmental co-ordination and harmonisation of policies, legislation and actions relating to the environment.

[24] Above n 1 at para. 17.

that the local authority has an obligation to consider need, desirability and sustainability when making a rezoning decision. The responsibility of the environmental authorities is to apply its mind to the question whether need and desirability had been addressed by the local authority. This they can do by having regard to the fact that rezoning had taken place and accepting that need and desirability was therefore considered by the local authority during the rezoning stage unless the rezoning decision is challenged, reasoned the Supreme Court of Appeal.

28. It accordingly concluded that having regard to the local authority's obligation, when considering an application for rezoning to consider need, desirability and sustainability, the environmental authorities had applied their mind to socio-economic considerations. In reaching its conclusion, the Supreme Court of Appeal had regard to the fact that the rezoning decision was not subject to attack and that there was no evidence that circumstances had subsequently changed.

29. Having found that there was no merit in the other grounds of review, the Supreme Court of Appeal dismissed the appeal with costs. Hence the present application for leave.

Issues Presented

30. In this Court, the applicant contended that the environmental authorities themselves were obliged to consider the socio-economic impact of constructing the proposed filling station. The applicant submitted that this obligation is wider than the requirement to assess the need and desirability of the proposed filling station under the Ordinance. This obligation requires the environmental authorities to assess, among other things, the cumulative impact on the environment brought about by the proposed filling station and all existing filling stations that are in close proximity to the proposed one. This in turn required the environmental authorities to assess the demand or necessity and desirability, not feasibility, of the proposed filling station with a view to fulfilling the needs of the targeted community, and its impact on the sustainability of existing filling stations. The applicant relied upon the provisions of section 24(b)(iii) of the Constitution,[25] as well as sections 2(4)(a),[26] 2(3), 2(4)(g), 2(4)(i),[27] 23[28] and 24[29] of NEMA.

[17] 31. The environmental authorities accepted that the socio-economic impact of the proposed filling station had to be considered.

---

[25] This provision is set out in full in para. 43. [26] This provision is set out in full in n 67 below.
[27] Sections 2(3), 2(4)(g) and 2(4)(i) are set out in full in para. 63.
[28] This provision is set out in full in para. 64. [29] This provision is set out in full in para. 65.

However, they contended that, consistently with the practice that is followed in Mpumalanga, need and desirability of the proposed filling station was considered by the local authority when it considered the rezoning of the property. They submitted that it was therefore not necessary for them to reconsider these factors. In support of this contention they relied upon section 56 of the Ordinance[30] read with Schedule 7 of

---

[30] Section 56 of the Ordinance provides:

(1) An owner of land who wishes to have a provision of a town-planning scheme relating to his land amended may, in such a manner as may be prescribed, apply in writing to the authorised local authority, and at the same time—

(a) he shall pay to the local authority such fees as may be levied by that local authority; and
(b) he shall give notice of the application—

  (i) by publishing once a week for 2 consecutive weeks a notice in such form and such manner as may be prescribed;
  (ii) by posting a notice in such form as may be prescribed in a conspicuous place on his land, and he shall maintain such notice for a period of at least 14 days from the date of the first publication of the notice contemplated in subparagraph (i): Provided that the local authority may, in its discretion, grant exemption from compliance with the provisions of this subparagraph.

(2) The authorised local authority may, in its discretion, give further notice of the application—

(a) by posting a notice in such form as may be prescribed in a conspicuous place on its notice board, and in such a case it shall maintain such notice for a period of at least 14 days from the date of the first publication of the notice contemplated in subsection (1)(b)(i);
(b) in any other manner.

(3) The applicant shall submit proof to the satisfaction of the authorised local authority that he has complied with the provisions of subsection (1).

(4) On receipt of an application in terms of subsection (1) the authorised local authority shall, subject to the provisions of subsection (5), forward—

(a) a copy thereof to—

  (i) The Transvaal Roads Department, where the land concerned or any portion thereof is situated outside an "urban area" as defined in section 1 of the Advertising on Roads and Ribbon Development Act, 1940;
  (ii) the National Transport Commission, where the land concerned or any portion thereof is situated within a "building restriction area" as defined in section 1 of the National Roads Act, 1971;
  (iii) the Director-General: Constitutional Development and Planning, where the application contemplates either the subdivision of land zoned for industrial purposes or the zoning of land for industrial purposes;
  (iv) every local authority or body providing any engineering service contemplated in Chapter V to the land concerned or to the local authority contemplated in subsection (1); and
  (v) any other department or division of the Transvaal Provincial Administration, any other state department which or any other person who, in the opinion of the local authority, may be interested in the application; and

(b) a copy of every objection lodged and all representations made in respect of the application to the applicant, and the applicant shall, within a period of 28 days from the date of receipt of the copy, forward his reply thereto to the local authority.

(5) An applicant may, in the stead of the authorised local authority and with its consent, forward a copy of the application to any person or body contemplated in subsection (4)(a) and submit proof to the satisfaction of the local authority that he has done so.

(6) Every person to whom or body to which a copy of the application has been forwarded in terms of subsection (4)(a) or (5) may, within a period of 60 days from the date on which the copy was forwarded to him or it, or such further period as the authorised local authority may allow, comment in writing thereon.

(7) Where objections have been lodged or representations have been made in respect of the application, the authorised local authority shall, subject to the provisions of section 131, hear the objections or representations.

[18] the Regulations[31] promulgated under the Ordinance.[32] The environmental authorities submitted that rezoning forms part and parcel of the process of an application for authorisation in terms of section 22 of ECA.

32. The applicant took issue with the submission that rezoning is part and parcel of the application for authorisation in terms of section 22 of ECA. The applicant submitted that the two processes are distinct and separate. The local authority considers an application for rezoning from a town-planning perspective. It focuses, in particular, on what land uses it will allow on a particular piece of land and is constrained by the applicable law to consider whether there is a need for the proposed land use and whether it is desirable. By contrast, the environmental authorities are required to consider the impact of the proposed development on the environment and socio-economic conditions.

33. The applicant also drew attention to the fact that the rezoning relied upon by the environmental authorities had taken place approximately eight years prior to the application for authorisation in terms of section 22 of ECA. It submitted that since the rezoning application was approved, there had been significant changes in the environment, including the construction of three new filling stations in the area.

34. It is therefore common cause that in considering an application for authorisation under section 22 of ECA, the environmental authorities were obliged to consider the socio-economic impact of the proposed filling station. The environmental authorities, however, equate the need and [19] desirability requirement under the Ordinance with the requirement to consider the social, economic and environmental impact of a proposed filling station. The questions which fall to be considered in

---

(8) After the provisions of subsection (7) have been complied with, the authorised local authority shall consider the application with due regard to every objection lodged and all representations made, and may for that purpose—

(a) carry out an inspection or institute any investigation;
(b) request any person to furnish such information, as it may deem expedient.

(9) Having considered the application in terms of subsection (8) the authorised local authority may—

(a) approve the application subject to such amendment which it may, after consultation with the applicant, deem fit or refuse it;
(b) postpone a decision on the application, either wholly or in part.

(10) The authorised local authority shall without delay and in writing notify the applicant, an objector or any person who has made representations, of its decision taken by virtue of the provisions of subsection (9).

[31] Above n 21.
[32] In terms of Schedule 7 of the Regulations promulgated under the Ordinance, an application for amendment of town-planning scheme must be accompanied by "a motivation for need and desirability". Item C 3(c).

this application are therefore, firstly, the nature and scope of the obligation to consider the social, economic and environmental impact of a proposed development; second, whether the environmental authorities complied with that obligation; and, if the environmental authorities did not comply with that obligation, the appropriate relief.

35. Before addressing these issues, it is necessary to consider two preliminary matters. The first is the proper cause of action in this application. The other is whether the application raises a constitutional matter, and if so, whether it is in the interests of justice to grant leave to appeal.

The Proper Cause of Action

36. In the founding affidavit, the applicant alleged that the review proceedings were being brought under section 36 of ECA,[33] alternatively the common law, alternatively PAJA. Neither the Supreme Court of Appeal nor the High Court considered the proper cause of action. They approached the matter on the footing that there was an overlap in the grounds of review under the common law, ECA and PAJA. It is apparent that the decision of this Court in *Bato Star Fishing (Pty) Ltd* v. *Minister of Environmental Affairs and Others* was not drawn to the attention of the courts below.[34] By the time the matter reached this Court, however, the applicant had made up its mind; it relied on PAJA, in particular, on subsections 6(2)(b), 6(2)(e)(iii) and 6(2)(i).[35] It is necessary to address this issue and put in context the provisions of section 36 of ECA which make provision for a person aggrieved by a decision made under ECA to approach a high court for review.

37. In *Bato Star* this Court held that "[t]he cause of action for the judicial review of administrative action now ordinarily arises from PAJA,

---

[33] See para. 20.   [34] 2004 (4) SA 490 (CC); 2004 (7) BCLR 687 (CC).
[35] Section 6(2) provides:

A court or tribunal has the power to judicially review an administrative action if—

...

(b) a mandatory and material procedure or condition prescribed by an empowering provision was not complied with;
...
(e) the action was taken—
　...
　(iii) because irrelevant considerations were taken into account or relevant considerations were not considered;
...
(i) if the action is otherwise unconstitutional or unlawful.

not from the common law as in the past".[36] Section 36 of ECA does no more than to provide for the review of decisions of environmental authorities. The grounds upon which decisions under ECA may be **[20]** reviewed are those set out in PAJA. The clear purpose of PAJA is to codify the grounds of review of administrative action. The fact that section 36 of ECA allows a person whose interests are affected by a decision of an administrative body under ECA to approach the High Court for review, does not detract from this. The provisions of section 36 must therefore be read in conjunction with PAJA which sets out the grounds on which administrative action may now be reviewed.

38. It is not in dispute that the decision by the environmental authorities to grant authorisation under section 22 of ECA is administrative action within the meaning of PAJA. It is a decision which was taken by an organ of state in the performance of a public function in terms of ECA. The environmental authorities did not contend otherwise. The applicant seeks to review the decision of the environmental authorities on three grounds. Firstly, the environmental authorities failed to comply with a mandatory material procedure or condition prescribed by ECA (subsection 6(2)(b)). Secondly, in granting the authorisation, the environmental authorities took into account irrelevant considerations and failed to consider relevant considerations (subsection 6(2)(e)(iii)). Thirdly, the decision by the environmental authorities is otherwise unconstitutional and therefore unlawful (subsection 6(2)(i)).

39. There is a significant overlap in these grounds. In the course of oral argument it became clear that the main ground of attack was that the environmental authorities failed to consider the impact of the proposed filling station on socio-economic conditions, a matter which they were required to consider. The central question in this application therefore is whether the environmental authorities failed to take into consideration matters that they were required to consider prior to granting the authorisation under section 22(1) of ECA.

Does the Application Raise a Constitutional Issue?

40. Section 24 of the Constitution guarantees to everyone the right to a healthy environment and contemplates that legislation will be enacted for the protection of the environment.[37] ECA and NEMA are legislation which give effect to this provision of the Constitution. The question to be considered in this application is the proper interpretation

---

[36] Above n 34 at para. 25.   [37] The text of section 24 is set out in full in para. 43.

of the relevant provisions of ECA and NEMA and, in particular, the nature of the obligations imposed by these provisions on the environmental authorities. The proper interpretation of these provisions raises a constitutional issue. So, too, does the application of PAJA. It follows therefore that the present application raises a constitutional issue.

Is it in the Interests of Justice to Grant Leave to Appeal?

41. This case raises an important question concerning the obligation of state organs when making decisions that may have a substantial impact on the environment. In particular, it concerns the nature and scope of the [21] obligation to consider socio-economic conditions. The need to protect the environment cannot be gainsaid. So, too, is the need for social and economic development. How these two compelling needs interact, their impact on decisions affecting the environment and the obligations of environmental authorities in this regard, are important constitutional questions. In these circumstances, it is therefore in the interests of justice that leave to appeal be granted to consider these issues.

42. In order to put the issues involved in this case in context and to evaluate the cogency of the constitutional challenge, it is necessary to understand both the constitutional and the legislative frameworks for the protection and management of the environment.

The Relevant Constitutional Provision

43. The Constitution deals with the environment in section 24 and proclaims the right of everyone—

(a) to an environment that is not harmful to their health or well-being; and
(b) to have the environment protected, for the benefit of present and future generations, through reasonable legislative and other measures that—
  (i) prevent pollution and ecological degradation;
  (ii) promote conservation; and
  (iii) secure ecologically sustainable development and use of natural resources while promoting justifiable economic and social development.

Sustainable Development

44. What is immediately apparent from section 24 is the explicit recognition of the obligation to promote justifiable "economic and social development". Economic and social development is essential to

the well-being of human beings.[38] This Court has recognised that socio-economic rights that are set out in the Constitution are indeed vital to the enjoyment of other human rights guaranteed in the Constitution.[39] But development cannot subsist upon a deteriorating environmental base. Unlimited development is detrimental to the environment and the destruction of the environment is detrimental to development. Promotion of development requires the protection of the environment. Yet the environment cannot be protected if development does not pay attention to the costs of environmental destruction. The environment and development are thus inexorably linked. And as has been observed—

[Environmental stresses and patterns of economic development are linked one to another. Thus agricultural policies may lie at the root of land, water, and [22] forest degradation. Energy policies are associated with the global greenhouse effect, with acidification, and with deforestation for fuelwood in many developing nations. These stresses all threaten economic development. Thus economics and ecology must be completely integrated in decision making and lawmaking processes not just to protect the environment, but also to protect and promote development. Economy is not just about the production of wealth, and ecology is not just about the protection of nature; they are both equally relevant for improving the lot of humankind.[40]

45. The Constitution recognises the interrelationship between the environment and development; indeed it recognises the need for the protection of the environment while at the same time it recognises the need for social and economic development. It contemplates the integration of environmental protection and socio-economic development. It envisages that environmental considerations will be balanced with socio-economic considerations through the ideal of sustainable development. This is apparent from section 24(b)(iii) which provides that the environment will be protected by securing "ecologically sustainable development and use of natural resources while promoting justifiable economic and social development". Sustainable development and sustainable use and exploitation of natural resources are at the core of the protection of the environment.

---

[38] *Declaration on the Right to Development* adopted by General Assembly Resolution 41/128 of 4 December 1986, www.un.org/documents/ga/res/41/a41r128.htm, accessed on 4 June 2007. Article 1 asserts that "[t]he right to development is an inalienable human right". The Preamble describes development as "a comprehensive economic, social, cultural and political process, which aims at the constant improvement of the well-being of the entire population".

[39] *Government of the Republic of South Africa and Others* v. *Grootboom and Others* 2001 (1) SA 46 (CC); 2000 (11) BCLR 1169 (CC).

[40] Report of the World Commission on Environment and Development: *Our Common Future* (Brundtland Report), www.un.org/esa/sustdev/documents/docs_key_conferences.htm. link: General Assembly 42nd Session: Report of the World Commission on Environment and Development, accessed on 4 June 2007. Chapter 1 at para. 42.

The Concept of Sustainable Development in International Law

46. Sustainable development is an evolving concept of international law. Broadly speaking its evolution can be traced to the 1972 Stockholm Conference. That Conference stressed the relationship between development and the protection of the environment, in particular, the need "to ensure that development is compatible with the need to protect and improve [the] environment for the benefit of their population".[41] The principles which were proclaimed at this conference provide a setting for the development of the concept of sustainable development.[42] Since then the concept of sustainable development has received considerable endorsement by the international community.[43] Indeed in 2002 people from over 180 countries gathered in our country for the Johannesburg World Summit on Sustainable Development (WSSD) to reaffirm that sustainable development is a world priority.[44]

47. But it was the report of the World Commission on Environment [23] and Development (the Brundtland Report)[45] which "coined" the term "sustainable development".[46] The Brundtland Report defined sustainable development as "development that meets the needs of the present without compromising the ability of future generations to meet their own needs".[47] It described sustainable development as—

[i]n essence . . . a process of change in which the exploitation of resources, the direction of investments, the orientation of technological development; and institutional change are all in harmony and enhance both current and future potential to meet human needs and aspirations.[48]

48. This report argued for a merger of environmental and economic considerations in decision-making[49] and urged the proposition that "the goals of economic and social development must be defined in terms of sustainability".[50] It called for a new approach to development—"a type of development that integrates production with resource conservation

---

[41] Principle 13 of the *Declaration of the United Nations Conference on the Human Environment*, held in Stockholm 1972, www.unep.org/Documents/Default.asp?DocumentID=97&ArticleID=1503, accessed on 4 June 2007.
[42] Separate Opinion of Vice-President Weeramantry in *Gabčikovo–Nagymaros Project (Hungary/Slovakia)* 37 ILM 162 (1998).
[43] Id.
[44] Segger and Weeramantry (eds.), *Sustainable Justice: Reconciling Economic, Social and Environmental Law* (Martinus Nijhoff, Leiden, 2005) 561.
[45] Above n 40.
[46] Sands, *Principles of International Environmental Law*, 2nd edn (Cambridge University Press, Cambridge, 2003) 252.
[47] Above n 40, Chapter 2 at para. 1. [48] Id. at para. 15. [49] Id. at paras. 72-80.
[50] Id. at para. 2.

and enhancement, and that links both to the provision for all of an adequate livelihood base and equitable access to resources".[51] The concept of sustainable development, according to the report, "provides a framework for the integration of environment[al] policies and development strategies".[52]

49. The 1992 Rio Conference made the concept of sustainable development a central feature of its Declaration.[53] The Rio Declaration is especially important because it reflects a real consensus in the international community on some core principles of environmental protection and sustainable development.[54] It developed general principles on sustainable development and provided a framework for the development of the law of sustainable development.[55]

50. At the heart of the Rio Declaration are Principles 3 and 4. Principle 3 provides that "[t]he right to development must be fulfilled so as to equitably meet developmental and environmental needs of present and future generations". Principle 4 provides that "[i]n order to achieve sustainable development, environmental protection shall constitute an integral part of the development process and cannot be considered in [24] isolation from it". The idea that development and environmental protection must be reconciled is central to the concept of sustainable development.[56] At the core of this Principle is the principle of integration of environmental protection and socio-economic development.

51. Commentators on international law have understandably refrained from attempting to define the concept of sustainable development. Instead they have identified the evolving elements of the concept of sustainable development.[57] These include the integration of environmental protection and economic development (the principle of

---

[51] Above n 40 at Chapter 1 para. 47.   [52] Id. at para. 48.

[53] The United Nations Conference on Environment and Development was held in Rio de Janeiro, Brazil on 3-14 June 1992, www.un.org/documents/ga/conf151/aconf15126-1annex1.htm, accessed on 4 June 2007. This Conference adopted among other instruments, the Rio Declaration on Environment and Development (the Rio Declaration).

[54] Boyle and Freestone (eds.), *International Law and Sustainable Development: Past Achievements and Future Challenges* (Oxford University Press, Oxford, 1999) 4.

[55] In this sense, the Rio Declaration provides a benchmark for measuring future developments and a basis for defining sustainable development.

[56] Above n 54 at 26.

[57] Above n 46 at 266. Sands identifies five recurring elements which appear to comprise the legal concept of sustainable development as reflected in international agreements. These are:

- the need to take into consideration the needs of present and future generations;
- the acceptance, on environmental protection grounds, of limits placed upon the use and exploitation of natural resources;
- the role of equitable principles in the allocation of rights and obligations;
- the need to integrate all aspects of environment and development; and
- the need to interpret and apply rules of international law in an integrated and systemic manner.

integration); sustainable utilisation of natural resources (the principle of sustainable use and exploitation of natural resources); the right to development; the pursuit of equity in the use and allocation of natural resources (the principle of intra-generational equity); the need to preserve natural resources for the benefit of present and future generations (the principle of inter-generational and intra-generational equity); and the need to interpret and apply rules of international law in an integrated systematic manner.[58]

52. The principle of integration of environmental protection and development reflects a—

... commitment to integrate environmental considerations into economic and other development, and to take into account the needs of economic and other social development in crafting, applying and interpreting environmental obligations.[59]

This is an important aspect of sustainable development because "its formal application requires the collection and dissemination of environmental information, and the conduct of environmental impact assessments". (Footnote omitted.)[60] The practical significance of the integration of the environmental and developmental considerations is that environmental considerations will now increasingly be a feature of economic and development policy.[61]

53. The principle of integration of environmental protection and socio-economic development is therefore fundamental to the concept of [25] sustainable development.[62] Indeed economic development, social development and the protection of the environment are now considered pillars of sustainable development. As recognised in the WSSD, States have assumed—

... a collective responsibility to advance and strengthen the interdependent and mutually reinforcing pillars of sustainable development—economic development, social development and environmental protection—at the local, national, regional and global levels.[63]

54. The concept of sustainable development has received approval in a judgment of the International Court of Justice. This much appears from the judgment of the International Court of Justice in *Gabčíkovo–Nagymaros Project (Hungary/Slovakia)* where the Court held—

---

[58] Above n 54 at 8-16. [59] Above n 46 at 263. [60] Id.
[61] Id. at 264. [62] Above n 44 at 564; above n 46 at 263.
[63] United Nations Department of Economic and Social Affairs—Division for Sustainable Development, *Johannesburg Declaration on Sustainable Development*, 2002 para. 5, www.un.org/esa/sustdev/documents/WSSD_POI_PD/English/POI_PD.htm, accessed on 4 June 2007.

Throughout the ages, mankind has, for economic and other reasons, constantly interfered with nature. In the past, this was often done without consideration of the effects upon the environment. Owing to new scientific insights and to a growing awareness of the risks for mankind—for present and future generations—of pursuit of such interventions at an unconsidered and unabated pace, new norms and standards have been developed, set forth in a great number of instruments during the last two decades. Such new norms have to be taken into consideration, and such new standards given proper weight, not only when States contemplate new activities but also when continuing with activities begun in the past. This need to reconcile economic development with protection of the environment is aptly expressed in the concept of sustainable development.[64]

55. The integration of economic development, social development and environmental protection implies the need to reconcile and accommodate these three pillars of sustainable development. Sustainable development provides a framework for reconciling socio-economic development and environmental protection. This role of the concept of sustainable development as a mediating principle in reconciling environmental and developmental considerations was recognised by Vice-President Weeramantry in a separate opinion in *Gabčíkovo–Nagymaros*, when he said—

The Court must hold the balance even between the environmental considerations and the development considerations raised by the respective Parties. The principle that enables the Court to do so is the principle of sustainable development.[65]

56. It is in the light of these developments in the international law of environment and sustainable development that the concept of sustainable development must be construed and understood in our law.

[26] *The Concept of Sustainable Development in Our Law*

57. As in international law, the concept of sustainable development has a significant role to play in the resolution of environmentally related disputes in our law. It offers an important principle for the resolution of tensions between the need to protect the environment on the one hand, and the need for socio-economic development on the other hand. In this sense, the concept of sustainable development provides a

---

[64] *Gabčíkovo–Nagymaros Project (Hungary/Slovakia)* 37 ILM 162 (1998) 200 at para. 140. In a Separate Opinion, Vice-President Weeramantry held that the concept of sustainable development is part of international customary law. See Separate Opinion at 207.

[65] Above n 42 at 204.

framework for reconciling socio-economic development and environmental protection.

58. Sustainable development does not require the cessation of socio-economic development but seeks to regulate the manner in which it takes place. It recognises that socio-economic development invariably brings risk of environmental damage as it puts pressure on environmental resources. It envisages that decision-makers guided by the concept of sustainable development will ensure that socio-economic developments remain firmly attached to their ecological roots and that these roots are protected and nurtured so that they may support future socio-economic developments.

59. NEMA, which was enacted to give effect to section 24 of the Constitution, embraces the concept of sustainable development. Sustainable development is defined to mean "the integration of social, economic and environmental factors into planning, implementation and decision-making for the benefit of present and future generations".[66] This broad definition of sustainable development incorporates two of the internationally recognised elements of the concept of sustainable development, namely, the principle of integration of environmental protection and socio-economic development, and the principle of inter-generational and intra-generational equity. In addition, NEMA sets out some of the factors that are relevant to decisions on sustainable development. These factors largely reflect international experience. But as NEMA makes it clear, these factors are not exhaustive.[67]

[27] 60. One of the key principles of NEMA requires people and their needs to be placed at the forefront of environmental

---

[66] Section 1(1)(xxix).
[67] Section 2(4)(a) of NEMA provides:

Sustainable development rquires the consideration of all relevant factors including the following:

(i) That the disturbance of ecosystems and loss of biological diversity are avoided, or, where they cannot be altogether avoided, are minimised and remedied;
(ii) that pollution and degradation of the environment are avoided, or, where they cannot be altogether avoided, are minimised and remedied;
(iii) that the disturbance of landscapes and sites that constitute the nation' s cultural heritage is avoided, or where it cannot be altogether avoided, is minimised and remedied;
(iv) that waste is avoided, or where it cannot be altogether avoided, minimised and reused or recycled where possible and otherwise disposed of in a responsible manner;
(v) that the use and exploitation of non-renewable natural resources is responsible and equitable, and takes into account the consequences of the depletion of the resource;
(vi) that the development, use and exploitation of renewable resources and the ecosystems of which they are part do not exceed the level beyond which their integrity is jeopardised;
(vii) that a risk-averse and cautious approach is applied, which takes into account the limits of current knowledge about the consequences of decisions and actions; and
(viii) that negative impacts on the environment and on people's environmental rights be anticipated and prevented, and where they cannot be altogether prevented, are minimised and remedied.

management—*batho pele*.[68] It requires all developments to be socially, economically and environmentally sustainable. Significantly for the present case, it requires that the social, economic and environmental impact of a proposed development be "considered, assessed and evaluated" and that any decision made "must be appropriate in the light of such consideration and assessment".[69] This is underscored by the requirement that decisions must take into account the interests, needs and values of all interested and affected persons.

61. Construed in the light of section 24 of the Constitution, NEMA therefore requires the integration of environmental protection and economic and social development. It requires that the interests of the environment be balanced with socio-economic interests. Thus, whenever a development which may have a significant impact on the environment is planned, it envisages that there will always be a need to weigh considerations of development, as underpinned by the right to socio-economic development, against environmental considerations, as underpinned by the right to environmental protection. In this sense, it contemplates that environmental decisions will achieve a balance between environmental and socio-economic developmental considerations through the concept of sustainable development.

62. To sum up therefore NEMA makes it abundantly clear that the obligation of the environmental authorities includes the consideration of socio-economic factors as an integral part of its environmental responsibility.[70] It follows therefore that the parties correctly accepted that the Department was obliged to consider the impact of the proposed filling station on socio-economic conditions. It is within this context that the nature and scope of the obligation to consider socio-economic factors [lies], in particular, whether it includes the obligation to assess the cumulative impact of the proposed filling station and existing ones, and the impact of the proposed filling station on existing ones. But first what are the relevant provisions of NEMA?

[28] A. *The Relevant Provisions of NEMA*

63. The provisions of NEMA which are relevant to this case and which were relied upon by the applicant are those that contain the national environmental management principles, the general objectives

---

[68] Section 2(2). [69] Section 2(4)(i).
[70] This principle was considered in the following cases: *BP Southern Africa (Pty) Ltd* v. *MEC for Agriculture, Conservation, Environment and Land Affairs* 2004 (5) SA 124 (W) at 140E-151H; *Turnstone Trading CC* v. *Director General Environmental Management, Department of Agriculture, Conservation & Development*, case no 3104/04 (T), 11 March 2005, unreported, at paras. 17-19; *MEC for Agriculture, Conservation, Environment and Land Affairs* v. *Sasol Oil (Pty) Ltd and Another* 2006 (5) SA 483 (SCA) at para. 15.

of integrated environmental management and those that deal with the implementation of these principles and objectives. The national environmental management principles that are relevant in this case are those contained in sections 2(2), 2(3), 2(4)(g) and 2(4)(i). The principles contained in these provisions require that:

Environmental management must place people and their needs at the forefront of its concern, and serve their physical, psychological, developmental, cultural and social interests equitably.[71]

Development must be socially, environmentally and economically sustainable.[72]

Decisions must take into account the interests, needs and values of all interested and affected parties, and this includes recognising all forms of knowledge, including traditional and ordinary knowledge.[73]

The social, economic and environmental impacts of activities, including disadvantages and benefits, must be considered, assessed and evaluated, and decisions must be appropriate in the light of such consideration and assessment.[74]

64. Section 23, which sets out the general objectives of integrated environmental management, proclaims as one of those objectives, the objective to—

identify, predict and evaluate the actual and potential impact on the environment, socio-economic conditions and cultural heritage, the risks and consequences and alternatives and options for mitigation of activities, with a view to minimising negative impacts, maximising benefits, and promoting compliance with the principles of environmental management set out in section 2 . . .[75]

65. Section 24,[76] which deals with the implementation of the general objectives of integrated environmental management, provides that—

In order to give effect to the general objectives of integrated environmental management laid down in this Chapter, the potential impact on—

(a) the environment;
(b) socio-economic conditions; and
(c) the cultural heritage,

---

[71] Section 2(2).   [72] Section 2(3).   [73] Section 2(4)(g).
[74] Section 2(4)(i).   [75] Section 23(2)(b).
[76] In dealing with NEMA in this case it is important to bear in mind that this statute has, since its enactment in 1998, been amended. Section 24(1) was amended in 2004 to delete the reference to social, economic and cultural impacts. However, in section 23(2)(b) the general objectives of integrated environmental management were not amended. This provision proclaims that one of the general objectives of integrated environmental management is "to identify, predict and evaluate the actual and potential impact on the environment, socio-economic conditions and cultural heritage". The provisions of NEMA that are relevant to this case are those that were in force at the time when the application for authorisation was made.

[29] of activities that require authorisation or permission by law and which may significantly affect the environment, must be considered, investigated and assessed prior to their implementation and reported to the organ of state charged by law with authorising, permitting, or otherwise allowing the implementation of an activity.[77]

66. The principles of NEMA that have been relied upon by the applicant must be understood in the context of the role of these principles in decisions affecting the environment, the general objectives of integration of environmental management and the procedures for the implementation of the NEMA principles.

67. NEMA principles "apply ... to the actions of all organs of state that may significantly affect the environment".[78] They provide not only the general framework within which environmental management and implementation decisions must be formulated,[79] but they also provide guidelines that should guide state organs in the exercise of their functions that may affect the environment.[80] Perhaps more importantly, these principles provide guidance for the interpretation and implementation not only of NEMA but any other legislation that is concerned with the protection and management of the environment.[81] It is therefore plain that these principles must be observed as they are of considerable importance to the protection and management of the environment.

68. Apart from these principles, NEMA contemplates the integration of environmental management activities and to this extent it outlines the general objectives of integrated environmental management. Section 23 of NEMA sets out these general objectives. These include the objectives to promote the integration of the national environmental management principles into decisions that may significantly affect the environment;[82] and to identify, predict and evaluate actual and potential impact on the environment, socio-economic conditions and cultural heritage.[83] Their apparent purpose is to minimise the negative impact

---

[77] Section 24(1) of NEMA.   [78] Section 2(1).   [79] Section 2(1)(b).
[80] Section 2(1)(c).   [81] Section 2(1)(e).
[82] Section 23(2)(a) provides:

The general objective of integrated environmental management is to promote the integration of the principles of environmental management set out in section 2 into the making of all decisions which may have a significant effect on the environment.

[83] Section 23(2)(b) provides:

The general objective of integrated environmental management is to identify, predict and evaluate the actual and potential impact on the environment, socio-economic conditions and cultural heritage, the risks and consequences and alternatives and options for mitigation of activities, with a view to minimising negative impacts, maximising benefits, and promoting compliance with the principles of environmental management set out in section 2.

on the environment and socio-economic conditions and to promote compliance with the principles of environmental management.[84]

[30] 69. The general objectives of integrated environmental management are furthered by section 24, which deals with the implementation procedures. These require, among other things, that the potential impact on the environment, socio-economic conditions and cultural heritage of activities that require authorisation under section 22(1) of ECA and which may significantly affect the environment "must be considered, investigated and assessed prior to their implementation and reported upon to the organ of state charged by law with authorising... the implementation of an activity".[85] To underscore the importance of this requirement, subsection 24(7) requires that any investigation "must, as a minimum" investigate the potential impact, including the cumulative effects of the proposed development on the environment, socio-economic conditions and cultural heritage.[86] The provisions of section 24(7) must of course be read and understood in the light of the regulations that the Minister is empowered to make concerning the scope and the contents of reports that must be submitted for authorisation required by section 22(1) of ECA.

70. Against this background, I now turn to consider the nature and the scope of the obligation to consider socio-economic conditions.

---

[84] Id. [85] See para. 65.
[86] Section 24(7) provides:

Procedures for the investigation, assessment and communication of the potential impact of activities must, as a minimum, ensure the following:

(a) Investigation of the environment likely to be significantly affected by the proposed activity and alternatives thereto;
(b) investigation of the potential impact, including cumulative effects, of the activity and its alternatives on the environment, socio-economic conditions and cultural heritage, and assessment of the significance of that potential impact;
(c) investigation of mitigation measures to keep adverse impacts to a minimum, as well as the option of not implementing the activity;
(d) public information and participation, independent review and conflict resolution in all phases of the investigation and assessment of impacts;
(e) reporting on gaps in knowledge, the adequacy of predictive methods and underlying assumptions, and uncertainties encountered in compiling the required information;
(f) investigation and formulation of arrangements for the monitoring and management of impacts, and the assessment of the effectiveness of such arrangements after their implementation;
(g) co-ordination and co-operation between organs of state in the consideration of assessments where an activity falls under the jurisdiction of more than one organ of state;
(h) that the findings and recommendations flowing from such investigation, and the general objectives of integrated environmental management laid down in this Act and the principles of environmental management set out in section 2 are taken into account in any decision made by an organ of state in relation to the proposed policy, programme, plan or project; and
(i) that environmental attributes identified in the compilation of information and maps as contemplated in subsection (2)(e) are considered.

The Nature and the Scope of the Obligation to Consider Socio-Economic Conditions

71. The nature and the scope of the obligation to consider the impact of the proposed development on socio-economic conditions must be [**31**] determined in the light of the concept of sustainable development and the principle of integration of socio-economic development and the protection of the environment. Once it is accepted, as it must be, that socio-economic development and the protection of the environment are interlinked, it follows that socio-economic conditions have an impact on the environment. A proposed filling station may affect the sustainability of existing filling stations with consequences for the job security of the employees of those filling stations. But that is not all; if the proposed filling station leads to the closure of some or all of the existing filling stations, this has consequences for the environment. Filling stations have a limited end use. The underground fuel tanks and other infrastructure may have to be removed and land may have to be rehabilitated.

72. Apart from this, the proliferation of filling stations in close proximity to one another may increase the pre-existing risk of adverse impact on the environment. The risk that comes to mind is the contamination of underground water, soil, visual intrusion and light. An additional filling station may significantly increase this risk and increase environmental stress. Mindful of this possibility, NEMA requires that the cumulative impact of a proposed development, together with the existing developments on the environment, socio-economic conditions and cultural heritage, must be assessed.[87] The cumulative effect of the proposed development must naturally be assessed in the light of existing developments. A consideration of socio-economic conditions therefore includes the consideration of the impact of the proposed development not only in combination with the existing developments, but also its impact on existing ones.

73. This approach to the scope of the obligation to consider socio-economic conditions is consistent with the concept of sustainable development under our legislation. In this regard it is necessary to refer to some of the principles of NEMA to illustrate the point.

74. First, NEMA requires all developments to be socially, economically and environmentally sustainable. Unsustainable developments are in themselves detrimental to the environment. This is particularly true of developments contemplated in section 21 of ECA, that is, developments

---

[87] Section 24(7)(b).

that may have substantial detrimental impact on the environment, such as a filling station. The proliferation of filling stations poses a potential threat to the environment. This threat arises from the limited end-use of filling stations upon their closure.[88] The proliferation of filling stations may [32] ultimately lead to the closure of one or some of the existing filling stations. The filling station infrastructure that lies in the ground may have an adverse impact on the environment. As observed by the Supreme Court of Appeal, "[t]he environment may well be adversely affected by unneeded, and thus unsustainable, filling stations that become derelict...".[89] The inherent danger in the proliferation of filling stations has led some governments to impose restrictions not only on where filling stations may be constructed, but also on the distance between filling stations.[90]

75. Second, NEMA requires that environmental authorities place people and their needs at the forefront of their concern so that environmental management can serve their developmental, cultural and social interests.[91] The continued existence of development is essential to the needs of the population, whose needs a development must serve. This can be achieved if a development is sustainable. The collapse of a development may have an adverse impact on socio-economic interests such as the loss of employment. The very idea of sustainability implies continuity. It reflects a concern for social and developmental equity between generations, a concern that must logically be extended to equity within each generation. This concern is reflected in the principles of

---

[88] The background to the Gauteng Guidelines alludes to the limited end-use of filling stations:

Property zoned for filling stations has limited end-use after closure. According to Gautrans' view, the property cannot have direct access to roads at the filling station access points should it be used for another purpose. Given the vast number of applications that the department received to date, it means that Gauteng would in future be sitting with "graveyard" sites due to the legacy of the petroleum industry. The department thus has to be guided by all types of developments presently to ensure that Gauteng's environment does not exceed a level beyond which its non-renewable resources are jeopardised. Furthermore, remediation costs are high. The reuse of existing sites must therefore be considered.

[89] Above n 1 at para. 17.
[90] The Gauteng Guidelines, for example, require a distance of 3 kilometres in urban areas and a 25 kilometre distance for rural areas. The imposition of distance or limitation criteria was based on a review of international approaches. The Guidelines indicate, for example, that in Dublin, guidelines have been published which indicate that new petrol stations will generally not be permitted on national roads or adjoining residential areas and will only be considered in rural areas if they are in the immediate environs of rural villages; in Singapore, existing filling stations located within 1 kilometre of an interchange are considered to be inappropriately located; in Germany, filling stations should only be erected on rural roads where there is a clear need and there should be 25 kilometres between filling stations; and in Denmark, drivers requiring high octane petrol will have access to a filling station within 30 kilometres.
[91] Section 2(2).

inter-generational and intra-generational equity which are embodied in both section 24 of the Constitution and the principles of environmental management contained in NEMA.[92]

76. It is, therefore, not enough to focus on the needs of the developer while the needs of the society are neglected. One of the purposes of the public participation provision of NEMA is to afford people the opportunity to express their views on the desirability of a filling station that will [33] impact on socio-economic conditions affecting them.[93] Indeed, if a development is to serve the developmental needs of the people, the impact of new developments on existing ones is a legitimate concern.

77. Third, NEMA requires the consideration, assessment and evaluation of the social, economic and environmental impact of proposed activities. This requires the assessment of the socio-economic benefits and disadvantages of proposed activities.[94] This clearly enjoins the environmental authorities to consider and assess the impact of a proposed activity on existing socio-economic conditions which must of necessity include existing developments. Any doubt on this score is removed by section 24(7)(b), which requires an "investigation of the potential impact, including cumulative effects, of the activity and its alternatives on ... socio-economic conditions ... and assessment of the significance of that potential impact ... ".[95] Subsection 23(2)(b) is to the same effect. One of the objectives of integrated environmental management is to identify the actual and potential impact on the environment and socio-economic conditions in order to minimise negative impacts. ECA, too, contemplates that the environmental impact report will include "an estimation of the nature and extent of the effect of the activity ... on the social and economic interests".[96]

78. What must be stressed here is that the objective of considering the impact of a proposed development on existing ones is not to stamp out competition; it is to ensure the economic, social and environmental sustainability of all developments, both proposed and existing ones. Environmental concerns do not commence and end once the

---

[92] Section 24(b) of the Constitution requires the environment to be protected "for the benefit of present and future generations ... ". Section 1(1)(xxix) of NEMA defines sustainable development to mean the integration of social, economic and environmental factors into planning implementation and decision-making so "as to ensure that development serves present and future generations".

[93] Section 2(4)(f) of NEMA provides:

The participation of all interested and affected parties in environmental governance must be promoted, and all people must have the opportunity to develop the understanding, skills and capacity necessary for achieving equitable and effective participation, and participation by vulnerable and disadvantaged persons must be ensured.

[94] Section 2(4)(i). [95] Section 24(7)(b). [96] Section 26(a) of ECA.

proposed development is approved. It is a continuing concern. The environmental legislation imposes a continuing, and thus necessarily evolving, obligation to ensure the sustainability of the development and to protect the environment. As the International Court of Justice observed—

in the field of environmental protection, vigilance and prevention are required on account of the often irreversible character of damage to the environment and of the limitations inherent in the very mechanism of reparation of this type of damage.[97]

79. There are two points that must be stressed here. First, the Constitution, ECA and NEMA do not protect the existing developments at the expense of future developments. What section 24 requires, and what NEMA gives effect to, is that socio-economic development must be justifiable in the light of the need to protect the environment. The Constitution and environmental legislation introduce a new criterion for [34] considering future developments. Pure economic factors are no longer decisive. The need for development must now be determined by its impact on the environment, sustainable development and social and economic interests. The duty of environmental authorities is to integrate these factors into decision-making and make decisions that are informed by these considerations. This process requires a decision-maker to consider the impact of the proposed development on the environment and socio-economic conditions.

80. Second, the objective of this exercise, as NEMA makes it plain, is both to identify and predict the actual or potential impact on socio-economic conditions and consider ways of minimising negative impact while maximising benefit. Were it to be otherwise, the earth would become a graveyard for commercially failed developments. And this in itself poses a potential threat to the environment. One of the environmental risks associated with filling stations is the impact of a proposed filling station on the feasibility of filling stations in close proximity. The assessment of such impact is necessary in order to minimise the harmful effect of the proliferation of filling stations on the environment. The requirement to consider the impact of a proposed development on socio-economic conditions, including the impact on existing developments, addresses this concern.

81. Finally NEMA requires "a risk averse and cautious approach" to be applied by decision-makers.[98] This approach entails taking into account the limitation on present knowledge about the consequences

---

[97] Above n 64 at para. 140.   [98] Section 2(4)(a)(vii).

of an environmental decision. This precautionary approach is especially important in the light of section 24(7)(b) of NEMA, which requires the cumulative impact of a development on the environmental and socio-economic conditions to be investigated and addressed. An increase in the risk of contamination of underground water and soil, and visual intrusion and light, for example, are some of the significant cumulative impacts that could result from the proliferation of filling stations. Sub-section 24(7)(b) specifically requires the investigation of the potential impact, including cumulative effects, of the proposed development on the environment and socio-economic conditions, and the assessment of the significance of that potential impact.[99]

82. What was required of the environmental authorities therefore was to consider the impact on the environment of the proliferation of filling stations as well as the impact of the proposed filling station on existing ones. This conclusion makes it plain that the obligation to consider the socio-economic impact of a proposed development is wider than the requirement to assess need and desirability under the Ordinance. It also [35] comprehends the obligation to assess the cumulative impact on the environment of the proposed development.

83. What remains to be considered now is whether the environmental authorities complied with this obligation.

Did the Environmental Authorities Comply with Their Obligations under NEMA?

84. It is common cause that the environmental authorities themselves did not consider need and desirability. They took the view that these were matters that must be "proven, argued and considered by the Local Council" when an application for rezoning is made in terms of section 56 of the Ordinance. As Dr Batchelor put it, these "... are town-planning factors which are taken into consideration by the Local Councils whenever they are confronted with an application for the change of land use either in terms of Section 56 of the ... Ordinance ... or an application in terms of the Development Facilitation Act of 1995".

85. There is a fundamental flaw in this approach. Need and desirability are factors that must be considered by the local authority in terms

---

[99] Section 24(7)(b) of NEMA provides:

Procedures for the investigation, assessment and communication of the potential impact of activities must, as a minimum, ensure ... investigation of the potential impact, including cumulative effects, of the activity and its alternatives on the environment, socio-economic conditions and cultural heritage, and assessment of the significance of that potential impact.

of the Ordinance. The local authority considers need and desirability from the perspective of town-planning and an environmental authority considers whether a town-planning scheme is environmentally justifiable. A proposed development may satisfy the need and desirability criteria from a town-planning perspective and yet fail from an environmental perspective. The local authority is not required to consider the social, economic and environmental impact of a proposed development as the environmental authorities are required to do by the provisions of NEMA. Nor is it required to identify the actual and potential impact of a proposed development on socio-economic conditions as NEMA requires the environmental authorities to do.

86. The environmental authorities assumed that the duty to consider need and desirability in the context of the Ordinance imposes the same obligation as the duty to consider the social, economic and environmental impact of a proposed development as required by the provisions of NEMA. They were wrong in that assumption. They misconstrued the nature of their obligations under NEMA and as a consequence failed to apply their minds to the socio-economic impact of the proposed filling station, a matter which they were required to consider. This fact alone is sufficient to warrant the setting aside of the decision.

87. But there are further considerations which militate against the decision of the environmental authorities. According to the environmental authorities, once an applicant for authorisation indicates that the property has been rezoned for the purposes for which it is intended to be used, the environmental authorities "accept that the need and desirability has indeed been considered by the Local Council" in accordance with the town-planning legislation. Their obligation, as they see it, is to apply their mind to the question of whether the property on which the proposed filling station is to be constructed has been rezoned for that [36] purpose and from the fact of rezoning, they conclude that need and desirability aspects have been addressed.

88. By their own admission therefore the environmental authorities did not consider need and desirability. Instead they relied upon the fact that (a) the property was rezoned for the construction of a filling station; (b) a motivation for need and desirability would have been submitted for the purposes of rezoning; and (c) the town-planning authorities must have considered the motivation prior to approving the rezoning scheme. Neither of the environmental authorities claims to have seen the motivation, let alone read its contents. They left the consideration of this vital aspect of their environmental obligation entirely to the local authority. This in my view is manifestly not a proper discharge of their statutory duty. This approach to their obligations, in effect, amounts

to unlawful delegation of their duties to the local authority. This they cannot do.

89. It is clear that the environmental authorities misconstrued what was required of them by NEMA. They considered that they did not have to take into account socio-economic considerations as required by NEMA. NEMA required the environmental authorities to consider the impact of the proposed filling station on socio-economic conditions and thereafter to make a decision that is appropriate in the light of such a consideration. The mandatory nature and the materiality of the requirement is manifest. The conclusion that the environmental authorities failed to comply with a mandatory and material condition for the granting of authorisation is therefore inescapable. As a result, their decision falls to be reviewed under section 6(2)(b) of PAJA as they did not comply with a mandatory and material condition set by NEMA.

90. Here NEMA specifically enjoins the environmental authorities to consider, assess and evaluate the social and economic impact of the proposed filling station, including its cumulative effect on the environment as well as its impact on existing filling stations, and thereafter to make a decision that is appropriate in the light of such assessment. This requirement was included in NEMA to guide the environmental authorities in making a decision that may affect the environment. In these circumstances, failure by the environmental authorities to comply with this requirement did not just have "formal rather than substantive significance", as my colleague, Sachs J, suggests in his dissenting judgment.[100] In my view, it is a failure which goes to the very function that the environmental authorities were required by statute to perform; the environmental authorities failed to perform the very function which they were required by law to perform.

91. What must be stressed here is that the question on review is not whether there is evidence that an additional filling station posed undue threat to the environment. The question is whether the environmental authorities considered and evaluated the social and economic impact of [37] the proposed filling station on existing ones and how an additional filling station would affect the environment. Indeed it is difficult to fathom how the environmental authorities could have assessed the threat of overtrading to the environment if they did not apply their minds to this question at all. They could have established such threats if they had applied their mind to this question. They did not do so. Their decision cannot therefore stand.

---

[100] Sachs J at para. 119.

92. It is no answer by the environmental authorities to say that had they themselves considered the need and desirability aspect, this could have led to conflicting decisions between the environmental officials and the town-planning officials. If that is the natural consequence of the discharge of their obligations under the environmental legislation, it is a consequence mandated by the statute. It is impermissible for them to seek to avoid this consequence by delegating their obligations to the town-planning authorities. What is of grave concern here is that the environmental authorities did not even have sight of the motivation placed before the local authority relating to need and desirability, let alone read it. Section 24(1) of NEMA makes it clear that the potential impact on socio-economic conditions must be considered by "the organ of state charged by law with authorising, permitting or otherwise allowing the implementation of [a proposed] activity".

93. Our Constitution does not sanction a state of normative anarchy which may arise where potentially conflicting principles are juxtaposed. It requires those who enforce and implement the Constitution to find a balance between potentially conflicting principles. It is founded on the notion of proportionality which enables this balance to be achieved. Yet in other situations, it offers a principle that will facilitate the achievement of the balance. The principle that enables the environmental authorities to balance developmental needs and environmental concerns is the principle of sustainable development.

94. There are further difficulties for the environmental authorities in relying on the prior rezoning. The record discloses that the environmental authorities had in mind the rezoning "from 'special' to 'Business 1'". This occurred sometime in 1996 or thereabout. It is however clear from the application for this rezoning that at the time, the property in question had already been rezoned "special" for the purposes of a filling station and hotel. If this is true, then the rezoning for the purposes of constructing a filling station had been approved earlier than 1996. In other words the town-planning authorities had already considered the need and desirability of the filling station by 1996. If this is so, then there would have been no need for the town-planning authorities to consider its need and desirability in the 1996 rezoning "from 'special' to 'Business 1'". If this is so, then certain difficulties arise.

95. The first is that reliance by the environmental authorities on the 1996 rezoning as being the occasion when the need and desirability of the proposed filling station was considered by the local authority may be misplaced, as need and desirability had been considered by then. [**38**] Second, the rezoning for the purposes of a filling station was probably approved sometime in 1995, that is some six years prior to the

application for authorisation and some eight years prior to the granting of authorisation under section 22(1) of ECA. Thirdly, the rezoning had taken place prior to NEMA coming into operation, a statute which establishes the principles which apply to all decisions of state organs that may affect the environment.

96. In these circumstances, even if the environmental authorities were entitled to rely on the prior rezoning, I am of the view that it was incumbent on the environmental authorities to consider the matter afresh in the light of the provisions of NEMA. During the intervening period, a significant change in the environment could have taken place. Indeed the record indicates that further filling stations were constructed in that period. It is significant to note that item 10(2)(i) of GN Rl 183 of 5 September 1997 contemplates that a decision granting authorisation in terms of section 22(1) of ECA will be valid for a limited period. This is a recognition that changes may occur in the environment after the authorisation is granted. Indeed the authorisation granted by the environmental authorities in this case is valid for two years from the date of its granting.

97. In any event, there is no suggestion that either the town-planning authorities or the environmental authorities applied their minds to the impact of the proposed filling station on socio-economic conditions. The scoping report was concerned primarily with the financial feasibility of the proposed filling station. In fact, it said nothing about the impact of the proposed filling station on the existing ones. In all the circumstances of this case, the environmental authorities took a narrow view of their obligations and misconstrued their obligations. As a consequence of this, the environmental authorities failed to apply their minds to the impact of the proposed filling station on socio-economic conditions.

98. Before concluding this judgment, there are two matters that should be mentioned in relation to the duty of environmental authorities which are a source of concern. The first relates to the attitude of Water Affairs and Forestry and the environmental authorities. The environmental authorities and Water Affairs and Forestry did not seem to take seriously the threat of contamination of underground water supply. The precautionary principle required these authorities to insist on adequate precautionary measures to safeguard against the contamination of underground water. This principle is applicable where, due to unavailable scientific knowledge, there is uncertainty as to the future impact of the proposed development. Water is a precious commodity; it is a natural resource that must be protected for the benefit of present and future generations.

99. In these circumstances one would have expected that the environmental authorities and Water Affairs and Forestry would conduct a thorough investigation into the possible impact of the installation of petrol tanks in the vicinity of the borehole, in particular, in the light of the **[39]** existence of other filling stations in the vicinity. The environmental authorities did not consider the cumulative effect of the proliferation of filling stations on the aquifer. The Geohydrology division of Water Affairs and Forestry was content with simply stating that the developer must ensure that there is no pollution of water and that there must be monitoring as proposed in the report and in accordance with the regulations. Neither the Water Quality Management nor the Water Utilization divisions of the Water Affairs and Forestry commented on the reports as they did not receive them. They became aware of the development after both the record of decision and the appeal from it had been issued.

100. The other matter relates to the attitude of the environmental authorities to the objection of the applicant to the construction of the proposed filling station. In the Supreme Court of Appeal they argued that the applicant's opposition to the application for authorisation was motivated by the desire to stifle competition which was "thinly disguised as a desire to protect the environment".[101] In this regard, they pointed to the fact that the main deponent on behalf of the applicant, Mr Le Roux, owns other filling stations in the area. The Supreme Court of Appeal found that "there appears to be some merit in the contention".[102] Whatever the merits of the criticism may be, a matter on which it is not necessary to express an opinion, an environmental authority whose duty it is to protect the environment should welcome every opportunity to consider and assess issues that may adversely affect the environment.

101. Similarly, the duty of a court of law when the decision of an environmental authority is brought on review is to evaluate the soundness or otherwise of the objections raised. In doing so, the court must apply the applicable legal principles. If upon a proper application of the legal principles, the objections are valid, the court has no option but to uphold the objections. That is the duty that is imposed on a court by the Constitution, which is to uphold the Constitution and the law which they "... must apply impartially and without fear, favour or prejudice". Neither the identity of the litigant who raises the objection nor the motive is relevant.

102. The role of the courts is especially important in the context of the protection of the environment and giving effect to the principle

---

[101] Above n 1 at para. 13.   [102] Id.

of sustainable development. The importance of the protection of the environment cannot be gainsaid. Its protection is vital to the enjoyment of the other rights contained in the Bill of Rights; indeed, it is vital to life itself. It must therefore be protected for the benefit of the present and future generations. The present generation holds the earth in trust for the next generation. This trusteeship position carries with it the responsibility to look after the environment. It is the duty of the court to ensure that this responsibility is carried out. Indeed, the Johannesburg Principles [40] adopted at the Global Judges Symposium underscore the role of the judiciary in the protection of the environment.[103]

103. On that occasion members of the judiciary across the globe made the following statement—

We affirm our commitment to the pledge made by world leaders in the Millennium Declaration adopted by the United Nations General Assembly in September 2000 "to spare no effort to free all of humanity, and above all our children and grandchildren, from the threat of living on a planet irredeemably spoilt by human activities, and whose resources would no longer be sufficient for their needs".[104]

In addition, they affirmed—

... that an independent Judiciary and judicial process is vital for the same implementation, development and enforcement of environmental law, and that members of the Judiciary, as well as those contributing to the judicial process at the national, regional and global levels, are crucial partners for promoting compliance with, and the implementation and the enforcement of, international and national environmental law.[105]

104. One of these principles expresses—

A full commitment to contributing towards the realization of the goals of sustainable development through the judicial mandate to implement, develop and enforce the law, and to uphold the Rule of Law and the democratic process...[106]

Courts therefore have a crucial role to play in the protection of the environment. When the need arises to intervene in order to protect the environment, they should not hesitate to do so.

---

[103] United Nations Environment Programme—Division of Policy Development and Law, *Global Judges Symposium on Sustainable Development and the Role of Law*—The Johannesburg Principles on the Role of Law and Sustainable Development adopted at the Global Judges Symposium held in Johannesburg, South Africa on 18-20 August 2002, www.unep.org/law/Symposium/Principles.htm, accessed on 4 June 2007.
[104] Id.   [105] Id.   [106] Id.

Conclusion

105. The considerations set out above make it clear that the decision of the environmental authorities is flawed and falls to be set aside as they misconstrued the obligations imposed on them by NEMA. In all the circumstances, the decision by the environmental authorities to grant authorisation for the construction of the filling station under section 22(1) of ECA cannot stand and falls to be reviewed and set aside. It follows that both the High Court and the Supreme Court of Appeal erred, the High Court in dismissing the application for review and the Supreme Court of Appeal in upholding the decision of the High Court.

[41] *The Relief*

106. The appropriate relief in this case is to send the matter back to the environmental authorities for them to consider the matter afresh in a manner that is consistent with this judgment.

Costs

107. Then there is the question of costs. This is a case, in my view, in which the costs should follow the result. However, I do not think that the Trust and its trustees must be saddled with costs. It is true that they opposed the matter—but this was to safeguard their interests. The contest, at the end of the day, was between the applicant and the first, second and third respondents. It is these respondents who should pay the cost of the applicant while the remaining respondents who opposed the matter will have to look after their own costs. The costs payable by the first, second and third respondents must include those that are consequent upon the employment of two counsel.

Order

108. In the event I make the following order:

(a) The application for leave to appeal is granted.
(b) The appeal is upheld.
(c) The order of the Supreme Court of Appeal is set aside.
(d) The order of the High Court is set aside.
(e) The decision of the first, second and third respondents granting authorisation for the construction of the filling station to be located on a portion of portion 1, Erf 216, Kingsview

extension 1, White River, Mpumalanga, under section 22(1) of the Environment Conservation Act 73 of 1989 is reviewed and set aside.

(f) The matter is remitted to the first, second and third respondents for them to consider afresh the application for authorisation for the construction of the filling station to be located on a portion of portion 1, Erf 216, Kingsview extension 1, White River, Mpumalanga, under section 22(1) of the Environment Conservation Act 73 of 1989.

(g) The first, second and third respondents are ordered to pay the applicant's costs including the costs incurred in the courts below, which includes the costs consequent upon the employment of two counsel.

Moseneke DCJ, Madala J, Mokgoro J, Navsa AJ, Nkabinde J, O' Regan J, Skweyiya J and Van der Westhuizen J concur in the judgment of Ngcobo J.

Sachs J

109. It is ironic that the first appeal in this Court to invoke the majestic protection provided for the environment in the Bill of Rights[1] comes not [42] from concerned ecologists but from an organised section of an industry frequently lambasted both for establishing world-wide reliance on non-renewable energy sources and for spawning pollution. So be it. The doors of the Court are open to all, and there is nothing illegitimate or inappropriate in the Fuel Retailers Association of Southern Africa seeking to rely on legal provisions that may promote its interests.

110. The brief dissent which follows is accordingly not based on factors related to the motivation of the applicant, but rather on how I believe the relevant law should be applied to the facts of this case. In this respect I would like to associate myself with the eloquent and comprehensive manner in which Ngcobo J highlights the importance of environmental law for our society and establishes the legal setting in which this matter is to be determined. I also support the way in

---

[1] Section 24 provides as follows:

Everyone has the right—

(a) to an environment that is not harmful to their health or well-being; and
(b) to have the environment protected, for the benefit of present and future generations, through reasonable legislative and other measures that—

   (i) prevent pollution and ecological degradation;
   (ii) promote conservation; and
   (iii) secure ecologically sustainable development and use of natural resources while promoting justifiable economic and social development.

which he alerts the Department of Water Affairs and Forestry to its legislative responsibilities in this area. I agree with his conclusion that it was not appropriate for the authorities simply to rely on an earlier zoning decision by the Council. They should indeed have looked at the matter more broadly and in a more up-to-date manner. Where I part ways with his judgment is in regard to the materiality of that failure.

111. Section 6(2) of the Promotion of Administrative Justice Act[2] authorises—

[a] court or tribunal . . . to judicially review an administrative action if—
. . .

(b) a mandatory *and material* procedure or condition prescribed by an empowering provision was not complied with. (My emphasis.)

As Hoexter observes:

It would of course be delightfully simple if the failure to comply with mandatory provisions inevitably resulted in invalidity while ignoring directory provisions never had this consequence, but the reality is not so clear-cut. From our case law one sees that some requirements classified as "mandatory" need not, in fact, be strictly complied with, but that "substantial" or "adequate" compliance may be sufficient. The reference in the PAJA to a "material" procedure or condition may indeed be read as recognising this.[3] (Footnote omitted.)

She goes on (correctly in my opinion) to support an approach which she believes sensibly links the question of compliance to the purpose of the **[43]** provision,[4] and quotes from *Maharaj and Others* v. *Rampersad* where Van Winsen AJA stated the following:

The enquiry, I suggest, is not so much whether there has been "exact", "adequate" or "substantial" compliance with [the] injunction but rather whether there has been compliance therewith. This enquiry postulates an application of the injunction to the facts and a resultant comparison between what the position is and what, according to the requirements of the injunction, it ought to be. It is quite conceivable that a court might hold that, even though the position as it is is not identical with what it ought to be, the injunction has nevertheless been complied with. In deciding whether there has been a compliance with the injunction *the object sought to be achieved by the injunction and the question whether this object has been achieved are of importance.*[5] (Her emphasis.)

---

[2] Act 3 of 2000.
[3] Hoexter, *Administrative Law in South Africa* (Juta & Co. Ltd, Cape Town, 2007) at 262.
[4] Id. at 263.   [5] 1964 (4) SA 638 (A) at 646C-E.

She notes with apparent approval the suggestion that this approach shows a trend away from the strictly legalistic to the substantive.[6]

112. It seems to me that while the majority judgment did not find it necessary to evaluate the facts because a mandatory procedure was not complied with, if the evidence before the Court suggests that the failure was not of a material nature, it should not lead to the decision being set aside. In my view the facts in the present matter as available from the record do not establish that having a competitor to the filling stations owned by an Executive Member of the applicant[7] posed any measurable threat to the environment that needed to be considered. On the contrary, the facts reveal that all the ordinary environmental controls were in place and that any potential deleterious effect of possible overtrading was speculative and remote, in a word, makeweight.

113. As I analyse the evidence, the procedural default could have had little bearing on the overall nature of an enquiry framed by the principles and objectives of the National Environmental Management Act (NEMA).[8] Running right through the preamble and guiding principles of NEMA is the overarching theme of environmental protection and its relation to social and economic development.[9] This theme is

---

[6] Hoexter above n 3 at 263 quoting Van Dijkhorst J in *Ex Parte Mothuloe (Law Society, Transvaal, Intervening)* 1996 (4) SA 1131 (T); [1996] 2 All SA 342 (T) at 1138D/E-E. See too Olivier JA in *Weenen Transitional Local Council* v. *Van Dyk* 2002 (4) SA 653 (SCA); [2002] 2 All SA 482 (SCA) at para. 13. The importance of avoiding a narrowly textual and legalistic approach was underlined by this Court in *African Christian Democratic Party* v. *Electoral Commission and Others* 2006 (3) SA 305 (CC) at para. 25.

[7] The Executive Member owns two filling stations in the White River area and had an interest in a third at the time of instituting proceedings in the High Court.

[8] Act 107 of 1998.

[9] See in particular the long title and preamble. The long title makes it clear that NEMA was adopted "[t]o provide for co-operative environmental governance by establishing principles for decision-making on matters affecting the environment". The preamble reads as follows:

...

Whereas... sustainable development requires the integration of social, economic and environmental factors in the planning, implementation and evaluation of decisions to ensure that development serves present and future generations;

everyone has the right to have the environment protected, for the benefit of present and future generations, through reasonable legislative and other measures that—

prevent pollution and ecological degradation;
promote conservation; and
secure ecologically sustainable development and use of natural resources while promoting justifiable economic and social development;

...

And whereas it is desirable—
that the law develops a framework for integrating good environmental management into all development activities;

...

that the law should establish principles guiding the exercise of functions affecting the environment;

...

repeated again and again. Economic sustainability is not treated as an independent [44] factor to be evaluated as a discrete element in its own terms. Its significance for NEMA lies in the extent to which it is interrelated with [45] environmental protection. Sustainable development presupposes accommodation, reconciliation and (in some instances) integration between economic development, social development and environmental protection.[10] It does not envisage social, economic and

Section 1(1)(xxix) defines "sustainable development" as "the integration of social, economic and environmental factors into planning, implementation and decision-making so as to ensure that development serves present and future generations".

Section 2, which establishes national environmental management principles, provides that—

(1) The principles set out in this section . . .

...

(b) serve as the general framework within which environmental management and implementation plans must be formulated;
(c) serve as guidelines by reference to which any organ of state must exercise any function when taking any decision in terms of this Act or any statutory provision concerning the protection of the environment;

...

The section further provides that—

(3) Development must be socially, environmentally and economically sustainable.

(4) (a) Sustainable development requires the consideration of all relevant factors including the following:

(i) That the disturbance of ecosystems and loss of biological diversity are avoided, or, where they cannot be altogether avoided, are minimised and remedied;
(ii) that pollution and degradation of the environment are avoided, or, where they cannot be altogether avoided, are minimised and remedied;
(iii) that the disturbance of landscapes and sites that constitute the nation's cultural heritage is avoided, or where it cannot be altogether avoided, is minimised and remedied;
(iv) that waste is avoided, or where it cannot be altogether avoided, minimised and re-used or recycled where possible and otherwise disposed of in a responsible manner;
(v) that the use and exploitation of non-renewable natural resources is responsible and equitable, and takes into account the consequences of the depletion of the resource;
(vi) that the development, use and exploitation of renewable resources and the ecosystems of which they are part do not exceed the level beyond which their integrity is jeopardised;
(vii) that a risk-averse and cautious approach is applied, which takes into account the limits of current knowledge about the consequences of decisions and actions; and
(viii) that negative impacts on the environment and on people' s environmental rights be anticipated and prevented, and where they cannot be altogether prevented, are minimised and remedied.

(b) Environmental management must be integrated, acknowledging that all elements of the environment are linked and interrelated, and it must take into account the effects of decisions on all aspects of the environment and all people in the environment by pursuing the selection of the best practicable environmental option.

The "best practicable environmental option" is defined in section 1(1)(iii) as "the option that provides the most benefit or causes the least damage to the environment as a whole, at a cost acceptable to society, in the long term as well as in the short term".

[10] See Segger and Weeramantry (eds.), *Sustainable Justice: Reconciling Economic, Social and Environmental Law* (Martinus Nijhoff Publishers, Leiden, 2005) at 2 where it is stated that—

It [sustainable development]identifies an imperative to meet the development needs of the present and future equitably, and to simultaneously meet environmental needs. Sustainable development provides a "conceptual

environmental sustainability as proceeding along three separate tracks, each of which has to be weighed separately and then somehow all brought together in a global analysis. The essence of sustainable development is balanced integration of socio-economic development and environmental priorities and norms.[11] Economic sustainability is thus not part of a check-list that has to be ticked off as a separate item in the sustainable development enquiry. Rather, it is an element that takes on significance to the extent that it implicates the environment. When economic development potentially **[46]** threatens the environment it becomes relevant to NEMA. Only then does it become a material ingredient to be put in the scales of a NEMA evaluation.

114. In the present matter the evidence does not indicate that opening a new filling station would pose or suggest any undue threat to the environment. On the contrary, the relevant environmental authorities made a finding to the effect that environmental criteria were met. First the High Court and then the Supreme Court of Appeal rejected challenges made to this finding, and in this Court the applicant chose not to continue with its earlier attacks on it. Furthermore, the feasibility study indicated that the project appeared to be economically sustainable. As the Supreme Court of Appeal pointed out, any suggestion of a future graveyard of disused filling stations was purely hypothetical. I might add that though the precautionary principle is an important one, particularly in relation to a potentially hazardous product such as petrol, it has little application where the threat to the environment is remote and any possible damage would be containable. We must accordingly proceed on the assumption that the normal question of sustainable development does not arise, that is, that this case does not require us to decide whether on balance the gains made in socio-economic development by

---

bridge" betwen the right to social and economic development, and the need to protect the environment. Accommodation, reconciliation and integration are emphasised.

At 561 it is stated that "[f]or sustainable development to be realised, there must be better accommodation, reconciliation and (in some instances) integration between economic development, social development and environmental protection".

[11] Id. at 8:

Social, environmental and eonomic developments can overlap, or even conflict. When they do, they are not sustainable. As witnessed in recent years, public protests and global tensions, popular struggles against the privatization of essential services, against new rules for trade and investment liberalization, against decisions of international financial institutions, are centered on this concern. Economic laws and policies which do not take social and environmental elements into account are unlikely to be successful in a democratic society. Similarly, environmental laws that ignore social and economic realities, and social laws that violate environmental or economic principles, can waste valuable political and material resources, also leading to failure. The need for a balanced integration of socio-economic development and environment priorities and norms permeates international law and policy on sustainable development.

opening up a new enterprise could appropriately permit a certain degree of negative impact on the environment.[12]

115. What the applicant's argument ultimately boiled down to was that the risk of overtrading was real and that this was an economic factor that should have been taken into account when the question of sustainable development was being considered. Absent some consequent threat to the environment, however, the question of possible overtrading is not one which I believe the decision-makers in this matter were called upon to consider.

[47] 116. In my view, commercial sustainability only becomes a relevant factor under NEMA when it touches on actual or potential threats to the environment. Thus, if there were a genuine risk that the introduction of a new industry would be ruinous to traditional forms of livelihood, thereby dramatically changing the character of the neighbourhood, that could be a significant socio-economic environmental factor. Similarly, if there were a real prospect of the landscape ending up as a disfigured and polluted graveyard replete with abandoned petrol tanks not easily removed, that would certainly require attention.

117. Conversely, if some damage to the environment were to be established, the economic sustainability of a proposed economic enterprise could be highly relevant as a countervailing factor in favour of a finding that on balance the development is sustainable. Thus, an enterprise that promised long-term employment and major social upliftment at relatively small cost to the environment, with damage reduced to the minimum, could well be compatible with NEMA. On the other hand to

---

[12] See Birnie and Boyle (eds.), *International Law and the Environment*, 2nd edn (Oxford University Press, New York, 2002) at 86:

Sustainable development contains both substantive and procedural elements ... They include the sustainable utilization of natural resources; the integration of environmental protection and economic development; the right to development; the pursuit of equitable allocation of resources both within the present generation and between present and future generations (intra- and inter-generational equity), and the internalization of environmental costs through application of the "polluter pays" principle.

See also *People United for Better Living in Calcutta—Public and Another* v. *State of West Bengal and Others* 1993 AIR Calcutta 215, quoted in Segger and Weeramantry above n 10 at 50, where Benerjee J stated:

While it is true that in a developing country there shall have to be developments, but that development shall have to be in closest possible harmony with the environment, as otherwise there would be development but no environment, which would result in total devastation, though, however, may not be felt in presenti but at some future point of time, but then it would be too late in the day, however, to control and improve the environment.

In the present matter the opening of a new filling station would in reality suggest economic development providing employment for several persons at no apparent environmental cost. Any potential social cost as a result of competition is purely speculative.

allow a fly-by-night undertaking either to spoil a pristine environment, or to use up scarce resources, or to introduce undue health hazards, will probably be in conflict with NEMA.

118. But there is no evidence, above the level of speculation, that the arrival of a new kid on the block doing the same business in the same way in competition with existing filling stations would give rise to the risk of unacceptable degradation either to the physical environment or to the socio-cultural environment. I am therefore not persuaded that the principles of sustainable development are engaged in this matter at all. The objective of NEMA, after all, is to preserve the environment for present and future generations, and not to maintain the profitability of incumbent entrepreneurs.

119. For these reasons, I would not set aside the determination of the decision-makers. In substance the decision-makers considered the factors to which NEMA required them to pay attention. Though the Fuel Retailers Association raised an objection that had technical merit, the failure by the decision-makers was innocuous as far as the environment was concerned and had formal rather than substantive significance. In my view the High Court and the Supreme Court of Appeal got it right in dismissing the applicant's challenge to the decision authorising the new filling station. I would accordingly refuse the appeal and uphold the decision of the Supreme Court of Appeal.

[Reports: 2007 (6) SA 4 (CC); [2008] 2 LRC 102; 2007 (10) BCLR 1059 (CC)]

Diplomatic relations — Diplomatic protection — Appellants requesting diplomatic protection from Government of South Africa against Government of Lesotho — Whether State having obligation to provide diplomatic protection — Position under international law — Whether South Africa entitled to afford appellants diplomatic protection — Whether appellants having right to diplomatic protection under South African law — South African Constitution — Responsibility of executive for conducting foreign relations — Discretion of executive with respect to diplomatic relations — Principle of equal sovereignty of States — Policy considerations — Lesotho cancelling and revoking mining leases without payment of compensation — Whether international delict — Whether violating international minimum standards — Whether expropriation — Nationality requirement — Exhaustion of local remedies requirement — Whether claim admissible before international tribunal

Nationality — Diplomatic protection — Nationality requirement for international delict — Whether nationality rule disqualifying South African Government from affording diplomatic protection to appellants — Continuous nationality rule

Claims — Exhaustion of local remedies — Diplomatic protection — Exhaustion of local remedies rule for international delict — Whether exhaustion of local remedies rule disqualifying South African Government from affording diplomatic protection to appellants — Whether Lesotho courts rectifying wrongs

Relationship of international law and municipal law — Conduct of foreign relations — Whether justiciable in municipal court — The law of South Africa

Van Zyl and Others v. Government of Republic of South Africa and Others[1]

South Africa, High Court. 20 July 2005

(Patel J)

---

[1] Before the High Court the appellants were represented by Mr J. Dugard SC, Mr A. Katz and Mr M. du Plessis, instructed by Couzyn, Hertzog & Horak Incorporated, Pretoria. The respondents

Supreme Court of Appeal. 20 September 2007

(Harms ADP; Heher and Cachalia JJA; Hurt and Mhlantla AJJA)

SUMMARY: *The facts*:—The appellants, Mr van Zyl, Mr and Mrs van Zyl in their capacity as trustees of two trusts, together with six diamond mining companies, requested diplomatic protection from the respondents, the Government of the Republic of South Africa, the President, the Minister of Foreign Affairs and the Deputy Minister, against the Government of Lesotho. The request arose from the alleged expropriation by the Government of Lesotho of the appellants' property rights in the execution of the Lesotho Highlands Water Project.[2]

The first appellant, Mr Josias van Zyl, and his wife were South African citizens. They were second and third appellants respectively in their capacity as trustees of two trusts, the Burmilla Trust and the Josias van Zyl Family Trust, both registered in South Africa. The six corporate appellants, most importantly Swissborough Diamond Mines (Pty) Ltd ("Swissborough"), were registered in Lesotho for the purpose of diamond mining. Mr van Zyl, the Burmilla Trust and the Family Trust owned 5, 90 and 5 per cent respectively of the issued shares in Swissborough. Swissborough and the Family Trust held 99 and 1 per cent respectively of the shares in the other companies. The directors of the companies were also South African citizens.

Following the commencement of construction work in the Rampai area, pursuant to the Lesotho Highlands Water Project, the Government of Lesotho and Swissborough concluded five mining leases. Four of those leases were subsequently cancelled and revoked by the Government of Lesotho without the payment of compensation—acts found to be unlawful by Lesotho courts.

The appellants alleged that the Government of Lesotho had thereby committed an international delict in Lesotho. In various letters they requested diplomatic protection from the Government of South Africa, alleging *inter alia* expropriation of their property rights, violation of the international minimum standard, corruption in the Government of Lesotho and improper collusion with the South African Government and asserting a right to effective diplomatic protection under the South African Constitution. They argued that the Constitution obliged the respondents to remedy this violation of their property rights and entrenched the right to citizenship as a basic human right. The respondents refused the request maintaining that the appellants were not entitled to diplomatic protection in the circumstances. The appellants applied to have the respondents' decisions reviewed and set aside.

---

were represented by Mr G. L. Grobler SC, Mr R. J. Raath SC and Mr M. Mphaga, instructed by the State Attorney, Pretoria. Before the Supreme Court of Appeal the appellants were represented by Mr Redelinghuys, the first appellant arguing in person.

[2] On 24 October 1986, the Republic of South Africa and the Kingdom of Lesotho concluded a Treaty concerning the Lesotho Highlands Project. The main purpose of the project was to supply water to Witwatersrand from a dam that had to be built in Lesotho.

Held (by the High Court):—The application was dismissed.

(1) The most fundamental aspect of diplomatic protection at an international level was the right for a State to bring a claim to an international tribunal on behalf of its nationals whose rights had been violated by another State. International law had not yet reached a point where States were under an international law duty to provide diplomatic protection to their nationals (paras. 17-21).

(2) The appellants were not subjects of international law and could not have international law applied in any claims they had against the Kingdom of Lesotho. Since there was no internationalization of the mining leases, there was no possibility of the application of international law as between the contracting parties on any dispute in terms of the mining leases (paras. 22-9).

(3) The extent of diplomatic protection was completely within the discretion of the State of nationality. Given the importance of the principle of equal sovereignty of States, any form of diplomatic protection was only lawful if the preconditions were satisfied; otherwise unwarranted interference with the sovereignty of the host State would result (paras. 30-6).

(4) International minimum standards pertaining to expropriation of property were not to be equated with the international minimum norms pertaining to international human rights violations. There was, however, an international norm not to deprive anyone of property except in terms of general principles of property law.[3] South Africa and Lesotho had ratified and were therefore bound by the Universal Declaration of Human Rights and the African Charter on Human and Peoples' Rights. The general rule of customary international law was that where the host State had expropriated specific property of a foreigner, then prompt, adequate and effective compensation must be paid. There was no international human right to the protection of property in international law. It was for States to protect by way of diplomatic protection the rights they enjoyed in respect of their nationals. Diplomatic protection was not a human right under international law (paras. 37-43).

(5) The executive was responsible for conducting foreign relations;[4] it had broad discretion with respect to diplomatic relations. The respondents' decisions were only reviewable on an extremely limited basis. The conduct of foreign relations, determined on sometimes sensitive policy considerations, could not be properly evaluated by the courts (paras. 44-58).

---

[3] See Article 17(2) of the Universal Declaration of Human Rights, Article 14 of the African Charter on Human and Peoples' Rights, Article 1 of the First Protocol: Enforcement of Certain Rights and Freedoms to the European Convention for the Protection of Human Rights and Fundamental Freedoms and Article 21(2) of the American Convention on Human Rights. However, neither the International Covenant on Civil and Political Rights nor the International Covenant on Economic, Social and Cultural Rights provided for the protection of property rights.

[4] Section 232 of the Constitution provided that customary international law was the law of the Republic unless it was inconsistent with the Constitution or an Act of Parliament. The Constitution recognized South Africa as a subject of international law and the executive as responsible for negotiating and signing international agreements, an important element in the conduct of foreign relations.

(6) The respondents refused to afford diplomatic protection to the appellants as of right. This resulted from an informed and carefully considered policy decision, not from a perception that diplomatic protection did not exist in international law. Under international law, States had the right but not the obligation to protect their nationals beyond their borders. There was no claimable right under the Constitution. There was no infringement of the appellants' fundamental rights. The respondents considered applicable policy considerations and rationally determined that they could not accede to the appellants' request (paras. 59-70).

(7) There was no international delict which would vest the right in South Africa to act against Lesotho on the basis of diplomatic protection for the appellants. For an international delictual claim, the wronged foreign person or company had to have South African nationality, the alleged expropriation had to violate international minimum standards and the national had to have exhausted all legal remedies available under Lesotho law. The mining leases, creating rights in property for Swissborough, were subject to Lesotho law; they were not internationalized and were not subject to South African law of which customary international law was a part under Section 232 of the Constitution. A breach of contract with no international element could not be elevated to an international wrong. There was no violation of minimum international standards and no expropriation. Since there was no indication that the parties to the leases intended to subject their concession agreements to international law, international law required that those agreements were subject to Lesotho law. Had Lesotho committed an international wrong, the nationality and exhaustion of local remedies requirements had not been satisfied for a claim to be admissible before an international tribunal (paras. 71-93).

(8) The nationality requirement was not satisfied. South Africa had no right of diplomatic protection against Lesotho in respect of acts performed within its own territory against companies incorporated in Lesotho. Neither did the cession of rights to the second appellant after the alleged violation secure diplomatic protection for its State of nationality since the claim had to belong to a person continuously. The first and third appellants were not entitled to diplomatic protection from South Africa by virtue of their shareholding in companies incorporated in Lesotho since none of their shares had been expropriated. Companies did not have the same constitutional entitlement as citizens who were nationals to request diplomatic protection. The ambit of discretion was prescribed by customary international law; the executive had the duty to consider requests for diplomatic protection but to promote South African interests. The fourth to ninth appellants were not South African nationals even though South Africans held some of the shares in them. The South African shareholders were not entitled to diplomatic protection (paras. 94-100).

(9) The appellants had not exhausted local remedies in Lesotho. The exhaustion of local remedies rule was based on respect for host State sovereignty. It was a customary international law precept and a substantive law rule. The standard of jurisprudence and justice in Lesotho courts was beyond question; to

undermine those courts would be tantamount to infringing Lesotho's sovereignty (paras. 101-5).

The appellants appealed to the Supreme Court of Appeal.

Held (by the Supreme Court of Appeal):—The appeal was dismissed.

(1) The appellants had no right under South African law to diplomatic protection, especially not in respect of protection of a particular kind. Nationals had a right to request and the Government to consider diplomatic protection rationally. The respondents had acted within the framework of the *Kaunda* judgment.[5] They had received the request, considered the matter properly and decided to decline to act on rational grounds. Courts should act with restraint when dealing with allegations of unlawful conduct ascribed to foreign States (paras. 1-59).

(2) The respondents were not entitled to intervene on behalf of the appellants because no international delict had been committed. Since the mining lease was concluded in Lesotho by the Government of Lesotho with a Lesotho company under Lesotho mining laws in respect of Lesotho diamond rights, its validity had to be determined by the Lesotho courts by reference to Lesotho law. Neither had the Government of Lesotho otherwise agreed to internationalize the agreement. This was not a case of expropriation contrary to international law (paras. 60-80).

(3) The nationality rule disqualified the Government of South Africa from affording any diplomatic protection to the appellants except, possibly, Mr van Zyl and the Family Trust. Since this case concerned a delict against the companies, not the shareholders, it was irrelevant that the State of nationality of the shareholders was entitled to exercise diplomatic protection in respect of its nationals. The cession by the corporate appellants to the Burmilla Trust disqualified both the corporate appellants and the Trust from diplomatic protection since nationality had to be continuous from the date of injury to the date of claim. The cessionary, who had not been wronged, could not be a victim deserving protection (paras. 81-6).

(4) The respondents were not entitled to grant the appellants diplomatic protection since all local legal remedies had not been exhausted. The exhaustion of local remedies rule, applicable where there was reasonable effective redress and no undue delay by the State, presupposed the existence of an international delict and compliance with the nationality rule. Although the acts of cancelling and revoking the mining leases were wrongful, Lesotho courts had rectified the wrongs by declaring the acts void and without effect. Swissborough had the option of pursuing an action for damages (paras. 87-92).

The text of the judgment of the Supreme Court of Appeal commences at p. 545. The text of the judgment of the High Court commences on the following page.

---

[5] *Kaunda and Others v. President of the Republic of South Africa and Others*, 136 ILR 452.

JUDGMENT OF THE HIGH COURT

[100] PATEL J

A. *General introduction*

Preface

1. This case is about the applicants' claim to an alleged right to diplomatic protection from the respondents.

2. I am strained by the sheer shipment of documents contained in forty-odd lever arch files comprising almost sixteen thousand paginated pages and argument that lasted no less than seven days in court.

3. A draft judgment was completed during the administrative recess of June–July 2004. However, the Constitutional Court's judgment in *Kaunda and Others* v. *President of the RSA and Others (2)*[1] was handed down on 4 August 2004. On studying the judgment, it became apparent that the judgment of the highest Court had some bearing on the present matter, thus I invited the parties to file written submissions. The applicants filed their submissions on 15 November 2004 and the respondents delivered their submissions on 26 November 2004. These submissions comprise about 425 pages in total. The submissions were requested and received so as to work on the draft judgment during the administrative recess of December 2004–January 2005. The first applicant, Josias van Zyl, during the recess delivered, on 15 December 2004, to the security officer at the Palace of Justice, three volumes of further submissions "in an attempt to correct the many inaccuracies and distortions of the facts and application of law as contained in the respondents' submissions . . . ". Each of these volumes comprise approximately 370 pages. They were received by me on 24 January 2005. It has been a daunting task, requiring rigour and industry to deal with the volume of material as well as the magnitude, novelty **[101]** and complexity of the issues concerning diplomatic protection and the breadth of the respondents' application to strike out.

Introduction

4. This is an application for the review and setting aside of decisions taken by certain organs of the South African State in declining to afford diplomatic protection or *effective* diplomatic protection to the applicants in their long-standing dispute with the Government of the Kingdom of Lesotho ("GoL") concerning the alleged expropriation without compensation of their properties in Lesotho by the GoL. The factual milieu

---

[1] 2004 (10) BCLR 1009 (CC); 2005 (4) SA 235 (CC).

that gave rise to the dispute between the applicants and the GoL are discernible from two comprehensive judgments.[2] This application does not involve an inquiry into or determination on the validity of action taken by GoL in Lesotho. It is fundamentally concerned with reviewing the decisions of the organs of the State and a direction to the executive of the Republic of South Africa to provide diplomatic protection and more so to provide *effective* diplomatic protection to the applicants.

Parties

5. The parties to these proceedings are nine applicants. They are the first applicant Josias van Zyl married to Gail van Zyl, both are South African citizens. They are the trustees of the second and third respondents, namely the Burmilla Trust and Josias van Zyl Family Trust. The fourth, fifth, sixth, seventh, eighth and ninth applicants are Swissborough Diamond Mines (Pty) Ltd, Patiseng Diamond (Pty) Ltd, Motete Diamonds (Pty) Ltd, Rampai Diamonds (Pty) Ltd, Matsoku Diamonds (Pty) Ltd and Orange Diamonds (Pty) Ltd. These latter six applicants are companies registered in terms of the Company Rules of the Kingdom of Lesotho and collectively referred to as *Swissborough*. The first applicant owns 5% of the issued shares in the fourth applicant. The Burmilla Trust, the second applicant, owns 90% of the issued shares in the fourth applicant and holds 99% of the issued shares in the fifth to ninth applicants. The Josias van Zyl Family Trust owns 5% of the issued shares in the fourth applicant and holds 1% of the issued shares in the fifth to ninth applicants. The directors and shareholders of the six companies in the Swissborough group are South African citizens. However, the six companies in the group are Lesotho companies incorporated in that country for purposes of diamond mining.

6. The first respondent is the Government of the Republic of South Africa. The second, third and fourth respondents are the President, the Minister of Foreign Affairs and the Deputy Minister of Foreign Affairs. They are collectively referred to as *the respondents* or *the executive* unless it is necessary to identify them in particular.

[102] *Preliminary issue*

7. At the outset of the hearing of the application there was an indication by the applicants' lead counsel Mr Dugard SC, appearing with

---

[2] *Attorney-General of Lesotho and Another* v. *Swissborough Diamond Mines (Pty) Ltd and Others* [1997] 8 BCLR 1122 (CA); *Swissborough Diamond Mines (Pty) Ltd and Others* v. *Government of the Republic of SA and Others* 1999 (2) SA 279 (T) at 287F-299H/I.

Mr Katz and Mr Du Plessis, that the respondents wish to introduce an application to strike out certain portions of the applicants' replying and supplementary replying affidavits. Mr Grobler SC, the respondents' lead counsel together with Mr Raath SC and Mr Mphaga, signified that he would do so and wished to hand up an application to amend the respondents' application to strike out which was served on the applicants on 24 October 2004 and which document did not find its way into the court file. Mr Grobler indicated that they were only informed in a cursory manner about the applicants' preliminary objection to the late filling of the respondents' application to strike out. Mr Dugara insisted that the applicants wish to argue the preliminary issue by contending that the respondents' application to strike out is not properly before the Court.

8. Thereafter, Mr Katz, for the applicants, handed up a document headed: "applicants' note on how this court should deal with the respondents' application to strike out applications". Counsel submitted that in terms of section 173 of the Constitution this Court has the inherent power to protect and regulate its own processes by having regard to the interest of justice. The emphasis was that the interest of justice required this Court not to entertain the respondents' striking-out application separately from the main application, because *first*, in order to determine the merits of the striking-out application the Court is required to consider the merits of the main application as well. This requires full ventilation of the international law, constitutional law and other submissions. *Secondly*, the manner and timing of the launching of the striking-out application constitutes an abuse of the process of the Court.

9. I shall deal first with the timing of the striking-out application. The applicants' replying affidavit was filed on 5 May 2003. Subsequently, on 11 June the applicants addressed a letter to the Deputy Judge President confirming, *inter alia*, that the matter is ripe for hearing and no supplementary papers have to be filed and also intimated that the respondents' attorney had confirmed that the duration of the proceedings and that the respondents' counsel were in a position to have the matter heard from 27 to 31 October 2003. In response to the applicants' attorney's letter, on 13 June, Stafford DJP directed that all the papers for the main application and any ancillary applications must be completed, paginated and indexed at least before 5 September 2003 and filed with the clerk of the third Court. By 5 September the respondents did not file any ancillary application, such as the application to strike out. However, a month later, on 6 October, the respondents served and filed their application to strike out together with their heads of argument. It was argued for the applicants that the respondents failed to comply with the

Deputy Judge President directive and they failed to tender any explanation for their failure to apply for condonation. Consequently, Mr Katz submitted that the respondents' failure to tender an explanation or to seek condonation constitutes an abuse of the process of court and the respondents' strike-out application should be dismissed with costs let alone hearing it separately from the main application.

[**103**] 10. Mr Katz also contended that in order to determine the merits of the strike-out application properly then there has to be full ventilation of the international law and constitutional laws issues. And for this Court to consider the arguments on the striking-out application, it would have to consider in some detail all the affidavits and supporting annexures. It was submitted that since the respondents would have it that the striking-out application is to be argued first, then a ruling on it would have to be given and only thereafter would the parties proceed to argue the main application. This procedure would be unfair to the applicants and certainly not in the interest of justice. Consequently, the approach advocated by the respondents would mean that the Court would effectively have the merits of the main application argued twice, first during the striking-out application and also during the hearing of the main application. Mr Katz in my view, rightly submitted that the main application and the striking-out application should be heard together rather than separately. Mr Grobler, on behalf of the respondents, conceded and it was not necessary to make a ruling. The entire application proceeded on the basis that the application to strike out would be considered together with the main application. The Court assured respondents' counsel that an opportunity would be afforded to them to highlight any aspects of the striking-out application.

11. Suffice to point out that the purpose of an *ad hoc* directive, such as the one issued by the Deputy Judge President, is to ensure proper case management and to facilitate full ventilation of the real issues so as to ensure that justice is done. A directive by its very nature is designed to meet the needs of a specific matter. It is in essence a refinement of the general procedures directing that litigants come to grips with the real issues between them so that they are fully ventilated in a just and a fair manner. An *ad hoc* directive should not be considered as something akin to a rule of law by virtue of section 173 of the Constitution and section 43 of the Supreme Court Act 59 of 1959. A court is empowered to protect and regulate its own processes by taking account of the interest of justice and it is competent to condone non-compliance with an *ad hoc* directive even where specific time limits are set for the delivery of any processes in respect of any particular matter. Whether a substantive application for condonation is required will depend upon the nature,

the importance and the complexity of the case. Even when there is no substantive application for condonation for non-compliance with a particular *ad hoc* directive the court's inherent power to regulate its own processes *may be* invoked in the interest of justice.

B. *Application for Review and Mandamus*

Salient underlying facts

12. Briefly, the salient underlying facts pertinent to the present purposes are in the decisions of the respondents as a consequence of the applicants' request for diplomatic protection. The request for diplomatic protection arose out of the alleged expropriation by the GoL of the applicants' property rights in execution of the Lesotho Highlands Water Projects. The alleged expropriation was effected by the GoL through various measures [104] which resulted in litigation in the Lesotho High Court and culminated in an appeal.[3]

13. As a consequence of the alleged expropriation of the applicants' property rights, they maintained that the GoL violated the International Minimum Standard in its treatment of the applicants *allegedly* with the knowledge and support of the first respondent. It is against this synoptic backdrop that the applicants initially from October 2000 to March 2001 requested diplomatic protection from the respondents.

14. On 3 April 2001, the fourth respondent advised the second applicant that the third respondent was unable to accede to their request for diplomatic protection or mediation in the second applicant's dispute with the GoL. On 7 August 2001, the applicants' renewed their request for diplomatic protection and the second respondent's legal adviser, Adv Gumbi, advised as follows:

...

> I have been directed to inform you that the South African Government is unable to grant your request for the "diplomatic protection" you asked for in relation to your private commercial dispute with the Government of Lesotho.
>
> The President has from time to time on request by South African companies raised matters of this nature with other Governments. This is done clearly for purposes of allowing the parties to explore possible settlement, not as a matter of right.
>
> The reason for the Government's inability to intervene as of right in this matter is that no such right to "diplomatic protection" of commercial transactions exists in law.

---

[3] *Attorney-General of Lesotho and Another v. Swissborough Diamond Mines (Pty) Ltd and Others* 1997 (8) BCLR 1122 (LesCA) at 1126E, 1129C-H.

You have, correctly, pursued this matter through the judicial system in Lesotho. We encourage you to continue in that manner.

We trust that this matter has now been settled.

15. Subsequently, the applicants again renewed their request for diplomatic protection to the second respondent. The latter informed the applicants in a letter of 20 July 2001 and again on 6 November 2001 that a *note verbale* was transmitted on 5 March 2002 by the first and third respondents, at the request of the second respondent, to the GoL. The *note* reads as follows:

The Department of Foreign Affairs of the Republic of South Africa presents its compliments to the High Commission of the Kingdom of Lesotho and has the honour to submit, for the attention of the Lesotho Government, copies of correspondence directed to the Presidency of the Republic of South Africa by Mr Josias van Zyl, Chairman of the Board of Trustees of the Burmilla Trust. The Department of Foreign Affairs has been requested by the Presidency to bring the matter to the attention of the Government of Lesotho.

The Department of Foreign Affairs of the Republic of South Africa avails itself of this opportunity to renew to the High Commission of the Kingdom of Lesotho the assurance of its highest consideration.

[105] *Relief sought by the applicants*

16. The substantive relief that the applicants seek [is]:

(1) Reviewing and setting aside the decision of second respondent taken on or about 6 November 2001 to refuse to afford diplomatic protection to applicants in their disputes with the government of the Kingdom of Lesotho concerning the cancellation of mining leases in Lesotho and what amounted to expropriation without compensation of applicants' mining leases by the government of the Kingdom of Lesotho ("the disputes");
(2) Reviewing and setting aside the decision of the second respondent taken on or about 6 July 2001 to refuse to afford diplomatic protection to applicants in the dispute;
(3) Reviewing and setting aside the decision of the third, alternatively fourth respondent taken on or about 3 April 2001 to refuse on behalf of the first respondent to accede to the applicants' request for diplomatic protection in the dispute;
(4) Declaring the above decisions to be null and void and of no force and effect;
(5) Directing the respondents to take all steps necessary to vindicate the rights and claims of the applicants, including but not limited to providing diplomatic protection to applicants as a consequence of the government of the Kingdom of Lesotho's violation of applicants' rights pertaining to the

mining leases granted to fourth applicant and registered in 1988 and the extension mining leases granted to fourth applicant during 1990;
(6) Granting further and/or alternative relief;
(7) Directing respondents to pay applicants' costs of suit.

What is diplomatic protection?

17. At the heart of this matter is the applicants' complaint that the decision by the respondents in refusing diplomatic protection is unlawful. This raises the question: What is diplomatic protection? The appellation *diplomatic protection* is not a precise term of art.[4] The classical formulation of diplomatic protection was enunciated by the Permanent Court of International Justice in the *Mavrommatis*[5] case that:

> It is an elementary principle of international law that a State is entitled to protect its subject[s], when injured by acts contrary to international law committed by another State, from which they have been unable to obtain satisfaction through ordinary channels. By taking up the case of one of its subjects and by resorting to diplomatic protection or international judicial proceedings on his behalf, a State is in reality asserting its own rights—its rights to ensure, in the person of its subject, respect for the rules of international law.[6]

18. At the request of the General Assembly of the United Nations, the International Law Commission (ILC) was tasked to examine the nature and scope of diplomatic protection because the exercise of diplomatic protection has generally been regarded as the right of the State and any **[106]** reliance on that right is within the absolute discretion of States.[7] This right is premised on the fiction that an injury to an individual is an injury to the State of nationality. The discretionary character of diplomatic protection has attracted trenchant criticism since it is regarded as incompatible with an international legal system committed to human rights.[8] Although free from controversy, it has been suggested that the right to diplomatic protection should be viewed as being the right of the individual with the State merely being the agent.[9] Presently, Professor John Dugard is tasked to initiate reports and codification proposals on the topic of diplomatic protection. He has submitted four

---

[4] *Kaunda* v. *President of the RSA* 2004 (10) BCLR 1009 (CC) para. 26 at 1018B-C.
[5] *Mavrommatis Palestine Concessions, Judgment No 2*, 1924 PCIJ, Ser. A, No 2.
[6] Id. at 12.
[7] Phoebe Okowa, Chapter 15: "Issues of Admissibility and the Law on International Responsibility" 472 at 477, in *International Law*, (2003) edited by Malcolm D. Evans.
[8] Id. at 478.
[9] M. Bennouna, "Preliminary report on Diplomatic Protection" (1998), United Nations Document A/CN. 4/485, paras. 34-7; 65-6; J. Dugard, "First Report on Diplomatic Protection" (2002), United Nations Document A/CN 4/506, paras. 17; 61-74.

reports on the subject dealing, *inter alia*, with the duty to extend diplomatic protection to nationals, the exhaustion of local remedies and the diplomatic protection of corporations and shareholders.[10] The most fundamental aspect of diplomatic protection at an international level is the right for a State to bring a claim to an international tribunal on behalf of its nationals whose rights have been violated by another State. Diplomatic protection is a hallmark of nationality status, an aspect I will consider later.

The Dugard proposal

19. In the "Report of the International Law Commission on the work of the fifty-second session",[11] the Special Rapporteur is of the view that the traditional position has changed or at least has been undermined by more modern state practice. Professor Dugard notes that:

Developments in international human rights law, which elevate the position of the individual in international law, have further undermined the traditional doctrine. If an individual has the right under human rights instruments to assert his basic human rights before an international body, against his own State of nationality or a foreign State, it is difficult to maintain that when a State exercises diplomatic protection on behalf of an individual it asserts its own right.[12]

The *Report* examines state practice on the conditions under which States exercise diplomatic protection[13] and concludes:

In sum, there are signs in recent State practice, constitutions and legal opinion of support for the view that states have not only a right but a legal obligation to protect their national abroad. This approach is clearly in conflict with the traditional view. It cannot, however, be dismissed out of hand as it accords with the principal goal of contemporary international law—the advancement of the human rights of the individual rather than the sovereign powers of the State. This issue is therefore one that needs to be considered, if necessary by way of progressive development.

[107] 20. In the *Report*, Professor Dugard proposed *de lege ferenda*, that is that a State should have a legal duty under general international law to exercise diplomatic protection on behalf of the injured national

---

[10] J. Dugard, "First Report on Diplomatic Protection" fn [9] above, para. 36. See: *Kaunda v. President of RSA, supra* para. 28.
[11] "*The Report*" 1 May-9 June and 10 July-18 August (2002) A/55/10.
[12] Id. at para. 66.
[13] Id. at paras. 78-86.

upon request, if the injury results from a grave breach of a *jus cogens* norm attributable to another State.[14] According to Professor Dugard,

> If a State party to a human rights convention is required to ensure to everyone within its jurisdiction effective protection against violation of the rights contained in the convention and to provide adequate means of redress, there is no reason why a State of nationality should not be obliged to protect its own national when his or her most basic human rights are seriously violated abroad.[15]

After debate, the ILC rejected the Dugard proposal regarding Article 4 and decided instead that:

> The issue was not yet ripe for the attention of the Commission and that there was a need for more State practice, and, particularly, more *opinio juris* before it could be considered.

21. The applicants' argument, in these proceedings, is not predicated on any international law obligation which the respondents may be under a duty to provide diplomatic protection, but flows instead from its basis in South African law and particularly constitutional law. It is contended that while international law may not have reached a point where States are under an international law duty to provide diplomatic protection to their nationals, the applicants submit that their case is part of the movement which Professor Dugard identified in his *Report* to the ILC. It is further submitted that this Court is at liberty to review the scope and ambit of diplomatic protection under the Constitution notwithstanding international law's slow state of progress.[16] The Dugard proposal has not received judicial imprimatur.

Applicants' claim to "right" to diplomatic protection

22. The applicants' claim to diplomatic protection is twofold. *Firstly*, that the Constitution imposes a positive obligation on the respondents to remedy the violation of the applicants' property rights by the GoL. It is contended that the first respondent is under a duty in terms of section 7 of the Constitution to promote, secure and protect the rights in the Bill of Rights. It was argued that the omission by respondents to exercise diplomatic protection on behalf of applicants against Lesotho bears a causal nexus with the continuing harm that applicants suffer in respect of their right to property under the Constitution. That omission

---

[14] Draft Article 4(1). [15] "*The Report*" fn [11] above, paras. 87-9.
[16] See *Kaunda v. President of RSA (supra)* para. 29 quoted at para. 43 below. See also: *Abbasi and Another v. Secretary of State for Foreign Affairs and Another* [2002] EWCA Civ 1598 paras. 41 and 69.

is particularly repugnant in respect of the second respondent, given his oath of office under the Constitution to "protect and promote the rights of all South Africans", to "do justice to all", and to devote himself "to the well-being of the Republic and all its people". The continued failure by the first respondent and its officials, since 1994, to diplomatically protect applicants **[108]** in their dispute with the GoL is a violation of the constitutional injunction in section 237 that the Government is to "diligently and without delay" carry out "all constitutional obligations". In support of this argument counsel for the applicants relied on *Mohamed and Another* v. *President of the Republic of South Africa*,[17] where the Constitutional Court held that the South African government should have acted positively by securing an undertaking from the US government that Mohamed would not risk being put to death and to protect his constitutional rights through the engagement of diplomatic channels. It was submitted that likewise the respondents ought to act positively to protect the applicants' rights through the exercise of effective diplomatic protection in terms of both the International Minimum Standard, as well as section 25(2)[18] of the Constitution, since the applicants have a right to compensation where their property rights have been expropriated.[19]

23. *Secondly*, that the Constitution entrenches the right to citizenship as a basic human right.[20] This right to citizenship is one of few rights expressly reserved for South Africans. It was contended that in a substantive sense the "rights, privileges and benefits of citizenship" include

---

[17] 2001 (3) SA 893 (CC). Reported at 2001 (7) BCLR 685 (CC).
[18] S 25(2) of the Constitution provides:

Property may be expropriated only in terms of law of general application.

(a) for a public purpose or in the public interest; and
(b) subject to compensation, the amount of which and the time and manner of payment of which have either been agreed to by those affected or decided or approved by a court.

[19] In respect of the right to compensation arising from an expropriation in breach of the international minimum standard: see Dugard, *International Law—A South African Perspective* (2000), 2nd edn, at 225. In respect of the right to compensation arising from an expropriation in breach of section 25 of the Constitution: see the judgment of Ackermann J in *First National Bank of SA Ltd t/a Wesbank* v. *Minister of Finance* 2002 (4) SA 768 (CC) at paras. 57-9; also reported at 2002 (7) BCLR 702 (CC).

[20] Section 3 read with section 20 provides as follows:

3. (1) There is a common South African citizenship.
  (2) All citizens are—

  (a) equally entitled to the rights, privileges and benefits of citizenship; and
  (b) equally subject to the duties and responsibilities of citizenship.

  (3) National legislation must provide for the requisition, loss and restoration of citizenship.
20. No citizen may be deprived of citizenship.

the right to remain in and return to South Africa, to enjoy the protection of its laws, the right to have a passport (which is expressly provided in section 21(4) of the Constitution)[21] and the right of adult citizens to vote and stand for office. At international law, not just any individual is entitled to diplomatic protection since nationality is a prerequisite. It is the bond of nationality between the State and the individual that confers the protection under customary international law. It was submitted that in a world consisting of nation States, citizenship (or nationality) creates a legal link between a State and the people who are its nationals.

24. Hence, it was argued that the vulnerability of applicants is plain since their rights are being violated and thereby entitling them to request and **[109]** receive diplomatic protection as citizens of South Africa fundamentally for three reasons. *One*, the applicants' right under customary international law (which as asserted is part of South African law through section 232 of the Constitution) regarding treatment by a foreign State, in that latter State in accordance with the International Minimum Standard, has been violated through the acts of expropriation by the GoL without compensation having been paid. *Two*, the applicants' right to property under the South Africa Constitution has been, and continues to be, violated by means of various stratagems to which the South African government has been involved in or acquiesced in the violation of applicants' property rights. After 1994, that continued involvement or acquiescence amounted to a violation of applicants' property rights under the interim, and the final Constitutions. *Three*, applicants' right to equality has also been violated.

25. On 20 July 2001, the second respondent's office addressed a letter to applicants in which it advised that:

[T]he South African government is unable to grant your request for the "diplomatic protection" you ask for in relation to your private commercial dispute with the Government of Lesotho.

The second respondent proceeded to indicate that on occasion on request by South African companies matters of this nature were raised with other governments. This was done purely for purposes for facilitating the parties to explore possible settlement. It is not as a matter of a right. Hence the applicants submitted that the exercise of public power in this fashion is discriminatory and unconstitutional since it gives the impression that the President exercises his public power in

---

[21] This section should be read with section 4 of the South African Passports and Travel Documents Act 4 of 1994.

order to protect the unlawful conduct of the first respondent in the execution of the Lesotho Highlands Water Project ("LHWP") Treaty to avoid paying compensation to the applicants. Such compensation is a water transfer cost-related expense in the LHWP Treaty for which the first respondent is liable and that it "would set an unhealthy precedent for other businesses to request diplomatic intervention from the South African government in their disputes with foreign governments".

26. It was also submitted that a democratic society based on a supreme Constitution, the advancement of human rights and freedoms, and which constitutionalises citizenship as a fundamental right indeed places a legal duty on the State to offer its citizens diplomatic protection against foreign powers. In this regard, the applicants find support in the views of Professors Erasmus and Davidson that:

Citizenship should, logically, also include entitlement to diplomatic protection. Without this dimension it will lose an essential part of its meaning and effect. Citizenship is also about the link between the state and its citizen *vis-à-vis* other states [this much is evidenced by the very existence under international customary law of the doctrine of diplomatic protection whereby states are entitled to advance claims against other states for violations of their nationals' rights]. It cannot have a restricted, internal meaning such as the right to vote ... South African constitutional law clearly does not relegate citizenship to an inferior status or a right to be "enjoyed" only with the leave and licence of state officials. Neither does it suggest that South Africans lose their rights or claims to their state's obligation to protect them if they engage in international **[110]** travel or commerce. As a matter of fact, the Constitution expressly recognises that they are entitled to travel and trade.[22]

Principles relevant to analyse the facts

27. For purposes of analysing the factual matrix of this matter it is necessary to allude broadly to the pertinent principles of international law. Private individuals or companies are not proper subjects of international law[23] and they benefit from the protection of international law when specific status is conferred upon them in treaties or agreements between States whereby rules of international law may sometimes govern the relationship between States and such individuals or companies.[24] The proper subjects of international law are sovereign States and international organisations with international legal personality. They are

---

[22] Erasmus and Davidson, "Do South Africans have a Right to Diplomatic Protection?", (2000) 25 SAYIL, 112, at 126. See: *Kaunda* v. *President of RSA* (*supra*) paras. 58-67; fn 47 at 1027 H-I.
[23] Cf: Dugard, *International Law*, at 1-2.   [24] Id. at 22.

designated of possessing international rights and duties and have procedural capacity to maintain their rights by bringing international claims before an international tribunal.[25]

28. Where a private individual or company enters into a mining lease with a sovereign State for the exploitation of mineral resources in that country, then that private individual or company acts on an equal footing with the sovereign State in terms of that State's private law as any of its citizens would do when concluding a contract with it. Its remedies for breach or enforcement of the contract are those which flow from the contract and are determined by the proper law of the contract. Such contract is not a treaty merely because one contracting party is a State. Consequently a breach of that contract *per se* by a contracting State does not incur international responsibility of the State party.[26] According to Professor Booysen:

> One may likewise say that there is a hypothesis that individuals usually contract on the basis of a particular national private law. This is also the case where they contract with foreign states. The particular national system is then determined by the rules of the conflict of laws. In the normal course, national law permits individuals to select the law which will govern their commercial contract ... Party autonomy to select the applicable law of an international contract is not only a feature of national laws, but has also been described as a general principle of law recognised by civilized states and thus a principle of international law.[27]

In contracts between States and individuals, the parties can select a non-national law like international law to govern their contract.[28]

29. The municipal law allows the parties to make a choice of law which may include international law or by agreement it may be internationalised so that the individual or company is entitled to take its dispute to an [111] international arbitration tribunal in terms of an arbitration clause contained in the contract or by virtue of special treaty arrangements between its State of nationality and the host State. In such arbitration tribunal, international law or a mixture of both will be applied, depending on the choice of law of the contract.[29] For example, where the Convention on the Settlement of Investment Disputes between States and Nationals of other State is applicable, the individual

---

[25] *Reparation for Injuries Suffered in the Service of the United Nations* 1949 ICJ Reports 174 at 179.
[26] Cf: Dugard, op. cit., at 229.
[27] Booysen, *Principles of International Trade Law as a Monistic System*, at 50 and at 201.
[28] Id. at pp. 201-3; see also Dugard, op. cit., at 229.   [29] Cf: Dugard, op. cit., at 229-30.

or company may act directly against the host State in the International Centre for Settlement of Investment Disputes (ICSID)[30] or where a Bilateral Investment Treaty provides for the investor to take up its claim against the host State to an international arbitration tribunal or the host State subjects itself in an arbitration clause to international arbitration and the application of international law as proper law of the contract. In the instant case, there is no internationalisation of the mining leases and there is no possibility of the application of international law as between the contracting parties on any dispute in terms of the mining leases. Therefore, the applicants are not subjects of international law and cannot have international law applied in any of their claims that they may have against the Kingdom of Lesotho.

30. However, there is a remote possibility that the Republic of South Africa may have a claim based on international law against the Kingdom of Lesotho if certain necessary preconditions exist. This will be alluded to later in this judgment. Nevertheless where the claim is neither based on the mining leases concluded between the fourth applicant and the Kingdom of Lesotho, then it is not a claim with expropriation as *causa*. The *causa* of such a claim may arise from a breach of the rules of international law applicable between two States and their relationships are governed by international law. That *causa* may arise since every State has an international law obligation to treat nationals of another State according to certain international minimum standards. Conversely, every State has the right in international law that its nationals shall be treated by a host State according to those standards. Should the host State treat a foreign national in breach of those minimum standards then the State of nationality has a claim against the host State. This claim is usually exercised by means of diplomatic protection. The person or company in respect of whom the minimum standards are infringed by the host State, the person or company has no right against the host State in this relationship. The State of nationality protects its own rights which it has in its nationals by insisting on the application of the international minimum standard by the host State.[31]

31. The essence of the relationship is between the State of nationality, the host State and the particular national, where the international minimum standards have been breached. The International Court in the *Barcelona Traction* case[32] described it as follows:

---

[30] Booysen, op. cit., at 562-3.   [31] Dugard, op. cit., at 217; Booysen, op. cit., at 566-7.
[32] *Barcelona Traction, Light and Power Co. Ltd Second Phase* (*Belgium* v. *Spain*) [1970] ICJ Reports, 3, at 44; 46 ILR 178.

The Court would here observe that, within the limits prescribed by international law, a State may exercise diplomatic protection by whatever means and [112] whatever extent it thinks fit, for it is its own right that the State is asserting. Should the natural or legal persons on whose behalf it is acting consider that their rights are not adequately protected, they have no remedy in international law. All they can do is to resort to municipal law, if means are available, with a view to furthering their cause or obtaining redress. The municipal legislator may lay upon the State an obligation to protect its citizens abroad, and may also confer upon the national a right to demand the performance of that obligation, and clothe the right with corresponding sanctions. However, all these questions remain within the province of municipal law and do not affect the position internationally.

The State must be viewed as the sole judge to decide whether its protection will be granted, to what extent it is granted, and when it will cease. It retains in this respect as discretionary power the exercise of which may be determined by considerations of a political or other nature, unrelated to the particular case. Since the claim of the State is not identical with that of the individual or corporate person whose cause is espoused, the State enjoys complete freedom of action.[33]

32. The rights of the State of nationality are relevant and it can decide on the basis of its national interests whether it will act upon the infraction of its international law rights. However, international law places no duty on such a State to protect its nationals abroad and in practice States often do not extend diplomatic protection to their nationals.[34] The applicants conceded that there is no such duty in international law. Thus, it follows that the extent of diplomatic protection is completely within the discretion of the State of nationality. According to Jennings and Watts[35] it may take the following forms:

It may often be sufficient to alert the local state to the interest of the alien's home state in the treatment being accorded the alien. Thus the protecting state may, with varying degrees of formality, make inquiries of the other state as to the facts of a particular incident, or seek an explanation, or lodge a protest, or require that the wrongdoers be punished or that damages be paid to its injured national. More forceful forms of protection, such as intervention, have sometimes been resorted to, although the legality of such action is now very questionable. Since protection may ultimately result in the presentation of an international claim, even in the earlier stages of exercising protection the protecting state will usually be guided by the law relating to the international claims, particularly in such matters as the rules as to nationality of claims and exhaustion of local remedies. Nevertheless, practice shows that in the preliminary stages

---

[33] Id. at paras. 78-9.
[34] Jennings and Watts, *Oppenheim's International Law*, vol. 1, para. 410 at 934.
[35] Jennings and Watts, op. cit., at 935.

[states] may take steps designed to protect or assist their nationals even when, strictly speaking, no entitlement to present an international claim has arisen: thus a state will sometimes (although usually with some diffidence) make diplomatic representations before local remedies have been exhausted, or where the national status of the injured individual might not be sufficiently clearly established to justify the formal presentation of a claim, particularly in cases involving dual nationality.

In consequence of the importance of the principle of equal sovereignty of States, any form of diplomatic protection will only be lawful if the preconditions or requirements for lawful diplomatic protection have been [113] complied with, otherwise such steps in international law constitute an unwarranted interference with the sovereignty of the host State.[36]

33. Mr Grobler on behalf of the respondent, argued that the applicants are seeking to have the principles of international law applicable between the Republic of South Africa and the Kingdom of Lesotho enforced as though they, the applicants, are subjects of international law by seeking a mandamus to force the executive to exercise an international law right which belongs to the Republic alone. In respect of which this Court has no certainty as to whether the preconditions for its existence indeed occurred.

34. The applicants, however, allege that the international minimum standards were violated by the Kingdom of Lesotho because certain mining leases were expropriated without compensation. It is critically important to draw a distinction between the initial acquisition of rights and the treatment of those rights after they came into existence. Insofar as the acquisition of property or patrimonial rights are concerned the receiving State may restrict the ability of a foreign national to own land or acquire rights and thereby treat them less favourably than its own nationals. Where the foreign entity is a commercial enterprise then the acquisition of property is likely to assume the character of an economic investment. The terms and conditions on which such an investment is permitted are usually for the determination of the State and may be subject to its treaty obligations. It is not obliged to accord national investor treatment to foreign investors. A differential treatment as between the national and foreign investment is permissible and it is not necessarily contrary to the State's international obligations.[37]

35. The acquisition of private rights of a patrimonial nature is governed exclusively by the municipal law of the receiving State in matters relating to ownership and other rights *in rem*, the *lex rei sitae* alone can

---

[36] Id. at 935.   [37] Id. at 933.

apply.[38] In this present case, the *lex loci actus* would be the same as the *lex rei sitae* since the deed's registry is in Maseru. This embraces the rule both in South African and Lesotho municipal law. The formal validity of any act or instrument creating rights pertaining to an immoveable is likewise also determined by the *lex rei sitae*. Thus, the proper law of the mining lease contracts was the municipal law of Lesotho. It would be the same as the *lex loci contractus* which would apply to formalities concerning ordinary commercial contracts.[39] The GoL granted mining rights by way of mining leases. These were registered in the deeds registry at Maseru. Therefore, the applicable law would certainly be the law of the Kingdom of Lesotho since these mining leases were not internationalised and thereby international law is not applicable as the proper law of choice.

36. Once a foreign national has acquired property within the host State or concluded an investment contract with that State, then that State is obliged to respect such rights in conformity with the requirements of international [**114**] law. The host State may by international law indeed expropriate such property lawfully:

Traditionally this right has been regarded as discretionary power inherent in the sovereignty and jurisdiction which the State exercises over all persons and things in its territory, or in the so-called right of "self-preservation" which allows it, *inter alia*, to further the welfare and economic progress of its population.[40]

International norms pertaining to expropriation

37. Traditionally international norms governing expropriation may be for public purposes but adequate and effective compensation should be paid and no discrimination should take place between foreigners and nationals of the host State. These norms, however, have been challenged by developing States by replacing the compensation standard with their own national standards.[41] The international minimum standards pertaining to expropriation of property are not to be equated to the international minimum norms pertaining to international human rights violations. This is what the applicants seem to be doing. However, the right not to be deprived of one's property *may* constitute an infringement of international human rights norm[s].

---

[38] Garcia-Amador *et al.*, *Recent Codification of the Law of State Responsibility for Injuries to Aliens*, at 38.
[39] *Ex parte Spinazze and Another NO* 1985 (3) SA 650 (A).
[40] Garcia-Amador *et al.*, op. cit., at 46. See: Dugard, op. cit., at 225-8; Jennings and Watts, op. cit., vol. 1, at 933.
[41] Brownlie, *Principles of International Law* (1973) at 518 et seq.

38. Article 17(2) of the Universal Declaration of Human Rights provides that:

No one shall be deprived of his property.

And article 14 of the African Charter on Human and Peoples' Rights provides that:

The right to property shall be guaranteed. It may only be encroached upon in the interest of public need or in the general interest of the community and in accordance with the provisions of appropriate laws.

Both the Republic of South Africa and the Kingdom of Lesotho are bound by the provisions of the Universal Declaration of Human Rights and the African Charter since they have ratified these fundamental instruments. Further, the first paragraph of article 1 of the First Protocol: Enforcement of Certain Rights and Freedoms to the European Convention for the Protection of Human Rights and Fundamental Freedoms reads:

Every natural or legal person is entitled to the peaceful enjoyment of his possessions. No one shall be deprived of his possessions except in the public interest and subject to the conditions provided for by law and by the general principles of international law.

In addition article 21(2) of the American Convention on Human Rights provides that:

No one shall be deprived of his property except upon payment of just compensation, for reasons of public utility or social interest, and in the cases and according to the forms established by law.

39. It is clear that there is an international norm not to deprive anyone of her or his property except in terms of general principles of property law. The fundamental instruments certainly contemplate the lawful deprivation of **[115]** property in the interest of the community or the public or for reasons of public utility or social interest. Only the Protocol to the European Human Rights Convention provides for "by law and by the general principles of international law". These are international human rights law principles pertaining to the confiscation or expropriation of property of foreign nationals and the compensation that must be paid for such deprivation. Nationalisation or expropriation in international law may take place by way of a judgment of a court, a legislative act or an executive act. If a court of law were to give effect to legislation and thereby deprive a foreigner of his or her title to property,

then the court order will be an act of expropriation.[42] It is characterised by its effect which may be the taking of the property, the destruction of a right or any act which destroys a right even if no physical property has been taken.[43]

40. The general rule of customary international law is that where the host State has expropriated property of a foreigner then prompt, adequate and effective compensation must be paid in the case of expropriation of specific property.[44] Full compensation including *lucrum cessans* and even *restitutio in intergrum* is required in the case of unlawful expropriations.[45] According to Professor Singh:[46]

International Covenant on Economic, Social and Cultural Rights of 1966 provides that developing countries, with due regard to human rights and their national economy, may determine to what extent they will guarantee to non-nationals the economic rights recognised in the Covenant. In its resolution on permanent sovereignty over natural resources, adopted on 17 December 1973, the United Nations General Assembly affirmed that each nationalising State, by virtue of its sovereignty to safeguard its natural resources, is entitled to determine the amount of possible compensation and the mode of payment, and that any disputes should be settled in accordance with the domestic legislation of that nationalising State. An affirmation in somewhat similar terms appears in the Charter of Economic Rights and Duties of States, adopted by the General Assembly in 1947; this contains a reference to the payment of "appropriate compensation", and provides for the settlement of any controversy by the domestic tribunals of the nationalising State, unless it is freely and mutually agreed by all States concerned that other peaceful means be sought on the basis of the sovereign equality of States and in accordance with the principle of free choice of means.

41. Neither the International Covenant on Civil and Political Rights nor the International Covenant on Economic, Social and Cultural Rights provides for the protection of property rights. The underlying reason for the weak protection of property rights on the international sphere is because of the New International Economic Order expressed in numerous resolutions of the **[116]** General Assembly of the United

---

[42] *Oilfields of Texas* v. *Iran* (1986) 12 Iran–US CTR 308 at 318 et seq.

[43] Christie, "What Constitutes a Taking of Property under International Law?" [1968] BYIL 307 at 310; See: *German Interests in Polish Upper Silesia* [1926] PCIJ, Ser. A, No 7; *Norwegian Shipowners Claims* [1922] 1 *United Nations Reports of International Arbitral Awards* 307 (1922).

[44] Bowett, "State Contracts of Aliens: Contemporary Developments in Compensation for Termination of Breach" [1988] 59 BYIL 48 at 73.

[45] *Chorzów Factory* [1928] PCIJ, Ser. A, No 17; *Topco* v. *Libya* [1979] 53 ILR 389 at 507.

[46] Gurdip Singh, *International Law* (2003), 1st edn, at 124-5; See also: Article 2, para. 2(c). Charter of Economic Rights and Duties of States (UN General Assembly Resolution 3281 (XXIX of 1974), [1975] 4 ILM 251.

Nations.[47] These resolutions emphasised the sovereignty of status of States over their natural resources. In principle, there is no support for the thesis that an international human right to protection of property is recognised as such in international law. However, it appears that it is for States to protect by way of diplomatic protection their rights which they enjoy in respect of their nationals. According to Phoebe Okowa:[48]

There is here a presumption that nationals were indispensable elements of a State's territorial attributes and a wrong done to the national invariably affects the rights of the State.

42. The question is, do the principles of the *Kaunda*[49] decision apply in respect of deprivation of property rights of a national in a foreign country? That decision is distinguishable from the issue in the present matter on several bases: *Firstly*, in the *Kaunda* case (*supra*) the alleged infringement was an egregious one, that is gross and flagrant infraction of international human rights such as physical abuse and torture which is different from expropriation of property. Chaskalson CJ stated:

When the request is directed to a material infringement of a human right that forms part of customary international law, one would not expect our government to be passive.[50]

In addition, the learned Chief Justice also indicated:

There may even be a duty on a government in extreme cases to provide assistance to its nationals against egregious breaches of international human rights which come to its knowledge. The victims of such breaches may not be in a position to ask for assistance, and in such circumstances, on becoming aware of the breaches, the government may well be obliged to take an initiative itself.[51]

Secondly, the true beneficiary of international human rights is the individual and such rights do not vest in juristic persons such as companies like the fourth to ninth applicants. *Thirdly*, there is indeed a fundamental difference between an infringement of international human rights on the one hand and breaches of international minimum standards in respect of property on the other. The latter essentially constitutes an international delict.

---

[47] Resolution on Permanent Sovereignty over Natural Resources (General Assembly Resolution 1803 [XVII] of 1962); The Declaration on the Establishment of the New International Economic Order of 1974 (General Assembly Resolution 3201 (S-VI); The Programme of Action on the Establishment of the New Economic Order of 1974 (General Assembly 3202 (S-VI)); Charter of Economic Rights and Duties of States of 1974 (General Assembly Resolution 3281 (XXIX)). See also: Booysen, op. cit.
[48] Phoebe Okowa, op. cit., at 477.   [49] 2004 (10) BCLR 1009 (CC); 2005 (4) SA 235 (CC).
[50] Id. para. 64.   [51] Id. para. 70. See also: para. 217.

43. On applying the principles of the *Kaunda* decision, one must be mindful of the important and crucial differences between the present matter and that case. In the final analysis, Chaskalson CJ was emphatic that:

[117] Currently the prevailing view is that diplomatic protection is not recognised by international law as a human right and cannot be enforced as such. To do so may give rise to more problems than it would solve.[52]

Therefore, in any application of the *Kaunda* principles, one must ensure some measure of caution because different emphases are discernible since the present matter is about *alleged* breaches of the applicants' property rights by the GoL and certainly not an egregious and material infringement of international human rights. On this particular aspect the two cases are distinguishable from each other.

Respondents' decision under review

44. The applicants requested the second respondent to afford diplomatic protection to them. The request was for the second respondent, in his executive capacity as the President, to take diplomatic action on behalf of the Republic of South Africa against the Kingdom of Lesotho. It was argued by Mr Dugard that the President was under a duty towards the applicants on the basis alleged by them to extend "*effective*" diplomatic protection. This argument is untenable because a further phase of the Lesotho Highlands Water Project is under construction in Lesotho in terms of the Treaty and it could possibly jeopardise its construction. Under the circumstances, the President would have had no choice but to act against his better judgment. The President dispatched a *Note Verbale* to the GoL drawing its attention to the applicants' claim and in doing so he adopted a nuanced approach upon having considered the applicants' request and reacted appropriately.[53] The government has a broad[54] and extremely wide discretion, and how best to provide and in what form diplomatic protection it can offer.[55] The choices and considerations open to the President were and are within the exclusive purview of foreign relations between the first respondent and the GoL. The exercise of the discretion is invariably influenced by political and economic considerations rather than the legal merits of the particular claim.[56] It is essentially a matter pertaining to foreign relations as will become apparent in this judgment.

---

[52] Id. para. 29. [53] Id. para. 79 at 1030A. [54] Id. para. 81 at 1030E-F.
[55] Id. para. 275 at 1083G. [56] See: *Barcelona Traction* fns 32 and 33 above.

45. Now, the pertinent question is whether the second respondent's decision and the decisions of the third and [fourth] respondents are reviewable and if so, on what basis and to what extent. This depends upon the nature of the powers and functions of the executive in conducting foreign relations on behalf of the Republic of South Africa and that invariably depends on the provisions of the Constitution since all public power and actions, whether executive or otherwise, are only legitimate if lawful:

The rule of law—to the extent at least that it expresses this principle of legality—is generally understood to be a fundamental principle of constitutional law.[57]

[118] 46. Central to our constitutional order is that both the legislature and executive in any sphere are constrained by the principle that they may exercise no power and perform no function beyond that conferred upon them by law. In this sense, the principle of legality is implied within the Constitution. Even pertaining to executive action, which does not constitute administrative action within the meaning of section 33 of the Constitution, the principle of legality is necessarily implicit in the Constitution.

47. The second respondent, as the President, is the Head of the State as well as the head of the national executive.[58] He has the powers entrusted to him by the Constitution and legislation, including those necessary to perform the functions of Head of State and head of the national executive.[59] The executive authority of the Republic is vested in the President[60] and he exercises that authority, together with the other members of the Cabinet, *inter alia* by performing any executive function[61] provided for in the Constitution or in national legislation.[62] In doing so, the President promotes that which will advance the aspirations and interests of the Republic.[63] This duty is a strong constitutional imperative in presidential decision-making and executive actions. Historically, the executive authority had the power and function to conduct foreign relations of the Republic with other States. This power and function is not specifically mentioned in the Constitution.[64]

---

[57] *Fedsure Life Assurance Ltd and Others* v. *Johannesburg Transitional Metropolitan Council and Others* 1999 (1) SA 374 (CC) para. 56 at 399D. Also reported at 1998 (12) BCLR 1458 (CC).
[58] S 83(a) of the Constitution.   [59] S 84(1) of the Constitution.
[60] S 85(1) of the Constitution.   [61] S 85(2)(a)-(d) of the Constitution.
[62] S 85(2)(e) of the Constitution.   [63] S 83(e) of the Constitution.
[64] By virtue of ss 84(1)(h) and (i) and section 231(1) the President is responsible for receiving and recognising foreign diplomatic and consular representatives and for appointing ambassadors, plenipotentiaries and diplomatic and consular representatives. Furthermore, the negotiating and signing of all international agreements is stated to be the responsibility of the national executive.

48. Section 232 of the Constitution provides that customary international law is law in the Republic unless it is inconsistent with the Constitution or an Act of Parliament. The Constitution recognises that the Republic of South Africa is a subject of international law and the executive is responsible for negotiating and signing international agreements, an important element in the conduct of foreign relations. This presupposes that the responsibility, power and function of the executive, with the President as its head, is responsible for foreign policy and to conduct foreign relations on behalf of the Republic. This responsibility, power and function indeed vest in the national executive by virtue of the Constitution through item 2(1) of Schedule 6 which provides that all law that was in force when the *new* Constitution took effect continues in force subject to any amendment or repeal and inconsistency with the Constitution. Consistency with the Constitution requires that the common-law powers are now regulated by the Constitution. The Constitutional Court in *Pharmaceutical* [119] *Manufacturers of South Africa: In re Ex parte the President of the Republic of South Africa*[65] categorically pronounced:

Powers that were previously regulated by the common law under the prerogative and the principles developed by the courts to control the exercise of public power are now regulated by the Constitution. Thus, in *President of the Republic of South Africa and Another* v. *Hugo* the power of the President to pardon or reprieve offenders had to be dealt with under s 82(1) of the interim Constitution, and not under the prerogative of the common law. In *Fedsure* the question of legality had to be dealt with under the Constitution and not under the common-law principle of *ultra vires*. In *SARFU 3* the President's power to appoint a commission and the exercise of that power had to be dealt with under s 84(2) of the 1996 Constitution and the doctrine of legality, and not under the common-law principles of prerogative and administrative law.

49. These common-law powers are now incorporated by virtue of section 84(1) read with section 85(2)(e) and item 2(1) of Schedule 6 of the Constitution as constitutional powers and functions and also as the common law cannot be seen as distinct from the Constitution. In this regard the Constitutional Court in *Pharmaceutical Manufacturers (supra)* observed:[66]

---

[65] 2000 (2) SA 674 (CC) para. 41 at 695C-E (footnotes omitted). Also reported at 2000 (3) BCLR 241 (CC).

[66] Id. para. 44 at 696B-C. In *President of the Republic of South Africa and Another* v. *Hugo* 1997 (4) SA 1 (CC) paras. 8-10, also reported at 1997 (6) BCLR 708 (CC), the Constitutional Court held that the prerogative powers under the previous constitutions were now those enumerated in the new Constitution (at 8B/C-9A).

There are not two systems of law, each dealing with the same subject-matter, each having similar requirements, each operating in its own field with its own highest Court. There is only one system of law. It is shaped by the Constitution which is the supreme law, and all law, including the common law, derives its force from the Constitution and is subject to constitutional control.

50. The nature of these powers and acts performed [is] essentially executive and not administrative and, therefore, section 33 of the Constitution and concomitantly the provisions of the Promotion of Administrative Justice Act 3 of 2000 are not the mechanisms of control regarding executive powers. A series of considerations may be pertinent in determining whether an action is administrative or executive. The source of the power is a relevant factor and so is the nature of the power as well as its subject matter. The question is whether it involves the exercise of a public duty and, if so, how closely it is related on the one hand to policy matters which are not administrative, and on the other to the implementation of legislation which is administrative.[67] Undoubtedly, the powers and functions to conduct foreign relations are by source, origin, nature and description essentially executive powers and intrinsically involved with foreign policy considerations. Professor Singh observed:

... foreign policy which is formulated by Government, not by diplomats. In order to carry out its policy, a government will need to manage and adjust its international relations by applying different forms of pressure. However, in [120] normal circumstances, it will conduct its international intercourse by negotiations. This is diplomacy. Persuasive argument, if applied skilfully and sensitively at the right time, certainly leads to better result[s] than pressure technique backed by the threat of force. The latter may provoke resistance and finally lead to war.[68]

Therefore, within the panoply of diplomatic protection and any intervention the executive has a reasonably wide choice to—

Consular action, negotiation, mediation, judicial and arbitral proceedings, reprisals, retortion, severance of diplomatic relations, [and] economic pressure.[69]

The executive in invoking the form of diplomatic protection or intervention is required to make an informed choice invariably exercising a discretion based on:

---

[67] *President of the Republic of South Africa* v. *South African Rugby Football Union* 2000 (1) SA 1 (CC) para. 143 at 67. Also reported at 1999 (10) BCLR 1059 (CC). See also: *Bato Star Fishing (Pty) Ltd* v. *Minister of Environmental Affairs and Others* 2004 (4) SA 490 (CC) para. 48 at 514F-G–515C, also reported at 2004 (7) BCLR 687 (CC).
[68] Singh, *International Law*, 210.   [69] Dugard, *The Report*, fn [9] above.

the application of intelligence and tact to the conduct of relations between the governments of independent States, ... or more briefly still, the conduct of business between States by peaceful means.[70]

This then raises the fundamental question to what extent is the exercise of executive powers, whether it is diplomatic or otherwise, subject to control by the court?

51. *Firstly*, it must not infringe any provision of the Bill of Rights and *secondly*, it is clearly constrained by the principle of legality and *thirdly*,

... it is implicit in the Constitution, the President must act in good faith and must not misconstrue the powers.[71]

These constraints arise from the *constitutionalisation* of administrative justice and moreover by virtue of the provisions of the Promotion of Administrative Justice Act 3 of 2000. This statute expressly disavows applicability to executive powers and functions including those mentioned in section 85(2)(e) of the Constitution. Undoubtedly, the Constitution is the supreme law of the Republic and any conduct inconsistent with it is certainly invalid.[72]

52. In England the prerogative powers were historically beyond the reach of the courts, however, the exercise of some powers, not all of them, has been subjected to judicial review. In the landmark case of *Council of Civil Service Unions and Others* v. *Minister of the Civil Service*[73] it was held that a decision-making power derived from the common law and not a statutory source is not "for that reason only" immune from judicial review and that is so in respect of prerogative powers.[74] It is not the source but the subject matter which determines whether the exercise of such a power is subject to review. Lord Roskill stated:

But I do not think that that right of challenge can be unqualified. It must, I think, depend upon the subject-matter of the prerogative power which is exercised. Many examples were given during the argument of prerogative **[121]** powers which as at present advised I do not think could properly be made the subject of judicial review. Prerogative powers such as those relating to the making of treaties, the defence of the realm ... are not, I think, susceptible to judicial review because their nature and subject-matter are such as not to be amenable to the judicial process. The Courts are not the place wherein to

---

[70] Singh, op. cit., 210.
[71] *President of the Republic of SA.* v. *South African Football Union* 2000 (1) SA 1 (CC), para. 48 at 70-1.
[72] S 2 of the Constitution.   [73] [1985] 3 AC 374 (HL).
[74] Id. at 410C-D; 411B-C; 417G-418B.

determine whether a treaty should be concluded or the armed forces disposed in a particular manner or parliament dissolved on one date rather than another.[75]

In *R* v. *Home Secretary, ex parte Bentley*[76] Watkins LJ restated the principle:

> The question is simply whether the nature and subject-matter of the decision is amenable to the judicial process. Are the Courts qualified to deal with the matter or does the decision involve such questions of policy that they should not intrude because they are ill-equipped to do so?

53. Our Constitutional Court, however, decided that the principle whereby the review of the exercise of prerogative powers is qualified by the question whether the subject-matter of the power is justiciable, does not apply in our constitutional dispensation. In *President of the Republic of South Africa and Another* v. *Hugo*[77] Goldstone J stated:

> The interim Constitution obliges us to test impugned action by any organ of State against the discipline of the interim Constitution and, in particular, the Bill of Rights. That is a fundamental incidence of the constitutional State which is envisaged in the Preamble to the interim Constitution ...
>
> ...
>
> In my view, it would be contrary to that promise if the exercise of the presidential power is above the interim Constitution and is not subject to the discipline of the Bill of Rights.

Nevertheless, the learned Justice alluded that it may well be that because of the nature of the executive power or the manner in which it is exercised, the provisions of the Constitution:

> provide no ground for an effective review of a presidential exercise of such a power. The result, in a particular case, may be the same as that in England, but the manner in which that result is reached in terms of the interim Constitution is a different one. On the English approach the Courts, in certain cases, depending on the subject matter of the prerogative power exercised, would be deprived of jurisdiction. Under the interim Constitution the jurisdiction would be there in all cases in which the presidential powers under s 82(1) are exercised.[78]

54. The conduct of foreign relations may be one of the rare instances where the Constitution and Bill of Rights provide no ground for an effective review. This will be the case where the decision does not limit

---

[75] Id. 418A-C; see also Lord Scarman at 407B-C.
[76] [1993] 4 All ER 442 at 452j-453c. See: *Minister for Arts, Heritage and Environment and Others* v. *Peko-Wallsend Ltd and Others* [1987] 75 ALR 218 at 224; *Burt* v. *Governor-General* [1992] 3 NZLR 672 (CA) at 678.
[77] 1997 (4) SA 1 (CC) para. 28 at 17B-C and D-E.   [78] Id. para. 28 at 17E-F/G.

any fundamental rights and is concerned primarily with the conduct of foreign relations. Even if a court may not agree with the merits of the decision or the grounds on which it was taken or its wisdom, then the basis for review lies in the principle of legality and the rule of law. There may be **[122]** cases when a decision may be set aside but that should not second-guess the exercise of executive discretion. In the Constitutional Court case of *Hugo* (*supra*) Goldstone J noted:

> This is what happened in *R* v. *Home Secretary, ex parte Bentley*, but even then the Court declined to issue a mandamus or a declaration. It simply invited the Home Secretary to consider the case again in the light of the decision that he had misconstrued his powers. As it was put by Wilson J in *Operation Dismantle Inc.* v. *The Queen*: "the courts should not be too eager to relinquish their judicial review function simply because they are called upon to exercise it in relation to weighty matters of State." Equally, however, it is important to realise that judicial review is not the same thing as substitution of the Court's opinion on the merits for the opinion of a person or body to whom a discretionary decision-making power has been committed. The first step is to determine who as a constitutional matter has the decision-making power; the second is to determine the scope (if any) of judicial review of the exercise of that power.[79]

55. The Canadian Supreme Court in *Operation Dismantle Inc.* v. *The Queen*[80] was asked to review and set aside the decision by the Government to allow the testing of United States cruise missiles in Canada. Wilson J said:

> I would conclude, therefore, that if we are to look at the Constitution for the answer to the question whether it is appropriate for the Courts to "second guess" the executive on matters of defence, we would conclude that it is not appropriate. However, if what we are being asked to do is to decide whether any particular act of the executive violates the rights of the citizens, then it is not only appropriate that we answer the question; it is our obligation under the Charter to do so.[81]

In addition, her Ladyship held that:

> ... the courts should not be too eager to relinquish their judicial review function simply because they are called upon to exercise it in relation to weighty matters of State. Equally, however, it is important to realise that judicial review is not the same thing as substitution of the court's opinion on the merits for the opinion of the person or body to whom discretionary decision-making power has been committed. The first step is to determine who as a constitutional matter has the decision-making power; the second is to determine the scope (if any) of judicial review of the exercise of that power.

---

[79] Id. para. 29 at 18B-C.   [80] [1985] 18 DLR (4th) 481.   [81] Id. at 504.

It might be timely at this point to remind ourselves of the question the court is being asked to decide. It is, of course, true that the federal legislature has exclusive legislative jurisdiction in relation to defence under section 91(7) of the Constitution Act, 1867 and that the federal executive has the powers conferred upon it in sections 9–15 of that Act. Accordingly, if the court were simply being asked to express its opinion on the wisdom of the executive's exercise of its defence powers in this case, the court would have to decline. It cannot substitute its opinion for that of the executive to whom the decision-making power is given by the Constitution.[82]

56. In the present matter, having regard to the dicta quoted above, the decisions attacked by the applicants will only be reviewable on an extremely limited basis pertaining to foreign policy and foreign relations. **[123]** However, a court should not be deterred in exercising review jurisdiction when necessary. The Constitutional Court in *Kaunda* (*supra*) stressed:

This does not mean that South African courts have no jurisdiction to deal with issues concerned with diplomatic protection. The exercise of all public power is subject to constitutional control. Thus even decisions by the President ... are justiciable. This also applies to an allegation that the government has failed to respond appropriately to a request for diplomatic protection.[83]

And Chaskalson CJ stated:

If government refuses to consider a legitimate request, or deals with it in bad faith or irrationality, a court should require government to deal with the matter properly. Rationality and bad faith are illustrations of grounds on which a court may be persuaded to review a decision. There may possibly be other grounds as well and these illustrations should not be understood as a closed list.[84]

57. Counsel for the respondents, in my view, rightly submitted that this Court should not substitute its decision for that of the President by issuing a mandamus because, *firstly*, the conduct of foreign relations and policy as well as matter[s] pertaining thereto cannot be properly evaluated or determined by this Court. *Secondly*, the functions and powers of decisions pertaining to the conduct of foreign relations are entrusted to the executive who has to determine foreign relations on policy considerations which at times may be sensitive. The executive has a broad discretion in such matters which must be respected by the courts. The courts surely cannot assume the role of a super-executive in matters which are peculiarly and exclusively within the domain of the executive. Chaskalson CJ, in *Kaunda*, stated:

---

[82] Id. at 503-4.   [83] Para. 78.   [84] Id. para. 80.

A decision as to whether protection should be given, and if so, what, is an aspect of foreign policy which is essentially the function of the Executive. The timing of representations if they are to be made, the language in which they should be couched, and the sanctions (if any) which should follow if such representations are rejected are matters with which courts are ill-equipped to deal. The best way to secure relief for the national in whose interest the action is taken may be to engage in delicate and sensitive negotiations in which diplomats are better placed to make decisions than Judges, and which could be harmed by court proceedings and the attendant publicity.[85]

And Ngcobo J said:

The conduct of foreign relations is a matter which is within the domain of the Executive. The exercise of diplomatic protection has an impact on foreign relations. Comity compels States to respect the sovereignty of one another; no [124] State wants to interfere in the domestic affairs of another. The exercise of diplomatic protection is therefore a sensitive area where both the timing and the manner in which the intervention is made are crucial. The State must be left to assess foreign policy considerations and it is a better judge of whether, when and how to intervene. It is therefore generally accepted that this is a province of the Executive, the State should generally be afforded a wide discretion in deciding whether and in what manner to grant protection in each case and the Judiciary must generally keep away from this area. That is not to say the Judiciary has no role in the matter.[86]

In the English case of *R* v. *Secretary of State for Foreign Affairs, ex parte Ferhut Butt*, Lightman J said.[87]

The general rule is well established that the courts should not interfere in the conduct of foreign relations by the Executive, most particularly, where such interference is likely to have foreign policy repercussions (see *R* v. *Secretary of State for Foreign and Commonwealth Affairs ex parte Everett* [1989] 1 QB 811 at 820). This extends to decisions whether or not to seek to persuade a foreign Government to take any action or remind a foreign Government of any international obligation (e.g. to respect human rights) which it has assumed.

58. The question to accede or not to accede to a request for diplomatic protection or intervention is pre-eminently within the province

---

[85] Id. para. 77. See: *Rudolph Hess* 90 ILR 386 at 395. According to Donald P. Kommers, *The Constitutional Jurisprudence of the Federal Republic of Germany*, 2nd edn, at 154: *Hess* underscores the broad discretion enjoyed by governmental organs in dealing with political matters:

The breadth of this discretion in foreign affairs has its basis in the nature of foreign relations", said the Second Senate ... In order to facilitate the realisation of the federation's political goal within the framework of what is constitutionally permissible ... the Constitution confers considerable discretion on foreign affairs agencies in assessing the practicality and feasibility of certain policies or actions. The First Senate reached a similar conclusion in *Schleyer Kidnapping* case (1977).

[86] Id. para. 172.   [87] [1999] EWHC Admin 624 (1 July 1999) 1, para. 12 at 6.

of the executive. Executive action in such matter[s] [. . .] is determined by material foreign policy considerations and is often of sensitive nature and invariably impact[s] on foreign relations. Thus, the courts should act with circumspection and a high degree of deference in matters of foreign relations conducted by the executive. Sir John Donaldson MR in *R* v. *Secretary of State for Foreign and Commonwealth Affairs, ex parte Pirbhai*[88] aptly cautioned:

It can rarely, if ever, be for judges to intervene where diplomats fear to tread.[89]

Basis of the respondents' decision

59. The applicants' requested diplomatic protection from the second respondent was based on an alleged right to effective diplomatic protection that was not attributable to an impression on the respondents' part that there existed no such thing as diplomatic protection in international law. A perusal of the various advices and submissions received by the respondents upon which they made their decisions shows this clearly. The applicants from the outset asserted that they were entitled to diplomatic protection as of right. In their letter of 15 December 2000 two bases were laid for this, *firstly*, that the first respondent (by way of the letter of the State Attorney of 15 May 1995):

. . . committed itself to mediation, thereby expressing its willingness to provide the diplomatic protection to the Swissborough group albeit for such mediation to be subject to certain conditions, which conditions have now been fulfilled.

Secondly, it was also contended in the letter that:

We have been advised that the State is under constitutional obligation to provide diplomatic protection to its citizens. He does, however, enjoy a **[125]** measure of discretion as to the methods it will employ to comply with that obligation. The discretionary element, under customary international law, of the decision is not whether to afford diplomatic protection, but rather what form of intervention is most appropriate and effective in the circumstances. The State is obliged to pursue the matter to a conclusion that will give effect to its citizens' rights.

60. This latter contention was repeated in further correspondence and memoranda, as well as at a meeting on 10 August 2001, to the second respondent's legal advisor Adv Gumbi, which was also attended by applicants' advisors on international law. The legal advice received by the

---

[88] 107 ILR 465 (1985).
[89] Id. 479, quoted in *Abbasi* v. *Secretary of State for Foreign Affairs*, op. cit., para. 37(1).

respondents was to the effect that international law does provide for the right on the part of a State to claim protection from another State under suitable circumstances and the claim, however, belongs to the State and not to its national on behalf of whom it may be acting. Such a national, therefore, does not have any right to diplomatic protection. Whether diplomatic protection should be afforded is a matter of discretion to be decided as a matter of policy.[90] The respondents were advised as to the considerations of policy, on the basis of which it was recommended not to exercise their discretion in favour of the applicants and to refuse to intervene. In this regard the first opinion was given by the Senior State Law Advisor, an expert on international law, of the Department of Foreign Affairs. In paragraph 3 he opined that:

The question relating to international law in this matter can be reduced to the following: is the South African Government under an obligation to provide diplomatic protection to the (applicants) ... all of them being South African citizens/nationals in their respective capacities of natural/juristic persons? If the [answer] is in the affirmative, the minister of the President will have to grant the relief sought by Mr Van Zyl and the two trusts ... If there is no such obligation under international law, the decision whether to accord diplomatic protection or not, will be a policy decision, on which we cannot comment.

The opinion in paragraph 4 stated:

It can be emphatically stated that a right to diplomatic protection does not exist in international law: "diplomatic protection of both an individual and a corporation lies within the sole discretion of the national state".[91]

According to Parry and Grant in *Encyclopedic Dictionary of International Law*:

It is an elementary principle of international law that a state is entitled to protect its subjects, when injured by acts contrary to international law committed by another state, from whom they have been unable to obtain satisfaction through the ordinary channels. By taking up the case of one of its subjects and by resorting to diplomatic protection or international judicial proceedings on its behalf, a state is in reality asserting its own rights—its rights to ensure, in the person of its subjects, respect for the rules of international law.[92]

---

[90] Phoebe Okowa, op. cit., at 477:

Since the exercise of diplomatic protection is generally viewed as a right of the State, the argument has consistently been made that reliance on that right is within the absolute discretion of States (Borchard, 1915, p. 29; Greig, 1976, p. 523; Oppenheim, 1992, p. 934). It is further accepted that the decision whether to exercise the discretion or not is invariably influenced by political considerations rather than legal merits of the particular claim.

And see also: *Barcelona Traction*, op. cit., paras. 78-9.

[91] It was with a reference to Dugard, *International Law*: at 213.   [92] At 93.

[126] 61. The advice was conveyed to the third respondent, the Minister of Foreign Affairs, on 22 March 2000. The legal advice and the fact that according to the opinion that there was no obligation on the part of the first respondent to afford diplomatic protection and any decision to intervene was a policy decision. In paragraph 2.5 it recommended that the policy decision should be based upon the following:

The Swissborough Group/Burmilla Trust has, by its own admission, "exhausted its local remedies". What they fail to mention is that these constituted court proceedings in Lesotho, which they lost. Therefore, mediation or intervention by the South African Government would imply a lack of faith in the judicial system of a sovereign state. This would be potentially damaging to the already sensitive nature of the relations between the two countries. Moreover, this would set an unhealthy precedent for other businesses to request diplomatic intervention from the South African Government.

The recommendation regarding the applicable policy considerations was repeated later in the submissions to the second respondent.

62. On the basis of the advice received the fourth respondent, the Deputy Minister of Foreign Affairs, in a letter stated that

... regrettably the South African Government is unable to accede to your request ...

This inability cannot be attributable to the view that it was legally impossible to accede to the applicants' request but the position taken was as a result of a policy decision. That decision was made within the ambit of exercising the relevant discretion.

63. Subsequently, the applicants approached the second respondent. Consequently, another advice was obtained from the Chief State Law Advisor in the Department of Justice. This opinion opens by stating the applicants' view that:

... both in international law and in terms of the South African Constitution, a right to diplomatic protection exists, and that the South African Government is under a legal obligation, both in terms of international and South African constitutional law, to accord diplomatic protection to them.

The applicants' assertion once again raised the question, whether a right to diplomatic protection exists in the sense contended by them in their earlier submissions to the respondents that they enjoy a claimable right to diplomatic protection. From this opinion it was clear that international law does provide for diplomatic protection as a right claimable by a State on behalf of its nationals *vis-à-vis* another State but not one claimable by its nationals themselves.[93]

[127] The Chief State Law Advisor's opinion to the respondents concluded by stating that:

It should be noted that there is a clear distinction between the right of diplomatic protection acknowledged by international law, and the right to diplomatic protection *as claimed by the applicants in this matter*. The international law acknowledges the right of diplomatic protection. As illustrated above that right lies with a state, and entails that when a national of a state suffers an injury at the hands of another state, the state of nationality may take up the claim. When taking up the claim, the claim becomes that of the state itself ... The decision to exercise the right of diplomatic protection lies within the discretion of the national state. The international law therefore recognises the right of diplomatic protection that lies with a state *and does not recognise a right to diplomatic protection as claimed in the present matter*.[94]

The opinion also stated:

We are ... of the opinion that the constitutional right to diplomatic protection as claimed by the applicants does not exist.[95]

Finally, in paragraph 15 of the opinion it was stated:

We therefore conclude that although a right of diplomatic protection that lies with a state exists in the international law, a "right to diplomatic protection" as averred by the applicants is not presently acknowledged in the international law. In the South African municipal positive law the alleged right has also not been acknowledged, and we have serious reservations whether such right will be acknowledged by a competent court. However, in view of the fact that this question is still "open" in our positive law, it cannot be excluded that a competent court may, in proper and particular circumstances and in terms of the Constitution, find that a "right to diplomatic protection" exists. Whatever the contents and scope of such a right may be, if acknowledged, is at this stage open to speculation.

---

[93] Dugard, *International Law: A South African Perspective*, 2nd edn, at 213-14:

Diplomatic protection of an individual and a corporation lies within the sole discretion of the national state. In deciding whether to exercise this discretion the national state obviously will be guided by political considerations, chief of which will be its relationship with the defendant state. Should a state refuse to intervene on behalf of its national, the latter has no remedy under international law. Municipal law may lay an obligation on the state to protect its nationals abroad and may confer upon a national to demand the performance of that obligation, but this is entirely a question of municipal law. Although there is no South African authority on this subject, Prof. Booysen has suggested that there is no obligation on the executive to protect a national in such case.

[94] Italics is not that of the writer but my emphasis.
[95] *Kaunda* v. *President of RSA (supra)* para. 35:

The Bill of Rights is extensive and covers conventional and less conventional rights in detail. A right to diplomatic protection is a most unusual right, which one expects to be spelt out expressly rather than be left to implication.

During argument Mr Grobler meticulously dealt with the various opinions upon which the respondents relied and submitted that the theme of "a right to protection" within the context of the claim asserted by the applicants, that is that they are entitled to diplomatic protection as of right exist (in the sense of a benefit claimable as of right) is indeed untenable.

64. The applicants, however, transmitted a further submission to the third and fourth respondents. The latter prepared a submission to the second respondent in which reference was made to the applicants' request and the fact that:

It is claimed that they are entitled to such diplomatic protection in terms of international law, as well as in terms of the Constitution of the Republic of South Africa...

This precipitated in a letter from the second respondent's legal advisor to applicants, dated 20 July 2001, in which she stated:

... the South African Government is unable to grant your request for "diplomatic protection"...

[128] 65. On an evaluation of the evidence it is clear that the respondents refused to afford diplomatic protection to the applicants as of right. It was an informed and carefully considered product of a policy decision and not simply based on a perception that diplomatic protection does not exist at all in international law. The decision was reached after receiving opinions from both the legal advisors of the Department of Foreign Affairs and Department of Justice.

66. This was then followed by the meeting of 10 August 2001 with Adv Gumbi, raising, *inter alia*, questions as to the effectiveness of any possible intervention on the part of the first respondent. Thus, further correspondence and submissions flowed from the applicants including a supplementary memorandum as well as more correspondence that culminated in the applicants' changed stance by asking the respondents to withhold the payment of all further royalties to the Kingdom of Lesotho:

... pending the Government of Lesotho's decision in respect of our settlement offer which expires on 30 November 2001. Should the settlement offer be accepted the payment of the settlement amount of R89,065,828.00 to be made from such royalties being withheld.

To this was added a threat that:

The refusal and/or failure by the RSA Government to withhold the payment of such royalties to the Government of Lesotho will leave us with no alternative but to launch an urgent application in the high court of Pretoria to freeze all royalties the Government of Lesotho is entitled to received (*sic*) from the RSA Government.

67. The applicants saw no limits to their *assumed* claimable right. They even sought to compromise the first respondent by asking him to act in breach of the Republic's international duties in terms of the treaty on the Lesotho Highlands Water Project with the GoL. Adv Gumbi properly and correctly advised the second respondent that the form of intervention which applicants sought to withhold the payment of royalties to the GoL was not permissible. Accordingly the second respondent again decided not to accede to the applicants' request and informed them in the letter of 6 November 2001 that

... such protection does not exist as a matter of law ...

68. The applicants made reference to diplomatic protection as of right but quite clearly the second respondent's refusal was not based upon the view that international law does not provide for diplomatic protection at all but upon the view that it does not provide for a right to diplomatic protection as sought for by the applicants. Nor does the Constitution provide for such a claimable right. International law acknowledges that States have the right to protect their nationals beyond their borders but are under no obligation to do so.[96]

69. The applicants also contend that the ground upon which the second respondent's decision is based was on a wrong understanding of the law insofar as diplomatic protection exists in international law. It is clear that the President fully appreciated his discretion in international law in terms of which he could take policy considerations into account which he did **[129]** by having proper and due regard to the nature of the relations between the Republic of South Africa and the Kingdom of Lesotho. This the President did in his decision of 6 July 2001 when he refused to act and later on reconsideration on 6 November 2001 he decided to despatch the *Note Verbale*. Thus, it is clear that the President acted fully within his powers, and Mr Grobler rightly submitted that the President did not misunderstand the power or discretion according to international law. What the President quite correctly understood was that the applicants did not have an *enforceable right to effective diplomatic protection as of right* asserted and sought for by the applicants. What is clear is that a request for diplomatic protection was received from the applicants, it was considered on the basis of policy and it was decided

---

[96] *Barcelona Traction*, op. cit., fn 32 above.

on that basis to despatch a *Note Verbale* to the GoL. This was certainly in compliance with what was decided in *Kaunda*.[97]

70. Like the President, the third respondent in her capacity as Minister of Foreign Affairs indeed had the power to take the decisions, which she did, and it was lawful for her to take into account policy considerations relevant to the relationship between the Kingdom of Lesotho and the Republic of South Africa. The submissions advanced on behalf of the applicants by Mr Katz that the decision of the third respondent was objectively irrational and not rationally related to the purpose for which the power was granted is wrong. The third respondent appreciated the international legal position. Further, the applicants' assertion that the respondents did not apply their minds to the request is also based on the supposition that the respondents wrongly understood the law. They, the respondents, were correctly advised and they certainly appreciated their powers and the extent of their discretion. They did not exercise their power on the basis of wrong understanding of the law. The exercise of their powers was certainly not arbitrary as alleged by the applicants. The applicants, furthermore, have not shown any limitation or infringement of their fundamental rights. Thus, having regard to the applicable policy considerations which were of such a nature that the respondents rationally determined that they could not accede to the applicants' request for diplomatic protection as of right. Therefore, none of the grounds upon which the applicants seek to have the decisions of the respondents set aside as prayed for in prayers 1, 2 and 3 and in seeking a declarator in terms of prayer 4 can be sustained.

Alleged international delict and violation of international minimum standards

71. It is common cause that for an international delictual claim entitling the Republic of South Africa to exercise diplomatic protection *vis-à-vis* the Kingdom of Lesotho two fundamental pre-requisites must objectively exist: The foreign person or company wronged by the Kingdom of Lesotho must have nationality of the Republic of South Africa and as a result of the wrong concomitantly the treatment by the Kingdom of Lesotho of the South African national regarding the alleged expropriations is in violation of international minimum standards and that national must have exhausted all legal remedies available in terms of the municipal law of Lesotho. **[130]** It is only then the Republic will be entitled to elevate the dispute to the international level on the

---

[97] At paras. 67, 69, 70, 80.

basis that the international law rights of the Republic with respect to the treatment of its national have been infringed upon. In this regard the respondents brought certain facts to the Court's attention in the answering affidavit. These facts are that out of the five mining leases four were cancelled by the fourth to ninth applicants claiming damages from the GoL and instituted an action which is still pending. The Rampai mining lease and the tributing agreement were expropriated in terms of legislation conforming to the international minimum standards for expropriation and any damages claimed [were] preserved by such legislation.

72. Justifiably the respondents' complaint is that the mining leases concluded between Swissborough and the GoL were not annexed to the applicants' founding papers. By its failure to do so the applicants seek to create the impression that the leases are international investment agreements or international concessions and that the principles of international law are applicable to the leases on that basis. What is crucial is to analyse the mining leases in order to determine the true nature thereof and also to determine whether the leases entered into between a company incorporated in the Kingdom of Lesotho and the GoL were subject to the municipal law of that country or some other municipal regime or an international law. The first applicant, the deponent on behalf of all the applicants, alleges that the five mining leases are identical, except for the areas to which they are applicable and the rental payable. The Rampai lease reveals that the law of the Kingdom of Lesotho was accepted by the parties as the law governing the contract. The heading states that it was entered into in terms of sections 6 and 15 of the Mining Rights Act 43 of 1967. Further, the meaning of certain terms in the contract shall have the meaning assigned to them by section 1 of the Mining Rights Act 1967. Swissborough as lessee undertook to faithfully comply with all the provisions and regulations of the Mineral Rights Act and the Constitution of Lesotho (clause 6.2). It also undertook to comply with all the regulations in respect of explosives (clause 11) and to pay compensation for any damage to the surface area in terms of section 19(5) of the Mineral Rights Act upon the expiration or termination of the lease (clause 13.3). It was further stipulated that the mining lease would be registered in the Deeds Registry of Maseru in accordance with the provisions of the Deeds Registry Act 1967 and provided that the plan relating to the lease area was endorsed by the Mining Board and framed and approved in accordance with the regulations (clause 16). Both parties choose their *domicilum citandi et executandi* in Maseru, Lesotho. The contract was signed at Maseru and was to be executed in Lesotho under supervision of Lesotho authorities (clauses 7, 8, 10 and

12). Clause 4 stipulated that the rental was to be paid in the currency of Lesotho, in the amount 100 Maloti per square kilometre of the lease area or part thereof per annum.

73. On an analysis of the mining lease it is apparent that there appears to be no internationalisation because *firstly*, the contract was to be registered and performed in terms of the laws of the Kingdom of Lesotho. *Secondly*, although there is an arbitration clause (clause 14) ... there is no reference to international arbitration or application of international law to the arbitration. Therefore, there is no foreign or international element whatsoever in the [131] contract. *Thirdly*, a real right in land is conferred by the lease. In the main clause it stipulated that "... the STATE hereby grants the LESSEE which accepts the sole and exclusive right to prospect for and to mine and dispose of Precious Stones in the RAMPAI area ... " the mineral rights. What was granted is a real right in land. It was registered against the land when the mining lease was registered in the Maseru deeds office, in terms of the Deeds Registries Act.[98] The exercise of these mineral rights entitles Swissborough to go onto the land to prospect for and if precious stones are found to mine and dispose of them. Swissborough becomes owner of all diamonds thus found.[99] From this exposition it is clear that the mining leases granted to Swissborough created rights in property. The mining leases and the real rights created in terms thereof were subjected to the municipal law of Lesotho which would apply in respect of the questions, *firstly*, whether the mining leases were valid; *secondly*, pertaining to any disputes arising from these mining leases such as the cancellation thereof and rights arising from breach of contract; and *thirdly*, whether any real rights indeed came into existence; and if so the expropriation thereof. Furthermore, the tributing agreements were nothing but subleases and for their existence dependent upon the validity of the mining leases and existence of the real rights. In essence these subleases conferred the right to exercise the mineral rights created by the mining leases. These leases were also entered into between companies incorporated in Lesotho. The analysis of the mining leases equally applies to the tributing agreements, or subleases, and [they] contain no foreign element in them.

74. With that contracted backdrop the first consideration is, was there any violation of international standard by the GoL? I am mindful of the following dicta of Lord Nicholls in *Kuwait Airways Corporation* v. *Iraqi Airways Co. (Nos 4 and 5)*:[100]

---

[98] *Trojan Exploration Co. (Pty) Ltd* v. *Rustenburg Platinum Mines Ltd* 1996 (4) SA 499 (SCA) at 509G-J where the nature of these rights [is] discussed. Also reported at [1996] 4 All SA 121 (A).
[99] Id. at 528J-529C; 534F-535B.   [100] [2002] 2 WLR 1353.

An English court will not sit in judgment on the sovereign acts of a foreign government or state. It will not adjudicate upon the legality, validity or acceptability of such acts, either under domestic law or international law. For a court to do so would offend against the principle that the courts will not adjudicate upon the transactions of foreign sovereign states. This principle is not discretionary. It is inherent in the very nature of the judicial process: see *Buttes Gas and Oil Co.* v. *Hammer (No 3)* [1982] AC 888, 932.[101]

But,

This is not to say an English court is disabled from ever taking cognisance of international law or from ever considering whether a violation of international law has occurred. In appropriate circumstances it is legitimate for an English court to have regard to the content of international law in deciding whether to recognise a foreign law. Lord Wilberforce himself accepted this in the *Buttes* case, at p. 931D. Nor does the "non-justiciable" principle mean that the judiciary must shut their eyes to a breach of an established principle of international law committed by one state against another when the breach is **[132]** plain and, indeed, acknowledged. In such a case the adjudication problems confronting the English court in the *Buttes* litigation does not arise. The standard being applied by the court is clear and manageable, and the outcome not in doubt. That is the present case.[102]

75. In principle our courts adopt the same position as the English courts. However this Court is invited by the applicants to determine whether or not an international delict has been committed by the Kingdom of Lesotho for the Republic of South Africa to invoke diplomatic protection. The applicants make vague allegations about the so-called "expropriation" of the mining leases and tributing agreements. The concept "expropriation" is used in an extremely wide sense so as to include the purported cancellations in October 1991 by the Commissioner of Mines of the five mining leases, which were set aside on 20 March 1995 by the High Court of Lesotho and also in respect of the four leases which were already cancelled by Swissborough on 11 March 1993, but excluded the Rampai mining lease. The Revocation of Specified Mining Leases Order revoked all the mining leases on 20 March 1992 and it was set aside by the Lesotho High Court on 27 September 1994 and the Lesotho Court of Appeal on 13 January 1995. The formal expropriation of the Rampai mining lease and the Rampai tributing agreement occurred on 17 August 1995 that was after the Lesotho Highlands Development Authority (Amendment) Act 5 of 1995 and had taken effect respectively on 16 August 1995 and 17 August 1995. In the order of the Lesotho High Court whereby the Rampai mining lease was

---

[101] Id. para. 24 at 1362. [102] Id. para. 26 at 1362.

declared to be void *ab initio* on 28 April 1999 and confirmed by the Appeal Court of Lesotho on 16 October 2000 remain unexplained.

76. It was argued on behalf of the respondents that there can be no possible expropriation without the relevant right or agreement having been expropriated at least in the sense of being terminated. It is common cause that the fourth applicant cancelled the four mining leases, excluding the Rampai mining lease after having accepted the purported cancellation by the Commissioner of Mines as a result of a material breach of contract. It is also common cause that the Rampai mining lease was declared void *ab initio* and that a formal expropriation of the Rampai mining lease had taken place. However, the dispute turns on the question whether the cancellation of the mining leases by the fourth applicant, the declaration of invalidity of the Rampai mining lease and its formal expropriation, all without the relevant applicants having received damages or compensation, amount to a violation of minimum international standards of treatment of the applicants by the GoL. The gist of the applicants' arguments was that the cancellation of the four mining leases "was nothing more than *a forced ex contractu* cancellation in response to the international wrong perpetrated by the GoL". These four leases were mining leases concluded in terms of the Lesotho Minerals Act 43 of 1967. They were made subject to the law of Lesotho. Under the Law of Contract of Lesotho, Swissborough had an election whether to accept the purported cancellations by the Commissioner of Mines of the mining leases as a material breach of contract in the form of repudiation and to cancel the [**133**] leases on the basis of such breach, or to retain these leases and to enforce the provisions thereof. In respect of the four leases Swissborough elected to cancel them and claim damages, whereas, in the case of the Rampai lease, it elected not to cancel and to enforce the terms thereof. Mr Grobler submitted that the argument advanced by Mr Dugard on behalf of the applicants that there was an international wrong perpetrated by the GoL in the purported cancellation of the leases is without legal substance because before such a wrong could be established, the internal remedies in terms of the municipal law of Lesotho had to be exhausted and that no damages would be paid by the GoL. To elevate a breach of contract to an international wrong in respect of a contract with no international element is certainly bad in law.

77. The third applicant issued summons for breach of contract on 2 June 1995. The applicants alleged that their "cancellation was nothing more than a *forced ex contractu* cancellation in response to the international wrong perpetrated by the GoL". This argument is also bad in law. It is also factually incorrect. The applicants' argument supposes

that an individual can in law avail itself on the national law level of any international law violation by the State. The argument also presupposes that international law relating to the responsibility of States is part of national private law and particularly of national law of contract. Such an argument obviously takes the theory that "international law is part of national law" to absurd extremes.

78. Thus, there is no authority that it was the intention with section 232 of our Constitution that all the rules of state liability must automatically form part of municipal private law.[103] If this were true, then it would mean that the entire private law and the law of contracts would be transformed drastically and concomitantly uncertainty would prevail. Such an intention cannot be attributed to the Constitution. The international rules of state liability are rules applying between States. If individuals and private legal entities are to apply these rules in respect of States, the nature of the rules is changed because the subjects are changed. This means that the rules are now applied by analogy. There is no reason why such an infusion of private law should be assumed. Section 232 provides that customary international law is part of the law of the Republic unless it is inconsistent with the Constitution or an Act of Parliament. There is, however, no indication that the leases of the applicants were ever subject to South African law. South African law cannot, therefore, be applied to the leases and to their cancellation. This also means that customary international law cannot through South African law become applicable to the leases and their cancellation. Section 232 is simply not applicable to these leases and their cancellation, neither can it be applicable to the Lesotho law of contract which regulated the cancellation of the mining leases.

79. In the applicants' heads of argument reference is made to the nature of their leases with the Lesotho Government. They are described as "concession agreements" or "long-term international economic agreements". **[134]** It is a general principle of international law that parties to an international transaction can select the law governing their transaction.[104] This rule is generally and widely adhered to and may also be regarded as a customary international law rule. It is also a rule recognised by South African law.[105] An international transaction is subject to the law chosen by the parties. If they have not expressly chosen a law, then there may be a tacit choice of law. According to our law, if there is a reference to an Act of Parliament of a particular country, this is taken as evidence

---

[103] Booysen, "The Administrative Law Implications of the 'Customary International Law is Part of South African Law' Doctrine" (1997) 22 SAYIL 46 at 51.
[104] Booysen, *International Trade Law*, 201.
[105] See Forsyth, *Private International Law*, 3rd edn (1996) 278ff and especially at 280.

of a tacit choice of that country's law.[106] If there is no tacit choice of law, the law of the place where the contract was concluded is applicable.[107] Whatever test is applied, it is clear that all leases were concluded subject to the law of Lesotho. The applicants could have chosen international law to govern their agreements with the GoL, but they chose not to do so. According to the principle of *pacta sunt servanda*, which is also a principle of international law, they are bound by the choice according to international law.[108] The parties to the leases, namely Swissborough Diamond Mines (Pty) Ltd and the Lesotho Government, have not internationalised their concession agreement. Although the leases can be regarded as long-term investment agreements, they do not contain any of the recognised features of an internationalised contract such as a stabilisation clause, international arbitration clause or the selection of international law as proper law.[109]

80. Further, the four cancelled leases are different contracts with an independent legal existence. They cannot merely be grouped together or be made dependent on what happened to another lease such as the Rampai lease. Their cancellation must have been followed with proper legal action in order to fulfil the requirements of the exhaustion of local remedies before any international wrong could have been committed by the GoL. In this regard the applicants' submissions are incorrect since the cancellation of the four leases brought them to an end without any violation of the minimum international standards. What is apparent is that there were no expropriations as the applicants seemed to contend.

81. The Rampai lease was void *ab initio*. However, the right that was granted to Swissborough was a *ius in rem*. It was the right to prospect for and to mine precious stones and dispose of them. Thus, it is the *lex situs* that is the municipal law of Lesotho which regulates whether this real right came into existence. The mining lease creates an obligation to deliver this real right by means of registration according to the Lesotho Deeds Registries Act. It is the law of Lesotho which determines whether this mining lease itself came into existence. According to international law these questions of initial acquisition have to be determined in accordance with the law of Lesotho. There is no international element in the contract in terms of which the real right was delivered and registered. Since the [135] initial contract was not internationalised and no foreign proper law was determined, therefore, the question whether international law or some other municipal system is the proper law of

---

[106] See *Strettoh* v. *Union Steamship Company Ltd* (1881) 1 EDC 315; Forsyth, op. cit., at 284.
[107] See *Standard Bank of South Africa Ltd* v. *Efroiken and Newman* 1924 AD 171 at 185; Forsyth, op. cit., at 287.
[108] *Amco* v. *Indonesia* 89 ILR 366 at 495.   [109] Booysen, op. cit., at 488.

the contract regulating the original conclusion of the mining lease or the grant of the real right certainly does not arise.

82. Arbitration tribunals appointed by consent of States to adjudicate their disputes act as international adjudicators. They are not subject to the legal constraints placed by public international law on States and their courts to adjudicate the sovereign acts of a foreign State. This would be the case with ICSID arbitration. In terms of the Convention on the Settlement of Investment Disputes Between States and Nationals of Other States, the jurisdiction of the Centre is based on double consent: consent of the State to the treaty and consent to submit the particular dispute to ICSID.[110] Principles of customary international law applied by such tribunals are, therefore, not necessarily apt to be applied by national courts. This is particularly true as far as the adjudication of the acts of a friendly foreign government is concerned.[111] The International Court of Justice in the *Barcelona Traction* case[112] echoed the principle that the awards of arbitration tribunals do not necessarily contain customary international law principles:

The Parties have also relied on the general arbitral jurisprudence which has accumulated in the last half-century. However, in most cases the decisions cited rested upon the terms of instruments establishing the jurisdiction of the tribunal or claims commission and determining what rights might enjoy protection; they cannot therefore give rise to generalisation going beyond the special circumstances of each case.[113]

83. Since there is no indication that the parties to the leases intended to subject their concession agreements to the principles of international law, thus international law requires that the concession agreement must be judged according to the law of Lesotho. Therefore, according to international law it is the law of Lesotho which must apply in determining the validity of the Rampai concession agreement. Hence, the applicants' argument based on *Amco* v. *Indonesia*[114] does not really enhance their case but actually supports respondents' view that Lesotho law should govern the validity of the Rampai lease. What the arbitration tribunal found in that case was that the authorisation given by the Indonesian Government to the investor was binding and that, according to Indonesia law, such binding authorisation could not be withdrawn. The authorisation was binding according to the principle of *pacta sunt servanda* and it

---

[110] Article 25 of the ICSID Convention. See also: Booysen, *International Trade Law*, 818 et seq.
[111] *Elettronica Sicula* case 1989 ICJ Reports 15 at 46 and 74 where the dichotomy between international tribunals and national courts and the difference in law they apply are considered.
[112] Fn 32 above, para. 63 at 40.   [113] Id. para. 63.   [114] 89 ILR 366.

could not be withdrawn by the Indonesian State except by law.[115] Thus, the ICSID arbitration tribunal noted:

These acquired rights could not be withdrawn by the Republic, except by observing the requisites of procedural conditions established by law and for [136] reasons admitted by the latter. In fact, the Republic did withdraw such rights, not observing the legal requisites of procedure, and for reasons which, according to law, did not justify the said withdrawal.

It is, therefore, a recognition that Indonesian law and its procedures govern the investment. Clear rights were acquired and these rights needed protection. It is tantamount to saying that a validly issued license cannot simply be withdrawn by the state because, by accepting the licence, the licensee has received vested rights. Such a proposition is not denied by the respondents. In the present case, however, to use the analogy again, no valid licence has ever been issued with the result that no rights could have been acquired.[116]

84. In the High Court of Lesotho in *Swissborough Diamond Mines and Others* v. *The Commissioner of Mines and Geology NO and Others*[117] Mr van Zyl characterised the counter-application by the LHDA for a declaratory order that the Rampai lease was *void ab initio* as a "procedural attack". It is of the essence that the Lesotho property law regarding all land and real rights in that country vest in the nation. All rights to the use of land or to the exploitation of mineral resources are granted by way of either a lease or a mining lease. The consent of the chiefs, under whose jurisdiction the land in question falls as being local custodians of the nation, is therefore of the essence of the Lesotho property law. Kheola CJ in the judgment in the counter application, stated:

It seems to me that the executive functions referred to in Order 1 of 1970 [were] only in regard to the upper echelons of government in the execution of particular acts. Such acts do not include allocation of land or grants of rights in land which is a function of the King and Chiefs under customary law. That these rights are derived from the customary law and not from their executive functions is confirmed by section 93(1)(ii) [*sic*] of the 1966 Constitution which reads as follows:

> (1) The power to allocate land that is vested in the Basotho Nation, to make grants of interests or rights in or over such land, to revoke or derogate from any allocation or grant that has been made or otherwise to terminate or restrict any interest or right that has been granted is vested in the King in trust for the Basotho Nation.
>
> (2) The power that is vested in the King by subsection (1) of this section shall be exercised by him and, on his behalf, by the Chiefs in

---

[115] Id. para. 247 at 497.   [116] Id. at 497.
[117] Case No: CIV/APN/394/91 (date of judgment 29 April 1999).

accordance with the provisions of this Constitution and any other law and the King and the Chiefs shall, in relation to the exercise of that power, be subject to such duties and have such further powers as may be imposed or conferred on them by this Constitution or any other law.

"Law" is defined in section 139 of the 1966 Constitution as including the "customary law of Lesotho and any other unwritten rule of law". "Any other law" in subsection (2) refers to customary law.

It is in view of this essential imperative of the Lesotho property law that section 6 of the Mining Rights Act provides that a mineral title may be granted in the manner prescribed in this Act, but not otherwise.

Kheola CJ then comes to the conclusion:

that the provisions of section 6 of MRA are mandatory and the "grant of the lease" which does not conform to the requirements of that subsection is no grant at all. It is in fact a nullity, and no duty to act can flow from such **[137]** nullity. See *Ondombo Beleggings Edms Bpk.* v. *Minister of Mineral and Energy Affairs* 1991 (4) SA 718 (A) at 725.[118]

85. The essential character of the Lesotho property law is also the basis of the judgment of the Court of Appeal in *Swissborough Diamond Mines (Pty) Ltd and Another* v. *LHDA*. Beck AJA said:

... the dictates of both common sense and of deeply rooted tradition enshrined in customary law concerning grants related to land point to prior consultation with, and agreement of, the relevant Chiefs being an absolute necessity.[119]

86. The Rampai lease did not come into existence because it was contrary to the very essence of the Lesotho property law which is the *lex situs* governing the acquisition of the real rights by Swissborough to prospect for and to mine precious stones and dispose thereof. Since the relevant real rights [have] not come into existence, in terms of the essence of the Lesotho property law, therefore no question of the expropriation can arise. As far as the so-called extension leases are concerned, the applicants' argument again breaks down at the acquisition stage, and they are in an even worse position. The evidence proffered by the applicants in the founding affidavit is in essence that they made a "reasonable" offer to settle the conflict arising from the fact that the Rampai lease was registered right across the area where the Katse Dam was to be constructed and the land was to be submerged by water. Kheola CJ held that no witness could answer how it came about that a 15-year mining lease was "granted" right in the dam basin which was

---

[118] Date of judgment 6 October 2000, at 432-57.   [119] Annexure AP15 at 1235.

planned to be filled with water within five years after the "grant" of the Rampai mining lease.[120]

87. Further, from the judgment of Joffe J in the *Swissborough*[121] case it is also clear that the LHDA had commenced its construction by July 1988 whereas the Rampai mining lease was signed a month later and registered in October 1989. The applicants waited until 1991 when the construction activities had progressed to an advanced stage before they brought their initial interdict application. It was this conflict which Mr van Zyl then sought to settle with the proposal that extension leases be granted in other areas in exchange for relinquishing the Rampai lease. The history of these so-called "extension leases" shows that negotiations to settle this conflict never went beyond the draft agreement or where some of the relevant authorities had indicated their willingness to conclude such an agreement. Mr van Zyl did not accept these terms and negotiations broke down. No extension leases were ever concluded and no meeting of minds took any final form.

88. According to the Mineral Rights Act of 1967, a mining lease can only take effect once it is signed and registered in the deeds office. Thus, the applicants' arguments that although there never came into existence any extension mining leases by final agreement or by Lesotho law, but that international law would recognise such "investment contract", are incomprehensible. Further, the evidence pertaining to the "extension leases" **[138]** which the applicants seek to adduce in their replying affidavit by means of documentary evidence should have been in the founding affidavit. The respondents are only required to answer the case in the founding affidavit. The disputes in this application are determined on the basis of the facts stated in the founding affidavit and answered to by the respondents. The applicants cannot make out a new case or attempt to adduce *facta probantia* in their replying affidavit which should have been alleged in the founding affidavit. This aspect is considered in determining the respondents' application to strike out below.

89. The applicants' further assertion that the GoL are liable for damages suffered to be determined by international law arbitration dispute resolution procedures is without substance. The applicants are not subjects of the international law. They are neither competent to hold the sovereign Kingdom of Lesotho liable in any international proceedings, nor can they seek to apply international law principles in their domestic dispute with the GoL. Their reliance on the Treaty on the LHWP and the protocols to that agreement is legally untenable.

---

[120] Annexure AP14.   [121] 1999 (2) SA 279 (T).

The applicants derive no rights from that Treaty since they are not international law subjects.[122]

90. The applicants contended that the expropriation of the Rampai mining lease and the tributing agreement was in terms of legislation not conforming to the international minimum standards for expropriation and any damages claim was preserved by such legislation. The facts pertaining to the expropriation on 17 August 1995 of the Rampai mining lease and the attendant tributary agreement in terms of Lesotho Highlands Development Authority (Amendment) Act 5 of 1995 as read with Lesotho Highlands Development Authority (Validation of the Activities in respect of Phase 1A and Phase 1B Scheme) Act 6 of 1995 are set out in the answering affidavit deposed to by the fourth respondent Mr Aziz Pahad. It is not necessary for me to consider this aspect in any great detail. The applicants argued that the expropriation was unnecessary because by encroaching upon the Rampai mining lease area, an expropriation had taken place in terms of the Lesotho Highlands Development Authority Order 23 of 1986 and compensation had to be paid in terms of the compensation regulations. It was submitted on behalf of the respondents that apart from being legally incorrect the applicants' argument is self-defeating as no unlawful encroachment on the Rampai lease area would then have resulted from the activities of the LHDA in construction of the dam. However, that order empowered the LHDA to acquire property and interests in land in accordance with the Land Act 1979. This statute did, however, not deal with mining leases or mineral rights since these were dealt with by the Mining Rights Act 1967. Consequently the Land Act did not empower the acquisition of the Rampai mining lease, hence, in April 1990 the Government of the Kingdom of Lesotho promulgated the Lesotho Highland Water Project Compensation Regulations, 1990. Joffe J in *Swissborough* described these regulations as follows:

The nature of the compensation claims envisaged by these regulations are those of a rural peasant community obliged to vacate their land.[123]

[139] 91. After the Revocation of Specific Mining Leases Order 7 of 1992 was set aside by the Lesotho High Court and confirmed on appeal by the Lesotho Court of Appeal and after the cancellation by the Mining Commissioner of the five mining leases was set aside, it was clear that the LHDA had to expropriate the Rampai mining lease and

---

[122] Id. at 327C-330C. See also: *Pan American World Airways Inc.* v. *SA Fire and Accident Insurance Co. Ltd* 1965 (3) SA 150 (A) at 161B-D.
[123] 1999 (2) SA 279 (T) at 291C.

the concomitant tributing agreement. This was done by means of Acts 5 and 6 of 1995 which authorised the LHDA to expropriate a mining lease. The compensation provisions in Act 5 of 1995 are clearly for proper compensation, namely for *full and prompt compensation*.[124] The formula by which this compensation was to be assessed is contained in the new section 46A(8). The formula for full compensation was that it shall not exceed the aggregate of an amount which a willing buyer would have paid to a willing seller in the open market immediately prior to the expropriation date, that is the market value thereof, and an amount to make good any actual financial loss caused directly by any activity of the authority. This formula of compensation is accepted in most open and democratic societies as the formula which should be applied in assessing equitable compensation and the rules in assessing such compensation in order to strike a balance between the interests of the community on the one hand and the expropriatee on the other, are usually also contained in expropriation legislation.[125] The rules for compensation found in section 46A(10) bear a resemblance to the internationally accepted rules for assessing compensation and contain the equitable *Pointe Guarde* principle[126] in section 46A(10)(g). In a nutshell "compensation for compulsory acquisition of land cannot include an increase in value which is due to the scheme underlying the expropriation". There is no doubt that Act 5 of 1995 conforms to the international minimum standards as far as the determination of compensation is concerned. The applicants conceded to this submission.

92. Mr van Zyl however detected a conspiracy in Act 5 of 1995. That conspiracy, according to him, lies in the definition of *holder* in relation to a mineral right, which is defined as "a person in whose favour a duly granted and executed mineral right is registered in terms of the Deeds Registries Act 1967", i.e. that by virtue of section 38A(3) and (8) only such a person will be entitled to compensation. Mr Grobler for the respondents argued that should Swissborough's mining lease thus prove to be void *ab initio* then no compensation will be claimable. Swissborough and the tributing companies waited until 22 July 1996 before instituting their claims for compensation, the former in the amount of R49,647,630 and the seventh applicant R475,198,918. These claims were never pursued and the LHDA, being the compensating authority

---

[124] S 38A(3) as inserted by s 4 of Act 5 of 1995. See: annexure AP8 at 1107.
[125] Cf the South African Expropriation Act 63 of 1975, s 12(1) as read with s 12(5) thereof. See also Gildenhuys, *Onteieningsreg*, 2nd edn, at 154-61 with respect to claims for compensation in western democracies and the origin of the rules of compensation from English law at 34.
[126] *Pointe Guarde Quarrying and Transport Co. v. Sub-Intendent of Crown Lands* [1947] AC 565 (Tri & To) at 572; see Gildenhuys, op. cit., para. 9, at 256.

in terms of Act 5 of 1996, had a clear interest in bringing the counter-application. LHDA had in consequence of the declaration of invalidity not paid compensation to Swissborough and Rampai Diamonds. However, any claim for **[140]** damages which Swissborough and Rampai Diamonds may have had against the GoL in respect of the invalidity of the Rampai mining lease was preserved by section 2 of Act 6 of 1995. This provides that the validation is subject to any accrued or vested right to damages. Indeed, a claim in this regard had been anticipated in the summons issued on 20 May 1996 for damages pertaining to the cancellation by Swissborough of the other four leases. This action has been pleaded to and is ripe for hearing. Thus, it is clear that no minimum international standards have been violated by the GoL regarding the expropriation of the Rampai lease.

93. Assuming that an international wrong has been committed by the GoL, then the litigant must satisfy two prerequisites, namely requirement of nationality and exhaustion of local remedies, to prosecute a claim before an international tribunal.

Requirement of nationality

94. The first is the requirement of nationality. Professor Singh noted that:

According to the practice of States, arbitral and judicial decisions and opinions of writers, nationality is a legal bond having as its basis a social fact of attachment, a genuine connection of existence, interests and sentiments, together with the existence of reciprocal rights and duties.[127]

Chaskalson CJ in *Kaunda (supra)*[128] said:

South African citizenship requirements are such that citizens invariably, if not always, will be nationals of South Africa. They are entitled, as such, to request the protection of South Africa in a foreign country in case of need. Nationality is an incident of their citizenship which entitles them to the privilege or benefit of making such a request. Should there ever be an exceptional case where the citizen's connection with South Africa is too remote to justify a claim of nationality, it would be a legitimate response to such a request to say that South Africa is not entitled to demand diplomatic protection for that person. But apart from that, the citizen is entitled to have the request considered and responded to appropriately.[129]

---

[127] Singh, op. cit., at 128-9.
[128] 2004 (10) BCLR 1009 (CC); 2005 (4) SA 235 (CC).   [129] Id. paras. 62-3.

95. The holders of the mineral leases and of the mineral rights conferred by those leases by registration in the deeds office in Maseru are nationals of the Kingdom of Lesotho, namely the fourth applicant who was the contracting party and the recipient of the real rights in respect of all five leases and the fifth to ninth applicants who concluded subleases namely tributing agreements respectively in respect of each of the mining leases held by the fourth applicant. In *Barcelona Traction*,[130] the International Court of Justice concluded that the nationality of a company had to be determined by reference to the laws of the State in which it is incorporated. The majority were of the view that the fact of incorporation under the law of a State was conclusive. Moreover, it was not necessary to lift the corporate veil in order to determine the economic reality of a company, and whether this indicated links with a State other than that of incorporation. Thus, the Court [rejected] Belgium's claim to exercise **[141]** diplomatic protection in respect of a wrong done to a Canadian company in circumstances where the majority shareholders were Belgian. The Court held that the reality was that the company as an institution of municipal law was an entity distinct from its shareholders. It stated:

Thus whenever shareholders' interests are harmed by an act done to the company, it is to the latter he must look to institute appropriate action; for although the separate entities may have suffered from the same wrong, it is only one entity whose rights have been infringed.[131]

The Republic of South Africa can on no basis have a right of diplomatic protection against the Kingdom of Lesotho in respect of acts performed within its own territory against companies incorporated in Lesotho.

96. Inasmuch as the second applicant may have taken cession of the rights of these Lesotho companies the second applicant does not thereby secure advantage of diplomatic protection of its State of nationality. According to Professor Brownlie:

... from the time of the occurrence of the injury until the making of the award the claim must continuously and without interruption have belonged to a person or to a series of persons (a) having the nationality of the State by whom it is put forward, and (b) not having the nationality of the State against whom it is put forward.[132]

The cession of the claim and concomitant actions arising from the alleged actions by the GoL and the LHDA, therefore, disqualifies the

---

[130] Fn 32. [131] Id. para. 44 at 3.
[132] Ian Brownlie, *Principles of Public International Law*, 4th edn at 481.

fourth to ninth applicants as well as the second applicant from claiming diplomatic protection. Further, none of the registered mining leases and tributing agreements were ceded to the second applicant. Except for the Rampai lease, in the other instances as Mr Dugard rightly acknowledged, the cessions were after the alleged violation. This then is fatal to the Republic's right to diplomatic protection.

97. The second basis upon which the requirement of nationality is not complied [with] is that the first and third applicants, who are nationals of the Republic of South Africa, are not entitled to diplomatic protection from the Republic of South Africa merely by virtue of their shareholding in the companies which are incorporated in Lesotho. None of their shares were expropriated. Nor is it alleged that the control of the companies [was] interfered with. Their only interest in the fourth to ninth applicants is their shareholding. They do not hold any mining leases, tributing agreements or mineral rights. No basis was alleged or proved for the corporate veil of the third to ninth applicants to be pierced in this regard. Inasmuch as an expropriation purportedly amounting to an alleged delict by the GoL [has] been proved, however, such delict has not been committed against the first and third applicants. They are accordingly not entitled to diplomatic protection.

98. Mr Grobler further submitted that it will be against the principle of the sovereign equality of States as enshrined in Article 2(1) of the Charter of the United Nations[133] for a South African court to force the South African government to follow an international practice *vis-à-vis* another State, such **[142]** as the Kingdom of Lesotho, to which neither State has explicitly consented or which is not a recognized practice between the two States. There is no proof tendered by the applicants that the Kingdom of Lesotho has recognised the right of diplomatic protection by the Republic of South Africa in respect of shareholders of companies incorporated in the Kingdom of Lesotho. The applicants' concession that the Government of the Kingdom of Lesotho did not answer the respondents' *Note Verbale* is an indication that the Kingdom of Lesotho does not recognise such a practice. In *Nduli and Another* v. *Minister of Justice and Others*[134] it was held that our courts only apply universally recognised customary international law rules or rules which have received the assent of South Africa. The fact that neither State to this dispute wishes to take the matter further, shows that there is no crystallisation of any practice between them. If the rights of shareholders are directly the subject of a State's injurious acts, the national State of

---

[133] "The Organization is based on the principle of the sovereign equality of all its members."
[134] 1978 (1) SA 893 (A) at 906. See also *S* v. *Petane* 1988 (3) SA 51 (C) at 64.

the shareholders will be entitled to diplomatic protection.[135] This will occur when a company is nationalised or if the rights of its shareholders are usurped.[136]

99. Mr Dugard submitted on behalf of the applicants that the applicants' "rights and interests" under the relevant mining leases were violated, but in response Mr Grobler pointed out that in this regard there is a lack of legal clarity and understanding of municipal and international law. The first to third applicants could not have had any rights or legal interests under the relevant mining leases, neither according to Lesotho law nor in terms of international law. Only the fourth to ninth applicants which are incorporated juristic *persona* according to Lesotho law could have had any possible legal rights or legal interests in the mining leases and/or tributing agreements. This flows from the fact that in international law, as well as in municipal law, shareholders have no rights or legal interests in the property or rights of their companies. The principle that a legal person such as a company has a personality distinct from that of the shareholders is clearly accepted by international law. In the *Standard Oil Company Tanker*[137] case the arbitration tribunal held that the injury inflicted on a property of a company cannot in law be regarded as an injury to the shareholders:

Whereas in fact the decisions of principle of the highest courts of most countries continue to hold that neither the shareholders nor their creditors have any right to the corporate assets other than to receive, during the existence of the company, a share of the profits, the distribution of which has been decided by a majority of the shareholders, and, after its winding-up, a proportional share of the assets.[138]

The arbitration tribunal further held that:

Whereas to state that a physical person, a legal person or a group of physical or legal persons exercise a preponderating influence over a given legal person is obviously not equivalent to declaring or admitting that they have a right of ownership in the property of the latter.[139]

[143] The arbitration tribunal emphasised that a shareholder has no right in the property of the company. This principle is unaffected by the number of shares which are owned.

100. In *Kaunda (supra)* Chaskalson CJ and the minority proceed from an analysis of section 3 of the Constitution pertaining to a national

---

[135] Booysen, *International Trade Law*, at 61 reached by Beyer in his study of this aspect, *Der Diplomatische Schutz der Aktionäre im Völkerrecht* (1977) at 194; *Barcelona Traction* case (*supra*) at 36, para. 47, at 41, para. 66.
[136] *El Triunfo* case 15 UNRIAA 467 at 476.   [137] (1926) UNRIAA 744 at 782.
[138] Id. at 787.   [139] Id. at 789.

seeking diplomatic protection. The learned Chief Justice indicated that a national has an entitlement to request diplomatic protection. This entitlement to request diplomatic protection is found to be part of the constitutional guarantee accorded by section 3 of the Constitution.[140] The finding proceeds from the premise that the requirements for citizenship under South African law are such that:

citizens invariably, if not always, will be nationals of South Africa. They are entitled as such to request the protection of South Africa in a foreign country in case of need.[141]

However, the same premise cannot be applied to companies who are legal persons, since they are not citizens and enjoy no rights or privileges in terms of section 3 of the Constitution. In consequence, the guarantee to citizens under section 3 of the Constitution which gives rise to the entitlement to citizens who are nationals to request diplomatic protection, does not apply to companies. Therefore, the ratio of the *Kaunda* judgment provides no basis upon which it can be found in the present case, that the companies that have been expropriated without compensation in Lesotho in contravention of the relevant international norms, have the same entitlement to request diplomatic protection as that held by a citizen. However, where a company is a national and that company seeks diplomatic protection, then the executive is obliged to consider the request and has to exercise its discretion whether to afford diplomatic protection or not. In that circumstance, the source of the duty to consider in the case of a company is constitutional accountability as evidenced by section 41(1)(a), (b) and (c) of the Constitution.[142]

---

[140] Cf para. 67; see paras. 58-63.   [141] Id. para. 62.
[142] Ss 41(1)(a), (b) and (c) provide as follows:

41. (1) All spheres of government and all organs of state within each sphere must—

    (a) preserve the peace, national unity and individuality of the Republic;
    (b) secure the well-being of the people of the Republic;
    (c) provide effective, transparent, accountable and coherent government for the Republic as a whole.

This section should be read with section 83(c) and section 85(1) and (2)(b) and (e) of the Constitution. S 83 (c) reads:

The President—

    (a) ...
    (b) ...
    (c) promotes the unity of the nation and that which will advance the Republic.

And section 85(1) and (2)(b) and (e) provide as follows:

Further, the ambit of [144] the discretion is prescribed by customary international law. This duty to consider and the ambit of the discretion are underscored by the responsibility of the President as head of the executive, to promote that which will advance the Republic of South Africa in conducting foreign relations with other States. Thus, in the final analysis, the fourth to ninth applicants which held the mining leases and tributing agreements are certainly not nationals of the Republic of South Africa even though some of the shares held in them are held by the first to third applicants who are South African nationals. These South African shareholders in those companies are not entitled to diplomatic protection.

Exhaustion of local remedies

101. The second prerequisite for admissibility of a claim at an international level is the rule on exhaustion of local remedies. This rule can be traced back to the aspect of sovereignty of the host State. Amerasinghe explains:

> The rule sprang up primarily as an instrument designed to ensure respect for the sovereignty of host states in a particular area of international dispute settlement. Basically this is the principle [*sic*] reason for its survival today and also for its projection into the international system of human rights protection. Whether in the modern law of diplomatic protection or in the conventional law of human rights protection, the *raison d'être* of the rule is a recognition given by members of the international community to the interest of the host state, flowing from its sovereignty, in settling international disputes of a certain kind by its own means before international mechanisms are invoked.[143]

The function of the rule is described as follows by the International Court of Justice in *Interhandel* case (*Switzerland* v. *United States*):[144]

> The "rule of local remedy" ensures that the State where the violation has occurred should have an opportunity to redress it by its own means, within the framework of its own domestic legal system.

---

(1) The executive authority of the Republic is vested in the President.
(2) The President exercises the executive authority, together with other members of the Cabinet, by—
  (a) ...;
  (b) developing and implementing national policy;
  (c) ...;
  (d) ...;
  (e) performing any other executive function provided for in the Constitution or in national legislation.

[143] *Local Remedies in International Law* 359, reproduced in Henkin, Pugh *et al., International Law*, at 588.
[144] 1959 ICJ 6.

102. The contention advanced by the applicants is that the exhaustion of local remedies is irrelevant. This reveals a clear lack of understanding of the concept of diplomatic protection. The rule of the exhaustion of local remedies is a customary international law precept.[145] It is also regarded as a substantive law rule. This means that an international wrong is only regarded as being committed when the injured person cannot obtain redress through local remedies. Even if it is regarded merely as a rule of a procedural nature, its effect remains the same as far as the facts of this case are concerned, namely the rule precludes recourse to diplomatic protection if its conditions are not fulfilled. The rule requires that all remedies must be exhausted. According to Doehring:[146]

Undisputed and long-standing international legal practice confirms the principle that the exercise of active diplomatic protection is precluded as long as [145] all the remedies available under domestic law have not been exhausted by the private party involved.

103. In *Panevezys–Saldutiskis Railway Case (Estonia v. Lithuania)*[147] it was argued that since there was a decision of the highest court of Lithuania that was adverse to the parties' case, it was not necessary to exhaust local remedies. But the Permanent Court of International Justice's response to this argument was:

[I]f the Esimene Company instituted proceedings in the Lithuanian court as to their right to be regarded as the owners and concessionaires of the Panevezys–Saldutiskis Railway, the parties to the suit would not be the same as those in the (appeal court case)—so that no question of *res judicata* could arise: nor is there anything to show that the Esimene Company would find itself confronted by a course of decisions . . . of the Lithuanian courts which would render the Company's suit hopeless, despite the difference of parties.[148]

The Court, therefore, found that the exhaustion of local remedies rule was applicable. In view of this decision, the applicants' argument pertaining to the non-applicability of the exhaustion of local remedies rule is unacceptable. Further, summons was issued for damages regarding the cancellation of four leases by Swissborough against the GoL. The action has been pleaded and the case is ripe for hearing and for that very reason the applicants have not exhausted local remedies in Lesotho.

---

[145] *Panevezys-Saldutiskis Case (Estonia v. Lithuania)*, 1939 PCIJ Reports, Series A/B No 764 at 18; *Interhandel Case* 1959 ICJ Reports 6 at 27; *Electricity Company of Sofia Case* 1939 PCIJ Series A/B No 77 at 78.
[146] Doehring, *Local Remedies, Exhaustion of*, in Bernhardt (ed.), *Encyclopaedia of Public International Law* vol. 3 (1997) 238 at 240.
[147] 1939 PCIJ Reports Series A/B No 764.   [148] Id. at 21.

104. Mr Grobler, in my view, rightly submitted that the first applicant, Mr van Zyl, was perfectly happy with the quality of jurisprudence and justice meted out by the Lesotho High Court and the Lesotho Court of Appeal when the judgments were in the applicants' favour. It is rather ironical that after having been afforded the opportunity of more than fifty court days of leading evidence on the validity of the Rampai mining lease, the Lesotho High Court and the Lesotho Court of Appeal declared the mining lease invalid, now those very same courts are berated as meting out injustice. There is simply no ground upon which it can be objectively found that the quality of justice dispensed by the Lesotho High Court and the Lesotho Court of Appeal does not meet the minimum international standard. The judgments of both courts are of exceptionally high quality and the standard of jurisprudence and justice is beyond question. There is no basis whatsoever for finding that the applicants can have no confidence in courts of Lesotho. Mr van Zyl in particular and the applicants generally are grossly mischievous in seeking this Court, as an organ of the Republic of South Africa, as well as the President, as head of the Executive, to critically undermine the courts of Lesotho. To answer to such a call would in essence [be] tantamount to infringing the sovereignty of the Kingdom of Lesotho.

Conclusion on international delict and the prerequisites to prosecuting a claim for diplomatic protection

105. The elements of an international delict which would vest the right in the Republic of South Africa to act against the Kingdom of Lesotho on the **[146]** basis of diplomatic protection for the applicants have not been satisfied by the applicants and no such right vests in the Republic of South Africa. Nor have they satisfied the two essential prerequisites for the admissibility of a claim for purposes of diplomatic protection. Thus, it follows that the mandamus requested by the applicants against the executive to act in providing diplomatic protection against the Kingdom of Lesotho in prayer 5 of the notice of motion cannot be granted.

Legitimate expectation

106. Briefly, one last aspect regarding the main application needs to be considered: the applicants' argument based upon legitimate expectation. It rests upon two bases. *Firstly*, reliance is placed on the letter of the State Attorney of 15 May 1995 and *secondly*, on various pronouncements of certain office-bearers of the first respondent regarding foreign

policy. However, this did not form part of the applicants' case at all. Counsel for the respondents rightly submitted that the State Attorney's letter did not constitute any representation which was clear, unambiguous and devoid of relevant qualification, however, no reasonable expectation could have been induced by the letter. Insofar as the pronouncements of foreign policy [are] concerned the applicants rely upon a *substantive* legitimate expectation. It was argued that this expectation arose from various expressions of foreign policy made on behalf of the first respondent. The applicants' counsel in their heads of argument submitted that:

At a minimum, the policy expressed creates a legitimate expectation that the respondents' commitment to promoting economic stability and increasing investor confidence will inform the respondents' exercise of discretion regarding the provision of diplomatic protection to applicants.

In response Mr Grobler rightly submitted that no such legitimate expectation is to be found in the application papers. The applicants' argument is simply to wax forth by simply adding new elements to an unpleaded case. The pronouncements of foreign policy relied upon did not give rise to a legitimate expectation in the true sense. Further, our law does not recognise a doctrine of legitimate expectation which gives rise to substantive rights as asserted by the applicants. Finally, the applicants' purported claim based on legitimate expectation does not advance their case for any of the relief sought in the notice of motion.

C. *Respondents' Strike-Out Application*

Introduction

107. The respondents served an application to strike out on 6 October 2003 notifying the applicants of their intention to move for the striking-out of certain paragraphs contained in the replying and supplementary replying affidavits as well as annexures thereto. Subsequently, a day prior to hearing of the matter the respondents served an amendment to the striking-out application intending to add further paragraphs under prayer 1 of the application to strike out and also tendered the costs for the ensuing amendment. The grounds, for the application to strike out, are set out in annexures "A" and "B". The respondents also served comprehensive heads of argument. Their papers comprise no less than 200 pages.

[147] 108. Prior to the hearing, the applicants neither filed any notice to oppose the strike-out application nor intimated their intention

to raise any preliminary issue. At the outset of the proceeding the applicants raised in essence a point *in limine* contending that the application to strike out was not before the Court and [the Court] should not entertain it separately to the consideration of the main application or at all since the respondents failed to comply with the time specified in the Deputy Judge President's directive. After some debate the issue was resolved that the matter proceed on the basis that the main application and the application to strike out should be heard simultaneously. Thus, it was not necessary to make a ruling.[149]

109. In deliberation of what was said earlier regarding *ad hoc* directives,[150] I am of the view, and without laying down a rule, that [in] any non-compliance with a directive, particularly an *ad hoc* one, a party ought not to take advantage by simply raising the issue of non-compliance without affording the other party to file a condonation application. In a matter of complexity and multiplicity of intricate issues such as this one, a party wishing to raise a preliminary issue ought to have the courtesy to timeously alert the other party of any intended point *in limine*. It is unreasonable for a party to wait until the last moment to stand upon his or her rights under the directive.[151]

Applicants introduced a new case in reply

110. The main thrust of the respondents' application to strike out is aimed at applicants' conduct in the presentation of their case in reply. It is characterised by a complete disdain of the most basic rules of procedure and of evidence as well as by a disdain of the censure previously meted out to them by the courts, both in Lesotho and this country, for exactly the same behaviour. The respondents submitted that the applicants' conduct smacked of contumacy. The respondents' counsel, Mr Raath, argued that the applicants' defiance of those rules, and of the previous judgments against them, finds expression, *inter alia*, in paragraph 32 of the founding affidavit that:

The merits of applicants' disputes with the Government of Lesotho are not directly in issue in this application ... What is in issue is the failure by the respondents to exercise their power (to decide to afford applicants diplomatic protection) in a constitutionally permissible manner.

I have been advised that it is, however, necessary to briefly describe the events in Lesotho which lead up to applicants' applications/requests for diplomatic protection.

---

[149] See para. [10] above.   [150] See para. [11] above.
[151] See *Gutman NO* v. *Standard General Insurance Co. Ltd* 1981 (4) SA 114 (C) at 122E-G; *Webster* v. *Webster* 1992 (3) SA 729 (E) at 734G.

This statement is prefatory to everything which followed in the remainder of the founding affidavit. It is submitted that it was calculated to bring the respondents under the impression that they were dealing with a case presented, as is normally done for purposes of review proceedings, on the basis that only the proper execution by a functionary of his or her duties is in issue, and not the merits, as if by way of an appeal. The respondents **[148]** were assured in the founding affidavit that they are not facing any further allegations of conspiracy on the part of the first respondent with the GoL. Thus, the applicants did not refer to the first respondent at all in their definition "combination" at paragraphs 92 and 93 of the founding affidavit. Furthermore, the founding affidavit is emphatic that the actions against the first respondent were withdrawn and that a press statement was made:

... in which it was stated that the African National Congress which controls the Government of the Republic of South Africa was not responsible for the harm caused to and the financial damages suffered by applicants resulting from the conduct from the GoL—and that this was done in order to "pave the way" for the first respondent to afford the applicants diplomatic protection.

However, in the replying affidavit new material is extensively introduced in an attempt to prove the merits of applicants' claim against the GoL as well as the first respondent's involvement in a conspiracy with the GoL. Mr Raath submitted that it is a blatant attempt to resurrect nothing less than a dominating theme and it pertains also to the first respondent under the ANC.

111. In *Swissborough*[152] Joffe J referred to *Imprefed (Pty) Limited* v. *National Transport Commission*[153] regarding the more complex the dispute between the parties the greater precision is required in the formulation of the issues even in motion proceedings. In *Imprefed*[154] the Appellate Division quoted with approval from *Kali* v. *Incorporated General Insurances Limited*[155] that:

... a pleader cannot be allowed to direct the attention of the other party to one issue and then, at the trial, attempt to canvass another.

This is precisely what applicants endeavoured to do in the founding affidavit by expressly moving away from the RSA conspiracy theme but the replying affidavit imports it in its full vigour. In this regard the following passage from *Triomf Kunsmis (Edms) Bpk* v. *AE&CI Bpk en andere*[156] is apposite:

---

[152] 1999 (2) SA 279 (T) at 324C-D.   [153] 1993 (3) SA 94 (A) at 106-7.
[154] Id. at 107H.   [155] 1976 (2) SA 179 (D) at 182A.
[156] 1984 (2) SA 261 (W) at 269B-G.

Hier is nie sprake van slegs 'n tydelike bevel *pendente lite* nie en dit is by uitnemendheid ook die soort geval waar die volgende stelling wat Regter Nestadt R in *Shephard* v. *Tuckers Land and Development Corporation (Pty) Ltd (1)* 1978 (1) SA 173 (W) at 177 aanhaal, van toepassing is:

> It is founded on the trite principle of our law of civil procedure that all the essential averments must appear in the founding affidavits or the Courts will not allow an applicant to make or supplement his case in his replying affidavits and will order any matter appearing therein which should have been in the founding affidavits to be struck out.

Verder aan:

> This is not however an absolute rule. It is not the law of Medes and Persians. The Court has a discretion to allow new matter to remain in a replying affidavit, giving the respondent the opportunity to deal with it in a second set of answering affidavits. This indulgence, however, will only be allowed in special or exceptional circumstances.

[149] Dit is interessant dat wanneer Nestadt R sê dat dit nie 'n absolute reël is nie, hy praat van 'n diskresie

> ... to allow new matter to remain in the replying affidavit.

My indruk is dat hierdie reëls soos aldus geformuleer hoofsaaklik van toepassing is op wat gewoonlik beskou word as "new matter", wat nie sinoniem is met 'n nuwe oorsaak van aksie nie. In die geval van 'n nuwe oorsaak van aksie wat die bestaande een vervang kan ek my kwalik omstandighede indink wat nie die onvermydelike gevolg het dat die proses, soos op daardie stadium, afgewys word nie. Dit is een ding om slegs ekstra feite ter ondersteuning van 'n bepaalde oorsaak van aksie, of te onderstreep, of vir die eerste keer aan te haal in 'n repliserende verklaring. Dit is 'n ander ding om geheel en al bollemakiesie te slaan ten opsigte van die gedingsoorsaak wat die gedingvoering in 'n totaal verskillende rigting stuur.

112. What is clearly apparent [is] that the applicants manifested procedural innocence by stating in paragraph 32 of the founding affidavit that the merits of their case against the GoL [were] not in issue, but what was to follow was merely presented as a brief outline of the history of the matter and thereby disavowing any reliance on the RSA conspiracy theme. Mr Raath submitted that the founding affidavit was marked by brevity rather than superfluity. The respondents, however, proceeded to put forward their case on that basis. But, what followed is a lengthy replying affidavit attempting to prove the merits of applicants' claims against the GoL by introducing the RSA conspiracy theme. (The founding affidavit comprised 91 pages, similarly the answering affidavit also comprised 91 pages, but in comparison, the replying affidavit runs for a full 535 pages.) What is also apparent [is] that the founding affidavit

was calculatedly offered in feigned procedural innocence from the outset as part of a ruse to snare the respondents so that the RSA conspiracy theme could surface in the replying affidavit without the respondents having an opportunity to deal with it. An applicant who wishes to rely upon exceptional circumstances in justification of introduction of new matter in the replying affidavit should do so by way of an application begging leave to supplement his or her papers. In the absence of such an application, not even an invitation to the other party to file a second set of affidavits will suffice,[157] nor is the respondent entitled to file further affidavits without the leave of the court.[158]

113. The applicants rather than seeking leave to supplement their founding affidavit chose to use their replying affidavit as a vehicle to introduce a new case mainly based upon the RSA conspiracy theme. The Deputy Minister of Foreign Affairs in his answering affidavit indicated:

Mr Van Zyl the deponent to the founding affidavit omits to mention material facts which are decisive of the matter. Nowhere in his affidavit or annexures thereto does he set out these material facts.

114. Mr Katz on behalf of the applicants argued that the applicants provided the respondents detailed documentation setting out all the material facts including those the fourth respondent contends that the applicants failed to mention. Counsel submitted that this [was a] failure by the respondents (at the time the impugned decisions were taken) to notice the material facts that **[150]** were disclosed in the applicants' request for diplomatic protection. This was made worse for the applicants by the fourth respondent's assertion in his answering affidavit that the former failed to mention the "material facts" in the founding affidavit and the annexures thereto. Mr Katz also submitted that the conspiracy theme is but one example of the background facts which may assist this Court in understanding the first respondent's decision-making process regarding the applicants' request for diplomatic protection and which may have relevance in confirming the irrationality of the decision-making process for the purposes of the review application. And for that reason alone, the conspiracy issue ought not to be struck out.

115. I am not persuaded by the convoluted argument advanced by Mr Katz that the conspiracy theme that pervades the replying affidavit should not be struck out for essentially those reasons. *Firstly*, the

---

[157] *Strauss* v. *Strauss and Another* [1998] 4 All SA 137 (A) at 141h-142a.
[158] See also *James Brown and Hamer (Pty) Ltd.* v. *Simmons NO* 1963 (4) SA 656 (A) at 660D-E.

applicants failed to heed what was said by Joffe J in *Swissborough*[159] that:

> Regard being had to the function of affidavits, it is not open to an applicant or a respondent to merely annex to its affidavit documentation and to request the Court to have regard to it. What is required is the identification of the portions thereof on which reliance is placed and an indication of the case which is sought to be made out on the strength thereof. If this were not so the essence of our established practice would be destroyed. A party would not know what case must be met. See *Lipschitz and Schwarz NNO* v. *Markowitz* 1976 (3) SA 772 (W) at 775H and *Port Nolloth Municipality* v. *Xahalisa and Others; Luwalala and Others* v. *Port Nolloth Municipality* 1991 (3) SA 98 (C) at 111B-C.

116. *Secondly*, the applicants latched onto some of the averments made in the answering affidavit, for example the fact that applicants did not mention therein that they themselves cancelled four of the five mining leases. They then proceed to deal over many pages as well as referring to voluminous documents to make out a case that these facts were known to the respondents' predecessors. They then introduced a new case mainly based upon the RSA conspiracy theme. It has no relevance to the aspects raised in the answering affidavit. A perusal of the replying affidavit reveals that an averment of a few lines in the answering affidavit triggered a substantial number of pages of response in the replying affidavit. It shows that in doing so the applicants attempted to generate a whirlwind of contentious issues, having little or no relation to the averments made in the answering affidavit, presumably in the hope of importing a new case in reply. And such a case may somehow be subsumed in the enormous breadth of the massive material (including speculation and argument) and voluminous annexures by which the respondents and the Court are inundated. Suffice to say that in comparison the applicants' founding affidavit is characterised by relative sparsity but the replying affidavit scatters as widely as possible in anticipation of reaping a brand new case with a crop of new matter which the respondents never had the opportunity to deal with. This is exactly what was done in *Swissborough* and drew criticism from the learned Judge. In spite of the criticism expressed in *Swissborough* and in flagrant disregard of the most basic rules of procedure and of evidence, the applicants rely in their heads of argument on new matter imported [151] into the replying affidavit by way of inadmissible evidence tendered in the proceedings in Lesotho in order to establish their case on the RSA conspiracy theme.

---

[159] 1999 (2) SA 279 (T) at 345-H.

117. *Thirdly*, it is remarkable that the "material facts" themselves are not in contention. What is apparent [is] that the parties are not in dispute with each other as far as the factual allegations are concerned. It concerns only two aspects: one, whether it was mentioned in the founding affidavit and/or annexures thereto, and two, that the respondents assert that they were not aware of those facts when they made their decisions. Despite this, applicants seek in hundreds of pages of the replying affidavit and a proliferation [of] annexures to offer material in order to demonstrate that those "material facts" are correct. It [is] tantamount to the applicants abusing the process. They could simply have indicated where these "material facts" were alluded to in the annexures to the founding affidavit. However, that would not have served applicants' purpose which is now to elevate their case to prove the actual merits of their case against the GoL, and especially to introduce the RSA conspiracy theme as the basis for their new cause of action, namely the unconstitutional behaviour on the part of the first respondent on South African soil which, *inter alia*, leads to their brand new case based upon section 25 of the Constitution on the basis that respondents thus acted unlawfully within the borders of South Africa. This is certainly a stratagem of abusing the process.

118. *Fourthly*, regarding any references to the annexures not mentioned in the founding affidavit, a deponent to an affidavit cannot simply append annexures and tell either the opponent or the Court to have regard thereto in order to find the applicants' case lurking somewhere. The deponent has to identify the specific portions of the annexure as well as the case sought to be made out on the strength thereof. It is no use for the applicants to point to some references which may be hidden somewhere in the voluminous annexures to the founding affidavit in order to respond to respondents' criticism in the answering affidavit.

119. The applicants, in their written submissions of 8 November 2003, indicated that the case put before this Court is the case made out in their founding affidavit and that is the case both Mr Dugard and Mr Katz argued on their behalf. The critical question is what is the purpose of a catena of paragraphs in 535 pages of the replying affidavit weighted by a chain of accompanying annexures? Was it a purposeless exercise on the applicants' part? I remain unpersuaded that the conspiracy theme is merely in the reply as an example of the factual background to assist the Court in understanding first respondent's decision-making process regarding the applicants' request for diplomatic protection. It is apparent that the applicants' deponent is certainly not candid because a substantial number of paragraphs deal with the conspiracy theme and a large number of paragraphs are utilized to change the character of the

application. The replying affidavit and its annexures are replete with new matter and which cannot be raised in the replying affidavit.[160] New matter falls under the rubric of irrelevant matter and is susceptible to be struck out.

[152] 120. The objectionable paragraphs in the applicants' replying affidavit and annexures thereto are:

(a) *conspiracy theme*

   (i) in the replying affidavit:
Paragraphs 11.2 and JVZ C1.15.12.7 and JVZ C29 and C30; 15.24 (specifically 15.24.6, 15.24.8 and 15.24.9); 19; 27.10 and JVZ C1; 31.3; 31.4 and JVZ C70 and C1; 31.5 and JVZ C70; 31.6 and JVZ C70 and C71; 31.7 and JVZ C71; 31.8 and JVZ 72; 31.9 and JVZ C73.7 and C73.8; 31.10; 31.11; 31.13; 31.14; 31.15; 31.16; 31.17; 31.18; 31.19; 32.1 (only insofar as relates to JVZ C1); 32.12; 32.13; 32.15; 32.16; 32.17; 32.18; 32.19; 32.20; 32.21; 38.1 (last sentence); 42 (excluding paragraph 42.9) and JVZ C75; 76.1 (except first two sentences); 135.2; 135.3 to 135.8 as well as 135.10 and JVZ C78; 135.9 and JVZ C103; C122; 135.11 to 135.29 (specifically 135.12; 135.16; 139.19 and JVZ C104; 139.20 to 139.22 and JVZ C1; C105; C105.1; C105.3; C105.4; C106; C107; C108; 135.25; 135.26; 135.29); 135.23; 135.27 to 135.8 and JVZ C109; 139; 144; 148.2 and JVZ C1; 154 and JVC1, C110, C111, C113, C114, C115, C116 and C117; 155.2 (only portion of page 1841); 165.2 (third last and second last sentence); 165.4; 166; 168.

   (ii) In the supplementary replying affidavit:
Paragraphs 2 to 3 and JVZ C1, C75 (K1); C140, C141, C142, C143, C144, C145, C146.

(b) *changing character of application* Paragraphs 6 and JVZ C1; 10.3 and JVZ C1; 14.4 and 14.5 and JVZ C9, C10, C11, C12, C13, C14, C15, C16, C17, C18, C19, C20, C21, C22, C23, C24, C25 and C26; 15.6; 15.2.2 to 15.12.7 and JVZ C29 and C30; 15.14 and JVZ C31; 15.15 and JVZ C32; 15.21; 25.1 (last sentence) and JVZ C1; 27.5.2 to 27.5.6; 27.5.8; 27.5.9 and JVZ C68 and 69; 27.10 and JVZ C1; 31.2 and JVZ C1; 31.3; 31.4 and JVZ C70 and C1; 31.6 and JVZ C70 and C71; 31.7 and JVZ C71; 31.12; 130.2 to 130.7 and JVZ C1; 132.1; 133.1 and

---

[160] Id. at 338F.

JVZ C27; 134.1 (from "I refer this Honourable Court to the evidence of Mr Labuschagne ... " at page 1763) and 134.2.

Other objectionable matter

121. Besides the new matter, there [is] other objectionable matter in the applicants' replying affidavit and annexures. [This] would be any matter which is "scandalous, vexatious or irrelevant".[161] The objectionable paragraphs that fall within any of those descriptions as well as inadmissible hearsay and another [are] enumerated hereunder.

(a) *scandalous and/or vexatious matter*
Paragraphs 17.3; 27.5 (introduction); 31.12 (last sentence at page 1522); 39.55.1 (pages 1642-5); 39.55.14 (pages 1645-6).

(b) **[153]** *irrelevant matter*
Paragraphs 7.1 (except first sentence); 10.2 to 10.8 and JVZ C2, C3 and C4; 14.5; 19; 15.13; 15.16 to 15.21; 22.2 to 22.12; 14.1 (last sentence); 27.4; 27.5.1; 27.8; 27.9; 135.24; 135.25; 135.26; 135.27-135.28 and JVZ C109; 135.29.

(c) *other new matter*
Paragraphs 143.3 (except first sentence) and JVZ C1 and C122; 153; 154.8; 158 and JVZ C118, C119, C120, C121, C122, C123, C124, C125, C126, C127, C128, C129, C130, C131, C132, C133, C134; 139.

(d) *inadmissible hearsay evidence*
It is trite that the courts have declined to countenance the admission of hearsay evidence unless there is urgency or special circumstances to warrant the acceptance of such evidence in application proceedings.[162]

Paragraphs 14.5.14; 15.4 (TV reports); 15.15 and JVZ C32 (newspaper reports); 27.5.4 (evidence of Labuschagne in Lesotho trial); 27.5.5 (Labuschagne's affidavit filed in case 18474/99); 27.5.6; 31.18 (evidence adduced in Lesotho litigation); 31.19; 31.20; 31.21; 32.4 (except first two sentences); 32.6; 32.12; 32.20; 32.21; 36.2 (only reference to Putsounce's evidence); 36.2.1; 36.2.2; 130.2 (evidence adduced in Lesotho litigation and GoL official documents at the top of page 1756); 135.23; 154.2; 154.3; 154.4; 154.5; 154.6; 154.9; 155.2 (on the portion of page 1841); 155.3; 165.4; 166.3.1 (Labuschagne's evidence quoted at pages 1879 to 1891).

---

[161] Rule 6(15) of the Uniform Rules of Court.
[162] *Swissborough Diamond Mines* v. *Government of RSA* 1999 (2) SA 279 (T) at 336G, 1-J; *Galp* v. *Tansley NO and Another* 1966 (4) SA 555 at 558, 560.

(e) *no case is made out for legitimate expectation*
Paragraphs 52 and JVZ C82, 83 and 84; 558.2 (third last and second last sentences).

Requirement of prejudice

122. A court will only grant an application to strike out until it is satisfied that the party bringing the application will be prejudiced in his or her case if an order is not granted.[163] In the instant case, the prejudice sustained by the respondents is to be found in the titanic proportion of new matter introducing the conspiracy theme with the professed motive to change the character of the main application as well as by introducing scandalous, vexatious and irrelevant matter and inadmissible hearsay evidence. It is overwhelming.[164] Both the main application and the striking-out application are woven with exhaustive and overwhelming new matter in the replying affidavit together with a train of annexures [which] required industry to deal with and was indeed prejudicial and certainly fall to be struck out.

[154] *Costs of striking-out application*

123. As far as costs are concerned, the respondents seek that the applicants pay the respondents' costs, including the costs of three counsel, on an attorney and own client scale. This form of order is such as to not only indicate extreme opprobrium but also the court's intention to allow the successful party to recoup more fully than would be the case in an ordinary attorney and client scale.[165]

124. I propose to order the applicants to pay the respondents' costs on an attorney and own client scale as a mark of disapproval of the applicants' conduct because there was a radical departure from and by disregarding the most basic rules of practice and procedure and the law of evidence. In my view this kind of conduct falls within the paradigm of abusing the process of court. Further, the applicants overwhelmed the respondents and this Court, literally and figuratively, with a shipment of documents in the hope of changing the character of the main application. The applicants and this Court were inundated with irrelevant new matter, scandalous and vexatious assertions and inexplicable hearsay evidence. Thus, the applicants' conduct not only smacks of

---

[163] *Syfrets Mortgage Nominees Ltd* v. *Cape St Francis Hotels (Pty) Ltd* 1991 (3) SA 276 (SE) at 282H-283C. See also: *Beinash* v. *Wixley* 1997 (3) SA 721 (SCA) at 733J-734C, also reported at [1997] 2 All SA 241 (A); *Vaatz* v. *Law Society of Namibia* 1991 (3) SA 563 (Nm) at 566J-567B.

[164] See: *Swissborough Diamond Mines* v. *Government of the RSA* 1999 (2) SA 279 (T) at 338C.

[165] *Cambridge Plan AG* v. *Cambridge Diet (Pty) Ltd and Another* 1990 (2) SA 574 (T) at 589D-E.

contumacy but shows utter disdain for the most fundamental rules of practice, procedure and evidence. Such conduct certainly merits censure and surely justifies an award of attorney and own client costs. Thus, in the circumstances of this particular case, it is fair and just to make such an order given the magnitude and complexity of the matter.

D. *Cost of Main Application*

125. Neither parties argued against the respondents' engagement of three counsel. The respondents were represented by two silks and a junior. The services of three counsel were certainly not extravagant having regard to the novelty, complexity and magnitude of the matter as well as numerous issues of international law and constitutional law and the importance of the matter to both sides. The respondents did not pray for any special order of costs. Thus, as ordinarily the costs should follow the result.

E. *Order*

126. Accordingly the following order is made:

(a) *application to strike out*

   (i) The respondents' application to amend their application to strike out is granted and the respondents pay the costs tendered occasioned by the amendment.
   (ii) The respondents' application to strike out is upheld and the applicants are jointly and severally, the one paying the others to be absolved, ordered to pay the costs thereof on an attorney and own client scale including the costs consequent upon the employment of three counsel.

(b) **[155]** *main application*
The application is dismissed and the first, second, third, fourth, fifth, sixth, seventh, eighth and ninth applicants are jointly and severally, the one paying the others to be absolved, ordered to pay the costs of the application including the costs consequent upon the employment of three counsel.

[Reports: [2005] 4 All SA 96; [2006] 4 LRC 18; 2005 (11) BCLR 1106 (T)]

The text of the judgment of the Supreme Court of Appeal, delivered by Harms ADP, with whom the others agreed, commences on the opposite page.

JUDGMENT OF THE SUPREME COURT OF APPEAL

[297] *Introduction*

1. This appeal relates to a claim for diplomatic protection, i.e., action by one State against another State in respect of an injury to the person or property of a national of the former State that has been caused by an international delict that is attributable to the latter State. Diplomatic protection includes, in a broad sense, consular action, negotiation, mediation, judicial and arbitral proceedings, reprisals, a retort, severance of diplomatic relations, and economic pressures.[1]

2. The appellants requested the Government of the RSA to provide them with diplomatic protection against the Government [298] of Lesotho. The international delict on which they relied was the cancellation and revocation of five mineral leases that had been granted by the Government of Lesotho.

3. The President of the RSA was advised that the Government was under no obligation to afford diplomatic protection to the appellants; that any decision to intervene would involve a policy and not a legal decision; that the decision is the sole prerogative of the Government; that the disputes between the appellants and the Government of Lesotho had been decided by the Lesotho courts; that mediation or intervention by the Government would imply a lack of faith in the judicial system of a sovereign State; and that diplomatic intervention would set an unhealthy precedent. The President in the result refused to accede to the appellants' request and they were informed that they were not, in the circumstances of the case, entitled to diplomatic protection.

4. Dissatisfied with this ruling, the appellants sought to review the Government's decision. They also applied for a mandamus directing the Government "to take all steps necessary to vindicate the rights of the applicants, including but not limited to providing diplomatic protection". The application was heard by Patel J in the Pretoria High Court. He dismissed the application but granted leave to appeal to this Court.

5. Courts should act with restraint when dealing with allegations of unlawful conduct ascribed to sovereign States.[2] Unfortunately, in order to decide this case it is necessary to deal with the allegations made by the appellants to determine whether or not Patel J was correct in dismissing their application.

---

[1] *Kaunda* v. *President of the RSA* 2004 (10) BCLR 1009 (CC), 2005 (4) SA 235 (CC) paras. 26-7.
[2] *Swissborough Diamond Mines (Pty) Ltd* v. *Government of the RSA* 1999 (2) SA 279 (T) at 330D and follows. Cf *Kuwait Airways Corp.* v. *Iraqi Airways Co.* [2002] UKHL 19, [2002] 3 All ER 209 (HL) paras. 24-6.

6. This judgment holds that the appellants have no right under South African law to diplomatic protection, especially not in respect of protection of a particular kind. Nationals have a right to request Government to consider diplomatic protection and Government has a duty to consider it rationally. Government received the request, considered the matter properly and decided to decline to act on rational grounds. This judgment further holds that the Government is not entitled under international law to afford the appellants diplomatic protection under the particular circumstances of the case. Accordingly, the appeal stands to be dismissed.

The Parties

7. There are nine appellants but the driving force behind the litigation is the first appellant, Mr Josias van Zyl. He and his wife are in their capacity as trustees of two trusts, the Burmilla Trust and the Josias van **[299]** Zyl Family Trust, the second and third appellants respectively. Both trusts are registered in South Africa. Mr and Mrs van Zyl are South African citizens.

8. There are six corporate appellants, all companies incorporated and registered in Lesotho. The important one is Swissborough Diamond Mines (Pty) Ltd. The issued shares in Swissborough belong to Mr van Zyl (5%), Burmilla Trust (90%) and the family trust (5%). Swissborough holds 99% of the shares in the other companies and the family trust holds the remaining 1%. The mineral leases were all held by Swissborough and the other appellant companies derived their interests from Swissborough by means of tributary agreements (effectively sub-leases). Because of this it will not be necessary to distinguish between the appellant companies and references to Swissborough will usually be in a generic sense to include a reference to all or most of the appellants. All the directors are also South African citizens.

9. The respondents are, respectively, the Government of the RSA, the President, the Minister of Foreign Affairs and, last, the Deputy Minister. It is for purposes of the judgment not important to distinguish between them and I shall refer to them (unless the context requires otherwise) as the Government. I also do not intend to distinguish between the State and the Government and will use the terms interchangeably.

The History

10. This case has a long and convoluted history. The appellants displayed an obsessive attention to peripheral facts and factoids and their affidavits raise speculation to the level of fact and thereafter raise

argument based on the speculation.[3] And as in the *Kaunda* case, this case has been complicated by the appellants' excessive demands and the form in which the notice of motion was framed.[4] In what follows I intend to limit myself to the salient facts. They are briefly related at this juncture to set the stage for a more detailed discussion where and when required.

11. The RSA and the Kingdom of Lesotho concluded a treaty concerning the Lesotho Highlands Project on 24 October 1986. The main purpose of the project was to supply water to the Witwatersrand from a dam that had to be built in Lesotho. Joffe J in previous proceedings between the appellants and the Government dealt with the detail of the treaty and what he said need not be repeated.[5] During June 1988, **[300]** construction operations by the Lesotho Highlands Development Authority, a Lesotho statutory body established pursuant to the treaty, began in the Rampai area.

12. Shortly thereafter, on 4 August 1988, the Government of Lesotho and Swissborough entered into five mining leases. One of these leases covered the Rampai area in the basin of the proposed dam. The terms of the Rampai lease are typical. The lease was entered into in Lesotho in terms of ss 6 and 15 of the Lesotho Mining Rights Act 1967. The Commissioner of Mines represented the Basotho Nation and Mr van Zyl represented Swissborough. Swissborough obtained the sole right to prospect for and mine and dispose of precious stones within the Rampai area for a period of ten years with a right of renewal for a further five years. Swissborough had to pay the Government of Lesotho a yearly rental of R13,600 (R100 per square kilometre) and a royalty of 14% on the value of the stones recovered. The agreement contained an arbitration clause. The lease had to be registered in terms of the Mining Rights Act, which happened soon thereafter. (For purposes of the rest of the judgment a distinction will be drawn between the Rampai lease and the other four because of subsequent events.)

13. The Authority proceeded with its work on the dam project until July 1991 when Swissborough obtained an interim interdict against the Authority preventing it from performing any work within the Rampai area. The rule was subsequently discharged by agreement but the final determination of the application was kept in abeyance pending settlement negotiations.

---

[3] As happened in *Swissborough Diamond Mines (Pty) Ltd* v. *Government of the RSA* 1999 (2) SA 279 (T) at 315E-F per Joffe J.

[4] *Kaunda* v. *President of the RSA* 2004 (10) BCLR 1009 (CC), 2005 (4) SA 235 (CC) at para. 128.

[5] In particular, he found (at 327C and follows) that the appellants did not derive any rights from the treaty.

14. Faced with the consequences of a grant of competing rights to Swissborough and the Authority as well as a breach of its treaty obligations, the Government of Lesotho took a number of steps which the Lesotho courts in due course found were unlawful.[6] These acts form the crux of the appellants' complaints against the Government of Lesotho.

15. The first step was the cancellation by the Commissioner of Mines of all the mining leases. This enabled the Authority to rely on the cancellation of the Rampai lease as a defence to the interdict application. (The other leases did not affect the construction activities.) However, on 20 November 1991, the court, at the behest of Swissborough, on an interim basis set aside the cancellation of the mining leases by the Commissioner. It also issued an interim interdict preventing the Authority from proceeding with its dam construction activities within the Rampai area. One may assume that this order must have had a devastating effect on the construction activities of the Authority.

16. In another attempt to undo the mining leases the governing Military Council issued the "Revocation of Specified Mining Leases Order" of 20 March 1992. This executive order revoked the five mining leases of [301] Swissborough; provided that no person would be entitled to compensation for loss or damage as a result of the cancellation; and prohibited the institution of any legal proceedings, including arbitration proceedings, resulting from or in connection with the order or the cancellation of the leases.

17. Another application to court followed immediately, this time for an order setting aside the revocation order and for another interim interdict.[7] Swissborough was successful and Cullinan CJ in his judgment of September 1994 had some harsh words about the actions of the Government of Lesotho, especially for the disrespect for the Constitution and the negation of the rule of law.

18. The subsequent appeal was not successful. During January 1995 the Court of Appeal held that the revocation order was in conflict with the provisions of the Lesotho Human Rights Act and consequently void.[8] The appeal against the interim interdict, however, succeeded on the ground that Cullinan CJ had not exercised a proper discretion. The

---

[6] How it came about that the Government of Lesotho granted conflicting rights at that stage has been the subject of much speculation in Lesotho but has never been explained.

[7] The terms of the order are quoted at *Swissborough Diamond Mines (Pty) Ltd* v. *Government of the RSA* 1999 (2) SA 279 (T) 297E-I.

[8] *Attorney-General of Lesotho* v. *Swissborough Diamond Mines (Pty) Ltd* 1997 (8) BCLR 1122 (L AC). The terms of the order are quoted in *Swissborough Diamond Mines (Pty) Ltd* v. *Government of the RSA* 1999 (2) SA 279 (T) 298A-D.

balance of convenience, the court found, did not favour Swissborough and that an award of damages would compensate Swissborough adequately. Swissborough was given time to do exploratory work in the Rampai area to quantify its damages.[9]

19. During March 1995, the Government of Lesotho and the Authority conceded that the cancellation of the mining leases by the Commissioner had been invalid. The Authority nevertheless lodged a counter-application for a declaration that the Rampai lease had been void ab initio because the required formalities had not been followed. The court consequently set the cancellation aside and referred the validity issue for oral evidence. This led to a 58-day trial before the Chief Justice, Mr Justice Kheola.

20. Kheola CJ found against Swissborough on 28 April 1999, holding that the Rampai lease was void ab initio. Swissborough appealed to the Court of Appeal but the appeal was dismissed on 6 October 2000.[10] The reasons are fairly basic. According to Lesotho customary law all land belongs to the Basotho Nation; this principle is entrenched in the Lesotho Constitution; any grant of rights in relation to land required the consent of the relevant Chiefs; since its promulgation the Lesotho Mining Rights Act 1967 (under which the mineral leases were granted) [302] required the Chiefs' consent for the grant of mineral rights; and the evidence established that no consent had been sought or granted.[11] The Rampai lease was accordingly void.

21. Less than three weeks later the appellants made the initial request for diplomatic protection, which led to these proceedings.

22. It is convenient to mention two intervening matters. The first relates to the other four leases that were not involved in the Rampai appeal. Faced with the revocation order, which denied it access to court, Swissborough decided to regard the Government of Lesotho's denial of the validity of these leases as a repudiation of contract and to accept the repudiation, thereby bringing to an end any contractual relationship between the parties. (Notably, probably for tactical reasons, Swissborough did not cancel the Rampai lease.) On 25 October 1993, Swissborough instituted action claiming R930m damages. There was an additional claim of R15m in respect of physical damage to plant and equipment.

23. On 16 September 1994, Swissborough ceded its rights in respect of the pending action and the contractual and delictual damages claims

---

[9] *Attorney-General* v. *Swissborough Diamond Mines (Pty) Ltd* 1995-6 Lesotho LR 173.
[10] *Swissborough Diamond Mines (Pty) Ltd* v. *LHDA* 2000 Lesotho LR 432 (CA).
[11] This explains why the lease [was] purported to have been entered into by the Basotho Nation and not by the Government of Lesotho.

to Burmilla Trust. Although the rights were valued at R2,637m, the consideration was a mere R1,000. Burmilla Trust has not yet been substituted as plaintiff and the action has not been pursued. Another action relating to the same or similar causes of action was instituted during May 1996 by Swissborough. This action is also in limbo.

24. Two years later Swissborough entered into another cession agreement with Burmilla Trust in amplification of the first one. It ceded all Swissborough's claims against the Government of Lesotho in the event of a declaration that any of the mining leases were invalid.

25. The second set of intervening facts concerns the adoption of legislation by the Government of Lesotho to place matters on a proper legal footing and to comply with its national and, coincidentally, its international obligations especially in relation to the treaty with the RSA. The Lesotho Act 5 of 1995, which came into effect on 16 August 1995, provided for the expropriation by the Authority of mineral rights for purposes of the water project. Thus far the Authority had been entitled to take "land" and pay compensation but the initial legislation did not deal with mineral rights and did not have adequate compensation provisions. This Act, however, provided for full compensation, properly determined, in respect of any such expropriation to a person in whose favour a "duly granted and executed mineral right" was registered. Pursuant to this Act, the Authority purported to expropriate the Rampai lease on 17 August 1995 but in the light of the Rampai judgment expropriation was unnecessary because there was nothing to expropriate.

[303] 26. On the same day another piece of legislation was promulgated, namely Lesotho Act 6 of 1995. It validated certain dam construction activities of the Authority "subject to any accrued or vested right to damages". Again, as a result of the Rampai judgment Swissborough had no accrued or vested rights, at least not in relation to the Rampai lease.

The Request for Diplomatic Protection

27. The first request for diplomatic protection was made per letter of 25 October 2000 to the Department of Foreign Affairs. It relied on the unlawful revocation of the mineral leases during 1992 and the destruction and confiscation of assets by the Government of Lesotho.[12] The appellants also complained about corruption "at the highest level" in the Government of Lesotho. In addition they alleged that Swissborough

---

[12] In a letter of 10 April 2001 it is referred to as a confiscation through the cancellation of the mineral leases.

had suffered a miscarriage of justice at the hand of the Lesotho courts. The appellants further said that they had "no faith in the independence and impartiality" of the Lesotho courts[13] and they "rejected" the Rampai judgment because the judges were "specially appointed" and their analysis of the evidence and their findings were "one-sided and manifested bias".

28. The next letter of consequence was dated 8 December 2000. Before dealing with its terms it is necessary to contextualise it. During 1993, Swissborough instituted action against the Government of the RSA for damages suffered as a result of the loss of their leases. The particulars of this action (and a related action against a local statutory body) need not be mentioned—they are to be found in the judgment of Joffe J. In summary, Swissborough alleged that the Government of the RSA interfered unlawfully with its mining rights, which caused it to suffer damages of R945m. Swissborough, in addition, claimed R507.8m from the statutory body on similar grounds. The unlawful interference, according to the particulars of claim, was done with the improper motive of obtaining an unlawful advantage for the joint water supply venture. The defendants in that case allegedly "procured" (followed by ten alternatives) the unlawful interference with Swissborough's rights by the Government of Lesotho.

29. The conspiracy issue also formed part of the case before Kheola CJ and was the main reason for the length of the trial. He found that the allegations were without any merit and made a special costs order against Swissborough. The Court of Appeal did not consider the merits of the issue because it became irrelevant in the light of the finding that the Rampai lease was invalid.

30. During 1995, Mr van Zyl approached the RSA Government with settlement proposals. This elicited a letter from the State Attorney **[304]** written on the instructions of the Minister of Water Affairs (under whose jurisdiction the dam project fell), dated 15 May 1995. It is necessary to quote from the letter 3/136

- The Minister is in principle not averse to endeavours aimed at settling legitimate claims against the Government.
- The manner in which you have conducted the pursuit of your interests as you perceive them, has, however, created the firm impression that you set out to coerce the Republic of South Africa to meet a claim which you may or may not have against the Government of the Kingdom of Lesotho and the Lesotho Highlands Development Authority. This you set

---

[13] The letter of 19 December 2000 repeated the statement.

out to do *inter alia* by calling upon the international community to take up your perceived cause against the Government of the Republic of South Africa, by widely publicizing allegations of immoral collusion and improper conduct on the part of the Government and by making similar allegations in respect of the present Government in your recent correspondence to the Minister.
- You have indeed succeeded in creating a situation where you have offended the dignity of the Republic of South Africa, not only under the previous Government, but also under the present one. The dispute is thus no longer a simple commercial dispute. Settlement of the actions with you may amount to an acknowledgement of the veracity of your allegations and may compromise the credibility of the present Government, not only in its international relations with the Kingdom of Lesotho, but also with the other states and international institutions whose assistance you sought to muster.
- As long as you persist in your allegations of improper collusion between the Government of the Republic of South Africa and the independent and sovereign Kingdom of Lesotho, no advances of settlement can be entertained.
- Should you withdraw the actions as well as the offensive allegations against the Government of the Republic of South Africa unreservedly and publicly, my Government may find itself in a position where it may consider attempts to facilitate mediation of the various disputes between yourself and the Government of the Kingdom of Lesotho and the Lesotho Highlands Development Authority.
- As matters presently stand this is, however, impossible without prejudicing the dignity of the Government of the Republic of South Africa and its credibility in the international community.

31. The appellants rejected the suggestion that they withdraw the allegations; instead, as mentioned, they proceeded to conduct a lengthy trial in order to prove the allegations of collusion and they harassed the Government in the local litigation as appears from the judgment of Joffe J. During July 1999 (shortly after the judgment of Kheola CJ), Mr van Zyl went yet further: he submitted a voluminous request for an inspection by the World Bank (a financier of the scheme) alleging that the Bank, the RSA Government, the Government of Lesotho and the Authority were involved in the "patently unlawful acts" surrounding the water project and the leases.

32. Having lost the Rampai appeal the appellants in the mentioned letter of 8 December 2001, rather cynically relied on the promises contained in the State Attorney's letter; they withdrew the South African **[305]** actions and the allegations "in respect of the ANC government's

involvement" in an unlawful conspiracy; and they released a press statement apologising to Government.

33. The next letter of importance, dated 15 December 2000, argued the existence of a "right to diplomatic protection" under the Constitution at length (an assertion repeated in later correspondence) and submitted that "the State is under a constitutional obligation to provide diplomatic protection to its citizens". The letter also requested the Government to "act in terms of its undertaking" contained in the letter of the State Attorney.

34. The appellants insisted that Government should provide them with diplomatic protection by mediating the dispute and convincing the Government of Lesotho to pay a "settlement" amount of R85.4m with interest within a given period. Otherwise Government had to institute legal proceedings against the Government of Lesotho in an international court or arbitration tribunal for payment of some R1,812.5m with interest on the appellants' behalf.

35. In spite of its refusal to grant the request, the Government sent a *Note Verbale* to the Government of Lesotho, informing that government of the complaint. The Government of Lesotho did not respond but its view appears forcefully from a letter dated 19 November 2001, by its attorneys to Swissborough in response to a parallel paper campaign against the Government of Lesotho. It rejected the allegations in no uncertain terms, stating that a number of premises of the arguments put forward were, to the knowledge of the claimants, fundamentally flawed; that the attacks on the judiciary were scurrilous; and that there was no prospect of any settlement. (A copy of the letter is annexed to this judgment.) This six-page letter drew a reply of 138 pages from Mr van Zyl. The Government of Lesotho responded by reiterating that it would not submit to any form of arbitration, international or otherwise.

The Court Application

36. Review applications, in the ordinary course of events, have to be brought under Uniform Rule 53 (unless covered by the Promotion of Administrative Justice Act 3 of 2000—PAJA). This one was not, and the failure to follow the rule caused much aggravation.

37. The founding affidavit of Mr van Zyl set out the nature of the application under a separate heading. He relied on a violation of the appellants' rights by the cancellation of the mining leases without payment of compensation (and nothing more). This, he said, constituted

an expropriation that did not comply with minimum international standards. The Government of Lesotho was accordingly obliged to pay the appellants some R3,089m damages.

38. Mr van Zyl proceeded to say, as foreshadowed in the correspondence, that the appellants have "a constitutional right to diplomatic protection" and that the Government has "a corresponding obligation to provide such protection"; the issue (he said) was the failure of Government [306] to exercise its power in a constitutionally permissible manner; the decision was irrational because it was based on a wrong understanding of its legal obligation; and that the merits of the disputes with the Government of Lesotho were not directly in issue.

39. Then followed 70 pages of "history and background" interspersed with legal argument. Two aspects need to be noted. The first concerns the Lesotho courts. After alleging that the appellants had exhausted their local remedies, Mr van Zyl proceeded to state (contrary to the line taken in the preceding correspondence) that the application was not "a reflection on the integrity of any of the judges in the Courts of Lesotho" or on those courts. The second is a one-liner based on the State Attorney's letter of 15 May 1995: this letter allegedly gave the appellants a legitimate expectation that the Government would afford them diplomatic protection should they withdraw their South African litigation, something they had now done.[14]

40. Attached to the founding affidavit are about 850 pages of exhibits. The allegations contained in these annexures were not confirmed in the founding affidavit and are therefore not evidence. Mr van Zyl and his legal advisers knew that it is not open to a party merely to annex documentation to an affidavit and during argument use its contents to establish a new case. A party is obliged to identify those parts on which it intends to rely and must give an indication of the case it seeks to make out on the strength thereof.[15] The fact that the appellants again have ignored the procedural rules dealt with by Joffe J is probably due to Mr van Zyl's belief, as he said during argument, that 50 per cent of all court rules are unconstitutional and can be ignored.

41. The main affidavit in answer was by the Deputy Minister, Mr Aziz Pahad. It dealt in 91 pages with the appellants' right to diplomatic protection and with the decision of Government in response to the

---

[14] I do not propose to deal with the legitimate expectation argument separately because the facts are destructive of any such argument. The expectation was not legitimate or reasonable. There is also something schizophrenic about the argument because, as will appear later, the replying affidavit resurrected the abandoned conspiracy argument.

[15] *Swissborough Diamond Mines (Pty) Ltd* v. *Government of the RSA* 1999 (2) SA 279 (T) 323F-325C.

request. He added that Mr van Zyl had failed to disclose five material facts. These facts, according to the deponent, went to the heart of the application.

42. This elicited a replying affidavit of about 550 pages and annexures of some 1,700 pages. The main "justification" proffered was that Mr van Zyl indeed had disclosed the five material facts in the founding affidavit. In other words, this mass of material was required to underpin five common cause facts. One illustration should suffice. Mr Pahad alleged that the cession of Swissborough's claims to Burmilla Trust was material and had not been stated in the founding affidavit. Mr van Zyl took Mr Pahad to task because, he pointed out, the fact of the cession appeared **[307]** from a note on two of the annexures to the founding affidavit. Instead of admitting the cession and giving the reference, Mr van Zyl now sought to traverse new ground. In addition, Mr van Zyl resurrected the conspiracy case in the reply because, he said, of the Government's allegations concerning his failure to disclose material facts. He also attacked the Government's decision on new grounds.

43. The Government applied for the striking out of major parts of the reply as either new matter or as otherwise objectionable, namely being scandalous, vexatious, irrelevant or inadmissible.

The Proceedings in the TPD

44. During the hearing before Patel J, the appellants were represented by three counsel. Patel J granted the Government's striking out application and dismissed the appellants' application. His judgment dealt in great detail with all the legal issues raised. As will appear in the course of this judgment, I agree in general terms with his reasoning but I do not find it necessary to decide all the issues he did.

45. It is convenient to deal at this stage with the application to strike out. Both sides filed lengthy heads dealing with each and every finding made by Patel J. The learned judge, it should be noted, took great pains to analyse the complaint. I do not think that a court of appeal could reasonably be asked to redo an exercise concerning an interlocutory matter, especially in the circumstances of this case. Schutz JA once made these pointed remarks:[16]

There is one other matter that I am compelled to mention—replying affidavits. In the great majority of cases the replying affidavit should be by far the shortest. But in practice it is very often by far the longest—and the most valueless. It

---

[16] *Minister of Environmental Affairs and Tourism* v. *Phambili Fisheries (Pty) Ltd* [2003] 2 All SA 616 (SCA), 2003 (6) SA 407 (SCA) at para. 80.

was so in these reviews. The respondents, who were the applicants below, filed replying affidavits of inordinate length. Being forced to wade through their almost endless repetition when the pleading of the case is all but over brings about irritation, not persuasion. It is time that the courts declare war on unnecessarily prolix replying affidavits and upon those who inflate them.

46. A reply in this form is an abuse of the court process and instead of wasting judicial time in analysing it sentence by sentence and paragraph by paragraph such affidavits should not only give rise to adverse costs orders but should be struck out as a whole. Since I am of the view that Patel J should have taken that route *mero motu*, I am not going to deal with those few instances where he quoted a wrong paragraph number (one of the grounds, as I understood from what Mr van Zyl volunteered during argument, that led to a complaint to the Judicial Services Commission against the late judge) or erred. I shall nevertheless have **[308]** regard to the reply to the extent that it contains relevant and admissible material that impacts on the merits of the case.[17]

The Hearing in the SCA

47. It is unfortunately necessary to say something (but not all) about the appeal hearing. Mr Redelinghuys, an attorney with the right of appearance, appeared for all appellants excepting Mr van Zyl. Mr Redelinghuys knows the case because he was Swissborough's attorney in Lesotho. Mr van Zyl argued in person but chose to follow Mr Redelinghuys.

48. The heads of argument filed by the appellants ran to 530 pages. A few days before the hearing, without explanation, another set of 325 pages was filed.[18] After a short and well prepared introductory argument, Mr Redelinghuys proceeded to deal with the additional heads. His main point was that the appellants had suffered a denial of justice at the hands of the Lesotho courts. The nub of the argument was that "national legal systems can be judged objectively for acts and omissions of its courts with respect to aliens" and that "a state incurs international responsibility if it administers justice to aliens in a fundamentally unfair way". He relied on art. 10 of the Universal Declaration of Human Rights, which provides that

---

[17] A party is in principle not entitled to rely on new matter, even if it has not been struck out: *Director of Hospital Services* v. *Mistry* 1979 (1) SA 626 (A) 635H-636B; *Bowman NO* v. *De Souza Roldao* 1988 (4) SA 326 (T).

[18] At the end of argument, when Mr van Zyl was told he could file further argument in reply, he immediately produced a third set of heads running to 65 pages that had nothing to do with the reply. The appellants also filed 2,600 pages of authorities.

everyone is entitled in full equality to a fair and public hearing by an independent and impartial tribunal, in the determination of his rights and obligations and of any criminal charge against him.

49. Mr Redelinghuys was asked on what basis could he argue this point since it did not form part of the case set out in the founding affidavit—indeed, the case of the appellants was, as mentioned, that the application was no reflection on the Lesotho courts—nor was it the case in the high court or in the main heads of argument. He sought in response to rely on unsupported allegations made against the judiciary in the attached correspondence to which he added *ex cathedra* allegations. It was pointed out to Mr Redelinghuys that he, as an officer of the court, could not make submissions that do not have an evidential basis. Mr Redelinghuys subsequently retracted and abandoned the point.

50. This gave Mr van Zyl the opportunity to attack this Court for having already decided the case; to lecture the Court about justice; and to renew the attack on the Lesotho judiciary.[19] Those courts, he said, were not only biased, they were manipulated. Mr van Zyl was given more than [309] one opportunity to identify the passages in the record where the allegation of a denial of justice had been made. He did not. I do not wish to belabour the point. Although the failure of justice was raised in the preceding correspondence, the appellants deliberately chose to omit it as a cause of complaint from the founding affidavit and, apart from a generalised statement, also from the replying affidavit. The appellants are not entitled in this manner to resurrect an abandoned case.[20]

The Review

51. The approach to Government and the Government's response occurred before the Constitutional Court delivered the *Kaunda* judgment,[21] which brought some clarity on the issue of the right to diplomatic protection. For purposes of this case the following principles there set out are relevant:

---

[19] Mr van Zyl's wrath was not limited to the judges of Lesotho. It spilled over to local judges who had held against him and counsel who appeared against him. All were involved in a Machiavellian plot. He even made snide remarks about a professor of law who, he said, was in court and advised Government.

[20] Relying on J. Paulsson's *Denial of Justice in International Law* (2005). The argument of a denial of justice at the hand of the Government of Lesotho was just a variation of the argument which will be dealt with later.

[21] *Kaunda and Others* v. *President of the RSA* 2004 (10) BCLR 1009 (CC), 2005 (4) SA 235 (CC).

11. Traditional international law acknowledges that States have the right to protect their nationals beyond their borders but they are under no obligation to do so (para. 23).
12. Diplomatic protection is not recognised by customary international law as a human right and cannot be enforced as such and it remains the prerogative of the State to exercise it at its discretion (para. 29).
13. It would be inconsistent with the principle of state sovereignty for South Africa to assume an obligation that entitles its nationals to demand, and obliges it to take action to ensure, that laws and conduct of a foreign State and its officials meet not only the requirements of the foreign State's own laws, but also the rights that our nationals have under our Constitution (para. 44).
14. Although there is no enforceable right to diplomatic protection, South African citizens are entitled to request South Africa for protection under international law against wrongful acts of a foreign State and the citizen is entitled to have the request considered and responded to appropriately (para. 60).
15. The entitlement to request diplomatic protection flows from citizenship and is part of the constitutional guarantee given by s 3 of the Constitution, which provides that all citizens are equally entitled to the rights, privileges and benefits of citizenship (paras. 67, 178, 188, 236).
16. The government has an obligation to consider the request and deal with it consistently with the Constitution (paras. 67, 192).
17. There may be a duty on government, consistent with its obligations under international law, to take action to protect one of its citizens against a gross abuse of international human rights norms. A request to the government for assistance in such circumstances **[310]** where the evidence is clear would be difficult, and in extreme cases possibly impossible to refuse (para. 69, cf 242).
18. A court cannot tell the government how to make diplomatic interventions for the protection of its nationals (para. 73).
19. A decision as to whether, and if so, what protection should be given, is an aspect of foreign policy that is essentially the function of the executive (para. 77).
20. If government refuses to consider a legitimate request, or deals with it in bad faith or irrationally, a court could require government to deal with the matter properly (paras. 80, 193). This does not mean that courts could substitute their opinion for that of the government or order the government to provide a particular form of diplomatic protection (para. 79).

52. The appellants' request was premised on a "right" to diplomatic protection and not on a right to have a request considered. It was further based on the duty of Government to provide a particular type of diplomatic protection. These demands were, in the light of the Constitutional Court's judgment, ill-founded.[22] A further demand (coupled with a threat of an urgent court application) that Government should withhold all royalties due to the Government of Lesotho under the treaty until the latter had agreed to mediate or arbitrate was not only ill-founded but also presumptuous.

53. I have at the outset of this judgment set out the advice given to the President.[23] From this (and further documentation attached to the answering affidavit) it appears that the Government acted within the framework of the principles of the *Kaunda* judgment: Government knew that the appellants did not have a "right" at international law; it recognised the fact that the Constitution might impact on the matter; it recognised the appellants' right to have a request considered; it was acutely aware of the appellants' serious attack on the Lesotho judiciary as evidenced by the first letter of request; and it realised that it had to make a policy decision bearing in mind what it called the sensitive relationship between the two countries. (Such decisions are always political and the prime consideration remains the relationship with the defendant State[24] and the grounds for refusing to act may be unrelated to the particular case.)[25] The Government obtained legal advice from different persons; it held meetings with Mr van Zyl and his delegation of lawyers and international legal experts; inter- and intra-departmental memoranda [311] were prepared; the Government considered the request carefully over a period of time; and it made a policy decision—first by the Deputy Minister, then by the Minister and, eventually, by the President himself who twice considered the matter.

54. Patel J dealt with the facts correctly and fairly there is no need to redo a job done well. Once again the appellants' position shifted in the replying affidavit. The justification for the new case was the fact that they did not have the Government's internal documents when the application was launched. The answer to this is that had they bothered to follow Uniform Rule 53, they would have had the documents before the answering affidavit was filed; they would have been entitled to

---

[22] The argument submitted at the end of the proceedings was that the appellants have an unwritten constitutional right to diplomatic protection and that Government has an unwritten duty to provide it. It is in conflict with the main submission that the appellants have a right to submit a request and have a right that the request should be properly considered.

[23] Because the President made the ultimate decision the preceding decisions were subsumed and do not require separate consideration.

[24] Dugard, *International Law: A South African Perspective* 3rd edn at 290.

[25] *Kaunda* v. *President of the RSA (2)* 2004 (10) BCLR 1009 (CC) para. 23.

amplify their founding affidavit; and the case would have proceeded in an orderly manner and without complications.

55. The appellants argue that the Government was not entitled to introduce a "new" reason during a judicial review, the new reason being the reliance on policy considerations. This reason was not mentioned to the appellants in the preceding correspondence. The first answer is that had the appellants followed Rule 53, the Government would have disclosed the policy reason. The second answer is that the case on which the appellants rely for the principle that an organ of State is not entitled to raise new reasons for an administrative decision in an answering affidavit was one where the new reasons were *ex post facto* reasons and, accordingly, not the true reasons for the decision.[26] The third answer is that the English line of cases[27] on which the principle is based applies where there is a statutory duty to give reasons (which is not the case in this instance because the decision is not covered by PAJA). A court is entitled to admit evidence that elucidates an administrative decision. In any event, Government had sufficient reason for not disclosing the policy considerations: international relations by their very nature are confidential.

56. There are a number of subsidiary points that have no merit. For instance, it is said that the evidence of Mr Pahad that the President received and accepted advice amounts to hearsay. Then there are "new" points, some raised in the reply and others in the heads. These include allegations of mala fides, a denial that the relations between the two countries are indeed sensitive, complaints of unequal treatment and the violation of the right to equal provision of diplomatic protection.

The Mandamus Sought

57. The prayer for an order requiring Government to afford the appellants diplomatic protection appears to be an independent prayer, and not conditional on the success of the review application. Whether this relief could be sought independently is an issue that need not be **[312]** decided. At this stage of the judgment I merely wish to mention that the founding affidavit did not spell out what is required of Government although, as stated, the appellants insisted in the correspondence that Government had to mediate or litigate in international *fora*. The replying affidavit dealt with the matter in some detail. It was

---

[26] *Jicama 17 (Pty) Ltd* v. *West Coast District Municipality* 2006 (1) SA 116 (C) at para. 12. The court nevertheless dealt with the additional reasons and found them bad.

[27] Discussed in *R* v. *Westminster City Council, ex parte Ermakov* [1996] 2 All ER 302 (CA), a case quoted in *Jicama* (supra).

no longer a matter of diplomatic protection—the appellants sought "effective" diplomatic protection in line with the demand set out in the correspondence.

58. The notice of appeal filed in this Court recited the relief sought in the notice of motion and, once again, gave no indication of what order was sought. Appellants' heads of argument were, however, of a different order. Government must be ordered to "demand" the payment of compensation. Should this demand not be met, Government must "require" of the Government of Lesotho to submit to international arbitration or to adjudication before the International Court of Justice. And, finally, if adequate compensation is not paid within 90 days, the Government of the RSA must pay these claims as constitutional damages.

59. The order now sought is procedurally out of order (the claim for constitutional damages was not anticipated in nor does it reasonably arise from the founding affidavit); it flies in the face of the *Kaunda* principle that a court cannot tell the Government how to conduct foreign affairs and make diplomatic interventions; and it ignores the fact that the Government of Lesotho has stated repeatedly and explicitly that it will not engage in international dispute settlement (its consent is required for both arbitration and engaging the International Court of Justice).

The Interface between National and International Law

60. A major problem with the appellants' case is the way they seamlessly move between national and international law, depending on what is convenient at any particular moment. They recognise that their application is based on South African municipal law because international law does not recognise a right of a national to diplomatic protection. However, when arguing their entitlement under local law, they rely on international law principles that deal with the power of States to provide diplomatic protection. Although customary international law is part of our law,[28] it is conceptually difficult to understand how an international law rule dealing with one relationship (State : State) can be transformed into a local rule regulating another relationship (citizen : State).

61. One example suffices. The right to ask for diplomatic protection derives from s 3 of the Constitution as an aspect of citizenship—and nothing else.[29] How then can the Lesotho companies claim diplomatic

---

[28] Constitution s 232.
[29] Gerhard Erasmus and Lyle Davidson, "Do South Africans Have a Right to Diplomatic Protection?" (2000) 25 *SAYIL* 113 at 130.

protection from Government? The appellants seek the answer in a **[313]** proposal of the International Law Commission[30] that the State of nationality of shareholders (the RSA) in a corporation is entitled to exercise protection "on behalf of" such shareholders (Mr van Zyl and the two Trusts) in the case of an injury to the corporation (Swissborough) if the corporation had, at the time of the injury, the nationality of the delinquent State (Lesotho) and incorporation under the "law" of Lesotho was required as a precondition of doing business there. Even if one accepts that this is a rule of international and, therefore, South African law, I fail to see how this "rule" can determine the corporate appellants' entitlement to diplomatic protection under municipal law.

62. Having said this, it remains necessary to consider whether Government is entitled in terms of international law to grant the appellants diplomatic protection. Unless the appellants are able to establish such a right vesting in Government their application has to fail for this further reason, both in relation to the review and the mandamus.

63. The appellants argue that they only have to make out a prima facie case of entitlement but this understates the position. An applicant must make out a clear case for a mandamus or a review. Whether an applicant has a right is a matter of substantive law and whether that right is clear depends on evidence. But the test is not really germane for present purposes. In this case the material and admissible facts are mainly common cause and the general principle applies that in motion proceedings the case has to be determined on the respondent's version.

64. It is necessary to state a number of trite international law principles in order to understand the debate that follows.

- The appellants are not subjects at international law and have, accordingly, no rights at international law.[31]
- Aliens in a foreign country are subject to the laws of that country to the same extent as the nationals of that country.
- Property rights are determined by municipal law. The questions whether any rights have been granted, exist or whether they have terminated are all questions that have to be determined according to local law:

---

[30] "Seventh Report on Diplomatic Protection" by John Dugard, Special Rapporteur (7 March 2006). The appellants laid great score on this report as setting out international law in spite of the fact that it has not yet been adopted. In what follows I shall assume in favour of the appellants the correctness of the supposition.

[31] Dugard, *International Law: A South African Perspective* 3rd edn and Booysen, *Principles of International Trade Law as a Monistic System* deal with most of the propositions that follow.

In principle, the property rights and the contractual rights of individuals depend in every State on municipal law and fall therefore more particularly within the jurisdiction of municipal tribunals.[32]

- [314] There is no universally acceptable concept of property rights because the Western concept based on Roman law principles does not apply everywhere. According to African customary law, as expressed in the Lesotho Constitution, land belongs to the nation, in this case the Basotho Nation, and all interests in land are granted by the nation, represented by the King and the Chiefs. Chinese law, for instance, has its own complexities.[33] The finding by Patel J that there is no support for the thesis that international law recognises the protection of property (at least in the Roman-Dutch legal sense) as a basic human right appears to have merit.[34]
- Contracts concluded between States and aliens are also governed by municipal law.[35]
- Contracts between States and aliens may be "internationalised", i.e., the contracts may be made subject to international law principles and international adjudication by agreement, expressly or by necessary implication.[36]
- Aliens are entitled to request the country of their nationality to protect them against a breach of international minimum standards such as the breach of a basic human right. These basic rights are defined in international human rights instruments:

    It is an elementary principle of international law that a State is entitled to protect its subject, when injured by acts contrary to international law committed by another State, from which they have been unable to obtain satisfaction through ordinary channels. By taking up the case of one of its subjects and by resorting to diplomatic protection or international judicial proceedings on his behalf, a State is in reality asserting its own rights—its rights to ensure, in the person of its subject, respect for the rules of international law.[37]

- A sending State that is willing to afford diplomatic protection can only do so if: (a) the victim has the nationality of the sending

---

[32] *Panevezys–Saldutiskis Railway Case (Estonia v. Lithuania)* 1939 PCIJ Reports Series A/B No 76 at 18.

[33] Cf *International Marine Transport SA v. MV "Le Cong" and Guangzhou Ocean Shipping Co.* (Case 080/05) unreported SCA judgment of 23 November 2005 at para. 9.

[34] Cf Annemarieke Vermeer-Künzli, "*A Matter of Interest: Diplomatic Protection and State Responsibility Erga Omnes*" 46 (2007) *International & Comparative Law Quarterly* 550.

[35] *Serbian and Brazilian Loans Case* [1929] PCIJ Series A No 20/21 at 41.

[36] *Revere Copper and Brass Inc. v. Overseas Private Investment Corp.* (1978) 56 ILR 258 at 275.

[37] *Mavrommatis Palestine Concessions* 1924 PCIJ Series A No 2.

State; (b) the victim has exhausted local remedies in the errant jurisdiction; and (c) an international delict whereby the victim has been injured by an unlawful act imputable to the other State has been committed.[38]
- An international delict presupposes the existence of a right because [315] without a right there cannot be a wrong.[39]
- A State may confiscate or expropriate the property of an alien provided it is in accordance with a law of general application, in the public interest and prompt and adequate compensation is paid.
- The responsible State is under an obligation to make full reparation for the injury caused by an internationally wrongful act.

International Rights and Wrongs

65. Before there can be an international wrong there must be an international right. In this case the appellants have to show that the Rampai mineral lease was subject to international law, i.e., that it had been internationalised. (Although I am limiting this part of the discussion to the Rampai lease, what follows applies equally to the other four leases save for the fact that their invalidity has not yet been determined by the Lesotho courts.)

66. As Patel J held, and is apparent from the terms of the lease discussed earlier, the Rampai lease was entered into in Lesotho by the Government of Lesotho with a Lesotho company under the Lesotho mining laws in respect of Lesotho diamond rights. Therefore, its validity had to be determined under Lesotho law by Lesotho courts.

67. It is important to emphasise that this is not a case of expropriation or confiscation of existing rights. The issue is whether rights had come into existence according to local law that requires compliance with prescribed formalities. All the authorities quoted by the appellants, and there were many, deal with a situation where a State that had agreed not to amend its laws in order to undo an international contract (so-called stabilisation clauses), reneges on its undertaking. This is not such a case. A State is as much bound by its own laws as are its citizens and I do not know of a principle whereby a State, when entering into contract with a corporation with alien shareholders, can ignore municipal law that governs that type of contract.[40]

---

[38] "Seventh Report on Diplomatic Protection" art. 1; Gerhard Erasmus and Lyle Davidson, "Do South Africans Have a Right to Diplomatic Protection?" (2000) 25 *SAYIL* 113 at 130.

[39] "Draft Articles on State Responsibility" provisionally adopted by the International Law Commission.

[40] Cf the approach of the arbitrator, Sir Herbert Sisnett, in the *Shufeldt Claim* (*United States of America* v. *Guatemala*) II RIAA 1080.

68. For the sake of completeness I proceed to consider whether the Government of Lesotho had otherwise agreed to internationalise the agreement, i.e., agreed that its validity would be determined according to international law and by an international tribunal. This depends on an interpretation of the lease, i.e., whether there are any tacit terms to that effect.

69. The appellants argue that the lease was not covered by the general principle that agreements between governments and aliens are governed by one or other municipal law[41] because (they submit) these leases were long-term international economic agreements or bilateral investment [316] treaties.[42] Such leases may by virtue of their "character" import international law by implication. In this regard they rely on the opinion of Prof. Dupuy referred to in the *Revere Copper* case.[43]

In this latter respect he refers to such characteristics of these agreements as their broad subject matter, their introduction into developing countries of investments and technical assistance, their importance in the development of the country concerned, their long duration implying "close cooperation between the State and the contracting party" and "requiring permanent installations as well as the acceptance of exclusive responsibilities by the investor", and the close association of the foreign contractor "with the realization of the economic and social progress of the host country". Because of the required cooperation between the contracting party and the State "and the magnitude of the investments to which it agreed", the contractual nature of the legal relation "is intended to bring about an equilibrium between the goal of the general interest sought by such relation and the profitability which is necessary for the pursuit of the task entrusted to the private enterprise".

70. The appellants' argument is opportunistic. The lease had hardly any of the characteristics referred to in the cited passage. Apart from the fact that the lease was of a relatively long duration, there was no "required cooperation" between the parties; there was no obligation to introduce any foreign investment (unless the R13,000 per annum can be regarded as foreign investment) or technical assistance; there is no evidence that the lease was important for the development of Lesotho; and there was no requirement of permanent installations or the acceptance of exclusive responsibilities by Swissborough.

---

[41] *Serbian and Brazilian Loans Case* [1929] PCIJ Series A No 20/21 at 41.
[42] See in general Wenhau Shan, "Is Calvo Dead?" 55 (2007) *American Journal of Comparative Law* 123. The appellants have mentioned concessions as another exception. Exactly what must be understood under a concession is unclear. It may refer to a unilateral administrative grant, which is not the case in this instance: *Amco-Asia Corp.* v. *Republic of Indonesia* (1985) 24 ILM 1022 at 1034.
[43] *Revere Copper and Brass Inc.* v. *Overseas Private Investment Corp.* (1978) 56 ILR 258 at 275.

71. Because the Rampai lease was invalid ab initio,[44] whatever the Government of Lesotho did by cancellation or revocation to undo the putative lease was without effect because there was nothing to undo. The acts of the Government of Lesotho at the time may have been wrong in the moral sense but they were not wrongful (at least not with full knowledge of the facts).

72. The appellants furthermore rely on the arbitration clause in the lease. According to the argument the clause, in spite of its minimalist terms, has far-reaching consequences: because it does not say that Lesotho law applies and because it does not say that the arbitration was to be a local one, it follows from the fact that Swissborough had foreign shareholders that international law applied and that the arbitration had [317] to be an international one. The argument need merely be stated to be rejected.

73. A related argument concerns the Convention on the Settlement of Investment Disputes between States and Nationals of other States (the Washington Convention of 18 March 1965), referred to as ICSID. The Government of Lesotho acceded to this Convention and enacted the Arbitration (International Investment Disputes) Act 23 of 1974. The appellants argue that because of this the Government of Lesotho is bound to submit the dispute to ICSID arbitration. The Convention (art. 25) provides that the jurisdiction of this arbitral court "extends to any legal dispute arising directly out of an investment, between a Contracting State... and a national of another Contracting State, which the parties to the dispute consent in writing to submit to the Centre".

74. Without delving any deeper into this murky argument it suffices to state that South Africa is not "another contracting party" to the Convention;[45] that the lease was not an investment contract; that Swissborough was not a South African national; and that the parties did not agree—in writing or otherwise—to submit to this form of arbitration.

75. There remains the issue concerning the so-called extension leases. According to Mr van Zyl, the Government of Lesotho undertook to extend the terms of the four leases in settlement of their dispute. He, in turn, agreed to cancel the Rampai lease. The extension leases were also to be subject to the provisions of the [Mining] Rights Act and required the

---

[44] *Swissborough Diamond Mines (Pty) Ltd.* v. *LHDA* 2000 Lesotho LR 432 (CA).

[45] The "failure" of Government to accede to the Convention became another bone of contention. The appellants argue that this violates their right to access to courts or other tribunals under s 34 of the Constitution. Apart from the fact that the respondents were never called upon to justify this neglect, the argument has no merit. The appellants had their days in court. They lost. Now they want another court. That is not what the Constitution guarantees.

same formalities as the original leases. The extension leases were never signed. The Government of Lesotho did not sign, why is irrelevant. Mr van Zyl says that he refused to sign because someone demanded a bribe in spite of an anti-corruption clause in the draft agreement. His refusal was noble but how this entitles him to relief in relation to non-existent leases is not understood. A promise to contract is not a contract.[46]

76. I accordingly conclude that the appellants did not establish that they had any rights and, accordingly, that no international wrong could have been committed against them which would have entitled the Government to afford diplomatic protection. It is, however, necessary to say something about the appellants' subtext. Their real complaint is that the Rampai judgment amounted to an expropriation without compensation committed by an organ of State (the courts) for which the Government of Lesotho was responsible; and this was an international wrong because of a denial of justice by the Lesotho courts.

[318] 77. I have already shown that this was not part of the appellants' case and that the underlying requirement of the existence of an international right is absent. As the appellants correctly accept, they have to show a fundamental failure of justice.[47] The main thrust of the argument was, however, directed at the merits of the judgment and because the appellants believe that the courts have reached a wrong conclusion they assume that the courts must have been biased, another fanciful proposition. But there are other attacks, which I shall mention briefly to illustrate the lack of merit of the appellants' case.

78. They allege that the Court of Appeal was manipulated because it consisted of acting judges and the permanent judges of the court did not sit in the matter.[48] Because this issue was not raised on the papers it was not possible for Government to respond with evidence. Nevertheless, the appellants knew (according to Mr van Zyl) a month in advance, of the composition of the bench. They did not complain. If they had a ground for complaint they were obliged to raise it then. They chose not to do so, maybe because four of the five judges were retired South African judges. (The fifth, according to the published report, was a permanent Lesotho appeal judge.) As far as the permanent judges are concerned, we know that Mr van Zyl was of the view that the President of the court

---

[46] Cf *Ondombo Beleggings (Edms) Bpk* v. *Minister of Mineral and Energy Affairs* 1991 (4) SA 718 (A).
[47] *Loewen* v. *USA* (ICSID case ARB (AF)/98/3) (2003) 42 ILM 811.
[48] The Court of Appeal judges are mostly part-time judges drawn from the ranks of retired South African judges and practising advocates. On the appointment of acting judges to hear specific cases see Morné Olivier, "The Appointment of Acting Judges in South Africa and Lesotho" 27 (2006) *Obiter* 554.

was disqualified to hear the matter.[49] Another member of the court (as appears from the law reports) acted as counsel for the Government of Lesotho in the revocation appeal and was therefore disqualified to sit.[50] There may have been similar explanations why the other two judges did not sit.

79. The appellants also complain about the amount of security they had to provide for the Rampai appeal and say that it was many times higher than the amount set for the revocation appeal. We do not know what evidence was before that court in relation to both matters but one could guess that security for an appeal on a 58-day trial and one for an appeal on an application could differ materially. In any event, the determination of security did not lead to a denial of justice because the appellants were [319] able to provide and did provide security.

80. The third point under this heading relates to the fact that the appellants allege that they discovered new evidence after judgment. They wrote a letter to the President of the court, insisting that he revoke the judgment. His refusal is said to be yet further evidence of the bias of the Lesotho courts.

Nationality[51]

81. I have therefore found that Government is not entitled to intervene on behalf of the appellants because no international delict had been committed. The claim of the corporate appellants and the trusts has to fail on an additional ground, namely the issue of nationality or citizenship.[52]

82. It is necessary to distinguish between an international wrongful act that causes "direct injury to the rights of shareholders as such" (in which event the State of nationality of the shareholders is entitled to exercise diplomatic protection in respect of its nationals) in contradistinction to injury to the rights "of the corporation itself" (where that State is not entitled to act on behalf of its national shareholders). This

---

[49] This is based on the allegation that the President, when he sat on the revocation appeal, was a director of the Development Bank of SA. The complaint is that he wrote the judgment dealing with the interdict (where Swissborough was not successful) but there is no complaint about him concurring with the favourable judgment on the invalidity of the revocation order. Swissborough had a local remedy which was not pursued: *R* v. *Bow Street Metropolitan Stipendiary Magistrate, ex parte Pinochet Ugarte (no 2)* [1999] 1 All ER 577 (HL).

[50] This illustrates the importance of procedural rules and the danger of relying on Mr van Zyl's assertions, whether on affidavit, in the annexed documents or during argument.

[51] Cf *Nottebohm Case (Liechtenstein* v. *Guatemala)* (1955) 22 ILR 349 (ICJ).

[52] "Seventh Report on Diplomatic Protection" arts. 3 and 9. F. S. Dunn, *The Protection of Nationals: A Study in the Application of International Law* (1932) 27-8.

case concerns a delict against the companies and not one against the shareholders "as such".[53]

83. As mentioned earlier, the appellants rely on draft art. 11 contained in the International Law Commission report. It bears quoting:

The State of nationality of the shareholders in a corporation shall not be entitled to exercise diplomatic protection on behalf of such shareholders in the case of an injury to the corporation unless:

(a) ...
(b) The corporation had, at the time of the injury, the nationality of the State alleged to be responsible for causing injury, and incorporation under the law of the latter State was required by it as a precondition for doing business there.

84. The shareholder appellants rely on art. 11 because the Government of Lesotho required the incorporation of Swissborough in Lesotho as a precondition for entering into the mining leases. Patel J, however, found that art. 11 does not reflect customary international law—it is but a recommendation that awaits acceptance by the international community. I tend to agree with his reasoning, which is partly based on the **[320]** *Barcelona Traction* case,[54] but do not find it necessary to decide the issue because the shareholders' claim fails for reasons stated and that follow.

85. The corporate appellants cannot rely on the rule as formulated. The rule is expressed in favour of shareholders who are nationals of the sending State, and not in favour of the corporation itself. Article 11 is not and does not purport to be an exception to the nationality rule (art. 3). (It is different with stateless persons and refugees; they are expressly stated to be exceptions to art. 3.)

86. Another aspect of the nationality rule is the continuing nationality rule. According to the amended proposal of the International Law Commission, a State is only entitled to exercise diplomatic protection in respect of a person who was a national of that State continuously from the date of the injury to date of claim.[55] As Patel J held, the cession by the corporate appellants to Burmilla Trust disqualified both the

---

[53] "Seventh Report on Diplomatic Protection" art. 12. See also *Standard Oil Co. Tanker* (1926) 2 RIAA 781 at 782 and *Agrotexim v. Greece* [1996] 21 ECRR 250 (ECHR).

[54] *The Barcelona Traction, Light and Power Co. Ltd (Belgium* v. *Spain)* 1970 ICJ 3 to which must now be added *Case concerning Ahmadou Sadio Diallo (Republic of Guinea* v. *Democratic Republic of the Congo)* Preliminary Objections 2007 ICJ General List no 103.

[55] "Seventh Report on Diplomatic Protection" art. 5 comments. *Loewen v. USA* (ICSID case no ARB(AF)/98/3) (2003) 42 ILM 811.

corporate appellants and the Trust from diplomatic protection.[56] The whole object of diplomatic protection is to protect a national against a wrong committed against that national. Someone who has not been wronged cannot, by virtue of a cession, become a victim. The cessionary may be entitled to the proceeds of any claim but that does not transform the cessionary into a victim. Likewise, a cedent cannot be entitled to diplomatic protection in relation to a right which that person no longer holds. It follows from this that the nationality rule disqualified the Government from affording any diplomatic protection to all the appellants save, possibly, Mr van Zyl and the family trust.

Exhaustion of Local Remedies

87. There is yet another reason why Government is not entitled to grant the appellants diplomatic protection. A State may not bring a claim for diplomatic protection before the injured person has exhausted all local legal remedies unless these do not provide a reasonable effective redress or there is undue delay attributable to the State concerned.[57]

88. The wrong, as defined in the founding affidavit, was the cancellation [321] and revocation of the mining leases without payment of compensation: initially the Commissioner of Mines cancelled the leases and they were then cancelled by means of the revocation order. (The Rampai judgment did not cancel any lease; it merely held that the Rampai lease was void from the beginning.)

89. It is common cause that these two acts were wrongful. This the Lesotho courts have held and the Government of Lesotho conceded in relation to the acts of the Commissioner and accepted by abiding by the revocation judgment. It means that the Lesotho courts have rectified the wrongs by declaring the acts void and without effect. One of the reasons for the existence of the "local remedy" rule is that it is necessary that the State where the violation occurred should have an opportunity to redress it by its own means, within the framework of its own domestic legal system.[58]

---

[56] The appellants rely on a report of the International Law Association (2006) according to which the rule may be dispensed with "in the context of global and financial markets". Why this possible exception is mentioned I fail to understand. The appellants also argue that the rule does not apply to a continuing wrong. There was no continuing wrong in this case although there may have been a series of wrongs.

[57] "Seventh Report on Diplomatic Protection" arts. 14 and 16. The other exceptions are not relevant. *Panevezys–Saldutiskis Railway Case (Estonia* v. *Lithuania)* 1939 PCIJ Reports Series A/B no 76. This rule presupposes the existence of an international delict and compliance with the nationality rule.

[58] *Interhandel Case (Switzerland* v. *United States)* 1959 ICJ 6 at 27, quoted with approval in the *Case concerning Ahmadou Sadio Diallo (Republic of Guinea* v. *Democratic Republic of the Congo)* Preliminary Objections 2007 ICJ General List no 103 at para. 42.

If this principle is applied the violation by the Government of Lesotho has been redressed within the framework of its domestic legal system. The appellants are not entitled to hark back, resurrect the past and ignore the supervening facts.

90. If the cancellation and revocation of the four leases was illegal, Swissborough would in principle be entitled to damages. As mentioned, Swissborough cancelled these leases and instituted action for breach of contract against the Government of Lesotho but the action has not been pursued by Swissborough.

91. The appellants argue that their acceptance of the repudiation must be discounted because they were forced by the actions of the Government of Lesotho to cancel the four leases. The argument is disingenuous because if that were the case they would also have had to cancel the Rampai lease, something they studiously avoided doing. Their second argument is that they cannot succeed in the case because of the Court of Appeal judgment on the Rampai lease. The argument lacks substance: that judgment is not *res judicata* in respect of the four leases and the appellants are entitled to use the "new" evidence, which they say they have since uncovered, to show that the Rampai judgment was wrongly decided. Furthermore, if they never had any valid mineral rights (on the supposition that Rampai was decided correctly) they can hardly have any cause of complaint.

92. Another claim to which their request relates is the claim for damages for the loss and destruction of Swissborough's plant. The cause of this is said (without any evidence) to have been unlawful acts committed by servants or agents of the Government of Lesotho. This cause of action, as mentioned, forms part of the litigation, which has been pending in Lesotho for more than ten years. There is no valid **[322]** explanation why these actions have not been pursued and local remedies exhausted.

Conclusion

93. The conclusion is therefore that the appeal must be dismissed with costs. The employment by the respondents of three counsel was fully justified.

94. Order: The appeal is dismissed with costs, including the costs consequent on the employment of three counsel.

ANNEX

Letter from the attorneys of the Government of Lesotho to the attorneys of the appellants dated 19 November 2001.

Dear Sir,

Re: *Settlement Offer in the Matter between the State of Lesotho and the Swissborough Group, Josias van Zyl, the Josias van Zyl Family Trust and the Burmilla Trust*

1. *Introduction*

1.1 We have now had an opportunity to study the voluminous documents in which your clients' offer of settlement has been set out and motivated and to consult with our client in that regard. The documents occupy some 1,600 pages in all and range from the two-page document left by your clients' counsel, Mr H. Louw, with the Deputy Attorney-General, Mr K. R. K. Tampi, on or about 2 May 2001, in which payment of M300,000.00 plus costs, coupled with some conditions is called for; to the "Financial Claims against the Kingdom of Lesotho and Claims in respect of the Extension Leases" handed to Mr Tampi on 3 May 2001, and five volumes of attachments thereto subsequently received; the "Proposed All in Settlement", dated 21 May 2001 and signed by Mr Louw, claiming M79,941,943.00, plus interest thereon; and, finally, the Supplementary Memorandum of 6 August 2001, explaining why the dispute must be settled—or adjudicated upon if settlement is not reached—according to the rules of Public International Law.

1.2 No useful purpose will be served, in view of the decision on the offer which has been reached by our client, in debating the various arguments advanced on behalf of your clients as to their entitlement to compensation. But there are a number of premises put forward for such arguments which are, to the knowledge of your clients, so fundamentally inaccurate that we can only believe that they are intended for readers who do not have knowledge of the facts, and must be corrected:

[323] 2. *Expropriation without compensation*
The oft repeated justification for the claims made on behalf of your clients is that their rights were expropriated without the payment of compensation. The following are the facts in this regard:

2.1 It is correct that the Revocation of Specified Mining Leases Order, No 7 of 1992, purported to deprive SDM and its associated companies, without compensation, of their rights in the mining leases they held. That legislation was passed by the military government which succeeded the military government of General Justin Lekhanya which had granted the leases. However, that legislation was struck down as unlawful by the High Court of Lesotho whose judgment was confirmed by the Lesotho Court of Appeal on 13 January 1995.

2.2 By the time the courts' judgments were delivered SDM and its subsidiaries (save for Rampai Diamonds (Pty) Limited) had already, on 15 March 1993, cancelled four of the mining lease agreements pertaining to them on the grounds that the Government of Lesotho ("GOL") had unlawfully repudiated its obligations under such agreements, *inter alia*, by passing the Revocation Order aforementioned.

2.3 Consequently, as far as four of the five leases in question are concerned there is no longer any question of expropriation without compensation. Expropriation by the Revocation Order was declared unlawful and there has been no subsequent expropriation. It is SDM and its subsidiary companies who terminated the leases by electing to cancel them and claim damages (as to which, see paragraph 3 below).

2.4 As to the Rampai lease, this was indeed, subsequent to the Revocation Order, expropriated. It lies largely in the catchment area of the Katse Dam and was expropriated under provisions providing for expropriation against payment of full compensation, appearing in the Lesotho Highlands Development Authority (Amendment) Act, No 5 of 1995. (It was to the introduction of this legislation that the Minister of Natural Resources was referring in the Memorandum to Cabinet quoted at pp. 18/19 of your clients' memorandum dated 6 August 2001.)

2.5 However, that Act provides for compensation (by LHDA) only to the holder of a "duly granted and executed mineral right registered in terms of the Deeds Registry Act 1967". Consequently the finding of the High Court and the Court of Appeal that the Rampai lease was not lawfully granted prevents SDM and Rampai from claiming compensation from LHDA. But it is not without remedy (see paragraph 4.3 below).

3. *Claimants have exhausted their remedies in the courts of Lesotho*
In paragraph 3.8 of your clients' Supplementary Memorandum of 6 August 2001 it is said:

> This also demonstrates that all judicial remedies have been exhausted. This requirement for diplomatic protection to be exercised has been met.

The averment that Claimants have exhausted their remedies in the courts of Lesotho is exactly contrary to the facts.

3.1 As to the Motsoku, Patisang, Orange and Motete lease areas, under Case No CIV/T/213/96, SDM and the four subsidiaries just mentioned instituted action against the Government of [324] Lesotho for damages amounting, in all, to M958,702,281.00 on 20 May 1996.

3.2 Further particulars to the claim were requested and supplied, and a Plea was filed on behalf of Defendant on 9 October 1996. The pleadings have been closed and the matter is ripe for hearing.

4. *As to the Rampai lease*

4.1 On 23 July 1996, SDM and Rampai filed a claim for compensation under the provisions of section 46A of the LHDA Order, as amended by Act 6 of 1995, in the amount of M521,846,548.00.

4.2 As pointed out in paragraph 2.5 above the provision for compensation by LHDA applies only to a lease duly granted and records have held that the lease in question was not lawfully granted to SDM or Rampai.

However, there is nothing to prevent SDM and Rampai from instituting action against GOL in the courts of Lesotho, claiming such damages as are alleged to have been suffered.

5. *Loss of confidence in the courts of Lesotho*
It is the courts of Lesotho which struck down, at the instance of your clients, the legislation which is repeatedly invoked as justification for turning to other *fora* for assistance, namely the Revocation of Specified Mining Leases Order, No 7 of 1992.

5.1 In a memorandum submitted to the Government of South Africa by SDM (before the result of its application to strike down the Revocation Order was known) and quoted in your clients' Supplementary Memorandum on settlement of 6 August 2001 it is said that:

> SDM has not yet exhausted the available judicial remedies in Lesotho. As the Lesotho Court of Appeal has a high reputation both for competence and independence it cannot seriously be suggested that if the application pending before Cullinan CJ, fails, it would be "obviously futile" to appeal against such decision.

Of course, not only were your clients successful before Cullinan CJ, but the Court of Appeal upheld his judgment.

5.2 Now that a judgment goes the other way, it is said by your clients that the Judges of Appeal were biased and their findings one-sided. In correspondence Mr van Zyl has gone further, insulting the President of the Court of Appeal and the present Chief Justice, who set aside the Rampai lease and whose decision was confirmed on appeal.

5.3 There is no foundation to these scurrilous remarks. The five judges who sat on the appeal, four of whom have held high judicial office in other Southern African countries and do not live in Lesotho, behaved throughout with perfect propriety. The distasteful accusations which you have seen fit to forward in this regard are rejected.

6. *The settlement offer*
Our client has carefully considered the settlement offer presented to it and has decided that it is not prepared to accept it. Naturally, the factual distortions dealt with above have contributed to that decision. Some additional considerations are mentioned below.

[325] 6.1 *The financial averments upon which the offer is based*:
Fundamental to the offer of settlement is that your clients have spent in the region of M18 million in developing the lease areas. Examination of the figures put forward in that regard, and knowledge of what occurred in the lease areas, gives rise to what appears to our client to be a well-founded

suspicion that they are fabricated. No original vouchers bearing witness to the expenditure allegedly incurred have ever been presented. The figures are all taken from financial statements prepared in respect of each company by a firm of chartered accountants, Messrs Glutz and Hlasa, practising in Maseru.

However, it is not Messrs Glutz and Hlasa who substantiate the correctness of the statements, but a Mr A. N. Walker, a chartered accountant conducting a one-man practice in the town of Potchefstroom in the Republic of South Africa. Mr Walker states that he has verified your clients' expenditure "from the audited accounts prepared by Messrs Glutz and Hlasa". That, in our client's respectful view, hardly constitutes reliable impartial substantiation of the claim.

6.2 *The reliability of Mr J. van Zyl, the chief source of information for the claim:*

The impression is created throughout the submissions made on behalf of your clients that one is dealing here with people and bodies of substance who have contributed very large amounts of money to mining development in Lesotho. That is misleading.

The driving and controlling force behind all the Plaintiffs is Mr Josias van Zyl. In the papers opposing the application for an interdict by SDM some idea of the chequered career of Mr van Zyl is provided, together with details of the trail of debt which his enterprises have left. Our clients have reason to doubt that the millions of Maloti it is claimed were spent were indeed either spent or, to the extent that expenditure may have been incurred, paid for by any of the Claimants. Mr van Zyl's word is not considered acceptable and it is felt that the only way to test the essentially unsupported contentions about expenditure upon which your clients' claims rest is by reference to proper documentary proof through the process of discovery for which the Court Rules provide, and by cross-examination of the witnesses who are called to substantiate them, chief of whom must be Mr van Zyl.

Defences to the claim:

The submissions motivating the settlement are based on the premise that no defence exists to the claims. That is not so. On the contrary, the latest information regarding the cession of the claims to the Burmilla Trust give rise to a further defence which will be raised in an amendment to the Plea in the aforementioned action instituted by SDM and four of its subsidiaries.

6.3 *Government's resistance to corruption*:

This elected Government has demonstrated, by word and deed, that it is implacably opposed to corruption. The manner in which the leases giving rise to your clients' claims were awarded, especially that in the Rampai area, by the Military Government of General Lekhanya give[s] rise to grave suspicion **[326]** of impropriety. Not only were none of the area chiefs consulted (the reason why the lease was set aside) but General Lekhanya did not provide a satisfactory explanation, when called as your clients' witness, as to how his government came to award a mining lease for, effectively, 15 years, in an area which was to be flooded in five years' time. On the information available to Government, no mining was done in that area until work on the Katse dam was well advanced, when there was an attempt to hold Government to ransom by a court interdict.

By the same token, while huge amounts are claimed for expenses and lost profits, no cent was ever paid by way of royalties to Government by any of your clients, who alleged that no profit had been made and, indeed, that the leases granted to them could not be viably mined without further rights to large tracts of land.

It is true that Government is not in possession of hard proof of corruption. But it is felt that the circumstances giving rise to these claims are such that they should be resisted and thoroughly tested. And it is Government's view that the best way to test them is by subjecting them to scrutiny in open court.

7. We have dealt herein with only the most glaring examples of misinformation contained in the documents put forward and some of the reasons for rejecting the proposals therein. As part of settlement negotiations, what is contained in that offer and this response is privileged from disclosure in further proceedings. But in case your clients should not abide by that rule of law we record that apart from what is set out herein, none of the averments made on your clients' behalf in the documents in which the settlement offer is contained are admitted.

8. Finally, as to the contention that the claims will be pursued in other *fora*, we are instructed to advise you that if that should occur our client will resist any such attempt to the extent that it may be advised that that is necessary. It is denied that any other forum has jurisdiction in the disputes which exist. Your clients' remedies lie in pursuing the claims already instituted and, if so advised, instituting fresh claims in the courts of Lesotho. (Subject, of course, to our client's right to raise whatever defences are available to it.)

[Reports: 2008 (3) SA 294; [2008] 1 All SA 102 (SCA)]

Diplomatic relations — Diplomatic protection — Applicant requesting diplomatic protection from Government of South Africa against Government of Zimbabwe — Whether applicant entitled to diplomatic protection — Whether State having obligation to provide diplomatic protection — Position under international law — Whether South Africa entitled to afford diplomatic protection — South African Constitution — Responsibility of executive for conducting foreign relations — Discretion of executive with respect to diplomatic relations — Zimbabwean expropriation of farmland — Whether violating international minimum standards

Nationality — Diplomatic protection — Nationality requirement for international delict — Whether nationality rule disqualifying South African Government from affording diplomatic protection to applicant — Applicant sole shareholder in companies incorporated in Zimbabwe — Whether expropriation of property of companies by Zimbabwe capable of giving rise to diplomatic protection by South Africa

Claims — Exhaustion of local remedies — Diplomatic protection — Exhaustion of local remedies rule for international delict — Whether effective local remedies available

Relationship of international law and municipal law — Conduct of foreign relations — Whether justiciable in municipal court — Nature of protection — Whether court entitled to question efficacy of steps taken by South African Government — The law of South Africa

Von Abo v. Republic of South Africa and Others[1]

South Africa, High Court (Transvaal Provincial Division).
29 July 2008

(Prinsloo J)

[1] Before the High Court in the original proceedings, the applicant was represented by Mr P. Hodes SC, Mr A. Katz and Mr M. Du Plessis, instructed by W. J. Herbst, and the respondents by Mr Mtshaulana SC and Mr Sello, instructed by the State Attorney. Before the Constitutional Court, the applicant was represented by Mr Hodes, Mr Katz and Mr Du Plessis and the respondents by Mr P. J. J. de Jager SC, Advocate Mphaga and Mr Sello. In the second hearing before the High Court, the applicant was represented by Mr Hodes and Mr Katz and the respondents by Mr de Jager, Advocate Mphaga and Mr Sello.

Constitutional Court. 5 *June* 2009

(Langa CJ; Moseneke DCJ; Cameron, Mokgoro, Ngcobo, Nkabinde, O'Regan, Sachs, Skweyiya, Van der Westhuizen and Yacoob JJ)

High Court (North Gauteng Division). 5 *February* 2010[2]

(Prinsloo J)

SUMMARY: *The facts*:—The applicant was a South African citizen who had invested in farmland in Zimbabwe. Title to the farms was vested in a number of private companies incorporated in Zimbabwe and a private trust registered there, all of which were controlled by the applicant. The farmland was expropriated without compensation by Zimbabwe, pursuant to a policy of expropriating farms owned by white farmers. The applicant sought the intervention of the Government of the Republic of South Africa, requesting that it exercise its right of diplomatic protection in his case by taking whatever steps were necessary to ensure that Zimbabwe afforded him a proper remedy for the losses he claimed to have suffered. Amongst the action he called for was that South Africa become party to the International Convention on the Settlement of Investment Disputes, 1965 ("the ICSID Convention"). The applicant maintained that he had received no satisfactory answer to his appeals for diplomatic protection. He therefore commenced proceedings against the Republic of South Africa, the President of South Africa and the Ministers for Foreign Affairs, Trade and Development and Justice and Constitutional Development ("the respondents"). The relief sought was orders that the failure to consider and decide upon his request was invalid and unconstitutional, that he had a right to diplomatic protection, that South Africa had a constitutional duty to accord him diplomatic protection and that South Africa should take all necessary steps to ensure that the violation of his rights by Zimbabwe was remedied. He also requested an order that, if such steps were not taken, South Africa be required to pay as damages such amount as he would have been entitled to receive by way of compensation for the violation of his property rights. A request for an order that South Africa become party to the ICSID Convention was abandoned during the proceedings.

The respondents maintained that attempts had been made to secure from the Government of Zimbabwe redress for South African owners of property which had been expropriated by Zimbabwe but that these steps had been unsuccessful. They contended that the right of diplomatic protection under international law could not be exercised in the present case, because the property had been vested in companies and the trust, all of which had the

---

[2] On 4 April 2011 the Supreme Court of Appeal upheld an appeal from the North Gauteng High Court and set aside the Order of 29 July 2008 (except for paragraphs 1 and 7) and the Order of 5 February 2010. This judgment, unavailable when the volume went to press, will be reported in a future volume of the *International Law Reports*.

nationality of Zimbabwe, and that, even if South Africa had had the right to exercise diplomatic protection, it was under no obligation to do so.

Held (by the High Court on 29 July 2008):—The applicant was entitled to an order for relief.

(1) Most of the evidence filed by the respondents was hearsay and therefore inadmissible. The record showed that the applicant had repeatedly attempted without any success to secure the intervention of the respondents with the Government of Zimbabwe. The respondents had given no adequate explanation of their failure to protect the applicant (paras. 39-53 and 94-132).

(2) Although the applicant had abandoned his prayer for specific relief regarding South African participation in the ICSID Convention, the consistent failure on the part of the respondents to make South Africa a party to the ICSID Convention or to conclude a bilateral investment treaty with Zimbabwe to protect South African nationals investing in Zimbabwe was relevant to an assessment of the rationality of their refusal to accord diplomatic protection (paras. 26-42).

(3) It was a principle of international law that a State was entitled to exercise diplomatic protection if three conditions were met: the person in respect of whom protection was exercised had to be a national of that State or a person with a genuine link with that State; that person had to have been the victim of a violation of his rights which amounted to an infringement of the international minimum standard at the hands of a foreign State; and the victim must have exhausted all available remedies against the delinquent State (paras. 62-8).

(a) The fact that the farmland had been vested in the companies and the trust did not prevent South Africa from exercising diplomatic protection. Although ordinarily diplomatic protection of a company had to be exercised by the State of nationality of that company, there was an exception which allowed the State of nationality of the shareholders to intervene where the company had the nationality of the State responsible for injuring the company. The companies and the trust in the present case had the requisite genuine link with South Africa. Accordingly, the first condition was satisfied (paras. 55-61).

(b) The expropriation of the farmland without compensation was unlawful under international law and constituted a clear violation of the international minimum standard, thus satisfying the second requirement (paras. 70-81).

(c) The applicant had also satisfied the third requirement of exhausting all available local remedies. In view of the disregard shown by the Government of Zimbabwe for judgments of the Zimbabwean courts concerning the expropriation of white-owned farmland, no purpose would be served by the applicant seeking further remedies in the courts of Zimbabwe (paras. 82-9).

(4) The applicant qualified for diplomatic protection. Such protection might take the form of effective diplomatic pressure on the Government of Zimbabwe to restore the land or pay compensation, facilitating the opportunity for the applicant to go to ICSID to seek relief or entering into a bilateral investment treaty which provided for compensation (paras. 90-3).

(5) The exercise of the right of diplomatic protection was not a matter falling solely within the domain of the executive. The applicant had a right to apply for diplomatic protection and the respondents, at a minimum, were under a constitutional duty rationally to apply their minds to the request. In the present case they had failed to do so and that failure was a breach of the applicant's constitutional rights (paras. 135-55).

(6) Accordingly, the Court would grant declarations that the respondents' failure to consider and decide upon the applicant's request for diplomatic protection was unconstitutional and invalid, that the applicant had a right to diplomatic protection and that the respondents had a constitutional obligation to provide such protection. The respondents were ordered forthwith, and in any event within sixty days of the order, to take all necessary steps to have the violation of the applicant's rights by the Government of Zimbabwe remedied and report to the Court on the steps taken (para. 161).

Proceedings in the Constitutional Court

The respondents did not appeal from the judgment of the High Court. However, the applicant commenced proceedings under Section 172(2)(a) of the Constitution[3] to have the Order of the High Court confirmed by the Constitutional Court in so far as it related to the conduct of the President of South Africa. Section 172(2)(a) of the Constitution provided that certain orders regarding constitutional invalidity required confirmation by the Constitutional Court.

Held (by the Constitutional Court):—The application was rejected. The Order of the High Court did not require confirmation as it did not concern the conduct of the President. The question of diplomatic protection concerned the foreign relations of South Africa and the Department of Foreign Affairs was seised of the matter. Any failure was, therefore, that of the Government of South Africa and the relevant minister and not of the President. It was for the Government to decide whether protection should be granted and, if so, what form it should take. If the Government failed rationally to consider a request for diplomatic protection, that was the constitutional responsibility of the minister concerned, not of the President (pp. 624-43).

Further Proceedings in the High Court

The High Court then considered whether the relevant respondents had complied with the Order that they take all necessary steps to have the violation of the applicant's rights by the Government of Zimbabwe remedied.

Held (by the High Court on 5 February 2010):—The respondents had not complied with the Order.

---

[3] For the text of Section 172(2)(a), see p. 631 below.

(1) Although a Deputy Director-General in the Department of Foreign Affairs had submitted an affidavit regarding the steps taken following the 2008 judgment of the Court, there was no indication that the Minister of Foreign Affairs or any other respondent had personally made any effort to comply with the Order of the Court. The respondents had not, therefore, complied with their reporting duty under the Order (pp. 643-9).

(2) In any event, the affidavit disclosed steps falling short of what was required by the Order. Although a request had been made to the Government of Zimbabwe to assist South African nationals who had been dispossessed, there was no indication that this request would ever yield any protection for the applicant. It was untenable for the respondents to contend that such action was sufficient because it was for the executive to determine what steps should be taken. There were many other steps open to the respondents, given the judgment by the Southern African Development Community Tribunal regarding the Zimbabwean expropriations[4] and the fact that Zimbabwe was dependent upon South Africa in so many respects (pp. 649-62).

(3) The appropriate remedy was that the Government of South Africa and the Minister of Foreign Affairs should pay to the applicant such damages as he had suffered as a result of the violation of his rights by the Government of Zimbabwe, the amount of these damages to be assessed in later proceedings (pp. 662-6).

The judgment of Moseneke DCJ (with whom the rest of the Court agreed) in the Constitutional Court appears at p. 624. The judgment of the High Court of 5 February 2010 appears at p. 643. The following is the text of the judgment of the High Court of 29 July 2008:

JUDGMENT OF THE HIGH COURT (29 JULY 2008)

[530] 1. This matter came before me as a special opposed application. Mr Hodes SC, assisted by Mr Katz and Mr Du Plessis, appeared for the applicant. Mr Mtshaulana SC, at times assisted by Mr Sello, appeared for the respondents.

Brief Synopsis

2. The applicant is a 75-year-old South Africa citizen. He hails from Bothaville in the Freestate, where he was born on 6 April 1933. He still lives in Bothaville.

3. More than fifty years ago, in 1954 or 1955, the applicant began to obtain farming interests, including farming landed property, in the Republic of Zimbabwe (then Southern Rhodesia, later Rhodesia and

---

[4] *Mike Campbell (Pvt) Ltd, William Michael Campbell and Others* v. *Republic of Zimbabwe* (Case No 2/2007), reported at 138 ILR 385.

now Zimbabwe, as it will be referred to throughout for the sake of convenience). For reasons of commercial expediency, the applicant, from time to time, floated private companies and procured the registration of the farming properties into the name of these private companies, for his ultimate benefit. In 1985 he also arranged for the registration of a trust (known as the Von Abo Trust—"the Trust"), which he also employed in the same manner as the private companies aforesaid. At present the [531] applicant is the sole beneficiary of this Trust with the right to appoint, in his sole discretion, further or other beneficiaries out of the group consisting of direct descendants born in legal wedlock of, or legally adopted by, the applicant.

4. The final control of all decisions of and actions by the relevant private companies and the Trust at all times vested in the applicant by virtue of the fact that he is, and always has been, the managing director of the companies and the trustee of the Trust.

5. Over the years, the applicant increased his financial and farming interests in Zimbabwe, accordingly also his involvement in the farming activities of the different companies and the Trust.

6. The applicant initially found it necessary to finance the activities in Zimbabwe by applying his own South African resources. Within a relatively short period he was, however, able to continue with the farming activities in Zimbabwe by using financial support available in Zimbabwe. He consistently over the past fifty years re-invested all profits and capital gains from the Zimbabwean activities, in Zimbabwe. This enabled him to reach the point, as referred to in greater detail below, of being the beneficial owner of a considerable farming empire in Zimbabwe.

7. The development of the applicant's Zimbabwean involvement obviously required not only financial ability, but also substantial personal sacrifices, business acumen, the ability to persist in correct decision taking, and unmitigated hard work.

8. Beginning in 1997 (but, as history shows, in more accelerated fashion since 2000), the Government of Zimbabwe violated the applicant's rights by destroying his property interests in a number of farms in Zimbabwe, or contributing to their destruction. This destruction of property rights was achieved as part of an overall scheme and/or policy of the Zimbabwean government to expropriate land owned by white farmers. The scheme and/or policy continues to this day in Zimbabwe, notwithstanding international condemnation and the fact that the expropriation of property rights in the manner perpetrated by the Zimbabwean government is a clear violation of international law, and, for that matter, South African law.

9. No compensation of any sort was paid. This action by the Government of Zimbabwe constituted expropriation without the payment of compensation, which action did not comply with the international minimum standard, which standard is to be afforded to all persons, citizens and aliens (foreign nationals) alike.

10. It is common cause that the applicant has attempted, without success, to protect his rights in Zimbabwe and the rights of the entities under his control, or at least to ameliorate the violation of such rights.

11. Those attempts failed and there was (and is) no effective recourse available to the applicant and countless others in Zimbabwe. This is not disputed. The applicant has exhausted all remedies available in Zimbabwe. This is also not disputed.

[532] 12. As a national and citizen of the Republic of South Africa, the applicant directed correspondence to the first respondent as represented by the second respondent (the president) and a number of different ministers and officials, which correspondence brought to the first respondent's attention the applicant's plight and that of other South Africans similarly situated in Zimbabwe. The cumbersome and futile journey travelled by the applicant in this process is detailed in the correspondence forming part of the papers.

13. It appears that the applicant embarked on these written appeals to government when it was plain that his efforts to persuade the Zimbabwean authorities to leave his property alone were unsuccessful. He describes in graphic detail how he attempted, through litigation, to protect his interests with the assistance of the Zimbabwean courts. These efforts failed dismally, there were broken promises, court orders were ignored and eviction notices came flooding in, thick and fast.

14. Already in March 2002, the applicant wrote to the second respondent in his capacity as Head of State, requesting diplomatic protection concerning the violation of his rights in Zimbabwe.

15. The protection envisaged consisted of diplomatic assistance in the furtherance of the protection of the applicant's rights *vis-à-vis* the State of Zimbabwe.

16. Early on in the correspondence, the applicant also requested the second respondent or the fourth respondent to become a party to the International Convention on the Settlement of Investment Disputes (ICSID), in order that the applicant might pursue a compensation claim against the Government of Zimbabwe pursuant to the ICSID complaint mechanisms, and requested a meeting with the second respondent in order to convince the latter of ICSID's importance from both a practical and legal perspective.

I pause to point out that part of the relief initially sought before me by the applicant was a *mandamus* directing the respondents to take up membership of ICSID. Apart from the fact whether it was open to me to grant mandatory relief of this nature, Mr Mtshaulana strongly argued, by referring to the rules of ICSID, that such an order, if granted, may turn out to be a *brutum fulmen*, because Zimbabwe would have to consent to take part in such dispute resolution proceedings. It was argued that there was no guarantee that such a consent would be forthcoming. This state of affairs, or perhaps other practical considerations, prompted the applicant, towards the end of the proceedings before me, to abandon the prayer for this special mandatory relief and only to pursue prayers for more general declaratory, mandatory and supervisory relief. An initial prayer for the reviewing and setting aside of the failure of the respondents to consider and decide the applicant's application for diplomatic protection was also abandoned.

17. The cumbersome correspondence journey, *supra*, came to naught. Eventually, the applicant placed the respondents on terms. They did not respond. This prompted the applicant to launch this application.

[533] *The Relief Sought*

18. The prayers contained in the original notice of motion were the following:

1. Reviewing and setting aside the failure of the Respondents to consider and decide the Applicant's application for diplomatic protection in respect of the violation of his rights by the Government of Zimbabwe;
2. Declaring that the failure of the Respondents to consider and decide the Applicant's application for diplomatic protection in respect of the violation of his rights by the Government of Zimbabwe is inconsistent with the Constitution, 1996 and invalid;
3. Declaring that the Applicant has the right to diplomatic protection from the Respondents in respect of the violation of his rights by the Government of Zimbabwe;
4. Declaring that the Respondents have a Constitutional obligation to provide diplomatic protection to the Applicant in respect of the violation of his rights by the Government of Zimbabwe;
5. Ordering the Respondents to forthwith, and in any event within 30 (thirty) days of date of this Order, take all necessary steps to have the Applicant's violation of his rights by the Government of Zimbabwe remedied, including, but not limited to, becoming a party to ICSID or consenting ad hoc to the Applicant's dispute with the Government of Zimbabwe (in respect of his claim that such Government has violated his rights) being submitted to

the International Centre for Settlement of Investment Disputes (ICSID) established under the Convention on the Settlement of Investment Disputes Between States and Nationals of Other States;
6. Directing the Respondents to report by way of affidavit to this Honourable Court within 30 (thirty) days of this Order, what steps they have taken in respect of prayer 5 above and providing a copy of such report to the applicant;
7. That, in the event of the Respondents failing to comply effectively with either the Order in terms of prayer 5 or in terms of prayer 6, ordering the Respondents jointly and severally (the one paying the other to be absolved) to pay to the Applicant such damages as he may prove that he has suffered as a result of the violation of his rights by the Government of Zimbabwe;
8. Directing that the Respondents, jointly and severally (the one paying the other to be absolved), pay the Applicant's costs of this Application.

19. After the relief sought was scaled down, as I have explained, the prayers now before me are the following:

1. Declaring that the failure of the Respondents to rationally, appropriately and in good faith consider and decide the Applicant's application for diplomatic protection in respect of the violation of his rights by the Government of Zimbabwe is inconsistent with the Constitution, 1996 and invalid;
2. Declaring that the Applicant has the right to diplomatic protection from the Respondents in respect of the violation of his rights by the Government of Zimbabwe;
3. Declaring that the Respondents have a Constitutional obligation to provide diplomatic protection to the Applicant in respect of the violation of his rights by the Government of Zimbabwe;
4. [534] Ordering the Respondents to forthwith, and in any event within 30 (thirty) days of date of this Order, take all necessary steps to have the Applicant's violation of his rights by the Government of Zimbabwe remedied;
5. Directing the Respondents to report by way of affidavit to this Honourable Court within 30 (thirty) days of this Order, what steps they have taken in respect of prayer 4 above and providing a copy of such report to the Applicant;
6. That, in the event of the Respondents failing to comply effectively with either the Order in terms of prayer 4 or in terms of prayer 5, ordering the Respondents jointly and severally (the one paying the other to be absolved) to pay to the Applicant such damages as he may prove that he has suffered as a result of the violation of his rights by the Government of Zimbabwe;
7. Directing that Respondents, jointly and severally (the one paying the other to be absolved), pay the Applicant's costs of this application.

20. As far as prayer 6 (the damages claim) is concerned, the applicant requested me, in the event of him being successful, to postpone this

prayer *sine die* pending compliance by the respondents with prayers 4 and 5, and granting all parties leave to supplement their papers prior to the hearing of the damages claim.

The Citation of the Respondents

21. The first respondent is the Government of the Republic of South Africa.

22. The second respondent is the President of the Republic of South Africa, cited as such in his official capacity. The second respondent is cited inasmuch as he is in terms of section 83(a) of the Constitution both the Head of State and Head of the National Executive. In terms of section 84 of the Constitution, he has been assigned certain powers and functions, and in terms of section 85 he, together with the other members of the Cabinet, exercises the executive authority of the Republic of South Africa.

23. The third respondent is the Minister of Foreign Affairs of the Republic of South Africa who is cited in her capacity as such. The third respondent is cited because on 6 April 2006, a letter from the second respondent's office was sent to the applicant's attorneys recording that—

it is the practice of the President's office to seek the comments and recommendations of the Ministry of Foreign Affairs as the responsible line functionary dealing with issues affecting Foreign Affairs. As soon as the latter's response is received, the presidency will take these (*sic*) into consideration and you will be advised of the outcome.

24. The fourth respondent is the Minister of Trade and Industry who is cited in his official capacity. He was also cited because of advice contained in some of the letters to the effect that he had an interest in the matter.

25. The fifth respondent is the Minister of Justice and Constitutional Development. She was only joined at a later stage. This came about when, in January 2007, an officer in the Department of Foreign Affairs **[535]** wrote to the applicant's attorney, telling him that it had been decided that the Department of Justice and Constitutional Development is the Government Department responsible for coordinating matters relating to ICSID.

Of Matters ICSID, BIPPA and BIT

26. I have recorded the applicant's later decision to abandon the prayer for mandatory relief that would force the respondents to join ICSID. I have mentioned the apparent reason for this late abandonment.

27. Nevertheless, I consider it convenient and appropriate to make a few brief remarks about ICSID as well as the other two structures mentioned above.

28. As indicated, ICSID is the International Convention on the Settlement of Investment Disputes. ICSID is a public international organisation created under a treaty with its head office in Washington DC, in the United States of America. ICSID provides facilities for the conciliation and arbitration of investment disputes between contracting States (Zimbabwe is a contracting State) and nationals of other contracting States. Its objective in making such facilities available is to promote an atmosphere of mutual confidence within States and foreign investors conducive to increasing the flow of private international investment.

29. South Africa is not a party to ICSID. However, should it join the other 136 States parties to ICSID (including Zimbabwe) by becoming a party to the treaty, it will at no financial or political cost to itself provide to its nationals an avenue to settle investment disputes with other nations (such as those at issue in this matter in respect of Zimbabwe).

30. Another avenue to assist the applicant would be for South Africa to make an *ad hoc* declaration of consent under the Additional Facility Rules of ICSID which allow for cases involving nationals of states not a party to ICSID (South Africa) and States parties to ICSID (Zimbabwe) to be arbitrated under ICSID rules.

31. The above constitute obvious reasons for the applicant to urge the respondents to either join ICSID or make the *ad hoc* declaration in order to open those obvious opportunities to the applicant and other aggrieved citizens in their quest for compensation.

32. Of course, both sides agreed, on a proper interpretation of the ICSID rules, that Zimbabwe would have to consent to such a process even if the Republic were to join ICSID. Hence the abandonment of the prayer for this particular relief.

33. Nevertheless, no reason was advanced for the refusal on the part of the respondents to join ICSID and, thereafter, bring pressure to bear on Zimbabwe to give the required consent. The paper trail journey to which I have referred reveals a constant failure on the part of the respondents to even debate the possibility of joining ICSID let alone disclosing reasons of the refusal to do so.

34. I add that the late Chief Justice I. Mahomed, when chairperson of the South African Law Commission ("the Commission") in the Commission's project report 94 of July 1998, directed to the then Minister of **[536]** Justice, made specific recommendations in regard to the ICSID convention, "the Washington Convention of 1965". The Commission discussed the purpose of ICSID and its special features and benefits

for South Africa and concluded that "the arguments in favour of South Africa ratifying the Convention are strongly persuasive".

Already at that stage, the Washington Convention enjoyed a high degree of international acceptance, particularly among African States. As at 30 June 1995 it had been ratified by 119 States and signed by a further fifteen States. The only States in the region yet to ratify the Convention were (at that stage) South Africa, Namibia and Angola. The Convention has also generally been positively received by developing countries.

35. I find it convenient to quote a few extracts from the aforesaid report of the Law Commission:

> 92.1.9 Although South Africa is a developing country, its relatively strong infrastructure and position as the major economic power in the region place South Africa in a somewhat unique position as a country which could get a dual benefit from ICSID membership.
>
> 92.1.10 On the other hand, the country is anxious to attract more foreign investment and some of the potential projects could benefit from the availability of arbitration or conciliation under the Washington Convention. Ratification of the Convention would therefore be another positive signal which South Africa could send out to indicate that the new Government is eager to create the necessary legal framework to encourage foreign investment. Bilateral investment treaties between States, particularly between a developed and a developing State, commonly contains a provision for arbitration under ICSID as a means of encouraging private investment in the developing country. As appears from the text below, such clauses are already being included in bilateral investment treaties recently entered into by the South Africa Government with the Governments of certain foreign States.
>
> 92.1.11 On the other hand, South African companies are eagerly looking for investment opportunities in other African countries, virtually all of which are members of ICSID. Ratification of the Convention by South Africa would facilitate such investment and further the economic development of the region.
>
> 92.1.12 Failure to ratify the Convention would leave South Africa as one of the very few African countries which have not done so and a continued failure to do so appears difficult to justify. Moreover, the inclusion of ICSID arbitration clauses in bilateral investment treaties recently entered into by the South African Government with the Governments of, for example, Germany, France, Switzerland, Denmark, Korea and Canada have created the expectation among potential investors in those countries that South Africa intends acceding to the Washington Convention.

92.1.13 Secondly, as appears from paragraphs ... above, the ICSID mechanism reduces the involvement of foreign State courts to an absolute minimum, thereby reducing sensitivity concerning national sovereignty.

92.1.14 **[537]** It is, however, necessary to consider what the possible additional costs of membership of ICSID would be, pursuant to ratification of the Convention.

92.1.15 South Africa would therefore incur no costs in joining ICSID, other than the cost of enacting the legislation to give effect to ratification to the Convention.

92.1.16 For the reasons set out in paragraphs ... above, it is submitted that South Africa should follow the example of most other African countries and ratify the Washington Convention. Draft legislation to give effect to this recommendation is contained in chapter 4 of the Draft Bill.

36. Against this background, counsel for the applicant, in their very comprehensive and well-crafted heads of argument, submitted that it was startling to discover that the advantages of ICSID are not unknown to the respondents. The first respondent, in concluding various bilateral investment treaties prior to the Commission's report of 1998, "created the expectation among potential investors in those countries that South Africa intends acceding to the Washington Convention". This much was stated in a report of the Law Commission, *supra*.

Counsel for the applicant submit that the aforesaid expectation created among potential investors, as alluded to by the Commission, is reflected in the fact that in each of a number of investment treaties concluded by the first respondent with foreign States, an ICSID arbitration is referred to as one of the options by which any investment dispute arising between the parties would be settled. Counsel then list seven such agreements or treaties, referring in each instance to the relevant article in the treaty designed to promote and protect reciprocal investments. For example, there was a bilateral agreement between the republic and Canada in 1995, a treaty with Germany in 1995, an agreement with Denmark, an agreement with France, an agreement with Korea and, lastly, an agreement with the Swiss Federal Council on the promotion and reciprocal protection of investments.

The last mentioned agreement, dated 27 June 1995, was handed up as an exhibit during the course of his diligent address by Mr Mtshaulana on behalf of the respondents. He did so to fortify his argument, *supra*, that an agreement from both sides was required in order to bring about, for example, an ICSID arbitration and, where the consent of Zimbabwe was by no means guaranteed, the original prayer for this court to order the respondents to take out ICSID membership ought not to be entertained.

37. The fact that the prayer for this specific relief was abandoned as a result, does not mean, in my view, that the consistent failure on the part of the respondents to join ICSID and make a serious attempt to enter into a Bilateral Investment Treaty ("BIT") with Zimbabwe with the view to protecting its nationals investing in that country should not come under the spotlight when consideration is given to the submissions by the applicant that the failure of the respondent to grant the applicant diplomatic protection is unconstitutional for its irrationality.

[538] Counsel for the applicant, in their heads of argument, put it as follows:

94. With respect, the above demonstrates that ICSID is in fact considered by the South African Government to be a plausible means by which South African nationals might settle their investment disputes with foreign states. To withhold such a means of dispute settlement from the applicant and similarly situated individuals in respect of investment disputes arising, and within Zimbabwe, is discriminatory, irrational and contrary to the foreign policy commitments made by the first respondent to which reference is made earlier.

95. The question remains unanswered by the respondents: if the South African Government's so-called efforts to assist the applicant (and others) in disputes with Zimbabwe around that Government's expropriation of property of South African nationals has "not met with great success, if any at all" then on what plausible rational and Constitutionally sufficient basis are the respondents denying the applicant and others similarly situated an opportunity to proceed under ICSID, a vehicle which, as the Dutch example demonstrates, may well meet with success?

38. The "foreign policy commitments made" alluded to by counsel is a reference, *inter alia*, to a written statement by the third respondent in answer to a written question by an opposition Member of Parliament, dated 27 March 2002, where she says, *inter alia*, the following:

The South African Government would continue to ensure the safety and security of all its citizens, their property as well as South African owned companies operating in foreign countries.

39. The "Dutch example" referred to by counsel relates to the fact that Zimbabwe, as a party of ICSID, had consented to the jurisdiction of the ICSID tribunal in relation to a compensation claim lodged by Dutch nationals arising out of the expropriation of their property rights by the Government of Zimbabwe. It is the case of *Bernardus Henricus Funnekotter and Others* v. *Republic of Zimbabwe*, Case No ARB/05/06, vol. 5, p. 496, CVA 143(i). The matter was registered with ICSID on

15 April 2005 and it concerns the expropriation without compensation of commercial farms in Zimbabwe. Counsel point out that it should be noted that Mr Funnekotter is a citizen or national of a State which is also a party to ICSID, and accordingly he was entitled to bring a case against the Republic of Zimbabwe under ICSID for that reason. Zimbabwe has consented to the arbitration.

On the subject of "foreign policy commitments made", *supra*, it is convenient, at this stage, to highlight further commitments made by the Foreign Minister (third respondent) in response to opposition questions in parliament. Already in June 2004 she said the following:

> Among the steps taken are the recommendations made to our Department of Trade and Industry (DTI) to discuss and conclude with their Zimbabwean counterparts the Bilateral Investment Promotion and Protection Agreement. BIPPA *has been concluded* and now awaits signature by our Minister of Trade and Industry and his Zimbabwean counterpart. **[539]** (Emphasis added.)

On the same occasion, she also said the following to Parliament:

> The future steps that the Government will take to ensure the protection of the property rights of South African citizens with agricultural interests and those citizens who own property and companies in Zimbabwe is through the signing of the Bilateral Investment Protection of Property [*sic*] Agreement. *Our Department of Trade and Industry and their Zimbabwean counterparts have concluded discussions on the agreement. The agreement is awaiting signature by the Ministers of both Governments once the calendars of the Ministers permit.* (Emphasis added.)

Later in June 2004, the Minister said the following:

> Furthermore, our DTI has together with the Zimbabwean Government concluded the Bilateral Investment Promotion and Protection Agreement (BIPPA) which is aimed at, among other issues, protecting the properties of South African nationals in Zimbabwe.

On the same occasion she also said the following in writing:

> Substantial progress has been made in concluding a Bilateral Investment Promotion and Protection Agreement (BIPPA). *In December 2003, our DTI and the Government of Zimbabwe met in Harare and concluded BIPPA.* (Emphasis added.)

40. It was common cause during the proceedings before me, that the much vaunted BIPPA was never signed. No one ever saw the BIPPA. Repeated appeals by the applicant, in the course of his cumbersome correspondence journey ("the journey") which I will deal with later, to have sight of the BIPPA, were turned down flat. The third respondent

never bothered to file a supporting or verifying affidavit to explain why the BIPPA, if it ever existed, was never signed. In fact, not one of the respondents took the trouble to sign a verifying or supporting affidavit to the opposing affidavit. Instead, they got Mr Pieter Andreas Stemmet ("Stemmet"), a Senior State Law Adviser at the Department of Foreign Affairs, to attest to the opposing affidavit. There were no verifying or explanatory or supporting affidavits by any of the respondents.

A replying affidavit, containing emphatic submissions to the effect that Stemmet's evidence is inadmissible because it amounts to hearsay and does not reflect his personal knowledge, was filed in May 2007. A year later, in May 2008 when the matter came before me, the respondents, without asking for condonation, handed up a feeble, one and a half page affidavit by Aziz Goolam Hoosein Pahad, the Deputy Minister of Foreign Affairs, who is neither a respondent nor a member of the cabinet, if one has regard to sections 91 and 93 of the Constitution. His affidavit does not advance the case of the respondents. On the contrary, it advances the case of the applicant that Stemmet's evidence amounts to hearsay. The affidavit of Pahad, such as it is, is riddled with hearsay evidence.

41. The unexplained failure on the part of any of the respondents to file personal affidavits to deal with the complaints of the applicant amounts, in my view, to a shocking dereliction of duty. It also flies in the face of the **[540]** requirements of section 165(4) of the Constitution which provides that organs of State, through legislative and other measures, must assist and protect the courts to ensure the independence, impartiality, dignity, accessibility and effectiveness of the courts.

42. While on the subject of dereliction of duty, it is convenient to return to another promise which the third respondent made to Parliament in a written reply to an opposition question in June 2004. She said the following:

The Zimbabwean Government has also indicated that properties belonging to nationals from SADC-Member States would be de-listed and that a cabinet task team had been established to develop a policy framework within which properties of foreign investors, including South Africans, would be resolved.

Appreciation is expressed by the Zimbabwean (*sic*) for the critical role South Africa is playing towards the resolution of the political and economic difficulties facing Zimbabwe *and that it was important that Zimbabwe reciprocate and assist South African nationals in Zimbabwe.* (Emphasis added.)

In the proceedings before me, it was common cause that no de-listing, as promised, ever took place. There was no explanation whatsoever from any of the respondents, let alone the third respondent, for their abject failure, over all these years, as members of the Executive of the power house of the region, to bring about the "reciprocity" promised by Zimbabwe and/or to employ a host of diplomatic measures, recognised worldwide, to protect its citizens.

The Admissibility, or Lack Thereof, of the Evidence Contained in the Respondents' Answering Affidavit

43. I have pointed out that the deponent to the respondents' opposing affidavit, Stemmet, had to make do on his own without any supporting affidavits from any of the respondents.

44. I have also pointed out that the applicant, in emphatic terms, already in his replying affidavit dated June 2007, submitted that, under the circumstances, Stemmet's evidence mainly amounts to hearsay. In the replying affidavit full details are recorded of the evidence considered to be hearsay and which falls to be struck out or ignored. I pointed out that the only reaction from the respondents was to hand up a short affidavit by the Deputy Minister a year later, when the proceedings commenced before me.

45. Stemmet, the deponent, is a Senior State Law Adviser (International Law) at the Department of Foreign Affairs. His evidence, unless confirmed by others who were privy to the meetings, documents, advice and/or information on which he comments, is limited to his personal and/or professional involvement therein.

46. The courts have long and consistently held that it is impermissible for a deponent to an affidavit to give evidence on behalf of another where the latter does not file a confirmatory affidavit to confirm the evidence.

In *Gerhardt* v. *State President and Others* 1989 2 SA 499 (T) the following is said at 504F-H:

[541] Clearly one person cannot make an affidavit on behalf of another and Mr Hattingh, who appears on behalf of the three respondents, concedes correctly that I can only take into account those portions of the second respondent's affidavit in which he refers to matters within his knowledge. Insofar as he imputes intentions or anything else to the State President, it is clearly hearsay and inadmissible.

In the unreported judgment of *Nasko Demirev Amaudova and Others* v. *Minister of Home Affairs and Director-General Home Affairs*, Case No 30035/2003, Patel J said:

It is trite law that only the first respondent could have dealt with what was within his knowledge and why he refused the applicant's representations and request for temporary permits, irrespective of any departmental arrangements in respect of any delegation of authority. No-one else could depose to that knowledge except the first respondent himself. Surely, one person cannot make an affidavit on behalf of another unless duly authorised to do so and such authority is either supported or confirmed by an affidavit. There is no supporting or confirmatory affidavit from the first respondent. Further, a court can only have regard to those parts of the affidavit in which he or she refers to matters within his or her knowledge, otherwise it is simply hearsay and inadmissible.

The same sentiments were expressed in *Tantoush* v. *Refugee Appeal Board and Others* 2008 1 SA 232 (TPD). In the same judgment, the learned judge makes the following remark at 256J to 257A:

Moreover, as I have already intimated, where new material was introduced in reply, the respondents could have relied upon the principle enunciated in *Sigaba* v. *Minister of Defence and Police and Another* 1980 3 SA 535 (TK) to seek leave to file additional affidavits in the sure likelihood that such leave would have been granted.

47. Counsel for the applicant developed this argument further by submitting that the respondents, not having furnished admissible evidence in rebuttal, in the process failed to rebut the applicant's allegations of irrational and unconstitutional conduct. In this regard I was referred to *Hurley and Another* v. *Minister of Law and Order and Another* 1985 4 SA 709 (D) 725-GH where the following passage from *R* v. *Jacobson and Levy* 1931 AD 466 at 479 is quoted:

If the party, on whom lies the burden of proof, goes as far as he reasonably can in producing evidence and that evidence "calls for an answer" then, in such case, he has produced *prima facie* proof, and, in the absence of an answer from the other side, it becomes conclusive proof and he completely discharges his onus of proof. If a doubtful or unsatisfactory answer is given it is equivalent to no answer and the *prima facie* proof, being undestroyed, again amounts to full proof.

48. In the light of this trite law the effect of this failure by any of the respondents to adduce evidence is that the evidence in Stemmet's affidavit regarding what was in the mind of any of the respondents as justification for their decisions to refuse diplomatic protection is hearsay and inadmissible. The Constitutional Court in *President of the Republic of South Africa* v. *South African Rugby Football Union and Others* **[542]** 2000 (1) SA 1 (CC) para. 105 accepted that hearsay evidence falls to be ignored, even in the absence of an objection or an application to strike out.

49. In his comprehensive replying affidavit, the applicant spells out, chapter and verse, details of all the evidence which falls to be disregarded for the reasons aforesaid. It is not necessary to repeat everything in this judgment.

One of the examples, however, is paragraph 20 of the opposing affidavit which, in my opinion, is the only paragraph in which the respondents attempt to give some information about efforts taken to afford diplomatic protection. It reads as follows:

20.2 Regarding the general request for diplomatic protection, the respondents responded in several ways.

> 20.2.1 The ambassador to Harare and his staff have consistently engaged the Zimbabwean Government on the question of the status of all South African farmers in Zimbabwe. During the last few years, meetings were held with several cabinet ministers including the Minister of Foreign Affairs, the Minister of Land Affairs, the Minister of Finance, the Minister of Agriculture, the Permanent Secretary of Land Affairs and the Permanent Secretary of Justice. In these meetings, the plight of South African farmers whose land had either been invaded by war veterans or expropriated by the state was raised.
> 20.2.2 The ambassador also met with the then Vice President of Zimbabwe, Honourable Vice President Mujuru as well as with Minister of Land Affairs, Mr D. Motasa in regard to the issue of expropriation of land belonging to South African farmers.
> 20.2.3 The embassy has also tried to intervene on behalf of farmers in trouble by engaging with the Zimbabwean foreign ministry requesting intervention on behalf of specific South African investors.

20.3 Regrettably, these efforts have not met with great success, if any at all.

Right at the end of his one-and-a-half page affidavit Deputy Minister Pahad says the following:

I further confirm that steps detailed in paragraph 20 of Stemmet's affidavit *are known to me from information provided to me*. (Emphasis added.)

50. For obvious reasons, Pahad's evidence also amounts to hearsay and does not come to the assistance of the respondents. Moreover, Stemmet's hearsay evidence, as quoted, is so vague that it can have no practical significance: it appears that only the ambassador may have met with some Zimbabwean officials. No details are given about when the meetings were held and what the outcome was. No details are given

of what efforts were made to bring pressure to bear, diplomatically speaking, on the perpetrators with the view to protecting the South African citizens.

51. Paragraph 20.4 of the opposing affidavit (also covered by the umbrella statement, such as it is, by Deputy Minister Pahad) deals with [543] earlier alleged efforts on the part of the South African High Commissioner to speak to some high ranking Zimbabweans about the plight of the South African farmers. The same remarks apply in this instance, and to the rest of the Pahad affidavit, for that matter.

52. The applicant's request for diplomatic protection by following the ICSID route is met with the following somewhat cryptic response in the opposing affidavit:

Applicant requested diplomatic protection under the auspices of ICSID. This was not acted upon because it was an unlawful request or a request which would have meant that the National Executive performed an unconstitutional act.

It is difficult to understand this approach in the light of the advice by the Law Commission, *supra*.

53. Most of the allegations in the founding affidavit are, in any event, admitted. Some are met with bare denials without controverting evidence being offered.

54. One "defence" offered is that the applicant's companies are Zimbabwean entities and this court has no jurisdiction to adjudicate on the matter. This issue will be dealt with in the following paragraphs.

Does the Duty to Afford Diplomatic Protection Fall Away because the Applicant's Companies and the Trust are Zimbabwean Entities?

55. In their opposing affidavit the respondents say the following:

The entities on whose behalf the applicant has approached the Court are Zimbabwean entities. Zimbabwe is a sovereign state and how it treats its citizens, companies and trusts is a matter for Zimbabwean Law and this Court has no jurisdiction to adjudicate on this matter.

56. The applicant has explained that during the fifty-year period, *supra*, he began to manage his farming interests through various companies that he formed. In 1985 the applicant also arranged for the registration of a Trust, known as the Von Abo Trust ("the Trust").

57. The final control of all decisions of and actions by the relevant private companies and the Trust at all times vested in the applicant by virtue of the fact that he is, and always has been, the managing director

of the companies and the senior trustee of the Trust. He also holds valid cessions in his favour by all these companies and the Trust as far as this particular application is concerned.

58. The stance adopted by the respondents, *supra*, appears to fly in the face of their statement that "the respondents responded to the request for diplomatic protection by taking such steps as were appropriate".

59. Nevertheless, the argument appears to be that nationality, one of the prerequisites for diplomatic protection by South Africa, is not satisfied in the sense that the companies and the Trust are nationals of Zimbabwe.

60. In response, counsel for the applicant, in their heads of argument, submit that the South African Government may assert diplomatic [544] protection on the applicant's behalf because of his rights in the companies and Trust that have been injured in Zimbabwe. They argue that it may do so on account of the following international law principles (their submissions are reflected hereunder in abbreviated form):

1. The companies and the Trust have a genuine link with South Africa. The director and sole member of the Zimbabwean companies and sole beneficiary of the Trust is a South African national (the applicant) and the business activities of the Zimbabwean companies and Trust are managed, financed and controlled from South Africa where the seat of management—such as it is—is now forced to be situated.
2. A State under international law is entitled to take up the protection of its nationals who have direct rights of control and management and/or shareholding in a company incorporated in a foreign State, which has been the victim of a violation of international law.
3. Ordinarily the State of nationality of a corporation must exercise diplomatic protection on behalf of the company. However, there is an important exception to this rule in international law which allows the State of nationality of the shareholders to intervene where the corporation has the nationality of the State responsible for causing injury to the corporation.
4. A State is entitled to take up the protection of its nationals, shareholders in a company incorporated in a foreign State, which has been the victim of a violation of international law, so long as there is a genuine link between the State exercising diplomatic protection and the natural person it seeks to protect—*Nottebohm* case 1955 ICJ Reports, 4 at 23.

   The companies and the Trust have a genuine link with South Africa.

5. In the present case there is accordingly a "close and permanent connection" between South Africa (through the applicant) and the companies and Trust, such that South Africa is entitled to exercise diplomatic protection on the applicant's behalf.

In such cases intervention on behalf of the corporation is not possible under the normal rule of International Law, as claims cannot be brought by foreign States on behalf of a national against its own Government. If the normal rule is applied foreign shareholders are at the mercy of the State in question; they may suffer serious loss, and yet be without redress. This is an extension in the international field of the situation which may arise in municipal law when those who should be defending the interest of the corporation fraudulently or wrongfully fail to do so (e.g. *Foss* v. *Harbottle*).

See the article by Mervyn Jones, "Claims on Behalf of Nationals who are Shareholders in Foreign Companies" (1949) 26 British Yearbook of International Law 225 at 236.

6. The United Kingdom and the United States have asserted the existence of such an exception—notably in the cases concerning the *Delagoa Bay Railway Company* (1888 to 1889) BFSP 691, Moore International Arbitrations (1898) vol. 2 at 1865, cited in Dugard, **[545]** *International Law—A South African Perspective*, 3rd edition, 2005, at 289 and other authorities.

7. In 2003 the International Law Commission gave its approval to the principle expressed in the *Delagoa Bay* case that the State of nationality of the shareholders in a corporation may exercise diplomatic protection on their behalf where the corporation has the nationality of the State responsible for causing injury to the corporation—Fourth Report on Diplomatic Protection (CA-CN. 4/530, at 27-37).

8. Moreover, Stemmet's legal response is contrary to a recent decision of the International Court of Justice in the *Case Concerning Ahmadou Sadio Diallo* (*Republic of Guinea* v. *Democratic Republic of Congo*) Preliminary Objections, decided on 27 May 2007. From the passage quoted by counsel, it appears that this court reaffirmed the principle described above, namely that the State of nationality of the shareholders in a corporation may exercise diplomatic protection on their behalf as already described.

9. In conclusion, counsel for the applicant argues that Stemmet's argument, advanced in the opposing affidavit, is in any event contrary to the Government's own stated policy. This is a reference to the third respondent's assurance to Parliament, quoted above, in

her written response to opposition questions, that "Government is committed to ensure the safety and security of all its citizens, their property *as well as South African owned companies operating in foreign countries*". (Emphasis added.)

61. I find myself in respectful agreement with these submissions. Accordingly, I hold that this court does have jurisdiction to entertain the application of the applicant.

Jurisdictional Facts to be Met for Diplomatic Protection

62. It is an elementary principle of International Law that a State is entitled to protect its nationals against the wrongs committed by other States contrary to International Law. The Permanent Court of International Justice described this principle in the *Mavrommatis Palestine Concessions* case (1924) PCIJ Reports series A(2) 12 as follows:

It is an elementary principle of International Law that a State is entitled to protect its subjects, when injured by acts contrary to International Law committed by another State, from whom they have been unable to obtain satisfaction through the ordinary channels. By taking up the case of one of its subjects and by resorting to diplomatic action or international judicial proceedings on his behalf, a State is in reality asserting its own rights—its right to ensure, in the person of its subjects, respect for the rules of International Law.

63. Legal scholars commonly use the term "diplomatic protection" to embrace consular action, negotiation, mediation, judicial and arbitral proceedings, reprisals, restorsion, severance of diplomatic relations, economic pressure and, in the final resort, the use of force—Dugard, First Report on Diplomatic Protection (March 2000) ILCA-CN. 4/506 p. 15 para. 43.

[546] For reasons already mentioned, and some still to be highlighted, I see very little evidence, if any, of the respondents having adopted any of these courses of action in defence of the applicant.

64. It is generally accepted that although a State is not obliged to admit foreigners, once it had done so, it was under an obligation towards the foreigners' State of nationality to provide a degree of protection to his or her person or property in accordance with the international minimum standard of treatment for foreigners—Dugard, op. cit., p. 11, para. 33.

65. A State may normally not intercede on behalf of a national before various jurisdictional facts relating to diplomatic protection are met.

66. The State may only intercede on behalf of one of its nationals or a person that has a genuine link with the State.

67. The victim must have suffered a violation of his rights at the hands of the foreign State which amounts to an infringement of international minimum standard.

68. The victim must have exhausted all the available remedies against the delinquent State.

69. The first jurisdictional fact, that of nationality, has already been dealt with, *supra*.

The Second Jurisdictional Fact: Violation of the International Minimum Standard

70. The applicant, in his founding affidavit, has set out the important acts by the Government of Zimbabwe which led to the destruction or "taking" of his property rights in Zimbabwe. These allegations are undisputed.

71. These acts are part of a pattern of notorious conduct by the Zimbabwean Government which amounts to large-scale expropriation of farmland owned by white farmers. Counsel for the applicant submit that it is beyond dispute, and not seriously open to refutation by the respondents, that the Government of Zimbabwe has since 1997 egregiously violated international law and international human rights laws, which has been the sole reason for the damages suffered by the applicant.

72. The above is common knowledge and has been the subject of intense criticism and scrutiny by the world community. The applicant took the trouble to incorporate, as part of the papers, a series of international reports which highlight all these transgressions and human rights violations. I do not deem it necessary to analyse any of the details contained in those reports. They include:

1. Human Rights Watch Briefing Paper, Under a Shadow: Civil and Political Rights in Zimbabwe, 6 June 2003;
2. Amnesty International's 2002, 2003, 2004 and 2005 Country Report on Zimbabwe; and
3. Zimbabwe, Country Reports on Human Rights Practices—2002, 2003, 2004 and 2005, released by the Bureau of Democracy, Human Rights, and Labour (US State Department).

[547] 73. In his founding affidavit, the applicant details certain actions which demonstrate the manner in which the Zimbabwean Government has either itself violated the applicant's property rights or has acquiesced in the violation thereof by individuals who have acted with Government support, whether tacit or express.

74. The Government of Zimbabwe published a "preliminary notice of compulsory acquisition" in that country's *Government Gazette* of 28 November 1997 under General Notice 737 of 1997, by virtue of the provisions of the Zimbabwean Land Acquisition Act 3/1992. This publication indicated that the Government of Zimbabwe intended compulsorily acquiring a number of the properties belonging to the applicant's legal personae detailed in his founding affidavit. This came like a bolt out of the blue because up to that stage the political situation in Zimbabwe was peaceful and, certainly from the point of view of a farmer/businessman, stable such as to allow economic activity in the interest of and to the benefit of the country as well as the active and hardworking agricultural farmer.

75. The applicant opposed the Government of Zimbabwe's intended acquisition of the farming properties in which he has an interest, using whatever legal and proper means available to him and was successful in these matters. All these matters were then satisfactorily disposed of in the course of the period immediately after December 1997, by way of judicial and/or administrative findings handed down by the relevant authorities. These findings notwithstanding, the Government of Zimbabwe continued its efforts to obtain the farming properties in their country, by publishing further notices and engineering further attachments of properties. In addition, the Government of Zimbabwe encouraged, aided and protected so-called "war veterans" in their action of infiltrating and settling on farms owned by the applicant's entities.

76. The applicant explained in his founding affidavit what happened to him in regard to his Trusts property, Fauna. As he makes clear, the actions of the Government of Zimbabwe in respect of this property (and movables on this property) and results flowing therefrom, are an example of what took place in Zimbabwe and his experience in respect of all the other relevant properties in similar and all material respects.

77. And, as the applicant points out, his experience in this regard is similar to the experience of a vast number of other active and full-time farmers in Zimbabwe at that time.

78. As the applicant testifies:

> The situation at present is that I have extremely limited access to Fauna Ranch (and all the other properties) and then only at the complete discretion of the unlawful squatters and occupants of the property. These squatters have killed off all the game and most of my herd of cattle and have simply confiscated all assets on the property.
>
> The above is a very brief history of my experience in respect of Fauna Ranch. My experience in respect of all the other properties is basically the same with exactly the same result; that my land has been settled by persons who have

no lawful right to occupation or possession thereof [548] and who, as a result of their settlement, have destroyed, pilfered and otherwise rendered unusable the land and the assets on the land.

79. In my view, the applicant demonstrates beyond any serious doubt (and certainly on a balance of probabilities) that his property rights in Zimbabwe have been expropriated unlawfully under international law. I add that, as will be described later, he was also arrested simply for being on one of his properties and had to appear in court many times before the charges were withdrawn.

80. Nationalisation or expropriation in international law may take place by any organ of the State whether by judgment of a court, Legislative Act or Executive Act. The expropriation is characterised by its effect which may be the taking of property, the destruction of a right or any act which destroys a right even if no physical property has been taken. See Christie, "What Constitutes a Taking of Property under International Law?" 38 (1962) BYIL 307 at 310.

81. It is not in issue that the expropriation of the properties in question was effected without compensation, a clear violation of the international minimum standard, which gives rise to State responsibility. See Dugard, *International Law—A South African Perspective*, 3rd edn, 2005, at 299.

The Third Jurisdictional Fact: Exhaustion of Local Remedies

82. Reference has already been made to the applicant's futile efforts to protect his interest by litigating against the Zimbabwean Government in that country. The applicant's allegations that he had exhausted his local remedies are not disputed on the papers.

83. The rule of public international law with respect to the exhausting of local remedies finds application in the context of the granting of diplomatic protection. A victim of an unlawful act by a foreign State may only invoke diplomatic protection and his or her State of nationality may only grant it *vis-à-vis* the wrongdoing State, if certain requirements such as the existence of nationality of the victim (*supra*) and exhaustion of local remedies have been satisfied.

84. However, a long-standing rule of customary international law is that if remedies are futile they need not be pursued. See Dugard, *International Law—A South African Perspective*, 3rd edn, 2005, at 293-5.

85. This rule [has] now been codified in article 10 of the International Law Commission's Rules on Exhaustion of Local Remedies (report

of the International Law Commission on the work of its 55th session, chapter V, 2003) and article 44 of the International Law Commission's Articles on State Responsibility, 2001.

86. No purpose will be served by seeking further remedies in the courts of Zimbabwe. Given the almost absolute disregard that Government shows even for the orders of its own courts, particularly in respect of the expropriation and taking of the farms of white farmers, there are no remedies available to the applicant.

87. To the extent that it may be suggested that there are any remedies left to exhaust in Zimbabwe, those remedies are not "effective", as that term is understood in international law.

[549] 88. It appears that on an objective assessment of the facts of the applicant's case, any remedies left to be pursued in Zimbabwe, such as they may be, would be futile.

89. Upon a realistic assessment of the facts and the history behind this matter, there is no reasonable prospect of the applicant securing damages or vindication of his rights in a Zimbabwean court. The rule about exhaustion of local remedies (which exists in the context of diplomatic protection) finds application in this case and the requirements of this rule have been met by the applicant.

90. In view of the aforegoing I have concluded that the jurisdictional facts for qualifying for diplomatic protection have been established by the applicant.

By way of example, such diplomatic protection may involve effective diplomatic pressure on the Zimbabwean Government to restore the properties to the applicant and his companies and to pay compensation for losses and damages. Another form of diplomatic protection may be to facilitate the opportunity for the applicant to go the ICSID route and get a proper hearing in front of an international arbitration tribunal. Another possibility might be for the respondents to enter into a BIT or a BIPPA with retrospective effect containing a clause providing for compensation by the errant State to the aggrieved party. A good example of such an agreement is the one between the Republic and the Swiss Federal Council which Mr Mtshaulana handed up as an exhibit. Article 3 of that agreement reads as follows:

Investments and returns of investors of each Contracting Party shall at all times be accorded fair and equitable treatment and shall enjoy full protection and security in the territory of the other Contracting Party. Neither Contracting Party shall in any way impair by unreasonable or discriminatory measures the management, maintenance, use, enjoyment, extension or disposal of investments in its territory of investors of the other Contracting Party.

Article 4(1) reads as follows:

Investors of one Contracting Party whose investments in the territory of the other Contracting Party suffer losses owing to war or other armed conflict, revolution, a state of national emergency, revolt, insurrection or riot in the territory of the latter Contracting Party shall be accorded by the latter Contracting Party treatment, as regards restitution, indemnification, compensation or other settlement, no less favourable than that which the latter contracting party accords to its own investors or investors of any third State whichever is more favourable to the investor concerned. Resulting payments shall be freely transferable at the rate of exchange applicable on the date of transfer pursuant to the exchange regulations in force.

Article 8, under the heading "Pre-agreement Investments", reads as follows:

The present agreement shall also apply to investments in the territory of a contracting party made in accordance with its laws and regulations by investors of the other Contracting Party prior to the entry into force of this Agreement.

[550] 91. I have already pointed out that over all these years the respondents have done absolutely nothing to assist the applicant, despite diligent and continued requests for diplomatic protection on the part of the latter. No explanation whatsoever has been forthcoming for this tardy and lacklustre behaviour. The few vague allegations made in the opposing affidavit, *supra*, referring to "meetings" and "engagements" between the ambassador and other officials are unspecified, contain no information about the details of the meetings and the outcome thereof and, in any event, amount to hearsay.

92. I have pointed out that the BIPPA, already promised to Parliament by the Foreign Minister in 2003, has remained nothing but a phantom on the horizon. The prospective Contracting Parties have been looking at their calendars for a suitable date for more than five years without success. The feeble excuse offered from time to time in the opposing papers that the South Africans are dependent on the whims and time frames of the Zimbabweans is nonsense. This is a powerful and a proud country and there is no reason why it cannot employ any of the effective internationally recognised diplomatic measures, *supra*, to bring about proper protection for its nationals. For this abject failure and dereliction of duty, there is no explanation whatsoever to be found in the papers filed on behalf of the respondents.

93. Before turning to what the Constitutional Court has had to say on the subject of diplomatic protection, it is necessary to traverse, in abbreviated form, the journey travelled by the applicant in his efforts

to get assistance and help from the respondents. It is a cumbersome exercise, but necessary, albeit in truncated form, because it illustrates the plight of the applicant and the main thrust of his grievance for not managing to elicit any form of protection from his own government.

The Journey

94. The applicant illustrated the details by means of correspondence attached to the founding affidavit and incorporated therein.

95. Under the heading "Efforts to obtain assistance" the applicant, firstly, attaches 54 letters written either by himself or others on his behalf. These include a Human Rights Commissioner, a Member of Parliament and the Chairman of Grain South Africa. After listing these letters he says "I have not summarised the contents of the aforementioned communications in order not to render this affidavit even more voluminous, but I pray that the contents of all the annexures to this affidavit be read as if therein incorporated."

96. The applicant then lists and describes 27 letters exchanged between his attorneys and (mainly) junior officials in the departments of the respondents. He then says the following:

The letters mentioned above are self-explanatory and manifest the litany of requests and applications I have made to the South African Government for assistance (diplomatic or otherwise) in relation to my predicament *vis-à-vis* the Zimbabwean Government. I pray that their contents be regarded as if herein incorporated.

[551] 97. In his able address, Mr Mtshaulana argued that this method of presenting this particular portion of the applicant's case, could fly in the face of the following dictum to be found in a well-known case of *Swissborough Diamond Mines* v. *Government of the RSA* 1999 2 SA 279 (TPD) at 324F-H:

Regard being had to the function of affidavits, it is not open to an applicant or a respondent to merely annexe to its affidavit documentation and to request the Court to have regard to it. What is required is the identification of the portions thereof on which reliance is placed and an indication of the case which is sought to be made out on the strength thereof. If this were not so the essence of our established practice would be destroyed. A party would not know what case must be met.

The learned judge there quotes a few authorities dealing with this subject and goes on to refer to two other cases, including *Van Rensburg* v. *Van Rensburg en Andere* 1963 1 SA 505 (A) at 509E-510B where it was held that a party in motion proceedings may advance legal argument in support of the relief or defence claimed by it even where such arguments are not specifically mentioned in the papers, provided they arise from the facts alleged.

98. As Mr Hodes convincingly argued on behalf of the applicant, there is no question whatsoever of these respondents not knowing what case they have to meet. The letters are generally short and to the point and, as is stated in the founding affidavit, self-explanatory. They illustrate the case made out in the founding affidavit. Their relevance is beyond question. To summarise each of the letters as part of the affidavit would be impractical and add to the voluminous nature of the papers. It would be entirely unnecessary in these particular circumstances.

99. I now turn to the contents of some of the letters. In my view it is neither practical nor necessary to analyse each and every letter. Details will be condensed, where possible, for the sake of brevity.

100. On 24 March 2002 (and when it was obvious that his efforts in the Zimbabwean courts were fruitless) the applicant wrote a long letter to the second respondent himself. He points out that he is a fifth generation South African citizen of Scandinavian and Scottish descent. He deals with the half a century of investments in Zimbabwe. All the dividends flowing from his investments were re-invested in that country. All companies had now been taken over by settlers and one by a high-profile politician, without any compensation. There is no legal system to which he can appeal in Zimbabwe. There is no law. The so-called war veterans are a law to themselves. The applicant has always believed in a fair and just society. Before the 1994 election he gave premises for the ANC in Bothaville even though he was branded as a sell out by his own society. He appealed to the State President (second respondent) for assistance.

101. Almost two months later, in May 2002, Administrative Secretary E. Ndlovu in the Presidency, acknowledged receipt of the letter and said that "since the matter you have raised falls under the jurisdiction of the Minister of Foreign Affairs, it has been forwarded to her for further attention. You may expect a reply from the Minister's office."

[552] 102. On 14 May 2002, Dr Boy Geldenhuys, a Member of Parliament, wrote to the President (second respondent) on behalf of the applicant. Part of the letter reads as follows:

Mr Von Abo is a well-known upstanding South African citizen fully committed to a non-racial democratic South Africa. Besides playing an influential role in the South African agricultural sector he also invested heavily in the farming industry of Zimbabwe with the full knowledge and assistance of the Reserve

Bank of Zimbabwe. Due to the unlawful occupation of industrial farms by so-called war veterans without any compensation, Mr Von Abo stands to lose millions of rands.

If Mr Von Abo as a South African citizen could be assisted by your good offices to a more just settlement, it will be highly appreciated.

103. On 22 May 2002 the presidency again acknowledge receipt of the first letter written in March and repeated the advice that the letter would be forwarded to the Minister for Foreign Affairs. This time the author of the letter was administrative assistant to the Legal Adviser Nonqaba Tshotsho. It is clear that she was unaware of the first letter written by Administrative Secretary E. Ndlovu.

104. On 6 June 2002, Deputy Minister Pahad replied to the letter of Dr Boy Geldenhuys MP in the following terms:

As soon as my department became aware of the fact that the re-settlement programme was affecting South African owned properties, companies and investments in Zimbabwe, it commenced to engage with the Zimbabwean authorities through diplomatic channels. The last discussions were held as recently as 11 June 2002 between the South African High Commissioner to Zimbabwe and Zimbabwean Principal of Lands. The possible protection of South African owned property and investments in Zimbabwe within the context of a Bilateral Agreement on the Protection of Investments was one of the issues discussed. In fact, the Department of Trade and Industry has been involved with the Zimbabwean authorities in this regard since 2001.

I would, therefore, wish to give my assurance that the South African Government is fully aware of the situation and will endeavour to do its utmost to safeguard South African owned property, companies and investments. As soon as it is possible to take up the specific case of Mr Von Abo, we shall do so. (Emphasis added.)

This letter is also riddled with hearsay evidence. Moreover, it is another example of a BIPPA, or similar agreement, already promised in 2002 but never becoming a reality.

105. On 27 June 2002 the applicant wrote to the South African High Commissioner in Harare appealing for assistance. He details the farming interests held by him, and asks for assistance by the Foreign Minister.

106. On 27 June 2002 the applicant writes to the second respondent, pointing out that to date he had not heard anything from the Foreign Minister (despite the consecutive promises made in writing by the Administrative Secretary and the Administrative Assistant to the Legal Adviser respectively).

[553] 107. On 17 July 2002 Administrative Secretary Maritz, in the office of the Ministry of Foreign Affairs, apologises for the delay and

says "I also wish to assure you that the matter is receiving attention and that you will shortly receive a formal response from our department."

108. On 24 July 2002 the applicant writes to the South African High Commissioner in Harare referring to his previous letter of 27 June. He complains about the confiscation of his property and singles out one property by saying:

The property, Duiker Flat, was taken by the governor of Mashonaland Central, Mr Elliot Manyaka. Please refer to appendix 2 which is a copy of a letter from the office of the district administrator, Vendura, advising that the ministry of lands, agriculture and rural resettlement had accepted Mr Manyaka's application to lease the farm from the Government—whilst this property still belongs to me.

The proposed acquisition of the Nuanetsi properties was opposed, and the matter was withdrawn by the Minister of Lands. Despite this, the ranches are fully occupied by settlers and their cattle. Poaching is rife.

My farm managers on the Mazoe properties have been evicted, and they have been barred from returning. It must be noted that due to the government not adhering to its own prescribed legal time frame in serving acquisition documents, all of the acquisition orders are null and void.

I therefore appeal to the South African Government to protect my rights as a South African citizen and intervene, on my behalf, to ensure that my rights are reinstated.

109. On 30 July 2002 the applicant again writes to the High Commissioner in the following terms:

Since our letter to you on the above I have received a letter from the invaders of Fauna Ranch addressed to my manager Mr Willem Kloppers.

I am sending you a copy of the letter, which I have typed for easier reading for your urgent attention. I have no doubt that you would agree that this is not just anarchy but that could be seen as pure piracy.

I also include a list of the names of the people who have invaded the ranch and the cattle that they have brought in.

110. On 30 July 2002 the applicant sent copies of the aforesaid letters to the High Commissioner to Administrative Secretary Maritz at the Ministry of Foreign Affairs in Cape Town. He concludes the letter in the following terms:

As you will see from the documentation it amounts to pure piracy. I would be grateful if this could receive your and your minister's most urgent attention.

111. On 30 August 2002 a reminder is sent to Administrative Secretary Maritz.

112. On 10 September 2002 Deputy Minister Pahad writes to Niewoudt and Partners in Bothaville, presumably the applicant's attorneys in that Free State town, in the following terms:

[554] I acknowledge receipt of your letter dated 6 September 2002.
The South African Government, through its High Commission in Zimbabwe, has been and will continue to, interact with the Zimbabwean Government in the protection of South African nationals' interests in Zimbabwe. In this regard, I attach herewith the press release on the actions that the South African Government has taken, with particular reference to Mr Von Abo's situation. As can be seen from the attached press statement the South African Government has in fact in its interactions with the Zimbabwe Government, *extended diplomatic protection to Mr Von Abo.* (Emphasis added.)

The press release is not in evidence. As I have indicated, no details of the so-called diplomatic protection and the effect thereof, have been forthcoming. I regret to say that it is difficult to resist the conclusion that the respondents were simply stringing the applicant along, and never had any serious intention to afford him proper protection. Their feeble efforts, if any, amounted to little more than quiet acquiescence in the conduct of their Zimbabwean counterparts and their "war veteran" thugs. As I understand the pronouncements of the Constitutional Court, *infra*, this conduct from the authorities will not pass constitutional muster.

113. On 11 September 2002, Dr P. J. Von Abo, a son of the applicant, writes to the Department of Foreign Affairs in the following terms:

As you are aware Mr C. L. Von Abo is to appear in Court at Mwenezi Zimbabwe on Wednesday the 18th of September 2002 since he has only been released on bail on the 20th of August 2002. The charges against him are unknown. We ask for the Department's help and assistance in this regard which had been offered previously but did not realise.
We ask for your assistance in particular to the following: all the properties that we own in Zimbabwe are illegally occupied and taken over by so-called war veterans. We ask that the businesses either be released or that we are fully compensated for what is due to us. Furthermore we ask for protection that we are not illegally arrested and harassed on our own properties. We also ask for the normal diplomatic protection and assistance that any South African citizen can expect from our Government.
I take this opportunity as citizen of South Africa to ask for your assistance since I will be travelling with him and we rely on your help in this regard. We will be leaving for Zimbabwe on 16 September 2002 via Beitbridge to attend to the matter.

114. On 12 September 2002 the applicant writes a reminder to the South African High Commissioner in Harare pointing out that no acknowledgment or response had been forthcoming from that office. I also point out that this letter, and others to the High Commissioner, were hand delivered and written receipts form part of the papers.

115. On 13 September 2002 the Acting Director-General of the Department of Foreign Affairs writes to the applicant's son, Dr P. J. Von Abo, in the following terms:

The South African High Commission in Harare has been notified accordingly and is in the process of attending to your request. They [555] have conveyed the contents thereof to the Zimbabwean authorities by means of a diplomatic note.

No reply has been received as yet from the Zimbabwean authorities about the charges laid against Mr C. L. Von Abo nor about what kind of assistance and protection is to be granted to both of you.

116. On 20 September 2002 the applicant writes another letter to the South African High Commissioner listing further details of damages suffered on other farms of his in the Glendale district. This letter was also delivered by hand.

117. On 30 September 2002 the applicant again writes to Administrative Secretary Maritz of the Ministry of Foreign Affairs pointing out that his request of 24 March 2002 had not yet been attended to.

118. On 22 October 2002 Deputy Minister Pahad writes to the applicant in the following terms (only extracts quoted):

I apologise for any misunderstanding that may have arisen from the perceived lack of response from the Department of Foreign Affairs to your letters requesting assistance regarding your properties in Zimbabwe. I would, however, like to draw your attention to the fact that there has been a steady flow of information between the Department of Foreign Affairs and persons who approached us on your behalf. In replying to these persons, it had been assumed that you were being kept informed by the recipients of our replies . . .

Please be assured that your request to the President has been noted and that South African Government through the High Commission in Harare has been and will continue to interact with the Zimbabwean Government on the protection of the interests of South African citizens in Zimbabwe.

119. On 25 October 2002 the applicant writes to the Deputy Minister telling him that the High Commissioner has not responded to his appeals and that movable property on his farms had been seized illegally. He also says the following to the Deputy Minister:

I, as an individual cannot force the Zimbabwean Government to uphold my rights, but the South African Government can do just that under International Law; but it needs the will to do just that; as land owners of other nationalities have been protected by their Governments. (Emphasis added.)

120. On 29 November 2002 the applicant writes to the second respondent, sending him details of earlier correspondence and saying the following:

I do believe Honourable President that you will agree that these responses are highly unsatisfactory responses to an urgent and very serious matter. To be informed by the Deputy Minister a full seven months after my initial appeal to you that the South African High Commissioner is interacting with the Zimbabwe authorities without specifying in any way what is meant thereby and what results have been obtained is grossly insufficient.

While recognising that comparisons are often odious, I still wish to draw your attention to the discrepancy between my own position and that of two neighbours, a Mr Piere Emrick and a Mr Rolf Saldan, respectively French **[556]** *and German nationals who have enjoyed the full protection of their Governments and whose properties have not been affected in any way. In the Mazoe Valley, a Ms Nisliv, a Danish national, and in the Centenary district the Austrian owner of Forester Estates comprising 65,000 acres is likewise enjoying the protection of their Government.*

These are merely a few examples of very many foreign investors whose agricultural property rights are still respected by the Zimbabwean authorities. In stark contrast to this, hundreds of South African investors have lost their entire livelihood in Zimbabwe including their agricultural equipment and even their household goods in some instances. It is quite clear that South African investors are being lumped together with white Zimbabwean farmers for expropriation without any compensation by the Zimbabwean Government.

I once again appeal to you Honourable President to take our plight to heart as many of us have already been ruined financially and others are on their way there. (Emphasis added.)

121. On 22 January 2003 Human Rights Commissioner Leon Wessels writes to Deputy Minister Pahad on behalf of the applicant, urging the Deputy Minister to provide diplomatic support. Commissioner Wessels follows this up with a reminder on 11 February 2003 because there was no response.

122. On 13 February 2003 Mr H. J. Botma, Chairman of Grain South Africa, writes a long letter to the second respondent. He deals with the whole saga and says *inter alia*

we repeatedly hear from our Government that the interest[s] of South African investors in Zimbabwe are in fact being protected, but in reality the processes to which they are being exposed indicate that there is a complete breakdown in the rule of law in that country.

He goes on to say that Grain South Africa is committed to a farmer development programme that already impacts positively on the livelihoods of over 10,000 black farmers and it will continue to be part of this programme that should ensure sustainable land and agricultural reform. He urges the State President to take a firm stand on this whole issue of the Zimbabwean atrocities and to protect the South African farmers. He points out that many South Africans have made commercial investments in agriculture in Zimbabwe in an industry that contributed 60% to the GDP of that country.

123. On 10 March 2003 Deputy Minister Pahad writes a short, cryptic letter to Human Rights Commissioner Wessels in the following terms:

Attached please find a copy of the letter forwarded to Mr Von Abo in this regard. As you will notice from the letter, the status of all South African owned farms in Zimbabwe is discussed as a single issue and not as individually owned properties by the South African Government during its interactions with the Zimbabwean Government.

124. On 12 March 2003 the applicant writes the following letter to Deputy Minister Pahad:

I thank you for your letter dated 10 March 2003, which is most assuring. I am very grateful to you and the South African Government **[557]** for the action taken to secure our investments in Zimbabwe. I can assure you that it is most appreciated and it certainly reassures me that we have future in a democratic South Africa.

I would, however, like to place on record what has happened to me and what is still happening to me in Zimbabwe.

1. Chief Chewezi moved into a house of mine on the farm Mshawa, part of Lochnagar Estates in Centenary district, 2002, cut the padlocks of the tobacco sheds and sold 30,000kg of my tobacco worth R1 million for his account. Told my manager that if he would report this to the police, he would regret it.
2. Elliot Manyika (Governor Mashonaland Central) took over Duiker Flats, a farm in the Dindura district, part of Linabo Estates belonging to me. Totally illegally even in Zimbabwean terms. Letter attached.
3. All the implements, tractors, fuel, vehicles equipment etcetera have been seized on Von Abo Estates and Brecon, Glendale district. List attached.
4. Fauna and Flora Ranches in the Mwenezi area have been taken over by more than 300 so-called settlers. They have totally decimated the ranches which is part of a conservancy area. They snared and killed off all the game namely the following:

400 Eland
150 Giraffe
70 Tsessebe
80 Sable
9 Oryx
15 Waterbuck (there are others)

The underground pipeline supplying water to the different paddocks has been dug up and vandalised for kilometres.

At present the 20% of my cattle that is still on the property is being slaughtered at the rate of four to five per week.

5. Dunbartom Estates Centenary district has been taken over completely. A high developed tobacco concern with 60 hectare of drip irrigation. Tobacco facilities worth millions is totally out of commission. The earning capacity was more than a US dollar million per year.

I am enclosing a list of the properties, their production figures, sworn valuation and loose assets taken, for your attention.

What is, however, of great concern to me is what is meant by "would be delisted in accordance with the laws and regulations of Zimbabwe" and who is going to be held responsible for my losses and how am I going to be compensated for that.

I have pointed out that promises that farms would be "delisted" never materialised. I have pointed out that not one of the respondents bothered to furnish an affidavit to explain their conduct, or lack thereof.

125. On 15 March 2003, Mr Wilfried Pabst, a German businessman, wrote a long e-mail message to the Deputy Foreign Minister. I quote a few short extracts:

By introduction kindly be advised that I am a German businessman with substantial investments in South Africa and in a wildlife Sanctuary on Zimbabwe. Your Minister of Tourism and Environment, Mr Valli **[558]** Moosa, has met with me and is informed about our venture in Zimbabwe, my trepidations about it and our hopes to be part of the Trans Frontier Conservation Area.

The problems I am facing in Zimbabwe are very similar to those experienced by Mr Von Abo. However, my German Government, my Parliament and my Ambassadors have all been most forthcoming in intervening on my behalf with Zimbabwean politicians and authorities. I personally have known President Mugabe for eight years and met half of the country's Ministers and Vice President of the last three or four years in the defence of my investment. My Ambassadors, German Politicians and I have taken numerous actions at ministerial and vice presidential level, which have ensured that my staff and my land are safe.

(He does, however, express reservations of what might happen still in future.) He then says:

With all due respect to the South African Government, Honourable Minister, the protection you have actively offered on the ground case by case [had] been most unsatisfactory. Your High Commission in Harare does not have remotely the same authority to deal case by case with politicians in Zimbabwe as do my ambassadors ... Your Minister of Foreign Affairs, Ms Zuma, visits Zimbabwe, spends no time with members of the opposition, farmers or other interest groups and returns to South Africa to accuse the media of having made up the problems facing Zimbabwe ...

126. On 12 May 2003 the applicant writes to the Deputy Foreign Minister enquiring about the promised delisting of properties and telling him that he is still out on bail after having been arrested on one of his properties in August 2002. He says "up to date I have had no assistance from your department regarding my arrest, and I would like to place that on record".

127. On 17 June 2003 the Deputy Minister writes to the applicant telling him that farms listed under the Zimbabwean Land Reform Programme owned by nationals from SADC Member States and/or countries with BIPPAs would be delisted. He ends the letter with his regulation promise that the Government will continue its endeavours to find the solution for the problems.

128. On 2 December 2003 the Deputy Minister writes to Mr Boy Geldenhuys MP telling him that the BIPPA was in the process of being negotiated.

129. On 11 December 2003 the applicant writes to the second respondent in the following terms:

The South African Government is well aware that despite the assurance and guarantees given by them, my total investment in Zimbabwe has been unlawfully confiscated by Zanu PF supporters, without any intervention by the South African Government. On the contrary, statements have been made by the South African authorities that actually condone the confiscation of property, assets and investments by the Mugabe regime.

I was arrested [in] August 2002 without a warrant on one of my properties, Fauna Ranch Mwenezi. I have had to attend court hearings five times **[559]** during the past eighteen months and have to be back in court on the 21st of January 2004 in Zimbabwe as I am still out on bail. I have repeatedly requested the South African Government to assist me to deal with this unlawful arrest. Up to this day I have had no assistance from the South African authority, despite the assurance that was given to this effect by the South African Government in March 2002.

I hereby place it on record that I hold the South African Government responsible for my losses in Zimbabwe which [were] valued by professional valuators as well as my loss of income all attributable to inaction on the part of the South African Government.

Should my personal safety be in jeopardy on my next court appearance in Zimbabwe I shall hold the South African Government directly responsible for neglecting to give me any diplomatic assistance despite assurances to the contrary.

130. On 5 January 2004 the Deputy Minister writes to the applicant telling him that he had noted the plight of the applicant and his next court appearance and he told the South African High Commission in Harare about this. He says "the latter will, from a consular point of view, continue to monitor and attend your court cases, *as and when possible*" (emphasis added). The Deputy Minister then assures the applicant that a BIPPA had been negotiated and that "the process is in its final stages". On 19 February 2004 the Deputy Minister again writes a letter to one Mr MacKenzie telling him that the BIPPA is in its final stages and that it is envisaged that the agreement would be signed within the first quarter of 2004.

131. I indicated that the process of dealing with all these letters is a cumbersome one and a full analysis of every letter is, in my view, unnecessary. In my opinion, what has already been quoted and analysed is a fair reflection of the whole sorry saga. Later requests for ICSID involvement were turned down flat. A request to inspect the draft BIPPA was refused. Many letters were acknowledged "with gratitude" by junior officials, but nothing of substance was forthcoming from the respondents.

132. Perhaps the applicant's tortured journey can be concluded, for present purposes, with the following startling concession made by Ambassador Mamabolo Deputy Director-General: Branch Africa on behalf of the Department of Foreign Affairs as late as March 2005:

In terms of the Zimbabwean Government's policy, land owned by nationals from countries with BIPPAs would be delisted. As these abovementioned agreements have been signed by a number of countries with Zimbabwe, it seems that the South African farmers, at present, do not enjoy the same level of protection as the farmers of such other countries which have signed agreements with Zimbabwean Government, a situation which the South African Government has been actively working to change. Hence the South African Government is ready to conclude and sign the BIPPA. Amen.

[560] *The Applicant's Damages*

133. In his founding affidavit, the applicant, in clear and emphatic terms, listed the estimated damages suffered by him. The damages were properly assessed and neatly specified in the founding affidavit.

134. The total conservatively calculated damages, in respect of six farming units, amount to between 9.6 million and 11.4 million US dollars, or something in the order of R50 to R60 million. The details are not disputed on the papers.

The Legal Position: Guidelines Received from the Constitutional Court

135. Understandably, counsel for the applicant, in their comprehensive argument, strongly relied on the judgment in *Kaunda and Others* v. *President of the Republic of South Africa and Others* 2005 4 SA 235 (CC) ("*Kaunda*").

136. *Kaunda* appears to be the leading South African authority on diplomatic protection and the State's duty under the Constitution towards its nationals who claim protection for injuries suffered abroad at the hands of a foreign government.

137. At the outset, counsel for the applicant point out that in *Kaunda*, paragraph 29, the majority, *per* Chaskalson CJ, states that "the prevailing view is that diplomatic protection is not recognised by international law as a human right and cannot be enforced as such" and, therefore, that claimants, such as the applicant, "cannot base their claims on customary international law".

138. It is then submitted on behalf of the applicant that he does not base his claims for relief on customary international law, although Customary International Law is relevant to the determination of the jurisdictional facts underpinning the applicant's claim, *supra*.

139. The applicant's claim was premised on the Constitution when the requests for diplomatic protection were made to the respondents.

140. In this regard it is convenient to quote the following words of the learned Chief Justice:

64. When the request is directed to a material infringement of a human right that forms part of customary international law, one would not expect our Government to be passive. Whatever theoretical disputes may still exist about the basis for diplomatic protection, it cannot be doubted that in substance the true beneficiary of the right that is asserted is the individual.

65. The founding values of our Constitution include human dignity, equality and the advancement of human rights and freedoms. Equality is reflected in the principle of equal citizenship demanded by section 3.

66. The advancement of human rights and freedoms is central to the Constitution itself. It is a thread that runs throughout the Constitution and informs the manner in which Government is required to exercise its powers. To this extent, the provisions of section 7(2) are relevant, not as giving our Constitution extraterritorial effect, but as showing that our **[561]** Constitution contemplates that Government will act positively to protect its citizens against human rights abuses.

67. The entitlement to request diplomatic protection which is part of the Constitutional guarantee given by section 3 has certain consequences. If, as I have held, citizens have a right to request Government to provide them with diplomatic protection, then Government must have a corresponding obligation to consider the request and deal with it consistently with the Constitution.

141. The applicant therefore had a right to apply for diplomatic protection, and the respondents, at a minimum, were under a constitutional duty at the very least to properly (that is rationally) apply their minds to the request for diplomatic protection. The learned Chief Justice puts it as follows in paragraph 69:

There may thus be a duty on government, consistent with its obligations under International Law, to take action to protect one of its citizens against gross abuse of international human rights norms. A request to the government for assistance in such circumstances where the evidence is clear would be difficult, and in extreme cases possibly impossible to refuse. It is unlikely that such a request would ever be refused by government, but if it were, the decision would be justiciable, and the court could order the government to take appropriate action.

142. Inasmuch as it may have been argued on behalf of the respondents (although not with great force) that the question of diplomatic protection falls in the domain of the executive, so that a court ought not to interfere, given the principle of the separation of powers, regard should be had to the following words of the learned Chief Justice:

77. A decision as to whether protection should be given, and if so, what, is an aspect of foreign policy which is essentially the function of the Executive. The timing of representations if they are to be made, the language in which they should be couched, and the sanctions (if any) which should follow if such representations are rejected are matter with which courts are ill-equipped to deal. The best way to secure relief for the national in whose interest the action is taken may be to engage in delicate and sensitive negotiations in which diplomats are better placed to make decisions than Judges, and which could be harmed by court proceedings and the attendant publicity.

78. This does not mean that South African courts have no jurisdiction to deal with issues concerned with diplomatic protection. The exercise of all public power is subject to Constitutional control. Thus even decisions by

the President to grant a pardon or to appoint a Commission of enquiry are justiciable. *This also applies to an allegation that Government has failed to respond appropriately to a request for diplomatic protection.*

79. For instance, if the decision were to be irrational, a court could intervene. This does not mean that courts would substitute their opinion for that of the Government or order the Government to provide a particular form of diplomatic protection ...

80. *If Government refuses to consider a legitimate request, or deals with it in bad faith or irrationally, a court could require Government to deal with the matter properly. Rationality and bad faith are illustrations of grounds on* **[562]** *which a court may be persuaded to review a decision. There may possibly be other grounds as well and these illustrations should not be understood as a closed list.* (Emphasis added.)

143. From these guidelines provided by the Constitutional Court it appears that there need not be an actual refusal on the part of Government to grant diplomatic protection before a court will intervene. In an appropriate case, a court can also come to the assistance of the aggrieved national where Government "fails to respond appropriately" or "deals with the matter in bad faith or irrationally".

In my view, and for all the reasons mentioned, the Government, in the present instance, failed to respond appropriately and dealt with the matter in bad faith and irrationally. For six years or more, and in the face of a stream of urgent requests from many sources, they did absolutely nothing to bring about relief for the applicant and hundreds of other white commercial farmers in the same position. Their "assistance", such as it is, was limited to empty promises. They exhibited neither the will nor the ability to do anything constructive to bring their northern neighbour to book. They paid no regard, of any consequence, to the plight of valuable citizens such as the fifth-generation applicant with a fifty-year track record in Zimbabwe, and other hardworking white commercial farmers making a substantial contribution to the GDP in Zimbabwe and providing thousands of people with work in that country.

144. In *Kaunda*, the learned Ngcobo J, in his concurring judgment, also provided valuable guidelines for purposes of adjudicating upon a case of this nature.

145. *Inter alia*, the learned judge concentrated on the construction of sections 3(2) and 7(2) of the Constitution in the context of cases of this nature. The relevant provisions in section 3 read as follows:

3(1) There is a common South African citizenship.
(2) All citizens are—

(a) Equally entitled to the rights, privileges and benefits of citizenship; and
(b) Equally subject to the duties and responsibilities of citizenship.

The relevant provisions in section 7 read as follows:

(1) The Bill of Rights is a cornerstone of democracy in South Africa. It enshrines the rights of all people in our country and affirms the democratic values of human dignity, equality and freedom.

(2) The state must respect, protect, promote and fulfil the rights in the Bill of Rights.

146. I find it convenient and helpful to quote extracts from the remarks made by the learned judge:

175. The starting point in the determination of the question whether there is a duty to provide diplomatic protection is section 3(2)(a). This section provides that all South African citizens are "equally entitled to [563] the rights, privileges and benefits of citizenship". This provision is the source of the rights, privileges and benefits of citizenship to which South African citizens are entitled under our Constitution.

176. What section 7(2) does, on the other hand, is to bind the state to respect, protect, promote and fulfil the rights in the Bill of Rights. Here it must be borne in mind that the right to citizenship is constitutionally entrenched in the Bill of Rights. It is clear from section 3(2)(a) that, in addition to certain rights, there are benefits and privileges to which South African citizens are entitled. *In this sense, sections 3(2) and 7(2) must be read together as defining the obligations of the Government in relation to its citizens.*

177. Section 3(2)(a) therefore confers a right upon every citizen to be accorded the rights, privileges and benefits of citizenship. This provision also makes it clear that citizenship should be treated equally in the provision of rights, privileges and benefits. This, of course, does not mean that citizens may not be treated differently where there are compelling reasons to do so . . .

178. Flowing from this, a citizen has the right under section 3(2)(a) to require the Government to provide him or her with rights, privileges and benefits of citizenship. The obligation of the Government is to consider rationally such request and decide whether to grant such request in relation to that citizen. If the Government decides not to grant such request its decision may be subject to judicial review. This is so because such a decision is taken in the exercise of public power and the exercise of public power must conform to the Constitution. The question whether the exercise of public power conforms to the Constitution must be determined by the courts.

179. The question that must be considered next is whether the rights, privileges and benefits comprehended in section 3(2)(a) include the right, privilege and benefit to request diplomatic protection . . .

188. *I conclude therefore that diplomatic protection is a benefit within the meaning of section 3(2)(a). It follows therefore that sections 3(2)(a) and 7(2) must be read as imposing a constitutional duty on the Government to ensure that all South African nationals abroad enjoy the benefits of public protection. The proposition that the Government has no constitutional duty in this*

regard must be rejected. Such a proposition is inconsistent with the Government's own declared policy and acknowledged constitutional duty. (Emphasis added.)

147. In her judgment in *Kaunda*, O'Regan J said the following about section 3:

242. In my view, therefore, to the extent that section 3 entitles citizens to the privileges and benefits of citizenship, this obliges the state to provide diplomatic protection to citizens at least in circumstances where citizens are threatened with or have experienced the egregious violation of International human rights norms binding on the foreign state that caused or threatened to cause the violation.

148. Against this background I debated with counsel for the applicant the remedy sought and the nature of the relief called for.

What is left, after the ICSID prayer and the review prayer had been abandoned, is **[564]** declaratory, mandatory and supervisory relief. This appears from the notice of motion, as it now stands, *supra*.

149. I enquired from counsel whether the provisions of section 38 of the Constitution could come into play. Section 38 provides that "anyone listed in this section has the right to approach a competent court, *alleging that a right in the Bill of Rights has been infringed or threatened*, and the court may grant appropriate relief, including a declaration of rights . . . " (emphasis added). My question was whether section 38 could be applied in view thereof that section 3 is, strictly speaking, not part of the Bill of Rights. I was referred to the words of Ngcobo J, *supra*, that section 3 and section 7 (which is part of the Bill of Rights) should be read together for purposes of deciding this issue of diplomatic protection. I was also referred to *Minister of Health and Others* v. *Treatment Action Campaign (No 1)* 2002 (5) SA 703 (CC) at 708D where the following is stated:

7. Section 38 of the Constitution empowers a court to grant appropriate relief when it concludes that a breach or threatened breach of a person's rights under the Bill of Rights has been established. *This provision is mirrored in section 172 of the Constitution, which similarly empowers a court when deciding a Constitutional matter within its jurisdiction to grant "just and equitable" relief.* (Emphasis added.)

If the application were to succeed, the provisions of section 172 must, for obvious reasons, come into play. From the aforementioned analysis, I must conclude that section 38 is applicable, and, even if it is not, section 172 is to be interpreted as providing the same wide discretion when it comes to deciding what "appropriate relief" or "any order that is just and equitable" would be in the specific circumstances of the case.

What may then serve as a useful guide, would be the well-known words of Ackermann J in *Fose* v. *Minister of Safety and Security* 1997 (3) SA 786 (CC) at 799F where the following is said with regard to the corresponding provisions in the interim Constitution:

19. Appropriate relief will in essence be relief that is required to protect and enforce the Constitution. Depending on the circumstances of each particular case the relief may be a declaration of rights, an interdict, a *mandamus* or such other relief as may be required to ensure that the rights enshrined in the Constitution are protected and enforced. If it is necessary to do so, the courts may even have to fashion new remedies to secure the protection and enforcement of these all-important rights.

150. On the same subject, it is convenient to quote what was said in *Mohamed and Another* v. *President of the Republic of South Africa and Others (Society for the Abolition of the Death Penalty in South Africa and Another Intervening)* 2001 (3) SA 893 (CC) at 921G-922H when it comes to the question of appropriate relief:

69. ... With regard to the prayer for mandatory relief in the form of an order on the Government to seek to intercede with the United States authorities regarding the wrong done to Mohamed, the Government's opposition to any form of order was even more forceful. More **[565]** specifically it was submitted that any such an order would infringe the separation of powers between the Judiciary and the Executive. In substance the stance was that Mohamed had been irreversibly surrendered to the power of the United States and, in any event, it was not for this Court, or any other, to give instructions to the Executive.

70. We disagree. It would not necessarily be futile for this Court to pronounce on the illegality of the Governmental conduct in issue in this case ...

71. Nor would it necessarily be out of place for there to be an appropriate order on the relevant organs of State in South Africa to do whatever may be within their power to remedy the wrong here done to Mohamed by their actions, or to ameliorate at best the consequence of prejudice caused to him. To stigmatise such an order as a breach of the separation of State power as between the Executive and the Judiciary is to negate a foundational value of the Republic of South Africa, namely supremacy of the Constitution and the rule of law. The Bill of Rights, which we find to have been infringed, is binding on all organs of State and it is our constitutional duty to ensure that appropriate relief is afforded to those who have suffered infringement of their constitutional rights.

151. The footnote introduced by that court after stating "the Bill of Rights, which we find to have been infringed, is binding on all organs of state and it is our constitutional duty ... " reads as follows:

Under section 7(2) read with sections 38 and 172(1)(a) of the Constitution. (Emphasis added.)

152. It can do no harm to bear the provisions of two other related sections in the Constitution in mind: Section 232 provides that customary international law is law in the Republic unless it is inconsistent with the Constitution or an Act of Parliament. Section 237 provides that all constitutional obligations must be performed diligently and without delay.

153. As to appropriate relief, the Constitutional Court has also been known to grant supervisory relief in the sense that the offending organ of State must report progress back to the court—see *Sibiya* v. *Director of Public Prosecutions, Johannesburg* 2005 (5) SA 315 (CC) at 337G-338G. In the judgment, Yacoob J says the following:

> 62. This Court has the jurisdiction to issue a *mandamus* in appropriate circumstances and to exercise supervisory jurisdiction over the process of the execution of its order. It is appropriate in this case for this to be done. The question of a supervisory order was raised with counsel at the hearing of the case. None raised any objection to a supervisory order.

See also *Kiliko and Others* v. *Minister of Home Affairs and Others* 2006 (4) SA 114 at 129C-130I.

154. In all the circumstances I have come to the conclusion that the applicant has made out a proper case for appropriate relief.

[566] 155. The certification process, as described by section 172(2)(a) of the Constitution, will be attended to, in the normal course, by the applicant in cooperation with the respondents.

Costs

156. Counsel for the applicant urged me, in the event of the applicant succeeding, to grant the costs flowing from the employment of three counsel and also to grant the costs on a punitive scale.

157. They made compelling submissions in this regard. They argued that the respondents failed to comply with the requirements of section 165(4) of the Constitution which instructs organs of State to assist and protect the courts to ensure the independence, impartiality, dignity, accessibility and effectiveness of the courts. The opposing affidavit of Stemmet was filed out of time. No diligent effort was made to deal with the argument as to inadmissibility of the evidence, *supra*, mentioned in the replying affidavit. The affidavit of Deputy Minister Pahad, such as it was, was handed up a year after the replying affidavit was filed

and on the morning when the proceedings commenced. There was no application for condonation. The South Africa/Swiss Bilateral Treaty, *supra*, was tendered for inspection on the second day of the hearing without compliance with the rules. The BIPPA was not shown to the applicant.

158. It was argued that the respondents' truancy in this litigation is cause for concern, given that they are no ordinary litigants, but organs of state, with unlimited resources available for the purposes of litigation.

159. Nevertheless, although these submissions are not without merit, it also occurs to me that a substantial portion of the time and costs flowing from these proceedings was devoted to the ICSID argument and the review portion of the initial relief sought. This was abandoned. Although the ICSID submissions were not without relevance, I consider it equitable to take this issue into account when deciding whether or not a punitive cost order would be appropriate.

160. In all the circumstances, I have decided against awarding the costs of three counsel and making a punitive cost order.

The Order

161. I make the following order:

1. It is declared that the failure of the respondents to rationally, appropriately and in good faith consider, decide and deal with the applicant's application for diplomatic protection in respect of the violation of his rights by the Government of Zimbabwe is inconsistent with the Constitution, 1996 and invalid.
2. It is declared that the applicant has the right to diplomatic protection from the respondents in respect of the violation of his rights by the Government of Zimbabwe.
3. It is declared that the respondents have a Constitutional obligation to provide diplomatic protection to the applicant in respect of the violation of his rights by the Government of Zimbabwe.
4. **[567]** The respondents are ordered to forthwith, and in any event within 60 days of the date of this order, take all necessary steps to have the applicant's violation of his rights by the Government of Zimbabwe remedied.
5. The respondents are directed to report by way of affidavit to this court within 60 (sixty) days of this order, what steps they have taken in respect of paragraph 4 above, and to provide a copy of such report to the applicant.

6. The applicant's claim for damages against the respondents, subject to effective compliance with paragraphs 4 and 5 above, and as formulated in the notice of motion, is postponed *sine die*. Leave is granted to all parties to supplement their papers prior to the hearing of this claim for damages, if appropriate.
7. The respondents are ordered, jointly and severally, to pay the costs of the applicant, which will include the costs flowing from the employment of two counsel.

[Report: 2009 (2) SA 526]

The following is the text of the judgment of the Constitutional Court, delivered by Moseneke DCJ:

JUDGMENT OF THE CONSTITUTIONAL COURT

[348] *Introduction*

1. Before us are confirmatory proceedings in terms of section 172(2)(a)[1] of the Constitution read with Rule 16 of the Constitutional Court Rules.[2] [349] The applicant, Mr Von Abo, seeks confirmation of an order of the North Gauteng High Court, Pretoria (High Court) made by Prinsloo J against the President of the Republic of South Africa. In that court, the President was cited, along with four other Cabinet

---

[1] Section 172(2)(a) states:

The Supreme Court of Appeal, a High Court or a court of similar status may make an order concerning the constitutional validity of an Act of Parliament, a provincial Act or any conduct of the President, but an order of constitutional invalidity has no force unless it is confirmed by the Constitutional Court.

[2] Rule 16 provides as follows:

1. The Registrar of a court which has made an order of constitutional invalidity as contemplated in section 172 of the Constitution shall, within 15 days of such order, lodge with the Registrar of the Court a copy of such order.

2. A person or organ of state entitled to do so and desirous of appealing against such an order in terms of section 172(2)(d) of the Constitution shall, within 15 days of the making of such an order, lodge a notice of appeal with the Registrar and a copy thereof with the Registrar of the Court which made the order, whereupon the matter shall be disposed of in accordance with the directions given by the Chief Justice.

3. The appellant shall in such notice of appeal set forth clearly the grounds on which the appeal is brought, indicating which findings of fact and/or law are appealed against and the order it is contended ought to have been made.

4. A person or organ of state entitled to do so or desirous of applying for the confirmation of an order in terms of section 172(2)(d) of the Constitution shall, within 15 days of the making of such order, lodge an application for such confirmation with the Registrar and a copy thereof with the Registrar of the Court which made the order, whereupon the matter shall be disposed of in accordance with directions given by the Chief Justice.

5. If no notice or application as contemplated in subrules (2) and (4), respectively, has been lodged within the time prescribed, the matter of the confirmation of the order of invalidity shall be disposed of in accordance with directions given by the Chief Justice.

Ministers and the government, as a respondent. The court order consists of declaratory and mandatory relief. However, only paragraph 1 of the declaratory orders has been brought to this court for confirmation and only the President has been cited as respondent. The essence of the order sought to be confirmed is that the failure of the President, as one of several government respondents, to consider and decide properly the request of Mr Von Abo for diplomatic protection against the violation of his property rights by the government of Zimbabwe, was inconsistent with the Constitution and invalid.[3]

2. Mr Von Abo is a South African citizen and businessman who held various properties and farming interests in Zimbabwe. His complaint against the government of South Africa flows from its alleged failure to afford him diplomatic protection against his proprietary interests being "violated" by the Government of Zimbabwe.

3. In the High Court the applicant cited as the first respondent the Government of South Africa, together with the President as second respondent and the Minister for Foreign Affairs, the Minister for Trade and Industry and the Minister for Justice and Constitutional Development as third, fourth and fifth respondents respectively. However, in this court, the applicant has cited only the President as respondent. This the applicant has done because, in his view, the failure by the President to afford him diplomatic protection constitutes "any conduct" of the President referred to in section 172(2)(a) of the Constitution and therefore an order of the High Court relating to the conduct of the President is binding only if it is confirmed by this court. Implicit in the stance the applicant has adopted is that the order of the High Court relating to the Cabinet Ministers, who were respondents before it, is not susceptible to confirmation by this court and that, if not reversed on appeal, is without more binding and final.

4. Before I identify the crisp issue for decision it is necessary to sketch the background facts and course of the litigation.

Background Facts and Litigation

5. As managing director of certain companies and sole trustee of the Von Abo Trust, Mr Von Abo established substantial financial and farming interests in Zimbabwe. This he did over the course of the last **[350]** 50 years. Initially, he financed the farming activities by applying his own resources drawn from his South African reserves. In time however, he funded the farming interests using finances available to him

---

[3] *Von Abo v. Government of the Republic of South Africa* 2009 (2) SA 526 (T) at para. 161.

in Zimbabwe. He set about re-investing profits and capital gains in his Zimbabwean interests. In this manner he became the beneficial owner of a "considerable farming empire" in that country.

6. From about 1997, the Government of Zimbabwe devised a legislative scheme to confiscate land owned by white farmers. This led to widescale expropriation of land and farming businesses without compensation. Many white-owned farms were taken over by the government or invaded by people who claimed to be repossessing farms under government authority. Owners of the farms, their workers and other occupants were forcibly evicted without due process of the law. The farming operations stalled and many farms were destroyed in the process. The same fate befell Mr Von Abo's farming interests.

7. Mr Von Abo was aggrieved that his farming operations had been ruined and, what is more, that the Government of Zimbabwe had not paid him compensation for the expropriation or damages he had suffered. Having exhausted all remedies available to him in Zimbabwe, he approached the South African Government for diplomatic protection related to his invaded land and now-compromised commercial interests. In March 2002 he wrote to the President requesting diplomatic protection concerning the "violation of his rights" in Zimbabwe. Mr Von Abo also requested that the President and the Minister for Trade and Industry accede on behalf of South Africa to the International Convention on the Settlement of Investment Disputes (ICSID), in order that he might, as a citizen of a party to this Convention, pursue a claim for compensation against the Zimbabwean Government under ICSID.[4] This would have been feasible because Zimbabwe had acceded to ICSID and could thus be held liable under its terms. To this end, he requested a meeting with the President in order to discuss the importance of the government becoming a party to ICSID.

8. Dissatisfied with the response of the government and what he termed its failure to "take diplomatic steps . . . to protect or fulfil [his] rights" and without "meaningful explanation for this failure and/or refusal", he decided to put it on terms, and threatened legal action. No response was forthcoming from the government. In January 2007 and nearly five years after his initial request to the government for diplomatic protection, Mr Von Abo approached the High Court. He sought an order declaring, amongst other prayers, that the failure of the government to consider and decide his application for diplomatic

---

[4] ICSID was entered into force on 14 October 1966. Zimbabwe deposited its ratification of ICSID on 20 May 1994.

protection in respect of the violation of his rights by the Government of Zimbabwe was inconsistent with the Constitution and invalid.

9. The government and the Cabinet Ministers cited opposed the relief sought. They contended that they had seriously considered the request **[351]** for diplomatic protection and that they had taken reasonable steps to provide the protection sought. They added that the Government of South Africa had made several diplomatic representations on Mr Von Abo's plight to the Government of Zimbabwe without success but had no means to coerce that government to heed the representations.

10. These averments were deposed to by an official in the Department of Foreign Affairs. None of the government respondents filed an affidavit to confirm the correctness of the answering affidavit put up on behalf of government. This the applicant took issue with in his replying affidavit. In its judgment, the High Court found the omission to be a material defect in the defence raised by the government and other respondents. It accordingly approached the facts on the basis that the government and other respondents had put up no credible facts to controvert Mr Von Abo's version.

The High Court

11. The High Court found that the requirements necessary for a State to assert a claim for diplomatic protection on behalf of its citizen were present. It found that the requirements are that the claimant must be a national of the country from which diplomatic protection is sought; that there had been a violation of an international minimum standard; and that the claimant had previously exhausted all available internal remedies. The High Court found that the long, drawn-out responses of the government to the applicant's numerous letters and requests had amounted to merely "stringing the applicant along" and that the respondents "never had any serious intention to afford him proper protection". As a result, the court held that the applicant did indeed have a right to diplomatic protection, and that the respondents had failed to take the necessary steps to afford Mr Von Abo diplomatic protection. The High Court concluded that the applicant had made out a proper case for declaratory and mandatory relief and granted the order sought against all respondents including the President.

12. For the sake of completeness, I reproduce the order of the High Court in full. [The Court quoted paragraph 161 of the order of the High Court of 29 July 2008, as reported at pp. 623-4 above.]

[352] 13. Neither the government nor any of the other respondents has assailed the correctness of the judgment or the validity of the order of the High Court by way of an appeal. The order was made nearly ten months ago and the time within which the respondents in that court may have sought leave to appeal has long elapsed. A party to confirmation proceedings in this court has an automatic right of appeal against the order sought to be confirmed. None of the government respondents has availed itself of this right of appeal. If anything, during the hearing in this court, counsel for the respondent sought to tender new evidence to show that the government respondents were taking active steps to comply with the order of the High Court. From the bar counsel for the respondent assured this court that neither the government nor any of the other respondents is minded to do anything other than comply with the order of the High Court.

Proceedings in this Court

14. I have explained earlier that Mr Von Abo has approached this court for an order confirming the order of the High Court but only insofar as it relates to the conduct of the President and only in relation to paragraph 1 of the order. He says that the order will be a limping one unless it is confirmed by this court in terms of section 172(2)(a) of the Constitution. The applicant's conviction that the order of the High Court is susceptible to confirmation appears to have been emboldened by the stance of the High Court. In its judgment, the High Court too is of the view that its order should be referred to this court for confirmation. The respondent does not agree with this characterisation and on this basis opposes the confirmation. He contends that the order in issue does not relate to his conduct as President as envisaged in section 172(2)(a) of the Constitution and thus it is not susceptible to confirmation.

New Evidence

15. Before I formulate the crisp issue to be determined, regrettably, I must stray to mention a matter that unduly obscured, if not sidetracked the determination of the core question. The matter relates to the abortive attempts on behalf of the respondent to introduce new evidence to the confirmatory proceedings in this court. This occurred in the following manner. Prior to the hearing of 11 November 2008 the respondent attached an annexure to his written argument. The contents of the annexure related to diplomatic exchanges between the Governments of South Africa and Zimbabwe as part of an effort by

our government to [353] comply with the order of the High Court in favour of Mr Von Abo. The respondent's attorney served the annexure on the applicant's attorney and filed it with the registrar of this court. The annexure contained a claim on behalf of the respondent that the evidence of the diplomatic exchanges was confidential and deserved to be protected from public disclosure by means of a court order. This court issued an interim ruling to protect the claimed confidentiality until the date of hearing when the parties would be heard on the confidentiality claim.[5]

16. However, on the day of the hearing, the respondent had still not brought a formal application for the admission of the new evidence contained in the annexure. The applicant's attitude was that it would not take the point that no formal application for admission of the evidence had been made but would oppose its admission on grounds of relevance. It was argued that the evidence was irrelevant as it had no bearing on the possible outcome of the confirmatory proceedings. The new evidence related to the conduct of the respondents after and in compliance with the order of the High Court.

17. Confronted by this difficulty, counsel for the President nonetheless requested a postponement of the confirmation hearing in order to bring a formal application to tender the new evidence. The hearing was postponed to 26 February 2009 and the respondent was ordered to pay the wasted costs occasioned by the postponement of the hearing and to file the requisite application no later than 28 November 2008. The deadline came and went and no application to tender new evidence was made. On 20 January 2009 the court issued directions requiring the parties to make representations on why this court should not withdraw its concession to keep the "confidential" documents away from public viewing.

18. It was only on 11 February 2009 that the respondent filed a belated application to tender new evidence, along with a request for condonation for his non-compliance with the court's directions of 11 November 2008. Mr Von Abo opposed the application for condonation and for leave to tender new evidence. He submitted that the new evidence was irrelevant to the confirmation proceedings. As matters turned out, at the hearing of 25 February 2009, this court did not reach the application to admit new evidence. This was so because by direction of this court the parties were enjoined to argue only the narrow question

---

[5] A similar ruling was adopted in *Independent Newspapers (Pty) Ltd* v. *Minister for Intelligence Services; Freedom of Expression Institute In re: Masetlha* v. *President of the Republic of South Africa and Another* 2008 (5) SA 31 (CC) (2008 (8) BCLR 771 (CC); [2008] ZACC 6).

whether the High Court order was susceptible to confirmation under section 172(2)(a) of the Constitution.

19. However, the wasted costs relating to the two interlocutory applications remain undetermined. It is thus now necessary to dispose of the costs of the two applications. In my view, both applications were destined to be dismissed. During the hearing counsel for the respondent conceded that the respondent should be ordered to pay all the wasted [354] costs related to the aborted application to introduce new evidence as well as the related application for condonation. That concession was properly made.

20. In *Van Wyk* v. *Unitas Hospital* this court warned that in an application for condonation the explanation of the delay must be full and frank and must demonstrate that the case of the applicant bears some prospect of success.[6] The application for condonation was bad on both counts. It lacked an adequate explanation for the failure of the respondent to bring an application for admission of fresh evidence within the time-frames stipulated by the directions of this court. What is more, the substantive application to introduce new evidence at this late stage bore no prospects of success because, as the applicants correctly submitted, the new evidence in issue bore no relevance to the confirmation proceedings. Instead it related to events that occurred after the High Court had made the order which is now the subject of the present confirmation proceedings. The new matter was not directed at challenging the order of the High Court but rather at displaying the steps the government had taken to satisfy the order. I propose to make an adverse order as to wasted costs relating to the two interlocutory applications against the respondent. I have said the respondent does not resist the adverse cost order being made. I will make the costs order at an appropriate stage of this judgment.

21. This of course means that the new testimony which was said to be confidential was not admitted as part of the papers in this matter. It must follow without more that any interim order intended to protect that confidentiality should fall away. Again, I will revert to this matter when I fashion an appropriate order.

Issues

22. This court's directions of 25 February 2009 required the parties to argue only the following issues:

---

[6] *Van Wyk* v. *Unitas Hospital and Another (Open Democratic Advice Centre as Amicus Curiae)* [2007] ZACC 24; 2008 (2) SA 472 (CC); 2008 (4) BCLR 442 (CC) at paras. 20 and 22.

(a) whether the order of the High Court that the conduct of the President is inconsistent with the Constitution and invalid, is subject to confirmation by this court in terms of section 172(2)(a) of the Constitution.
(b) if this court were to find that the order of the High Court is not subject to confirmation what order should this court make in relation to costs.
(c) if this court were to find that the order of the High Court is not subject to confirmation what order should this court make regarding its own order made on 4 November 2008 regarding the confidentiality of certain documents claimed on behalf of the respondents.

23. At the hearing, the sole question of substance that came up for debate was whether the failure to provide diplomatic protection by the [355] President constitutes "conduct" as envisaged in section 172(2)(a) of the Constitution. If it does, this court is obliged to consider and determine the merits of the decision of the court *a quo* in order to decide whether the order of the High Court should be confirmed. However, if the President's failure does not constitute the envisaged conduct, that finding would be dispositive of the matter and the application for confirmation would be struck off the roll.

Contentions of the Parties

24. Before I briefly describe the submissions of the parties, it is expedient to set out the wording of section 172(2)(a) in full:

The Supreme Court of Appeal, a High Court or a court of similar status may make an order concerning the constitutional validity of an Act of Parliament, a provincial Act or *any conduct of the President*, but an order of constitutional invalidity has no force unless it is confirmed by the Constitutional Court. (My emphasis.)

25. The applicant has asked this court to confirm the order of the High Court because it relates to the conduct of the President. He contended that the words "any conduct of the President" in section 172(2)(a) must be accorded a generous meaning. Read widely, the provision renders a court order relating to "any conduct" of the President susceptible to confirmation. He submitted that "any conduct" so envisaged in the section certainly includes the conduct of the President in relation to Mr Von Abo's request for diplomatic protection. In another submission the applicant says that the mere fact that the order of the High Court has declared the conduct of the President unconstitutional is sufficient to render it "conduct" for the purposes of section 172(2)(a). The declaration of invalidity compels confirmation of the order by this court so as to dispel any uncertainty.

26. In addition, the applicant submitted that the line between the concurrent jurisdiction provided for by section 172(2)(a) read with section 167(5) of the Constitution, and the exclusive jurisdiction conferred by section 167(4)(e) of the Constitution must be drawn in the light of *Doctors for Life*.[7] There, this court held that the nature of the conduct envisaged in section 167(4)(e) is that which involves decisions relating to crucial political questions, and necessarily implicates separation of powers issues.[8] Those decisions may only be made by this court.[9] However, presidential conduct in terms of sections 172(2)(a) and 167(5) does not necessarily involve crucial political questions but must still be confirmed by this court. Although, so the argument goes, sections 172(2)(a) and 167(5) cannot include each and every action of the President, a determination on whether conduct of the President is "conduct" for the purposes of these sections, should be made on a case-by-case basis. It requires a context-sensitive enquiry.

[356] 27. The respondent has urged us to refuse the application for confirmation. Stated pithily, the respondent's attitude is that the failure to provide proper diplomatic intervention in issue does not amount to the "conduct of the President" as envisaged in section 172(2)(a). The failure to act found by the High Court, in truth, is not that of the President but of the government including certain of its ministers. The duty to consider properly whether to furnish diplomatic protection rests on the government acting through the national executive which is headed by the President. However, the respondent exercises executive authority together with other members of the Cabinet. For this contention the respondent advanced several reasons in law and fact which, given the conclusion I reach, I need not now re-state.

Constitutional Jurisdiction

28. This court, like other courts in our land, is a progeny of our democratic Constitution and so too is its jurisdiction. However, unlike other courts it occupies a special place in our new constitutional order. It is the highest court on all constitutional matters and is clothed with both exclusive and concurrent jurisdiction. It enjoys exclusive jurisdiction in regard to specified constitutional matters and makes the final decision on other constitutional issues that are also within the jurisdictions of other superior courts and in particular, the Supreme Court of Appeal

---

[7] *Doctors for Life International v. Speaker of the National Assembly and Others* [2006] ZACC 11; 2006 (6) SA 416 (CC); 2006 (12) BCLR 1399 (CC).
[8] Id. at paras. 21 and 24.   [9] Id.

and the High Court. The exclusive and supervisory jurisdictions of this court may be properly gathered from three constitutional provisions. They are sections 172(2)(a) and 167(5) of the Constitution, which regulate concurrent jurisdiction with the High Court and the Supreme Court of Appeal, and section 167(4), which carves out jurisdictional exclusivity for this court. I look at the remit of each of the provisions with reference to our jurisprudence.

29. It is plain from the wording of section 172(2)(a) that an order of the Supreme Court of Appeal or of the High Court concerning the constitutional validity of "any conduct of the President" has no force unless this court confirms it. In reviewing the meaning of the phrase "any conduct" this court in *Pharmaceutical Manufacturers* held that it must be accorded a generous and wide meaning.[10] The court explained that the purpose of the section is to ensure that the highest court in constitutional matters should supervise declarations of constitutional invalidity against the conduct of the President who as Head of State and head of the national executive is the highest organ of the State. The court warned that this purpose would be defeated if the constitutional validity of the conduct of the President in that case could be characterised as not falling within the bounds of section 172(2)(a).[11]

30. I must instantly add that in that case this court was called upon to decide whether to confirm an order of the High Court that had declared [357] invalid a proclamation by the President to bring into force an Act of Parliament. The Act concerned had provided that it would come into operation on a date to be determined by the President. The national legislation concerned required the President to take the positive step of issuing a proclamation. Clearly, only the President could exercise the power specially conferred on him by legislation. In other words, the President did not exercise executive authority together with other members of the Cabinet. It is that conduct which the court considered to be susceptible to confirmation. It must be said that whilst *Pharmaceutical Manufacturers* considered the conduct of the President to be a proper subject for confirmation in that case, it does not furnish the answer to the crisp question of which conduct of the President, if any, is not susceptible to confirmation under section 172(2)(a).

31. Another provision of the Constitution that regulates confirmation by this court of orders relating to "conduct of the President" is section 167(5). It provides that:

---

[10] *Pharmaceutical Manufacturers Association of SA and Another: In Re Ex Parte President of the Republic of South Africa and Others* [2000] ZACC 1; 2000 (2) SA 674 (CC); 2000 (3) BCLR 241 (CC) at para. 56.
[11] Id.

The Constitutional Court makes the final decision whether an Act of Parliament, a Provincial Act or *conduct of the President* is constitutional, and must confirm any order of invalidity made by the Supreme Court of Appeal, a High Court, or a court of similar status, before that order has any force. (My emphasis.)

32. In substance the provisions of sections 172(2)(a) and 167(5) serve separate but complementary purposes. Both sections map out the respective areas of jurisdiction of the Supreme Court of Appeal and the High Court, on the one hand, and of this court, on the other. They may be said to be two sides of the same coin. Put differently, section 172(2)(a) forms part of a collection of provisions that confer constitutional jurisdiction on the Supreme Court of Appeal and High Courts subject to the express oversight of this court in relation to orders on the constitutional validity of national and provincial legislation and conduct of the President. On the other hand, section 167(5) delineates the power of this court in relation to the same class of orders of constitutional invalidity made by the Supreme Court of Appeal and the High Court. This suggests that the "conduct of the President" envisaged in the two provisions ordinarily bears the same meaning. In other words, if particular conduct of the President is liable to be confirmed under the one provision, ordinarily it should also be so under the other provision. Both provisions serve the vital purpose of ensuring that orders of invalidity directed at the appropriate class of the President's conduct have no force unless confirmed by this court. This complementary relationship between these two provisions was recognised by this court in *Doctors for Life*.[12] In that case we held that through sections 167(5) and 172(2)(a), the Constitution contemplates that disputes on whether provincial or national legislation or conduct of the President is constitutional will be considered in the first instance by the **[358]** High Courts, which are given the power to declare such laws or conduct invalid, subject to confirmation by this court.[13]

33. This does not however mean that every dispute about the conduct of the President falls within the jurisdiction of the High Court or the Supreme Court of Appeal. The first prominent exclusion is found in the provisions of section 167(4)(e), which expressly confers exclusive jurisdiction by providing that, only this court may "decide that Parliament or the *President has failed to fulfil a constitutional obligation*" (my emphasis).

34. The Constitution distinguishes disputes related to the "conduct of the President" from those where he has "failed to fulfil a constitutional

---

[12] Above n 7.   [13] Id. at para. 23.

obligation". In *SARFU*[14] this court pointed out that the words "fulfil a constitutional obligation" must be given a narrow meaning in order to avoid any conflict with the power given to the High Court and the Supreme Court of Appeal on all questions concerning the constitutional validity of conduct of the President. There the court recognised that it would be difficult to determine what that narrow meaning should be in each case. This court in *Doctors for Life*,[15] and previously the Supreme Court of Appeal in *King* v. *Attorneys' Fidelity Fund*,[16] resorted to a narrow construction of section 167(4)(e) in order not to constrict the powers of lower courts to test legislation and the conduct of the President for constitutional compliance.

35. It seems plain to me that where the conduct of the President does not pass muster as a "constitutional obligation" envisaged in section 167(4)(e), ordinarily it would be susceptible to the jurisdiction of the Supreme Court of Appeal or the High Court. That jurisdiction is conferred by the Constitution through the provisions of section 167(5) read with section 172(2)(a) and must be given full effect.

36. In *Doctors for Life*, Ngcobo J, writing for the court, observed that the word "obligation" connotes a duty specifically imposed by the Constitution on parliament to perform specified conduct.[17] It seems to me that by parity of reasoning the same consideration applies to an "obligation" relating to the President. The main thrust of these decisions seems to be that section 167(4)(e) which provides for the exclusive jurisdiction of the Constitutional Court should be construed restrictively in order to give full recognition to the power of the Supreme Court of Appeal and the High Court to determine whether conduct of the President is constitutionally valid. On the other hand, the Constitution does contemplate that certain duties are pointedly reserved for the President. This class of **[359]** obligations is derived from the Constitution itself or from legislation. It includes specified duties that the President as Head of State and head of the national executive must fulfil.[18]

37. It however remains a complex question whether a specific power exercised by the President under the Constitution or other law amounts to a "constitutional obligation" which only this court may decide. It

---

[14] *President of the Republic of South Africa and Others* v. *South African Rugby Football Union and Others* [1998] ZACC 21; 1999 (2) SA 14 (CC); 1999 (2) BCLR 175 (CC) at para. 25.

[15] Above n 7 at para. 19.

[16] *King and Others* v. *Attorneys' Fidelity Fund Board of Control and Another* 2006 (1) SA 474 (SCA); 2006 (4) BCLR 462 (SCA) at para. 23.

[17] Above n 7 at paras. 25-6.

[18] See section 84(1) of the Constitution which provides that:

The President has the powers entrusted by the Constitution and legislation, including those necessary to perform the functions of Head of State and head of the national executive.

is neither prudent nor pressing to describe what amounts to a constitutional obligation under section 167(4)(e) any more so than I have done. Even so, ready examples of constitutional obligations specifically entrusted to the President may be found in section 84(2) of the Constitution.[19] Many of the powers and obligations in section 84(2) vest in the President as Head of State and head of the national executive. These duties may correctly be described as functions the Constitution requires him or her to perform. Ordinarily they would be matters that have important political consequences and which call for a measure of comity between the judicial and executive branches of the State. Some of the obligations do relate to decisions on crucial political questions, referred to in *Doctors for Life*,[20] and necessarily implicate separation of powers issues. Moreover, the decisions to be tested for constitutional compliance are those of the highest office of the Head of State and the head of the national executive. [360] And for that reason the Constitution provides that disputes of that order must be decided by this court only.

38. I need say nothing more about exclusive jurisdiction of this court because none of the parties in this case contended that this is a matter which falls within the exclusive power of this court under section 167(4)(e). Both accepted that the High Court had jurisdiction to deal with the matter in terms of section 172(2)(a) and section 167(5). That approach to this matter is the correct one. That simply means that the residual question is whether the dispute over the alleged failure to deal with the applicant's requests for diplomatic protection against the violation of his property rights by the Zimbabwean government can properly be characterised as relating to conduct of the President under section 172(2)(a).

---

[19] Section 84(2) of the Constitution provides as follows:

The President is responsible for—

(a) assenting to and signing Bills;
(b) referring a Bill back to the National Assembly for reconsideration of the Bill's constitutionality;
(c) referring a Bill to the Constitutional Court for a decision on the Bill's constitutionality;
(d) summoning the National Assembly, the National Council of Provinces or Parliament to an extraordinary sitting to conduct special business;
(e) making any appointments that the Constitution or legislation requires the President to make, other than as head of the national executive;
(f) appointing commissions of enquiry;
(g) calling a national referendum in terms of an Act of Parliament;
(h) receiving and recognising foreign diplomatic and consular representatives;
(i) appointing ambassadors, plenipotentiaries, and diplomatic and consular representatives;
(j) pardoning or reprieving offenders and remitting any fines, penalties or forfeitures; and
(k) conferring honours.

[20] Above n 7 at para. 24.

39. In order to answer this question, it is expedient to describe briefly the nature of the executive authority envisaged by the Constitution. It vests in the President the executive authority which he or she must exercise together with other members of the Cabinet.[21] These powers include implementing national legislation, developing and implementing national policy, co-ordinating functions of State departments, and preparing and initiating legislation. And more significantly for the present case, section 85(2)(e)[22] requires the President, acting together with Cabinet, to perform any other executive function provided for in the Constitution or in national legislation. In my view, the exercise of all of these powers under section 85 does not necessarily constitute an "obligation" as used in section 167(4)(e).

40. There may be appropriate instances where conduct of the President constitutes "conduct" that is susceptible to the jurisdiction of the High Court and the Supreme Court of Appeal under sections 172(2)(a) and 167(5). However, it is important to keep in mind the provisions of sections 91(1) and (2)[23] and 92(1) and (2).[24] In terms of these provisions the Cabinet is [361] made up of the President, the Deputy President and Ministers who are all appointed by the President. He assigns to them their powers and functions. Once the powers and functions have been assigned, the Deputy President and Ministers are responsible for the executive powers and functions assigned to them. These provisions make plain that members of the Cabinet are accountable independently and collectively to Parliament for the exercise of their powers and performance of their functions. For good measure, section 92(3) of the Constitution restates the obvious which is that, when they exercise the powers assigned to them, members of the Cabinet must act in

---

[21] Section 85 of the Constitution provides that:

(1) The executive authority of the Republic is vested in the President.
(2) The President exercises the executive authority together with the other members of the Cabinet.

[22] Section 85(2)(e) provides that "the President exercises the executive authority, together with the other members of the Cabinet by performing any other executive function provided for in the Constitution or in national legislation".

[23] These provisions state the following:

(1) The Cabinet consists of the President, as head of the Cabinet, a Deputy President and Ministers.
(2) The President appoints the Deputy President and Ministers, assigns their powers and functions, and may dismiss them.

[24] These provisions state the following:

(1) The Deputy President and Ministers are responsible for the powers and functions of the executive assigned to them by the President.
(2) Members of the Cabinet are accountable collectively and individually to Parliament for the exercise of their powers and the performance of their functions.

accordance with the Constitution.[25] This is significant because once Cabinet ministers are assigned powers and functions by the President they are not mere vassals of the President. They bear the duty and the responsibility to fulfil the duties and functions so assigned which in practice take the form of political and executive leadership of specified State departments. The Constitution makes the point that besides the duty to account to the head of the national executive, cabinet ministers bear the responsibility to report and account to Parliament on how they execute their executive duties.

41. Relevant here, in my opinion, is the collaborative nature of the national executive function, on the one hand, and the individual accountability of every Minister in the Cabinet, on the other. The President is head of Cabinet. Thus, where a national executive function is impugned or where the conduct of a Minister is challenged, it may be said, loosely speaking, that the conduct of the President as head of the national executive is in issue. However, to categorise all national executive functions at cabinet level as "conduct of the President" for the purposes of sections 167(5) and 172(2)(a), by mere virtue of the fact that the President is head of the national executive, is to misconstrue the true nature of the national executive function envisaged by Chapter 5 of the Constitution. It may well be that the President has some residual authority as head of the national executive, but the primary responsibility lies with the government, and with the Ministers to whom a specific task has been assigned in accordance with sections 91 and 92 of the Constitution.

42. It seems to me, therefore, that it is impermissible to hold that when the conduct of the government as represented by the national executive or of one or more members of the Cabinet, is impugned on the ground that it is inconsistent with the Constitution and thus invalid, that dispute relates to the conduct of the President and therefore that the ensuing order of constitutional invalidity must be confirmed by this court on the ground that it relates to the conduct of the President. If that were so, it would mean that in theory every order against the government or a member of the Cabinet must be confirmed before it has any force or effect. As I have demonstrated earlier, that would defeat the scheme of **[362]** Chapter 5 of the Constitution; it would blur the careful jurisdictional lines between this court and other superior courts drawn

---

[25] Section 92(3) provides:

Members of the Cabinet must—

(a) act in accordance with the Constitution; and
(b) provide Parliament with full and regular reports concerning matters under their control.

by Chapter 8 of the Constitution; and would lead to an unwarranted increase of confirmation proceedings in this court.

43. It is now convenient to return to the context of the present case. It is clear that the Government of South Africa was the first and main respondent in the High Court proceedings, and that diplomatic protection could have been considered by any of the Ministers empowered by the President to do so under section 92 of the Constitution. This being a matter which relates to the foreign relations of the Republic, it is clear from the papers that the Department of Foreign Affairs was seized with the matter and that each time correspondence was sent to the President, it was forwarded to that Department for its attention. Consequently, any failure to consider the applicant's request for diplomatic protection would have been the failure of the Government of South Africa or indeed of a specific Minister, in this case the Minister for Foreign Affairs. As I have concluded earlier, it does not follow that a constitutionally reprehensible failure of a Minister or of the government in a generic sense amounts to a failure by the President to fulfil his constitutional obligations.

44. In addition, on a reading of the correspondence between the applicant and the Office of the Presidency, it is clear that the latter's response indicated that Mr Von Abo's concerns had been forwarded to the Ministry for Foreign Affairs. Moreover, much of the remaining correspondence brought before this court as evidence of the applicant's attempts to secure diplomatic protection was directed by Mr Von Abo to certain executive officials, namely the South African High Commissioner in Zimbabwe and the Minister for Foreign Affairs. Moreover, the responses to his various requests were authored by these executive officials.

45. In *Kaunda*[26] the majority held that the provision of diplomatic protection at the request of a citizen whose rights are violated in and by a foreign State is a matter which forms part of the executive function of government. Thus, it is up to the government to decide whether protection should be given, and if so, what form the diplomatic intervention should take. This court stated that "if government refuses to consider a legitimate request, or deals with it in bad faith or irrationally, a court could require government to deal with the matter properly".[27] This duty and function to give proper consideration to a legitimate request for diplomatic intervention by government is one carried out in terms of section 85(2) read together with section 92(1) of the Constitution which makes it clear that the Minister concerned bears the

---

[26] *Kaunda and Others v. President of the Republic of South Africa and Others* 2005 (4) SA 235 (CC); [2004] ZACC 5; 2004 (10) BCLR 1009 (CC).

[27] Id. at para. 80.

constitutional responsibility to execute the assigned powers and functions. Thus, any failure of the national executive or one of its members to discharge its [363] obligations must be remedied accordingly and a court is entitled to require the government or the Minister concerned to fulfil its constitutional responsibilities. It would, however, be inappropriate to attribute the conduct of the government or of a member of the Cabinet to the President, for no reason other than that he or she is the head of the national executive. The primary responsibility rests upon the appropriate member of the Cabinet, and although the President may bear residual responsibility, it cannot be said that where the primary obligation is not fulfilled by the Cabinet member, that that failure constitutes "conduct of the President" within the meaning of section 172(2)(a).

46. There is an additional consideration. In *Liebenberg*[28] this court foreshadowed the difficulties associated with imprecise and open-ended citing of the President in litigation. It observed that when declaring conduct of the President unconstitutional it is necessary to indicate precisely which conduct is attributable to the President, and falls foul of the Constitution.[29] This requirement is important for at least two reasons. One important reason is that a concisely worded order would disclose the character of the conduct of the President in issue and thereby indicate whether the court concerned was properly clothed with jurisdiction to resolve the dispute. Also the President, as respondent, is entitled to know which conduct has offended in order to decide whether to appeal or to correct the constitutionally recalcitrant conduct in issue.

47. The High Court, in its judgment, regrettably does not specify the conduct of the President it found to be inconsistent with his constitutional obligations. We will do well to keep in mind the actual finding of the High Court that it was in fact confronted with conduct of the government and not of the President. The passage below is one of several that consistently decry the conduct of the government:

In my view, and for all the reasons mentioned, the Government, in the present instance, failed to respond appropriately and dealt with the matter in bad faith and irrationally. For six years or more, and in the face of the stream of urgent requests from many sources, they did absolutely nothing to bring about relief for the applicant and hundreds of other white commercial farmers in the same position. Their "assistance" such as it is, was limited to empty promises.[30]

48. This and other findings against the government are followed through in the order the High Court made. Its order does not single

---

[28] *Minister of Home Affairs* v. *Liebenberg* [2001] ZACC 3; 2002 (1) SA 33 (CC); 2001 (11) BCLR 1168.
[29] Id. at para. 15.   [30] Above n 3 at para. 143.

out the offending conduct on the part of the President in particular. The order we are called upon to confirm does not even refer to the President. It does no more than make a declaration that "the failure of the respondents" is inconsistent with the Constitution. It must be added that the President is one of five respondents, the others being the government and three other Cabinet ministers.

[364] 49. In light of the above, I find that the applicant has approached this court erroneously. The portion of the order of the High Court that declares the conduct of the respondents to be invalid does not concern the conduct of the President within the meaning of section 172(2)(a) of the Constitution and is therefore not subject to confirmation, despite the fact that he was cited as a party to the proceedings. At this stage, it is in order to restate the importance of claimants in litigation identifying the exact entity, State organ or Minister whose conduct is being impugned. Increasingly practitioners and litigants cite and sue the President and the government in litigation as generic representatives of a State organ, or Minister or other State functionary. This practice is unhelpful and often leads not only to imprecise pleading, but also to difficulties in identifying appropriate State officials to respond to the claims made.

50. The Constitution carefully apportions powers, duties and obligations to organs of State and its functionaries. It imposes a duty on all who exercise public power to be responsive and accountable and to act in accordance with the law. This implies that a claimant, who seeks to vindicate a constitutional right by impugning the conduct of a State functionary, must identify the functionary and its impugned conduct with reasonable precision. Courts too, in making orders, have to formulate orders with appropriate precision.

51. I also keep in mind that neither the government nor any of the respondents have appealed against the decision of the High Court. If anything, as I have explained earlier, counsel for the government has confirmed with this court that the government has taken steps to comply with the order of the High Court. It was open to the government to appeal the decision of the High Court. It did not do so. It has chosen to abide. It follows that the order made by the High Court is of full force and effect and in substance accords with the relief which Mr Von Abo sought before that court.

52. The view we take that the order of the High Court in relation to the President is not susceptible to confirmation by this court does not in any way diminish the relief granted and consequently does not harbour any prejudice of any type for Mr Von Abo. Put otherwise the government's liability towards Mr Von Abo cannot be said to be in any way diminished only by reason of paragraph 1 of the High Court order

not having been confirmed by this court. It also follows that absent any appeal to this court, it is unnecessary to traverse any of the merits. Accordingly, this court expresses no view whatsoever on the correctness or otherwise of the judgment of the High Court. What is clear is that the order of the High Court has not been assailed and it stands unblemished.

53. I have made it clear that in this matter we do not reach the merits of the dispute which was before the High Court. The import of the conclusions that we reach is that the application for confirmation is misconceived because it does not concern conduct of the President within the meaning of section 172(2)(a) of the Constitution. In the circumstances, the order of the High Court does not need to be confirmed by this court. It embodies no competent claim and should therefore not have come to this **[365]** court in the first instance. In the event, the application for the confirmation of the order of the High Court stands to be struck off the roll.

Costs

54. The applicant came to this court in the honest belief that he was required by the provisions of section 172(2)(a) of the Constitution to submit the order of the High Court for confirmation. As I have intimated earlier, the High Court held the same belief. I have found that the application for confirmation must fail. The application has raised matters of considerable constitutional importance. Mr Von Abo came to this court only because he thought that the step was necessary before he could properly vindicate the final order of the High Court in his favour. In any event, this was constitutional litigation against the government and ordinarily an order of costs against the applicant would be plainly inappropriate. This court has consistently eschewed burdening with costs unsuccessful litigants who honestly sought to vindicate their constitutional rights against the government. The proper course to adopt here is to make no order as to costs.

55. In relation to the two interlocutory applications the respondent properly conceded that he is liable to pay all the wasted costs which must include the cost of two counsel.

Order

56. The following order is made:

(a) The application by the applicant in terms of section 172(2)(a) of the Constitution and Rule 16 of the rules of this court for confirmation of paragraph 1 of the order issued by the North

Gauteng High Court, Pretoria, under case No 3106/2007, on 29 July 2008, to the extent that it refers to the President, is struck off the roll.
(b) No order as to costs is made in relation to the application for confirmation.
(c) The respondent is ordered to pay the costs of the applicant occasioned by the applications for leave to adduce new evidence and for condonation of the late filing of the application to adduce new evidence.
(d) The interim order of this court that annexures to the respondent's written submission shall not be made accessible to the public is set aside.
(e) The respondent is also ordered to pay all costs occasioned by the application to declare certain evidentiary material confidential and inaccessible to the public.
(f) The costs orders in paragraphs (c) and (e) above shall include costs consequent upon the employment of two counsel.

Langa CJ, Cameron J, Mokgoro J, Ngcobo J, Nkabinde J, O'Regan J, Sachs J, Skweyiya J, Van der Westhuizen J and Yacoob J concur in the judgment of Moseneke DCJ.

[Reports: 2009 (5) SA 345; 2009 (10) BCLR 1052 (CC)]

The following is the text of the judgment of the High Court of 5 February 2010:

JUDGMENT OF THE HIGH COURT (5 FEBRUARY 2010)

[272] 1. This judgment concerns a hearing which flowed from certain supervisory relief which I granted in a judgment reported as *Von Abo* v. *Government of the Republic of South Africa and Others* 2009 (2) SA 526 (T) (the main judgment).

2. Before me Mr Hodes SC assisted by Mr Katz appeared for the applicant, and Mr De Jager SC assisted by Mr Mphaga and Ms Sello appeared for the respondents.

The Main Judgment

3. Where this judgment is a sequel to the main judgment, it must inevitably be read in conjunction with that judgment. It will be neither necessary nor practicable to embark upon lengthy and unnecessary

repetition of the contents of that judgment. Brief references and quotes will suffice.

4. It is, however, convenient to revisit the order I made in the main judgment as it is reported at 566H-567D: [The Court quoted paragraph 161 of the order of the High Court of 29 July 2008, as reported at p. 623 above.]

[273] 5. The damages claim referred to in para. 6 of the order was crafted as follows in the notice of motion which formed the basis of the application which resulted in the main judgment:

6. That, in the event of the respondents failing to comply effectively with either the order in terms of prayer 4 or in terms of prayer 5, ordering the respondents jointly and severally (the one paying and the other to be absolved) to pay to the applicant such damages as he may prove that he has suffered as a result of the violation of his rights by the Government of Zimbabwe.

6. In purported compliance with paras. 4 and 5 of the order the respondents indeed reported back to this court by means of an affidavit dated 19 October 2008, the main judgment having been handed down on 29 July 2008. At that stage the application which came before the Constitutional Court, to which reference is made hereunder, had not yet been finalised.

7. When the Constitutional Court judgment, dated 5 June 2009, was handed down, and in view of the outcome thereof, the parties made arrangements for this further hearing, which inevitably had to flow from the provisions of paras. 4 and 5 of my order in the main judgment, to take place.

8. At a meeting with representatives of both parties in chambers I enquired from both parties whether they felt that I was seized with the matter and, in any event, whether I should preside over the follow-up hearing, particularly in view of some unflattering remarks I had made [274] about the conduct of the respondents during the course of the main judgment. Counsel from both sides indicated that they felt I should conduct the follow-up hearing and urged me to do so. After due reflection I obliged.

9. The essence of the enquiry which came before me in the follow-up hearing was to establish whether or not the respondents had effectively complied with para. 4 of my order in the main judgment—at 567A. A positive finding, from the point of view of the respondents, would signal the end of the matter. A negative finding would result in declaratory relief to the effect that the respondents were liable to compensate the applicant for his damages. A quantum trial would then come into play.

The Judgment in Von Abo v. President of the Republic of South Africa 2009 (5) SA 345 (CC) (the Constitutional Court Judgment)

10. During the course of the proceedings before me, which led up to the main judgment, there was agreement between the parties that an adverse finding about the conduct of the State President, who was the second respondent in those proceedings, would require a certification process by the Constitutional Court as intended by the provisions of s 172(2) (a) of the Constitution—see the main judgment at 566A.

11. Such an adverse finding is contained in para. 1 of the order in the main judgment—at 566H.

12. It is convenient to quote the text of s 172(2)(a) of the Constitution:

The Supreme Court of Appeal, a High Court, or a court of similar status may make an order concerning the constitutional validity of an Act of Parliament, a provincial Act or *any conduct of the President*, but an order of constitutional invalidity has no force unless it is confirmed by the Constitutional Court. [Emphasis added.]

13. The applicant duly launched such an application before the Constitutional Court, seeking confirmation of the order contained in para. 1 supra.

14. In the event, the Constitutional Court found that the application for confirmation was misconceived because the matter does not concern conduct of the President within the meaning of s 172(2)(a) of the Constitution—Constitutional Court judgment at 364I-J.

15. In the result, the application for confirmation was struck from the roll, but some costs orders were made against the respondents—Constitutional Court judgment at 365E-I.

16. The Constitutional Court also held that it was necessary to identify the particular government minister responsible for alleged unconstitutional conduct and the Minister for Foreign Affairs, the third respondent, was earmarked in the process. The following is said in the Constitutional Court judgment in this regard:

Consequently, any failure to consider the applicant's request for diplomatic protection would have been the failure of the Government of South Africa or indeed of a specific minister, in this case the Minister **[275]** for Foreign Affairs. As I have concluded earlier, it does not follow that a constitutionally reprehensible failure of a minister or of the government in a generic sense amounts to a failure by the President to fulfil his constitutional obligations. [Constitutional Court judgment at 362C-E.]

17. It was this finding that inspired the applicant to seek relief only against the Government of South Africa (first respondent) and the Minister for Foreign Affairs (third respondent) in the follow-up hearing.

18. For present purposes, it is convenient to quote paras. 51 and 52 of the Constitutional Court judgment reported at 364E-T [reported at p. 623 above].

19. In view of these remarks I am of the opinion that care must be taken not to revisit the merits of the case, for purposes of this follow-up hearing. The horse has bolted. The crisp issue to decide, as explained above, is whether or not the respondents have complied with para. 4 of the order in the main judgment. The main source of information on which the aforesaid issue must be decided, is the report submitted by the respondents (for present purposes, read the first and third respondents) in purported compliance with paras. 4 and 5 of the order in the main judgment.

The Report Submitted by the Respondents (the Report)

20. The report consists of an affidavit, running into some 12 pages, with annexures.

21. The deponent to the affidavit names himself as "ambassador J. N. K. Mamabolo". He is a deputy director-general in the Department of Foreign Affairs. He states that he is duly authorised to depose to the affidavit. This authority flows from the following:

A confirmatory affidavit of the Director-General: Department of Foreign Affairs is annexed to this affidavit. As Director-General does not **[276]** have personal knowledge of the issues raised in this affidavit, he has therefore delegated the authority to depose to this affidavit to me.

22. There is a confirmatory affidavit by Ayanda Ntsaluba who identifies himself as the Director-General of the Department of Foreign Affairs, and says "I have authorised Ambassador J. N. K. Mamabolo, a deputy director-general in the Department of Foreign Affairs to depose to the main affidavit". He confirms the contents of Ambassador J. N. K. Mamabolo's affidavit "insofar as it refers to me". In the process he confirms the ambassador's statement, supra, that he has no personal knowledge of the issues raised "in this affidavit".

23. The Director-General does not say what the source of his authority is to delegate authority to the ambassador.

24. In his affidavit the ambassador says that, following the main judgment which was handed down on 29 July 2008 (incorrectly stated by the ambassador to have been 24 July) a meeting was held on

6 August 2008 between officials of the Department of Foreign Affairs, the Department of Trade and Industry, the Presidency and counsel to discuss the way forward. The ambassador did not attend the meeting but he was "informed" by Advocate Stemmet, Senior State Law Advisor also mentioned in the main judgment, who represented the Department of Foreign Affairs at the meeting and who also deposed to a confirmatory affidavit, attached to the report.

25. According to the ambassador, counsel at the meeting emphasised the importance of "order 4" which is para. 4 of the order made in the main judgment, and which description I shall also adopt for the sake of convenience. Of course order 4, stripped to its essentials, reads that "the respondents are ordered to forthwith take all necessary steps to have the applicant's violation of his rights by the Government of Zimbabwe remedied". Order 5 (para. 5 of the order in the main judgment), also stripped to essentials, provides that the respondents are directed to report by way of affidavit to this court within 60 days what steps they have taken in respect of order 4, and to provide a copy of such report to the applicant.

26. Not one of the respondents, let alone the third respondent, who was singled out particularly in the Constitutional Court judgment, as described, "reported by way of affidavit", as instructed in order 5. There is no direct indication, as far as I can see, that the third respondent (or any other respondent) personally made any effort to comply with orders 4 and 5.

27. The order in the main judgment was directed at the respondents, not at Ambassador Mamabolo or anybody else. The abject failure on the part of the respondents, and particularly the third respondent, to demonstrate any visible sign of even taking notice of these orders, amounts, in my view, to contempt of court. Counsel for the applicant put it as follows in their comprehensive heads of argument:

It is submitted that the absence and/or failure of the respondents to be involved personally in the discussion of options and possible actions in [277] order to give effect to the Court order is unacceptable and borders on the contemptuous.

With these sentiments I agree. At 539I-540B of the main agreement I already expressed the view that the unexplained failure on the part of any of the respondents to file personal affidavits to deal with the complaints of the applicant amounts to a dereliction of duty and flies in the face of the requirements of s 165(4) of the Constitution, which provides that organs of State, through legislative and other measures, must assist and protect the courts to ensure the independence, impartiality, dignity, accessibility and effectiveness of the courts.

28. The failure on the part of the respondents to file affidavits, or to even explain the failure to do so, or to show any demonstrable interest in the orders, effectively, in my view, amounts to non-compliance with the orders, more particularly orders 4 and 5. The subject of the inadmissibility for one person to make an affidavit on behalf of another, without the latter filing at least a verifying or supporting affidavit, was extensively dealt with in the main judgment at 540E-543D. Against this background, it was argued before me during this follow-up hearing on behalf of the applicant that where the respondents had not filed an affidavit confirming the contents of the report, the contents of the report constitute inadmissible hearsay and I should have no regard thereto. On behalf of the applicant reliance was placed on the well-known authorities already quoted in the main judgment, including *Gerhard* v. *State President and Others* 1989 (2) SA 499 (T) at 504F-H and *Tantoush* v. *Refugee Appeal Board and Others* 2008 (1) SA 232 (T) at 256D-F. Where the respondents (and nobody else) were directed to report by way of affidavit as to the steps they had taken in respect of their duty to have the applicant's violation of his rights by the Government of Zimbabwe remedied, it meant that they were obliged to report on what steps were taken since the grant of the order on 29 July 2008, and not what they had done prior to the grant of the order (as will appear from a further analysis of the report hereunder). Where the respondents failed to file affidavits in compliance with the order, it follows, in my view, that they have not complied with their reporting duty. On the same subject, it was also argued an behalf of the applicant, correctly in my view, that it was not for the Director-General of the Department of Foreign Affairs, who is not a respondent, to authorise Ambassador Mamabolo to make any affidavit at all. It was for the respondents, and the respondents alone, to authorise someone to make an affidavit in respect of the report, and then only if a confirmatory affidavit by the relevant respondent was filed of record. This is in line with the authorities quoted supra. The opposing argument offered, in this regard, on behalf of the respondents, was that the Director-General is the most senior official in the department of the third respondent. By virtue of his office he is intimately involved in and accountable for all conduct of officials of the department, including ambassadors to foreign States. He is entitled to depose to affidavits on behalf of the Minister, as the accountable officer of that department. This entitlement does not derive from being cited as a respondent, but from his position within the department. He is in law empowered to delegate [278] any power or function he may have to other officials, unless he is specifically precluded thereto by legislation. No authority in support of this proposition was submitted to me. The Director-General

in his affidavit did not even mention the third respondent or indicate that she authorised him to delegate his authority, such as it may be, to the ambassador. The court order is directed against the third respondent (and other respondents). Her complete silence and failure of involvement in these proceedings remain unexplained. I cannot agree with the argument submitted on behalf of the respondents.

29. Nevertheless, on the assumption that my conclusion that the report falls to be disregarded for lack of compliance with orders 4 and 5 due to the absence of involvement by the respondents, is wrong, I now turn to a further analysis of the report.

Further Analysis of the Report

30. Following the first meeting of 6 August 2008, supra, there was another meeting on 27 August 2008 "with a view to discuss options and possible actions to propose to the Department of Foreign Affairs' principals in order to give effect to the court order". It is not stated who the "principals" are. According to the minute of that meeting, the ambassador was not present. Neither did he apologise for his absence. In fairness, it must be observed that the minute suggests that Advocate De Wet, Chief State Law Advisor, did discuss the main judgment with the Minister. Certain directives, possibly flowing from the meeting with the Minister, who, of course, was not at the meeting, were discussed. These included the following: a diplomatic note had to be sent by the ambassador in Harare to seek an appointment with "relevant ministers" to meet with them as a matter of urgency; the Zimbabwean ambassador in Pretoria had to be called in by the deputy director-general: Africa "to make representations on behalf of Mr Von Abo"; and a high-level delegation had to be composed to travel to Zimbabwe to meet with the relevant Zimbabwean authorities as soon as possible.

31. At the meeting, further resolutions were passed to implement these directives. Included amongst these was a decision to hold a meeting "between all departmental stake holders" on 1 September 2008 "in order to develop the strategy for engaging the Zimbabweans to be followed during the meetings". It was also decided that a strategy be developed on how to deal with similar requests from other South African landowners whose farms were expropriated in Zimbabwe. According to the minute, the meeting lasted for 1 hour and 20 minutes.

32. On 2 September 2008 a follow-up meeting was held. Again Ambassador Mamabolo was absent. The meeting was attended by State Law Advisors De Wet and Stemmet, the South African ambassador to Harare, the Chief Director: Consular Services, the Director: Malawi,

Zimbabwe, Zambia, Mozambique and Tanzania, and one Mr Reed of the Zimbabwe desk. It was reported that a meeting had been held with the Zimbabwean ambassador who indicated the willingness of his government to engage the South African Government on the matter, and [**279**] undertook to bring the matter immediately to the attention of the relevant Zimbabwean authorities. An aide-mémoire and a diplomatic note requesting a meeting for a South African delegation with the "Zimbabwean authorities" had also been handed over. It was decided that the South African delegation had to be led by a deputy director-general. No explanation is given for the decision not to involve more senior officials such as any of the respondents. As regards strategy, the possibility of "the resurrection" of the Bilateral Investment Promotion and Protection Treaty, "although it will not have retrospective effect", and the delisting of properties of nationals of SADC States were mooted. These subjects were extensively dealt with in the main judgment and I do not propose revisiting a full discussion thereon. Significantly, it was also decided that "in order to prevent further negative publicity on the matter" the applicant's attorneys would be informed that the department was attending to the matter.

33. A confidential report of a meeting between Mr M. Nkosi: Deputy Director-General: Africa Bilateral and ambassador K. Moyo of Zimbabwe was also tabled. According to this report, the deputy director-general told the ambassador that "given the order of the High Court regarding the expropriation without compensation of the properties in Zimbabwe belonging to Mr Crawford Lindsay Von Abo, the Government of South Africa is legally obliged to engage with the Government of Zimbabwe to resolve the matter". It was recorded that the discussions took place in a cordial atmosphere and ambassador Moyo assured Mr Nkosi that the matter would be dealt with by the relevant authorities and that the DFA (Department of Foreign Affairs) delegation of senior officials would be welcome in Zimbabwe.

34. Significantly, and perhaps rather ominously, this confidential report concludes with the following comment:

As expected ambassador Moyo commented during the discussions that Zimbabwe has no land problems any longer; implying that the Land Reform Process was complete. In this regard, he says South Africa has serious land problems which will take years to deal with.

35. There was also a report, in the form of a telex, dated 1 September 2008, on a meeting, of the same date, between the chargé d'affaires and Mr Chifamba, Zimbabwean Divisional Head for Africa: Economics, when the former handed over the diplomatic note and aide-mémoire

to the latter. Mr Chifamba undertook to forward the documentation to the Ministry of Land Affairs of his government.

36. It appears from this telex that Mr Chifamba made some outspoken comments about the Von Abo case. He said that in the absence of a Bilateral Investment Agreement (BIPPA, discussed fully in the main judgment) there was no legal framework in existence to address these complaints. He said the applicant, Mr Von Abo's, interaction with the Government of Zimbabwe "and his involvement in politics" played a role in the fact that all his properties were acquired in terms of the land reform process. He said Mr Von Abo was a multiple farm owner and Zimbabwean legislation allows only one farm per individual. He also **[280]** relied on the, in my view somewhat jaded, arguments about colonial excesses of the past and said that any serious amendments to the Land Reform Process would "not only be untenable but indeed unthinkable". He said, however, that Zimbabwe "realises the predicament of the South African Government as a result of the Von Abo case and would assist where possible".

37. This telex, created by Mr Geerlings, First Secretary Political of the Department of Foreign Affairs in Harare (he is obviously a South African official) was addressed to a number of Foreign Affairs officials, including ambassador Mamabolo, State Law Advisors De Wet and Stemmet and some others. The addressees do not include any of the respondents. This telex concludes with the following, in my view somewhat despondent, comment:

It became evident during the meeting that the Von Abo case has created some embarrassment to the Zimbabwean Government. It is, however, very unlikely that the Zimbabwean Government will take any steps in favour of Mr Von Abo. *The best that the South African Government could hope for is that the Zimbabwean Government would give its co-operation in making it easier to convince the judge that indeed enough diplomatic protection was given to Von Abo, but that the Zimbabwean Government did not want to respond to these pleas as it is convinced about the merits of its own Land Reform Process.* [Emphasis added.]

38. This comment, in what I will describe as "the Geerlings telex of 1 September 2008", represents, in my view, the typical approach adopted by the relatively junior South African officials (the respondents never got involved) in their purported efforts to afford diplomatic protection to the applicant: the applicant's case, and that of other South African farmers who met the same fate, was "raised" or "discussed" with the Zimbabwean officials at cordial meetings or in even more cordial diplomatic notes, but when resistance was encountered from Zimbabwe, nothing whatsoever was done to counter that resistance or to employ any

of the internationally recognised diplomatic measures already identified in the main judgment. See for example the main judgment at 545I-J. In this regard I take the liberty to revisit, for easy reference, what was said there:

> 63. Legal scholars commonly use the term "diplomatic protection" to embrace consular action, negotiation, mediation, judicial and arbitral proceedings, reprisals, retorsion, severance of diplomatic relations, economic pressure and, in the final resort, the use of force—Dugard "First Report on Diplomatic Protection" (March 2000) ILCA-CN 4/506 p. 15 para. 43.

39. In the main judgment I already expressed serious reservations and displeasure at the lacklustre conduct of the respondents when it came to considering the applicant's request for diplomatic protection. I concluded that they did not act in good faith. See for example the remarks at 539E-G, 540D-E, 550C-E, 554C-E, 562A-F, and order 1 at 566H-I.

40. Regrettably matters did not improve, despite the main judgment and the supervisory mandamus therein contained: with due respect to the relatively junior South African officials saddled with the task, their **[281]** efforts remained unconvincing. They never went beyond raising the issue in diplomatic notes or at cordial meetings. No pressure was brought to bear on the Zimbabwean Government to bring about diplomatic protection for the applicant. This is in stark contrast with the more vigorous and effective approach adopted by the embassies of other foreign nationals threatened by the same land reform programme. See for example the reference in the main judgment to the "Dutch example" at 538F-H and the evidence of the German businessman, Mr Pabst, referred to at 557I-558E. As far as the "Dutch example" is concerned, namely the case of *Bernardus Henricus Funnekotter and Others v. Republic of Zimbabwe*, I was informed during the follow-up hearing that the ICSID tribunal, in the ensuing arbitration, awarded considerable amounts in damages to Mr Funnekotter and other Dutch nationals. By agreement between the parties, a copy of this ICSID judgment was presented to me after the follow-up proceedings were concluded. As stated in the main judgment, the case was conducted as ICSID case No ARB/05/6 and it was concluded in April 2009.

41. Of course, as already explained, the South African officials had to make do without the direct intervention of the respondents themselves. The latter, as senior ministers and members of the Executive, are far more influential and would, on the probabilities, have been able to exert more pressure and employ the recognised diplomatic measures, supra,

more effectively, had they elected to do so. I have already found that their inexplicable failure to get involved in these proceedings constitutes non-compliance with orders 4 and 5.

42. Mr De Jager in his able and enthusiastic address on behalf of the respondents reminded me that a court cannot tell the government how to make diplomatic interventions for the protection of its nationals—see *Kaunda and Others* v. *President of the Republic of South Africa and Others* 2005 (4) SA 235 (CC) (2005 (1) SACR 111; 2004 (10) BCLR 1009) at 260E-G. See also the restatement of the principles laid down in *Kaunda* in *Van Zyl and Others* v. *Government of the Republic of South Africa and Others* 2008 (3) SA 294 (SCA) at 309B-310C.

43. In the light of these authorities Mr De Jager's submission is technically speaking correct. However, order 4 of the main judgment was not designed to tell the government how to make the diplomatic interventions. It was designed to direct the government to deal with the matter properly and in good faith. This subject was dealt with, at some length, in the main judgment, and, more particularly, at 561B-566A. I do not propose revisiting the whole debate, but it may be convenient to remember the following remarks from *Kaunda* at 262D-E:

> 80. If government refuses to consider a legitimate request, or deals with it in bad faith or irrationally, a court could require government to deal with the matter properly . . .

This is what order 4 was intended to achieve. As already stated, the main enquiry in these follow-up proceedings is to determine whether or not order 4 was complied with.

[282] 44. Also relevant to this enquiry, in my view, are the principles defining "appropriate relief" as intended by the provisions of s 38 of the Constitution—see the remarks made in the main judgment at 564A-565E. In my view it is clear from the dicta in cases like *Fose* v. *Minister of Safety and Security* 1997 (3) SA 786 (CC) (1997 (7) BCLR 851) at 799F and *Mohamed and Another* v. *President of the Republic of South Africa and Others (Society for the Abolition of the Death Penalty in South Africa and Another Intervening)* 2001 (3) SA 893 (CC) (2001 (2) SACR 66; 2001 (7) BCLR 685) at 922G, that the appropriate relief granted to vindicate the infringement of an entrenched right must be effective relief to ensure that the breach is effectively vindicated.

45. Against this background, it is necessary to continue with the analysis of the report to pursue the enquiry as to whether or not order 4 has been effectively complied with.

Further Analysis of the Report

46. The aide-mémoire, referred to in the Geerlings telex of 1 September 2008, and which was handed over to Mr Chifamba from the Zimbabwean Foreign Ministry, was attached to that telex. At the foot thereof the following acknowledgement is contained:

The South African Government intends to give effect to the court order. It is foreseen that, amongst others, the following interventions will be made with the Zimbabwean authorities:

- a meeting between the ambassador, Harare with the relevant ministers be requested;
- a delegation of senior officials from the (*sic*) South Africa to meet with the relevant Zimbabwean authorities;
- the Zimbabwean ambassador to South Africa be summoned by the Department of Foreign Affairs.

The aim of these interventions will be to adhere to the court order and to provide Mr Von Abo with diplomatic protection as requested by him.

Despite these good intentions expressed, it has always been common cause that the applicant has received absolutely no relief in the form of diplomatic protection.

47. In another telex from Harare, this time created by the South African ambassador, Mr Makalima, and dated 22 September 2008, the possibility was mooted of calling for an extension of the 60-day period contained in order 5. The following was stated at the foot of this telex:

While it may be true that the formation of the new government could impact on the speed with which the Government of Zimbabwe responds to our request for a high level meeting to discuss the Von Abo case, it bears noting that the envisaged discussions are meant to take place at the level of senior officials rather than political heads of government ministries. It is on this account that the Mission feels strongly that the South African Government should be insistent on its request for a meeting with the Zimbabwean officials. It is the Mission's guess that the judge in this case would be unlikely to entertain a request for postponement on the grounds that the Zimbabwean Government is currently undergoing reconfiguration.

[283] No request for postponement was submitted. During argument before me, Mr De Jager indicated that the respondents were no longer relying on the need for a postponement. He indicated, if I understood him correctly, that an extension of the 60-day period would have made no difference.

48. Attached to the ambassador's affidavit as annexure H, is "President's Minute No 648" dated 30 October 2006 containing the then State President's approval for an attached draft Promotion and Reciprocal Protection of Investments Agreement (BIPPA) to be entered into with Zimbabwe. The draft BIPPA is attached. Article 11 thereof reads as follows:

This agreement shall apply to all investments, whether made before or after the date of entry into force of this agreement, but shall not apply to any dispute which arose before entry into force of this agreement.

It is common cause that the BIPPA was never signed. It is also clear that the BIPPA, if signed in 2006, would not have assisted the applicant whose dispute with the Zimbabwean authorities had by then long since arisen. These details with regard to the BIPPA were never disclosed during the proceedings leading up to the main judgment. Failure to do so remains unexplained. The issue of, inter alia, the entering into of an effective BIPPA was dealt with in the main judgment at 535B-540E. The belated disclosure of an unsigned and ineffectual draft BIPPA so long after the event is in any case an exercise in futility. It can have no bearing on the duty resting on the respondents to bring about effective compliance with orders 4 and 5. What is of relevance is what was done by the respondents after the orders were issued, in order to bring about diplomatic protection for the applicant, and to remedy the unconstitutional conduct of the respondents as was found in the main judgment.

49. Annexure I to the ambassador's affidavit is the minute of the long-awaited meeting between the two government delegations. It took place in Harare on 26 September 2008. The South African delegation was led by ambassador Mamabolo. The rest of his delegation consisted of ambassador Makalima, Chief Director Consular Service Naidoo, State Law Advisors De Wet and Stemmet, Director of Southern Africa Makaya and First Secretary Geerlings. The Zimbabwean delegation was led by Mr Chifamba, Acting Secretary for Foreign Affairs, and a host of deputy divisional heads, desk officers, a consular officer, deputy directors, a legal advisor and representatives from the President's office.

50. According to the minute Mr Chifamba acknowledged that the South African Embassy had pursued "the matters relating to South African farmers in Zimbabwe" since 2000, and undertook "to avail copies of relevant correspondence to South Africa". No such correspondence was in evidence before me, and, if it was, it would have been irrelevant for reasons already mentioned. Mr Chifamba "explained the political and socio-economic context in which the Land Reform

Program was implemented and underscored that the Land Reform Program was ongoing and irreversible".

51. Ambassador Mamabolo emphasised the need for the South African Government to comply with the court order, in respect of Mr Van Abo. **[284]** He added that the meeting should also address issues relating to all affected South African farmers in Zimbabwe. The meeting should in this respect also agree on the way to handle these matters in future. He emphasised the interconnection between the South African and Zimbabwean economies and South Africa's commitment to contribute to a sustainable economic recovery for Zimbabwe. In this respect, he emphasised the urgency of signing the Bilateral Investment Promotion and Protection Agreement (BIPPA).

52. For the sake of brevity I shall attempt to summarise the rest of the minute. In total, it runs into three pages containing 13 paragraphs. The Zimbabwean delegation briefed the meeting on Zimbabwe's policy and legal framework with regard to the land reform programme. The South African delegation "explored the possible remedies available under Zimbabwean legislation in the Von Abo matter". The Zimbabwean delegation indicated that the law provides for compensation for improvements on land and equipment acquired. This whole issue was fully canvassed in the main judgment. There it was held that the applicant had exhausted all possible remedies available to him in Zimbabwe, with no success at all. The magnitude of the applicant's losses was illustrated in the main judgment. A nebulous suggestion of possible "compensation for improvements" could not, under any circumstances, represent effective diplomatic protection for the applicant. The meeting noted the decision of the 2008 SADC summit on operational questions relating to the SADC tribunal. There was a suggestion that prosecution of former owners of commercial farms would be stayed pending finalisation of the case before the SADC tribunal. Further reference to this event will be made hereunder. Possible remedies available to nationals of other countries under the International Convention for the Settlement of Investment Disputes (ICSID) and BIPPAs were not available in the case of South Africa since South Africa was not a party to ICSID and BIPPA had not yet been signed. This whole issue was canvassed fully in the main judgment. The dereliction of duty on the part of the respondents in this regard contributed to the finding that they had acted unconstitutionally. Details relating to other South African farmers who suffered the same fate as the applicant were exchanged. Rather cryptically, "the meeting noted that there were legal processes in place to deal with illegal farm occupations". The Zimbabwean side further noted that affected farmers should act within the legal provisions. Then follows, as

far as I can gather, the high-water mark of the South African delegation's efforts to comply with order 4 and to achieve diplomatic protection for the applicant:

> The South African side requested that the Zimbabwean Government should assist where representations are made by the South African Embassy on behalf of South African farmers who are victims of illegal land occupation.

The only response was another reference to the "fact" that "compensation for acquired equipment is also available to affected farmers". It was then resolved that the issue of affected South African farmers in Zimbabwe "would also in future be discussed within the framework of the Joint Permanent Commission between the two countries". Then there was yet [285] another agreement noted about the importance and necessity of the signing of BIPPA. Article 11 of the 2006 draft BIPPA, supra, was also mentioned. The meeting also noted "the provisions of article 5 of the power sharing agreement signed on 15 September 2008 between the political parties of Zimbabwe as it relates to the land reform program in Zimbabwe". Nothing further was mentioned about this power-sharing agreement and the document was not in evidence during the proceedings before me. The minute ends on this rather endearing note:

> The South African delegation thanked the Zimbabwean Government for the warm hospitality and cordial manner in which the discussions were conducted.

53. Annexure K is yet another telex, this time from Mr Ndou, former High Commissioner of South Africa in Harare, and now the ambassador in Tripoli. It is dated 26 September 2008 and addressed, inter alia, to Deputy Director-General: Africa, Nkosi, and Director-General Ntsaluba. This appears to be an account of ambassador Ndou's recollections of meetings and other contacts which purportedly took place over the years between South African officials (notably the High Commissioner) and Zimbabwean officials, with regard to the plight of South African farmers following the land invasions. For reasons mentioned, I consider this to be totally irrelevant because it deals with alleged events which took place prior to the supervisory mandamus being granted in terms of order 4 and order 5. Moreover, it is nothing more than a vague recollection. It concludes with the following words:

> This report was compiled from the High Commissioner's recollection of events during his tenure in Zimbabwe from June 1999 to June 2005. The report might not be in a chronological order but reflects events as they happened. The Business Unit should feel free to consult the High Commissioner to seek further clarity and any specific detail regarding the matter.

There are also no supporting documents such as minutes of meetings and the like attached to this vague account. I fail to see how this document can be of any meaningful assistance for purposes of deciding the issue at hand.

54. The final annexure to the ambassador's affidavit which may require some comment is an affidavit by one Randall Williams, Director: Legal-International Trade and Investment at the Department of Trade and Industry. He says he is responsible for negotiating Bilateral Investment Treaties (BITs). He refers to the 2006 draft BIPPA, supra, and President's Minute No 648, supra. He also refers to an earlier draft BIPPA dated December 2003 under the blessing of President's Minute 514. None of these were disclosed during the main proceedings before me. I repeat my view that these disclosures are irrelevant for purposes of deciding whether orders 4 and 5 were effectively complied with. In any event, no BIPPA had been signed by the time this affidavit was deposed to. The controversial art. 11 is also alluded to in the affidavit of Mr Williams. There is reference to disagreement between the two governments about the wording of art. 11. The last word, evidently, came from Zimbabwe which proposed that art. 11 should exclude investments [286] relating to agricultural land made before the entry of the proposed agreement. Of course this whole debate is irrelevant and academic for present purposes because the proposed South African wording, supra, and the proposed Zimbabwean wording both excluded any hope of diplomatic protection for the applicant. The events covered in the affidavit, such as they are, are irrelevant because they predate orders 4 and 5. This Williams affidavit, in my view, does nothing to enhance the case of the respondents. If anything, given the disclosure of earlier BIPPAs which came to naught, it fortifies conclusions expressed in the main judgment that the government failed to respond appropriately to the plight of its citizens and never showed any real intention to comply with its constitutional obligations in this regard—see for example the remarks in the main judgment at 562C-E.

Conclusionary Remarks about the Report and Related Matters

55. For the reasons I have mentioned, I find that the respondents have failed to comply with orders 4 and 5.

56. In the first place, such failure flows from the fact that the respondents, and particularly the third respondent, exhibited no interest whatsoever in attempting to comply with the orders of this court. Her conduct borders on the contemptuous. Her conduct corresponds with the lack of interest exhibited by all respondents in the main proceedings.

Her conduct also flies in the face of s 165(4) of the Constitution—see the main judgment at 539I-540A.

57. Where the respondents, against whom orders 4 and 5 were directed, took no part in the proceedings, and failed to report by affidavit as they were instructed to do, and where no proper basis was laid for the "authority" ultimately passed on to Ambassador Mamabolo to deal with the matter, the report falls to be disregarded for that reason alone, and in view of the relevant authorities as dealt with in the main judgment—at 540E-543D.

58. In the second place, and on the assumption that my conclusions about the disqualification of the report are wrong, I find that, on a proper consideration of the report, such as the one I conducted, orders 4 and 5 were still not complied with:

1. In an aide-mémoire Ambassador Mamabolo and his team expressed the intention "to adhere to the court order and to provide Mr Von Abo with diplomatic protection as requested by him." They did absolutely nothing of this sort. The highwater mark of their efforts, at the meeting between the delegations, was that they "requested that the Zimbabwean Government should assist where representations are made by the South African Embassy on behalf of South African farmers who are victims of illegal land occupation". There is no indication that this "request", such as it was, would ever yield any form of protection for the applicant.
2. There are no signs whatsoever of the respondents, through their junior delegation, contemplating the employment of any of the recognised diplomatic measures, which could have brought about [287] diplomatic protection. These measures were mentioned earlier in this judgment and also listed in the main judgment at 545I-J. There is no explanation for the abject failure to employ these recognised measures, or any other effective measures which may have brought about protection for the applicant.
3. In the celebrated words of the learned Chief Justice in *Kaunda*, at 262D, this court was entitled to require the government to deal with the matter properly. The respondents failed to do so.
4. In their comprehensive heads of argument counsel for the respondents made the following submission:

    In the premises it is submitted that the respondents have fully complied with the supervisory order. As stated in *Kaunda*, they have exercised such diplomatic measures as they deemed, in their prerogative, were appropriate. The fact that such measures did not yield the desired result, we submit, does not detract from the fact that they discharged their constitutional obligation and consequently fully complied with the court's order.

For the reasons mentioned, I disagree. On this argument offered by the respondents, if I understand it correctly, it would mean that a government, which has the prerogative to decide on the nature of the diplomatic interventions to be made, can opt for the most ineffective and weak measures, which have no prospect of achieving the desired result, and still insist that their feeble efforts pass constitutional muster because they have the prerogative to decide what measures to adopt. To use the present example, the best the Mamabolo delegation did was to "[request] that the Zimbabwean Government should assist where representations are made by the South African Embassy on behalf of South African farmers who are victims of illegal land occupation". This was a hopeless request with no prospect of inviting any protection for the applicant. The same feeble attitude emerges from the Geerlings telex of 1 September 2008 that—

the best that the South African Government could hope for is that the Zimbabwean Government would give its co-operation in making it easier to convince the judge that indeed enough diplomatic protection was given to Von Abo, but that the Zimbabwean Government did not want to respond to these pleas as it is convinced about the merits of its own Land Reform Process.

To argue that these measures comply with the court order because it is the prerogative of the government to decide what measures to adopt, is untenable. It does not pass the test as expressed in *Kaunda, Mohamed* and *Fose* supra. The task must be performed properly. The remedy afforded to an aggrieved individual whose fundamental rights have been impaired (in this case by his government) must be an effective one. It did not happen in the present case.

5. The "efforts" of the South African delegation, such as they are, are also not in compliance with the declared policy of the South African government, as repeatedly expressed in assurances to Parliament by [**288**] the third respondent, from 2002 onwards. For example, in a written reply to Parliament, she said the following in March 2002:

The South African Government would continue to ensure the safety and security of all its citizens, their property as well as South African owned companies operating in foreign countries.

Record vol. 6 p. 522. See also the discussion on the subject in the main judgment at 538D-539E.

6. I am also of the view that the respondents, had they wished to do so, could have taken advantage of the judgment by the Southern African, Development Community (SADC) Tribunal in Windhoek as fortification for effective diplomatic interventions on behalf of the applicant. The judgment, reported as SADC (T) case No 2/2007, was handed to me for consideration during the follow-up proceedings.* It was a case between 79 farmers (including farming companies) and the Republic of Zimbabwe as respondent. The court consisted of five members presided over by Mr Justice Pillay. The members included Justices Mtambo and Mondlane and members Dr Kambovo and Dr Tshosa. Already in October 2007 some of the applicants filed an application with the tribunal challenging the acquisition by the respondent of their agricultural land in Zimbabwe. They also applied for, and were granted, interim relief on 13 December 2007, pending the determination of the main case. In terms of the interim order the Republic of Zimbabwe was restrained from taking any steps or permitting any steps to be taken directly or indirectly to evict the applicants from the peaceful residence on and beneficial use of their properties. Subsequently, 77 other persons applied to intervene in the proceedings. As far as I can make out, some of them are South African citizens. According to the final judgment, the applicants were, in essence, challenging the compulsory acquisition of their agricultural lands by the respondent. The acquisitions were carried out under the land reform programme undertaken by the respondent. Some of the conclusions arrived at by the tribunal are the following:

(a) by unanimity, the Tribunal has jurisdiction to entertain the application;
(b) by unanimity, the applicants have been denied access to the courts in Zimbabwe;
(c) by a majority of 4 to 1, the applicants have been discriminated against on the ground of race; and
(d) by unanimity, fair compensation is payable to the applicants for their lands compulsorily acquired by the respondent.

The tribunal, by unanimity, then ordered the respondent to take all necessary measures to protect the possession, occupation and ownership of the lands of all the applicants, except three of them who had already been evicted from their lands, and to take all

---

* *Campbell* v. *Zimbabwe* (main decision) case No 2 of 2007.

appropriate measures to ensure that no action was taken to evict [289] these applicants or interfere with their peaceful occupation and use of their farms. In respect of the three that had been evicted, the respondent was ordered to pay compensation on or before 30 June 2009, which was long before the follow-up proceedings came before me in October 2009. As I pointed out, it also appears from the minute of the meeting of the two delegations in Harare in September 2008 that these proceedings were taken note of. The copy of the judgment of the tribunal handed to me is undated, but it is clear, for the reasons mentioned, that the final order must have been handed down before June 2009 (the date when compensation had to be paid to those evicted), and well before the matter came before me for purposes of the follow-up proceedings. Although this may be somewhat of a peripheral issue, I am of the view that diligent government ministers, in the position of the respondents, facing the task to comply with orders 4 and 5, could also have relied on the judgment of the tribunal to fortify their efforts to employ effective diplomatic interventions on behalf of the applicant They failed to do so.

59. In all the circumstances I have come to the conclusion that the respondents have failed to effectively comply with orders 4 and 5, so that the applicant's claim for damages, as contemplated in order 6 (main judgment at 567B-C), must come into play.

Constitutional Damages

60. It was held in the main judgment (more particularly at 560C-566I) that the respondents had acted unconstitutionally and, in the process, had violated the applicant's right to diplomatic protection as entrenched in the Constitution.

61. On behalf of the applicant it was argued before me, during the follow-up proceedings, that the applicant is entitled to be compensated for this breach of his constitutional right and that, in the circumstances of this case, payment of damages, as compensation, would be the appropriate relief to be granted.

62. In my view a consideration of the following words by the then learned Chief Justice, Centlivres, in *Minister of the Interior and Another v. Harris and Others* 1952 (4) SA 769 (A) at 780H-781B would be appropriate:

(I)n other words the individual concerned whose right was guaranteed by the Constitution would be left in the position of possessing a right which would be of no value whatsoever. To call the rights entrenched in the Constitution constitutional guarantees and at the same time to deny to the holder of those rights any remedy in law would be to reduce the safeguards enshrined in sec. 152 to nothing. There can to my mind be no doubt that the authors of the Constitution intended that those rights should be enforceable by the Courts of Law. They would never have intended to confer a right without a remedy. The remedy is, indeed, part and parcel of the right. *Ubi jus, ibi remedium* ... In *Dixon* v. *Harrison*, 124 ER 958 at p. 964, it was stated that the greatest absurdity imaginable in law is:

> [290] that a man hath a right to a thing for which the law gives him no remedy; which is in truth as great an absurdity, as to say, the having of right, in law, and having no right, are in effect the same.

63. The translation of *ubi ius, ibi remedium*, offered by Hiemstra and Gonin, *Trilingual Dictionary* 2nd edn at 294 is: "Where there is a right, there is a remedy."

64. In *MEC, Department of Welfare, Eastern Cape* v. *Kate* 2006 (4) SA 478 (SCA) ([2006] 2 All SA 455) the following is said at paras. 23–5:

> 23. ... *Fose* v. *Minister of Safety and Security* [1997 (3) SA 786 (CC)] *recognised that, in principle, monetary damages are capable of being awarded for a constitutional breach*. In that case Ackermann J made the following general, but important, observation in the context of the interim Constitution:
>
>> I have no doubt that this Court has a particular duty to ensure that, within the bounds of the Constitution, effective relief be granted for the infringement of any of the rights entrenched in it. In our context, an appropriate remedy must mean an effective remedy, for without effective remedies for breach, the values underlying and the right entrenched in the Constitution cannot properly be upheld or enhanced. Particularly in a country where so few have the means to enforce their rights through the courts, it is essential that, on those occasions when the legal process does establish that an infringement of an entrenched right has occurred, it be effectively vindicated. The courts have a particular responsibility in this regard and are obliged to "forge new tools" and shape innovative remedies, if needs be, to achieve this goal.

Earlier, the learned judge said the following [at para. 60 of the report]:

> *It seems to me that there is no reason in principle why "appropriate relief" should not include an award of damages, where such an award is necessary to protect and enforce ch 3 rights*. Such awards are made to compensate persons who have suffered loss as a result of the breach of a statutory right if, on a proper construction of the statute in question, it was the Legislature's intention that such damages should be payable, *and it would be strange if damages could not be claimed for, at least, loss occasioned by the breach of a right vested in the claimant by the supreme law. When it would be appropriate to do so, and what the measure of damages should be will*

depend on the circumstances of each case and the particular right which has been infringed.

24. Monetary damages for a constitutional breach have since been awarded by this Court, and endorsed by the Constitutional Court in *Modderfontein Squatters, Greater Benoni City Council* v. *Modderklip Boerdery (Pty) Ltd (Agri SA and Legal Resources Centre, Amici Curiae); President of the Republic of South Africa and Others* v. *Modderklip Boerdery (Pty) Ltd (Agri SA and Legal Resources Centre, Amici Curiae)* [the references are 2004 (6) SA 40 (SCA) (2004 (8) BCLR 821; [2004] 3 All SA 169) and 2005 (5) SA 3 (CC) (2005 (8) BCLR 786)]. In the decision of this Court Harms, JA said the following:

> [291] Courts should not be overawed by practical problems. They should "attempt to synchronise the real world with the ideal construct of a constitutional world" *and they have a duty to mould an order that will provide effective relief to those affected by a constitutional breach.* [In para. 42.]

25. *In* Fose *the Constitutional Court emphasised that it was "not required to answer the question ... whether an action for damages in the nature of constitutional damages exists in law, nor whether an order for the payment of damages qualifies as appropriate relief ... in respect of a threat to or infringement of any of the rights in ch 3" but was concerned only with the much narrower task of deciding whether an award of damages was appropriate in relation to the particular breach that was there in issue. Similarly, in this case, we are not called upon to answer those questions broadly and in the abstract—and I do not do so—but only to decide whether the particular breach that is now in issue is deserving of relief in the form of the monetary damages that are now claimed. Whether relief in that form is appropriate in a particular case must necessarily be determined casuistically, with due regard to, among other things, the nature and relative importance of the rights that are in issue, the alternative remedies that might be available to assert and vindicate them, and the consequences of the breach for the claimant concerned.* [Emphasis added.]

65. In *Kate* an appropriate award of damages was made. In the present case the nature of the damages sustained by the applicant was illustrated in the main judgment. Through the as yet unexplained failure of the respondents to assist him properly, the applicant lost the fruits of the hard work of a lifetime. Had the respondents properly performed their constitutional duty of awarding diplomatic protection to the applicant, when they were first approached to do so almost a decade ago, these damages would not have been sustained. I cannot see how any relief, other than a damages award, can be "appropriate relief" as explained in *Fose, Kate* and other authorities, and as intended by the provisions of the Constitution, notably, perhaps, the provisions of s 38 thereof. I see no alternative relief: this court cannot, for lack of jurisdiction, for

example order the reinstatement of the applicant on his properties. The nature and importance of the rights of the applicant that were infringed and that are in issue, were illustrated in the main judgment. The same applies to the consequences of the breach on the part of the respondents for the applicant concerned. A damages award, would, in my view, be in line with the principles laid down by the learned judge of appeal in the above-quoted passage to be found in *Kate* at 490G-491B.

66. It remains for me to deal with the argument presented on behalf of the respondents in opposing the notion of a damages award. By way of illustration, I quote the following extract from the heads of argument offered by counsel for the respondents:

A temporary neglect to assist Mr Von Abo as was found by this honourable court, does not create any causal link between what the Zimbabwean Government did and the fact that Mr Von Abo had not yet received redress in any material form. Diplomacy is an ongoing process and it is for the respondents now to assist Mr Von Abo as far as they can. A finding that the respondents failed to perform their constitutional responsibility in regard to diplomatic assistance to **[292]** Mr Von Abo, as the court found *in casu*, does not and cannot automatically give rise to damages especially not in the event where it is clear that whatever they may have done in the past up until this moment would not have persuaded the Zimbabwean Government to abandon or reverse their execution of the Land Reform Program.

67. I cannot agree with these submissions. The internationally recognised forms of diplomatic intervention, supra, have been designed to force offending States to toe the line. There is no room for an argument that diplomatic intervention becomes toothless, simply because the offending State exhibits no intention ever to co-operate. It is precisely under those circumstances when the recognised interventions, supra, come into play: the strength of the intervention, as illustrated, depends on the level of resistance. South Africa is the powerhouse of the region. It is common knowledge that Zimbabwe is dependent on South Africa for almost every conceivable form of aid and assistance. I see no reason why the respondents cannot apply the necessary pressure, under these circumstances, to assist their valuable and long-suffering citizens, such as the applicant. In breach of their constitutional duties, the respondents have refrained from affording such assistance for almost a decade. To date, they have brought about no meaningful assistance for the applicant whatsoever. This state of affairs may well continue into the future. The time has arrived for this court to afford the applicant appropriate and effective relief as illustrated in *Fose, Kate* and other judgments.

The Order

68. I make the following order:

1. It is declared that the first and third respondents, jointly and severally, the one paying the other to be absolved, are liable to pay to the applicant such damages as he may prove that he has suffered as a result of the violation of his rights by the Government of Zimbabwe.
2. The question of the quantum of the damages is referred to oral evidence.
3. The usual rules will apply with regard to discovery, expert evidence and the holding of a pre-trial conference.
4. The respondents, jointly and severally, are ordered to pay the applicant's costs arising from this follow-up hearing, including the costs of two counsel.

[Reports: 2010 (3) SA 269; 2010 (7) BCLR 712]

NOTE.—On 4 April 2011 the Supreme Court of Appeal set aside the Order of 29 July 2008 (except for the declaration in paragraph 1 and the costs order in paragraph 7) and the Order of 5 February 2010 (*Republic of South Africa and Others* v. *Von Abo* [2011] ZASCA 65).

Human rights — Right to life — Death penalty — Constitutionality of death penalty — International instruments — Whether abolishing death penalty — Freedom from torture, cruel, inhuman or degrading punishment — Whether two issues to be dealt with separately — Whether imposition of death penalty in Uganda constituting cruel, inhuman or degrading punishment — Whether framers of Constitution of Uganda purposefully providing for death penalty — Constitutional interpretation — Reading death penalty provisions as whole and in relation to relevant international instruments — Uganda's history and background — Punishment for political purposes — Whether conflict between Articles 22(1) and 44(a) of Constitution of Uganda — Whether death penalty inconsistent with Articles 20, 21, 22(1), 24, 28, 44(a) and 45 of Constitution of Uganda

Human rights — Right to life — Death penalty — Constitutionality of mandatory death penalty — Inherency of individual's right — Right to equality before and under law — Right to fair, speedy and public hearing before independent and impartial tribunal — Right to legal representation at State's expense for offence carrying death sentence — Whether sentencing part of trial — Whether Ugandan laws providing for mandatory death sentence inconsistent with Articles 20, 21, 22, 24, 28 and 44(a) of Constitution of Uganda

Human rights — Right to life — Death penalty — Long delay between death sentence pronouncement and execution — Whether unreasonable delay rendering execution unconstitutional — Death-row syndrome — Whether constituting cruel, inhuman and degrading treatment contrary to Articles 24 and 44 of Constitution

Human rights — Right to life — Death penalty — Mode of hanging — Constitutionality — Whether causing excessive pain and suffering — Whether constituting cruel, inhuman and degrading treatment contrary to Articles 24 and 44 of Constitution — The law of Uganda

ATTORNEY-GENERAL v. KIGULA AND OTHERS[1]

Uganda, Supreme Court. 21 *January* 2009

[1] The appellant was represented by Angela Kiryabwire Kanyima, Acting Commissioner for Civil Litigation, Margaret Nabakooza, Senior State Attorney, and Rashid Kibuuka, State Attorney. The respondents were represented by John Katende, Professor Frederick Sempebwa, Soozi Katende and Sim Katende.

(Odoki CJ; Tsekooko, Mulenga, Kanyeihamba and Katureebe JJSC; Kitumba and Egonda Ntende JJSC (Acting))

SUMMARY: *The facts*:—The respondents were sentenced to death for capital offences under Ugandan law. They petitioned the Constitutional Court challenging the constitutionality of the death penalty. They contended that the imposition of the death penalty was inconsistent with Articles 24[2] and 44[3] of the 1995 Constitution of Uganda. In the alternative, they argued that Ugandan laws providing for a mandatory death sentence were inconsistent with Articles 20,[4] 21,[5] 22,[6] 24, 28[7] and 44(a) of the Constitution, denying the convict rights to appeal against sentence, equality before the law and a fair hearing. The respondents also maintained that the long delay between sentence pronouncement and execution resulting in death-row syndrome, and the mode of hanging, constituted cruel, inhuman and degrading treatment contrary to Articles 24 and 44 of the Constitution.

The Constitutional Court held that the imposition of the death penalty did not constitute cruel, inhuman or degrading punishment; nor were Ugandan laws prescribing it inconsistent with Articles 24 and 44 of the Constitution. Ugandan laws prescribing the mandatory death sentence were, however, unconstitutional. The mode of hanging was constitutional but a delay of three years or more from death sentence by the highest appellate court to execution was inordinate, rendering any execution cruel, inhuman and degrading treatment contrary to Article 24 of the Constitution. The Attorney-General appealed and the respondents cross-appealed.

Held:—The appeal and cross-appeal were dismissed.

---

[2] Article 24 of the Constitution provided that: "No person shall be subjected to any form of torture or cruel, inhuman or degrading treatment or punishment."

[3] Article 44(a) of the Constitution provided that: "Notwithstanding anything in this Constitution, there shall be no derogation from the enjoyment of the freedom from torture, and cruel, inhuman or degrading treatment or punishment."

[4] Article 20 provided that: "(1) Fundamental rights and freedoms of the individual are inherent and not granted by the State. (2) The rights and freedoms of the individual and groups enshrined in this Chapter shall be respected, upheld and promoted by all organs and agencies of Government and by all persons."

[5] Article 21(1) provided that: "All persons are equal before and under the law in all spheres of political, economic, social and cultural life and in every other respect and shall enjoy equal protection of the law."

[6] Article 22(1) of the Constitution provided that: "No person shall be deprived of life intentionally except in execution of a sentence passed in a fair trial by a court of competent jurisdiction in respect of a criminal offence under the laws of Uganda and the conviction and sentence have been confirmed by the highest appellate court."

[7] Article 28(1) provided that: "In the determination of civil rights and obligations or any criminal charge, a person shall be entitled to a fair, speedy and public hearing before an independent and impartial court or tribunal established by law."

Article 28(3)(e) of the Constitution provided that: "Every person who is charged with a criminal offence shall, in the case of any offence which carries a sentence of death or imprisonment for life, be entitled to legal representation at the expense of the state."

(1) The imposition of the death penalty in Article 22(1) was not inconsistent with Articles 20, 24, 28, 44(a) and 45 of the Constitution.

(a) Since the right to life was the most fundamental of all rights, its withdrawal deserved serious consideration by the makers and interpreters of Constitutions. While Constitutions differed according to a country's philosophy and circumstances, they all intended to implement common standards of humanity (p. 677).

(b) International instruments did not abolish the death penalty but rather governed the framework for its imposition. While States were urged to aim for the abolition of capital punishment by guaranteeing an unqualified right to life, its retention did not violate international law.

(i) The Universal Declaration of Human Rights, 1948 provided separately for the right to life and freedom from torture, cruel, inhuman or degrading punishment. The International Covenant on Civil and Political Rights, 1966 ("the Covenant") prohibited the arbitrary deprivation of life, recognized the retention of the death penalty in certain countries and provided safeguards. There was no conflict between Articles 6 and 7 of the Covenant, provisions in *pari materia* with Articles 22(1) and 24 of the Constitution (pp. 677-9).

(ii) Although carrying out a death sentence in Uganda could constitute a cruel punishment, it did not in the context of Article 24 since there was express provision for it in Article 22(1). Uganda could introduce legislation to amend the Constitution and abolish the death sentence (pp. 679-80).

(iii) The United Nations human rights treaties dealt with the need to abolish the death penalty in the Covenant's Second Optional Protocol, 1990, and separately with matters of torture, cruel or inhuman punishment in the Convention Against Torture and Other Cruel, Inhuman or Degrading Treatment or Punishment, 1984. The Convention's Article 1 definition of torture confirmed that it did not apply to a lawful death sentence (p. 680).

(iv) The African Charter on Human and Peoples' Rights, 1981 also dealt with the death penalty and torture matters separately and used the word "arbitrarily"; a 1984 resolution adopted by the United Nations Economic and Social Council contained safeguards for those facing the death penalty (pp. 681-2).

(c) The framers had provided for the death penalty in the Constitution. They were aware of the United Nations instruments, particularly those to which Uganda was a party. The death penalty provisions had to be considered together with and in relation to the relevant international instruments. Article 22(1) of the Constitution conformed to the international instruments, particularly the Covenant, to which Uganda was a party. Additional safeguards were provided in Articles 28 and 121[8] of the Constitution. International instruments dealt with the death penalty separately from freedom from torture, cruel, inhuman

---

[8] Article 121(5) of the Constitution provided that: "Where a person is sentenced to death for an offence, a written report of the case from the trial judge or judges or person presiding over the court or tribunal, together with such other information derived from the record of the case or elsewhere as may be necessary, shall be submitted to the Advisory Committee on the Prerogative of Mercy."

or degrading punishment; provisions relating to those two subjects did not conflict. There was no conflict between Articles 22(1) and 44(a) of the Constitution. Article 44(a) was not meant to apply to Article 22(1) as long as the death sentence was passed by a competent court after a fair trial and confirmed by the highest appellate court. The framers could have provided expressly for a non-derogable right to life had they intended. In light of Uganda's history and background, the effect and purpose of the two provisions was to treat the right to life with qualification but with necessary safeguards, while totally outlawing all other forms of torture, cruel and degrading punishments as had been used in Uganda for political purposes (pp. 682-9).

(2) Ugandan laws providing for a mandatory death sentence were inconsistent with Articles 20, 21, 22, 24, 28 and 44(a) of the Constitution.

(a) According to the constitutional provisions, each individual's rights were inherent, all persons were equal before and under the law, a person was entitled to a fair, speedy and public hearing before an independent and impartial tribunal, and the accused was entitled to legal representation at the State's expense if the offence carried the death sentence (pp. 690-4).

(b) Sentencing was part of the trial as the court weighed the evidence, the nature of the offence and the circumstances of the case to arrive at an appropriate sentence. A sentence pre-ordained by legislature, as in capital cases, compromised the principle of a fair trial (p. 694).

(c) A mandatory death sentence was inconsistent with the right of equality before and under the law. There was no option for presenting mitigating factors or making inquiries under Sections 94 and 98 respectively of the Trial on Indictments Act—curious, given the report requirement in Article 121(5) of the Constitution. The removal by Parliament of the power of the courts to determine sentence was also inconsistent with Article 126 of the Constitution; the administration of justice was a function of the judiciary. Any law fettering the discretion of courts to confirm, or not, both conviction and sentence was unconstitutional (pp. 694-6).

(3) An unreasonable delay in carrying out a lawful death sentence rendered it inhuman and degrading treatment contrary to Article 24 of the Constitution. A death sentence was commuted to life imprisonment three years after confirmation of the sentence by the highest appellate court, failing presidential pardon.

(a) A condemned person retained his other rights as a human being, including his dignity, until execution. Living with the natural fear of death for a long period in poor prison conditions led to mental suffering resulting in death-row syndrome and treatment that was cruel and inhuman (pp. 696-8).

(b) A condemned person did not seek a quick execution but rather an exhaustion of appellate processes; this accorded with evolving standards of common decency provided for in the various international instruments. It was important given the finality of the death sentence and wrong convictions. Prison conditions should conform to the law and international standards. The law envisaged that the President would decide without unreasonable delay upon the prerogative of mercy pursuant to Article 121; this accorded with the spirit of the Constitution (pp. 698-703).

(4) Given that the death penalty was constitutional, hanging as a mode of execution was not unconstitutional under Article 24 of the Constitution. Suffering was necessarily part of the death process. Although a method causing instant death was preferable, hanging caused death within minutes, meeting the standard of not causing excessive pain and suffering (pp. 703-6).

(5) Debate on the desirability of the death penalty should be re-opened by the legislature. The failure, refusal or neglect by the executive to decide the fate of death-row prisoners appeared to indicate a desire to discontinue the death penalty (pp. 706-7).

Per Egonda Ntende JSC (Acting) (dissenting in part): (1) The death penalty was permitted under Article 22(1) of the Constitution. Articles 24 and 44 of the Constitution did, however, apply to Article 22(1). These three articles, relating to the punishment and treatment of offenders, had to be read together (pp. 707-13).

(2) This approach was supported by European Court of Human Rights and United Nations Human Rights Committee jurisprudence.[9] Articles 2(1) and 3 of the European Convention on Human Rights and Articles 6 to 7 of the International Covenant on Civil and Political Rights were *in pari materia* with Articles 22(1), 24, 21(1) and 24 respectively of the Constitution. Given Uganda's accession to the Covenant in 1995 and First Optional Protocol in 1996, Committee decisions were particularly persuasive. Ugandan law was to be interpreted so as not to conflict with Uganda's international law obligations (pp. 714-21).

(3) Hanging as a method of execution as practised in Uganda was cruel, inhuman and degrading treatment contrary to Article 24 of the Constitution. It failed to meet the least possible physical and mental suffering test set by the Human Rights Committee (pp. 721-8).

The following is the text of the judgments delivered in the Court:

The respondents/cross-appellants (the respondents) filed their Petition in the Constitutional Court under Article 137(3) of the Constitution challenging the constitutionality of the death penalty under the Constitution of Uganda.

The respondents were all persons who at different times had been convicted of diverse capital offences under the Penal Code Act and had been sentenced to death as provided for under the laws of Uganda. They contended that the imposition on them of the death sentence was inconsistent with Articles 24 and 44 of the Constitution. To the respondents

---

[9] *Soering* v. *United Kingdom*, 98 ILR 270 and *Ng* v. *Canada*, 98 ILR 479.

the various provisions of the laws of Uganda which prescribe the death sentence are inconsistent with Articles 24 and 44. The respondents also further petitioned in the alternative as follows:

> First, that the various provisions of the laws of Uganda which provide for a mandatory death sentence are unconstitutional because they are inconsistent with Articles 20, 21, 22, 24, 28 and 44(a) of the Constitution. They contended that the provisions contravene the Constitution because they deny the convicted person the right to appeal against sentence, thereby denying them the right of equality before the law and the right to fair hearing as provided for in the Constitution.
> Second, that the long delay between the pronouncement by court of the death sentence and the actual execution allows for the death-row syndrome to set in. Therefore the carrying out of the death sentence after such a long delay constitutes cruel, inhuman and degrading treatment contrary to Articles 24 and 44(a) of the Constitution.
> Third, that Section 99(1) of the Trial on Indictments Act, which provides for hanging as the legal mode of carrying out the death sentence, is cruel, inhuman and degrading contrary to Articles 24 and 44 of the Constitution.

Accordingly they sought various reliefs, orders and declarations.

The Attorney-General (the appellant) opposed the Petition in its entirety, contending that the death penalty was provided for in the Constitution of Uganda and its imposition, whether as a mandatory sentence or as a maximum sentence, was constitutional. Both parties filed affidavits in support of their respective cases.

The Constitutional Court heard the petition and decided as follows:

> 1. The imposition of the death penalty does not constitute cruel, inhuman or degrading punishment in terms of Articles 24 and 44 of the Constitution, and therefore the various provisions of the laws of Uganda prescribing the death sentence are not inconsistent with or in contravention of Articles 24 and 44 or any provisions of the Constitution.
> 2. The various provisions of the laws of Uganda which prescribe a mandatory death sentence are inconsistent with Articles 21, 22(1), 24, 28, 44(a) and 44(c) of the Constitution and, therefore, are unconstitutional.
> 3. Implementing the carrying out of the death sentence by hanging is constitutional as it operationalizes Article 22(1) of the Constitution. Therefore Section 99(1) of the Trial on Indictments Act

is not unconstitutional or inconsistent with Articles 24 and 44(a) of the Constitution.
4. A delay beyond three years after a death sentence has been confirmed by the highest appellate court is an inordinate delay. Therefore for those condemned prisoners who have been on death row for three years and above after their sentences had been confirmed by the highest appellate court, it would be unconstitutional to carry out the death sentence as it would be inconsistent with Articles 24 and 44(a) of the Constitution.

Consequently, the court made the following orders:

1. For those Petitioners whose appeal process is completed and their sentence of death has been confirmed by the Supreme Court, their redress will be put on halt for two years to enable the Executive to exercise its discretion under Article 121 of the Constitution. They may return to court for redress after the expiration of that period.
2. For the Petitioners whose appeals are still pending before an appellate court:

    (a) they shall be afforded a hearing in mitigation on sentence,
    (b) the court shall exercise its discretion whether or not to confirm the sentence,
    (c) therefore, in respect of those whose sentence of death will be confirmed, the discretion under Article 121 should be exercised within three years.

The Attorney-General was not wholly satisfied by the above decision and orders, hence this appeal. The respondents were also dissatisfied with parts of the decision of the Constitutional Court, hence the cross-appeal.

In this Court the Attorney-General filed eight grounds of appeal as follows:

1. The Learned Justices of the Constitutional Court erred in law in holding that the various provisions of the law that prescribe mandatory death sentences are inconsistent with Articles 21, 22(1), 24, 28, 44(a) and 44(c) of the Constitution.
2. The Learned Justices of the Constitutional Court erred in law in holding that Section 132 of the Trial on Indictments Act (Cap 23) is inconsistent with Articles 21, 22(1), 24, 28, 44(a) and 44(c) of the Constitution.
3. The Learned Justices of the Constitutional Court erred in law and fact in holding that delay in carrying out the death sentence after it has been

confirmed by the highest appellate court is inconsistent with Articles 24 and 44(a) of the Constitution.
4. The Learned Justices of the Constitutional Court erred in law and in fact in holding that a delay in carrying out a death sentence beyond 3 years after the highest court has confirmed the death sentence is inordinate.
5. The Learned Justices of the Constitutional Court erred in law and in fact in ordering that the petitioners whose death sentence has been confirmed by the Supreme Court shall have their redress put on halt for two years to enable the Executive to exercise its discretion under Article 121 of the Constitution.
6. The Learned Justices of the Constitutional Court erred in law and in fact in ordering that for the petitioners whose appeals are still pending before an appellate court they shall be heard in mitigation on sentence.
7. The Learned Justices of the Constitutional Court erred in law in ordering that the appellate courts shall exercise discretion whether or not to confirm the death sentence.
8. The Learned Justices of the Constitutional Court erred in law and in fact in ordering that where the death sentence has been confirmed the discretion under Article 121 of the Constitution should be exercised within three years.

The appellant seeks orders to allow the appeal, overrule the Judgment of the Constitutional Court and costs of the appeal.

On the other hand, the respondents cross-appealed on the following grounds:

1. That the Learned Justices of the Constitutional Court erred in law when they held that Articles 24 and 44(a) of the Constitution of the Republic of Uganda 1995 as amended (hereafter referred to as "The Constitution") which prohibit any forms of torture, cruel, inhuman and degrading treatment or punishment were not meant to apply to Article 22(1) of the Constitution.
2. That the Learned Judges of the Constitutional Court erred in law when they held that the death penalty was not inconsistent with Articles 20, 21, 22(1), 24, 28, 44(a) and 45 of the Constitution.
3. That in the alternative but without prejudice to the above, that the Learned Justices of the Constitutional Court erred in law when they found as a question of fact and law that hanging was a cruel, inhuman and degrading treatment or punishment but held that it was a permissible form of punishment because the death penalty was permitted by the Constitution.

The respondents seek orders and declarations as follows:
Declarations to the effect that:

    (a) the death penalty, in its nature, and in the manner, process and mode in which it is or can be implemented in Uganda, is a form of

torture, cruel, inhuman or degrading treatment or punishment prohibited under Articles 24 and 44(a) of the Constitution;
(b) the imposition of the death penalty is a violation of the right to life protected under Articles 22(1), 20 and 45 of the Constitution;
(c) Sections 25(1), 25(2), 25(3), 25(4), 118, 123(1), 129(5), 184, 273(2), 301 B(2) and 235(1) of the Penal Code Act (Cap 120) and Sections 7(1)(a), 7(1)(b), 8, 9(1) and 9(2) of the Anti-Terrorism Act (Act No 14 of 2002) and any other laws that prescribe a death penalty in Uganda are inconsistent with and in contravention of Articles 20, 21, 22(1), 24, 28, 44(a), 44(c) and 45 of the Constitution to the extent that they permit or prescribe the imposition of death sentences;
(d) the carrying out of a sentence of death is inconsistent with Articles 20, 21, 22(1), 24, 28, 44(a), 44(c) and 45 of the Constitution;
(e) the method of carrying out a death sentence by hanging is cruel, inhuman and degrading and inconsistent with the provisions of Articles 20, 21, 22(1), 24, 44(a) and 45 of the Constitution.

Orders:

(a) that the death sentences imposed on the respondents be set aside;
(b) that the orders of the Constitutional Court granting the cross-appellants' Petition be affirmed and those refusing the cross-appellants' Petition be set aside and substituted with orders prayed for in the Petition in the Constitutional Court.
(c) that the Court exercise its jurisdiction to grant such other orders, redress or relief to the respondents/cross-appellants as are appropriate in the circumstances of the case and in the interests of justice;
(d) that the respondents/cross-appellants be granted costs of the cross-appeal.

Both parties filed what they termed "summary submissions" but also made oral submissions in support of their respective cases.

The appellant was represented by Angela Kiryabwire Kanyima, Ag. Commissioner for Civil Litigation, assisted by Margaret Nabakooza, Senior State Attorney and Rashid Kibuuka, State Attorney. The respondents were represented by John Katende together with Prof. Frederick Sempebwa, Soozi Katende and Sim Katende.

The appellant's counsel argued grounds 1, 2, 6 and 7 together, and then grounds 3, 4, 5 and 8 also together. On the other hand, counsel for the respondents argued that ground 1 of the cross-appeal should be argued first as it was the main issue of contention, the others being argued in the alternative. In their view, if the Court upholds this ground it would be unnecessary to adjudicate on the other grounds. They therefore argued that ground alone, and argued the others also separately.

We agree with counsel for the respondents that the first ground of the cross-appeal is the main issue in this case, and that logically it should be argued first. The alternative issues can then be considered after the disposal of that ground.

The first issue for determination arising out of the cross-appeal is whether the death penalty is inconsistent with Articles 20, 21, 22(1), 24, 28, 44(a) and 45 of the Constitution.

The Constitutional Court found that the death penalty was not inconsistent with the above provisions of the Constitution and that Articles 24 and 44 of the Constitution did not apply to Article 22(1) of the Constitution. The respondents disagree.

Counsel for the respondents argued that the death penalty by itself is a cruel, inhuman and degrading punishment and therefore violates Article 24 of the Constitution. Counsel relies on the decision of this Court in *Attorney-General* v. *Abuki* [2001] 1 LRC 63 in interpreting what amounts to "cruel, inhuman and degrading punishment". Counsel argued that if the case of banishment [was] found to be such punishment, then [the] death penalty which is much severer must also be judged cruel, inhuman and degrading. Counsel also relies on the Tanzania case of *Republic* v. *Mbushuu* [1994] 2 LRC 335 where the death penalty was adjudged to be "cruel, inhuman and degrading". He also relied on the South African case of *State* v. *Makwanyane* [1995] 1 LRC 269 where the court considered provisions in the South African Constitution similar to Article 24 of the Uganda Constitution and declared the death sentence to be cruel, inhuman and degrading and therefore unconstitutional in South Africa.

In arguing whether Articles 24 and 44 were meant to apply to Article 22(1) of the Constitution, counsel argues that the freedom from cruel, inhuman and degrading punishment, as contained in Article 24, is absolute from which derogation is prohibited by Article 44(a). If the makers of the Constitution had intended that Article 24 would not apply to Article 22(1) they would have provided so expressly. Since Article 44(a) provides that "Notwithstanding anything in this Constitution, there shall be no derogation from the enjoyment of the freedom from torture, and cruel, inhuman or degrading treatment or punishment", it follows that any provision of the Constitution which provides for a punishment that is cruel, inhuman and degrading, like the death penalty, is inconsistent with Article 44(a) and would be unconstitutional. In counsel's opinion, Article 22(1) was in conflict with Article 24 and the Court, relying on *Ssemogerere* v. *Attorney-General* (Constitutional Appeal No 1 of 2002) [2005] 1 LRC 50, can proceed to interpret one article against the other to resolve the conflict. In counsel's view, the conflict is resolved by Article 44(a). Counsel states in his written submission: "The purpose and wording of Article 44(a) was to resolve any anomaly in *any* part of the Constitution and it allows no exceptions or qualifications even those impliedly or expressly envisaged by Article 22(1). The death penalty is therefore not saved by Article 22(1) [Counsel's emphasis]." Counsel urged this Court not to rely on case law from jurisdictions that did not have the equivalent of Article 44(a) in their constitutions. He particularly singled out the Nigerian case of *Kalu* v. *The State* (1998) 13 NWLR 531 which had allowed the death sentence as constitutional in Nigeria. Counsel contends that the Constitutional Court was wrong to follow that decision.

On the other hand, counsel for the appellant fully supported the decision of the Constitutional Court that Articles 24 and 44 were not meant to apply to Article 22(1) of the Constitution, and that the death penalty as provided for in Article 22(1) was constitutional in Uganda.

In dealing with this matter we wish to start from what appears to be a common position, namely that the right to life is the most fundamental of all rights. The taking away of such a right is, therefore, a matter of great consequence deserving serious consideration by those who make constitutions as well as those who interpret those constitutions. One must also bear in mind that different constitutions may provide for different things precisely because each constitution is dealing with a philosophy and circumstances of a particular country. Nevertheless there are common standards of humanity that all constitutions set out to achieve. In discussing this matter we will make reference to international instruments on the subject.

The death penalty appears to have existed for as long as human beings have been on earth. Sometimes it was arbitrarily imposed and carried out in all sorts of manner as for example burning on the stake, crucifixion, beheading, shooting, etc. During World War II, the crimes committed by the Nazis in Germany, whereby millions of people were put to death, clearly shocked the world. This was one of the reasons why the Universal Declaration of Human Rights was adopted and proclaimed by the United Nations General Assembly on 10 December 1948. The preamble to that declaration provides in part:

Whereas disregard and contempt for human rights have resulted in barbarous acts which have outraged the conscience of mankind, and the advent of a world in which human beings shall enjoy freedom of speech and belief and freedom from fear and want has been proclaimed as the highest aspiration of the common people...

Now, therefore, The General Assembly:

Proclaims this Universal Declaration of Human Rights as a common standard of achievement for all peoples and all nations, to the end that every individual and every organ of society, keeping this Declaration constantly in mind, shall strive by teaching and education to promote respect for those rights and freedoms and by *progressive measures*, national and international, to secure their universal and effective recognition and observance, both among the peoples of Member States themselves and among the peoples of territories under their jurisdiction. (Emphasis added.)

With the above background and objectives in mind, the Assembly proceeded to set out international standards to be achieved by all member states.

Article 3 states: "Everyone has the right to life, liberty and security of person."

Article 5 states: "No one shall be subjected to torture or to cruel, inhuman or degrading treatment or punishment."

It may be noted that the right to life is provided for separately, and the freedom from torture, cruel, inhuman or degrading punishment is also treated separately. It cannot be argued therefore that by these provisions, the Universal Declaration of Human Rights had thereby abolished the death penalty in the world. Indeed this could not have been so, for even as the Declaration was being proclaimed, death sentences passed by International Tribunals were being carried out against war criminals in Germany and Japan.

The next instrument is the International Covenant on Civil and Political Rights which was adopted and opened for signature, ratification and accession by the General Assembly on 16 December 1966, and came into force on 23 March 1976.

Article 6(1) thereof states: "Every human being has the inherent right to life. This right shall be protected by law. No one shall be arbitrarily deprived of his life."

This article amplifies Article 2 of the Universal Declaration of Human Rights (supra) by adding on that the right to life must be protected by law and may not be *arbitrarily* taken away. In our view, the introduction of the word "arbitrarily" is significant because it recognizes that under certain acceptable circumstances a person may be lawfully deprived of his life. This is further acknowledged in Article 6(2) which states:

In countries which have not abolished the death penalty, sentence of death may be imposed only for the most serious crimes in accordance with the law in force at the time of the commission of the crime and not contrary to the provisions of the present covenant and to the Convention on the Prevention and Punishment of the Crime of Genocide. This penalty can only be carried out pursuant to a trial judgment rendered by a competent court.

This provision recognised the reality that there were still countries that had not yet abolished capital punishment. It also seeks to set out safeguards that should be followed in the imposition of death sentences. Article 6(4) provides thus:

Anyone sentenced to death shall have the right to seek pardon or commutation of the sentence. Amnesty, pardon or commutation of the death sentence may be granted in all cases.

These safeguards are not to be construed as intended to delay or prevent the abolition of capital punishment, but they have to be followed by those countries which, for one reason or other peculiar to their circumstances, have not yet abolished the death penalty.

It is also significant to note that having so comprehensively provided for the death penalty in Article 6, the convention proceeds to provide separate sections for torture, cruel, inhuman or degrading treatment or punishment. Thus Article 7 provides thus:

No one shall be subjected to torture or to cruel, inhuman or degrading treatment or punishment. In particular no one shall be subjected without his free consent to medical or scientific experimentation.

It is noteworthy that the above provisions of the Covenant are *in pari materia* with Articles 22(1) and 24 of the Constitution of Uganda.

We do not see nor can we find any conflict between Articles 6 and 7 of this Covenant. This issue was considered by the Human Rights Committee of the United Nations in *Ng* v. *Canada* (Communication No 469/1991 [98 ILR 479]) where the majority of the committee held that because the International Covenant contained provisions that permitted the imposition of capital punishment for the most serious crimes, but subject to certain qualifications, and notwithstanding the view of the committee that the execution of a sentence of death may be considered to constitute cruel and inhuman treatment within the meaning of Article 7 of the Covenant, the extradition of a fugitive to a country which enforces the death sentence in accordance with the requirements of the International Covenant could not be regarded as a breach of the obligations of the extraditing country.

As Twinomujuni JA observed, in his judgment, executing a death sentence in Uganda may constitute a cruel punishment, but not in the context of Article 24 because the death penalty has been expressly provided for in Article 22(1). The International Covenant provides that nothing in its provisions should be construed as delaying or preventing the abolition of capital punishment. In Uganda, although the Constitution provides for the death sentence, there is nothing to stop Uganda as a member of the United Nations from introducing legislation to amend the Constitution and abolish the death sentence. Indeed, the Constitutional Review Commission showed by Odoki JSC (as he then was), and referred to in this judgment (Annexture B) did recommend for a periodic review of the subject.

Internationally, the campaign and efforts to abolish the death penalty as such continue. On 15 December 1989, the General Assembly adopted the Second Optional Protocol to the International Covenant on Civil and Political Rights, aiming at the abolition of the death penalty (15 December 1989; UN GA Res. 44/128).

By this Protocol, each of the States Parties to it undertakes to "take all necessary measures to abolish the death penalty within its jurisdiction".

The United Nations having dealt with the need to abolish the death sentence in the above protocol proceeded to deal with matters of torture, cruel or inhuman punishment separately. Thus the United Nations General Assembly in December 1975 adopted the Declaration on the Protection of All Persons from being Subjected to Torture and Other Cruel, Inhuman or Degrading Treatment or Punishment. Subsequently on 10 December 1984, the United Nations General Assembly adopted the Convention Against Torture and Other Cruel, Inhuman or Degrading Treatment or Punishment. This Convention came into force on 26 June 1987.

This Convention offers a definition of what constitutes torture, which, in our opinion, leaves no doubt that it does not apply to a lawful death sentence. Article 1 thereof states:

For the purposes of this Convention, the term "torture" means any act by which severe pain or suffering, whether physical or mental, is intentionally inflicted on a person for such purposes as obtaining from him or a third person information or a confession, punishing him for an act he or a third person has committed or is suspected of having committed, or intimidating or coercing him or a third person, or for any reason based on discrimination of any kind, when such pain or suffering is inflicted by or at the instigation of or with the consent or acquiescence of a public official or other person acting in an official capacity. *It does not include pain or suffering arising only from, inherent in or incidental to lawful sanctions.* (Emphasis added.)

The General Assembly on 18 December 2002 adopted the Optional Protocol to the Convention Against Torture and Other Cruel, Inhuman or Degrading Treatment or Punishment, whose objective is "to establish a system of regular visits undertaken by independent international and national bodies to places where people are deprived of their liberty in order to prevent torture and other cruel, inhuman or degrading treatment or punishment".

There are other International Instruments containing similar provisions on the right to life and on freedom from torture, cruel, inhuman or degrading treatment or punishment. The African Charter on Human and Peoples' Rights of 1981 in Article 4 provides:

Human beings are inviolable. Every human being shall be entitled to respect for his life and the integrity of his person. No one may be *arbitrarily* deprived of this right. (Emphasis added.)

In this charter, again the freedom from cruel, inhuman or degrading treatment is treated separately. Once again, one must note the use of the word "arbitrarily".

It may further be pointed out that the United Nations Economic and Social Council on 25 May 1984 adopted a Resolution containing the safeguards guaranteeing protection of the rights of those facing the death penalty. Again some of the provisions of the Resolution are instructive. Paragraph 1 states as follows: "In countries which have not abolished the death penalty, capital punishment may be imposed only for the most serious crimes, it being understood that their scope should not go beyond intentional crimes with lethal or other extremely grave consequences." Paragraphs 4-9 are as follows:

4. Capital punishment may be imposed only when the guilt of the person charged is based upon clear and convincing evidence leaving no room for an alternative explanation of the facts.
5. Capital punishment may only be carried out pursuant to a final judgment rendered by a competent court after legal process which gives all possible safeguards to ensure a fair trial...
6. Anyone sentenced to death shall have the right to appeal to a court of higher jurisdiction, and steps should be taken to ensure that such appeals shall become mandatory.
7. Anyone sentenced to death shall have the right to seek pardon, or commutation of sentence; pardon or commutation of sentence may be granted in all cases of capital punishment.
8. Capital punishment shall not be carried out pending any appeal or other recourse procedure or other proceeding relating to pardon or commutation of the sentence.
9. Where capital punishment occurs, it shall be carried out so as to inflict the minimum possible suffering.

The above instruments are some of those that lay out the framework governing the imposition of capital punishment. States are urged to strive to achieve the goal of the abolition of capital punishment by guaranteeing an unqualified right to life. But it is also recognised that for various reasons some countries still consider it desirable to have capital punishment on their statute books. The retention of capital punishment by itself is not illegal or unlawful or a violation of international law. It is in that context that we now proceed to discuss the constitutional provisions regarding capital punishment in Uganda.

We take judicial notice of the fact that the debate and subsequent promulgation of the Constitution of Uganda 1995 came after a long period of strife in the country—a period when there had been gross violations of human rights by various organs of the state, particularly the army and other security agencies. This was a period when there were thousands of extra-judicial killings, as well as wanton torture of people. It is for this reason that the preamble to the Constitution states:

We the People of Uganda:
Recalling our history which has been characterised by political and constitutional instability;
Recognising our struggles against the forces of tyranny, oppression and exploitation...

The Constituent Assembly debated a draft Constitution that was prepared by the Constitutional Review Commission, which had travelled the width and breadth of Uganda encompassing people's views on various aspects of the Constitution. One of the subjects on which the Commission specifically sought and received views was the death penalty. In its Report (Annexture B) the Commission had this to say in paragraph 7.106:

We have seriously considered arguments of both sides, critically analysed the international attitude to capital punishment, the praiseworthy campaign of Amnesty International for the abolition of the death penalty and consideration of the fact that the death penalty has been abolished in several countries, including a few African countries. We fully understand the need for a change of attitude to capital punishment. We have, however, not found sufficient reasons to justify going against the majority views expressed and analysed.

The Commission then recommended as follows:

7.107

(a) Capital punishment should be retained in the new Constitution.
(b) Capital punishment should be the maximum sentence for extremely serious crimes, namely murder, treason, aggravated robbery, and kidnapping with intent to murder.

(c) It should be in the discretion of the Courts of Law to decide whether a conviction on the above crimes should deserve the maximum penalty of death or life imprisonment.
(d) The issue of maintaining the death penalty should be regularly reviewed through national and public debates to discover whether the views of the people on it have changed to abolition or not.

Clearly, inclusion of the death penalty in the Constitution was therefore not accidental or a mere afterthought. It was carefully deliberated upon.

The concern about torture, cruel and inhuman treatment was considered as a separate subject as there were also reports of people having been subjected to all sorts of torture, cruel and inhuman treatments by various agencies of the state. Uganda is a Member of the United Nations. The framers of the Constitution were aware of the various United Nations Instruments, particularly those to which Uganda is a party. That is why Article 287 provided for the continuation of treaties and conventions to which Uganda is a party.

With this background in mind, one should look at all the relevant provisions regarding the death penalty in their totality and how they relate to the International Instruments hereinabove referred to. Furthermore, it is well settled by this Court in *Ssemogerere v. AG* (Constitutional Appeal No 1 of 2002) [2005] 1 LRC 50 that in interpreting the Constitution, provisions should not be looked at in isolation. The Constitution should be looked at as a whole with no provision destroying another, but provisions sustaining each other. This has been said to be the rule of harmony or completeness. It has also been settled by this Court that provisions bearing on a particular issue should be considered together to give effect to the purpose of the Constitution.

The death penalty is not only provided for in Article 22(1) of the Constitution but also in several other places. First, Article 22(1) provides:

No person shall be deprived of life intentionally except in execution of a sentence passed in a fair trial by a court of competent jurisdiction in respect of a criminal offence under the laws of Uganda and the conviction and sentence have been confirmed by the highest appellate court.

Clearly this conforms to the international instruments already alluded to above, particularly the International Covenant on Civil and Political Rights to which Uganda is a party. In Uganda, the death sentence can only be carried out in execution of a sentence passed by a competent court after a fair hearing. Article 28(3)(e) states:

Every person who is charged with a criminal offence shall, *in the case of any offence which carries a sentence of death* or *imprisonment for life*, be entitled to legal representation at the expense of the state. (Emphasis added.)

This further gives an extra safeguard to a person who is sentenced to death, i.e. legal representation at the expense of the state. It is to be noted here that Article 28 comes after Article 24. So the framers must have known what was provided in Article 24.

Furthermore, Article 121 which deals with the prerogative of mercy has a special provision regarding the death sentence. Article 121(5) states:

Where a person is sentenced to death for an offence, a written report of the case from the trial judge or judges or person presiding over the court or tribunal, together with such other information derived from the record of the case or elsewhere as may be necessary, shall be submitted to the Advisory Committee on the Prerogative of Mercy.

Here it is clear that the framers of the Constitution were concerned about an extra safeguard for a person sentenced to death, i.e. that the Committee on the Prerogative of Mercy should take into account a report about the case from the judge or judges who presided over the case. The rationale for this is that the judge in his report may reveal whether or not the convicted person showed remorse or contrition during the trial or whether there may be extenuating circumstances upon which mercy may be extended to the convicted person.

In our view these are deliberate provisions in the Constitution which can only point to the view that the framers of the Constitution purposefully provided for the death penalty in the Constitution of Uganda.

Counsel for the respondents argues that the death penalty is a cruel, inhuman and degrading punishment and it, therefore, is inconsistent with Articles 24 and 44(a) of the Constitution.

Article 24 of the Constitution states:

No person shall be subjected to any form of torture or cruel, inhuman or degrading treatment or punishment.

This is *in pari materia* with Article 5 of the Universal Declaration of Human Rights. It is also *in pari materia* with Article 7 of the International Covenant on Civil and Political Rights. In the foregoing discussion, [we] have endeavoured to show that the International Instruments have tended to deal with the death penalty separately from the freedom from torture, cruel, inhuman or degrading punishment. The provisions relating to those two subjects do not conflict with one another. Counsel for the appellant contends that there is a conflict between

Articles 22(1) and 24 because Article 44(a) provides for no derogation from the right to freedom from torture, cruel, inhuman or degrading punishment.

Counsel further argues that Article 44 is unique and overrides all other provisions of the Constitution that may provide anything to the contrary, including Article 22(1). In his view, had the framers of the 1995 Constitution intended to save punishments that would otherwise offend Article 44, they would have re-enacted a provision similar to Article 12(2) of the 1967 Constitution which provided thus:

> Nothing contained in or done under the authority of any law shall be held to be inconsistent with or in contravention of this article to the extent that the law in question authorises the infliction of any punishment that was lawful in Uganda immediately before 9 October 1962.

Clearly, counsel's argument is based on the assumption that the death penalty *per se* amounts to "cruel, inhuman or degrading treatment" which is outlawed by Article 44(a). He further argues in his written submission that:

> On the basis of the *Abuki* case, each of these words have to be read and interpreted in isolation, not conjunctively, so that any one element if proved must not be allowed to stand.

So the question that we must answer is whether the framers of the Constitution deliberately intended to exclude Article 22(1) from the operation of Article 44(a) or whether they inadvertently created confusion and conflict between two important provisions of the Constitution. It is also noteworthy that the Constitution itself did not define the terms "torture, cruel, inhuman or degrading punishment". Courts have tried to define them depending on the context.

As counsel for the respondents submitted, the right to life is the most fundamental of all rights. It is therefore curious that the framers of the Constitution did not have it included within Article 44(a) as one of those rights that are non-derogable under any circumstances. Or could it be that they regarded the right to life to be so fundamental and chose to deal with it separately and provide for exceptions to it in a self-contained provision which was supposed to stand alone to the exclusion of Article 44(a)? We have already pointed out that the death penalty is referred to in several provisions of the Constitution. In our view, the framers of the Constitution did not regard the death penalty as qualifying for the classification of "cruel, unusual, inhuman or degrading treatment or punishment" for purposes of the Constitution, as long as it was passed by a competent court, in a fair trial and confirmed by the highest court as provided for in Article 22(1). Paul Sieghart in his article published in *The International Law of Human Rights* (1983) p. 130, and cited by the Court of Appeal in the Tanzanian case of *Republic* v. *Mbushuu* [1995] 1 LRC 216 at page 232, seems to support the view that provisions about torture, cruel or inhuman punishment are intended to apply to the process of living. He writes as follows:

> As human rights can only attach to living human beings, one might expect the right to life itself to be in some sense primary, since none of the other rights would have any value or utility without it. But the international instruments do not in fact accord it any formal primacy: on the contrary ... contain qualifications rendering the right less than absolute, and allowing human life to be deliberately terminated in certain specific cases ... The right to life thus stands in marked contrast to some of the other rights protected by the same instruments; for example, the freedom from torture and other ill-treatment ... and the freedom from slavery and servitude ... are both absolute, and subject to no exception of any kind. *It may therefore be said that international human rights law assigns a higher value to the quality of living as a process, than to the existence of life as a state ... the law tends to regard acute or prolonged suffering* (at all events in cases where it is inflicted by others, and so it is potentially avoidable) *as a greater evil than death*, which is ultimately unavoidable for everyone. (Emphasis added.)

The phrase "cruel, unusual, inhuman or degrading punishment" has its history in the English Bill of Rights of 1688. According to *Death Penalty Cases: Leading US Supreme Court Cases on Capital Punishment* (2nd edn, 2002), p. 2, the English Bill was a response to the cruelty of King James II. In a revolt against him which he savagely suppressed, hundreds of captured rebels were taken before special courts (the "Bloody Assizes"), convicted and then brutally executed by such methods as hanging, being cut down before death, being disembowelled, beheaded, or being hacked to pieces. It is also said that even in Europe at that time there was "use of the rack, drawing and quartering and burning alive". The authors continue:

> When the United States Constitution was adopted in 1789, some of these barbaric punishments still were used abroad, and the framers of the Constitution apparently were determined to prohibit their imposition in America. However, branding, whipping, and the cropping of ears were commonly used in the United States before and after the adoption of the Eighth Amendment, until, by 1850, they were virtually abolished by the state legislatures.
>
> It is clear that the Cruel and Unusual Punishments clause was *not* intended to abolish capital punishment. Some proof of this is provided by other language in the Constitution; the Fifth Amendment in particular implies that the death penalty was constitutionally acceptable. It was intended (in part) to forbid the infliction of more pain than was necessary to extinguish life. Therefore, the

focus of the few death penalty cases before the Supreme Court in the 19th Century was not whether a death sentence could be imposed, but how it was to be carried out.

The Supreme Court of the United States has interpreted the Eighth Amendment and struck down sentences found to be "excessive" in the circumstances of a particular case. In *Trop* v. *Dulles* (1958) 356 US 86 the majority were of the opinion that the Eighth Amendment must draw its meaning from "the evolving standards of decency that mark the progress of a maturing society", and therefore held that it was cruel and unusual punishment to take away the citizenship of a wartime deserter. This was not even a death penalty case. The problem has been how to determine and measure what [are] to be "contemporary standards of decency".

The Supreme Court considered the Eighth Amendment in *Furman* v. *Georgia* (1972) 408 US 238, which has also been cited in this court by counsel for the respondents. For the first time, the US Supreme Court, by majority, declared that the death penalty was a cruel and unusual punishment. However, barely four years later, the same court, again by majority, in *Gregg* v. *Georgia* (1976) 428 US 153 rejected the decision in *Furman* that the death penalty is *per se* cruel and unusual and went on to uphold a Georgian law that permitted capital punishment but provided for certain trial procedures and appeals designed to prevent the penalty being imposed arbitrarily. In his opinion which was joined in by Justices Powell and Stevens, Justice Stewart stated thus ((1976) 428 US 153 at 168-80):

We address initially the basic contention that the punishment of death for the crime of murder is, under all circumstances, "cruel and unusual" in violation of the Eighth and Fourteenth Amendments of the Constitution... The Petitioners in the capital cases before the court today renew the "standards of decency" argument, but developments during the four years since *Furman* have undercut substantially the assumptions upon which their argument rested. Despite the continuing debate, dating back to the 19th Century, over the morality and utility of capital punishment, it is now evident that a larger proportion of American society continues to regard it as an appropriate and necessary criminal sanction.

The most marked indication of society's endorsement of the death penalty for murder is the legislative response to *Furman*. The legislatures of at least 35 states have enacted new statutes that provide for the death penalty for at least some crimes that result in the death of another person. And the congress of the United States, in 1974, enacted a statute providing the death penalty for aircraft piracy that results in death. These recently adopted statutes have attempted to address the concerns expressed by the court in *Furman* primarily:

(i) by specifying the factors to be followed in deciding when to impose a capital sentence, or
(ii) by making the death penalty mandatory for specified crimes. But all of the post-*Furman* statutes make clear that capital punishment itself has not been rejected by the elected representatives of the people...

The above cases illustrate the debate that has raged, and continues to rage, in the United States regarding aspects of the death sentence, and what constitutes "evolving standards of decency". We cannot say that those states in the United States of America, or indeed anywhere else in the world who retain the death penalty, have not evolved standards of decency. Each situation must be examined on its own merits and in its context.

In Uganda, we have already alluded to the concerns of the framers of the Constitution at the time when these provisions were enacted. Although counsel for the respondents has sought to rely on the omission of the equivalent of Article 12(2) of the 1967 Constitution from the 1995 Constitution, he did not advert to the fact that the preamble to the 1967 Constitution did not include the equivalent of the following recital in the 1995 Constitution:

Recalling our history which has been characterised by political and constitutional instability;
Recognising our struggles against the forces of tyranny, oppression and exploitation.

Secondly, the Court cannot fail to recollect that the debate and passing of the 1995 Constitution was proceeded by two important commissions of inquiry. The first was the commission of inquiry into the violations of Human Rights in Uganda, headed by Oder JSC (RIP). The second was the Constitutional Review Commission headed by Odoki JSC (as he then was).

The first Commission established that there had been gross violation of human rights including numerous extra-judicial killings, or many cases where people simply disappeared. Indeed, even during the rule of Idi Amin, there was a Judicial Commission set up to look into "missing persons". Its report listed many people as "missing, presumed dead". The Oder Commission reported numerous instances of torture, where people were burned with molten plastic materials, shocked with electricity, buried alive, hacked to death, put in boots of cars etc. This Commission made certain recommendations some of which were later to be considered by the Odoki Commission and included in the draft Constitution that was presented to the Constituent Assembly in 1993.

Therefore in debating it, the framers of the Constitution had in mind the recent history of Uganda, characterised by gross abuses of human rights. This explains the promulgation of the Constitution with a full Bill of Rights but including clear exceptions where those were found necessary, and modelled on international instruments.

Article 22(1) is clearly meant to deal with and do away with extra-judicial killings by the state. The article recognises the sanctity of human life but recognises also that under certain circumstances acceptable in the country, that right might be taken away. The framers also were aware that the Constitutional Commission had specifically sought and analysed views from the public in Uganda about the retention of the death penalty.

The framers of the Constitution were also aware of the numerous instances of torture and other cruel punishments that had characterised our recent history. They seem to have come out on these two aspects of our history and dealt with them by providing that life is sacrosanct and may only be taken away after due process up to the highest court, and after the President has had opportunity to exercise the prerogative of mercy. On the other hand, there must not be torture or cruel, inhuman or degrading punishment under any circumstances.

In our view there is no conflict between Articles 22(1) and 44(a). Article 44(a) was not meant to apply to article 22(1) as long as the sentence of death was passed by a competent court after a fair trial and it had been confirmed by the highest appellate court. Such a sentence could not be torture, cruel or degrading punishment in the context of Article 24. Had the framers intended to provide for the non-derogable right to life, they would have so provided expressly. But in light of the history and background they had at the time, it is clear to us that the effect and purpose of the two provisions was to treat the right to life with qualification but with the necessary safeguards, while totally outlawing all other forms of torture, cruel and degrading punishments as had been found to have taken place in Uganda. Many of the instances of extra-judicial killing and torture were found to have been meted out to perceived political opponents. It is instructive that Article 43 on general derogation specifically states that "public interest" shall not permit political persecution or detention without trial.

We therefore agree with the Constitutional Court on this ground that the imposition of the death penalty in Article 22(1) is not inconsistent with Articles 20, 24, 28, 44(a) and 45 of the Constitution. Grounds 1 and 2 of the cross-appeal must fail.

We wish to add that the right to life is so important that the abolition of the death penalty requires specific progressive measures by the state to eventually expressly effect such abolition. This has been done by many countries all over the world who have specifically provided for no death penalty in their Constitutions, or who have acceded to the Optional Protocol on the Abolition of the Death Penalty. Some Constitutions have not qualified the right to life and it has been easy for the courts to rule that the death sentence is unconstitutional as happened in South Africa with the *Makwanyane* case (supra) upon which the respondents have put so much reliance.

In our view, the *Makwanyane* case, so well and ably reasoned, is a good authority for the abolition of the death sentence in its entirety, where the Constitution itself has not dealt with it. Indeed, Chaskalson P, in his comprehensive judgment, after reviewing the background to the promulgation of the South African Constitution, stated as follows (at page 289):

The death sentence was, in terms, neither sanctioned or excluded, and it was left to the Constitutional Court to decide whether the provisions of the pre-Constitutional law making the death penalty a competent sentence for murder and other crimes are consistent with chap. 3 of the Constitution. If they are, the death sentence remains a competent sentence for murder in cases in which those provisions are applicable, unless and until Parliament otherwise decides; if they are not, it is our duty to say so, and to declare such provisions to be unconstitutional.

Later, the learned President further states with regard to the right to life (at page 309):

The unqualified right to life vested in every person by section 9 of our Constitution is another factor crucially relevant to the question whether the death sentence is cruel, inhuman or degrading punishment within the meaning of Section 11(2) of our Constitution. In this respect our Constitution differs materially from the Constitutions of the United States and India. It also differs materially from the European Convention and the International Covenant. (Emphasis added.)

The distinguished Judge reviewed many cases, and indeed found that some judges in those jurisdictions had argued for the unconstitutionality of the death penalty notwithstanding provisions permitting it, but he reaches his conclusion in the context of the South African Constitution when he states:

I am satisfied that in the context of our constitution the death penalty is indeed a cruel, inhuman and degrading punishment.

Sachs J, in his concurring judgment, also agrees that Section 9 of the South African Constitution guarantees an unqualified right to life. He states (at page 389):

This Court is unlikely to get another case which is emotionally and philosophically more elusive, and textually more direct. Section 9 states: "every person shall have the right to life". These *unqualified and unadorned* words are binding on the state... and, on the face of it, outlaw capital punishment. Section 33 does allow limitations on fundamental rights; yet, in my view, executing someone is not limiting that person's life, but extinguishing it. (Emphasis added.)

It appears to us clear enough that the situation and the Constitution in South Africa are materially different from those obtaining in Uganda. The Constitution of Uganda does not include the right to life under the general provision dealing with derogation under Articles 43 and 44 of the Constitution. In Tanzania, the Court of Appeal in *Mbushuu* (supra) saved the death penalty under the general provisions on derogation from fundamental human rights. But in Uganda the Constitution specifically provides for it under a substantive article of the Constitution, i.e. Article 22(1). The subject of the death penalty was not left for the Constitutional Court to fill in gaps as in the case of South Africa. The courts cannot now take on the role of the Legislature to abrogate a substantive provision of the Constitution by a process of interpreting one provision against another. In our view, this is the work of the Legislature who should indeed further study the issue of the death penalty with a view to introducing appropriate amendments to the Constitution.

The next issue for determination concerns the provisions, in various laws, for the imposition of the *mandatory* death sentence for certain offences in those laws. The Commissioner for Civil Litigation who represented the appellant combined grounds 1, 2, 6 and 7 of the appeal.

She argues that the various laws of Uganda which prescribe the mandatory death sentence are not inconsistent with nor do they contradict Articles 21, 22(1), 24, 28, 44(a) and 126(1) of the Constitution. To her, the mandatory death sentence is like any other mandatory sentence under the laws of Uganda, and being mandatory does not make it unconstitutional. She relies on Article 22(1) which provides for the death penalty, and on Article 21(4) which provides that nothing shall prevent Parliament from enacting laws necessary for making provisions that are required to be made under the Constitution. To the learned Commissioner, the death penalty and the laws that provide for it are made under Article 21. Therefore, she contended, prescribing for a death penalty upon conviction is not inconsistent with Article 21 nor does it contravene any provision of the Constitution.

She further contends that the mandatory sentence is justifiable and demonstrably necessary in Uganda within the context of Articles 21(4) and 43 as it reflects the views of the people of Uganda. Since under Article 43 Parliament is allowed to derogate from the various rights and freedoms, prescribing for the mandatory death penalty is within its mandate. The mandatory sentence ensures that different people who have committed a similar offence do not get different sentences. She invoked Article 21(1), 21(2) and 21(3) to fortify her argument. She further contended that the criminal justice system in Uganda did not provide for various degrees of an offence as in some other jurisdictions, and there are no equivalents of our Articles 21 and 126. She supported the dissenting judgment of Mpagi-Bahigeine JA in that regard.

Counsel further argued that since the court has a discretion to determine the appropriateness of the sentence even before conviction, the mandatory sentence does not deprive the court of its discretion.

On the other hand, Prof. Sempebwa, who argued the case for the respondents on this point, supported the decision of the Constitutional Court that the mandatory death sentence was unconstitutional. He submitted that the provisions of the Penal Code which provide for the mandatory death sentence for murder and aggravated robbery were inconsistent with the Constitution notwithstanding that there may have been a fair trial before conviction. But, to him, fair trial as envisaged in Article 22(1) included conviction and sentencing. Pleading mitigation was part of fair trial in all other non-mandatory sentences. The fact that mitigation was not expressly mentioned as a right in the Constitution does not deprive it of its essence as a right because the rights in the Constitution are not exhaustive. Mitigation is an element of fair trial. He relied on *Mithu* v. *State of Punjab* [1983] 2 SCR 690 and *Reyes* v. *Queen* [2002] UKPC 11, [2002] 2 LRC 606.

Counsel further argued that the second element in Article 22(1) relates to confirmation of sentence. The conviction and sentence of death must, before its execution, be confirmed by the highest appellate court, in this case the Supreme Court. In counsel's view to confirm implies a discretion whether to confirm or not. A sentence which has been fixed by law to be passed upon conviction deprives the court of that sentencing discretion. Therefore the mandatory sentence becomes inconsistent with the Constitution and therefore unconstitutional. Even in jurisdictions like the United States which prescribe for various degrees of murder, for example, the mandatory sentences have been adjudged to be unconstitutional. He cited *Woodson* v. *North Carolina* (1976)

426 US 280. Furthermore, he argued, mandatory death sentences were cruel and inhuman because they do not differentiate between offenders, thereby offending Article 24. Murder may be committed under different circumstances. He further cited the Malawian case of *Kafantayeni v. Attorney-General* [2007] MWHC 1, [2007] 5 LRC 353 in support. Finally, counsel submitted that sentencing is a matter of law and part of the administration of justice which under Article 126 is a preserve of the Judiciary. Parliament should only prescribe the maximum sentence and leave the courts to administer justice by sentencing offenders according to the gravity and circumstances of the case. He prayed the court to confirm the judgment of the Constitutional Court on this issue.

In considering the constitutionality of the mandatory death sentence, we think it is important to consider certain provisions of the Constitution. Article 20 states that fundamental rights and freedoms are inherent and not granted by the state, and directs all organs and agencies of Government and all persons to respect, uphold and promote those rights and freedoms. Article 21(1) states as follows:

All persons are equal before and under the law in all spheres of political, economic, social and cultural life and *in every other respect and shall enjoy equal protection of the law.* (Emphasis added.)

Article 28 guarantees the right to a fair hearing. In particular the following deserve note. Article 28(1) states:

In the determination of civil rights and obligations or any criminal charge, a person shall be entitled to a fair, speedy and public hearing before an independent and impartial court or tribunal established by law.

Article 28(3)(e) states:

Every person who is charged with a criminal offence shall—

(e) In the case of any offence which carries a sentence of death or imprisonment for life, be entitled to legal representation at the expense of the state.

In our view, these provisions bring out a number of important factors. First the rights of each individual are inherent. Secondly, all persons are equal before and under the law. Thirdly, a person is entitled to a fair, speedy and public hearing before an independent and impartial tribunal. Fourthly, in a case that carries a death sentence, the state must provide legal representation to the accused person. This can only be because the framers of the Constitution deemed that an offence carrying a death penalty is so heavy and so important that all help and latitude must be given to the accused person for that person to have a fair trial.

A trial does not stop at convicting a person. The process of sentencing a person is part of the trial. This is because the court will take into account the evidence, the nature of the offence and the circumstances of the case in order to arrive at an appropriate sentence. This is clearly evident where the law provides for a *maximum* sentence. The court will truly have exercised its function as an impartial tribunal in *trying and sentencing* a person. But the court is denied the exercise of this function where the sentence has already been pre-ordained by the Legislature, as in capital cases. In our view, this compromises the principle of fair trial.

Then there is the other aspect of the right of equality before and under the law. Two provisions stand out. Section 94 of the Trial on Indictments Act provides:

If the accused person is found guilty or pleads guilty, the judge shall ask him or her whether he or she has anything to say why sentence should not be passed upon him or her according to law, but the omission so to ask him or her shall have no effect on the validity of the proceedings.

It would appear that the reason why the accused person is given this right is so that he may present some mitigating factors, even at this late stage, which may affect the sentence to be passed on him or her.

Then there is Section 98 which allows the court to make inquiry before passing sentence, in all cases except when the sentence to be passed is of death. The section states:

The Court, before passing any sentence *other than a sentence of death*, may make such inquiries as it thinks fit in order to inform itself as to the proper sentence to be passed, and may inquire into the character and antecedents of the accused person either at the request of the prosecution or the accused person and may take into consideration in assessing the proper sentence to be passed such character and antecedents including any other offences committed by the accused person whether or not he or she has been convicted of those offences: except that:

(a) the accused person shall be given an opportunity to confirm, deny or explain any statement made about him or her and in any case of doubt the court shall in the absence of legal proof of the statement ignore the statement.

(b) No offence of which the accused person has not been convicted shall be taken into consideration in assessing proper sentence unless the accused person specifically argues that the offence shall be taken into consideration and a note of that request shall have been recorded in the proceedings...

We find this provision troubling. First it provides in essence that a person accused of stealing a chicken may not only be heard in mitigation, but may actually request the court to inquire into his character and antecedents for purposes of assessing appropriate sentence for him, while on the other hand, a person accused of murder and whose very life is at stake may not do likewise. We think this is inconsistent with the principle of equality before and under the law. Not all murders are committed in the same circumstances, and all murderers are not necessarily of the same character. One may be a first offender, and the murder may have been committed in circumstances that the accused person deeply regrets and is very remorseful. We see no reason why these factors should not be put before the court before it passes the ultimate sentence.

We also find this provision curious in light of Article 121(5) of the Constitution, which states:

Where a person is sentenced to death for an offence, written report of the case from the trial judge or judges or person presiding over the court or tribunal, together with such other information derived from the record of the case or elsewhere as may be necessary, shall be submitted to the Advisory Committee on the Prerogative of Mercy.

The question that arises from this is: If the judge will have been prevented by Section 98 of the Trial on Indictments Act from carrying out an inquiry when the accused person is still before him, on what basis will he write the report required of him under Article 121(5) of the Constitution? It is reasonable to deduce that in fact by virtue of Article 121(5) the judge is obliged to conduct an inquiry and that Section 98 of the Trial on Indictments Act is inconsistent with that article of the Constitution.

In our view if there is one situation where the framers of the Constitution expected an inquiry, it is the one involving a death penalty. The report of the Judge is considered so important that it forms a basis for advising the President on the exercise of the prerogative of mercy. Why should it not have informed the Judge in passing sentence in the first place?

Furthermore, the administration of justice is a function of the Judiciary under Article 126 of the Constitution. The entire process of trial from the arraignment of an accused person to his/her sentencing is, in our view, what constitutes administration of justice. By fixing a mandatory death penalty Parliament removed the power to determine sentence from the courts and that, in our view, is inconsistent with Article 126 of the Constitution.

We do not agree with learned counsel for the Attorney-General that because Parliament has the powers to pass laws for the good governance of Uganda, it can pass such laws as those providing for a mandatory death sentence. In any case, the laws passed by Parliament must be consistent with the Constitution as provided for in Article 2(2) of the Constitution.

Furthermore, the Constitution provides for the separation of powers between the Executive, the Legislature and the Judiciary. Any law passed by Parliament which has the effect of tying the hands of the Judiciary in executing its function to administer justice is inconsistent with the Constitution. We also agree with Prof. Sempebwa, for the respondents, that the power given to the court under Article 22(1) does not stop at confirmation of conviction. The court has power to confirm both conviction and sentence. This implies a power *not* to confirm, implying that the court has been given discretion in the matter. Any law that fetters that discretion is inconsistent with this clear provision of the Constitution.

We are of the view that the learned Justices of the Constitutional Court properly addressed this matter and came to the right conclusion. We therefore agree with the Constitutional Court that all those laws on the statute book in Uganda which provide for a mandatory death sentence are inconsistent with the Constitution and therefore are void to the extent of that inconsistency. Such mandatory sentence can only be regarded as a maximum sentence. In the result, grounds 1, 2, 6 and 7 of the appeal must fail.

We now turn to the issue of delay in execution of the sentence of death. Counsel for the appellant argued grounds 3, 4, 5 and 8 together. She contended that Articles 24 and 44(a) of the Constitution, or any other provision thereof, do not set a time limit within which the sentence of death must be carried out after the judicial process. She argued that Article 121 of the Constitution confers on the President the Prerogative of Mercy without setting out the time frame within which he is to exercise that mercy. Therefore any delay in execution of the sentence of death is not unconstitutional. She cited *De Freitas* v. *Benny* (1976) AC 239 in support of the argument that delay is not unconstitutional. She further argued that it would be unconstitutional to impose time limits within which an execution should be carried out, or within which the President must exercise the Prerogative of Mercy. To her any delay allows the convicted person to live longer in hope of a reprieve, and that executions should not be rushed.

On the other hand, counsel for the respondents argued that staying on death row for a long time causes the suffering of the "death-row syndrome" which itself amounts to a cruel and inhuman or degrading treatment or punishment. He submitted that all the respondents had been on death row for a long time, and that in Uganda the average length of stay on death row was ten years. He clarified that by arguing that long delay was unconstitutional, the respondents were not seeking early execution, but were contending that having been kept on death row for a long time, to execute them would amount to a cruel, inhuman punishment contrary to Articles 24 and 44(a) of the Constitution. He submitted that *Riley* v. *Attorney-General of Jamaica* [1982] 3 All ER 469, cited by the appellant, had been overruled by *Pratt* v. *Attorney-General of Jamaica* [1993] 2 LRC 349. Counsel sought to rely on *Catholic Commission for Justice and Peace in Zimbabwe* v. *Attorney-General* [1993] 2 LRC 279, which decided that a long delay on death-row causes the death-row syndrome which is cruel and inhuman. The case of *De Freitas*, cited by the appellant, had also been overruled by *Lewis* v. *Attorney-General of Jamaica* [2000] 5 LRC 253 which held, inter alia, that to execute a person who had been on death row for over six years after conviction would amount to inhuman treatment.

Counsel therefore supported the findings and decision of the Constitutional Court on these issues and prayed for the dismissal of these grounds of appeal.

These grounds raise one fundamental question: where a death sentence has been passed lawfully, can there be supervening events which can render the carrying out of such death sentence on the condemned prisoners to constitute inhuman and degrading treatment contrary to Article 24 of the Constitution? The Constitutional Court held that to execute a condemned person after three years on death row from the time when the last appellate court confirmed the sentence is cruel and inhuman and therefore a violation of Article 24 of the Constitution.

Perhaps we should start with establishing the legal status of a person who has been sentenced to death and the sentence has been confirmed. A condemned person does not lose all his other rights as a human being. He is still entitled to his dignity within the confines of the law until his sentence is carried out strictly in accordance with the law. There are many authorities to that effect cited in the judgment of the Constitutional Court. Some key features seem to underline what is regarded as the death-row syndrome. There is, first, the element of delay between when the prisoner is sentenced to death and when the execution actually takes place. There is the natural fear of death that the prisoner has to live with constantly for a long time.

The second element that has been considered by courts in other jurisdictions is that of prison conditions under which the prisoner is kept pending execution. In the *Catholic Commission* case (supra), the Supreme Court of Zimbabwe set aside the death sentences because the appellants had been on death row for five years, in "demeaning conditions". It was held that the prolonged delay in those conditions caused prolonged mental suffering which amounted to cruel and inhuman treatment, and that a period of more than two years tended to be inordinate delay.

The Constitutional Court, in our view, correctly addressed the issue and correctly analysed the evidence. Okello JA, who wrote the lead judgment, after reviewing the evidence stated ([2006] 3 LRC 388 at 440):

The above evidence has not been controverted. It portrays a very grim picture of the conditions in the condemned section of Luzira Prison. They are demeaning physical conditions. Such conditions coupled with the treatment meted out to the condemned prisoners during their confinement, as depicted by the above evidence, are not acceptable by Ugandan standards and also by the civilised international communities. Inordinate delays in such conditions indeed constitute cruel, inhuman or degrading treatment prohibited by Articles 24 and 44(a) of the Constitution of Uganda.

To determine whether there has been an inordinate delay, the period [which] the condemned prisoner has spent on the death row, in my view, should start from when his/her sentence has been confirmed by the highest appellate court. Appeal process for a prisoner convicted of a capital offence is mandatory. In Uganda, there is a two steps appeal system. An appellant has no control over the time the appeal process should take. While the appeal process is on, a condemned prisoner has hope of his conviction and sentence being revised. It is the time taken between the confirmation of his/her sentence and execution, when the condemned prisoner has virtually lost all hopes of surviving execution, that should determine whether or not there has been an inordinate delay.

We fully agree. However, one must remember the concerns of the condemned persons that they do not seek a quick execution when they argue against inordinate delay. Indeed, it would be a contradiction in terms for one to argue against the death penalty while at the same time arguing that it must be carried out with speed.

According to various international instruments already cited in this judgment, a person who has been sentenced to death must be given as much latitude as possible to exhaust not only the court appellate processes but even all appeals for clemency before the sentence of death is carried out. For example in the Safeguards Guaranteeing the Protection of the Rights of Those Facing the Death Penalty, Resolution 1984/50 of 25 May 1984 of the United Nations Economic and Social Council, paragraphs 7 and 8 thereof state as follows:

7. Anyone sentenced to death shall have the right to seek pardon or commutation of sentence; pardon or commutation of sentence may be granted in all cases of capital punishment.
8. Capital punishment shall not be carried out pending any appeal or other recourse procedure or other proceeding relating to pardon or commutation of the sentence.

We believe these provisions are part of the evolving standards of common decency, namely that society should not wish to put a person to death expeditiously. The rationale for this must be because the death sentence is final. It extinguishes life. It should therefore not be carried out in a hurry. There have been reported too many instances where persons who have spent many years on death row are finally found to have been wrongly convicted and been released or had their sentences commuted. Had such persons been executed so as to avoid their suffering of the death-row syndrome, it would have been gross miscarriage of justice, far worse than death-row syndrome. In our view it calls for a balance so that while a person exercises his rights under the law to exhaust all avenues under the law before he is executed, he at the same time is not unduly kept in prison serving a sentence that he was not sentenced to. We must also add that persons sentenced to death need not be held in demeaning conditions as has been testified to. The government and all those who inspect prisons must ensure that the conditions under which all prisoners are kept strictly conform to the law and to international standards.

The Constitution provides for the Prerogative of Mercy exercised by the President under Article 121. This is based on the English model where the Sovereign could exercise mercy over a person convicted by the courts. Many countries have adopted this system, including the United States whose Constitution has, in some respects, influenced the Constitution of Uganda. The Supreme Court of the United States has expounded on the matter of executive clemency in the case of *Herrera* v. *Collins* (1993) 506 US 390. In his judgment cited in *Death Penalty Cases: Leading US Supreme Court Cases on Capital Punishment* (2nd edn, 2002), at page 301, Chief Justice Rehnquist states thus ((1993) 506 US 390 at 412-13):

Our Constitution adopts the British model and gives to the President the "Power to grant Reprieves and Pardons for offences against the United States"... In *United States* v. *Wilson*... Chief Justice Marshall expounded on the President's pardon power:

As this power had been exercised from time immemorial by the executive of that nation whose language is our language, and to whose judicial institutions ours bear a close resemblance; we adopt their principles respecting the operation and effect of a pardon, and look into their books for the rules prescribing the manner in which it is to be used by the person who would avail himself of it.

A pardon is an act of grace, proceeding from the power entrusted with the execution of all laws, which exempts the individual on whom it is bestowed from punishment the law inflicts for a crime he has committed. It is the private, though official act of the executive magistrate, delivered to the individual for whose benefit it is intended, and not communicated officially to the court. It is a constituent part of the judicial system, that the judge sees only with judicial eyes, and knows nothing respecting any particular case, of which he is not informed judicially. A private deed, not communicated to him, whatever may be its character, whether a pardon or release, is totally unknown and cannot be acted on. The looseness which would be introduced into judicial proceedings, would prove fatal to the great principles of justice, if the judge might notice and act upon facts not brought regularly into the cause. Such a proceeding, in ordinary cases, would subvert the best established principles, and overturn those rules which have been settled by the wisdom of ages.

The learned Chief Justice observes that although the Constitution vests in the President a pardon power, it did not require the states to enact a clemency mechanism. He continued thus:

Executive clemency has provided the "fail safe" in our criminal justice system . . . It is an unalterable fact that our judicial system, like the human beings who administer it, is fallible. But history is replete with examples of wrongfully convicted persons who have been pardoned in the wake of after-discovered evidence establishing their innocence.

Our Constitution provides for more or less the same position as the American one on the matter of Prerogative of Mercy. Learned Counsel for the Attorney-General argued that since the Constitution itself does not provide for a time limit within which to exercise the Prerogative of Mercy, it is not up to the courts to impose such time limits as this would [be] tantamount to interference with executive privilege.

There is sympathy for that view. However, one should look at the Constitution as a whole to determine the purpose and effect of the various provisions. The right to fair hearing provided for in Article 28 envisages a fair, speedy and public trial. The right to liberty in Article 23 envisages that one's liberty may be compromised in execution of a court order. In our view, these provisions mean that a person who has had a speedy trial should only have his liberty compromised in execution of a sentence of court *without delay*. The person would thereby serve his due sentence and regain his liberty. In the case of a sentence of death it would mean that after the trial, the processes provided for under Article 121 should be put in motion as quickly as possible so that the person knows his fate, i.e. whether he is pardoned, given a respite or remission or whether the sentence is to be carried out. It could not have been envisaged by the Constitution makers that Article 121 could be used to keep persons on death row for an indefinite period. This in effect makes them serve a long period of imprisonment which they were not sentenced to in the first place. Evidence was given of persons who have spent as long as eighteen or twenty years on death row without decisions by the Executive as to their fate. This could not have been envisaged by the Constitution.

Although the Constitution does not provide for a time limit within which the President may exercise the Prerogative of Mercy, one has to take, by analogy, the provisions of the Interpretation Act. Section 34(2) thereof provides thus:

Where no time is prescribed or allowed within which anything shall be done, that thing *shall be done without unreasonable delay* and as often as due occasion arises. (Emphasis added.)

Article 121 sets up a permanent body called the Advisory Committee on the Prerogative of Mercy which is chaired by the Attorney-General. We see no reason why this committee, charged with advising the President, should not process the cases of all persons sentenced to death as a matter of priority and without unreasonable delay and advise the President accordingly. Likewise, once advised, we see no reason why the President may not make his decision without unreasonable delay. One has to bear in mind that a person's life and liberty is at stake here. In our view, the President must not delay to take a decision whether to pardon, grant a respite, substitute a lesser sentence or remit the whole or part of the sentence. The law envisages that even the President will act without unreasonable delay. To hold otherwise would mean that the President could withhold his decision indefinitely or for many years, and the person would remain on death row at the pleasure of the President. In our view this would be contrary to the spirit of the Constitution.

The Constitutional Court held that a period of more than three years from the time when the death sentence was confirmed by the highest court would constitute inordinate delay. We agree. As soon as the highest court has confirmed sentence, the Advisory Committee on the Prerogative of Mercy and the prisons authorities should commence to process the applications of condemned persons so that the President is advised without unreasonable delay. In that way, a person sentenced to death would spend considerably less time on death row without knowing conclusively his fate. The appeal process itself will in all probability have taken several years. If the President decides that the death sentence be carried out, so be it.

In the circumstances, we agree with the Constitutional Court that to hold a person beyond three years after the confirmation of sentence is unreasonable.

Although it has been suggested as in the *Makwanyane* case (supra) that the period of delay should be counted from when the sentence of death is first pronounced, we have taken the view, as the Constitutional Court did, that the period of trial and appeal, i.e. the judicial process, should be counted out. From the time a person is charged with a capital offence carrying a mandatory death sentence as has been the case, that person knows that he may be convicted. His anxiety and worry about the death sentence would start from there. One may even add that he knew or should have known the consequences when he committed the offence. But he knows that he is entitled to put his defence before a court and the prosecution has the burden of proving the case beyond a reasonable doubt. He therefore has a real chance of getting acquitted or being found guilty of a lesser offence like manslaughter, if the offence charged was murder, and get a lesser sentence. Even after conviction and sentence of death has been imposed, in Uganda, the convicted person has a constitutional right to appeal to a higher court and legally argue against his conviction even at the expense of the state in terms of legal representation. He has a constitutional right to appeal to the highest court which has to confirm his conviction and sentence before that sentence can be carried out. It is after the last highest court has confirmed both conviction and sentence that the person now realistically faces the death penalty, as he is now at the mercy of the President. We are of the view that it is this stage which should count for the purposes of the argument about the delay in execution of the death sentence. The delay must be in respect of the execution of a death sentence that has been confirmed by the highest appellate court as provided by Article 22(1) of the Constitution. Before that, the sentence cannot be carried out.

We have already said in this judgment that the right to life is so fundamental that there should be no rush to extinguish it. The accused person must be given all reasonable time to prepare his defence, or appeal as the case may be. There may be inherent delays in the process of trial and appeal, but the person still has his right to life and has hope of succeeding legally in the courts. For that reason it is only reasonable that the period to be regarded as delay in execution of the sentence must only start when the sentence of death is executable, i.e. after it has been confirmed by the highest court.

What is the effect of an unreasonable delay on an otherwise constitutional death sentence? This, in our view, was adequately answered by the High Court in the *Mbushuu* case ([1994] 2 LRC 335 at 349) where the court stated thus:

When a prisoner who has been on death row for several years approaches the courts for relief, he is not seeking to be put to death expeditiously, but rather, he is saying that the long period he has spent on death row, coupled with the agony and anguish of death row endured for several years, plus the horrible conditions under which he is kept, is such as to render his execution at that particular time cruel and inhuman as to offend the constitutional prohibition against cruel and inhuman punishments... *he would not be challenging the legality or appropriateness of the original sentence of death. He would be accepting the validity of that original sentence but merely arguing that the juxtaposition of the intervening delay, and prolonged anguish of death row, which has been appropriately described as the "living hell" is such as to render it particularly inhuman to execute him at that stage.* (Emphasis added.)

This passage was quoted with approval by Twinomujuni JA. We agree with it. We observe that the Constitutional Court exhaustively considered the subject of inordinate delay in carrying out a death sentence, and we fully concur with the court in that respect. We would agree that a delay carrying out sentence beyond three years from the date when the sentence of death was confirmed by the highest court constitutes unreasonable delay.

At the end of a period of three years after the highest appellate court confirmed the sentence, and if the President shall not have exercised his prerogative one way or the other, the death sentence shall be deemed to be commuted to life imprisonment without remission. In the result, grounds 3, 4, 5 and 8 of the appeal must fail.

The next issue for determination is the constitutionality of hanging as a method of carrying out the death sentence which is contained in ground 3 of the cross-appeal. Mr Sim Katende argued this issue on behalf of the respondents. He criticised the Constitutional Court for holding that hanging was constitutional because the death penalty was allowed by Article 22 of the Constitution. Counsel argued that if the reasoning of the Constitutional Court were to be upheld it would mean that any method of execution would be constitutionally acceptable. He submitted that hanging is provided for by Section 99 of the Trial on Indictments Act. It is not provided for in the Constitution itself. Therefore, he argued it can be challenged if it is inconsistent with or in contravention of any provision of the Constitution. In this respect he submitted that hanging had been stated to be a cruel, inhuman and degrading punishment in the *Mbushuu* and *Makwanyane* cases. The evidence of experts and other witnesses, particularly the affidavit of Antony Okwanga and Ben Ogwang, had shown that hanging was cruel, inhuman and degrading in the manner it was carried out, the way it affected other prisoners and the way it affected even the executioners themselves. This was inconsistent with and in contravention of Articles 24 and 44(a) of the Constitution. He relied on the *Abuki* case for the proposition that in interpreting the Constitution purpose and effect must be looked at, and that there can be no derogation whatsoever from the freedom from torture, cruel, inhuman or degrading punishment. He also cited the *Catholic Commission* case where Gubby CJ observed as follows ([1993] 2 LRC 279 at 289):

It cannot be doubted that prison walls do not keep out fundamental rights and protections. Prisoners are not, by mere reason of a conviction, denuded of all the rights they otherwise [possess]. No matter the magnitude of the crime, they are not reduced to non-persons. They retain all basic rights, save those inveritably removed from them by law, expressly or by implication. Thus, a prisoner who has been sentenced to death does not forfeit the protection afforded by Section 15(i) of the Constitution in respect of his treatment while under confinement.

Counsel conceded that every punishment involves pain, but submitted that the degree of pain in hanging was excessive. He further relied on *Abuki* for the proposition that rights and freedoms guaranteed by the Constitution are to be interpreted having regard to evolving standards of common decency. Hanging violated those standards and should therefore be held to be unconstitutional.

This issue no doubt raises some difficulty. This difficulty arises from the fact, as already found, that the Constitution itself permits the death penalty, even though some other jurisdictions have decided that the death penalty itself violates those standards of common decency and have outlawed it. Those who have outlawed it are no longer concerned with the manner of carrying out the death sentence. In the *Mbushuu* case (supra) the High Court considered the totality of the death penalty, i.e. the sentence itself *and* the manner of carrying it out, in coming to the conclusion that the death penalty was a cruel punishment. If the Constitution permits the death penalty, the difficulty must be to identify that method of carrying it out that will extinguish the life of the condemned person without causing excessive pain and suffering.

In the instant case, counsel for the appellant have argued the issue of hanging in the alternative. Their argument is that even if it is found that the death penalty is provided for in the Constitution, then the manner of carrying it out by hanging is unconstitutional as it constitutes a cruel and degrading punishment.

As indicated above, counsel relied on the *Abuki* case. In our view, the *Abuki* case must be put in its proper context. In that case the Penal Code provided for the offence of practising witchcraft, and for the sentence of imprisonment and/or banishment as punishment upon conviction for that offence. The court ordered that the accused serve a period of ten years of banishment from his home after serving the term of imprisonment. It is that punishment that was found to be cruel, inhuman and degrading and therefore unconstitutional.

In this case, the punishment prescribed for capital offences is death. In this judgment we have said that provided the conditions stated in Article 22(1) of the Constitution are fulfilled, the death penalty is constitutional. Therefore what remains to be determined is the *manner* of carrying out the constitutionally permitted punishment.

The UN resolution on safeguards guaranteeing the rights of those facing the death penalty (supra) states in paragraph 9 thereof:

Where capital punishment occurs, it shall be carried out so as to inflict the *minimum possible suffering*. (Emphasis added.)

What is recognised is that suffering must necessarily be part of the death process, but that it must be minimised. In our view one would need to make a comparative scientific study of the various methods of carrying out the death sentence to determine which one imposes less suffering than the others.

As the Constitutional Court observed, hanging has been used in Uganda to carry out death sentences since 1938. The framers of the Constitution were aware of the method used when they provided for the death sentence. It is not in dispute that fear, anguish, etc. must accompany a sentence of death by hanging. But then which method of carrying out a death sentence does not invoke these natural instincts in a normal human being?

Counsel for the respondents argued in their written submissions that: "Most jurisdictions which still retain the death penalty, including the USA and China which carry out the most executions in the world today, have moved away from hanging to the more humane lethal injection." They urged the Court to "compel the Legislature to prescribe a more humane method of execution".

While we appreciate the argument of learned counsel, there is no evidence on record to show that in fact the lethal injection method is any more humane than hanging, that it produces no pain, nor that it does not produce any mishaps as may happen during hanging. There is no evidence to show that the persons who do the injection are any less traumatised than those that carry out the hanging. There are also many countries that still use hanging. We do not know whether lethal injection causes any less anguish, fear or pain. Nonetheless, since the law requires that execution be done in a manner authorised by law, it must have been envisaged that the Legislature would continue to study scientifically the available methods of execution and adopt and provide for one which conforms to the "evolving standards" of decency. We would indeed urge our Legislature to do just that. But for now we are inclined to the view that the pain and suffering experienced during the hanging process is inherent in the punishment of the death penalty which has been provided for in the Constitution. We would therefore not say it is unconstitutional in the context of Article 24 of the Constitution. We have considered the affidavit evidence of Dr Harold Hillman and Dr Albert C. Hunt in support of the respondents. Although both dispute the notion that hanging causes instantaneous death, they agree that death occurs within a fairly short time, i.e. "over several minutes". Dr Hunt refers to a scientific article published by Drs Ryle James and Nasmight Jmith (Exhibit AHI) which also casts doubt on the notion that hanging causes instant death. But that article concludes as follows:

However, hanging, even without cord damage, usually causes death rapidly either by compression of the carotid arteries, reflex cardiac arrest due to carotid sinus stimulation, various obstruction or airway obstruction. "Dancing" on the end of the rope may, in many cases, be decerebrate twitching or "fitting" rather than struggling and whilst death may not be instantaneous, unconsciousness is probably usually rapid.

In our view, the issue is not whether the method of execution causes instant death, but whether it causes minimum possible pain and suffering. If there is a proved method that causes instant death, it would certainly be preferable. But in these circumstances, a method that causes death within minutes would, in our view, meet the standard of not causing excessive pain and suffering.

Before we leave this subject, we wish to urge that the Legislature should re-open debate on the desirability of the death penalty in our Constitution, particularly in light of findings that for many years no death sentences have been executed yet the individuals concerned continue to be incarcerated on death row without knowing whether they were pardoned, had their sentences remitted, or are to be executed. The failure, refusal or neglect by the Executive to decide on those death sentences would seem to indicate a desire to do away with the death penalty.

In the result, by unanimous decision we dismiss the appeal, and by majority decision we dismiss the cross-appeal.

We confirm the declarations made by the Constitutional Court and we would modify the orders made by that court as follows:

1. For those respondents whose sentences were already confirmed by the highest court, their petitions for mercy under Article 121 of the Constitution must be processed and determined within three years from the date of confirmation of the sentence. Where after three years no decision has been made by the Executive, the death sentence shall be deemed commuted to imprisonment for life without remission.
2. For those respondents whose sentences arose from the mandatory sentence provisions and are still pending before an appellate court, their cases shall be remitted to the High Court for them to be heard only on mitigation of sentence, and the High Court may pass such sentence as it deems fit under the law.
3. Each party shall bear its own costs.

JUDGMENT OF EGONDA-NTENDE AG. JSC

I have had the benefit of reading the majority judgment in draft. I agree that the death penalty is constitutionally permitted but regretfully do not agree that Articles 24 and 44 of the Constitution do not apply to Article 22(1). For that reason I shall in the judgment below deal with grounds no 1 and no 3 of the cross-appeal. However, I agree with the majority judgment that this appeal and the cross-appeal (save for grounds no 1 and no 3) should fail for the reasons set forth in the majority judgment.

Ground No 1 of the Cross-Appeal

Ground no 1 of the cross-appeal states:

1. That the learned justices of the Constitutional Court erred in law when they held that Articles 24 and 44(a) of the Constitution of the Republic of Uganda 1995 as amended (hereinafter referred to as "the Constitution") which prohibit any forms of torture, cruel, inhuman and degrading

treatment or punishment were not meant to apply to Article 22(1) of the Constitution.

Connected to this ground is ground no 3 of the cross-appeal which is stated as follows:

3. That in the alternative but without prejudice to the above, that the learned justices of the Constitutional Court erred in law when they found as a question of fact and law that hanging was a cruel, inhuman and degrading treatment or punishment but held that it was a permissible form of punishment because the death penalty was permitted by the Constitution.

In the court below the issue that was decided and gives rise to the above grounds in the cross-appeal was framed in the following manner:

4. Whether Section 99(1) of the Trial on Indictments Act which prescribes hanging as the legal method of implementing the death penalty is inconsistent with and in contravention of Articles 24 and 44 or any other provisions of the Constitution.

This issue was argued in the court below in the alternative to the first two issues that dealt with whether the death penalty was constitutionally permissible. The findings and holding of the Constitutional Court on those two issues are therefore of some interest to the findings and holding of the Court on its issue no 4. I will set out below what the majority of the Constitutional Court held and the reasons therefor in respect to whether or not Articles 24 and 44(a) of the Constitution applied to Article 22(1) of the Constitution.

Okello JA (as he then was) stated (at 422-3):

Article 22(1) recognises death penalty in execution of a sentence passed in a fair trial by a court of competent jurisdiction in respect of a criminal offence under the laws of Uganda and the conviction and sentence have been confirmed by the highest appellate court in Uganda. This is an exception to the enjoyment of the right to life. To that extent, death penalty is constitutional. Article 24 outlaws any form of torture, cruel, inhuman or degrading treatment or punishment. The imposing question to answer is whether the framers of the Constitution intended to take away, by Article 24, the right they recognised in Article 22(1).

The learned Justice of Appeal discussed some comparative jurisprudence and then continued (at 424):

In our case, Article 22(1) recognises death penalty as an exception to the enjoyment of the right to life. There is well-known rule of interpretation that to take away a right given by common law or statute, the legislature should do that in clear terms devoid of any ambiguity. It is important to note that the right to life is not included in Article 44 on the list of the non-derogable rights. Accordingly Articles 24 and 44 could not have been intended to apply to the death penalty permitted in Article 22(1). When Articles 24 and 44 were being enacted, Article 22 was still fresh in the mind of the framers. If they (framers of our constitution) had wanted to take away, by Article 24, the rights recognised in Article 22(1), they would have done so in clear terms, not by implication. Imposition of death penalty therefore, constitutes no cruel, inhuman or degrading punishment. The various provisions of the laws of Uganda which prescribe death sentence are, therefore, not inconsistent with or in contravention of Articles 24 and 44 or any provisions of the Constitution.

In deciding issue no 4 he held as follows (at 433):

Execution by hanging may be cruel, but I have found that Articles 24 and 44(a) were not intended to apply to death sentence permitted in Article 22(1). Therefore, implementing or carrying out death penalty by hanging cannot be held to be cruel, inhuman and degrading. Articles 24 and 44(a) do not apply to it. Punishment by its nature must inflict some pain and unpleasantness, physically or mentally to achieve its objective. Section 99(1) of the Trial on Indictments Act is therefore constitutional as it operationalises Article 22(1). It is not inconsistent with Articles 24 and 44(a).

Twinomujuni JA reasoned as follows before he answered issue no 1 in the negative (at 450):

This article [24] makes no reference to Article 22(1)! Did the framers of the Constitution forget that they had just authorised a death sentence in Article 22(1)? Is a death sentence something they could have forgotten so easily and so quickly? Personally, I think not. The framers of the Constitution could not have in one breath authorised a death sentence and in another outlawed it. They must have meant that all forms of torture, cruel, inhuman or degrading treatment or punishment are prohibited except as authorised in Article 22(1) of the Constitution. We must remember that unlike in *Abuki* and *Kyamanywa* cases where the court was interpreting a statute against a provision of the Constitution, in this petition we are dealing with the interpretation of Article 22(1) against Article 24 both provisions of the Constitution. Where a Constitution creates derogation in clear language to a right or freedom guaranteed under the Constitution, then derogation will stand despite the provisions of Articles 43 and 44 of the Constitution. The only exception is where derogation purports to take away a fundamental right or freedom guaranteed [in] Chapter IV of this Constitution. In the instant case, Article 22(1) provides for derogation to the right to life. The derogation is an exception to acts of torture, or cruel, inhuman or degrading treatment or punishment under Article 24 of the Constitution. The language used is very clear and unambiguous. Therefore, it is clear to me that a death sentence in Uganda cannot be one of the acts prohibited under Article 24 of the Constitution. It is an exception to the article. I would hold that it is not cruel, inhuman or degrading treatment or punishment within the meaning of Article 24 of the Constitution. I would answer the first issue in the negative.

With regard to hanging the learned Justice of Appeal stated (at 466):

Whether you call hanging cruel, inhuman, degrading, sadistic, barbaric, primitive, outmoded, etc., as long as the people of Uganda still think that it is the only suitable treatment or punishment to carry out a death sentence, their values norms and aspirations must be respected by the courts. I also think that it is trite that every sentence must involve pain and suffering if it is to achieve its purpose as a punishment. A death sentence is not merely designed to remove from this earth, blissfully and peacefully, those people who have committed heinous crimes like murder, genocide and crimes against humanity etc. It is intended to punish them here on earth before they go. It is not a one-way ticket to Sugar Candy Mountains of George Orwell's *Animal Farm*. Once it is accepted that the death sentence is authorised by the Constitution, it is an exception to Article 24 and all Parliament has to do is to provide a balanced method of carrying it out, between blissful and peaceful methods of dispatch like the lethal injection and more barbaric methods like stoning or public beheading. In that context, hanging is a modest method of carrying out the death sentence and therefore, Section 99 of Trial on Indictment Act does not offend Articles 24 and 44(a) of the Constitution.

Byamugisha JA agreed with the judgment of Okello JA and added (at 404-5):

The framers of the Constitution were aware of the provisions of Articles 24 and 44 when they enacted Article 22. In my view, they would not have permitted a death sentence in one article and prohibited it in another. This means that the right to life is a derogation of a fundamental human right which provides an exception to acts of torture, cruel, inhuman and degrading form[s] of punishment prohibited by Article 24 (supra). It is therefore my considered opinion that the death penalty is not a cruel, inhuman and degrading treatment or punishment within the meaning of the article. Consequently, I would answer the first issue in the negative.

The second issue is almost related to the first one. Having held that the Constitution authorises the death sentence that is carried out in execution of a court order, it goes without saying that it is not affected by Article 24. The various laws of Uganda that prescribe the death sentence upon conviction are therefore not inconsistent with or in contravention of Articles 24 and 44(a) of the Constitution. They are also not affected by Article 44(a). I would answer the second issue in the negative.

Mr Sim Katende, learned counsel who argued this aspect of the cross-appeal, submitted, in effect summarising the written submissions filed in the appeal/cross-appeal, that the Constitutional Court erred when it held that since the death penalty was constitutionally permissible, the method of carrying out that sentence could not be challenged. The Constitution does not provide for the manner of carrying out of the death penalty. He submitted that hanging as the method of carrying out the death penalty is provided for in the Trial on Indictments Act which was subject to constitutional review. He argued that hanging was unconstitutionally cruel. Firstly that there are unchallenged judicial decisions to that effect, citing *Republic* v. *Mbushuu* [1994] 2 LRC 335, a decision of the Court of Appeal of Tanzania, and *State* v. *Makwanyane* [1995] 1 LRC 269, of the Constitutional Court of South Africa.

Secondly Mr Katende submitted that there was on record the unchallenged evidence of Dr Hillman and Dr Hunt that hanging was cruel and inhuman. Thirdly there was the evidence of Antony Okwonga, a former prisons officer, Vincent Oluka and Ben Ogwang which was unchallenged that proved that hanging as practised in Uganda was a cruel, inhuman and degrading punishment. He referred to the cases of *Attorney-General* v. *Abuki* [2001] 1 LRC 63 and *Catholic Commission for Justice and Peace in Zimbabwe* v. *Attorney-General* [1993] 2 LRC 279 in support of the cross-appeal.

Ms Angela Kiryabwire Kanyima, learned counsel for the appellant, the Attorney-General, opposed the cross-appeal. She submitted that the death penalty allowed under Article 22(1) of the Constitution does not constitute torture, cruel or inhuman or degrading treatment within the meaning of Articles 24 and 44 of the Constitution as those articles did not apply to a sentence of death passed by a competent court.

With regard to hanging, she submitted that the death penalty is saved by law, and therefore Section 99(1) of the Trial on Indictments Act merely puts into effect the Constitution and is not therefore unconstitutional. It cannot amount to torture, cruel, inhuman or degrading treatment. Secondly that hanging as a form of carrying out the death penalty is acceptable to the people of Uganda. The Trial on Indictments Act is a reflection of the people's will as it was made by their Parliament.

It may be useful at this stage to bring into view the provisions of the Constitution that touch on the question at hand. Article 22(1) of the Constitution, whose title is "Protection of right to life", states:

No person shall be deprived of life intentionally except in execution of a sentence passed in a fair trial by a court of competent jurisdiction in respect of a criminal offence under the laws of Uganda and the conviction and sentence have been confirmed by the highest appellate court.

Article 24 has a heading, "Respect for human dignity and protection from inhuman treatment". It reads:

No person shall be subjected to any form of torture or cruel, inhuman or degrading treatment or punishment.

Article 44 is entitled "Prohibition of derogation from particular human rights and freedoms". It states:

Notwithstanding anything in this Constitution, there shall be no derogation from the enjoyment of the following rights and freedoms—

(a) freedom from torture and cruel, inhuman or degrading treatment or punishment;
(b) freedom from slavery or servitude;
(c) the right to a fair hearing;
(d) the right to an order of habeas corpus.

It is clear, in my view, that the Constitution does authorise the death penalty under Article 22(1) of the Constitution. A literal reading of Article 22(1) leaves one with no other possible meaning.

What I do not find justified is the view that Articles 24 and 44(a) do not apply to Article 22(1). Or expressed in different words that Article 22(1) is an exception to Articles 24 and 44(a).

As was noted by Twinomujuni JA, in his judgment, some of the accepted principles in interpreting a Constitution include the following:

(c) The entire Constitution has to be read as an integrated whole, and no one particular provision destroying the other but each sustaining the other. This is the rule of harmony, rule of completeness and exhaustiveness and the rule of paramountcy of the written Constitution.
(d) The words of the written Constitution prevail over all unwritten conventions, precedents and practices.
(e) No one provision of the Constitution is to be segregated from the others and be considered alone, but all the provisions bearing upon a particular subject are to be brought into view and be interpreted as to effectuate the greater purpose of the instrument.

In *Ssemogerere* v. *Attorney-General* (Constitutional Appeal No 1 of 2002) [2005] 1 LRC 50 this Court had opportunity to consider this rule in interpretation of the Constitution. Chief Justice Odoki put it in the following words (at 59):

The second question is harmonisation. The Constitutional Court was in error to hold that it did not have jurisdiction to construe one provision against another in the Constitution. It is not a question of construing one provision as against another but of giving effect to all the provisions of the Constitution. This is because each provision is an integral part of the Constitution and must be given meaning or effect in relation to the others. Failure to do so will lead to an apparent conflict with the Constitution.

Oder JSC stated (at 75):

Another important principle governing interpretation and enforcement of the Constitution, which is applicable to the instant case, is that all the provisions of the Constitution touching on an issue are considered all together. The Constitution must be looked at as a whole.

Mulenga JSC, discussing the same rule, stated (at 94):

To my mind, the clause does not thereby preclude the court from interpreting or construing two or more provisions of the Constitution brought before it, which may appear to be in conflict. In my opinion, the court has, not only the jurisdiction, but also the responsibility to construe such provisions, with a view to harmonise them, where possible, through interpretation. It is a cardinal rule in constitutional interpretation, that provisions of a constitution concerned with the same subject should, as much as possible, be construed as complementing, and not contradicting one another. The Constitution must be read as an integrated and cohesive whole.

Applying the above rule to the task at hand, Article 22(1) if read together with Articles 24 and 44 would, in my view, mean that whereas the death penalty is authorised by the Constitution the same Constitution does ordain that it must not be carried out in a manner that is in violation of Articles 24 and 44. Death penalty is authorised but must be in compliance with Articles 24 and 44(a) as these provisions render cruel, inhuman and degrading treatment or punishment unconstitutional. This, in my view, is the only way to read all those provisions together, in harmony, without segregating one provision from the other, or any one particular provision destroying the other.

All these three articles relate to the subject of punishment or treatment of offenders. They must be read together. Article 22(1) makes the death penalty lawful as an exception to the right to life. Article 24 outlaws cruel, inhuman, degrading treatment or punishment. Article 44 makes Article 24 non-derogable. The death penalty authorised in Article 22(1) must conform to criteria for punishment set out in Article 24. It is not that framers in writing Article 24 had forgotten what they had just written in Article 22(1). No, the framers were aware and required that all the provisions be read together, and not one against the other. I am unable to find any justification for the view that the constituent assembly intended that Articles 24 and 44 would not apply to Article 22(1). If that had been their intention, given the precedent available in the Constitution (1967) preceding the one that they were enacting, they would have stated so clearly.

The approach I have taken of reading all the relevant provisions together in harmony finds persuasive support from a decision of the European Court of Human Rights in *Soering* v. *United Kingdom* (1989) 11 EHRR 439. The US government sought to extradite Mr Soering, a German national living in the United Kingdom, for the murder of two people in Virginia, US. The Secretary of State, after the necessary proceedings in the courts in UK, issued an extradition warrant. Mr Soering brought an application before the European Court of Human Rights seeking a declaration that the United Kingdom was in breach of its treaty obligations under Article 3 of the European Convention on Human Rights in light of the fact that should he be extradited to the US, tried and convicted he was likely to be sentenced to a death penalty, which would violate his charter rights, inter alia, Article 3 that forbids torture, inhuman and or degrading treatment or punishment to any person. It was the argument for Mr Soering that if convicted and sentenced to death, it was likely that he would spend a long period of time on death row without being executed, inflicting pain and suffering to him, known as the death-row phenomenon.

Article 3 of the European Convention states:

No one shall be subjected to torture, or to inhuman or degrading treatment or punishment.

The European Court held that under Article 2(1) of the Convention capital punishment was permitted. Article 2(1) states:

Everyone's right to life shall be protected by law. No one shall be deprived of his life intentionally save in execution of a sentence of a court following his conviction of a crime for which the death penalty is provided by law.

It then went on to say:

103. The Convention is to be read as a whole and Article 3 should therefore be construed in harmony with the provisions of Article 2 (see, mutatis mutandis, the *Klass and Others* judgment of 6 September 1978, Series A no 28, p. 31, para. 68). On this basis Article 3 evidently cannot have been intended by the drafters of the Convention to include a general prohibition of the death penalty since that would nullify the clear wording of Article 2(1) . . .

104. That does not mean however that circumstances relating to a death sentence can never give rise to an issue under Article 3. The manner in which it is imposed or executed, the personal circumstances of the condemned person and a disproportionality to the gravity of the crime committed, as well as the conditions of detention awaiting execution, are examples of factors capable of bringing the treatment or punishment received by the condemned person within the proscription under Article 3 . . .

The Court went on to observe and hold:

111. For any prisoner condemned to death, some element of delay between imposition and execution of the sentence and the experience of severe stress in conditions necessary for strict incarceration are inevitable. The democratic character of the Virginia legal system in general and the positive features of Virginia trial, sentencing and appeal procedures in particular are beyond doubt. The Court agrees with the Commission that the machinery of justice to which the applicant would be subject in the United States is in itself neither arbitrary nor unreasonable, but, rather respects the rule of law and affords not inconsiderable procedural safeguards to the defendant in a capital trial. Facilities are available on death row for the assistance of inmates, notably through provision of psychological and psychiatric services... However, in the Court's view, having regard to the very long period of time spent on death row in such extreme conditions, with the ever present and mounting anguish of awaiting execution of the death penalty, and to the personal circumstances of the applicant, especially his age and mental state at the time of the offence, the applicant's extradition to the United States would expose him to a real risk of treatment beyond the threshold set by Article 3. A further consideration of relevance is that in the particular instance the legitimate purpose of extradition could be achieved by another means which would not involve suffering of such exceptional intensity or duration.

Accordingly, the Secretary of State's decision to extradite the applicant to the United States would, if implemented, give rise to a breach of Article 3.

Article 2(1) of the European Convention on Human Rights is *in pari materia* with Article 22(1) of our Constitution. So is Article 3 with Article 24 of our Constitution. The approach by the European Court to read the said provisions in harmony is in line with the established approach to constitutional interpretation here in Uganda. Reading the provisions together is essential in order to grasp the full meaning of the provisions bearing upon the same subject.

The reasoning of the European Court is very persuasive. The European Convention on Human Rights is the forerunner of the bill of rights found in many independence constitutions and post-independence constitutions. The jurisprudence of the European Court is therefore quite persuasive.

Further authority for this approach is found in the decision of the Human Rights Committee in *Ng* v. *Canada*, Communication No 469 of 1991 [98 ILR 479] delivered on 7 January 1994. This decision is quoted by the majority in support of the proposition that there is no conflict between Article 22(1) and Articles 24 and 44(a) of our Constitution. In that case the applicant, a British citizen, who had been living in Canada, had been extradited to the United States for trial on several counts of murder. He brought an action against Canada that his extradition to the United States would result in breach of his rights under Articles 6 and 7 of the International Covenant on Civil and Political Rights as he would face the death penalty, and be subject to not only the death-row phenomenon but also the mode of execution (gas asphyxiation) which was cruel, inhuman and degrading treatment or punishment.

Articles 6 and 7 of the International Covenant on Civil and Political Rights are *in pari materia* with Articles 21(1) and 24 of our Constitution as noted by the majority judgment.

The Committee decided that Mr Ng was not a victim of the violation by Canada of Article 6 of the Covenant but found that he was a victim of Canada's violation of Article 7. It went on to say,

16.1 In determining whether, in a particular case, the imposition of capital punishment constitutes a violation of Article 7, the Committee will have regard to the relevant personal factors regarding the author, the specific conditions of detention on death row, and whether the proposed method of execution is particularly abhorrent. In the instant case, it is contended that execution by gas asphyxiation is contrary to internationally accepted standards of humane treatment, and that it amounts to treatment in violation of Article 7 of the Covenant. *The Committee begins by noting that whereas Article 6, paragraph 2, allows the imposition of the death penalty under certain limited circumstances, any method of execution provided by law must be designed in such a way as to avoid conflict with Article 7.*

16.2 The Committee is aware that, by definition, every execution of a sentence of death may be considered to constitute cruel and inhuman treatment within the meaning of Article 7 of the Covenant; on the other hand, Article 6, paragraph 2, permits the imposition of capital punishment for the most serious crimes. *Nonetheless, the Committee reaffirms, as it did in its General Comment 20[44] on Article 7 of the Covenant (CCPR/21/Add.3, paragraph 6), that, when imposing capital punishment, the execution of the sentence "... must [be] carried out in such a way as to cause the least possible physical and mental suffering".*

It is clear that the Committee treated Articles 6 and 7 of the International Covenant as not in conflict as noted by the majority judgment. It is also very clear that the Committee read and interpreted both articles in harmony, without separating them, or ignoring one provision in preference to the other, an aspect of the decision ignored by the majority judgment. The approach of the Committee is very persuasive as it is clearly consistent with our rule of harmony in constitutional interpretation as espoused by this Court in *Ssemogerere* v. *Attorney-General* (Constitutional Appeal No 1 of 2002) [2005] 1 LRC 50. It is worthwhile noting that Uganda acceded to the International Covenant on Civil and Political Rights on 21 September 1995 and to the First Optional

Protocol on 14 February 1996. At the very least the decisions of the Human Rights Committee are therefore very persuasive in our jurisdiction. We ignore the same at peril of infringing our obligations under that treaty and international law. We ought to interpret our law so as not to be in conflict with the international obligations that Uganda assumed when it acceded to the International Covenant on Civil and Political Rights.

What the Constitutional Court has done is in effect to write back into law, with regard to the death penalty, Article 12(2) of the 1967 Constitution which was specifically omitted in the 1995 Constitution. Article 12 reads:

(1) No person shall be subjected to torture or to inhuman or degrading punishment or other like treatment.

(2) *Nothing contained in or done under the authority of any law shall be held to be inconsistent with or in contravention of this article to the extent that the law in question authorises the infliction of any punishment that was lawful in Uganda immediately before 9 October 1962.* (Emphasis is mine.)

Article 24 of the 1995 Constitution does not include the exception that was provided in Article 12(2) of the 1967 Constitution and the omission of that provision was deliberate. As noted by Mulenga JSC in *Attorney-General* v. *Abuki* [2001] 1 LRC 63 at 108:

The prohibition of such treatment and punishment is absolute. *It is instructive, in my opinion, to recall that the 1967 Constitution of Uganda in art. 12 similarly provided for the protection from inhuman treatment but with a qualification in clause (2) which provided: [sets out Article 12(2) of the 1967 Constitution] When the current constitution was framed and promulgated on 8 October 1995, that provision was deliberately omitted. That alone, in my view, should leave no doubt in anyone's mind about the intention of the framers of the Constitution to make the prohibition absolute.* Therefore while the Privy Council's decision in *Riley* may have been strong persuasive authority in Uganda prior to the 1995 Constitution, it is today irrelevant and inapplicable. With effect from 8 October 1995, validity of any punishment prescribed by existing law ceased to depend on its existence prior to Uganda's independence. The validity depends on conformity with the Constitution. (Emphasis is mine.)

It is reasonable to infer that the omission in the 1995 Constitution of an equivalent provision to Article 12(2) of the 1967 Constitution and Article 21(2) of the 1962 Constitution was intended to make prohibition in Article 24 absolute as noted by Mulenga JSC in *Attorney-General* v. *Abuki*. Not only was there no specific derogation against Article 24 as was previously the case prior to the 1995 Constitution but the Constitution under Article 44 protects Article 24 from derogation. The wording of Article 44 is instructive. It starts with the words, "Notwithstanding anything in this Constitution...". The framers were aware of what they had enacted in Article 22(1). The framers decided, notwithstanding that the death penalty was constitutionally permissible, to subject it to Article 24 without derogation.

I am strengthened in that view in light of the nature of the legislative or constitutional history of the proviso or rider in all our earlier constitutions. Its omission can only be significant. Constitutional history of the provision may, as in this instance, provide strong inference as to why a particular interpretation may be preferable to the other. The omission of that rider coupled with the non-derogation clause in Article 44, points, in my view, to only one conclusion. That the framers of the Constitution raised the threshold of Article 24 to apply to all existing punishments, rather than exclude all existing punishments or any punishment stipulated in the law at the time of enacting of the 1995 Constitution.

The Constitutional Court declined to follow *Attorney-General* v. *Abuki*, distinguishing it on the ground that in the *Abuki* decision what the court was considering was an Act of Parliament as against the Constitution, while in the case before it, the court was considering one provision of the Constitution against another provision of the Constitution. In my view this is not strictly correct with regard to the consideration of whether hanging as provided for in the Trial on Indictments Act was a cruel, inhuman or degrading treatment or punishment. Hanging, as a method of execution of a death penalty, is not provided for by the Constitution. It is provided for by an Act of Parliament. It is the provisions of that Act that were challenged (in the alternative). *Attorney-General* v. *Abuki* is therefore applicable.

The Constitutional Court is bound by the decisions of the Supreme Court, sitting as an appellate court in constitutional matters. And so is the Supreme Court itself bound by its earlier decisions, though it may depart from them, if it appears right to do so. Article 132(4) states:

> 4. The Supreme Court may, while treating its own previous decisions as normally binding, depart from a previous decision when it appears to it right to do so; and all other courts shall be bound to follow the decisions of the Supreme Court on questions of law.

Mulenga JSC stated in *Attorney-General* v. *Abuki* (at 109):

> This prohibition is directed, without exception, to everyone capable of causing or effecting derogation from observance, respect and/or enforcement of the freedoms and rights specified in the article. It applies not only to the law makers but also to those who interpret, apply, or enforce the law. A subjective view that

some of the penalties, still on our statute books, which are inflicted daily by the courts of law, are cruel or inhuman may be understandable. However, that cannot be a basis for the contention that the courts of law are excepted from the clear prohibitions under Articles 24 and 44 of the Constitution. If any existing law prescribes a penalty which is inconsistent with Article 24, or any other provisions of the Constitution, it is liable to be interpreted in accordance with Article 274, which provides in clause (1)

> Subject to the provisions of this article, the operation of the existing law after the coming into force of this Constitution shall not be affected by the coming into force of this Constitution but the existing law shall be construed with such modifications, adaptations, qualifications and exceptions as may be necessary to bring it into conformity with this Constitution.

Kanyeihamba JSC stated in part, in the same case of *Attorney-General* v. *Abuki* (at 115-16):

Article 24 is doubly entrenched by Article 44 to the extent that it is unalterable. In other words, there are no conceivable circumstances or grave facts by which the rights protected in Article 44 can ever be altered to the disadvantage of anyone even if that person has been charged [with] a serious offence. Parliament may not pass any law whose provisions derogate from Article 44. Courts cannot pass any sentence that derogates from the same article.

Further on he stated:

In my opinion, even an Act passed unanimously by Parliament and any judgment of any court, whatever its position in the hierarchy of the courts' system, which derogates from Articles 24 and 44 is unconstitutional, and therefore, null and void.

Attorney-General v. *Abuki* clearly establishes the reach of Articles 24 and 44 of the Constitution. The said provisions apply to all punishments and/or treatment meted out by a state actor inclusive of the courts. The protection against torture, cruel or degrading treatment and punishment is absolute.

What the Constitutional Court had to determine was whether hanging passes constitutional muster with regard to the provisions of Articles 24 and 44 of the Constitution. The Court took the view that hanging was definitely cruel but concluded that it was not subject to the provisions of Articles 24 and 44 of the Constitution. This was, with due respect, an error.

For the reasons set out above I would find that the Constitutional Court erred in law when it held that Articles 24 and 44 of the Constitution did not apply to Article 22(1) of the Constitution of Uganda.

I would hold that Articles 22(1), 24 and 44 must be read together, in so far as they relate to sentencing and punishment, to provide a harmonious interpretation that does not do violence to the meaning of any one provision. Capital penalty is clearly authorised by Article 22(1) but to give effect to Articles 24 and 44 such capital penalty as may be authorised by law must not infringe Articles 24 and 44 of the Constitution. Parliament is free to enact laws that provide for the execution of the death penalty but such laws are subject to Articles 24 and 44(a) of the Constitution of Uganda. It is suggested in the majority opinion that international human rights instruments treat the right to life including the derogation in respect of capital punishment separately from the provision against torture, inhuman and degrading treatment or punishment. And that therefore one provision is not intended to affect the other. In my view this approach is inconsistent with the rule of harmony in constitutional interpretation. And authority to the contrary is [abundant]. I will refer to only two decisions in relation to the European Convention on Human Rights and the International Covenant on Civil and Political Rights.

As demonstrated by *Soering* v. *UK* (supra) and *Ng* v. *Canada* (supra) this cannot be true with regard to the European Convention on Human Rights and the International Covenant on Civil and Political Rights. The approach to interpretation is that all the provisions be read together in harmony, rather than one against the other, in order to elicit the true intent of the framers of the Convention.

The Constitutional Court held, and the majority now affirm, that Articles 24 and 44(a) do not apply to the death penalty authorised under Article 22(1) of our Constitution. That imposition and or execution (i.e. mode of carrying out) of the death penalty cannot be questioned under Article 24 of the same Constitution. The Constitutional Court held, and the majority of this Court now affirm, that delay in the execution of the death penalty in Uganda creates "death-row phenomenon" that amounts to "cruel, inhuman and degrading treatment or punishment" under Article 24 of the Constitution.

It is odd, in my view, that delay in executing the death penalty can amount to "cruel, inhuman and degrading treatment" under Article 24 while at the same time the same provision cannot be used to determine whether the mode of implementing the death penalty meets the threshold provided by Article 24 of the Constitution. I am unable to find any justification for this approach.

As pointed out in *Soering* v. *UK* (supra) there are several factors, including the one accepted and the one rejected by the Constitutional Court, that are available to determine whether the death penalty may infringe the equivalent of our Article 24 of the Constitution. The Court put it in the following words:

104. That does not mean however that circumstances relating to a death sentence can never give rise to an issue under Article 3. The manner in which it is imposed or executed, the personal circumstances of the condemned person and a disproportionality to the gravity of the crime committed, as well as the conditions of detention awaiting execution, are examples of factors capable of bringing the treatment or punishment received by the condemned person within the proscription under Article 3 . . .

It is somewhat incongruous that one factor or circumstance surrounding the death penalty was found to be a violation of Article 24 while another factor or circumstance related to the death penalty could not even be examined to determine whether or not it may trigger Article 24 into operation.

I would allow ground no 1 of the cross-appeal.

Ground No 3 of the Cross-Appeal

I now turn to ground no 3 of the cross-appeal. It states:

3. That in the alternative but without prejudice to the above, that the learned justices of the Constitutional Court erred in law when they found as a question of fact and law that hanging was a cruel, inhuman and degrading treatment or punishment but held that it was a permissible form of punishment because the death penalty was permitted by the Constitution.

In considering this ground the words of Oder JSC in *Attorney-General v. Abuki* [2001] 1 LRC 63 at 86 are instructive. He stated in part:

Article 24 of the Ugandan Constitution provides: "No person shall be subjected to any form of torture, cruel, inhuman or degrading treatment or punishment." It seems clear that the words emphasised [*sic*] have to be read disjunctively. Thus read, the article seeks to protect the citizens from seven different conditions: (i) torture; (ii) cruel treatment; (iii) cruel punishment; (iv) inhuman treatment; (v) inhuman punishment; (vi) degrading treatment and (vii) degrading punishment. Under Article 44 the protection from the seven conditions is absolute.

He continued to consider the meaning of what is protected under Article 24. He stated (at 88):

The treatment or punishment prescribed by Article 24 of the Constitution is not defined therein. According to the Concise Oxford Dictionary they have the following meaning: Torture—"the infliction of severe bodily pain, especially as a punishment or a means of persuasion; severe physical or mental suffering;

force out of natural position or state; deform; pervert". Cruel—"causing pain or suffering, especially deliberately; pervert".

Inhuman—"brutal, unfeeling, barbarous, not of a human type; inhumanly".

Degrading—"humiliating; causing loss of self-respect". Treatment—"a process or manner of behaving towards or dealing with a person; customary way of dealing with a person". Punishment—"the act of punishing; the condition of being punished; the loss or suffering inflicted; severe treatment or suffering".

As I have already said, the prohibitions under Article 24 are absolute. The state's obligations are therefore absolute and unqualified. All that is therefore required to establish a violation by a state organ falls within one or other of the seven permutations of Article 24 set out above. No question of justification can ever arise.

European Convention on Human Rights jurisprudence on Article 3 is helpful in throwing light on what may constitute cruel, inhuman and degrading treatment or punishment, given that the wording of Article 3 of the Convention and our Article 24 is virtually the same save for the inclusion of the word "cruel" in our Article 24 which is not present in Article 3 of the Convention.

In *Ireland* v. *United Kingdom* [1978] ECHR 5310/71 the European Court stated in paragraph 162:

... ill treatment must attain a minimum level of severity if it is to fall within the scope of Article 3. The assessment of this minimum is in the nature of things relative; it depends on all the circumstances of the case, such as the duration of the treatment, its physical or mental effects and, in some cases, the sex, age and state of health of the victim, etc.

In *Soering* v. *United Kingdom* (supra) the Court stated in paragraph 100:

... Treatment has been held by the Court to be both "inhuman" because it was premeditated, was applied for hours at a stretch and "caused, if not actual bodily injury, at least intense physical and mental suffering" and also "degrading" because it was "such as to arouse in [its] victims feelings of fear, anguish and inferiority capable of humiliating and debasing them and possibly breaking their physical or moral resistance"....

In order for a punishment or treatment associated with it to be "inhuman" or "degrading", the suffering or humiliation involved must in any event go beyond that inevitable element of suffering or humiliation connected with a given form of legitimate punishment...

In this connection, account is to be taken not only of the physical pain experienced but also, where there is a considerable delay before execution of the punishment, of the sentenced person's mental anguish of anticipating the violence he is to have inflicted on him.

Regard may be given to the jurisprudence of the Human Rights Committee on provisions that are *in pari materia* with Article 24 of the Constitution. Article 7 of the International Covenant on Civil and Political Rights (to which Uganda acceded as noted above) is *in pari materia* with Article 24 of the Constitution. I refer to the decision in *Ng* v. *Canada* (supra) where the Committee stated:

16.3 In the instant case, the author has provided *detailed information that execution by gas asphyxiation may cause prolonged suffering and agony and does not result in death as swiftly as possible, as asphyxiation by cyanide gas may take over 10 minutes. The State party had the opportunity to refute these allegations on the facts; it has failed to do so.* Rather, the State party has confined itself to arguing that in the absence of a norm of international law which expressly prohibits asphyxiation by cyanide gas, "it would be interfering to an unwarranted degree with the internal laws and practices of United States to refuse to extradite a fugitive to face the possible imposition of the death penalty by cyanide gas asphyxiation".

16.4 In the instant case and on the basis of the information before it, the Committee concludes that execution by gas asphyxiation, should the death penalty be imposed on the author, would not meet the test of "least possible physical and mental suffering", and constitutes cruel and inhuman treatment, in violation of Article 7 of the Covenant. Accordingly, Canada, which could reasonably foresee that Mr Ng, if sentenced to death, would be executed in a way that amounts to a violation of Article 7, failed to comply with its obligations under the Covenant, by extraditing Mr Ng without having sought and received assurances that he would not be executed.

16.5 The Committee need not pronounce itself on the compatibility, with Article 7, of methods of execution other than that which is at issue in this case.

The question to be decided is whether hanging as practised in this jurisdiction infringes Article 24 of the Constitution. The Constitutional Court found that hanging is indeed cruel. The evidence produced in that court to support this conclusion was as compelling as it was chilling. Dr Harold Hillman of the United Kingdom and Dr Albert Hunt from Scotland swore affidavits in this matter that detail medical explanation of the process of hanging. It is clear that in the majority of cases and or studies that they have come across, death is not instantaneous. In Dr Hillman's opinion death by hanging was humiliating because (i) the person is masked; (ii) the person's wrists and ankles are bound to restrain him; (iii) the person cannot react to pain, distress and feeling of asphyxia by the usual physiological responses of crying out or moving violently (although he sometimes twitches late in execution, usually attributed to the effect of lack of oxygen on the spinal cord); and (iv) the person hanged often sweats, drools, the eyes bulge and he micturates and defecates.

Mr Okwanga in his affidavit stated in part,

8. From my experience, this is the procedure that takes place when the prisoners were to be executed:

(a) When the President of the Republic signs the death warrants, the executions are supposed to be carried out within 1 (one) week.
(b) The warrants are then handed over to the Commissioner of Prisons who hands them over to the Officer in Charge, Luzira Upper Prison, who then liaises with the Officer in Charge, Condemned Section.
(c) No notice is given to the prisoners as to whether there was going to be an execution.
(d) The Officer in Charge then starts the repair of the execution machine, the cleaning of the gallows, the restriction of the prisoners' movements, the making of coffins in the prison carpentry workshop and the making of lists of which particular cells the prisoners are resident.
(e) The warders selected to take part in the execution as well as the Executioner are normally brought from outside the condemned section of Luzira. This is because the prison warders who are stationed in the condemned section are normally close to the inmates and would not feel comfortable helping in the execution of the prisoners. These different prison warders are paid a special allowance to participate in the executions.
(f) When the initial preparations are complete, the condemned prisoners selected to be executed are taken from their cells. This is usually done very early in the morning. The prison warders go from cell to cell, calling out names of prisoners and forcefully ordering them out of the cells. All the prisoners are terrified, as they suspect that this removal from their cells is about execution but do not know for sure whether this [is] to be an execution.
(g) The selected prisoners are handcuffed and leg-irons are put on their legs. They say their last goodbyes to their fellow condemned prisoners. Some prisoners are taken kicking and screaming. Many of them soil themselves in the process.
(h) The prisoners are taken to the Officer in Charge's office. The prisoners are then arrested before execution. The Officer in Charge announces to each individual prisoner the crime he was convicted of, as well as the date and time of his execution, which is normally 3 (three) days thereafter. At that stage, most of the prisoners collapse, soil themselves, cry and wail and start praying to the Lord.
(i) The prisoners are then taken to the death chamber/gallows in Section E of the prison and locked up in individual cells.
(j) The prisoners' heights and weights are recorded. The recording of the heights and weights is part of a formula to measure how far the prisoners would drop when the lever of the execution table is released. The formula

is supposed to help the condemned prisoners to drop without their heads being plucked off. It also helps in measuring coffins.
(k) After recording the weights and heights, the prisoners are then given 3 (three) days period before their executions. This 3 (three) day period is to enable the prison authorities to get in touch with the prisoners' relatives and for the prisoners to make their wills and make peace with God.
(l) In the meantime, preparations for the execution continue. Coffins are made in the courtyard of the upper prison directly next to Section A of the condemned section. The prisoners in Section A can hear the sounds of the coffins being made, and this puts them on notice that an execution is imminent. This increases the terror, horror and apprehension of the rest of the prisoners in the condemned section.
(m) Prisoners in Luzira Prison who are not in the condemned section are deployed to make the hoods and clothing that the soon-to-be-executed prisoners are to wear. This is done in the tailoring section of the prison, and this process ensures that all the inmates of Luzira Prison know that an execution is imminent. The number of hoods and clothes made also informs the other prisoners of the number of prisoners due to be executed. This adds to the general unease, fear, alarm and dread in the Prison.
(n) For the 3 (three) days, while the prisoners await their respective executions a dark cloud of death descends upon and engulfs the whole prison. Everyone is tense especially the prisoners slated to be executed, the warders and everyone connected to Luzira Prison.
(o) During the 3 (three) days wait, some of the prisoners confess that they are guilty but that they are now ready to meet their Maker as they had become born again. Others insist that they are innocent but that they had found peace in God and forgiveness for the people that had falsely or maliciously caused all this misery upon their lives. At this time, the priests and imams are present, giving the prisoners solace and comfort in this most trying of times.
(p) *During these 3 (three) days, the lights in the cells are left on all day and night and the prisoners are under 24 (twenty-four) hour surveillance. The prison warders ensure that there are no instruments that can assist such prisoners to commit suicide during those 3 (three) days.*
(q) *During those 3 (three) days, a prison warder reminds each prisoner hour after hour of the crime he was convicted of, the sentence imposed upon him and the number of hours remaining to the carrying out of the death sentence by hanging.*
(r) During those 3 (three) days, the prisoners normally write notes/chits/letters to their fellow condemned prisoners who are not scheduled to be executed that day. These notes/chits/letters normally serve as their last Wills and Testaments. The prisoners are normally pitifully poor and all they have to will are items like flasks, bedroom slippers, soap and their threadbare clothes. These are usually willed to their death row colleagues. These notes/chits/letters are given to the prison warders who pass them on to the intended recipients.

(s) During those 3 (three) days, the prisoners usually keep singing hymns, to comfort themselves. The words of the hymns are normally changed by the prisoners to be executed, so as to keep the rest of the condemned prisoners informed of their fates.
(t) During those 3 (three) days, the prisoners are also given a last chance to be visited by their friends and relatives, but hardly any prisoners receive family visits. This is because many prisoners are poor peasants whose families cannot afford the fare to Kampala, or the prisoners have spent such long periods in prison that their families have forgotten or abandoned them.
(u) During these 3 (three) days, the prisoners' skins normally appear faded, wan and washed-out. Their faces appear ashy, pale and white.
(v) On the day of execution, in the middle of the night the prisoners are herded to the Pinion room and the Officer in Charge reads the execution order for their respective executions. The shaken prisoners at this time usually turn whitish with popped out eyes. Some start wailing afresh while others sing hymns and accept Jesus Christ as their personal Saviour.
(w) The prisoners to be executed are taken to the dressing room and dressed in an unusual overall-like outfit and are covered from head to toe without any openings for the hand or feet. They are also hand and leg cuffed to avoid incidences of violence. Black hoods are passed over the prisoners' heads. Weights are placed in the overalls of the smaller and lighter prisoners to make them heavier.
(x) The execution chamber is capable of hanging 3 (three) prisoners at a time. The prisoners can be led singly or in threes, supported by warders.
(y) With black hoods over their heads, the prisoners cannot see or tell how they are going to be executed, or who is present to witness their executions.
(z) At that time, the priests and imams normally read to the prisoners their last rites, and bless them. Most of the prisoners are usually still wailing, bawling and lamenting. Some of them admit their guilt and ask for forgiveness, but many others maintain that they are innocent until the very end.
(aa) From the time the prisoners are led to the dressing room and hence to the gallows themselves, their colleagues in the death chamber are, through hymns, recounting the proceedings to the rest of the prisoners in the condemned section below. Graphic details are given out through these songs, telling the other condemned prisoners of who is being taken for dressing, or for execution and what is being done to him at every moment.
(bb) At the execution chambers, the prisoners' legs are tied-up and the noose pushed over their heads to their necks. At the back of the prisoners' heads the noose is tightened, cutting off their breathing.
(cc) The metal loop is normally on the right hand side of the prisoners' necks so that when they drop the loop would be directly under their cheeks and it would quickly break the cervical bone and kill them instantly.
(dd) The prisoners are then put atop a table, 3 (three) at a time. The table is one that opens at the bottom when a certain gear-like lever is pressed. The aim is to place the noose around the prisoner's head, press the lever

so that the table opens and let the prisoner hang from the neck until he is dead.
(ee) When all is set, the executioner releases a gear-like lever and the table opens into two, each side gets stuck against the rubber under the table leaving the space of the two joined tables open and the 3 (three) prisoners drop down.
(ff) There is an extremely loud thud when the two sides of the table get stuck against the rubber, and an even bigger one when the prisoners hit a table in the basement room directly below the gallows.
(gg) After the bodies drop, the Officer in Charge and the priest go down to the ground and enter the basement where the bodies are hanging to ensure that the prisoners have been executed. The prison doctor is normally already in the basement.
(hh) The doctor examines the corpses to confirm that the prisoners are dead before the corpses are placed in poorly made ceiling board coffins ready for burial in shallow unmarked mass graves.
(ii) *In case the prisoners are not certifiably dead, they are then killed by hitting them at the back of the head with a hammer or a crow-bar.*
(jj) This process is repeated until all the prisoners due to be executed that day are executed.
(kk) The shallow mass grave is situated next to the Women's Prison, Luzira and the prisoners' families have no access to the corpse. They are not even told where the grave is situated.
(ll) The corpses are deposited into the mass graves and sprayed with acid to help them decompose faster. Subsequently, cabbages and other vegetables are grown over the mass graves to feed the remaining prisoners.

9. *I have on several occasions witnessed the heads of prisoners being plucked off during executions. This occurred mainly in old inmates who were aged above 60 years old. Witnessing human heads being plucked off is a very shocking and harrowing experience indeed as both the skin and cervical break off leading to blood gushing out like pressure pipe water. When the heads are plucked off, blood spills all over the place and even onto the prison warders assisting in the execution.* (Emphasis is mine.)

The evidence put forth by the respondents on this issue was not challenged by the appellants in the court below. Neither was it contradicted. The appellants did not adduce any evidence to put in doubt what Mr Okwanga sets out in his affidavit as to what occurs in this country during execution of the death penalty.

I accept the evidence of the respondents that hanging as a method of execution as it is carried out in this country, is a process that is cruel, inhuman and degrading treatment and punishment. In situations where the head is plucked off this is like killing an insect or a bird. It is inhuman to decapitate persons in the name of punishment. To subject those who do not die instantly to death by bludgeoning is likewise not only cruel, it is inhuman and degrading as well. This is akin to the times when the order for death by hanging included quartering and disembowelling! This is definitely beyond the pain, suffering or humiliation that should be associated with the death penalty.

In the last three days before hanging a prisoner is continually reminded every hour for twenty-four hours by a prison warder that he is to die by hanging and the remaining number of hours before the hanging is to occur. This consistent and round-the-clock reminder of the violence that is to be visited upon him must surely cause the same amount of mental suffering as that experienced under the death-row phenomenon. It is entirely unnecessary but no doubt imposes extreme mental suffering.

The evidence adduced by the parties clearly shows that hanging as practised in Uganda fails to meet the test of "the least possible physical and mental suffering" that has been set by the Human Rights Committee under the International Covenant on Civil and Political Rights.

I would agree with the respondents that hanging as a method of execution as it is carried out in Uganda is a cruel, inhuman and degrading treatment and punishment.

In my view it is the duty of Parliament to legislate the manner in which the death penalty should be carried out. In doing so, Parliament is obliged to take into account the dictates of the Constitution, including ensuring that the method it establishes is not a cruel, inhuman and degrading treatment and or punishment. It is not for this Court at this stage to suggest what method should be acceptable as no evidence has been adduced for consideration by this Court. That point is moot. There is no evidence before this Court with regard to other methods of implementation of the death penalty for this Court to say at this stage that method X or Y or Z is, or is not, cruel, inhuman or degrading treatment and punishment.

I would allow ground No 3 of the cross-appeal.

[Report: [2009] 2 LRC 168]

INDEX

For references to particular articles of treaties, see the Table of Treaties.

Abbreviations used in the index
ACC (African Children's Charter (1990))
ACHPR (African Charter on Human and Peoples' Rights (1981))
ACHR (American Convention on Human Rights (1969))
CARPA (Convention on Aspects of Refugee Problems in Africa (1969))
CC (Criminal Code)
CEDAW (Convention on the Elimination of All Forms of Discrimination Against Women (1979))
CRC (UN Convention on the Rights of the Child (1989))
CSC (Continental Shelf Convention (1958))
ECA (Environment Conservation Act 1989 (South Africa))
ECHR (European Convention on Human Rights (1950))
EEZ (Exclusive Economic Zone)
EIA (environmental impact assessment)
ICCPR (International Covenant on Civil and Political Rights (1966))
ICESCR (International Covenant on Economic, Social and Cultural Rights (1966))
ICJ ((Statute of the) International Court of Justice)
ILO No 169 (ILO Convention on Indigenous and Tribal Peoples in Independent Countries (No 169) (1989))
ITLOS (International Tribunal for the Law of the Sea)
NEMA (National Environmental Management Act 1998 (South Africa))
RC (Convention Relating to the Status of Refugees (1951))
SC (Slavery Convention (1926))
TC (Torture Convention (1984))
UDHR (Universal Declaration of Human Rights (1948))
UNC (UN Charter (1945))
UNCLOS (United Nations Law of the Sea Convention (1982))
UNHRC (UN Human Rights Committee)
VCLT (Vienna Convention on the Law of Treaties (1969))
WSSD (World Summit on Sustainable Development)

admissibility of evidence (municipal law/general)
  evidence obtained in manner infringing human rights 144-211
  evidence obtained through search and seizure in breach of fundamental rights 144-211
  evidence obtained through search and seizure in third State 144-211
  hearsay evidence, as recorded in affidavit 593-6
admissibility of evidence obtained by torture/confession, third party torture 243-8
African Children's Charter (1990) (ACC)
  best interests of the child (ACC 4) 306
  implementing legislation/incorporation 301, 312-13
  marital status of parents, relevance (ACC 18(3)) 306
  non-discrimination obligation (ACC 3) 306
  parental responsibility (ACC 20(1)) 306
age discrimination, prohibition, omission from legislation 309

alien, rights and obligations
protection, constitution 310-11, 361-2
respect for laws of receiving State 365
Australia
crimes against humanity, requirements
actus reus (physical elements of offence)
as act or state of affairs 97
commission of act proscribed under municipal law 88
mens rea, intentional exercise of powers leading to commission of crime 94-9, 101-12, 115-32
Criminal Code
Ch 2 (general principles of criminal responsibility)
applicability to s 270.3(1)(a) (slavery, sexual servitude and deceptive recruiting) 94-9, 100-4, 114, 116, 127-8
text (extracts) 81-3
Ch 2 s 5.1(1) (fault elements) 83, 97, 101, 103, 117-18, 119-20
Ch 2 s 5.2(2) (intention) 83, 95, 97, 101-12, 115-32
Ch 2 s 5.2(3) (knowledge) 83, 95, 97
Criminal Code Amendment (Slavery and Sexual Servitude) Act 1999 (repeal of Imperial Acts relating to slavery) 80, 89
criminal responsibility (general principles) (CC Ch 2) 81-3, 94-9, 100-4, 114, 116, 127-8
external affairs power (Constitution, s 51(xxix)), slavery legislation 87
law of, Criminal Code, s 270.3(1)(a) (slavery, sexual servitude and deceptive recruiting): *see* slavery, sexual servitude and deceptive recruiting (CC 270) *below*
legislation, interpretation, guidelines
ordinary and natural meaning 130-1
text/literal approach 111, 122-3
legislation, interpretation, presumption of conformity with international law 122-3
slavery, sexual servitude and deceptive recruiting (CC 270) 79-139
actus reus, commission of act proscribed under municipal law 88, 136
burden/standard of proof 86-7, 90, 98-9, 103-12, 114, 127-8
'chattel slavery' 78 n. 6, 87-8, 90-4, 95, 111
Criminal Code Amendment (Slavery and Sexual Servitude) Act 1999 (repeal of Imperial Acts relating to slavery) 80, 89
criminal responsibility (general principles) (CC Ch 2) and 81-3, 94-9, 100-4, 114, 116, 127-8
customary international law 105
debt bondage (CC 271.8) 81, 91, 108, 124-5
debt or contract, relevance 84-7, 90, 92-4, 97, 109, 110-11, 137
as implementation/incorporation of Slavery Convention (1926) 87-8, 108, 113-14, 122
mens rea
intentional exercise of powers resulting in condition of slavery 83, 94-9, 101-12, 115-32
knowledge of basis of powers, relevance 94-9
overlapping nature of offences/definitions 77 n. 3, 91
penalty, relevance 81, 123
possessing a slave/using a slave (CC 270.3(1)(a)) 79-139
'powers of *ownership*'/'in possession' 88, 89-90, 91-4, 97, 98, 111, 116, 121, 122, 129-33, 135-9
prohibition (CC 270.2) 80
sex industry, development in the law on 125-6

INDEX 731

'slave'/'slavery'
  CC 270.1 ('condition of person over whom ... powers attaching to the right of ownership are exercised') 80, 88-94, 109, 113-14, 129-32, 136
  'condition' of 92-3
  consent/absence of choice test 84, 90-4, 105-6, 107, 109-10, 125, 133-6, 138
  de jure vs de facto status as 89-94
  exploitation/harsh conditions of employment distinguished 87, 92, 95-6, 98, 108-9, 111, 118-19, 122, 123-4, 127-8
  Slavery Convention (1926) ('status or condition of a person over whom ... powers ... of ownership are exercised') (SC 1(1)) 88-94, 101-2, 105, 108, 113-14, 122, 129-32
  Slavery Convention (Supplementary Convention) (1956) 88-94, 101-2, 105
  'slave trading' (CC 270.3(3)) 81
  slavery offences (CC 270.3) 80-1
  'Slavery, the Slave Trade, and Other Forms of Servitude' (Report of UN Secretary-General (1953)) (list of powers of ownership) 90
  text 80-2
  treaties, implementing legislation/incorporation, interpretation
  language of treaty, divergence 92-3
  treaty as aid 92-3, 101-2, 105, 108, 113-14, 122-3

Bangalore Principles of Judicial Conduct (1989)
  international obligations as aid to interpretation [in case of ambiguity] 307, 308, 317-18, 323, 366
  primacy in case of conflict 323
  text (extracts) 366
BITs (bilateral investment treaties), South Africa–Zimbabwe BIT, failure to conclude 590-3, 655-8
Botswana, personal law, definition 313-14
Brundtland Report (2007) 443-4, 455-6

Canada
  admissibility of evidence
    evidence obtained in manner infringing human rights 144-211
    evidence obtained through search and seizure in breach of fundamental rights 144-211
    evidence obtained through search and seizure in third State 144-211
  Charter of Rights and Freedoms
    extraterritorial application, jurisprudence
      Cook 148, 150-1, 152, 165, 168-78, 181-2, 185, 188-9, 190-3, 195-8, 199-200, 202, 206, 207-11
      Hape 218, 220, 221, 236-7, 267
      Harrer 148, 149, 168-78, 179-80, 183-5, 192, 203-4, 206, 208, 211
      Khadr (2008) 232-3, 236-7, 240-1, 243-4, 246, 252, 265, 267-8, 270-1
      Schreiber 169-70, 175, 191, 198, 206, 211
      Suresh 244, 268
      Terry 148, 149, 150, 159, 166, 167, 168-78, 180, 185, 187, 189, 191, 192-3, 195, 206, 208
    extraterritorial application (s 7 (fundamental justice))
      applicability of divergent local law and standards 174-85, 198-211
      continued questioning of detainee by Canadian officers aware of previous torture as breach 243-7, 269-71, 272

Canada (*cont.*)
  ex post facto scrutiny 176-7, 205, 206-7
  fundamental justice (s 7) 144-211
  Guantánamo Bay Naval Base detainees (Canadian nationals) 214-24, 243-76
  non-Canadian officials outside Canada 167-78, 198
  extraterritorial application (s 8 (search and seizure)), *Hape* (search and seizure in Turks and Caicos) 185-211
  extraterritorial application (s 8 (search and seizure in third State)) 144-211
  extraterritorial jurisdiction, disclosure obligation 214-15, 216-24
  Guantánamo Bay Naval Base detainees (Canadian nationals): *see* Guantánamo Bay Naval Base detainees (Canadian), applicability of Charter of Rights and Freedoms *below*
  interpretation
    customary international law and 153-8
    presumption of conformity with international obligations 160-2
    principles vs rules approach 200-6
  Charter of Rights and Freedoms by section
    s 1 (rights and freedoms subject to reasonable limits prescribed by law), 'reasonable limits prescribed by law ... demonstrably justified in a free and democratic society' 247-8
    s 7 (right to life, liberty and security/fundamental justice), extraterritorial jurisdiction and: *see* Charter of Rights and Freedoms, extraterritorial application (s 7 (fundamental justice)) *above*
    s 8 (unreasonable search and seizure), undertaken outside Canada/extraterritorial 144-211
    s 11(d) (presumption of innocence), use of evidence obtained outside the jurisdiction and 150, 169, 176-7, 180-1, 183, 205-6
    s 24(1) (enforcement of guaranteed rights and freedoms) 149, 229
      applicability to extraterritorial activities 149, 181, 205, 210
      repatriation of Guantánamo Bay detainees, appropriateness as remedy 248-50, 259-64, 271-6
    s 24(2) (exclusion of evidence obtained in manner infringing Charter rights and freedoms) 144-211
    s 32(1) (applicability) 152-3
    text 142 n. 2, 152
  comity
    customary international law distinguished 159-60
    definition 158-60
    non-obligatory nature 158
    as principle of interpretation 158-60
    sovereign equality of States (UNC 2(1)) (*par in parem non habet jurisdictionem*) (with particular reference to extraterritorial jurisdiction) 158-60, 164-5, 167, 169, 175, 176, 178, 180-1, 188-9, 198, 203-5, 214-15, 218-20, 267
  Criminal Code 1970-85-87-94-97-01, offences 'deemed to have been committed' within territory (s 7) 167
  Criminal Code 1970-85-87-94-97-01 by section
    s 6(2) (territorial principle) 167
    s 269.1 (prohibition of torture by peace officer or public officer) 244-5
  customary international law 'as part of' municipal law
    automaticity 153-6
    compliance obligation 158
    conflict with legislation and 154
      legislation contrary to, right to adopt 155-6

INDEX 733

derogations ('reasonable limits prescribed by law as demonstrably justified in a free and democratic society') 247-8
disclosure obligation
 exculpatory disclosure 221-3
 Guantánamo Bay detainees and 214-24
 public interest privilege, balance of interests 223-4
extraterritorial effect of legislation
 clear intent/express provision, need for 153, 167
 examples of Canadian legislation 166-7
extraterritorial enforcement of legislation by legislating State
 applicable law 174-85, 198-211
 sovereign equality of States (UNC 2(1)) (*par in parem non habet jurisdictionem*) and 167-8, 171-3, 195-207
extraterritorial jurisdiction, right to life, liberty and security of person and 149, 150, 176-7, 180-1, 205-6, 242
foreign relations, responsibility for
 DFAIT Act 1985 provisions 241-2
 repatriation request 241-2, 251-2
fundamental justice, balance of interests 183-4, 188-9, 200-6
Guantánamo Bay Naval Base detainees (Canadian), applicability of Charter of Rights and Freedoms
 detention conditions as breach of international law, relevance 219-20
 diplomatic protection and 231-2, 235-6
 disclosure obligation (s 7 (fundamental justice)) 214-24
 repatriation, obligation to request 239-76
  appropriateness as remedy for breach of Charter (Charter 24(1)) 241-2, 248-50, 259-64, 271-6
  as responsibility of DFAIT 241-2, 251-2
 judicial review/justiciability (matters relating to foreign relations or prerogative power)
  jurisprudence, *Burns* 246-7, 274, 275
  repatriation of Guantánamo Bay detainees request, decision on 234-5, 236, 241-2, 251-2, 260-3, 264, 273-5
jurisdiction, 'deemed to have been committed' within territory 167
law of
 Controlled Drugs and Substances Act 1996, s 9 (money laundering) 144
 Crimes against Humanity and War Crimes Act 2000
  s 6(1) (universal jurisdiction) 166
  s 8 (nationality principle) 166
 Department of Foreign Affairs and International Trade (DFAIT) Act 1985 (including amendments), s 10 (powers and duties of Minister), text 241-2
 Evidence Act 1985, ss 38 *et seq.* (disclosure obligation: balance of interests) 223-4
 Geneva Conventions Act 1985 220
legislation, interpretation, presumption of conformity with international obligations 160-2
money-laundering, measures to prevent, search and seizure outside forum State/extraterritorial 144-211
nationality principle (jurisdiction over national for acts committed abroad)
 act committed abroad, concurrent territorial jurisdiction 171-2
 presence within the jurisdiction, need for 164
nexus for purposes of jurisdiction, extraterritorial criminal jurisdiction and 164-5
prescriptive/enforcement jurisdiction 162-5, 166, 174

Canada (*cont.*)
  presumption of innocence, use of evidence obtained outside the jurisdiction and 150, 169, 176-7, 180-1, 183, 205-6
  search and seizure on territory of third State ('extraterritorial')
    human/fundamental rights and
      divergent law and standards, relevance 174-85, 198-211
      ex post facto scrutiny of compliance 176-7, 205, 206-7
    prevention of international crime 144-211
    sovereign equality of States (UNC 2(1)) (*par in parem non habet jurisdictionem*) and 167-8, 195-207
      applicability of forum State law, relevance 197-8
      control of investigation by forum State officials, relevance 197
      cooperative investigation with local authorities, applicable rules 148-9, 151, 169, 176, 179, 185, 187-8, 189-91, 192-5
      initiation of investigation by forum State officials, relevance 196
  sovereign equality of States (UNC 2(1)) (*par in parem non habet jurisdictionem*)
    comity (with particular reference to extraterritorial jurisdiction) 158-60, 164-5, 167, 169, 175, 176, 178, 180-1, 188-9, 198, 203-5, 214-15, 218-20, 267
    as customary international law/general principle of international law 156-8
  territorial jurisdiction (criminal and tort) (including cross-border offences) 162-88
    applicable law, cross-border offences 178-85
    basis
      comity 159-60
      sovereign integrity/avoidance of infringement on third State 163
    objective territorial principle (State where injury occurred) vs subjective territorial principle (State where act took place) 163, 172
  torture or cruel, inhuman or degrading treatment or punishment (CRC 37(a)) 245, 251, 252, 256
  torture, definition/classification as
    Criminal Code 245
    'severe pain or suffering . . . intentionally inflicted . . . for such purposes as obtaining . . . information or a confession' (TC 1) 245
    sleep deprivation 234, 238-9, 240, 243-4, 251, 256, 259, 265, 271
  torture (municipal law/general)
    Criminal Code provisions 244-5
    prohibition on use to obtain information/evidence, third party torture 243-8
    Suresh 244
  universal jurisdiction, doctrine/theory, narrow ambit 164
CEDAW (1979), non-discrimination obligation (CEDAW 2(f)) 307
child rights
  'best interests of the child' obligation 301, 305-6, 320, 326
  marital status of parents, relevance 306-7, 309, 327-9
  parental responsibility
    ACC 20(1) 306
    CRC 18(1) 305-6
  jus cogens/peremptory norm considerations 314, 315-16
  personal law, whether 313-14
Child Rights Convention (1989)
  implementing legislation, need for 305

INDEX   735

non-discrimination obligation (CRC 2(1)) 305
  differential treatment, justification 320-3
  parental responsibility (CRC 18(1)) 305-6
  torture or other cruel, inhuman or degrading treatment or punishment (CRC 37(a)) 245,
    251, 252, 256
citizenship
  as human right 487-8
  rights appertaining to 487-8
comity
  customary international law distinguished 159-60
  definition 158-60
  non-obligatory nature 158
  as principle of interpretation 158-60
  source/norm of international law, whether 197
  sovereign equality of States (UNC 2(1)) (*par in parem non habet jurisdictionem*) (with
    particular reference to extraterritorial jurisdiction) 158-60, 164-5, 167, 169, 175,
    176, 178, 180-1, 188-9, 198, 203-5, 214-15, 218-20, 267
**compensation for failure to meet constitutional obligation to exercise diplomatic
  protection** 662-6
concession agreement
  applicable law
    law of State party 520
    parties' right to choose as principle of international law 518-19
confiscation, of ships contravening EEZ rules 49-50, 52-6, 66, 67-9, 70-2
constitution (State), alien, applicability to 347, 361-2
constitution (State), interpretation
  aids
    human rights treaties 677-84
    legislative history 682-3, 688-9
  guidelines/principles
    clear language/absence of ambiguity 316-17
    natural and ordinary sense 316-17
    text as a whole/avoidance of conflict 683-5, 712-16, 720
  international law and
    customary international law 153-8
    presumption of conformity [in absence of express counter-indication] 400-8
  jurisprudence
    Abuki 685, 704-5, 709, 717-18, 721
    El Mann 316-17, 318
    Ngobit 317
    Ssemogerere 677, 683, 712-13
  'living tree'/purposive principle 309, 311-12, 315, 318, 329
crimes against humanity, requirements
  actus reus
    as act or state of affairs 97
    commission of act proscribed under municipal law 88
  mens rea
    intentional exercise of powers leading to commission of crime 94-9, 101-12, 115-32
    jurisprudence, *Kunarac* 96

cruel and unusual treatment or punishment, classification as
death penalty: *see* death penalty as inhuman or degrading treatment *headings*
history of concept (British Bill of Rights/US Constitution) 686-8
customary international law 'as part of' municipal law
automaticity 153-6
compliance obligation 158
conflict of legislation and, legislation contrary to, right to adopt 155-6
incorporation/implementing legislation, need for
'assent', need for 528-9
implementation/adoption by court as 413-15
legislation duplicating existing common law 500-1
jurisprudence
Bouzari 155
Mack 155
Nduli 528
Reference re Foreign Legations 155
Reference re US Forces in Canadian Criminal Courts 155
The Ship 'North' 154-5
Trendtex 154
customary international law, evidence of, judicial decisions 417-18
customary international law, formation/requirements, general acceptance 528

death penalty, abolition (ICCPR, Second Optional Protocol) 680
death penalty as inhuman or degrading treatment (ICCPR 7)
conditions of detention and 715-17
incorporation of principle in municipal law 684
method, relevance 723
death penalty as inhuman or degrading treatment (municipal law/general) 672
customary international law and 384, 394-5, 413-18
hanging as method 672, 674-5, 703-6, 708-11, 718-20, 721-8
mandatory death penalty and 377-93, 395-418, 424-5, 672, 673, 687-8, 691-701
death penalty as inhuman or degrading treatment/torture (municipal law/general) 76-85, 671-5, 689, 691-3, 695-8, 703-28
death penalty, jurisprudence
Abuki 676, 704
Boyce 384-5, 386, 388, 393, 404
Catholic Commission for Peace and Justice 697, 698, 704, 711
Makwanyane 676, 690, 702, 703-4, 711
Mbushuu 676, 686, 691, 703, 704, 711
Mithu 389, 392, 396-8, 408-12, 417
Ng 679, 715-16, 720, 723
Nguyen 376-7, 379, 382, 383-7, 388-90, 393, 394-5, 398, 412, 415, 420-1
Ong Ah Chuan 376-7, 379, 380-3, 385-6, 387, 388-90, 393, 395, 396, 398-9, 408, 410, 412, 419, 421-2, 424
Reyes 384-7, 390, 397, 399-402, 404, 407
Soering 714-15
Watson 389, 484-6
death penalty (municipal law/general)
abolition, progressive, desirability 689-90
constitutionality 377

INDEX 737

as matter for determination by Constitutional Court 671-728
public opinion, relevance 692
separation of powers and 695-6
equality before the law and 418-25, 692-4, 716
history 677-83
international law norms including human rights treaties in general and 677-83
  absence of specific provision 677-9
procedural fairness/due process
  legal representation, right to 668 n. 7, 683-4, 693-4
  mandatory death penalty 376-418
  mitigating factors in determining penalty, right to plead 692, 694-5, 707
  prompt and public hearing before an independent tribunal 683-4, 689, 693-4, 700-1
State practice 415-17
UNESCO Resolution 1984/50 on safeguards guaranteeing protection of rights of those facing death penalty 681, 698-9, 705
death penalty (pardon/commutation/prerogative of mercy) (municipal law/general)
constitutional provisions 673, 674, 684, 695, 696, 699-701, 707
delay in exercise of/death-row syndrome 673, 674
right to seek
  human rights treaties provision for 698-9
  UNESCO Resolution 1984/50 on safeguards guaranteeing protection of rights of those facing death penalty 681, 698-9, 705
death penalty and the right to life (ICCPR 6), arbitrary deprivation of life, whether 678
death penalty and the right to life (municipal law/general), 'in accordance with the law' requirement 376-418
death penalty and the right to life (pardon/commutation/amnesty, right to seek) (ICCPR 6(4)), abolition of death penalty and 679
death row as inhuman or degrading treatment (ECHR 3)
conditions of detention and 714-15
Soering 714-15
death row as inhuman or degrading treatment/torture (municipal law/general) 672, 673, 697-703, 706-7, 710: *see also* death penalty (pardon/commutation/prerogative of mercy) (municipal law/general)
conditions of detention and 698-9, 714-17, 721-8
constitutionality 377-93, 395-418, 424-5
'reasonable' length of detention 701-3
repeated reading of death warrant 728
debt bondage: *see* slavery or forced labour, prohibition (including UDHR 4/ECHR 4)
Denmark, expropriation/nationalization, legality, requirements/relevant factors, due process/administrative propriety (rule of law), treaty provision 295
deportation/expulsion of alien, applicability to, prohibited immigrant 337-48
deportation/expulsion of alien, enforceability of expulsion order, impossibility of return to country of origin because of travel and documentary difficulties, effect on order 341-4
diplomatic protection, alternatives/supporting measures/means 491-3
BIT 591-2, 603-4
referral to ICSID, facilitation of 596, 603
diplomatic protection, concept and basis
as declining/residual concept, ICSID provisions and 596, 603
definition 484-5
  Diplomatic Protection, ILC Articles on (2000/2006) 484

diplomatic protection, concept and basis (*cont.*)
Dugard Report on Diplomatic Relations (2002) 484-6
foreign affairs considerations 498-507
human right, whether 497-8
intervention in the affairs of another State, whether 493
Diplomatic Protection, ILC Articles on (2000/2006)
'diplomatic protection', definition and scope 484
Dugard Report (2002) and 484-6
Dugard Report (2006) and 561-2
exhaustion of local administrative or judicial remedies 484-5
Diplomatic Protection, ILC Articles on (2000/2006) by article, Art. 11 (diplomatic protection of shareholders of company having nationality of State causing injury) 568-9
diplomatic protection, jurisprudence
Barcelona Traction 491-2, 512, 527, 569
Diallo 569 n. 54, 570 n. 58, 598
Kaunda 478, 484-5, 497-8, 505-6, 510, 513, 526, 529-30, 545, 557-9, 561, 616-20, 639-40, 653, 659
Mavrommatis 484, 563, 599
Nottebohm 568 n. 51, 597
diplomatic protection of
corporation incorporated in third State but controlled by nationals of protecting State, against country of nationality 527-8
corporation with nationality of protecting State, genuine link requirement 597-9
investment/investors
Van Zyl 478-576
Von Abo 581-666
shareholders in foreign corporation 528
genuine link requirement 597-9
injury to corporation and injury to shareholders distinguished 568-9
injury to shareholder, need for 528
diplomatic protection, requirements: *see also* nationality of claims with particular reference to nationality as the basis of the right to exercise diplomatic protection
acceptability of action when requirement not/not yet met 492-3
exhaustion of local administrative or judicial remedies: *see* exhaustion of local administrative or judicial remedies (diplomatic protection)
injury under international law/international delict, breach of minimum international standard of treatment/expropriation 497, 513-26, 528, 533, 545, 564-8, 600-2
diplomatic protection, right to/duty of State to provide
compensation for failure to carry out constitutional obligation 662-6
discretion/margin of appreciation 484-5, 491-4, 498-513
as exercise of State's own right 484-5
international investment and: *see* diplomatic protection of, investment/investors
judicial review/justiciability 557-71, 616-22
legitimate expectation and 533-4, 554
State's responsibility for conduct of foreign relations and 498-507
obligation to explain failure/refusal to exercise right including State responsibility for 594-6, 604, 605-16, 625-8, 632-43, 646-62
unlikelihood of favourable response to, relevance 665
under [customary] international law 507-13

under municipal law
  diligent performance of constitutional obligations requirement 487-9, 622
  fundamental rights (constitutional provisions) 486, 487-9, 616-22
disclosure obligation
  Guantánamo Bay detainees and 214-24
  public interest privilege, balance of interests 223-4
  self-discrimination/exculpatory disclosure and 221-3
drugs-trafficking
  money-laundering: *see* money-laundering, measures to prevent
  non-discrimination obligation/equality before the law, penalties based on minor differentials 418-25
  presumption of, constitutionality/fundamental rights and 380-2
due process, 'fair, just and reasonable' requirement 410-11

EEZ (UNCLOS 53-75 (Part V))
  enforcement of coastal State laws and regulations (UNCLOS 73)
    administrative proceedings 12, 37, 46-8, 66, 72
    criminal proceedings 13-17, 45-6, 48, 59, 65, 72, 73
    penalties (UNCLOS 73(3)), confiscation of vessel and 49-50, 52-6, 66, 67-9, 70-2
effective remedy before national authority, need for (ECHR 13), breach of ECHR right, need for 237
effective remedy before national authority, need for (ICCPR 2(3))
  appeal against refusal of work permit 359
  prohibited immigrant and 359
environmental impact assessment (EIA), need for
  activities which may have detrimental effect, legislative provision 429-31
  Gabčíkovo/Nagymaros Project 447-8, 456-7
  petrol filling station 429-72
environmental impact assessment (EIA), scope/requirements
  continuous nature 456-7
  cumulative effect/existing developments 438, 450, 453, 454-60, 463
  scoping report, definition 431 n. 13
  standard of assessment
    'real threat' 468-72
    risk averse and cautious approach 457-8
environmental protection obligations
  constitutional provision for 442, 443-4, 445-6
  Gauteng Guidelines (2002) 434, 455
  public participation 456
  sustainable development: *see* sustainable development principle
environmental protection/socio-economic interests, need to balance (integration principle) 431-2, 436-41, 442-62, 468-72
  Brundtland Report (2007) 443-4, 445-6
  responsibility for determining
    courts 463-4
    town planning vs environmental authorities 458-65, 466-7
  WSSD and 447
equality before the law (UDHR 7) 324
Eskimology, definition 290

exhaustion of local administrative or judicial remedies (diplomatic protection) 531-3, 570-1
  customary international law 532
  deficient or ineffective local machinery 533
  effective remedy, need for 570-1, 602-3
  jurisprudence
    Interhandel 531, 570
    Panevezys–Saldutiskis Railway 532
exhaustion of local administrative or judicial remedies (ECHR 35(1) [26/27(3)]), purpose, opportunity for State party to rectify situation 571
expropriation/nationalization, classification as/de facto
  breach of contract, distinguished 516-17
  restrictions on hunting and catches resulting from treaty 295
expropriation/nationalization, compensation
  customary international law 496
  prompt, just and effective compensation, obligation to pay, customary international law 496
expropriation/nationalization, legality, requirements/relevant factors, due process/administrative propriety (rule of law), treaty provision 295
expropriation/nationalization of property of national abroad, diplomatic protection and 497-8, 581-666
extraterritorial effect of legislation: *see also* territorial jurisdiction (criminal and tort) (including cross-border offences)
  clear intent/express provision, need for 153, 167
  examples of Canadian legislation 166-7
  Statute of Westminster 1931 166
extraterritorial enforcement of legislation by legislating State
  applicable law 174-85, 198-206
  jurisprudence
    Lotus 165-6
    Military and Paramilitary Activities (Nicaragua v. USA) 166
  sovereign equality of States (UNC 2(1)) (*par in parem non habet jurisdictionem*) and 167-8, 171-3, 195-207
extraterritorial jurisdiction, right to life, liberty and security of person and 149, 150, 176-7, 180-1, 205-6, 242

family life, respect for (ICCPR 17), refusal of work permit and 359
family life, respect for (municipal law/general)
  human dignity and 367-8
  work, right to and 367-8
family, right to found, UN Declaration on human rights of individuals who are not citizens of the country in which they live (1985) 364-5
fisheries, conservation and management measures (EEZ) (UNCLOS 61-8), monitoring/reporting obligations 27, 33-4
flag State
  change or loss of flag 54
  flag, right to determine right to (UNCLOS 91(1)) 54
foreign relations
  executive responsibility, diplomatic protection 498-507
  responsibility for, repatriation request 241-2, 251-2
freedom of movement, passport: *see* passport, freedom of movement and

Gabčíkovo/Nagymaros Project
environmental impact assessment 456-7
sustainable development and 447-8
General Comments (UNHRC), 18 (non-discrimination), differential treatment, requirements 324, 326
genuine link, need for: *see* diplomatic protection of, corporation with nationality of protecting State, genuine link requirement
Greenland
collective land rights tradition 286
law of, Home Rule Act 1978, s 8(1) (natural resources: fundamental right of resident population) 286
Guantánamo Bay, procedures as breach of international obligations 219-20
Guantánamo Bay Naval Base detainees
applicable law (non-US nationals), extraterritorial application of home State law 214-24, 243-76
diplomatic protection and, Khadr detention 231-2, 235-6
habeas corpus proceedings
disclosure of records provided by non-US investigating officers 214-24
exculpatory disclosure 221-3
jurisprudence
Boumediene 254, 268
Hamdan 219-20, 233, 239, 254, 267-8, 270
Khadr (2008) 232-3, 236-7, 240-1, 243-4, 246, 252, 265, 267-8, 270-1
Rasul 219, 239, 267-8
repatriation of non-US detainees 239-76
torture, sleep deprivation 234, 238-9, 240, 243-4, 251, 256, 259, 265, 271
Guantánamo Bay, US Presidential Order of 13 November 2001 (Detention, treatment and trial of certain non-citizens in the war against terrorism), 'military tribunals shall have exclusive jurisdiction . . . ' (s 7(b)(1)) 216-17

habeas corpus (other than USA), Geneva Conventions (1949) 219-20
The Hoshinmaru (**Japan v. Russian Federation**)
admissibility 19-21
amount and form of bond, Tribunal's decision 26-8
applications/submissions
correction 10
Japan 8, 9-10
Russia 8-9, 10
decisions of Tribunal 28-9
exhaustion of local administrative or judicial remedies 72-5
factual background 10-18
jurisdiction 18-19
monitoring/reporting obligations, failure to observe 27, 33-4
procedural history 5-10
reasonableness of bond 21-6
human/fundamental rights and freedoms (municipal law/general)
derogation/restrictions
balance of interests of State and individual 183-4, 188-9, 201-6
prescribed by law 247-8

human/fundamental rights and freedoms (municipal law/general) (*cont.*)
proportionality requirement 368
reasonable and necessary in a democratic society 247-8
indivisibility 369
inherent nature 693
human rights of individuals who are not citizens of the country in which they live, UN Declaration (1985), right to marry/found a family 364-5
human rights legislation, principles vs rules approach 200-6
human rights treaties
balance with public interest/national security 345
incorporation/implementing legislation, need for 400-12
continuity of treaties and 683

ICSID Convention (1965)
diplomatic protection and, as waiver of/replacement for 596
South·Africa, failure to join 586-90
immigration controls/procedures
discretionary powers 360
prohibited immigrant
deportation/expulsion of 337-48
refusal of entry permit 352-4, 356-7, 367
India, Constitution 1950 by article, Art. 21 (protection of life and liberty) 411
indigenous people: *see* Thule Tribe (Greenland), compensation claim for 1953 Dundas Area resettlement
Indigenous and Tribal Peoples in Independent Countries (ILO Convention No 169) (1989)
coordinated and systematic action to protect rights, governments' responsibility for (ILO No 169 2(1)) 285-6
dispute settlement procedures, obligation to establish (ILO No 169 14(3)) 286
ILO's monitoring role 285
peoples in independent countries regarded as indigenous on account of descent from populations at time of conquest or colonization who retain some or all of their own institutions (ILO No 169 1(1)(b)) 292-3, 296
right to return to traditional lands once grounds for relocation cease (ILO No 169 16(3)) 281, 286-7
expropriation, effect 295-6
provision of lands of equal status to those previously occupied or compensation (ILO No 169 16(4)) 286-7
self-identification as indigenous or tribal (ILO No 169 1(2)) 285
traditional lands, governments' obligation to identify and to guarantee protection (ILO No 169 14(2)) 285-6
transmission of land rights, respect for established procedures (ILO No 169 17(1)) 286
tribal peoples in independent countries whose social, cultural and economic conditions distinguish them . . . from national community (ILO No 169 1(1)(a)) 284-5, 288-92, 293-4, 296
individual in international law, diplomatic protection and 486-91
inhuman or degrading treatment (ICCPR 7), death penalty: *see* death penalty as inhuman or degrading treatment (ICCPR 7)

INDEX 743

integration principle: *see* environmental protection/socio-economic interests, need to balance (integration principle)
intergenerational rights and responsibilities: *see also* sustainable development principle
  municipal law provisions 449, 455-6, 471
  as principle of sustainable development 446-7
International Covenant on Economic, Social and Cultural Rights (ICESCR) (1966)
  applicability, alien 366-7, 370-1
  foundational nature of rights 369-70
  progressive realization (ICESCR preamble) 369-71
international delict, breach of minimum international standard of treatment/ expropriation as 497, 513-26, 528, 533, 545, 564-8, 600-2
intragenerational equity/equitable sharing of resources, sustainable development principle and 446-7, 449, 455-6, 471 n. 12
Inughuit: *see* Thule Tribe (Greenland), compensation claim for 1953 Dundas Area resettlement
ITLOS, Rules of the Tribunal
  45 6, 7, 41, 42
  63(1) 6, 7, 42
  64(3) 6, 7, 42
  65(4) 7
  67(2) 7, 42
  71 7
  73 6, 7, 41, 42
  110 19
  111 19
  111(4) 6, 41
  112(3) 6

Japan–Russia Fisheries Commission 27
  agreed minute/Protocol, effect 23-4
judicial review/justiciability (matters relating to foreign relations or prerogative power)
  diplomatic protection: *see* diplomatic protection, right to/duty of State to provide, judicial review/justiciability
  immigration authorities 360
  jurisprudence
    Bentley 503
    Council of Civil Service Unions (CSSU) 502-3
    Ferhut Butt 506-7
    Hugo 503-4
    Kaunda 505-6, 616-20
    Operation Dismantle 504-5
    Pirbhai 507
  material failure requirement 467-72
  planning authorization 442, 467-72
  police powers 360-1
  repatriation of Guantánamo Bay detainees request, decision on 234-5, 236, 241-2, 251-2, 260-3, 264, 273-5
***jus cogens*/peremptory norm**, derogation, prohibition 314, 315-16

Kenya
age discrimination, prohibition, omission from legislation 309
alien, rights and obligations
  protection of the constitution 310-11, 361-2
  respect for laws of receiving State 365
child rights
  parental responsibility
    ACC 20(1) 306
    jus cogens/peremptory norm considerations 314, 315-16
    personal law, whether 313-14
  Children Act No 8 2001
    African Children's Charter (1990), as implementation of 301, 312-13
    CEDAW (1979) and 306-7
    Child Rights Convention (1989), as implementation of 305, 312-13
    Constitution s 82(2) and 301
  Children Act No 8 2001 by section
    s 5 (non-discrimination obligation)
      birth and status, inclusion 316
      Constitution 82(3) distinguished 316
    s 24 (parental responsibility), text 304
    s 24(3) (parental responsibility for child born out of wedlock), whether discriminatory 301-30
    constitutionality 310-11, 319-20, 329-30
    CRC 2 and 3 and 301
    s 25 (parental responsibility of father for child born out of wedlock), text 304
Constitution (1963 with amendments prior to adoption of 2010 constitution), alien, applicability to 347, 361-2
Constitution (1963 with amendments prior to adoption of 2010 constitution) by section
  s 70(a) (life, liberty, security of person and protection of the law)
    illegal immigrant/refugee, applicability to 336, 345-6
    text 336
  s 71 (right to life) 369
  s 72(1) (liberty of person), passport as part of the right to 359-60, 363, 372
  s 74(1) (torture or inhumane treatment or degrading punishment) 359, 361-3
  s 75(1) (compulsory taking of property: prohibition), deprivation of passport and travel documents and 359-60, 363, 372
  s 81(1) (freedom of movement), passport and 363
  s 82(2) (discrimination in performance of public officer or authority)
    Children Act 2001 and 301, 316
    judicial enlargement of categories, rejection as judicial activism 316-17
  s 82(4)(b) (discriminatory legislation: exclusion with respect to adoption, marriage, divorce, burial, devolution of property on death or other matters of personal law) 315
  s 84(1) (right of individual redress/representative actions: exclusion) 309, 314, 335-6
    precise indication of rights allegedly contravened, need for 308, 309, 336
  s 123 (definitions), 'person' 314-15
Constitution, interpretation
  guidelines/principles
    clear language/absence of ambiguity 316-17
    natural and ordinary sense 316-17

INDEX 745

jurisprudence: *see* constitution (State), interpretation, jurisprudence
'living tree'/purposive principle 311-12, 315, 318, 329
deportation/expulsion of alien, applicability to, prohibited immigrant 337-8
deportation/expulsion of alien, enforceability of expulsion order, impossibility of return to
    country of origin because of travel and documentary difficulties, effect on order 341-4
effective remedy before national authority, need for (ICCPR 2(3))
  appeal against refusal of work permit 359
  prohibited immigrant and 359
family life, respect for (ICCPR 17), refusal of work permit and 359
family life, respect for (municipal law/general)
  human dignity and 367-8
  work, right to and 367-8
family, right to found, UN Declaration on human rights of individuals who are not citizens
    of the country in which they live (1985) 364-5
human/fundamental rights and freedoms (municipal law/general), indivisibility 369
human rights of individuals who are not citizens of the country in which they live, UN
    Declaration (1985)
  alien's obligation to observe laws of home State 365
  right to marry/found a family 364-5
human rights treaties 336-41, 345
  balance with public interest/national security 345
  incorporation/implementing legislation, need for 400-12
ICESCR rights
  alien and 366-7, 370-1
  direct effect 369-71
  foundational nature 369-70
  progressive realization (ICESCR preamble) 369-71
Immigration Act 1967 (including amendments), constitutionality of s 3 (prohibited
    immigrants) and s 8 (removal of person unlawfully present) 335, 337-8
Immigration Act 1967 (including amendments) by section
  s 3 (prohibited immigrants)
    constitutionality 337-8
    text (extracts) 337
  s 5(1) (classes of entry permit) 353
  s 5(2) (issue of entry permit to non-prohibited immigrant) 353
    as discretionary act 353-4, 356-7
  s 5(3) (appeal against refusal of entry permit) 353
  s 8 (removal of person unlawfully present) 353
    constitutionality 337-8
    text (extracts) 337-8
immigration controls/procedures
  discretionary powers 360
  prohibited immigrant
    deportation/expulsion of 337-48
    refusal of entry permit 352-4, 356-7, 367
judicial review/justiciability (matters relating to foreign relations or prerogative power)
  immigration authorities 360
  police powers 360-1
jus cogens/peremptory norm, derogation, prohibition 314, 315-16
law of, Police Act, s 14 (functions of police force) 360-1

Kenya (*cont.*)
law and order, responsibility for, discretionary powers 360-1
legislation, interpretation, aids
  context, social and economic 309, 311-12, 315
  dictionary 308
legislation, interpretation, presumption of conformity with international obligations
  Bangalore Principles (1989) 307, 308, 317-18, 323, 366
  clear meaning of legislation and 307
national security defence
  admissibility, responsibility for determining 372-3
  work permit, right to refuse 368
non-discrimination obligation (CRC 2(1)), differential treatment, justification/grounds 320-3
non-discrimination obligation (UDHR) 323-5
non-discrimination obligation/equality before the law (municipal law/general)
  age, relevance 309
  derogations, 'personal law' 313-14, 315
  differential treatment, justification, child rights 320-3
  differential treatment, justification/grounds
    non-arbitrary distinction 320-1
    reasonableness 320-3
  marital status, relevance 306-7, 309, 327-9
  of public officer or authority (Constitution 82(2)) 301
passport
  freedom of movement and 359-60, 363, 372
  'property' of holder, whether 359-60, 363, 372
personal law
  child rights and 313-14
  definition (with reference to Constitution 82(4)(b)) 313-14, 315
refugee status, determination/verification, procedural requirements, public interest/interests of individual, balance 345-8
refugees, unlawful entry or presence, non-penalization (RC 31(1)), failure to comply with immigration/entry requirements and 345-8
res judicata/non bis in idem principle (including double jeopardy rule), identity of subject matter, need for 354-6
torture or cruel, inhuman or degrading treatment or punishment (municipal law/general), derogation, exclusion 671-7, 684-5, 689, 691-2, 696-8, 703-28
torture (ICCPR 7), burden/standard of proof 362-3
torture (municipal law/general), alien and 359, 361-3
treaties, direct effect/self-executing, ICESCR (1966) 369-71
treaties, implementing legislation/incorporation
  margin of appreciation 312-13, 317, 327-30
  need for/examples of
    human rights treaties 400-12
    ICESCR 369-70
treaties, implementing legislation/incorporation, interpretation
  primacy in case of conflict 314, 317, 323
    Bangalore Principles (1989) 323
women, 'personal law', applicability 313-14
work permit, right to refuse 367

INDEX 747

national security and 368
proportionality requirement 368
work, right to
 ACHPR 15 365
 Constitution and 355, 364, 365, 369, 371
 family life and 367-8
 ICESCR 6 355, 360, 363-4, 365, 369

law and order, responsibility for, discretionary powers 360-1
Law of the Sea Convention (1982): Part XV: Section 2 (settlement of disputes: compulsory procedures entailing binding decisions: jurisdiction (UNCLOS 288)), prompt release proceedings: *see* prompt release of vessels and crews, jurisdiction (UNCLOS 292(1))
Law of the Sea Convention (1982): Part XV: Section 2 (settlement of disputes: compulsory procedures entailing binding decisions: procedural matters), admissibility, prompt release proceedings (Art. 292): *see* prompt release of vessels and crews (UNCLOS 292 proceedings), procedural issues/nature of proceedings, admissibility
legislation, constitutionality, presumption of 318-20
legislation, interpretation, aids
 context, social and economic 309, 311-12, 315
 dictionary 308
legislation, interpretation, guidelines
 ordinary and natural meaning 130-1
 text/literal approach 111, 122-3
legislation, interpretation, presumption of
 conformity with international law 122-3
 conformity with international obligations 160-2
  Bangalore Principles (1989) 307, 308, 317-18, 323, 366
  clear meaning of legislation and 307
 constitutionality 318-20
Lesotho
 Constitution 1966, s 139 ('law') 522
 law of
  Deeds Registry Act 1967 514
  Highlands Development Authority (Amendment) Act 5 of 1995 516-17, 524
   full and prompt compensation 525-6
  Highlands Development Authority (validation of activities) Act 6 of 1995 524, 526, 550
  Mining Rights Act 1967 549, 566-7
   s 1 (definitions) 522
   s 6 (grant of mineral title) 514, 522, 547
   s 15 522, 547
life, right to (ACHPR 4), death penalty and 681
life, right to (ICCPR 6)
 arbitrary deprivation (ICCPR 6(1)) 678
 death penalty and: *see* death penalty and the right to life (ICCPR 6)
life, right to (municipal law/general), derogation, possibility of 685, 689, 691-2, 708-10, 712, 713, 717-20

measure of damages/compensation including valuation of company/property/assets, relevant factors, hunting and fishing losses/increased costs 296-7

money-laundering, measures to prevent, search and seizure in third State/extraterritorial 144-211

national security defence, admissibility, responsibility for determining, ministerial affidavit 372-3
nationality of claims with particular reference to nationality as the basis of the right to exercise diplomatic protection 487-8, 526-31
 continuity of nationality, cession of rights covered by claim to person having nationality of protecting State 527-8, 569-70
 diplomatic protection as right of citizenship 487-9, 619-20
 genuine link requirement 597-9
nationality of corporation, citizenship, right to 330
nationality principle (jurisdiction over national for acts committed abroad)
 act committed abroad, concurrent territorial jurisdiction 171-2
 presence within the jurisdiction, need for 164
natural resources, equitable sharing/intragenerational equity: *see* intragenerational equity/equitable sharing of resources
natural resources, UNGA resolutions relating to, 3201 (S-VI) (Declaration on the Establishment of a New International Economic Order (NIEO)) 496
Netherlands, law of, Military Penal Code, Art. 4 (applicability of Penal Code to offences committed by members of armed forces abroad) 194-5
nexus for purposes of jurisdiction, extraterritorial criminal jurisdiction and 164-5
non-discrimination obligation, child rights: *see* African Children's Charter (1990) (ACC); Child Rights Convention (1989), non-discrimination obligation (CRC 2(1))
non-discrimination obligation (ECHR 14), jurisprudence, *Belgian Linguistic Case* 317
non-discrimination obligation (UDHR 2) 324
non-discrimination obligation/equality before the law (municipal law/general)
 derogations, 'personal law' 313-14, 315
 differential treatment, justification/grounds
  child rights 320-3
  requirements
   non-arbitrary distinction 320-1
   reasonableness 320-3
 drugs-trafficking, penalties based on minor differentials 418-25
 judicial enlargement of categories, rejection as judicial activism 316-17
non-discrimination obligation/equality before the law (UNHRC General Comment 18), differential treatment, requirements, legitimate aim 324, 326

passport
 deprivation by authorities
  compulsory taking of property, whether 359-60, 363, 372
  liberty of the person and 359-60, 363, 372
 freedom of movement and 359-60, 363, 372
 liberty of the person and 359-60, 363, 372
 'property' of holder, whether 359-60, 363, 372
personal law
 child rights and 313-14
 definition 313-14, 315
precautionary principle, EIAs and 457-8
precedent in municipal courts, decisions of human rights tribunals 714-17, 722-3

INDEX 749

prescriptive/enforcement jurisdiction 162-5, 166, 174
presumption of innocence (municipal law/general), use of evidence obtained outside the jurisdiction and 150, 169, 176-7, 180-1, 183, 205-6
procuring: *see* slavery or forced labour, prohibition (including UDHR 4/ECHR 4)
prompt release of vessels and crews, jurisdiction (UNCLOS 292(1)) 18-19
    agreement to submit to another court or tribunal and 19
    'detention' of crew 21-2, 29-30
    determination/declaration of non-compliance with Art. 73(2) 19
        limitation to 20-1, 31
    terms and conditions of release, exclusion 20
prompt release of vessels and crews on posting of reasonable bond or financial security (UNCLOS 73(2))
    applicability, administrative proceedings 66-7
    'bond or other financial security'
        agreement of parties on form/procedure, need for 23-4
        bank guarantee 27-8
        as criminal law concept 30
    jurisprudence
        Camouco 22, 29, 30-1, 32
        Juno Trader 22-3, 31, 74-5
        Monte Confurco 22, 35, 55, 57-8
        Volga 22, 35
    legislative provisions, in Russia 17-18, 58-60
    purpose/basis of provision
        balance between interests of coastal State and flag State 30
        as guarantee of return to court 30
    'reasonable'
        determination as responsibility of Tribunal 20
        relevant factors 22-6
            gravity of offence/proportionality 22, 24-5, 29, 30-1, 34-5
            value of ship 23-4, 25-6
    time-limits for setting of bond 21-2, 31-3
prompt release of vessels and crews (UNCLOS 292 proceedings), procedural issues/nature of proceedings
    additional statements 9
    admissibility
        alleged non-compliance with Art. 73(2), need for 19, 51-2
        critical date 20
        exhaustion of local administrative or judicial remedies, need for 72-5
        mootness and 20, 54-6, 69-70
    confiscation of vessel, effect 49-50, 52-6, 70-1
    municipal court proceedings and
        due process requirement 56, 69
        'without prejudice to the merits of any case before the appropriate domestic forum' (UNCLOS 292(3)) 52-6, 57-8, 68-9
    specific complaint, need for 20, 69
    time-limit for application, 'without delay' 58, 67-9
property, arbitrary deprivation/interference with, prohibition (international norms other than specific treaty provisions) 494-7
    as human rights norm 494-6
    lawful deprivation 494-6

property, definition/classification as, future or contingent interest, responsibility for 414-15
property, real/immovable, applicable law, *lex situs* 493-4, 519
property, right to (ACHPR 14), encroachment 'in accordance with the appropriate laws' 495
property, right to (ACHR 21), as human rights norm 495
property, right to (ICCPR), absence of specific provision 496-7
property, right to (ICESCR), absence of specific provision 496-7

refugee status, determination/verification, procedural requirements, public interest/interests of individual, balance 345-8
Refugees in Africa Convention (1969)
  regional complement to Refugees Convention (1951) (CARPA 8) 345
  voluntary repatriation (CARPA 5) 345
refugees, unlawful entry or presence, non-penalization (RC 31(1)), failure to comply with immigration/entry requirements and 345-8
repatriation of refugees, CARPA 5 345
res judicata/non bis in idem **principle (including double jeopardy rule)**, identity of subject matter, need for 354-6
restitutio in integrum, as measure of damages/compensation, customary international law 496
Rio Declaration on Environment and Development (1992), sustainable development principle 446
Rome Statute (1998), 'enslavement' 89
Russian Federation (1991-)
  EEZ, enforcement of coastal State laws and regulations (UNCLOS 73)
    administrative proceedings 12, 37, 46-8, 66, 72
    criminal proceedings 13-17, 45-6, 48, 59, 65, 72, 73
  fisheries laws and regulations
    Anadromous Stocks Regulations, text (extracts) 13-14
    Criminal Code (Art. 253(2): exploitation of natural resources in EEZ without permission) 45-6
      text 46
    Criminal Code (Art. 256: illegal fishing with grave damage and use of self-propelled transport) 13-14
      text 16
    EEZ Law No 191-FZ of 17 December 1998 (Art. 12(2)), text 14
    Wildlife Law No 52-FZ of 24 April 1995 13-14
      text 15-16
  law of
    Administrative Offences Code
      Art. 8.17(2) (violation of fishing rules) 12-13, 46-7, 49-50
      Art. 29.10(3) (disposal of seized items and documents) 48-9
    Criminal Procedure Code, Art. 82 (material evidence) 46
  prompt release of vessels and crews on posting of reasonable bond or financial security (UNCLOS 73(2))
    applicability, administrative proceedings 66-7
    complexity of procedures 58-9
    due process requirement 56, 69

search and seizure outside forum State: *see* money-laundering, measures to prevent, search and seizure in third State/extraterritorial

INDEX 751

search and seizure on territory of third State ('extraterritorial')
human/fundamental rights and
divergent law and standards, relevance 174-85, 198-211
ex post facto scrutiny of compliance 176-7, 205, 206-7
prevention of international crime and 144-211
sovereign equality of States (UNC 2(1)) (*par in parem non habet jurisdictionem*) and 167-8, 195-207
applicability of forum State law, relevance 197-8
control of investigation by forum State officials, relevance 197
cooperative investigation with local authorities, applicable rules 148-9, 151, 169, 176, 179, 185, 187-8, 189-91, 192-5
initiation of investigation by forum State officials, relevance 196
separation of powers, mandatory death sentence and 695-6
ships, nationality (including UNCLOS 91)
confiscation of ship for breach of fisheries legislation, effect 54, 71-2
registration (flag State), relevance 54
right to determine (UNCLOS 91(1)), State's exclusive jurisdiction 54
Singapore
Constitution 1963 (including amendments)
ECHR provisions, exclusion 402-3
Malaysian Constitution as basis 402-3
Constitution 1963 (including amendments) by article
Art. 2(1) (definitions) ('law') 379-82
'custom or usage' 379-80
customary international law 379-80, 384, 394-5, 413-18
'written law' 379-80
Art. 9(1) (right to life and personal liberty: due process/'in accordance with the law' requirement) 376-418
'fair, just and reasonable' requirement 410-11
text 379
Art. 12(1) (equality before the law/judicial protection) 376-9, 418-25
constitution, interpretation, presumption of conformity with international obligations [in absence of express counter-indication] 400-8
customary international law 'as part of' municipal law, incorporation/ implementing legislation, need for, implementation/adoption by court as 413-15
customary international law, evidence of, judicial decisions 417-18
death penalty as inhuman or degrading treatment (municipal law/general)
customary international law and 384, 394-5, 413-18
mandatory death penalty and 377-93, 395-418, 424-5
death penalty, jurisprudence
Nguyen 376-7, 379, 382, 383-7, 388-90, 393, 394-5, 398, 412, 415, 420-1
Ong Ah Chuan 376-7, 379, 380-3, 385-6, 387, 388-90, 393, 395, 396, 398-9, 408, 410, 412, 419, 421-2, 424
death penalty (municipal law/general)
constitutionality 377
continuity of law relating to 411-12
equality before the law and 418-25
procedural fairness/due process (mandatory death penalty) 376-418
State practice, relevance 415-17

Singapore (*cont.*)
death penalty and the right to life (municipal law/general), 'in accordance with the law' requirement 376-418
drugs-trafficking
Misuse of Drugs Act (MDA)
constitutionality (equality before the law) 418-25
constitutionality (right to life and liberty) 379-418
as 'law' 379-80
Misuse of Drugs Act (MDA) by section
s 5(2) (presumption of trafficking) 380-3
s 17 (presumption of trafficking), constitutionality/fundamental rights and 380-3
s 33 and Schedule 2 (punishments) 376-7
ECHR
applicability prior to independence (1963/1965) 402
omission of provisions from Constitution 402-3
law of, Penal Code, s 302 (murder: mandatory death penalty) (adopted 1883) 411-12
torture or cruel, inhuman or degrading treatment or punishment, rejection of proposal for inclusion in constitution (Wee Commission (1966)) 403-8
Wee Constitutional Commission (1966) 403-8
slave trade, definition 81
slavery or forced labour, prohibition (including UDHR 4/ECHR 4): *see also* Australia, slavery, sexual servitude and deceptive recruiting (CC 270)
actus reus
commission of act proscribed under municipal law 88, 136
as act or state of affairs 97
burden/standard of proof 86-7, 90, 98-9, 103-12, 114, 127-8
'chattel slavery' 78 n. 6, 87-8, 90-4, 95, 111
as crime against humanity 90-1
Criminal Code Amendment (Slavery and Sexual Servitude) Act 1999 (repealing Imperial Acts relating to slavery) 80
criminal responsibility (general principles) and 81-3, 94-9, 100-4, 114, 116, 127-8
debt bondage 81, 91, 108, 124-5
description of practice 84-7
debt or contract, relevance 84-7, 90, 92-4, 97, 109, 110-11, 137
jurisprudence
Kozminski 135
Kunarac 90-1, 93-4
Mussry 134-5
Shackney 133-4
Siliadin 91-2
mens rea
intentional exercise of powers resulting in condition of slavery 94-9, 101-12, 115-32
knowledge of basis of powers, relevance 94-9
municipal law provisions 80
overlapping nature of offences/definitions 77 n. 3, 91
penalty, relevance 81, 123
possessing/using a slave 79-139
sex industry, development in the law on 125-6
'slave'/'slavery'
consent/absence of choice test 84, 90-4, 105-6, 107, 109-10, 125, 133-6, 138

INDEX 753

customary international law 105
de jure vs de facto status as 89-94
exploitation/harsh conditions of employment distinguished 87, 92, 95-6, 98, 108-9, 111, 118-19, 122, 123-4, 127-8
municipal law 80, 88, 92-3, 97-8, 109, 113-14, 129-32, 136
'powers of *ownership*'/'in possession' 88, 89-90, 91-4, 97, 98, 111, 116, 121, 122, 129-33, 135-9
'Slavery, the Slave Trade, and Other Forms of Servitude' (Report of UN Secretary-General (1953)) (list of powers of ownership) 90
'status or condition of a person over whom . . . powers . . . of ownership are exercised' (SC 1(1)) 88-94, 101-2, 105, 108, 113-14, 122, 129-32
US Constitution, Thirteenth Amendment 133-5
slavery offences 81
slavery, sexual servitude and deceptive recruiting 79-139
trafficking in persons and 123-4
slavery, treaties and other international instruments relating to in date order
Brussels Conference 1889-90, General Act 88
Treaty of St-Germain-en-Laye (1919) 88
Slavery Convention (1926): *see also* slavery or forced labour, prohibition (including UDHR 4/ECHR 4), 'slave'/'slavery', 'status or condition of a person over whom . . . powers . . . of ownership are exercised' (SC 1(1))
implementing legislation/incorporation 87-8, 108, 113-14, 122
object and purpose 89-90
travaux préparatoires 89
Supplementary Convention on the Abolition of Slavery (1956) 89, 101-2
Rome Statute (1998) 89
sources of international law (ICJ 38)
judicial and arbitral decisions (ICJ 38(1)(d))
mandatory death penalty 417-18
subsidiary nature 417-18
teachings of publicists (ICJ 38(1)(d))
mandatory death penalty 417-18
subsidiary nature 417-18
South Africa
admissibility of evidence (municipal law/general), hearsay evidence, as recorded in affidavit 593-6
BITS (Zimbabwe)
failure to sign 590-3, 655-8
failure to give reasons 591-2
citizenship: *see also* nationality *below*
as human right 487-8
rights appertaining to 487-8
compensation for failure to meet constitutional obligation to exercise diplomatic protection 662-6
concession agreement
applicable law
law of State party 520
parties' right to choose as principle of international law 518-19
Constitution Act 108 of 1996 (including amendments) by section, Chapter 1 (Founding Provisions)

South Africa (*cont.*)
s 3 (citizenship)
corporations and 530
text 487 n. 19, 618
s 3(2)(a) (citizens: equal entitlement to rights, privileges and benefits of citizenship), diplomatic protection and 487-9, 619-20
Constitution Act 108 of 1996 (including amendments) by section, Chapter 2 (Bill of Rights)
s 7 (Rights), text 619
s 7(2) (obligation to respect, protect, promote and fulfil Bill of Rights), extraterritorial applicability/right to diplomatic protection 486, 617, 618-22
s 24 (right to environment), text 443, 466 n. 1
s 24(b)(iii) (sustainable development principle) 443-4, 455-6
s 25(2) (expropriation) 487
text 487 n. 18
s 38 (enforcement of rights) 620
s 39(3) (consistent rights and freedoms under common law, customary law or legislation) 500-1
Constitution Act 108 of 1996 (including amendments) by section, Chapter 5 (President and National Executive)
s 83(a) (President as head of State/National Executive) 499, 586
s 83(c) (President's obligation to promote unity of nations) 499
s 84(1) (Presidential powers) 499, 500, 586
s 84(2) (powers and functions of President) 500, 636
text 636 n. 19
s 85(1) (executive authority of President) 499, 586
s 85(2)(a-d) (functions of President) 499
s 85(2)(e) (functions of President) 499, 637
judicial review, exclusion 502
text 637 n. 22
s 91 (Cabinet) 592, 637
text 637 n. 23
s 92(1) (accountability of Ministers) 639-40
s 92(3) (Cabinet members: obligation to act in accordance with Constitution) 637-8
text 638 n. 25
s 93 (Deputy Ministers) 592
Constitution Act 108 of 1996 (including amendments) by section, Chapter 8 (Courts and Administration of Justice)
s 165(4) (obligation of organs of State to protect independence of courts) 592
s 167(4) (Constitutional Court: exclusive jurisdiction) 633
s 167(4)(e) (Constitutional Court: exclusive jurisdiction: failure to fulfil constitutional obligation) 633, 635-7
s 167(5) (Constitutional Court: final authority on constitutionality) 632-9
s 172(1)(b) (constitutional matters: court's power to make any order that is just and equitable) 620-2
s 172(2)(a) (order of constitutional invalidity) 622, 625, 628, 629-30, 631-43, 645-6
text 624 n. 1, 631
s 173 (inherent right of court to regulate own procedures) 480, 481-2
Constitution Act 108 of 1996 (including amendments) by section, Chapter 14 (general provisions)

INDEX 755

s 232 (customary international law as law in the Republic) 488, 500, 622
s 237 (diligent performance of obligations) 487-9, 622
Constitutional Court, jurisdiction, 'any conduct of the President' 632-43
Constitutional Court Rules, r 16 (order of unconstitutionality: procedure), text 624 n. 2
'constitutional matter', President's conduct in relation to diplomatic protection 632-43
customary international law 'as part of' municipal law 488
customary international law, formation/requirements, general acceptance 528
death penalty, jurisprudence, *Makwanyane* 676, 690, 702, 703-4, 711
death row as inhuman or degrading treatment/torture (municipal law/general) 672, 673, 697-703, 706-7, 710
diplomatic protection, alternatives/supporting measures/means 491-3
 BIT 591-2, 603-4
 referral to ICSID, facilitation of 596, 603
diplomatic protection, concept and basis
 as declining/residual concept, ICSID provisions and 596, 603
 human right, whether 497-8
 intervention in the affairs of another State, whether 493
diplomatic protection of
 corporation
  against country of nationality 527-8
  genuine link requirement 597-9
 investment/investors
  Van Zyl 478-576
  Von Abo 581-666
 shareholders in foreign company, injury to shareholder, need for 528
 shareholders in foreign corporation, genuine link requirement 597-9
diplomatic protection, requirements, injury under international law/international delict,
  breach of minimum international standard of treatment/expropriation 497, 513-26, 528, 533, 545, 564-8, 600-2
diplomatic protection, right to/duty of State to provide
 compensation for failure to carry out constitutional obligation 662-6
 discretion/margin of appreciation 484-5, 491-4, 498-513
 failure to press Zimbabwe for failure to delist properties of SADC-Member State nationals 592-3, 646-62
 human rights/treaty violations and 497-8
 judicial review/justiciability 557-71, 616-22
  legitimate expectation and 533-4, 554
  State's responsibility for conduct of foreign relations and 498-507
 obligation to explain failure/refusal to exercise right including State responsibility for 594-6, 604, 605-16, 625-8, 632-43, 646-62
  unlikelihood of favourable response to, relevance 665
 President's responsibility for 624-45
 under customary international law 507-13
 under municipal law, diligent performance of constitutional obligations requirement 487-9, 622
EIA, need for
 activities which may have detrimental effect (NEMA 2(4)(1)) 429-31
 petrol filling station (Mpumalanga) 429-72
EIA, scope/requirements (scoping report), definition 431 n. 13
Environment Conservation Act 1989 (ECA)

756   INDEX

South Africa (*cont.*)
  s 2(4)(i) (EIAs) 430-1
  s 21 (detrimental activities)
    integration principle (NEMA 23(2)(a)) and 456
    petrol filling station as 430
    priority of peoples' interests principle (NEMA 2(2)) and 455-6
    sustainable development principle (NEMA 24(7)(b)) and 454-5
    text 430 n. 2
  s 21 (detrimental activities: relevant considerations)
    cumulative effects (NEMA 24(7)(b)) 456
    risk averse and cautious approach (NEMA 2(4)(a)(vii)) 457-8
  s 22 (authorization of ECA s 21(1) activity)
    judicial review of authorization under 442
    limited duration of authorization 462
    rezoning and 439-40
    socio-economic considerations and 437-8, 440-1, 453
    text 429 n. 4
  s 26 (scope and content of EIA) 431 n. 13
  s 36 (right to request reasons for decision), text 435 n. 18
  environmental impact assessment (EIA), scope/requirements
    continuous nature 456-7
    standard of assessment
      'real threat' 468-72
      risk averse and cautious approach 457-8
  environmental legislation/regulation other than ECA: *see also* Constitution Act 108 of 1996 by section, Chapter 2 (Bill of Rights), s 24 (right to environment) *above*
    Gauteng Guidelines (2002) 434, 455
    NEMA 1998 (National Environmental Management Act): *see* NEMA 1998 (National Environmental Management Act) *below*
    Town-Planning and Townships Ordinance 1986, s 56 (application procedure), text 439 n. 30
    Town-Planning and Townships Ordinance 1986 Regulations, Schedule VII (specimen application form)
      'need and desirability' test (Part C(c)) 431, 434, 436-41, 458-62
      text 436 n. 21
  environmental protection obligations, public participation 456
  environmental protection/socio-economic interests, need to balance (integration principle) 431-2, 436-41, 442-62, 468-72
    responsibility for determining
      courts 463-4
      town planning vs environmental authorities 458-65, 466-7
exhaustion of local administrative or judicial remedies (diplomatic protection) 531-3, 570-1
  customary international law 532
  deficient or ineffective local machinery 533
  effective remedy, need for 570-1, 600-2
expropriation/nationalization, classification as/de facto, breach of contract, distinguished 516-17
expropriation/nationalization of property of national abroad, diplomatic protection and 497-8, 581-666
foreign relations, executive responsibility

INDEX 757

diplomatic protection 498-507
President's powers 499
fundamental rights (constitutional provisions), diplomatic protection, right to/duty of State to provide and 486, 616-22
ICSID and 586-90
incorporation in Constitution 500
individual in international law, diplomatic protection and 486-91
intergenerational rights and responsibilities 446-7, 449, 455-6, 471 n. 12
international delict, breach of minimum international standard of treatment as 497, 513-26, 528, 533, 545, 564-8
intragenerational equity/equitable sharing of resources, sustainable development principle and 446-7, 449, 455-6, 471 n. 12
judicial review/justiciability (matters relating to foreign relations or prerogative power), planning authorization 442, 467-72
law of: *see also* environment legislation/regulation other than ECA *above*
   Promotion of Administrative Justice Act 2000 441-2, 501
      s 1(i)(b)(aa) (administrative actions excluded from judicial review) 502
      s 6(2) (reviewable decisions), text (extracts) 457, 467
      s 6(2)(a) (mandatory and material decision) 441-2, 467-72
      s 6(2)(e)(iii) (judicial review, grounds: failure to consider relevant considerations) 442
      s 6(2)(i) (unconstitutionality of decision) 442
   Supreme Court Act 59 of 1959, s 43 (inherent power of court to regulate its own procedures) 481-2
Mpumalanga filling station rezoning application, background
   alternatives to proposal, adequacy 432-4
   judicial review 435-8
   decision on application, appeal 434-5
   Geo3 report 432
   scoping report 431-2
   Water Affairs and Forestry requests 435
nationality of claims with particular reference to nationality as the basis of the right to exercise diplomatic protection 487-8, 526-31
   continuity of nationality, cession of rights covered by claim to person having nationality of protecting State 527-8, 569-70
   diplomatic protection as right of citizenship 487-9, 619-20
NEMA 1998 (National Environmental Management Act) 458-72
   Long Title, text 468 n. 9
   Preamble, text (extracts) 468
   s 1(1)(xxix) (sustainable development: definition), text 456 n. 92, 469 n. 9
   s 2 (environmental management principles), text (extracts) 449 n. 67, 451, 469 n. 9
   s 2(1) (applicability to actions of all State organs) 452
   s 2(1)(b) (environmental management: general framework) 452
   s 2(1)(c) (environmental management: guidance principles/interpretation of environmental legislation) 452-3
   s 2(2) (peoples' needs as priority) 451
   s 2(3) (sustainable development principle) 451
   s 2(4)(a) (sustainable development: relevant factors) 449-50
   s 2(4)(a)(vii) (risk averse and cautious approach) 457-8
   s 2(4)(f) (public participation) 456

South Africa (*cont.*)
  s 2(4)(g) (interests, needs and values of all parties including traditional and ordinary knowledge) 431
  s 2(4)(i) (EIAs) 430-1, 451
  s 23(2)(a) (integration principle) 456
    text 452 n. 82
  s 23(2)(b) (environmental management objectives: identification of impact) 456
    text 451, 452 n. 83
  s 24 (implementation procedures) 452, 453
  s 24(1) (environmental impact, responsibility for determining), text 451-2
  s 24(7) (EIAs: investigation, assessment and communication procedures), text 453 n. 86
  s 24(7)(b) (EIAs: investigation, assessment and communication procedures: inclusion of cumulative effects) 456
  precautionary principle, EIAs and 457-8
property, arbitrary deprivation/interference with, prohibition (international norms other than specific treaty provisions) 494-7
  as human rights norm 494-6
  lawful deprivation 494-6
property, real/immovable, applicable law, *lex situs* 519
standard of treatment of alien (with particular reference to foreign investment)
  minimum international standard 491-2
    breach as international delict 497, 513-26, 528, 533, 545, 564-8, 600-2
    human rights and expropriation distinguished 494
State contract
  applicable law, public international law 490-1
  classification as 514-15
  'internationalization', arbitration clause/BITs provisions 490-1, 565-7
State responsibility, law relating to, applicable law, international law as part of municipal law 517-18
strike-out application, procedure 534-44, 555-6, 557-61
sustainable development principle
  development of principle 445-50
  equitable sharing/intragenerational equity and 446-7, 449, 455-6, 471 n. 12
  petrol filling stations, oversupply 434-9, 454-8, 462-5
sovereign equality of States (UNC 2(1)) (*par in parem non habet jurisdictionem*)
  comity (with particular reference to extraterritorial jurisdiction) 158-60, 164-5, 167, 169, 175, 176, 178, 180-1, 188-9, 198, 203-5, 214-15, 218-20, 267
  as customary international law/general principle of international law 156-8
  extraterritorial enforcement of legislation by legislating State and 167-8, 171-3, 195-207
sovereignty, extraterritorial effect of legislation and: *see* extraterritorial enforcement of legislation by legislating State, sovereign equality of States (UNC 2(1)) (*par in parem non habet jurisdictionem*) and; sovereign equality of States (UNC 2(1)) (*par in parem non habet jurisdictionem*)
standard of treatment of alien (with particular reference to foreign investment)
  minimum international standard 491-2
    breach as international delict 497, 513-26, 528, 533, 545, 564-8, 600-2
    human rights and expropriation distinguished 494, 497
State contract
  applicable law, public international law 490-1
  classification as 514-15
  'internationalization', arbitration clause/BITs provisions 490-1, 565-7

INDEX 759

State responsibility, law relating to, applicable law, international law as part of municipal law
517-18
Stockholm Declaration on the Human Environment (1972), sustainable development
principle 445
sustainable development principle
development of principle 445-50
equitable sharing/intragenerational equity and 446-7, 449, 455-6, 471 n. 12
Gabčíkovo/Nagymaros Project 447-8, 456-7
in South Africa 429-72
integration principle: *see* environmental protection/socio-economic interests, need to balance
(integration principle)
petrol filling stations, oversupply 434-9, 454-8, 462-5
treaties and other international instruments reflecting
Brundtland Report (2007) 443-4, 445-6
Rio Declaration on Environment and Development (1992) 446
Stockholm Declaration on the Human Environment (1972) 445

territorial jurisdiction (criminal and tort) (including cross-border offences)
162-88: *see also* extraterritorial effect of legislation; nationality principle
(jurisdiction over national for acts committed abroad); universal jurisdiction,
doctrine/theory
applicable law, cross-border offences 178-85
basis
comity 159-60
sovereign integrity/avoidance of infringement on third State 163
'deemed to have been committed' within territory 167
jurisprudence, *Lotus* 163
objective territorial principle (State where injury occurred) vs subjective territorial principle
(State where act took place) 163, 172
Thule Tribe (Greenland), compensation claim for 1953 Dundas Area resettlement
280-98
amounts claimed 280-1
claim for compensation for lost and impaired hunting grounds, decision 296-7
measure of damages 296-7
claims for individual relocation costs and losses 297-8
claims for loss of occupation, access and hunting rights (claims 1 and 2), decision 294-6
collective right of access to land for subsistence and traditional hunting and fishing activities
286
collective right to use territory of Greenland 286
coordinated and systematic action to protect rights, governments' responsibility for (ILO
No 169 2(1)) 285-6
Denmark–USA Defence Agreement (1951)
legislative approval 282-3, 295
restriction on hunting and catches as expropriation 295
validity 294-5
dispute settlement procedures, obligation to establish (ILO No 169 14(3)) 286
ILO's monitoring role 285
ILO Convention on Indigenous and Tribal Peoples in Independent Countries (No 169)
(1989), ILO committee Report on complaint by SIK (Sulinermik
Inuussutissarsiutequartut Kattuffiat) (1999) 284-7
ILO No 169, government's compliance with, Home Rule Act 1978 285-6

Thule Tribe (Greenland), compensation claim for 1953 Dundas Area resettlement (*cont.*)
Memorandum of Understanding relating to Removal of Tribe from Dundas Defence Area (2003) 281, 296
  extracts 287-9
people in independent countries regarded as indigenous on account of descent from populations at time of conquest or colonization who retain some or all of their own institutions (ILO No 169 1(1)(b)) 292-3, 296
right to return to traditional lands once grounds for relocation cease (ILO No 169 16(3)) 281, 286-7
  expropriation, effect 295-6
  provision of lands of equal status to those previously occupied or compensation (ILO No 169 16(4)) 286-7
self-identification as indigenous or tribal (ILO No 169 1(2)) and 285
standing in Danish courts (Hingitaq 53) 294
traditional lands, governments' obligation to identify and to guarantee protection (ILO No 169 14(2)) 285-6
transmission of land rights, respect for established procedures (ILO No 169 17(1)) 286
tribal people in independent countries whose social, cultural and economic conditions distinguish them ... from national community (ILO No 169 1(1)), whether 284-5, 296
  current conditions as basis for determination 293
  expert evidence 288-92
  Greenland people as a whole 292-3
  technological developments, impact 285
The Tomimaru
admissibility 45-56
applications/submissions
  Japan 41-2, 43, 44
  Russia 43-4
breach of Administrative Offences Code 49-50
confiscation 49-50, 52-6, 67-9, 70-2
factual background 44-50
jurisdiction 50-1
mootness 54-6, 69-70
procedural history 41-4
torture or cruel, inhuman or degrading treatment or punishment (CRC 37(a)) 245, 251, 252, 256
torture or cruel, inhuman or degrading treatment or punishment (municipal law/general)
derogation, exclusion 671-7, 684-5, 689, 691-2, 696-8, 703-28
prohibition, rejection of proposal for inclusion in constitution 403-8
torture, definition/classification as
death penalty 680-1
definitions
  'infliction of intense pain to the body or mind to punish, extract a confession or information or to obtain sadistic pleasure' (*Black's Law Dictionary*) 362
  'severe pain or suffering ... intentionally inflicted ... for such purposes as obtaining ... information or a confession' (TC 1) 245, 251, 252, 256
municipal law, Canada 245
sleep deprivation 234, 238-9, 240, 243-4, 251, 256, 259, 265, 271

INDEX 761

torture (ICCPR 7): *see also* death penalty as inhuman or degrading treatment (ICCPR 7)
 alien, applicability to 361-2
 burden/standard of proof 362-3
torture (municipal law/general)
 alien and 361-3
 prohibition on use to obtain information/evidence, third party torture 243-8
trafficking in persons, slavery compared 123-4
travaux préparatoires **as supplementary means of interpretation (VCLT 32)**, in respect of
 Slavery Convention, Art. 1 89
treaties, definition/form (VCLT 2(1)(a)), agreed minute, Japan–Russia Fisheries Commission
 23-4
treaties, direct effect/self-executing, ICESCR (1966) 369-71
treaties, implementing legislation/incorporation
 jurisprudence, *Mithu* 408-12
 margin of appreciation 312-13, 317, 327-30
 need for/examples of
  African Children's Charter 301, 312-13
  Child Rights Convention (1989) 305, 312-13
  human rights treaties 400-12
  ICESCR 369-70
  Slavery Convention (1926) 87-8, 108, 113-14, 122
treaties, implementing legislation/incorporation, interpretation
 language of treaty, divergence 92-3
 primacy in case of conflict 314, 317, 323
 treaty as aid 92-3, 101-2, 105, 108, 113-14, 122-3

Uganda
 Constitution 1967 by article, Art. 12(2) (infliction of punishment lawful before October
  1962) 685, 717-18
 Constitution 1995 by article 692
  Art. 20 (fundamental rights), text 668 n. 4
  Art. 20(1) (inherent nature of fundamental rights and freedoms) 693
  Art. 21(1) (equality before the law) 693-4, 716
   text 668 n. 5, 693
  Art. 22(1) (deprivation of life: fair trial)
   constitutionality 672-728
   decision to retain provision 682-3
   text 668 n. 6
  Art. 24 (torture or cruel, inhuman or degrading treatment: prohibition)
   death penalty and 671-85, 689, 691-3, 696-8, 703-28
   text 668 n. 2
  Art. 28(1) (determination of civil rights and obligations: fair, speedy and public hearing
   before independent and impartial tribunal) 700-1
   text 668 n. 7, 693
  Art. 28(3)(e) (offence carrying sentence of death: right to legal representation), text 668
   n. 7, 683-4, 693
  Art. 43 (fundamental rights: public interest), fair hearing obligation and 689
  Art. 44(a) (torture/cruel, inhuman or degrading treatment prohibition: non-derogation)
   death penalty and 671-7, 684-5, 689, 691-2, 696-8, 703-28
   text 668 n. 3

Uganda (*cont.*)
    Art. 44(c) (right to fair hearing: non-derogation) 673, 675
    Art. 45 (human rights not specifically mentioned), death penalty and 674, 675, 676, 689
    Art. 121(5) (death sentence: prerogative of mercy) 673, 674, 684, 695, 696, 699-701, 707
        text 669 n. 8
    Art. 126 (administration of justice as judicial function) 695-6
    Art. 132(4) (binding effect of Supreme Court decisions) 718-19
    Art. 173(3) (challenge to constitutionality of legislation or official action) 671
    Art. 273(1) (interpretation of existing law) 718-19
    Art. 287 (treaties: continuity) 683
    constitution, interpretation
        aids
            human rights treaties 677-84
            legislative history 682-3, 688-9
        guidelines/principles, text as a whole/avoidance of conflict 683-5, 712-16, 720
    Constitutional Court, binding effect of decisions 718-19
    death penalty as inhuman or degrading treatment/torture (municipal law/general) 76-85, 671-5, 689, 691-3, 695-8, 703-28
        hanging as method 672, 674-5, 703-6, 708-11, 718-20, 721-8
        mandatory death penalty and 672, 673, 687-8, 691-701
    death penalty (municipal law/general)
        abolition, progressive abolition, desirability 689-90
        constitutionality
            as matter for determination by Constitutional Court 671-728
            public opinion, relevance 692
            separation of powers and 695-6
        decision to retain in 1995 Constitution 682-3
        equality before the law and 692-4, 716
        history 677-83
        international law norms including human rights treaties in general and 677-83
            absence of specific provision 677-9
        procedural fairness/due process
            legal representation, right to 668 n. 7, 683-4, 689, 693-4
            mitigating factors in determining penalty, right to plead 692, 694-5, 707
            prompt and public hearing before an independent tribunal 683-4, 689, 693-4, 700-1
    death penalty (pardon/commutation/prerogative of mercy) (municipal law/general)
        constitutional provisions 673, 674, 684, 695, 696, 699-701, 707
        right to seek
            human rights treaties provision for 698-9
            Safeguards Guaranteeing the Protection of the Rights of Those Facing the Death Penalty (UNESCO resolution 1984/50) 681, 698-9, 705
    death row as inhuman or degrading treatment/torture (municipal law/general) 698-9
        conditions of detention and 698-9, 714-17, 721-8
        'reasonable' length of detention 701-3
        repeated reading of death warrant 728
    human/fundamental rights and freedoms, inherent nature 693
    human rights treaties
        consistency with Uganda Constitution 714-17
        incorporation/implementing legislation, need for, continuity of treaties and 683

INDEX 763

law of
  Interpretation Act, s 34(2) ('without unreasonable delay'), text 701
  Trial on Indictments Act
    s 94 (accused's right to plead mitigating circumstances) 694
    s 98 (court's right to consider mitigating circumstances in cases not incurring death penalty) 694-5
    s 99(1) (hanging as prescribed mode for execution of death penalty), constitutionality 672, 674-5, 703-6, 708-11, 718-20, 721-8
life, right to (ICCPR 6), arbitrary deprivation (ICCPR 6(1)) 678
life, right to (municipal law/general), derogation, possibility of 685, 689, 691-2, 708-10, 712, 713, 717-20
precedent in municipal courts
  binding effect of Supreme Court decisions 718-19
  decisions of human rights tribunals 714-17, 722-3
torture, definition/classification as, death penalty 680-1
UNESCO Resolution 1984/50 on Safeguards Guaranteeing Protection of the Rights of Those Facing the Death Penalty 681, 698-9, 705
United States of America (USA)
  Constitution, Amendments, Fourth (search and seizure), exclusion of evidence and 215-17
  death penalty (pardon/commutation/prerogative of mercy) (municipal law/general), right to seek 699-700
Universal Declaration of Human Rights (1948) (UDHR), 'rights' not specifically included, death penalty 677-8, 684
universal jurisdiction, doctrine/theory, narrow ambit 164
Uummannaq community: *see* Thule Tribe (Greenland), compensation claim for 1953 Dundas Area resettlement

women: *see also* CEDAW (1979)
  'personal law', applicability 313-14
work permit, right to refuse 367-8
  national security and 368
  proportionality requirement 368
work, right to
  ACHPR 15 365
  family life and 367-8
  ICESCR 6 355, 360, 363-4, 365, 366, 367, 369, 371
  municipal law/general 355, 364, 365, 369, 371

Zambia, law of, Penal Code, s 145 (bigamy) 158-9
Zimbabwe, expropriation/nationalization of property of alien within the jurisdiction 581-666